MAIL/FAX BID SHEET

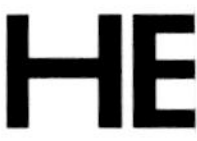

Auction # 818
Submit Your Bids By Fax
FAX HOTLINE: 214-443-8425

Heritage Galleries & Auctioneers
Direct Customer Service Line—Toll Free:
1-866-835-3243 (24 hour VM)
www.HeritageGalleries.com
3500 Maple Avenue, 17th Floor
Dallas, Texas 75219-3941

(All information must be completed.)

NAME ______________________________ CUSTOMER # (if known) ______________________________

ADDRESS ______________________________ E-MAIL ADDRESS ______________________________

CITY/STATE/ZIP ______________________________

DAYTIME PHONE (A/C) ______________________________ EVENING PHONE (A/C) ______________________________

Would you like a FAX or e-mail confirming receipt of your bids? If so, please print your FAX # or e-mail address here: ______________________________

REFERENCES: New bidders who are unknown to us must furnish satisfactory industry references or a valid credit card in advance of the sale date.

Dealer References (City, State) and/or Credit Card Information

____

____

____

____

____

You are authorized to release payment history information to other dealers and auctioneers so that I may establish proper credit in the industry. (Line out this statement if you do not authorize release).

Non-Internet bids (including but not limited to, podium, fax, phone and mail bids) may be submitted at any time and are treated similar to floor bids. These types of bids must be on-increment or at a half increment (called a cut bid). Any podium, fax, phone or mail bids that do not conform to a full or half increment will be rounded up or down to the nearest full or half increment and will be considered your high bid.

Current Bid	Bid Increment	Current Bid	Bid Increment
< $10	$1	$3,000 - $4,999	$250
$10 - $29	$2	$5,000 - $9,999	$500
$30 - $59	$3	$10,000 - $19,999	$1,000
$60 - $99	$5	$20,000 - $29,999	$2,000
$100 - $199	$10	$30,000 - $49,999	$2,500
$200 - $299	$20	$50,000 - $99,999	$5,000
$300 - $499	$25	$100,000 - $249,999	$10,000
$500 - $999	$50	$250,000 - $499,999	$25,000
$1,000 - $1,999	$100	$500,000 - $1,499,999	$50,000
$2,000 - $2,999	$200	> $1,500,000	$100,000

(Bid in whole dollar amounts only.)

LOT NO.	AMOUNT	LOT NO.	AMOUNT	LOT NO.	AMOUNT	LOT NO.	AMOUNT

PLEASE COMPLETE THIS INFORMATION:

1. IF NECESSARY, PLEASE INCREASE MY BIDS BY:
   ❑ 10% ❑ 20% ❑ 30%
   Lots will be purchased as much below bids as possible.

2. ❑ I HAVE BOUGHT COINS FROM YOU BEFORE (references are listed above)

I have read and agree to all of the Terms and Conditions of Sale: inclusive of paying interest at the lesser of 1.5% per month (18% per annum) or the maximum contract interest rate under applicable state law from the date of sale (if the account is not timely paid), and the submission of disputes to arbitration.

____

(Signature required) Please make a copy of your bid sheet for your records.

SUBTOTAL	
TOTAL from other side	
TOTAL BID	

FAX HOTLINE: 214-443-8425

REV. 7/21/05

LOT NO.	AMOUNT	LOT NO.	AMOUNT	LOT NO.	AMOUNT	LOT NO.	AMOUNT
						TOTAL this side	

Please make a copy of your bid sheet for your records.

HERITAGE COMICS AUCTIONS *presents*

Comics and Comic Art Signature Auction #818

October 14-15, 2005

3500 MAPLE AVENUE, 17TH FLOOR • DALLAS, TX 75219-3941

LOT VIEWING

Tuesday, October 11 thru Friday, October 14
9:00 AM - 5:00 PM CT

In Heritage's Dallas offices by appointment
3500 Maple Avenue, 17th Floor
Dallas, Texas 75219-3941
800-872-6467

FAX BIDDING

Deadline Wednesday, October 13, 2005
12 noon CT • 214-443-8425 • Attn. Kathy Eilers (Ext. 392)

INTERNET BIDDING

HeritageComics.com
Closes at 10:00 pm CT, the night prior to session on sale

TELEPHONE BIDDING

Must be arranged on or before
Wednesday, October 12, 2005
Toll Free: 1-866-835-3243 (24 hour VM)

LOT PICK UP

Monday, October 17, 2005, • 9 AM - 5 PM CT

AUCTIONEERS

Sam Foose, TX License #00011727

PUBLIC, INTERNET & MAIL BID AUCTION #818

SESSION I:
Silver Age, Bronze Age & Modern Age Comics
Friday, October 14, 2005 at 1:00 PM CT
Lots 1001-1475

SESSION II:
Golden Age Comics
Friday, October 14, 2005 at 6:00 PM CT
Lots 2001-2558

SESSION III:
The Aviator Collection
The Random House Archives
ECs, Undergrounds, Bound Comic Volumes, Magazines, Memorabilia, Books, Big Little Books
Saturday, October 15, 2005 at 1:00 PM CT
Lots 3001-xxxx

SESSION IV:
Original Art & Animation Art
Saturday, October 15, 2005 at 6:00 PM CT
Lots 4001-4535

AUCTION RESULTS

Immediately available at: HeritageGalleries.com

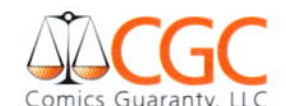

Lon Allen
Director of Sales
LonA@HeritageComics.com

HeritageComics.com
3500 Maple Avenue, 17th Floor
Dallas, TX 75219-3941
214-528-3500 • 800-872-6467 • 214-443-8425 (fax)

Ed Jaster
Director of Acquisitions
EdJ@HeritageGalleries.com

Catalogers: Barry Sandoval, Mark Stokes, David Tosh, Don Mangus, Jim Steele, Gary Dowell, Ben Samuels, and Mark Walters

Special Thanks to: Jim Amash, Gary Colabuono, Scotty Moore, Matt Nelson, Ken Quattro, Charlie Roberts, Simon Sanchez, Robin Snyder, Rob Stolzer, Roy Thomas, Jim Vadeboncoeur, Jr., and Dr. Michael Vassallo

Production and Design by: Mandy Bottoms, Cindy Brenner, Keith Craker, Cathy Hadd, Mary Hermann, Matt Pegues, Michael Puttonen, Debbie Rexing, Jim Steele, Marsha Taylor, David Tosh, Colette Warren and, Carl Watson

Photography by: Jody Garver, Lucas Garritson, Bea Faustino, Jamie Graham, Steve Robinson, Deign Rook, Matt Roppolo, Tony Webb, Jason Young, Butch Ziaks and Shaun Zokaie

Imaging and Pre-cataloging by: Estella Berumen, Lorena Camarillo, Charlotte Duncan, Kelly Faulkner, Rosa Faustino, Nancy Reyes, and Ricky Torres

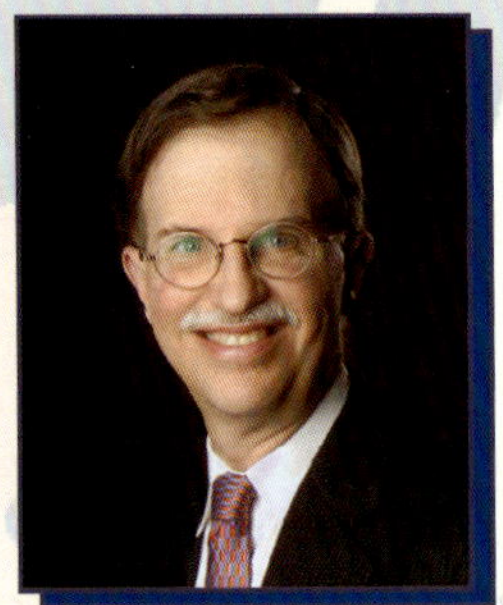

Steve Ivy
CEO
Co-Chairman
of the Board

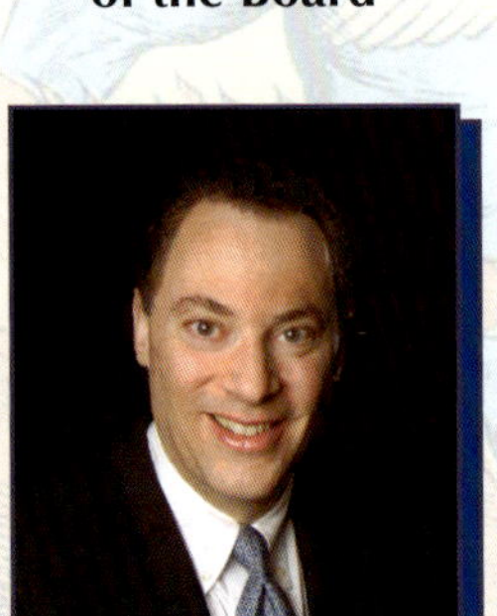

Jim Halperin
Co-Chairman
of the Board

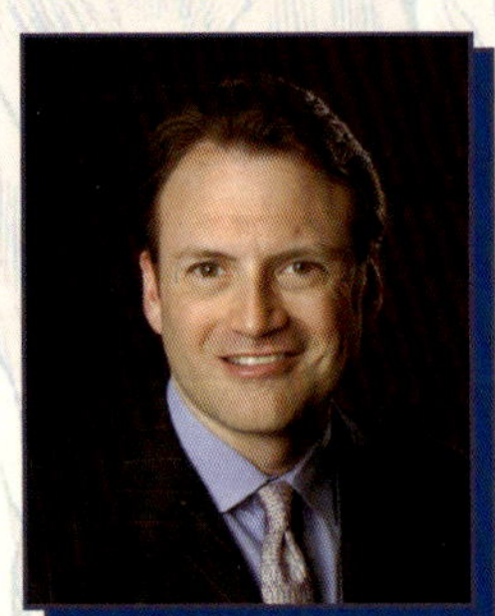

Greg Rohan
President

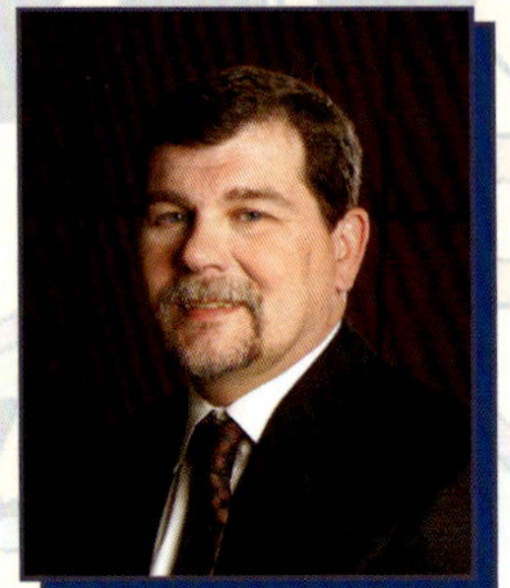

Ed Jaster
Director of
Acquisitions

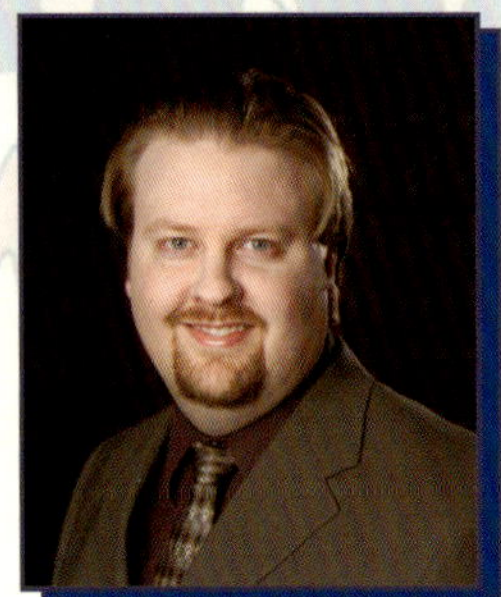

Lon Allen
Director
of Sales

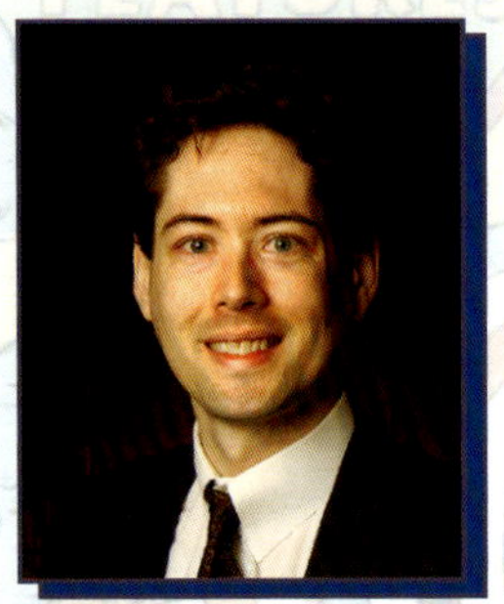

Ben Samuels
Consignment Director

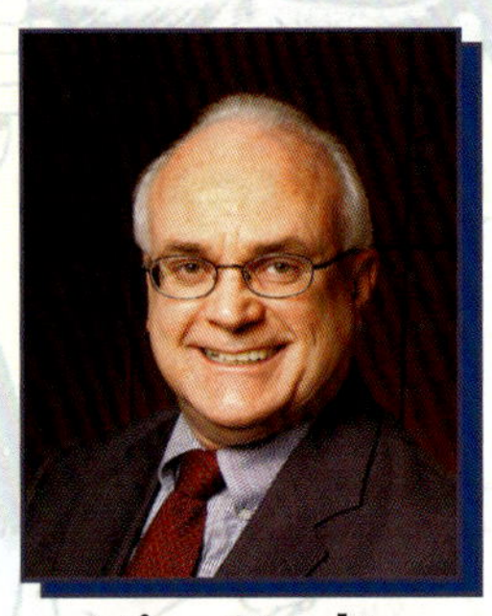

Jim Steele
Chief Cataloger for
Comics and Comic Art

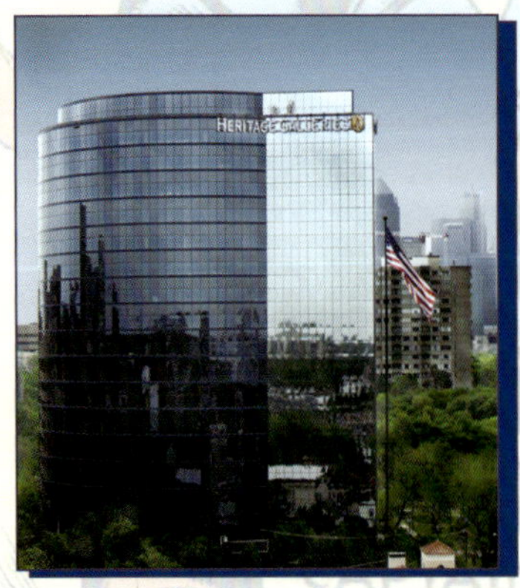

Jared Green
Vice President of
Business Development

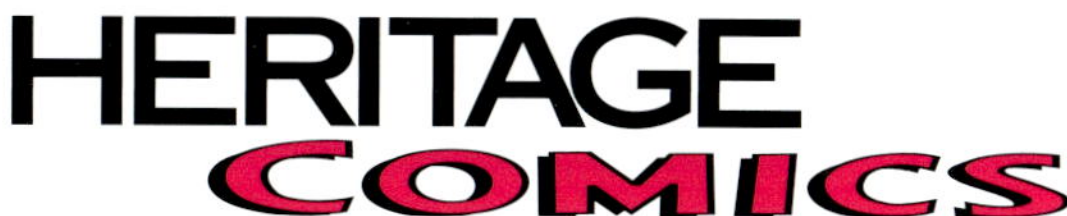

Dear Fellow Collector,

The big question around here since our last auction in August has been "How do we follow that one?" That one, Signature Auction #817, just happened to be one of the highest-grossing Comics/Comic Art auctions in our four years of bringing these specialty events to you, the highlight being the Fred Ray/Jerry Robinson original art for the cover of **Batman #11**, which set a world record in bringing the highest price ever for original comic art offered at auction. As for comics, we nearly broke our own record for highest price realized to date for a comic book with our sale of the Denver Copy of **Marvel Comics #1**.

With just two months between that sale and our upcoming one October 14-15, perhaps you'll forgive our not offering quite so many lots this time around. What isn't compromised is the quality of our offerings, as you will see throughout this catalog.

We spotlight the art of John Byrne and Terry Austin's original cover art for **X-Men #138** in a colorized version on the front of our catalog, and we feature the real thing in our auction. Other outstanding pieces by Neal Adams, Johnny Craig, Jack Davis, Al Feldstein, Frank Frazetta, Jack Kirby, and John Romita Sr. give even the most exacting collectors plenty of choices.

As for comics, copies of **Marvel Comics #1** in VF/NM 9.0 (the highest-certified grade to date), the Mile High copy of **More Fun Comics #53** in NM+ 9.6, the Pay Copy of **Motion Picture Funnies Weekly #1** in VF/NM 9.0, the Windy City copy of **Captain America Comics #1** in VF+ 8.5, **Justice League of America #1** in NM 9.4, and **Flash #105** in NM 9.4 are just a few of the exciting array awaiting your bidding. For you Mile High aficionados, we have nearly 200 comics from that esteemed pedigree, as well as representatives from the other most renowned pedigrees in collectible comic books.

On the following pages you will find tips from the catalogers who get to see these treasures up close. And besides the obvious higher-dollar items, there are plenty of unique collectibles in every section of our catalog. Check out our continuing offers from the Random House Archives and a wonderful Golden Age comic collection, the Aviator Collection. A wide assortment of high-grade Big Little Books, more super-nice bound volumes of comics... as usual I'm running out of space before I run out of items to talk about!

Happy bidding!

Jim Steele

Jim Steele
Chief Cataloger

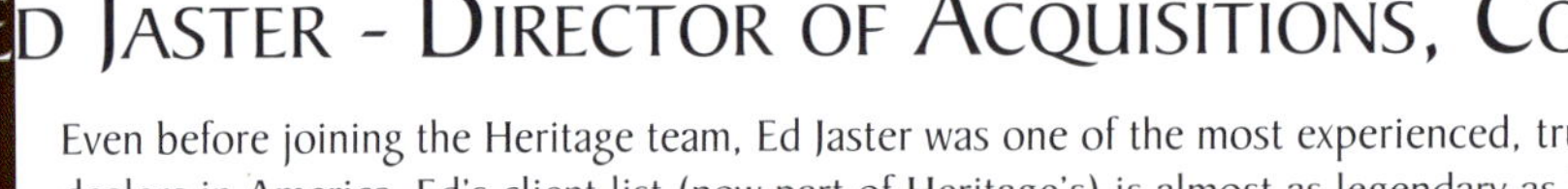

ED JASTER - DIRECTOR OF ACQUISITIONS, COMICS

Even before joining the Heritage team, Ed Jaster was one of the most experienced, trusted and well-known comics dealers in America. Ed's client list (now part of Heritage's) is almost as legendary as his knowledge of comics. He has bought and sold complete runs of Mile Highs, multiple copies of Detective #27, Captain America #1, Batman #1, and Amazing Fantasy #15, to name just a few. Ed is a Senior Overstreet Advisor, has won several CBG Customer Service Awards, and served as an AACC Grading and Certification panelist for Christie's auctions in 1994 and 1995. He has been published in the Overstreet Comic Book Price Guide, Comic Book Marketplace and The Comics Buyer's Guide.

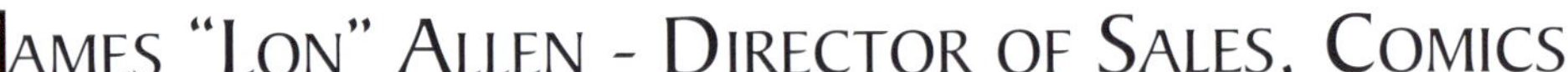

JAMES "LON" ALLEN - DIRECTOR OF SALES, COMICS

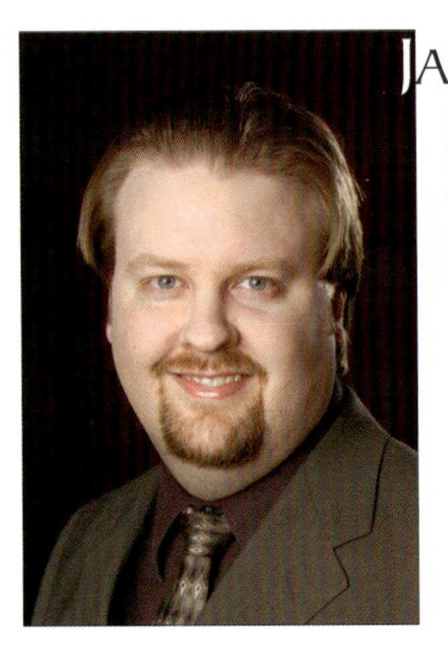

Lon attended Truman State University from 1991-1995, and, while there, turned his love of comics into a part-time business. His successful part-time business became an even more successful full-time business when he started J.L.A. Comics in 2000. In 2002, Lon joined Heritage Comics as Auction Coordinator, and was promoted to Director of Sales in 2005. He is an advisor to both the Overstreet Comic Book Price Guide and to GPAnalysis.com, and is a confirmed fan of both the Atlanta Braves and the Kansas City Chiefs.

Lon sez: "Check out our high-grade copy of Captain America Comics #1 in this auction. It's from the prestigious Windy City Collection and one of the finest copies of this legendary book known to exist. "Unlike most other high-grade copies, including the Mile High copy, this book is unrestored, making it particularly desirable for the advanced collector."

BEN SAMUELS - CONSIGNMENT DIRECTOR

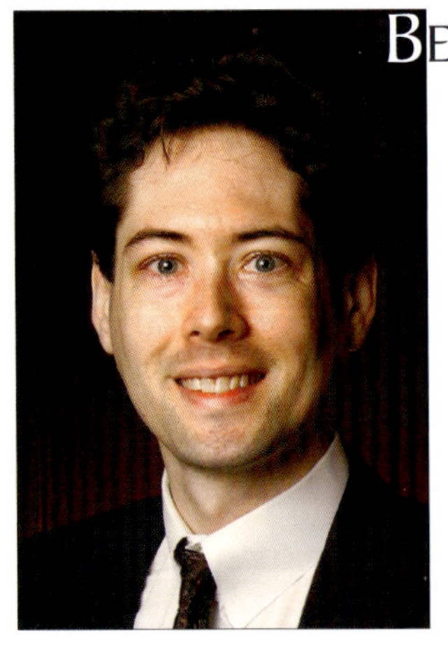

Ben received a BA in English from the University of Missouri (Columbia), and then worked in a variety of jobs in the graphic design field for several different companies. Later, he taught English in Japan and Thailand before finding a job doing graphic design for a newspaper in Bangkok. After returning to the USA, he found a position providing technical support for an internet hosting company, then web design and programming for a software company. He joined Heritage full-time in 2003 after several turns as a guest cataloger for comics. Ben has been a passionate comic book collector for over 25 years, and has recently expanded his collecting interests to include art, pulps, and anything else that strikes him as 'cool'. He also maintains www.samuelsdesign.com/comics <http://www.samuelsdesign.com/comics> in his spare time.

Ben sez: I'm particularly pleased with the collection of Marvel and DC bound volumes we're offering. Especially impressive are volumes like Tales of Suspense #39-60, Tales to Astonish #26-40 plus Incredible Hulk #1-6, Fantastic Four #1-20, and Batman #101-120 -- in all there are over 50 beautifully bound volumes, all bound in green boards with embossed title and issue numbers. Also of interest is the original cover artwork for Batman #231 by Neal Adams. The artwork was never inked, and the published cover was taken directly from Adams' tight pencils, making this a very unusual piece. We've also got several more excellent original Dick Tracy strips by Chester Gould, from the Larry Doucet collection. While it's hard to pick a favorite, that item I'm probably most excited about is an early, original airbrush painting by the legendary Alex Schomburg. It has impeccable provenance, and looks to date from his time working at the National Screen Service, before he began doing work for the comic book industry.

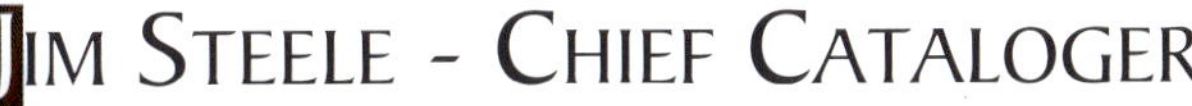

Jim Steele - Chief Cataloger

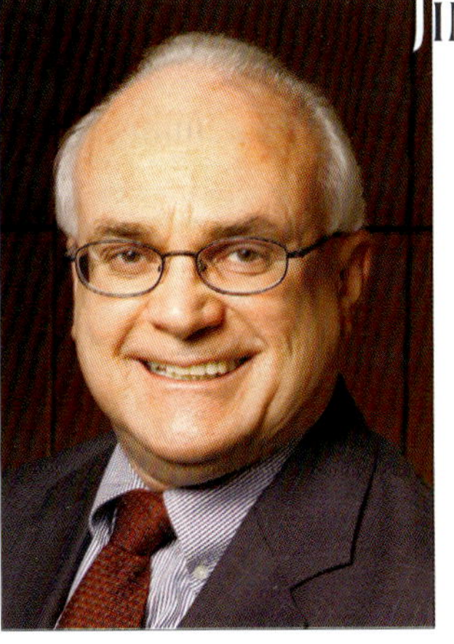

Native Dallasite Jim Steele can't remember a time he wasn't collecting something - rocks, coins, stamps, records, sports cards, and comics. By age nine, he was keeping his comics in orderly piles that eventually took over most of his chest of drawers, then most of his closet. When his letter to DC was published in The Atom #2, the 14-year old began receiving letters from collectors across the country, and became acquainted with entrepreneurs selling and trading back issues. A whole new world opened up to him - the Golden Age of Comics! His favorite era was still the early Marvel Age years of the early 1960s, followed by pre-Code ECs, Golden Age Fiction House, and mid-1950s DCs. After high school in Ruidoso, New Mexico, Jim studied Pre-Med, English, and Music, and earned track letters at San Bernardino Valley College in California. As for work experience, Jim was a radio DJ from 1963-1965 while still in high school. After college he began a long stint in the life and health insurance business, specializing in insurance claims. He owned his own bookstore from 1978-1985, and began setting up as a dealer at local comic book shows in 1978. That same year he started a mobile DJ service, returning briefly to radio in 1984-1985. Insurance company mergers and the search for a more fun full-time job led Jim to Heritage in 2002. Besides collecting, Jim enjoys attending concerts, following college and professional sports, karaoke-ing, and snow skiing.

Don Mangus - Comic Art Cataloger

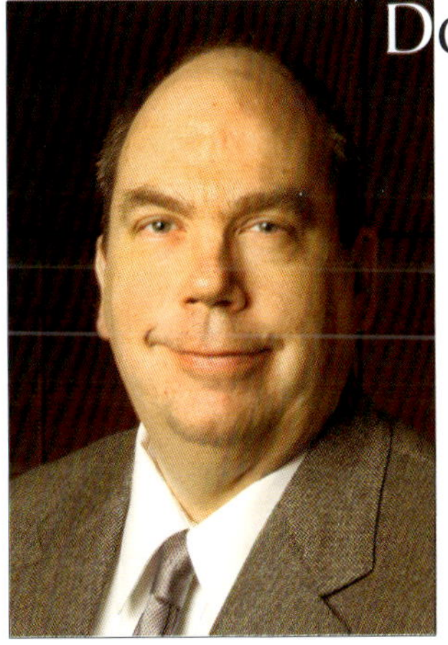

Don began collecting comic books in Anchorage, Alaska in 1964. This stirred a lifelong interest in art, which led him to acquire a BFA in 1978 and an MFA in painting in 1981, both from Southern Methodist University. From 1981 through 1996, he taught as an adjunct Professor of Design at Eastfield College in Mesquite, Texas. It was during this time that Don discovered original comic art, which quickly became his primary collecting interest, particularly non-superhero art circa 1950-80. In his spare time, Don enjoys painting, drawing, walking and hiking, as well as collecting and listening to mainstream jazz.

Don sez: "Be sure to check out these beauties: a rare Frank Frazetta Sweet Adeline daily, an early George McManus Spare Ribs and Gravy Sunday, the sensational covers by EC legends Johnny Craig, Jack Davis, Al Feldstein, and Wally Wood, and the two Alex Schomburg pieces!"

Barry Sandoval - Collectibles Specialist / Cataloger

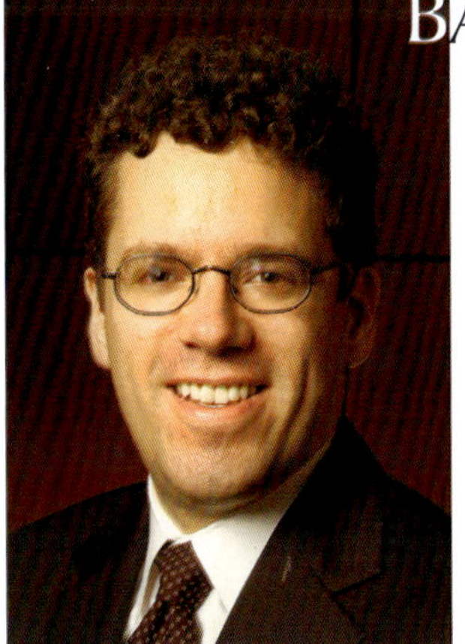

After receiving a BA in Journalism from Southern Methodist University, Barry relocated to Europe to begin a career in book publishing. He edited "The Encyclopedia of Photographers, 1900 to Present" (which won the Kodak Prize for best photography book of the year) as well as books on digital and conventional photography, a German-English dictionary, and other foreign-language reference works before returning to the USA and his native state of Texas. He has been interested in comics since the day his parents bought him a copy of Amazing Spider-Man #148. Barry also enjoys football, history, international travel, and the novels of Rex Stout and Len Deighton

Barry sez: "No matter if you started reading comics when they cost 12 cents, 35 cents (my favorite era!), or $2.75, a sense of history is a must; that's why you've got to doff your cap to Famous Funnies #1, the first monthly newsstand comic book. It paved the way for everything that followed! And of course, the reason I'm bringing it up is because we've got a copy of that scarce comic in this very auction. And while you can hardly miss the Pay Copy of Motion Picture Funnies Weekly #1 (one of eight copies known to exist), don't let it escape your attention that we've also got the covers of the unpublished issues #2-4 in another section of the catalog."

David Tosh - Collectibles Specialist / Cataloger

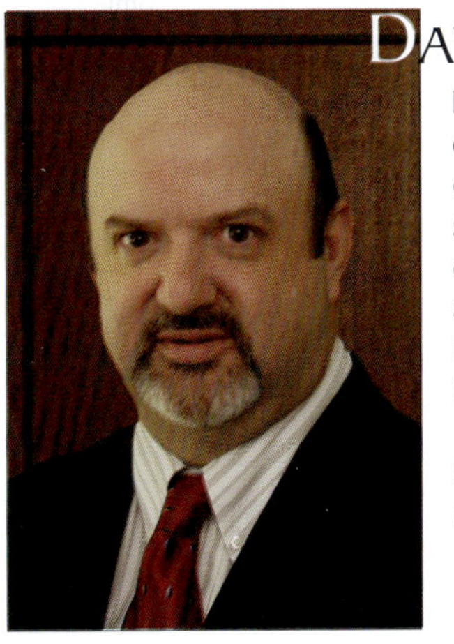

David began collecting comics in 1971, a hobby which colored many other aspects of his life. A former Nostalgia store owner and comic/movie poster dealer, David is also a graphic designer with over twenty-five years professional experience, and holds an Associates Degree from the Southwest Technical Institute in East Camden, Arkansas. In 1985, he started creating and publishing his own line of mini-comics, and has since had his work published in several nationally distributed magazine. He is particularly proud of the opportunity he has had to work with the likes of Robert Crumb and other Underground artists. David joined Heritage in 2003, and is currently co-authoring a book on the history of Harvey Comics. His hobbies include collecting comic books, movie posters, and related memorabilia, and playing bass in a small combo.

Dave sez: "Check out the incredible Gaines File Copy ECs in this auction, many of which are among the finest known examples. Of special interest is the copy of Weird Fantasy #13 (#1) in astounding NM/MT 9.8 condition!

TERMS & CONDITIONS OF SALE

AUCTIONEER AND AUCTION:

1. This auction is presented by Heritage Numismatic Auctions. Inc. or its subsidiary Currency Auctions of America, Inc. or their affiliate, Heritage Auctions, Inc. through its divisions Heritage Comic Auctions, or Heritage Sports Collectibles Auctions, as identified with the applicable licensing information either on the title page of the catalog or on the Internet site (the "Auctioneer"). The auction is conducted under these Terms and Conditions of Auction and applicable state and local law.

BUYER'S PREMIUM:

2. On bids placed through Heritage, a Buyer's Premium of fifteen percent (15%) for Heritage Vintage Movie Posters, Heritage Numismatic Auctions Inc, Heritage-CAA, Heritage-Slater Americana and Heritage Comics Auctions or nineteen and one-half percent (19.5%) for Heritage Sports Collectibles, Heritage-Odyssey and Heritage Galleries & Auctioneers of the hammer price will be added to the successful bid. If the bid is placed through eBay Live a Buyer's Premium equal to the normal Buyer's Premium plus an additional five percent (5%) of the hammer price will be added to the successful bid. There is a minimum Buyer's Premium of $9.00 per lot.

AUCTION VENUES:

3. Exclusively Internet, CurrencyAuction.com, Amazing Comics Auctions, Continuously Internet and OnLine Session are auctions conducted on the Internet. Signature auctions accept bids on the Internet first, followed by a floor bidding session. Bids may be placed prior to the floor bidding session by Internet, telephone, fax, or mail.

BIDDERS:

4. Any person participating in or who registers for the auction agrees to be bound by and accepts these Terms and Conditions of Auction ("Bidder(s)").
5. All Bidders must meet Auctioneer's qualifications to bid. Any Bidder who is not a customer in good standing of the Auctioneer may be disqualified at Auctioneer's sole option and will not be awarded lots. Such a determination may be made by Auctioneer in its sole and unlimited discretion, at any time prior to, during, or even after the close of the auction.
6. If an entity places a bid, then the person executing the bid on behalf of the entity agrees to personally guarantee payment for any successful bid.
7. Auctioneer reserves the right to exclude any person it deems in its sole opinion is disruptive to the auction or is otherwise commercially unsuitable.

CREDIT REFERENCES:

8. Bidders who do not have established credit with the Auctioneer must either furnish satisfactory credit information including two collectibles-related references well in advance of the auction date or supply valid credit card information. All Bidders must meet Auctioneer's qualifications to bid. Any Bidder who is not a customer in good standing at Auctioneer may be disqualified and will not be awarded lots. Auctioneer reserves the right to disqualify any Bidder even after the close of the auction. Bids placed through our Interactive Internet program will only be accepted from pre-registered Bidders. Bidders who are not members of HeritageGalleries.com should pre-register at least two business days before the first session to allow adequate time to contact references.

BIDDING OPTIONS:

9. Bids may be placed for a Signature Sale as set forth in the printed catalog section entitled "Choose your bidding method." For Exclusively Internet, CurrencyAuction. Com, Amazing Comics Auctions, Continuously Internet and OnLine Session auctions see the alternatives shown on each website. Review at HeritageCoin.com/Auctions/howtobid.asp.

10A. **Presentment of Bids: Non-Internet bids (including but not limited to podium, fax, phone and mail bids) are treated similar to floor bids. These types of bids must be on-increment or at a half increment (called a cut bid). Any podium, fax, phone, or mail bids that do not conform to a full or half increment will be rounded up or down to the nearest full or half increment and will be considered your high bid.**

10B. Auctioneer's Execution of Certain Bids. The Auctioneer cannot be responsible for your errors in bidding, so carefully check that your bid is entered correctly. When identical mail or FAX bids are submitted, preference is given to the first received. The decision of the Auctioneer and declaration of the winning Bidder is final. The Auctioneer is not responsible for executing mail bids or FAX bids received on or after the day the first lot is sold, nor Internet bids submitted after the published closing time; nor is the Auctioneer responsible for proper execution of bids submitted by telephone, mail, FAX, e-mail, Internet, or in person once the auction begins. Internet bids may not be withdrawn until your written request is received and acknowledged by Auctioneer (FAX: 214-443-8425); such requests must state the reason, and may constitute grounds for withdrawal of bidding privileges. To ensure the greatest accuracy, your written bids should be entered on the standard bid sheet form and be received at the Auctioneer's place of business at least two business days in advance of the auction' start. Lots won by mail Bidders will not be delivered at the auction unless prearranged in advance. Bid increments determine the lowest amount you may bid on a particular lot. Bids greater than one increment over the current bid can be any whole dollar amount.

10C. Caveat as to Bids. Bid increments determine the lowest amount you may bid on a particular lot. Bids greater than one increment over the current bid can be any whole dollar amount. It is possible under several circumstances for winning bids to be between increments, sometimes only $1 above the previous increment. Please see: "How can I lose by less than an increment?" </common/web_tips.php>

10D. Bidding Increments: The following chart governs current bidding increments.

Current Bid	Bid Increment	Current Bid	Bid Increment
< $10	$1	$3,000 - $4,999	$250
$10 - $29	$2	$5,000 - $9,999	$500
$30 - $59	$3	$10,000 - $19,999	$1,000
$60 - $99	$5	$20,000 - $29,999	$2,000
$100 - $199	$10	$30,000 - $49,999	$2,500
$200 - $299	$20	$50,000 - $99,999	$5,000
$300 - $499	$25	$100,000 - $249,999	$10,000
$500 - $999	$50	$250,000 - $499,999	$25,000
$1,000 - $1,999	$100	$500,000 - $1,499,999	$50,000
$2,000 - $2,999	$200	> $1,500,000	$100,000

CONDUCTING THE AUCTION:

11. Notice of the consignor's liberty to place reserve bids on his lots in the auction is hereby made in accordance with Article 2 of the Texas Uniform Commercial Code. A reserve is an amount below which the lot will not sell. THE CONSIGNOR OF PROPERTY MAY PLACE WRITTEN RESERVE BIDS ON HIS LOTS IN ADVANCE OF THE AUCTION. ON LOTS SUBJECT TO A RESERVE, IF THE LOT DOES NOT MEET THE RESERVE THE CONSIGNOR MAY PAY A REDUCED COMMISSION ON THOSE LOTS. Reserves are generally posted online about 3 days prior to the auction closing on Internet-Only auctions, and 7 days prior to the auction on Signature auctions. IF THERE IS AN UNMET RESERVE BID POSTED ON A LOT, THE CURRENT BID DISPLAYED ONLINE WILL AUTOMATICALLY BE SET AT ONE INCREMENT BELOW THE RESERVE BID. The Auctioneer will not knowingly accept (and reserves the right to reject) live telephone or floor bids from consignors. Any successful bid placed by a consignor on his consigned lot on the auction floor or by telephone during the live session, or after the reserves for an auction have been posted, will be considered an unqualified bid, and in such instances the consignor agrees to pay full Buyer's Premium and Seller's Commissions on the lot(s) even if (s)he buys them back.
12. The highest qualified Bidder shall be the buyer. In the event of any dispute between floor Bidders at a Signature Sale, the Auctioneer may at his sole discretion put the lot up for auction again. The Auctioneer's decision shall be final and binding upon all Bidders.
13. The Auctioneer reserves the right to refuse to honor any bid or to limit the amount of any bid which, in his sole discretion, is not submitted in "Good Faith," or is not supported by satisfactory credit, numismatic references, or otherwise. A bid is considered not made in "Good Faith" when an insolvent or irresponsible person, or a person under the age of eighteen makes it. Regardless of the disclosure of his identity, any bid by a consignor or his agent on a lot consigned by him is deemed to be made in "Good Faith".
14. All items are to be purchased per lot as numerically indicated and no lots will be broken. The Auctioneer reserves the right to withdraw, prior to the close, any lot or lots from the auction. Bids will be accepted in whole dollar amounts only.
15. No "buy" or "unlimited" bids will be accepted. Bidders will be awarded lots at approximately the increment of the next highest bid. No additional commission is charged for executing bids other than the Buyer's Premium applied to all successful bids. Off-increment bids may be accepted by the Auctioneer at Signature auctions.
16. Estimates will be given upon written request. It is recommended that Bidders approach or exceed the estimates in order to increase the chances of bidding successfully.
17. Auctioneer reserves the right to rescind the sale in the event of nonpayment, breach of a warranty, disputed ownership, auctioneer's clerical error or omission in exercising bids and reserves, or otherwise.
18. Outage Policy: Auctioneer occasionally experiences Internet and/or Server outages during which Bidders cannot participate or place bids. If such outage occurs, we may at our discretion extend bidding for the auction up to 24 hours. At our discretion, Auctioneer may consider two outages that occur very closely to one another to be one outage when extending such auction. This policy applies only to widespread outages and not to isolated problems that occur in various parts of the country from time to time.
19. Scheduled Downtime: Auctioneer periodically schedules system downtime for maintenance and other purposes; this scheduled downtime is not covered by the Outage Policy.
20. The Auctioneer or its affiliates may consign items to be sold in the auction sale, and may bid on those items or any other items in the sale. The Auctioneer or affiliates expressly reserve the right to modify any such reserve bids on these items or any others at any time prior to the live auction or the online closing based upon data made known to the Auctioneer or its affiliate.
21. The Auctioneer may extend advances, guarantees, or loans to certain consignors, and may extend financing or other credits at varying rates to certain Bidders in the auction.

PAYMENT:

22. All sales are strictly for cash in United States dollars. Cash includes: U.S. currency, bank wire, cashier checks, travelers checks, and bank money orders, all subject to reporting requirements. Credit Card (Visa or Master Card only) and PayPal payments may be accepted up to $10,000 from non-dealers at the sole discretion of the auctioneer, subject to the following limitations: a) sales are only to the cardholder, b) purchases are shipped to the cardholder's registered and verified address, c) Auctioneer may preapprove the cardholder's credit line, d) a credit card transaction may not be used in conjunction with any other financing or extended terms offered by the Auctioneer, and must transact immediately upon invoice presentation, e) rights of return are governed by these Terms and Conditions, which supersede those conditions promulgated by the card issuer, f) floor Bidders must present their card. Personal or corporate checks may be subject to clearing before delivery of the purchases.
23. Payment is due upon closing of the auction session, or upon presentment of an invoice. The Auctioneer reserves the right to void a sale if payment in full of the invoice is not received within 7 days after the close of the auction.
24. Lots delivered in the States of Texas, California, or other states where the auction may be held, are subject to all applicable state and local taxes, unless appropriate permits are on file with us. In the event that sales tax is not properly collected due to: 1) an expired, inaccurate, inappropriate tax certificate or declaration, 2) an incorrect interpretation of the applicable statute, 3) or any other reason, bidder agrees to pay Auctioneer the actual amount of tax due. Lots from different auctions may not be aggregated for sales tax purposes.
25. In the event that a Bidder's payment is dishonored upon presentment(s), Bidder shall pay the maximum statutory processing fee set by applicable state law.
26. If the auction invoice(s) submitted by the Auctioneer is not paid in full when due, the unpaid balance will bear interest at the highest rate permitted by law from the date of invoice until paid. If the Auctioneer refers the invoice(s) to an attorney for collection, the buyer agrees to pay attorney's fees, court costs, and other collection costs incurred by the Auctioneer. If Auctioneer assigns collection to its in-house legal staff, such attorney's time expended on the matter shall be compensated at a rate comparable to the hourly rate of independent attorneys.
27. In the event a successful Bidder fails to pay all amounts due, the Auctioneer reserves the right to resell the merchandise, and such Bidder agrees to pay for the reasonable costs of resale, including a 10% seller's commission, and also to pay any difference between the resale price and the price of the previously successful bid.
28. The Auctioneer reserves the right to require payment in full in good funds before delivery of the merchandise to the buyer.
29. The Auctioneer shall have a lien against the merchandise purchased by the buyer to secure payment of the auction invoice. Auctioneer is further granted a lien and the right to retain possession of any other property of the buyer then held by the Auctioneer or its affiliates to secure payment of any auction invoice or any other amounts due the Auctioneer from the buyer. With respect to these lien rights, the Auctioneer shall have all the rights of a secured creditor under Article 9 of the Texas Uniform Commercial Code. In addition, with respect to payment of the auction invoice(s), the buyer waives any and all rights of offset he might otherwise have against the Auctioneer and the consignor of the merchandise included on the invoice.
30. If a Bidder owes Auctioneer or its affiliates on any account, the Auctioneer and its affiliates shall have the right to offset such unpaid account by any credit balance due Bidder, and it may secure by possessory lien any unpaid amount by any of the Bidder's property in their possession.
31. Title shall not pass to the successful Bidder until all invoices are paid in full. It is the responsibility of the buyer to provide adequate insurance coverage for the items once they have been delivered.

RETURN POLICY:

A. MEMORABILIA

32A. A MEMORABILIA lot (Autographs, Sports Collectibles, or Music, Entertainment, Political, Americana and/or Pop Culture memorabilia) when the lot is accompanied by a Certificate of Authenticity, or its equivalent, from an independent third party authentication provider, has no right of return. Under extremely limited circumstances, not including authenticity (e.g. gross cataloging error), a purchaser, who did not bid from the floor, may request Auctioneer to void a sale. Such request for evaluation must be made in writing detailing the alleged gross error, and submission of the lot to the Auctioneer must be pre-approved by the Auctioneer. A bidder must notify the appropriate department head (check the inside front cover of the catalog or our website for a listing of department heads) in writing of the purchaser's request and such notice must be mailed within three (3) days of the mail bidder's receipt of the lot. Any lot that is to be evaluated for return must be received in our offices with 30 days. AFTER THAT 30 DAY PERIOD, NO LOT MAY BE RETURNED FOR ANY REASONS. Lots returned must be in the same condition as when sold and must include the Certificate of Authenticity, if any. No lots purchased by floor bidders may be returned (including those bidders acting as agents for others). Late remittance for purchases may be considered just cause to revoke all return privileges.

B. COINS, CURRENCY, COMICS AND SPORTSCARDS

32B. COINS, CURRENCY, COMICS AND SPORTSCARDS Signature Sales: The auction is not on approval. No certified material may be returned because of possible differences of opinion with respect to the grade offered by any third-party organization, dealer, or service. There are absolutely no exceptions to this policy. Under extremely limited circumstances, (e.g. gross cataloging error) a purchaser, who did not bid from the floor, may request Auctioneer to void a sale. Such request for evaluation must be made in writing detailing the alleged gross error, and submission of the lot to the Auctioneer must be pre-approved by the Auctioneer. A bidder must notify Ron Brackemyre, (ext. 312) in writing of the bidder's request and such notice must be mailed within three (3) days of the mail bidder's receipt of the lot. Any lot that is to be evaluated must be in our offices within 30 days. Grading or method of manufacture do not qualify for this evaluation process nor do such complaints constitute a basis to challenge the authenticity of a lot. AFTER THAT 30-DAY PERIOD, NO LOTS MAY BE RETURNED FOR REASONS OTHER THAN AUTHENTICITY. Lots returned must be housed intact in the original holder. No lots purchased by floor Bidders may be returned (including those Bidders acting as agents for others). Late remittance for purchases may be considered just cause to revoke all return privileges.

33. Exclusively Internet, CurrencyAuction.com, Amazing Comics Auctions,™ Continuously Internet and OnLine Session auctions: THREE (3) DAY RETURN POLICY. All lots (Exception: Third party graded notes are not returnable for any reason whatsoever) paid for within seven days of the auction closing are sold with a three (3) day return privilege. You may return lots under the following conditions: Within three days of receipt of the lot, you must first notify Auctioneer by contacting Customer Service by phone (1-800-872-6467) or e-mail (Bid@HeritageGalleries.com), and immediately mail the lot(s) fully insured to the attention of Returns, Heritage, 3500 Maple Avenue, 17th Floor, Dallas TX 75219-3941. Lots must be housed intact in their original holder and condition. You are responsible for the insured, safe delivery of any lots. A non-negotiable return fee of 5% of the purchase price ($10 per lot minimum) will be deducted from the refund for each returned lot or billed directly. Postage and handling fees are not refunded. After the three-day period (from receipt), no items may be returned for any reason. Late remittance for purchases revokes all Return-Restock privileges.

34. All Bidders who have inspected the lots prior to the auction will not be granted any return privileges, except for reasons of authenticity.

DELIVERY:

35. Postage, handling and insurance charges will be added to invoices. Please either refer to Auctioneer's web site HeritageGalleries.com for the latest charges or call Auctioneer.

COMPLETE SHIPPING AND HANDLING CHARGES:

36. Auctioneer is unable to combine purchases from other auctions or Heritage Rare Coin Galleries into one package for shipping purposes. Successful overseas Bidders shall provide written shipping instructions, including specified customs declarations, to the Auctioneer for any lots to be delivered outside of the United States.

37. All shipping charges will be borne by the successful Bidder. Any risk of loss during shipment will be borne by the buyer following Auctioneer's delivery to the designated common carrier.

38. Regardless of domestic or foreign shipment, risk of loss shall be borne by the buyer following Auctioneer's delivery to a shipper.

39. Any claims for undelivered packages must be made within 30 days of shipment by the auctioneer.

40. In the event an item is damaged either through handling or in transit, the Auctioneer's maximum liability shall be the amount of the successful bid including the Buyer's Premium.

CATALOGING:

41. The descriptions provided in any catalog are intended solely for the use of those Bidders who do not have the opportunity to view the lots prior to bidding.

42. Any description of the lots contained in this auction is for the sole purpose of identifying the items. Translations of foreign language documents are provided as a convenience to interested parties. Heritage makes no representation as to the accuracy of those translations and will not be held responsible for errors in bidding arising from inaccuracies in translation.

43. In the event of an attribution error, the Auctioneer may, at the Auctioneer's sole discretion, correct the error on the Internet, or, if discovered at a later date, to refund the buyer's money without further obligation. Under no circumstances shall the obligation of the Auctioneer to any Bidder be in excess of the purchase price for any lot in dispute.

WARRANTIES AND DISCLAIMERS:

44. NO WARRANTY, WHETHER EXPRESSED OR IMPLIED, IS MADE WITH RESPECT TO ANY DESCRIPTION CONTAINED IN THIS AUCTION. Any description of the items contained in this auction is for the sole purpose of identifying the items, and no description of items has been made part of the basis of the bargain or has created any express warranty that the goods would conform to any description made by the Auctioneer.

45. Auctioneer is selling only such right or title to the items being sold as Auctioneer may have by virtue of consignment agreements on the date of auction and disclaims any warranty of title to the coins.

46. Auctioneer disclaims any warranty of merchantability or fitness for any particular purposes.

47. Auctioneer disclaims all liability for damages, consequential or otherwise, arising out of or in connection with the sale of any property by Auctioneer to Bidder. No third party may rely on any benefit of these Terms and Conditions and any rights, if any, established hereunder are personal to the Bidder and may not be assigned. Any statement made by the Auctioneer is a statement of opinion and does not constitute a warranty or representation. Any employee of Auctioneer may not alter these Terms and Conditions, and, unless signed by a principal of Auctioneer, any alteration is null and void.

48A. **COINS, CURRENCY, COMICS AND SPORTSCARDS** – Coins sold referencing a third-party grading service ("Certified Coins") are sold "as is" without any express or implied warranty, except for a guarantee by Auctioneer that the Certified Coins are genuine. Certain warranties may be available from the grading services and the Bidder is referred to the following services for details of any such warranties: ANACS, P.O. Box 182141, Columbus, Ohio 43218-2141; Numismatic Guaranty Corporation (NGC), P.O. Box 4776, Sarasota, FL 34230; Professional Coin Grading Service (PCGS), PO Box 9458, Newport Beach, CA 92658 and ICG, 7901 East Belleview Ave., Suite 50, Englewood, CO 80111. Comic books sold referencing a third-party grading service ("Certified Comics") are sold "as is" without any express or implied warranty, except for a guarantee by Auctioneer that the Certified Comics are genuine. Certain warranties may be available from the grading services and the Bidder is referred to the following services for details of any such warranties: Comics Guaranty Corporation (CGC), P.O. Box 4738, Sarasota, FL 34230. Sportscards sold referencing a third-party grading service ("Certified Sportscards") are sold "as is" without any express or implied warranty, except for a guarantee by Auctioneer that the Certified Sportscards are genuine. Certain warranties may be available from the grading services and the Bidder is referred to the following services for details of any such warranties: Professional Sports Authenticator (PSA), P.O. Box 6180 Newport Beach, CA 92658; Sportscard Guaranty LLC (SGC) P.O. Box 6919 Parsippany, NJ 07054-6919; Global Authentication (GAI), P.O. Box 57042 Irvine, Ca. 92619; Beckett Grading Service (BGS), 15850 Dallas Parkway, Dallas TX 75248. Currency sold referencing a third-party grading service ("Certified Currency") are sold "as is" without any express or implied warranty, except for a guarantee by Auctioneer that the Certified Currency are genuine. Certain warranties may be available from the grading services and the Bidder is referred to the following services for details of any such warranties: Currency Grading & Authentication (CGA), PO Box 418, Three Bridges, NJ 08887.

48B. **MEMORABILIA** – Auctioneer does not warrant authenticity of a memorabilia lot (Autographs, Sports Collectibles, or Music, Entertainment, Political, Americana and/or Pop Culture memorabilia), when the lot is accompanied by a Certificate of Authenticity, or its equivalent, from an independent third party authentication provider. Bidder shall solely rely upon warranties of the authentication provider issuing the Certificate or opinion. For information as to such authentication provider's warranties the bidder is directed to: SCD Authentic, 4034 West National Ave., Milwaukee, WI 53215 (800) 345-3168; JO Sports, Inc., P.O. Box 607 Brookhaven, NY 11719 (631) 286-0970; PSA/DNA; 130 Brookshire Lane, Orwigsburg, Pa. 17961; Mike Gutierrez Autographs, 8150 Raintree Drive Suite A, Scottsdale, AZ. 85260; or as otherwise noted on the Certificate.

49. All non-certified coins and comics and currency are guaranteed genuine, but are not guaranteed as to grade, since grading is a matter of opinion. Grading is an art, not a science, and therefore the opinion rendered by the Auctioneer or any third party grading service may not agree with the opinion of others (including trained experts), and the same expert may not grade the same coin with the same grade at two different times. Auctioneer has graded the non-certified items, in the Auctioneer's opinion, to their current interpretation of the American Numismatic Association's standards as of the date the catalog was prepared. There is no guarantee or warranty implied or expressed that the grading standards utilized by the Auctioneer will meet the standards of ANACS, NGC, PCGS, ICG, CGC, CGA or any other grading service at any time in the future.

50. Auctioneer offers no opinion as to the validity of a grade assigned by any third-party grading service. Since we cannot examine C.G.A. encapsulated notes or Comics Guaranty Corporation (CGC) encapsulated comics, they are sold "as is" without our grading opinion, and may not be returned for any reason. Auctioneer shall not be liable for any patent or latent defect or controversy pertaining to or arising from any encapsulated collectible. In any such instance, purchaser's remedy, if any, shall be solely against the certification service certifying the collectible.

51. Due to changing grading standards over time and to possible mishandling of items by subsequent owners, the Auctioneer reserves the right to grade items differently than shown on certificates from any grading service that accompany the items. For the same reasons as stated above, the Auctioneer reserves the right to grade items differently than the grades shown in the catalog should such items be reconsigned to any future auction.

52. Although consensus grading is employed by most grading services, it should be noted as aforesaid that grading is not an exact science. In fact, it is entirely possible that if a lot was broken out of a plastic holder and was resubmitted to another grading service or even the same service, the lot could come back a different grade. Certification does not guarantee protection against the normal risks associated with potentially volatile markets.

53. The degree of liquidity for certified coins and collectibles will vary according to general market conditions and the particular lot involved. For some lots there may be no active market at all at certain points in time.

RELEASE:

54. In consideration of participation in the auction and the placing of a bid, a Bidder expressly releases Auctioneer, its affiliates, the Consignor, or Owner of the Lot from any and all claims, cause of action, chose of action, whether at law or equity or any arbitration or mediation rights existing under the rules of any professional society or affiliation based upon the assigned grade or a derivative theory, breach of warranty express or implied, representation or other matter set forth within these Terms and Conditions of Auction or otherwise, except as specifically declared herein; e.g., authenticity, typographical error, etc., and as to those matters, the rights and privileges conferred therein are strictly construed and is the exclusive remedy. Purchaser by non-compliance to its express terms of a granted remedy, shall waive any claim against Auctioneer.

DISPUTE RESOLUTION AND ARBITRATION PROVISION:

55. By placing a bid or otherwise participating in the auction, such person or entity accepts these Terms and Conditions of Auction, and specifically agrees to the alternative dispute resolution provided herein. Arbitration replaces the right to go to court, including the right to a jury trial.

56A. COINS & CURRENCY; If any disputes arise regarding payment, authenticity, grading or any other matter pertaining to the auction, the Bidder or a participant in the auction and/or the Auctioneer agree that the dispute shall be submitted, if otherwise mutually unresolved, to binding arbitration in accordance with the rules of the Professional Numismatists Guild (PNG) or American Arbitration Association (A.A.A.). The A.A.A. arbitration shall be conducted under the provisions of the Federal Arbitration Act with locale in Dallas, Texas. If an election is not made within ten (10) days of an unresolved dispute, Auctioneer may elect either PNG or A.A.A. Arbitration. Any claim made by a Bidder has to be presented within one (1) year or it is barred. An award granted in arbitration is enforceable in any court. No claims of any kind (except for reasons of authenticity) can be considered after the settlements have been made with the consignors. Any dispute after the settlement date is strictly between the Bidder and consignor without involvement or responsibility of the Auctioneer.

56B. ALL OTHER AUCTIONS; If any dispute arises regarding payment, authenticity, grading, description, provenance or any other material pertaining to the auction, the Bidder or the participant in the auction and/or the Auctioneer agree that the dispute shall be submitted, if otherwise mutually unresolved, to binding arbitration in accordance with the commercial rules of the American Arbitration Association (A.A.A.). The A.A.A. arbitration shall be conducted under the provisions of the Federal Arbitration Act with locale in Dallas, Texas. The prevailing party may be awarded his reasonable attorney's fees and costs. An arbitrator's award is enforceable in any court of competent jurisdiction. Any claim made by a Bidder has to be presented within one (1) year or it is barred. Any claim as to provenance or authenticity must be first transmitted to Auctioneer by credible and definitive evidence and there is no assurance such presentment that Auctioneer will validate the claim. Authentication is not an exact science and other contrary opinions may not be recognized by Auctioneer. Auctioneer in no event shall be responsible for consequential and incidental damages and the value of any item is determined by its high bid, which is Auctioneer's maximum liability. Provenance and authenticity are not guaranteed by the Auctioneer, but rather are guaranteed by the consignor. Any action or claim shall include the consignor with Auctioneer acting as interpleador or nominal party. While every effort is made to determine provenance and authenticity, it is up to the Bidder to arrive at that conclusion prior to bidding.

57. In consideration of his participation in or application for the auction, a person or entity (whether the successful Bidder, a Bidder, a purchaser and/or other Auction participant or registrant) agrees, that all disputes in any way relating to, arising under, connected with, or incidental to these Terms and Conditions and his purchases or default in payment thereof shall be arbitrated pursuant to the arbitration provision. In the event that any matter including actions to compel arbitration, construe the agreement, actions in aid or arbitration or otherwise needs to be litigated, such litigation shall be exclusively in the Courts of the State of Texas, in Dallas County, Texas, and if necessary the corresponding appellate courts. The successful Bidder, purchaser, or Auction participant also expressly submits himself to the personal jurisdiction of the State of Texas.

MISCELLANEOUS:

58. Agreements between Bidders and consignors to effectuate a non-sale of an item at auction, inhibit bidding on a consigned item to enter into a private sale agreement for an item, or to utilize the Auctioneer's auction to obtain sales for non-selling consigned items subsequent to the auction are strictly prohibited. If a subsequent sale of a previously consigned item occurs in violation of this provision, Auctioneer reserves the right to charge Bidder the applicable Buyer's Premium and consignor a Seller's Commission as determined for each auction venue and by the terms of the seller's agreement.

59. Acceptance of these terms and conditions qualifies Bidder as a Heritage customer who has consented to be contacted by Heritage in the future. In conformity with "do-not-call" regulations promulgated by the Federal or State regulatory agencies, participation by the Bidder is affirmative consent to being contacted at the phone number shown in his application and this consent shall remain in effect until it is revoked in writing. Heritage may from time to time contact Bidder concerning sale, purchase and auction opportunities available through Heritage and its affiliates and subsidiaries.

60. Storage of purchased coins: Purchasers are advised that certain types of plastic may react with the coin's metal and may cause damage to the coins. Caution should be used to avoid storage of coins in materials that are not inert.

STATE NOTICES:

61. Notice as to an Auction Sale in California. Auctioneer has in compliance with Title 2.95 of the California Civil Code as amended October 11, 1993 Sec. 1812.600, posted with the California Secretary of State its bonds for it and its employees and the auction is being conducted in compliance with Sec. 2338 of the Commercial Code and Sec. 535 of the Penal Code.

Rev. 7/12/05

CHOOSE YOUR BIDDING METHOD

Mail Bidding at Auction

Mail bidding at auction is fun and easy and only requires a few simple steps.

1. Look through the catalog, and determine the lots of interest.
2. Research their market value by checking price lists and other price guidelines.
3. Fill out your bid sheet, entering your maximum bid on each lot using your price research and your desire to own the lot.
4. Verify your bids!
5. Mail Early. Preference is given to the first bids received in case of a tie. When bidding by mail, you frequently purchase items at less than your maximum bid.

Bidding is opened at the published increment above the second highest mail or Internet bid; we act on your behalf as the highest mail bidder. If bidding proceeds, we act as your agent, bidding in increments over the previous bid. This process is continued until you are awarded the lot or you are outbid.

An example of this procedure: You submit a bid of $100, and the second highest mail bid is at $50. Bidding starts at $51 on your behalf. If no other bids are placed, you purchase the lot for $51. If other bids are placed, we bid for you in the posted increments until we reach your maximum bid of $100. If bidding passes your maximum: if you are bidding through the Internet, we will contact you by e-mail; if you bid by mail, we take no other action. Bidding continues until the final bidder wins.

Mail Bidding Instructions

1. **Name, Address, City, State, Zip**
   Your address is needed to mail your purchases. We need your telephone number to communicate any problems or changes that may affect your bids.

2. **References**
   If you have not established credit with us from previous auctions, you must send a 25% deposit, or list dealers with whom you have credit established.

3. **Lot Numbers and Bids**
   List all lots you desire to purchase. On the reverse are additional columns; you may also use another sheet. Under "Amount" enter the maximum you would pay for that lot (whole dollar amounts only). We will purchase the lot(s) for you as much below your bids as possible.

4. **Total Bid Sheet**
   Add up all bids and list that total in the appropriate box.

5. **Sign Your Bid Sheet**
   By signing the bid sheet, you have agreed to abide by the Terms of Sale listed in the auction catalog.

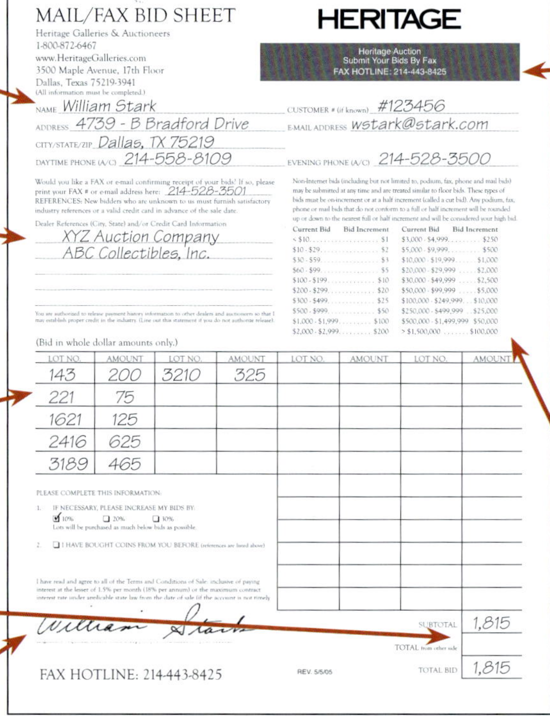

MAIL/FAX BID SHEET

HERITAGE

Heritage Galleries & Auctioneers
1-800-872-6467
www.HeritageGalleries.com
3500 Maple Avenue, 17th Floor
Dallas, Texas 75219-3941
(All information must be completed.)

Heritage Auction
Submit Your Bids By Fax
FAX HOTLINE: 214-443-8425

NAME William Stark — CUSTOMER # (if known) #123456
ADDRESS 4739 - B Bradford Drive — E-MAIL ADDRESS wstark@stark.com
CITY/STATE/ZIP Dallas, TX 75219
DAYTIME PHONE (A/C) 214-558-8109 — EVENING PHONE (A/C) 214-528-3500

Would you like a FAX or e-mail confirming receipt of your bids? If so, please print your FAX # or e-mail address here: 214-528-3501
REFERENCES: New bidders who are unknown to us must furnish satisfactory industry references or a valid credit card in advance of the sale date.

Dealer References (City, State) and/or Credit Card Information
XYZ Auction Company
ABC Collectibles, Inc.

You are authorized to release payment history information to other dealers and auctioneers so that I may establish proper credit in the industry. (Line out this statement if you do not authorize release).

Non-Internet bids (including but not limited to, podium, fax, phone and mail bids) may be submitted at any time and are treated similar to floor bids. These types of bids must be on-increment or at a half increment (called a cut bid). Any podium, fax, phone or mail bids that do not conform to a full or half increment will be rounded up or down to the nearest full or half increment and will be considered your high bid.

Current Bid	Bid Increment	Current Bid	Bid Increment
< $10	$1	$3,000 - $4,999	$250
$10 - $29	$2	$5,000 - $9,999	$500
$30 - $59	$3	$10,000 - $19,999	$1,000
$60 - $99	$5	$20,000 - $29,999	$2,000
$100 - $199	$10	$30,000 - $49,999	$2,500
$200 - $299	$20	$50,000 - $99,999	$5,000
$300 - $499	$25	$100,000 - $249,999	$10,000
$500 - $999	$50	$250,000 - $499,999	$25,000
$1,000 - $1,999	$100	$500,000 - $1,499,999	$50,000
$2,000 - $2,999	$200	> $1,500,000	$100,000

(Bid in whole dollar amounts only.)

LOT NO.	AMOUNT	LOT NO.	AMOUNT	LOT NO.	AMOUNT	LOT NO.	AMOUNT
143	200	3210	325				
221	75						
1621	125						
2416	625						
3189	465						

PLEASE COMPLETE THIS INFORMATION:
1. IF NECESSARY, PLEASE INCREASE MY BIDS BY: ☑ 10% ☐ 20% ☐ 30%
   Lots will be purchased as much below bids as possible.
2. ☐ I HAVE BOUGHT COINS FROM YOU BEFORE (references are listed above)

I have read and agree to all of the Terms and Conditions of Sale: inclusive of paying interest at the lesser of 1.5% per month (18% per annum) or the maximum contract interest rate under applicable state law from the date of sale (if the account is not timely

William Stark

SUBTOTAL 1,815
TOTAL from other side
TOTAL BID 1,815

FAX HOTLINE: 214-443-8425 — REV. 5/5/05

The official prices realized list that accompanies our auction catalogs is reserved for bidders and consignors only. We are happy to mail one to others upon receipt of $1.00. Written requests should be directed to Customer Service.

6. **Fax Your Bid Sheet**
   When time is short submit a Mail Bid Sheet on our exclusive Fax Hotline. There's no faster method to get your bids to us *instantly*. Simply use the **Heritage Fax Hotline number: 214-443-8425**.

When you send us your original after faxing, mark it "Confirmation of Fax" (preferably in red!)

7. **Bidding Increments**
   To facilitate bidding, please consult the following chart. Bids will be accepted on the increments or on the half increments.

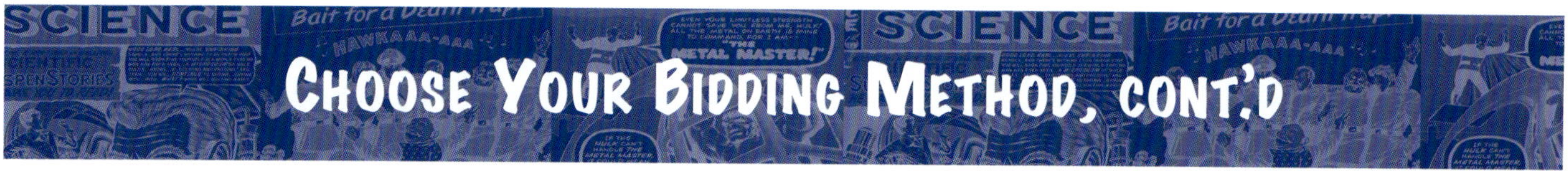

Choose Your Bidding Method, cont'd

Interactive Internet™ Bidding

You can now bid with Heritage's exclusive *Interactive Internet*™ program, available only at our web site: HeritageGalleries.com. It's fun, and it's easy!

1. Register on-line at: **HeritageGalleries.com**
2. View the full-color photography of every single lot in the on-line catalog!
3. Construct your own personal catalog for preview.
4. View the current opening bids on lots you want; review the prices realized archive.
5. Bid and receive immediate notification if you are the top bidder; later, if someone else bids higher, you will be notified automatically by e-mail.
6. The *Interactive Internet*™ program opens the lot on the floor at one increment over the second highest bid. As the high bidder, your secret maximum bid will compete for you during the floor auction, and it is possible that you may be outbid on the floor after Internet bidding closes. Bid early, as the earliest bird wins in the event of a tie bid.
7. After the sale, you will be notified of your success. It's that easy!

Interactive Internet™ Bidding Instructions

1. Log Onto Website

Log onto **HeritageGalleries.com** and chose the portal you're interested in (i.e., coins, comics, movie posters, fine arts, etc.).

2. Search for Lots

Search or browse for the lot you are interested in. You can do this from the home page, from the Auctions home page, or from the home page for the particular auction in which you wish to participate.

3. Select Lots

Click on the link or the photo icon for the lot you want to bid on.

4. Enter Bid

At the top of the page, next to a small picture of the item, is a box outlining the current bid. Enter the amount of your secret maximum bid in the textbox next to "Secret Maximum Bid." The secret maximum bid is the maximum amount you are willing to pay for the item you are bidding on (for more information about bidding and bid increments, please see the section labeled "Bidding Increments" elsewhere in this catalog). Click on the button marked "Place Absentee Bid." A new area on the same page will open up for you to enter your username (or e-mail address) and password. Enter these, then click "Place Absentee Bid" again.

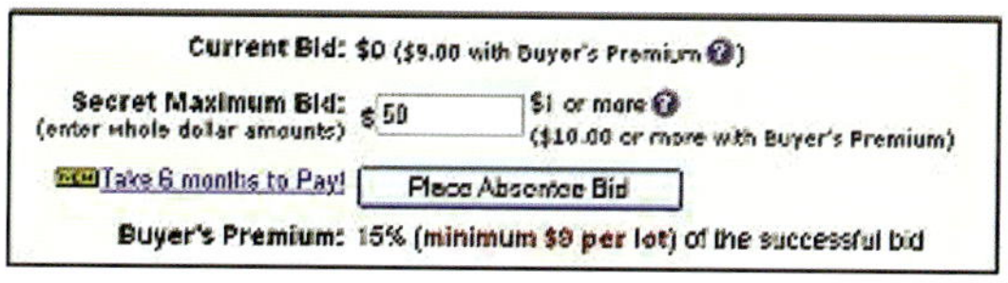

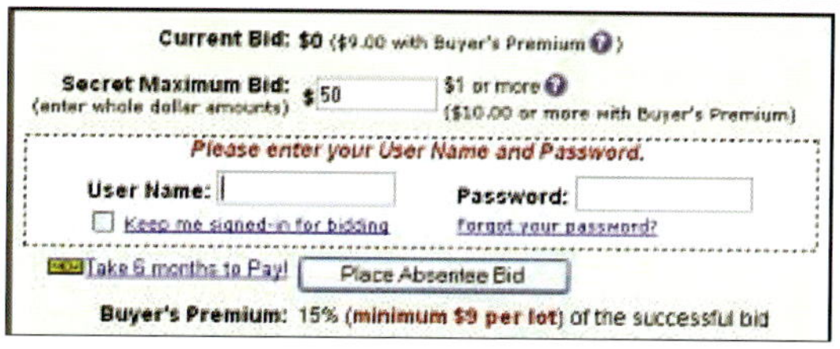

5. Confirm Absentee Bid

You are taken to a page labeled, "Please Confirm Your Bid." This page shows you the name of the item you're bidding on, the current bid, and the maximum bid. When you are satisfied that all the information shown is correct, click on the button labeled, "Confirm Bid."

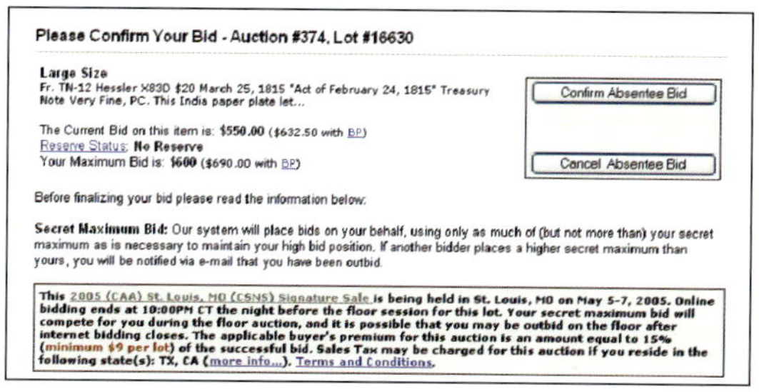

6. Bidding Status Notification

One of two pages is now displayed.

a. If your bid is the current high bid, you will be notified and given additional information as to what might happen to affect your high bidder status over the course of the remainder of the auction. You will also receive a Bid Confirmation notice via email.

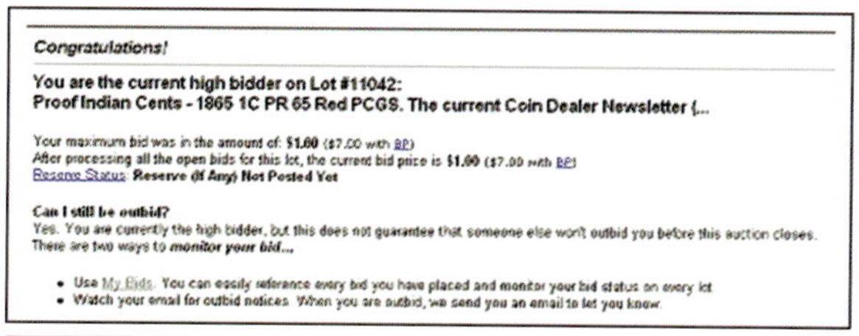

b. If your bid is not the current high bid, you will be notified of that fact and given the opportunity to increase your bid.

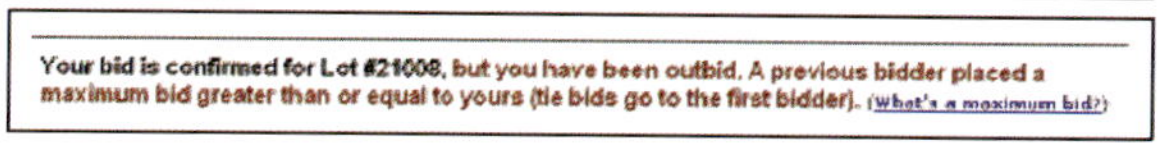

Current Bid: $0 ($9.00 with Buyer's Premium)
Secret Maximum Bid: (enter whole dollar amounts) $ 50 — $1 or more ($10.00 or more with Buyer's Premium)
Take 6 months to Pay! [Place Absentee Bid]
Buyer's Premium: 15% (minimum $9 per lot) of the successful bid

Current Bid: $0 ($9.00 with Buyer's Premium)
Secret Maximum Bid: (enter whole dollar amounts) $ 50 — $1 or more ($10.00 or more with Buyer's Premium)
Please enter your User Name and Password.
User Name: **Password:**
Keep me signed-in for bidding — Forgot your password?
Take 6 months to Pay! [Place Absentee Bid]
Buyer's Premium: 15% (minimum $9 per lot) of the successful bid

Please Confirm Your Bid - Auction #374, Lot #16630

Large Size
Fr. TN-12 Hessler X83D $20 March 25, 1815 "Act of February 24, 1815" Treasury Note Very Fine, PC. This India paper plate let...

The Current Bid on this item is: **$550.00** ($632.50 with BP)
Reserve Status: **No Reserve**
Your Maximum Bid is: **$600** ($690.00 with BP)

[Confirm Absentee Bid] [Cancel Absentee Bid]

Before finalizing your bid please read the information below:

Secret Maximum Bid: Our system will place bids on your behalf, using only as much of (but not more than) your secret maximum as is necessary to maintain your high bid position. If another bidder places a higher secret maximum than yours, you will be notified via e-mail that you have been outbid.

This 2005 (CAA) St. Louis, MO (CSNS) Signature Sale is being held in St. Louis, MO on May 5-7, 2005. Online bidding ends at 10:00PM CT the night before the floor session for this lot. Your secret maximum bid will compete for you during the floor auction, and it is possible that you may be outbid on the floor after internet bidding closes. The applicable buyer's premium for this auction is an amount equal to 15% (minimum $9 per lot) of the successful bid. Sales Tax may be charged for this auction if you reside in the following state(s): TX, CA (more info...). Terms and Conditions.

Congratulations!

You are the current high bidder on Lot #11042:
Proof Indian Cents - 1865 1C PR 65 Red PCGS. The current Coin Dealer Newsletter (...

Your maximum bid was in the amount of: **$1.00** ($7.00 with BP)
After processing all the open bids for this lot, the current bid price is **$1.00** ($7.00 with BP)
Reserve Status: **Reserve (If Any) Not Posted Yet**

Can I still be outbid?
Yes. You are currently the high bidder, but this does not guarantee that someone else won't outbid you before this auction closes. There are two ways to ***monitor your bid...***

- Use My Bids. You can easily reference every bid you have placed and monitor your bid status on every lot
- Watch your email for outbid notices. When you are outbid, we send you an email to let you know.

Your bid is confirmed for Lot #21008, but you have been outbid. A previous bidder placed a maximum bid greater than or equal to yours (tie bids go to the first bidder). (What's a maximum bid?)

INDEX

SESSION ONE

MARVEL SILVER AGE to MODERN AGE COMICS 1
DC SILVER AGE to MODERN AGE 21
OTHER SILVER AGE to MODERN AGE 36

SESSION TWO

TIMELY/ATLAS 41
DC GOLDEN AGE 50
OTHER GOLDEN AGE COMICS 97

SESSION THREE

THE AVIATOR COLLECTION 142
EC 153
UNDERGROUNDS 165
THE RANDOM HOUSE ARCHIVES
Comics 166
Original Art 167
Other Cool Stuff 176
OTHER BOUND COMICS VOLUMES 178
MAGAZINES 184
MEMORABILIA 189
BIG LITTLE BOOKS 191
BOOKS 193

SESSION FOUR

ORIGINAL ART 197
ANIMATION ART 277

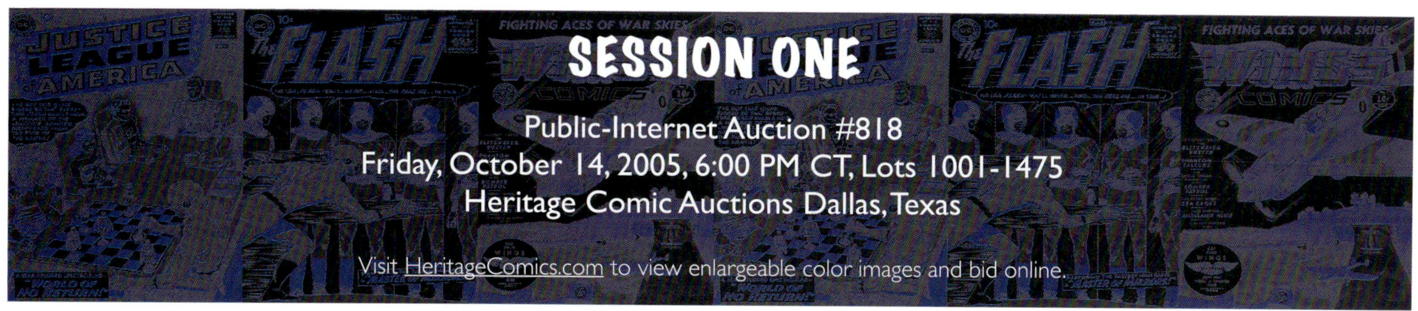

MARVEL SILVER AGE TO MODERN AGE

1001 Amazing Fantasy #15 (Marvel, 1962) CGC Apparent VG/FN 5.0 Slight (A) Off-white pages. This historic issue boasts the origin and first appearances of Spider-Man, Uncle Ben, and Aunt May. The cover is by Jack Kirby, and the interior art by Steve Ditko. CGC notes: "Restoration includes: small amount of color touch on cover. (Top and right edge trimmed.)" Overstreet 2005 GD 2.0 value = $1,400; VG 4.0 value = $2,800; FN 6.0 value = $4,200.

1002 The Amazing Spider-Man #1 (Marvel, 1963) CGC Apparent FN 6.0 Slight (A) Off-white pages. Spider-Man's origin is retold in the first issue of his first regular series. Other "firsts" include the first Fantastic Four crossover and the first appearances of John Jameson, J. Jonah Jameson, and the Chameleon. Steve Ditko cover (Jack Kirby layout) and art. CGC notes: "Restoration includes: small amount of color touch on cover." Overstreet 2005 GD 2.0 value = $875; VG 4.0 value = $1,750; FN 6.0 value = $2,625.

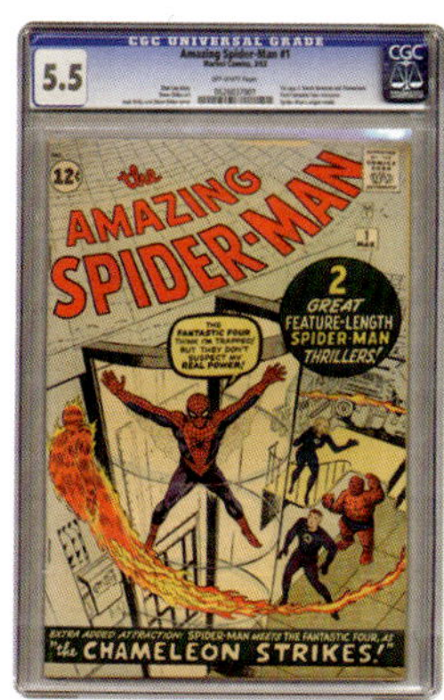

1003 The Amazing Spider-Man #1 (Marvel, 1963) CGC FN- 5.5 Off-white pages. Spider-Man makes his second appearance, this time in the premiere issue of his own title (with a special appearance by the Fantastic Four). Jack Kirby and Steve Ditko worked on this cover together, and Ditko handled all of the interior artwork. Two of Spidey's longtime foils — the Chameleon and J. Jonah Jameson — make their first appearances here. Overstreet 2005 FN 6.0 value = $2,625. CGC census 9/05: 43 in 5.5, 182 higher.

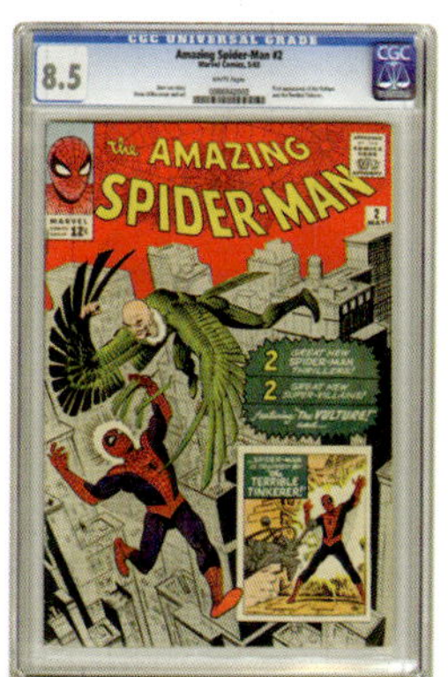

1004 The Amazing Spider-Man #2 (Marvel, 1963) CGC VF+ 8.5 White pages. Spidey's second issue features the first appearances of the Vulture and the Terrible Tinkerer. Steve Ditko provided the cover and interior art. Overstreet 2005 VF 8.0 value = $2,790; VF/NM 9.0 value = $4,745. CGC census 9/05: 12 in 8.5, 26 higher.

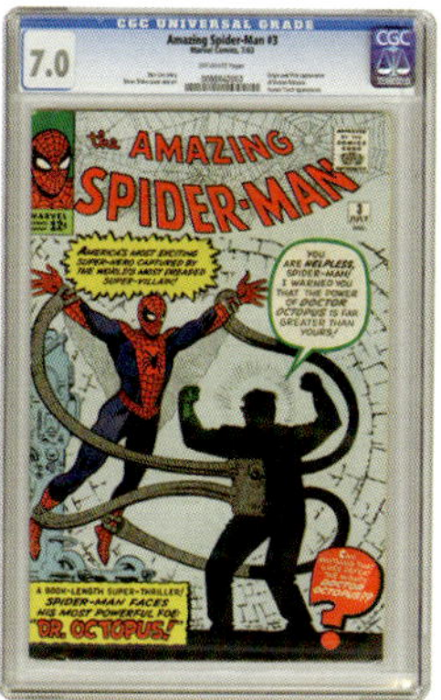

1005 The Amazing Spider-Man #3 (Marvel, 1963) CGC FN/VF 7.0 Off-white pages. Doctor Octopus, arguably Spidey's second-greatest arch-nemesis, makes his debut in the classic issue, which is also the title's first full-length story. The Human Torch makes an appearance. Steve Ditko provides the cover, interior art, and pin-up page. Overstreet 2005 FN 6.0 value = $672; VF 8.0 value = $1,960. CGC census 9/05: 33 in 7.0, 93 higher.

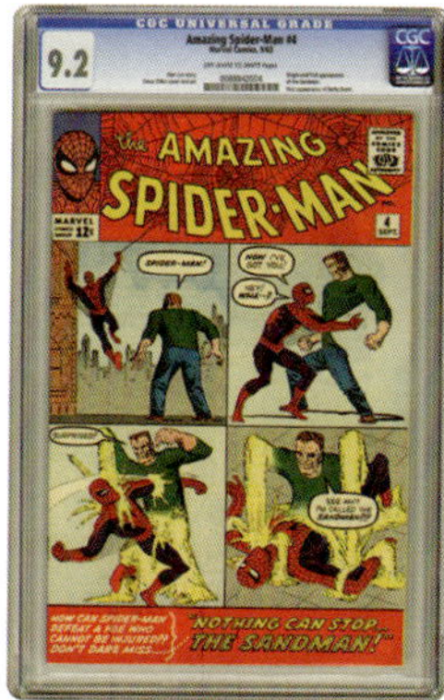

1006 The Amazing Spider-Man #4 (Marvel, 1963) CGC NM- 9.2 Off-white to white pages. The sinister Sandman makes his first appearance here, as do supporting love interests Betty Brant and Liz Allen. Steve Ditko cover and art. Overstreet 2005 NM- 9.2 value = $3,800. CGC census 9/05: 13 in 9.2, 8 higher.

1007 The Amazing Spider-Man #6 (Marvel, 1963) CGC VF/NM 9.0 Cream to off-white pages. Dr. Curt Connors appeared in the movie "Spider-Man 2," so does that mean that the Lizard will be appearing in the next sequel? That speculation is reason enough to consider going after this issue, the first appearance of the Lizard, aka Dr. Connors. The issue has a story by Stan Lee and art by Steve Ditko. Overstreet 2005 VF/NM 9.0 value = $2,162; NM- 9.2 value = $3,000. CGC census 8/05: 23 in 9.0, 28 higher.

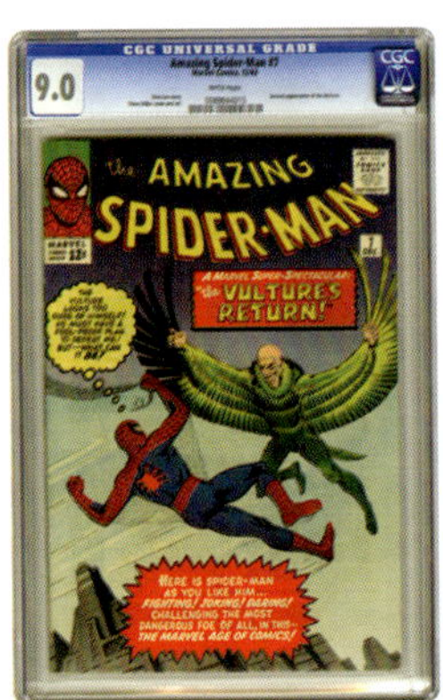

1008 The Amazing Spider-Man #7 (Marvel, 1963) CGC VF/NM 9.0 White pages. This issue marked the second appearance of the Vulture, as well as the title's first monthly issue. Steve Ditko cover and art. Overstreet 2005 VF/NM 9.0 value = $1,375; NM- 9.2 value = $1,900. CGC census 9/05: 1 in 9.0, none higher.

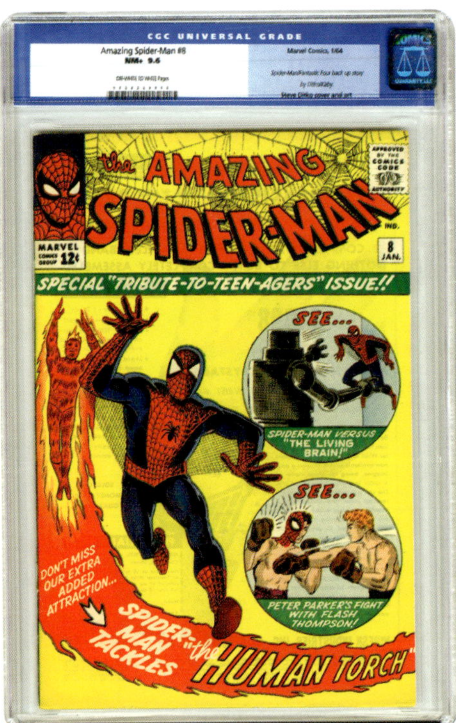

1009 The Amazing Spider-Man #8 (Marvel, 1964) CGC NM+ 9.6 Off-white to white pages. We give you Flash Thompson: football star, adored by the girls, Big Man On Campus. Didn'tcha *hate* him? The moment fans had waited eight issues for came in #8, as Peter Parker actually had a boxing match with the big bully (unfortunately, a robot attack interrupted matters). The art on the lead story is by Steve Ditko, who also drew the cover. The backup feature guest-stars the Fantastic Four, and offers an artistic team we really love: Ditko inking Jack Kirby! Surprisingly, Spidey shows amorous inclinations in the tale — he tries to hit on the Human Torch's girlfriend Dorrie, and even makes a web-valentine for the Invisible Girl (who was still single at the time, we hasten to add). Overstreet 2005 NM- 9.2 value = $1,900. CGC census 9/05: 7 in 9.6, 2 higher.

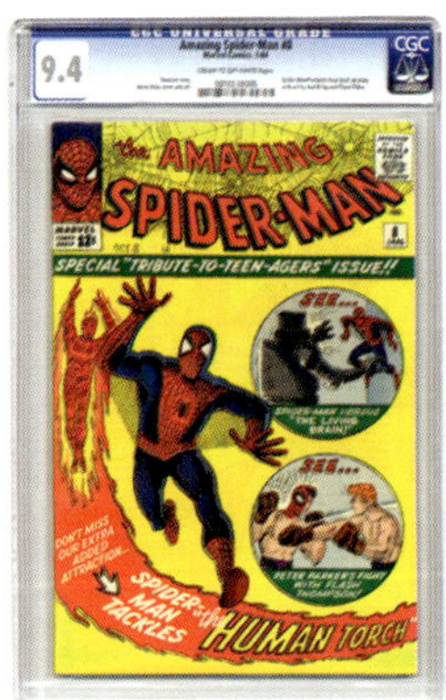

1010 The Amazing Spider-Man #8 (Marvel, 1964) CGC NM 9.4 Cream to off-white pages. Peter Parker gets a chance to box Flash Thompson, but alas, a robot interrupts the fisticuffs. Steve Ditko provided cover and interior art for the issue. There's also a backup feature that guest-stars the Fantastic Four and has art by Jack Kirby and Ditko. Overstreet 2005 NM-9.2 value = $1,900. CGC census 7/05: 19 in 9.4, 9 higher.

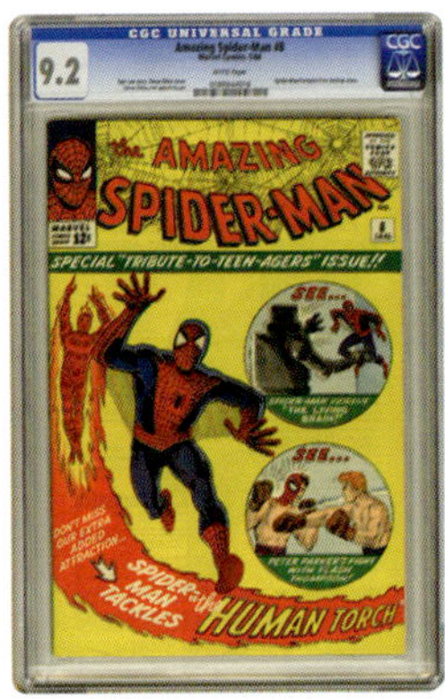

1011 The Amazing Spider-Man #8 (Marvel, 1964) CGC NM- 9.2 White pages. This action-packed "Tribute to Teenagers" issue features Spider-Man's battle with the Living Brain, and also a Jack Kirby/Steve Ditko Fantastic Four backup story. Also, there's a boxing match between Peter Parker and Flash Thompson. Cover by Steve Ditko. Overstreet 2005 NM- 9.2 value = $1,900. CGC census 9/05: 19 in 9.2, 28 higher.

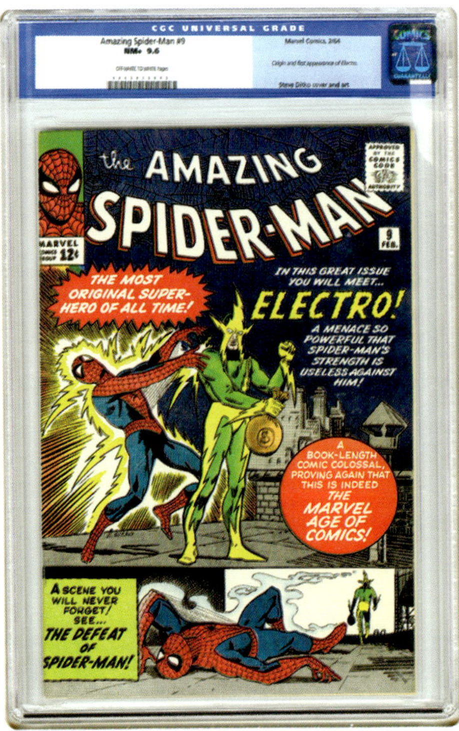

1012 The Amazing Spider-Man #9 (Marvel, 1964) CGC NM+ 9.6 Off-white to white pages. We get to see the best copies of this title month in and month out, but we had never gotten our hands on this issue in 9.6 condition before! It's the origin and first appearance of Electro, with a story by Stan Lee and cover and interior art by Steve Ditko. Note that the CGC slab has a two-inch crack at the top rear. Overstreet 2005 NM- 9.2 value = $2,025. CGC census 9/05: 6 in 9.6, none higher.

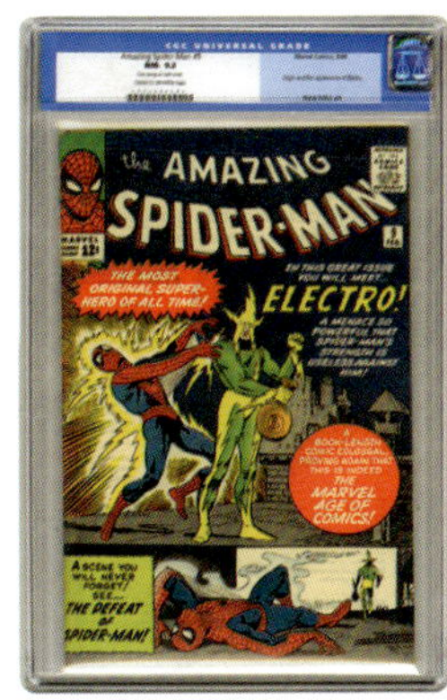

1013 The Amazing Spider-Man #9 (Marvel, 1964) CGC NM- 9.2 Cream to off-white pages. Electro makes his first appearance in this issue, which also relates his origin story. And Spider-Man not only has to tangle with Electro, he has other problems as well: in a shocking turn of events, Aunt May falls ill. The cover and interior art are by Steve Ditko. CGC notes, "date stamp on back cover." Overstreet 2005 NM- 9.2 value = $2,025. CGC census 8/05: 22 in 9.2, 15 higher.

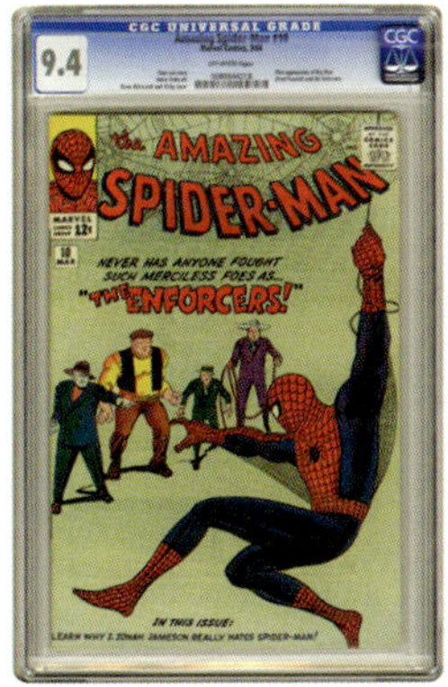

1014 The Amazing Spider-Man #10 (Marvel, 1964) CGC NM 9.4 Off-white pages. Big Man and the Enforcers make their first appearance. Steve Ditko cover and art. Overstreet 2005 NM- 9.2 value = $1,900. CGC census 9/05: 14 in 9.4, 8 higher.

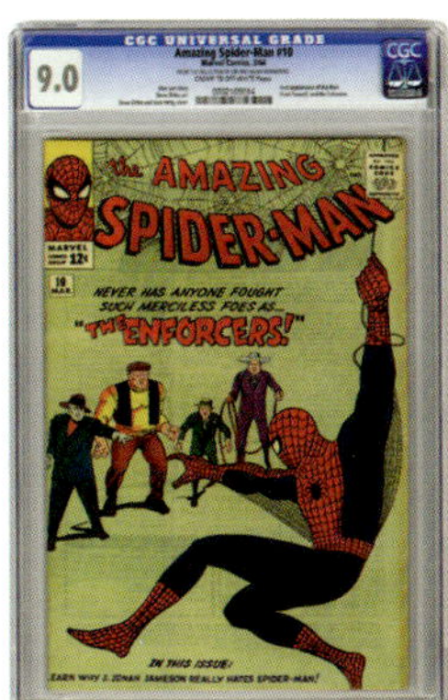

1015 The Amazing Spider-Man #10 (Marvel, 1964) CGC VF/NM 9.0 Cream to off-white pages. Big Man and the Enforcers (the Ox, Fancy Dan, and Montana) made their first appearance here to give Spider-Man a hard time. Steve Ditko drew the issue as well as the cover (the latter with a Jack Kirby assist). Overstreet 2005 VF/NM 9.0 value = $1,375; NM- 9.2 value = $1,900. CGC census 8/05: 26 in 9.0, 38 higher. *From the collection of Joe and Nadia Mannarino.*

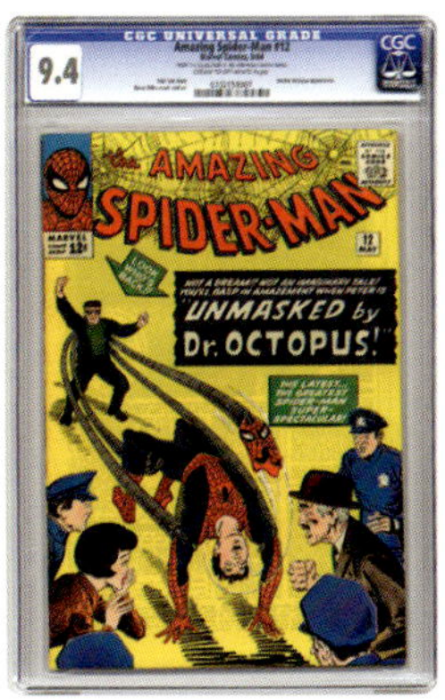

1016 The Amazing Spider-Man #12 (Marvel, 1964) CGC NM 9.4 Cream to off-white pages. Doctor Octopus returns for his third appearance, written by Stan Lee and drawn by Steve Ditko. And Spider-Man really does get unmasked — it's not a dream, hoax, or imaginary story! Overstreet 2005 NM- 9.2 value = $1,275. CGC census 8/05: 11 in 9.4, 3 higher. *From the collection of Joe and Nadia Mannarino.*

1017 The Amazing Spider-Man #12 (Marvel, 1964) CGC FN/VF 7.0 Off-white pages. Spidey versus Doctor Octopus in this, Doc Ock's third appearance. Steve Ditko cover and art. Overstreet 2005 FN 6.0 value = $201; VF 8.0 value = $570. CGC census 9/05: 18 in 7.0, 127 higher.

1018 The Amazing Spider-Man #13 (Marvel, 1964) CGC VF/NM 9.0 White pages. Steve Ditko drew the first appearance of Mysterio in this issue. Overstreet 2005 VF/NM 9.0 value = $1,266; NM- 9.2 value = $1,750. CGC census 9/05: 24 in 9.0, 29 higher.

1019 The Amazing Spider-Man #18 (Marvel, 1964) CGC NM+ 9.6 Off-white pages. This issue sees the first appearance of Ned Leeds who, Overstreet notes, "later becomes the Hobgoblin." Granted, that transformation of 20 years later is of earth-shaking import to many a Modern Age Marvelite, but back in '64 Ned posed an even greater threat: he was making time with Betty Brant! As far as the superhero action is concerned, the Sandman puts Spidey on the run; has our red-and-blue hero turned yellow? Pretty much, until a pep talk from Aunt May has him ready to kick some sandy butt. Also of note: great Steve Ditko art and a Fantastic Four cameo. Overstreet 2005 NM- 9.2 value = $800. CGC census 9/05: 8 in 9.6, 1 higher.

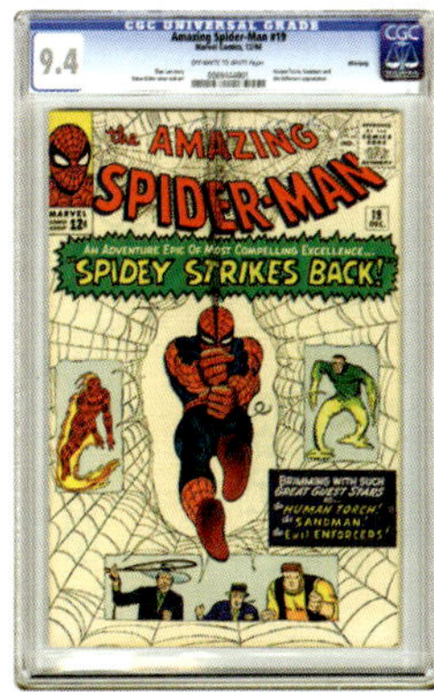

1020 The Amazing Spider-Man #19 Winnipeg pedigree (Marvel, 1964) CGC NM 9.4 Off-white to white pages. Sandman and the Enforcers have the Human Torch in their clutches, and in typically villainous fashion, decide they'll use him as bait to settle an old score with Spidey! The issue's cover and interior art are by Steve Ditko. Overstreet 2005 NM- 9.2 value = $650. CGC census 9/05: 17 in 9.4, 11 higher.

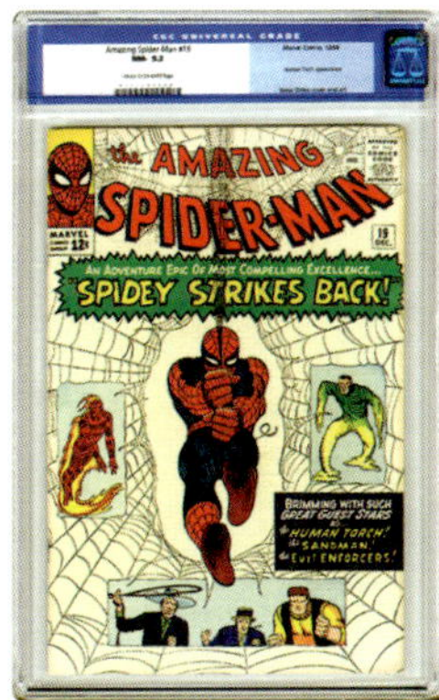

1021 The Amazing Spider-Man #19 (Marvel, 1964) CGC NM- 9.2 Cream to off-white pages. Spidey's sometime ally the Human Torch guest-stars in this issue, with the Sandman and the Enforcers seeing to bad-guy duties. The issue's cover and art are by Steve Ditko. Overstreet 2005 NM- 9.2 value = $650. CGC census 9/05: 24 in 9.2, 28 higher.

1022 The Amazing Spider-Man #61 Oakland pedigree (Marvel, 1968) CGC NM 9.4 Off-white pages. This pedigreed copy is a real keeper — sharp and glossy. John Romita Sr. provides the cover and story art. Overstreet 2005 NM- 9.2 value = $120. CGC census 9/05: 27 in 9.4, 9 higher.

1023 The Amazing Spider-Man #85 (Marvel, 1970) CGC NM 9.4 Cream to off-white pages. The Schemer is revealed to be the Kingpin's son. John Romita Sr. cover. Interior art by John Buscema (layouts), Romita (finished pencils), and Jim Mooney (inks). Overstreet 2005 NM- 9.2 value = $100. CGC census 8/05: 19 in 9.4, 14 higher. *From the collection of Joe and Nadia Mannarino.*

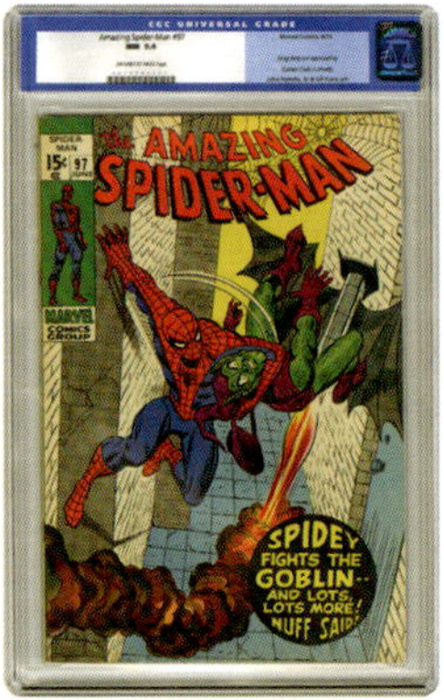

1024 The Amazing Spider-Man #97 (Marvel, 1971) CGC NM 9.4 Off-white to white pages. Green Goblin cover/story appearance. This is one of three famous Anti-Drug issues that Marvel chose to publish without the Comics Code Authority approval or seal. John Romita Sr. drew the cover; Gil Kane handled the interior art. Overstreet 2005 NM- 9.2 value = $145. CGC census 9/05: 65 in 9.4, 32 higher.

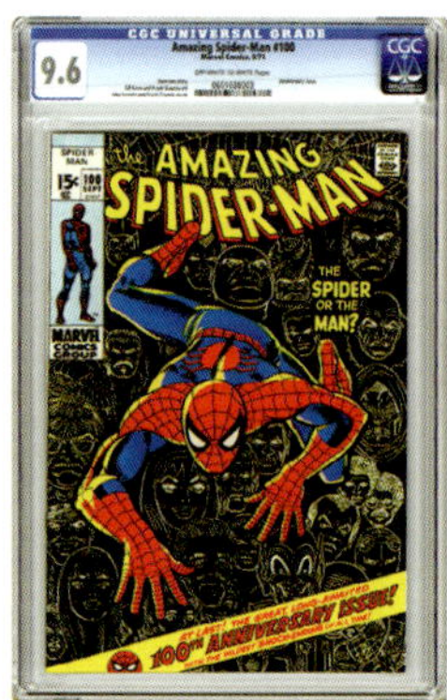

1025 The Amazing Spider-Man #100 (Marvel, 1971) CGC NM+ 9.6 Off-white to white pages. Anniversary issue, with cameos by the Green Goblin, Vulture, Lizard, Doctor Octopus, and the Kingpin (all in a dream sequence). John Romita Sr. cover, Gil Kane interior art. Overstreet 2005 NM- 9.2 value = $250. CGC census 9/05: 59 in 9.6, 10 higher.

1026 The Amazing Spider-Man #100 (Marvel, 1971) CGC NM+ 9.6 White pages. Not a dream! Not a ho..., well, actually this issue ***does*** have Peter Parker's dream, in which he meets Green Goblin, Vulture, Lizard, Doctor Octopus, and the Kingpin all appearing. But then he wakes up and has six arms, and ***that*** part's not a dream, not a hoax, ***not*** an imaginary story! The issue has a John Romita Sr. cover and Gil Kane interior art. Overstreet 2005 NM- 9.2 value = $250. CGC census 9/05: 59 in 9.6, 10 higher.

1027 The Amazing Spider-Man #100 (Marvel, 1971) CGC NM+ 9.6 White pages. Things tended to go from bad to worse for Peter Parker, and it was no different in his 100th outing here. When he tries drinking a potion to rid himself of his spider-powers, he has a horrible dream with the Green Goblin, Vulture, Lizard, Doctor Octopus, and the Kingpin all appearing. And when he wakes up, the reality is worse — he has six arms! The issue has a John Romita Sr. cover and Gil Kane interior art. Overstreet 2005 NM- 9.2 value = $250. CGC census 9/05: 59 in 9.6, 10 higher.

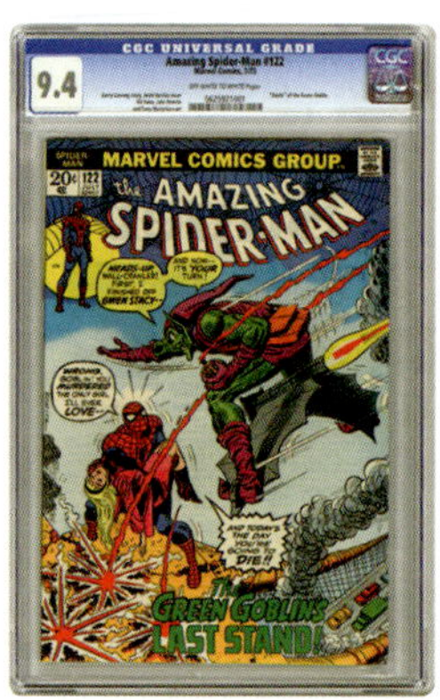

1028 The Amazing Spider-Man #122 (Marvel, 1973) CGC NM 9.4 Off-white to white pages. The death of the Green Goblin at the climax of this issue marked the end of Spider-Man's most memorable villain, in a scene that was copied almost exactly in the first "Spider-Man" movie. The comic is the work of creators at the top of their games, with Gerry Conway turning in perhaps his best writing ever, Gil Kane penciling the high-impact tale, and John Romita Sr. inking Kane's pencils as well as drawing the cover. Overstreet 2005 NM- 9.2 value = $290. CGC census 9/05: 111 in 9.4, 34 higher.

1029 The Amazing Spider-Man #156 Pacific Coast pedigree (Marvel, 1976) CGC NM- 9.2 Off-white pages. The wedding of Betty Brant and Ned Leeds. John Romita Sr. cover. Ross Andru art. Overstreet 2005 NM- 9.2 value = $28. CGC census 9/05: 18 in 9.2, 36 higher.

1030 The Amazing Spider-Man #160 Pacific Coast pedigree (Marvel, 1976) CGC NM 9.4 Cream to off-white pages. Gil Kane and John Romita Sr. cover. Ross Andru art. Last appearance of the Spider-Mobile. Overstreet 2005 NM- 9.2 value = $28. CGC census 9/05: 21 in 9.4, 20 higher.

1031 The Amazing Spider-Man #162 Pacific Coast pedigree (Marvel, 1976) CGC NM 9.4 Off-white pages. Nightcrawler and the Punisher appear. First full appearance of Jigsaw (first time face is shown). Ross Andru and John Romita Sr. cover. Interior art by Andru. Overstreet 2005 NM- 9.2 value = $35. CGC census 9/05: 40 in 9.4, 39 higher.

1032 The Amazing Spider-Man #168 Pacific Coast pedigree (Marvel, 1977) CGC NM 9.4 Off-white pages. Ross Andru art. Ed Hannigan cover. Overstreet 2005 NM- 9.2 value = $22. CGC census 9/05: 41 in 9.4, 82 higher.

1033 The Amazing Spider-Man #173 Pacific Coast pedigree (Marvel, 1977) CGC NM 9.4 Off-white pages. Ross Andru and John Romita Sr. cover. Interior art by Andru. Overstreet 2005 NM- 9.2 value = $22. CGC census 9/05: 14 in 9.4, 14 higher.

1034 The Amazing Spider-Man Annual #11 Pacific Coast pedigree (Marvel, 1977) CGC NM 9.4 Off-white pages. Gil Kane cover. Don Perlin art. Backup feature with John Romita Jr. art. Overstreet 2005 NM- 9.2 value = $15. CGC census 9/05: 9 in 9.4, 9 higher.

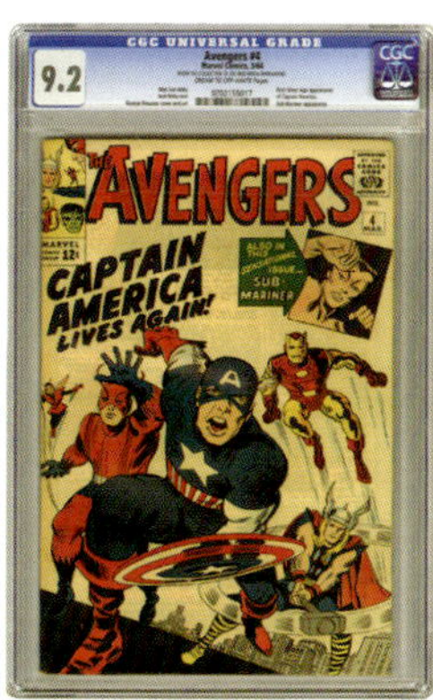

1035 The Avengers #4 (Marvel, 1964) CGC NM- 9.2 Cream to off-white pages. Here's a big one for you, boys and girls — the first Silver Age appearance of Captain America, who joins the Avengers in this issue. Sub-Mariner makes an important appearance — he's the one who tosses the big chunk of ice containing Cap into the water, where Cap's frozen body eventually gets rescued and revived by the Avengers. Jack Kirby drew the historic cover and story art, as well he should have; after all, "King" Kirby was, along with Joe Simon, the co-creator of the character! Overstreet 2005 NM- 9.2 value = $2,500. CGC census 6/05: 22 in 9.2, 17 higher. *From the collection of Joe and Nadia Mannarino.*

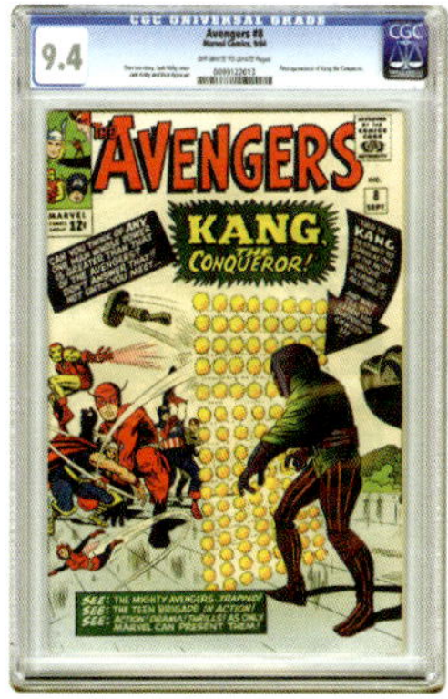

1036 The Avengers #8 (Marvel, 1964) CGC NM 9.4 Off-white to white pages. This issue's got the first appearance of Kang the Conqueror... sort of. He did appear in **Fantastic Four** #19, but he was calling himself Rama-Tut back then! The fact that they're one and the same is the surprise alluded to in the cover blurb. At any rate, Kang would reappear to menace the Avengers many times over the years; since his specialty was time travel, you never knew *when* he was going to show up (groan)! The cover and interior art are by Jack Kirby. Overstreet 2005 NM- 9.2 value = $350. CGC census 9/05: 8 in 9.4, 3 higher.

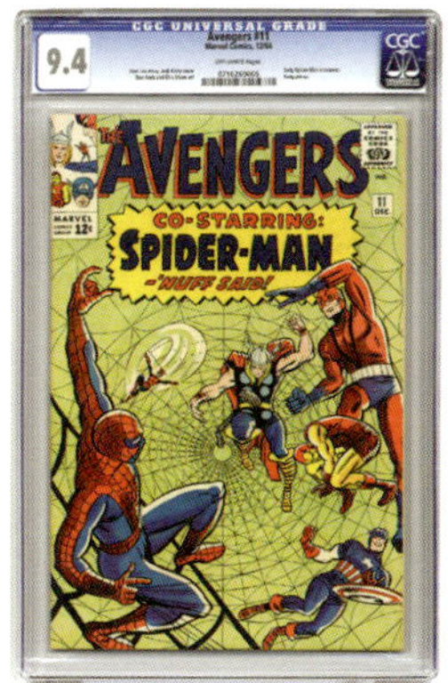

1037 The Avengers #11 (Marvel, 1964) CGC NM 9.4 Off-white pages. Kang sics a "Spider-Man robot" on the Avengers, but the time-traveling baddie doesn't reckon with the real Spider-Man crashing the party! It's one of the Webhead's earlier crossover appearances. The issue has a Jack Kirby cover and Don Heck interior art. Overstreet 2005 NM- 9.2 value = $400. CGC census 8/05: 13 9.4, 7 higher.

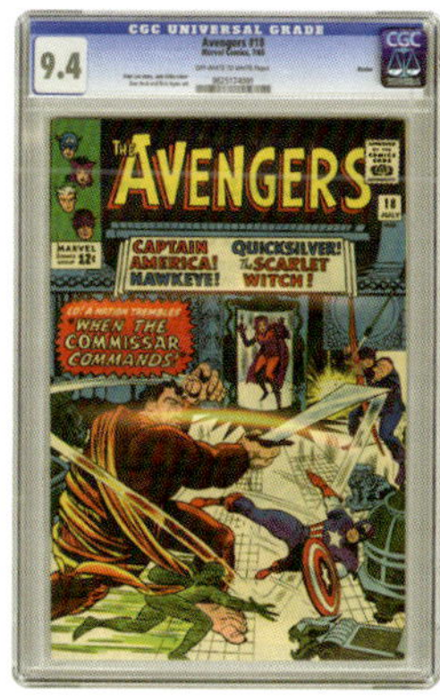

1038 The Avengers #18 Boston pedigree (Marvel, 1965) CGC NM 9.4 Off-white to white pages. This pedigreed copy looks newsstand fresh. Jack Kirby drew the cover, while Don Heck and Dick Ayers did the story art honors. Overstreet 2005 NM- 9.2 value = $170. CGC census 9/05: 15 in 9.4, 3 higher.

1039 The Avengers #24 (Marvel, 1966) CGC NM 9.4 Off-white to white pages. Jack Kirby cover. Don Heck and Dick Ayers art. Overstreet 2005 NM- 9.2 value = $85. CGC census 9/05: 27 in 9.4, 28 higher.

1040 The Avengers #37 (Marvel, 1967) CGC NM+ 9.6 White pages. Black Widow appearance. Gil Kane cover. Don Heck art. Overstreet 2005 NM- 9.2 value = $65. CGC census 8/05: 3 in 9.6, 1 higher.

1041 The Avengers #53 (Marvel, 1968) CGC NM 9.4 Off-white to white pages. The Avengers battle the X-Men. Magneto and the Toad also appear. John Buscema cover and art. Overstreet 2005 NM- 9.2 value = $85. CGC census 9/05: 17 in 9.4, 20 higher.

1042 The Avengers #64 (Marvel, 1969) CGC NM+ 9.6 Off-white pages. The "death" of Barney Barton is featured. Gene Colan art. Overstreet 2005 NM- 9.2 value = $55. CGC census 9/05: 7 in 9.6, 1 higher.

1043 The Avengers #100 Pacific Coast pedigree (Marvel, 1972) CGC NM 9.4 Off-white to white pages. Featuring everyone who had been an Avenger to that point. Barry Smith cover and art. Overstreet 2005 NM- 9.2 value = $110. CGC census 9/05: 27 in 9.4, 18 higher.

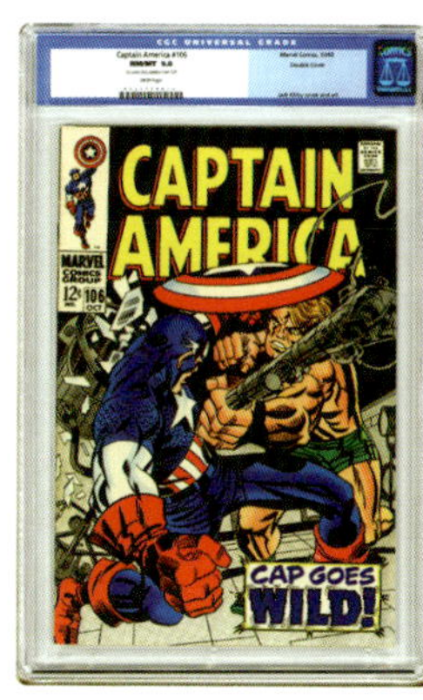

1044 Captain America #106 Double Cover (Marvel, 1968) CGC NM/MT 9.8 White pages. While thrilling to Jack Kirby's cover, you may be asking, "Who's the blond fellow trading punches with Cap, anyway?" Well, it's a Steve Rogers LMD, and as any S.H.I.E.L.D. fan can tell you, that stands for Life Model Decoy. CGC notes, "1st cover 9.6, interior cover 9.8." Overstreet 2005 NM- 9.2 value = $65. CGC census 9/05: 2 in 9.8, none higher.

1045 Captain America #109 Boston pedigree (Marvel, 1969) CGC NM 9.4 White pages. Cap's origin is retold. Jack Kirby cover and art. Comes with the Boston certificate of authenticity. Overstreet 2005 NM- 9.2 value = $100. CGC census 8/05: 49 in 9.4, 33 higher.

1046 Captain America #110 (Marvel, 1969) CGC NM+ 9.6 White pages. The Hulk has never been more fearsome than on this awesome Jim Steranko cover! And what's Bucky Barnes doing there? Well, it's actually Marvel's favorite teen Rick Jones, who becomes Captain America's partner in the issue. And to top it all off, there's the first appearance of Madame Hydra (later known as Viper). The interior art is by Steranko as well. Overstreet 2005 NM- 9.2 value = $130. CGC census 8/05: 28 in 9.6, 5 higher.

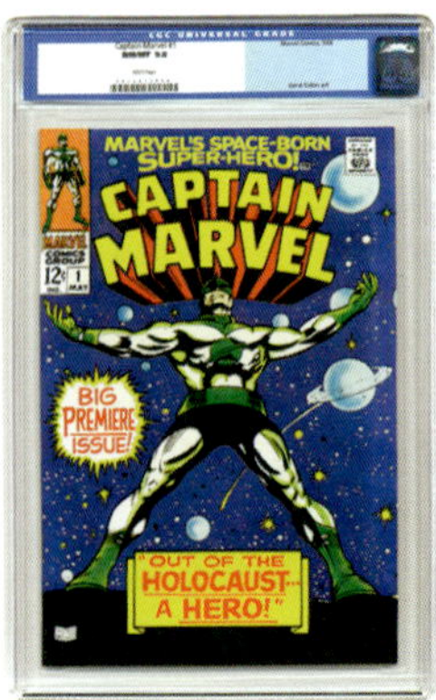

1047 Captain Marvel #1 (Marvel, 1968) CGC NM/MT 9.8 White pages. Mar-Vell of the Kree, Marvel's space-born super-hero, got his own title after debuting in **Marvel Super-Heroes**. Gene Colan provided the art-work. Overstreet 2005 NM- 9.2 value = $130. CGC census 9/05: 15 in 9.8, none higher.

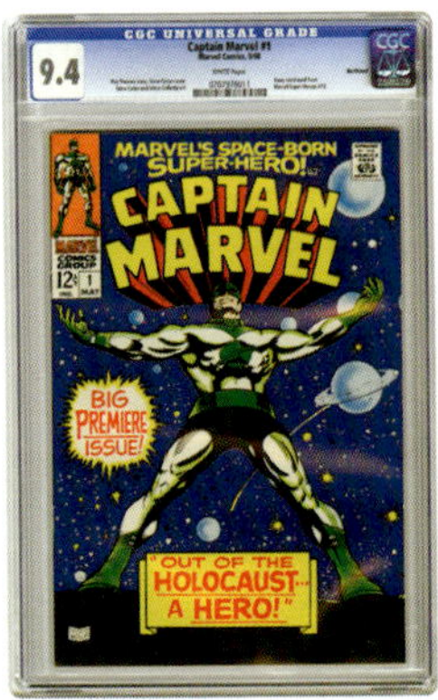

1048 Captain Marvel #1 Northland pedigree (Marvel, 1968) CGC NM 9.4 White pages. There have been a number of Captain Marvels in comics over the years, but this character was the first *Marvel* Captain Marvel! And this was only his third appearance after debuting in **Marvel Super-Heroes** #12 and 13. The cover and interior art are by Gene Colan. Comes with the Northland certificate of authenticity. Overstreet 2005 NM- 9.2 value = $130. CGC census 8/05: 68 in 9.4, 48 higher.

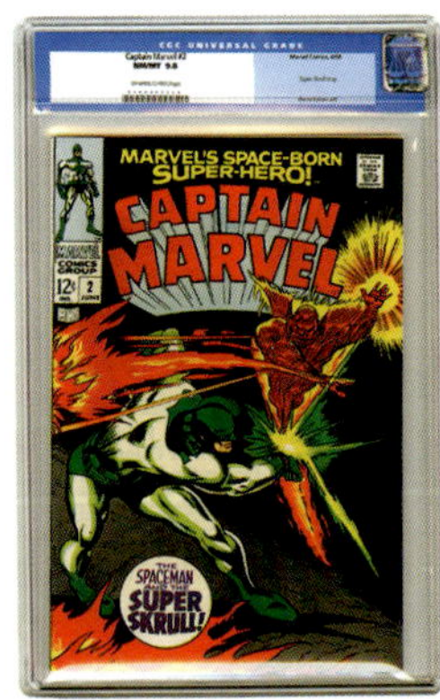

1049 Captain Marvel #2 (Marvel, 1968) CGC NM/MT 9.8 Off-white to white pages. Super spaceman Mar-Vell battles the Super-Skrull (looking just a bit like the Human Torch) in this issue. This gem of a copy, displaying tons of cover gloss and rich, deep colors against a black back-ground, looks like the real winner here. Gene Colan provides the cover and interior art. Overstreet 2005 NM- 9.2 value = $50. CGC census 8/05: 17 in 9.8, none higher.

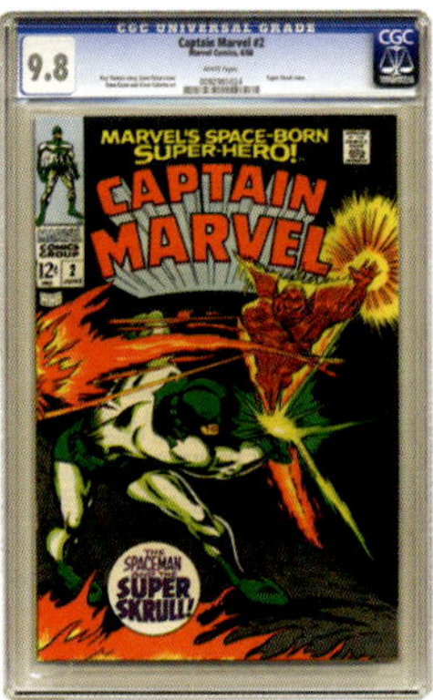

1050 Captain Marvel #2 (Marvel, 1968) CGC NM/MT 9.8 White pages. Gene Colan wasn't known for drawing cosmic adventures, but when called upon to deliver outer-space action, he handled it with aplomb. As this was just the title's second issue, Mar-Vell was still resplendent in his original costume! Overstreet 2005 NM- 9.2 value = $50. CGC census 9/05: 17 in 9.8, none higher.

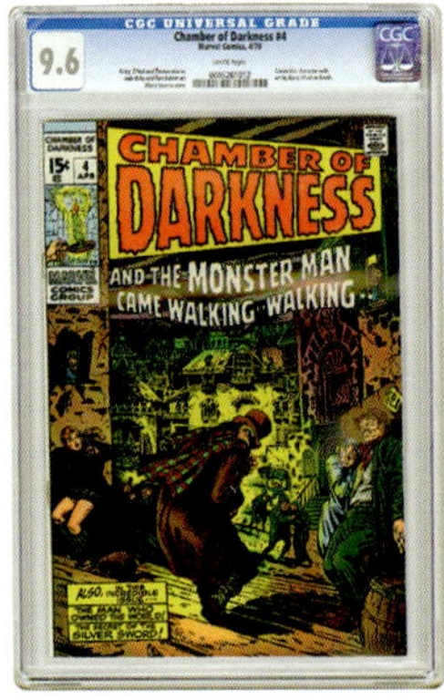

1051 Chamber of Darkness #4 (Marvel, 1970) CGC NM+ 9.6 White pages. This is by far the most valuable issue of this series' run thanks to a story featuring the Conan-like character Starr the Slayer, with a story by Roy Thomas and art by Barry Smith (i.e., the team that brought you **Conan The Barbarian** shortly thereafter). The rest of the book isn't exactly chopped liver — Jack Kirby drew one of the stories, with Tom Sutton rendering the third tale. The cover's by Marie Severin. Overstreet 2005 NM- 9.2 value = $90. CGC census 8/05: 5 in 9.6, 1 higher.

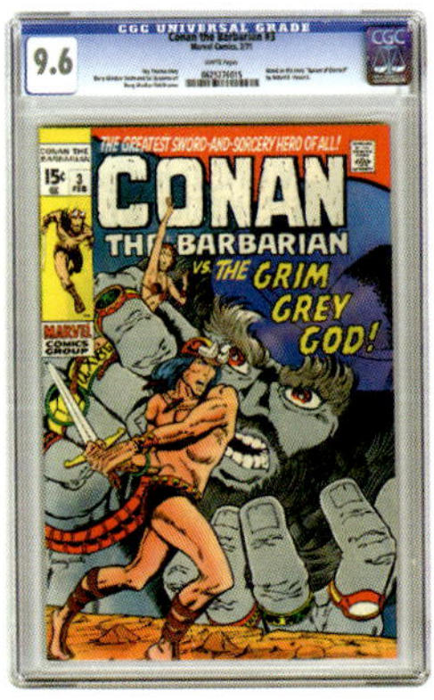

1052 Conan the Barbarian #3 (Marvel, 1971) CGC NM+ 9.6 White pages. Barry Smith, back in his pre-"Windsor" days, drew what many comic fans still think of as the definitive Conan. Here's a great early issue, adapted from the story "Spears of Clontarf" by Robert E. Howard. This issue experienced low distribution in some areas according to Overstreet. Overstreet 2005 NM- 9.2 value = $150. CGC census 8/05: 9 in 9.6, 1 higher.

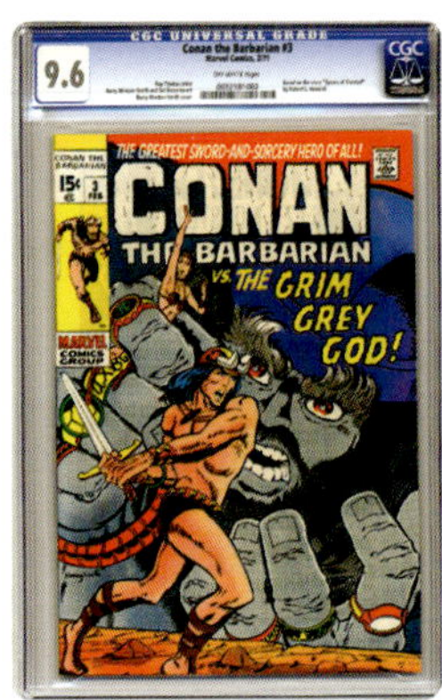

1053 Conan the Barbarian #3 (Marvel, 1971) CGC NM+ 9.6 Off-white pages. Barry Smith cover and interior art (with Sal Buscema). The Roy Thomas-scribed story was based on Robert E. Howard's "Spears of Clontarf." This issue experienced low distribution in some areas, according to Overstreet. Overstreet 2005 NM- 9.2 value = $150. CGC census 8/05: 9 in 9.6, 1 higher.

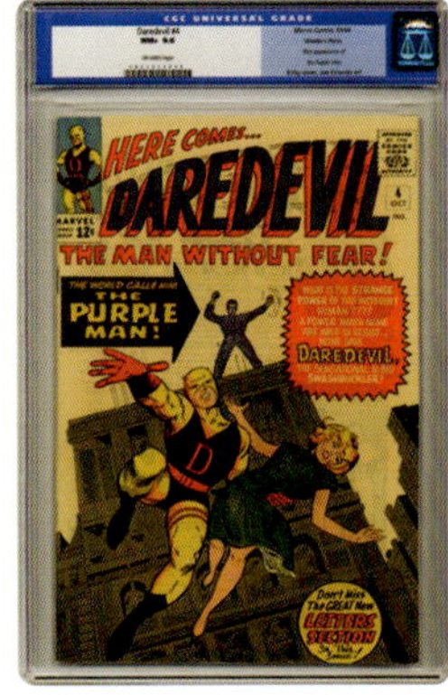

1054 Daredevil #4 Western Penn pedigree (Marvel, 1964) CGC NM+ 9.6 Off-white pages. To date, CGC hasn't certi-fied a higher grade for #4. This issue has the origin and first appearance of the Purple Man, the villain nobody seems to be able to resist! Jack Kirby only drew Daredevil a couple of times, so enjoy his take on DD (and Karen Page) on this issue's cover. The interior art is by Joe Orlando. Overstreet 2005 NM- 9.2 value = $575. CGC census 9/05: 5 in 9.6, none higher.

1055 Daredevil #6 (Marvel, 1965) CGC NM- 9.2 Cream to off-white pages. Daredevil, the "Man Without Fear", meets Mr. Fear himself! This was the origin and first appearance of Mr. Fear, aka Zoltan Drago (which is a pretty cool name in itself). Wally Wood provides excellent cover and interior art. Overstreet 2005 NM- 9.2 value = $275. CGC census 8/05: 17 in 9.2, 17 higher.

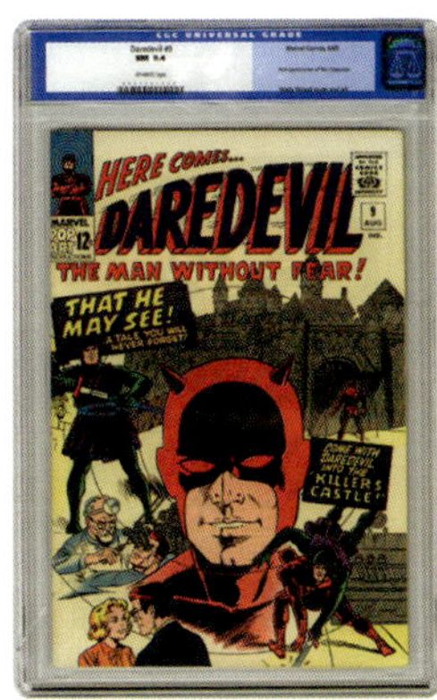

1056 Daredevil #9 (Marvel, 1965) CGC NM 9.4 Off-white pages. "That He May See" is this issue's epic feature. A Wally Wood cover is complemented by Wood and Bob Powell interior art. Overstreet 2005 NM- 9.2 value = $230. CGC census 9/05: 30 in 9.4, 15 higher.

1057 Daredevil #36 (Marvel, 1968) CGC NM+ 9.6 White pages. Daredevil battles the Trapster (formerly Paste-Pot Pete). Doctor Doom, the Human Torch, the Invisible Girl, and Mr. Fantastic appear. Gene Colan cover and art. Overstreet 2005 NM- 9.2 value = $60. CGC census 8/05: 4 in 9.6, 2 higher.

1058 Daredevil #40 (Marvel, 1968) CGC NM+ 9.6 Off-white pages. Daredevil takes on Ape Man, Bird Man, and Cat Man. Gene Colan cover and art. Overstreet 2005 NM- 9.2 value = $60. CGC census 6/05: 9 in 9.6, 1 higher.

1059 Daredevil #45 Curator pedigree (Marvel, 1968) CGC NM+ 9.6 White pages. Partial photo cover. Gene Colan interior art. Overstreet 2005 NM- 9.2 value = $45. CGC census 8/05: 12 in 9.6, 3 higher.

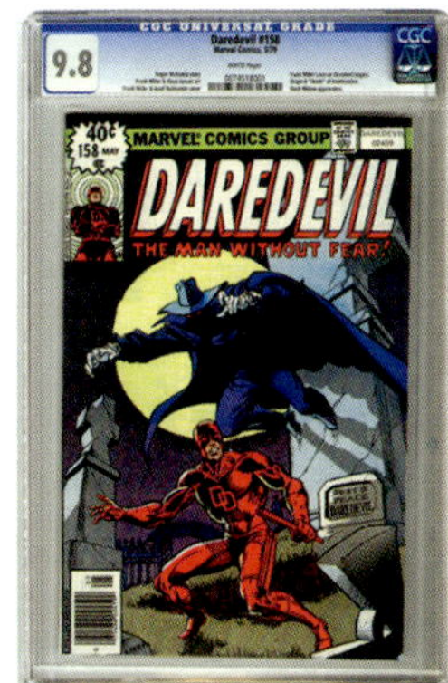

1060 Daredevil #158 (Marvel, 1979) CGC NM/MT 9.8 White pages. Here's the beginning of Frank Miller's legendary run as artist of this title. This issue has the origin of Deathstalker (it turns out he's the Exterminator from way back in issue #39) as well as the death of the character. The book also has a Black Widow appearance. Oh yeah, and it's in NM/MT condition! Even Daredevil could see that this copy is well worth going after. Overstreet 2005 NM- 9.2 value = $90. CGC census 6/05: 12 in 9.8, none higher.

1061 Daredevil Annual #1 (Marvel, 1967) CGC NM/MT 9.8 White pages. A square bound book with a white cover in this condition is quite a prize! DD's first annual has the Man Without Fear taking on Electro and his Emissaries of Evil. The cover and interior art are by Gene Colan. There's also a host of pinups and other backup features, including one showing a story conference between Colan and Stan Lee. Overstreet 2005 NM- 9.2 value = $70. CGC census 8/05: 1 in 9.8, none higher.

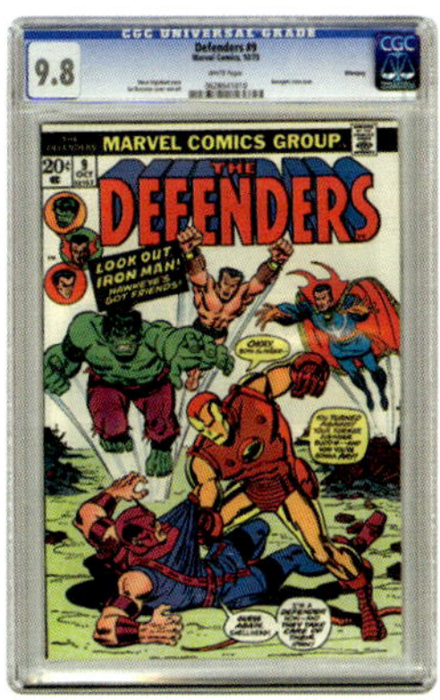

1062 The Defenders #9 Winnipeg pedigree (Marvel, 1973) CGC NM/MT 9.8 White pages. Large-scale comic crossovers may be commonplace today, but in 1973, it was unheard-of to have a crossover spanning eight issues of two different titles! Yet that's exactly what writer Steve Englehart and editor Roy Thomas pulled off to produce the "Avengers/Defenders War." This issue has the third installment of the storyline, with art by Sal Buscema. A side note for you No-Prize types: Buscema's cover pictures the Hulk and the Sub-Mariner, who don't appear in the issue! No copy of this Bronze Age winner has been graded higher by CGC to date. Overstreet 2005 NM- 9.2 value = $30. CGC census 9/05: 3 in 9.8, none higher.

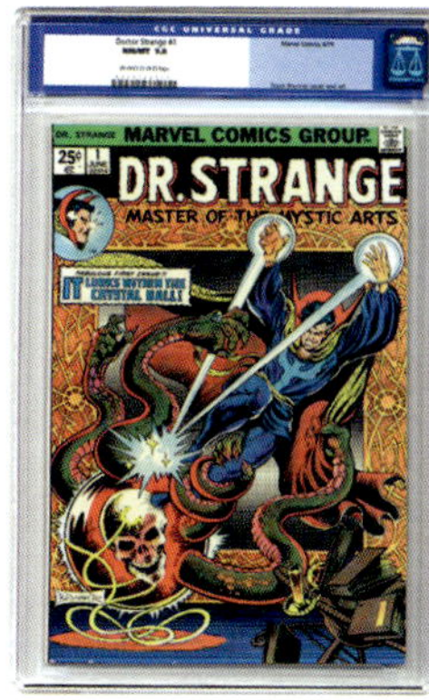

1063 Doctor Strange #1 (Marvel, 1974) CGC NM/MT 9.8 Off-white to white pages. Some five years after the demise of his previous series, the Master of the Mystic Arts got another shot at his own title. Frank Brunner drew the cover and the story, and is even credited as co-plotter along with ace writer Steve Englehart. Overstreet 2005 NM- 9.2 value = $80. CGC census 9/05: 11 in 9.8, none higher.

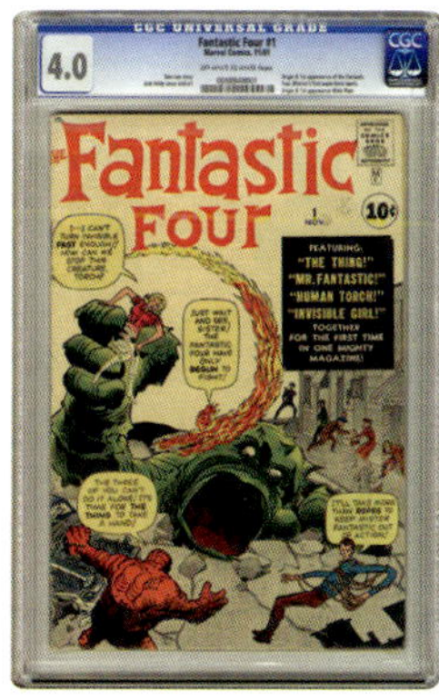

1064 Fantastic Four #1 (Marvel, 1961) CGC VG 4.0 Off-white to white pages. The book that ushered in the Marvel Age of Comics, with the first appearance of the Fantastic Four and their long-standing foe the Mole Man, all lovingly rendered in cover and story art by Jack Kirby. Overstreet 2005 VG 4.0 value = $1,750. CGC census 9/05: 39 in 4.0, 114 higher.

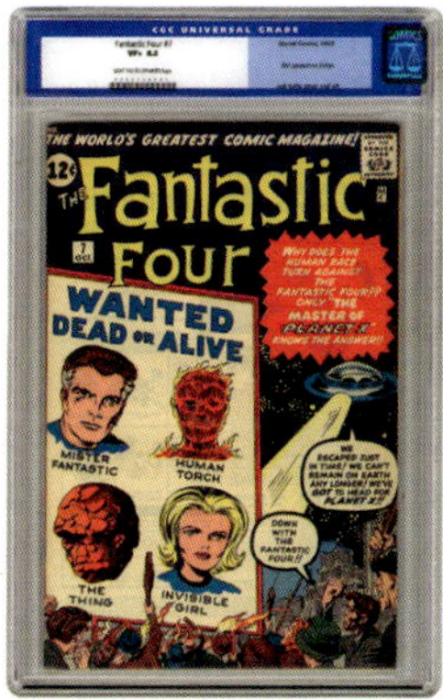

1065 Fantastic Four #7 (Marvel, 1962) CGC VF+ 8.5 Light tan to off-white pages. Though the Marvel Age of Comics had already started up, this Jack Kirby cover hearkens back to the days of Atlas monster mags! The story is in that vein as well, courtesy of Kirby and Stan Lee. The fate of a planet hangs in the balance, natch! Overstreet 2005 VF 8.0 value = $876; VF/NM 9.0 value = $1,413. CGC census 8/05: 9 in 8.5, 14 higher.

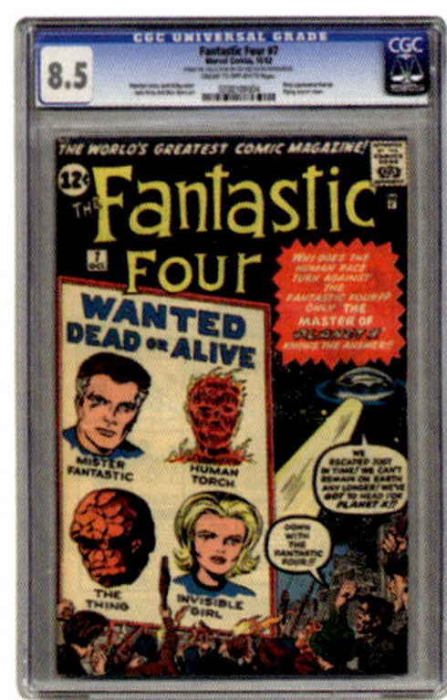

1066 Fantastic Four #7 (Marvel, 1962) CGC VF+ 8.5 Cream to off-white pages. This cover has the feel of one of those Atlas monster or mystery mags, but why shouldn't it, with Jack Kirby drawing it and Stan Lee providing the words? In this Stan-and-Jack tale, the fate of a planet hangs in the balance. Overstreet 2005 VF 8.0 value = $876; VF/NM 9.0 value = $1,413. CGC census 7/05: 9 in 8.5, 14 higher. ***From the collection of Joe and Nadia Mannarino.***

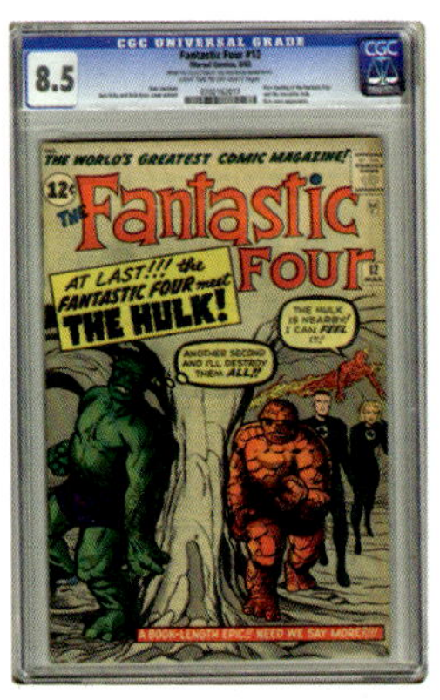

1067 Fantastic Four #12 (Marvel, 1963) CGC VF+ 8.5 Light tan to off-white pages. The Fantastic Four met the Hulk for the first time in this issue, a book which is tied with **The Amazing Spider-Man** #1 as the first Marvel crossover. The cover and art are by a fellow who knew all about drawing the Hulk, namely Jack Kirby. Overstreet 2005 VF 8.0 value = $1,750; VF/NM 9.0 value = $2,875. CGC census 8/05: 12 in 8.5, 21 higher. ***From the collection of Joe and Nadia Mannarino.***

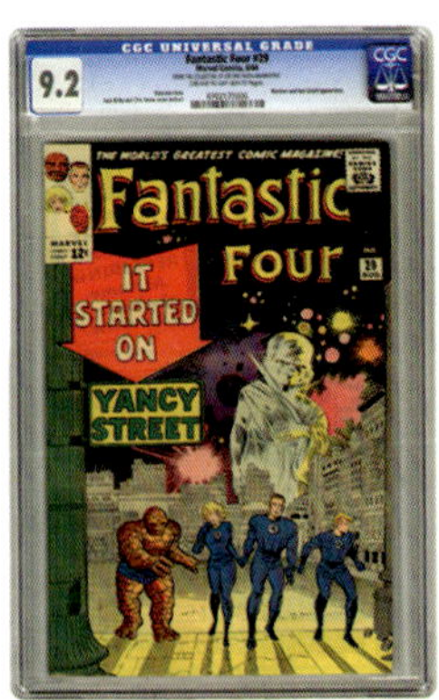

1068 Fantastic Four #29 (Marvel, 1964) CGC NM- 9.2 Cream to off-white pages. Only four copies of this issue outgrade our offering as of this writing! The issue has the Fantastic Four battling the Red Ghost and his Super-Apes, all under the watchful eye of the Watcher. The issue's cover and art are by Jack Kirby. Overstreet 2005 NM- 9.2 value = $360. CGC census 8/05: 8 in 9.2, 4 higher. ***From the collection of Joe and Nadia Mannarino.***

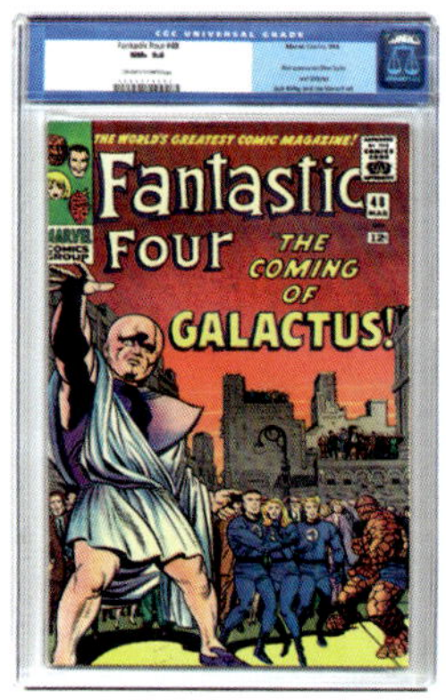

1069 Fantastic Four #48 (Marvel, 1966) CGC NM+ 9.6 Off-white to white pages. The first appearances of the Silver Surfer and Galactus make this one of the best-remembered and most-desired issues of this series. The Inhumans and the Watcher also appear. The epic is the work of writer Stan Lee and artist Jack Kirby. Overstreet 2005 NM- 9.2 value = $1,000. CGC census 7/05: 43 in 9.6, 9 higher.

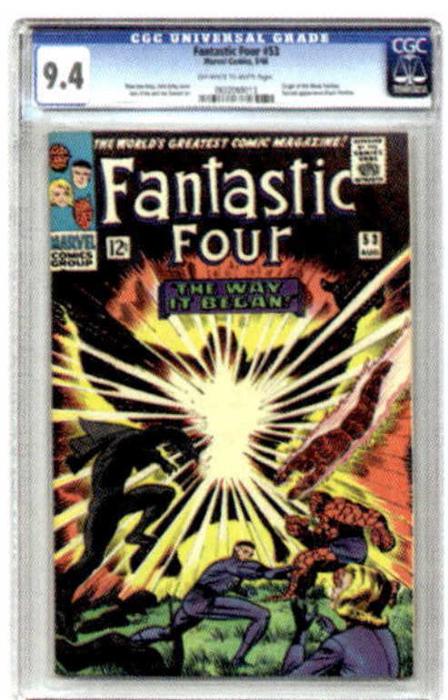

1070 Fantastic Four #53 (Marvel, 1966) CGC NM 9.4 Off-white to white pages. The Black Panther's second appearance was also the issue that revealed his origin story. Also in this issue is the first appearance of the villainous Klaw, and the first mention of that precious metal known as vibranium. It's from the era when writer Stan Lee and artist Jack Kirby were at the top of their form. Overstreet 2005 NM- 9.2 value = $200. CGC census 9/05: 16 in 9.4, 3 higher.

1071 Fantastic Four #74 (Marvel, 1968) CGC NM 9.4 Cream to off-white pages. Galactus and the Silver Surfer appear. Jack Kirby cover and art. Overstreet 2005 NM- 9.2 value = $100. CGC census 8/05: 14 in 9.4, 8 higher.

1072 Fantastic Four #107 Pacific Coast pedigree (Marvel, 1971) CGC NM+ 9.6 White pages. Ben Grimm gets the power to transform himself back and forth. John Buscema cover and art. Overstreet 2005 NM- 9.2 value = $48. CGC census 9/05: 7 in 9.6, 1 higher.

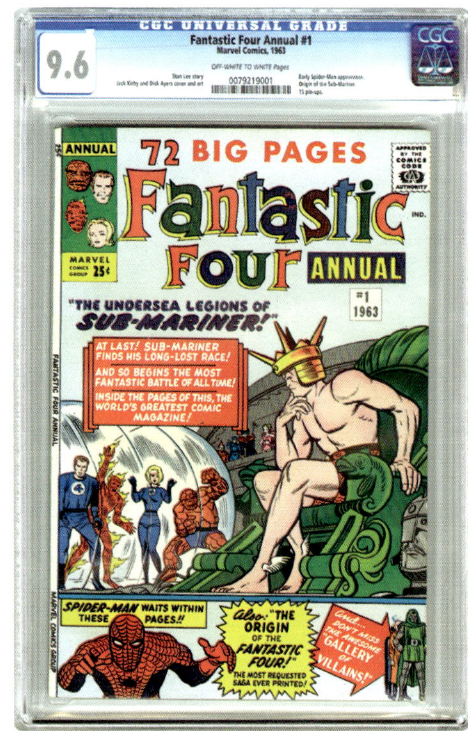

1073 Fantastic Four Annual #1 (Marvel, 1963) CGC NM+ 9.6 Off-white to white pages. Now and then you'll find a silver-haired Silver Age fan who will tell you that this is the best comic he ever read. And no matter when you first caught the "comic bug" yourself, how could you disagree that this is on the short list of the very best? Start with the loooong epic (37 pages!) that had the Sub-Mariner attacking the human race, a story that has been reprinted many times, and deservedly so, with visuals that only Jack Kirby could provide. Then there's an early Spider-Man appearance in a backup feature, with Kirby's pencils inked by Steve Ditko. Then there's another backup feature reprinting the Fantastic Four's origin. And let's not forget that this issue has the first appearance of Krang, and the first Silver Age appearance of Lady Dorma. The fresh look of this copy is really striking (check out the pristine white back cover) — no wonder it's tied for the highest grade that CGC has certified to date. Overstreet 2005 NM- 9.2 value = $1,300. CGC census 9/05: 5 in 9.6, none higher.

1074 Fantastic Four Annual #4 (Marvel, 1966) CGC NM 9.4 Off-white to white pages. First Silver Age appearance of the Golden Age Human Torch. The original Torch's origin is retold. First appearance of Quasimodo. Jack Kirby cover and art. Also contains reprints of the stories from **Fantastic Four** #25 and 26. Overstreet 2005 NM- 9.2 value = $165. CGC census 9/05: 11 in 9.4, 10 higher.

1075 Fantasy Masterpieces V2#12 (Marvel, 1980) CGC NM/MT 9.8 White pages. Featuring the Silver Surfer and Warlock. Overstreet 2005 NM- 9.2 value = $4. CGC census 8/05: 1 in 9.8, none higher.

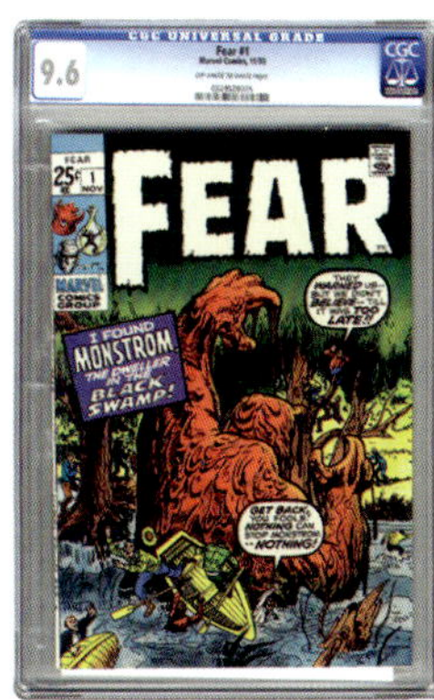

1076 Fear #1 (Marvel, 1970) CGC NM+ 9.6 Off-white to white pages. Square bound comics get dinged up pretty easily, so we're not surprised that this 9.6 copy is the highest-graded that CGC has certified to date. This collection of late 1950s/early 1960s mystery yarns has a Jack Kirby cover and interior art by the likes of Kirby, Don Heck, and Steve DItko. Overstreet 2005 NM- 9.2 value = $55. CGC census 7/05: 3 in 9.6, none higher.

1077 Frankenstein #1 Pacific Coast pedigree (Marvel, 1973) CGC NM 9.4 Off-white pages. Mike Ploog cover and art. Overstreet 2005 NM- 9.2 value = $75. CGC census 9/05: 35 in 9.4, 15 higher.

1078 Ghost Rider #1 (Marvel, 1967) CGC NM- 9.2 Off-white pages. Origin and first appearance of Ghost Rider. Dick Ayers cover and art. Overstreet 2005 NM- 9.2 value = $120. CGC census 8/05: 1 in 9.2, 5 higher.

1079 Giant-Size Spider-Man #3 Pacific Coast pedigree (Marvel, 1975) CGC NM+ 9.6 Off-white pages. Doc Savage co-stars. Gil Kane cover. Ross Andru art. Also reprints the Daredevil appearance from **Amazing Spider-Man** #16, with Daredevil's yellow costume re-colored red. Overstreet 2005 NM- 9.2 value = $42. CGC census 9/05: 12 in 9.6, none higher.

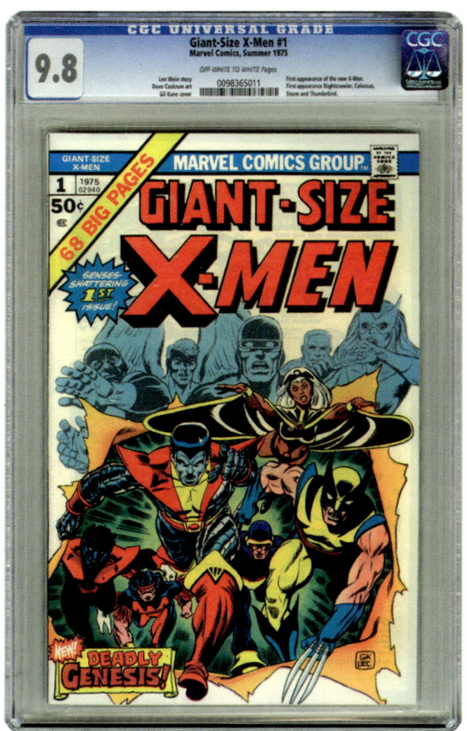

1081 Giant-Size X-Men #1 (Marvel, 1975) CGC NM+ 9.6 Off-white to white pages. The first appearance of the new X-Men is now the second most-valuable Bronze Age comic book. And what comic fan wouldn't treasure a 9.6 copy of this issue, especially considering it's a square bound issue with a white cover? While the new group's co-creators Len Wein and Dave Cockrum provided the issue's story and art respectively, cover art chores fell to Marvel's most prolific cover artist of the era, Gil Kane. Overstreet 2005 NM- 9.2 value = $1,100. CGC census 8/05: 100 in 9.6, 10 higher.

1082 Giant-Size X-Men #1 Winnipeg pedigree (Marvel, 1975) CGC NM+ 9.6 Off-white to white pages. Canada's Wolverine, Germany's Nightcrawler, the U.S.S.R.'s Colossus, and Africa's Storm (she's from Kenya or Tanzania depending on which account you read) joined with American Indian Thunderbird to form the new X-Men in this issue, which occupies the #2 spot in Overstreet's ranking of the most valuable Bronze Age comic books. Dave Cockrum drew that first story as well as inking Gil Kane's cover pencils. Overstreet 2005 NM- 9.2 value = $1,100. CGC census 9/05: 100 in 9.6, 10 higher.

1080 Giant-Size X-Men #1 (Marvel, 1975) CGC NM/MT 9.8 Off-white to white pages. Why do we like this copy so much? Well, here's the thing about square bound comics: even the ones certified with really high grades tend to have some sort of abrasion, bindery tear, or other peccadillo. And we found ***no*** such "downer" while scrutinizing this copy. And since we're talking about the second most-valuable comic of the 1970s, the first appearance of the new X-Men, that's great news indeed. Check the high-res scan on our website for yourself and you'll see why no copy of the issue has been certified with a higher grade by CGC to date. Overstreet 2005 NM- 9.2 value = $1,100. CGC census 9/05: 10 in 9.8, none higher.

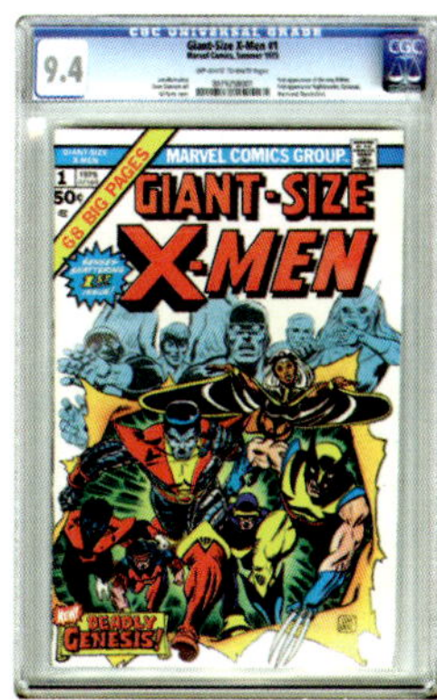

1083 Giant-Size X-Men #1 (Marvel, 1975) CGC NM 9.4 Off-white to white pages. The new X-Men made their first appearance in this issue, which was produced by the team's co-creators, writer Len Wein and artist Dave Cockrum. Gil Kane penciled the cover of what has become one of the key Marvel comics of the 1970s. Overstreet 2005 NM- 9.2 value = $1,100. CGC census 9/05: 178 in 9.4, 110 higher.

1084 Groovy #1 (Marvel, 1968) CGC NM 9.4 Off-white to white pages. Includes "Freak-Out Funnies" featuring the Mamas and Papas, Bob Dylan, the Monkees, and Sonny and Cher photos. Not CCA-approved. Overstreet 2005 NM- 9.2 value = $120. CGC census 8/05: 2 in 9.4, 1 higher.

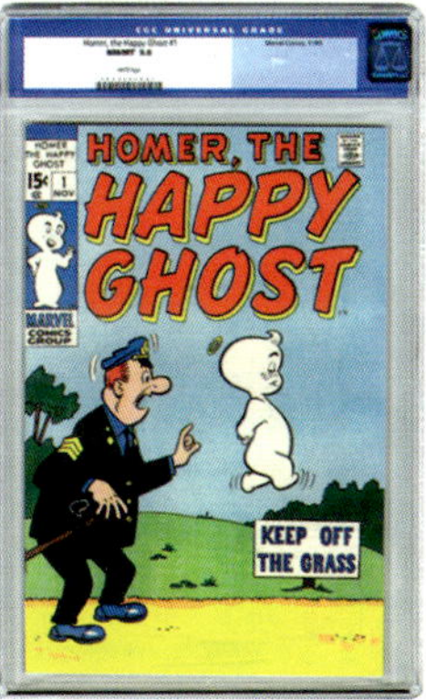

1085 Homer, the Happy Ghost #1 (Marvel, 1969) CGC NM/MT 9.8 White pages. No, you didn't accidentally flip to the Harvey section of the catalog! This ghost isn't just friendly, he's ***happy***, and so were his readers, because he was portrayed by a top writer (Stan Lee) and a top artist (Dan DeCarlo). This Silver Age issue reprints that duo's stories from the Atlas Comics years. Overstreet 2005 NM- 9.2 value = $150. CGC census 9/05: 1 in 9.8, none higher.

1086 Homer, the Happy Ghost #1 (Marvel, 1969) CGC VF/NM 9.0 Off-white to white pages. Stan Goldberg cover art. Overstreet 2005 VF/NM 9.0 value = $114; NM- 9.2 value = $150. CGC census 8/05: 4 in 9.0, 4 higher.

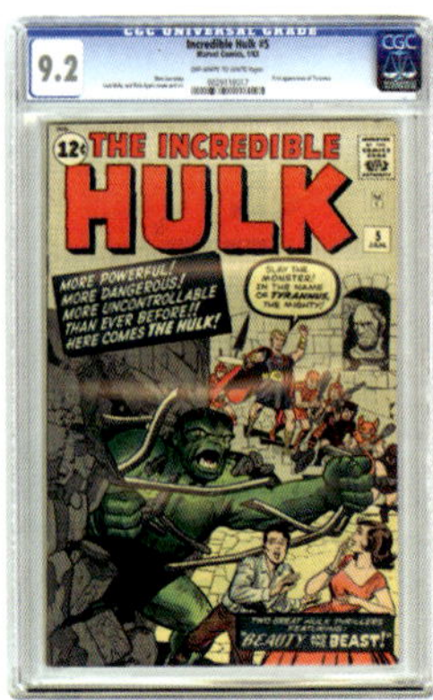

1087 The Incredible Hulk #5 (Marvel, 1963) CGC NM- 9.2 Off-white to white pages. Of the main Silver Age Marvel superhero titles, Hulk seems to be the hardest to find in top grades. That's certainly true for this issue — although we see this book quite often, this is the highest-graded copy we've ever offered! In the comic, the Hulk battles Tyrannus. The cover and interior art are by Jack Kirby. Overstreet 2005 NM- 9.2 value = $2,600. CGC census 9/05: 6 in 9.2, 4 higher.

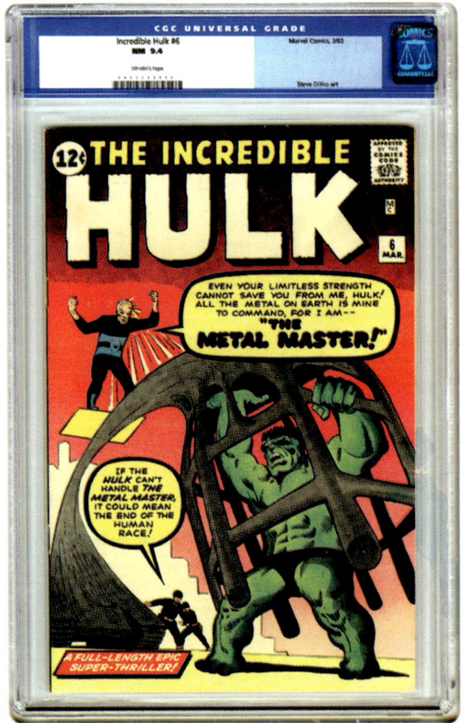

1088 The Incredible Hulk #6 (Marvel, 1963) CGC NM 9.4 Off-white pages. It sometimes seems that Marvel could do no wrong in the early 1960s, but one of their goof-ups was giving up too soon on the Hulk the first time around, canceling his series after only six issues. This last issue of the original run is notable for having the first appearance of the Teen Brigade. It's also the only issue of the first six to be penciled by Steve Ditko. Overstreet 2005 NM- 9.2 value = 3,400. CGC census 9/05: 3 in 9.4, 3 higher.

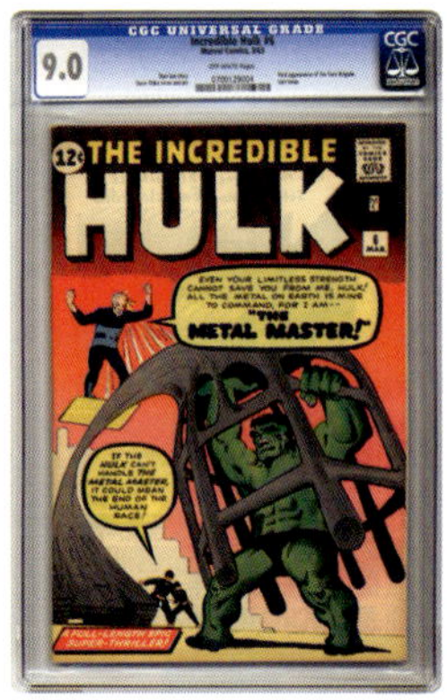

1089 The Incredible Hulk #6 (Marvel, 1963) CGC VF/NM 9.0 Off-white pages. This final issue of the original **Hulk** series has the first appearance of the Teen Brigade, the group of young ham radio buffs formed by the Hulk's buddy Rick Jones. The youngsters would pop up in many a Silver Age issue thereafter. Both this issue's cover and the interior art are by Steve Ditko. Overstreet 2005 VF/NM 9.0 value = $2,444; NM- 9.2 value = $3,400. CGC census 9/05: 6 in 9.0, 11 higher.

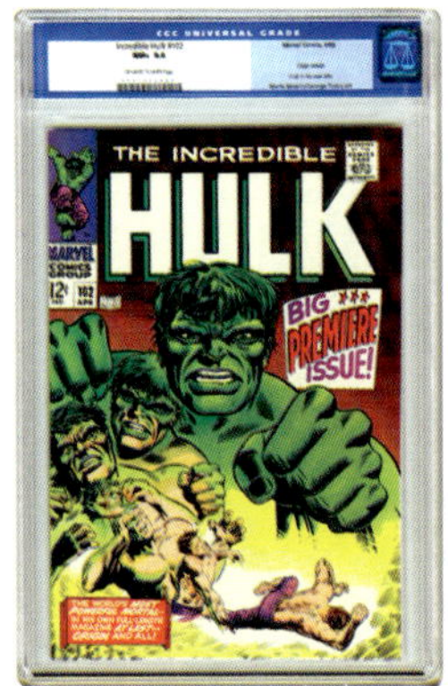

1090 The Incredible Hulk #102 (Marvel, 1968) CGC NM+ 9.6 Off-white to white pages. You know what's *really* hard to find? Those **Hulk** issues from #7-101! Just kidding — after canceling the original series after #6, Marvel didn't give the Hulk his own book again until five years later, and when they did so, they continued the numbering from **Tales to Astonish** #101. Marie Severin drew the issue's cover and teamed with George Tuska on the interior art. Overstreet 2005 NM- 9.2 value = $350. CGC census 9/05: 39 in 9.6, 5 higher.

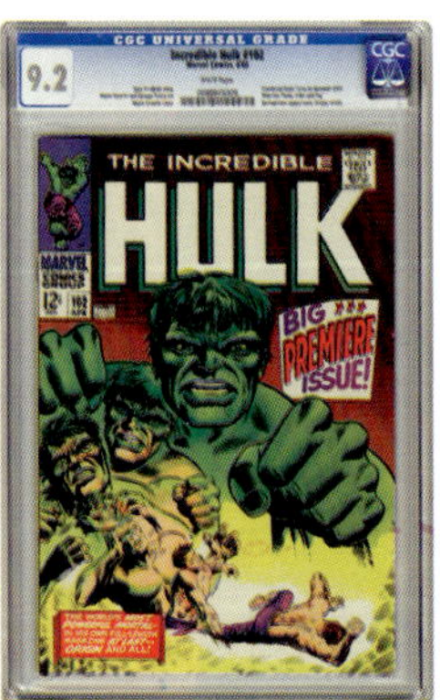

1091 The Incredible Hulk #102 (Marvel, 1968) CGC NM- 9.2 White pages. The origin of the Hulk is retold in this story, continued from **Tales to Astonish** #101. Warriors Three, Odin, and the Enchantress all make appearances. Cover by Marie Severin, interior art by Severin and George Tuska. Overstreet 2005 NM- 9.2 value = $350. CGC census 9/05: 73 in 9.2, 102 higher.

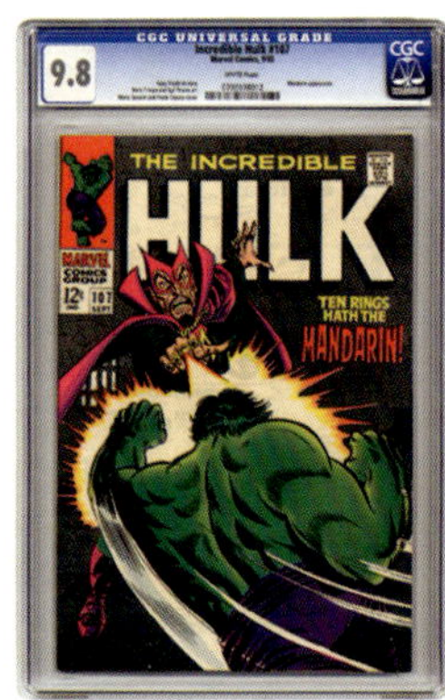

1092 The Incredible Hulk #107 (Marvel, 1968) CGC NM/MT 9.8 White pages. The Hulk takes on the Mandarin in this issue, and Nick Fury and S.H.I.E.L.D. are in the mix as well. The art's by "Happy" Herb Trimpe, the cover's by "Mirthful" Marie Severin, and we can't resist mentioning that the story's by "Groovy" Gary Friedrich. Groovy's certainly the word for this issue's grade of 9.8; it's tied for the highest certified to date! Overstreet 2005 NM- 9.2 value = $95. CGC census 8/05: 4 in 9.8, none higher.

1093 The Incredible Hulk #115 (Marvel, 1969) CGC NM+ 9.6 Off-white to white pages. The Leader makes an appearance. Cover and art by Herb Trimpe and Dan Adkins. Overstreet 2005 NM- 9.2 value = $60. CGC census 9/05: 7 in 9.6, 1 higher.

1094 The Incredible Hulk #175 (Marvel, 1974) CGC NM/MT 9.8 White pages. The Inhumans guest-star. Cover by Marie Severin, Herb Trimpe, and John Romita Sr. Interior art by Trimpe. Overstreet 2005 NM- 9.2 value = $20. CGC census 8/05: 7 in 9.8, none higher.

1095 The Incredible Hulk #181 (Marvel, 1974) CGC NM+ 9.6 Off-white pages. How nice is it to have a 9.6 of this key? Well, as of this writing, 2,502 copies of this issue have been certified by CGC, including three Apparent PRs and two Apparent FRs (oo-kay....), and of those 2,502, a mere seven have been certified with a higher grade than our offering! This issue, the first full appearance of Wolverine, is still the most valuable comic of the Bronze Age, and since its two nearest competitors, **Giant-Size X-Men** #1 and **X-Men** #94, actually took a slight *dip* in value with this year's Guide, we would say Hulk #181 is in no danger of losing its top-of-the-heap status. Overstreet 2005 NM- 9.2 value = $1,300. CGC census 9/05: 100 in 9.6, 7 higher.

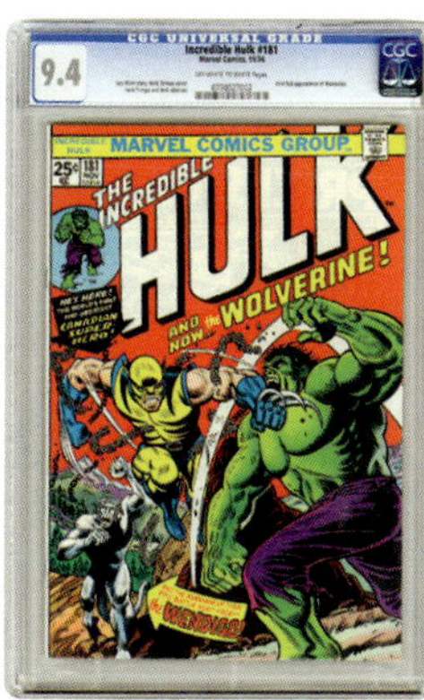

1096 The Incredible Hulk #181 (Marvel, 1974) CGC NM 9.4 Off-white to white pages. If Bronze Age books are your thing, you can't do any better than this issue, the most valuable comic of that era thanks to the first full appearance of Wolverine. The Hulk's main artist of the 1970s, Herb Trimpe, handled art chores. Overstreet 2005 NM- 9.2 value = $1,300. CGC census 5/05: 164 in 9.4, 107 higher.

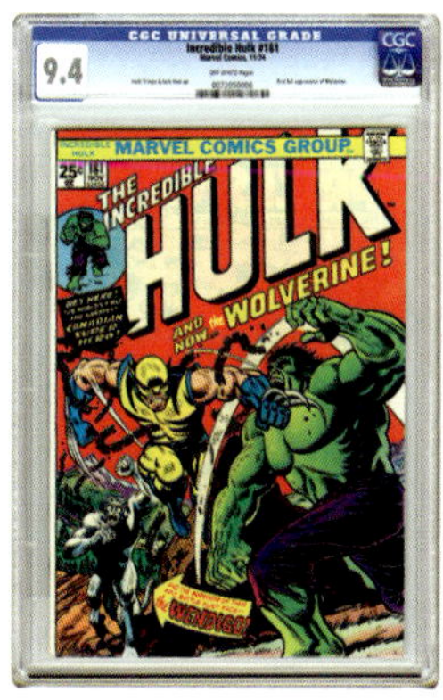

1097 The Incredible Hulk #181 (Marvel, 1974) CGC NM 9.4 Off-white pages. Some collectors didn't pluck this issue off the newsstands when it came out, others read their copies so many times that they're well-worn, and others still cut out the Shanna the She-Devil Marvel Value Stamp — sorry if any of those apply to you! But here's your chance to make up for any of those missteps by acquiring a sharp NM copy of this key issue, the first full appearance of Wolverine and the most valuable Bronze Age comic book. Overstreet 2005 NM- 9.2 value = $1,300. CGC census 9/05: 164 in 9.4, 107 higher.

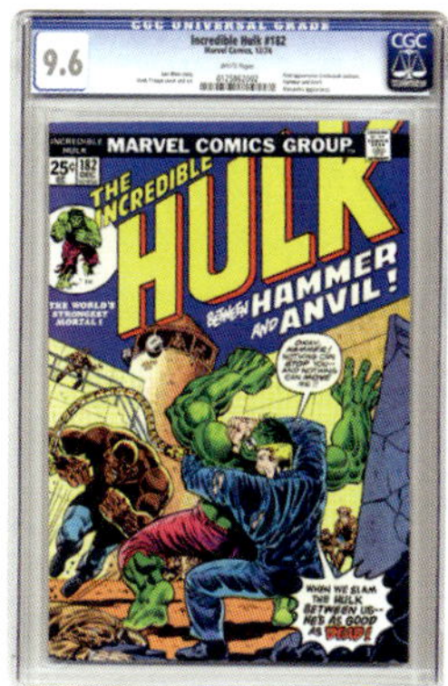

1098 The Incredible Hulk #182 (Marvel, 1974) CGC NM+ 9.6 White pages. It's the third appearance of Wolverine, who went on to become the most popular character in comics! It's also the *first* appearance of Hammer and Anvil, who went on to... appear in a **Marvel Team-Up** once. Well, you can't win 'em all. But back to Wolvie, this cameo was the last time he was seen before **Giant-Size X-Men** #1. The issue's cover and art are by Herb Trimpe. Overstreet 2005 NM- 9.2 value = $150. CGC census 9/05: 22 in 9.6, 3 higher.

1099 The Incredible Hulk #200 Pacific Coast pedigree (Marvel, 1976) CGC NM 9.4 Off-white pages. Rich Buckler cover, inked by John Romita Sr. Sal Buscema art. Overstreet 2005 NM- 9.2 value = $32. CGC census 9/05: 49 in 9.4, 59 higher.

1100 The Invaders #1 Pacific Coast pedigree (Marvel, 1975) CGC NM 9.4 Off-white pages. John Romita Sr. cover. Frank Robbins art. Overstreet 2005 NM- 9.2 value = $55. CGC census 9/05: 57 in 9.4, 68 higher.

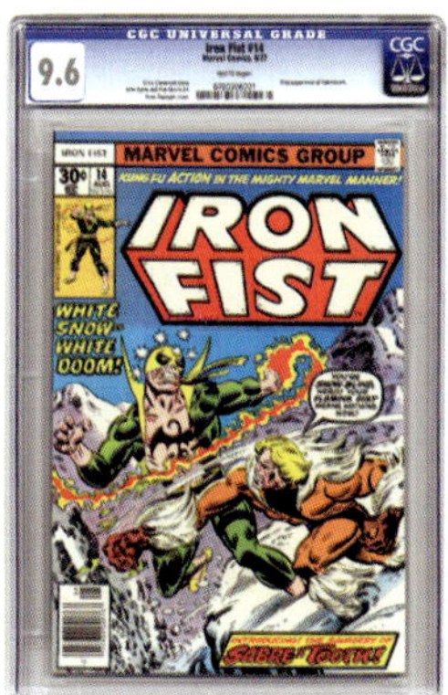

1101 Iron Fist #14 (Marvel, 1977) CGC NM+ 9.6 White pages. The first appearance of Sabretooth, this comic is one that fans just didn't appreciate until years later. In fact, the letters page of this issue announces that the next issue was to be the last because of poor sales! But now this is one of the more valuable issues of Marvel's Bronze Age, mostly because of the debut of the aforementioned villain, but also because it's a Chris Claremont and John Byrne collaboration that pre-dates Byrne's tenure on **X-Men**. Overstreet 2005 NM- 9.2 value = $160. CGC census 8/05: 78 in 9.6, 17 higher.

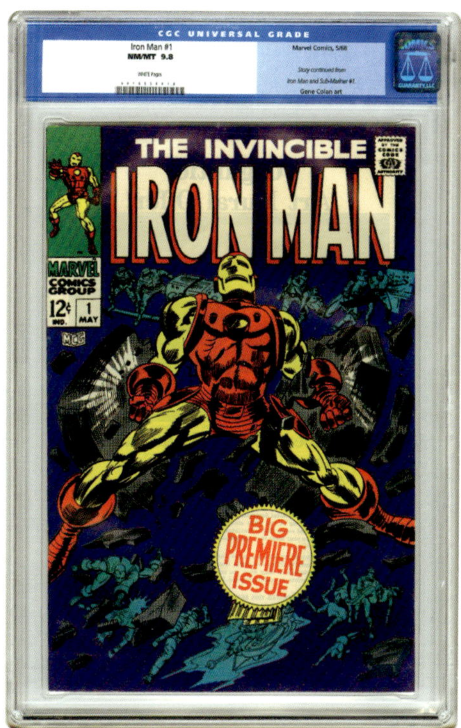

1102 Iron Man #1 (Marvel, 1968) CGC NM/MT 9.8 White pages. Iron Man finally got his own title in 1968 after sharing **Tales of Suspense** stardom with Captain America. In this story, continued from the one-shot **Iron Man and Sub-Mariner**, Shellhead takes on AIM and the Maggia. There's also a brief backup feature that retells Iron Man's origin. Gene Colan supplied the art for the cover and both stories. Overstreet 2005 NM- 9.2 value = $575. CGC census 9/05: 18 in 9.8, 2 higher.

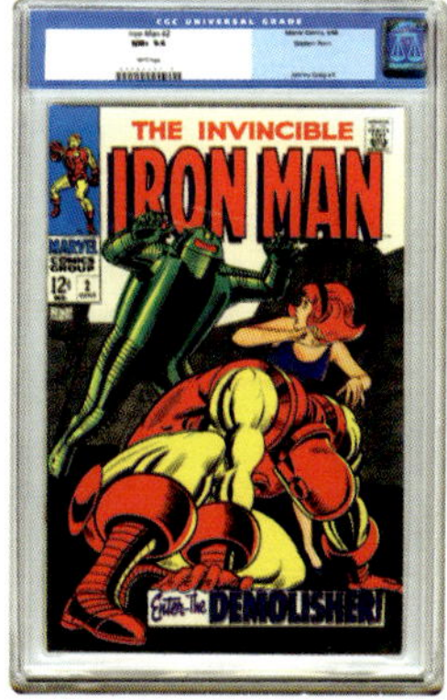

1103 Iron Man #2 Western Penn pedigree (Marvel, 1968) CGC NM+ 9.6 White pages. Every Iron Man fan goes through two stages. When you're a kid, you wish you had super-powered armor like Tony Stark's, and when you're a bit older, you wish you had girlfriends like Tony Stark's! One of the superhero/industrialist/playboy's many love interests, Janice Cord, made her first appearance in this issue. The cover and interior art are by Johnny Craig. Overstreet 2005 NM- 9.2 value = $180. CGC census 9/05: 55 in 9.6, 25 higher.

1104 Iron Man #54 Pacific Coast pedigree (Marvel, 1973) CGC NM+ 9.6 Off-white pages. First appearance of Moondragon (as Madame MacEvil). Sub-Mariner appearance. Story and partial pencils by Bill Everett. Remaining pencils by George Tuska. Gil Kane cover. Overstreet 2005 NM- 9.2 value = $35. CGC census 9/05: 7 in 9.6, none higher.

1105 Journey Into Mystery #96 (Marvel, 1963) CGC NM+ 9.6 White pages. Thor takes on Merlin in this issue, which has a Jack Kirby cover and Joe Sinnott interior art. This being a book with **Mystery** in the title, it's appropriate that there are two eerie backup features with art by Steve Ditko and Paul Reinman respectively. By the way, the Thor yarn even has an appearance by John F. Kennedy and his daughter Caroline. Ask not what your comic collection can do for you, ask what you can do for your comic collection! Overstreet 2005 NM- 9.2 value = $490. CGC census 9/05: 4 in 9.6, none higher.

1106 Journey Into Mystery #96 (Marvel, 1963) CGC NM 9.4 Off-white pages. The Mighty Thor takes on Merlin, and if that's not enough mythology for you, there's Camelot of another sort as John F. Kennedy and his young daughter Caroline put in an appearance. In fact, when Merlin goes searching for the leader of the U.S., he passes right by JFK because Kennedy looks too young! Speaking of the best and the brightest, this cover's by another brilliant Jack — Kirby, that is. The interior art is by Joe Sinnott (Thor story), Steve Ditko (mystery backup feature) and Paul Reinman (more mystery). Overstreet 2005 NM- 9.2 value = $490. CGC census 9/05: 4 in 9.4, 4 higher.

1107 Journey Into Mystery #102 (Marvel, 1964) CGC NM 9.4 Cream to off-white pages. Thor's number one love interest, the beautiful Sif, made her first appearance in this issue, and if that's not enough for you, there's also the first appearance of Hela, Goddess of Death! Both figure in a "Tale of Asgard" about Thor's boyhood. In the main feature, Thor takes on the Tomorrow Man. There's even a third story here, a "mystery" feature with Larry Lieber art. The Thor story and the cover were the work of the great Jack Kirby. Just two copies of #102 have received higher grades from CGC to date. Overstreet 2005 NM- 9.2 value = $280. CGC census 9/05: 5 in 9.4, 2 higher.

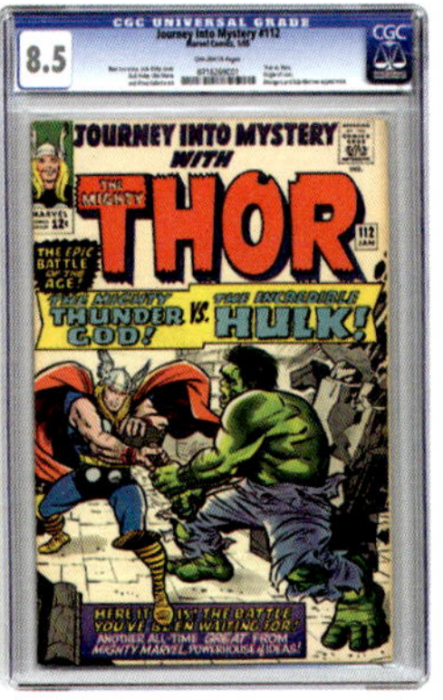

1108 Journey Into Mystery #112 (Marvel, 1965) CGC VF+ 8.5 Off-white pages. The tale of the Hulk-versus-Thor battle in **Avengers** #3 is told in much-expanded form in this issue. There's also a Tales of Asgard backup feature detailing the origin of Loki. Both of the features as well as the cover were drawn by Jack Kirby. Overstreet 2005 VF 8.0 value = $330; VF/NM 9.0 value = $515. CGC census 8/05: 17 in 8.5, 35 higher.

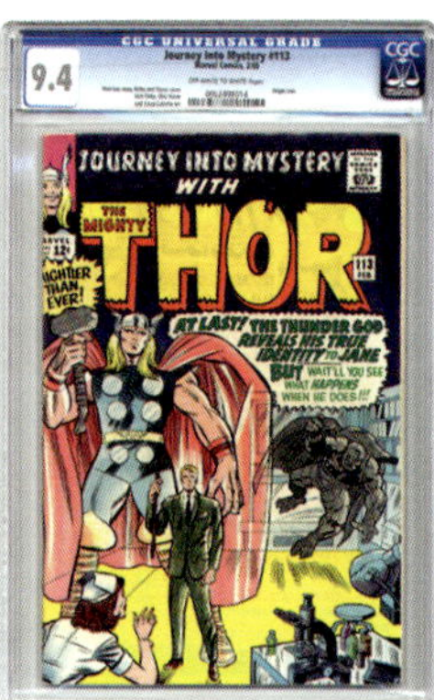

1109 Journey Into Mystery #113 (Marvel, 1965) CGC NM 9.4 Off-white to white pages. In this issue, Thor makes the momentous decision to reveal his identity to Jane Foster, but when it's time to show some proof, it turns out Odin has taken away his powers! Will he give 'em back in time for Thor to fight the Grey Gargoyle? Also in the issue, a backup feature continues the origin of Loki. The cover and interior art are by Jack Kirby. Overstreet 2005 NM- 9.2 value = $220. CGC census 9/05: 7 in 9.4, 2 higher.

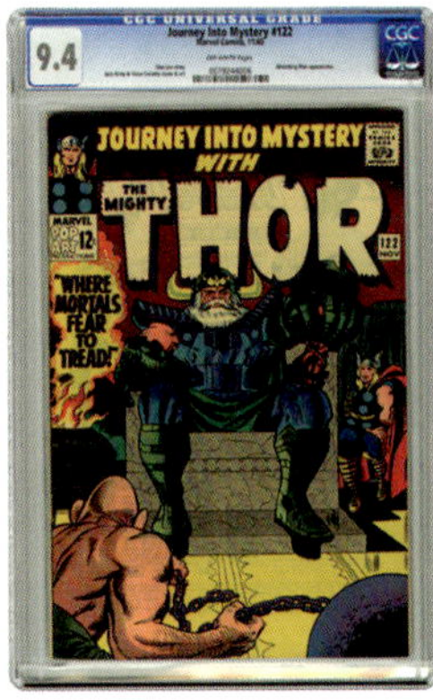

1110 Journey Into Mystery #122 (Marvel, 1965) CGC NM 9.4 Off-white pages. In this Stan Lee/Jack Kirby production, the Absorbing Man has the audacity to take on Odin himself! And the treacherous Loki is pulling the strings, natch. Kirby drew the entire issue, including the cover and the "Tales of Asgard" backup feature. Overstreet 2005 NM- 9.2 value = $190. CGC census 9/05: 5 in 9.4, 2 higher.

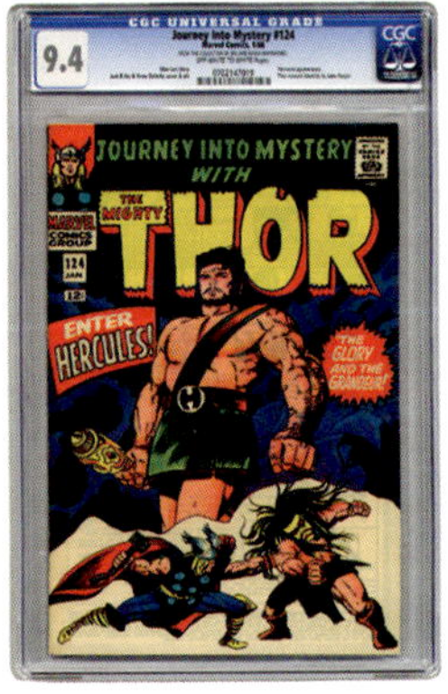

1111 Journey Into Mystery #124 (Marvel, 1966) CGC NM 9.4 Off-white to white pages. Thor reveals his secret identity to Jane Foster. There's also a Tales of Asgard backup feature. The cover and art are by Jack Kirby. Overstreet 2005 NM- 9.2 value = $200. CGC census 7/05: 18 in 9.4, 18 higher. *From the collection of Joe and Nadia Mannarino.*

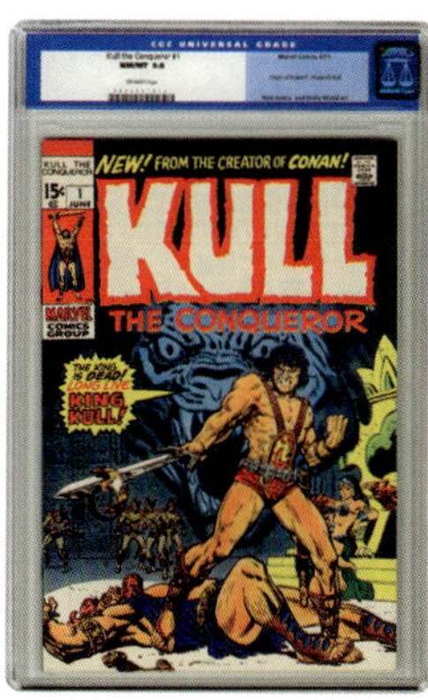

1112 Kull the Conqueror #1 (Marvel, 1971) CGC NM/MT 9.8 Off-white pages. After Conan became a smash success, Marvel gave Robert E. Howard's Kull a one-issue try-out in **Creatures On The Loose**, and shortly thereafter the man from Atlantis got his own series. Marvel started things off by telling the character's origin story. Ross Andru and Wally Wood drew the story, and Andru teamed up with Marie Severin for the cover. Overstreet 2005 NM- 9.2 value = $50. CGC census 9/05: 9 in 9.8, none higher.

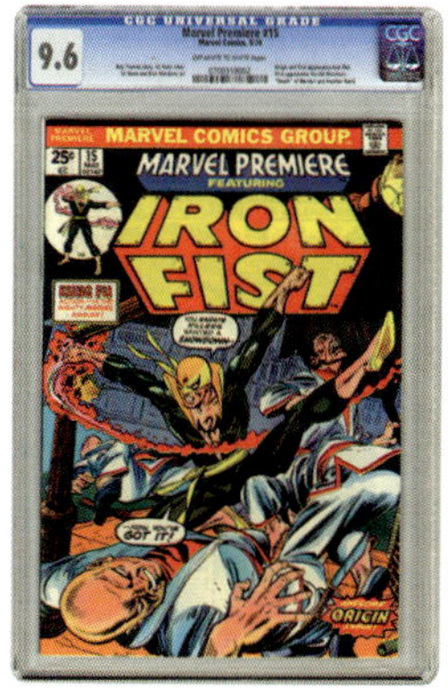

1113 Marvel Premiere #15 Iron Fist (Marvel, 1974) CGC NM+ 9.6 Off-white to white pages. We know it's been said before, but in 1974, *everybody* was kung-fu fighting! That includes Iron Fist, whose origin and first appearance are found in this very issue. Since the character went on to have his own series, and co-starred with Power Man in another series thereafter, it's no wonder that this is the most valuable issue of **Marvel Premiere**'s run. Overstreet 2005 NM- 9.2 value = $100. CGC census 9/05: 28 in 9.6, 6 higher.

1114 Marvel Tales #2 Boston pedigree (Marvel, 1965) CGC NM 9.4 Off-white to white pages. This square bound mag reprinted X-Men, Avengers, Hulk, and Dr. Strange stories, with art by Jack Kirby and Steve Ditko. Overstreet 2005 NM- 9.2 value = $160. CGC census 9/05: 8 in 9.4, 2 higher.

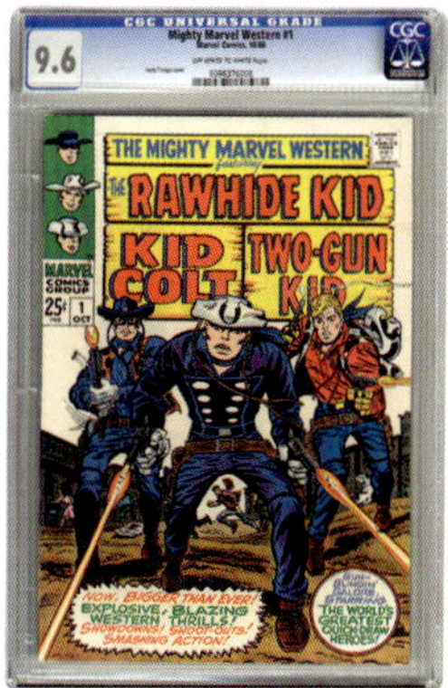

1115 Mighty Marvel Western #1 (Marvel, 1968) CGC NM+ 9.6 Off-white to white pages. Marvel brought out this series to give fans reprints of the company's best Western heroes: the Rawhide Kid, Kid Colt Outlaw, and the Two-Gun Kid. Alas, the gunfighters didn't bother to stand underneath their respective logos — Two-Gun Kid is the one on the ***left***, and oddly enough, he's the only one of the three on Herb Trimpe's cover who's ***not*** wielding two guns! The issue has Jack Kirby, Dick Ayers, and Jack Keller interior art. Overstreet 2005 NM- 9.2 value = $70. CGC census 7/05: 3 in 9.6, none higher.

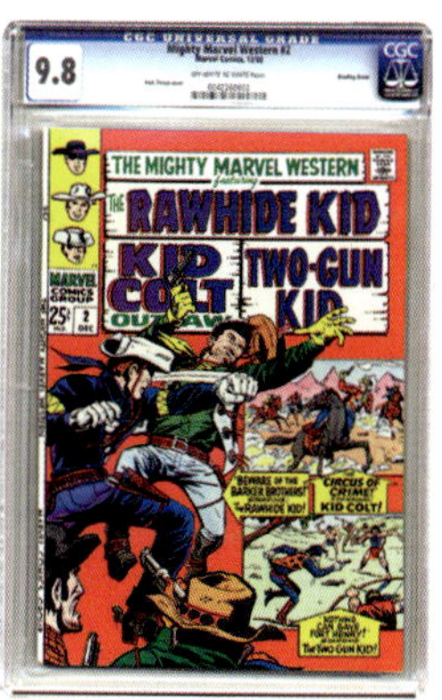

1116 Mighty Marvel Western #2 Bowling Green pedigree (Marvel, 1968) CGC NM/MT 9.8 Off-white to white pages. This square bound issue reprints Western yarns starring the Rawhide Kid, Kid Colt Outlaw, and the Two-Gun Kid. Jack Kirby, Dick Ayers, and Jack Keller are the interior artists; Herb Trimpe drew the cover. Overstreet 2005 NM- 9.2 value = $45. CGC census 7/05: 2 in 9.8, none higher.

1117 Millie the Model Annual #4 (Marvel, 1965) CGC NM+ 9.6 Off-white pages. Stan Goldberg cover and art. Overstreet 2005 NM- 9.2 value = $120. CGC census 7/05: 19 in 9.6, 1 higher.

1118 Millie the Model Annual #5 (Marvel, 1966) CGC NM+ 9.6 Off-white pages. Stan Goldberg cover and art. Overstreet 2005 NM- 9.2 value = $175. CGC census 7/05: 6 in 9.6, none higher.

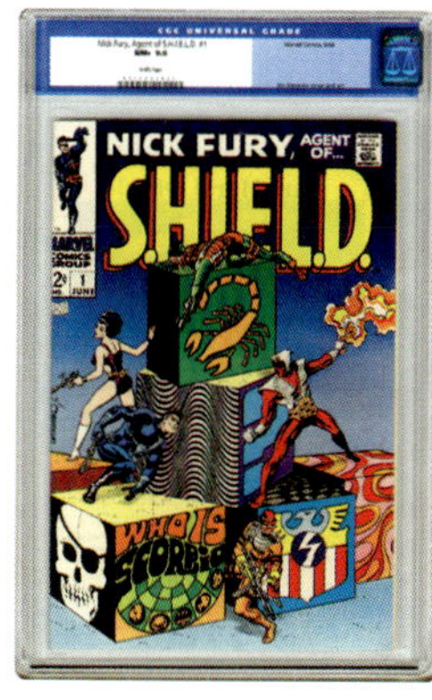

1119 Nick Fury, Agent of SHIELD #1 (Marvel, 1968) CGC NM+ 9.6 White pages. Jim Steranko wrote, penciled, and even colored this issue — check out Steranko's work on the cover in all its pop-art glory. Also seen on the cover is the villain Scorpio, who made his first appearance here. Overstreet 2005 NM- 9.2 value = $140. CGC census 9/05: 80 in 9.6, 17 higher.

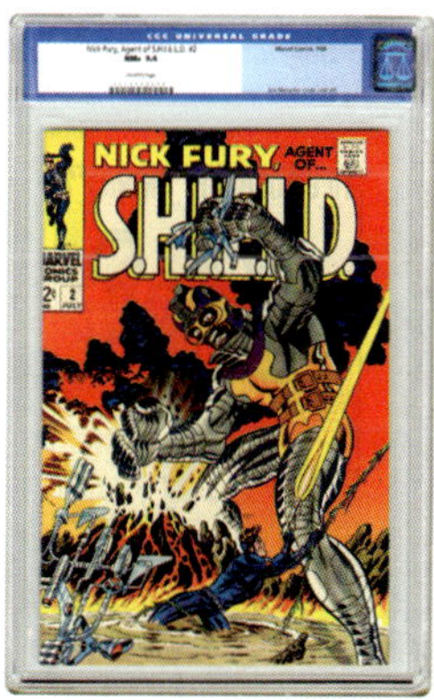

1120 Nick Fury, Agent of SHIELD #2 (Marvel, 1968) CGC NM+ 9.6 Off-white pages. Check out Jim Steranko in full "Jack Kirby" mode! Steranko drew the interior story as well. Overstreet 2005 NM- 9.2 value = $70. CGC census 9/05: 15 in 9.6, 3 higher.

1121 Not Brand Echh #1 (Marvel, 1967) CGC NM 9.4 Off-white to white pages. First Marvel parody book. First appearance of Forbush-Man. Jack Kirby cover. Kirby, John Severin, Marie Severin, Ross Andru, and Bill Everett art. Overstreet 2005 NM- 9.2 value = $80. CGC census 9/05: 16 in 9.4, 6 higher.

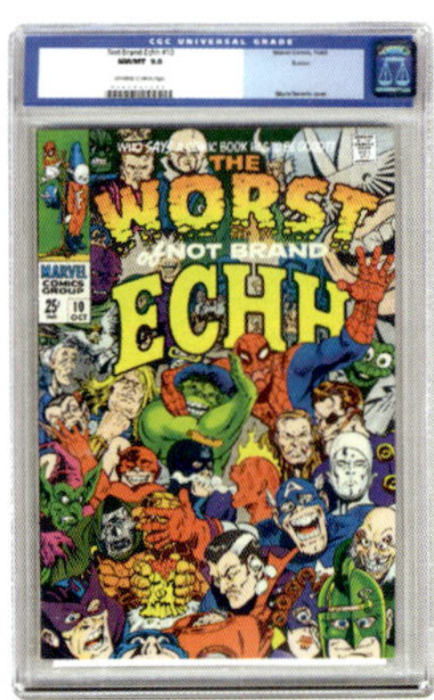

1122 Not Brand Echh #10 Boston pedigree (Marvel, 1968) CGC NM/MT 9.8 Off-white to white pages. Here's the highest-graded copy CGC has certified to date of this humor comic. You can't beat Marie Severin's cover, with wacky versions of just about every character in the Marvel Universe (even the long-johns-clad Forbush-Man)! Ms. Severin even slips in an homage to Gil Kane with a Kane-like "nostril shot" at the far bottom! Inside the issue, Marvel parodies abound: take the Silver Burper, Charlie America, and Knock Furious, Agent of SHEESH. But the issue also satirizes the likes of Batman and Robin and even those out-of-work EC GhouLunatics, the Old Witch, the Crypt Keeper, and the Vault Keeper! The interior art is by Severin, Jack Kirby, and Tom Sutton. Overstreet 2005 NM- 9.2 value = $55. CGC census 7/05: 1 in 9.8, none higher.

1123 Sgt. Fury and His Howling Commandos #13 (Marvel, 1964) CGC VF/NM 9.0 Cream to off-white pages. This is one of the key issues of this series: Captain America and Bucky guest-star, and it's only Cap's second solo appearance outside of The Avengers. The cover and art are by Jack Kirby. Overstreet 2005 VF/NM 9.0 value = $398; NM- 9.2 value = $540. CGC census 8/05: 22 in 9.0, 22 higher.

1124 Sgt. Fury and His Howling Commandos Annual #6 (Marvel, 1970) CGC NM/MT 9.8 Off-white to white pages. John Severin cover. CGC notes, "Date stamp on cover." Overstreet 2005 NM- 9.2 value = $24. CGC census 7/05: 1 in 9.8, none higher.

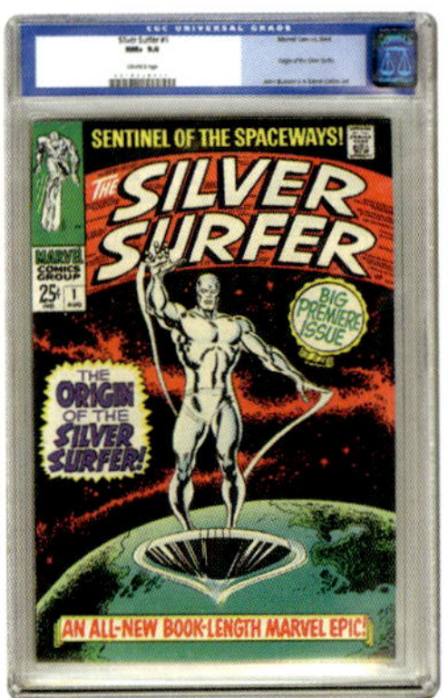

1125 The Silver Surfer #1 (Marvel, 1968) CGC NM+ 9.6 Off-white pages. The Sentinel of the Spaceways, the Silver Surfer stars in his first solo title; his cosmic origin is expanded upon. John Buscema provides the cover and interior art on the lead story. The Watcher stars in a backup feature, with art by Gene Colan. Overstreet 2005 NM- 9.2 value = $675. CGC census 8/05: 14 in 9.6, 1 higher.

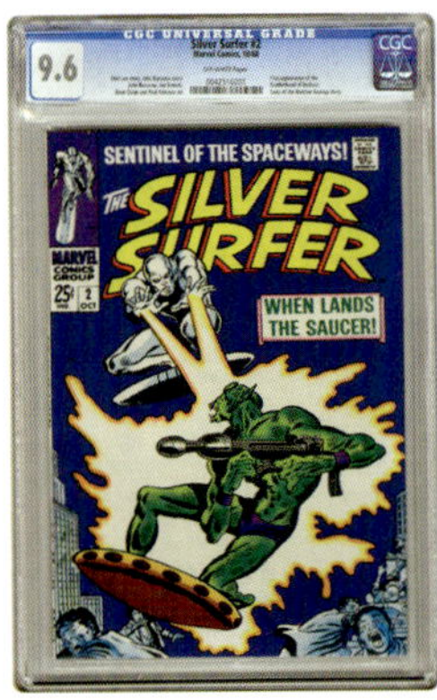

1126 The Silver Surfer #2 (Marvel, 1968) CGC NM+ 9.6 Off-white pages. This is the nicest copy we've seen to date of this square bound issue. It's got the first appearance of the alien race known as the Badoon (whom **Guardians of the Galaxy** fans might be familiar with). The issue's cover and interior art are by John Buscema. There's also a Watcher backup story with Gene Colan art. Overstreet 2005 NM- 9.2 value = $275. CGC census 9/05: 24 in 9.6, 3 higher.

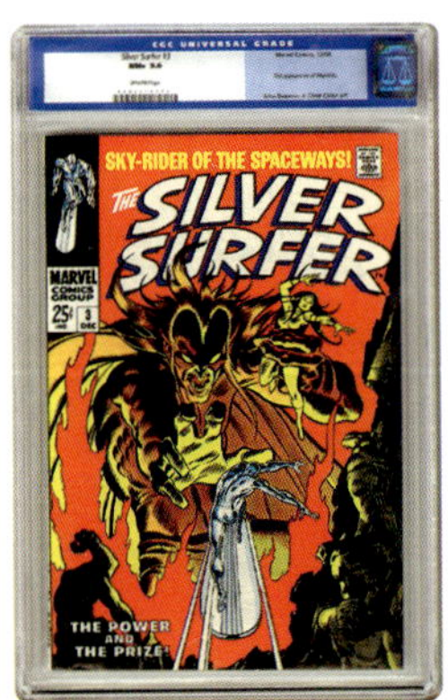

1127 The Silver Surfer #3 (Marvel, 1968) CGC NM+ 9.6 Off-white pages. This neat square bound issue features the first appearance of Mephisto. John Buscema cover and Surfer story art; the Watcher backup feature is by Gene Colan. Overstreet 2005 NM- 9.2 value = $235. CGC census 8/05: 8 in 9.6, none higher.

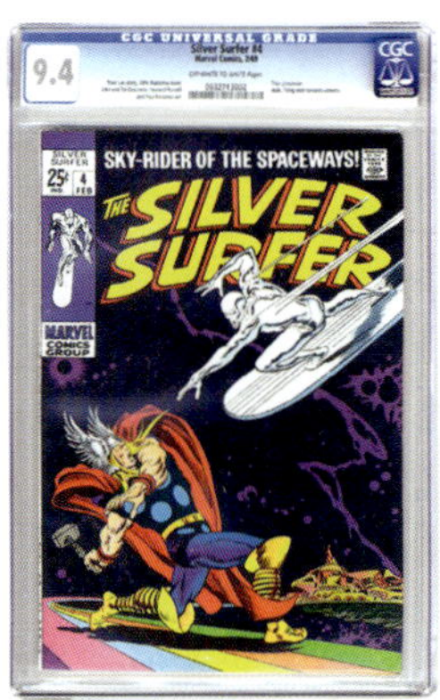

1128 The Silver Surfer #4 (Marvel, 1969) CGC NM 9.4 Off-white to white pages. Thor battles the Silver Surfer in this issue, and there are cameos by the Hulk, the Thing, and Hercules. John Buscema drew the cover as well as all of the story action. Issue #4 had lower distribution than other issues according to Overstreet. There's also a Watcher backup feature, retelling the story "The Terror of Tim Boo Ba." Overstreet 2005 NM- 9.2 value = $600. CGC census 7/05: 47 in 9.4, 18 higher.

1129 The Silver Surfer #4 (Marvel, 1969) CGC NM 9.4 Off-white pages. Thor encounters the Silver Surfer, and cosmic chaos ensues. The Hulk, the Thing, and Hercules are all along for the ride. John Buscema's art graces the cover and interiors. This issue had lower distribution than others, according to Overstreet. The Watcher backup feature retells the story "The Terror of Tim Boo Ba." Overstreet 2005 NM- 9.2 value = $600. CGC census 8/05: 47 in 9.4, 18 higher.

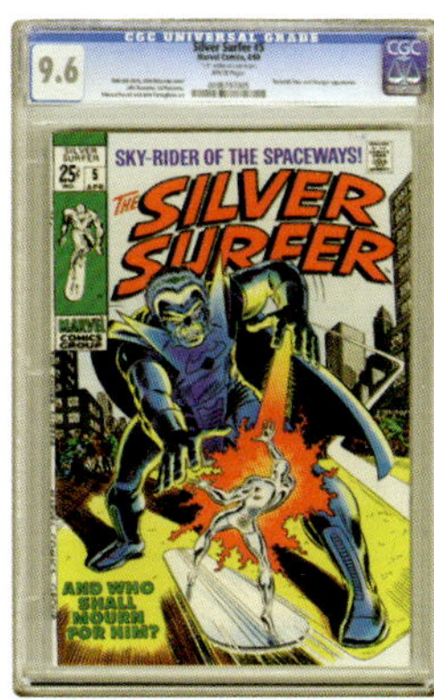

1130 The Silver Surfer #5 (Marvel, 1969) CGC NM+ 9.6 White pages. The Silver Surfer battles the Stranger. The Thing, Mr. Fantastic, and the Human Torch appear. John Buscema cover and art. Backup feature is a re-done version of the story from **Tales to Astonish** #26, featuring the Watcher in this version and drawn by Howard Purcell. CGC notes, "'1-9' written on cover in pen." Overstreet 2005 NM- 9.2 value = $150. CGC census 9/05: 9 in 9.6, 1 higher.

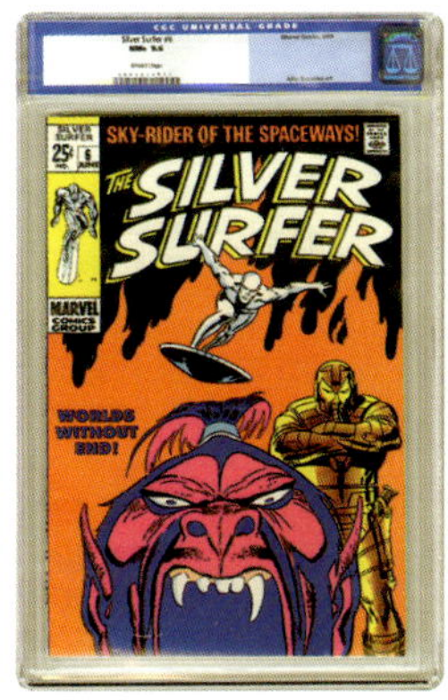

1131 The Silver Surfer #6 (Marvel, 1969) CGC NM+ 9.6 Off-white pages. The Cosmic Crestrider encounters "Worlds Without End!" John Buscema provides the cover and story art. The Watcher backup feature includes Syd Shores and Frank Brunner art. Overstreet 2005 NM- 9.2 value = $150. CGC census 8/05: 11 in 9.6, 1 higher.

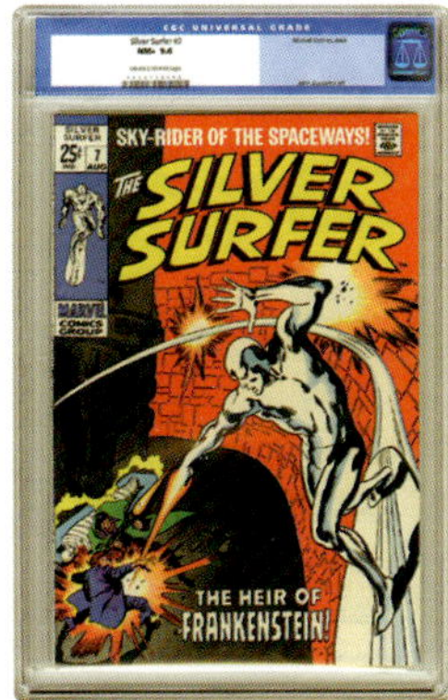

1132 The Silver Surfer #7 (Marvel, 1969) CGC NM+ 9.6 Off-white to white pages. Our run of superb **Silver Surfer**s continues with this unusual issue, which features the first Marvel Universe appearance of Frankenstein's monster. John Buscema, Sal Buscema, and Dan Adkins provide the art. "Tales of the Watcher" backup feature is by Howard Purcell. This is the last square bound issue of the original series. Overstreet 2005 NM- 9.2 value = $150. CGC census 8/05: 6 in 9.6, none higher.

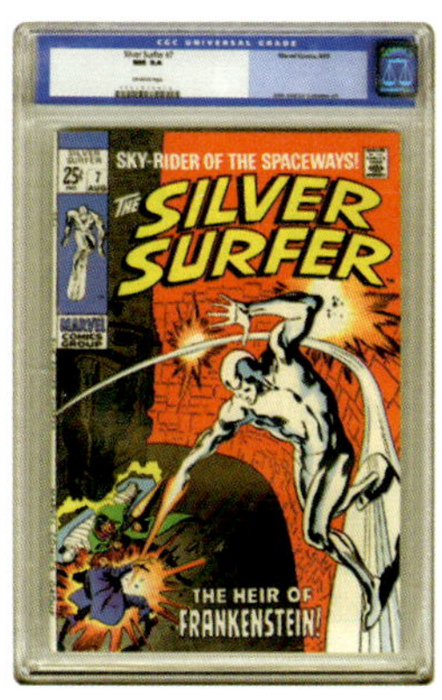

1133 The Silver Surfer #7 (Marvel, 1969) CGC NM 9.4 Off-white pages. This attractive square bound comic features the first Marvel Universe appearance of Frankenstein's monster. John Buscema provides the cover and is joined by Sal Buscema and Dan Adkins for the story art. A "Tales of the Watcher" backup feature is drawn by Howard Purcell. This is the last 25 cent issue. Overstreet 2005 NM- 9.2 value = $150. CGC census 8/05: 16 in 9.4, 6 higher.

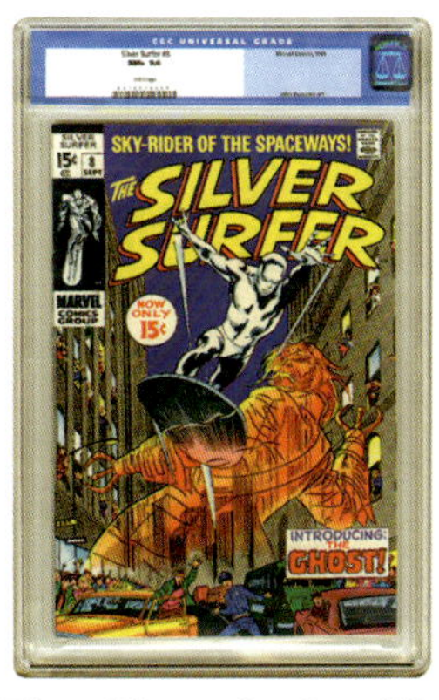

1134 The Silver Surfer #8 (Marvel, 1969) CGC NM+ 9.6 White pages. The Sky-Rider of the Spaceways confronts the Flying Dutchman's Ghost, with Mephisto tagging along for good measure. John Buscema's cover and story art is featured. This beautiful glossy copy is highlighted by supple white pages. Overstreet 2005 NM- 9.2 value = $110. CGC census 8/05: 8 in 9.6, none higher.

1135 The Silver Surfer #9 (Marvel, 1969) CGC NM+ 9.6 Off-white to white pages. The Sky-Rider of the Spaceways, as portrayed by John Buscema's cosmic cover and story art. This attractive copy is unsurpassed in the current CGC census for issue #9. Overstreet 2005 NM- 9.2 value = $110. CGC census 8/05: 10 in 9.6, none higher.

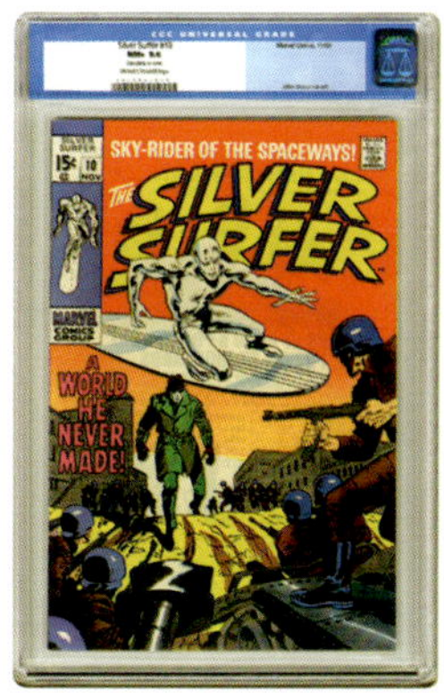

1136 The Silver Surfer #10 (Marvel, 1969) CGC NM+ 9.6 Off-white to white pages. The Cosmic Crestrider faces "A World He Never Made!" — it happens only in Marvelland! John Buscema drew the cover and story art. A great looking copy, despite a light date stamp on the cover. Overstreet 2005 NM- 9.2 value = $110. CGC census 8/05: 5 in 9.6, 1 higher.

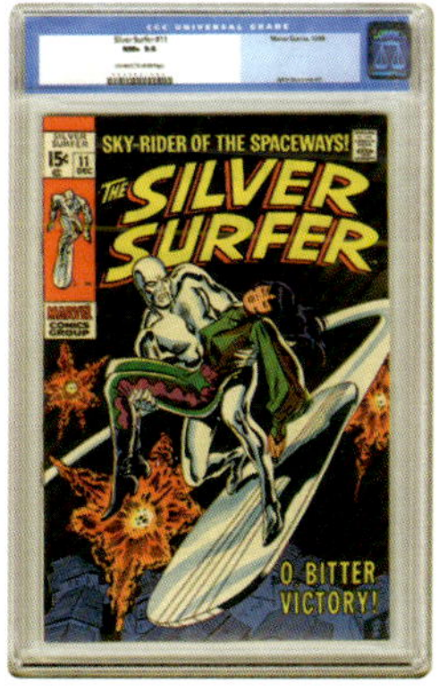

1137 The Silver Surfer #11 (Marvel, 1969) CGC NM+ 9.6 Off-white to white pages. The Sky-Rider of the Spaceways soars again, courtesy of John Buscema's gorgeous cover and interior art. A beautiful black background gives this sharp issue's cover an extra bit of pizzazz. Overstreet 2005 NM- 9.2 value = $100. CGC census 8/05: 7 in 9.6, 1 higher.

1138 The Silver Surfer #12 (Marvel, 1970) CGC NM 9.4 Off-white to white pages. The Silver Surfer battles the Abomination. John Buscema cover and art. Overstreet 2005 NM- 9.2 value = $100. CGC census 8/05: 15 in 9.4, 8 higher.

1139 The Silver Surfer #13 (Marvel, 1970) CGC NM 9.4 Off-white pages. John Buscema cover and art. Overstreet 2005 NM- 9.2 value = $100. CGC census 8/05: 10 in 9.4, 6 higher.

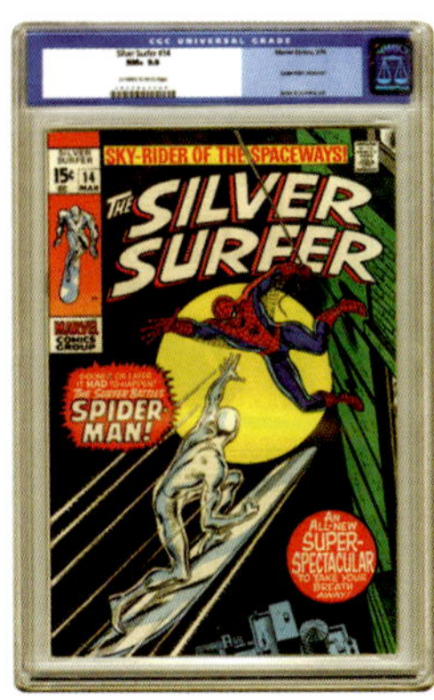

1140 The Silver Surfer #14 (Marvel, 1970) CGC NM+ 9.6 Off-white to white pages. Spider-Man drops by to trade a few well-placed blows with the Surfer. Chill out, guys! You're both on the same team! Art by John Buscema, inked by Dan Adkins. Overstreet 2005 NM- 9.2 value = $165. CGC census 8/05: 5 in 9.6, 1 higher.

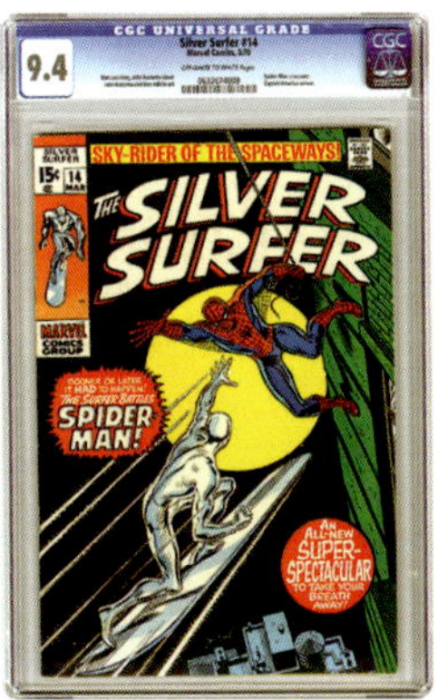

1141 The Silver Surfer #14 (Marvel, 1970) CGC NM 9.4 Off-white to white pages. Spider-Man guest-stars in this "Super-Spectacular" issue, and he's not alone; Captain America puts in a cameo appearance as well. Art is provided by John Buscema on pencils, inked by Dan Adkins. Overstreet 2005 NM- 9.2 value = $165. CGC census 8/05: 20 in 9.4, 6 higher.

1142 The Silver Surfer #15 (Marvel, 1970) CGC NM 9.4 Off-white to white pages. The Silver Surfer battles the Human Torch. The Thing and Mr. Fantastic also appear. John Buscema and Dan Adkins interior art. Marie Severin cover. Overstreet 2005 NM- 9.2 value = $100. CGC census 8/05: 17 in 9.4, 3 higher.

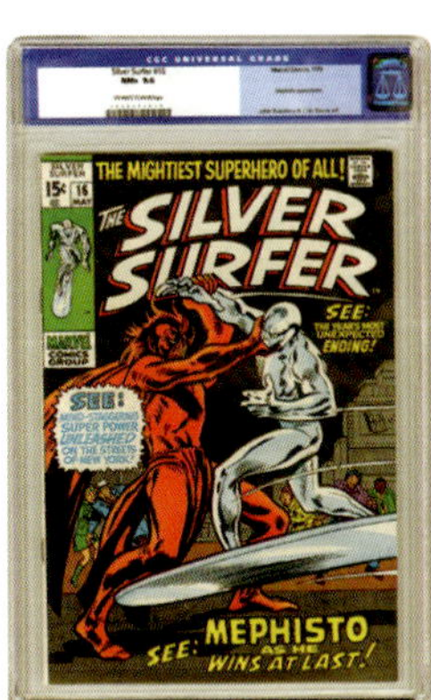

1143 The Silver Surfer #16 (Marvel, 1970) CGC NM+ 9.6 Off-white to white pages. The Silver Surfer battles Mephisto — who will win? Nick Fury and Dum-Dum Dugan make a brief appearance. John Buscema provides cover and story art. Overstreet 2005 NM- 9.2 value = $100. CGC census 8/05: 7 in 9.6, 1 higher.

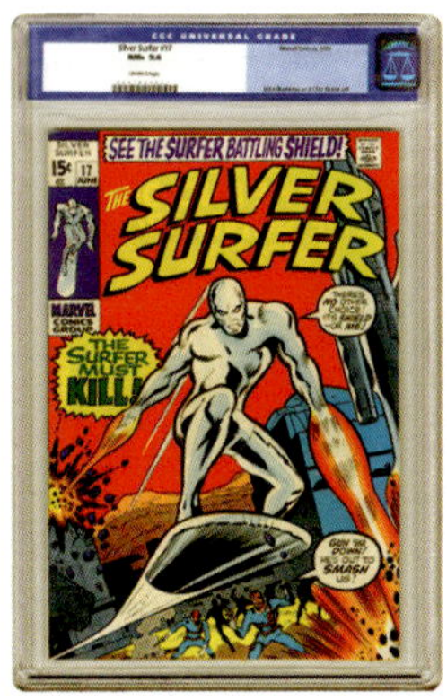

1144 The Silver Surfer #17 (Marvel, 1970) CGC NM+ 9.6 Off-white pages. Nick Fury guest-stars in this issue, which also includes a brief Fantastic Four appearance. Barry Smith provides the cover; John Buscema handles the interior art. This sparkling copy is unsurpassed in the current CGC census for this issue. Overstreet 2005 NM- 9.2 value = $100. CGC census 8/05: 7 in 9.6, none higher.

1145 The Silver Surfer #17 (Marvel, 1970) CGC NM 9.4 Off-white pages. Nick Fury guest-stars. Fantastic Four appearance. Art by Barry Smith (cover) and John Buscema (story). Overstreet 2005 NM- 9.2 value = $100. CGC census 8/05: 18 in 9.4, 7 higher.

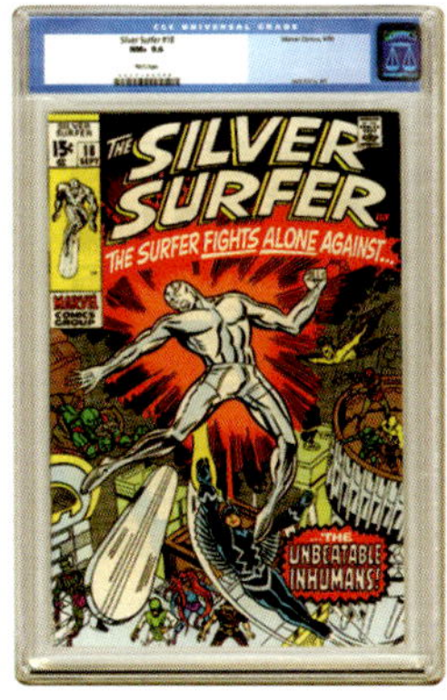

1146 The Silver Surfer #18 (Marvel, 1970) CGC NM+ 9.6 White pages. Jack Kirby provided the cover and interior art for this final issue of the original series. The Inhumans appear as guest-stars. Overstreet 2005 NM- 9.2 value = $100. CGC census 8/05: 6 in 9.6, 1 higher.

1147 The Silver Surfer V2#1 (Marvel, 1982) CGC NM/MT 9.8 Off-white pages. John Byrne cover and art. Overstreet 2005 NM-9.2 value = $10. CGC census 9/05: 28 in 9.8, none higher.

1148 Special Marvel Edition #15 Master of Kung Fu (Marvel, 1973) CGC NM/MT 9.8 Off-white to white pages. Every Bronze Age Marvel fan remembers the series **Master of Kung Fu**, but only possessors of a black belt in the Marvel arts know that the character of Shang-Chi first appeared in this title. And since the kung fu fighter is so closely associated with the Doug Moench/Paul Gulacy team, you might have forgotten that he was created by Steve Englehart and Jim Starlin. Starlin provided cover and interior art for the issue, which details the origin of Shang-Chi, the son of Fu Manchu. No copy has been graded higher than this one by CGC to date, and the black cover might tend to preclude any from doing so. Overstreet 2005 NM- 9.2 value = $120. CGC census 9/05: 10 in 9.8, none higher.

1149 Special Marvel Edition #15 (Marvel, 1973) CGC NM+ 9.6. First appearance of Shang-Chi, Master of Kung Fu. Jim Starlin cover and art. Overstreet 2005 NM- 9.2 value = $120. CGC census 8/05: 40 in 9.6, 10 higher.

1150 Spectacular Spider-Man #1 (Marvel, 1976) CGC NM/MT 9.8 Off-white to white pages. Sal Buscema cover and art. Overstreet 2005 NM- 9.2 value = $60. CGC census 9/05: 2 in 9.8, none higher.

1151 Strange Tales #101 (Marvel, 1962) CGC VF+ 8.5 Off-white to white pages. This issue marked the title's change to a superhero format (at least as far as the lead story was concerned). The Human Torch began a regular feature here, and the origin of the Fantastic Four was retold. Jack Kirby drew the cover and the Torch story; there are also some "strange" backup features drawn by Steve Ditko and Don Heck. Overstreet 2005 VF 8.0 value = $808; VF/NM 9.0 value = $1,304. CGC census 9/05: 5 in 8.5, 11 higher.

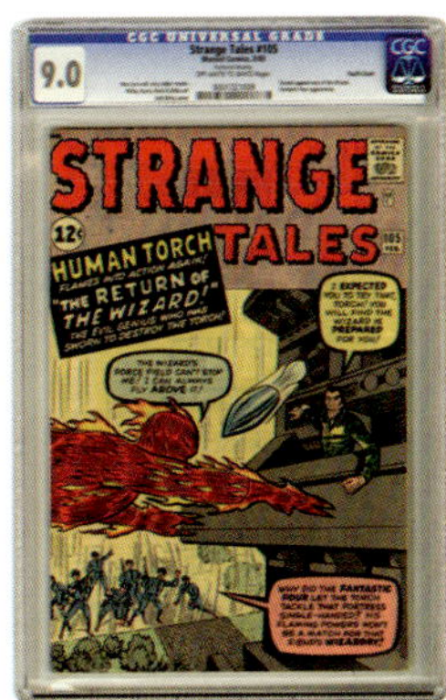

1152 Strange Tales #105 Pacific Coast pedigree (Marvel, 1963) CGC VF/NM 9.0 Off-white to white pages. The Wizard was a wealthy inventor who had accomplished everything there was to accomplish... except defeating the Human Torch. He gives it another go in this second appearance. The Torch gets some help from his sister, the Invisible Girl, in the story, which has Jack Kirby art. The issue's other two stories were drawn by Steve Ditko and Don Heck respectively. The cover's by Kirby. CGC notes, "Pre-Marvel chipping." Overstreet 2005 VF/NM 9.0 value = $342; NM- 9.2 value = $460. CGC census 9/05: 7 in 9.0, 6 higher.

1153 Strange Tales #145 Pacific Coast pedigree (Marvel, 1966) CGC NM+ 9.6 Off-white to white pages. Marvel's top two artists, Jack Kirby and Steve Ditko, saw to the art in this issue, with Kirby drawing the cover and the S.H.I.E.L.D. story, and Ditko drawing the Doctor Strange tale. Overstreet 2005 NM- 9.2 value = $55. CGC census 9/05: 5 in 9.6, 1 higher.

1154 Strange Tales #153 Pacific Coast pedigree (Marvel, 1967) CGC NM+ 9.6 White pages. The "Nick Fury, Agent of S.H.I.E.L.D." feature was the first strip that Jim Steranko worked on for Marvel, and to teach the newcomer the ropes, editor Stan Lee had Steranko work over layouts by Jack Kirby. This is the third issue of that Kirby/Steranko team-up. The book also has a Doctor Strange feature with Marie Severin art. The cover is by Steranko. Overstreet 2005 NM- 9.2 value = $65. CGC census 9/05: 5 in 9.6, 1 higher.

1155 The Sub-Mariner #1 (Marvel, 1968) CGC NM+ 9.6 Off-white to white pages. The first issue of Subby's own book includes a recap of his origin. The cover and interior art are by John Buscema. Overstreet 2005 NM- 9.2 value = $250. CGC census 7/05: 73 in 9.6, 16 higher.

1156 The Sub-Mariner #2 (Marvel, 1968) CGC NM+ 9.6 White pages. The Sub-Mariner battles Triton. The Inhumans appear. John Buscema cover and art (CGC header lists Sal Buscema as artist). Overstreet 2005 NM- 9.2 value = $100. CGC census 8/05: 56 in 9.6, 14 higher.

1157 Superman's Pal Jimmy Olsen #118 (DC, 1969) CGC NM- 9.2 Off-white to white pages. It doesn't get much wilder than this — "Hippie Olsen's Hate-In!" Lex Luthor appearance; Neal Adams cover art. Overstreet 2005 NM- 9.2 value = $40. CGC census 9/05: 1 in 9.2, 5 higher.

1158 Tales of Suspense #70 Boston pedigree (Marvel, 1965) CGC NM+ 9.6 White pages. In a World War II flashback story, the Nazis have a rocket aimed right at 10 Downing Street, and only Captain America can stop them! The story has George Tuska art over Jack Kirby layouts. The double-feature also has an Iron Man story with Don Heck art. The cover's by Kirby. Overstreet 2005 NM- 9.2 value = $120. CGC census 9/05: 4 in 9.6, 1 higher.

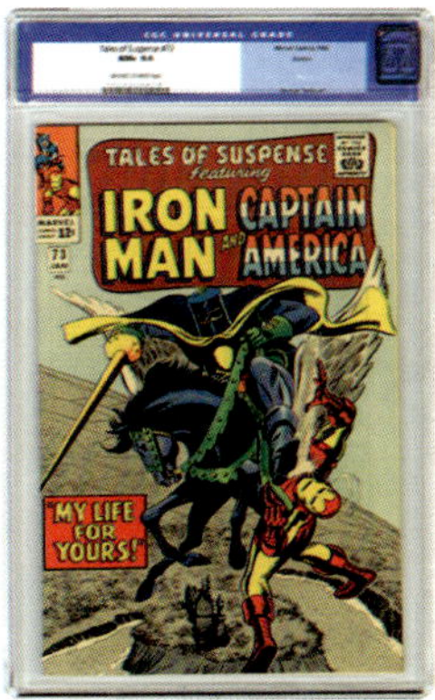

1159 Tales of Suspense #73 Boston pedigree (Marvel, 1966) CGC NM+ 9.6 Off-white to white pages. The very Gene Colan-like Adam Austin (wink, wink) drew this issue's cover as well as the Iron Man story. Also in the issue is an installment of the memorable "Sleeper" storyline, in which a Nazi robot that lay dormant for years has awoken, and Captain America has to try to stop it from hooking up with the other two parts. The Cap story has George Tuska art over Jack Kirby layouts. Overstreet 2005 NM- 9.2 value = $80. CGC census 9/05: 7 in 9.6, 2 higher.

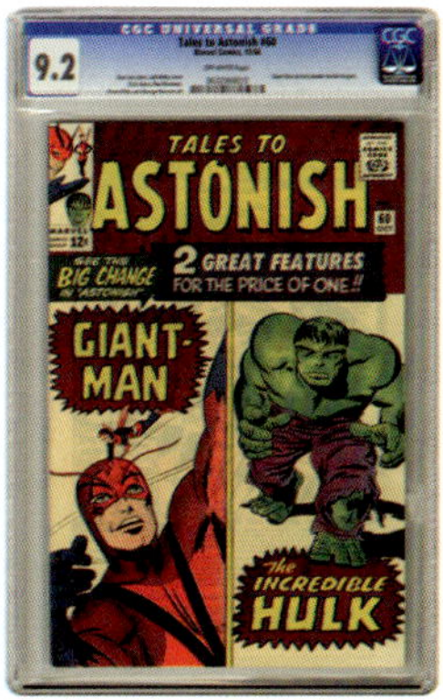

1160 Tales to Astonish #60 (Marvel, 1964) CGC NM- 9.2 Off-white pages. Giant-Man and Hulk began a double-feature arrangement with this issue. Jack Kirby drew both characters on the cover, while inside the book Dick Ayers drew Dr. Pym's story while Steve Ditko portrayed Dr. Banner in action. Overstreet 2005 NM- 9.2 value = $300. CGC census 9/05: 8 in 9.2, 6 higher.

1161 Tales to Astonish #64 (Marvel, 1965) CGC NM+ 9.6 Off-white to white pages. Jack Kirby cover. Hulk story with Steve Ditko art. Giant-Man story with Carl Burgos art. This is currently the highest grade awarded by CGC for this issue. Overstreet 2005 NM- 9.2 value = $140. CGC census 8/05: 5 in 9.6, none higher.

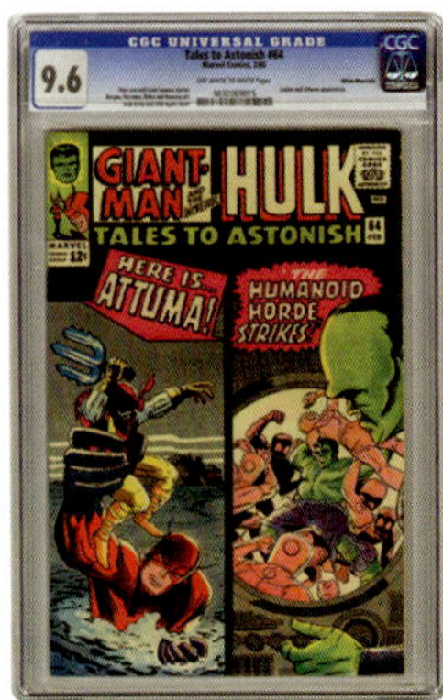

1162 Tales to Astonish #64 White Mountain pedigree (Marvel, 1965) CGC NM+ 9.6 Off-white to white pages. Legend has it that the owner of the White Mountain collection, which consisted primarily of horror and science fiction books, had no interest in superheroes, and that when a series like this one changed to a superhero format, he only continued buying them for a few issues out of force of habit. Perhaps he never even read this one after buying it, which would explain the superb condition! The issue has a Jack Kirby cover, with interior art by Steve Ditko (Hulk story) and Carl Burgos (Giant-Man story). Overstreet 2005 NM- 9.2 value = $140. CGC census 9/05: 5 in 9.6, none higher.

1163 Tales to Astonish #97 (Marvel, 1967) CGC NM 9.4 Off-white pages. X-Men cameo. Marie Severin and Herb Trimpe cover. Severin, Trimpe, Werner Roth, and Dan Adkins art. Overstreet 2005 NM- 9.2 value = $70. CGC census 9/05: 6 in 9.4, 3 higher.

1164 Thor #132 Double Cover (Marvel, 1966) CGC NM 9.4 White Pages. First appearance of Ego, the Living Planet (cameo). First appearance of the Recorder. Tales of Asgard backup feature. Jack Kirby cover and art. CGC notes, "1st cover 9.2, interior cover 9.4." Overstreet 2005 NM- 9.2 value = $90. CGC census 9/05: 58 in 9.4, 88 higher.

1165 Thor #165 (Marvel, 1969) CGC NM 9.4 White pages. This issue features the first full appearance of Him (Warlock). Jack Kirby cover and art. Overstreet 2005 NM- 9.2 value = $90. CGC census 9/05: 7 in 9.4, 4 higher.

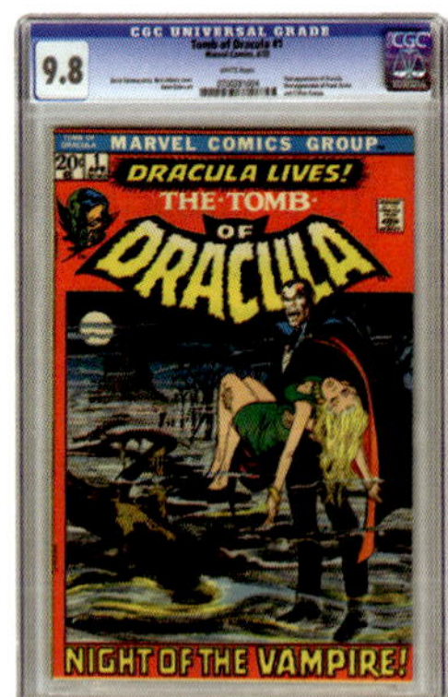

1166 Tomb of Dracula #1 (Marvel, 1972) CGC NM/MT 9.8 White pages. This issue marked the first appearance of Marvel's Dracula, and if you're wondering why it took so long, blame the Comics Code, which at one time had a restriction forbidding vampires in comics. Also making his first appearance was Drac's descendant (and enemy), Frank Drake. This series has become quite a collector's favorite, in large part because of the moody art of Gene Colan, who drew the series' entire run. And this first issue has the added bonus of a Neal Adams cover! Overstreet 2005 NM- 9.2 value = $220. CGC census 8/05: 4 in 9.8, none higher.

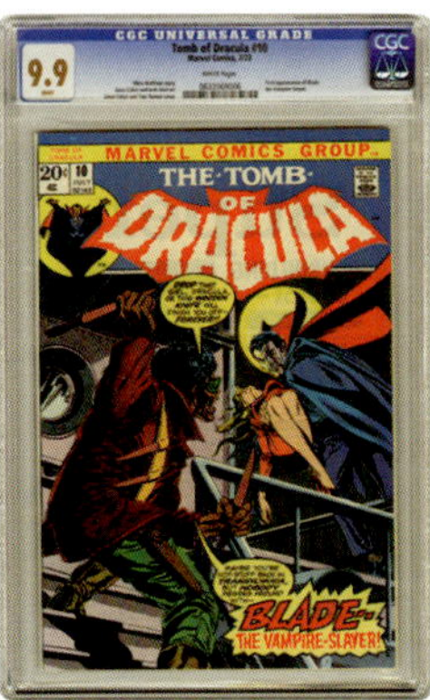

1167 Tomb of Dracula #10 (Marvel, 1973) CGC MT 9.9 White pages. Here's the only 9.9 yet certified of this key Bronze Age book, the first appearance of Blade, Vampire Slayer. It's a comic that soared in demand once Blade became the star of a movie, in fact he has now surpassed all other Marvel characters, being the first to star in *three* motion pictures! The story is by the character's creator Marv Wolfman, and the moody art is by the always excellent Gene Colan. Overstreet 2005 NM- 9.2 value = $175. CGC census 9/05: 1 in 9.9, none higher.

1168 Tomb of Dracula #10 (Marvel, 1973) CGC NM 9.4 White pages. This issue contains the first appearance of Blade the Vampire Slayer. Gene Colan handles the art chores, with assists from Tom Palmer and Jack Abel. Overstreet 2005 NM- 9.2 value = $175. CGC census 9/05: 14 in 9.4, 28 higher.

1169 Two-Gun Kid #83 (Marvel, 1966) CGC NM+ 9.6 White pages. Dick Ayers cover and art. Overstreet 2005 NM- 9.2 value = $35. CGC census 9/05: 2 in 9.6, none higher.

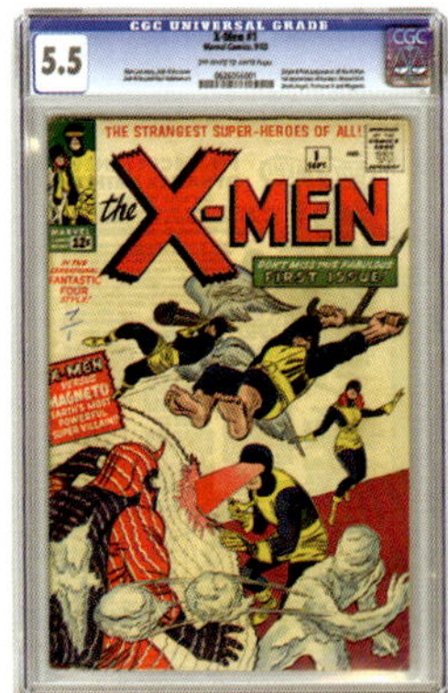

1170 X-Men #1 (Marvel, 1963) CGC FN- 5.5 Off-white to white pages. It all begins here, X-fans: the origin and first appearance of the original X-Men (the Angel, the Beast, Cyclops, Iceman, and Marvel Girl); the first appearances of Professor X and Magneto... all this and Jack Kirby cover and interior art, too! What a book! And what a copy for the grade: just a modest bit of wear (and a small inked seven-over-one mark, no doubt made by the newsstand agent). Overstreet 2005 FN 6.0 value = $1,950. CGC census 8/05: 31 in 5.5, 201 higher.

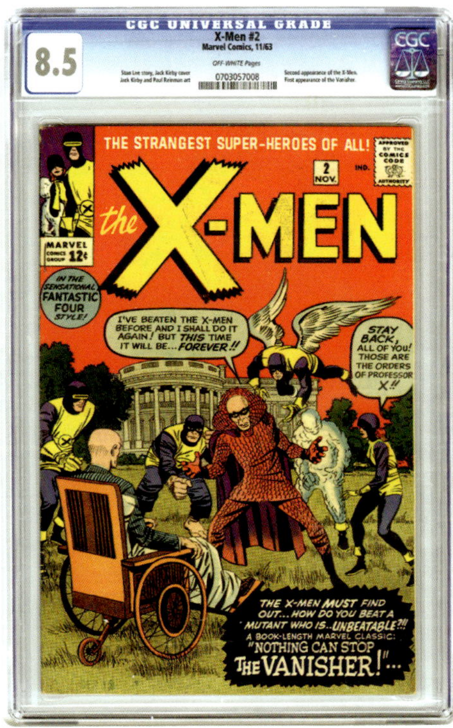

1171 X-Men #2 (Marvel, 1963) CGC VF+ 8.5 Off-white pages. Here's the skinny on this second issue: Stan Lee story. Jack Kirby cover. Jack Kirby and Paul Reinman art. Second appearance of the X-Men. First appearance of the Vanisher. And this copy? It's a beauty! 'Nuff said, true believer? Bid! Overstreet 2005 VF 8.0 value = $6,000; VF/NM 9.0 value = $10,000. CGC census 9/05: 16 in 8.5, 37 higher.

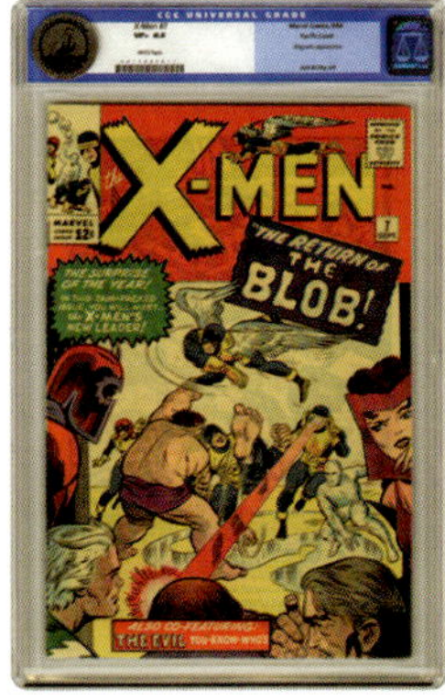

1172 X-Men #7 Pacific Coast pedigree (Marvel, 1964) CGC VF+ 8.5 White pages. This early issue has the first appearance of Cerebro, Professor X's mutant-detecting machine that was seen throughout the series and even played a major role in the "X-Men" movies. Also, Cyclops was named deputy leader of the X-Men in this issue. The villains are the X-Men's arch-foes, the Brotherhood of Evil Mutants. The issue's cover and art are by Jack Kirby. Overstreet 2005 VF 8.0 value = $407; VF/NM 9.0 value = $641. CGC census 9/05: 12 in 8.5, 28 higher.

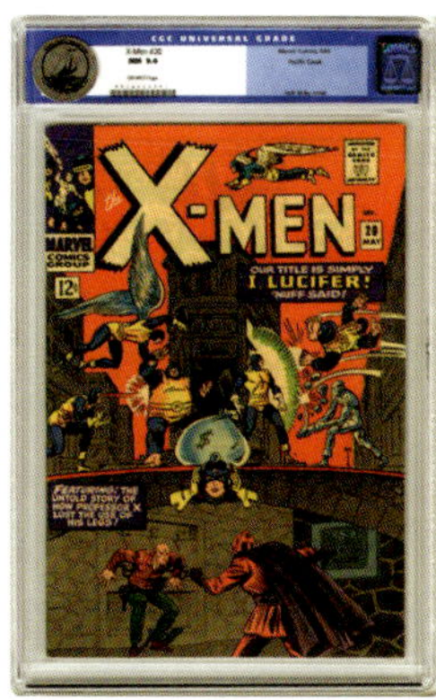

1173 X-Men #20 Pacific Coast pedigree (Marvel, 1966) CGC NM 9.4 Off-white pages. In this issue, wheelchair-bound Professor X tells the tale of how he lost his legs at the hands of Lucifer. And the X-Men have to battle not only Lucifer, but the Blob and Unus as well. The cover and interior art are by Werner Roth and Dick Ayers. Overstreet 2005 NM- 9.2 value = $270. CGC census 8/05: 13 in 9.4, 5 higher.

1174 X-Men #26 Pacific Coast pedigree (Marvel, 1966) CGC NM- 9.2 Off-white to white pages. The X-Men battle Kukulcan. Werner Roth and Dick Ayers art. Overstreet 2005 NM- 9.2 value = $190. CGC census 9/05: 25 in 9.2, 27 higher.

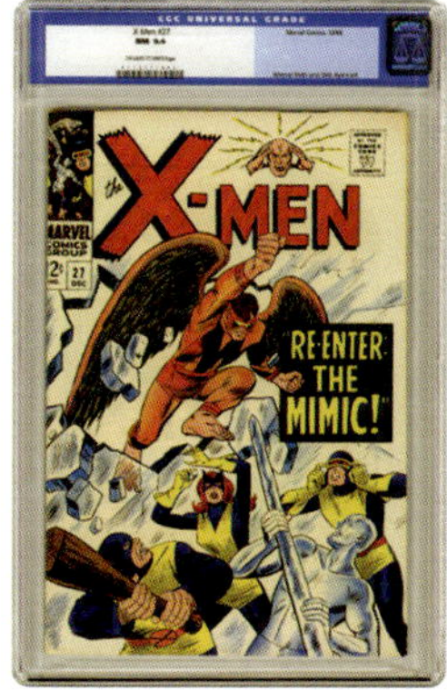

1175 X-Men #27 (Marvel, 1966) CGC NM 9.4 Off-white to white pages. This issue features the return of the mutant Mimic. Spider-Man drops by for a cameo appearance. Art by Werner Roth and Dick Ayers. Overstreet 2005 NM- 9.2 value = $190. CGC census 9/05: 4 in 9.4, 2 higher.

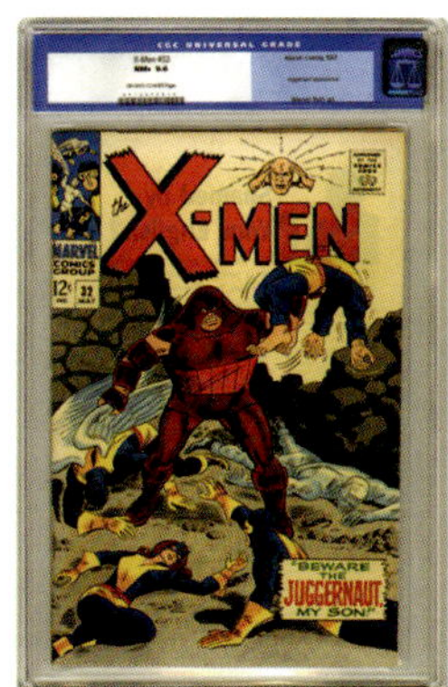

1176 X-Men #32 (Marvel, 1967) CGC NM+ 9.6 Off-white to white pages. In this issue, Professor X tries to cure the Juggernaut of his evilness — he *is* Xavier's stepbrother, after all. But as you can see from Werner Roth's cover, things don't quite work out that way, and a battle with the X-Men ensues! Roth provided interior art for the issue as well. Overstreet 2005 NM- 9.2 value = $150. CGC census 8/05: 8 in 9.6, 1 higher.

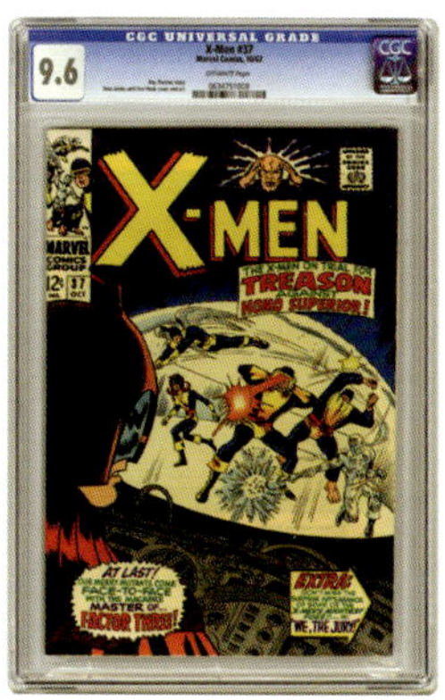

1177 X-Men #37 (Marvel, 1967) CGC NM+ 9.6 Off-white pages. The X-Men take on Factor Three, that's the Changeling, the Vanisher, the Blob, Unus the Untouchable, and their mysterious leader the Mutant-Master. The issue has Jack Kirby layouts and Don Heck finished art. Ross Andru supplied the interior art. Overstreet 2005 NM- 9.2 value = $150. CGC census 8/05: 7 in 9.6, 1 higher.

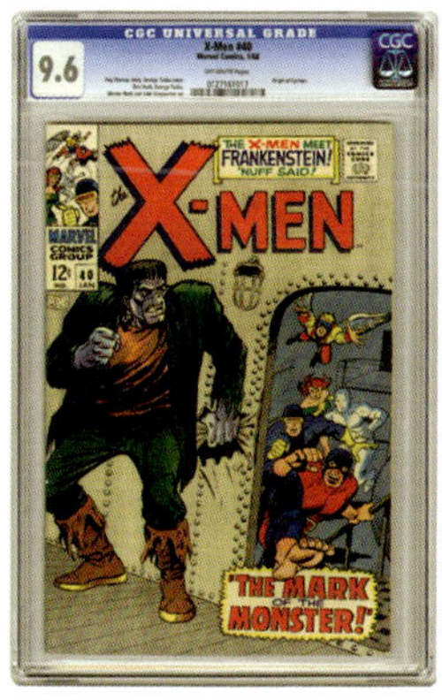

1178 X-Men #40 (Marvel, 1968) CGC NM+ 9.6 Off-white pages. The X-Men meet the Frankenstein android, and a backup feature continues the story of how Professor X recruited Cyclops. George Tuska drew the cover in addition to inking Don Heck's pencils on the main story. Werner Roth drew the backup feature. Overstreet 2005 NM- 9.2 value = $160. CGC census 8/05: 16 in 9.6, 1 higher.

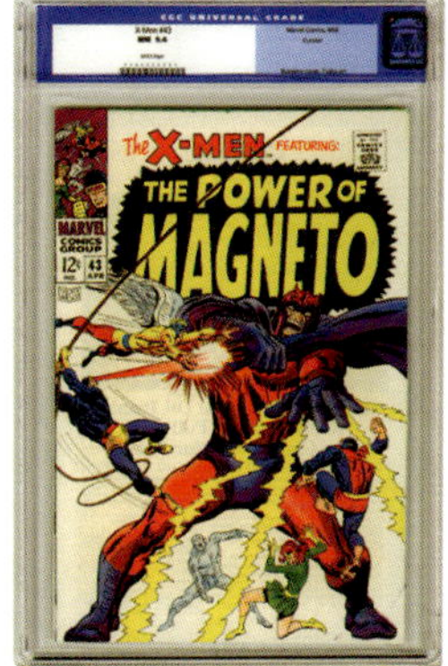

1179 X-Men #43 Curator pedigree (Marvel, 1968) CGC NM 9.4 White pages. The X-Men take on Magneto and the Toad in this issue. Quicksilver and the Scarlet Witch appear as well. The dynamic poses on the cover could only be the work of John Buscema (who didn't draw the X-Men very often!). The interior art is by George Tuska (main story) and Werner Roth (backup feature). Overstreet 2005 NM- 9.2 value = $125. CGC census 8/05: 13 in 9.4, 10 higher.

1180 X-Men #44 (Marvel, 1968) CGC NM 9.4 Cream to off-white pages. First Silver Age appearance of Red Raven. Magneto, Scarlet Witch, and Quicksilver appear. Backup feature begins origin of Iceman. Don Heck cover. Heck and Werner Roth art. Backup feature with George Tuska art. Overstreet 2005 NM- 9.2 value = $125. CGC census 8/05: 16 in 9.4, 2 higher.

1181 X-Men #44 (Marvel, 1968) CGC NM 9.4 Off-white pages. First Silver Age appearance of Red Raven is featured. Magneto, Scarlet Witch, and Quicksilver appear. The origin of Iceman appears in a back-up story with George Tuska art. Don Heck cover. Heck and Werner Roth art. Overstreet 2005 NM- 9.2 value = $125. CGC census 9/05: 16 in 9.4, 2 higher.

1182 X-Men #45 (Marvel, 1968) CGC NM+ 9.6 Off-white to white pages. Quicksilver appearance. Magneto also appears. Origin of Iceman. Art by Don Heck, Werner Roth, and John Tartaglione. Overstreet 2005 NM- 9.2 value = $125. CGC census 8/05: 29 in 9.6, 3 higher.

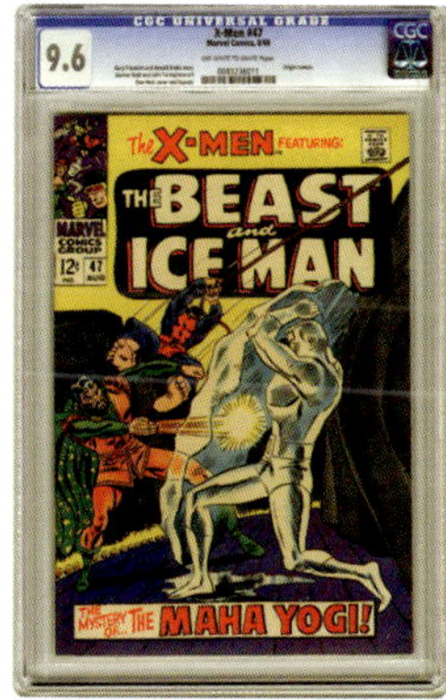

1183 X-Men #47 (Marvel, 1968) CGC NM+ 9.6 Off-white to white pages. With Professor X dead (or so everyone thought) and the X-Men disbanded by the FBI, Iceman and Beast have to go it alone against the Warlock, who's now calling himself the Maha Yogi. Plus, they get in a dust-up with four thugs, who are worthy of mention for their eclectic names: Cairo, Studs, O'Hara, and Hymie! Writer Gary Friedrich came up with this far-out stuff, and Don Heck drew it. Werner Roth provided finished pencils in addition to drawing a backup feature that explains Iceman's powers. Overstreet 2005 NM- 9.2 value = $125. CGC census 8/05: 7 in 9.6, 1 higher.

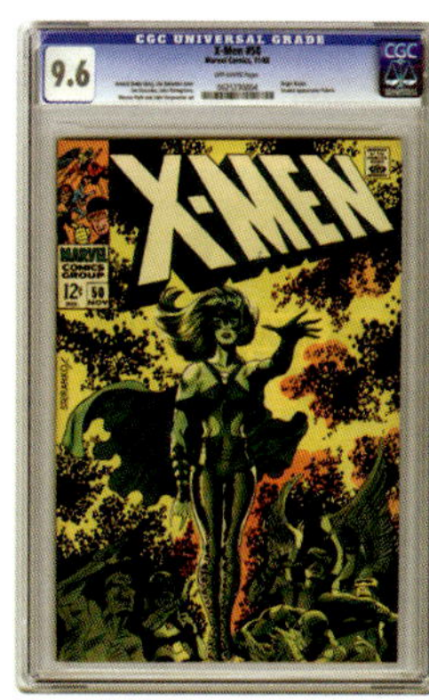

1184 X-Men #50 (Marvel, 1968) CGC NM+ 9.6 Off-white pages. This was the first issue of this series to have Jim Steranko interior art, and only the second issue with a Steranko cover. It's also the first issue with the familiar three-dimensional logo that was used for the next 33 years! The story features Polaris as well as Mesmero and Magneto. The backup feature tells the story of the Beast's childhood. Overstreet 2005 NM- 9.2 value = $130. CGC census 8/05: 14 in 9.6, 1 higher.

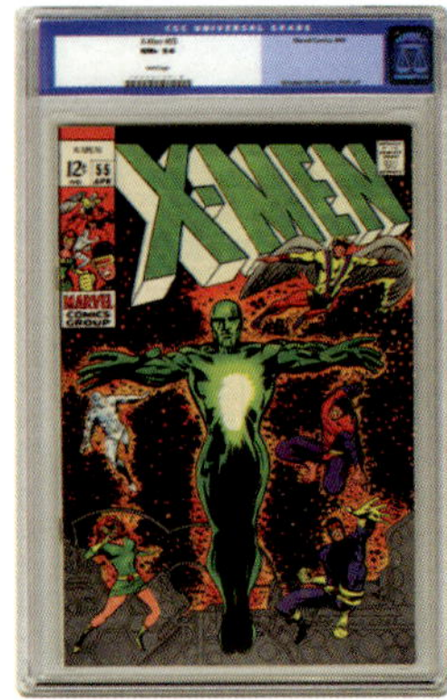

1185 X-Men #55 (Marvel, 1969) CGC NM+ 9.6 White pages. Alex Summers (soon to become Havok) discovers he has mutant powers in this issue. The cover is by Barry Smith (one of his first comic covers), and the interior art is by Werner Roth. A backup feature tells how the Angel joined the X-Men. Overstreet 2005 NM- 9.2 value = $135. CGC census 8/05: 12 in 9.6, none higher.

1186 X-Men #61 (Marvel, 1969) CGC NM 9.4 Off-white pages. Sauron appearance. Neal Adams cover. Adams and Tom Palmer art. Overstreet 2005 NM- 9.2 value = $130. CGC census 9/05: 19 in 9.4, 5 higher.

1187 X-Men #89 (Marvel, 1974) CGC NM 9.4 White pages. Reprints issue #41. Overstreet 2005 NM- 9.2 value = $85. CGC census 9/05: 12 in 9.4, 13 higher.

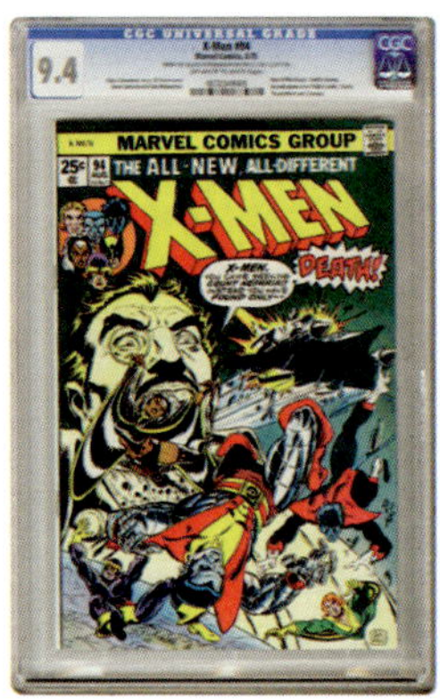

1188 X-Men #94 (Marvel, 1975) CGC NM 9.4 Off-white to white pages. This issue had key events aplenty. Not only was it the second appearance of the New X-Men, it showed the original members promptly packing their bags to leave the team (one "new" X-Man, Japanese mutant Sunfire, also said *sayonara* here, after only one adventure with the group). This issue, the first appearance of the new team in the regular **X-Men** title, is #3 on Overstreet's list of the most valuable Bronze Age books. The cover is by Gil Kane, and the interior art is by Dave Cockrum. CGC notes, "From the Dallas Stephens collection." Overstreet 2005 NM- 9.2 value = $1,000. CGC census 9/05: 84 in 9.4, 17 higher.

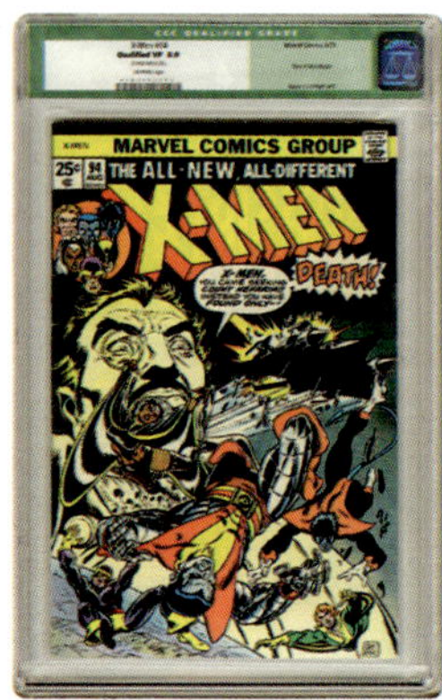

1189 X-Men #94 (Marvel, 1975) CGC Qualified VF 8.0 Off-white pages. The debut of the modern X-Men team is featured in this series, which includes the second appearance of Colossus, Nightcrawler, Storm, and Thunderbird, following **Giant-Size X-Men** #1. The old-guard heroes Angel, Marvel Girl, and Iceman resign; Sunfire leaves the group as well. Gil Kane and Dave Cockrum drew the dynamic cover, with interior art by Cockrum. CGC notes, "Staples replaced." Overstreet 2005 GD 2.0 value = $53; VG 4.0 value = $106; FN 6.0 value = $159; VF 8.0 value = $451.

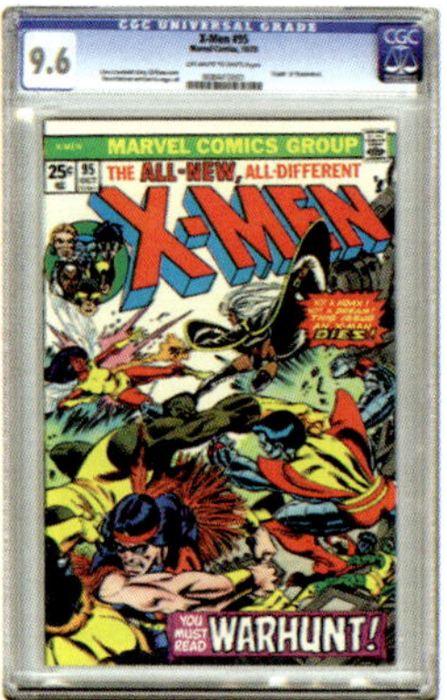

1190 X-Men #95 (Marvel, 1975) CGC NM+ 9.6 Off-white to white pages. Thunderbird, we hardly knew ye. The third appearance of the X-Men's Native American member was also his last, but at least he died knowing that he lasted longer than Sunfire as a member of the group, and also that his demise added drama to this Chris Claremont yarn with Dave Cockrum art. The cover is by Gil Kane. Overstreet 2005 NM- 9.2 value = $200. CGC census 9/05: 31 in 9.6, 6 higher.

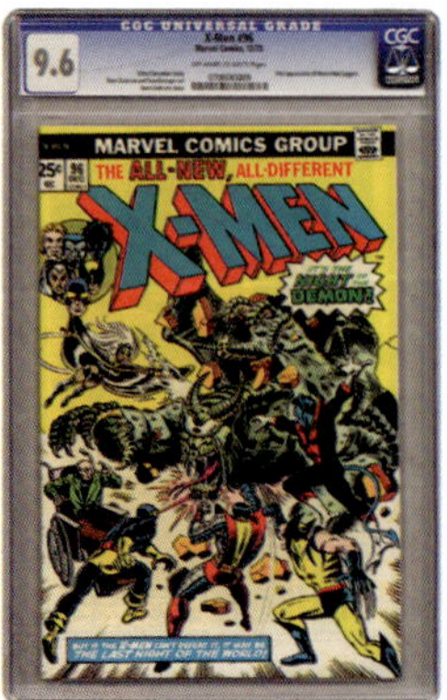

1191 X-Men #96 (Marvel, 1975) CGC NM+ 9.6 Off-white to white pages. Moira MacTaggert, sometime love interest of Professor X (and later of the Banshee), made her first appearance in this issue. It's also the first appearance of Sentinel-making mastermind Steven Lang. And for all you X-Maniacs out there, we'll note that the N'Garai demons seen on this cover would next appear to terrorize Kitty Pryde in a memorable tale in #143! The new X-Men's co-creator Dave Cockrum drew this issue's story, while Marie Severin provided the cover art. Overstreet 2005 NM- 9.2 value = $110. CGC census 8/05: 31 in 9.6, 2 higher.

1192 X-Men #96 (Marvel, 1975) CGC NM+ 9.6 Off-white to white pages. The new X-Men's third appearance in their regular series featured the first appearance of Dr. Moira MacTaggert, who in addition to helping the X-Men with her scientific acumen would be a love interest for both Professor X and the Banshee over the course of the series. The interior art is by the new group's co-creator Dave Cockrum, and the cover's by Bullpen vet Marie Severin. Overstreet 2005 NM- 9.2 value = $110. CGC census 9/05: 31 in 9.6, 2 higher.

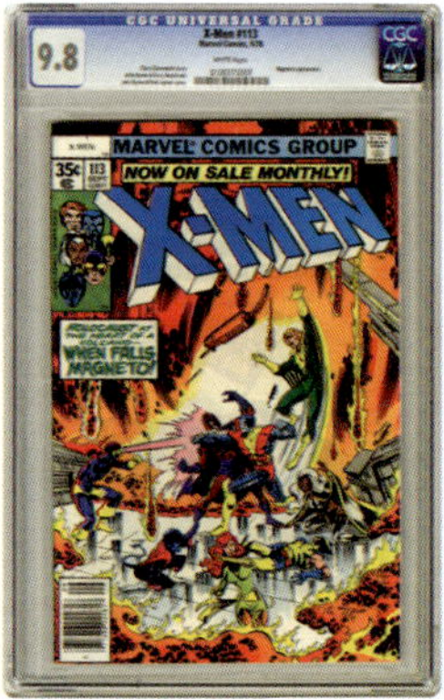

1193 X-Men #113 (Marvel, 1978) CGC NM/MT 9.8 White pages. While John Byrne had been penciling this series since #108, this issue has Byrne's first cover for the series. In the story, drawn by Byrne and Terry Austin, the X-Men's battle with Magneto in the Savage Land ends up with Phoenix and the Beast believing the rest of the X-Men dead and vice versa! Overstreet 2005 NM- 9.2 value = $50. CGC census 8/05: 7 in 9.8, 1 higher.

1194 X-Men #127 (Marvel, 1979) CGC NM/MT 9.8 White pages. Cover and interior art by John Byrne and Terry Austin. Overstreet 2005 NM- 9.2 value = $35. CGC census 8/05: 31 in 9.8, none higher.

1195 X-Men #135 (Marvel, 1980) CGC NM/MT 9.8 White pages. John Byrne and Terry Austin cover and art. Overstreet 2005 NM- 9.2 value = $35. CGC census 8/05: 34 in 9.8, 1 higher.

DC SILVER AGE TO MODERN AGE

1196 Action Comics #354 (DC, 1967) CGC NM 9.4 Off-white to white pages. Curt Swan cover. Al Plastino and Jim Mooney art. Overstreet 2005 NM- 9.2 value = $55. CGC census 9/05: 1 in 9.4, none higher.

1197 Adventure Comics #346 (DC, 1966) CGC NM 9.4 Cream to off-white pages. First appearance of Karate Kid, Princess Projectra, Ferro Lad, and Nemesis Kid. Curt Swan cover. Sheldon Moldoff art. Overstreet 2005 NM- 9.2 value = $95. CGC census 8/05: 3 in 9.4, none higher.

1198 All-Star Western #1 (DC, 1970) CGC NM+ 9.6 Off-white to white pages. Carmine Infantino art. Overstreet 2005 NM- 9.2 value = $60. CGC census 9/05: 1 in 9.6, none higher.

1199 All-Star Western #2 (DC, 1970) CGC NM+ 9.6 White pages. Neal Adams cover. Tony DeZuniga and Gray Morrow art. Overstreet 2005 NM- 9.2 value = $50. CGC census 9/05: 1 in 9.6, none higher.

1200 All-Star Western #4 (DC, 1971) CGC NM+ 9.6 Off-white to white pages. Neal Adams cover. Gil Kane and Gray Morrow art. Overstreet 2005 NM- 9.2 value = $35. CGC census 9/05: 2 in 9.6, none higher.

1201 All-Star Western #5 (DC, 1971) CGC NM/MT 9.8 Off-white to white pages. Neal Adams cover. Jim Aparo and Alan Weiss art. Overstreet 2005 NM- 9.2 value = $35. CGC census 9/05: 1 in 9.8, none higher.

1202 All-Star Western #6 (DC, 1971) CGC NM+ 9.6 Off-white to white pages. Tony DeZuniga cover. DeZuniga and Gil Kane art. Overstreet 2005 NM- 9.2 value = $35. CGC census 9/05: 2 in 9.6, none higher.

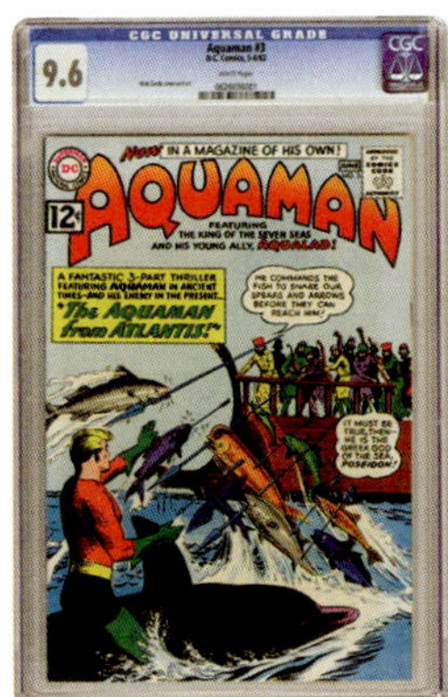

1203 Aquaman #3 (DC, 1962) CGC NM+ 9.6 White pages. No copy of this issue has been certified with a higher grade by CGC to date. Nick Cardy provided both cover and interior art. Overstreet 2005 NM- 9.2 value = $275. CGC census 9/05: 3 in 9.6, none higher.

1204 Aquaman #19 (DC, 1965) CGC NM 9.4 Off-white pages. Nick Cardy art; underwater cover. This copy is currently unsurpassed in CGC's census report for issue #19. Overstreet 2005 NM- 9.2 value = $130. CGC census 8/05: 2 in 9.4, none higher.

1205 Aquaman #45 (DC, 1969) CGC NM+ 9.6 Off-white to white pages. The terrific art of Nick Cardy (cover) and Jim Aparo (story) made **Aquaman** one of the best DC titles of the late Silver Age — this issue being the last with a 12¢ cover price. Overstreet 2005 NM- 9.2 value = $50. CGC census 8/05: 2 in 9.6, 1 higher.

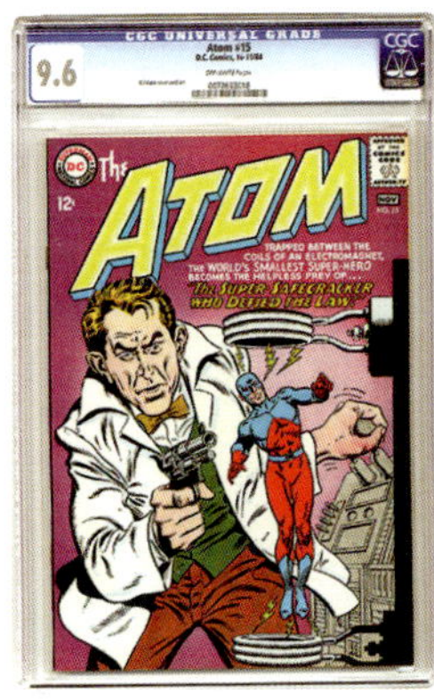

1206 The Atom #15 (DC, 1964) CGC NM+ 9.6 Off-white pages. Gil Kane art is featured on the cover and interior story. This is a sharp, attractive copy, currently unsurpassed in CGC's census report for this issue. Overstreet 2005 NM- 9.2 value = $125. CGC census 8/05: 2 in 9.6, none higher.

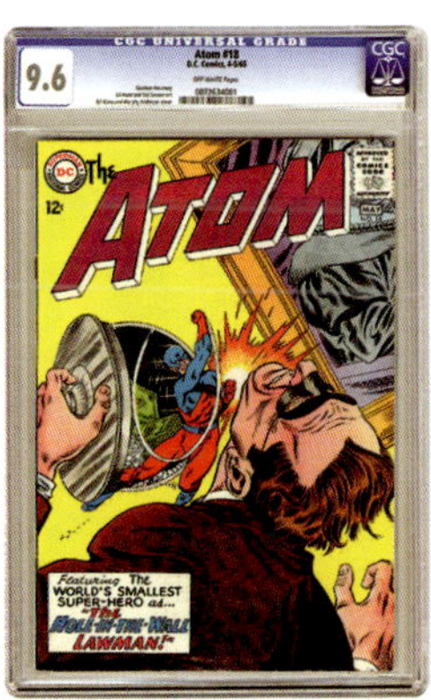

1207 The Atom #18 (DC, 1965) CGC NM+ 9.6 Off-white pages. The World's Smallest Hero scores a knock-out punch with this incredible copy. This one's got cover gloss galore; the bright yellow of the cover practically glows! Art by Gil Kane, Murphy Anderson, and Sid Greene. Overstreet 2005 NM- 9.2 value = $95. CGC census 8/05: 1 in 9.6, 1 higher.

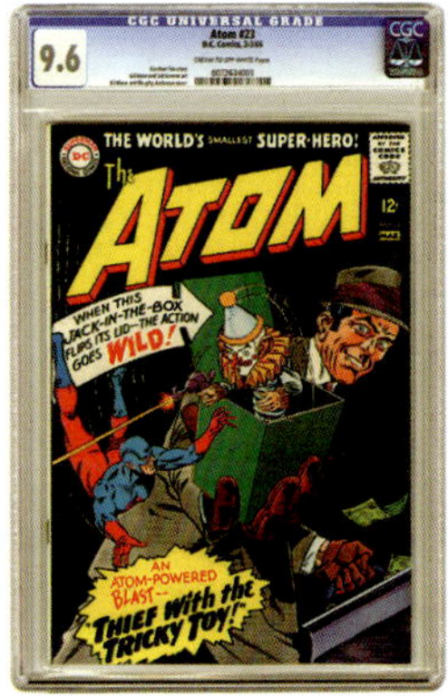

1208 The Atom #23 (DC, 1966) CGC NM+ 9.6 Cream to off-white pages. The Atom encounters "The Thief With the Tricky Toys" in this issue, which features art by Gil Kane with Murphy Anderson and Sid Greene. This superb copy sports a smooth black-background cover. Overstreet 2005 NM- 9.2 value = $80. CGC census 8/05: 2 in 9.6, none higher.

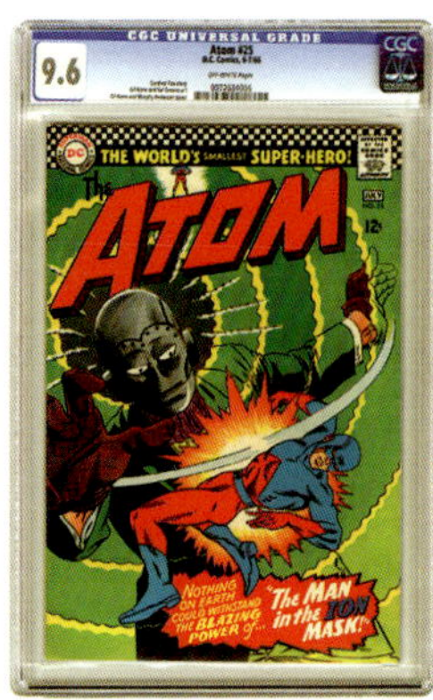

1209 The Atom #25 (DC, 1966) CGC NM+ 9.6 Off-white pages. The Atom faces off against *"The Man in the Ion Mask"* on this Gil Kane cover. Sharp and glossy copy, with none higher graded in the current CGC census. Overstreet 2005 NM- 9.2 value = $80. CGC census 8/05: 3 in 9.6, none higher.

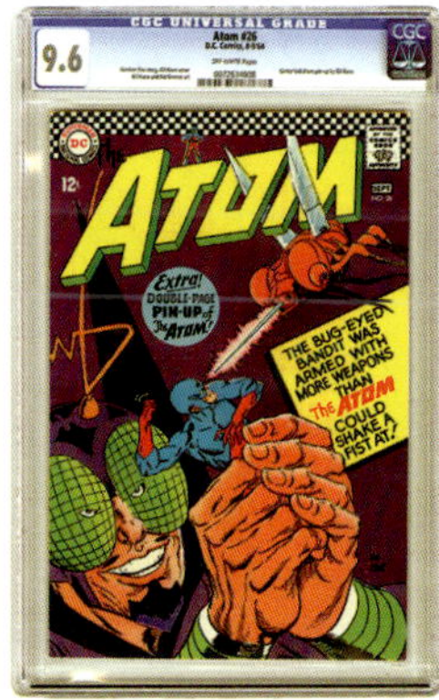

1210 The Atom #26 (DC, 1966) CGC NM+ 9.6 Off-white pages. Here's something you don't see every day — a robot mosquito! Art is by Gil Kane and Sid Greene. This exceptional comic is also unique, at least as far as 9.6 copies of issue #26 appear in the current CGC census! Overstreet 2005 NM- 9.2 value = $80. CGC census 8/05: 1 in 9.6, none higher.

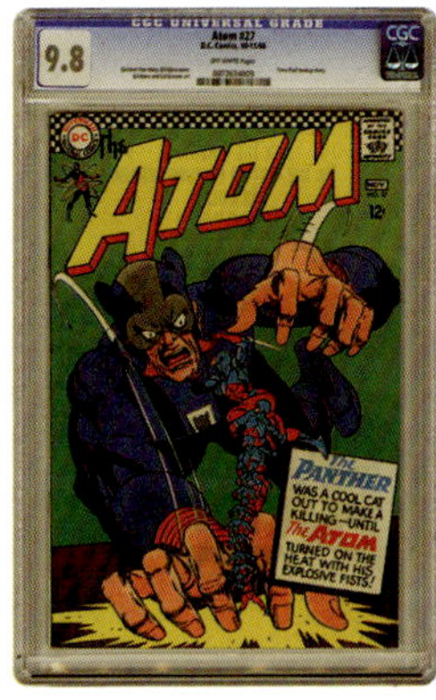

1211 The Atom #27 (DC, 1966) CGC NM/MT 9.8 Off-white pages. A Time Pool backup story is featured in this issue. Gil Kane and Sid Greene provide the artistic thrills. The biggest thrill will be in seeing this gem copy up close — it's fantastic! Overstreet 2005 NM- 9.2 value = $80. CGC census 8/05: 1 in 9.8, none higher.

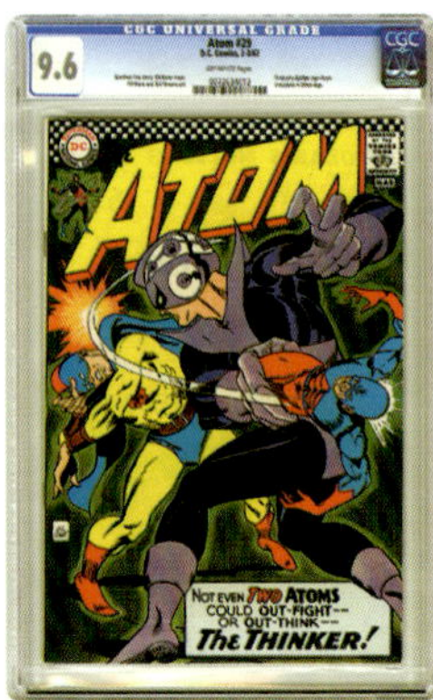

1212 The Atom #29 (DC, 1967) CGC NM+ 9.6 Off-white pages. The Golden Age Atom makes his first Silver Age crossover appearance. Gil Kane and Sid Greene supply the art. An outstanding copy of a great DC "Go-Go Check" comic. Overstreet 2005 NM- 9.2 value = $220. CGC census 8/05: 2 in 9.6, 1 higher.

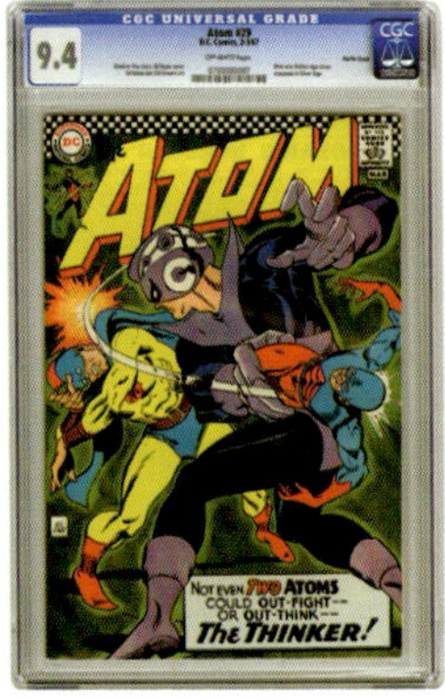

1213 The Atom #29 (DC, 1967) CGC NM 9.4 Off-white pages. The Golden Age Atom makes his first Silver Age appearance and teams up with his younger counterpart to battle the Thinker. Cover and art by Gil Kane. Overstreet 2005 NM- 9.2 value = $220. CGC census 9/05: 4 in 9.4, 3 higher.

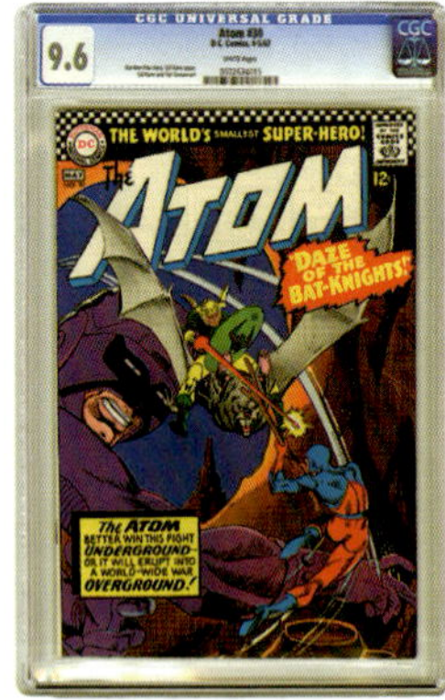

1214 The Atom #30 (DC, 1967) CGC NM+ 9.6 White pages. Our run of exceptional **Atom**s continues with this later issue, featuring "Daze of the Bat-Knights." Gil Kane handles the art chores, with an able assist from inker Sid Greene. Overstreet 2005 NM- 9.2 value = $80. CGC census 8/05: 2 in 9.6, none higher.

1215 Batman #212 (DC, 1969) CGC NM 9.4 Off-white pages. Last 12¢ issue, featuring art by Irv Novick and Joe Giella, and story by Frank Robbins. Overstreet 2005 NM- 9.2 value = $55. CGC census 7/05: 2 in 9.4, 4 higher.

1216 Batman #232 (DC, 1971) CGC NM/MT 9.8 White pages. DC comics in the seventies just did not get any better than the milestone "Daughter of the Demon." A brand-new villain debuted — and what an adversary Ra's al Ghul turned out to be. Not another super-powered goon, Ra's just had that certain evil presence that said he was not a man you'd want to mess with — Neal Adams' art certainly saw to that. Add to that some genuinely surprising twists courtesy of Denny O'Neil's plot, and extra eye candy in the form of Dick Giordano's inks (did anyone embellish Adams better?). It all adds up to a Bronze Age classic. Overstreet 2005 NM- 9.2 value = $185. CGC census 9/05: 4 in 9.8, none higher.

1217 Batman #237 (DC, 1971) CGC NM 9.4 Off-white to white pages. Classic "Night of the Reaper" story. Neal Adams cover and art. Overstreet 2005 NM- 9.2 value = $100. CGC census 9/05: 13 in 9.4, 4 higher.

1218 The Brave and the Bold #48 Strange Sports Stories (DC, 1963) CGC NM 9.4 Cream to off-white pages. Carmine Infantino cover and art. Overstreet 2005 NM- 9.2 value = $125. CGC census 9/05: 3 in 9.4, 2 higher.

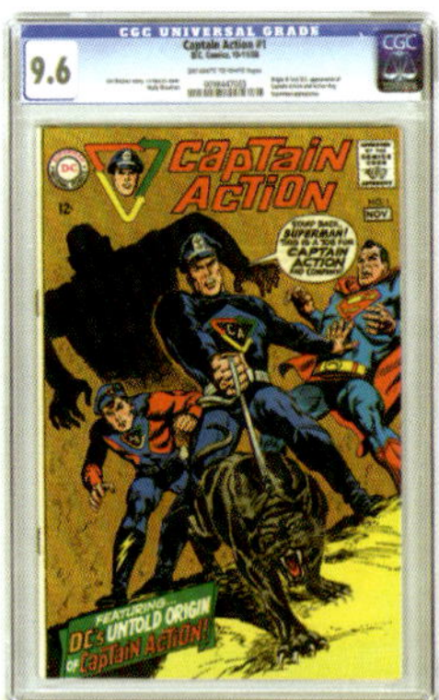

1219 Captain Action #1 (DC, 1968) CGC NM+ 9.6 Off-white to white pages. The origin of Captain Action is featured in this debut issue, inspired by the toy action figure. Superman makes a cover appearance. Irv Novick drew the cover, while Wally Wood handled the interior art. Overstreet 2005 NM- 9.2 value = $110. CGC census 9/05: 11 in 9.6, 1 higher.

1220 Challengers of the Unknown #24 (DC, 1962) CGC NM- 9.2 Cream to off-white pages. The only copy graded above 8.5 by CGC to date. Overstreet 2005 NM- 9.2 value = $100. CGC census 9/05: 1 in 9.2, none higher.

1221 Challengers of the Unknown #29 Pacific Coast pedigree (DC, 1963) CGC NM+ 9.6 Off-white to white pages. This pedigree copy is the only 9.6, and highest-graded copy overall, that CGC has certified for this issue to date. Overstreet 2005 NM- 9.2 value = $100. CGC census 9/05: 1 in 9.6, none higher.

1222 Challengers of the Unknown #30 Pacific Coast pedigree (DC, 1963) CGC NM 9.4 Off-white pages. The Challs battle Multi-Man. Overstreet 2005 NM- 9.2 value = $100. CGC census 9/05: 1 in 9.4, none higher.

1223 Challengers of the Unknown #31 Pacific Coast pedigree (DC, 1963) CGC NM- 9.2 Off-white to white pages. Origin of the Challengers retold. Overstreet 2005 NM- 9.2 value = $105. CGC census 9/05: 1 in 9.2, 1 higher.

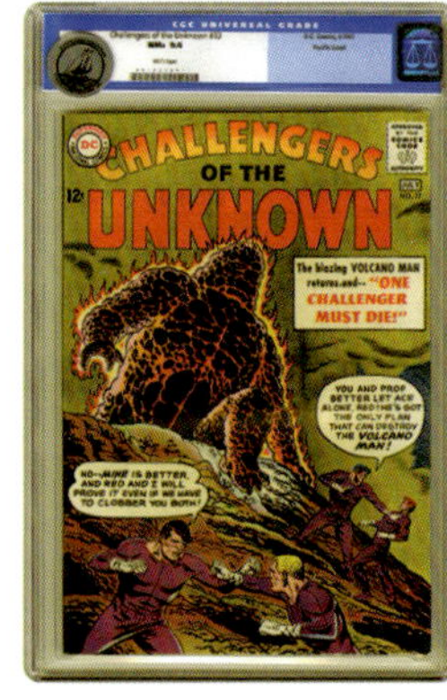

1224 Challengers of the Unknown #32 Pacific Coast pedigree (DC, 1963) CGC NM+ 9.6 White pages. The Challs take on Volcano Man, with Bob Brown providing the art. This is the only copy graded above VF- by CGC as of this writing. Overstreet 2005 NM- 9.2 value = $60. CGC census 9/05: 1 in 9.6, none higher.

1225 Challengers of the Unknown #33 Pacific Coast pedigree (DC, 1963) CGC NM- 9.2 Off-white pages. Overstreet 2005 NM- 9.2 value = $60. CGC census 9/05: 1 in 9.2, none higher.

1226 Challengers of the Unknown #34 Pacific Coast pedigree (DC, 1963) CGC NM 9.4 Off-white to white pages. Bob Brown art. Overstreet 2005 NM- 9.2 value = $60. CGC census 9/05: 1 in 9.4, none higher.

1227 Challengers of the Unknown #35 Pacific Coast pedigree (DC, 1964) CGC NM 9.4 White pages. Bob Brown art. Overstreet 2005 NM- 9.2 value = $60. CGC census 9/05: 1 in 9.4, none higher.

1228 Challengers of the Unknown #36 Pacific Coast pedigree (DC, 1964) CGC NM 9.4 Off-white to white pages. Bob Brown art. Overstreet 2005 NM- 9.2 value = $60. CGC census 9/05: 1 in 9.4, none higher.

1229 Challengers of the Unknown #38 Pacific Coast pedigree (DC, 1964) CGC NM+ 9.6 Off-white to white pages. The Challengers take on the Ooze, in an issue drawn by Bob Brown. Overstreet 2005 NM- 9.2 value = $60. CGC census 9/05: 1 in 9.6, none higher.

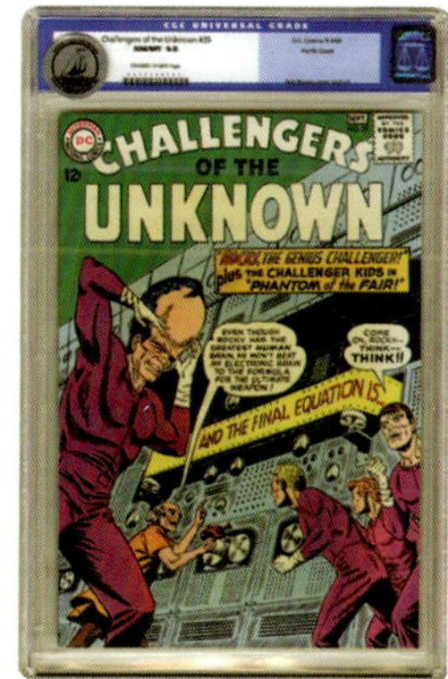

1230 Challengers of the Unknown #39 Pacific Coast pedigree (DC, 1964) CGC NM/MT 9.8 Off-white to white pages. Rocky Davis gets a super-brain in this issue, which features the art of Bob Brown. This is the only copy of the issue graded above VF+ by CGC to date! Overstreet 2005 NM- 9.2 value = $60. CGC census 9/05: 1 in 9.8, none higher.

1231 Challengers of the Unknown #40 Pacific Coast pedigree (DC, 1964) CGC NM+ 9.6 Off-white pages. Multi-Man's back to menace the Challengers yet again! Bob Brown handled art chores. Overstreet 2005 NM- 9.2 value = $60. CGC census 9/05: 1 in 9.6, none higher.

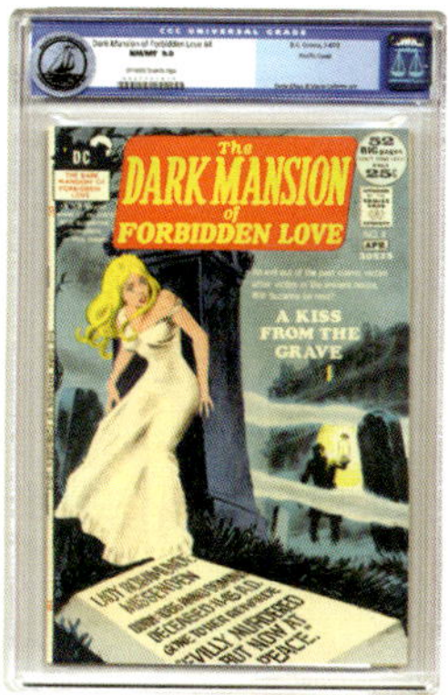

1232 Dark Mansion of Forbidden Love #4 Pacific Coast pedigree (DC, 1972) CGC NM/MT 9.8 Off-white to white pages. This experimental title may have been short-lived (this was the last issue) but it's a collector's favorite now. It's got a Nick Cardy cover and interior art by Ernie Chua (aka Ernie Chan). Overstreet 2005 NM- 9.2 value = $100. CGC census 7/05: 3 in 9.8, none higher.

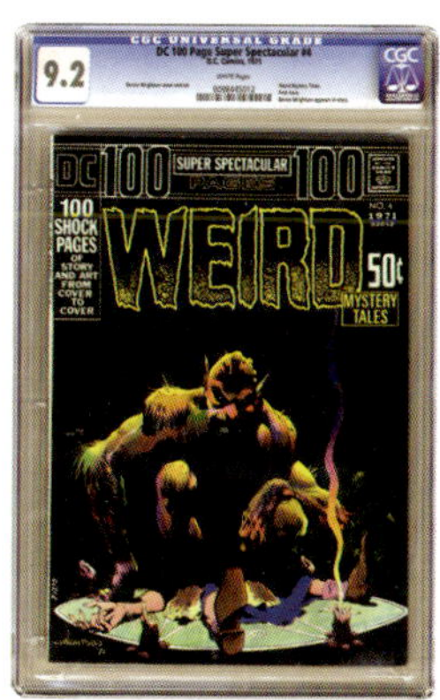

1233 DC 100-Page Super Spectacular #4 Weird Mystery Tales (DC, 1971) CGC NM- 9.2 White pages. The cover art by Master of the Macabre Bernie Wrightson is more than enough reason to go after this issue, but it also has much more to offer, including the interior art of Wrightson, Mort Drucker, Mort Meskin, Carmine Infantino, Jim Mooney, and Nick Cardy. Characters include Johnny Peril and the Phantom Stranger. Another "weird mystery" is why DC began this title with issue #4, but whatever the reason, this is the first issue of the square bound **Super Spectacular** series. Overstreet 2005 NM- 9.2 value = $260. CGC census 9/05: 3 in 9.2, 3 higher.

1234 DC 100-Page Super Spectacular #6 World's Greatest Super-Heroes (DC, 1971) CGC NM- 9.2 White pages. Neal Adams' wraparound cover for this issue is one of the best and most memorable covers of the 1970s! It depicts every major DC superhero, with Silver Agers on the front cover and the Golden Age crowd on the back (though the Earth-Two Wonder Woman keeps the front cover from being an all-Earth-One affair). A highlight of the interior is a previously unpublished Golden Age Wildcat story with Chet Kozlak art. Overstreet 2005 NM- 9.2 value = $260. CGC census 9/05: 9 in 9.2, 5 higher.

1235 Detective Comics #359 (DC, 1967) CGC NM+ 9.6 White pages. The new Batgirl, Barbara Gordon, burst onto the scene in this issue! Though there had been a "Bat-Girl" before, this new gal is the character everyone remembers, thanks partly to her slinky 60s costume and partly to the tantalizing fact that she was the daughter of Commissioner Gordon. Carmine Infantino drew the story, Murphy Anderson handled art chores on a backup feature, and the two collaborated on the irresistible cover. Speaking of irresistible, this copy is second to none in CGC's current census report! Overstreet 2005 NM- 9.2 value = $190. CGC census 9/05: 5 in 9.6, none higher.

1236 Detective Comics #387 (DC, 1969) CGC NM 9.4 Off-white to white pages. 30th anniversary issue. Irv Novick cover featuring the Joker and the Penguin. Reprints the first Batman story from issue #27. Overstreet 2005 NM- 9.2 value = $90. CGC census 9/05: 8 in 9.4, 8 higher.

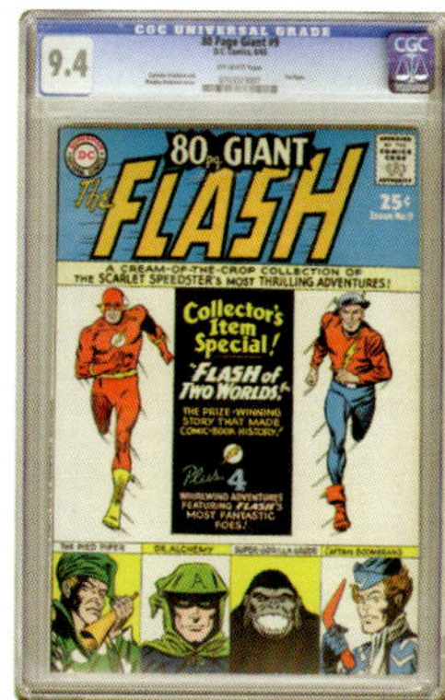

1237 80 Page Giant #9 The Flash (DC, 1965) CGC NM 9.4 Off-white pages. This square bound issue reprints the famous "Flash of Two Worlds" story from **Flash** #123, as well as key stories from #106, 108, and 117 and the fourth appearance of Barry Allen in **Showcase** #14. Overstreet 2005 NM- 9.2 value = $245. CGC census 9/05: 3 in 9.4, 3 higher.

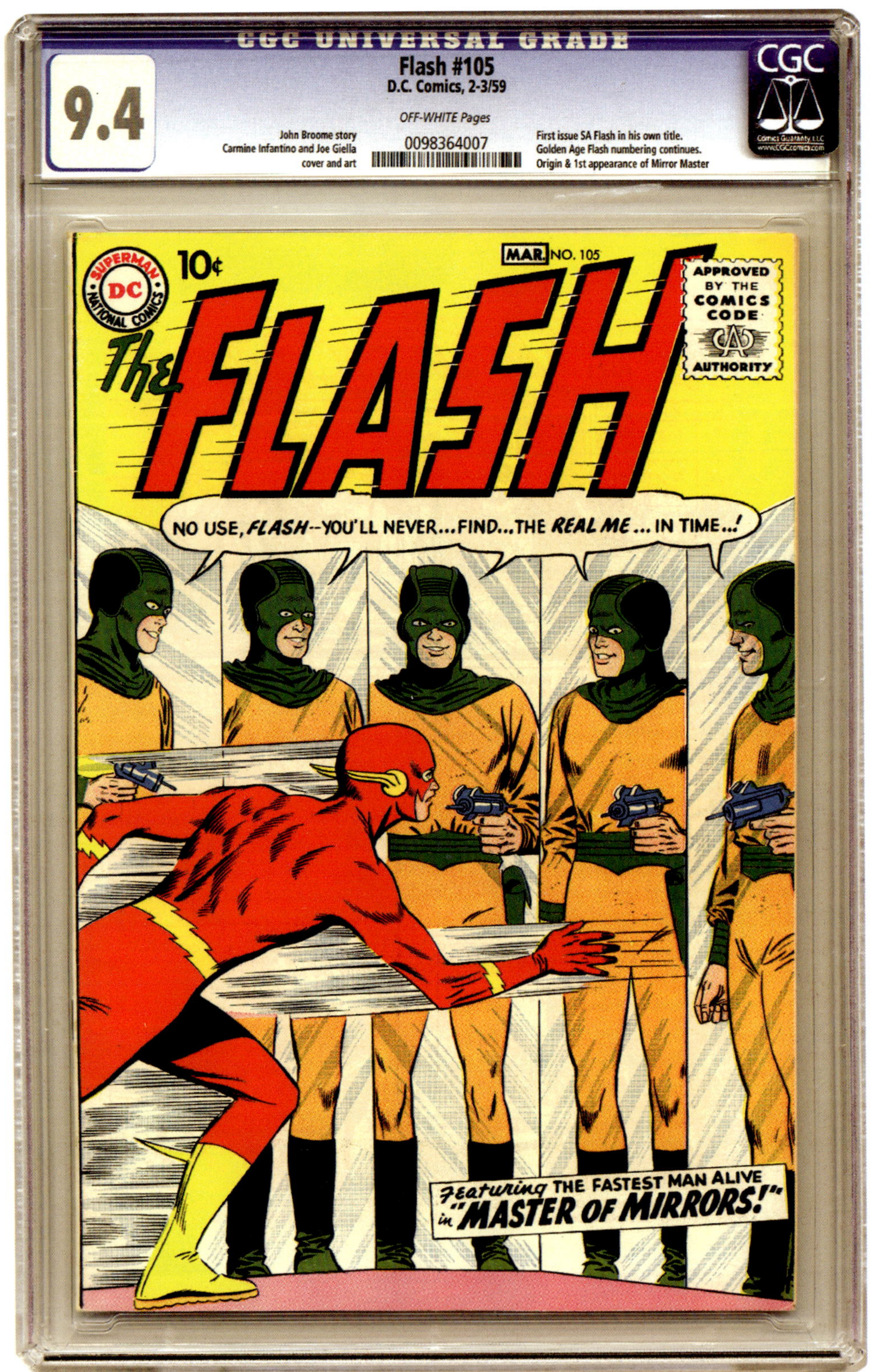

1238 The Flash #105 (DC, 1959) CGC NM 9.4 Off-white pages. This is the sole highest-graded copy of this issue as of this writing, and there aren't even many close runners-up - only four copies have been graded above VF 8.0 by CGC to date! And this is a key issue, the first issue featuring the Silver Age Flash in his own title (with numbering that continued where the Golden Age series had left off a decade earlier). This is one of the ten most valuable Silver Age comics according to Overstreet, and the only DCs from that era that top it are **Showcase** #'s 4, 8, and 9. This debut issue is also notable for having the origin and first appearance of the Mirror Master, plus a retelling of the Flash's origin. Carmine Infantino provided both cover and interior art. Overstreet 2005 NM- 9.2 value = $9,300. CGC census 9/05: 1 in 9.4, none higher.

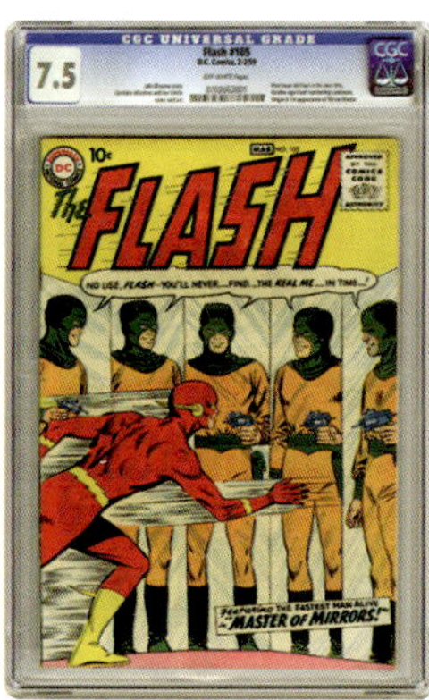

1239 The Flash #105 (DC, 1959) CGC VF- 7.5 Off-white pages. This is one of the ten most valuable Silver Age comics according to Overstreet — it's the first issue of the series, continuing the numbering from the Golden Age **Flash Comics**. The new Flash character had earned his own title after being a smash success in his first few appearances in the pages of **Showcase**. The origin of the new character is retold here, and in the villain department there's the origin and first appearance of the Mirror Master. The cover and interior art are by Carmine Infantino. Overstreet 2005 VF 8.0 value = $3,871. CGC census 8/05: 5 in 7.5, 7 higher.

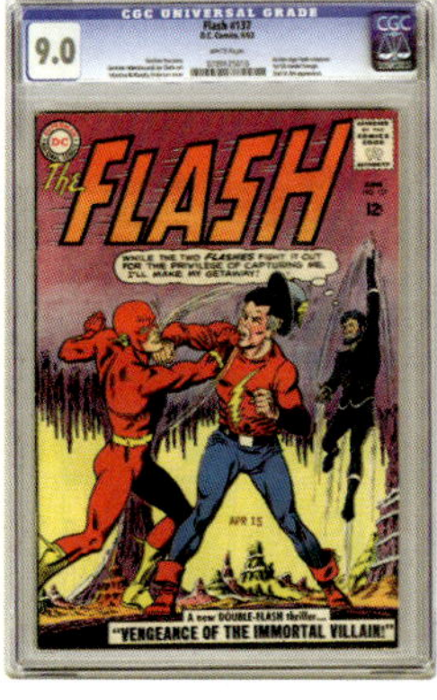

1240 The Flash #137 (DC, 1963) CGC VF/NM 9.0 White pages. Key stuff here for the multiple-Earths DC fan! It's the first "real" Silver Age appearance of the Justice Society (the only previous glimpse of them was in a flashback a few issues previously). The JSA decides to get back together, and that sets the stage for the great run of JLA/JSA team-ups which every red-blooded DC fan cherishes. The issue's also got the first Silver Age appearance of Johnny Thunder, as well as the Silver Age debut of Golden Age baddie Vandal Savage. And by the way, it's only the third meeting of the Flashes of Earth-One and Earth-Two! The cover and interior art are by Carmine Infantino. Overstreet 2005 VF/NM 9.0 value = $497; NM- 9.2 value = $675. CGC census 9/05: 4 in 9.0, 3 higher.

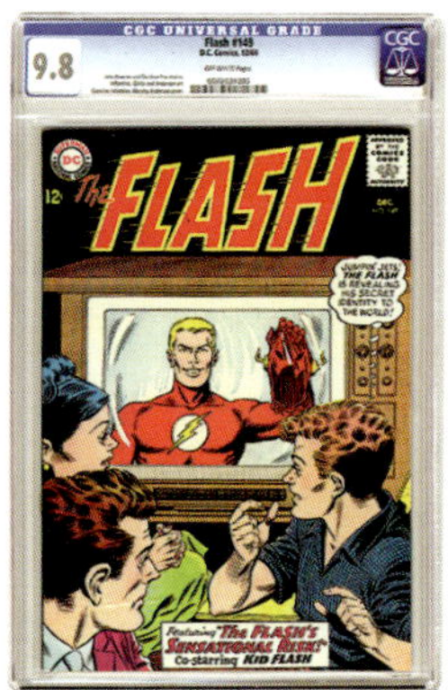

1241 The Flash #149 (DC, 1964) CGC NM/MT 9.8 Off-white pages. Remember this story? Flash unmasks on TV to jog Kid Flash's memory and cure his amnesia, but he does it so quickly that only Kid Flash and his "super-fast vision" will see it... at least that's the plan! Carmine Infantino drew this issue's irresistible "hook" cover in addition to the accompanying story. Overstreet 2005 NM- 9.2 value = $140. CGC census 8/05: 3 in 9.8, none higher.

1242 The Flash #156 (DC, 1965) CGC NM+ 9.6 Off-white pages. The Fastest Man Alive — Earth Enemy No. 1? Say it ain't so, Flash! This eye-popping copy features a flawless black-background cover. Overstreet 2005 NM- 9.2 value = $120. CGC census 8/05: 2 in 9.6, none higher.

1243 The Flash #159 (DC, 1966) CGC NM/MT 9.8 Off-white pages. The Flash calls it quits on this colorful cover — will he really walk out on his superhero career? Golden Age character Dr. Mid-Nite makes a rare Silver Age appearance. Carmine Infantino and Joe Giella supply the art. This incredible copy will magically transport you back in time to 1966 — have a nice trip! Overstreet 2005 NM- 9.2 value = $120. CGC census 8/05: 3 in 9.8, none higher.

1244 The Flash #161 (DC, 1966) CGC NM+ 9.6 Off-white pages. In addition to Flash's tussle with the Mirror Master, this issue features a new story based on the cover of #159 (which is mistakenly called "last issue" on the cover blurb). Robert Kanigher wrote the new tale, which like the first story was drawn by Carmine Infantino. Overstreet 2005 NM- 9.2 value = $100. CGC census 8/05: 1 in 9.6, none higher.

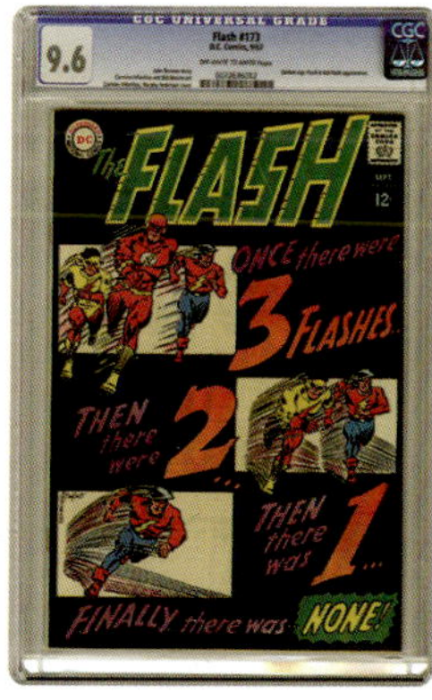

1245 The Flash #173 (DC, 1967) CGC NM+ 9.6 Off-white to white pages. The Golden Age Flash joins the Scarlet Speedster and Kid Flash — that's three Flashes for the price of one! A super-sharp copy, sporting a spotless black background cover. Overstreet 2005 NM- 9.2 value = $100. CGC census 8/05: 3 in 9.6, none higher.

1246 The Flash #175 (DC, 1967) CGC VF/NM 9.0 Off-white to white pages. Second Superman vs. Flash race. Justice League appearance. Carmine Infantino cover. Ross Andru art. Overstreet 2005 VF/NM 9.0 value = $178; NM- 9.2 value = $240. CGC census 9/05: 16 in 9.0, 21 higher.

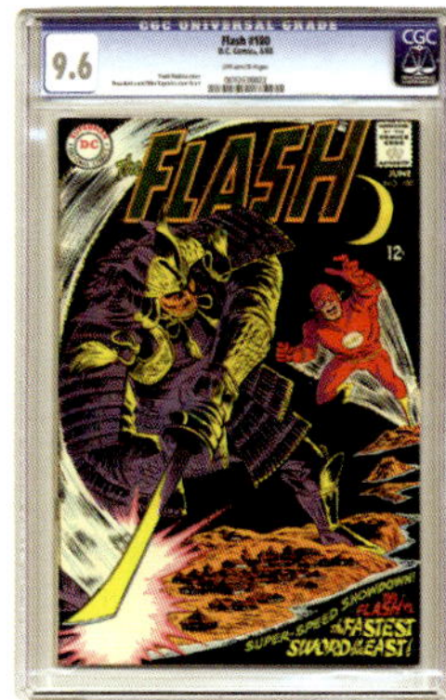

1247 The Flash #180 (DC, 1968) CGC NM+ 9.6 Off-white pages. The Flash takes on the Samuroids in this issue. Ross Andru provided both cover and interior art. Overstreet 2005 NM- 9.2 value = $90. CGC census 7/05: 5 in 9.6, 1 higher.

1248 The Flash #186 (DC, 1969) CGC NM 9.4 Off-white pages. First Silver Age appearance of Sargon the Sorcerer. Ross Andru cover and art. Overstreet 2005 NM- 9.2 value = $75. CGC census 7/05: 5 in 9.4, 1 higher.

1249 The Flash #191 (DC, 1969) CGC NM+ 9.6 White pages. Green Lantern appearance. Joe Kubert cover. Ross Andru art. Overstreet 2005 NM- 9.2 value = $55. CGC census 7/05: 3 in 9.6, none higher.

1250 The Flash #192 (DC, 1969) CGC NM+ 9.6 White pages. Carmine Infantino and Murphy Anderson cover. Ross Andru art. Overstreet 2005 NM- 9.2 value = $55. CGC census 7/05: 3 in 9.6, none higher.

1251 The Flash #194 (DC, 1970) CGC NM+ 9.6 White pages. Neal Adams cover. Ross Andru art. Overstreet 2005 NM- 9.2 value = $55. CGC census 7/05: 3 in 9.6, none higher.

1252 The Flash #195 (DC, 1970) CGC Qualified NM/MT 9.8 Off-white to white pages. Neal Adams cover. Gil Kane art. CGC notes, "cover detached from bottom staple." Overstreet 2005 GD 2.0 value = $5; VG 4.0 value = $10; FN 6.0 value = $15; VF 8.0 value = $33; VF/NM 9.0 value = $44; NM- 9.2 value = $55.

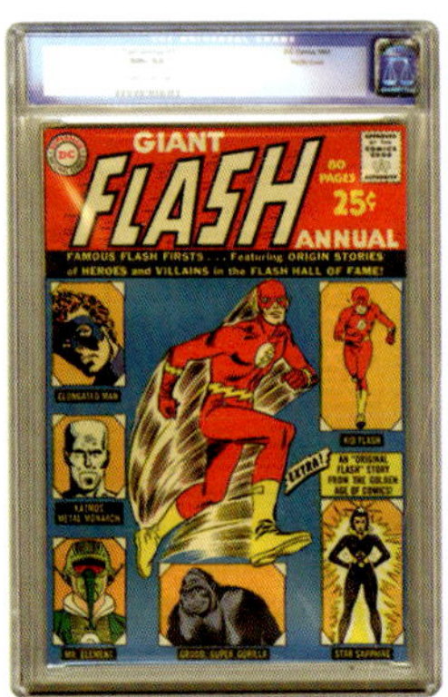

1253 Flash Annual #1 Pacific Coast pedigree (DC, 1963) CGC NM+ 9.6 Off-white to white pages. This incredible specimen, an 80-Page Giant, is the first Silver Age collection of stories featuring the Scarlet Speedster, with Carmine Infantino cover and art. Reprints include the first appearances of the Elongated Man, Gorilla Grodd, and Kid Flash. Bonus features include a Golden Age Flash reprint with Lee Elias art, and an index of all Silver Age Flash stories, writers, and artists up to issue #140. Square bound comics rarely turn up in this kind of near-perfect condition, so don't pass this one up, Flash-fans! Overstreet 2005 NM- 9.2 value = $625. CGC census 9/05: 2 in 9.6, none higher.

1254 The Forever People #1 (DC, 1971) CGC NM+ 9.6 White pages. First appearance of the Forever People. First full appearance of Darkseid. Superman appearance. Jack Kirby story, cover, and art. Overstreet 2005 NM- 9.2 value = $100. CGC census 9/05: 21 in 9.6, 3 higher.

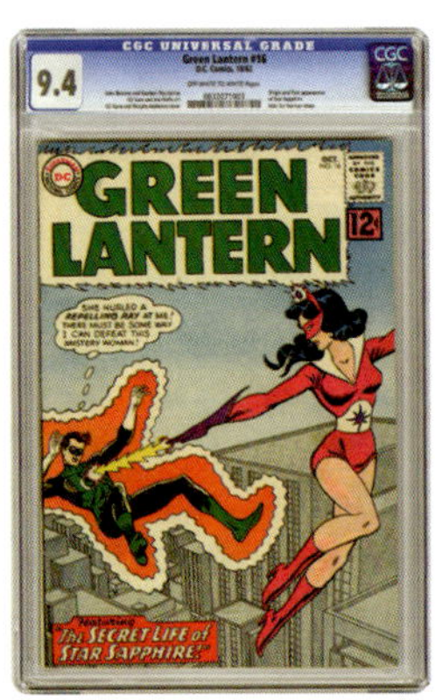

1255 Green Lantern #16 (DC, 1962) CGC NM 9.4 Off-white to white pages. It's the origin and first appearance of Star Sapphire, who looks remarkably like Hal Jordan's love interest Carol Ferris... wait a minute, she *is* Carol Ferris! A backup feature stars Abin Sur, who you may recall is the alien who gave Green Lantern his powers. The issue's cover and interior art are by Gil Kane. Overstreet 2005 NM- 9.2 value = $240. CGC census 9/05: 2 in 9.4, 1 higher.

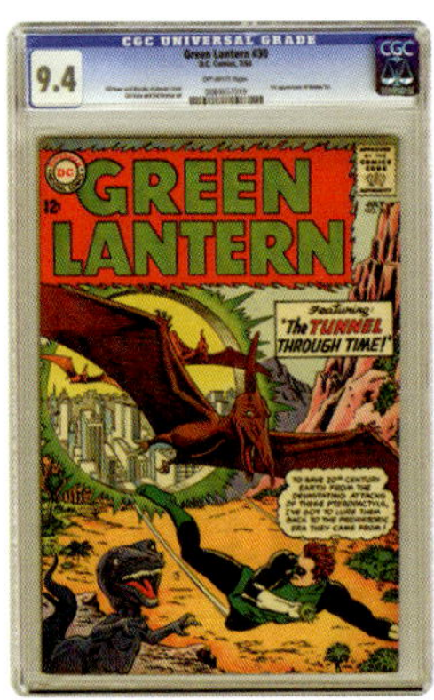

1256 Green Lantern #30 (DC, 1964) CGC NM 9.4 Off-white pages. This issue features the first appearance of Katma Tui, whom GL fans will remember as the lovely red-skinned guardian of another corner of the universe. The dinosaur cover as well as the interior art are by Gil Kane. Overstreet 2005 NM- 9.2 value = $190. CGC census 9/05: 2 in 9.4, 2 higher.

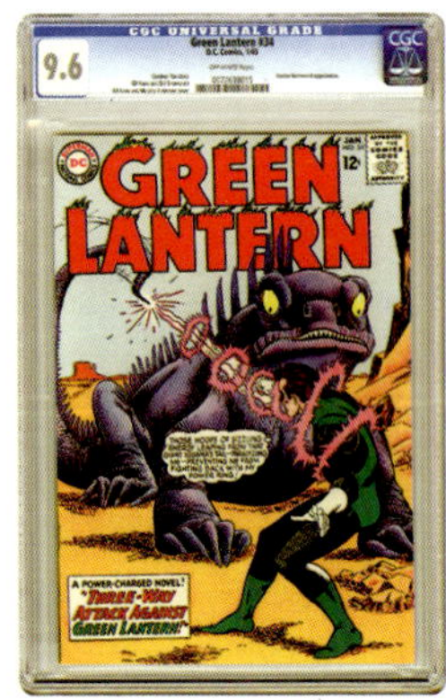

1257 Green Lantern #34 (DC, 1965) CGC NM+ 9.6 Off-white pages. This copy's tied for the highest grade that CGC has assigned for this issue to date. Big-brained Hector Hammond is the foe of the issue for Green Lantern. Gil Kane handled art chores on the cover and the interior. Overstreet 2005 NM- 9.2 value = $160. CGC census 8/05: 2 in 9.6, none higher.

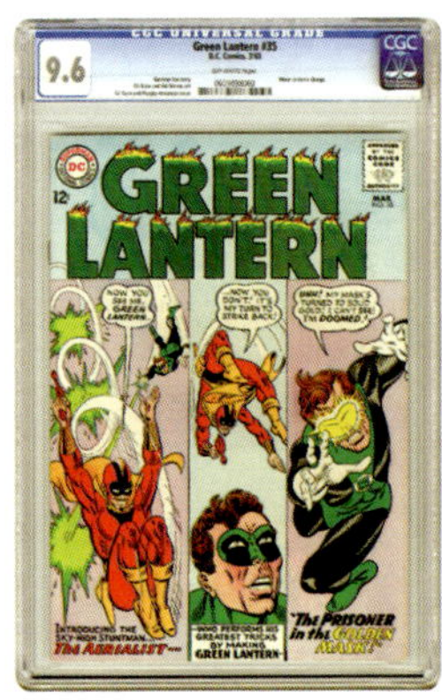

1258 Green Lantern #35 (DC, 1965) CGC NM+ 9.6 Off-white pages. This dynamite copy's tied for the highest grade that CGC has assigned for this issue to date. In the issue, Green Lantern battles... Batroc the Leaper?? Naww, it's the Aerialist, who made his first appearance here (pre-dating the aforementioned Marvel baddie, we hasten to add). Gil Kane provided both cover and interior art. Overstreet 2005 NM- 9.2 value = $160. CGC census 8/05: 2 in 9.6, none higher.

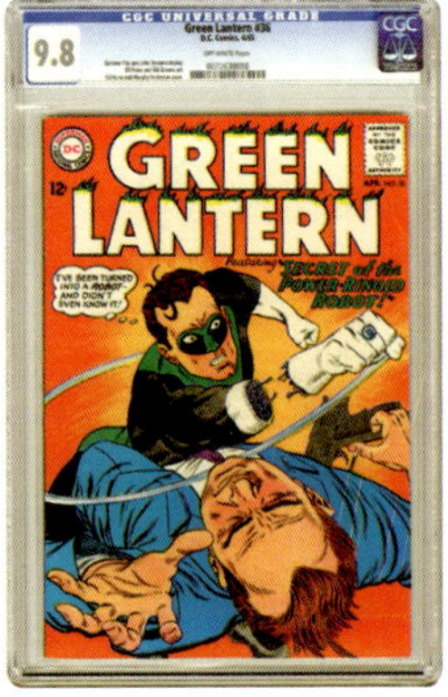

1259 Green Lantern #36 (DC, 1965) CGC NM/MT 9.8 Off-white pages. Just as Green Lantern recoils from the color yellow, we recoil from comics with dinged-up spines. So this 9.8 copy is just our style — it's tied for the highest grade that CGC has assigned to date. The issue's cover and interior art are by Gil Kane. Overstreet 2005 NM- 9.2 value = $160. CGC census 8/05: 2 in 9.8, none higher.

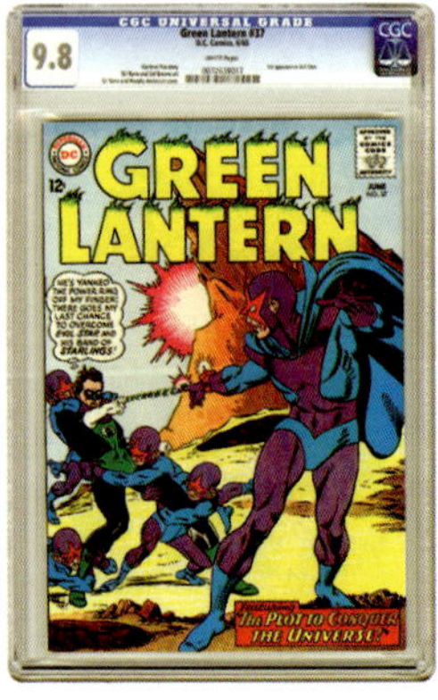

1260 Green Lantern #37 (DC, 1965) CGC NM/MT 9.8 White pages. Evil Star made his first appearance in this issue — he's a villain who was a worthy foe for Green Lantern, as the "star-band" Evil Star wore on his wrist was pretty similar to GL's power ring. Gil Kane handled cover and interior art chores here. Overstreet 2005 NM- 9.2 value = $160. CGC census 8/05: 1 in 9.8, none higher.

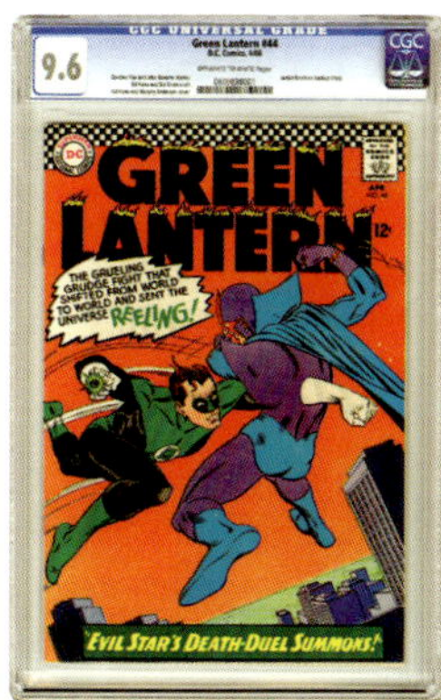

1261 Green Lantern #44 (DC, 1966) CGC NM+ 9.6 Off-white to white pages. Green Lantern takes on Evil Star. A backup feature has a tale of the Jordan brothers. Gil Kane cover and art. Overstreet 2005 NM- 9.2 value = $130. CGC census 8/05: 2 in 9.6, none higher.

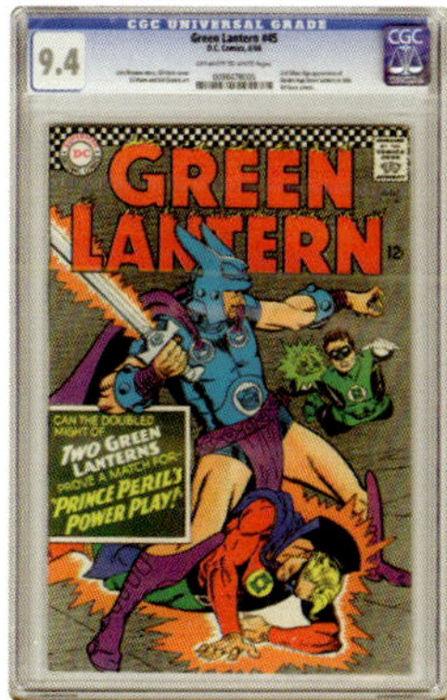

1262 Green Lantern #45 (DC, 1966) CGC NM 9.4 Off-white to white pages. The Golden Age Green Lantern, Alan Scott, made only his second Silver Age appearance in this issue of Hal Jordan's comic. Drawing both the cover and the interior action was Gil Kane. Overstreet 2005 NM- 9.2 value = $215. CGC census 9/05: 9 in 9.4, none higher.

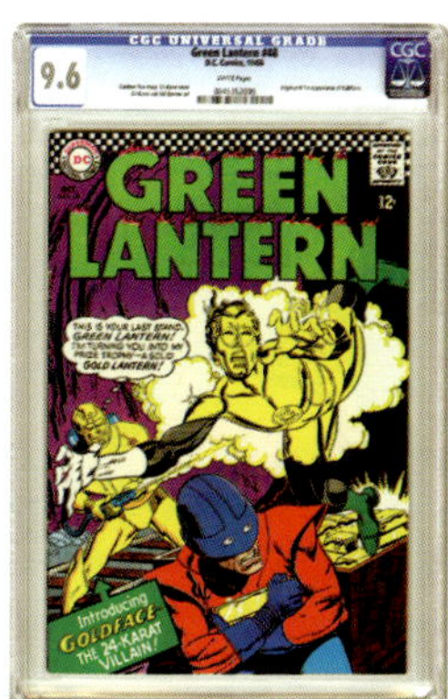

1263 Green Lantern #48 (DC, 1966) CGC NM+ 9.6 White pages. This issue's got the second appearance of Keith Kenyon, who becomes Goldface for the first time. The cover and interior art are by Gil Kane. Overstreet 2005 NM- 9.2 value = $130. CGC census 8/05: 5 in 9.6, none higher.

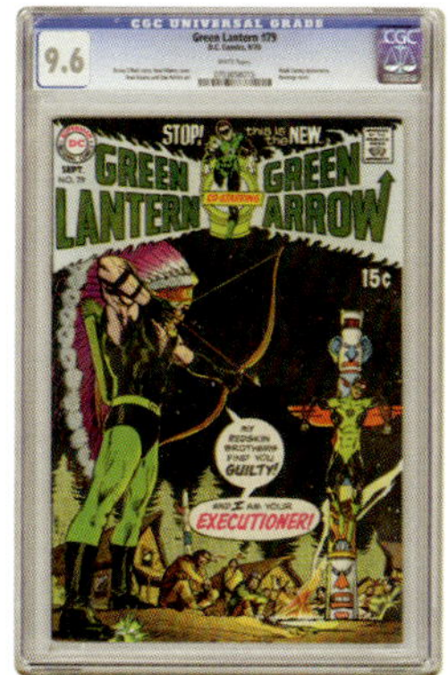

1264 Green Lantern #79 (DC, 1970) CGC NM+ 9.6 White pages. This freshly slabbed copy is the first 9.6 that has been certified for this issue! Contrast that with the other Neal Adams **Green Lantern** issues, most of which have multiple 9.6 copies on the census (some even show a 9.8 or two). Perhaps the dark cover colors are to blame for the paucity of top-grade specimens, but whatever the case, bring a healthy bidding budget for this census-topper! Black Canary guest-stars in the issue. Overstreet 2005 NM- 9.2 value = $90. CGC census 9/05: 1 in 9.6, none higher.

1265 Green Lantern #85 (DC, 1971) CGC NM 9.4 Off-white pages. Anti-drug issue. Neal Adams cover and art. Overstreet 2005 NM- 9.2 value = $110. CGC census 9/05: 27 in 9.4, 12 higher.

1266 Hawk and the Dove #1 (DC, 1968) CGC NM- 9.2 Off-white to white pages. Steve Ditko cover and art. Overstreet 2005 NM- 9.2 value = $120. CGC census 9/05: 7 in 9.2, 1 higher.

1267 Hawk and the Dove #5 (DC, 1969) CGC NM 9.4 Off-white to white pages. Gil Kane cover and art. Overstreet 2005 NM- 9.2 value = $70. CGC census 9/05: 4 in 9.4, none higher.

1268 Hawk and the Dove #6 (DC, 1969) CGC NM+ 9.6 Off-white pages. Gil Kane cover and art. Overstreet 2005 NM- 9.2 value = $70. CGC census 9/05: 1 in 9.6, none higher.

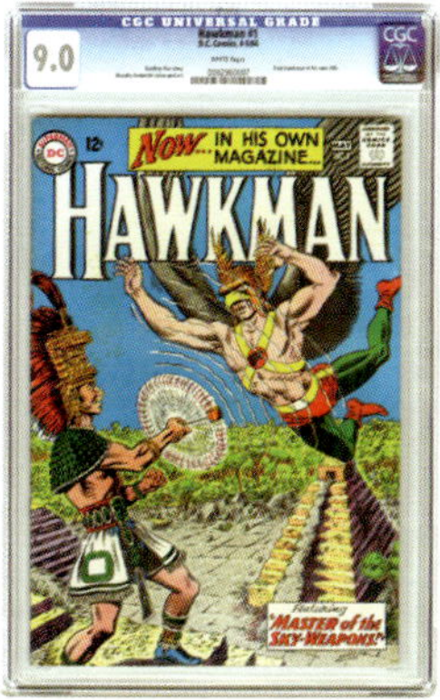

1269 Hawkman #1 (DC, 1964) CGC VF/NM 9.0 White pages. Murphy Anderson had a great run drawing Hawkman, and the Mayan temple and headdress on this first issue's cover are a fine showcase for the artist's draftsmanship. Incredibly, this was the first time the popular Hawkman had headlined his own title, but it wouldn't be the last. Overstreet 2005 VF/NM 9.0 value = $705; NM- 9.2 value = $975. CGC census 9/05: 12 in 9.0, 16 higher.

1270 Hawkman #11 Boston pedigree (DC, 1966) CGC NM 9.4 Off-white pages. First and only appearance of the Shrike. Murphy Anderson cover and art. Overstreet 2005 NM- 9.2 value = $85. CGC census 8/05: 1 in 9.4, 3 higher.

1271 Hawkman #12 Boston pedigree (DC, 1966) CGC NM 9.4 White pages. Murphy Anderson cover and art. Overstreet 2005 NM- 9.2 value = $85. CGC census 8/05: 6 in 9.4, 4 higher.

1272 Hawkman #17 Boston pedigree (DC, 1967) CGC NM 9.4 Off-white to white pages. Murphy Anderson cover and art. Overstreet 2005 NM- 9.2 value = $65. CGC census 8/05: 4 in 9.4, 4 higher.

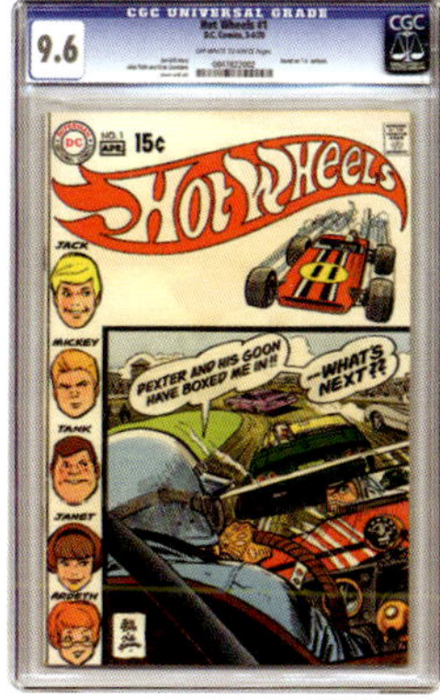

1273 Hot Wheels #1 (DC, 1970) CGC NM+ 9.6 Off-white to white pages. This issue can be a pain to find, probably because not only comic collectors, but fans of the Hot Wheels toys and of the cartoon show are in the market for a copy. DC found the perfect artist for the series, Alex Toth, a master at drawing cars and car racing. No copy of this white-cover issue has been graded higher by CGC to date. Overstreet 2005 NM- 9.2 value = $140. CGC census 8/05: 4 in 9.6, none higher.

1274 House of Mystery #124 (DC, 1962) CGC NM 9.4 White pages. Mort Meskin cover and art. Note that this is the only copy graded above VF+ by CGC as of this writing. Overstreet 2005 NM- 9.2 value = $110. CGC census 9/05: 1 in 9.4, none higher.

1275 House of Mystery #130 (DC, 1963) CGC NM 9.4 Off-white to white pages. Mort Meskin, George Roussos, and Howard Sherman art. Cover by Roussos. Overstreet 2005 NM- 9.2 value = $110. CGC census 9/05: 1 in 9.4, 1 higher.

1276 House of Mystery #145 (DC, 1964) CGC NM 9.4 Off-white pages. Martian Manhunter story. Joe Certa cover and art. Overstreet 2005 NM- 9.2 value = $85. CGC census 9/05: 1 in 9.4, none higher.

1277 House of Secrets #44 (DC, 1961) CGC NM 9.4 Off-white pages. Featuring Mark Merlin. Dick Dillin cover. Mort Meskin and Lee Elias art. Overstreet 2005 NM- 9.2 value = $125. CGC census 9/05: 1 in 9.4, none higher.

1278 House of Secrets #69 Massachusetts pedigree (DC, 1964) CGC NM 9.4 Off-white pages. Mark Merlin and Eclipso are featured. Dick Dillin cover. Jack Sparling and Mort Meskin art. Overstreet 2005 NM- 9.2 value = $85. CGC census 9/05: 1 in 9.4, 1 higher.

1279 Jonah Hex #1 (DC, 1977) CGC NM 9.4 White pages. Jose Luis Garcia-Lopez cover and art. Overstreet 2005 NM- 9.2 value = $150. CGC census 9/05: 53 in 9.4, 43 higher.

1280 Justice League of America #1 (DC, 1960) CGC NM 9.4 Off-white pages. This #1 issue is currently 13th in Overstreet's ranking of the most valuable Silver Age comics, and our offering is tied for the highest grade yet assigned! You'll notice that #1 doesn't appear on the cover anywhere — this comic is from the time when a #1 was considered a negative, even for tried-and-true characters like the JLA, who had had a successful debut in the pages of **The Brave and The Bold**. Murphy Anderson's cover image is one of the more famous covers of the Silver Age, and the story is by the creative team that produced every early JLA appearance: writer Gardner Fox and artist Mike Sekowsky. The issue is also notable for having the first appearance of three-eyed villain Despero. With the JLA still appearing in comics and cartoons to this day, demand for this key book can only increase. Overstreet 2005 NM- 9.2 value = $8,000. CGC census 9/05: 2 in 9.4, one higher.

1281 Justice League of America #11 (DC, 1962) CGC NM- 9.2 Off-white to white pages. The JLA journeys into the far future to battle the Lord of Time, in a tale from the typewriter of Gardner Fox via the pencil of Mike Sekowsky. Of the 30 copies that CGC has slabbed of this issue to date, only one has received a higher grade than this lovely copy. Overstreet 2005 NM- 9.2 value = $325. CGC census 9/05: 4 in 9.2, 1 higher.

1282 Justice League of America #38 (DC, 1965) CGC NM- 9.2 Off-white to white pages. It's a Justice Society crossover in "Crisis on Earth-A." Now, even a semi-obsessed DC fan would be forgiven for saying, "I know Earth-One, Two, S, X, and Prime, but which one's Earth-*A* again? Long story short: the Johnny Thunder of Earth-One is a ***villain***, and he creates an alternate Earth in which the JLA are bad guys known as the Lawless League. A tall order for the JSA as well as for Mike Sekowsky, who had to draw tons of characters on every page of this crossover issue. Overstreet 2005 NM- 9.2 value = $175. CGC census 9/05: 4 in 9.2, 7 higher.

1283 Justice League of America #41 (DC, 1965) CGC NM 9.4 Off-white to white pages. First appearance of the Key. Hawkgirl guest-stars. Mike Sekowsky cover and art. Overstreet 2005 NM- 9.2 value = $125. CGC census 9/05: 5 in 9.4, 2 higher.

1284 Legion of Super-Heroes #3 (DC, 1973) CGC NM+ 9.6 White pages. Curt Swan cover. Reprints Legion story from **Adventure Comics** #340 and Tommy Tomorrow story from **Action Comics** #340. Overstreet 2005 NM- 9.2 value = $16. CGC census 9/05: 2 in 9.6, 1 higher.

1285 The Many Loves of Dobie Gillis #13 (DC, 1962) CGC VF- 7.5 White pages. The late Bob Denver appears on the (line-drawn) cover. Overstreet 2005 VF 8.0 value = $60. CGC census 9/05: 1 in 7.5, none higher.

1286 Metamorpho #5 Pacific Coast pedigree (DC, 1966) CGC NM- 9.2 White pages. Joe Orlando cover and art. Overstreet 2005 NM- 9.2 value = $65. CGC census 9/05: 3 in 9.2, 5 higher.

1287 Mister Miracle #1 (DC, 1971) CGC NM+ 9.6 Off-white pages. First appearances of Mister Miracle and Oberon. Jack Kirby story, cover, and art. Overstreet 2005 NM- 9.2 value = $95. CGC census 9/05: 24 in 9.6, 2 higher.

1288 My Greatest Adventure #65 (DC, 1962) CGC NM 9.4 Off-white to white pages. Dick Dillin cover. Ruben Moreira, George Roussos, and Bill Ely art. Overstreet 2005 NM- 9.2 value = $95. CGC census 9/05: 1 in 9.4, none higher.

1289 My Greatest Adventure #75 Pacific Coast pedigree (DC, 1963) CGC NM- 9.2 Off-white to white pages. Gene Colan cover. Colan and Howard Purcell art. This is the highest-graded copy of this issue that CGC has certified to date. Overstreet 2005 NM- 9.2 value = $95. CGC census 9/05: 1 in 9.2, none higher.

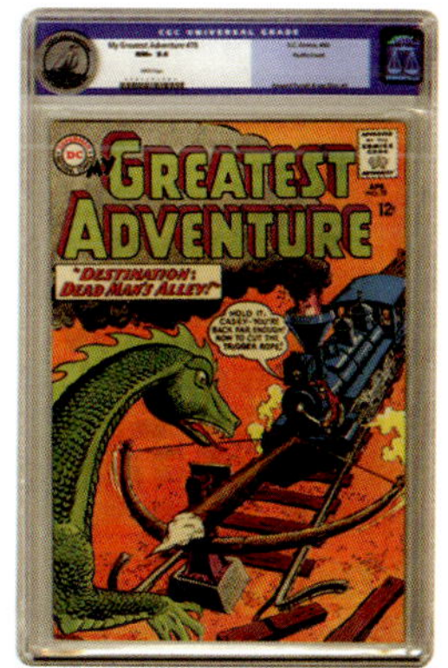

1290 My Greatest Adventure #78 Pacific Coast pedigree (DC, 1963) CGC NM+ 9.6 White pages. Lee Elias provides a dramatic dinosaur vs. train cover; with Elias and Howard Purcell supplying the interior art. This is a beautiful, sharp-looking copy, with fresh white pages and vivid cover colors; it's the highest-graded copy of the issue yet certified by CGC. Overstreet 2005 NM- 9.2 value = $95. CGC census 9/05: 1 in 9.6, none higher.

1291 The New Gods #1 Boston pedigree (DC, 1971) CGC NM+ 9.6 White pages. First appearances of Orion, Lightray, Metron, Highfather, and Kalibak. Jack Kirby story, cover, and art. Overstreet 2005 NM- 9.2 value = $130. CGC census 9/05: 59 in 9.6, 8 higher.

1292 The New Gods #2 (DC, 1971) CGC NM/MT 9.8 White pages. Early Darkseid appearance. Jack Kirby cover and art. Overstreet 2005 NM- 9.2 value = $65. CGC census 7/05: 1 in 9.8, none higher.

1293 The Phantom Stranger #6 Pacific Coast pedigree (DC, 1970) CGC NM+ 9.6 Cream to off-white pages. Neal Adams cover. Mike Sekowsky art. Overstreet 2005 NM- 9.2 value = $50. CGC census 9/05: 3 in 9.6, none higher.

1294 The Phantom Stranger #14 (DC, 1971) CGC NM 9.4 White pages. Neal Adams cover. Jim Aparo art. Overstreet 2005 NM- 9.2 value = $32. CGC census 9/05: 6 in 9.4, 2 higher.

1295 Sea Devils #9 Pacific Coast pedigree (DC, 1963) CGC NM+ 9.6 White pages. Russ Heath drew this issue's grey tone cover and the accompanying story as well. Overstreet 2005 NM- 9.2 value = $160. CGC census 9/05: 1 in 9.6, none higher.

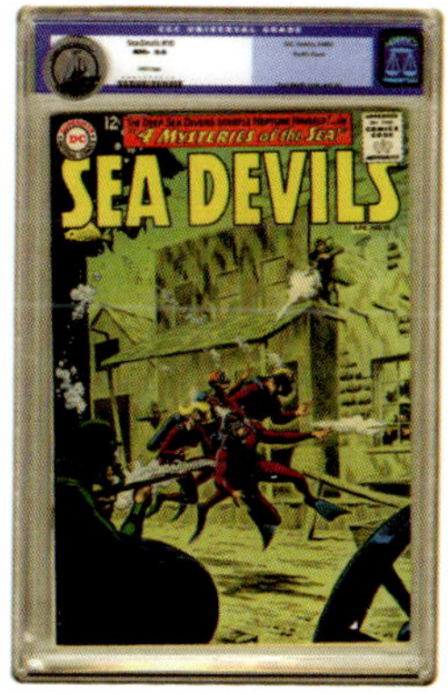

1296 Sea Devils #10 Pacific Coast pedigree (DC, 1963) CGC NM+ 9.6 White pages. This grey tone underwater scene by Russ Heath would have to be considered one of the best covers of the title's run. Overstreet 2005 NM- 9.2 value = $160. CGC census 9/05: 1 in 9.6, none higher.

1297 Sea Devils #11 Pacific Coast pedigree (DC, 1963) CGC NM 9.4 Off-white to white pages. This issue's cover and interior art are credited to Irv Novick. Overstreet 2005 NM- 9.2 value = $110. CGC census 9/05: 1 in 9.4, none higher.

1298 Sea Devils #12 Pacific Coast pedigree (DC, 1963) CGC VF/NM 9.0 Off-white pages. Irv Novick cover and art. Overstreet 2005 VF/NM 9.0 value = $85; NM- 9.2 value = $110. CGC census 9/05: 4 in 9.0, 1 higher.

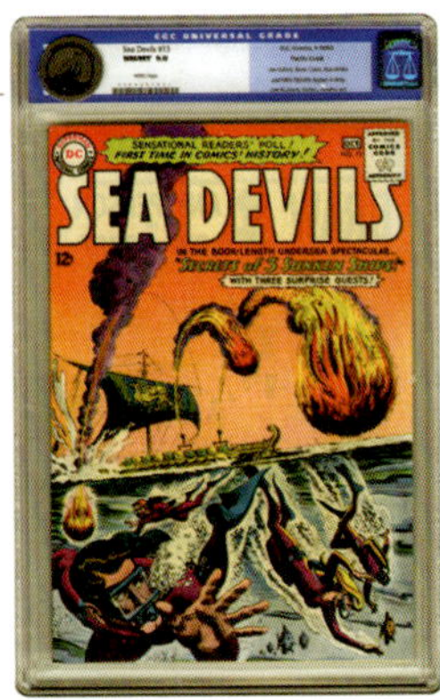

1299 Sea Devils #13 Pacific Coast pedigree (DC, 1963) CGC NM/MT 9.8 White pages. This issue's artists Joe Kubert, Gene Colan, Ross Andru, and Mike Esposito all make appearances as characters in the story as well! This is the only copy of the issue graded above 9.2 by CGC to date. Overstreet 2005 NM- 9.2 value = $115. CGC census 9/05: 1 in 9.8, none higher.

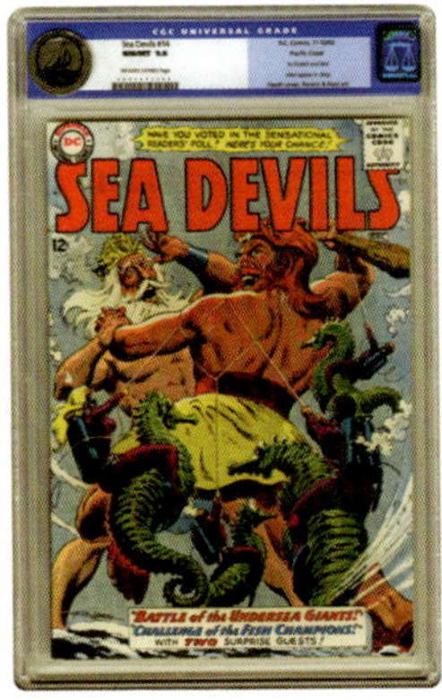

1300 Sea Devils #14 Pacific Coast pedigree (DC, 1963) CGC NM/MT 9.8 Off-white to white pages. In addition to providing the interior art for this issue, Irv Novick and Jack Abel appear as characters in the story! The cover is by Russ Heath. Overstreet 2005 NM- 9.2 value = $110. CGC census 9/05: 1 in 9.8, none higher.

1301 Sea Devils #15 Pacific Coast pedigree (DC, 1964) CGC NM 9.4 Off-white to white pages. Irv Novick provided the art for this story, which guest-stars... Irv Novick! The cover is by Russ Heath. Overstreet 2005 NM- 9.2 value = $110. CGC census 9/05: 1 in 9.4, none higher.

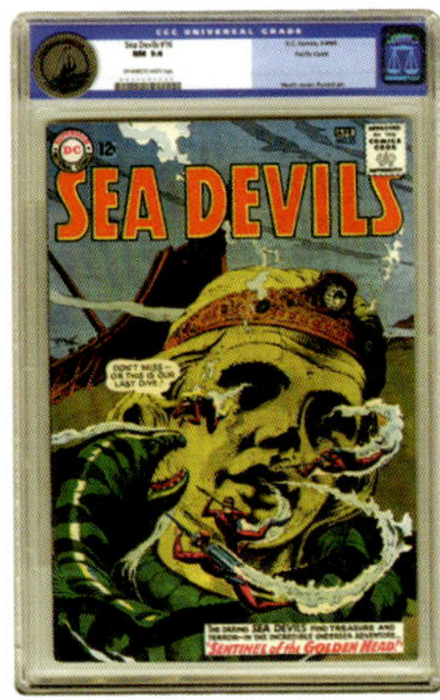

1302 Sea Devils #16 Pacific Coast pedigree (DC, 1964) CGC NM 9.4 Off-white to white pages. Russ Heath drew this issue's cover, and veteran Howard Purcell provided the interior art. Overstreet 2005 NM- 9.2 value = $110. CGC census 9/05: 1 in 9.4, none higher.

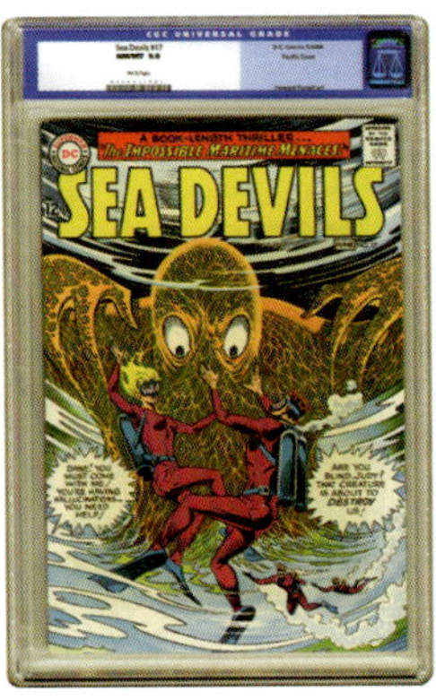

1303 Sea Devils #17 Pacific Coast pedigree (DC, 1964) CGC NM/MT 9.8 White pages. Howard Purcell handled art chores for this issue. Overstreet 2005 NM- 9.2 value = $110. CGC census 9/05: 1 in 9.8, none higher.

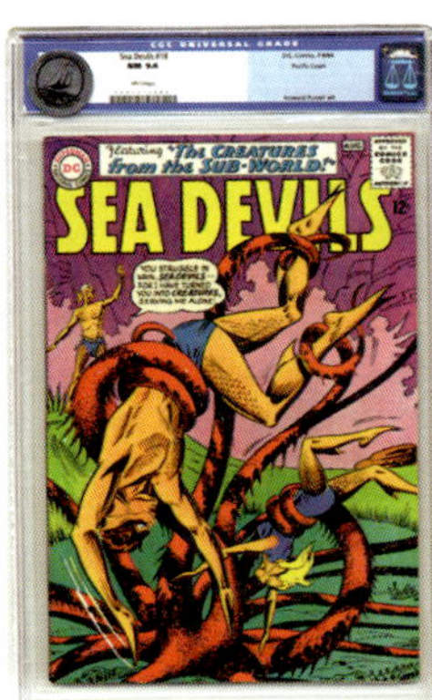

1304 Sea Devils #18 Pacific Coast pedigree (DC, 1964) CGC NM 9.4 White pages. This issue features Howard Purcell art. Overstreet 2005 NM- 9.2 value = $110. CGC census 9/05: 1 in 9.4, 1 higher.

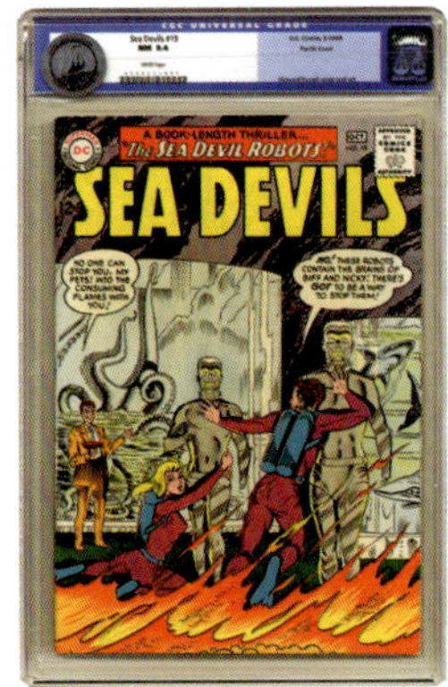

1305 Sea Devils #19 Pacific Coast pedigree (DC, 1964) CGC NM 9.4 White pages. Biff Bailey and Nicky Walton are in a jam, and Dane and Judy will have to think of something fast! Howard Purcell drew the cover scene as well as the story art. Overstreet 2005 NM- 9.2 value = $110. CGC census 9/05: 3 in 9.4, none higher.

1306 Sea Devils #20 Pacific Coast pedigree (DC, 1964) CGC VF/NM 9.0 Off-white to white pages. Howard Purcell cover and art. Overstreet 2005 VF/NM 9.0 value = $85; NM- 9.2 value = $110. CGC census 9/05: 2 in 9.0, 1 higher.

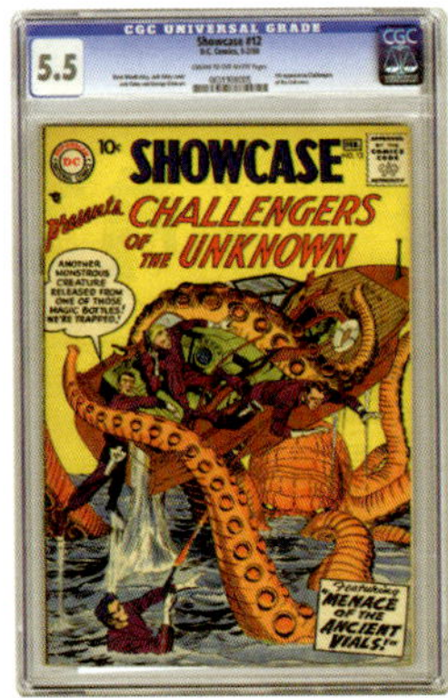

1307 Showcase #12 Challengers of the Unknown (DC, 1958) CGC FN- 5.5 Cream to off-white pages. The Challengers of the Unknown made their fourth appearance here. Providing the cover and interior art were a man who needs no introduction, Jack Kirby. Overstreet 2005 FN 6.0 value = $417. CGC census 9/05: 2 in 5.5, 7 higher.

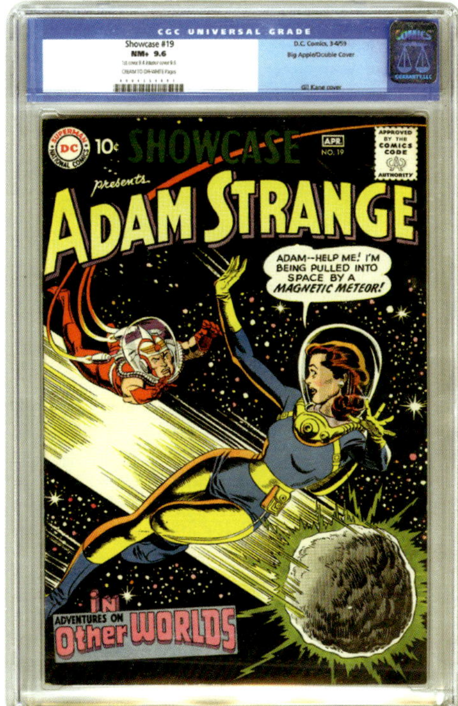

1308 Showcase #19 Adam Strange - Big Apple pedigree - Double Cover (DC, 1959) CGC NM+ 9.6 Cream to off-white pages. This was Adam Strange's third appearance in DC's foremost tryout title (he was next seen in **Mystery in Space**). This highest-graded copy of #19 to pass through CGC's offices to date has earned the outlandish certification of NM+ 9.6. The cover is by Gil Kane; the interior art is by Mike Sekowsky. CGC notes, "1st cover 9.4, interior cover 9.6." Overstreet 2005 NM- 9.2 value = $2,100. CGC census 9/05: 1 in 9.6, none higher.

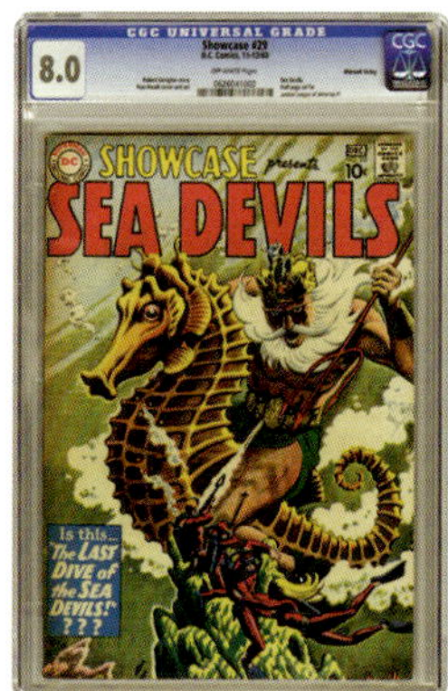

1309 Showcase #29 Sea Devils - Mohawk Valley pedigree (DC, 1960) CGC VF 8.0 Off-white pages. Russ Heath executed this striking grey tone cover as well as the book's interior art. This lot comes with the Mohawk Valley certificate of authenticity. Overstreet 2005 VF 8.0 value = $300. CGC census 9/05: 4 in 8.0, 3 higher.

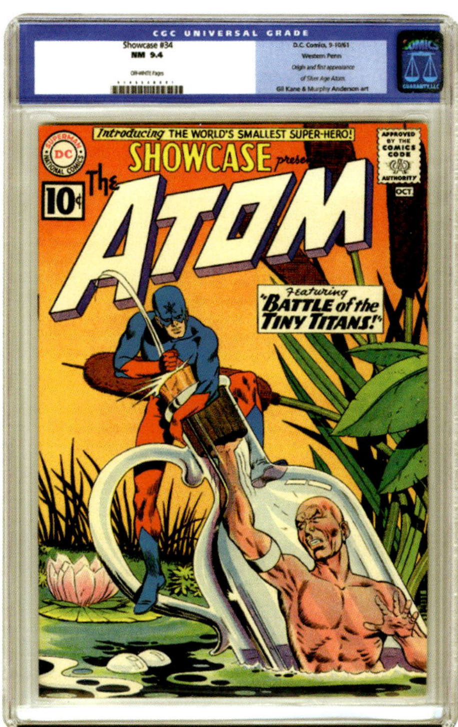

1310 Showcase #34 The Atom - Western Penn pedigree (DC, 1961) CGC NM 9.4 Off-white pages. This is the origin and first appearance of the Silver Age Atom, and our offering is a pedigree copy that's ties for the highest grade that CGC has assigned to date! The issue's cover and interior art are by Gil Kane and Murphy Anderson. Overstreet 2005 NM- 9.2 value = $2,200. CGC census 8/05: 2 in 9.4, none higher.

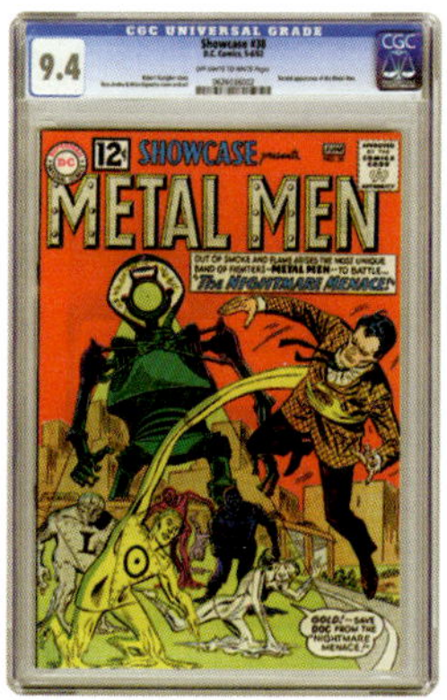

1311 Showcase #38 The Metal Men (DC, 1962) CGC NM 9.4 Off-white to white pages. This comic featured the second appearance of the Metal Men, brought to you by the team that created the scrappy bunch: writer Robert Kanigher and artists Ross Andru and Mike Esposito. Overstreet 2005 NM- 9.2 value = $640. CGC census 9/05: 3 in 9.4, 1 higher.

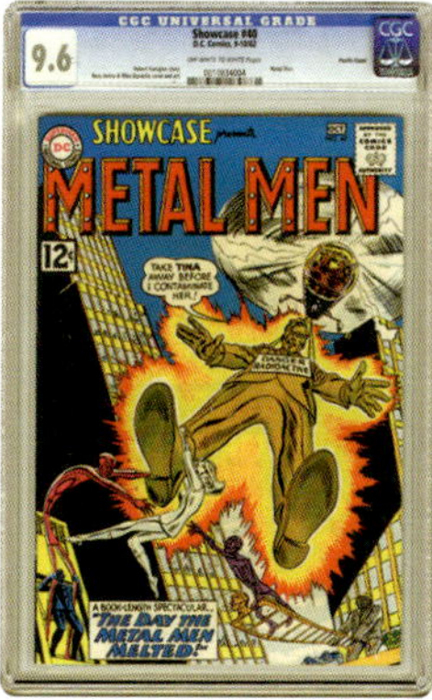

1312 Showcase #40 The Metal Men - Pacific Coast pedigree (DC, 1962) CGC NM+ 9.6 Off-white to white pages. This isn't just the highest-graded copy of the issue, it's the only one graded above 9.2 by CGC as of this writing! It's the fourth appearance of the Metal Men, by the group's original and best creative team, writer Bob Kanigher, penciler Ross Andru, and inker Mike Esposito. Overstreet 2005 NM- 9.2 value = $425. CGC census 8/05: 1 in 9.6, none higher.

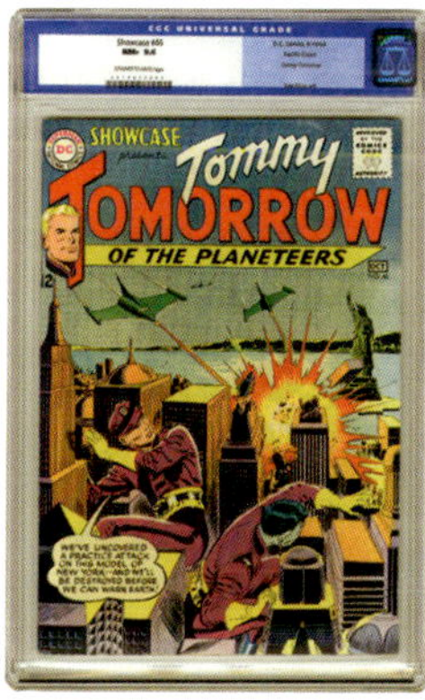

1313 Showcase #46 Tommy Tomorrow - Pacific Coast pedigree (DC, 1963) CGC NM+ 9.6 Off-white to white pages. We think it's safe to say that this issue's "attack on New York" cover scene is even more chilling today than back in 1963. The art is by Lee Elias. This is the highest-graded copy that CGC has certified to date. Overstreet 2005 NM- 9.2 value = $150. CGC census 8/05: 1 in 9.6, none higher.

1314 Showcase #83 Nightmaster (DC, 1969) CGC NM 9.4 Off-white to white pages. Joe Kubert cover. Bernie Wrightson art (with assists by Jeff Jones and Mike Kaluta). Overstreet 2005 NM- 9.2 value = $90. CGC census 9/05: 3 in 9.4, 1 higher.

1315 The Spectre #1 (DC, 1967) CGC NM 9.4 Off-white to white pages. After a successful run in the pages of **Showcase**, DC's ghostly hero finally got his own book here, drawn with panache by Murphy Anderson. The character, of course, dates back to the early days of the Golden Age in the pages of **More Fun Comics**. Overstreet 2005 NM- 9.2 value = $195. CGC census 9/05: 12 in 9.4, 1 higher.

1316 Strange Adventures #184 Boston pedigree (DC, 1966) CGC NM+ 9.6 White pages. Animal Man made only his second appearance here, in fact he hadn't even donned a costume yet. Gil Kane drew A-Man on the cover and inside the comic. Howard Purcell drew a backup feature. Overstreet 2005 NM- 9.2 value = $170. CGC census 9/05: 1 in 9.6, none higher.

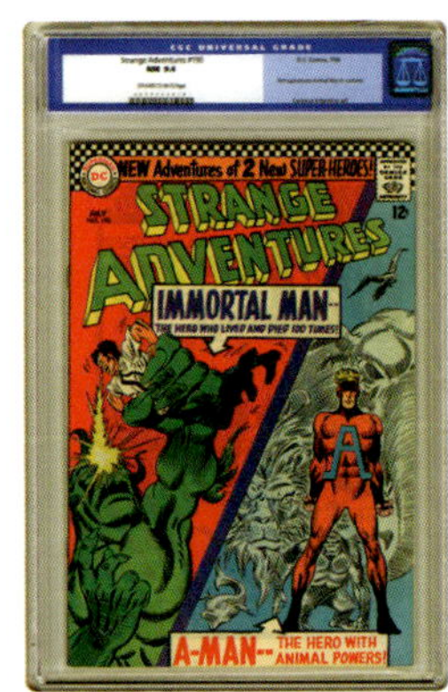

1317 Strange Adventures #190 (DC, 1966) CGC NM 9.4 Off-white to white pages. Animal Man, who first appeared in #180, donned a costume for the first time in this issue. Co-starring is Immortal Man, who first appeared in #177. The issue has Carmine Infantino art. Overstreet 2005 NM- 9.2 value = $220. CGC census 8/05: 5 in 9.4, 1 higher.

1318 Superboy #178 (DC, 1971) CGC NM+ 9.6 Off-white to white pages. Neal Adams cover. Murphy Anderson and Bob Brown art. Overstreet 2005 NM- 9.2 value = $32. CGC census 9/05: 4 in 9.6, none higher.

1319 Super DC Giant #15 Western Comics (DC, 1970) CGC NM+ 9.6 White pages. Also known as issue S-15. Joe Kubert cover. Gil Kane art. Overstreet 2005 NM- 9.2 value = $60. CGC census 9/05: 3 in 9.6, none higher.

1320 Superman #154 (DC, 1962) CGC NM 9.4 White pages. Mr. Mxyzptlk appears. Curt Swan cover and art. Overstreet 2005 NM- 9.2 value = $140. CGC census 9/05: 2 in 9.4, none higher.

1321 Superman #159 (DC, 1963) CGC VF/NM 9.0 Off-white to white pages. Curt Swan cover and art. Overstreet 2005 VF/NM 9.0 value = $107; NM- 9.2 value = $140. CGC census 9/05: 2 in 9.0, 1 higher.

1322 Superman #172 (DC, 1964) CGC VF/NM 9.0 Cream to off-white pages. Curt Swan cover and art. Lex Luthor, Brainiac, and the Legion of Super-Heroes appear. Overstreet 2005 VF/NM 9.0 value = $85; NM- 9.2 value = $110. CGC census 9/05: 2 in 9.0, 4 higher.

1323 Superman #173 Ohio pedigree (DC, 1964) CGC NM 9.4 Cream to off-white pages. Batman, Brainiac, and Lex Luthor appear. Curt Swan cover. Swan, Al Plastino, and George Papp art. Overstreet 2005 NM- 9.2 value = $110. CGC census 9/05: 3 in 9.4, none higher.

1324 Superman #220 (DC, 1969) CGC NM+ 9.6 Off-white to white pages. The Flash guest-stars. Curt Swan cover and art. Overstreet 2005 NM- 9.2 value = $50. CGC census 9/05: 3 in 9.6, 1 higher.

1325 Superman #233 (DC, 1971) CGC NM+ 9.6 Off-white to white pages. Everything changed for Superman in this issue, a landmark book which some even point to as the beginning of the Bronze Age of comics. Clark Kent becomes a TV newscaster (on orders from boss Morgan Edge, who makes his second appearance), Superman's powers are scaled back a bit, and all Kryptonite on Earth is destroyed. Neal Adams' cover for the issue is one of the more famous covers of the 1970s. The story art is by Superman vets Curt Swan and Murphy Anderson. Overstreet 2005 NM- 9.2 value = $90. CGC census 9/05: 4 in 9.6, none higher.

1326 Superman's Girl Friend Lois Lane #13 (DC, 1959) CGC VF/NM 9.0 Off-white pages. Curt Swan cover. Kurt Schaffenberger and Wayne Boring art. Overstreet 2005 VF/NM 9.0 value = $205; NM- 9.2 value = $275. CGC census 9/05: 2 in 9.0, none higher.

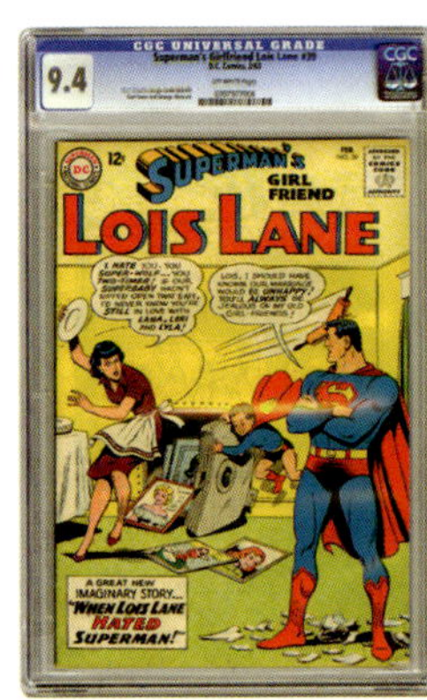

1327 Superman's Girl Friend Lois Lane #39 (DC, 1963) CGC NM 9.4 Off-white pages. If you loved DC's "imaginary stories," your favorite comic had to be **Lois Lane**! And if you like that old comic book standby the love triangle, how about a love ***pentagon***, with Smallville sweetie Lana Lang, mermaid Lori Lemaris, and Kryptonian cutie Lyla Lerrol also in the mix? The issue has a Kurt Schaffenberger cover, with interior art by Schaffenberger and Curt Swan. Overstreet 2005 NM- 9.2 value = $120. CGC census 9/05: 1 in 9.4, 1 higher.

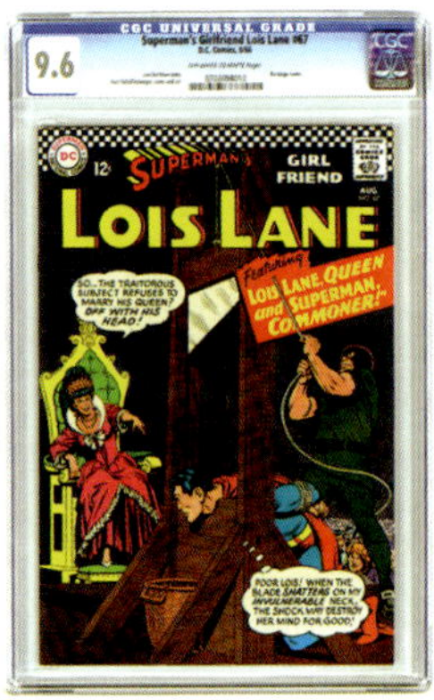

1328 Superman's Girl Friend Lois Lane #67 (DC, 1966) CGC NM+ 9.6 Off-white to white pages. Lois goes crazy again; this time, she believes she's a Queen, and demands Superman's head! The incredible luster and sharp edges of this well-kept book may well make you doubt your sanity; the cover's dark background shows absolutely no wear or stress. Overstreet 2005 NM- 9.2 value = $90. CGC census 9/05: 3 in 9.6, none higher.

1329 Superman's Girl Friend Lois Lane #70 (DC, 1966) CGC VF/NM 9.0 Off-white pages. Holy Crossover — this issue features the first Silver Age appearance of the Catwoman, as well as appearances by Batman, Robin, and the Penguin. Overstreet 2005 VF/NM 9.0 value = $278; NM- 9.2 value = $375. CGC census 9/05: 6 in 9.0, 10 higher.

1330 Superman's Girl Friend Lois Lane #119 (DC, 1972) CGC NM 9.4 White pages. Lois shows off her groovy hot pants on this issue's cover. Now *that's* a fashion idea worth reviving! Overstreet 2005 NM- 9.2 value = $40. CGC census 9/05: 3 in 9.4, 2 higher.

1331 Superman's Pal Jimmy Olsen #109 (DC, 1968) CGC NM+ 9.6 Off-white pages. Looks like Jimmy has teamed up with Lex Luthor to turn the tables on Superman — can it really be? Neal Adams supplies the dramatic cover illustration. Overstreet 2005 NM- 9.2 value = $40. CGC census 9/05: 4 in 9.6, none higher.

1332 Superman's Pal Jimmy Olsen #115 (DC, 1968) CGC NM 9.4 Off-white to white pages. Aquaman appearance. Neal Adams cover. Pete Costanza art. Overstreet 2005 NM- 9.2 value = $40. CGC census 9/05: 2 in 9.4, 3 higher.

1333 Superman's Pal Jimmy Olsen #136 (DC, 1971) CGC NM+ 9.6 Off-white pages. Neal Adams cover. Jack Kirby story and art. Origin of the new Guardian. Overstreet 2005 NM- 9.2 value = $45. CGC census 9/05: 6 in 9.6, 1 higher.

1334 Superman's Pal Jimmy Olsen #137 (DC, 1971) CGC NM+ 9.6 Off-white to white pages. The Newsboy Legion co-stars. Jack Kirby story, cover, and art. Overstreet 2005 NM- 9.2 value = $45. CGC census 9/05: 4 in 9.6, 2 higher.

1335 Superman's Pal Jimmy Olsen #138 (DC, 1971) CGC NM+ 9.6 White pages. Jack Kirby and Neal Adams cover (partial photo cover). Kirby interior art. Overstreet 2005 NM- 9.2 value = $45. CGC census 9/05: 7 in 9.6, 5 higher.

1336 Superman's Pal Jimmy Olsen #138 (DC, 1971) CGC NM 9.4 Off-white pages. Jack Kirby and Neal Adams cover (partial photo cover). Kirby interior art. Overstreet 2005 NM- 9.2 value = $45. CGC census 9/05: 7 in 9.4, 12 higher.

1337 Superman's Pal Jimmy Olsen #139 (DC, 1971) CGC NM+ 9.6 White pages. "Goody Rickles" storyline with Don Rickles cameo. Jack Kirby cover and art. Overstreet 2005 NM- 9.2 value = $45. CGC census 9/05: 5 in 9.6, none higher.

1338 Superman's Pal Jimmy Olsen #144 (DC, 1971) CGC NM+ 9.6 White pages. Jack Kirby and Neal Adams cover. Story and interior art by Kirby. Overstreet 2005 NM- 9.2 value = $40. CGC census 9/05: 3 in 9.6, none higher.

1339 Superman's Pal Jimmy Olsen #144 (DC, 1971) CGC NM 9.4 White pages. Jack Kirby and Neal Adams cover. Story and art by Kirby. Overstreet 2005 NM- 9.2 value = $40. CGC census 9/05: 9 in 9.4, 3 higher.

1340 Superman's Pal Jimmy Olsen #145 (DC, 1972) CGC NM+ 9.6 Off-white to white pages. Jack Kirby cover and art. The Newsboy Legion appears. Overstreet 2005 NM- 9.2 value = $40. CGC census 9/05: 3 in 9.6, 3 higher.

1341 Superman's Pal Jimmy Olsen #147 (DC, 1972) CGC NM+ 9.6 Off-white pages. Neal Adams cover. Jack Kirby story and art. Overstreet 2005 NM- 9.2 value = $40. CGC census 9/05: 12 in 9.6, 1 higher.

1342 Superman Annual #2 (DC, 1960) CGC VF+ 8.5 Off-white pages. Curt Swan and Stan Kaye cover. Overstreet 2005 VF 8.0 value = $318; VF/NM 9.0 value = $497. CGC census 9/05: 4 in 8.5, 4 higher.

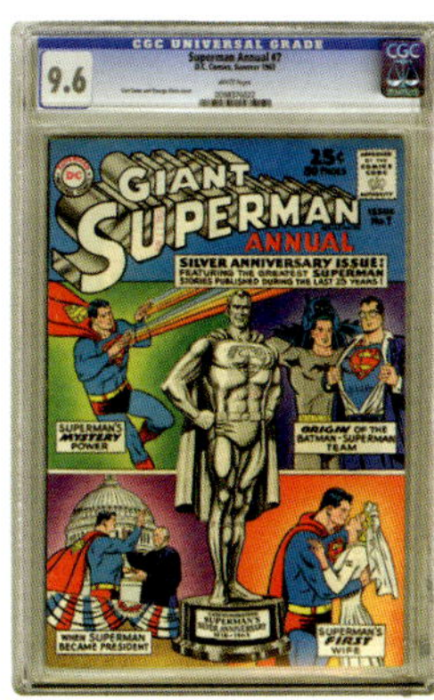

1343 Superman Annual #7 (DC, 1963) CGC NM+ 9.6 White pages. Curt Swan cover. Overstreet 2005 NM- 9.2 value = $190. CGC census 9/05: 2 in 9.6, none higher.

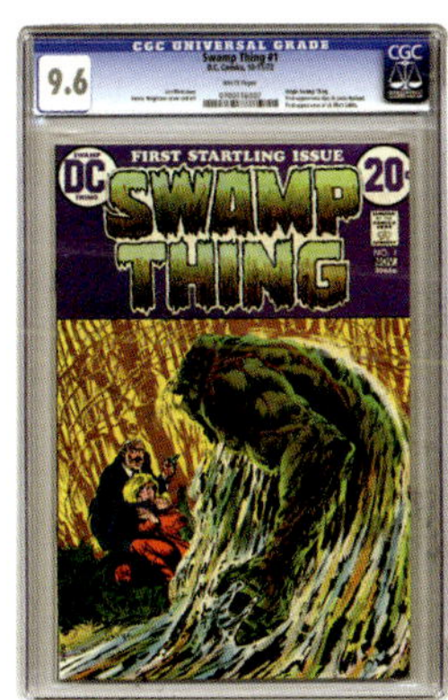

1344 Swamp Thing #1 (DC, 1972) CGC NM+ 9.6 White pages. You could call this the true first appearance of Swamp Thing, since the character who had appeared in **House of Secrets** #92 had a different name (Alex Olsen then, Alec Holland here) and a different origin story (19th century then, 20th century here). Not only does this issue introduce Alex and the new origin, it's the first appearance of supporting character Matt Cable, who would become a villain in years to come and even go on to appear in Neil Gaiman's **Sandman** series. The issue is by the character's co-creators, writer Len Wein and artist Bernie Wrightson. Overstreet 2005 NM- 9.2 value = $180. CGC census 8/05: 28 in 9.6, 3 higher.

1345 Tales of the Unexpected #100 Boston pedigree (DC, 1967) CGC NM 9.4 Off-white to white pages. Carmine Infantino cover. Bernard Baily art. Overstreet 2005 NM- 9.2 value = $75. CGC census 9/05: 1 in 9.4, none higher.

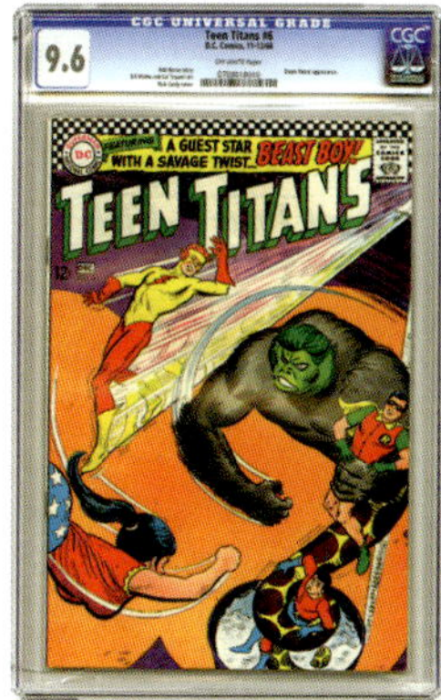

1346 Teen Titans #6 (DC, 1966) CGC NM+ 9.6 Off-white to white pages. Long before Beast Boy became a charter member of the New Teen Titans (changing his name to Changeling), he was a member of the Doom Patrol, which guest-stars here. Dissatisfied with his role in the Doom Patrol, he tries to join the Titans, but they reject him! The issue has a Nick Cardy cover and Bill Molno interior art. Overstreet 2005 NM- 9.2 value = $80. CGC census 9/05: 3 in 9.6, none higher.

1347 Teen Titans #9 (DC, 1967) CGC NM 9.4 Off-white to white pages. Nick Cardy cover. Irv Novick art. Overstreet 2005 NM- 9.2 value = $80. CGC census 9/05: 3 in 9.4, 3 higher.

1348 Teen Titans #38 (DC, 1972) CGC NM+ 9.6 Off-white pages. Nick Cardy cover. George Tuska art. Backup features reprint a Green Arrow story from **Adventure Comics** #260 and an Aquaman story from **Adventure Comics** #278. Overstreet 2005 NM- 9.2 value = $30. CGC census 9/05: 4 in 9.6, none higher.

1349 The Three Mouseketeers #1 (DC, 1970) CGC NM 9.4 Off-white to white pages. Sheldon Mayer art. Overstreet 2005 NM- 9.2 value = $75. CGC census 9/05: 4 in 9.4, none higher.

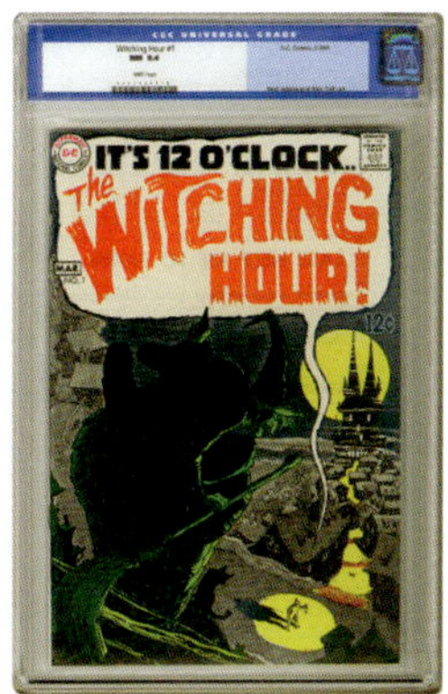

1350 Witching Hour #1 (DC, 1969) CGC NM 9.4 White pages. DC made sure this series got off to a good start by assigning art duties to A-listers Neal Adams and Alex Toth. And even in the pitch black of midnight (which we all know is the Witching Hour) you can make out the "NC" of cover artist Nick Cardy. Overstreet 2005 NM- 9.2 value = $170. CGC census 9/05: 11 in 9.4, 3 higher.

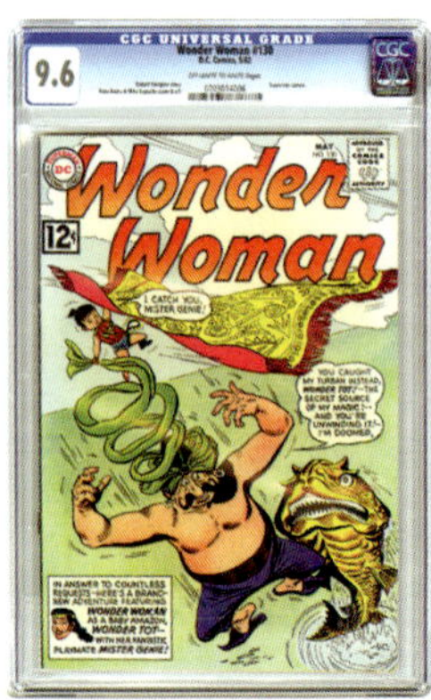

1351 Wonder Woman #130 (DC, 1962) CGC NM+ 9.6 Off-white to white pages. Superman makes a cameo appearance in this issue, which features a tale starring the Baby Amazon, Wonder Tot. This beautiful copy is currently unsurpassed in CGC's census report for this issue. Overstreet 2005 NM- 9.2 value = $125. CGC census 9/05: 1 in 9.6, none higher.

1352 Wonder Woman #130 Pacific Coast pedigree (DC, 1962) CGC NM 9.4 Off-white pages. Wonder Tot story. Ross Andru cover and art. Overstreet 2005 NM- 9.2 value = $125. CGC census 9/05: 2 in 9.4, 1 higher

1353 Wonder Woman #131 Pacific Coast pedigree (DC, 1962) CGC VF/NM 9.0 Off-white pages. Ross Andru cover and art. Overstreet 2005 VF/NM 9.0 value = $78; NM- 9.2 value = $100. CGC census 9/05: 1 in 9.0, none higher.

1354 Wonder Woman #132 Pacific Coast pedigree (DC, 1962) CGC NM 9.4 Off-white pages. Ross Andru cover and art. Overstreet 2005 NM- 9.2 value = $100. CGC census 9/05: 2 in 9.4, none higher.

1355 Wonder Woman #133 Pacific Coast pedigree(DC, 1962) CGC NM 9.4 Off-white pages. Includes one of the "Impossible Tales" featuring the Wonder Woman Family. Overstreet 2005 NM- 9.2 value = $100. CGC census 9/05: 2 in 9.4, none higher.

1356 Wonder Woman #135 Pacific Coast pedigree (DC, 1963) CGC NM 9.4 White pages. Ross Andru art. Overstreet 2005 NM- 9.2 value = $100. CGC census 9/05: 2 in 9.4, none higher.

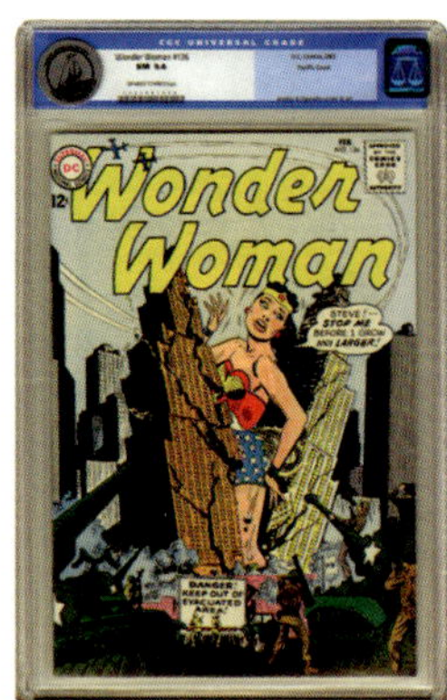

1357 Wonder Woman #136 Pacific Coast pedigree (DC, 1963) CGC NM 9.4 Off-white to white pages. This is the only copy of this issue graded above VF/NM by CGC to date! The art is by Ross Andru. Overstreet 2005 NM- 9.2 value = $100. CGC census 9/05: 1 in 9.4, none higher.

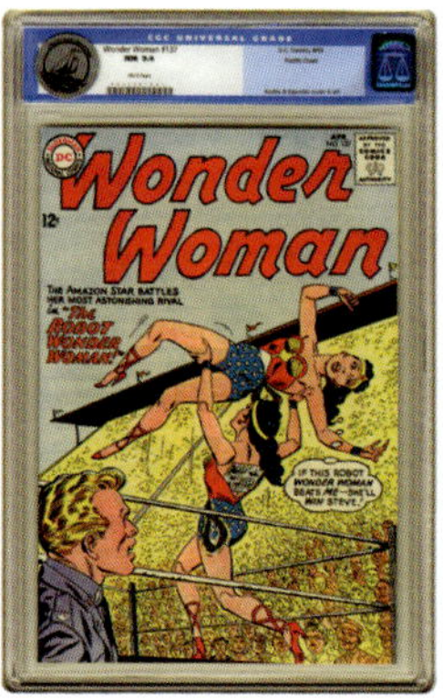

1358 Wonder Woman #137 Pacific Coast pedigree (DC, 1963) CGC NM 9.4 White pages. Ross Andru and his ever-present inking pal Mike Esposito provided the art for this issue. Overstreet 2005 NM- 9.2 value = $100. CGC census 9/05: 1 in 9.4, none higher.

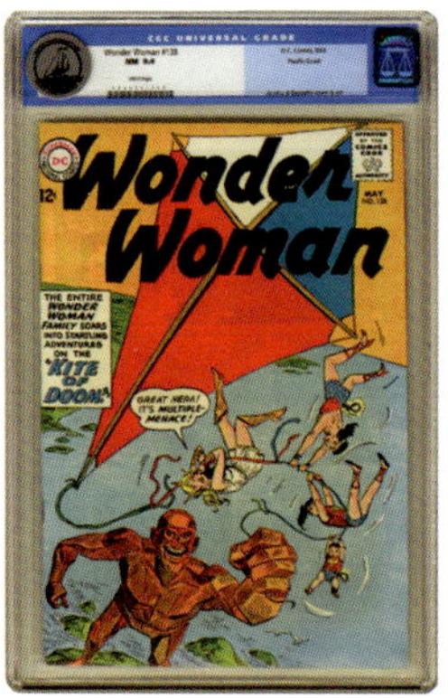

1359 Wonder Woman #138 Pacific Coast pedigree (DC, 1963) CGC NM 9.4 White pages. Ross Andru illustrated this issue, which features an Impossible Tale starring the whole "Wonder Woman Family." Overstreet 2005 NM- 9.2 value = $100. CGC census 9/05: 1 in 9.4, none higher.

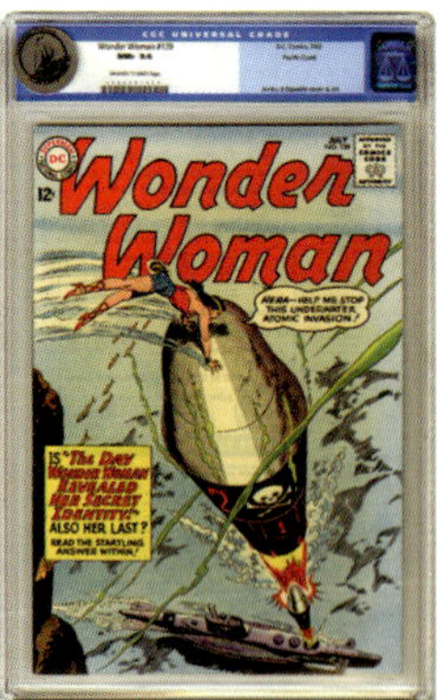

1360 Wonder Woman #139 Pacific Coast pedigree (DC, 1963) CGC NM+ 9.6 Off-white to white pages. This is the only 9.6, and the highest-graded copy overall, that CGC has certified for this issue to date. The cover and interior art are by Ross Andru. Overstreet 2005 NM- 9.2 value = $100. CGC census 9/05: 1 in 9.6, none higher.

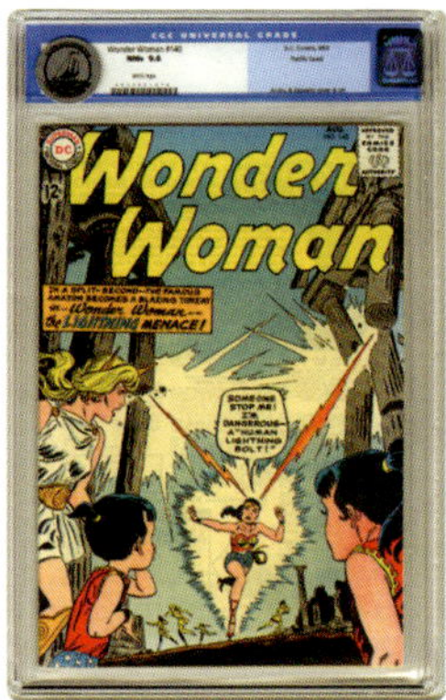

1361 Wonder Woman #140 Pacific Coast pedigree (DC, 1963) CGC NM+ 9.6 White pages. The "Impossible Tales" were the stories that featured Wonder Woman as a tot, an adolescent, and a grown woman all in the same story (impossibly enough!), and this is the sixth of those tales. The issue's cover and interior art are by Ross Andru. Overstreet 2005 NM- 9.2 value = $100. CGC census 9/05: 1 in 9.6, none higher.

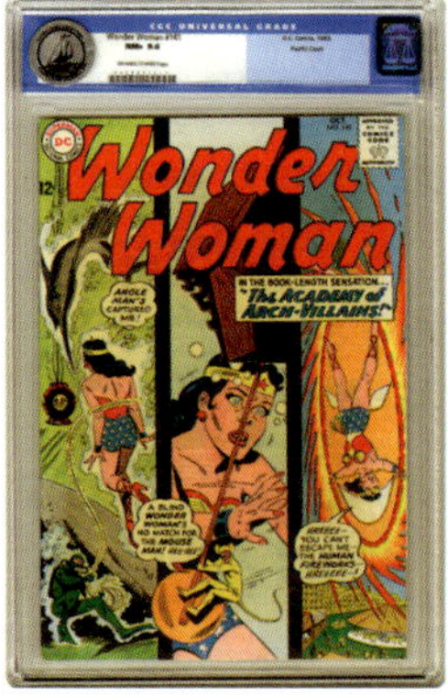

1362 Wonder Woman #141 Pacific Coast pedigree (DC, 1963) CGC NM+ 9.6 Off-white pages. It's surprising how seldom we see these Silver Age **Wonder Woman**s in any grade, and we're fortunate to offer the best copy yet certified right here. The issue's cover and interior art are by Ross Andru. Overstreet 2005 NM- 9.2 value = $100. CGC census 9/05: 1 in 9.6, none higher.

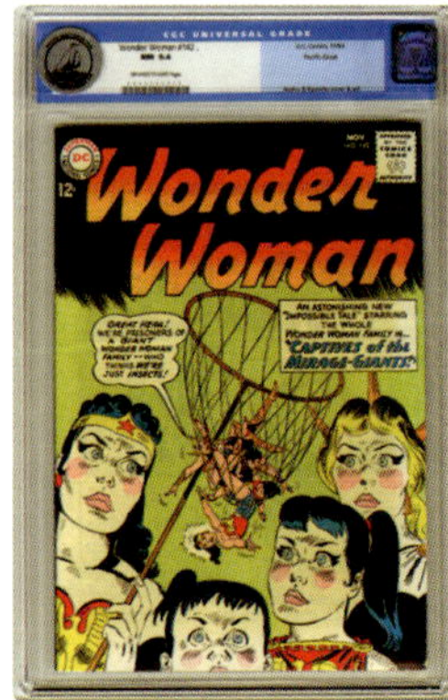

1363 Wonder Woman #142 Pacific Coast pedigree (DC, 1963) CGC NM 9.4 Off-white to white pages. The concept of the "Wonder Woman family" is weird enough, considering that it's the same character at three different ages, but when you throw in a giant Wonder Woman family... hey, the Sixties were wild, man! The "Impossible Tale" was drawn by Ross Andru. Overstreet 2005 NM- 9.2 value = $100. CGC census 9/05: 1 in 9.4, none higher.

1364 Wonder Woman #144 Pacific Coast pedigree (DC, 1964) CGC NM- 9.2 Off-white pages. Ross Andru cover and art. Overstreet 2005 NM- 9.2 value = $100. CGC census 9/05: 3 in 9.2, 1 higher.

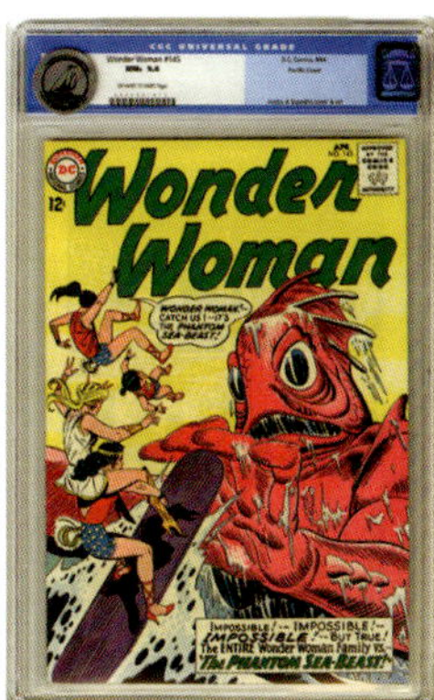

1365 Wonder Woman #145 Pacific Coast pedigree (DC, 1964) CGC NM+ 9.6 Off-white to white pages. It's impossible to have Wonder Woman at three different ages all appearing together at the same time, and yet DC came up with a number of the imaginary yarns. And speaking of impossible things, finding a nicer copy than this one might well fall into that category. CGC hasn't seen one that equals (let alone betters) it as of this writing. Overstreet 2005 NM- 9.2 value = $100. CGC census 9/05: 1 in 9.6, none higher.

1366 Wonder Woman #146 Pacific Coast pedigree (DC, 1964) CGC NM 9.4 Off-white to white pages. Ross Andru cover and art. Overstreet 2005 NM- 9.2 value = $100. CGC census 9/05: 3 in 9.4, none higher.

1367 Wonder Woman #147 Pacific Coast pedigree (DC, 1964) CGC NM 9.4 Off-white to white pages. Ross Andru cover and art. Overstreet 2005 NM- 9.2 value = $100. CGC census 9/05: 5 in 9.4, none higher.

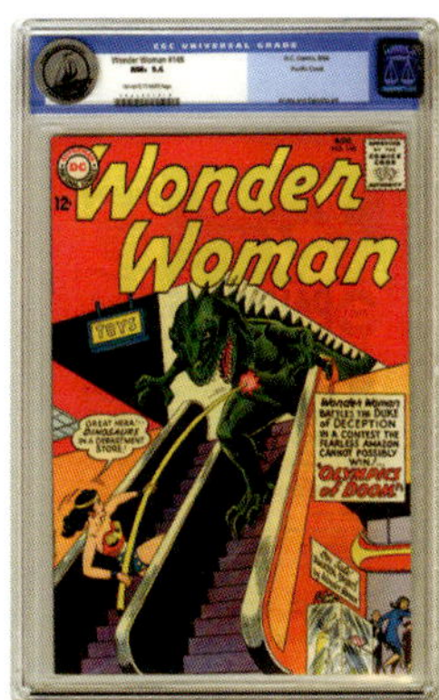

1368 Wonder Woman #148 Pacific Coast pedigree (DC, 1964) CGC NM+ 9.6 Off-white to white pages. This Pacific Coast copy has not been equaled according to CGC's most recent census report. The issue's art is by Ross Andru. Overstreet 2005 NM- 9.2 value = $100. CGC census 9/05: 1 in 9.6, none higher.

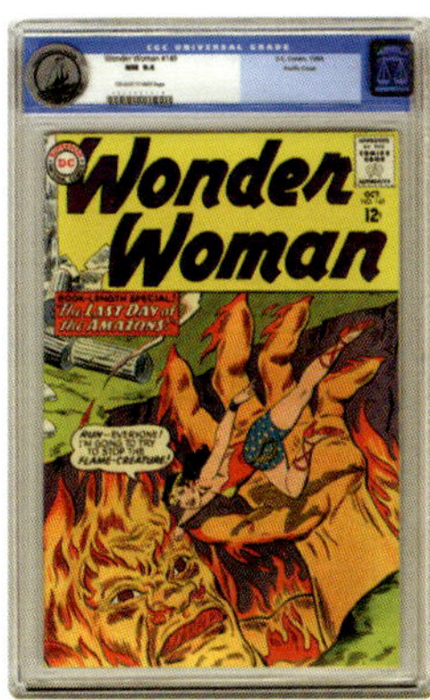

1369 Wonder Woman #149 Pacific Coast pedigree (DC, 1964) CGC NM 9.4 Off-white to white pages. It seems that the Pacific Coast copy of a given Silver Age DC book is the highest-graded copy more often than not. That's certainly the case here. The cover and interior art are by Ross Andru. Overstreet 2005 NM- 9.2 value = $100. CGC census 9/05: 1 in 9.4, none higher.

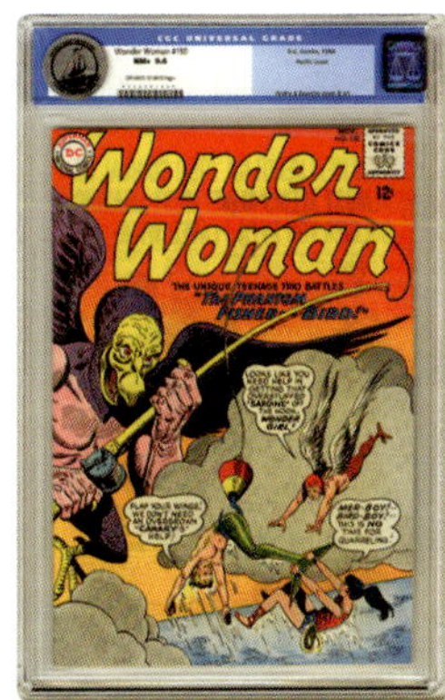

1370 Wonder Woman #150 Pacific Coast pedigree (DC, 1964) CGC NM+ 9.6 Off-white to white pages. Wonder Girl stars in this issue, and we don't mean Donna Troy — it's actually a younger version of Wonder Woman herself. Ross Andru provided cover and interior art. Overstreet 2005 NM- 9.2 value = $100. CGC census 9/05: 2 in 9.6, none higher.

1371 Wonder Woman #151 Pacific Coast pedigree (DC, 1965) CGC NM- 9.2 Off-white to white pages. Ross Andru cover and art. Overstreet 2005 NM- 9.2 value = $80. CGC census 9/05: 3 in 9.2, 1 higher.

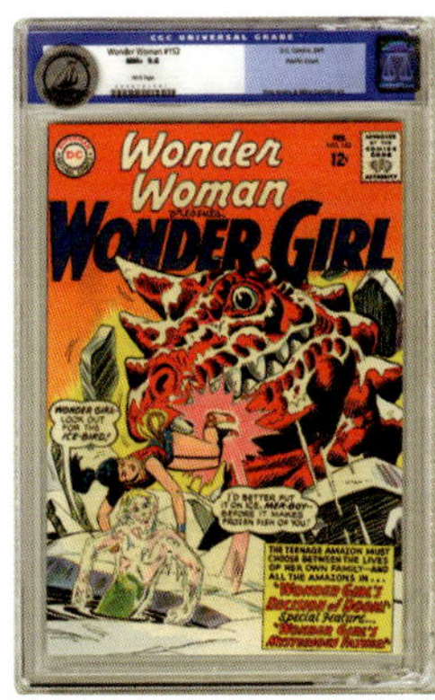

1372 Wonder Woman #152 Pacific Coast pedigree (DC, 1965) CGC NM+ 9.6 White pages. Wonder Girl (Wonder Woman when she was a girl) stars in this issue. The cover and interior art are by Ross Andru. Overstreet 2005 NM- 9.2 value = $80. CGC census 9/05: 1 in 9.6, none higher.

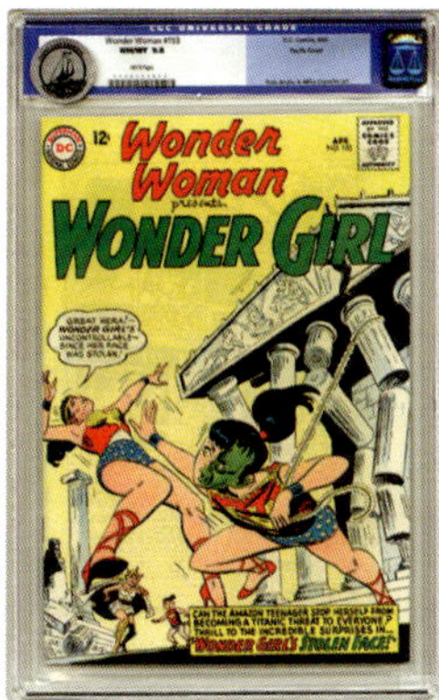

1373 Wonder Woman #153 Pacific Coast pedigree (DC, 1965) CGC NM/MT 9.8 White pages. The brief stretch in which Wonder Girl got star billing (with her name in larger type than Wonder Woman's) came to an end with this issue. The book's cover and interior art are by Ross Andru. Overstreet 2005 NM- 9.2 value = $80. CGC census 9/05: 2 in 9.8, none higher.

1374 Wonder Woman #154 Pacific Coast pedigree (DC, 1965) CGC NM 9.4 Off-white pages. Ross Andru cover and art. Overstreet 2005 NM- 9.2 value = $80. CGC census 9/05: 1 in 9.4, none higher.

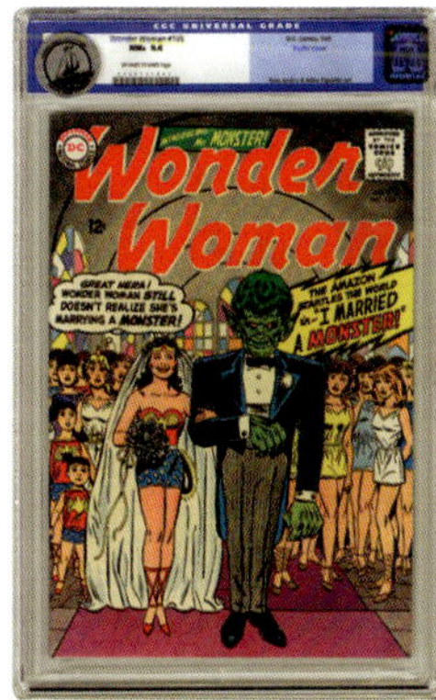

1375 Wonder Woman #155 Pacific Coast pedigree (DC, 1965) CGC NM+ 9.6 Off-white to white pages. This is the only 9.6, and highest-graded copy overall, that CGC has certified for this issue to date. The cover and interior art are by Ross Andru. Overstreet 2005 NM- 9.2 value = $80. CGC census 9/05: 1 in 9.6, none higher.

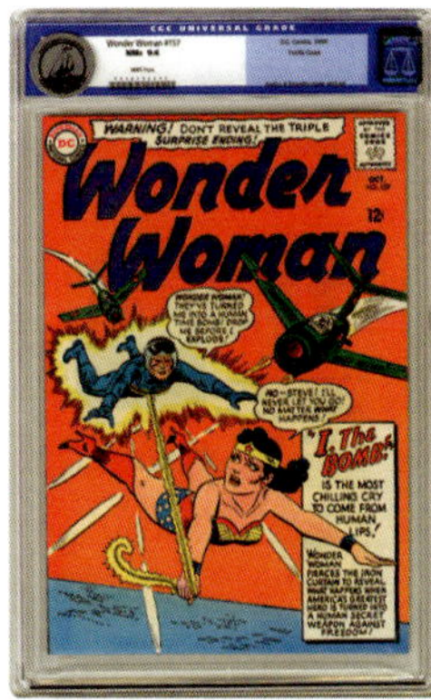

1376 Wonder Woman #157 Pacific Coast pedigree (DC, 1965) CGC NM+ 9.6 White pages. A costume change for Wonder Woman is seen in this issue, as superheroine's boots take the place of the somewhat dressier high heels she sported previously. The issue's cover and interior art are by Ross Andru. Overstreet 2005 NM- 9.2 value = $80. CGC census 9/05: 2 in 9.6, none higher.

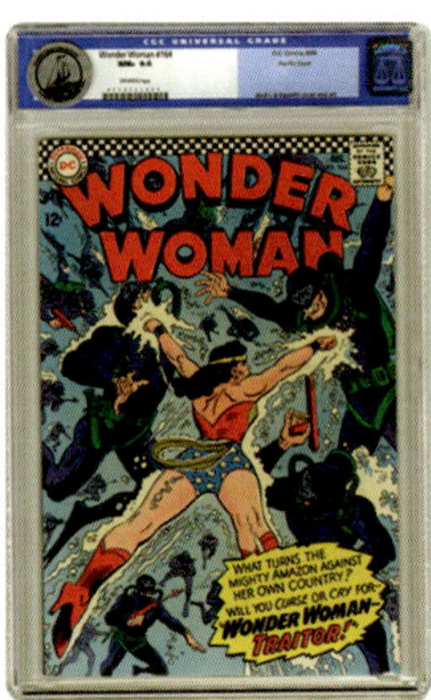

1377 Wonder Woman #164 Pacific Coast pedigree (DC, 1966) CGC NM+ 9.6 Off-white pages. Wonder Woman takes on Angle Man in this issue, which has art in a "Golden Age" style by Ross Andru. Overstreet 2005 NM- 9.2 value = $80. CGC census 9/05: 1 in 9.6, 1 higher.

1378 Wonder Woman #166 Pacific Coast pedigree (DC, 1966) CGC VF/NM 9.0 Off-white to white pages. Ross Andru cover and art. Overstreet 2005 VF/NM 9.0 value = $63; NM- 9.2 value = $80. CGC census 9/05: 2 in 9.0, 1 higher.

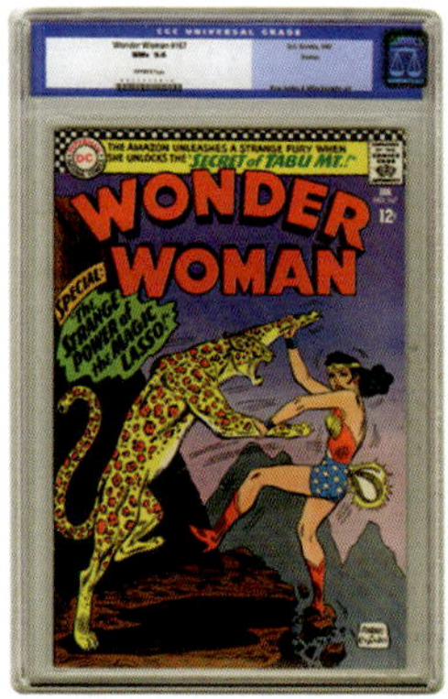

1379 Wonder Woman #167 Boston pedigree (DC, 1967) CGC NM+ 9.6 Off-white pages. This Silver Age adventure of the Amazon is brought to you by penciler Ross Andru and his erstwhile embellisher, Mike Esposito. Overstreet 2005 NM- 9.2 value = $80. CGC census 8/05: 1 in 9.6, 1 higher.

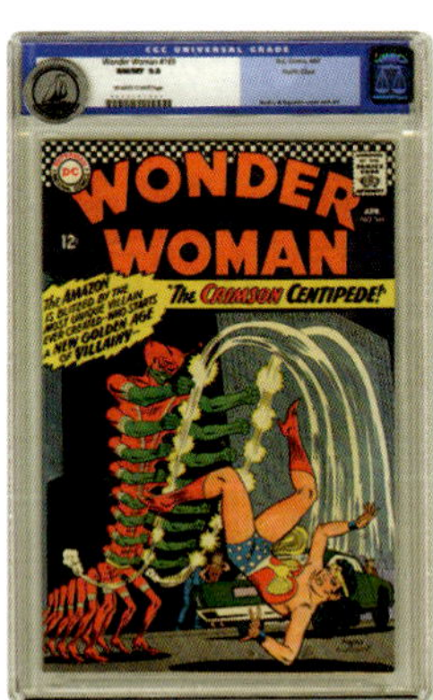

1380 Wonder Woman #169 Pacific Coast pedigree (DC, 1967) CGC NM/MT 9.8 Off-white to white pages. Check out the creepiness of the Crimson Centipede, who menaces Wonder Woman in this issue (he's doing the bidding of the war god Mars, by the way). Ross Andru provided cover and interior art for the issue. These **Wonder Woman** issues don't seem to change hands often in any grade, never mind a 9.8 copy! Overstreet 2005 NM- 9.2 value = $80. CGC census 9/05: 2 in 9.8, none higher.

1381 Wonder Woman #171 Pacific Coast pedigree (DC, 1967) CGC NM 9.4 Off-white pages. Wonder Woman takes on a Man-Fish and the Mouse Man. Ross Andru cover and art. Overstreet 2005 NM- 9.2 value = $60. CGC census 9/05: 1 in 9.4, 2 higher.

1382 Wonder Woman #172 Pacific Coast pedigree (DC, 1967) CGC NM+ 9.6 Off-white to white pages. Irv Novick cover and art. Overstreet 2005 NM- 9.2 value = $60. CGC census 9/05: 1 in 9.6, 1 higher.

1383 Wonder Woman #173 Pacific Coast pedigree (DC, 1967) CGC NM 9.4 Off-white to white pages. Irv Novick cover and art. Overstreet 2005 NM- 9.2 value = $60. CGC census 9/05: 4 in 9.4, none higher.

1384 Wonder Woman #176 Pacific Coast pedigree (DC, 1968) CGC NM 9.4 Off-white to white pages. Irv Novick cover. Ric Estrada art. Overstreet 2005 NM- 9.2 value = $60. CGC census 6/05: 6 in 9.4, 1 higher.

1385 Wonder Woman #182 Pacific Coast pedigree (DC, 1969) CGC VF/NM 9.0 Off-white pages. Mike Sekowsky cover and art. Overstreet 2005 VF/NM 9.0 value = $36; NM- 9.2 value = $45. CGC census 9/05: 1 in 9.0, 9 higher.

1386 Wonder Woman #183 Pacific Coast pedigree (DC, 1969) CGC NM 9.4 Off-white to white pages. Mike Sekowsky cover and art. Overstreet 2005 NM- 9.2 value = $45. CGC census 9/05: 2 in 9.4, 4 higher.

1387 Wonder Woman #186 Pacific Coast pedigree (DC, 1970) CGC NM 9.4 White pages. Mike Sekowsky cover and art. Overstreet 2005 NM- 9.2 value = $45. CGC census 9/05: 3 in 9.4, 1 higher.

1388 Wonder Woman #188 Pacific Coast pedigree (DC, 1970) CGC NM+ 9.6 White pages. Bondage cover. Mike Sekowsky story, cover, and art. Overstreet 2005 NM- 9.2 value = $45. CGC census 9/05: 2 in 9.6, 1 higher.

1389 Wonder Woman #189 (DC, 1970) CGC NM+ 9.6 Off-white to white pages. Mike Sekowsky cover and art. Overstreet 2005 NM- 9.2 value = $45. CGC census 9/05: 2 in 9.6, 1 higher.

1390 Wonder Woman #190 Pacific Coast pedigree (DC, 1970) CGC NM- 9.2 White pages. Mike Sekowsky cover and art. Overstreet 2005 NM- 9.2 value = $45. CGC census 9/05: 1 in 9.2, 4 higher.

1391 Wonder Woman #191 Pacific Coast pedigree (DC, 1970) CGC VF/NM 9.0 White pages. Mike Sekowsky cover and art. Overstreet 2005 VF/NM 9.0 value = $36; NM- 9.2 value = $45. CGC census 9/05: 3 in 9.0, 3 higher.

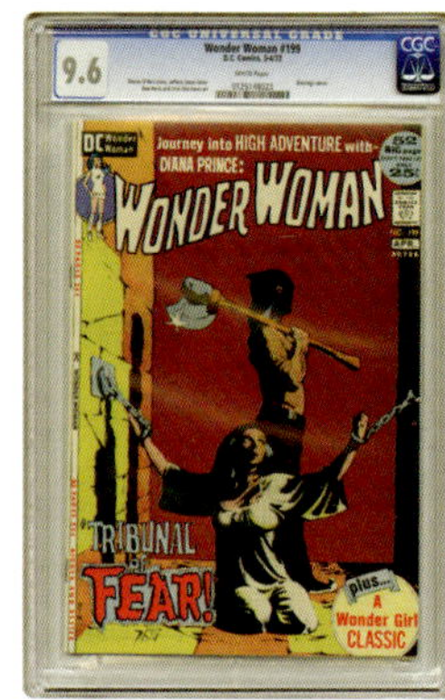

1392 Wonder Woman #199 (DC, 1972) CGC NM+ 9.6 White pages. A bondage cover by Jeff Jones... and the Comics Code was OK with it! Despite the remarkable cover, this issue has about the same Guide value as the preceding issues; look for that to change as more and more collectors lay eyes on this standout comic. Overstreet 2005 NM- 9.2 value = $75. CGC census 9/05: 9 in 9.6, 3 higher.

OTHER SILVER AGE TO MODERN AGE COMICS

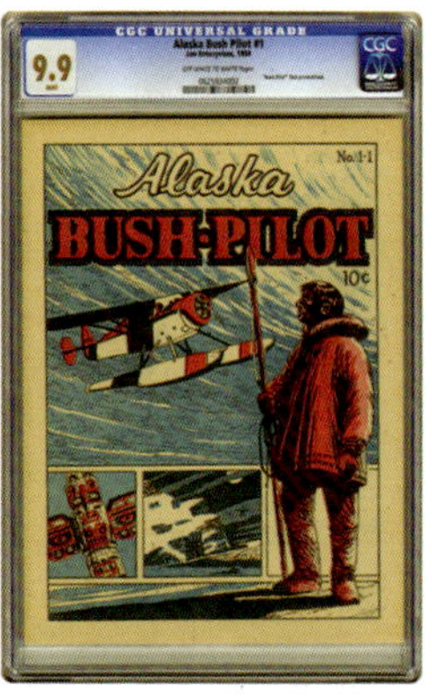

1393 Alaska Bush Pilot #1 (Jan Enterprises, 1959) CGC MT 9.9 Off-white to white pages. Here's a promotional comic for the collector who thought he had everything! We'd be remiss if we didn't recount this comic's backstory: the entire print run of 100 copies was found at a defunct printer's shop in Portland, Oregon, and 72 of them were water-damaged or otherwise unsalvageable. So here's one of the 28 surviving copies, and you certainly won't find one in a nicer grade! Not listed in Overstreet. CGC census 8/05: 1 in 9.9, none higher.

1394 Black Cat #64 Pacific Coast pedigree (Harvey, 1963) CGC NM 9.4 White pages. This giant issue offered encore presentations of Black Cat tales from earlier issues. A square bound book in this condition merits a long look! Overstreet 2005 NM- 9.2 value = $200. CGC census 6/05: 1 in 9.4, none higher.

1395 Black Cat #65 Pacific Coast pedigree (Harvey, 1963) CGC NM 9.4 Off-white to white pages. This is the last issue of the title. The square bound book includes one page of Bob Powell art. Overstreet 2005 NM- 9.2 value = $200. CGC census 6/05: 1 in 9.4, none higher.

1396 Blue Beetle #1 (Charlton, 1967) CGC NM 9.4 White pages. First appearance of the Question. Steve Ditko cover and art. Overstreet 2005 NM- 9.2 value = $160. CGC census 9/05: 4 in 9.4, 6 higher.

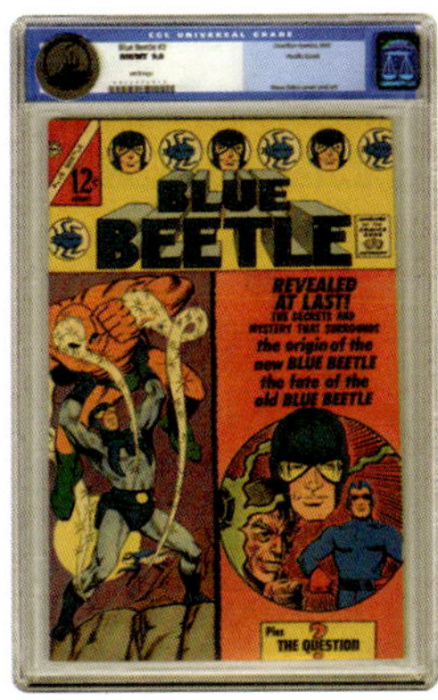

1397 Blue Beetle #2 Pacific Coast pedigree (Charlton, 1967) CGC NM/MT 9.8 White pages. This issue revealed the origin of Ted Kord, the new Blue Beetle, and finally told readers what had happened to the previous Beetle, Dan Garrett! The whole tale was plotted and drawn by the great Steve Ditko. Overstreet 2005 NM- 9.2 value = $75. CGC census 6/05: 2 in 9.8, none higher.

1398 Captain Atom #79 Pacific Coast pedigree (Charlton, 1966) CGC NM 9.4 Off-white to white pages. First appearance of Doctor Spectro. Steve Ditko cover and art. Overstreet 2005 NM- 9.2 value = $75. CGC census 6/05: 5 in 9.4, 4 higher.

1399 Captain Atom #85 Pacific Coast pedigree (Charlton, 1967) CGC NM+ 9.6 White pages. Steve Ditko cover and art. CGC notes, "2 siamese pages." Overstreet 2005 NM- 9.2 value = $70. CGC census 6/05: 2 in 9.6, none higher.

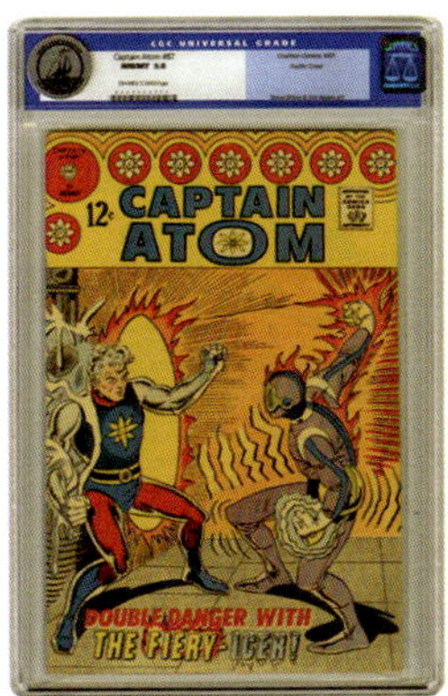

1400 Captain Atom #87 Pacific Coast pedigree (Charlton, 1967) CGC NM/MT 9.8 Off-white to white pages. Charlton's best artist Steve Ditko drew this issue's cover and the Captain Atom story, and the ultra-underrated Jim Aparo chipped in with a Nightshade adventure. Overstreet 2005 NM- 9.2 value = $70. CGC census 6/05: 2 in 9.8, none higher.

1401 Choo-Choo Charlie #1 (Gold Key, 1969) CGC NM 9.4 Off-white pages. The only issue of the title. John Stanley art. Overstreet 2005 NM- 9.2 value = $140. CGC census 8/05: 4 in 9.4, none higher.

1402 Darkness (second series 2002) V2#1 (Image, 2002) CGC MT 10.0 White pages. Holofoil edition. Mark Silvestri cover; Dale Keown art. Gem Mint copy. Overstreet 2005 NM- 9.2 value = $3. CGC census 9/05: 1 in 10.0, none higher.

1403 Dell Giant Comics Marge's Lulu and Tubby Halloween Fun #2 (Dell, 1958) CGC VF/NM 9.0 Off-white pages. Overstreet 2005 VF/NM 9.0 value = $159; NM- 9.2 value = $230. CGC census 9/05: 1 in 9.0, 1 higher.

1404 Flash Gordon #1 (King Features Syndicate, 1966) CGC NM+ 9.6 Off-white to white pages. First Silver Age appearance of Flash Gordon. Al Williamson cover and art. Overstreet 2005 NM- 9.2 value = $90. CGC census 8/05: 3 in 9.6, 2 higher.

1405 Flash Gordon #2 Pacific Coast pedigree (King Features Syndicate, 1966) CGC NM+ 9.6 Off-white pages. Gil Kane's dashing **Flash** cover kicks off this issue, which features interior art by Frank Bolle and Don Heck, and a story by Archie Goodwin. Super-sharp copy. Overstreet 2005 NM- 9.2 value = $45. CGC census 6/05: 2 in 9.6, none higher.

1406 Flash Gordon #4 Pacific Coast pedigree (King Features Syndicate, 1967) CGC NM 9.4 Off-white pages. Al Williamson cover and interior art. Archie Goodwin story. Overstreet 2005 NM- 9.2 value = $45. CGC census 6/05: 1 in 9.4, 1 higher.

1407 Flash Gordon #5 Pacific Coast pedigree (King Features Syndicate, 1967) CGC NM 9.4 Off-white to white pages. Al Williamson cover and interior art; Archie Goodwin story. Overstreet 2005 NM- 9.2 value = $45. CGC census 6/05: 3 in 9.4, none higher.

1408 Flying Saucers #1 Pacific Coast pedigree (Dell, 1967) CGC NM 9.4 Off-white to white pages. Frank Springer cover and art. Overstreet 2005 NM- 9.2 value = $50. CGC census 6/05: 2 in 9.4, 3 higher.

1409 Forbidden Worlds #144 Boston pedigree (ACG, 1967) CGC NM 9.4 Off-white to white pages. Cover by Kurt Schaffenberger (using the pseudonym Lou Wahl). Overstreet 2005 NM- 9.2 value = $40. CGC census 8/05: 1 in 9.4, none higher.

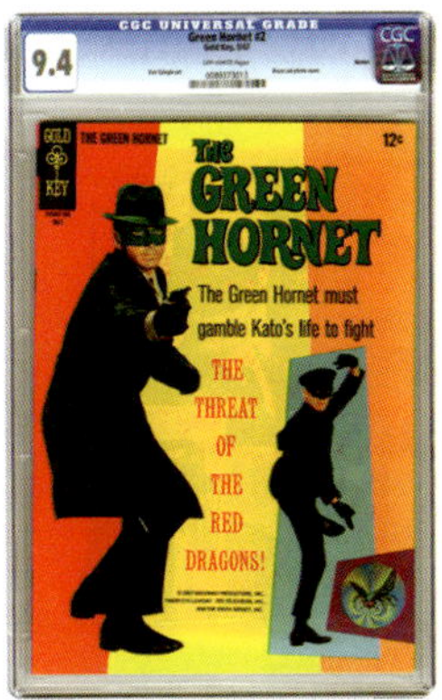

1410 The Green Hornet #2 Boston pedigree (Gold Key, 1967) CGC NM 9.4 Off-white pages. Photo cover featuring Bruce Lee and Van Williams. Dan Spiegle art. Overstreet 2005 NM- 9.2 value = $220. CGC census 9/05: 7 in 9.4, 1 higher.

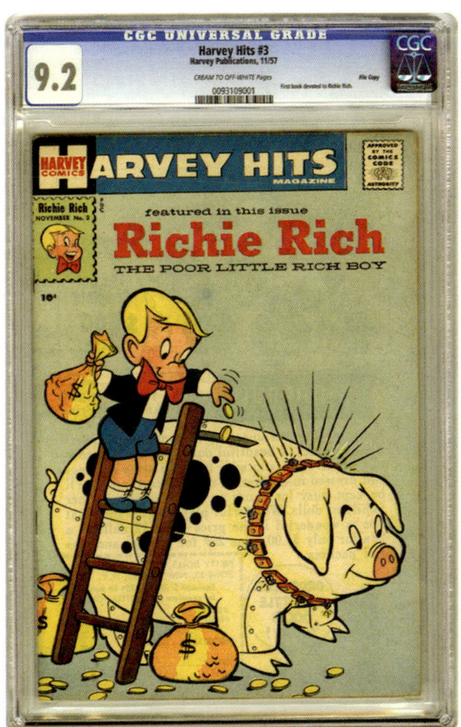

1411 Harvey Hits #3 Richie Rich - File Copy (Harvey, 1957) CGC NM- 9.2 Cream to off-white pages. This issue of Harvey Hits — sort of Harvey's equivalent of DC's tryout series **Showcase** — is the first comic book devoted to everyone's favorite "poor little rich boy," Richie Rich. Before long, of course, Richie would headline a fleet of long-running titles, making this appearance even more significant. To top it off, this high-grade beauty is a Harvey file copy! Overstreet 2005 NM- 9.2 value = $2,000. CGC census 9/05: 2 in 9.2, 2 higher.

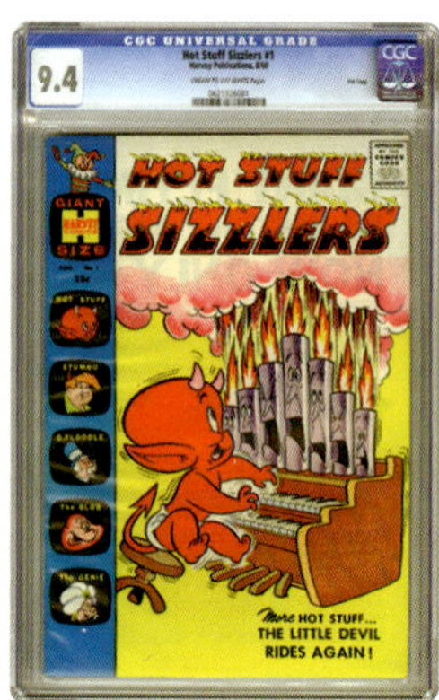

1412 Hot Stuff Sizzlers #1 File Copy (Harvey, 1960) CGC NM 9.4 Cream to off-white pages. Only Harvey could get away with a comic book starring a devil! And indeed, most surviving copies of this issue look like they've been to you-know-where and back. Not so with this issue, it's the only 9.4, and highest-graded copy overall, that CGC has certified to date. Overstreet 2005 NM- 9.2 value = $220. CGC census 8/05: 1 in 9.4, none higher.

1413 Hot Stuff Sizzlers #2 File Copy (Harvey, 1960) CGC NM 9.4 Cream to off-white pages. Overstreet 2005 NM- 9.2 value = $95. CGC census 8/05: 1 in 9.4, none higher.

1414 Hot Stuff Sizzlers #3 File Copy (Harvey, 1961) CGC NM 9.4 Cream to off-white pages. Overstreet 2005 NM- 9.2 value = $95. CGC census 8/05: 1 in 9.4, none higher.

1415 Hot Stuff Sizzlers #4 File Copy (Harvey, 1961) CGC NM+ 9.6 Cream to off-white pages. Overstreet 2005 NM- 9.2 value = $65. CGC census 8/05: 1 in 9.6, none higher.

1416 Hot Stuff Sizzlers #5 File Copy (Harvey, 1961) CGC VF/NM 9.0 Cream to off-white pages. Overstreet 2005 VF/NM 9.0 value = $52; NM- 9.2 value = $65. CGC census 8/05: 1 in 9.0, none higher.

1417 Hot Stuff Sizzlers #6 File Copy (Harvey, 1961) CGC NM+ 9.6 Cream to off-white pages. Overstreet 2005 NM- 9.2 value = $65. CGC census 8/05: 1 in 9.6, none higher.

1418 Hot Stuff Sizzlers #9 File Copy (Harvey, 1962) CGC NM 9.4 Off-white pages. Overstreet 2005 NM- 9.2 value = $65. CGC census 8/05: 1 in 9.4, none higher.

1419 Hot Stuff Sizzlers #10 File Copy (Harvey, 1962) CGC NM- 9.2 Off-white to white pages. Overstreet 2005 NM- 9.2 value = $65. CGC census 8/05: 1 in 9.2, none higher.

1420 Hot Stuff Sizzlers #12 File Copy (Harvey, 1963) CGC NM- 9.2 Off-white pages. Overstreet 2005 NM- 9.2 value = $48. CGC census 8/05: 1 in 9.2, none higher.

1421 Hot Stuff Sizzlers #13 File Copy (Harvey, 1963) CGC NM 9.4 Off-white pages. Overstreet 2005 NM- 9.2 value = $48. CGC census 8/05: 1 in 9.4, none higher.

1422 Hot Stuff Sizzlers #14 File Copy (Harvey, 1963) CGC NM+ 9.6 Off-white pages. Overstreet 2005 NM- 9.2 value = $48. CGC census 8/05: 1 in 9.6, none higher.

1423 Hot Stuff Sizzlers #16 File Copy (Harvey, 1964) CGC NM 9.4 Cream to off-white pages. Overstreet 2005 NM- 9.2 value = $48. CGC census 8/05: 1 in 9.4, none higher.

1424 Hot Stuff Sizzlers #17 File Copy (Harvey, 1964) CGC NM- 9.2 Off-white pages. Overstreet 2005 NM- 9.2 value = $48. CGC census 8/05: 1 in 9.2, none higher.

1425 Hot Stuff Sizzlers #18 File Copy (Harvey, 1964) CGC NM+ 9.6 Off-white pages. Overstreet 2005 NM- 9.2 value = $48. CGC census 9/05: 1 in 9.6, none higher.

1426 Hot Stuff Sizzlers #19 File Copy (Harvey, 1965) CGC NM+ 9.6 Off-white to white pages. Overstreet 2005 NM- 9.2 value = $48. CGC census 9/05: 1 in 9.6, none higher.

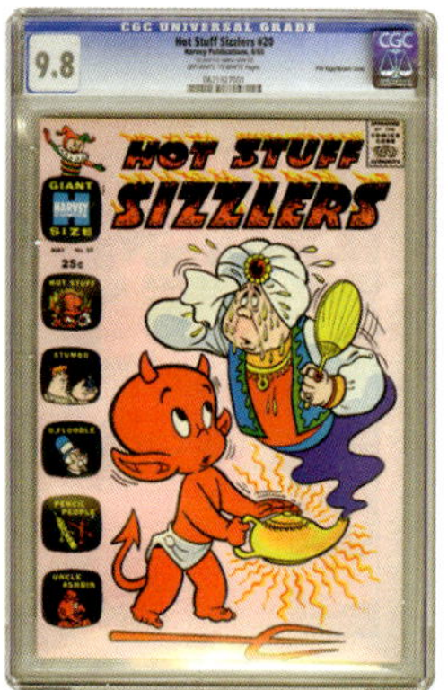

1427 Hot Stuff Sizzlers #20 Double Cover - File Copy (Harvey, 1965) CGC NM/MT 9.8 Off-white to white pages. Not only is this the highest-graded copy yet certified of this issue, it's got a double cover to add to the desirability. In addition to the devilish title character, this one's got backup features ranging from well-known (Stumbo the Giant) to ultra-obscure (Uncle Ashbin and the Pencil People). CGC notes, "1st cover 9.6, interior cover 9.8." Overstreet 2005 NM- 9.2 value = $48. CGC census 8/05: 1 in 9.8, none higher.

1428 Hot Stuff Sizzlers #21 File Copy (Harvey, 1965) CGC NM- 9.2 Off-white to white pages. Overstreet 2005 NM- 9.2 value = $32. CGC census 8/05: 1 in 9.2, none higher.

1429 Hot Stuff Sizzlers #22 File Copy (Harvey, 1966) CGC NM+ 9.6 Off-white to white pages. Overstreet 2005 NM- 9.2 value = $32. CGC census 8/05: 1 in 9.6, none higher.

1430 Hot Stuff Sizzlers #26 File Copy (Harvey, 1966) CGC NM 9.4 Off-white to white pages. Overstreet 2005 NM- 9.2 value = $32. CGC census 8/05: 1 in 9.4, none higher.

1431 Hot Stuff Sizzlers #28 File Copy (Harvey, 1967) CGC VF/NM 9.0 Off-white to white pages. Overstreet 2005 VF/NM 9.0 value = $25; NM- 9.2 value = $32. CGC census 8/05: 1 in 9.0, none higher.

1432 Hot Stuff Sizzlers #29 File Copy (Harvey, 1967) CGC NM+ 9.6 Off-white to white pages. Overstreet 2005 NM- 9.2 value = $32. CGC census 8/05: 1 in 9.6, none higher.

1433 Hot Stuff Sizzlers #30 File Copy (Harvey, 1967) CGC NM- 9.2 Off-white to white pages. Overstreet 2005 NM- 9.2 value = $32. CGC census 8/05: 1 in 9.2, none higher.

1434 Hot Stuff Sizzlers #31 File Copy (Harvey, 1967) CGC NM+ 9.6 Off-white to white pages. Overstreet 2005 NM- 9.2 value = $32. CGC census 9/05: 1 in 9.6, none higher.

1435 Hot Stuff Sizzlers #32 File Copy (Harvey, 1968) CGC NM 9.4 Off-white to white pages. Overstreet 2005 NM- 9.2 value = $32. CGC census 9/05: 1 in 9.4, none higher.

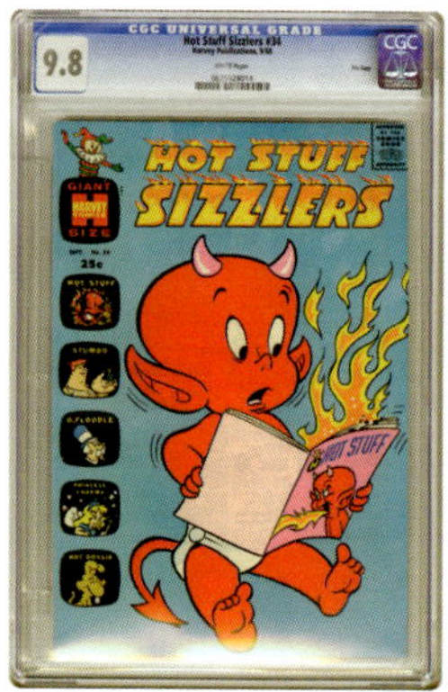

1436 Hot Stuff Sizzlers #34 File Copy (Harvey, 1968) CGC NM/MT 9.8 White pages. Overstreet 2005 NM- 9.2 value = $32. CGC census 9/05: 1 in 9.8, none higher.

1437 Hot Stuff Sizzlers #35 File Copy (Harvey, 1968) CGC NM 9.4 White pages. Overstreet 2005 NM- 9.2 value = $32. CGC census 9/05: 1 in 9.4, none higher.

1438 Hot Stuff Sizzlers #36 File Copy (Harvey, 1969) CGC NM+ 9.6 Off-white to white pages. Overstreet 2005 NM- 9.2 value = $32. CGC census 9/05: 1 in 9.6, none higher.

1439 Hot Stuff Sizzlers #37 File Copy (Harvey, 1969) CGC NM+ 9.6 Off-white to white pages. Overstreet 2005 NM- 9.2 value = $32. CGC census 9/05: 1 in 9.6, none higher.

1440 Hot Stuff Sizzlers #38 File Copy (Harvey, 1969) CGC NM+ 9.6 Off-white to white pages. Overstreet 2005 NM- 9.2 value = $32. CGC census 9/05: 1 in 9.6, none higher.

1441 Hot Stuff Sizzlers #38 File Copy (Harvey, 1969) CGC NM- 9.2 Off-white to white pages. Overstreet 2005 NM- 9.2 value = $32. CGC census 9/05: 1 in 9.2, none higher.

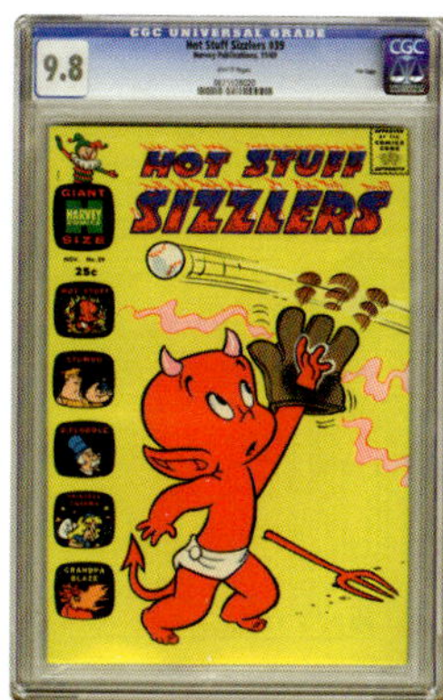

1442 Hot Stuff Sizzlers #39 File Copy (Harvey, 1969) CGC NM/MT 9.8 White pages. Overstreet 2005 NM- 9.2 value = $32. CGC census 9/05: 1 in 9.8, none higher.

1443 Hot Stuff Sizzlers #40 File Copy (Harvey, 1970) CGC NM+ 9.6 Off-white to white pages. Overstreet 2005 NM- 9.2 value = $32. CGC census 9/05: 1 in 9.6, none higher.

1444 Hot Stuff Sizzlers #41 File Copy (Harvey, 1970) CGC NM- 9.2 Off-white to white pages. Overstreet 2005 NM- 9.2 value = $32. CGC census 9/05: 1 in 9.2, none higher.

1445 Hot Stuff Sizzlers #42 File Copy (Harvey, 1970) CGC NM+ 9.6 Off-white to white pages. Overstreet 2005 NM- 9.2 value = $32. CGC census 9/05: 1 in 9.6, none higher.

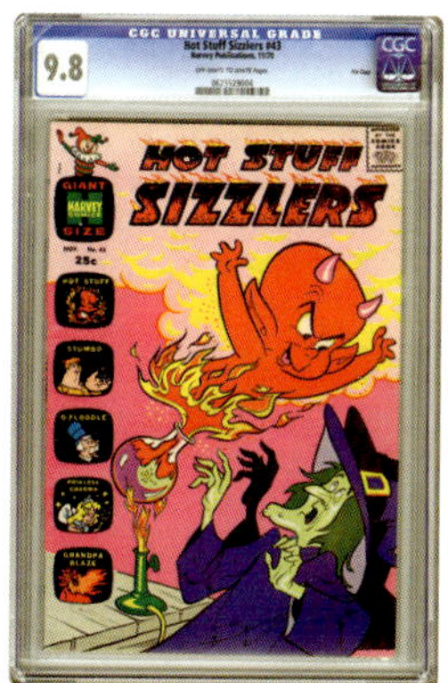

1446 Hot Stuff Sizzlers #43 File Copy (Harvey, 1970) CGC NM/MT 9.8 Off-white to white pages. Overstreet 2005 NM- 9.2 value = $32. CGC census 9/05: 1 in 9.8, none higher.

1447 Hot Stuff Sizzlers #44 File Copy (Harvey, 1971) CGC NM+ 9.6 Off-white to white pages. Overstreet 2005 NM- 9.2 value = $32. CGC census 9/05: 1 in 9.6, none higher.

1448 Hot Stuff Sizzlers #45 File Copy (Harvey, 1971) CGC NM+ 9.6 Off-white to white pages. Overstreet 2005 NM- 9.2 value = $32. CGC census 9/05: 1 in 9.6, none higher.

1449 Hot Stuff Sizzlers #46 File Copy (Harvey, 1971) CGC NM+ 9.6 Off-white to white pages. Overstreet 2005 NM- 9.2 value = $24. CGC census 9/05: 1 in 9.6, none higher.

1450 Hot Stuff Sizzlers #47 File Copy (Harvey, 1971) CGC NM+ 9.6 White pages. Overstreet 2005 NM- 9.2 value = $24. CGC census 9/05: 1 in 9.6, none higher.

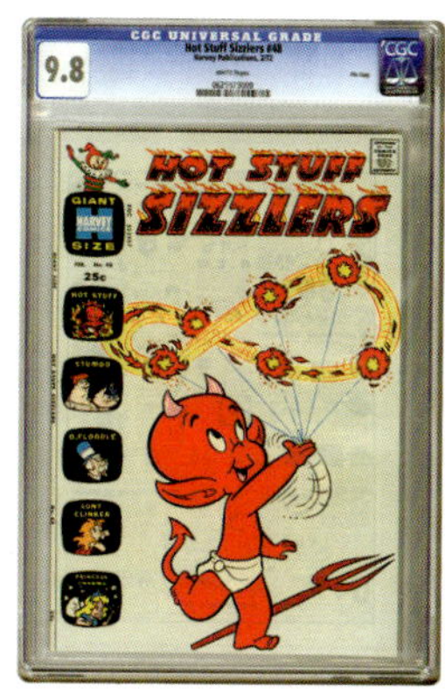

1451 Hot Stuff Sizzlers #48 File Copy (Harvey, 1972) CGC NM/MT 9.8 White pages. Overstreet 2005 NM- 9.2 value = $32. CGC census 9/05: 1 in 9.8, none higher.

1452 Hot Stuff Sizzlers #49 File Copy (Harvey, 1972) CGC NM- 9.2 Off-white to white pages. Overstreet 2005 NM- 9.2 value = $24. CGC census 9/05: 1 in 9.2, none higher.

1453 Hot Stuff Sizzlers #50 File Copy (Harvey, 1972) CGC NM 9.4 Off-white to white pages. Overstreet 2005 NM- 9.2 value = $24. CGC census 9/05: 1 in 9.4, none higher.

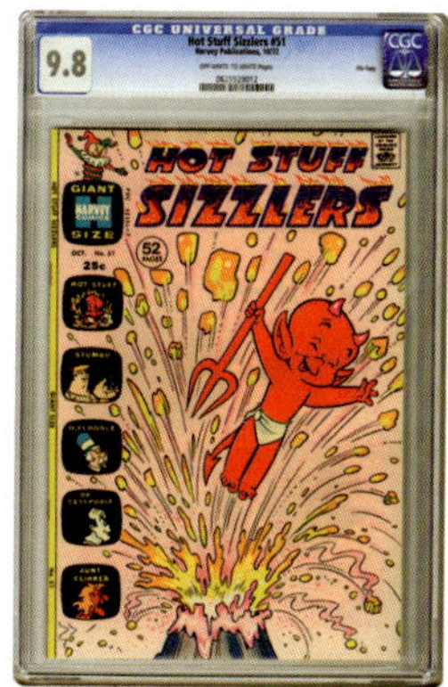

1454 Hot Stuff Sizzlers #51 File Copy (Harvey, 1972) CGC NM/MT 9.8 Off-white to white pages. Overstreet 2005 NM- 9.2 value = $24. CGC census 9/05: 1 in 9.8, none higher.

1455 Hot Stuff Sizzlers #52 File Copy (Harvey, 1972) CGC VF/NM 9.0 Off-white to white pages. Overstreet 2005 VF/NM 9.0 value = $20; NM- 9.2 value = $24. CGC census 9/05: 1 in 9.0, none higher.

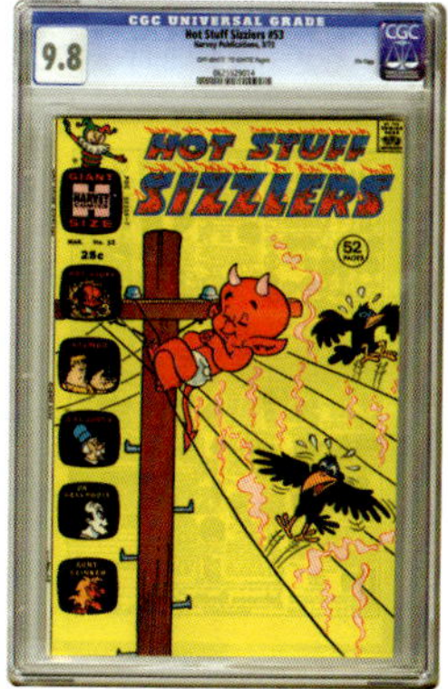

1456 Hot Stuff Sizzlers #53 File Copy (Harvey, 1973) CGC NM/MT 9.8 Off-white to white pages. Overstreet 2005 NM- 9.2 value = $16. CGC census 9/05: 1 in 9.8, none higher.

1457 Hot Stuff Sizzlers #55 File Copy (Harvey, 1973) CGC NM+ 9.6 White pages. Overstreet 2005 NM- 9.2 value = $16. CGC census 9/05: 1 in 9.6, none higher.

1458 Hot Stuff Sizzlers #57 File Copy (Harvey, 1973) CGC NM 9.4 White pages. Overstreet 2005 NM- 9.2 value = $16. CGC census 9/05: 1 in 9.4, none higher.

1459 Hot Stuff Sizzlers #59 File Copy (Harvey, 1974) CGC NM+ 9.6 Off-white to white pages. Overstreet 2005 NM- 9.2 value = $16. CGC census 9/05: 1 in 9.6, none higher.

1460 Hot Stuff Sizzlers File Copies Group (Harvey, 1962-73) Condition: Average VF. This group includes #7, 8, 15, 23, 24, 25, 27, 33, 54, 56, and 58. Approximate Overstreet value for group = $230.

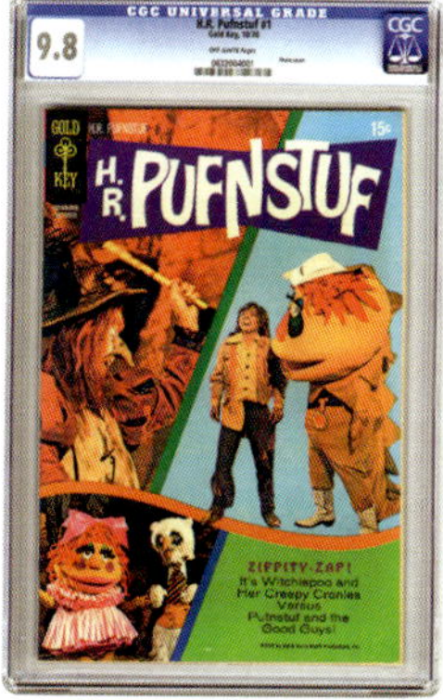

1461 H.R. Pufnstuf #1 (Gold Key, 1970) CGC NM/MT 9.8 Off-white pages. Sid and Marty Krofft — you either "get" them or you don't, and legions of fans have fond memories of the bizarre Krofft characters. This first issue commands higher prices with each passing year, and no copy has been graded higher than our offering to date. Overstreet 2005 NM- 9.2 value = $310. CGC census 7/05: 2 in 9.8, none higher.

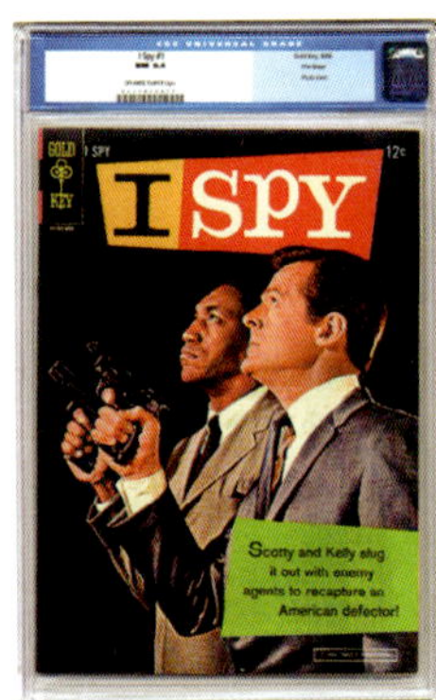

1462 I Spy #1 File Copy (Gold Key, 1966) CGC NM 9.4 Off-white to white pages. This issue, with a photo cover featuring Robert Culp and Bill Cosby, is one of the most valuable of the Gold Key TV tie-in books. To date, CGC hasn't awarded a higher grade for this issue. Overstreet 2005 NM- 9.2 value= $340. CGC census 9/05: 9 in 9.4, none higher.

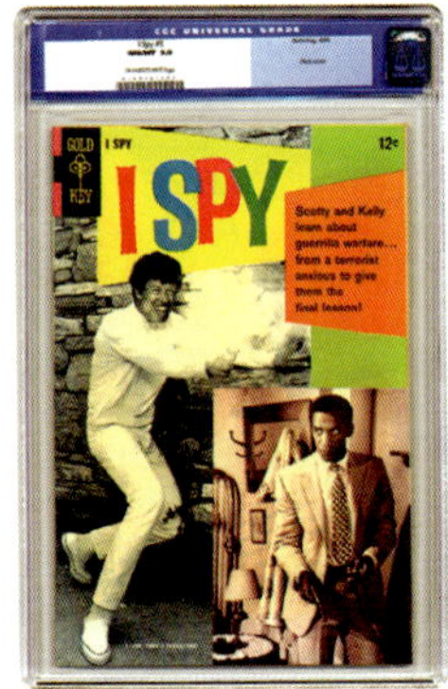

1463 I Spy #5 (Gold Key, 1968) CGC NM/MT 9.8 Off-white to white pages. If you think Robert Culp's all-white tennis outfit looks sharp, have a look at the condition of this all but perfect copy. Overstreet 2005 NM- 9.2 value = $200. CGC census 9/05: 2 in 9.8, none higher.

1464 Magilla Gorilla #1 File Copy (Gold Key, 1964) CGC VF/NM 9.0 Off-white pages. First comic book appearance of this Hanna-Barbera cartoon character. Overstreet 2005 VF/NM 9.0 value = $120; NM- 9.2 value = $160. CGC census 8/05: 1 in 9.0, none higher.

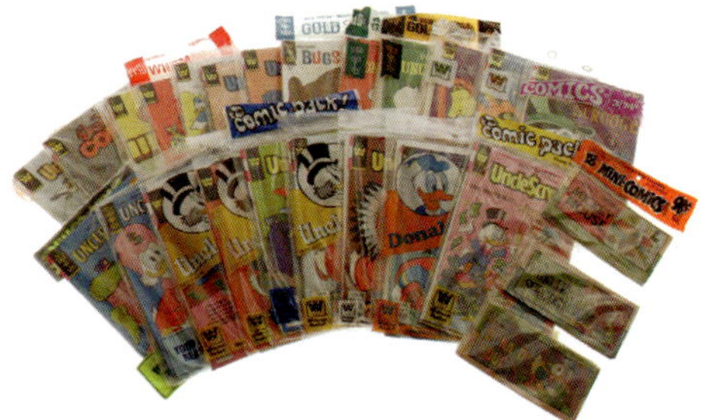

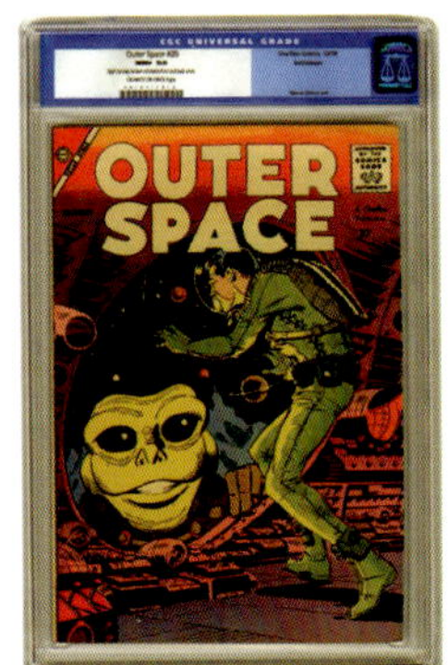

1465 Outer Space #20 Bethlehem pedigree (Charlton, 1958) CGC NM+ 9.6 Cream to off-white pages. Steve Ditko art graces the interior of this science fiction comic. The cover art, obviously "inspired by" Wally Wood, may be the work of Charlton stalwart Dick Giordano. This is one of only two copies of this issue that CGC has certified to date, with the other one a light year behind at 6.0. Overstreet 2005 NM- 9.2 value = $255. CGC census 9/05: 1 in 9.6, none higher.

1466 Peanuts #10 (Dell, 1961) CGC NM 9.4 Off-white pages. Charles Schulz cover. Overstreet 2005 NM- 9.2 value = $115. CGC census 8/05: 1 in 9.4, 1 higher.

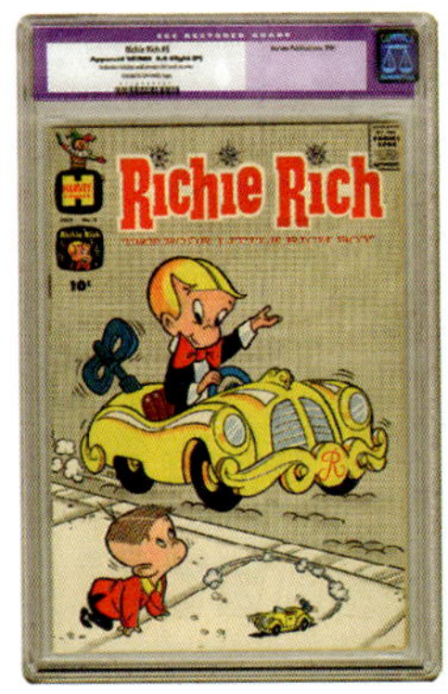

1467 Richie Rich #5 (Harvey, 1961) CGC Apparent VF/NM 9.0 Slight (P) Cream to off-white pages. Richie shows off his latest toy on the cover to this early issue. CGC notes, "Restoration includes: small amount of color touch on cover." Overstreet 2005 GD 2.0 value = $34; VG 4.0 value = $68; FN 6.0 value = $102; VF 8.0 value = $255; VF/NM 9.0 value = $403; NM- 9.2 value = $550.

1468 Roy Rogers & Trigger #127 (Dell, 1958) CGC NM 9.4 Off-white pages. Photo cover. CGC notes, "From the Dallas Stephens collection." Overstreet 2005 NM- 9.2 value = $75. CGC census 8/05: 1 in 9.4, none higher.

1469 The Spirit #1 Pacific Coast pedigree (Harvey, 1966) CGC NM+ 9.6 Off-white to white pages. Square bound. Will Eisner art (new material and reprints). Overstreet 2005 NM- 9.2 value = $110. CGC census 9/05: 5 in 9.6, none higher.

1470 The Spirit #1 Pacific Coast pedigree (Harvey, 1966) CGC NM- 9.2 Off-white to white pages. Square bound. Will Eisner art (new material and reprints). Overstreet 2005 NM- 9.2 value = $110. CGC census 6/05: 1 in 9.2, 8 higher.

1471 The Spirit #2 Pacific Coast pedigree (Harvey, 1967) CGC NM+ 9.6 Off-white to white pages. Square bound. Will Eisner art (new stories and reprints). Overstreet 2005 NM- 9.2 value = $80. CGC census 9/05: 4 in 9.6, none higher.

1472 Tarzan #207 (DC, 1972) CGC NM/MT 9.8 Off-white pages. First issue published by DC (numbering continued from Gold Key series). First part of origin. Joe Kubert cover and art. John Carter backup feature with Murphy Anderson art. Overstreet 2005 NM- 9.2 value = $60. CGC census 9/05: 6 in 9.8, none higher.

1473 Tarzan of the Apes #155 Curator pedigree (Gold Key, 1965) CGC NM+ 9.6 White pages. Origin retold. Painted cover by Russ Manning. Interior art also by Manning. Overstreet 2005 NM- 9.2 value = $55. CGC census 8/05: 2 in 9.6, none higher.

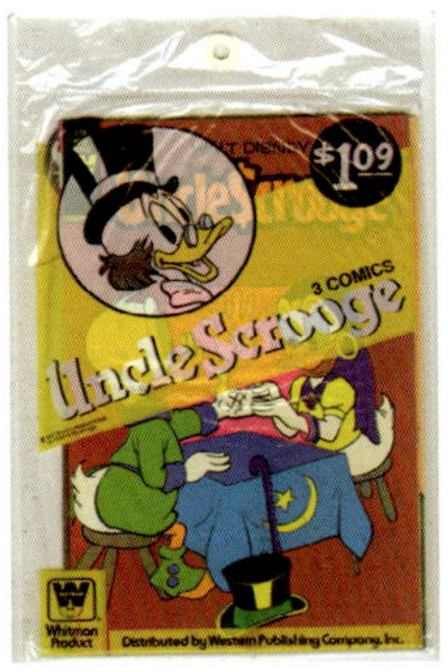

1474 Uncle Scrooge #179 and More Bagged 3-Pack (Whitman, 1980) Condition: Unopened. An unopened Whitman 3-Pack is quite a find no matter what's inside, but our jaws dropped when we saw that this one includes the ultra-hard-to-find **Uncle Scrooge** #179, which is listed among the 10 most valuable Bronze Age comics by Overstreet! That's because for many years, this issue was the "Holy Grail" to the hardcore Uncle Scrooge comic book completist. It was available only in bagged Whitman 3-Packs, which were only distributed to non-newsstand outlets (department stores and the like). Less than 30 copies have been confirmed to exist, and two NM unbagged copies sold for over $1,200 in 2001. This is the only example of an unopened bagged copy that we have ever seen or heard of. What are the other two comics in the bag? Sorry, there's no way to find out short of cutting open the 3-Pack (sorry if you just fainted) or otherwise manhandling the comics, so we'll leave it up to the winning bidder to try and figure it out. Also note that unlike many 3-Packs, only the top comic (#179) has the front cover facing outward. That same problem makes the comics impossible to grade in the normal manner, but as there are no defects visible except a few very light spine stress lines, we would put the condition of #179 at VF/NM or better. This would be the crown jewel in anyone's Uncle Scrooge collection, and in fact it might be the rarest Bronze/Modern Age comic book of all, so pass it up at your peril! Overstreet 2005 VF/NM 9.0 value (for #179 only) = $443; NM- 9.2 value = $600.

1475 Whitman and Gold Key 3-Packs and other Unopened Pre-Packs Group (Whitman and Gold Key, 1967-84). Here are the most bagged Whitman 3-Packs you're ever going to see in one place, and all of them are unopened! One in particular will be a real eye-opener for the Uncle Scrooge collector, it's the earliest known Uncle Scrooge pre-packed comic book (issue #69) dating from May 1967 - consider that until now, it was an accepted fact among collectors that the first Uncle Scrooge pre-pack originated around late 1972 or early 1973! In addition to that amazing find (which is a 5-Pack), we've got 15 3-Packs, four 2-Packs, two 4-Packs, and even an 18-Pack! The latter is a bag with three pouches, each containing six mini-comics, with a printed price of 98¢ for the bunch -- the comics are the 1976 Mini Comics measuring 3 1/4 by 6 1/2 inches (**Mickey Mouse, Donald Duck, Uncle Scrooge**, etc.). The majority of these pre-packs are from the early 1980s. As for the various bag styles, not to mention the different logo styles on the comics, they're too numerous to mention. And do we need to mention that many of these Whitman issues were only released in these pre-packs, and only sold in department stores, supermarkets, etc., not on newsstands? Due to the nature of these pre-packs, we can't determine every comic included in them, but we can confirm that the following comics are in there: **Uncle Scrooge** #69, 103, 104, 114, 117, 130, 154, 155, 162-170, 174, 176-178, 185-187, 191, 193, 195, 197, 200, 201, 204, and 205; Looney Tunes #43; Donald Duck #216, 219, 221, 234, and 236; **Walt Disney's Comics and Stories** #130, 493, and 495; and **Huey, Dewey, and Louie** #74. Since these Whitman issues are extremely difficult to find "in grade," you'll be pleased to know that the condition of the comics inside is excellent. Bid on 'em, enjoy 'em, but whatever you do, don't cut 'em open!

TIMELY/ATLAS

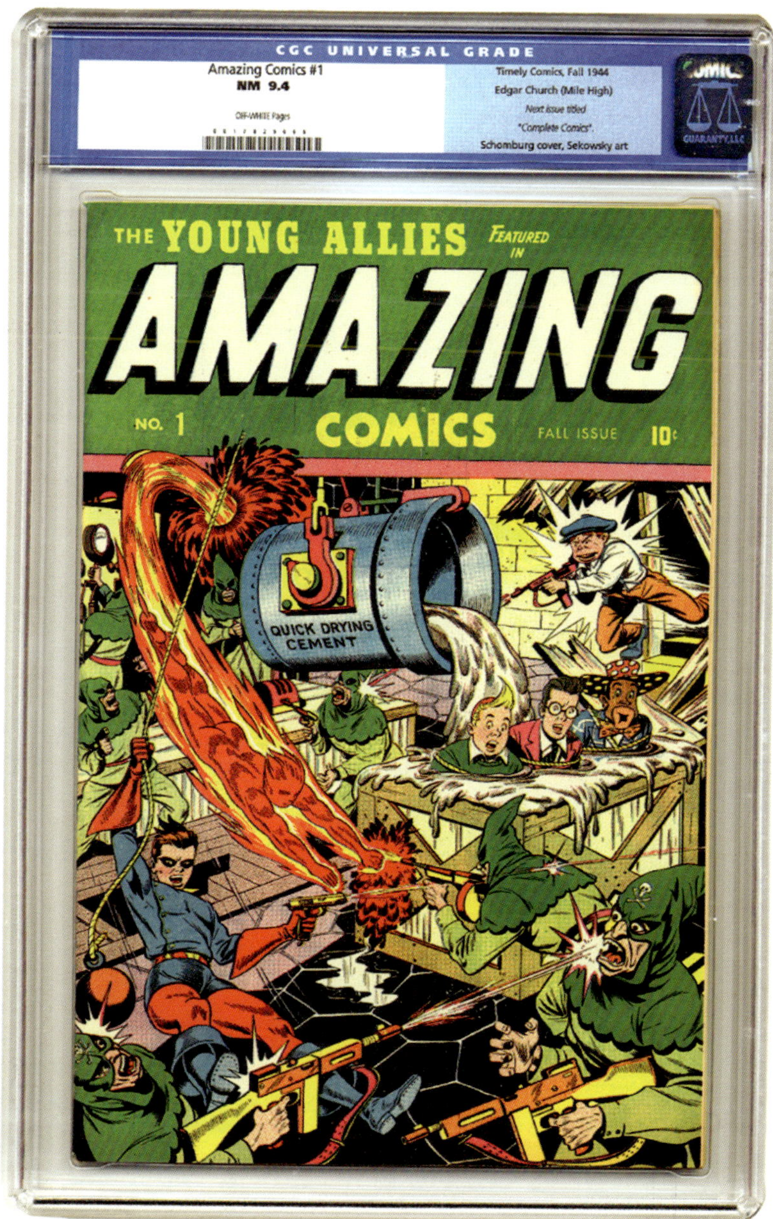

2001 Amazing Comics #1 Mile High pedigree (Timely, 1944) CGC NM 9.4 Off-white pages. This is the one and only issue of this title, and we've got the one and only 9.4 copy (the highest-graded copy overall as of this writing, natch). The issue starred the Young Allies, with the Whizzer and the Destroyer also appearing. The cover is by Alex Schomburg. Overstreet 2005 NM- 9.2 value = $3,000. CGC census 9/05: 1 in 9.4, none higher.

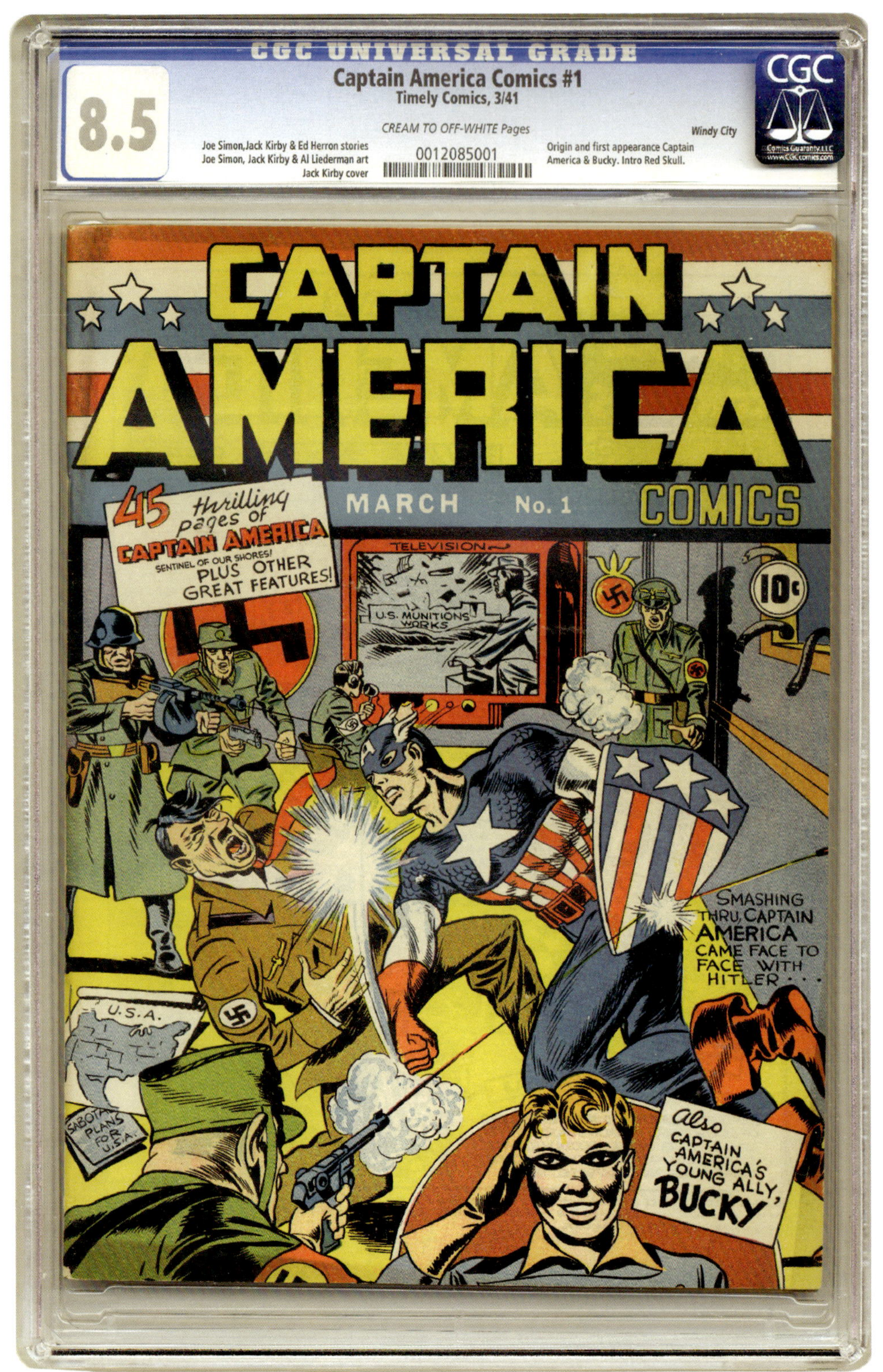

2002 Captain America Comics #1 Windy City pedigree (Timely, 1941) CGC VF+ 8.5 Cream to off-white pages. The only thing nicer than seeing the 8.5 on the slab of this key book was seeing the blue "universal" label signifying an unrestored copy! That's because this is one of the most frequently restored comic issues around, with many of the nicest copies (the Mile High copy, for one) bearing purple labels. A mere three unrestored copies of the issue have been certified with higher grades than this gem. This premiere issue is currently #6 in Overstreet's ranking of the most valuable comic books. It's the origin and first appearance of Captain America, written and drawn by the immortal duo of Joe Simon and Jack Kirby, and graced by one of the most famous and influential comic book covers of all. It also has the first appearances of Cap's sidekick Bucky and the villainous Red Skull. This particular copy has an interesting story behind it: the Windy City collection was assembled by a mailman who liked collecting #1 issues. He amassed a large collection indeed, extending from **Famous Funnies** #1 (1934) through the early 1960s. While the collection was assembled in Pennsylvania, it was Chicago dealer Gary Colabuono who introduced the books to the market, thus the "Windy City" moniker. The **Captain America Comics** #1 stands as one of the real gems of the Windy City hoard — here's your chance to make it yours! Overstreet 2005 VF 8.0 value = $50,000; VF/NM 9.0 value = $95,000. CGC census 9/05: 1 in 8.5, 3 higher.

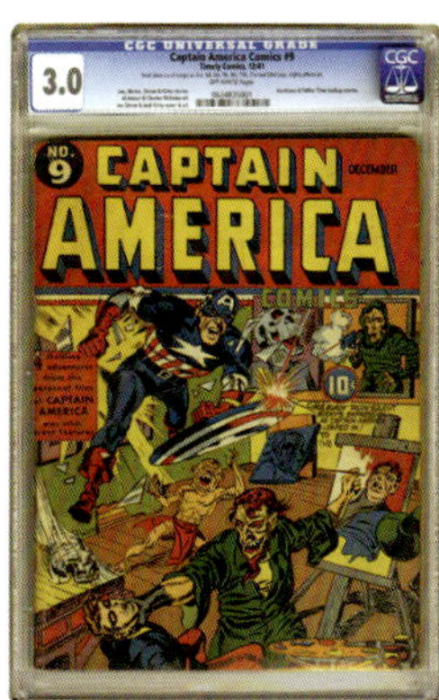

2003 Captain America Comics #9 (Timely, 1941) CGC GD/VG 3.0 Off-white pages. That distinctive Simon and Kirby pizzazz is evident on this cover featuring a twisted fiend known as the Black Talon. Inside, there's more S&K art, as Cap and Bucky fight that baddie and some others as well. CGC notes, "Small piece out of margin on 2nd, 5th, 6th, 7th, 9th, 17th, 21st, and 22nd page(s), slightly affects art." Overstreet 2005 GD 2.0 value = $439; VG 4.0 value = $878. CGC census 9/05: 1 in 3.0, 12 higher.

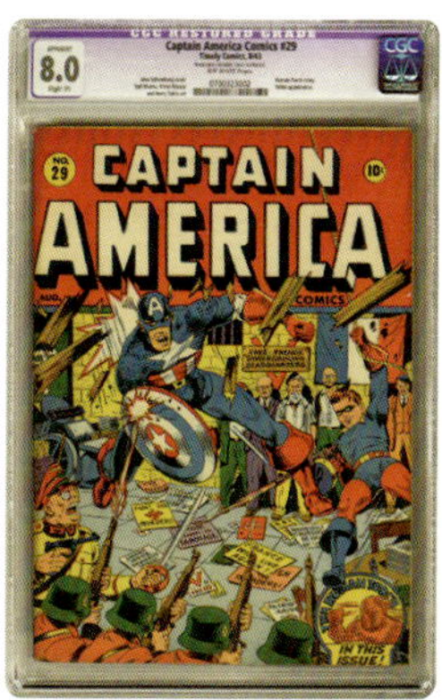

2004 Captain America Comics #29 (Timely, 1943) CGC Apparent VF 8.0 Slight (P) Off-white pages. Cap and Bucky come to the aid of the French Resistance on this stirring World War II cover by Alex Schomburg. Inside, the Human Torch shares space with none other than Adolph Hitler himself! This copy looks clean and sharp; it's from the "single staple" era, and this is where the minor restoration work has been done. CGC notes, "Restoration includes: cover reinforced." Overstreet 2005 GD 2.0 value = $246; VG 4.0 value = $492; FN 6.0 value = $738; VF 8.0 value = $1,538.

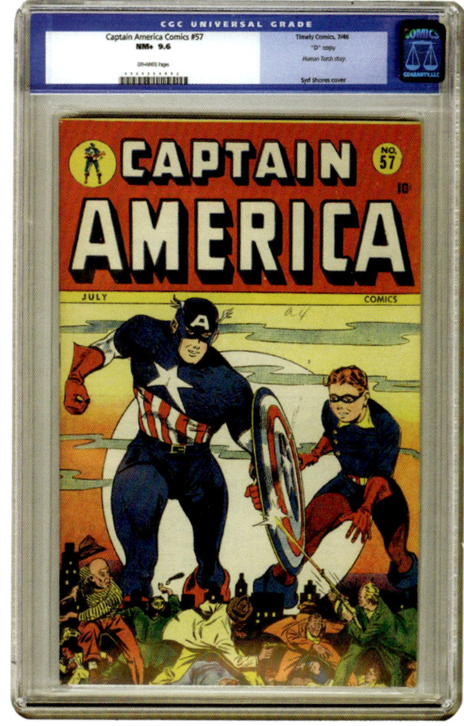

2005 Captain America Comics #57 "D" Copy pedigree (Timely, 1946) CGC NM+ 9.6 Off-white pages. This copy's the best one in CGC's census report — the only one graded above 9.0, in fact. On Vince Alascia's cover, Captain America and Bucky take a page out of the Sub-Mariner's book, swelling to giant size. Cap stars in three stories inside the comic, one each drawn by Alascia, Al Avison, and Bob Powell. The Human Torch stars in a backup feature, drawn by Carmine Infantino. Overstreet 2005 NM- 9.2 value = $1,800. CGC census 8/05: 1 in 9.6, none higher.

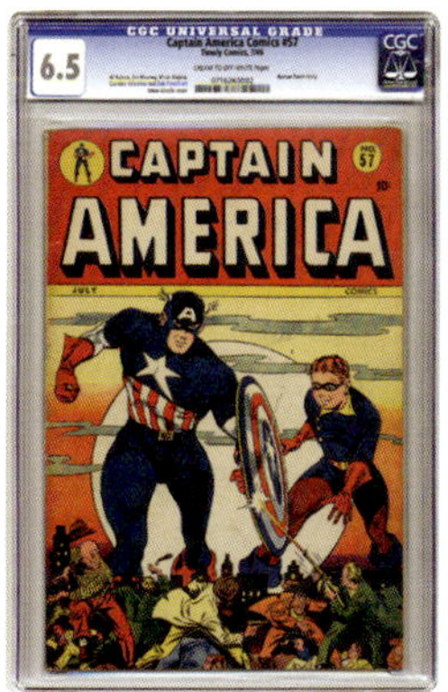

2006 Captain America Comics #57 (Timely, 1946) CGC FN+ 6.5 Cream to off-white pages. This Cap outing has a Vince Alascia cover, with interior art by Al Avison, Jim Mooney, Carmine Infantino, and Bob Powell. There's also a Human Torch backup feature. Overstreet 2005 FN 6.0 value = $414; VF 8.0 value = $863. CGC census 8/05: 1 in 6.5, 14 higher.

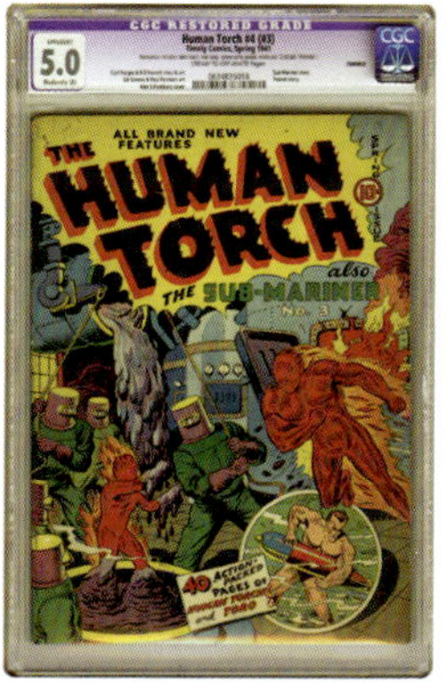

2007 The Human Torch #4 (#3) (Timely, 1941) CGC Apparent VG/FN 5.0 Moderate (A) Cream to off-white pages. Many a perplexed comic fan will wonder why this comic is called #4 (#3) since the cover clearly says "No. 3." The answer is that the indicia call it number 4. The issue's got an Alex Schomburg cover, with interior art by Bill Everett, Carl Burgos and others. A text feature reveals the origin of the Patriot. CGC notes, "Restoration includes: color touch, tear seals, spine splits sealed, reinforced (2 edges trimmed)." Overstreet 2005 GD 2.0 value = $423; VG 4.0 value = $846; FN 6.0 value = $1,269.

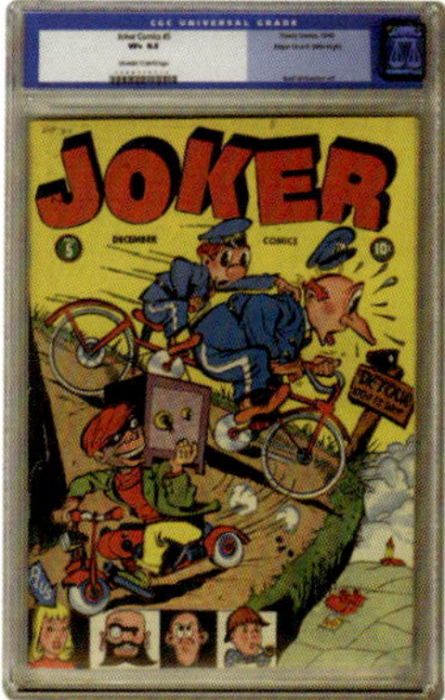

2008 Joker Comics #5 Mile High pedigree (Timely, 1942) CGC VF+ 8.5 Off-white to white pages. We now know that this issue's cover artist is none other than that master of the Fold-In, Al Jaffee! The cops on the tandem bicycle are the duo known as the Squat Car Squad. Basil Wolverton contributed interior art to the issue. This is the only copy of this issue that CGC has certified to date. Overstreet 2005 VF 8.0 value = $340; VF/NM 9.0 value = $520. CGC census 5/05: 1 in 8.5, none higher.

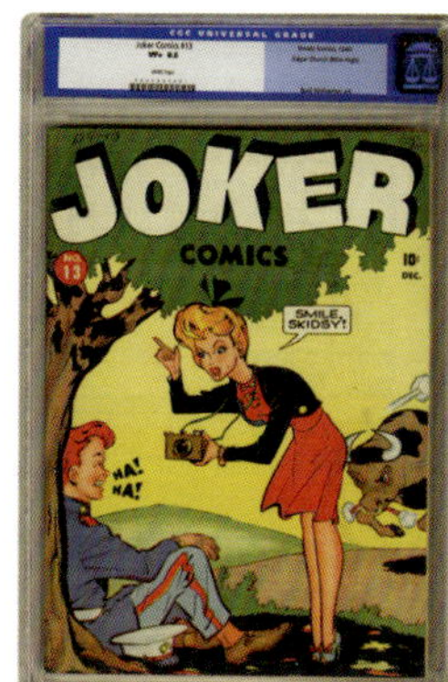

2009 Joker Comics #13 Mile High pedigree (Timely, 1943) CGC VF+ 8.5 White pages. Basil Wolverton's Powerhouse Pepper is among the characters in this funnybook. This is the only copy of the issue that CGC has certified as of this writing. Overstreet 2005 VF 8.0 value = $222; VF/NM 9.0 value = $324. CGC census 5/05: 1 in 8.5, none higher.

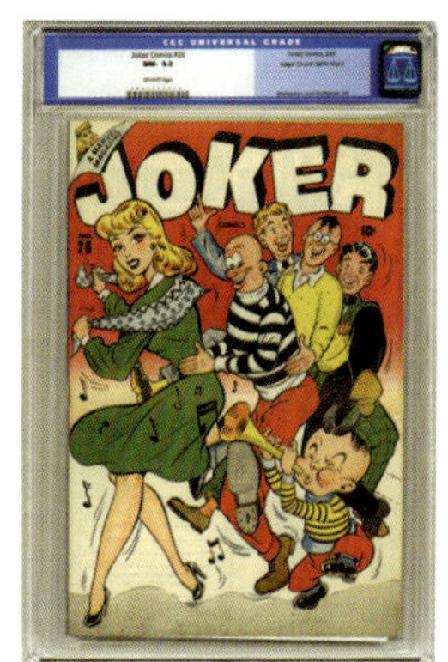

2010 Joker Comics #26 Mile High pedigree (Timely, 1947) CGC NM- 9.2 Off-white pages. A fun time was had by all (especially by Powerhouse Pepper!) on this cover. The Powerhouse Pepper story has Basil Wolverton art. There's also a "Hey Look" one-pager by Harvey Kurtzman. Overstreet 2005 NM- 9.2 value = $360. CGC census 5/05: 1 in 9.2, none higher.

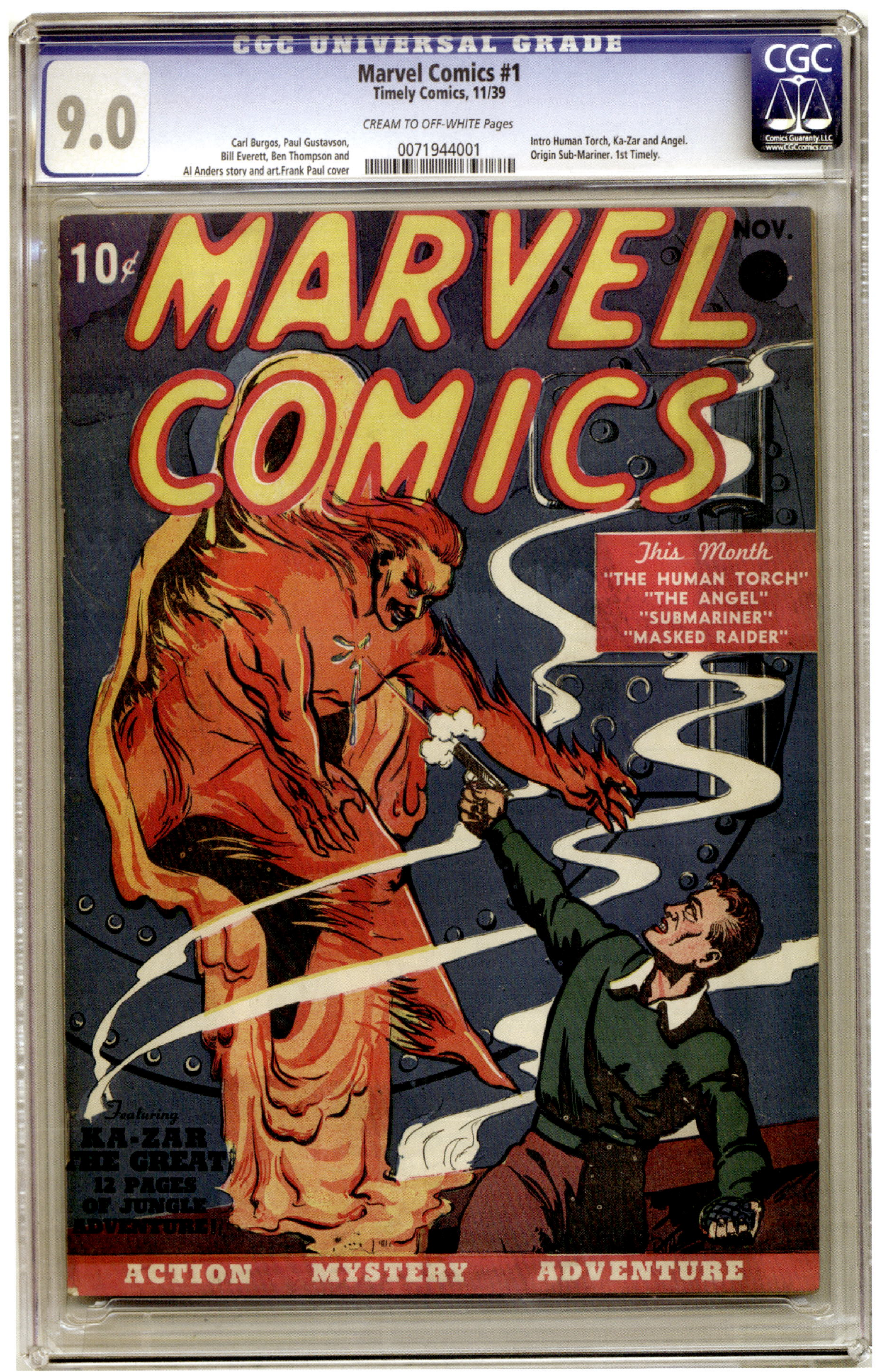

CGC UNIVERSAL GRADE
9.0
Marvel Comics #1
Timely Comics, 11/39
CREAM TO OFF-WHITE Pages
Carl Burgos, Paul Gustavson, Bill Everett, Ben Thompson and Al Anders story and art.Frank Paul cover
0071944001
Intro Human Torch, Ka-Zar and Angel. Origin Sub-Mariner. 1st Timely.
CGC
10¢
MARVEL COMICS
NOV.
This Month
"THE HUMAN TORCH"
"THE ANGEL"
"SUBMARINER"
"MASKED RAIDER"
Featuring
KA-ZAR THE GREAT
12 PAGES OF JUNGLE ADVENTURE!
ACTION MYSTERY ADVENTURE

2011 Marvel Comics #1 (Timely, 1939) CGC VF/NM 9.0 Cream to off-white pages. Have a look at the best of the best — the highest grade yet assigned for the most sought-after Marvel comic book. For many years, **Marvel Comics** #1 was listed as *the* most valuable comic book by Overstreet, and while it has since ceded that spot to **Action Comics** #1, for the Marvel fan there's no topping this issue here. Certainly no comic book can claim two first appearances as significant as those of the Human Torch and the Sub-Mariner, who both made their debuts here (the latter had been used in a promotional comic previously, but hadn't appeared in a newsstand publication until this issue). And that made this comic the start of the Marvel Universe, a set of characters that left its mark on American popular culture, selling millions of comic books and starring in TV shows, movies, and more. The publisher that produced the issue used many different company names over the years and is usually referred to as Timely, but it's only fitting that when the publisher finally had one official name years later, it took its name from this very comic. And the fact that both of the issue's stars were more rebellious anti-heroes than do-gooder types set this comic apart and would characterize Marvel in years to come. The range of characters here includes other familiar names besides the Torch and Sub-Mariner; for one, there's the first comic book appearance of pulp hero Ka-Zar, who would go on to star in several comic series of his own in later years and was a fixture of the Marvel Universe in the Silver Age and beyond. For another, there's the first appearance of the original Angel. The cover, showing the Human Torch, is by science fiction pulp illustrator Frank R. Paul. The interior material was the work of the artistic "shop" known as Funnies, Inc., the best-known artists of which are Bill Everett (who created the Sub-Mariner and drew the character's story in this issue) and Carl Burgos (who did the same for the Human Torch). Those fortunate few who ever acquire a copy of this issue usually have to make do with one that's restored or low-grade, or one that's printed a bit askew. None of the above applies to this nicely centered specimen which is tied with only one other copy for the highest grade CGC has assigned. There's no comic book collection that this wouldn't be the centerpiece of! Overstreet 2005 VF/NM 9.0 value = $254,500; NM- 9.2 value = $365,000. CGC census 8/05: 2 in 9.0, none higher.

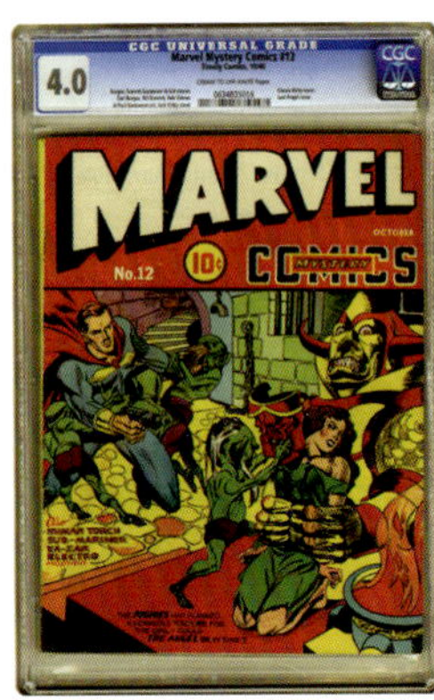

2012 Marvel Mystery Comics #12 (Timely, 1940) CGC VG 4.0 Cream to off-white pages. Overstreet calls Jack Kirby's cover "classic." Not only do we agree wholeheartedly with that, it makes us wish King Kirby had been a more prolific cover artist for Timely back in the Golden Age. Starring in the issue are the Sub-Mariner (by Bill Everett) and the Human Torch (by Carl Burgos). This is a much more appealing copy than the modest grade might indicate; it was evidently bumped down because of a water stain, but we had to look closely to notice the stain at all, and we think most collectors will agree. Overstreet 2005 VG 4.0 value = $800. CGC census 9/05: 1 in 4.0, 13 higher.

2013 Marvel Mystery Comics #17 (Timely, 1941) CGC Apparent GD+ 2.5 Moderate (A) Off-white pages. Alex Schomburg cover. Interior art by Simon and Kirby, Bill Everett, and Carl Burgos. CGC notes, "Restoration includes: pieces added, spine splits sealed, reinforced, staples replaced." Overstreet 2005 GD 2.0 value = $300.

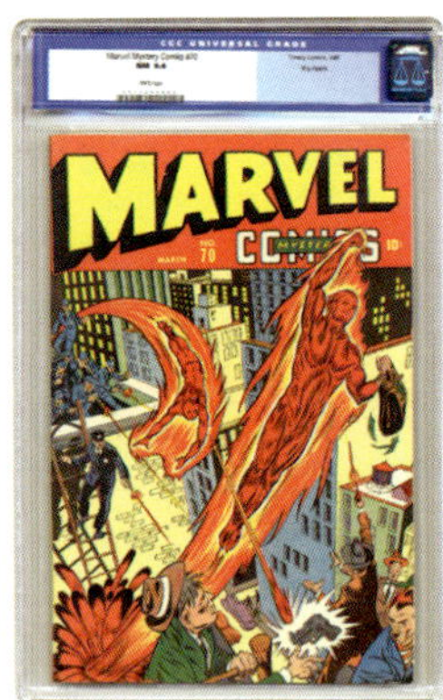

2014 Marvel Mystery Comics #70 Big Apple pedigree (Timely, 1946) CGC NM 9.4 White pages. For those of us born after the 1940s, snapping up a NM copy of this Timely treasure fresh off the newsstand can only be a dream. Until someone can perfect a time-travel machine, it ain't gonna happen. The next best thing will be winning this magnificent copy in this auction, which will be easy — if you place the right bid! Overstreet 2005 NM- 9.2 value = $1,500. CGC census 7/05: 2 in 9.4, none higher.

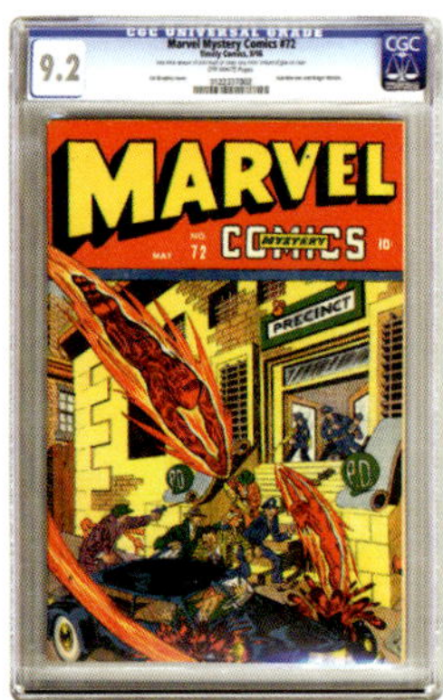

2015 Marvel Mystery Comics #72 (Timely, 1946) CGC NM- 9.2 Off-white pages. Sol Brodsky's illustration of a shoot-out at police headquarters for this issue's cover is priceless — check out the expression of the man in the car as Toro flames his way completely through the engine! Sub-Mariner and Angel stories are featured inside. Although this attractive copy bears a Universal Grade tag, CGC does note, "Very minor amount of color touch on cover, very minor amount of glue on cover." We'll be darned if we can spot it, however! Overstreet 2005 NM- 9.2 value = $1,500. CGC census 7/05: 3 in 9.2, 4 higher.

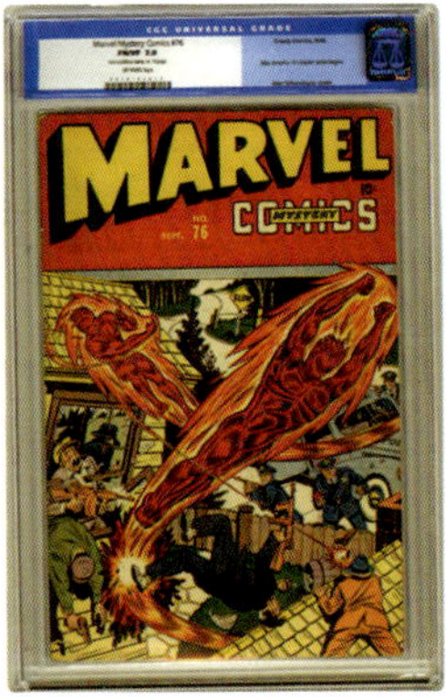

2016 Marvel Mystery Comics #76 (Timely, 1946) CGC FN/VF 7.0 Off-white pages. Alex Schomburg's last cover for the title marked the end of a spectacular run of over 50 covers on Timely's flagship series. In this issue a 10-chapter Miss America serial begins. CGC notes, "Name/address stamp on 1st page." Overstreet 2005 FN 6.0 value = $345; VF 8.0 value = $719. CGC census 7/05: 1 in 7.0, 9 higher.

2017 Marvel Tales #96 (Atlas, 1950) CGC VF- 7.5 Cream to off-white pages. Syd Shores contributes a great monster cover to this issue. Mike Sekowsky art is also featured. Overstreet 2005 VF 8.0 value = $406. CGC census 9/05: 3 in 7.5, 4 higher.

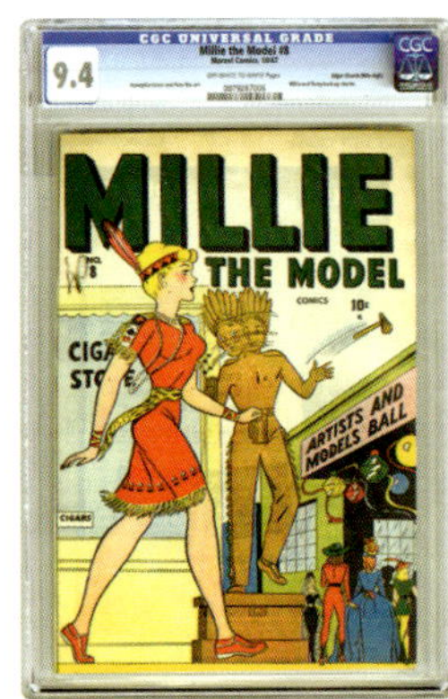

2018 Millie the Model #8 Mile High pedigree (Marvel, 1947) CGC NM 9.4 Off-white to white pages. Even a statue has to do a double-take when the statuesque Millie sashays past on the way to the models' ball. No, we don't know how to get invited to a models' ball (or we'd be there ourselves), but if you want to look at something pretty, do your best to acquire this superb NM copy, which by the way has a "Hey Look" backup feature by Harvey Kurtzman. This is the only copy of this issue that CGC has certified to date. Overstreet 2005 NM- 9.2 value = $330. CGC census 9/05: 1 in 9.4, none higher.

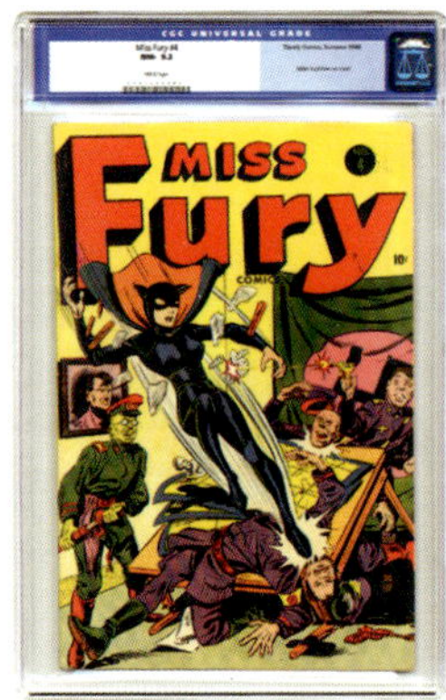

2019 Miss Fury #4 (Timely, 1944) CGC NM- 9.2 White pages. Tarpe Mills' shapely superhero shakes things up for the assorted Axis thugs found on this fun World War II cover. Check out the handsome, rugged portrait of Adolph Hitler hanging on the wall — even the office decorations are lies in Naziland! This honey of a copy will sure look sweet in your collection! Overstreet 2005 NM- 9.2 value = $1,525. CGC census 7/05: 2 in 9.2, 1 higher.

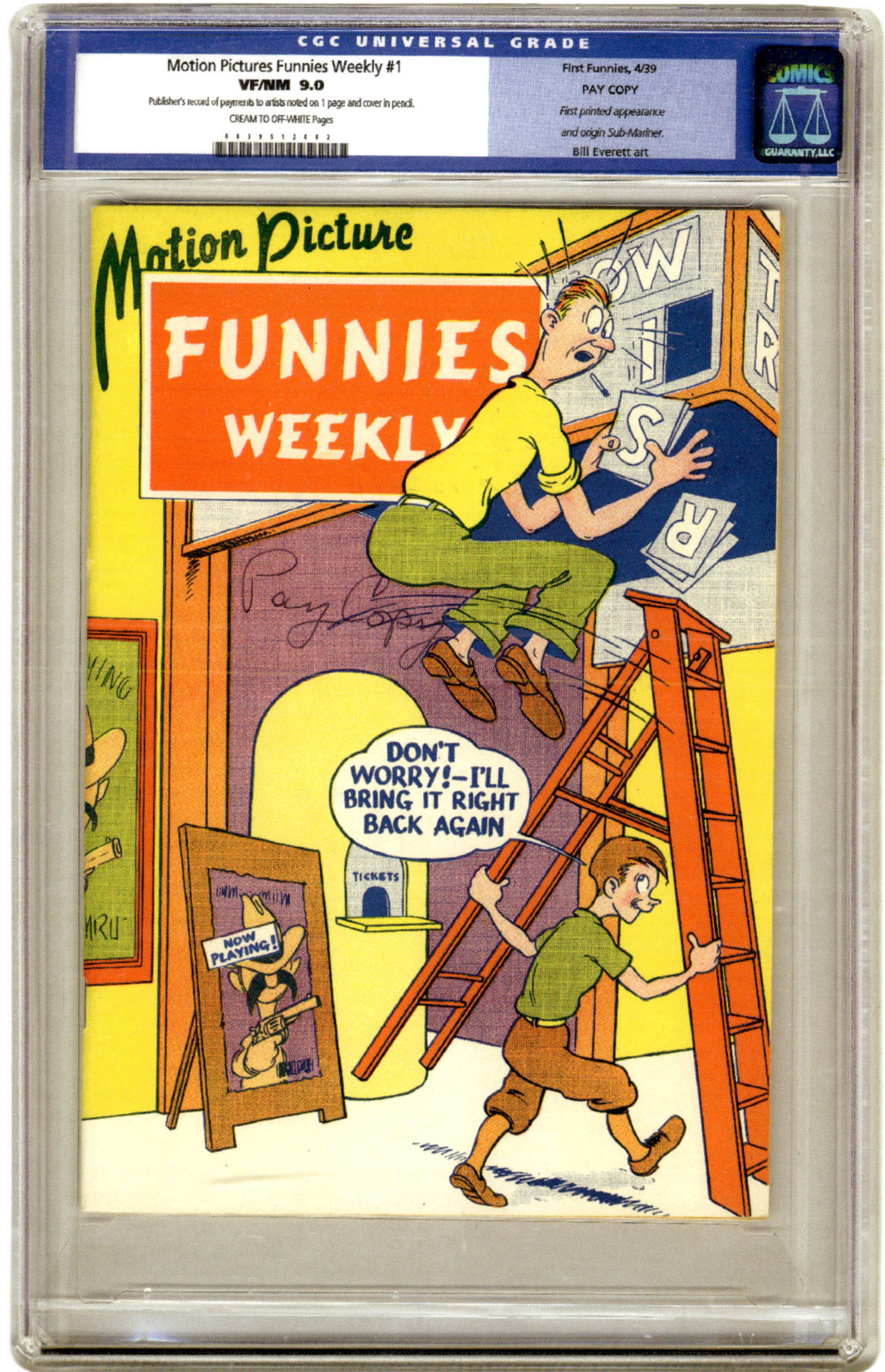

2020 Motion Picture Funnies Weekly #1 Pay Copy (First Funnies, Inc., 1939) CGC VF/NM 9.0 Cream to off-white pages.

This is one of the most famous single copies of a comic book in existence. And here's the most surprising thing about it when you see it up close: you've got to marvel at what a *great-looking* copy it is! Give our scan a look and you will agree that the issue has earned its VF/NM grade — the fresh cover colors stack up well even against comics from the famous pedigree collections. Now, terms like "holy grail" are used for collectibles quite a bit, but we feel that nobody could dispute that the **Motion Picture Funnies** Pay Copy has that status. Its significance and uniqueness make it so. And the reason it is so hotly sought-after is that it has the very first printed appearance of the Sub-Mariner. The comic was never released to newsstands — it was created as a promotional item by the Lloyd Jacquet studio (or "shop") of artists also known as Funnies Inc. It was intended to be a giveaway to be distributed weekly at movie theatres (as demonstrated by the back-cover ad which elaborates on the concept). The Sub-Mariner story even has a box on the last page saying "continued next week," but the concept did not catch on, and no second issue was printed. In fact, the very existence of this comic book was not known to comic fandom until the 1970s. As it stands today, only eight copies of the issue are known to exist. And the most desirable one of the bunch is the Funnies Inc. "pay copy," the office copy in which the amounts paid to the creators of the issue were noted in longhand. The copy came to light as part of Jacquet's estate and has been a storied collectible ever since. It's that Sub-Mariner connection that accounts for the great historical significance of this comic milestone. While this is not a Timely/Marvel publication, we have chosen to include it in the Timely section of this catalog because of the historical significance of the Sub-Mariner in the history of Timely. When the giveaway series didn't get off the ground, Jacquet simply re-used Bill Everett's Sub-Mariner story for **Marvel Comics** #1 (produced for Timely in its entirety by Funnies Inc.). The "continued next week" box was removed and Everett added four pages to the story. And the rest is history! As for the rest of the content of the issue (it's all black-and-white inside), it consists of various humor and adventure features. As a matter of fact, the Sub-Mariner story was not the only one to later see publication in a newsstand comic - the "Spy Ring" story was later seen in **Silver Streak Comics** #1, which was published by a forerunner of the publisher we know as Lev Gleason but was produced in its entirety by Jacquet's Funnies, Inc. As for the cover of this issue, it has been credited to Fred Schwab. To date, only two other copies of the issue have been certified by CGC, and the only other unrestored copy in the census was graded far below, at 7.0. To own the copy used by some of the "founding fathers" of comic books at this key moment in the history of the medium... well, it's thrilling enough just to lay eyes on the Pay Copy, and we will be envious indeed of whichever collector ends up taking this one home. CGC notes, "Publisher's record of payments to artists noted on 1 page and cover in pencil." Overstreet 2005 VF/NM 9.0 value = $22,250; NM- 9.2 value = $28,000. CGC census 9/05: 1 in 9.0, none higher.

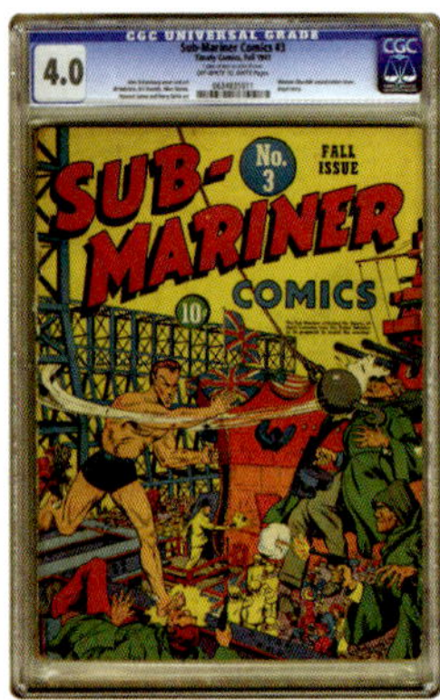

2021 Sub-Mariner Comics #3 (Timely, 1941) CGC VG 4.0 Off-white to white pages. Some Axis types are trying to assassinate Winston Churchill! Since the Sub-Mariner doesn't have a word balloon on this cover, let us provide one: "Here's some blood, toil, tears, and sweat for ya, Rat-zi!" The cover scene's by Alex Schomburg, of course. Inside the comic, Subby's story is a whopping 40-pager; we wish comics today even *had* 40 pages! CGC notes, "1 piece of tape on spine of cover." Overstreet 2005 VG 4.0 value = $846. CGC census 9/05: 1 in 4.0, 8 higher.

2022 Sub-Mariner Comics #21 (Timely, 1946) CGC Qualified FN/VF 7.0 Off-white to white pages. Last appearance of the Angel in this series. Syd Shores cover. Bill Everett and Carmine Infantino interior art. CGC notes, "Centerfold detached." Overstreet 2005 GD 2.0 value = $108; VG 4.0 value = $216; FN 6.0 value = $324; VF 8.0 value = $675.

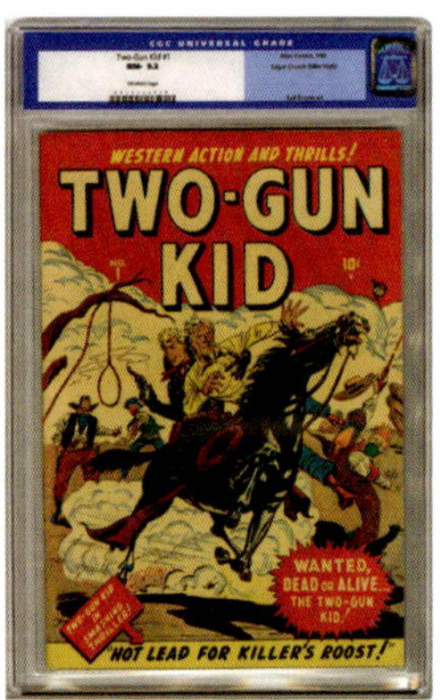

2023 Two-Gun Kid #1 Mile High pedigree (Atlas, 1948) CGC NM- 9.2 Off-white pages. The first Marvel Western comic book was this one right here, with the first appearance of the Two-Gun Kid. The various incarnations of the Kid were very good to Atlas/Marvel, with his title in publication on and off all the way up until the late 1970s. This is the best copy you'll find of this #1 issue; it's the only one graded above 7.5 by CGC to date. The cover and interior art are by Syd Shores. Overstreet 2005 NM- 9.2 value = $1,400. CGC census 9/05: 1 in 9.2, none higher.

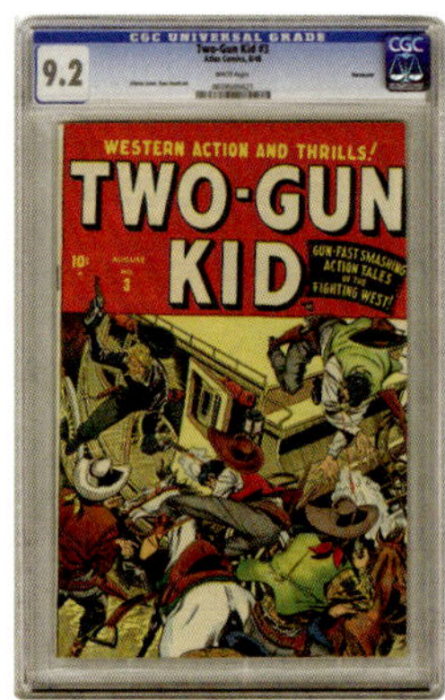

2024 Two-Gun Kid #3 Vancouver pedigree (Atlas, 1948) CGC NM- 9.2 White pages. The Two-Gun Kid's third cover is the first one to show him wielding... *two guns*! The gunslingin' action is credited to Syd Shores; Russ Heath provided interior art for the issue. Overstreet 2005 NM- 9.2 value = $400. CGC census 5/05: 1 in 9.2, 1 higher.

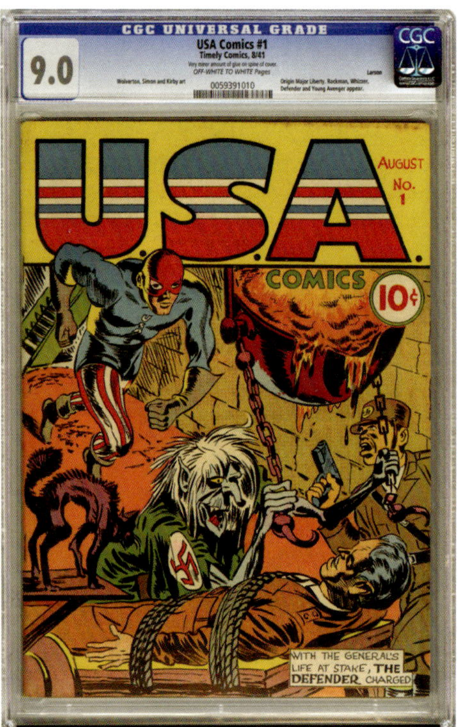

2025 USA Comics #1 Larson pedigree (Timely, 1941) CGC VF/NM 9.0 Off-white to white pages. No higher grade has been assigned by CGC to date for this Timely #1, and this copy has impeccable provenance going for it, being from the collection of Lamont Larson. The issue is on Overstreet's list of the 100 most valuable Golden Age books, and well it should be — the first appearance of the Whizzer is the most notable of a whole bunch of debuts; the others are Mister Liberty (later Major Liberty), Rockman, the Defender, and Jack Frost. No doubt you recognize the art of Simon and Kirby on the cover; the duo contributed a page of interior art as well. Basil Wolverton drew the aforementioned subterranean hero, Rockman. Overstreet 2005 VF/NM 9.0 value = $14,052; NM- 9.2 value = $19,500. CGC census 9/05: 3 in 9.0, none higher.

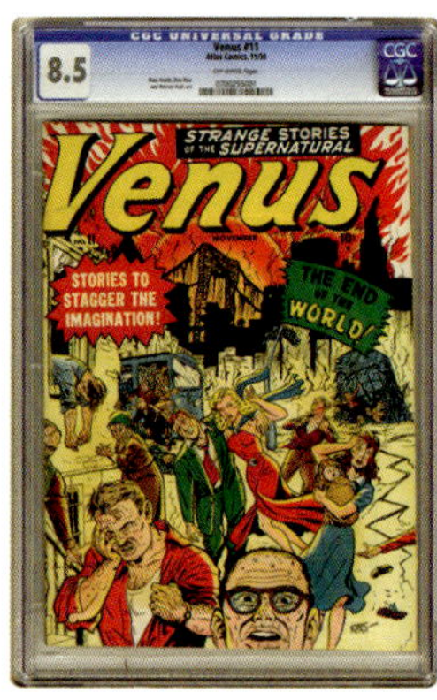

2026 Venus #11 (Atlas, 1950) CGC VF+ 8.5 Off-white pages. This issue's "End of the World" cover makes it one of the most valuable of this series' run. Russ Heath contributed interior art to the issue. Overstreet 2005 VF 8.0 value = $531; VF/NM 9.0 value = $816. CGC census 8/05: 1 in 8.5, none higher.

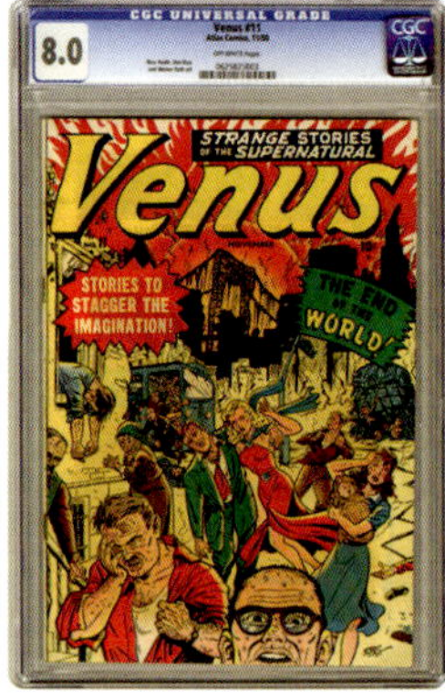

2027 Venus #11 (Atlas, 1950) CGC VF 8.0 Off-white pages. This issue's "End of the World" cover makes it one of the most valuable of this series' run. Russ Heath contributed interior art to the issue. Some staple rust evidently prevented this copy from grading out higher, but the great cover colors make this an extremely attractive specimen overall; only one copy has been graded higher by CGC to date. Overstreet 2005 VF 8.0 value = $531. CGC census 9/05: 1 in 8.0, 1 higher.

2028 Wisco/Klarer Comic Book (Miniature) Little Aspirin #2 (Marvel/Vital, 1950) CGC NM/MT 9.8. Off-white to white pages. The derby-wearing Timely comics character Little Aspirin stars in this paper-cover giveaway as the "Crook Catcher" — a detective without a badge! Overstreet 2005 NM-9.2 value = $28. CGC census 9/05: 1 in 9.8, none higher.

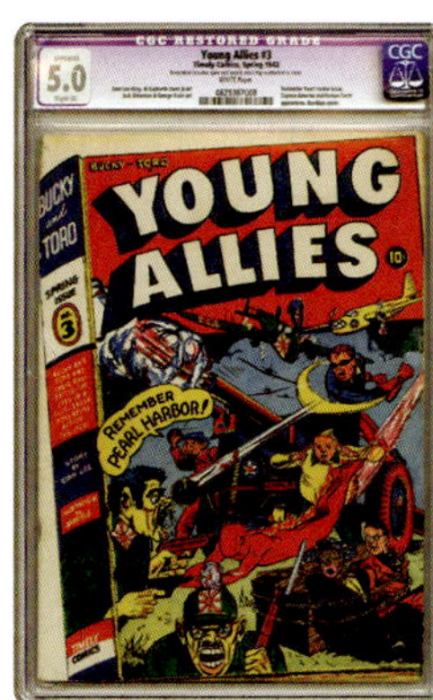

2029 Young Allies Comics #3 (Timely, 1942) CGC Apparent VG/FN 5.0 Slight (A) White pages. This classic "Remember Pearl Harbor" issue is on everybody's want list. Father Time, Captain America, and the Human Torch appear in this book-length epic. The creative faux book-cover image gave Stan Lee (a shy, retiring type if there ever was one) the opportunity to put his name on the cover (along with that of artist Al Gabriele). CGC notes, "Restoration includes: spine split sealed, small chip re-attached to cover." Overstreet 2005 GD 2.0 value = $296; VG 4.0 value = $592; FN 6.0 value = $888.

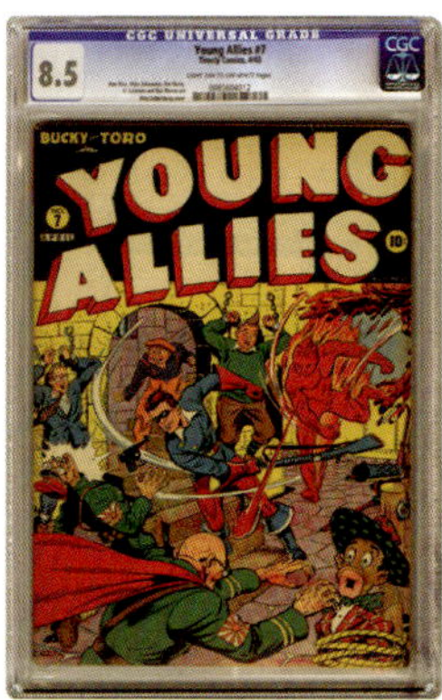

2030 Young Allies Comics #7 (Timely, 1943) CGC VF+ 8.5 Light tan to off-white pages. Alex Schomburg never failed to find a new and interesting variation on the "Bucky and Toro rescue their chums" cover theme! In addition to the Schomburg cover, this issue has art by Syd Shores and Mike Sekowsky. Overstreet 2005 VF 8.0 value = $844; VF/NM 9.0 value = $1,297. CGC census 5/05: 1 in 8.5, 3 higher.

2031 Young Allies Comics #18 (Timely, 1945) CGC VF+ 8.5 Cream to off-white pages. It happens every time — Tubby and Whitewash are captured and in imminent danger, leaving the rest of the Young Allies gang to rescue them! All that and more happens on the action-packed Alex Schomburg cover to this great issue. This attractive copy is flat and tight, with excellent cover color. Overstreet 2005 VF 8.0 value = $638; VF/NM 9.0 value = $982. CGC census 7/05: 2 in 8.5, 3 higher.

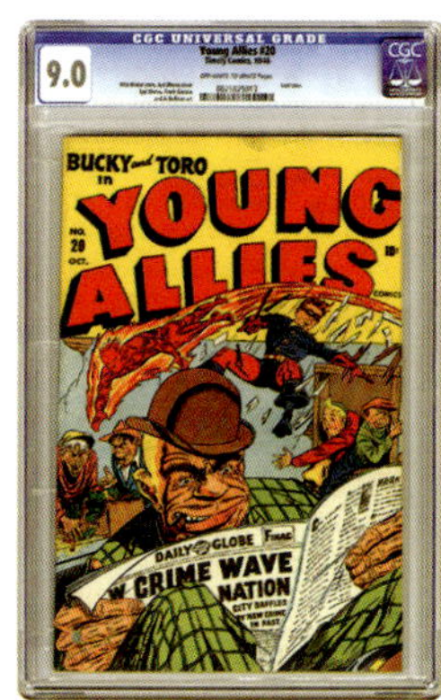

2032 Young Allies Comics #20 (Timely, 1946) CGC VF/NM 9.0 Off-white to white pages. It all has to end sometime; for the **Young Allies**, this issue wraps up this title's run. However, all is not lost for the plucky young team; they meet again in **Marvel Mystery** #77. Syd Shores supplies the "ugly mugs" cover; he's joined by Frank Giacoia and Al Bellman inside. Overstreet 2005 VF/NM 9.0 value = $982; NM- 9.2 value = $1,325. CGC census 8/05: 2 in 9.0, 1 higher.

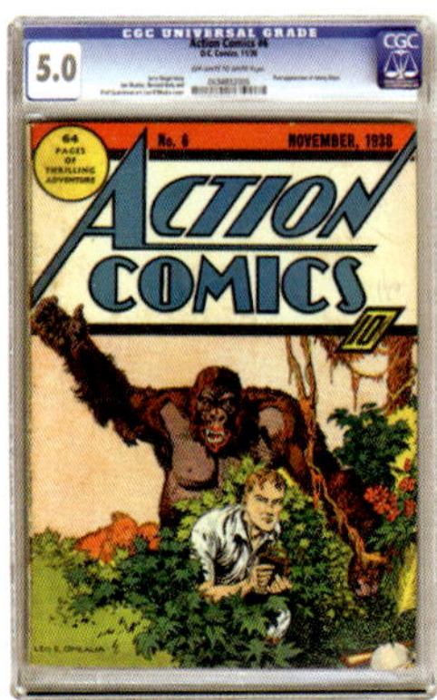

2033 Action Comics #6 (DC, 1938) CGC VG/FN 5.0 Off-white to white pages. This very early Superman adventure has the debut of an unnamed "office boy," who according to Overstreet as well as DC's own **Who's Who** is none other than Jimmy Olsen. It's a pretty important first appearance, considering that Superman's Pal later starred in his own comic that ran for twenty years! Neither Jimmy nor Superman made the cover, but Leo O'Mealia's absolutely superb cover illustration more than makes up for that. In fact, we regret that O'Mealia, who was best known as a sports cartoonist, wasn't much more prolific in the comic book field. We'd be remiss if we didn't note that this may be DC's first-ever gorilla cover — a theme the publisher would return to over and over in later decades, to the delight of many fans including us. Overstreet 2005 VG 4.0 value = $2,714; FN 6.0 value = $4,070. CGC census 8/05: 1 in 5.0, 3 higher.

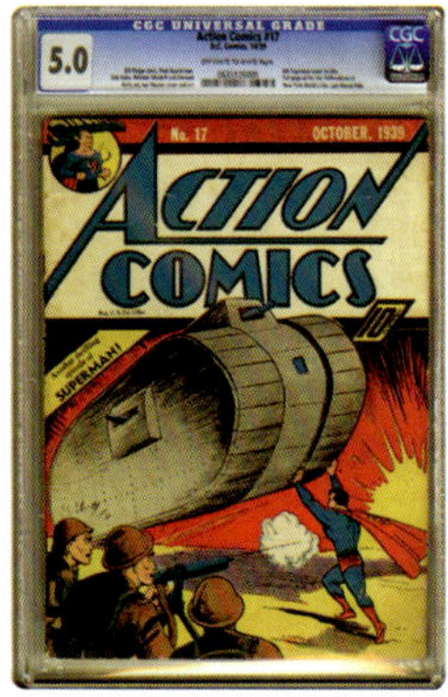

2034 Action Comics #17 (DC, 1939) CGC VG/FN 5.0 Off-white to white pages. This issue's war cover was only the sixth cover appearance overall for Superman! The cover is by the character's co-creator Joe Shuster, who along with writer Jerry Siegel produced this issue's Superman story. The issue's other artists include Bob Kane, Bernard Baily, George Papp, and Fred Guardineer. Note that the highest-graded copy in CGC's census is only a 7.0 as of this writing, so this mid-grade offering is one of the better ones you're going to find. Overstreet 2005 VG 4.0 value = $994; FN 6.0 value = $1,490. CGC census 9/05: 1 in 5.0, 7 higher.

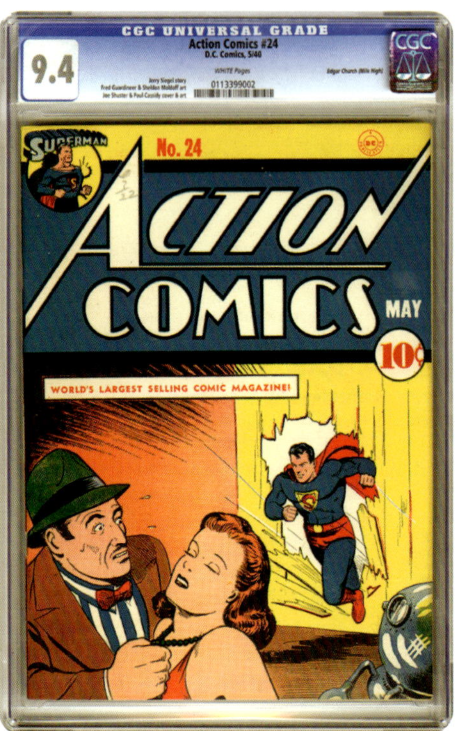

2035 Action Comics #24 Mile High pedigree (DC, 1940) CGC NM 9.4 White pages. Clark Kent's place of employment is mentioned as being the Daily Planet (formerly known as the Daily Star) for the first time in this issue. The Man of Steel never looked better than on the cover to this remarkable copy. That "dry, dark basement" belonging to Edgar Church was the perfect environment to store his vast collection of comics; this beautiful example comes complete with exceptionally nice, white paper and rich cover color. This one is "Super" in every way! Overstreet 2005 NM- 9.2 value = $4,000. CGC census 8/05: 1 in 9.4, none higher.

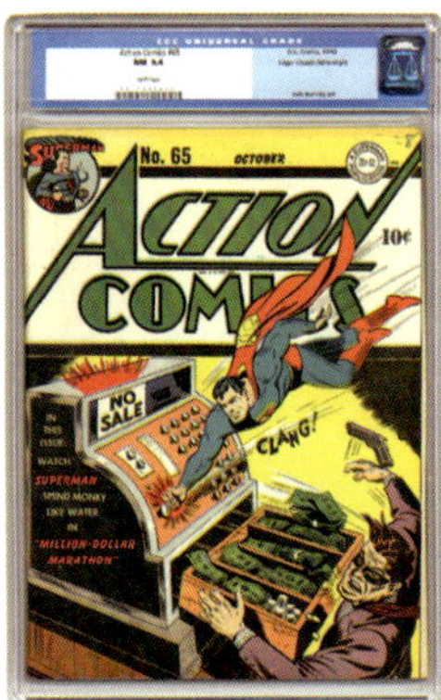

2036 Action Comics #65 Mile High pedigree (DC, 1943) CGC NM 9.4 White pages. This Mile High copy has lapped the competition and stands as the only one graded above 7.5 by CGC as of this writing. In the issue, Superman has to spend a million dollars in one day! No problem if you've got Heritage catalog #818, but back in '43 Superman had to do it the hard way, and it's all to help a humanitarian type fulfill the terms of an eccentric multimillionaire's will. The unusual "cha-ching" cover is by Jack Burnley. Other features include a Vigilante story (Mort Meskin art), a Congo Bill yarn (John Daly art) and an adventure of the Americommando (drawn by Bernard Baily). Overstreet 2005 NM- 9.2 value = $1,250. CGC census 7/05: 1 in 9.4, none higher.

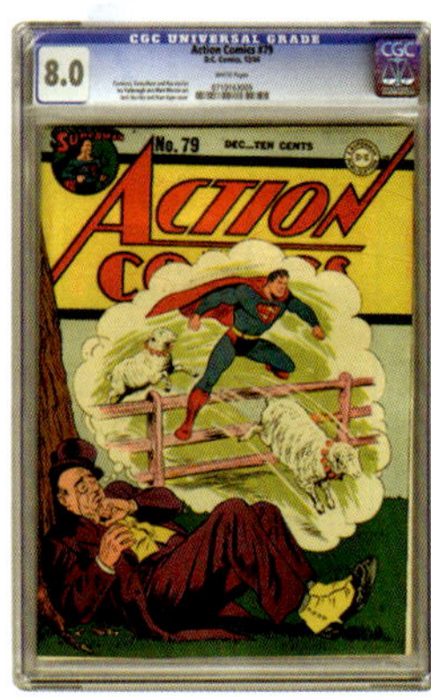

2037 Action Comics #79 (DC, 1944) CGC VF 8.0 White pages. Considering that the copy that tops CGC's current census is only a 9.0, our VF offering is in the upper tier of available copies. The issue's got a Jack Burnley cover. In addition to the Superman story (drawn by Ira Yarbrough), there are adventures of the Vigilante (drawn by Mort Meskin), Zatara, and Congo Bill. Overstreet 2005 VF 8.0 value = $506. CGC census 8/05: 1 in 8.0, 5 higher.

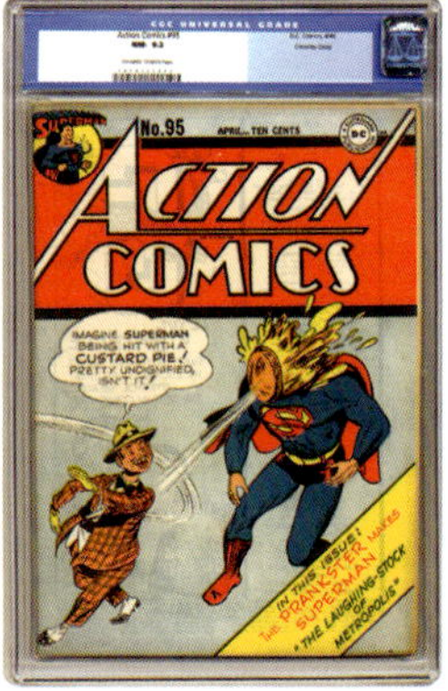

2038 Action Comics #95 Crowley Copy pedigree (DC, 1946) CGC NM- 9.2 Off-white to white pages. The Prankster's back to try to defeat Superman, and this time his scheme is to drive the Man of Steel out of town by making him look like a fool again and again. And it works, too... until Superman resolves to fight funny with funny! The issue has a Wayne Boring cover; interior artists include Jon Smalle (Superman story) and Mort Meskin (Vigilante story). Overstreet 2005 NM- 9.2 value = $925. CGC census 7/05: 1 in 9.2, 1 higher.

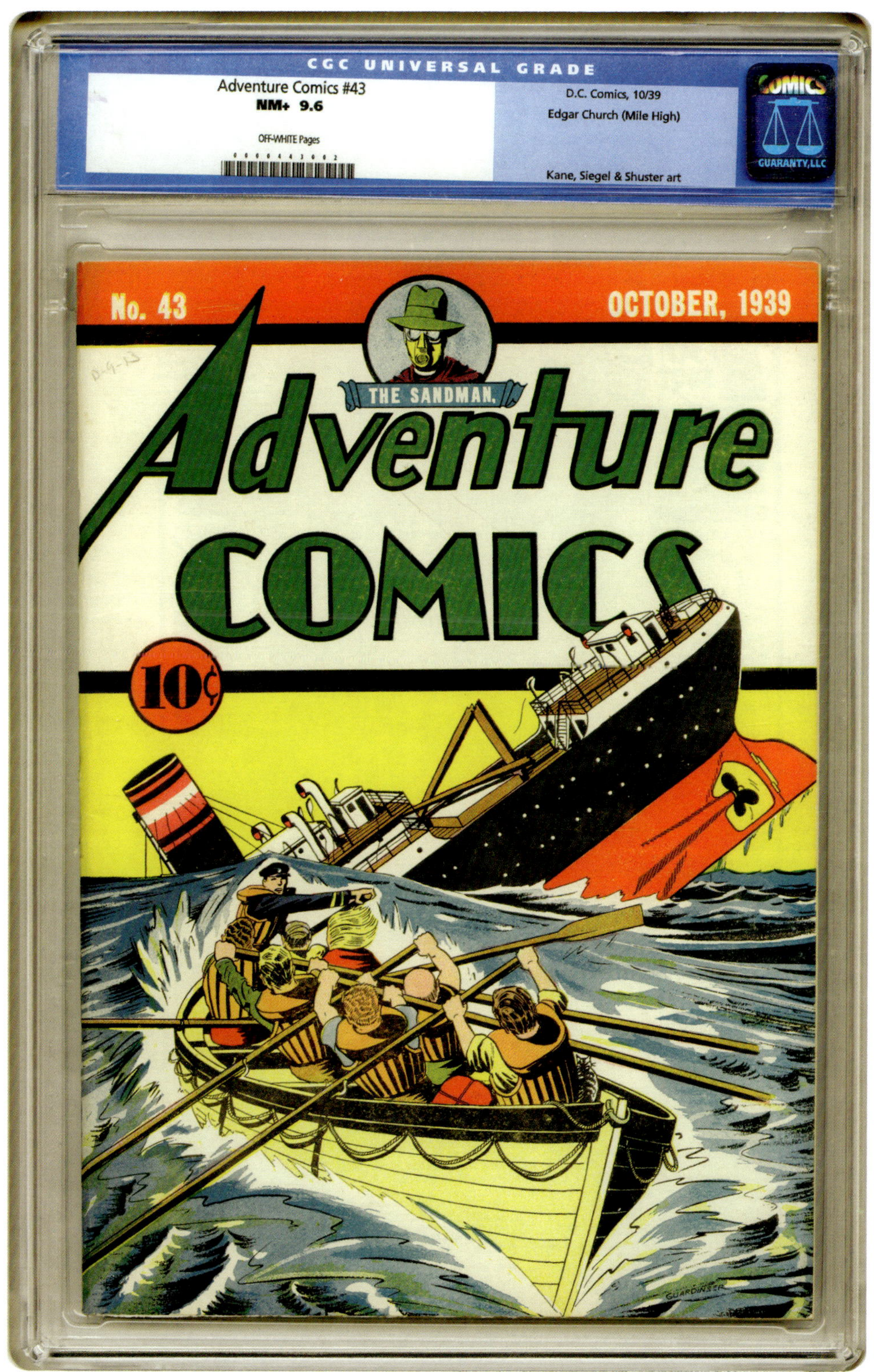

2039 Adventure Comics #43 Mile High pedigree (DC, 1939) CGC NM+ 9.6 Off-white pages. As you gaze upon this pristine Mile High copy, keep in mind how old this comic is — though the issue number sounds high, this came out at the same time as **Action** #17, and titles like **All Star Comics** hadn't even hit the stands yet! Our copy of this **Adventure** issue is the only one graded above 6.5 that CGC has certified to date. The seafaring cover by Fred Guardineer was an appetizer for an issue packed with adventure yarns. The key character is the Sandman, who made one of his earliest appearances in this story drawn by Bert Christman. Also on hand are characters such as playboy adventurer Barry O'Neill, amiable boxer Socko Strong, and the Federal Men (written by Superman co-creator Jerry Siegel). Bob Kane added a humor feature. Overstreet 2005 NM- 9.2 value = $4,500. CGC census 7/05: 1 in 9.6, none higher.

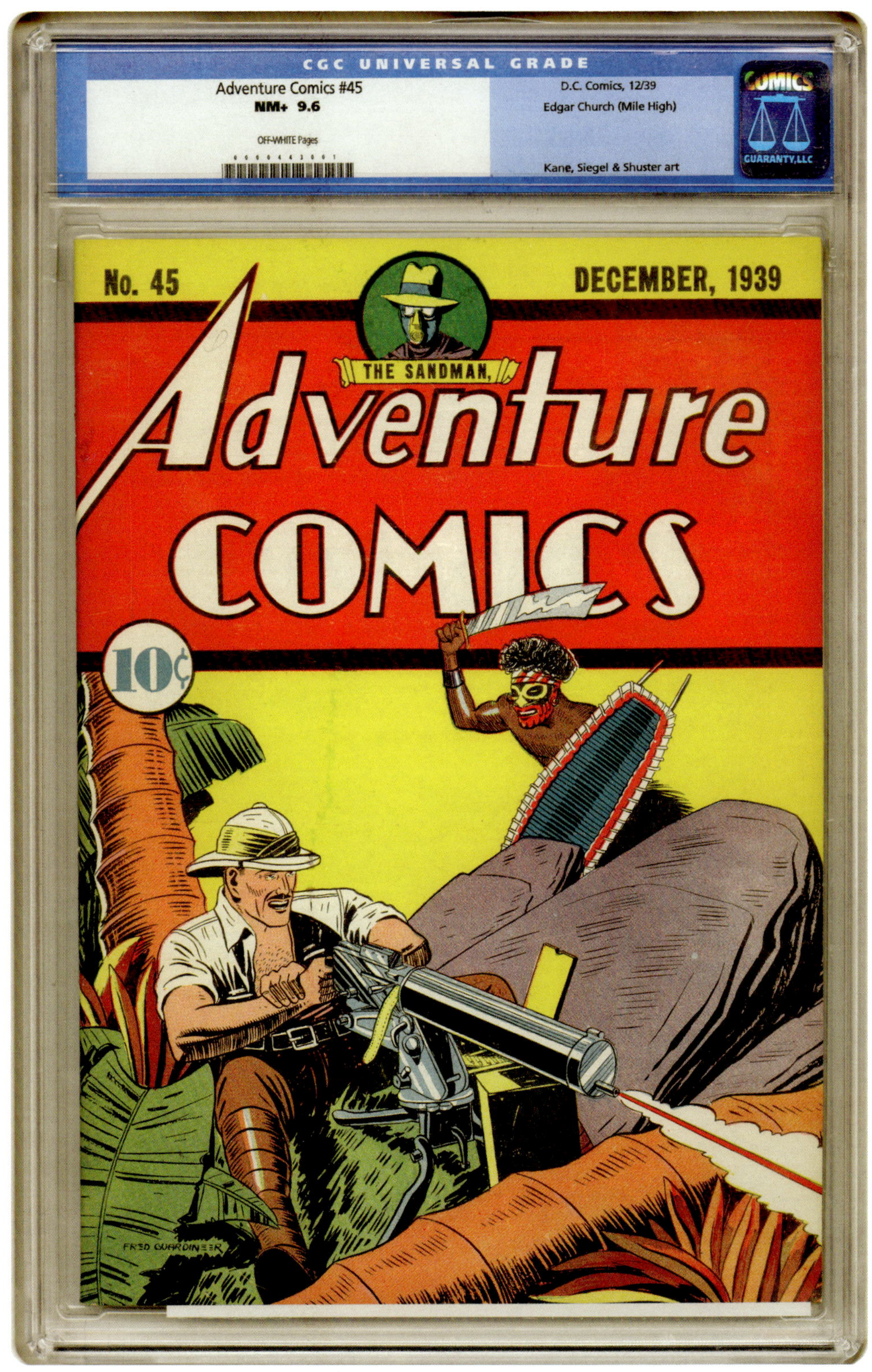

2040 Adventure Comics #45 Mile High pedigree (DC, 1939) CGC NM+ 9.6 Off-white pages. The spectacular Mile High colors are the first thing you'll notice about this copy... and *only* this copy, as it's the only one graded above 7.5 by CGC to date. This issue's cover, credited to Fred Guardineer, certainly lives up to the title of this series. Of course, the star of the book is the Sandman, drawn inside this issue by Creig Flessel. Bob Kane contributed both humor and adventure features to the comic. Overstreet 2005 NM- 9.2 value = $4,500. CGC census 7/05: 1 in 9.6, none higher.

2041 Adventure Comics #47 (DC, 1940) CGC Apparent GD- 1.8 Slight (A) Off-white to white pages. Sandman story. Creig Flessel cover. Bob Kane and Ogden Whitney art. CGC notes, "Restoration includes: cover cleaned, interior lightened," and adds, "Cover detached." Overstreet 2005 GD 2.0 value = $477.

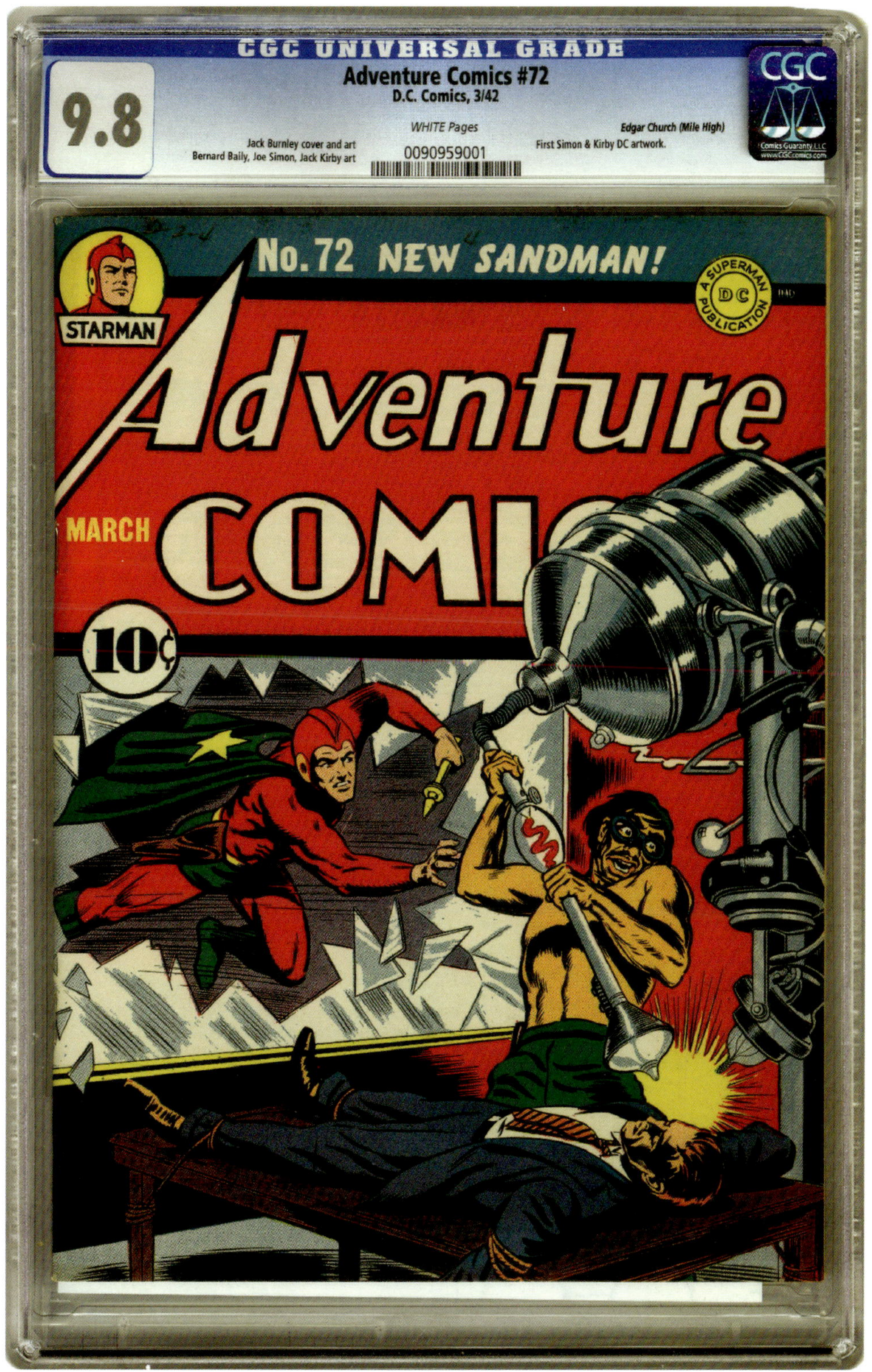

2042 Adventure Comics #72 Mile High pedigree (DC, 1942) CGC NM/MT 9.8 White pages. A 9.8 Mile High copy is a lovely sight to see no matter what the comic, but especially so for a significant book like this one, the first work for DC by the acclaimed team of Joe Simon and Jack Kirby. S&K wrote and drew the Sandman story in this issue, and they soon made the character their own with their dynamic interpretation. Other heroes seen in this issue are Hourman (with art by Bernard Baily) and the Shining Knight (drawn by Creig Flessel). Cover billing went to Starman, with outstanding art by Jack Burnley. This comic's status as the best existing copy of a comic ranked among the 100 most valuable Golden Age books by Overstreet makes it a desirable prize indeed! Overstreet 2005 NM- 9.2 value = $17,500. CGC census 9/05: 1 in 9.8, none higher.

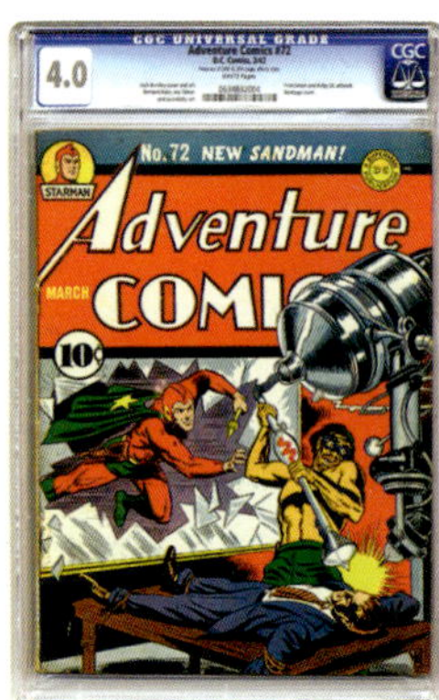

2043 Adventure Comics #72 (DC, 1942) CGC VG 4.0 White pages. When Simon and Kirby joined DC, it was quite a landmark event. This issue's Sandman story has S&K's very first work for the company, coming just a couple of issues after the character had been revamped (getting a more superhero-like costume and the addition of sidekick Sandy). The other artists (and characters in the issue) are certainly no slouches — among them are Jack Burnley (Starman), Creig Flessel (the Shining Knight) and Bernard Baily (Hourman). CGC notes, "Piece out of 28th and 29th page, affects story." Overstreet 2005 VG 4.0 value = $2,058. CGC census 8/05: 1 in 4.0, 5 higher.

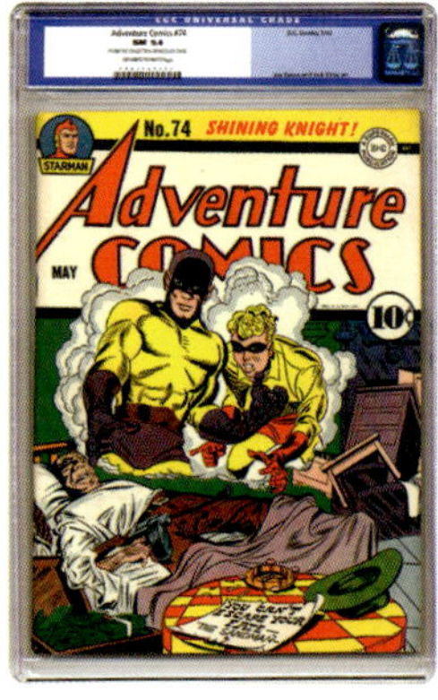

2044 Adventure Comics #74 (DC, 1942) CGC NM 9.4 Off-white to white pages. Simon and Kirby's Sandman stars in this issue, and S&K also collaborated on the Manhunter feature. The book also has a change for Hourman in the sidekick department, as Thorndyke Tompkins replaces Jimmy "Minute Man" Martin. Other heroes in the issue include Starman (drawn by Jack Burley) and the Shining Knight (drawn by Bernard Baily). CGC notes, "From the collection of Nicolas Cage." Overstreet 2005 NM- 9.2 value = $2,400. CGC census 7/05: 2 in 9.4, none higher.

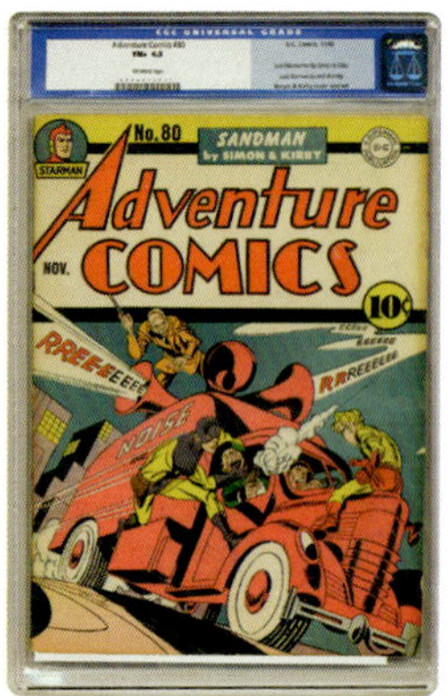

2045 Adventure Comics #80 (DC, 1942) CGC FN+ 6.5 Off-white pages. Two great runs of an artist and a character came to an end with this issue — it was Joe Simon and Jack Kirby's last Manhunter story and Jack Burnley's last Starman story. The issue also features an action-packed Sandman cover (and story) by S&K, an Hourman story by Bernard Baily, and a Shining Knight tale drawn by Louis Cazeneuve. Overstreet 2005 FN 6.0 value = $555; VF 8.0 value = $1,156. CGC census 7/05: 2 in 6.5, 6 higher. *From the Northern Lights Collection.*

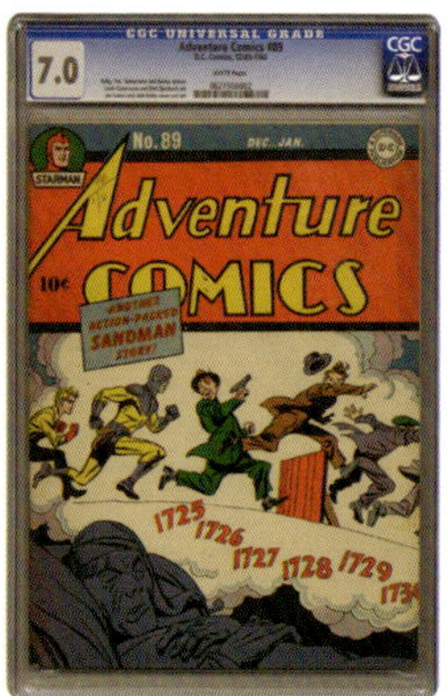

2046 Adventure Comics #89 (DC, 1944) CGC FN/VF 7.0 White pages. Why count sheep when you can count crooks? And count on the Sandman and Sandy to round 'em up. The distinctive style of Joe Simon and Jack Kirby graces both this issue's cover and the accompanying story. The book also has adventures of the Shining Knight, Starman, Manhunter, and more. Overstreet 2005 FN 6.0 value = $357; VF 8.0 value = $744. CGC census 7/05: 2 in 7.0, 2 higher. *From the Northern Lights Collection.*

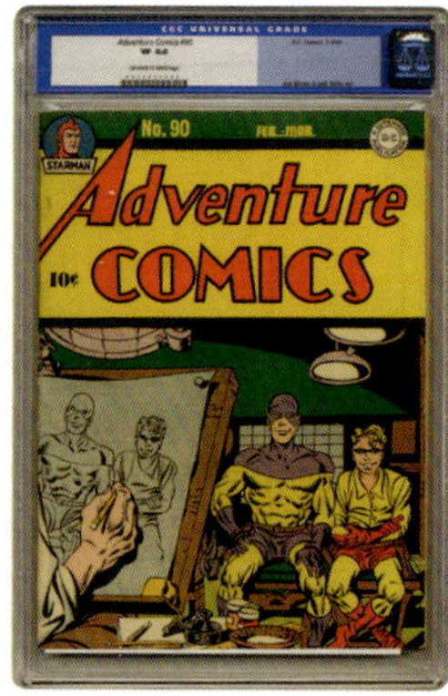

2047 Adventure Comics #90 (DC, 1944) CGC VF 8.0 Off-white to white pages. Crimefighting team Sandman and Sandy take time out to pose for artist Jack Kirby is his studio — that's the "King" pushing the pencil on this issue's cover. Inside, there's a Sandman tale by S & K (their next-to-last turn on the Dreamweaving Duo), in addition to Starman and others. Overstreet 2005 VF 8.0 value = $744. CGC census 7/05: 2 in 8.0, 2 higher. *From the Northern Lights Collection.*

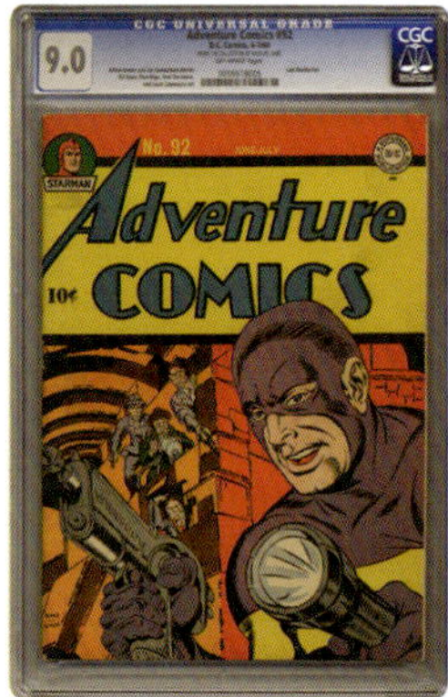

2048 Adventure Comics #92 (DC, 1944) CGC VF/NM 9.0 Off-white pages. DC's second incarnation of Manhunter had enjoyed a nice run in this title, but this issue was his last appearance of the Golden Age. However, the book's star, the Sandman, continued to fight crime, drawn on the cover by Simon and Kirby and inside the book by Gil Kane. Other features include Starman and the Shining Knight. CGC notes, "From the collection of Nicolas Cage." Overstreet 2005 VF/NM 9.0 value = $925; NM- 9.2 value = $1,250. CGC census 7/05: 1 in 9.0, 3 higher. *From the Northern Lights Collection.*

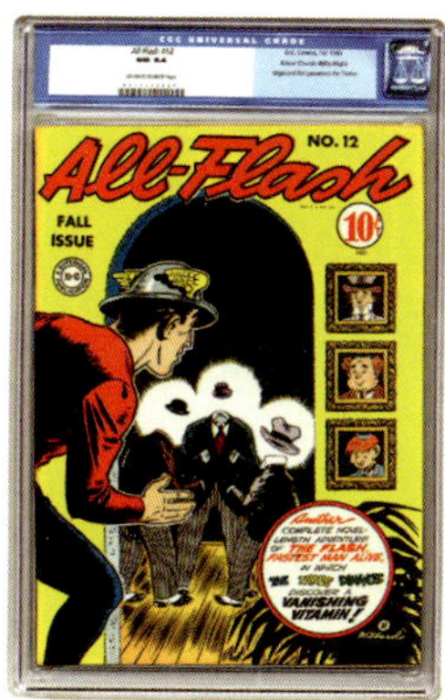

2064 All-Flash #12 Mile High pedigree (DC, 1943) CGC NM 9.4 Off-white to white pages. Remember the Thinker? No, we don't mean Rodin's (or Stan Lee's), but a brainy villain who tangled with Flash, the Atom, and others, and whose origin and first appearance are in this issue. E. E. Hibbard drew the cover as well as the interior. As for this Mile High copy, you don't have to be the Thinker to figure out that it's the best around! Overstreet 2005 NM- 9.2 value = $1,175. CGC census 7/05: 1 in 9.4, none higher.

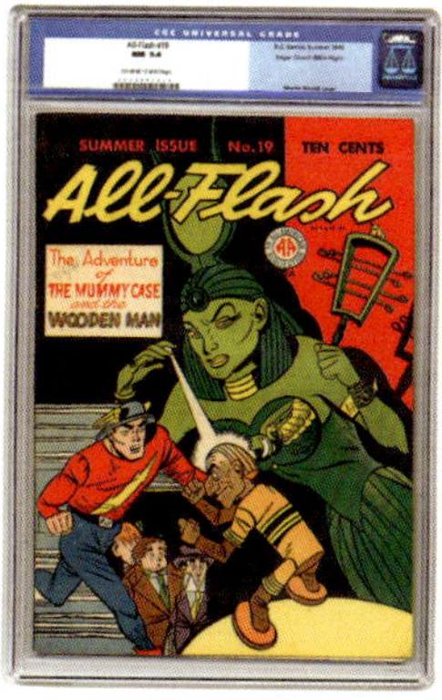

2065 All-Flash #19 Mile High pedigree (DC, 1945) CGC NM 9.4 Off-white to white pages. This issue's partially black cover is probably the reason why this is the only truly high-grade copy in CGC's census (the only one graded above 8.0, in fact). Speaking of the cover, it's by Martin Naydel, who drew the Flash tales inside the issue as well. Winky, Blinky, and Noddy guest-star. Overstreet 2005 NM- 9.2 value = $975. CGC census 7/05: 1 in 9.4, none higher.

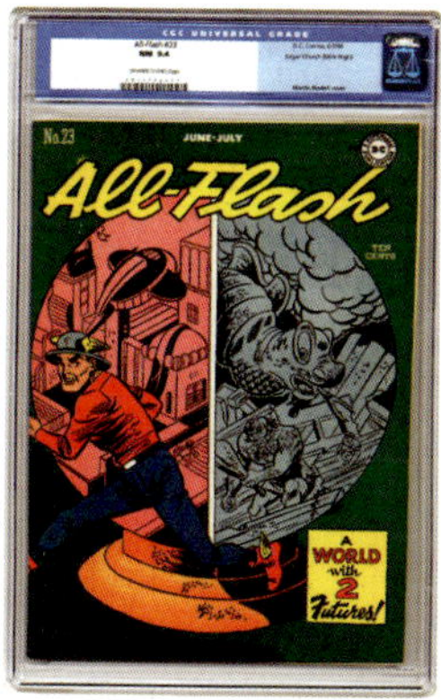

2066 All-Flash #23 Mile High pedigree (DC, 1946) CGC NM 9.4 Off-white to white pages. Ace **Flash** Martin Naydel lent his cartoony style to both this issue's cover and the interior story art. Overstreet 2005 NM- 9.2 value = $800. CGC census 9/05: 1 in 9.4, none higher.

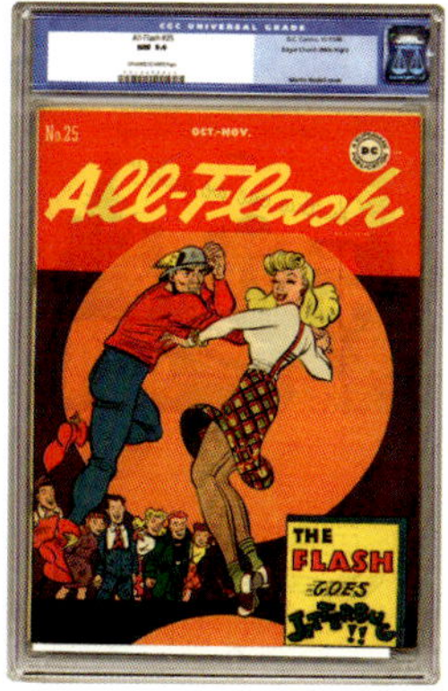

2067 All-Flash #25 Mile High pedigree (DC, 1946) CGC NM 9.4 Off-white to white pages. If you thought super speed was the Flash's only exceptional talent, watch him do the jitterbug with a 1940s lovely on Martin Naydel's cover! This Mile High copy is the only copy of the issue graded above VF/NM by CGC to date. Overstreet 2005 NM- 9.2 value = $800. CGC census 9/05: 1 in 9.4, none higher.

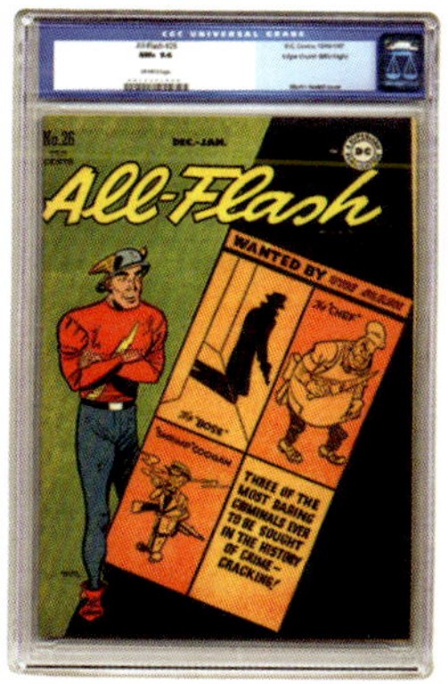

2068 All-Flash #26 Mile High pedigree (DC, 1946) CGC NM+ 9.6 Off-white pages. A mere four copies of this issue from late in the title's run have been slabbed to date, and this one's the highest-graded of the bunch... quite an impressive grade considering the partially black cover. The cover art is the work of Martin Naydel. Overstreet 2005 NM- 9.2 value = $800. CGC census 7/05: 1 in 9.6, none higher.

2069 All-Flash #29 (DC, 1947) CGC FN/VF 7.0 Off-white pages. Lee Elias cover. Elias and Martin Naydel art. Overstreet 2005 FN 6.0 value = $186; VF 8.0 value = $388. CGC census 9/05: 1 in 7.0, 3 higher.

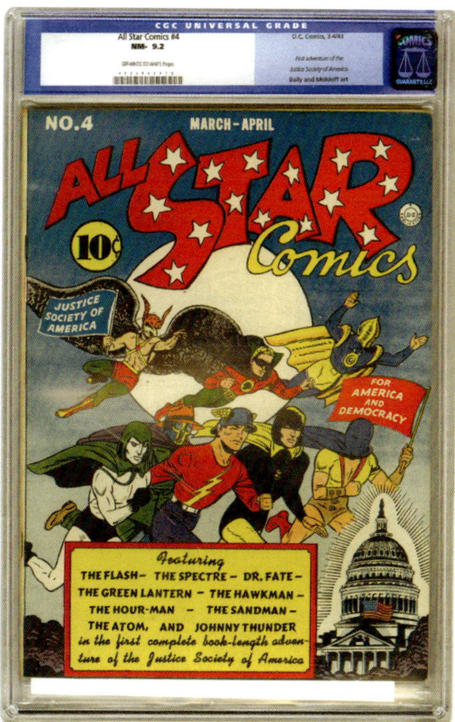

2070 All Star Comics #4 (DC, 1941) CGC NM- 9.2 Off-white to white pages. After the pomp and circumstance of the origin and first appearance of the JSA in the previous issue, the superheroes get down to business and enjoy their first adventure. E. E. Hibbard provided the inspiring cover, while Bernard Baily and Sheldon Moldoff did the interior art. This beauty is currently tied with one other copy as the highest-graded in CGC's census. Overstreet 2005 NM- 9.2 value = $8,100. CGC census 9/05: 2 in 9.2, none higher.

2071 All Star Comics #4 (DC, 1941) CGC Apparent GD+ 2.5 Moderate (A) Off-white pages. First adventure of the Justice Society (second appearance overall). E. E. Hibbard cover. Sheldon Moldoff, Bernard Baily, and Martin Nodell art. CGC notes, "Restoration includes: color touch, pieces added, reinforced, staples replaced." Overstreet 2005 GD 2.0 value = $523.

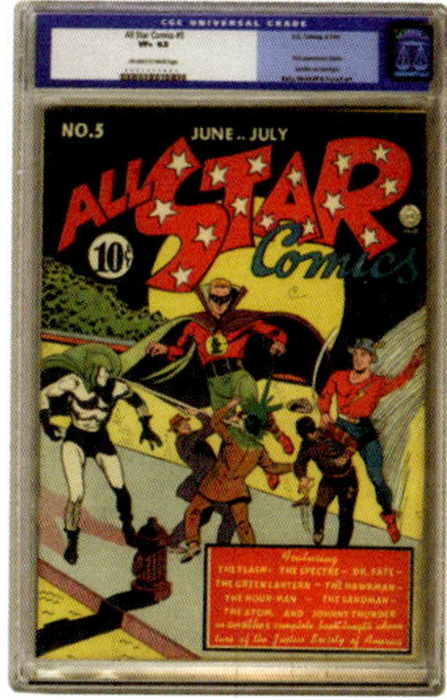

2072 All Star Comics #5 (DC, 1941) CGC VF+ 8.5 Off-white to white pages. Howard Purcell's covers were fewer and further between than those of other "name" DC artists, but his creations were invariably impressive. Sheldon Moldoff and Bernard Baily backed up Purcell with classic art on the Justice Society. This is a very pretty copy with rich, bright cover colors and just a bit of edge wear to prevent an even higher grade from CGC. Overstreet 2005 VF 8.0 value = $3,073; VF/NM 9.0 value = $4,937. CGC census 9/05: 3 in 8.5, 4 higher.

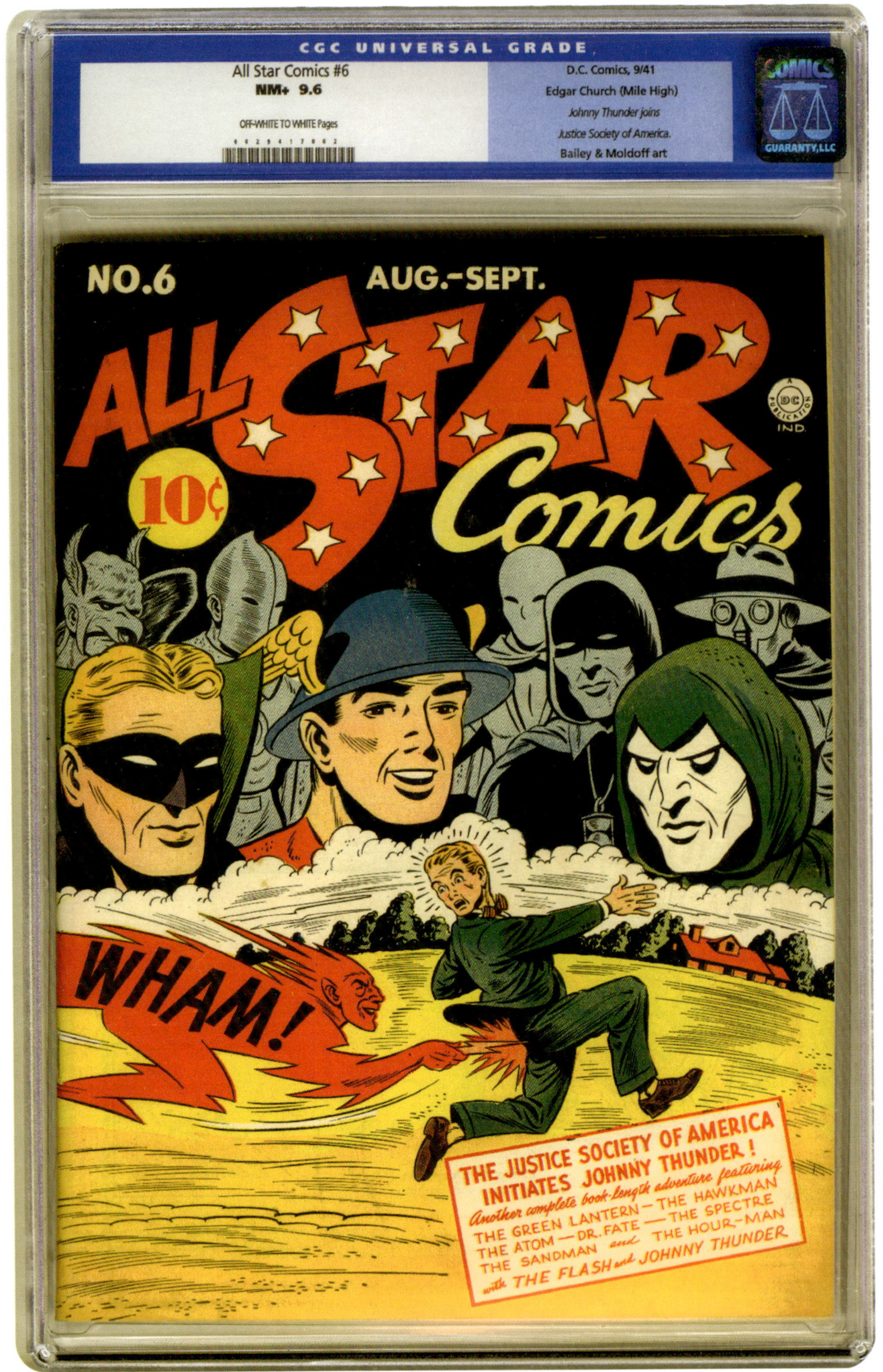

2073 All Star Comics #6 Mile High pedigree (DC, 1941) CGC NM+ 9.6 Off-white to white pages. One of the most prestigious titles to collect is **All Star**, and the most prestigious copy to have is the Mile High! And this copy looks newsstand-fresh despite the partially black cover. In the issue, Johnny Thunder joins the Justice Society, but not before the JSAers have a little fun with Johnny by sending him on a fake mission! Johnny replaces the Flash in the super-team. The book has an E. E. Hibbard cover, with interior art by the likes of Bernard Baily and Sheldon Moldoff. Note that the CGC slab has a small (3/4 inch) crack on the back right. Overstreet 2005 NM- 9.2 value = $4,000. CGC census 7/05: 1 in 9.6, none higher.

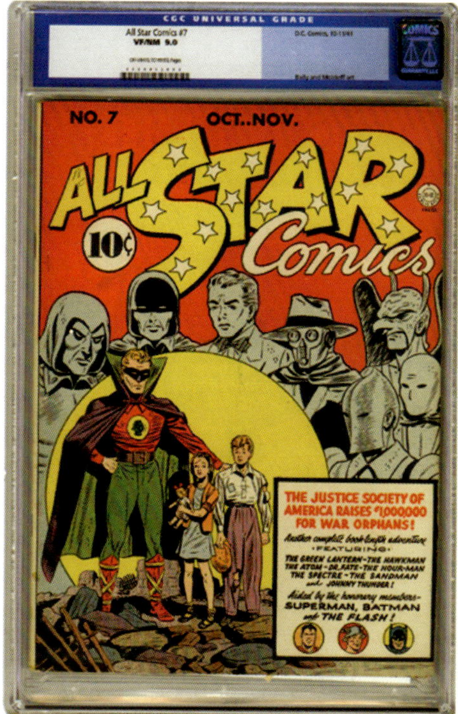

2074 All Star Comics #7 (DC, 1941) CGC VF/NM 9.0 Off-white to white pages. Just a shade below the highest grade (NM-9.2) that CGC has certified to date for issue #7, this copy sparkles. E. E. Hibbard created the cover, and Bernard Baily and Sheldon Moldoff offered story art. Overstreet 2005 VF/NM 9.0 value = $3,441; NM- 9.2 value = $4,750. CGC census 9/05: 3 in 9.0, 3 higher.

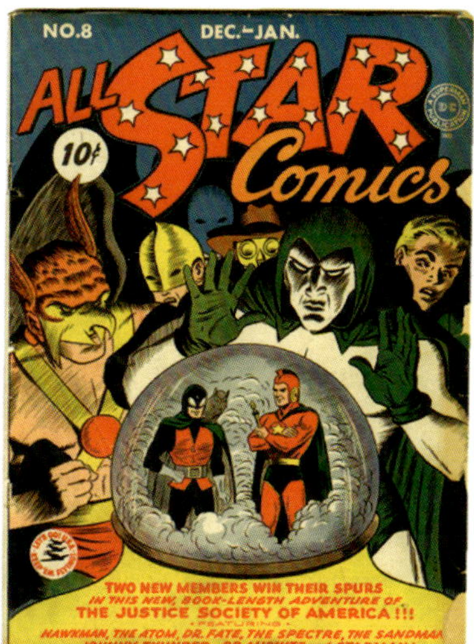

2075 All Star Comics #8 (DC, 1942) Condition: GD. It's the first appearance and origin of Wonder Woman, it's one of the 30 most valuable comic books according to Overstreet, and it's a copy that hasn't been sealed up in a slab, so you can actually *look* at it! This GD copy has cream pages; the cover is still attached at both staples (though hanging by a thread from the bottom one), and while there's a chunk missing from the margin of an interior page, no story panels are affected. When you give this a read, you can marvel at the fact that Wonder Woman wasn't mentioned in the JSA story, let alone the cover, supporting the theory held by some that the story was originally intended for **Sensation Comics** #1 and added here at the last minute. As for that JSA story, we'll note that Starman and Dr. Mid-Nite became members in this issue. The book has E. E. Hibbard cover art, with interior art by Sheldon Moldoff, Jack Burnley, Bernard Baily, and H. G. Peter. Overstreet 2005 GD 2.0 value = $2,825.

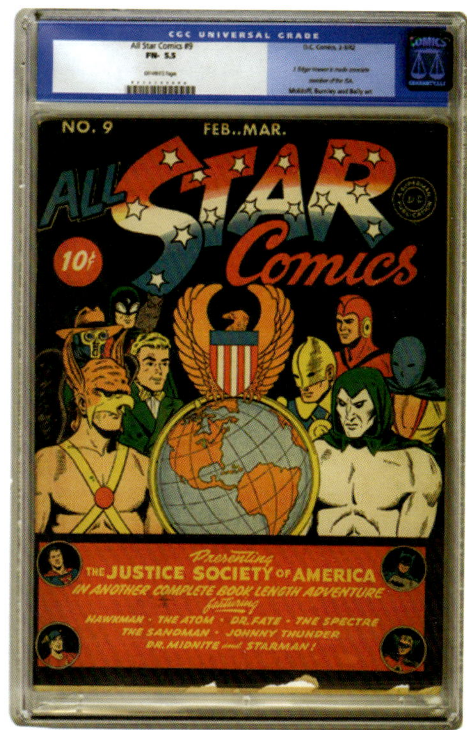

2076 All Star Comics #9 (DC, 1942) CGC FN- 5.5 Off-white pages. In this issue: J. Edgar Hoover is made an associate member of the Justice Society of America! One stipulation, however, J. Ed, no trying on the superheroes' costumes - especially Hawkgirl's! The artists are E. E. Hibbard on the cover, and Sheldon Moldoff, Jack Burnley, and Bernard Baily on the inside. Overstreet 2005 FN 6.0 value = $876. CGC census 9/05: 1 in 5.5, 8 higher.

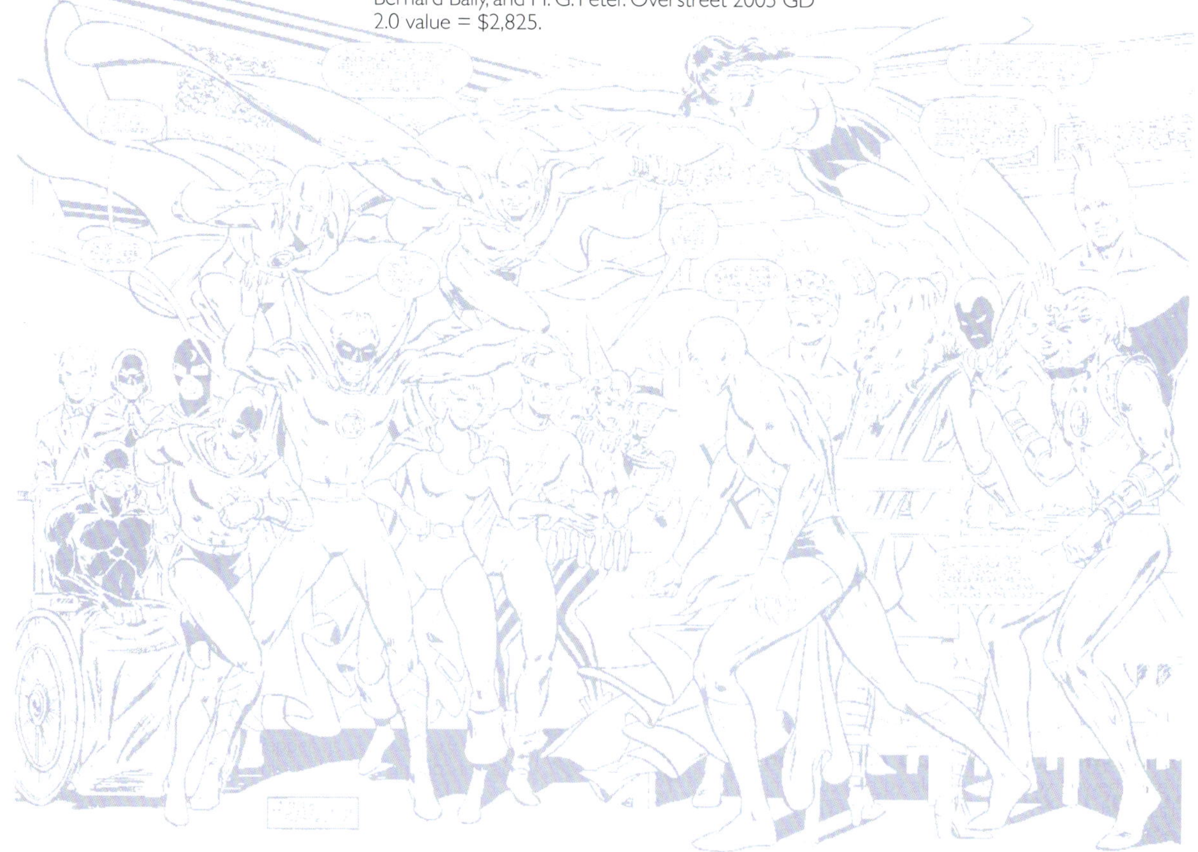

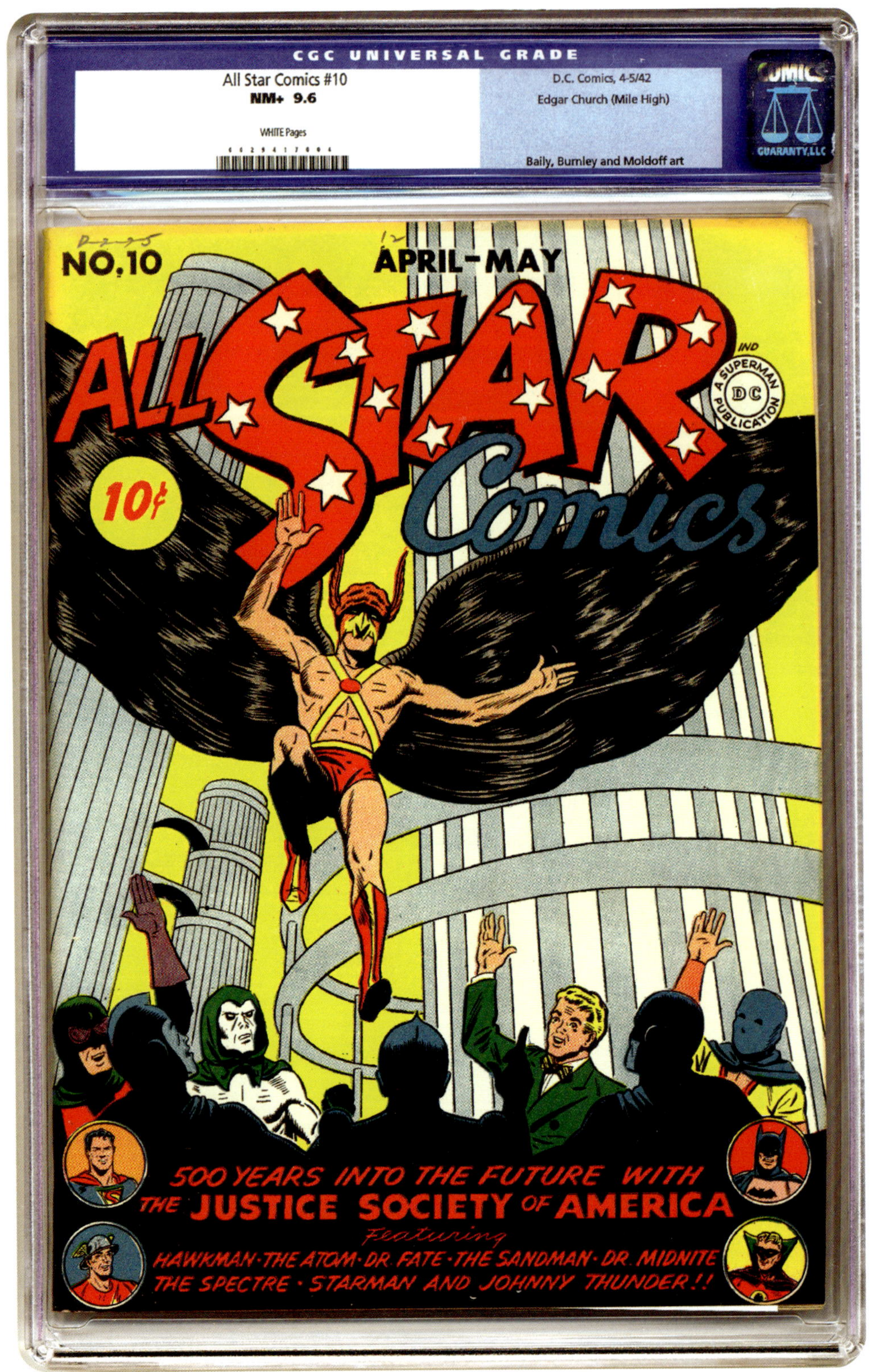

2077 All Star Comics #10 Mile High pedigree (DC, 1942) CGC NM+ 9.6 White pages. A glorious Hawkman cover never looked better than on this spectacular Mile High copy, the highest-graded that CGC has certified to date. This time-travel adventure for the Justice Society has art by E. E. Hibbard, Sheldon Moldoff, Jack Burnley, and Bernard Baily. Hibbard is credited with the cover, which has probably the only time you'll ever see Hawkman wearing shorts, and also offers a glimpse of "honorary members" Superman, Batman, Flash, and Green Lantern. Overstreet 2005 NM- 9.2 value = $3,800. CGC census 7/05: 1 in 9.6, none higher.

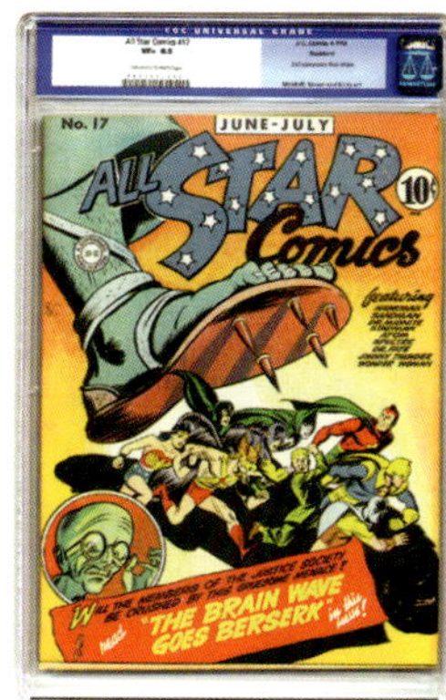

2081 All Star Comics #17 Rockford pedigree (DC, 1943) CGC VF+ 8.5 Off-white to white pages. JSA master villain Brain Wave "goes berserk" in his second **All-Star** appearance. This issue is notable for the inclusion of Joe Simon and Jack Kirby art on the Sandman chapter. This copy is very nice, with flat, tight surfaces, and great paper quality. Overstreet 2005 VF 8.0 value = $1,131; VF/NM 9.0 value = $1,741. CGC census 7/05: 1 in 8.5, 3 higher.

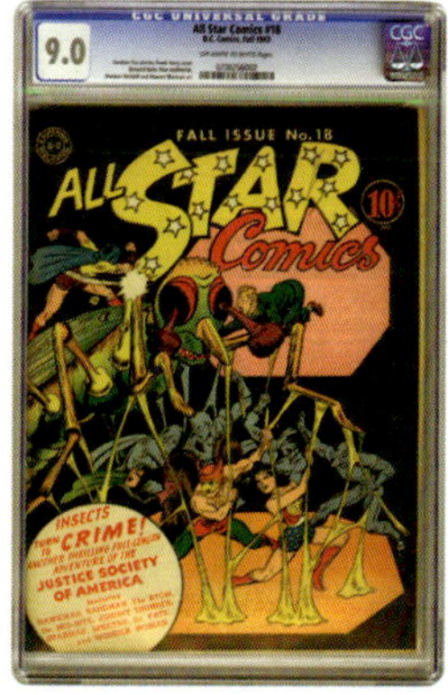

2082 All Star Comics #18 (DC, 1943) CGC VF/NM 9.0 Off-white to white pages. This issue's black cover would tend to preclude many high-grade copies existing, and indeed, only two have been graded higher than our offering by CGC as of this writing. In this issue, Justice Society takes on criminals who have the powers of insects, and yes, there are even some "spider men" among 'em (yeah, we know spiders are arachnids, but we didn't write the story!). The issue has a Frank Harry cover and interior art by the likes of Sheldon Moldoff, Bernard Baily, Howard Sherman, and Pierce Rice. Overstreet 2005 VF/NM 9.0 value = $1,741; NM- 9.2 value = $2,350. CGC census 8/05: 2 in 9.0, 2 higher.

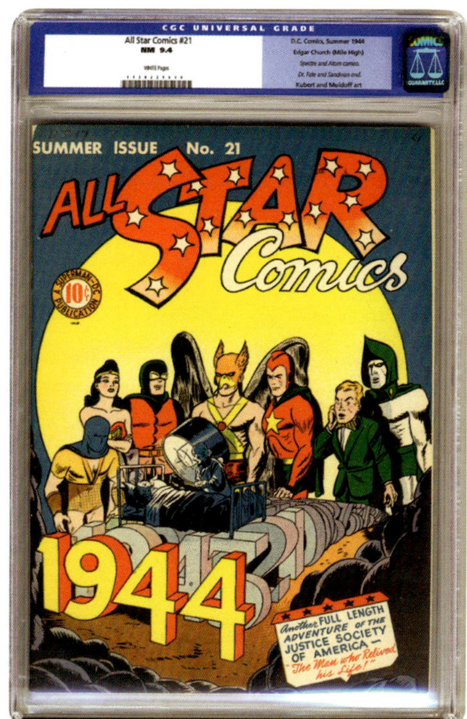

2083 All Star Comics #21 Mile High pedigree (DC, 1944) CGC NM 9.4 White pages. The sharp edges and great colors of this copy are exactly what you look for in a Mile High; it appears that only a corner "ding" at the top left kept this one from a higher grade. This issue marked the last appearance in the series for two founding members of the Justice Society, Dr. Fate and Sandman (to add insult to injury, they don't even appear on Joe Gallagher's cover). Also in these pages is Joe Kubert's work on this title, not drawing Hawkman, but rather Dr. Fate. Not to worry though, the Hawkman chapter was in the capable hands of Sheldon Moldoff. Overstreet 2005 NM- 9.2 value = $2,050. CGC census 7/05: 2 in 9.4, none higher.

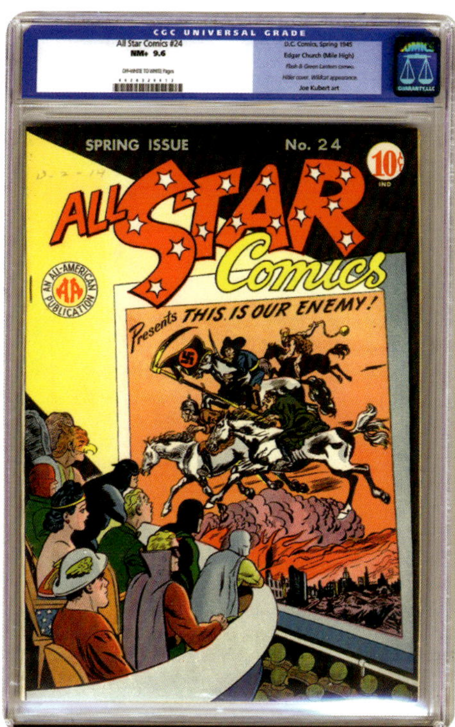

2084 All Star Comics #24 Mile High pedigree (DC, 1945) CGC NM+ 9.6 Off-white to white pages. We've seen Hitler covers before, but why is *Otto von Bismarck* joining him? It's because wartime propaganda was the order of the day for this issue, which features a look at all German aggressors throughout history. There's a whole bunch of extra JSA members here too, with Mr. Terrific making his only appearance with the group, and his **Sensation Comics** cohort, Wildcat, making one of only two appearances. The Flash and Green Lantern rejoin the group in this issue. Also of note is that Joe Kubert drew the issue's Hawkman chapter. And we can't resist mentioning C. C. Beck's Captain Tootsie ad on the back cover, featuring a blatant Sivana ripoff named Dr. Narsty! Overstreet 2005 NM- 9.2 value = $2,050. CGC census 9/05: 1 in 9.6, none higher.

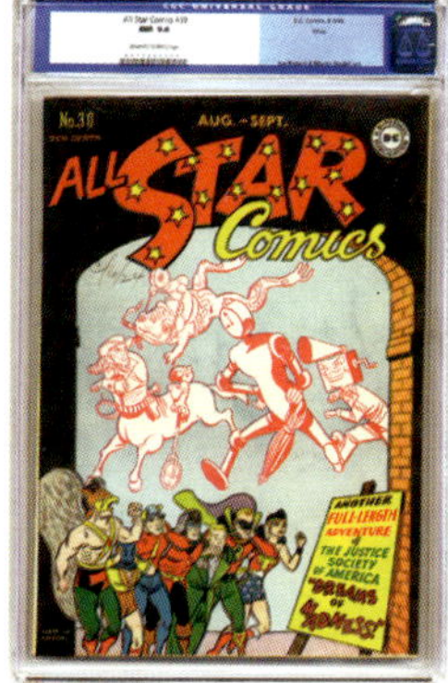

2085 All Star Comics #30 Ohio pedigree (DC, 1946) CGC NM 9.4 Off-white to white pages. The Justice Society doubts its sanity in this issue's "Dreams of Madness" story. This pedigreed dream of a copy, with its perfect black background cover, is not to be missed; you would have to be insane to have passed this gem by! Overstreet 2005 NM- 9.2 value = $1,575. CGC census 7/05: 1 in 9.4, 1 higher.

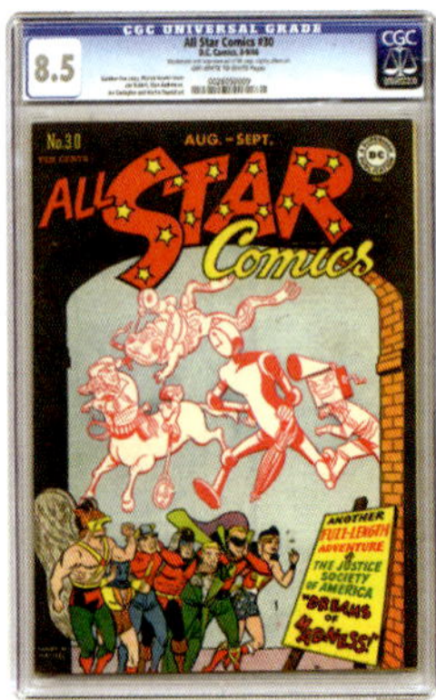

2086 All Star Comics #30 (DC, 1946) CGC VF+ 8.5 Off-white to white pages. This copy, with its stunning black-background cover by Martin Naydel, looks much nicer than the CGC-assigned grade. This is due to a bindery defect; CGC notes, "Manufactured with a large piece out of 5th page, slightly affects art." Our advice is to snap up this beauty, leave it in its holder, and use some of the money you saved to buy a copy of **All Star Archives** #7 to read! Overstreet 2005 VF 8.0 value = $756; VF/NM 9.0 value = $1,166. CGC census 9/05: 1 in 8.5, 3 higher.

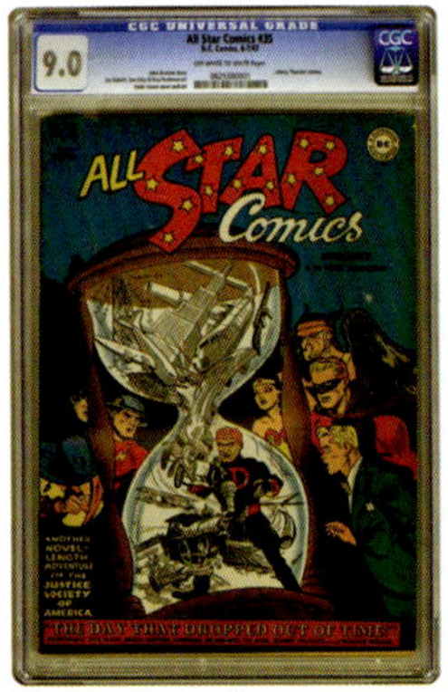

2087 All Star Comics #35 (DC, 1947) CGC VF/NM 9.0 Off-white to white pages. Per Degaton made his first appearance in this issue — he was a villain who would crop up again in the Bronze Age, and he even played a role in the **Crisis**! The issue has an Irwin Hasen cover, with interior art by Hasen, Lee Elias, Joe Kubert, and others. Overstreet 2005 VF/NM 9.0 value = $1,128; NM- 9.2 value = $1,525. CGC census 9/05: 2 in 9.0, 3 higher.

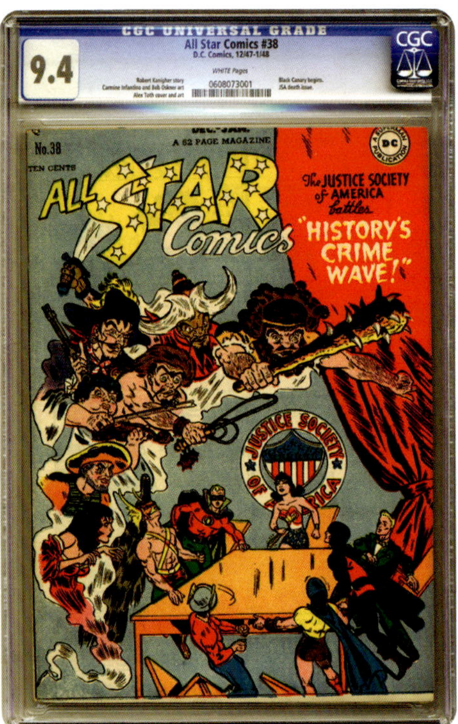

2088 All Star Comics #38 (DC, 1947) CGC NM 9.4 White pages. Roy Thomas calls this issue "the weirdest **All-Star** ever" — it begins with the male JSAers all being killed! Saving the day is left up to Black Canary (who makes her debut in this title) and Wonder Woman (who rarely played a prominent role in a JSA story, but takes center stage here). The issue is also notable for having early Alex Toth art — the great one was still a teenager when he drew this issue's cover. Toth also drew the beginning and end of the story; the middle portions are the work of Carmine Infantino and Bob Oksner respectively. Only one copy of this issue has been certified with a higher grade by CGC to date. Overstreet 2005 NM- 9.2 value = $2,400. CGC census 8/05: 1 in 9.4, 1 higher.

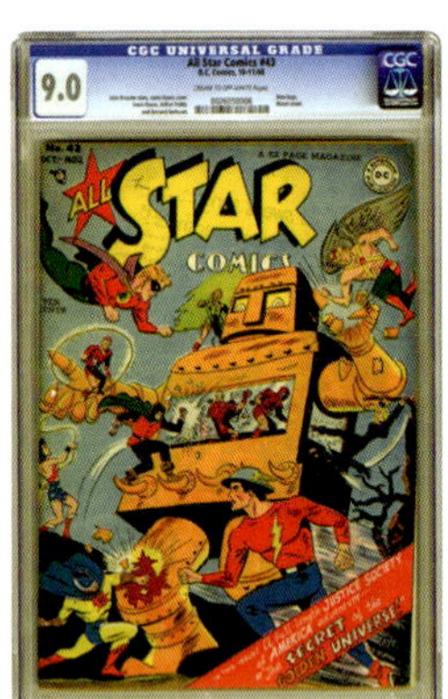

2089 All Star Comics #43 (DC, 1948) CGC VF/NM 9.0 Cream to off-white pages. Robot covers are always in demand, and here's one which will look familiar to Silver Age fans, as it was paid homage to years later on the cover of **The Brave and the Bold** #29. But even if mechanical menaces aren't your thing, feast your eyes on the Justice Society's lineup, which shows once again how aptly named this title is. The roll call includes the Atom, Wonder Woman, Black Canary, Hawkman, Green Lantern, Dr. Mid-Nite, and the Flash. The cover is by Irwin Hasen; the interior artists include Bob Oksner. Overstreet 2005 VF/NM 9.0 value = $1,091; NM- 9.2 value = $1,475. CGC census 9/05: 2 in 9.0, 2 higher.

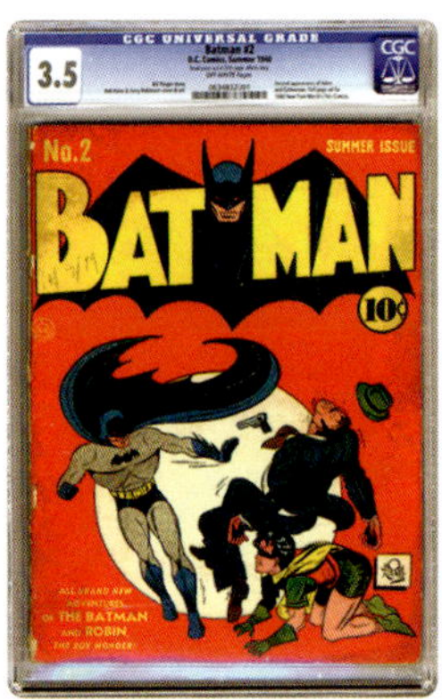

2090 Batman #2 (DC, 1940) CGC VG- 3.5 Off-white pages. Two of DC's villainous VIPs made only their second appearances in this issue. Not only does that jocund jack-of-all-crimes, the Joker, pop up for only the second time, he has purr-fect accompaniment in the form of Catwoman. In fact, this issue had the debut of the name "Catwoman," as the lady was called "the Cat" in her previous appearance. The art is by Bob Kane with the assistance of his lieutenants Jerry Robinson and George Roussos. CGC notes, "Small piece out of 20th page, affects story." Overstreet 2005 VG 4.0 value = $2,470. CGC census 8/05: 5 in 3.5, 17 higher.

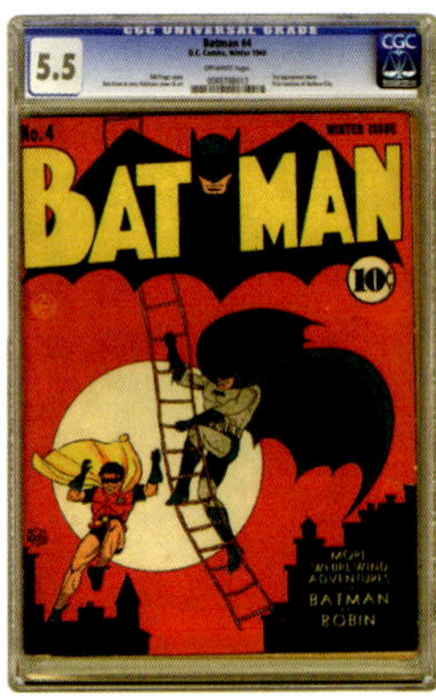

2091 Batman #4 (DC, 1940) CGC FN- 5.5 Off-white pages. Virtually every early issue of this title merits special notation in Overstreet; no wonder they continue to be in high demand by collectors year after year, generation after generation. The Joker makes his third appearance in this issue, which also occasions the first mention of Gotham City in a Batman comic book. Bob Kane and Jerry Robinson collaborate on the cover and story art. Overstreet 2005 FN 6.0 value = $2,031. CGC census 9/05: 3 in 5.5, 16 higher.

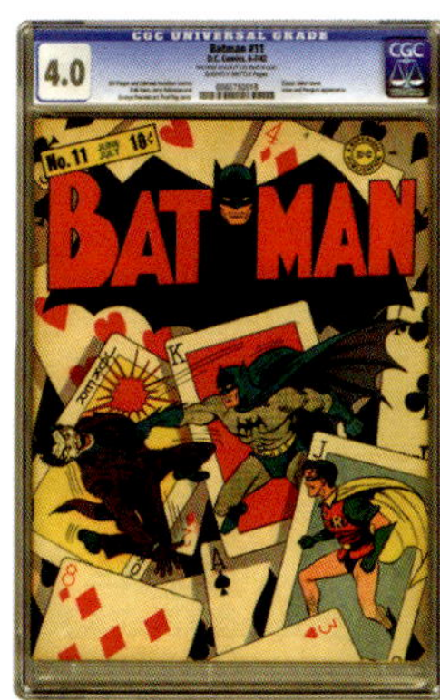

2092 Batman #11 (DC, 1942) CGC VG 4.0 Slightly brittle pages. In honor of his perennial foe's third cover appearance, Batman feeds the Joker a knuckle sandwich in this classic cover by Fred Ray and Jerry Robinson (although the CGC fails to note Robinson's contribution). Featured inside are appearances by the Joker and the Penguin, as well as art by Robinson, Bob Kane, and George Roussos. CGC notes: "Very minor amount of color touch on cover." Overstreet 2005 VG 4.0 value = $1,354. CGC census 9/05: 1 in 4.0, 38 higher.

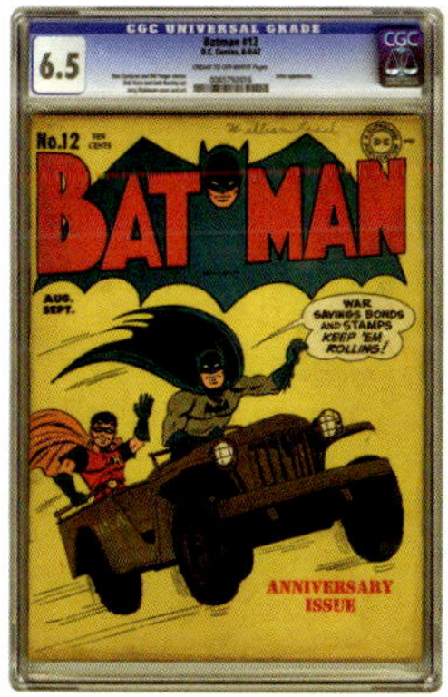

2093 Batman #12 (DC, 1942) CGC FN+ 6.5 Cream to off-white pages. The Joker makes an appearance in this issue, which features a cover by Jerry Robinson, and story art by Bob Kane and Jack Burnley. Overstreet 2005 FN 6.0 value = $900; VF 8.0 value = $1,892. CGC census 5/05: 6 in 6.5, 11 higher.

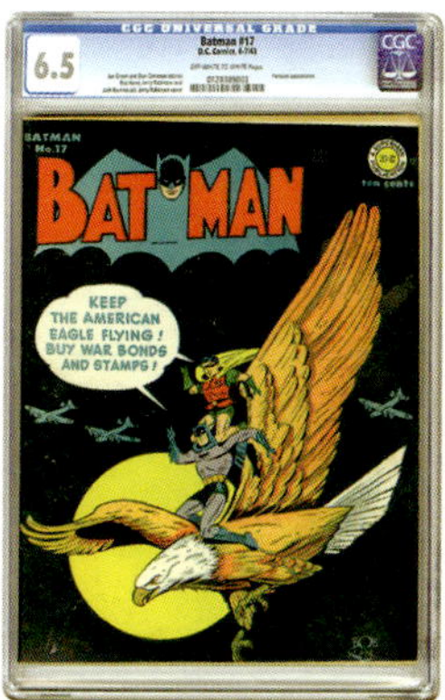

2094 Batman #17 (DC, 1943) CGC FN+ 6.5 Off-white to white pages. Jerry Robinson got this issue off to an impressive start with a dynamite "buy war bonds" cover. The issue's main story features the Penguin; in the tale, the Bumbershoot Bandit hears someone say he's nothing without his trick umbrellas, so he actually tries using other gadgets for his crimes for a while! The issue's interior artists include Robinson, Bob Kane, and Jack Burnley. Overstreet 2005 FN 6.0 value = $693; VF 8.0 value = $1,444. CGC census 7/05: 1 in 6.5, 25 higher.

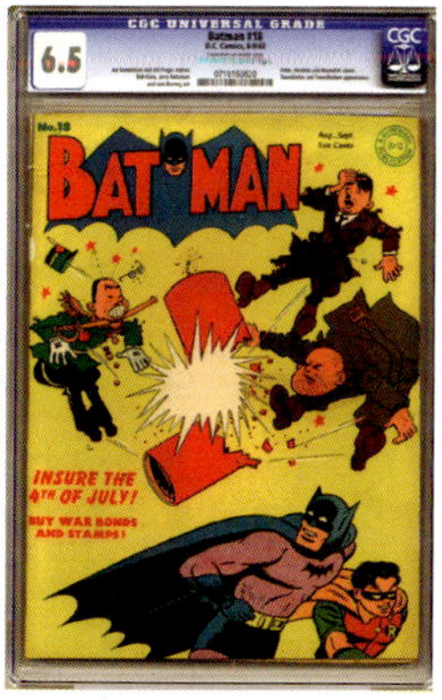

2095 Batman #18 (DC, 1943) CGC FN+ 6.5 Off-white to white pages. Hitler, Hirohito, and Mussolini get knocked on their Axis, and we have cover artist Stan Kaye to thank for it! Inside the comic, the Dynamic Duo takes on Tweedledum and Tweedledee. Also in these pages is the death of the entertaining villain known as the "Crime Surgeon," Matthew Thorne. Jerry Robinson and Jack Burnley contributed interior art. CGC notes, "3 tape stains on interior cover." Overstreet 2005 FN 6.0 value = $876; VF 8.0 value = $1,825. CGC census 8/05: 3 in 6.5, 8 higher.

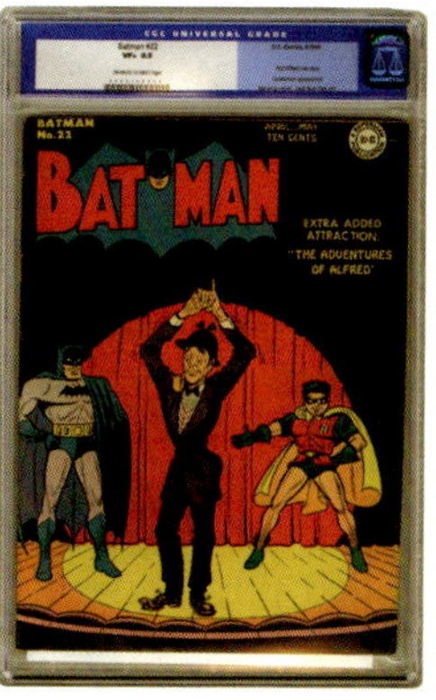

2096 Batman #22 (DC, 1944) CGC VF+ 8.5 Off-white to white pages. Alfred takes center stage on this Dick Sprang cover, and is featured in his first solo story. Jack Burnley and Jerry Robinson contribute interior art. This is an exceptional copy of an issue that, owing to the cover's black background, often displays even very minor blemishes. Overstreet 2005 VF 8.0 value = $963; VF/NM 9.0 value = $1,482. CGC census 9/05: 3 in 8.5, 7 higher.

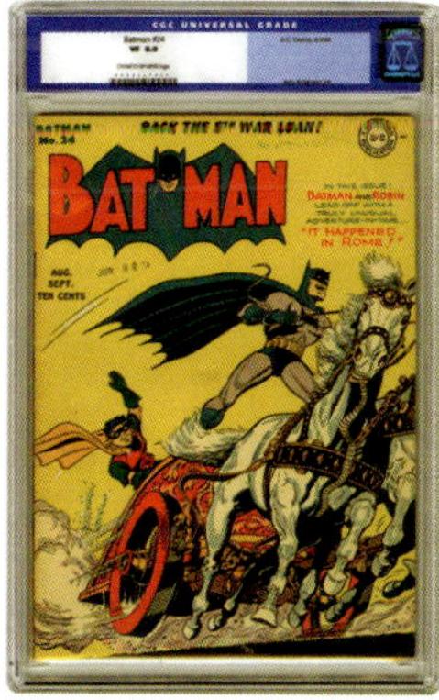

2097 Batman #24 (DC, 1944) CGC VF 8.0 Cream to off-white pages. Thanks to their pal Professor Carter Nichols, the Dynamic Duo are time-traveling, with ancient Rome their destination. Jerry Robinson is listed as artist for this issue. This World War II-era comic seems to be time-traveling as well; it certainly doesn't look its age! The cover colors are particularly bright on this sharp example. Overstreet 2005 VF 8.0 value = $963. CGC census 6/05: 3 in 8.0, 14 higher.

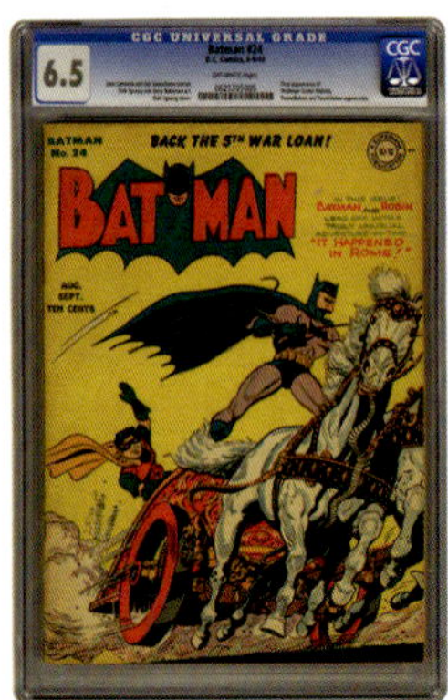

2098 Batman #24 (DC, 1944) CGC FN+ 6.5 Off-white pages. This issue marks the first appearance of Professor Carter Nichols, who can send people through time by using hypnosis! Make sense? Well, even if it doesn't, he was a character who reappeared on many occasions in the Golden and Silver Age, with a time travel story the invariable result. This time around, the Prof sends Bruce Wayne and Dick Grayson to ancient Rome, as seen on this Dick Sprang-drawn cover. Another story in this issue features those rotund rascals, Tweedledum and Tweedledee. The interior art is by Sprang and Jerry Robinson. Overstreet 2005 FN 6.0 value = $462; VF 8.0 value = $963. CGC census 7/05: 7 in 6.5, 22 higher. *From the Northern Lights Collection.*

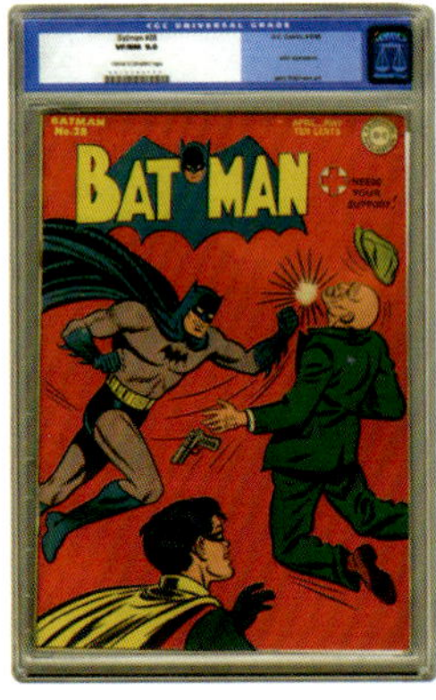

2099 Batman #28 (DC, 1945) CGC VF/NM 9.0 Cream to off-white pages. The Dark Knight Detective comes out swinging on this action cover. Jerry Robinson illustrates the stories inside, which include one starring that Clown Prince of Crime, the Joker. The deep, rich cover colors will really knock you out; this is one sharp-looking Golden Age comic. Overstreet 2005 VF/NM 9.0 value = $1,482; NM- 9.2 value = $2,000. CGC census 9/05: 4 in 9.0, 5 higher.

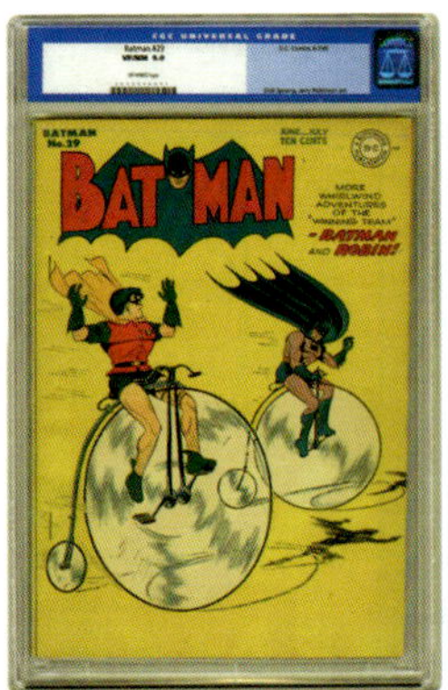

2100 Batman #29 (DC, 1945) CGC VF/NM 9.0 Off-white pages. A Dick Sprang cover gets this issue rolling; Jerry Robinson continues the thrill with his artistic skills inside. This flat, sharp copy looks as if it was opened only once or twice — very carefully! The staples show very little stress from reading. Overstreet 2005 VF/NM 9.0 value = $1,482; NM- 9.2 value = $2,000. CGC census 9/05: 5 in 9.0, 1 higher.

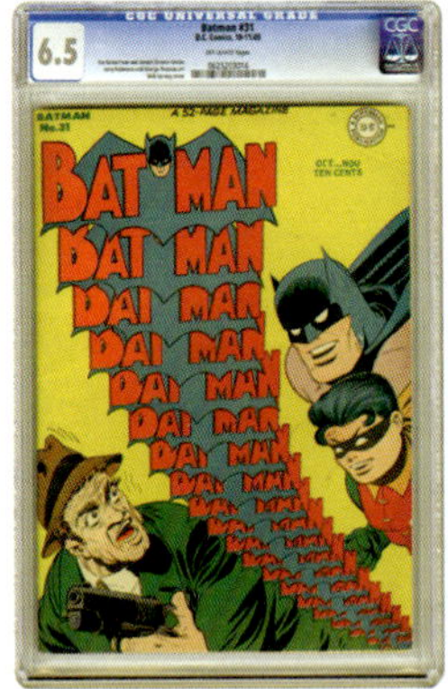

2101 Batman #31 (DC, 1945) CGC FN+ 6.5 Off-white pages. A complement of fine Bat-artists teamed up for this issue — Dick Sprang delivered the optical effects on the cover, while Jerry Robinson and George Roussos pitched in with interior art. Overstreet 2005 FN 6.0 value = $342; VF 8.0 value = $713. CGC census 9/05: 3 in 6.5, 15 higher.

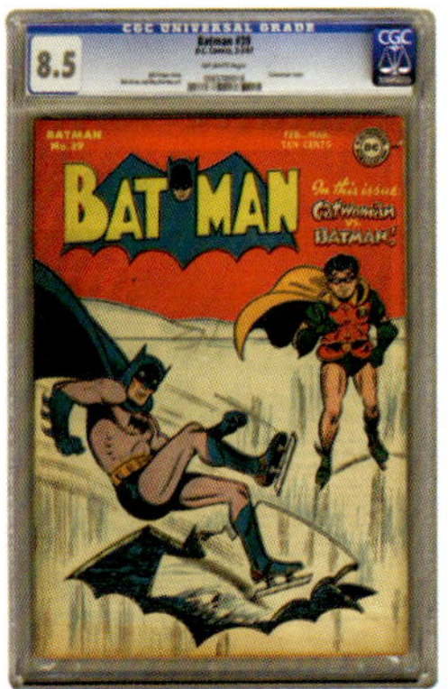

2102 Batman #39 (DC, 1947) CGC VF+ 8.5 Off-white pages. What set Catwoman apart from other super-villainesses was the undeniable attraction between her and her do-gooder foe Batman. And this issue has one of their best exchanges, as the Crime Queen purrs, "Join up with me... we can be king and queen of crime!" and the Caped Crusader quips, "How could we — with me *outside* and you *inside* a jail cell!" Great stuff, expertly drawn by Ray Burnley. The cover's by Ray's brother Jack Burnley. Overstreet 2005 VF 8.0 value = $713; VF/NM 9.0 value = $1,094. CGC census 6/05: 7 in 8.5, 4 higher.

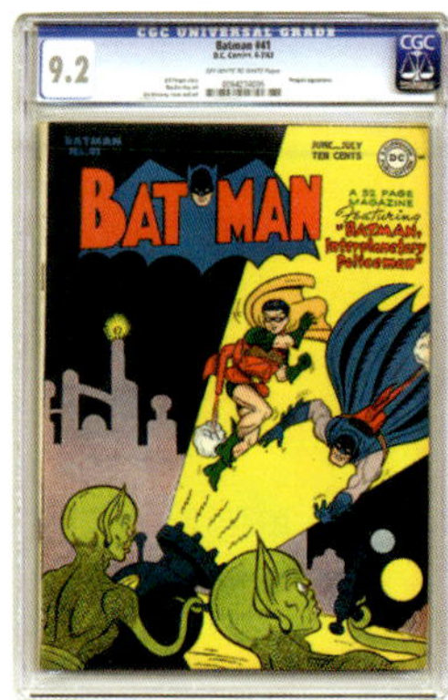

2103 Batman #41 (DC, 1947) CGC NM- 9.2 Off-white to white pages. This issue signaled an unusual change in the kind of stories featured in **Batman**. For the next fifteen years or so, the Dark Knight Detective would face all kinds of Outer Space creatures and situations. This first science fiction cover by Jim Mooney looks a bit like something from a pulp magazine, with its green-skinned aliens pointing ray guns at the Dynamic Duo. Inside the book, the Penguin made sure things weren't entirely out of this world. This is a superb example, with exceptional cover color and great page quality. Overstreet 2005 NM- 9.2 value = $1,075. CGC census 7/05: 2 in 9.2, 4 higher.

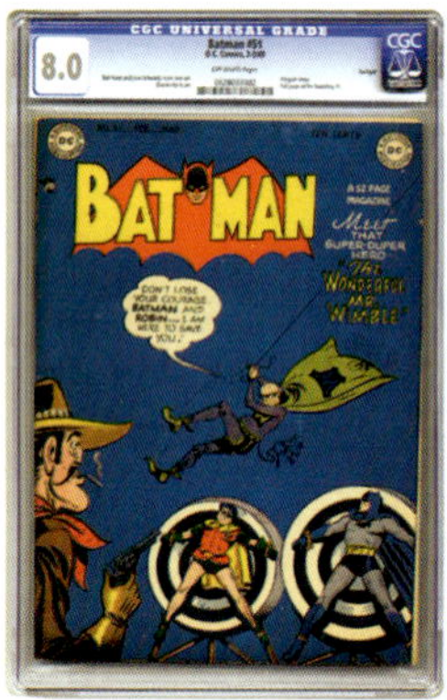

2104 Batman #51 Twilight pedigree (DC, 1949) CGC VF 8.0 Off-white pages. The Penguin is the featured villain in this issue; this time the Umbrella Rogue claims to have given up a life of crime in favor of the straight and narrow. A likely story! As for the skinny fellow on the cover, that's a certain Mr. Wimble, a working stiff who idolizes Batman and Robin and manages to lend them a hand. The book has a cover by Bob Kane and Lew Schwartz; the interior art is by Charles Paris. Comes with the Twilight certificate of authenticity. Overstreet 2005 VF 8.0 value = $494. CGC census 8/05: 1 in 8.0, 3 higher.

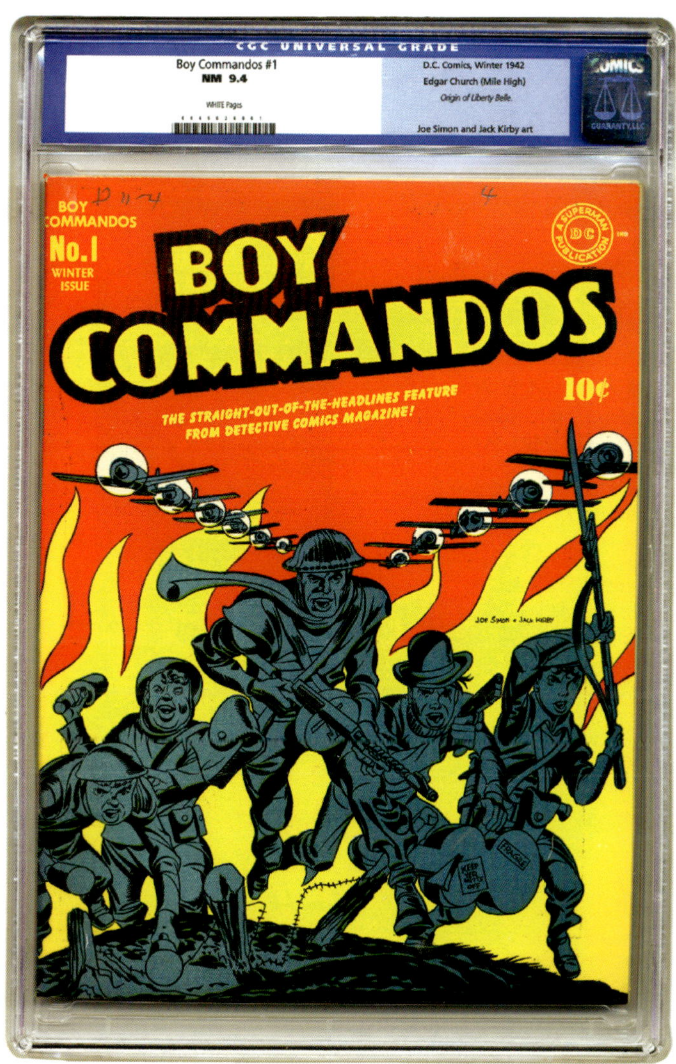

2105 Boy Commandos #1 Mile High pedigree (DC, 1942) CGC NM 9.4 White pages. While Joe Simon and Jack Kirby had already contributed to many comics by the time of this issue, this was only the second title (after **Captain America Comics**) that was all S&K. Of course, the kid group was a specialty of the duo. The group got its own title here after a successful debut in **Detective Comics**. The issue has a guest-appearance by the Sandman, whom Simon & Kirby were drawing in **Adventure Comics**'s by this time. And of course, it's also got a classic patriotic cover to recommend it. We can't imagine that any serious DC collector would pass on this Mile High copy! Overstreet 2005 NM- 9.2 value = $8,200. CGC census 9/05: 2 in 9.4, none higher.

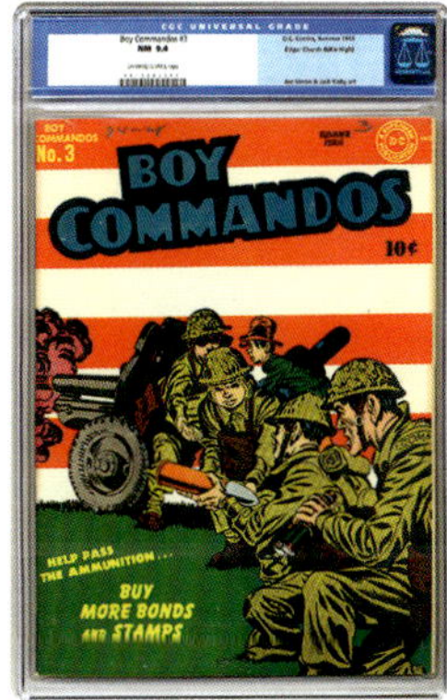

2106 Boy Commandos #3 Mile High pedigree (DC, 1943) CGC NM 9.4 Off-white to white pages. While the Boy Commandos were a Simon and Kirby creation, only a handful of issues of this title actually had S&K art, and this is one of em — the duo contributed a whopping 45 pages here. A patriotic buy-war-bonds cover is another plus. This Edgar Church copy is the only one graded above VF by CGC to date. Overstreet 2005 NM- 9.2 value = $1,450. CGC census 8/05: 1 in 9.4, none higher.

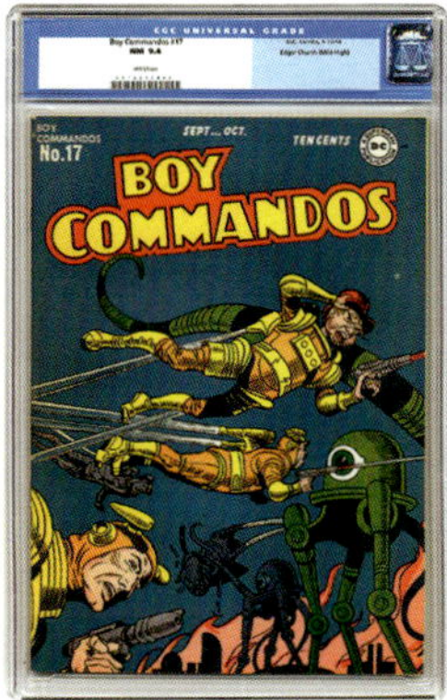

2107 Boy Commandos #17 Mile High pedigree (DC, 1946) CGC NM 9.4 White pages. The Boy Commandos in outer space? Well, with no Nazi menace left to fight in 1946, why not? The team's creators Joe Simon and Jack Kirby teamed up on one story in this issue, and there's also some Kirby solo work in these pages. Overstreet 2005 NM- 9.2 value = $385. CGC census 8/05: 1 in 9.4, none higher.

Oops! See more Boy Commandos on Page 103!

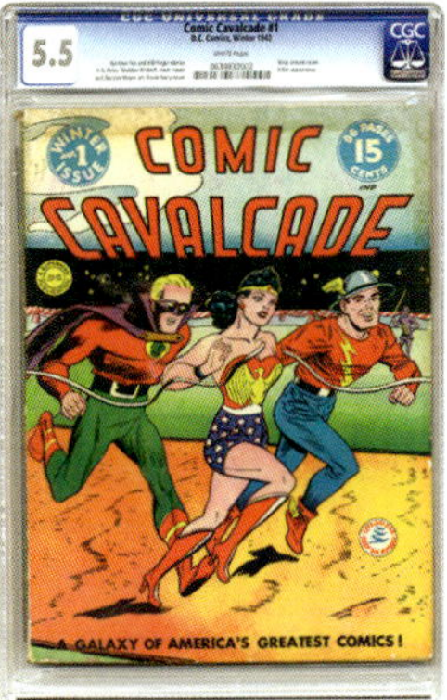

2108 Comic Cavalcade #1 (DC, 1942) CGC FN- 5.5 White pages. After **World's Finest** proved a success, DC brought out this companion title, a whopping 96-pager headlined (as were all the early issues) by stars Green Lantern, Wonder Woman, and the Flash... and don't miss the other half of the wraparound cover, which shows the supporting cast, including Wildcat and the Ghost Patrol. The issue's artists include Sheldon Moldoff (drawing the Black Pirate), Sheldon Mayer (drawing the semiautobiographical "Scribbly" feature), E. E. Hibbard (drawing the Flash) and H. G. Peter (drawing Wonder Woman). Overstreet 2005 FN 6.0 value = $2,805. CGC census 8/05: 1 in 5.5, 7 higher.

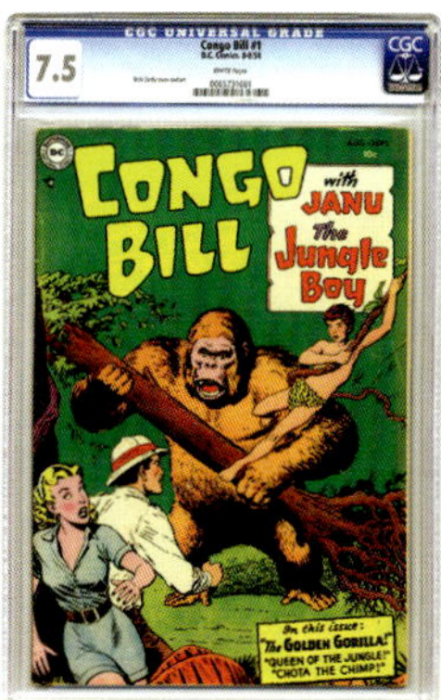

2109 Congo Bill #1 (DC, 1954) CGC VF- 7.5 White pages. A giant "Golden Gorilla" wrecks jungle havok on the Nick Cardy-drawn cover to this debut issue. All seven issues of this obscure DC title rank as "scarce" by Overstreet. This copy features great cover color and excellent page quality. Overstreet 2005 VF 8.0 value = $1,200. CGC census 7/05: 1 in 7.5, 1 higher.

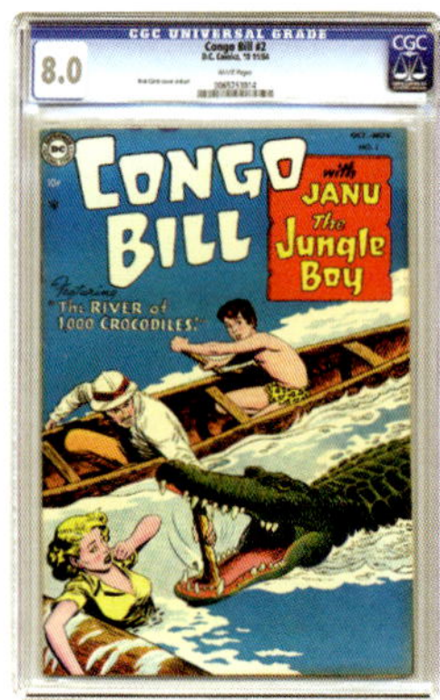

2110 Congo Bill #2 (DC, 1954) CGC VF 8.0 White pages. Bill comes to the rescue of a lovely lady in "the River of 1,000 Crocodiles!" Nick Cardy gets cover and interior art credit for this hard-to-find second issue. Overstreet 2005 VF 8.0 value = $880. CGC census 7/05: 2 in 8.0, none higher.

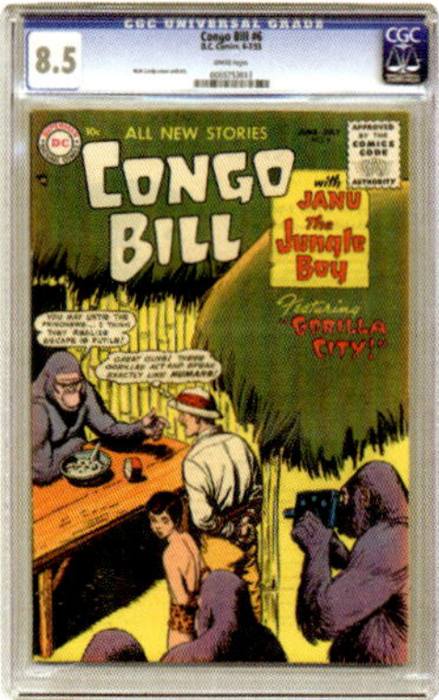

2111 Congo Bill #6 (DC, 1955) CGC VF+ 8.5 White pages. Bill and Janu the Jungle Boy encounter "Gorilla City" in this seldom-seen issue, featuring a nifty Nick Cardy cover and interior art. All seven issues of this title are considered so scarce, Overstreet doesn't even list values beyond VF 8.0! This attractive copy is topped only by the Mile High example (which is graded 9.0) in CGC's current listings. Overstreet 2005 VF 8.0 value = $680. CGC census 7/05: 1 in 8.5, 1 higher.

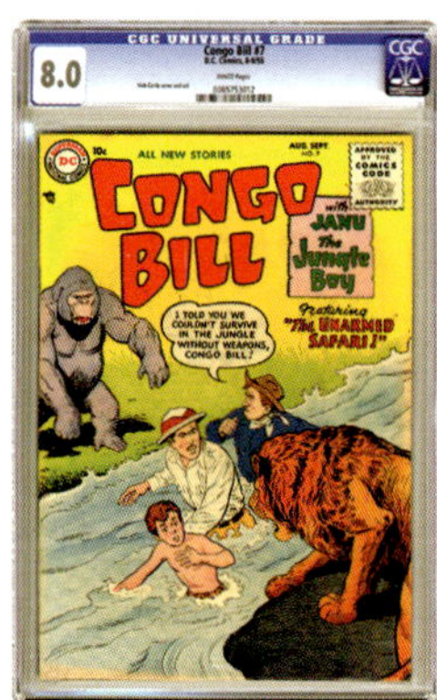

2112 Congo Bill #7 (DC, 1955) CGC VF 8.0 White pages. Here's the last issue of this scarce series, featuring art by DC titan Nick Cardy. Of the mere three copies currently certified by CGC, this one ranks highest by a long shot. It's a real keeper, even if you don't happen to specialize in collecting "gorilla covers" (but of course, who doesn't love DC's kooky simian stars?). Overstreet 2005 VF 8.0 value = $680. CGC census 7/05: 1 in 8.0, none higher.

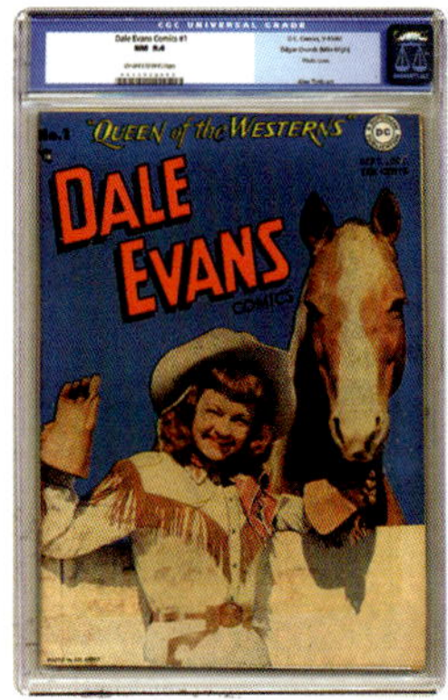

2113 Dale Evans Comics #1 Mile High pedigree (DC, 1948) CGC NM 9.4 Off-white to white pages. Dale Evans began a four-year DC run here, in a series that preceded her term as **Queen of the West** over at Dell. This premiere issue also has a Sierra Smith backup feature with Alex Toth art. Overstreet 2005 NM- 9.2 value = $1,250. CGC census 8/05: 1 in 9.4, none higher.

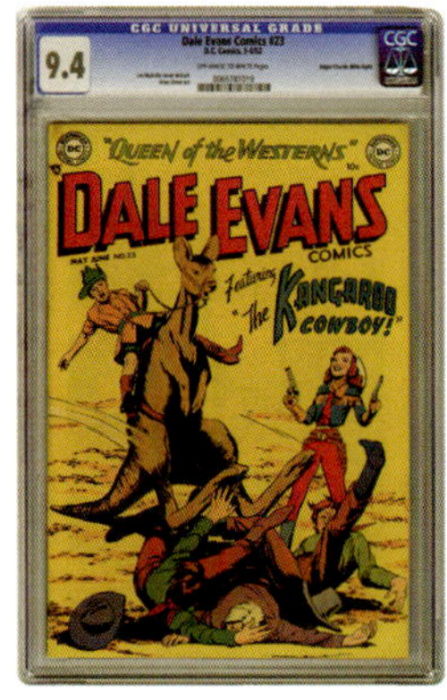

2114 Dale Evans Comics #23 Mile High pedigree (DC, 1952) CGC NM 9.4 Off-white to white pages. This Edgar Church copy of the next-to-last issue has to be the best available copy in existence. It's quite possibly the only Western comic to feature a kangaroo on the cover as well! You'll want to saddle up and hop off into the sunset if you miss out on this gem! Overstreet 2005 NM- 9.2 value = $200. CGC census 9/05: 1 in 9.4, none higher.

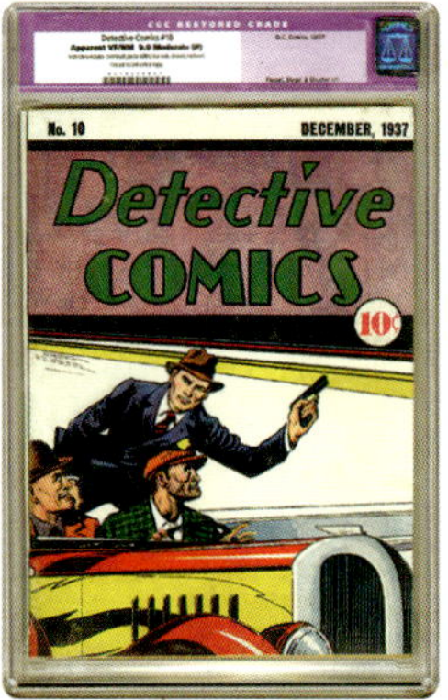

2115 Detective Comics #10 (DC, 1937) CGC Apparent VF/NM 9.0 Moderate (P) Cream to off-white pages. This pre-Golden Age DC issue sports a great Creig Flessel cover. The book's interior artists include Flessel, Joe Shuster, and Sven Elven. True detectives ruled the series in these pre-Batman days; featured characters included Slam Bradley, Speed Saunders, and Handcuff Hawkins. CGC notes, "Restoration includes: color touch, pieces added, tear seals, cleaned, reinforced." Overstreet 2005 GD 2.0 value = $688; VG 4.0 value = $1,376; FN 6.0 value = $2,064; VF 8.0 value = $3,440; VF/NM 9.0 value = $4,620.

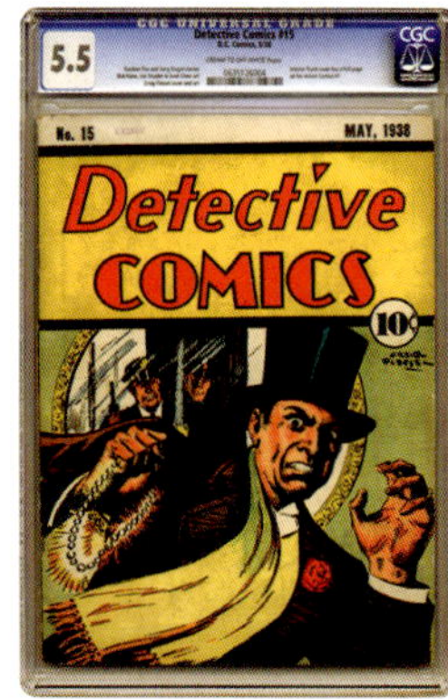

2116 Detective Comics #15 (DC, 1938) CGC FN- 5.5 Cream to off-white pages. An indication of just how early in the history of comics this issue was is the inside front cover — it's a full-page ad for **Action Comics** #1! And though Batman was still just a twinkle in Bob Kane's eye at this time, Kane was already contributing to **Detective** — he drew a one-page humor feature for this very issue. Other artists in the issue include Creig Flessel (who also drew the cover) and Joe Shuster (whose **Action** duties didn't keep him from penciling Spy and Slam Bradley stories here). Overstreet 2005 FN 6.0 value = 1,575. CGC census 9/05: 2 in 5.5, 1 higher.

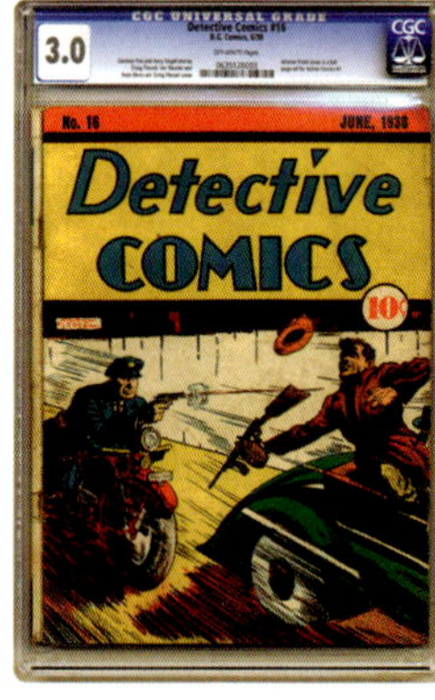

2117 Detective Comics #16 (DC, 1938) CGC GD/VG 3.0 Off-white pages. This early **Detective** boasts a great Creig Flessel cover. Flessel also contributed interior art, as did Joe Shuster, who teamed up with writer Jerry Siegel on the Slam Bradley story. Oh, speaking of that duo, the inside front cover of this book has a full-page ad for **Action Comics** #1, you may recall that Siegel and Shuster did some work for that one as well. Overstreet 2005 GD 2.0 value = $525; VG 4.0 value = $1,050. CGC census 9/05: 1 in 3.0, 5 higher.

2118 Detective Comics #26 (DC, 1939) Condition: PR. "The **Batman**! This new thrilling adventure strip starts in the May issue of **Detective Comics**! Don't miss it!" So reads the announcement at the top of a gag page, making this possibly the first printed mention of Batman. Note that this comic is complete, but it's somewhat brittle, with several staples added and tape repair all along the spine. Overstreet 2005 GD 2.0 value = $375.

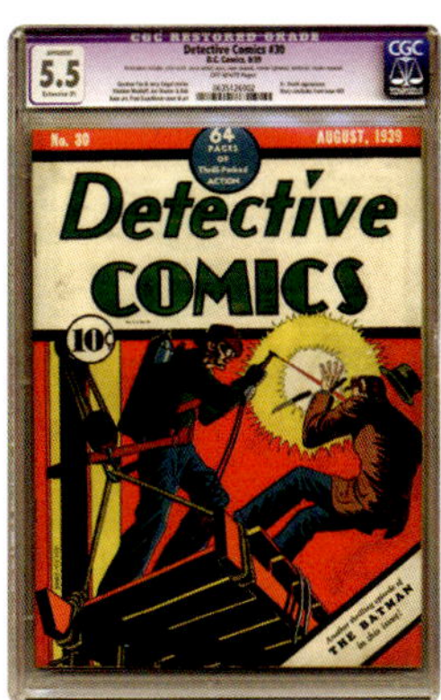

2119 Detective Comics #30 (DC, 1939) CGC Apparent FN- 5.5 Extensive (P) Off-white pages. This is the first time we've had a copy of this early Batman appearance! And the character's fourth outing already saw the start of some continuity; the previous issue's story had ended with the villainous Dr. Death apparently perishing in a fire, but in this issue he's back. Overstreet mentions the "classic Batman splash panel" — it's a grim Batman looming over the top third of the first page. Bob Kane collaborated with Sheldon Moldoff on the Batman story. Meanwhile, Jerry Siegel and Joe Shuster teamed up for a Slam Bradley adventure, and Fred Guardineer drew both a Speed Saunders story and the issue's dramatic cover. CGC notes, "Restoration includes: color touch, pieces added, seals, cover cleaned, interior lightened, reinforced, staples replaced." Overstreet 2005 GD 2.0 value = $710; VG 4.0 value = $1,420; FN 6.0 value = $2,130.

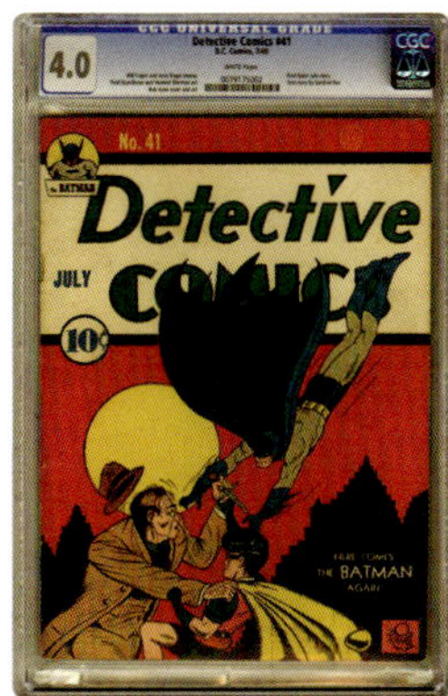

2120 Detective Comics #41 (DC, 1940) CGC VG 4.0 White pages. The modest overall grade assigned by CGC doesn't suggest the rich cover colors or page quality you will find with this offering. Robin's first solo adventure is featured, as is the art of Fred Guardineer, Howard Sherman, and co-creator Bob Kane, who also drew the cover. Overstreet 2005 VG 4.0 value = $690. CGC census 9/05: 2 in 4.0, 11 higher.

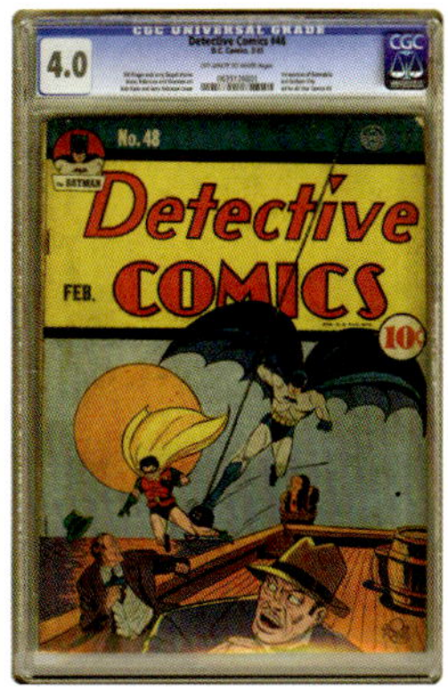

2121 Detective Comics #48 (DC, 1941) CGC VG 4.0 Off-white to white pages. Batman's creator Bob Kane drew this issue's cover with the help of able assistants Jerry Robinson and George Roussos. The same is true for the lead story inside the book. According to Overstreet, that Batman tale was the first time that the Batmobile was referred to as such! As for backup features, the usual Detective stalwarts (Slam Bradley, the Spy, Speed Saunders et al) are on hand. Overstreet 2005 VG 4.0 value = $462. CGC census 9/05: 2 in 4.0, 10 higher.

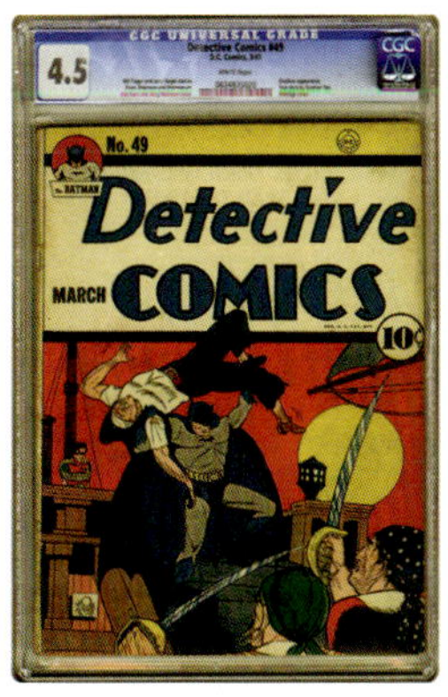

2122 Detective Comics #49 (DC, 1941) CGC VG+ 4.5 White pages. Clayface, made his last *Golden Age* appearance in this issue, but of course he's made quite a comeback in the intervening years! Bob Kane and Jerry Robinson saw to both the cover and the interior art. Overstreet 2005 VG 4.0 value = $462. CGC census 9/05: 2 in 4.5, 3 higher.

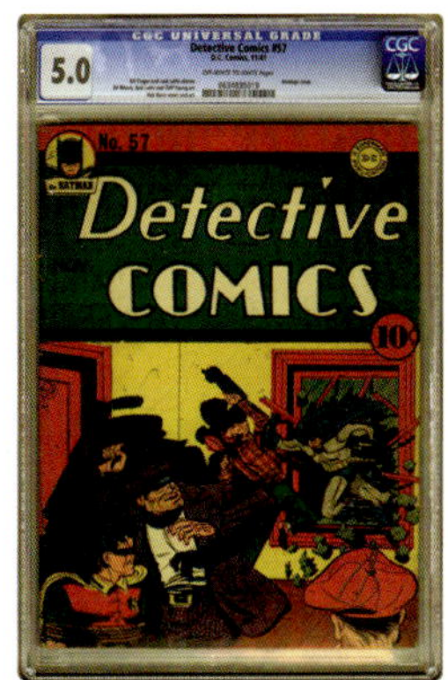

2123 Detective Comics #57 (DC, 1941) CGC VG/FN 5.0 Off-white to white pages. In this issue, the Darknight Detective tackles the case of two feuding brothers with a mind for murder, or as the thugs on Bob Kane's cover might put it, "moida!" OverstreetS 2005 VG 4.0 value = $308; FN 6.0 value = $462. CGC census 9/05: 1 in 5.0, 6 higher.

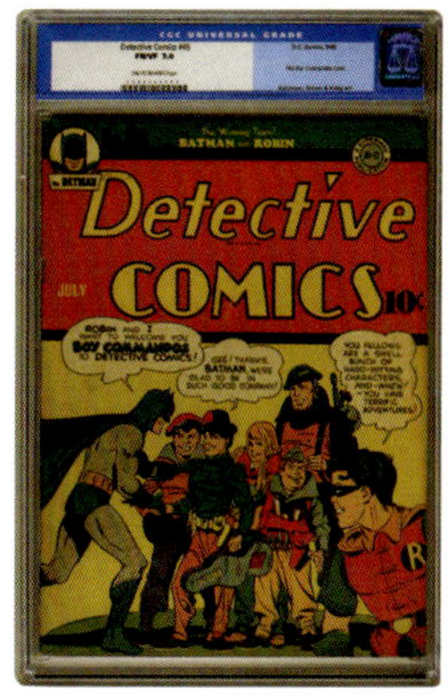

2124 Detective Comics #65 (DC, 1942) CGC FN/VF 7.0 Tan to off-white pages. This great cover was created by two noted teams - Joe Simon/Jack Kirby (on the Boy Commandos), and Fred Ray/Jerry Robinson (on Batman and Robin). Of further significance: it's the first cover featuring the Boy Commandos, and is presented here at the highest grade yet certified by CGC for issue #65. Overstreet 2005 FN 6.0 value = $900; VF 8.0 value = $1,925. CGC census 9/05: 3 in 7.0, 1 higher.

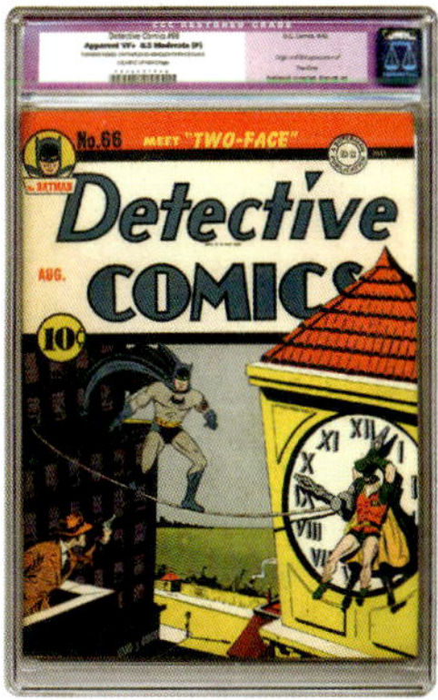

2125 Detective Comics #66 (DC, 1942) CGC Apparent VF+ 8.5 Moderate (P) Cream to off-white pages. The origin and first appearance of Two-Face makes this a key issue for anyone who loves those classic Batman villains. Jerry Robinson drew the cover as well as contributing interior art, and there's also a Boy Commandos story with art by the great Simon and Kirby. CGC notes, "Restoration includes: color touch, pieces added, spine reinforced, cleaned." Overstreet 2005 GD 2.0 value = $372; VG 4.0 value = $744; FN 6.0 value = $1,116; VF 8.0 value = $2,418; VF/NM 9.0 value = $3,909.

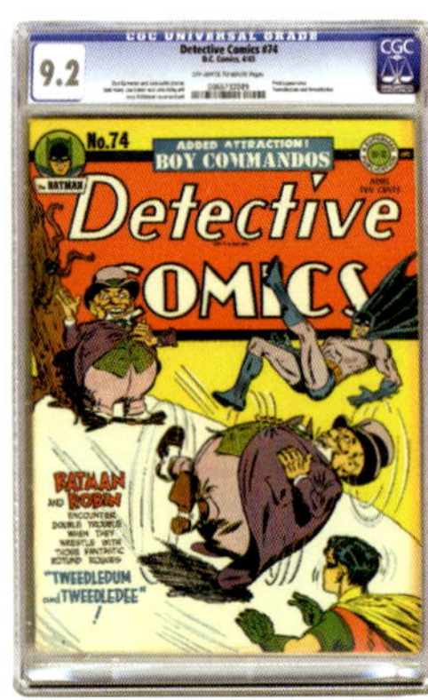

2126 Detective Comics #74 (DC, 1943) CGC NM- 9.2 Off-white to white pages. Tweedledum and Tweedledee, two lookalike cousins with a love for all things criminal, made their first appearance in this issue. Jerry Robinson drew the Dynamic Duo (and the Corpulent Duo) on the cover and inside the issue. The great condition of this copy makes it easy to forget it's a pretty early issue, so early that Batman still shared the book with a multitude of other features. The Boy Commandos (by Simon and Kirby, no less), Air Wave, Slam Bradley, and the Crimson Avenger are among the other features. Overstreet 2005 NM- 9.2 value = $1,425. CGC census 7/05: 1 in 9.2, 1 higher.

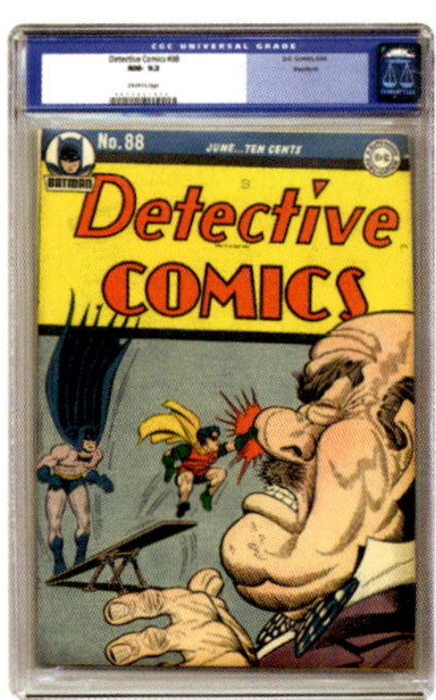

2127 Detective Comics #88 Rockford pedigree (DC, 1944) CGC NM- 9.2 Off-white pages. Bat-artist extraordinaire Dick Sprang handled art chores on both this cover and the accompanying story. The book's other detectives include Air Wave (drawn by George Roussos), the Crimson Avenger (drawn by John Daly), Slam Bradley (drawn by Martin Naydel) and the Boy Commandos (drawn by Louis Cazeneuve). Overstreet 2005 NM- 9.2 value = $1,200. CGC census 7/05: 1 in 9.2, 2 higher.

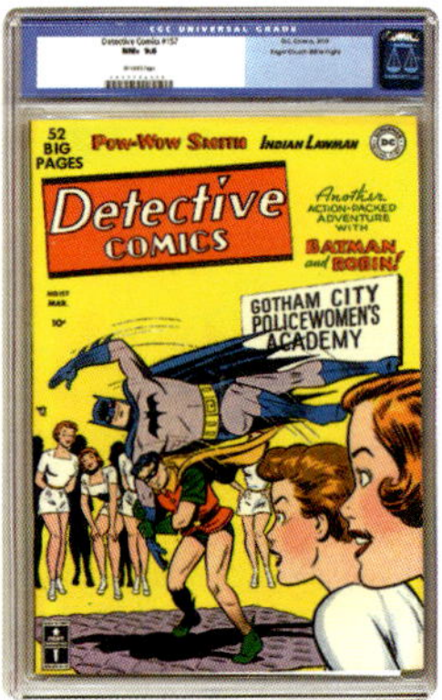

2128 Detective Comics #157 Mile High pedigree (DC, 1950) CGC NM+ 9.6 Off-white pages. Have a look at the bright yellows on the front and back covers of this beaut. Speaking of beauties, this is about as close to a "good girl" **Detective** cover as you're going to find (it's by Win Mortimer). In addition to a Batman tale, this issue has an adventure of Pow-Wow Smith, Indian Lawman, drawn by Carmine Infantino. Overstreet 2005 NM- 9.2 value = $800. CGC census 8/05: 1 in 9.6, none higher.

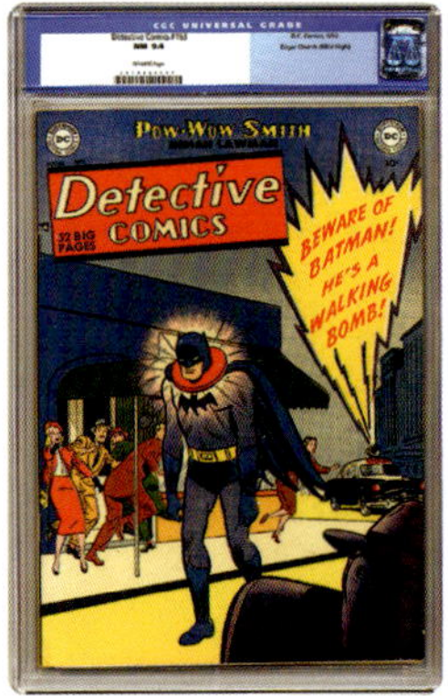

2129 Detective Comics #163 Mile High pedigree (DC, 1950) CGC NM 9.4 Off-white pages. We're fortunate enough to have oodles of **Detective** issues in our auctions, but this is the first time we've gotten our finned gloves on a copy of #163 — have a look at the unusual Win Mortimer cover! In addition to the Batman story (with Jim Mooney art), there's a bunch of other characters including Pow-Wow Smith and Dover and Clover. This is the only copy of this issue to be certified with a grade above 8.0 to date. Overstreet 2005 NM- 9.2 value = $725. CGC census 8/05: 1 in 9.4, none higher.

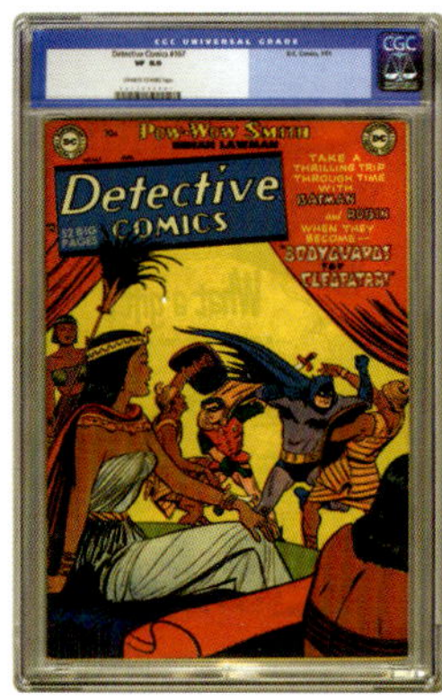

2130 Detective Comics #167 (DC, 1951) CGC VF 8.0 Off-white to white pages. Why the heck does an ancient Egyptian frieze have a picture of the Bat-Signal? It's reason enough for Batman and Robin to have their pal Carter Nichols send them back in time to investigate. And wouldn't you know it, they meet Cleopatra — Caesar and Marc Antony can't hold a candle to Batman and Robin! Pow-Wow Smith and Robotman star in backup features. The cover art is by Win Mortimer. Overstreet 2005 VF 8.0 value = $350. CGC census 9/05: 1 in 8.0, 3 higher.

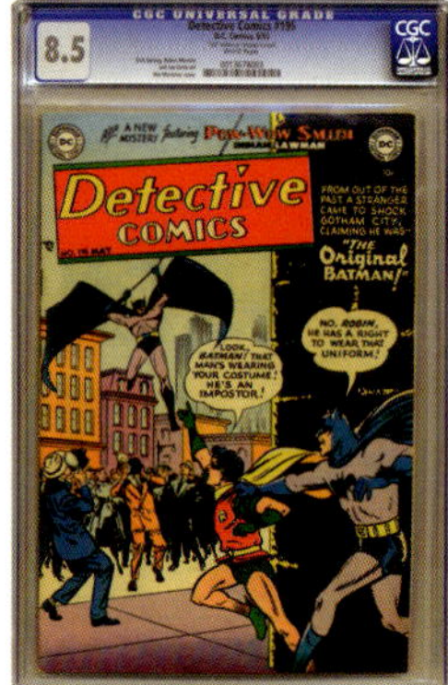

2131 Detective Comics #195 (DC, 1953) CGC VF+ 8.5 White pages. There's Batman, there's "the Bat-Man" (circa **Detective** #27), and then there's "Bat Man," a circus performer who says he had the name and costume before our favorite superhero even got started! Grounds for a lawsuit? No, but more than sufficient grounds for an entertaining yarn drawn by Dick Sprang. Backup features include Robotman and Pow-Wow Smith. The cover's by Win Mortimer. No copy of this issue has been graded higher by CGC to date. CGC notes, "'150' written on 1st page in pencil." Overstreet 2005 VF 8.0 value = $317; VF/NM 9.0 value = $484. CGC census 9/05: 1 in 8.5, none higher.

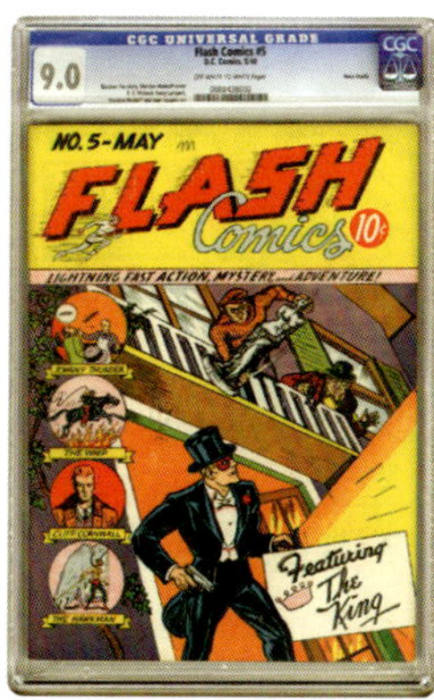

2132 Flash Comics #5 Nova Scotia pedigree (DC, 1940) CGC VF/NM 9.0 Off-white to white pages. "King" Standish, aka the King, appeared in this title for years, but this was the one and only time he was the main cover feature! That's him about to get the Venus De Milo conked on his head on Jon Blummer's cover. Also appearing are the Flash (naturally), Hawkman, Johnny Thunder, and many more. Sheldon Moldoff drew both the Hawkman and Cliff Cornwall features. Overstreet 2005 VF/NM 9.0 value = $3,622; NM- 9.2 value = $5,000. CGC census 8/05: 3 in 9.0, none higher.

2133 Flash Comics #7 (DC, 1940) CGC Qualified VG- 3.5 Off-white pages. Sheldon Moldoff's first Hawkman cover. Moldoff and E. E. Hibbard art. CGC notes, "Centerfold missing. Affects story. Incomplete." Overstreet 2005 GD 2.0 value = $439; VG 4.0 value = $878.

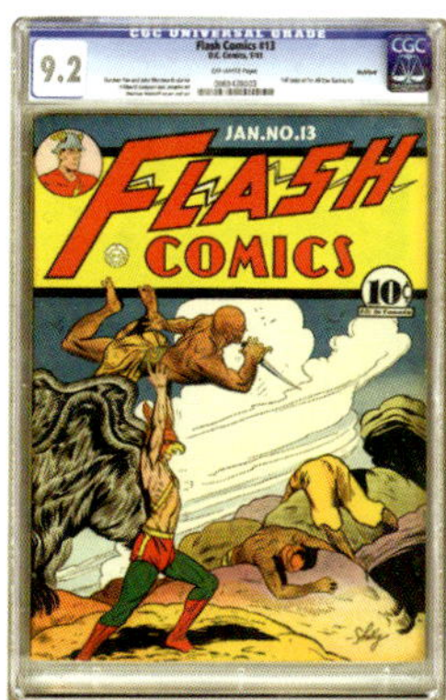

2134 Flash Comics #13 Rockford pedigree (DC, 1941) CGC NM- 9.2 Off-white pages. This copy tops CGC's current census report by a healthy margin; it's the only one graded above 8.0 as of this writing. We hadn't seen this particular issue before here at Heritage; we were missing out on a sensational Sheldon Moldoff cover! Moldoff drew Hawkman inside the issue as well. The Flash, Johnny Thunder, and many others also appear. Overstreet 2005 NM- 9.2 value = $2,700. CGC census 8/05: 1 in 9.2, none higher.

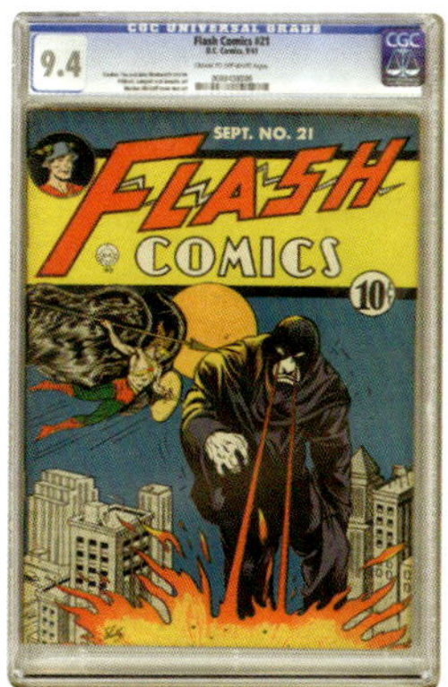

2135 Flash Comics #21 (DC, 1941) CGC NM 9.4 Cream to off-white pages. Sheldon Moldoff drew this issue's Hawkman cover as well as the story starring that Winged Wonder. Other characters in the issue include the Flash, Hawkman, the Whip, and "King" Standish. And saving the best news for last, no copy of this issue has been graded higher by CGC to date. Overstreet 2005 NM- 9.2 value = $2,650. CGC census 8/05: 2 in 9.4, none higher.

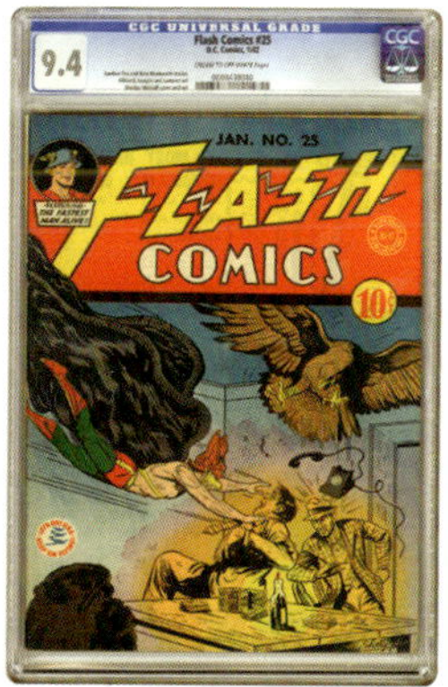

2136 Flash Comics #25 (DC, 1942) CGC NM 9.4 Cream to off-white pages. This copy soars above the others in CGC's census — it's the only copy of the issue graded above 8.5 as of this writing. Sheldon Moldoff drew the cover as well as the Hawkman story inside the issue. Other heroes on hand are the Flash (drawn by E. E. Hibbard), King Standish (drawn by Harry Lampert) and that humorous klutz, Johnny Thunder. Overstreet 2005 NM- 9.2 value = $1,550. CGC census 8/05: 1 in 9.4, none higher.

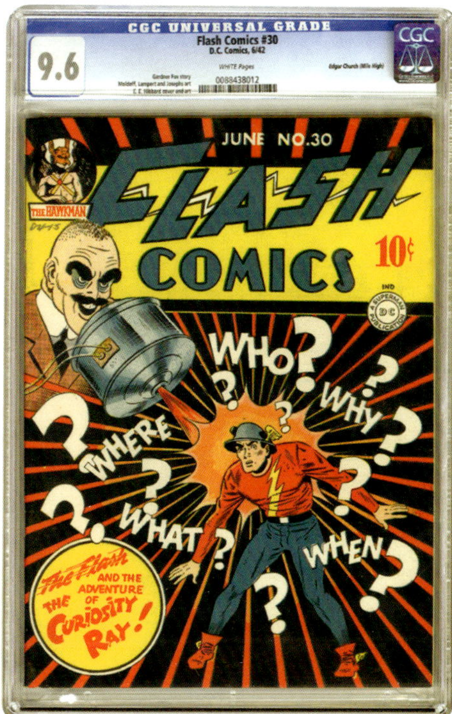

2137 Flash Comics #30 Mile High pedigree (DC, 1942) CGC NM+ 9.6 White pages. Edgar Church's collection produced this gem, the highest-graded copy of the issue that CGC has certified to date. The issue stars the Flash (drawn by E. E. Hibbard on the cover and inside the comic), Hawkman (drawn by Sheldon Moldoff), and Johnny Thunder. Overstreet 2005 NM- 9.2 value = $1,550. CGC census 8/05: 1 in 9.6, none higher.

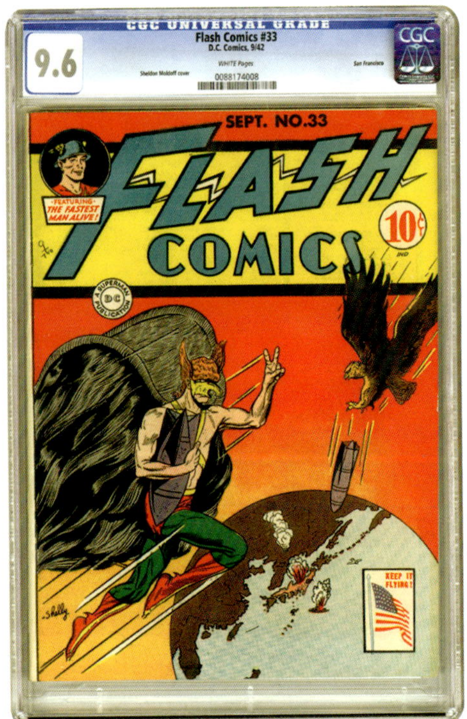

2138 Flash Comics #33 San Francisco pedigree (DC, 1942) CGC NM+ 9.6 White pages. This issue's memorable war cover is called "classic" by Overstreet — the Japanese war scene is the work of Sheldon Moldof, who also drew the Hawkman story inside the issue. The Flash, Johnny Thunder, and others also appear. This copy from the famed Tom Reilly collection is the highest-graded copy of the issue that CGC has certified to date. Overstreet 2005 NM- 9.2 value = $1,550. CGC census 8/05: 1 in 9.6, none higher.

2139 Flash Comics #39 San Francisco pedigree (DC, 1943) CGC NM 9.4 White pages. Sheldon Moldoff drew this issue's cover — check out Shiera Sanders letting her hair down! In addition to the Hawkman story drawn by Moldoff, there are also tales of the Flash, Johnny Thunder and others. As of this writing, this San Francisco treat is the only high-grade copy of the issue in CGC's current census — the only one graded above 6.5, in fact! Overstreet 2005 NM- 9.2 value = $1,425. CGC census 8/05: 1 in 9.4, none higher.

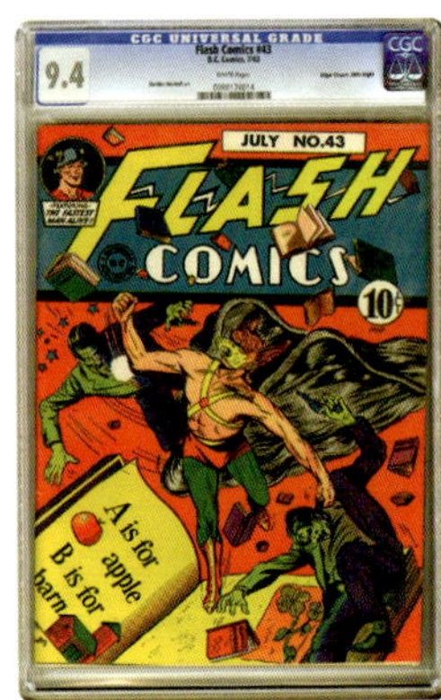

2140 Flash Comics #43 Mile High pedigree (DC, 1943) CGC NM 9.4 White pages. Sheldon Moldoff drew Hawkman both on this issue's cover and inside the comic. The unusual cover scene involving a child's primer ties into the story "Crime's First Reader." Hawkman isn't the only hero here who's mastered the ABCs of kicking butt — the Flash, Johnny Thunder, and other crimefighters also appear. Overstreet 2005 NM- 9.2 value = $1,250. CGC census 8/05: 2 in 9.4, 1 higher.

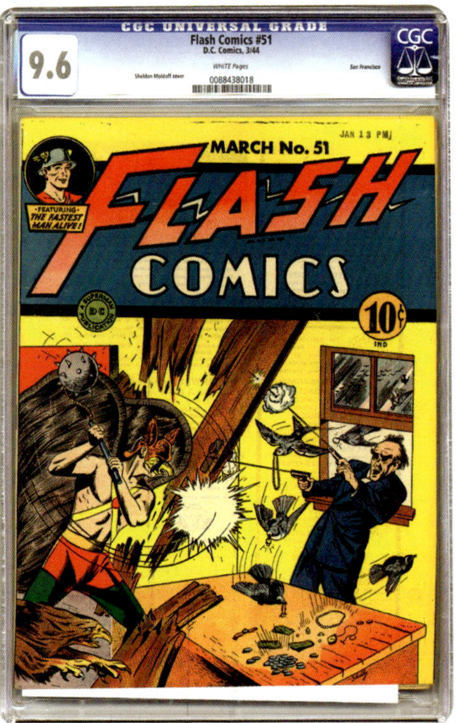

2141 Flash Comics #51 San Francisco pedigree (DC, 1944) CGC NM+ 9.6 White pages. No doubt you recognize the distinctive style of Sheldon Moldoff on this issue's cover — the question of whether "Shelly" or Joe Kubert is the best Hawkman artist would be an occasion for spirited debate. As usual, the Winged Wonder is joined by Flash and Johnny Thunder inside the comic. Overstreet 2005 NM- 9.2 value = $1,125. CGC census 9/05: 1 in 9.6, none higher.

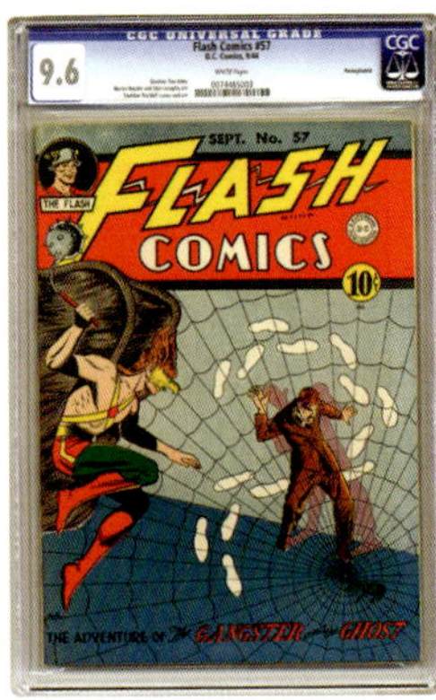

2142 Flash Comics #57 Pennsylvania pedigree (DC, 1944) CGC NM+ 9.6 White pages. The Pennsylvania collection hasn't gotten as much publicity as some of the other pedigrees, but you'll be a believer once you've had a look at this copy. The issue has a Sheldon Moldoff cover, with interior art by Moldoff (Hawkman), Martin Naydel (the Flash), and Stan Aschmeier (Johnny Thunder). Overstreet 2005 NM- 9.2 value = $1,125. CGC census 8/05: 1 in 9.6, 1 higher.

2143 Flash Comics #71 Pennsylvania pedigree (DC, 1946) CGC NM 9.4 White pages. Joe Kubert drew Hawkman both on the cover and in the accompanying story. The Winged Wonder is joined by the Flash and Johnny Thunder in the issue. Overstreet 2005 NM- 9.2 value = $1,000. CGC census 8/05: 1 in 9.4, none higher.

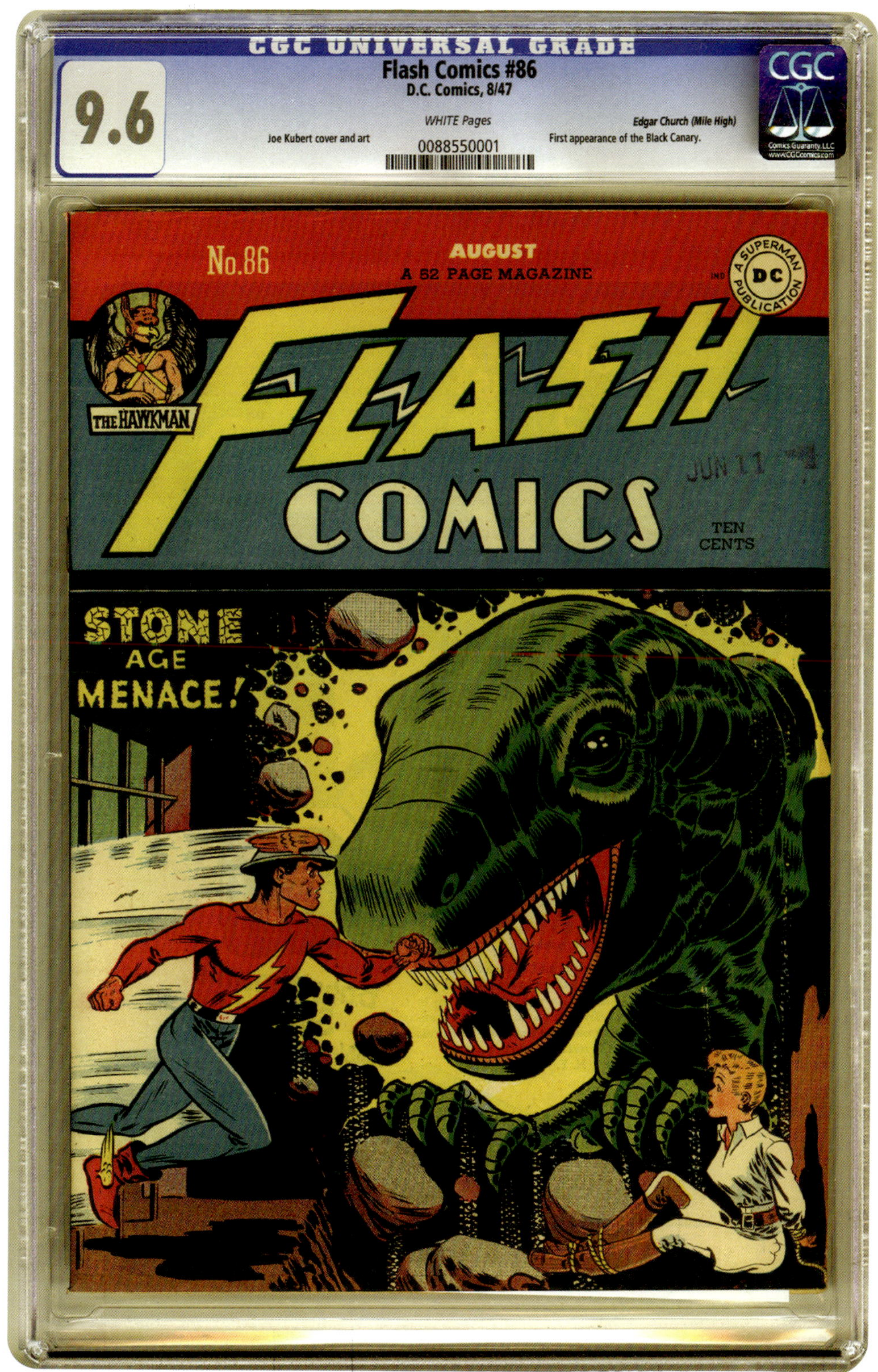

2144 Flash Comics #86 Mile High pedigree (DC, 1947) CGC NM+ 9.6 White pages. The first appearance of the Black Canary makes this an issue that stands out from the rest in this later part of the title's run. She debuts in the Johnny Thunder feature, and when we first see her she's persuading a lovestruck Johnny to steal for her! But even here it's left in doubt whether she's a villainess or a heroine, as the people she steals from are shown to be crooks themselves. The story's by the character's co-creators, writer Robert Kanigher and artist Carmine Infantino. The issue also boasts a Hawkman story with Joe Kubert art and cover art by Lee Elias. This is the only copy graded above 8.0 by CGC as of this writing. Overstreet 2005 NM- 9.2 value = $3,700. CGC census 7/05: 1 in 9.6, none higher.

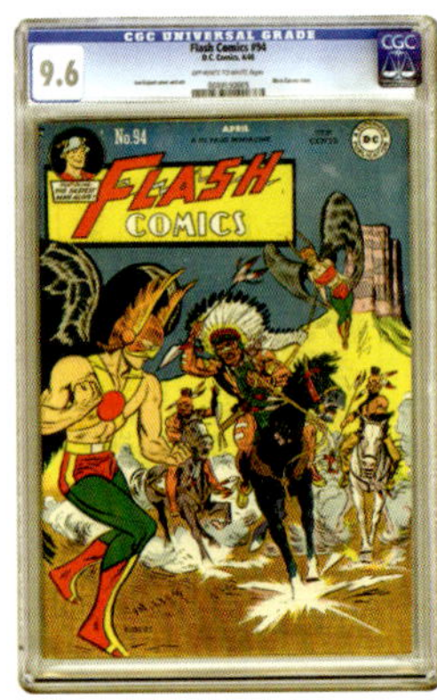

2145 Flash Comics #94 (DC, 1948) CGC NM+ 9.6 Off-white to white pages. An outstanding array of big-name artists awaits the winning bidder for this book: try Joe Kubert (Hawkman, on the cover and inside), Lee Elias (the Flash), Bernard Krigstein (the Atom), Bob Oksner (Ghost Patrol), and Carmine Infantino (Black Canary)! This is the highest-graded copy of this issue that CGC has certified to date. Overstreet 2005 NM- 9.2 value = $1,700. CGC census 8/05: 1 in 9.6, none higher.

2146 Flash Comics #100 (DC, 1948) CGC VF 8.0 Off-white pages. This issue's "scarce" according to Overstreet. Joe Kubert drew the cover as well as the Hawkman story, featuring one of the character's earliest appearances in his new costume. CGC has awarded a higher grade to just one other copy of #100 to date. Also featured are the Flash, Black Canary, the Atom, and the Ghost Patrol. Overstreet 2005 VF 8.0 value = $1,892. CGC census 9/05: 3 in 8.0, 1 higher.

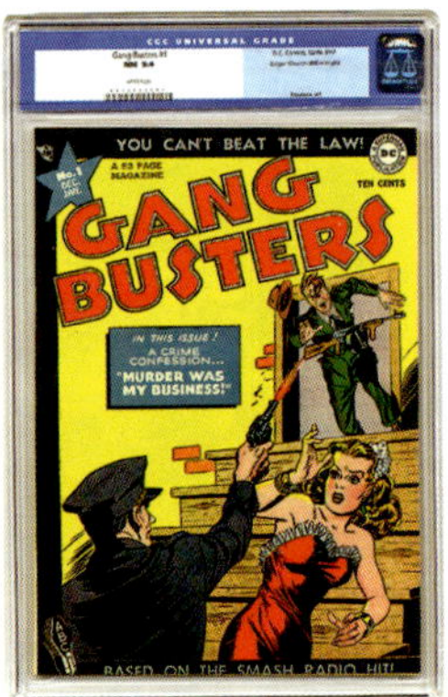

2147 Gang Busters #1 Mile High pedigree (DC, 1947) CGC NM 9.4 White pages. Our Mile High specimen is the highest-graded copy of this issue in CGC's census report as of this writing; given the comic's black border, don't expect a better one to come along! Note that the date on the CGC slab is incorrect; the comic is actually dated December 1947/January 1948. Overstreet 2005 NM- 9.2 value = $1,150. CGC census 8/05: 1 in 9.4, none higher.

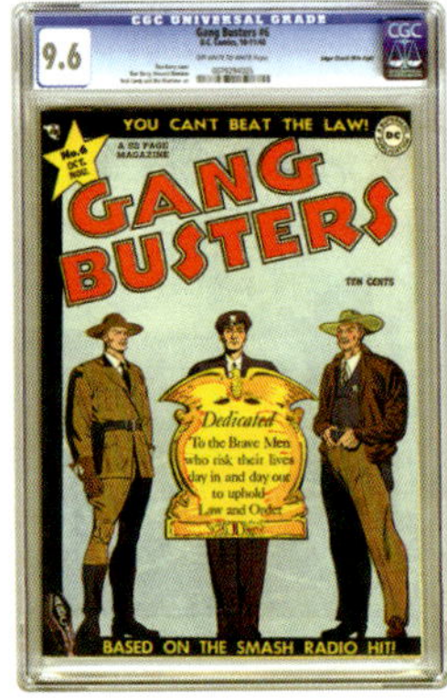

2148 Gang Busters #6 Mile High pedigree (DC, 1948) CGC NM+ 9.6 Off-white to white pages. A whole "gang" of good artists contributed to this issue: Dan Barry, Howard Sherman, Nick Cardy and Win Mortimer all drew stories, with Barry rendering the cover. The comic is of course a tie-in with the radio show of the same name. This is the highest-graded copy overall, and the only one graded above 8.5, that CGC has certified to date. Overstreet 2005 NM- 9.2 value = $275. CGC census 9/05: 1 in 9.6, none higher.

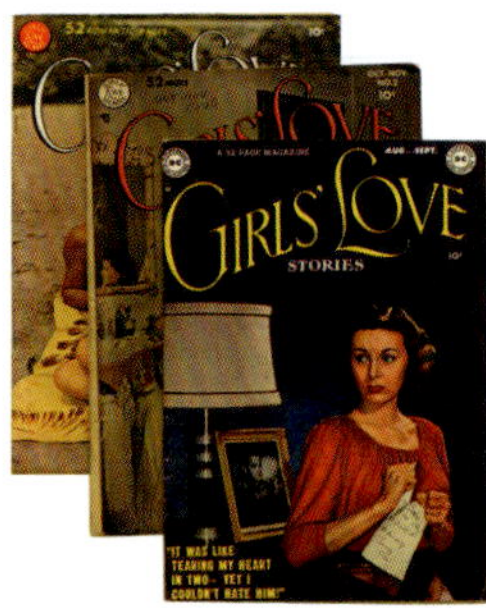

2149 Girls' Love Stories Group (DC, 1949-54) Condition: Average FN-. Included here are #1, 2, 3, 4, 9, 10, 11, 12, 14, 15, and 29. Most have photo covers. Artists include Alex Toth and Everett Raymond Kinstler. Approximate Overstreet value for group = $675.

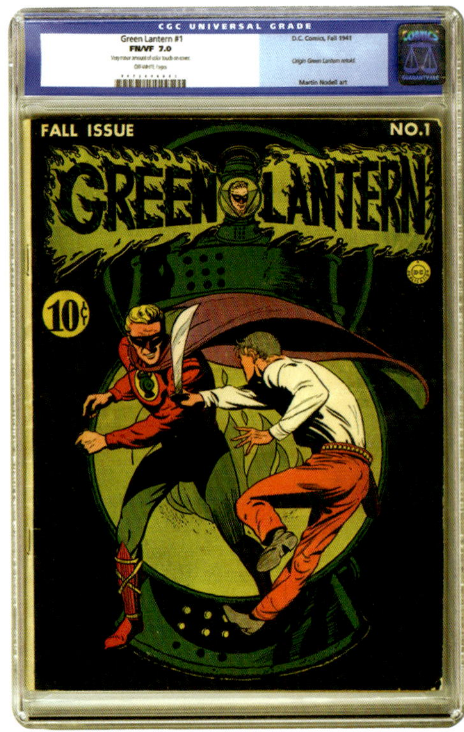

2150 Green Lantern #1 (DC, 1941) CGC FN/VF 7.0 Off-white pages. This issue's one of the most valuable DC comics. In fact, it's listed among the 20 most valuable comic books of all by Overstreet. This issue's story retells the origin of Alan Scott, the Golden Age GL, for kids who might have missed his earliest appearances in the pages of **All-American Comics**. GL's creator Martin Nodell drew the stories, Bill Finger supplied the scripts, and the cover is by Howard Purcell. CGC notes, "Very minor amount of color touch on cover." Overstreet 2005 FN 6.0 value = $8,925; VF 8.0 value = $23,800. CGC census 9/05: 5 in 7.0, 7 higher.

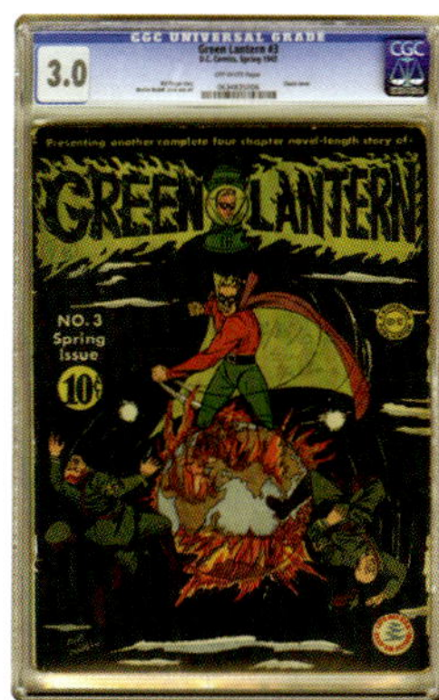

2151 Green Lantern #3 (DC, 1942) CGC GD/VG 3.0 Off-white pages. This issue's Martin Nodell cover earned Overstreet's "classic" designation. All of the interior art is also by Nodell, the character's creator. Overstreet 2005 GD 2.0 value = $484; VG 4.0 value = $968. CGC census 9/05: 1 in 3.0, 8 higher.

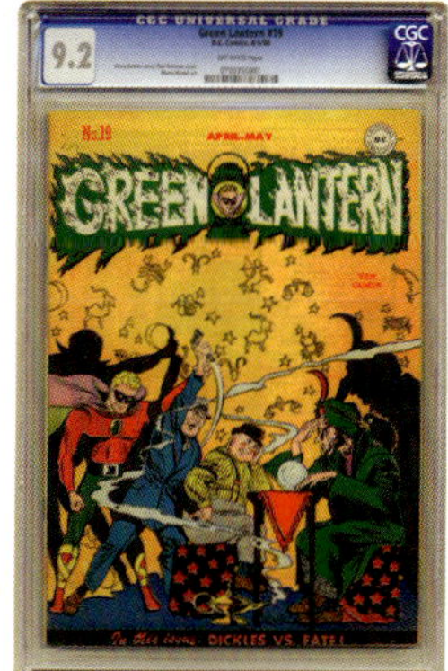

2152 Green Lantern #19 (DC, 1946) CGC NM- 9.2 Off-white pages. Looks like Doiby's in trouble again — good thing he's best pals with Green Lantern! This attractive copy is heavy on the eye-appeal, with great cover colors and a cool zodiac cover illustration by Paul Reinman. Inside, there's work by the original GL artist, Martin Nodell. This clean copy is topped by only one higher in the current CGC census. Overstreet 2005 NM- 9.2 value = $1,750. CGC census 9/05: 1 in 9.2, 1 higher.

2153 House of Mystery #3 Spokane pedigree (DC, 1952) CGC VF/NM 9.0 White pages. Decades before Chucky of "Child's Play" came along, this haunted dummy on this Bob Brown cover gave kids nightmares! The book's interior stories were drawn by Ruben Moreira, George Roussos, and Curt Swan. Overstreet 2005 VF/NM 9.0 value = $628; NM- 9.2 value = $850. CGC census 9/05: 3 in 9.0, 2 higher.

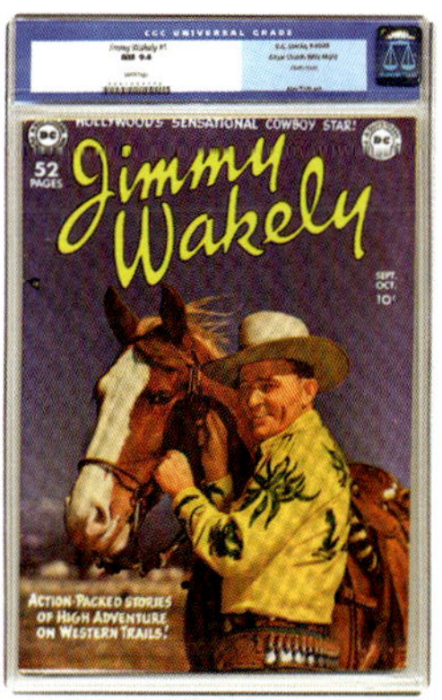

2154 Jimmy Wakely #1 Mile High pedigree (DC, 1949) CGC NM 9.4 White pages. Every time we'd seen this issue before, it was a well-thumbed "reading copy," so it's quite a pleasure to offer a NM Mile High. The title character benefited from Alex Toth art, while backup feature "Kit Colby, Girl Sheriff" has the work of Carmine Infantino. Overstreet 2005 NM- 9.2 value = $1,450. CGC census 8/05: 1 in 9.4, none higher.

2155 Jimmy Wakely #11 (DC, 1951) CGC VF+ 8.5 Cream to off-white pages. Gil Kane cover. Kane, Alex Toth, and Carmine Infantino art. This is the only copy of the issue that CGC has certified as of this writing. Overstreet 2005 VF 8.0 value = $222; VF/NM 9.0 value = $324. CGC census 8/05: 1 in 8.5, none higher.

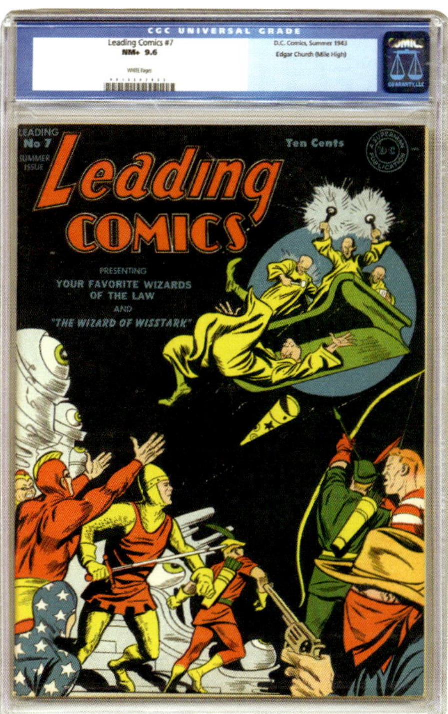

2156 Leading Comics #7 Mile High pedigree (DC, 1943) CGC NM+ 9.6 White pages. Our Edgar Church copy is the only one graded above 8.0 as of this writing, and the comic's black cover probably has a lot to do with that. The *eight* heroes on the cover are known as the *Seven* Soldiers of Victory, with the eighth member being the Crimson Avenger's sidekick Wing. The issue has a Jon Smalle cover and Pierce Rice art. Overstreet 2005 NM- 9.2 value = $1,025. CGC census 8/05: 1 in 9.6, none higher.

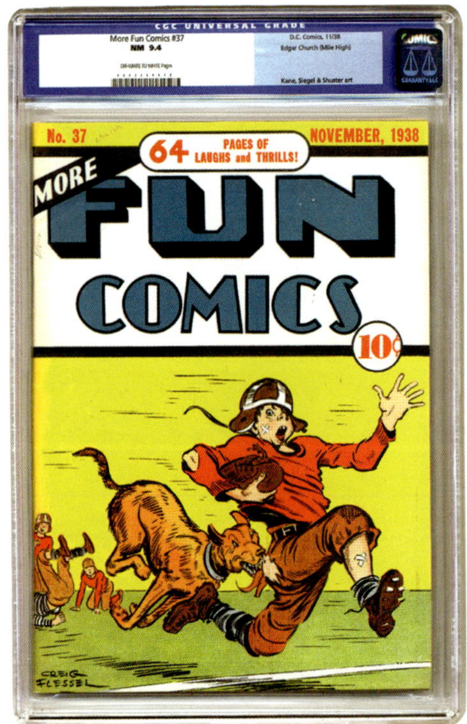

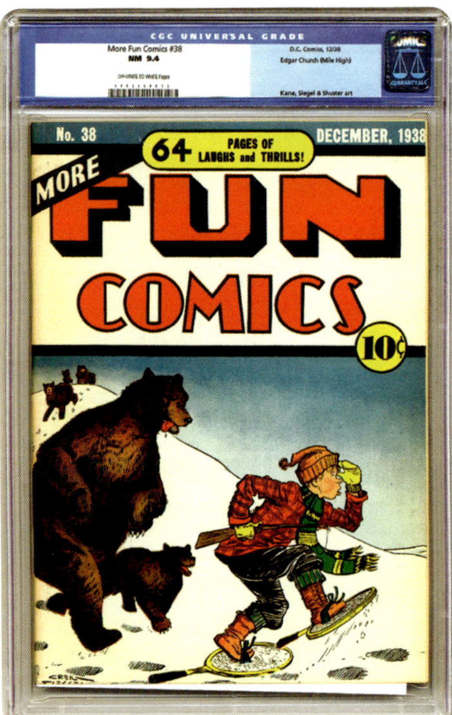

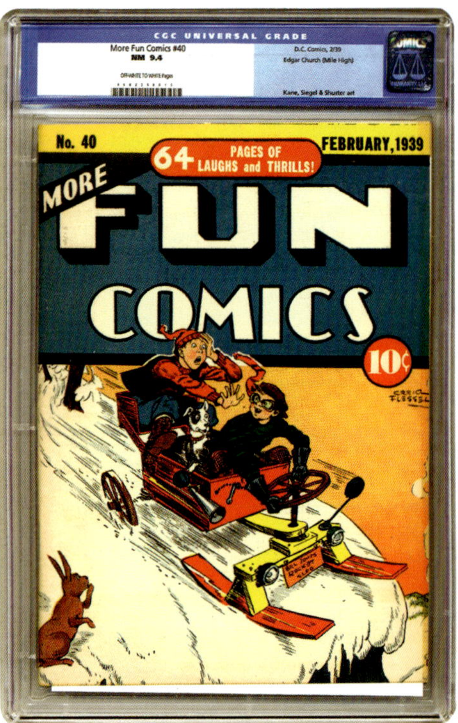

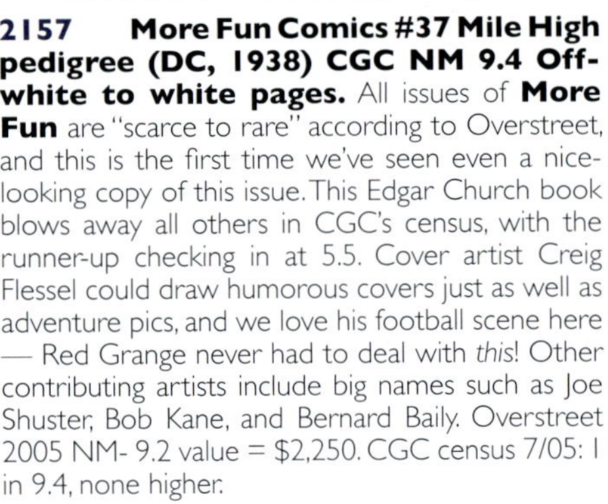

2157 More Fun Comics #37 Mile High pedigree (DC, 1938) CGC NM 9.4 Off-white to white pages. All issues of **More Fun** are "scarce to rare" according to Overstreet, and this is the first time we've seen even a nice-looking copy of this issue. This Edgar Church book blows away all others in CGC's census, with the runner-up checking in at 5.5. Cover artist Creig Flessel could draw humorous covers just as well as adventure pics, and we love his football scene here — Red Grange never had to deal with *this*! Other contributing artists include big names such as Joe Shuster, Bob Kane, and Bernard Baily. Overstreet 2005 NM- 9.2 value = $2,250. CGC census 7/05: 1 in 9.4, none higher.

2158 More Fun Comics #38 Mile High pedigree (DC, 1938) CGC NM 9.4 Off-white to white pages. This is the only unrestored copy of this tough-to-find issue that CGC has certified to date. Considering the December 1938 cover date, it's amazing that any of these were saved at all, never mind in such nice condition! This one's especially remarkable because the pre-1940 Edgar Church copies aren't always in the outstanding condition that characterizes the later books. No worries here, as this 9.4 copy has everything you could hope for. The comic has a Creig Flessel cover; the mix of interior features includes the Radio Squad by Jerry Siegel and Joe Shuster, the Buccaneer by Bernard Baily, a gag feature by Bob Kane, and much more. Overstreet 2005 NM- 9.2 value = $2,250. CGC census 7/05: 1 in 9.4, none higher.

2159 More Fun Comics #40 Mile High pedigree (DC, 1939) CGC NM 9.4 Off-white to white pages. Not only is this the only copy of this issue we've seen to date, it's the only copy that has been submitted to CGC for certification. No wonder Overstreet says "all issues are scarce to rare," and Gerber gave issue #40 a "7" rating. The issue's cover is by Creig Flessel, who could do humor scenes just as well as adventure fare! There's Flessel interior art in the issue as well, plus the Buccaneer by Bernard Baily, Radio Squad by Jerry Siegel and Joe Shuster, and a humor feature by Bob Kane. Overstreet 2005 NM- 9.2 value = $2,250. CGC census 9/05: 1 in 9.4, none higher.

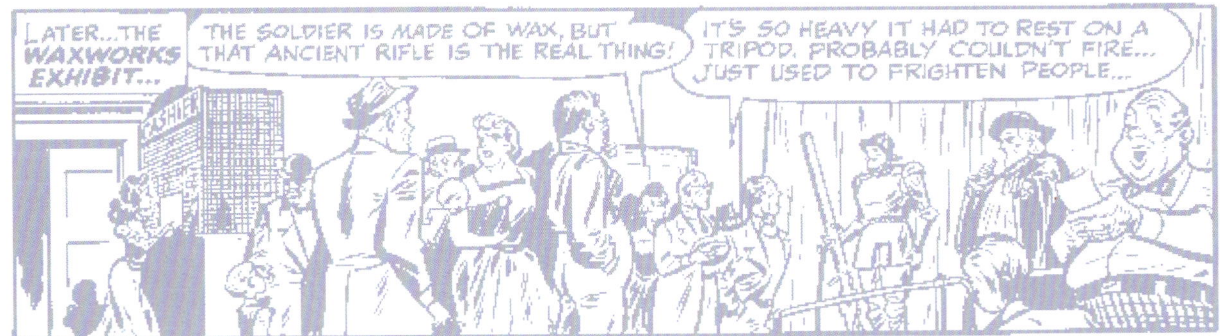

2160 More Fun Comics #46 (DC, 1939) CGC Apparent GD/VG 3.0 Slight (P) Cream to off-white pages. This book contains a full page ad of the 1939 New York World's Fair comic. Cover by Creig Flessel. Interior art by Joe Shuster, Bernard Baily, and Jack Lehti. CGC notes, "Restoration includes: color touch, cover cleaned, staples replaced. (3 edges trimmed, 12 pieces of tape on cover and centerfold)" Overstreet 2005 GD 2.0 value = $212; VG 4.0 value = $424.

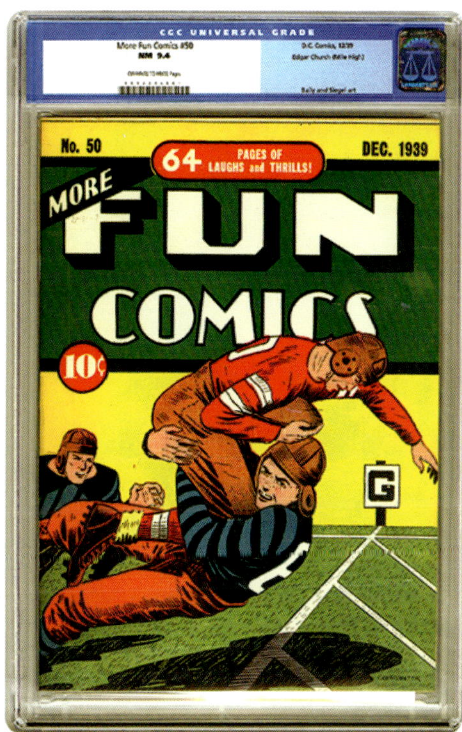

2161 More Fun Comics #50 Mile High pedigree (DC, 1939) CGC NM 9.4 Off-white to white pages. The early issues of **More Fun** often featured sports-oriented covers like this issue's football scene. This would turn out to be the last such cover; after one more non-heroic issue, the Spectre took over as cover feature. One of the highly-treasured Edgar Church Mile High books, this one lives up to its reputation — it's a champion copy all the way! Of the three unrestored copies currently listed by CGC, this one is miles above the next-best example, which rates a 7.5 grade. Overstreet 2005 NM- 9.2 value = $2,000. CGC census 8/05: 1 in 9.4, none higher.

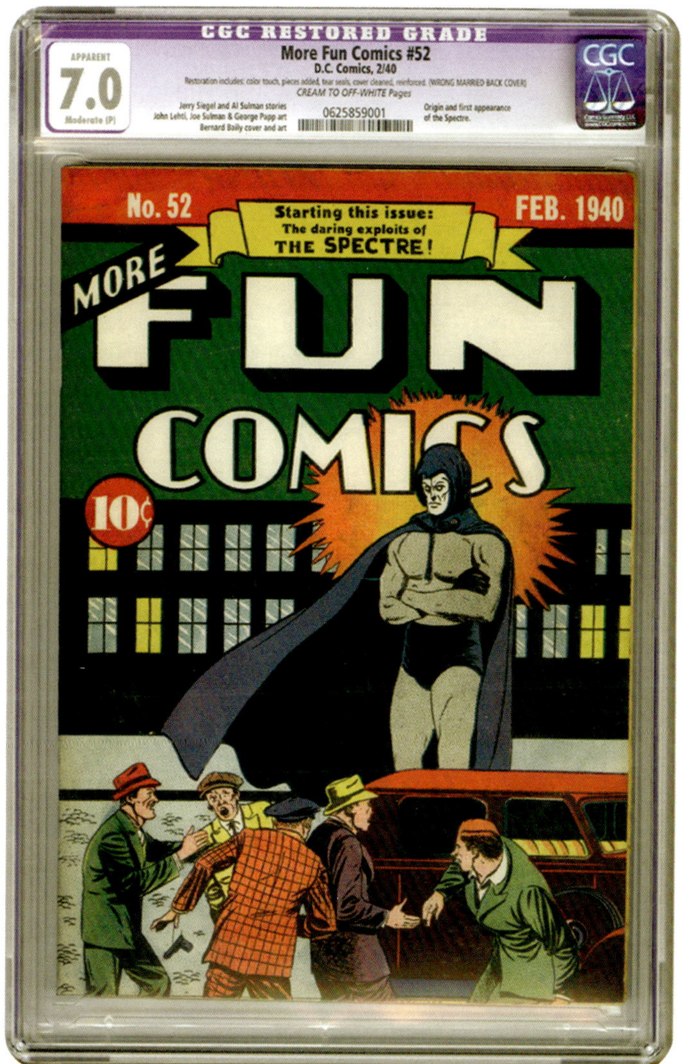

2162 More Fun Comics #52 (DC, 1940) CGC Apparent FN/VF 7.0 Moderate (P) Cream to off-white pages. This book contains the origin and first appearance of the Spectre, who is in costume in the first splash panel. Spectre cover by Bernard Baily. Stories by Jerry Siegel and Al Sulman, with interior art by Baily, John Lehti, Joe Sulman, and George Papp. CGC notes, "Restoration includes: color touch, pieces added, tear seals, cover cleaned, reinforced. (Wrong married back cover)" Overstreet 2005 GD 2.0 value = $5,350; VG 4.0 value = $10,700; FN 6.0 value = $16,050; VF 8.0 value = $40,400.

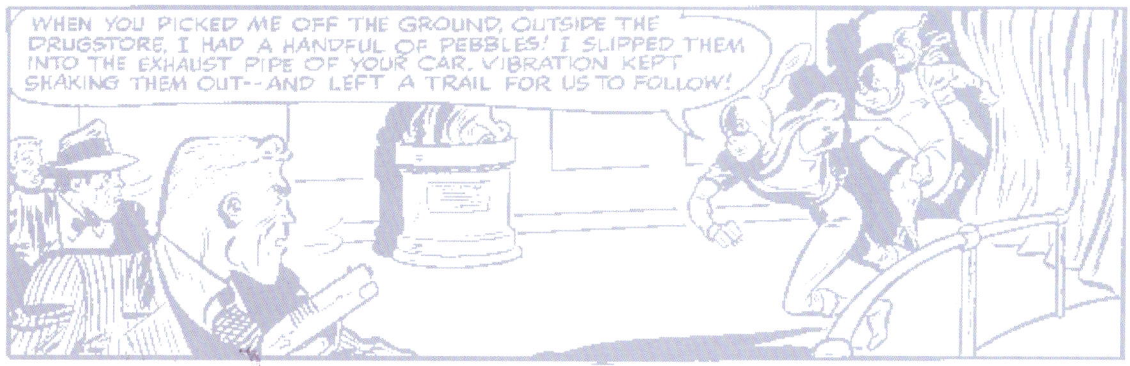

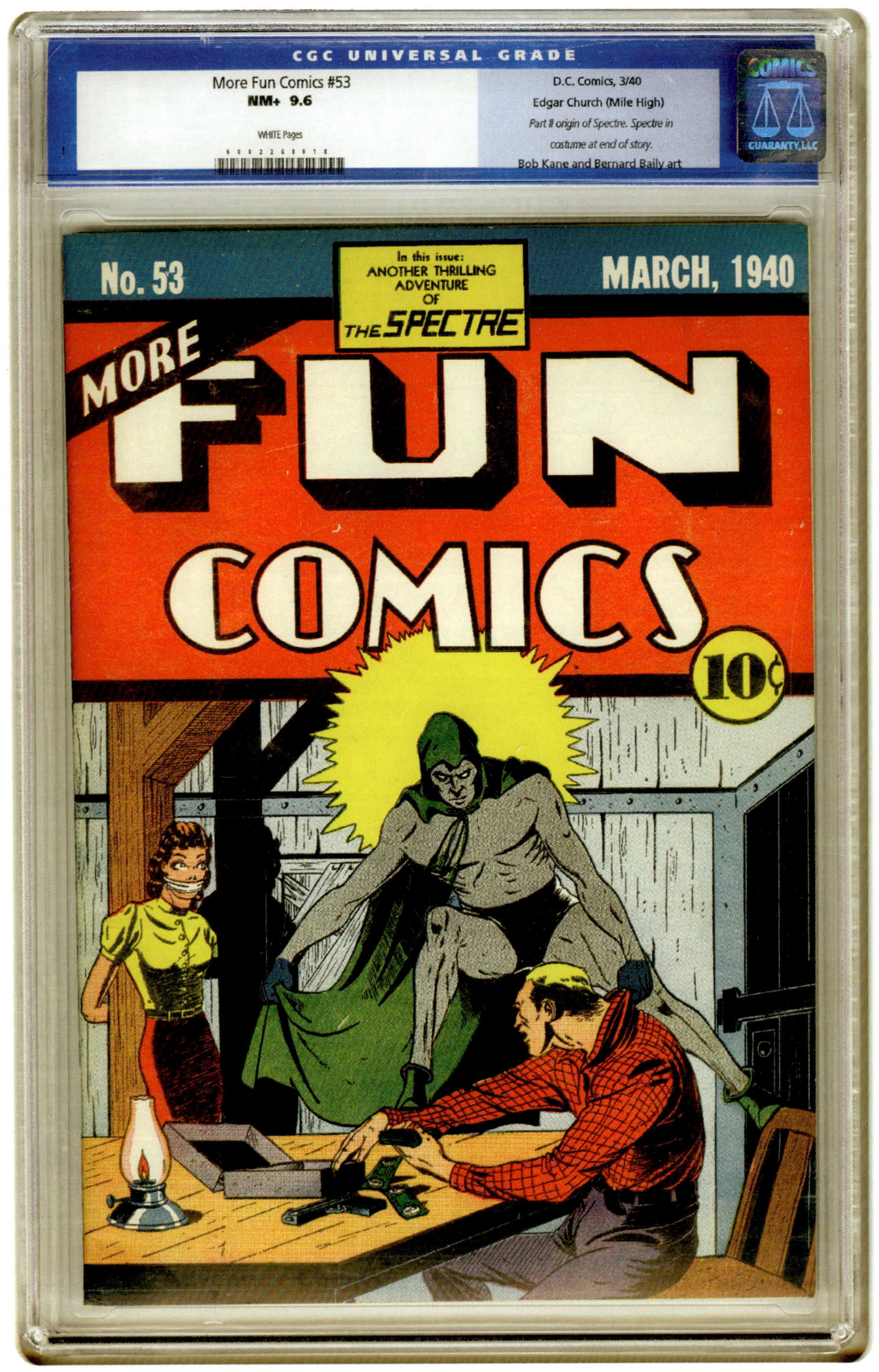
CGC UNIVERSAL GRADE
More Fun Comics #53
NM+ 9.6
WHITE Pages
D.C. Comics, 3/40
Edgar Church (Mile High)
Part II origin of Spectre. Spectre in
costume at end of story.
Bob Kane and Bernard Baily art
No. 53
In this issue:
ANOTHER THRILLING
ADVENTURE
OF
THE SPECTRE
MARCH, 1940
MORE
FUN
COMICS
10¢

2163 More Fun Comics #53 Mile High pedigree (DC, 1940) CGC NM+ 9.6 White pages. This issue, the second appearance of the Spectre, is currently #23 in Overstreet's ranking of the most valuable comic books, and the high ranking has to do with the hero's presence as well as the scarcity of the book — it's a Gerber "8." The Spectre appears in costume on the bondage cover and again at the end of the story, both of which were drawn by Bernard Baily. Only two copies of this issue have been graded above VF as of this writing, and while the Rockford pedigree copy tied this one for the highest grade yet assigned, that one's respectable page quality (cream to off-white) can't match the white pages of this Edgar Church copy. Once again, the Mile High copy stands as the best around — don't let it pass you by! Overstreet 2005 NM- 9.2 value = $46,000. CGC census 8/05: 2 in 9.6, none higher.

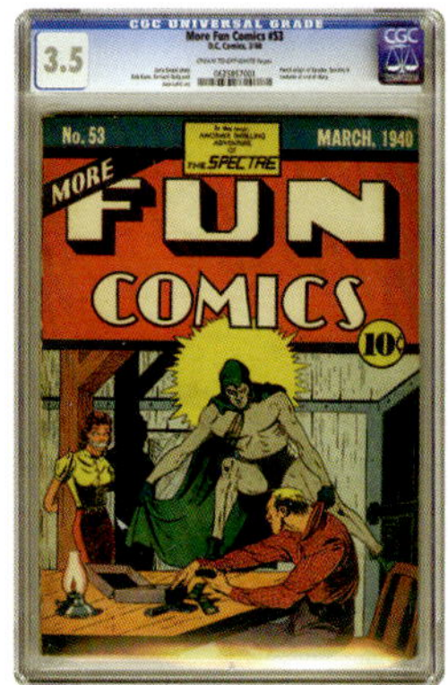

2164 More Fun Comics #53 (DC, 1940) CGC VG- 3.5 Cream to off-white pages. The second part of the Spectre's origin is featured here. He even shows up in costume at the end of the story. Cover by Bernard Baily. This issue features a story by Jerry Siegel, and interior art by **Batman** creator Bob Kane, Baily, and Jack Lehti. Captain Desmo stories also begin. Overstreet 2005 VG 4.0 value = $5,150. CGC census 8/05: 1 in 3.5, 4 higher.

2165 More Fun Comics #59 Mile High pedigree (DC, 1940) CGC NM 9.4 Off-white to white pages. See next page

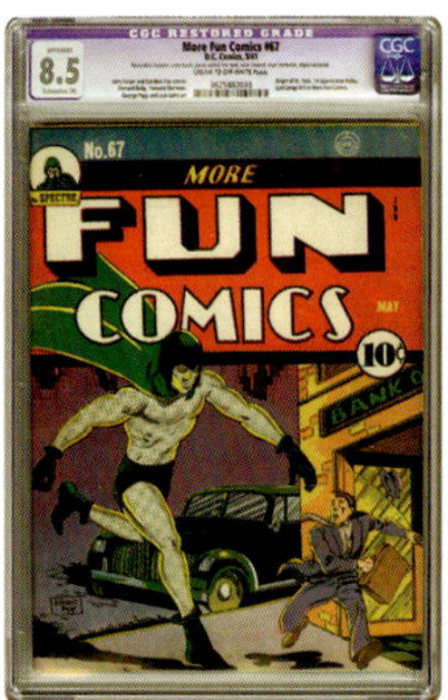

2166 More Fun Comics #67 (DC, 1941) CGC Apparent VF+ 8.5 Extensive (P) Cream to off-white pages. This book contains the origin Dr. Fate. Other notable features include the first appearance of Nabu, and the last Congo Bill in this title. Cover by Bernard Baily. Stories by Jerry Siegel and Gardner Fox, with interior art by Howard Sherman, George Papp, and Jack Lehti. CGC notes, "Restoration includes: color touch, pieces added, tear seal, cover cleaned, cover reinforced, staples replaced." Overstreet 2005 VG 4.0 value = $1,354; FN 6.0 value = $2,031; VF 8.0 value = $4,739.

2167 More Fun Comics #69 (DC, 1941) CGC Apparent VG+ 4.5 Slight (A) Off-white pages. Howard Sherman cover. Fred Ray, Bernard Baily, and George Papp art. CGC notes, "Restoration includes: small amount of color touch on cover, glue on spine of cover (1 piece of tape on spine of cover)." Overstreet 2005 GD 2.0 value = $246; VG 4.0 value = $492.

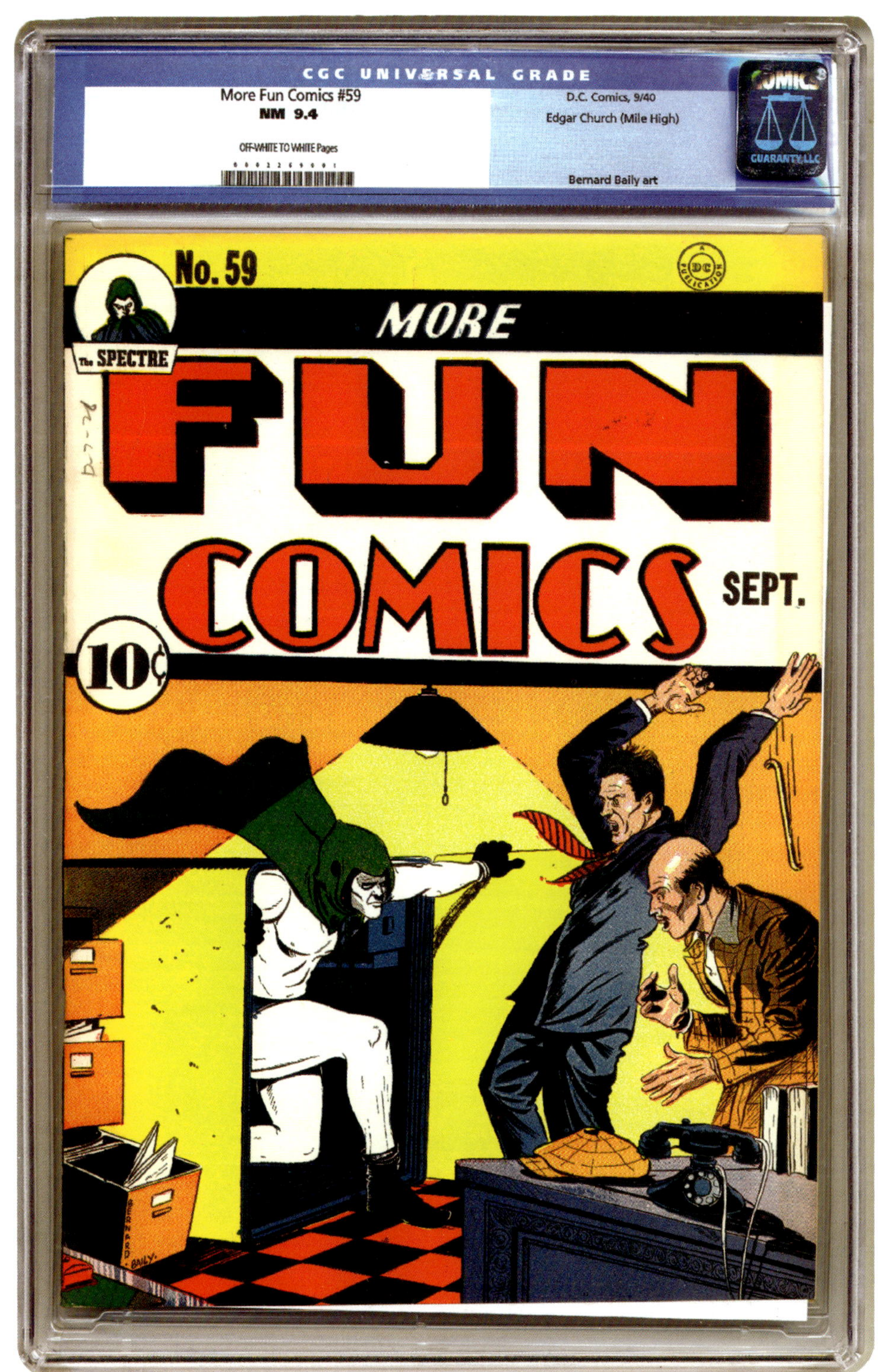

2165 More Fun Comics #59 Mile High pedigree (DC, 1940) CGC NM 9.4 Off-white to white pages. This Mile High copy has everything you could ask for in a comic book, and you're not ever going to find a nicer copy. The fearsome Spectre appears on the cover, drawn by Bernard Baily. Other features include Doctor Fate, Congo Bill, and the Radio Squad. Overstreet 2005 NM- 9.2 value = $5,300. CGC census 7/05: 1 in 9.4, none higher.

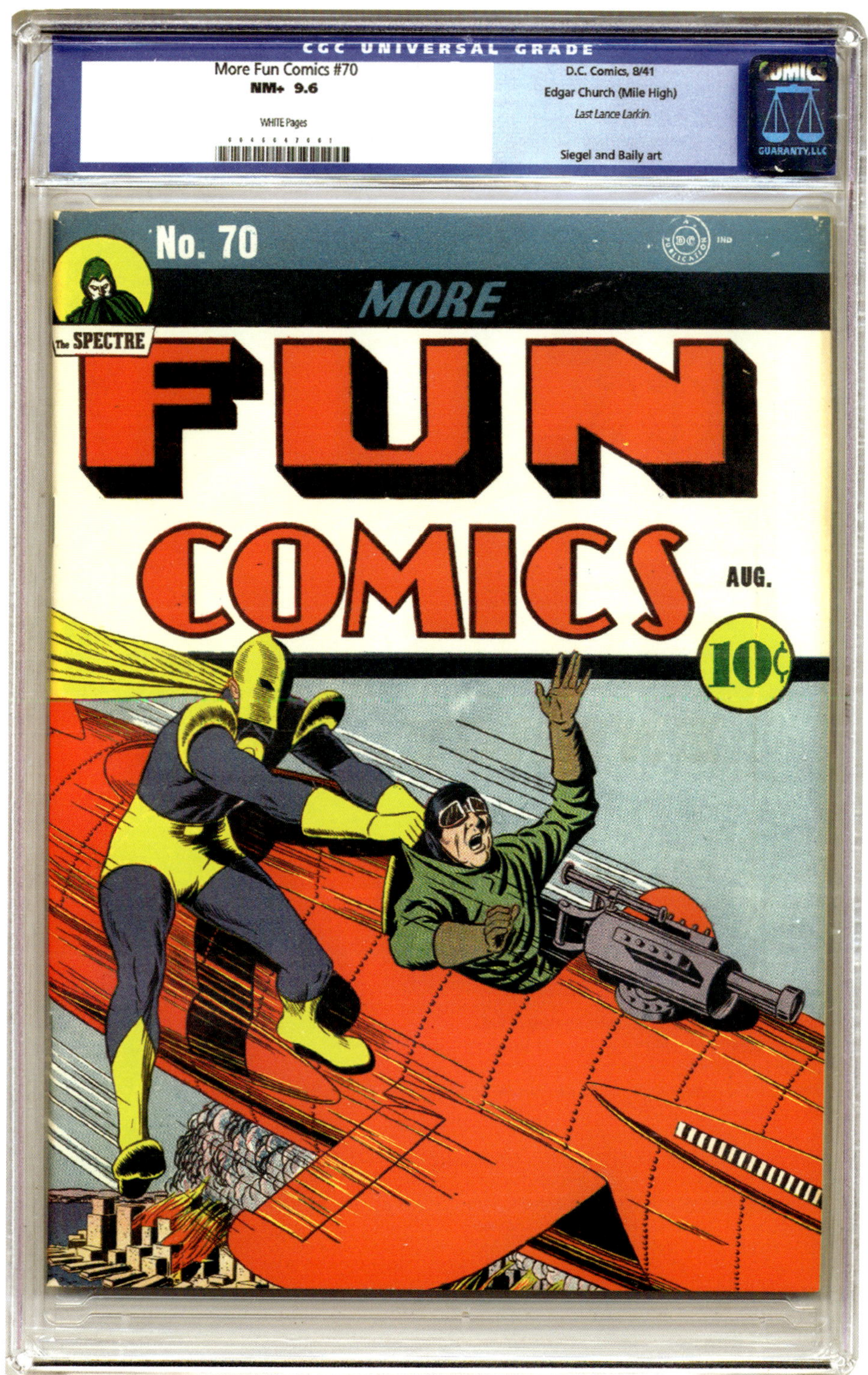

2168 More Fun Comics #70 Mile High pedigree (DC, 1941) CGC NM+ 9.6 White pages. Putting together a run of **More Fun** is a difficult endeavor indeed, especially if you're particular about condition. But we're doing our best to help you reach that goal; here's the highest-graded copy of this issue that CGC has certified to date. The lineup of characters includes Doctor Fate (Howard Sherman art), the Spectre (by Bernard Baily), and the Radio Squad (written by Jerry Siegel and drawn by Fred Ray). Also of note is the last installment of the Lance Larkin backup feature. The cover is by Sherman. Overstreet 2005 NM- 9.2 value = $3,200. CGC census 7/05: 1 in 9.6, none higher.

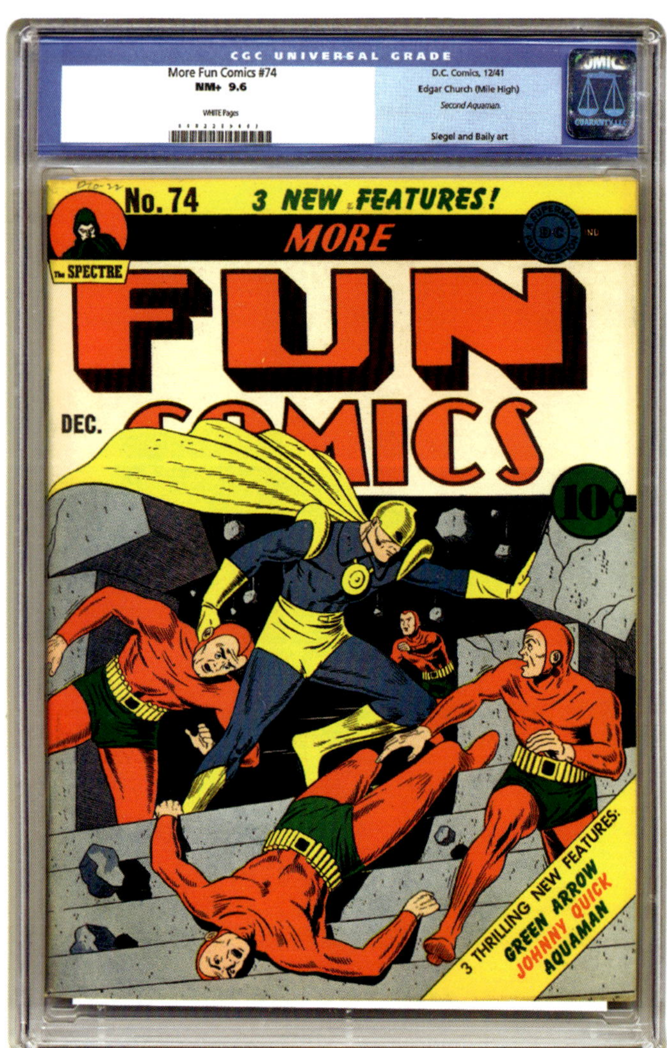

2169 More Fun Comics #74 Mile High pedigree (DC, 1941) CGC NM+ 9.6 White pages. Here are the second appearances of two super-famous superheroes, namely Aquaman and Green Arrow! Other highlights are Dr. Fate (drawn on the cover and inside the comic by Howard Sherman), and the fleet-footed Johnny Quick. The Spectre feature (drawn by Bernard Baily) is notable for having the first appearance of Percival Popp, the Supercop. Now, some would dispute whether the grim Spectre really needed a comic-relief partner, but that was the trend of the day, and the Spectre's Golden Age tales definitely changed with Mr. Popp around. This beautiful Mile High book is the only copy of the issue certified with a grade above VF/NM by CGC to date. Overstreet 2005 NM- 9.2 value = $3,850. CGC census 9/05: 1 in 9.6, none higher.

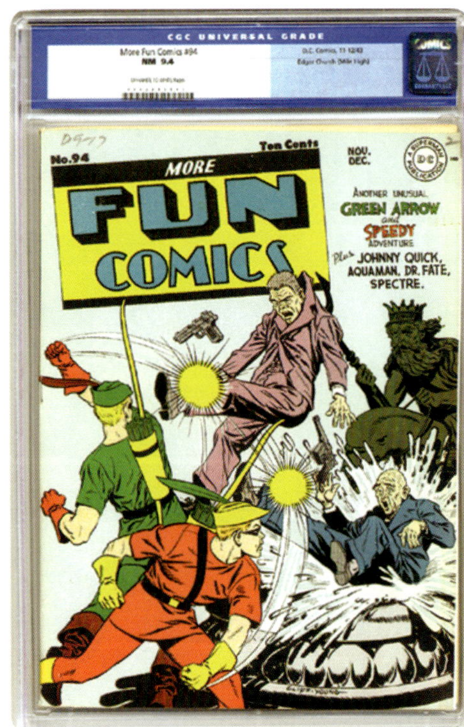

2170 More Fun Comics #94 Mile High pedigree (DC, 1943) CGC NM 9.4 Off-white to white pages. It's amazing that more copies of **More Fun** haven't survived considering the outstanding roster of heroes that populated the book. This issue's got Green Arrow and Speedy, Aquaman, the Spectre, Doctor Fate, and Johnny Quick. Comic relief is provided by funny twins Dover and Clover. This Mile High copy is one you simply can't go wrong with! Overstreet 2005 NM- 9.2 value = $1,125. CGC census 7/05: 1 in 9.4, 1 higher.

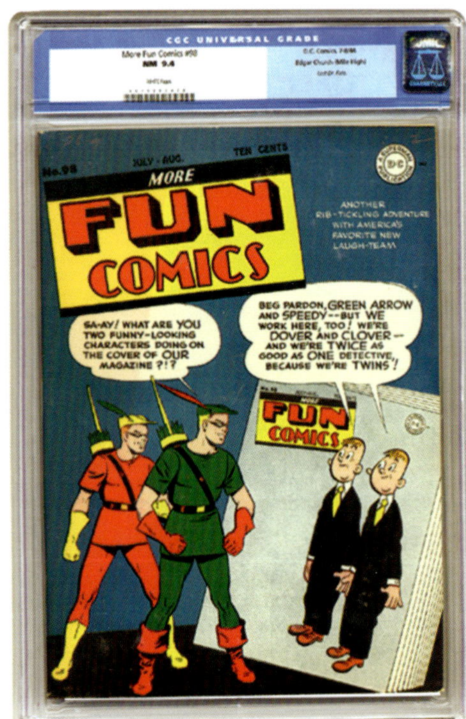

2171 More Fun Comics #98 Mile High pedigree (DC, 1944) CGC NM 9.4 White pages. Not that any issue of this title's *easy* to find, but this one's a Gerber "8" and called "scarce" by Overstreet! And as a matter of fact, we've got the highest-graded copy in CGC's census to offer you right here. Check out the funny cover — Dover and Clover should be glad it's not the Spectre staring them down! The issue also has an Aquaman story, plus the last appearance of Doctor Fate in this series. Overstreet 2005 NM- 9.2 value = $1,350. CGC census 7/05: 1 in 9.4, none higher.

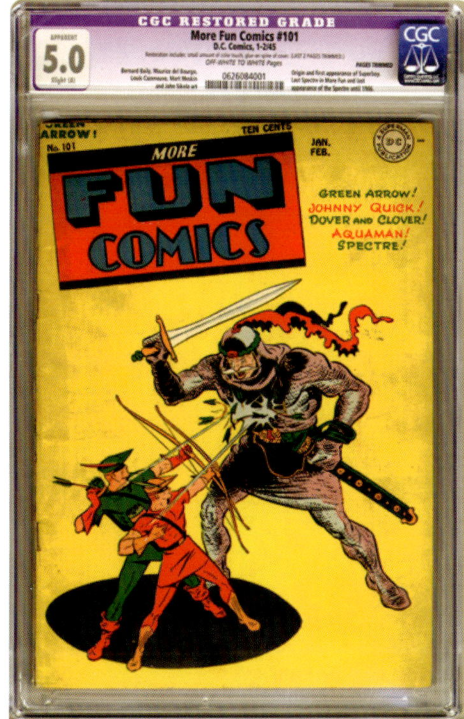

2172 More Fun Comics #101 (DC, 1945) CGC Apparent VG/FN 5.0 Slight (A) Off-white to white pages. History is made with this landmark issue, as DC adds to their growing Superman franchise by introducing the adventures of Superboy. Some have claimed Superman co-creators Jerry Siegel and Joe Shuster produced this initial Superboy tale; not so, says Overstreet. Oh well! This does appears to have been a last-minute addition, as no mention is made on the Green Arrow-starring cover; in fact, the cover lists a Dover and Clover story which is absent. There are stories featuring Green Arrow, Aquaman, Johnny Quick, and the Spectre (the last Golden Age appearence of this ghostly hero), though. CGC notes, "Restoration includes: small amount of color touch, glue on spine of cover, last two pages trimmed." Overstreet 2005 GD 2.0 value = $839; VG 4.0 value = $1,678; FN 6.0 value = $2,517.

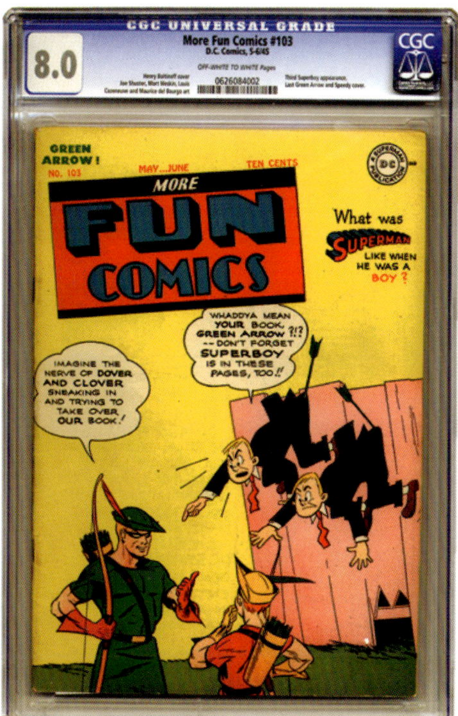

2173 More Fun Comics #103 (DC, 1945) CGC VF 8.0 Off-white to white pages. Green Arrow seems a wee bit over-protective of his **More Fun** cover-star rating, even pinning those wacky twin detectives Dover and Clover to a fence with a couple of well-place arrows! Stunts like this have to be addressed; Superboy (making his third appearance here) nabbed that coveted cover spot with the very next issue! This attractive copy currently ranks as the highest CGC-graded unrestored example of this issue. Artists include Mort Meskin, Joe Shuster, and Henry Boltinoff. Overstreet notes, "All issues are scarce to rare." Overstreet 2005 VF 8.0 value = $613. CGC census 8/05: 1 in 8.0, none higher.

2175 Mystery in Space #3 (DC, 1951) CGC VF- 7.5 Off-white pages. A signature cover for this long-running title is this early creation by Carmine Infantino. This copy's front displays as a higher grade, with colors and action leaping from a black background. Infantino and Gil Kane interior art is featured. Overstreet 2005 VF 8.0 value = $604. CGC census 9/05: 2 in 7.5, 8 higher.

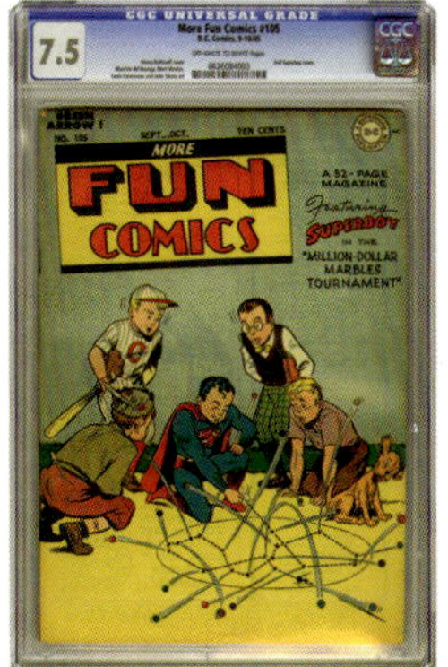

2174 More Fun Comics #105 (DC, 1945) CGC VF- 7.5 Off-white to white pages. Superboy is the star here, in his second-ever cover appearance. Artists include Henry Boltinoff, Mort Meskin, and John Sikela. Overstreet states, "all issues (of this title) are scarce to rare." Overstreet 2005 VF 8.0 value = $494. CGC census 8/05: 1 in 7.5, 1 higher.

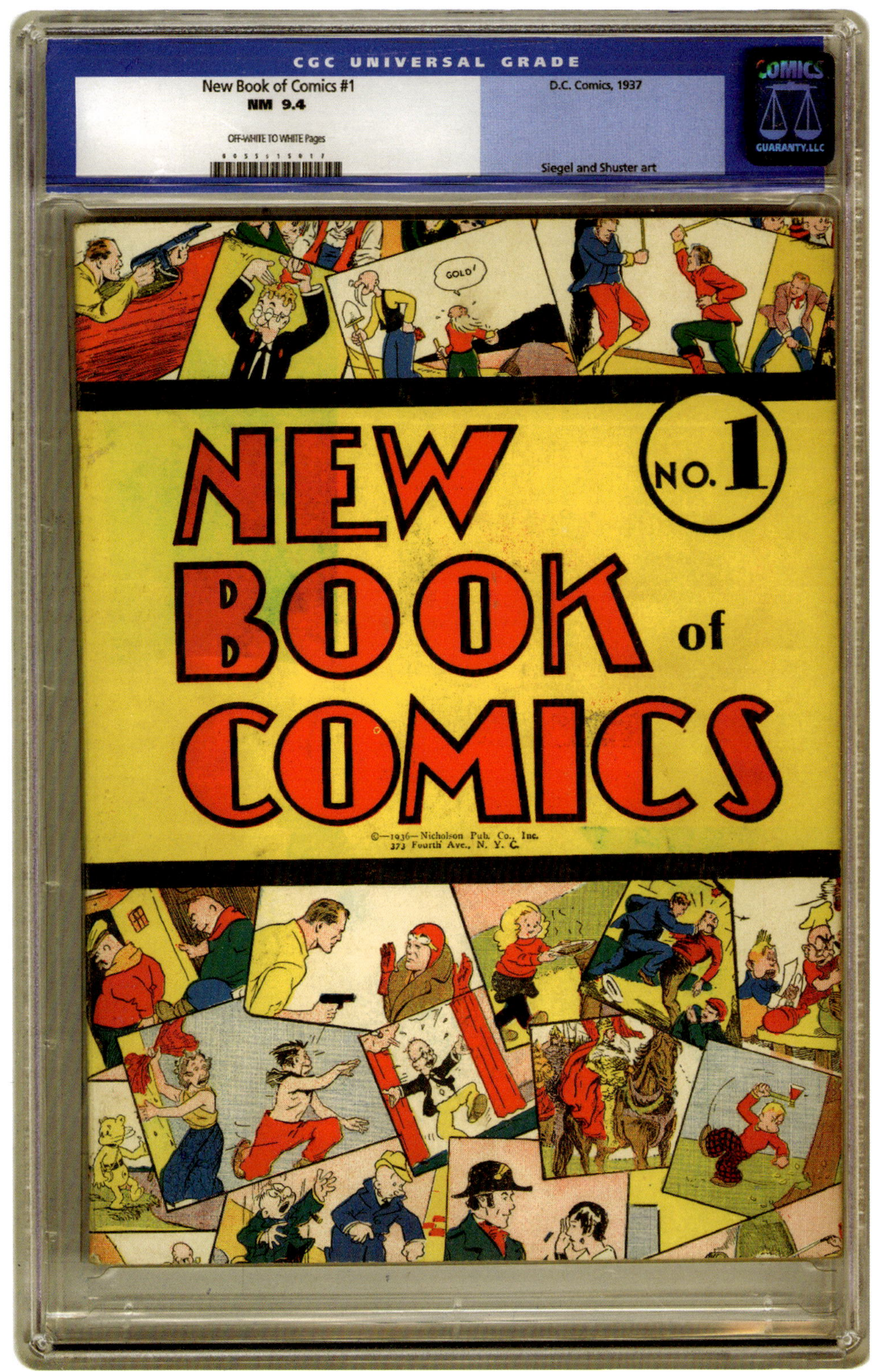

2176 New Book of Comics #1 (DC, 1937) CGC NM 9.4 Off-white to white pages. The Overstreet Guide added a NM- price for this issue for the first time this year, and that rocketed the book onto the Guide's list of the 50 most valuable Golden Age comics. Our offering is the proof that a top-grade copy does exist, yet ours remains the only one graded above 8.0 in CGC's census. Though we've got this one in our Golden Age section, it's technically a *Platinum Age* book, and the fact that the cover bears the copyright "Nicholson Pub. Co." shows how old the book is — Malcolm Wheeler-Nicholson was the founder of DC, but didn't run the company for very long. Overstreet lists this as the first regular-size comic annual, and the second DC annual of any size. The issue has reprinted material from **New Comics** #1-4 and **More Fun Comics** #9. The issue's a coveted Gerber "8," and it's dubbed "rare" by Overstreet as well. Considering the age of this book and its rarity, this copy is an absolute wonder, *especially* since it's a square bound comic! The features inside date from 1935 and 1936 and include Dr. Occult and the Federal Men, both by future Superman creators Jerry Siegel and Joe Shuster. There's also artwork by Sheldon Moldoff, Sheldon Mayer, and many other notable names from the earliest days of comics. Overstreet 2005 NM- 9.2 value = $27,000. CGC census 7/05: 1 in 9.4, none higher.

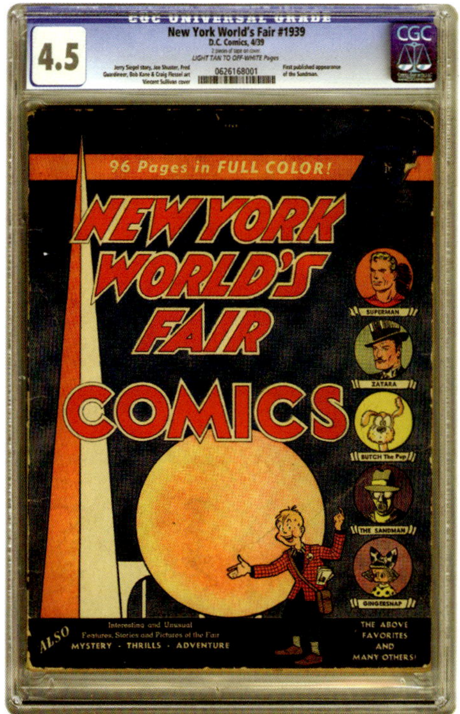

2177 New York World's Fair Comics 1939 (DC, 1939) CGC VG+ 4.5 Light tan to off-white pages. This issue is listed at number 36 in Overstreet's ranking of the most valuable Golden Age books, and the chief reason for the book's high desirability is that it's got the first published appearance of the Sandman. There are other stars on hand as well — if you don't recognize the blond fellow on the right, that's actually Superman (either the Man of Steel found some Super-Peroxide or there was a coloring goof at DC)! The book's stories were set at the World's Fair; the crimefighting visitors included the aforementioned Sandman and Superman, plus gumshoe Slam Bradley (written and drawn by Jerry Siegel and Joe Shuster, as was the Superman feature) and Zatara the Magician (drawn by Fred Guardineer). The roster of artists also included Bob Kane (drawing humor material), Creig Flessel, and Sheldon Moldoff. The cover was a team effort between Vincent Sullivan and Fred Guardineer. CGC notes, "2 pieces of tape on cover." Overstreet 2005 VG 4.0 value = $4,200. CGC census 9/05: 3 in 4.5, 7 higher.

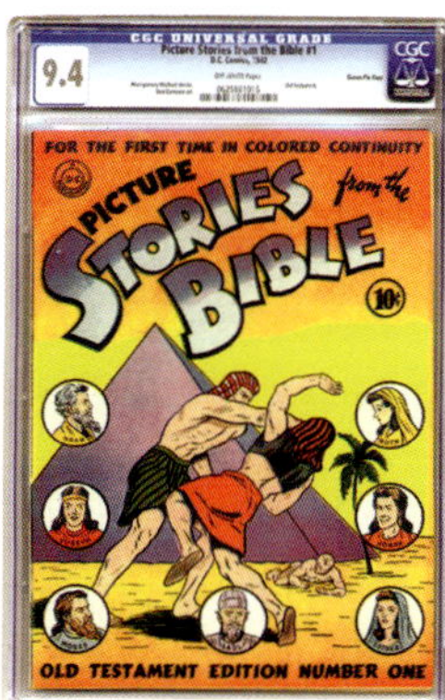

2178 Picture Stories from the Bible #1 Gaines File pedigree (DC, 1944) CGC NM 9.4 Off-white pages. This "graphic novel" version of the Old Testament was the brainchild of Max Gaines, and was found among the file copies stashed away by Max's son, EC publisher William Gaines. Although listed on the CGC header as a 1942 edition, this is really a 1944 reprint from Educational Comics with a DC cover logo; the back cover shows an order form (with a coupon addressed to M. C. Gaines, Publisher) for all four Old Testament books (you can see the "Fall 1943" date on the cover of the fourth volume). At any rate, this is still a very beautiful and historic item. Although CGC recognizes this as a Gaines File copy, no certificate accompanies this book. Overstreet 2005 NM- 9.2 value for 1942 edition = $270; NM- value for 1944 edition = $200. CGC census 8/05: 2 in 9.4, 1 higher.

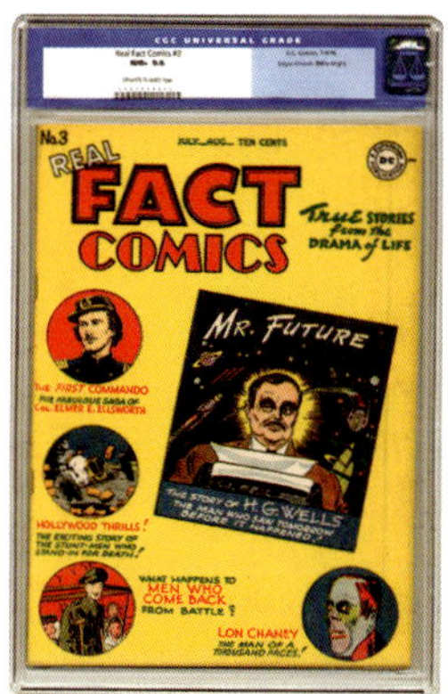

2179 Real Fact Comics #3 Mile High pedigree (DC, 1946) CGC NM+ 9.6 Off-white to white pages. According to Overstreet, this book has the first letter column in a DC comic! It also has features on H. G. Wells and Lon Chaney. Overstreet 2005 NM- 9.2 value = $400. CGC census 9/05: 1 in 9.6, none higher.

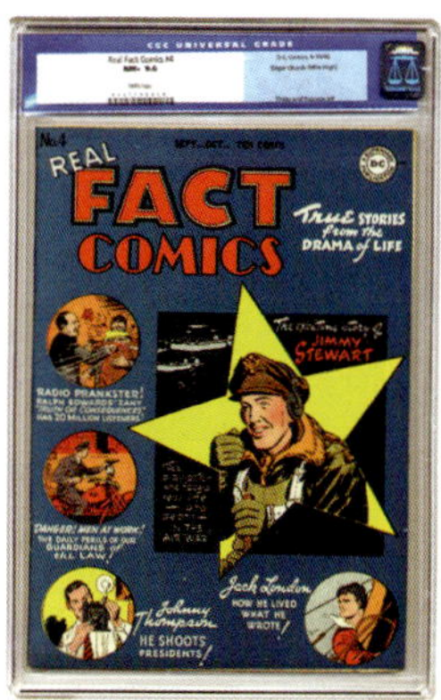

2180 Real Fact Comics #4 Mile High pedigree (DC, 1946) CGC NM+ 9.6 White pages. Virgil Finlay and George Roussos are among the contributors to this issue, which gave kids facts about actor Jimmy Stewart, writer Jack London, and even the radio game show "Truth Or Consequences." Here's a real fact for you: this is the highest-graded copy of the issue that CGC has certified to date. Overstreet 2005 NM- 9.2 value = $450. CGC census 9/05: 1 in 9.6, none higher.

2181 Real Fact Comics #11 Mile High pedigree (DC, 1947) CGC VF+ 8.5 White pages. Annie Oakley and FBI features. Everett Raymond Kinstler art. Overstreet 2005 VF 8.0 value = $89; VF/NM 9.0 value = $127. CGC census 9/05: 3 in 8.5, none higher.

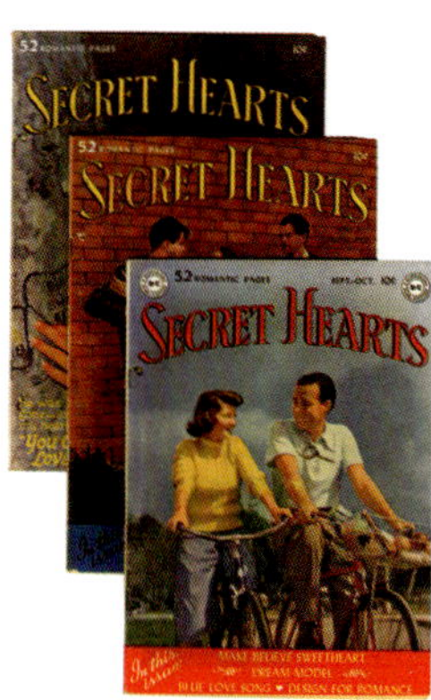

2182 Secret Hearts Golden Age Group (DC, 1949-57) Condition: Average VG/FN. This group includes #1, 2, 4, 5, 6, 7 (a rare issue according to Overstreet), 8, 9, 10, 20, 38, 41, and 43. Artists include Alex Toth and Everett Raymond Kinstler. Approximate Overstreet value for group = $750.

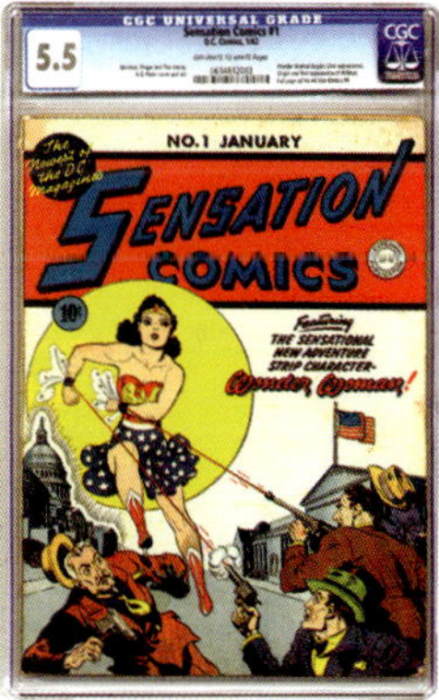

2183 Sensation Comics #1 (DC, 1942) CGC FN- 5.5 Off-white to white pages. This issue's listed among the 30 most valuable comics by Overstreet thanks to the second appearance of the number one superheroine in comics, Wonder Woman. The issue came out just one month after the character was first seen in **All Star Comics** #8, and this can be said to be Part Two of Wonder Woman's origin, as it shows her arriving in America for the first time and also introduces her "Diana Prince" secret identity. The story is by the creative team that defined the character in the Golden Age, namely writer William Moulton Marston and artist H. G. Peter. Making their first appearances in this issue were Mr. Terrific and Wildcat, both of whom have had stints with the Justice Society over the years) as well as Little Boy Blue and the Blue Boys, three kid pals who don costumes. There's also the Black Pirate feature by Sheldon Moldoff, which Moldoff reportedly called his personal favorite of the features he drew. The famous cover is the work of Jon Blummer. Overstreet 2005 FN 6.0 value = $7,725. CGC census 8/05: 2 in 5.5, 7 higher.

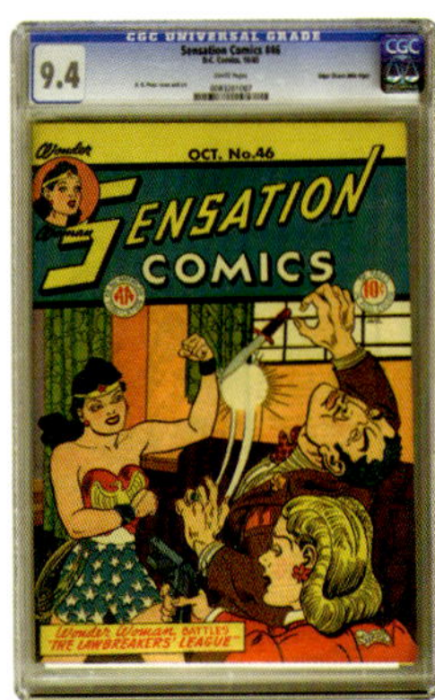

2184 Sensation Comics #46 Mile High pedigree (DC, 1945) CGC NM 9.4 White pages. Foolish villains — don't they realize that guns and knives won't help them against **Wonder Woman**? That should be as obvious as the fact this is an Edgar Church Mile High copy, and it's magnificent! And as is often the case with Mr. Church's books, this copy is the highest-graded in the current CGC census report for this issue. Overstreet 2005 NM- 9.2 value = $600. CGC census 9/05: 1 in 9.4, none higher.

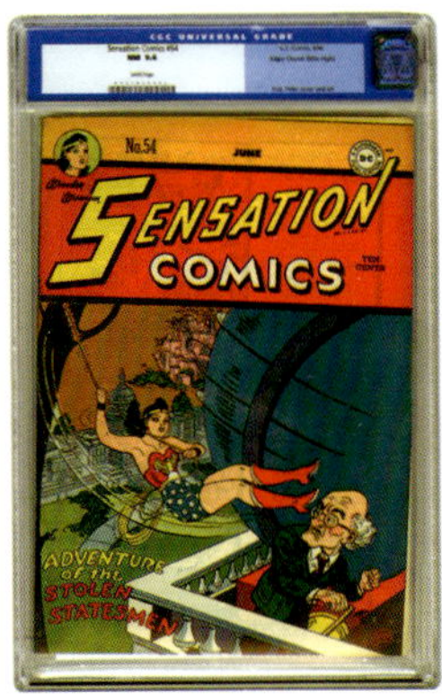

2185 Sensation Comics #54 Mile High pedigree (DC, 1946) CGC NM 9.4 White pages. Wonder Woman takes on the villainy of Dr. Fiendo in this issue. How bad of a guy is the Doctor? Well, he takes over the U.S. government, turns America into a police state, and has his kangaroo court sentence Wonder Woman and her pals to death for treason! A tall order indeed for the Amazon. H. G. Peter drew this issue's cover as well as the Wonder Woman story. Overstreet 2005 NM- 9.2 value = $550. CGC census 5/05: 1 in 9.4, 1 higher.

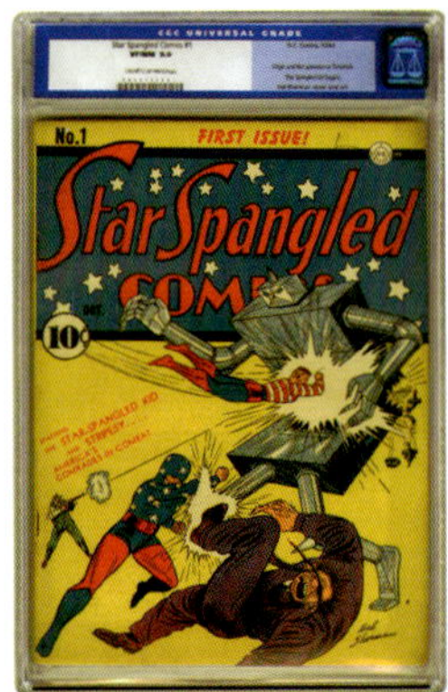

2186 Star Spangled Comics #1 (DC, 1941) CGC VF/NM 9.0 Cream to off-white pages. He's a superhero who can walk up walls and shoot webs; yes, we're talking about the Tarantula, whose origin and first appearance are in this issue. The character, who had suction cups in his boots and carried a web-gun, was a regular in the early run of this title. The stars of the issue are the Star-Spangled Kid and his adult sidekick Stripesy; that's them on this robot cover by Hal Sherman. Note that the CGC slab has a two-inch crack at the top rear, not affecting the integrity of the holder or the comic itself. Overstreet 2005 VF/NM 9.0 value = $5,661; NM- 9.2 value = $7,800. CGC census 6/05: 1 in 9.0, 1 higher.

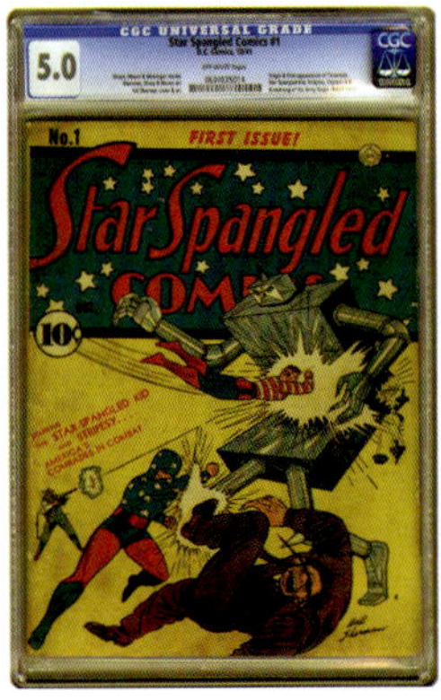

2187 Star Spangled Comics #1 (DC, 1941) CGC VG/FN 5.0 Off-white pages. The Star-Spangled Kid and his adult sidekick Stripesy are the stars of this first issue; that's them on this robot cover by Hal Sherman. Also of note is the origin and first appearance of the Tarantula. Overstreet 2005 VG 4.0 value = $1,006; FN 6.0 value = $1,509. CGC census 9/05: 1 in 5.0, 9 higher.

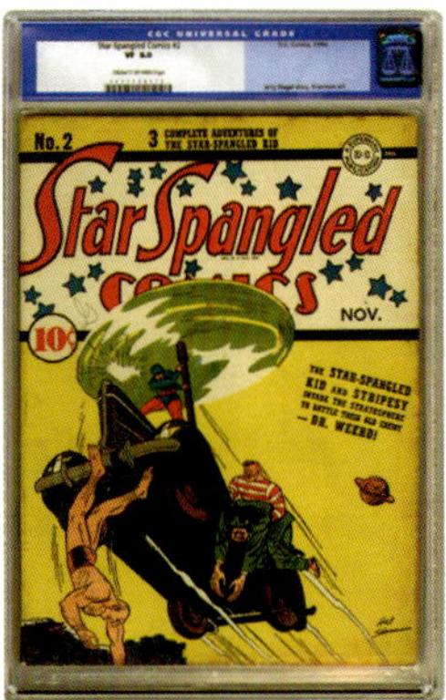

2188 Star Spangled Comics #2 (DC, 1941) CGC VF 8.0 Cream to off-white pages. The Star-Spangled Kid and Stripesy tangle with their aptly-named nemesis Dr. Weerd in this issue. Hal Sherman drew the cover as well as multiple stories featuring the duo; the stories were written by none other than Superman's co-creator Jerry Siegel. Overstreet 2005 VF 8.0 value = $1,056. CGC census 6/05: 1 in 8.0, 2 higher.

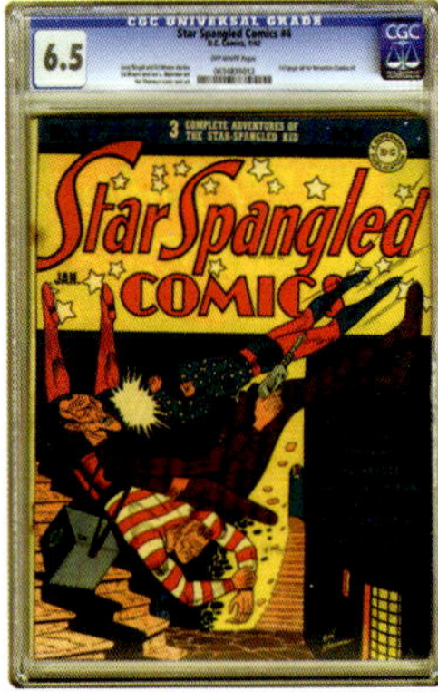

2189 Star Spangled Comics #4 (DC, 1942) CGC FN+ 6.5 Off-white pages. Writer Jerry Siegel and artist Hal Sherman teamed up to present the adventures of the Star Spangled Kid and his grown-up sidekick Stripesy. The Tarantula appears in a backup feature. Overstreet 2005 FN 6.0 value = $324; VF 8.0 value = $675. CGC census 9/05: 1 in 6.5, 4 higher.

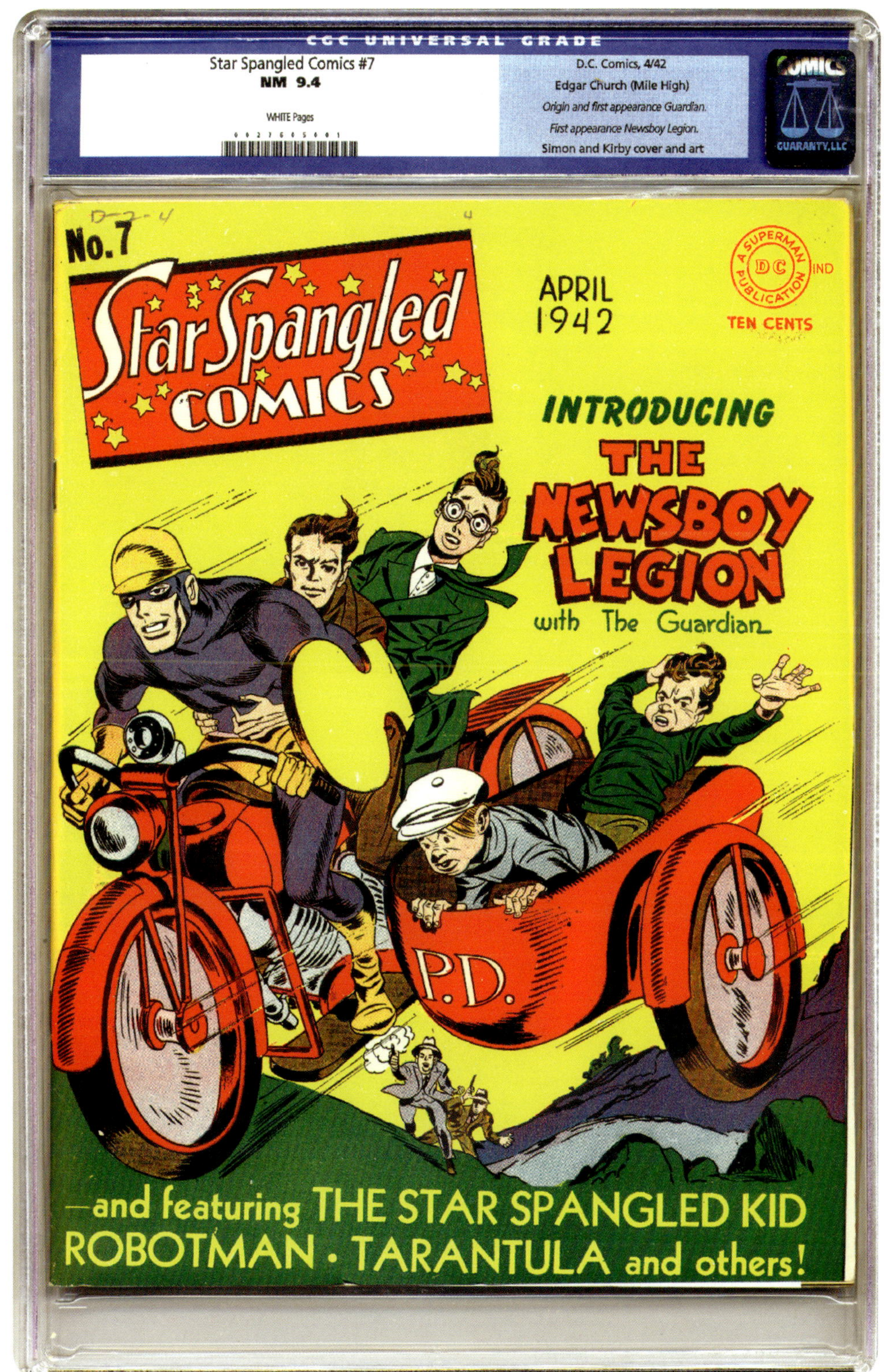

2190 Star Spangled Comics #7 Mile High pedigree (DC, 1942) CGC NM 9.4 White pages. Here's the origin and first appearance of the Newsboy Legion! Joe Simon and Jack Kirby created the group, four kids from Suicide Slum who had some brushes with the law, but whom patrolman Jim Harper took into his custody. Aided by Harper (and his alter-ego the Guardian, who also makes his first appearance), the group used its street smarts for good instead of evil, and the kids who bought comics couldn't get enough of the group's adventures. The issue also has the first appearance of Robotman (not the Doom Patrol guy, but a character who enjoyed a long run in this series and later appeared in the All-Star Squadron). This copy's got the amazing colors you associate with a Mile High, so it's no surprise that this is the highest-graded copy in CGC's census. Overstreet 2005 NM- 9.2 value = $9,700. CGC census 8/05: 1 in 9.4, none higher.

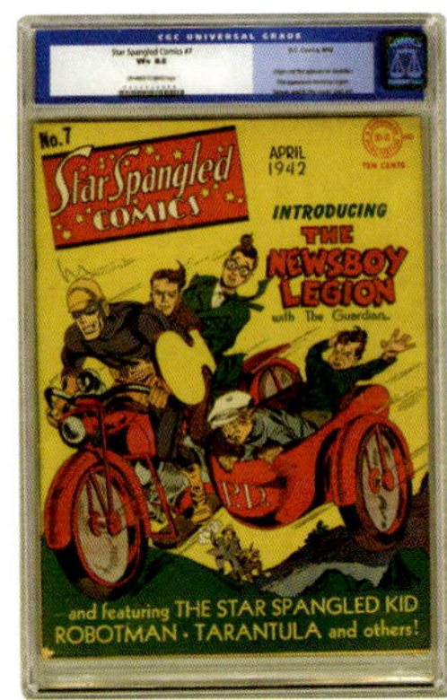

2191 Star Spangled Comics #7 (DC, 1942) CGC VF+ 8.5 Off-white to white pages. Any Simon and Kirby lover will want to pick this one up, it's the first appearance of the Newsboy Legion! And the story also has the origin and first appearance of the Guardian, who the newsboys always *suspected* was really Officer Jim Harper (we readers knew for sure). A couple of other new features debuted here as well, namely Robotman (not the guy from Doom Patrol, but the Jerry Siegel creation who later joined the All-Star Squadron) and TNT (plus the latter's sidekick Dan the Dyna-Mite). Overstreet 2005 VF 8.0 value = $4,382; VF/NM 9.0 value = $7,041. CGC census 6/05: 1 in 8.5, 1 higher.

2192 Star Spangled Comics #9 (DC, 1942) CGC GD/VG 3.0 Slightly brittle pages. Simon and Kirby cover. CGC notes, "Moderate amount of tape on 20th, 21st & 22nd page(s)." Overstreet 2005 GD 2.0 value = $165; VG 4.0 value = $330. CGC census 9/05: 1 in 3.0, 6 higher.

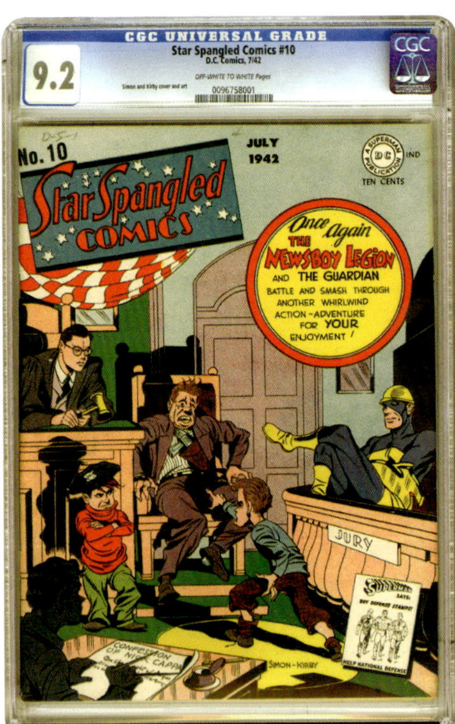

2193 Star Spangled Comics #10 Mile High pedigree (DC, 1942) CGC NM- 9.2 Off-white to white pages. Joe Simon and Jack Kirby continued their successful "Newsboy Legion" series with this issue, which features S & K cover and story art for this fourth tale featuring the kids. This Edgar Church Mile High copy may not match the through-the-roof ultra high grades of some from this pedigree, but it's still at the top of CGC's current census report for this issue. Other than a very minor amount of edge and corner wear, this one still looks great. Overstreet 2005 NM- 9.2 value = $2,150. CGC census 9/05: 1 in 9.2, none higher.

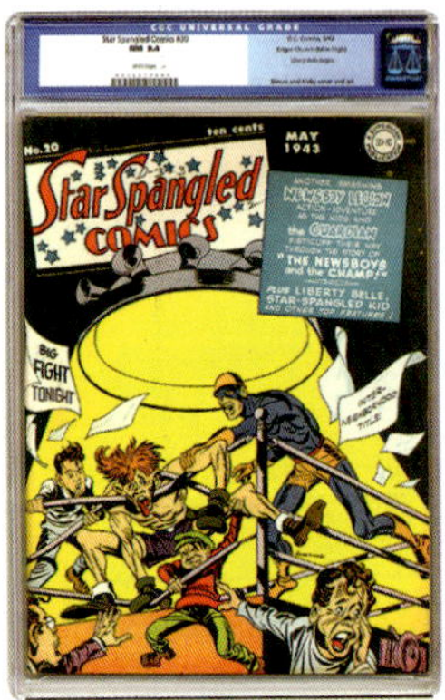

2194 Star Spangled Comics #20 Mile High pedigree (DC, 1943) CGC NM 9.4 White pages. Do you have issues with black-cover issues? No such worries if you've got the Mile High copy. The Newsboy Legion stars in this issue. On the cover, Simon and Kirby showed their skill at comedic scenes, as a gangly pugilist needs all the help he can get. Maybe Scrapper, Big Words and the rest can turn things around for this rope-a-dope. This issue also saw Liberty Belle's debut. Overstreet 2005 NM- 9.2 value = $1,725. CGC census 8/05: 1 in 9.4, none higher.

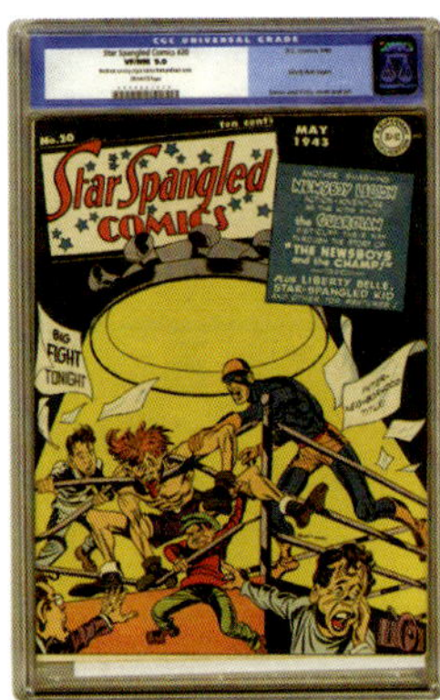

2195 Star Spangled Comics #20 (DC, 1943) CGC VF/NM 9.0 Off-white pages. Simon and Kirby's cover shows the duo's skill at comedic scenes, as a gangly pugilist needs all the help he can get. Maybe the streetwise Newsboy Legion can turn things around for this rope-a-dope. Joining the roster of characters in this issue was the Liberty Belle, who appeared in **Boy Commandos** previously. CGC notes, "Moderate tanning (at) edges (of) interior front and back cover." Overstreet 2005 VF/NM 9.0 value = $1,278; NM- 9.2 value = $1,725. CGC census 6/05: 1 in 9.0, 1 higher.

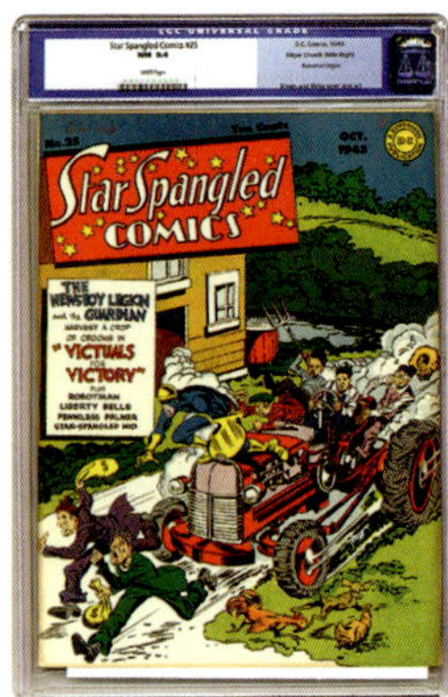

2196 Star Spangled Comics #25 Mile High pedigree (DC, 1943) CGC NM 9.4 White pages. To find a Golden Age book in this condition... well, even Big Words himself would be hard-pressed to come up with appropriate adjectives! The book stars Simon and Kirby's Newsboy Legion (Big Words, Gabby, Scrapper, and Tommy), with a cover by S&K. Robotman, who first appeared in #7, is among the backup features. Overstreet 2005 NM- 9.2 value = $1,350. CGC census 8/05: 1 in 9.4, 1 higher.

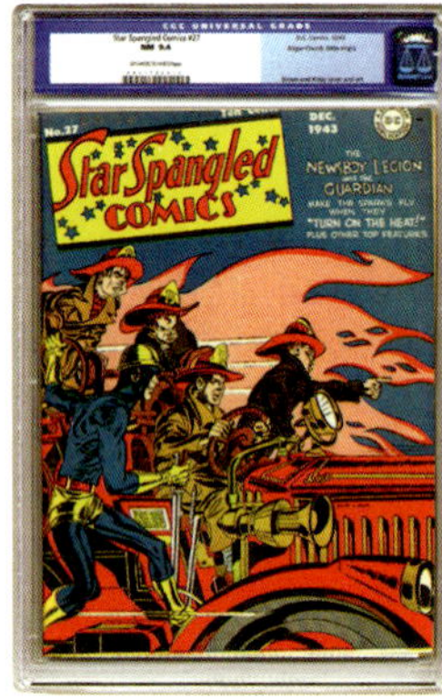

2197 Star Spangled Comics #27 Mile High pedigree (DC, 1943) CGC NM 9.4 Off-white to white pages. This was one of the last issues of Simon and Kirby's run on this title's Newsboy Legion feature — after #29 they turned over the reins to others who imitated their style (though S&K did return to contribute a cover now and then). The issue's other characters include the Star Spangled Kid and Robotman. This copy is up to the usual Edgar Church standard, i.e. near-perfect! Overstreet 2005 NM- 9.2 value = $1,350. CGC census 9/05: 2 in 9.4, none higher.

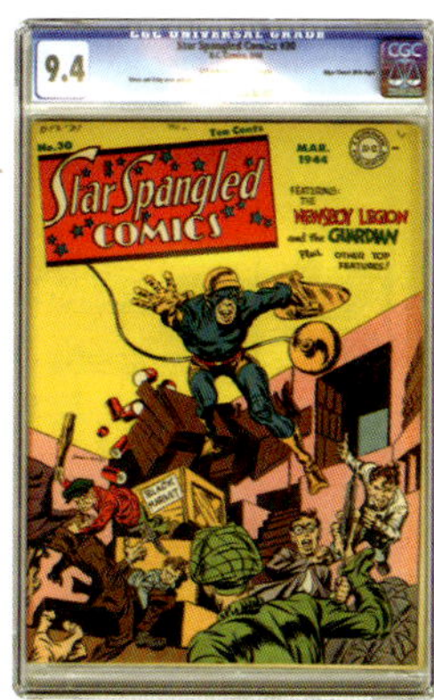

2198 Star Spangled Comics #30 Mile High pedigree (DC, 1944) CGC NM 9.4 Off-white to white pages. Simon and Kirby's creation the Newsboy Legion are the stars of the issue here, and they're backed up by the Star Spangled Kid, Robotman, and more. Overstreet 2005 NM- 9.2 value = $750. CGC census 9/05: 2 in 9.4, 1 higher.

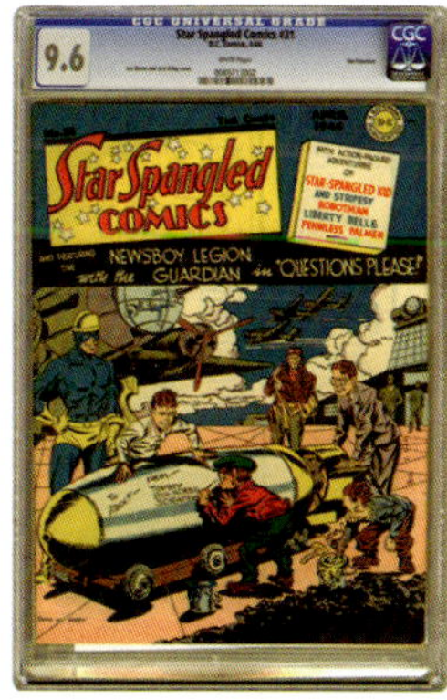

2199 Star Spangled Comics #31 San Francisco pedigree (DC, 1944) CGC NM+ 9.6 White pages. As the story of the "San Francisco" collection goes, many of the comics that were saved for young Tom Reilly were never actually read by him, and we don't doubt that's true for this comic, judging by the amazing condition and page quality. Simon and Kirby portray the mood of the times on the cover, with the Newsboy Legion dedicating a bomb to Herr Hitler himself. Overstreet 2005 NM- 9.2 value = $750. CGC census 6/05: 1 in 9.6, none higher.

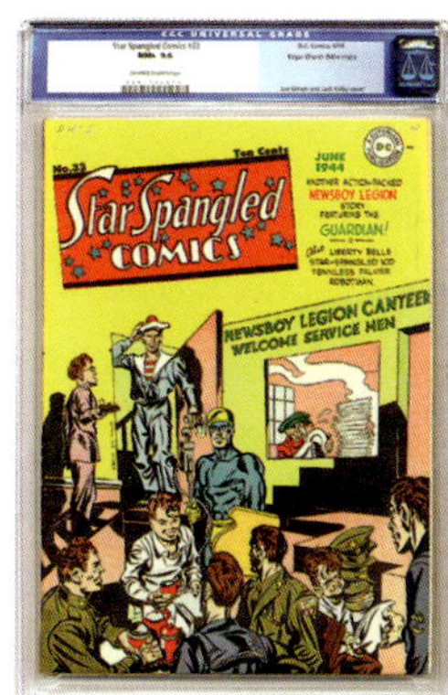

2200 Star Spangled Comics #33 Mile High pedigree (DC, 1944) CGC NM+ 9.6 Off-white to white pages. This superb Edgar Church specimen is the only copy of the issue that has been graded above 8.5 by CGC as of this writing. The Newsboy Legion stars on the cover (drawn by an unknown hand in the style of the group's creators Simon and Kirby). The issue's other features include Robotman and the Star-Spangled Kid. Overstreet 2005 NM- 9.2 value = $750. CGC census 8/05: 1 in 9.6, none higher.

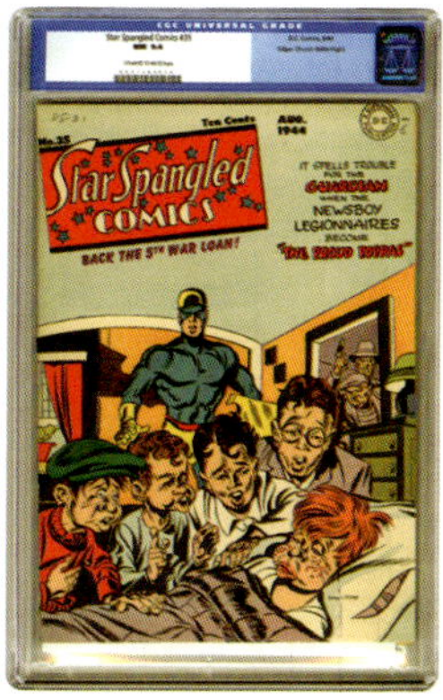

2201 Star Spangled Comics #35 Mile High pedigree (DC, 1944) CGC NM 9.4 Off-white to white pages. The Newsboy Legion and the Guardian are cover stars in this issue. Although signed as Simon and Kirby, this cover is actually the work of longtime DC artist Fred Ray. Of course, the real star here is the book's wonderful condition, thanks to the Edgar Church Mile High pedigree. This is by far the nicest copy in the current CGC census for this issue. Overstreet 2005 NM- 9.2 value = $750. CGC census 8/05: 1 in 9.4, none higher.

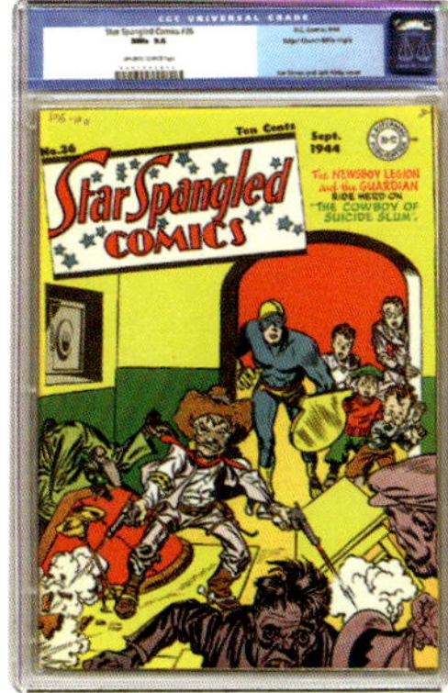

2202 Star Spangled Comics #36 Mile High pedigree (DC, 1944) CGC NM+ 9.6 Off-white to white pages. This super-sharp Edgar Church copy is the only one to be graded above 8.5 by CGC as of this writing. The Newsboy Legion stars; other characters in the issue include Robotman and the Star-Spangled Kid. Overstreet 2005 NM- 9.2 value = $750. CGC census 8/05: 1 in 9.6, none higher.

2203 Star Spangled Comics #43 (DC, 1945) CGC VF+ 8.5. Off-white to white pages. Art by Stan Kaye, Chuck Winter, and Jimmy Thompson. Overstreet 2005 VF 8.0 value = $323; VF/NM 9.0 value = $494. CGC census 9/05: 1 in 8.5, 1 higher.

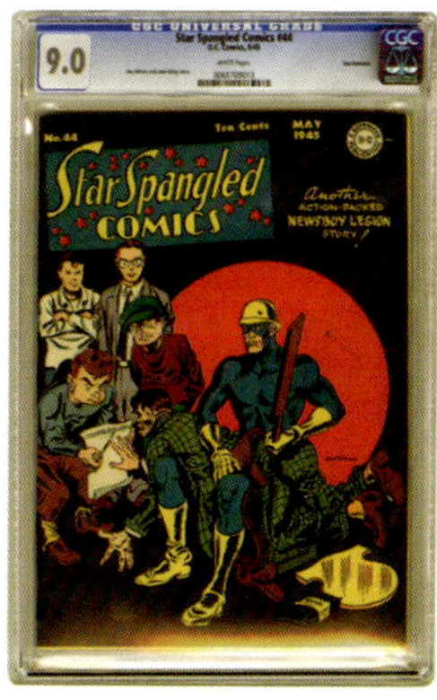

2204 Star Spangled Comics #44 San Francisco pedigree (DC, 1945) CGC VF/NM 9.0 White pages. This is a beautiful book, so we were a bit nonplused that two copies could possibly be graded higher than this San Francisco copy, and a bit befuddled by the conservative grade as well. Reaching for our microscopes, we then finally noticed an almost imperceptible black-on-black ball-point pen circle around the cover date that presumably accounted for the modest grade. But when you factor in the page quality, the pedigree, and the overall look of this black-cover issue, we find it hard to believe there's a more attractive copy out there. The cover bears the signature "Simon and Kirby," though Overstreet notes, "Most all issues after #29 signed by Simon & Kirby are not by them." Some point to Gil Kane as the actual artist. Of course, S&K's creation, the Newsboy Legion, was the stars of the book. Overstreet 2005 VF/NM 9.0 value = $494; NM- 9.2 value = $665. CGC census 6/05: 1 in 9.0, 2 higher.

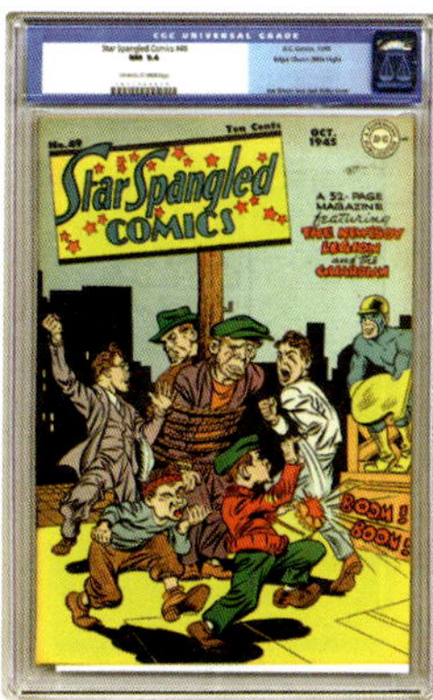

2205 Star Spangled Comics #49 Mile High pedigree (DC, 1945) CGC NM 9.4 Off-white to white pages. The Newsboy Legion is, as they've been known to say, "a *foist*-rate outfit," and they're the stars of this issue. Various sources attribute this issue's cover to Simon and Kirby, Jack Kirby by himself, or neither of the two! Other characters include the Star Spangled Kid and Robotman. Overstreet 2005 NM- 9.2 value = $665. CGC census 8/05: 1 in 9.4, none higher.

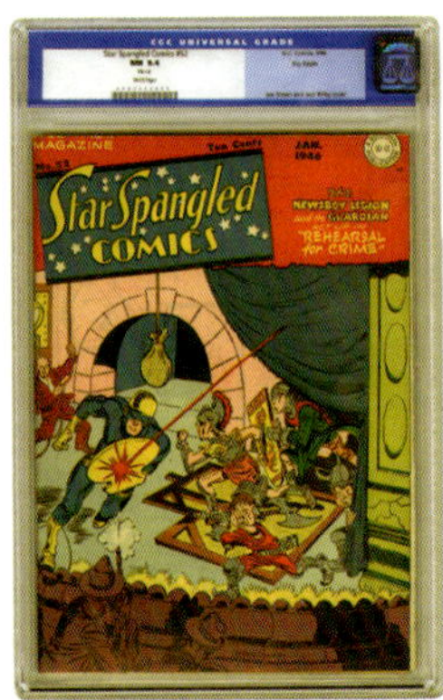

2206 Star Spangled Comics #52 Big Apple pedigree (DC, 1946) CGC NM 9.4 White pages. Joe Simon and Jack Kirby provide this Newsboy Legion and Guardian cover. This copy is noted on the CGC label as being mis-cut, but it's still a very attractive and desirable pedigreed example, with no better copies currently listed by CGC. Overstreet 2005 NM- 9.2 value = $600. CGC census 7/05: 1 in 9.4, none higher.

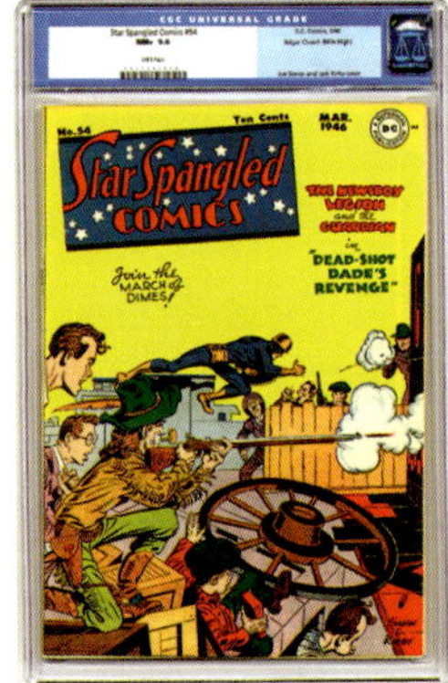

2207 Star Spangled Comics #54 Mile High pedigree (DC, 1946) CGC NM+ 9.6 White pages. This copy looks absolutely flawless to us — find something wrong with it, we *dare* ya! The book has a Simon and Kirby cover. In addition to S&K's creation, the Newsboy Legion, the book's got adventures of Robotman and the Star Spangled Kid. Overstreet 2005 NM- 9.2 value = $600. CGC census 8/05: 1 in 9.6, none higher.

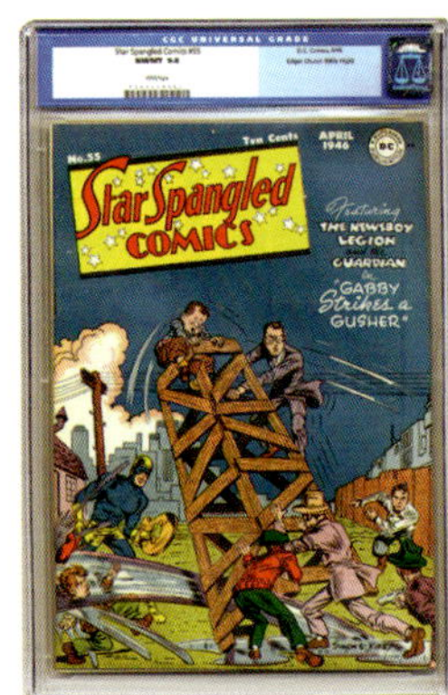

2208 Star Spangled Comics #55 Mile High pedigree (DC, 1946) CGC NM/MT 9.8 White pages. There's oil in them thar... *city*? Trust the Newsboy Legion to find it, and trust the Golden Guardian to get them out of the jam they're in. This issue's cover bears the signature of Simon and Kirby, though Overstreet warns, "Most all issues after #29 signed by Simon and Kirby are not by them." The Star Spangled Kid and Robotman are also featured. And of course, a 9.8 Mile High copy with white pages is one that will never be topped! Overstreet 2005 NM- 9.2 value = $600. CGC census 8/05: 2 in 9.8, none higher.

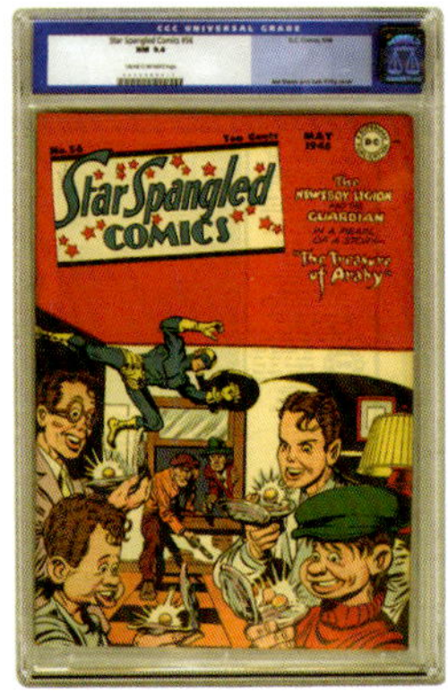

2209 Star Spangled Comics #56 (DC, 1946) CGC NM 9.4 Cream to off-white pages. The Newsboy Legion find their oyster dinner decorated with pearls on this cute cover by Joe Simon and Jack Kirby. The boys would soon be vacating their spot in this title to make way for a certain Boy Wonder, whose solo stories begin in issue #65. This copy is a pearl in itself; it's very fresh and attractive. Overstreet 2005 NM- 9.2 value = $600. CGC census 7/05: 1 in 9.4, none higher.

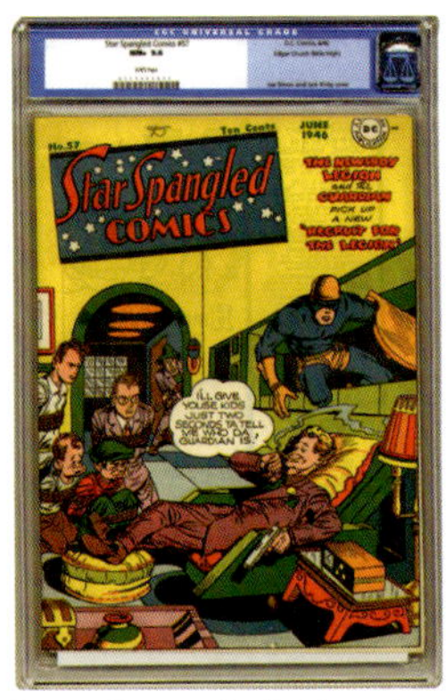

2210 Star Spangled Comics #57 Mile High pedigree (DC, 1946) CGC NM+ 9.6 White pages. Those crafty lads from Suicide Slum, the Newsboy Legion, star in this issue, which also has adventures of the Star Spangled Kid, Robotman, and more. Overstreet credits the cover to Simon and Kirby. Overstreet 2005 NM- 9.2 value = $600. CGC census 8/05: 2 in 9.6, none higher.

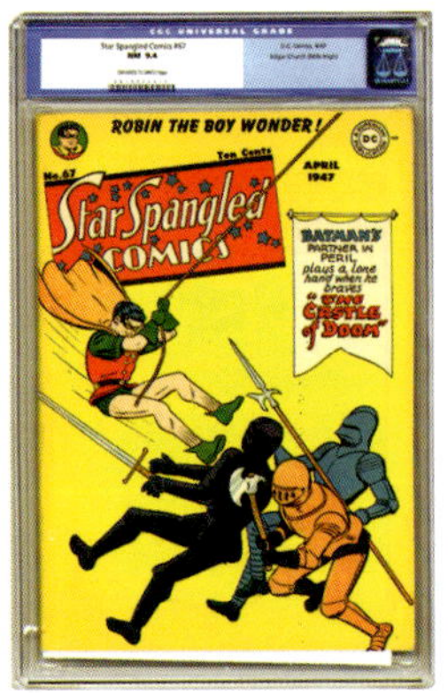

2211 Star Spangled Comics #67 Mile High pedigree (DC, 1947) CGC NM 9.4 Off-white to white pages. Where *are* all of the copies of this comic? This is the first one we've offered here at Heritage, and it's the only one that CGC has certified to date! Robin the Boy Wonder is the star of the show, and he's drawn by Win Mortimer both on the cover and inside the issue. Overstreet 2005 NM- 9.2 value = $875. CGC census 8/05: 1 in 9.4, none higher.

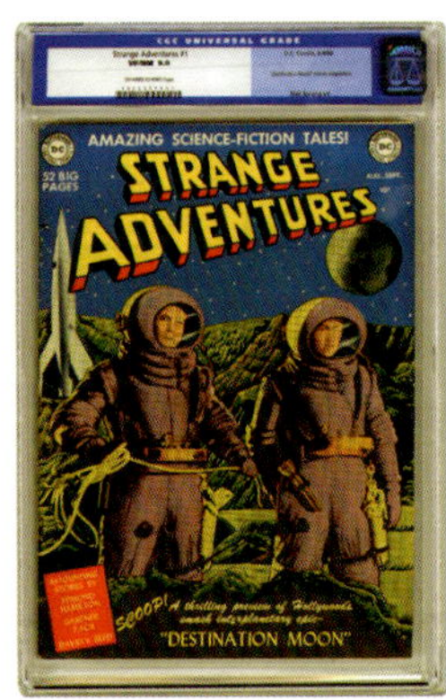

2212 Strange Adventures #1 (DC, 1950) CGC VF/NM 9.0 Off-white to white pages. This unique cover is one you can recognize from across the room thanks to its hybrid photo/grey tone look. This key first issue of the long-running series contains an adaptation of "Destination Moon," with a preview of the movie. With stories by Edmond Hamilton, David Reed, and Gardner Fox (who are credited on the cover, a rare honor for writers), this seminal issue got **Strange Adventures** off to a good start — good enough that it would eventually become one of the most successful sci-fi titles of the 1950s. The additional attraction of art by Dick Sprang (of **Batman** fame) didn't hurt either. Overstreet 2005 VF/NM 9.0 value = $3,420; NM- 9.2 value = $4,800. CGC census 7/05: 4 in 9.0, none higher.

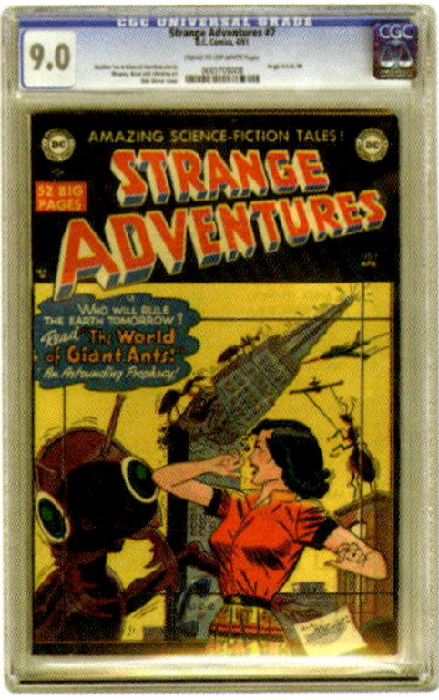

2213 Strange Adventures #7 (DC, 1951) CGC VF/NM 9.0 Cream to off-white pages. Bob Oksner's creepy cover predicts "Who will rule the Earth tomorrow" — how about giant purple ants? The reds, blues, and yellows practically glow against the black frame on this eye-catching cover. Inside, there's more great art by Jim Mooney, Gil Kane, and Carmine Infantino, plus the origin story of Kris KL-99. Overstreet 2005 VF/NM 9.0 value = $897; NM- 9.2 value = $1,240. CGC census 7/05: 3 in 9.0, none higher.

2214 Strange Adventures #10 (DC, 1951) CGC NM 9.4 Cream to off-white pages. Captain Comet makes his second appearance in this issue. What a gorgeous copy — flat, tight, with vibrant color and a big green monster on the cover! What more could you want? Bid! Overstreet 2005 NM- 9.2 value = $1,240. CGC census 9/05: 2 in 9.4, 2 higher.

2215 Strange Adventures #10 (DC, 1951) CGC NM- 9.2 Off-white to white pages. This was only the second outing for Captain Comet, who first appeared in the previous issue. The Captain's adventure was drawn by Carmine Infantino; also contributing were Murphy Anderson and Gil Kane. Overstreet 2005 NM- 9.2 value = $1,240. CGC census 8/05: 3 in 9.2, 4 higher.

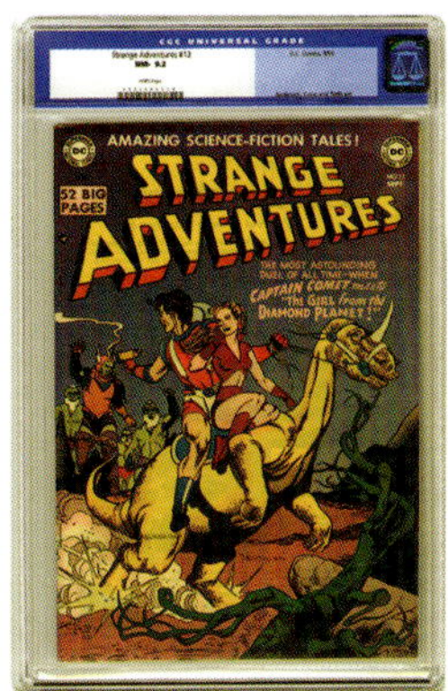

2216 Strange Adventures #12 (DC, 1951) CGC NM- 9.2 White pages. These early 1950s science fiction comics are so much fun! This choice example sports a cool Captain Comet cover, with the good Captain and a curvacious cutie riding a yellow dinosaur-type creature. Very colorful! And the art on these DC issues was always top-notch — Alex Toth, Murphy Anderson, and Gil Kane are featured in this issue. Overstreet 2005 NM- 9.2 value = $800. CGC census 9/05: 2 in 9.2, none higher.

2217 Strange Adventures #13 White Mountain pedigree (DC, 1951) CGC VF/NM 9.0 Off-white to white pages. It's Captain Comet to the rescue when Stone Men from the stars invade! Artists include Carmine Infantino, Alex Toth, and Gil Kane — not a half-bad line-up of talent! This pedigreed copy exhibits wonderful color and great paper quality. CGC notes: "Date stamp on first page." Overstreet 2005 VF/NM 9.0 value = $588; NM- 9.2 value = $800. CGC census 9/05: 2 in 9.0, 1 higher.

2218 Strange Adventures #16 (DC, 1952) CGC NM- 9.2 Off-white pages. Ever wonder what was behind those huge stone heads found on Easter Island? Apparently, someone found out — and now their doom awaits! Or so this wild cover will lead you to believe! This issue is filled with fantastic art from Murphy Anderson, Carmine Infantino, and Gil Kane. The cover colors simply pop off the page, especially the vibrant red of the stone head. As the cover blurb reads — Amazing! Overstreet 2005 NM- 9.2 value = $800. CGC census 9/05: 2 in 9.2, 1 higher.

2219 Strange Adventures #20 (DC, 1952) CGC NM- 9.2 Off-white pages. The wide-eyed little orange-skinned aliens on this cover conquer the Earth with their freeze ray — apparently it's more startling (and effective) than just flying around in saucers! This issue has a great line-up of artists, including Murphy Anderson, Carmine Infantino, and Gil Kane. This high-grade, colorful copy is surely one of the best in existence. To date, no other copies of this issue have been graded higher by CGC. Overstreet 2005 NM- 9.2 value = $800. CGC census 9/05: 1 in 9.2, none higher.

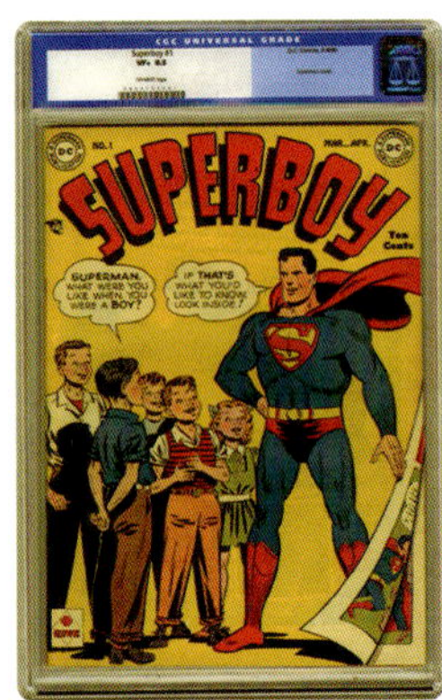

2220 Superboy #1 (DC, 1949) CGC VF+ 8.5 Off-white pages. This key debut issue doesn't even feature the title character on the cover — instead, it's the grown-up Superman who is seen enticing kids to turn the pages. The adventures of Superman as a boy was a natural idea. Joe Shuster and Jerry Siegel, fresh from a stint in the military, created the first Superboy stories, which originally saw print in **More Fun Comics** before this spinoff title was released in 1949. A thirty-year run was the result. This sharp copy is sure to please, with no major problems or defects to report. Overstreet 2005 VF 8.0 value = $5,418; VF/NM 9.0 value = $8,709. CGC census 9/05: 3 in 8.5, 2 higher.

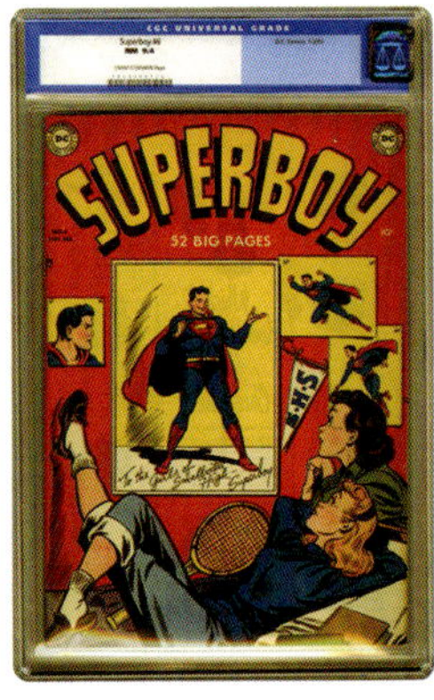

2221 Superboy #6 (DC, 1950) CGC NM 9.4 Cream to off-white pages. Smallville's greatest star really shines on this remarkable copy. It's currently one of only two copies of this issue certified by CGC, with the second rating only a distant FN- 5.5. Just the slightest hint of age around the right edge keeps this issue from looking as if it rolled off the presses last week, instead of fifty-five years ago. If only the best will do, this is the one for you! Overstreet 2005 NM- 9.2 value = $1,225. CGC census 9/05: 1 in 9.4, none higher.

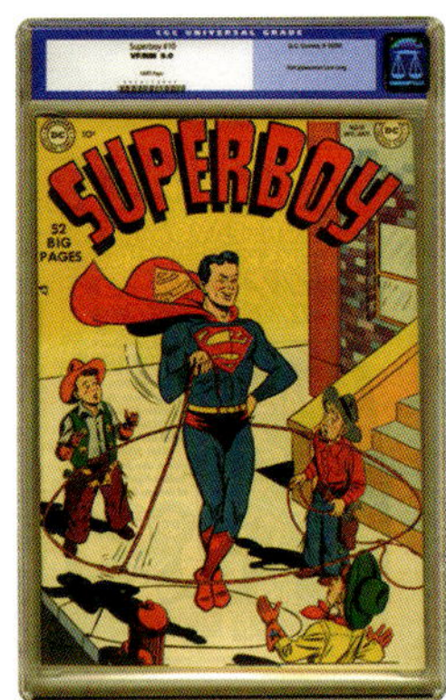

2222 Superboy #10 (DC, 1950) CGC VF/NM 9.0 White pages. This issue introduces Lana Lang to Smallville, and Superboy's world will be forever altered by this ravishing red-haired teen queen. Superman's affairs of the heart always seemed to involve a lady with "LL" initials, a trend that started at this moment in his life. This attractive copy has plenty of eye-appeal, with great cover color and excellent paper quality. Currently, it ranks at the top of the CGC census, with the next highest copy coming in at only 7.0. Overstreet 2005 VF/NM 9.0 value = $907; NM- 9.2 value = $1,225. CGC census 9/05: 1 in 9.0, none higher.

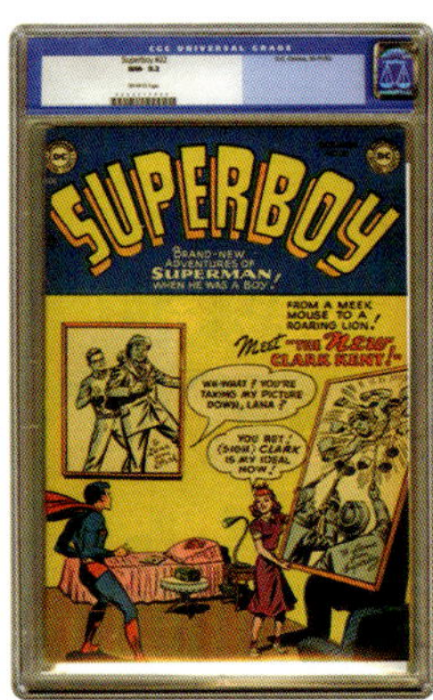

2223 Superboy #11 (DC, 1950) CGC VF/NM 9.0 Cream to off-white pages. Lana Lang, in her second appearance (and first cover — with *brown hair*, no less) wastes little time in her quest to prove Clark Kent is secretly the Boy of Steel. Looks like Clark better get used to this! Here's another gorgeous high-grade copy that is currently unsurpassed in the CGC census report for this issue. Overstreet 2005 VF/NM 9.0 value = $703; NM- 9.2 value = $950. CGC census 9/05: 1 in 9.0, none higher.

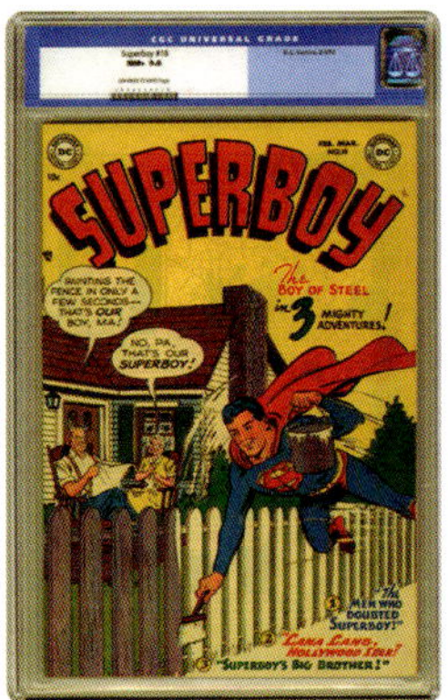

2224 Superboy #18 (DC, 1952) CGC NM+ 9.6 Off-white to white pages. Better grab those Foster Grants before you take a look at this impeccable peach of a copy — the cover colors are so bright, it might be too much for your peepers! Of the four copies of this issue currently certified by CGC, this one is far and away the finest. Overstreet 2005 NM- 9.2 value = $625. CGC census 9/05: 1 in 9.6, none higher.

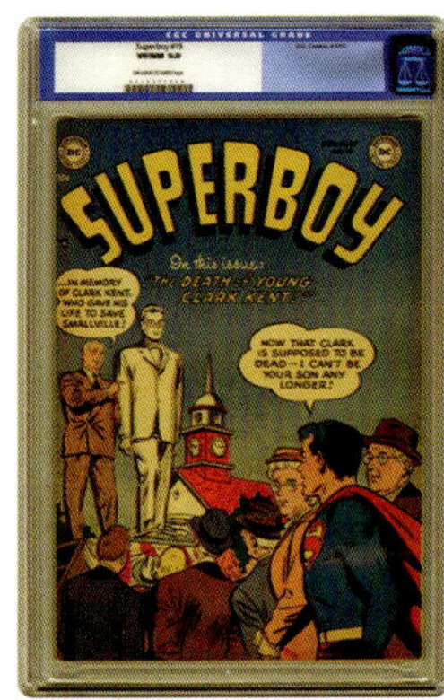

2225 Superboy #19 (DC, 1952) CGC VF/NM 9.0 Off-white to white pages. The Boy of Steel finds himself in a sticky wicket in this issue's cover story, entitled "The Death of Young Clark Kent." There's nothing sticky about this superb copy, though; it's rock-solid. And if you're thinking of waiting for a higher-graded copy to come along, be advised the wait may be long; to date, this is the only copy of issue #19 certified by CGC. Overstreet 2005 VF/NM 9.0 value = $465; NM- 9.2 value = $625. CGC census 9/05: 1 in 9.0, none higher.

2226 Superboy #20 (DC, 1952) CGC VF/NM 9.0 Off-white pages. A spooky-looking Jor-El makes a cover appearance (his second of the series) on this issue, as "The Ghost That Haunted Smallville." This copy is flat, clean, and very attractive; however, CGC notes: "Small tear on 5 pages." And although the CGC header doesn't reflect this, a certificate of authenticity claiming this book as part of the "Crestoh/Ross Collection" accompanies the book. Please note that there is a crack in the CGC holder, visible from the back. Overstreet 2005 VF/NM 9.0 value = $465; NM- 9.2 value = $625. CGC census 9/05: 1 in 9.0, 1 higher.

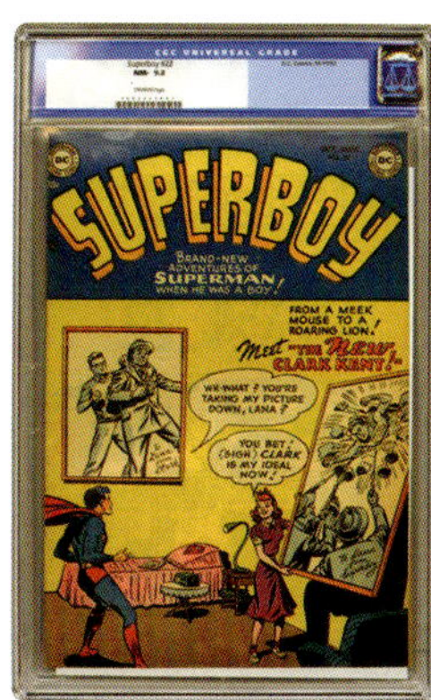

2227 Superboy #22 (DC, 1952) CGC NM- 9.2 Off-white pages. There's nothing quite like a near-mint copy when it comes to collecting comic books. Here's just such a book, yet at first glance, the logo's subtle color scheme of yellow and light orange may appear faded. Trust us, there is no fading; check out the vivid red in Superboy's cape, shorts, and boots. This is a very sharp copy. And to top it off, there's an early Lana Lang cover appearance, too. Overstreet 2005 NM- 9.2 value = $475. CGC census 9/05: 1 in 9.2, none higher.

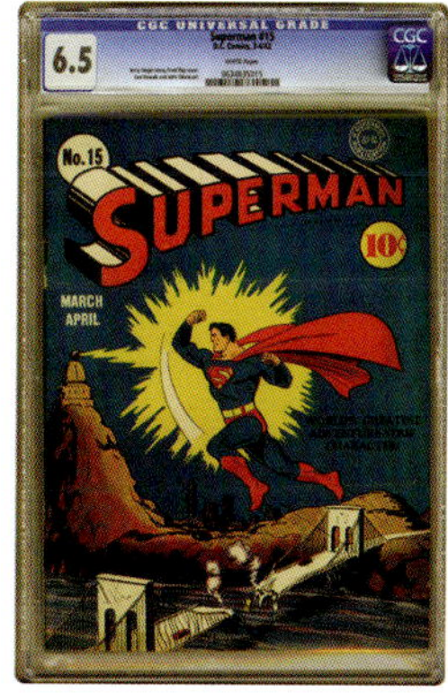

2228 Superman #15 (DC, 1942) CGC FN+ 6.5 White pages. The highest-graded copy of this issue to date is an 8.0, that means our offering numbers among the very best on the market. The issue's got great cover art by the underappreciated Fred Ray. Overstreet 2005 FN 6.0 value = $693; VF 8.0 value = $1,444. CGC census 9/05: 1 in 6.5, 2 higher.

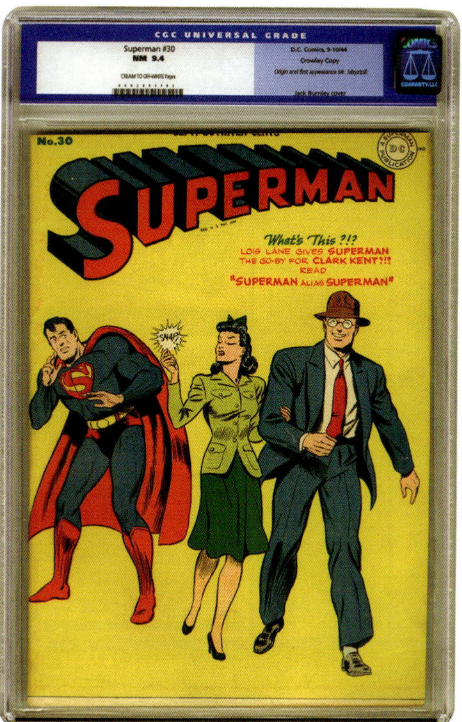

2229 Superman #30 Crowley pedigree (DC, 1944) CGC NM 9.4 Cream to off-white pages. That exasperating imp, Mr. Mxyztplk, made his first appearance in this issue! The origin story of that prankster from the land of Zrfff is also told here. The comic-relief villain didn't earn cover billing, but we'll excuse that oversight since what did make the cover is a great character piece by Jack Burnley, with Clark Kent being number one in Lois Lane's heart for a change. This book is from the collection of Wendell Crowley, who was an editor at Fawcett... obviously he made sure to check out what the competition was doing. Then again, he may have filed this one away without thumbing through it, explaining the amazing condition the book is in. This is the highest-graded copy of this issue that CGC has certified to date. Overstreet 2005 NM- 9.2 value = $3,200. CGC census 9/05: 1 in 9.4, none higher.

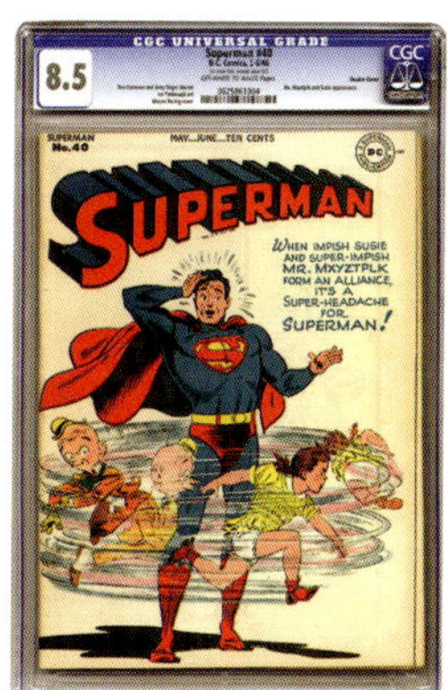

2230 Superman #40 Double Cover (DC, 1946) CGC VF+ 8.5 Off-white to white pages. The Man of Steel finds himself in double trouble, in the form of super-prankster Mr. Mxyztplk and irrepressible brat Susie, on this Wayne Boring-drawn cover. The happy high-bidder for this copy will find himself doubly delighted–this is one of those rare copies featuring a double cover. CGC notes "first cover 8.0, interior cover 8.5". Overstreet 2005 VF 8.0 value = $663; VF/NM 9.0 value = $1,019. CGC census 8/05: 1 in 8.5, 4 higher.

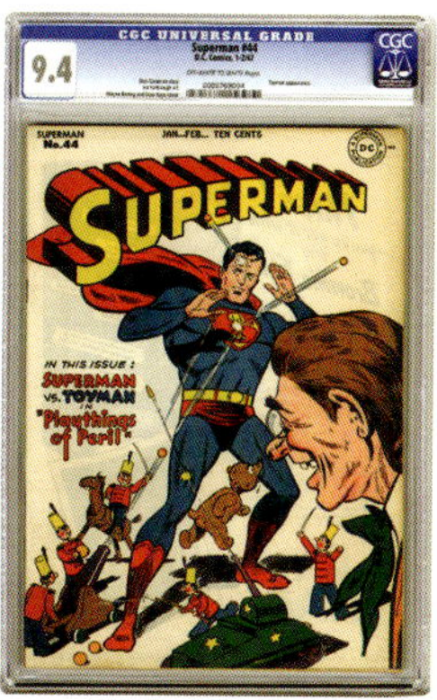

2231 Superman #44 (DC, 1947) CGC NM 9.4 Off-white to white pages. Superman tussles with the Toyman in this issue, as previewed on the Wayne Boring cover, but that's all just a warm-up for the story that has Supes traveling through time to meet William Shakespeare! And the Man of Steel even helps out by using his super-memory to co-write **Macbeth** and thus help the Bard meet a deadline. When the hurlyburly's done and the battle's lost and won, only the high bidder will go home with this copy, and no copy has been graded higher by CGC to date! Overstreet 2005 NM- 9.2 value = $1,100. CGC census 8/05: 2 in 9.4, none higher.

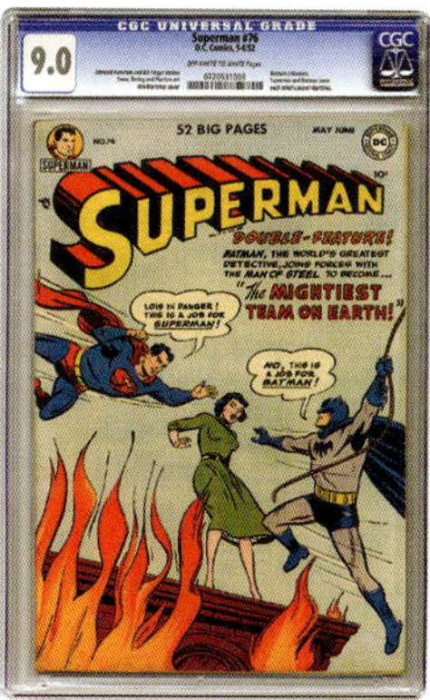

2232 Superman #76 (DC, 1952) CGC VF/NM 9.0 Off-white to white pages. There's no higher-graded copy in CGC's census to date of this key issue, in which Batman and Superman learn each other's secret identities for the first time! The famous scene takes place in a cabin aboard ship, which as fate (or writer Edmond Hamilton) would have it, is being shared by Clark Kent and Bruce Wayne. Flames light up the dark room just as the two are changing to Superman and Batman, and the rest is DC history, as the two would soon begin appearing in the same story in the pages of **World's Finest**. The story is also notable for being only the second time Curt Swan drew Superman — he would go on to be one of the definitive artists for the character. Wayne Boring drew one of the issue's other Superman stories, and Win Mortimer provided the cover art. Overstreet 2005 VF/NM 9.0 value = $1,741; NM- 9.2 value = $2,350. CGC census 8/05: 3 in 9.0, none higher.

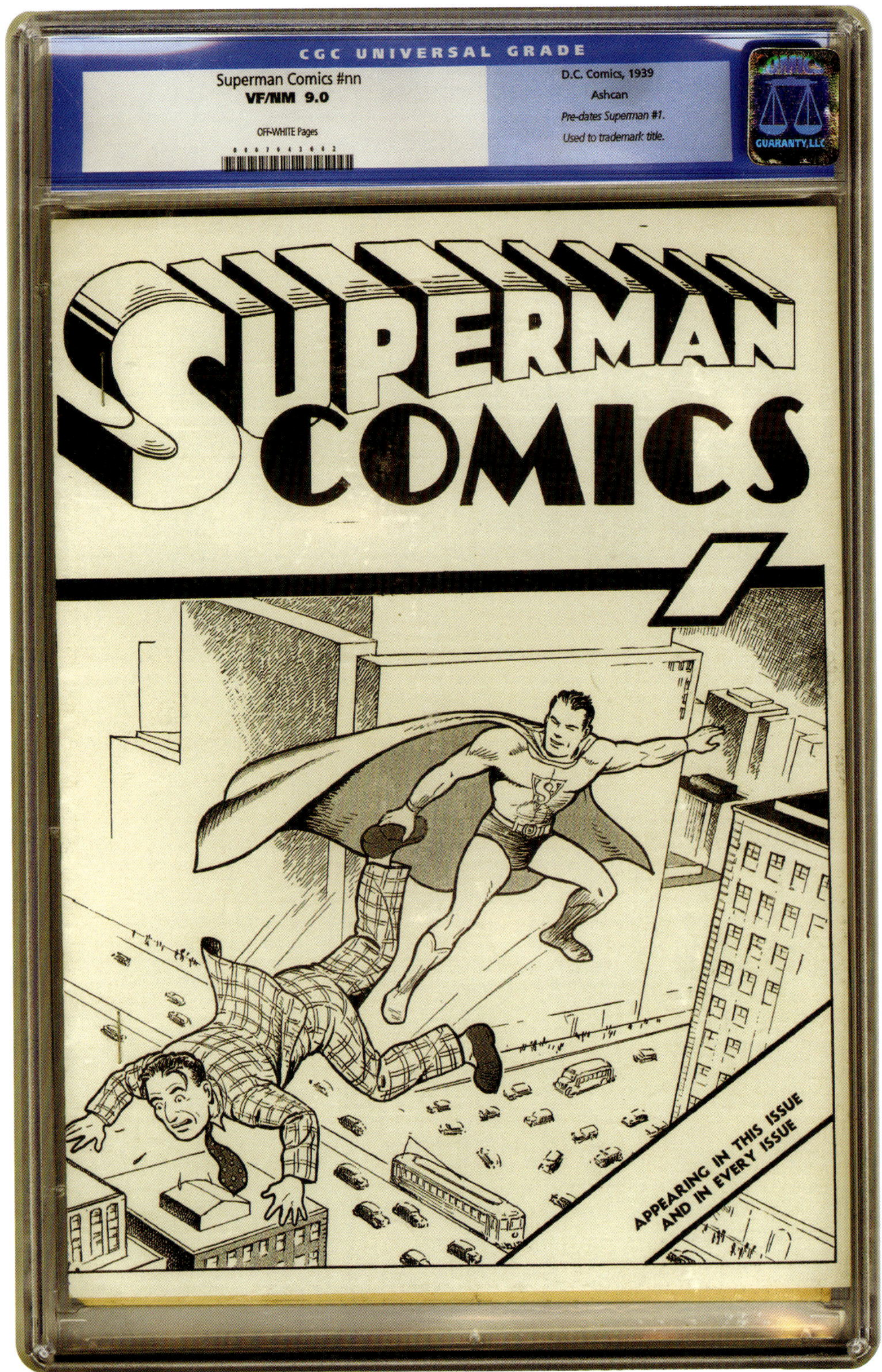

2233 Superman Comics #nn Ashcan (DC, 1939) CGC VF/NM 9.0 Off-white pages. Here's a Superman item that's harder to find than **Action Comics** #1, or any other published Superman comic for that matter! It's DC's ashcan for its planned **Superman** title (an ashcan is a mock-up of a comic, produced by hand in very small quantities, for purposes of securing a copyright for a title and/or a logo). Since the danger of Superman rip-offs was very much warranted in 1939, DC's urgency in wanting to secure rights to the title is understandable! There are only two known copies of this ashcan, and both were purchased from Sol Harrison, who became president of DC Comics; this is the higher-graded of the two, we might add. As is typical for ashcans, this one features re-used art — it's the cover art from **Action Comics** #7 (by Joe Shuster) and part of the interior of **Action Comics** #8. That makes this the first time that the now ultra-famous Superman logo appeared on a cover! And that's quite significant, since this is undoubtedly the most famous logo in comics. This item was bound, trimmed, and stapled by hand (and of course never intended to be a collectible) so the fact that there's a VF/NM copy in existence is amazing stuff. Note that if our back-cover scan appears dark, it's because the CGC holder has a couple of extra layers of reinforcing plastic behind the comic, no doubt to make up for this ashcan's having a much lower page count than a standard comic book. Ashcans are not listed in Overstreet. CGC census 7/05: 1 in 9.0, none higher.

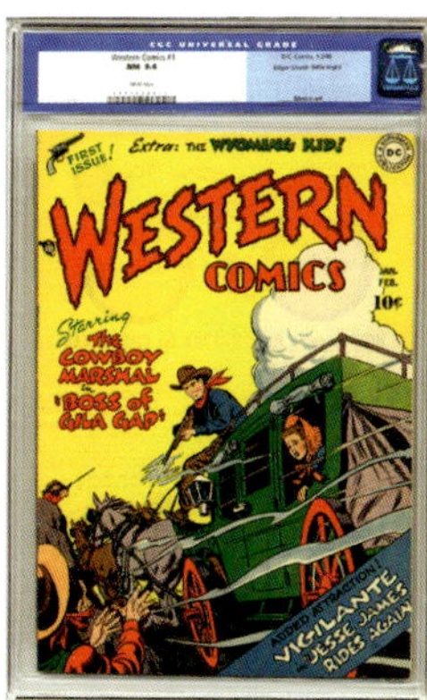

2234 Western Comics #1 Mile High pedigree (DC, 1948) CGC NM 9.4 White pages. DC's flagship Western title rode into town in 1948 and it didn't head off into the sunset until 1961. The posse of artists in this debut issue includes Howard Sherman (who also drew the cover), Mort Meskin, and Howard Post. Overstreet 2005 NM- 9.2 value = $1,050. CGC census 9/05: 1 in 9.4, none higher.

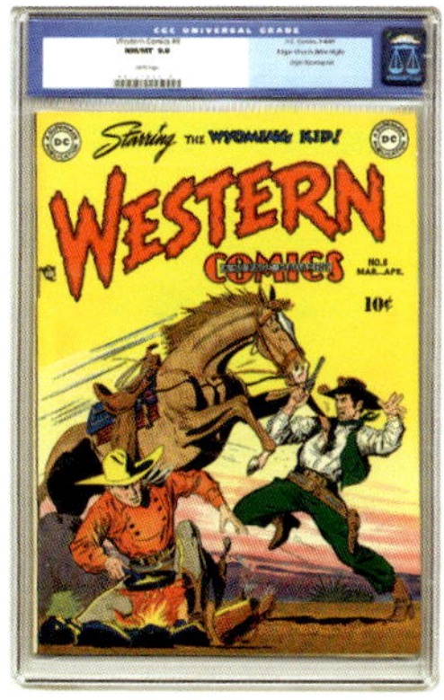

2235 Western Comics #8 Mile High pedigree (DC, 1949) CGC NM/MT 9.8 White pages. This issue tells the origin of the Wyoming Kid (he's a sheep rancher's son on a never-ending search for the man who killed his pop). Other characters in the issue are Rodeo Rick, Nighthawk, and the Cowboy Marshal. This is the best copy west of the Pecos, or east of it for that matter, in fact it's the only one graded above 7.5 by CGC to date. Overstreet 2005 NM- 9.2 value = $390. CGC census 9/05: 1 in 9.8, none higher.

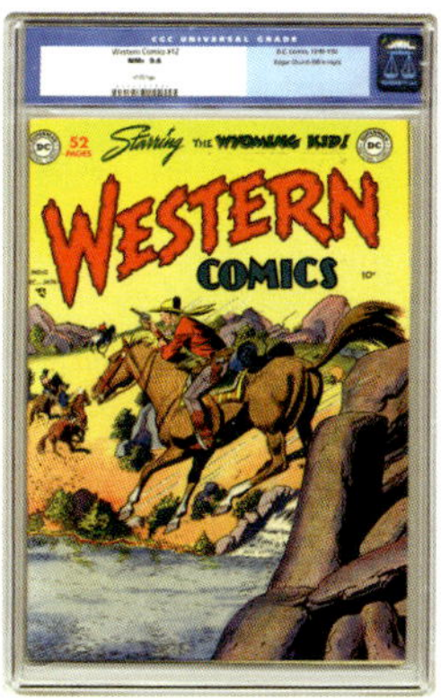

2236 Western Comics #12 Mile High pedigree (DC, 1950) CGC NM+ 9.6 White pages. The Nighthawk was just one of the pistol-packing heroes in this series, the others being Rodeo Rick, the Cowboy Marshal, and the fellow you see on the cover, who goes by the Wyoming Kid. This is the only copy of the issue graded above VF/NM by CGC as of this writing. Overstreet 2005 NM- 9.2 value = $210. CGC census 9/05: 1 in 9.6, none higher.

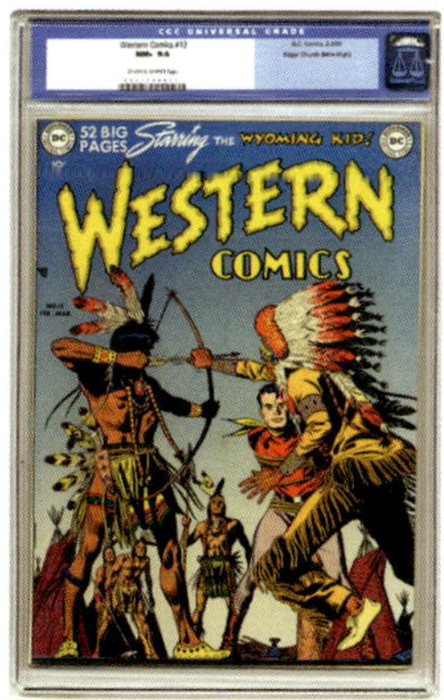

2237 Western Comics #13 Mile High pedigree (DC, 1950) CGC NM+ 9.6 Off-white to white pages. You can almost hear the beat of the tom-toms when you examine this issue's dramatic cover featuring the Wyoming Kid. And of course, there's no better way to enjoy any Golden Age cover than by owning the Mile High copy. It's an impeccably preserved book. Overstreet 2005 NM-9.2 value = $210. CGC census 9/05: 1 in 9.6, none higher.

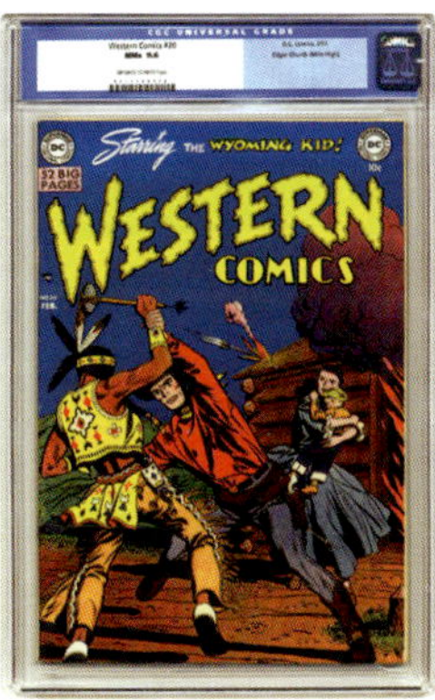

2238 Western Comics #20 Mile High pedigree (DC, 1951) CGC NM+ 9.6 Off-white to white pages. The Wyoming Kid, the Nighthawk, Rodeo Rick, and the Cowboy Marshal star in this DC western. Our offering is the only copy of the issue that CGC has certified as of this writing. Overstreet 2005 NM- 9.2 value = $210. CGC census 9/05: 1 in 9.6, none higher.

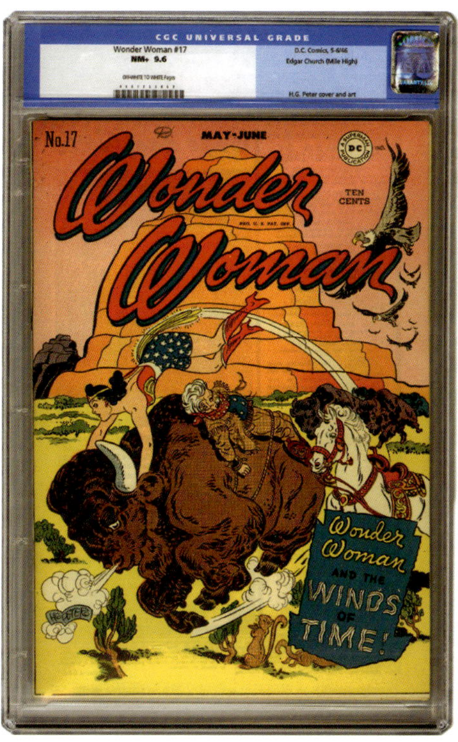

2239 Wonder Woman #17 Mile High pedigree (DC, 1946) CGC NM+ 9.6 Off-white to white pages. While it's often been said that there's nothing quite like a Mile High comic, we find extra joy in viewing one of Edgar Church's **Wonder Woman** books! This one has a sweet pink and orange cover, dominated by a rampaging buffalo. That big orange mountain in the background looks a lot like a yummy gelatin mold! This tasty copy tops the current CGC charts for this issue. Overstreet 2005 NM- 9.2 value = $1,450. CGC census 9/05: 1 in 9.6, none higher.

2240 Wonder Woman #174 Pacific Coast pedigree (DC, 1968) CGC NM+ 9.6 Off-white to white pages. Steve Trevor gains super powers. Irv Novick cover and art. Overstreet 2005 NM- 9.2 value = $60. CGC census 9/05: 2 in 9.6, none higher.

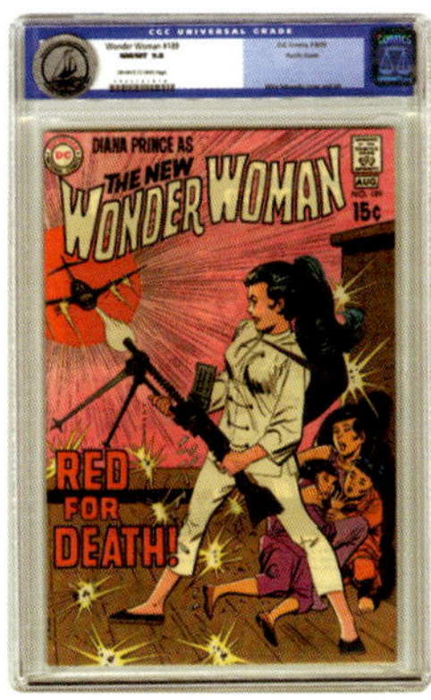

2241 Wonder Woman #189 Pacific Coast pedigree (DC, 1970) CGC NM/MT 9.8 Off-white to white pages. Wonder Woman heads for Red China in an issue from DC's "social relevance" period. Mike Sekowsky wrote the story and drew the entire issue. This perfect copy is the only 9.8 in CGC's census as of this writing. Overstreet 2005 NM- 9.2 value = $45. CGC census 9/05: 1 in 9.8, none higher.

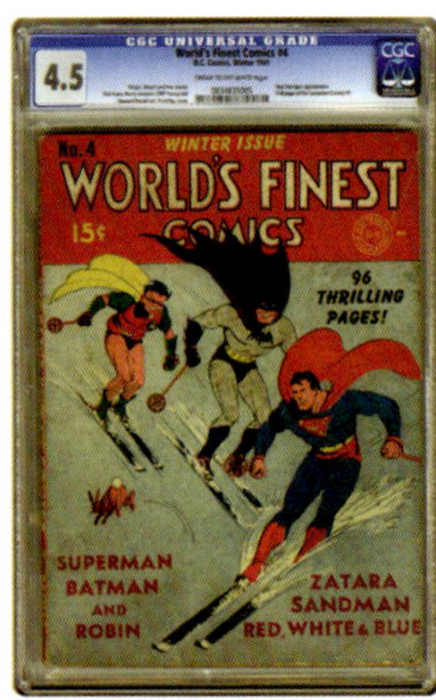

2242 World's Finest Comics #4 (DC, 1941) CGC VG+ 4.5 Cream to off-white pages. Yes, this cost a nickel more than other comics of the day, but the kid who could persuade mom to cough up the extra five cents got a huge 96-pager to read and reread. Stars Superman and Batman are joined by the Sandman, Hop Harrigan, Zatara, the Crimson Avenger, and too many other features to mention. The cover of this Winter issue is by Fred Ray. Overstreet 2005 VG 4.0 value = $524. CGC census 9/05: 1 in 4.5, 19 higher.

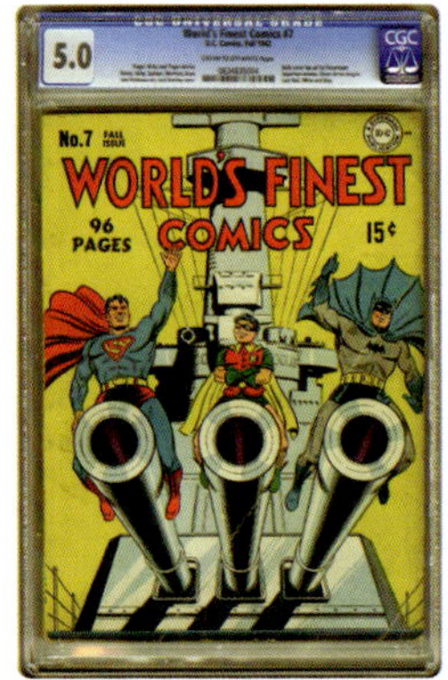

2243 World's Finest Comics #7 (DC, 1942) CGC VG/FN 5.0 Cream to off-white pages. Here's a nice "Nazi's-eye view" of American naval firepower courtesy of cover artist Jack Burnley. Inside the book, the obligatory Superman and Batman features are only the beginning — there's a Sandman story with Simon and Kirby art, plus stories starring Zatara, the Star-Spangled Kid and Stripesy, the equally patriotic Red, White, and Blue (who make their last appearance in this title), and Green Arrow (who makes his *first* appearance in the title). Overstreet 2005 VG 4.0 value = $384; FN 6.0 value = $576. CGC census 9/05: 1 in 5.0, 19 higher.

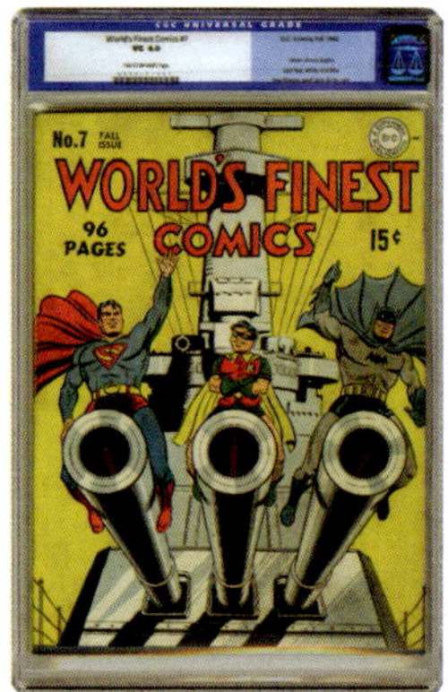

2244 World's Finest Comics #7 (DC, 1942) CGC VG 4.0 Tan to off-white pages. Jack Burnley's cover gives us a superb "Nazi's-eye view" of American naval firepower! Inside the book, the obligatory Superman and Batman features are only the beginning — there's also a Sandman story with Simon and Kirby art, plus stories starring Zatara, the Star-Spangled Kid and Stripesy, the equally patriotic Red, White, and Blue (who appears in this series for the *last* time), and Green Arrow (who does so for the *first* time). Overstreet 2005 VG 4.0 value = $384. CGC census 7/05: 2 in 4.0, 22 higher.

2245 World's Finest Comics #11 (DC, 1943) CGC VF 8.0 Cream to off-white pages. The concept of a "Victory Garden" was that citizens on the home front would do their civic duty by growing as much of their own produce as possible, thereby freeing up food supplies to be shipped to the fighting men overseas. And DC's heroes showed how it was done here, as illustrated by Jack Burnley and Jerry Robinson. Batman and Superman were just two of the many characters appearing in the issue. Only two copies (the best being VF/NM) are above ours in CGC's census as of this writing. Overstreet 2005 VF 8.0 value = $863. CGC census 9/05: 1 in 8.0, 2 higher.

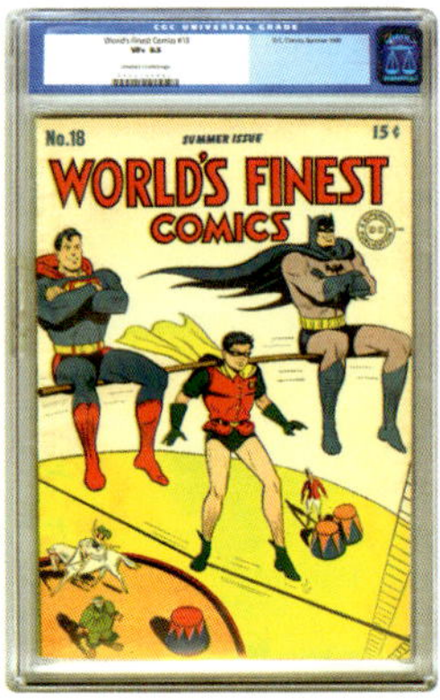

2246 World's Finest Comics #18 (DC, 1945) CGC VF+ 8.5 Off-white to white pages. A square bound book with a white cover isn't easy to find "in grade!" Jack Burnley drew this issue's death-defying cover scene (well, it's death-defying for Robin and Batman anyway, since they can't fly!). Batman and Superman appear in separate features inside the issue, and they're backed up by tales of Zatara, Green Arrow, the Boy Commandos, and making their last appearance in this title, the Star Spangled Kid and Stripesy. Overstreet 2005 VF 8.0 value = $756; VF/NM 9.0 value = $1,166. CGC census 9/05: 1 in 8.5, 2 higher.

2247 Adventures Into the Unknown #12 Northford pedigree (ACG, 1950) CGC NM- 9.2 Cream to off-white pages. As we look into our crystal ball, we sense an emptiness in your pre-Code horror collection. We sense that you are troubled because you lack a copy of **Adventures in the Unknown** #12. We also sense that many a season will change before you find another copy for sale that's as nice as this one. The book has an Ogden Whitney cover; the interior artists include Ken Bald, John Celardo, and Charles Sultan. Overstreet 2005 NM- 9.2 value = $310. CGC census 9/05: 1 in 9.2, none higher.

2248 Air Ace V2#8 Crowley Copy pedigree (Street & Smith, 1945) CGC NM 9.4 Off-white pages. Overstreet 2005 NM- 9.2 value = $180. CGC census 9/05: 1 in 9.4, none higher.

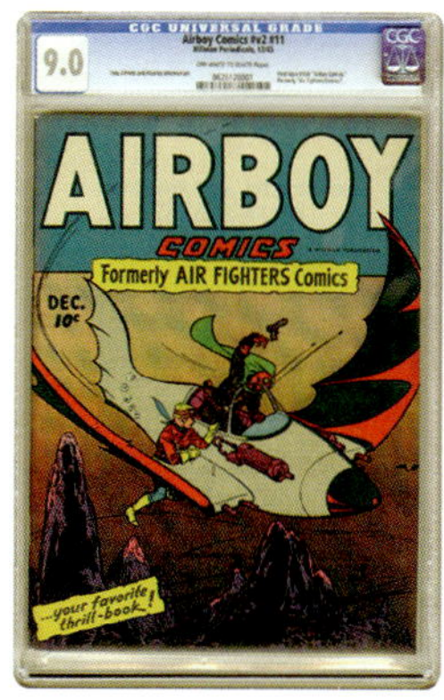

2249 Airboy Comics V2#11 (Hillman Fall, 1945) CGC VF/NM 9.0 Off-white to white pages. No copy of this first issue has been graded higher by CGC to date! Airboy, arguably the most popular of the Golden Age aviator heroes, got the series **Air Fighters Comics** renamed in his honor starting with this issue. Of course, the most awesome thing about Airboy was his Bird-Plane — check it out on this cover, which may be the work of Fred Kida. Tony DiPreta and Maurice Whitman contributed interior art to the issue. Overstreet 2005 VF/NM 9.0 value = $703; NM- 9.2 value = $950. CGC census 8/05: 1 in 9.0, none higher.

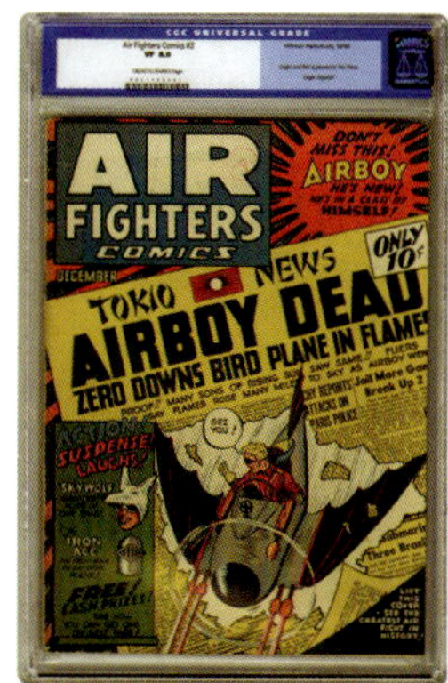

2250 Air Fighters Comics #3 (Hillman Fall, 1942) CGC VF 8.0 Cream to off-white pages. Bombastic, patriotic covers were a staple of the title. In this issue: origin and first appearance of the Heap, the origin of Skywolf, and the second appearance of Airboy. Surpassed in CGC grade by just one other copy. Charles Biro cover, with Fred Kida and Bob Fujitani art. Overstreet 2005 VF 8.0 value = $1,156. CGC census 5/05: 1 in 8.0, 1 higher.

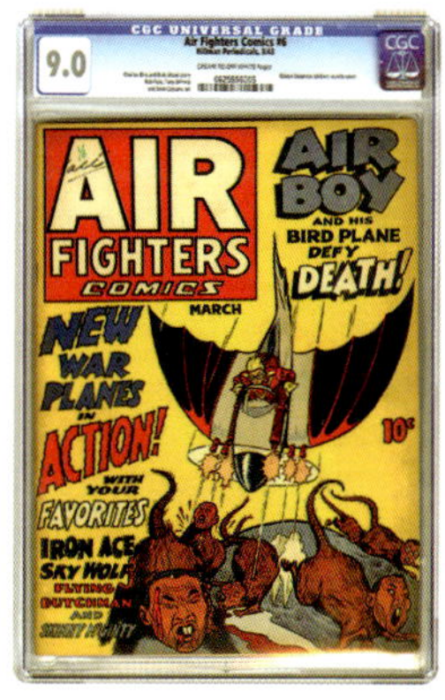

2251 Air Fighters Comics #6 (Hillman Fall, 1943) CGC VF/NM 9.0 Cream to off-white pages. We certainly don't wish to offend our many friends in Japan, but this issue's wild World War II cover, listed as "classic" by CGC, shows Airboy in his plane, gunning down rodents with the faces of Japanese soldiers! Artists include Bob Fuje, Tony DiPreta, and John Cassone. Overstreet 2005 VF/NM 9.0 value = $1,260; NM- 9.2 value = $1,700. CGC census 8/05: 1 in 9.0, 3 higher.

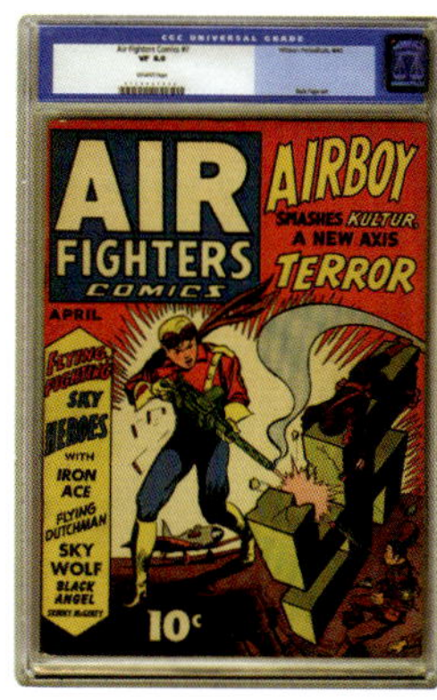

2252 Air Fighters Comics #7 (Hillman Fall, 1943) CGC VF 8.0 Off-white pages. This WWII cover has earned an Overstreet "classic Nazi swastika cover" designation. The Grand Comics Database Project credits Al Camy with the cover. Bob Fujitani, Tony DiPreta, and Fred Kida contributed story art. CGC has awarded a higher grade to just one other copy of this issue. Overstreet 2005 VF 8.0 value = $769. CGC census 5/05: 2 in 8.0, 1 higher.

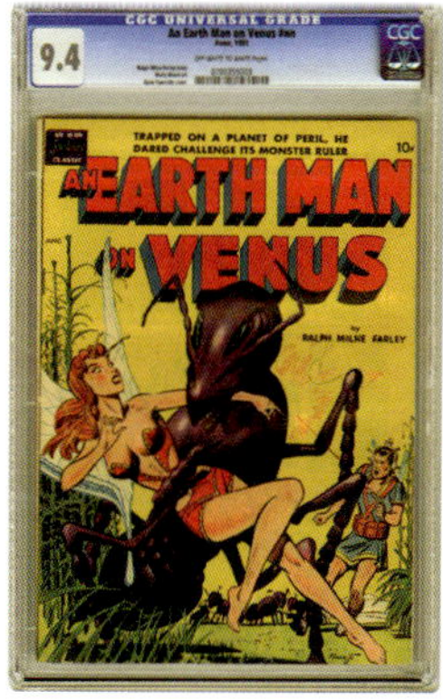

2253 An Earth Man on Venus #nn (Avon, 1951) CGC NM 9.4 Off-white to white pages. Man vs. giant insects was a popular theme of the Atomic Age, but in this landmark example, our valiant spaceman hero is wearing a kilt! A scantily clad, winged Venusian lass in peril adds another bonus to this outstanding Gene Fawcette cover; the interior art is by the legendary Wally Wood, ensuring this specimen's must-have status. This recently-slabbed specimen tops CGC's current census for this book. Overstreet 2005 NM- 9.2 value = $1,700. CGC census 9/05: 1 in 9.4, none higher.

2254 The Beyond #9 Bethlehem pedigree (Ace, 1952) CGC NM- 9.2 Off-white pages. This is the highest-graded copy that CGC has certified to date. Comes with the Bethlehem certificate of authenticity. Overstreet 2005 NM- 9.2 value = $215. CGC census 9/05: 1 in 9.2, none higher.

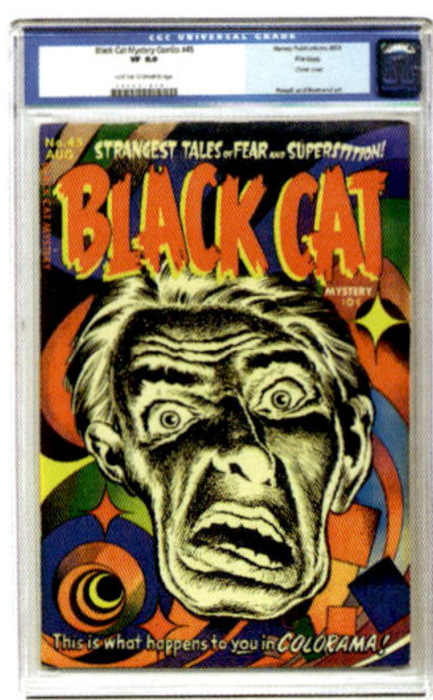

2255 Black Cat Mystery #39 Spokane pedigree (Harvey, 1952) CGC NM 9.4 White pages. This issue's story "The Body Maker," with art by Warren Kremer, was featured prominently in **Seduction of the Innocent** — in fact, it figures in the title of the last chapter of Fredric Wertham's book: "The Triumph of Dr. Payn." Also of note in this issue is a hanging cover and the art of Rudy Palais. This copy is the highest-graded certified by CGC to date, with the next-highest clocking in at a mere 8.0. Overstreet 2005 NM- 9.2 value = $315. CGC census 9/05: 1 in 9.4, none higher.

2256 Black Cat Mystery #45 File Copy (Harvey 1953) CGC VF 8.0 Light tan to off-white pages. This issue features two "classics": the "Colorama" story with Bob Powell art and Howard Nostrand's surreal cover. Nostrand also provided some interior art of his own. Overstreet 2005 VF 8.0 value = $239. CGC census 8/05: 3 in 8.0, 3 higher.

2258 Black Cat Mystery #48 Northford pedigree (Harvey, 1954) CGC NM 9.4 Off-white pages. This installment of pre-Code creepiness is brought to you by cover artist Lee Elias and interior artists Howard Nostrand and Bob Powell. Overstreet 2005 NM- 9.2 value = $270. CGC census 7/05: 1 in 9.4, none higher.

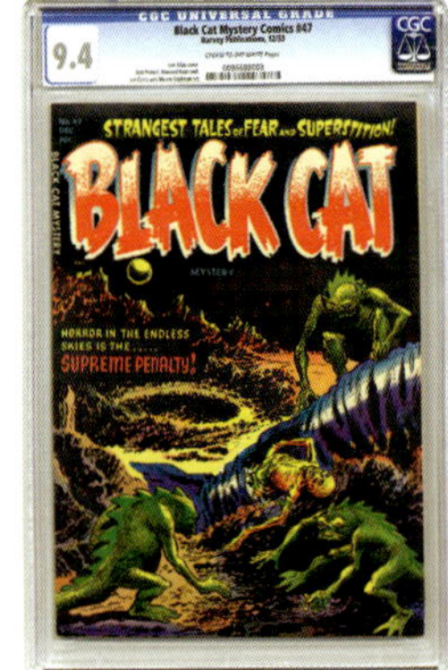

2257 Black Cat Mystery #47 (Harvey, 1953) CGC NM 9.4 Cream to off-white pages. This is the highest-graded copy CGC has certified to date of this black-cover issue! And the book's artists are a real Who's Who of Harvey horror, with Bob Powell, Howard Nostrand, Manny Stallman, and Joe Certa all contributing. Overstreet 2005 NM- 9.2 value = $270. CGC census 7/05: 1 in 9.4, none higher.

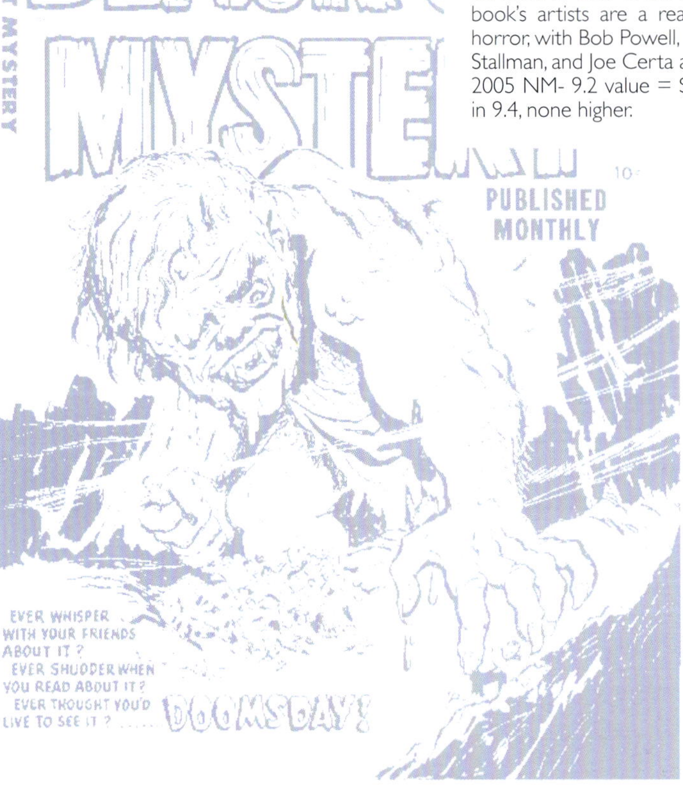

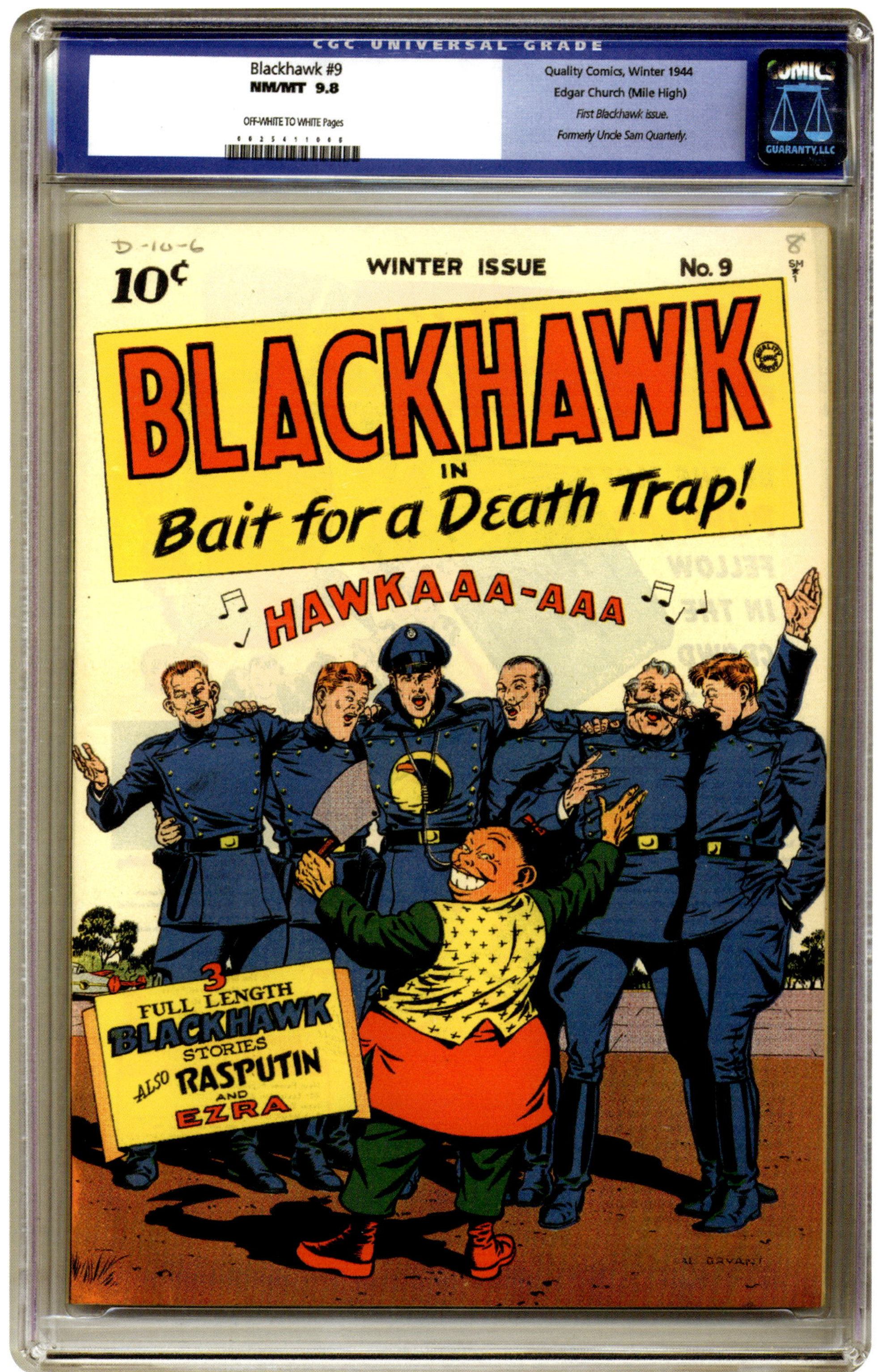

2259 Blackhawk #9 Mile High pedigree (Quality, 1944) CGC NM/MT 9.8 Off-white to white pages. We present to you the best known copy of a key first issue! And this is indeed the first **Blackhawk** issue, with numbering continued from the title **Uncle Sam Quarterly**. Legend has it that this new title was originally intended to have various backup features filling up much of the page count, but this debut issue reportedly sold so well that the series quickly became an almost all-Blackhawk affair. The cover is by Al Bryant. As for a white-cover issue in 9.8 condition, if you can acquire this beauty you'll be a happy collector indeed! Overstreet 2005 NM- 9.2 value = $5,400. CGC census 8/05: 1 in 9.8, none higher.

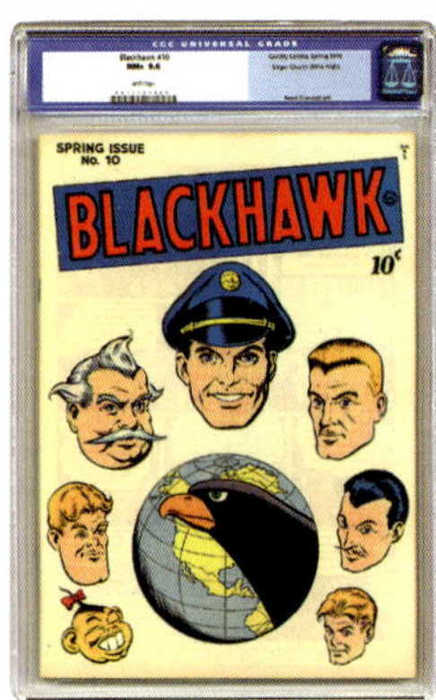

2260 Blackhawk #10 Mile High pedigree (Quality, 1946) CGC NM+ 9.6 White pages. This issue (only the second of the title, which took over the numbering from **Uncle Sam Quarterly**) features the first solo adventure of the redoubtable Chop Chop. We don't ever expect to see a better copy of this issue, especially considering the white cover. Overstreet 2005 NM- 9.2 value = $1,650. CGC census 8/05: 1 in 9.6, none higher.

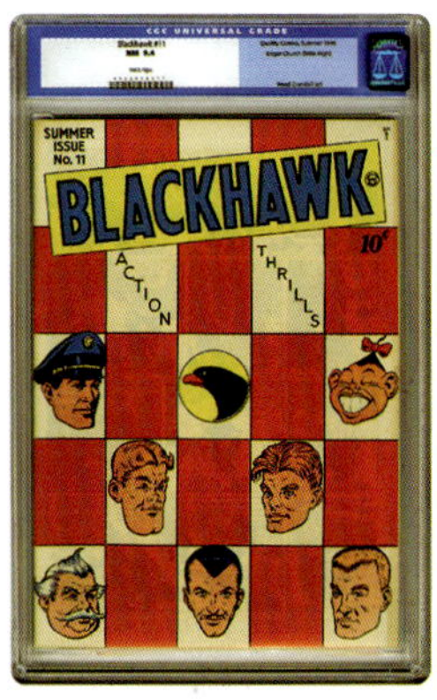

2261 Blackhawk #11 Mile High pedigree (Quality, 1946) CGC NM 9.4 White pages. This was only the third issue of the title (which had begun its numbering as **Uncle Sam**). Reed Crandall provided art for the issue. Overstreet 2005 NM- 9.2 value = $1,125. CGC census 8/05: 2 in 9.4, 1 higher.

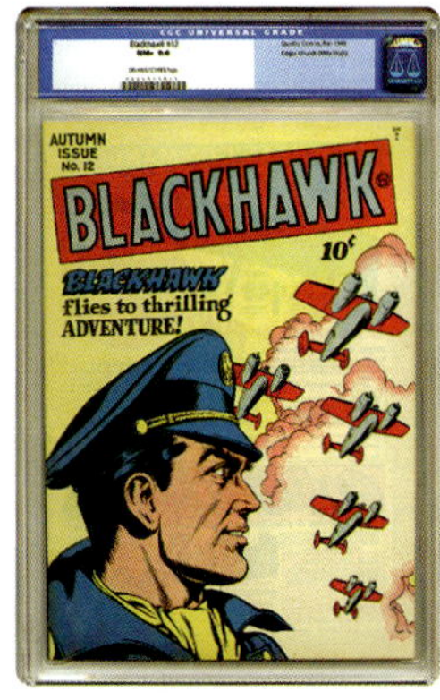

2262 Blackhawk #12 Mile High pedigree (Quality, 1946) CGC NM+ 9.6 Off-white to white pages. This is the first time we've offered this issue here at Heritage, and we've got a pedigree copy that soars above the rest. It's the only one graded above 6.5 by CGC as of this writing. Overstreet 2005 NM- 9.2 value = $1,125. CGC census 8/05: 1 in 9.6, none higher.

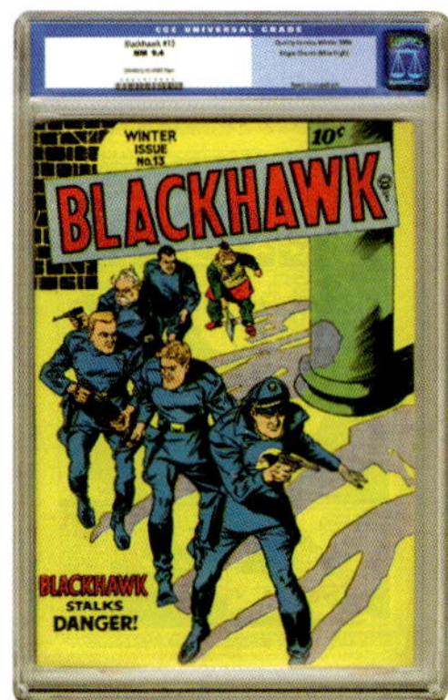

2263 Blackhawk #13 Mile High pedigree (Quality, 1946) CGC NM 9.4 Off-white to white pages. The radiant colors that are the trademark of the Edgar Church books are on display here, no wonder our offering is the highest-graded copy of the issue that CGC has certified to date. Reed Crandall provided interior art. Overstreet 2005 NM- 9.2 value = $1,125. CGC census 8/05: 1 in 9.4, none higher.

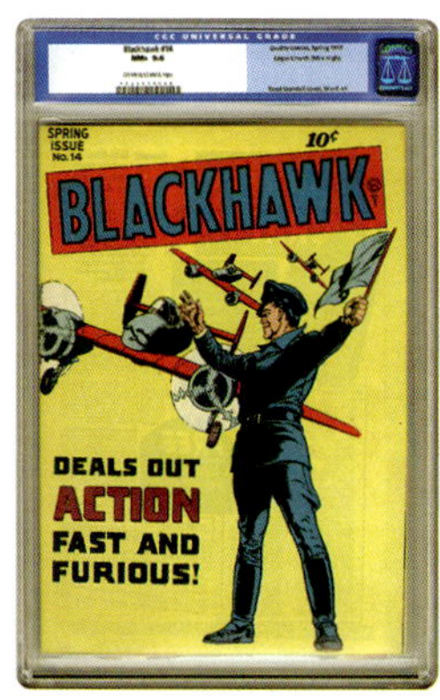

2264 Blackhawk #14 Mile High pedigree (Quality, 1947) CGC NM+ 9.6 Off-white to white pages. This Mile High copy is the one against which all others are measured! The issue has a Reed Crandall cover and Bill Ward interior art. Overstreet 2005 NM- 9.2 value = $1,125. CGC census 8/05: 1 in 9.6, none higher.

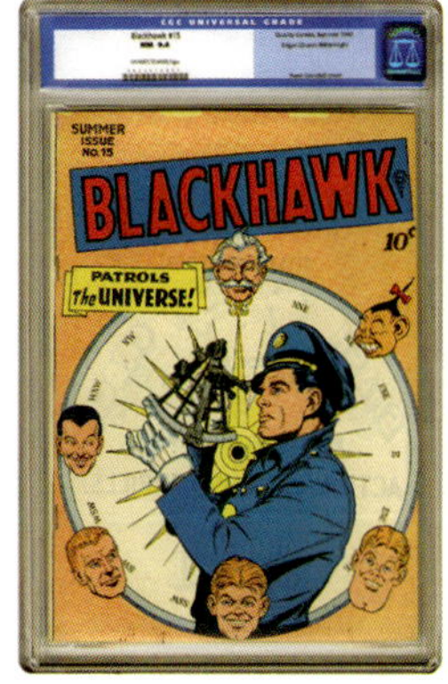

2265 Blackhawk #15 Mile High pedigree (Quality, 1947) CGC NM 9.4 Off-white to white pages. This sterling Mile High copy is the best around — the only one graded above 7.0 by CGC to date. By the way, while the top edge might appear on first glance to have chips missing, what you're seeing are light-colored blotches which were obviously nothing more than a printing quirk. This issue's cover is by Reed Crandall. Overstreet 2005 NM- 9.2 value = $1,125. CGC census 8/05: 1 in 9.4, none higher.

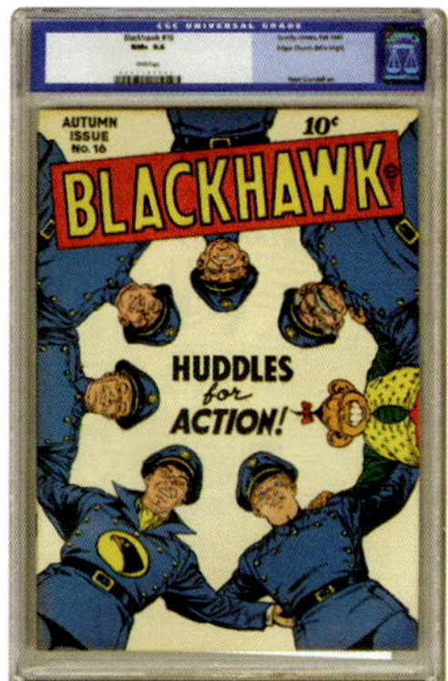

2266 Blackhawk #16 Mile High pedigree (Quality, 1947) CGC NM+ 9.6 White pages. Huddle up, comic fans — it's time to run the play known as "place a high bid." At stake is the nicest copy in CGC's current census report. The issue has an Al Bryant cover, with interior art by Bill Ward and Reed Crandall. Overstreet 2005 NM- 9.2 value = $900. CGC census 8/05: 1 in 9.6, none higher.

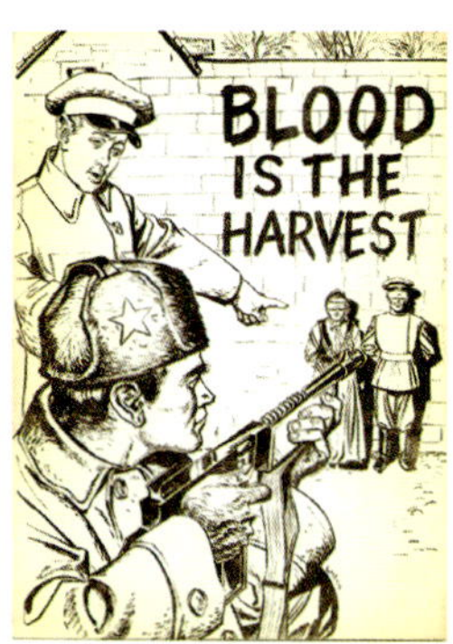

2267 Blood Is the Harvest #nn Black and White Edition (Catechetical Guild, 1950) Condition: NM-. One of the most notorious give-away comics ever, this anti-Communist propaganda comic was produced at the height of the Cold War. Overstreet says there are only five known copies of this black-and-white version. In the story, a bystander, hearing that a "young martyr" is being honored by the Soviets, tells the reader the true story of that boy, namely that he turned in his own father to the police state, resulting in the execution of his family and everyone who lived on his street. The bystander concludes the issue by wryly asking, "What if the whole world were Soviet?" A letter detailing the provenance of this copy is included. Overstreet 2005 NM- 9.2 value = $700.

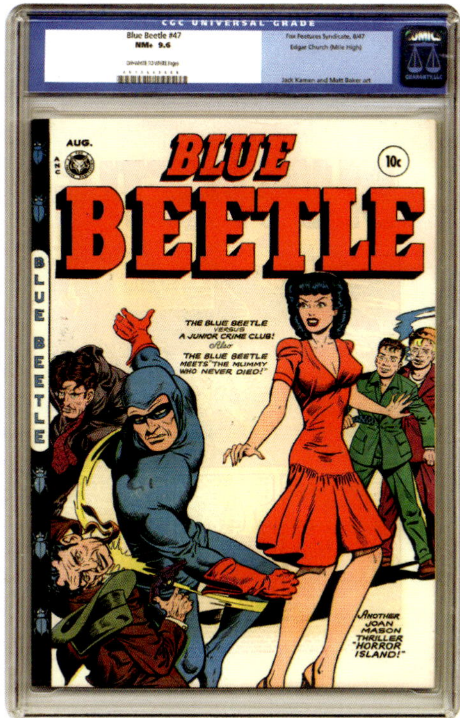

2268 Blue Beetle #47 Mile High pedigree (Fox Features Syndicate, 1947) CGC NM+ 9.6 Off-white to white pages. Some comic titles have one watershed issue. With **Detective Comics** it was #27, with **Journey Into Mystery** it was #83, and with Blue Beetle it was #47 — that's when the fairly average superhero fare of previous issues gave way to sex and violence (mostly the former) as only Jack Kamen and Matt Baker could deliver it! Kamen's cover offers a taste of what we're talking about — the two mugs in the background are dazed by what they're seeing, and we don't mean the Beetle's pugilistic prowess! And speaking of that cover, the white background on this Mile High copy is something special to behold. We were surprised to see that only three copies of this issue have been slabbed by CGC to date; ours is the best of the bunch by far. Overstreet 2005 NM- 9.2 value = $1,575. CGC census 7/05: 1 in 9.6, none higher.

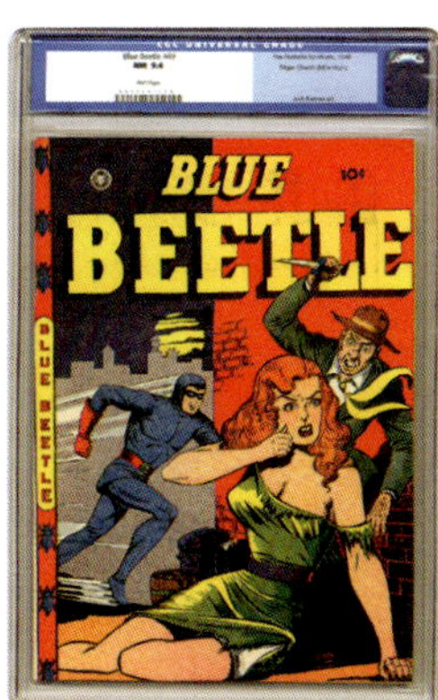

2269 Blue Beetle #49 Mile High pedigree (Fox Features Syndicate, 1947) CGC NM 9.4 White pages. Cover artist Jack Kamen relegated the Blue Beetle to the background in favor of a red-haired beauty — no complaints here. In fact, Kamen liked his rendition so much, he re-used the lovely lady for the cover of **Brenda Starr** #14 six months later! We think it's safe to say that "good girl" books will always be collectors' favorites, and since this is the Mile High copy, you just can't go wrong with it. Overstreet 2005 NM- 9.2 value = $1,250. CGC census 7/05: 1 in 9.4, none higher.

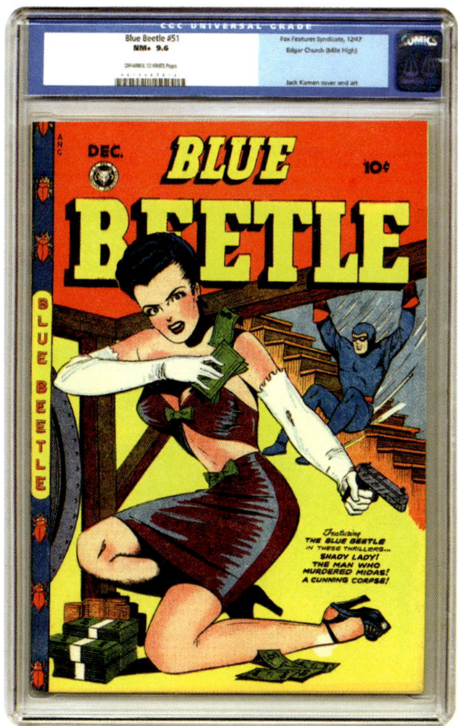

2270 Blue Beetle #51 Mile High pedigree (Fox Features Syndicate, 1947) CGC NM+ 9.6 Off-white to white pages. Jack Kamen was a giant in the world of "good girl" art, and the lovely lady on this cover has similar stature; she somehow seems to tower above the cellar ceiling on this eye-catching cover! The condition of this Mile High copy is impressive indeed, considering Fox wasn't exactly known for using the highest-quality paper around. The runner-up in CGC's census checks in at 8.5 as of this writing. Overstreet 2005 NM- 9.2 value = $1,050. CGC census 7/05: 1 in 9.6, none higher.

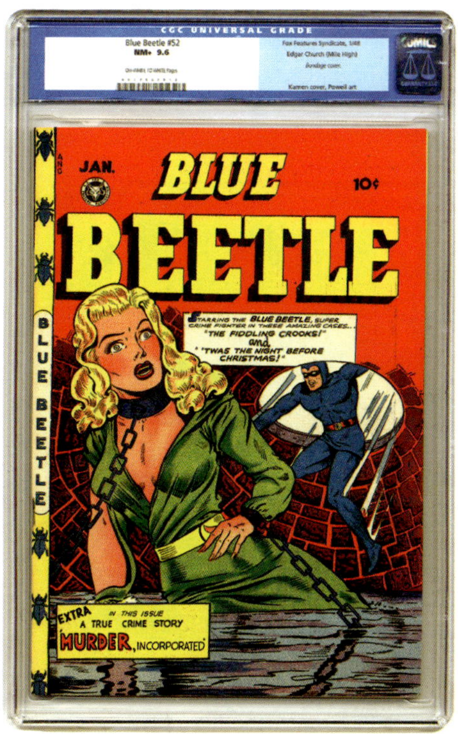

2271 Blue Beetle #52 Mile High pedigree (Fox Features Syndicate, 1948) CGC NM+ 9.6 Off-white to white pages. A bondage cover by Jack Kamen kicks off the exploitation fare on offer here. The issue includes interior art by Bob Powell as well as the series' first true crime tale. This copy from Edgar Church's collection is the highest-graded that CGC has certified to date. Overstreet 2005 NM- 9.2 value = $1,575. CGC census 7/05: 1 in 9.6, none higher.

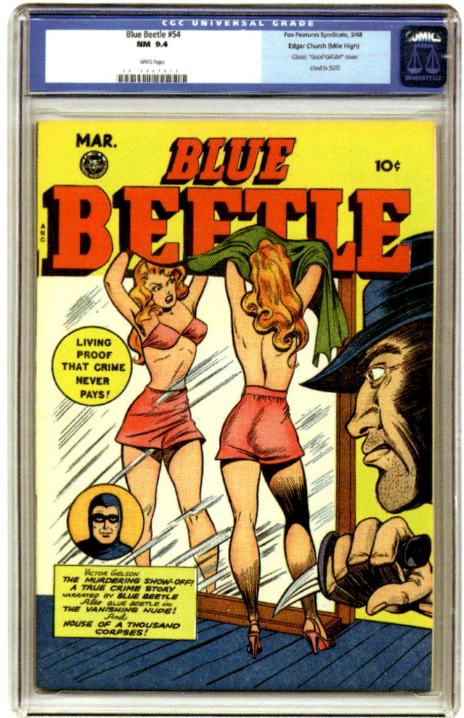

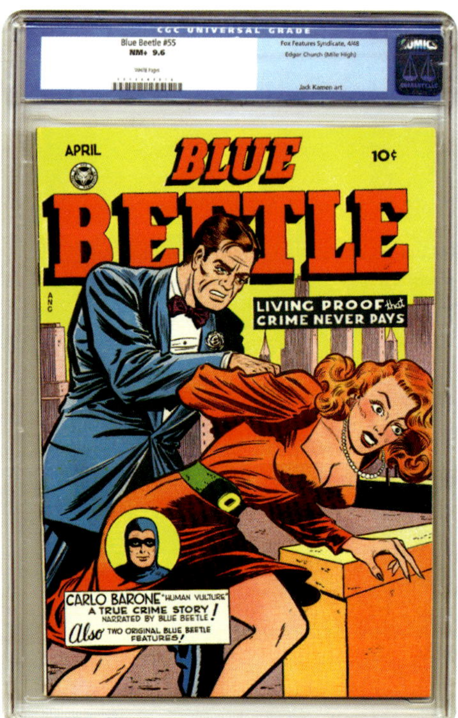

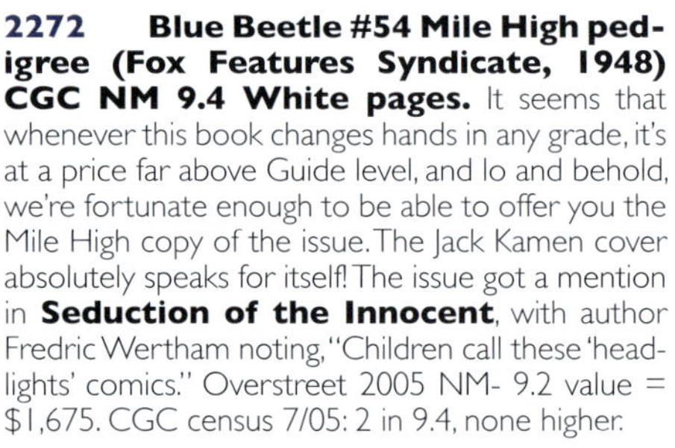

2272 Blue Beetle #54 Mile High pedigree (Fox Features Syndicate, 1948) CGC NM 9.4 White pages. It seems that whenever this book changes hands in any grade, it's at a price far above Guide level, and lo and behold, we're fortunate enough to be able to offer you the Mile High copy of the issue. The Jack Kamen cover absolutely speaks for itself! The issue got a mention in **Seduction of the Innocent**, with author Fredric Wertham noting, "Children call these 'headlights' comics." Overstreet 2005 NM- 9.2 value = $1,675. CGC census 7/05: 2 in 9.4, none higher.

2273 Blue Beetle #55 Mile High pedigree (Fox Features Syndicate, 1948) CGC NM+ 9.6 White pages. Jack Kamen contributed interior art to this issue, and whoever the cover artist was, Kamen made sure to leave the "headlights" on for him! Our Mile High copy is as super-sharp as you would expect. Overstreet 2005 NM- 9.2 value = $1,025. CGC census 7/05: 1 in 9.6, none higher.

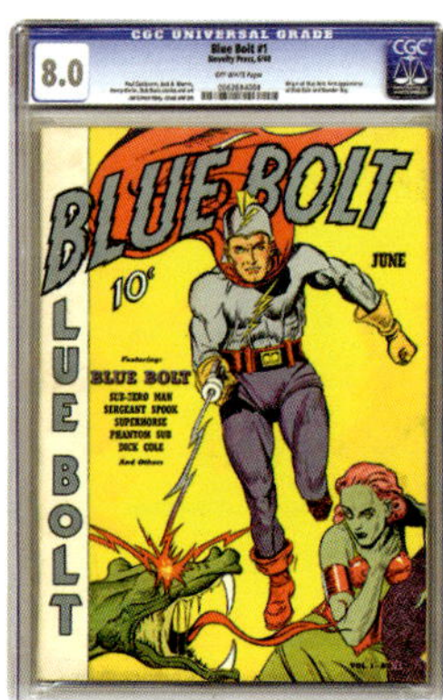

2274 Blue Bolt #1 (Novelty Press, 1940) CGC VF 8.0 Off-white pages. One of Novelty Press' first titles, this one was produced by the "shop" of artists known as Funnies Inc., with Joe Simon the most prominent of the contributors. Simon drew the cover as well as the Blue Bolt story. This issue also has the first appearance of Dick Cole (aka Wonder Boy), who would later have his own series. Overstreet 2005 VF 8.0 value = $2,015. CGC census 8/05: 1 in 8.0, 1 higher.

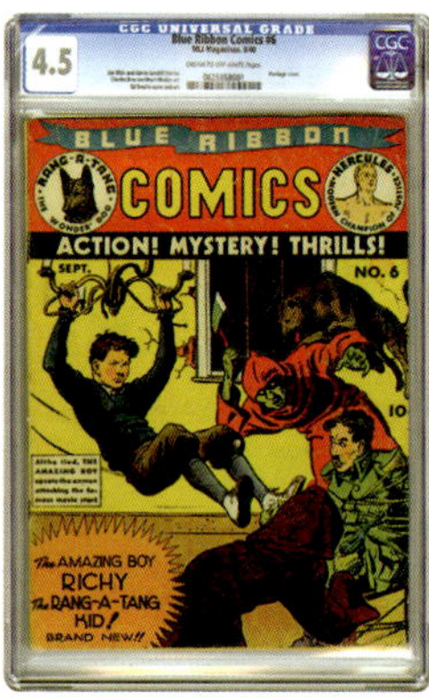

2275 Blue Ribbon Comics #6 (MLJ, 1940) CGC VG+ 4.5 Cream to off-white pages. This is the first time we've ever seen this issue here at Heritage! The star character is Rang-A-Tang the Wonder Dog, assisting (or assisted by) his kid pal Richy Waters. That's them on the cover rescuing an unnamed "famous movie star" whom we take to be Charlie Chaplin! That cover was drawn by Ed Smalle; the book also has art by Mort Meskin and Charles Biro. Overstreet 2005 VG 4.0 value = $130. CGC census 8/05: 1 in 4.5, 1 higher.

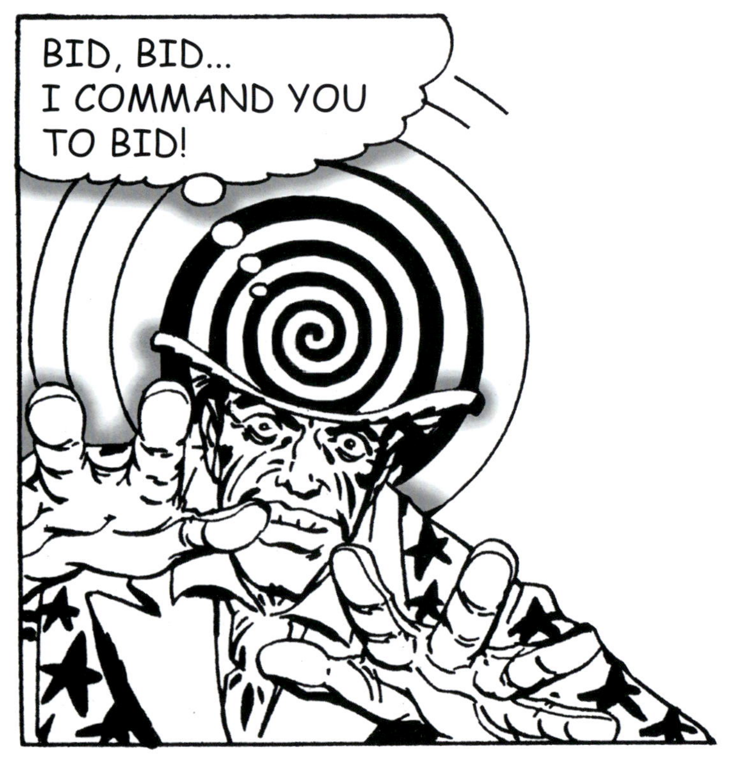

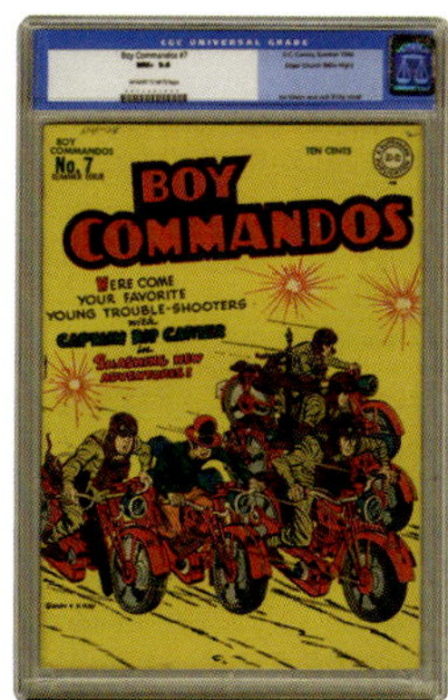

2276 Boy Commandos #7 Mile High pedigree (DC, 1944) CGC NM+ 9.6 Off-white to white pages. Here they come, roaring your way — it's the Boy Commandos, riding to victory on this cool World War II cover by Joe Simon and Jack Kirby. The brilliant cover colors, silky-smooth surfaces, and sharp edges tell you this must be from the legendary Edgar Church Mile High collection; now it's time to add it to yours with a winning bid! Overstreet 2005 NM- 9.2 value = $675. CGC census 6/05: 2 in 9.6, none higher.

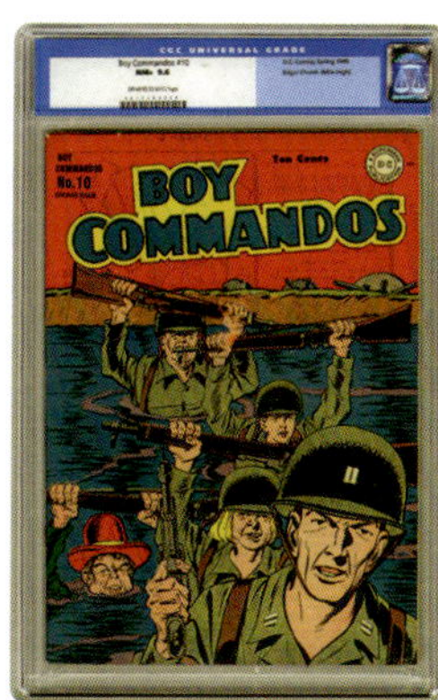

2278 Boy Commandos #10 Mile High pedigree (DC, 1945) CGC NM+ 9.6 Off-white to white pages. The boys are in deep as they wade through this World War II cover — Brooklyn looks like he might need some help! You'll need no help recognizing this as a choice example of an Edgar Church Mile High comic, as it is absolutely gorgeous! It's far and away the highest-graded copy to date according to CGC. Overstreet 2005 NM- 9.2 value = $675. CGC census 6/05: 1 in 9.6, none higher.

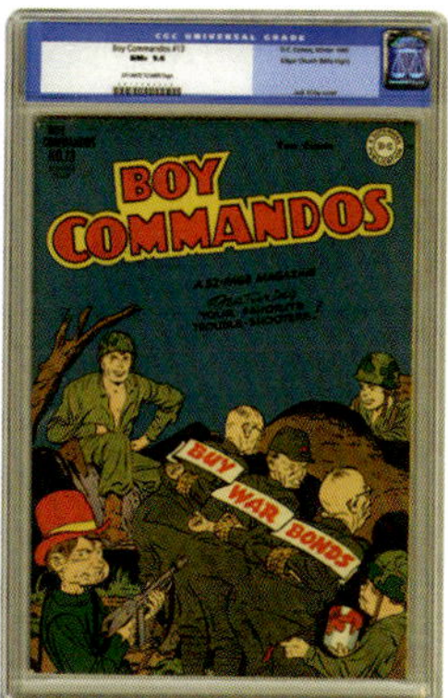

2280 Boy Commandos #13 Mile High pedigree (DC, 1945) CGC NM+ 9.6 Off-white to white pages. Joe Simon and Jack Kirby are credited in Overstreet for this odd World War II POW cover (which CGC has noted as only by Kirby). This is a typical Edgar Church Mile High copy, which of course means it's as good a copy as is likely to ever turn up. It's a good thing Edgar never let the neighborhood kids near his huge stash of comics! Overstreet 2005 NM- 9.2 value = $450. CGC census 6/05: 1 in 9.6, none higher.

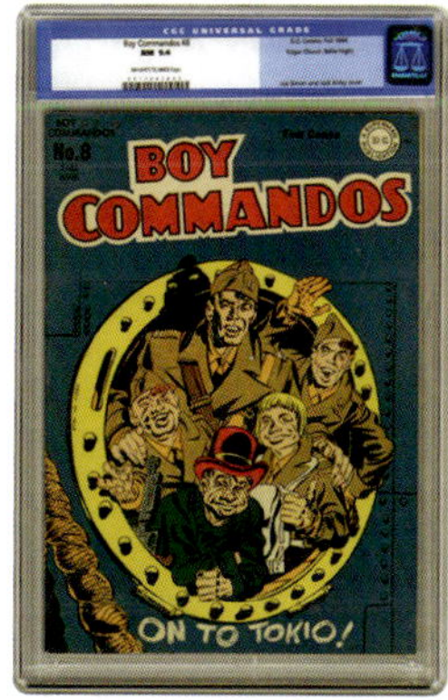

2277 Boy Commandos #8 Mile High pedigree (DC, 1944) CGC NM 9.4 Off-white to white pages. The boys are "on to Tokio" (sic) on this great World War II cover by Joe Simon and Jack Kirby. Deep, rich color makes this cover really "pop" — you know you've got an Edgar Church Mile High book with this one! CGC currently lists no higher-graded copies of this issue. Overstreet 2005 NM- 9.2 value = $675. CGC census 6/05: 1 in 9.4, none higher.

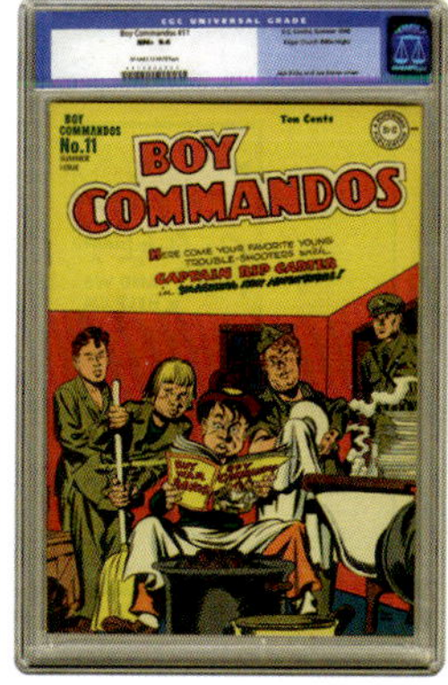

2279 Boy Commandos #11 Mile High pedigree (DC, 1945) CGC NM+ 9.6 Off-white to white pages. This infinity cover carries the Simon and Kirby signature, and CGC does list it as by Joe Simon and Jack Kirby, although Overstreet does not recognize it as such. At any rate, it's a stupendous example of the Mile High pedigree, that little ol' collection of Golden Age comics from a certain Mr. Edgar Church. The cover colors are absolutely astounding. Overstreet 2005 NM- 9.2 value = $450. CGC census 6/05: 1 in 9.6, none higher.

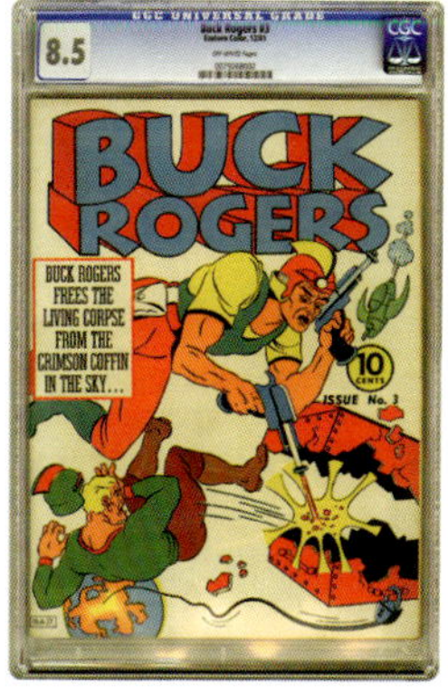

2281 Buck Rogers #3 (Eastern Color, 1941) CGC VF+ 8.5 Off-white pages. There's no oxygen in space, but there are oxymorons, as Buck Rogers finds out when he encounters "the living corpse." Comics with a white background are notoriously hard to find in top condition, but the whites here are unblemished — this is the second-highest graded copy that CGC has certified to date. Overstreet 2005 VF 8.0 value = $706; VF/NM 9.0 value = $1,091. CGC census 9/05: 1 in 8.5, 1 higher.

Oops! These Boy Commandos should be in our DC Golden Age section! See more on Page 67!

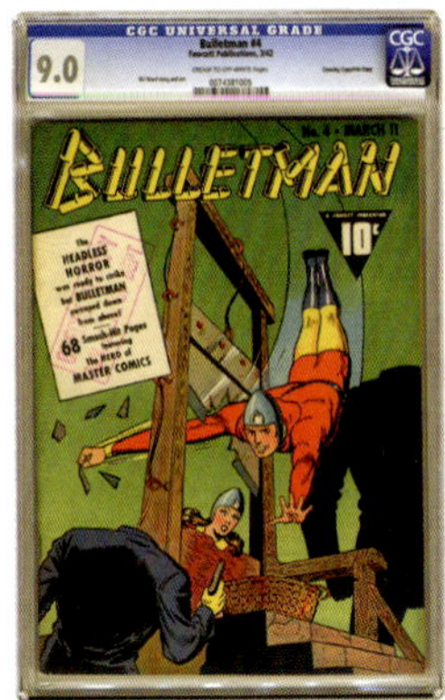

2282 Bulletman #4 Crowley Copy pedigree - File Copy (Fawcett, 1942) CGC VF/NM 9.0 Cream to off-white pages. In many an instance, the best copy known to exist of a particular Fawcett book is the one from the collection of Fawcett editor Wendell Crowley. And this is one of those instances! In addition to the adventure of Bulletman and Bulletgirl, there's a backup feature with Bill Ward art. Overstreet 2005 VF/NM 9.0 value = $925; NM- 9.2 value = $1,250. CGC census 8/05: 1 in 9.0, none higher.

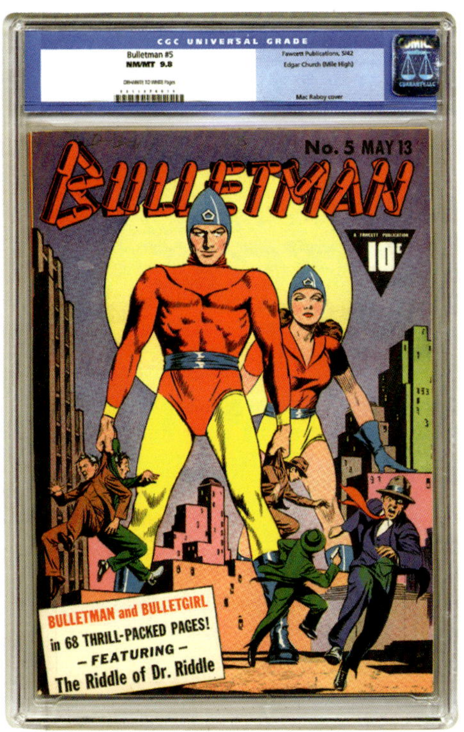

2283 Bulletman #5 Mile High pedigree (Fawcett, 1942) CGC NM/MT 9.8 Off-white to white pages. We've never had an opportunity to offer any copy of this issue, so we thought we'd rectify that by dishing up the best copy in existence, a 9.8 Mile High! One of Fawcett's best, Mac Raboy, provided the cover art. Overstreet 2005 NM- 9.2 value = $1,425. CGC census 9/05: 1 in 9.8, none higher.

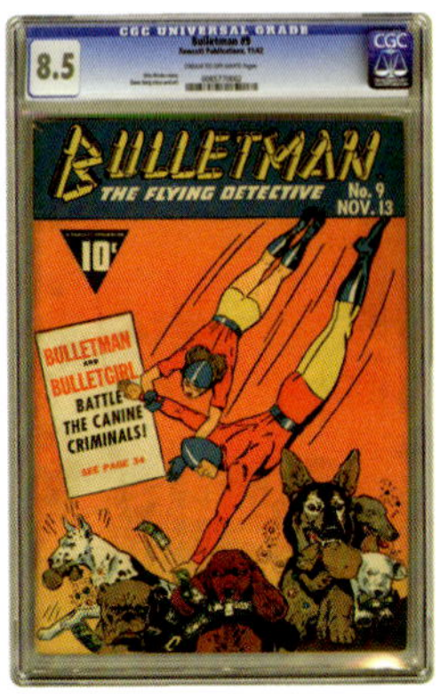

2284 Bulletman #9 (Fawcett, 1942) CGC VF+ 8.5 Cream to off-white pages. In addition to the adventures of Bulletman and Bulletgirl, this issue has a relatively unknown feature, "Ghost Stories," narrated by the night watchman of a cemetery and penciled by none other than future **Mad** guy Dave Berg! Overstreet 2005 VF 8.0 value = $506; VF/NM 9.0 value = $778. CGC census 9/05: 3 in 8.5, 2 higher.

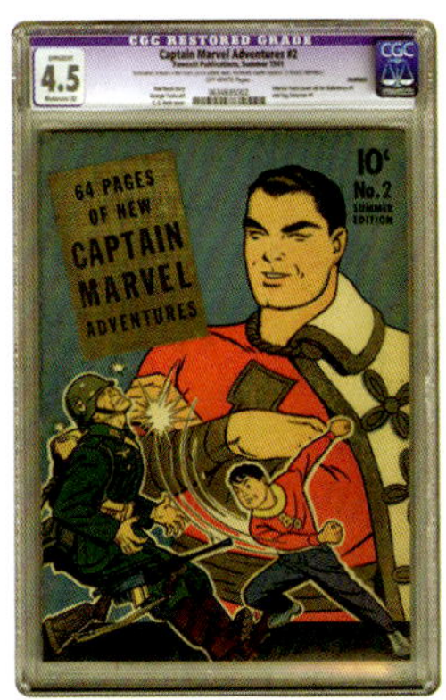

2285 Captain Marvel Adventures #2 (Fawcett, 1941) CGC Apparent VG+ 4.5 Moderate (A) Off-white pages. B. B. and C. C. take center stage here, and by that we mean Billy Batson (identifiable by his monogrammed shirt) and cover artist C. C. Beck. George Tuska contributed interior art to the issue. CGC notes, "Restoration includes: color touch, pieces added, seals, reinforced, staples replaced (3 edges trimmed)." Overstreet 2005 GD 2.0 value = $423; VG 4.0 value = $846.

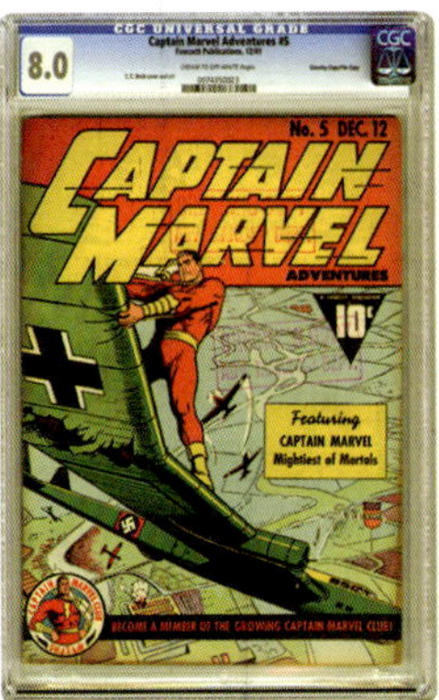

2286 Captain Marvel Adventures #5 Crowley Copy pedigree - File Copy (Fawcett, 1941) CGC VF 8.0 Cream to off-white pages. C. C. Beck drew both this issue's vertigo-inducing cover and the interior art. And though the Nazi menace is battled on the cover, it's archfoe Sivana who bedevils Captain Marvel in the stories. Though comics featuring the Big Red Cheese were among the top-selling books of their era, they're tough to find in a decent grade — as of this writing, only two copies of this issue have been graded higher by CGC. Overstreet 2005 VF 8.0 value = $963. CGC census 8/05: 1 in 8.0, 2 higher.

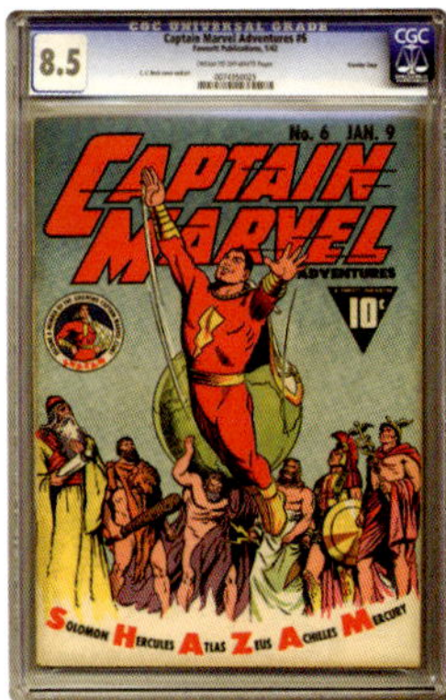

2287 Captain Marvel Adventures #6 Crowley Copy pedigree (Fawcett, 1942) CGC VF+ 8.5 Cream to off-white pages. This is the nicest copy we've ever offered of this particular issue, and frankly we would expect no less from the Crowley copy! If you need a refresher course on what the acronym SHAZAM stands for, have a look at C. C. Beck's cover. Beck also contributed interior art to the issue. Overstreet 2005 VF 8.0 value = $731; VF/NM 9.0 value = $1,128. CGC census 8/05: 1 in 8.5, 1 higher.

2288 Captain Marvel Adventures #11 Crowley Copy pedigree - File Copy (Fawcett, 1942) CGC VF/NM 9.0 Cream to off-white pages. Fans of the Big Red Cheese not only got to see their hero in war action on the cover, they also thrilled to Cap's battle with his arch-nemesis Sivana inside the issue. The cover and interior art are by C. C. Beck. Overstreet 2005 VF/NM 9.0 value = $888; NM- 9.2 value = $1,200. CGC census 8/05: 2 in 9.0, 3 higher.

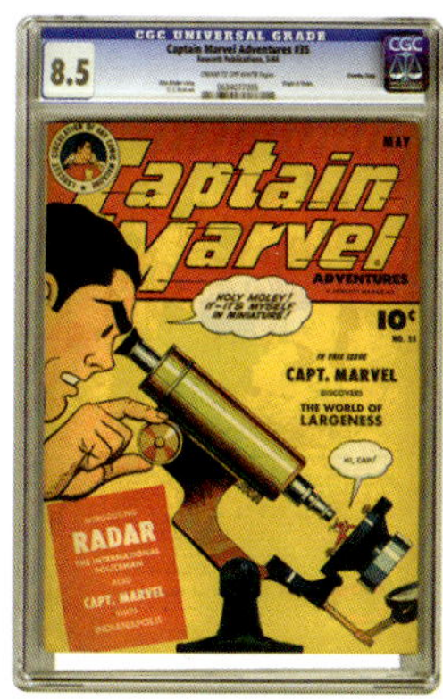

2289 Captain Marvel Adventures #35 Crowley Copy pedigree (Fawcett, 1944) CGC VF+ 8.5 Cream to off-white pages. Longtime Fawcett stalwart Radar has his origin revealed in this issue. But the star is of course Captain Marvel, who visits Indianapolis as part of the "city story" series. The issue has C. C. Beck interior art. Overstreet 2005 VF 8.0 value = $311; VF/NM 9.0 value = $473. CGC census 8/05: 1 in 8.5, 3 higher.

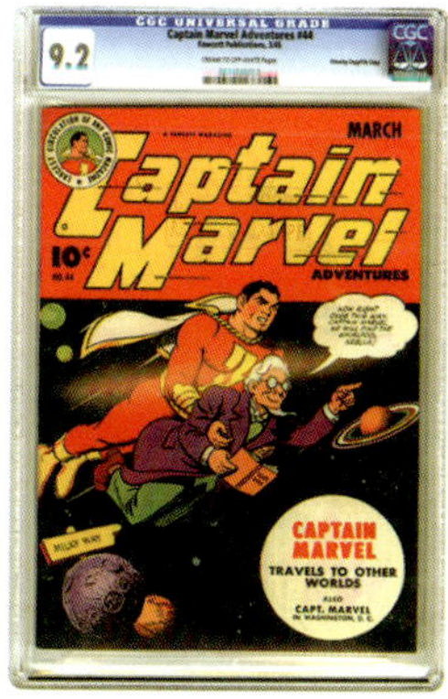

2290 Captain Marvel Adventures #44 Crowley Copy pedigree - File Copy (Fawcett, 1945) CGC NM- 9.2 Cream to off-white pages. The Big Red Cheese was one busy guy in this issue — first and foremost he had to deal with the malevolent worm Mr. Mind in one of the last installments of the long-running serial. Then he journeyed to other worlds (as seen on the cover), plus he headed for Washington D. C. in this issue's "city story." The cover art is by C. C. Beck. Overstreet 2005 NM- 9.2 value = $465. CGC census 8/05: 1 in 9.2, 2 higher.

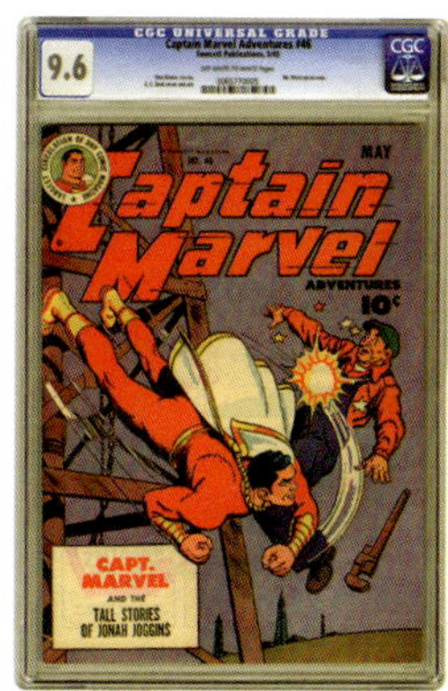

2291 Captain Marvel Adventures #46 (Fawcett, 1945) CGC NM+ 9.6 Off-white to white pages. The death of Mr. Mind in this issue brought to a close a serialized story that had fascinated fans for two years! This series' huge readership loved the ongoing battles between our hero and Mr. Mind (who was a worm, in case you didn't know!), but in this 25th installment of the story, Mr. Mind was tried, executed, and stuffed. The issue's cover and art are by C. C. Beck. Overstreet 2005 NM- 9.2 value = $465. CGC census 9/05: 1 in 9.6, none higher.

2292 Captain Marvel Adventures #50 (Fawcett, 1945) CGC NM 9.4 Cream to off-white pages. Role-reversal covers were always hard to resist — take this one by C. C. Beck, with Billy Batson rather than Captain Marvel punching out the baddies. The interior art is by Pete Costanza. Overstreet 2005 NM- 9.2 value = $425. CGC census 9/05: 3 in 9.4, 1 higher.

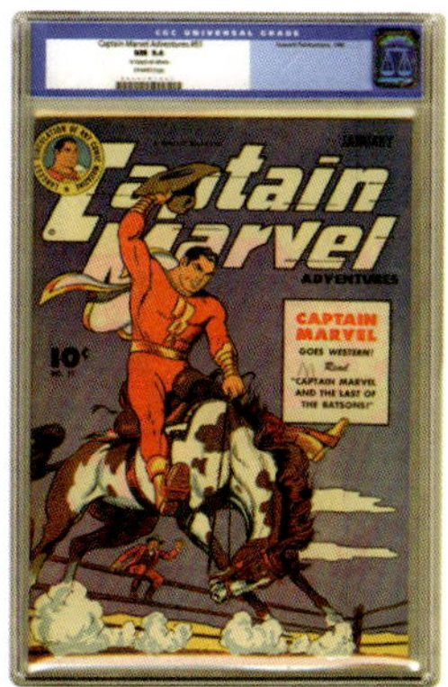

2293 Captain Marvel Adventures #51 (Fawcett, 1946) CGC NM 9.4 Off-white pages. This jaw-dropping copy will satisfy even the most discriminating collector! The issue's got a C. C. Beck cover and Pete Costanza interior art. CGC notes, "First four pages are Siamese." Overstreet 2005 NM- 9.2 value = $360. CGC census 9/05: 4 in 9.4, 1 higher.

2294 Captain Marvel Adventures #72 Crowley Copy pedigree - File Copy (Fawcett, 1947) CGC VF/NM 9.0 Cream to off-white pages. Partial photo cover. C. C. Beck art. Overstreet 2005 VF/NM 9.0 value = $237; NM- 9.2 value = $310. CGC census 8/05: 3 in 9.0, 1 higher.

2295 Captain Marvel Adventures #122 Crowley Copy pedigree (Fawcett, 1951) CGC NM 9.4 Off-white to white pages. Here's a pristine copy from the collection of Wendell Crowley (who edited the Marvel Family books at Fawcett). The issue has a C. C. Beck cover, with interior art by Beck and Pete Costanza. Overstreet 2005 NM- 9.2 value = $260. CGC census 8/05: 2 in 9.4, none higher.

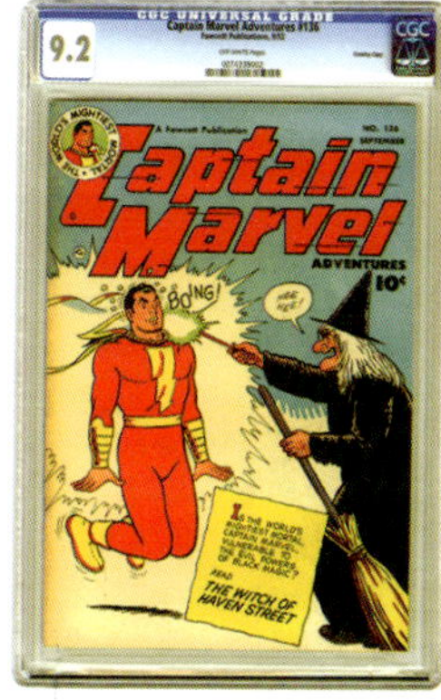

2296 Captain Marvel Adventures #136 Crowley Copy pedigree (Fawcett, 1952) CGC NM- 9.2 Off-white pages. Captain Marvel's signature artist C. C. Beck contributed cover and interior art to this issue. This copy's from the collection of former Fawcett editor Wendell Crowley. Overstreet 2005 NM- 9.2 value = $260. CGC census 8/05: 1 in 9.2, 1 higher.

2297 Captain Marvel Adventures #140 Crowley Copy pedigree (Fawcett, 1953) CGC NM- 9.2 Off-white pages. Horror cover. C. C. Beck interior art. Overstreet 2005 NM- 9.2 value = $260. CGC census 8/05: 1 in 9.2, 1 higher.

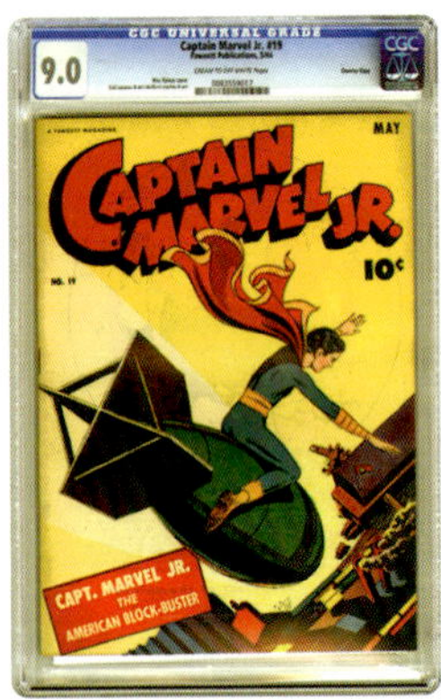

2298 Captain Marvel Jr. #19 Crowley Copy pedigree (Fawcett, 1944) CGC VF/NM 9.0 Cream to off-white pages. Years before "Dr. Strangelove," Captain Marvel Jr. learned to stop worrying and love the bomb — at least when one's heading for a Nazi munitions factory. The issue's cover is by Mac Raboy. Overstreet 2005 VF/NM 9.0 value = $548; NM- 9.2 value = $740. CGC census 8/05: 1 in 9.0, 1 higher.

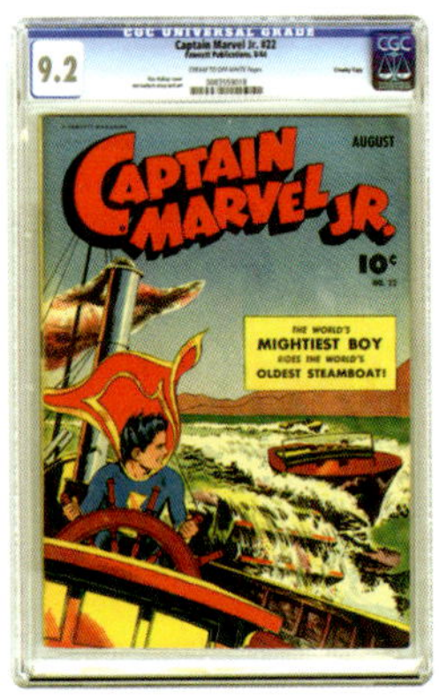

2299 Captain Marvel Jr. #22 Crowley Copy pedigree (Fawcett, 1944) CGC NM- 9.2 Cream to off-white pages. Captain Marvel Jr. got to ride the real-life steamboat known as the Clermont in this issue. The ship was already well over 100 years old when this comic came out — not the kind of vessel that's going to outrace a motorboat, unless Junior has some tricks up his sleeve! The cover scene's by the great Mac Raboy. Overstreet 2005 NM- 9.2 value = $585. CGC census 8/05: 2 in 9.2, 1 higher.

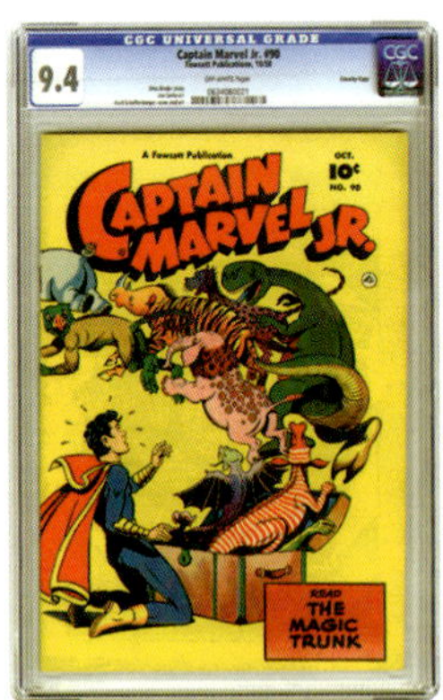

2300 Captain Marvel Jr. #90 Crowley Copy pedigree (Fawcett, 1950) CGC NM 9.4 Off-white pages. Kurt Schaffenberger drew the cover for this issue, which has interior art by Schaffenberger and Joe Certa. Overstreet 2005 NM- 9.2 value = $210. CGC census 8/05: 3 in 9.4, 1 higher.

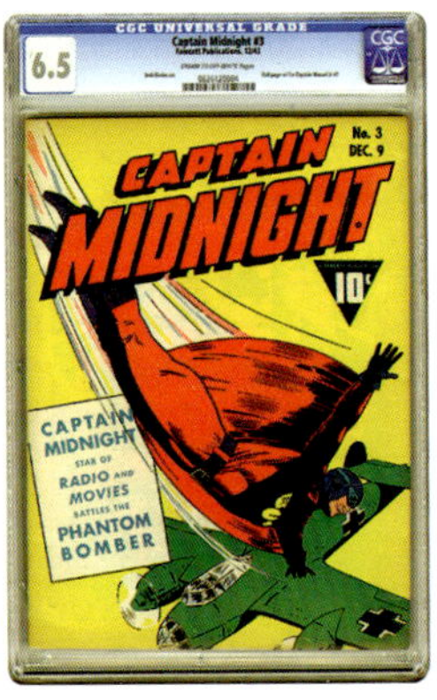

2301 Captain Midnight #3 (Fawcett, 1942) CGC FN+ 6.5 Cream to off-white pages. Overstreet lauds this issue's "classic Nazi war cover." The book's artists include Jack Binder. Overstreet 2005 FN 6.0 value = $393; VF 8.0 value = $819. CGC census 8/05: 1 in 6.5, 5 higher.

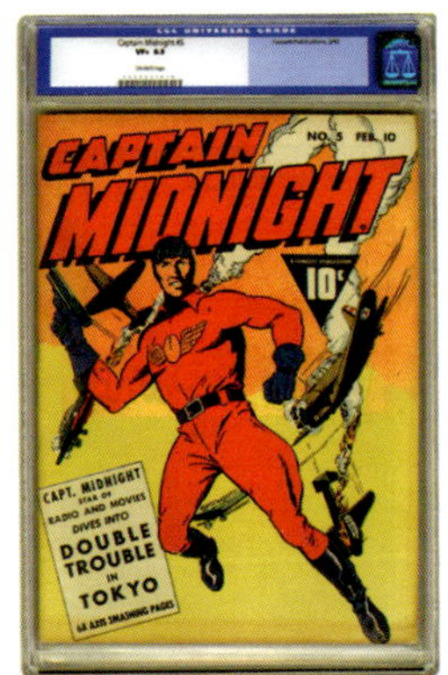

2302 Captain Midnight #5 (Fawcett, 1943) CGC VF+ 8.5 Off-white pages. Radio star Captain Midnight had a nice career in the comics as well, appearing in Dell's **The Funnies** and **Popular Comics** before getting his own series at Fawcett. This cover hasn't been conclusively attributed, but what a nicely rendered dogfight scene it is. Overstreet 2005 VF 8.0 value = $345; VF/NM 9.0 value = $719. CGC census 9/05: 1 in 8.5, 3 higher.

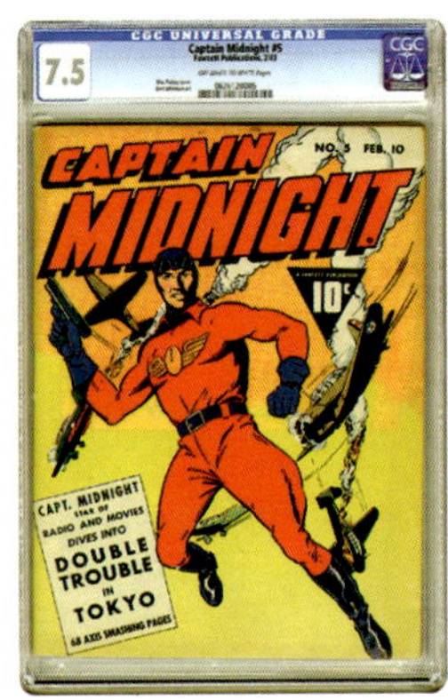

2303 Captain Midnight #5 (Fawcett, 1943) CGC VF- 7.5 Off-white to white pages. This issue's cover has been credited to the great Mac Raboy. The book stars Captain Midnight, who debuted in radio, but was a success in comics and movies as well. Overstreet 2005 VF 8.0 value = $719. CGC census 8/05: 1 in 7.5, 4 higher.

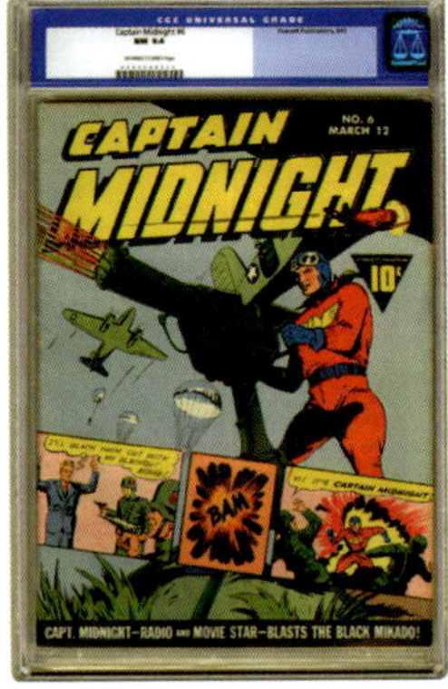

2304 Captain Midnight #6 (Fawcett, 1943) CGC NM 9.4 Off-white to white pages. This war cover offers a glimpse of our hero in his civilian identity, Captain Red Albright. Our copy is tied for the highest grade that CGC has assigned to date. Overstreet 2005 NM- 9.2 value = $1,000. CGC census 9/05: 2 in 9.4, one higher.

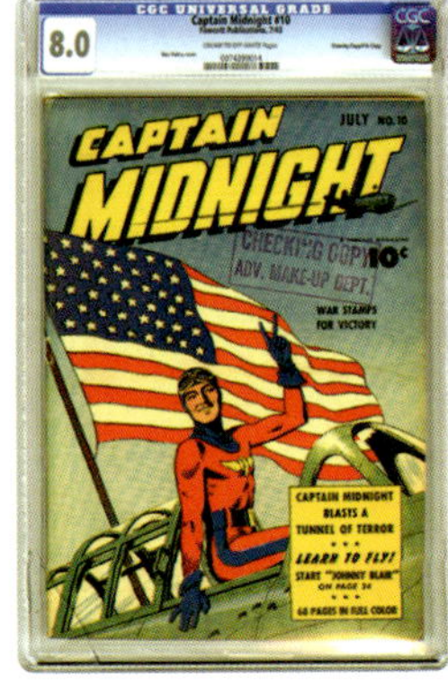

2305 Captain Midnight #10 Crowley Copy pedigree - File Copy (Fawcett, 1943) CGC VF 8.0 Cream to off-white pages. A patriotic flag cover by Mac Raboy makes this one of the more desirable issues of the series' run. Captain Midnight is joined by another high-flying hero in this issue, as the "Johnny Blair in the Air" backup feature begins. Overstreet 2005 VF 8.0 value = $506. CGC census 8/05: 1 in 8.0, 2 higher.

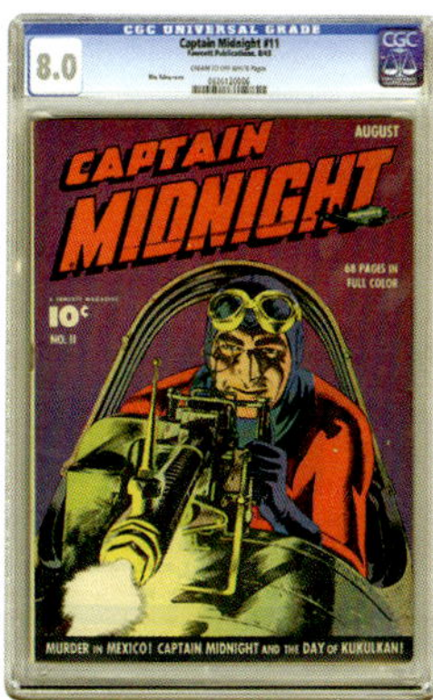

2306 Captain Midnight #11 (Fawcett, 1943) CGC VF 8.0 Cream to off-white pages. Overstreet credits this cover to Mac Raboy — it's a bit more hard-hitting than we're used to from Fawcett; it even has a bit of a pulp feel about it! Overstreet 2005 VF 8.0 value = $350. CGC census 8/05: 1 in 8.0, 1 higher.

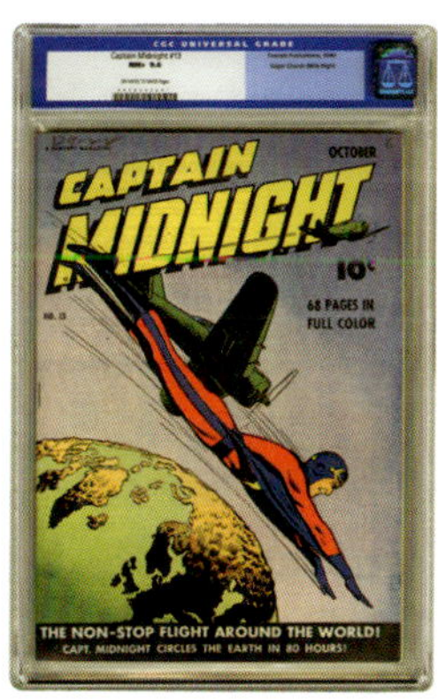

2307 Captain Midnight #13 Mile High pedigree (Fawcett, 1943) CGC NM+ 9.6 Off-white to white pages. This Mile High happens to be the copy pictured in Gerber's **Photo-Journal**, but the pic in Gerber's book hardly does it justice — have a look at it in all its glory here in our catalog, or better yet, put in an aggressive bid and enjoy it in your own living room! Overstreet 2005 NM- 9.2 value = $725. CGC census 9/05: 2 in 9.6, none higher.

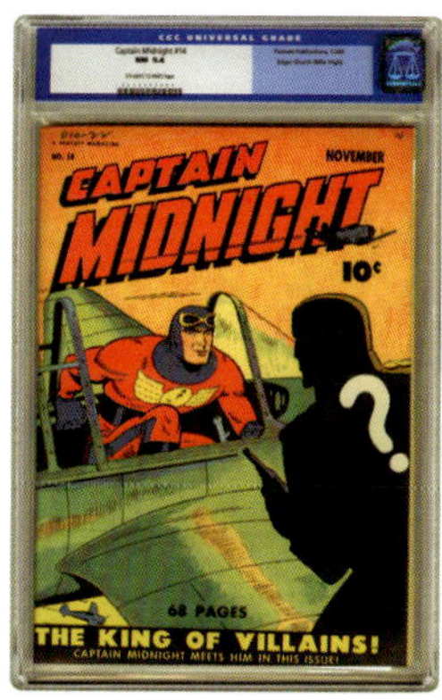

2308 Captain Midnight #14 Mile High pedigree (Fawcett, 1943) CGC NM 9.4 Off-white to white pages. This issue's baddie is billed as "The King of Villains" — the man enveloped in shadow is none other than (cover your eyes if you want to be surprised)... Storm Von Kloud! This issue's colors and page quality are what you'd expect from a Mile High book; i.e., the best you'll find. Overstreet 2005 NM- 9.2 value = $725. CGC census 9/05: 4 in 9.4, none higher.

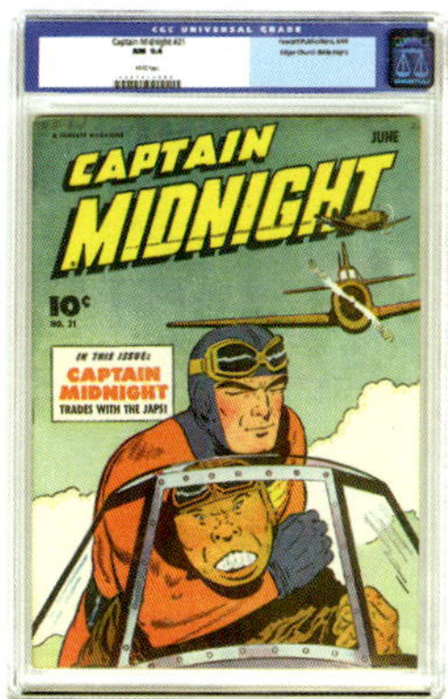

2309 Captain Midnight #21 Mile High pedigree (Fawcett, 1944) CGC NM 9.4 White pages. The high-flying Captain keeps the skyways safe in this World War II-era comic. This 60+ year-old comic still looks newsstand fresh. Overstreet 2005 NM- 9.2 value = $560. CGC census 8/05: 1 in 9.4, none higher.

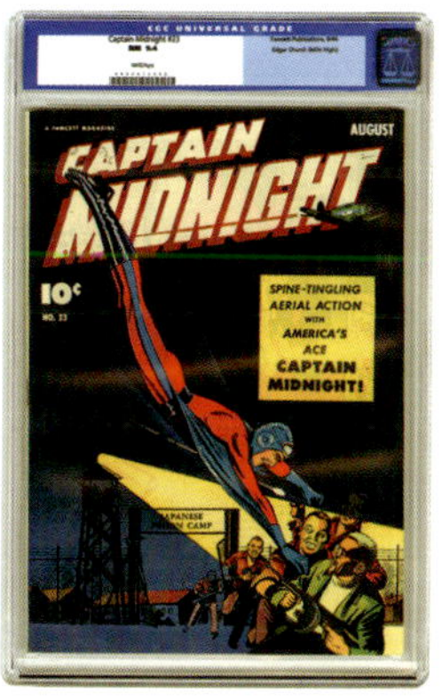

2310 Captain Midnight #23 Mile High pedigree (Fawcett, 1944) CGC NM 9.4 White pages. This Mile High beauty features a striking midnight-blue background cover. Edgar Church, our eternal thanks for keeping your comics in such superb condition all those many years! Absolutely fantastic. Overstreet 2005 NM- 9.2 value = $560. CGC census 8/05: 3 in 9.4, none higher.

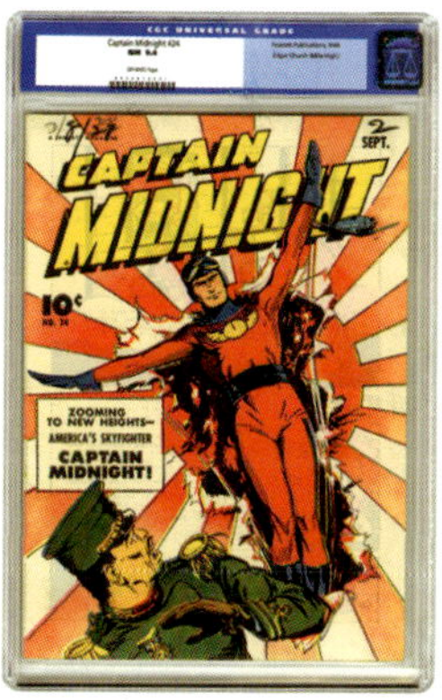

2311 Captain Midnight #24 Mile High pedigree (Fawcett, 1944) CGC NM 9.4 Off-white pages. America's Skyfighter smashes through the Japanese Rising Sun flag in this stirring World War II cover. The comic's fresh appearance is due to the Edgar Church Mile High pedigree; although this copy carries some heavier markings than most Mile Highs (graphite and grease pencil arrival dates near the top of the book), there's still plenty of great eye-appeal here. Overstreet 2005 NM- 9.2 value = $585. CGC census 8/05: 1 in 9.4, none higher.

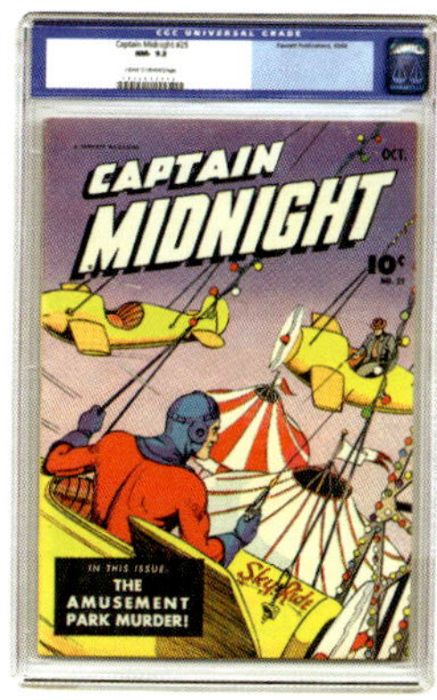

2312 Captain Midnight #25 (Fawcett, 1944) CGC NM- 9.2 Cream to off-white pages. He made his mark in radio (sponsored by the makers of Ovaltine), then made his way to the comics for a successful run: yes, we're talking about Captain Midnight. No copy of this issue has been certified with a higher grade by CGC to date. Overstreet 2005 NM- 9.2 value = $560. CGC census 9/05: 2 in 9.2, none higher.

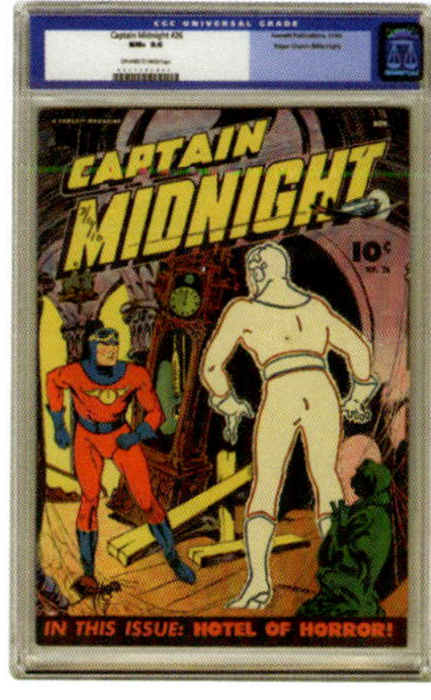

2313 Captain Midnight #26 Mile High pedigree (Fawcett, 1944) CGC NM+ 9.6 Off-white to white pages. Captain Midnight checks into the "Hotel of Horror" in this issue. This Mile High copy is the highest-graded copy of the issue that CGC has certified to date. Overstreet 2005 NM- 9.2 value = $560. CGC census 9/05: 1 in 9.6, none higher.

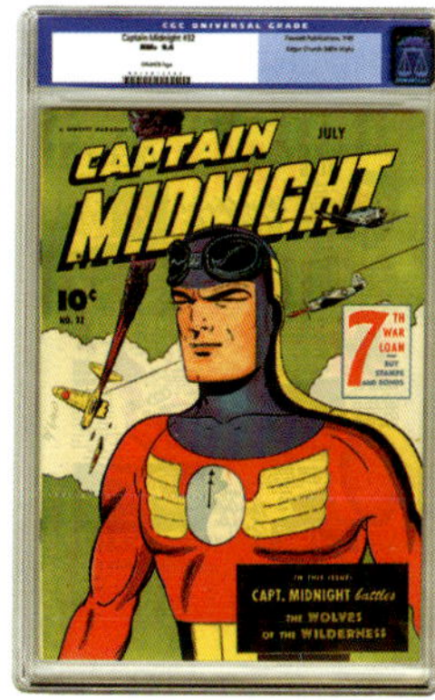

2314 Captain Midnight #32 Mile High pedigree (Fawcett, 1945) CGC NM+ 9.6 Off-white pages. The good Captain strikes a heroic pose on the cover to this issue, one of the last from the World War II era. It's a comic from the Edgar Church Mile High collection, so that means this little beauty looks like new. A winner all the way; it's clearly the best of the two copies currently graded by CGC. Overstreet 2005 NM- 9.2 value = $370. CGC census 8/05: 1 in 9.6, none higher.

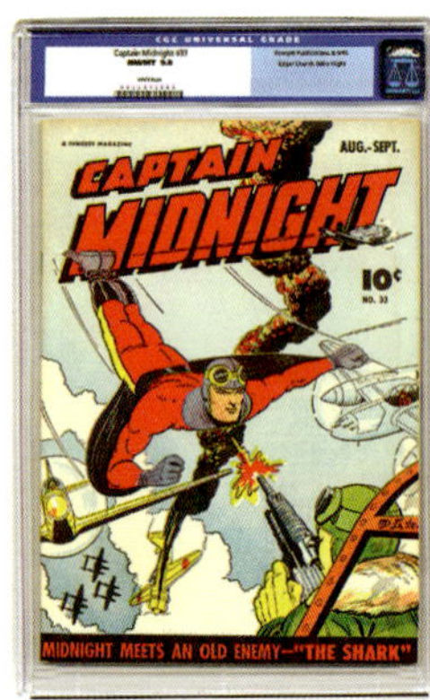

2315 Captain Midnight #33 Mile High pedigree (Fawcett, 1945) CGC NM/MT 9.8 White pages. This copy's got that "untouched" look that makes the nicest Mile High books so exciting! In this issue, Captain Midnight takes on his archfoe Ivan Shark, who bedeviled him on his radio show and in the movie serials as well. Overstreet 2005 NM- 9.2 value = $370. CGC census 8/05: 1 in 9.8, none higher.

2316 Captain Midnight #52 Mile High pedigree (Fawcett, 1947) CGC NM 9.4 Off-white pages. A cover scene set at the stroke of midnight may fit the title character, but it causes fits for collectors who want a black-cover issue that's not all dinged up. This Mile High copy is the best you're going to find. Overstreet 2005 NM- 9.2 value = $310. CGC census 9/05: 1 in 9.4, none higher.

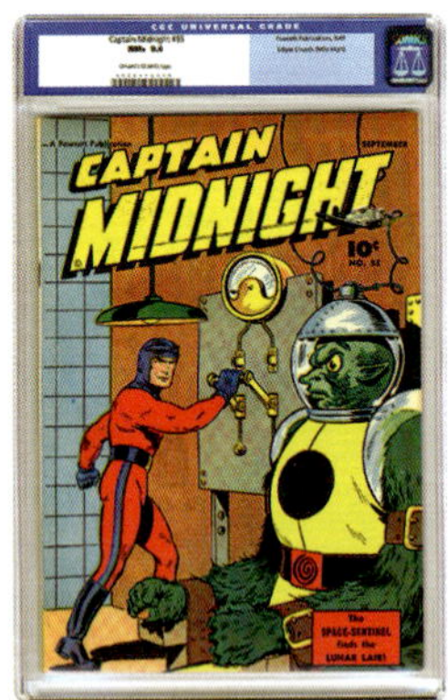

2317 Captain Midnight #55 Mile High pedigree (Fawcett, 1947) CGC NM+ 9.6 Off-white to white pages. Outer-space aliens thoughtfully put off menacing Earth while World War II was going on, but after the war it was open season on superheroes for the little green men of the universe. This sci-fi outing for Captain Midnight is best enjoyed by owning the best copy available, namely our Mile High offering! Overstreet 2005 NM- 9.2 value = $310. CGC census 8/05: 1 in 9.6, none higher.

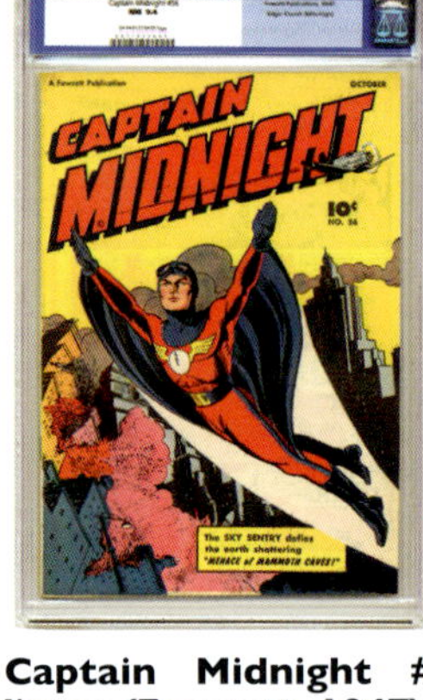

2318 Captain Midnight #56 Mile High pedigree (Fawcett, 1947) CGC NM 9.4 Off-white to white pages. Captain Midnight couldn't fly, but he could glide with the best of them, as seen on this cover which has been attributed to Dan Barry. Overstreet 2005 NM- 9.2 value = $310. CGC census 6/05: 1 in 9.4, none higher.

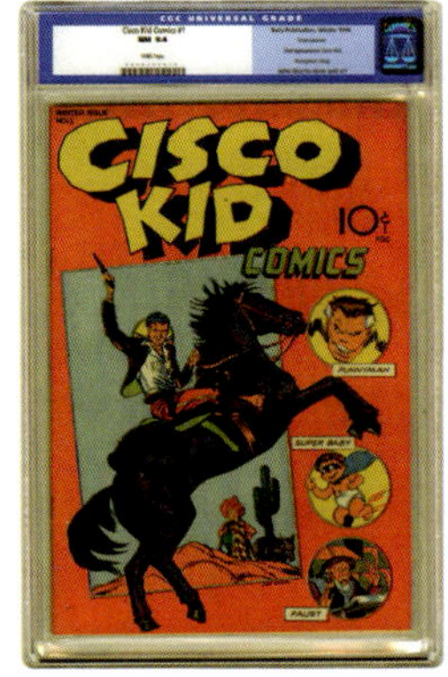

2319 Cisco Kid Comics #1 Vancouver pedigree (Baily Publication, 1944) CGC NM 9.4 White pages. The Cisco Kid, star of movies and later of TV, rode into his first comic book appearance here, several years before his long-running Dell series began. And appearing in the same comic as the Western star is... *Faust?* Yes, *that* Faust! Actually, considering that Bernard Baily is the publisher it's less surprising, as Baily had published **Illustrated Stories of the Operas** previously. Among the other characters is Funnyman (not the Jerry Siegel and Joe Shuster character), drawn by John Giunta. Giunta drew this issue's cover as well. Overstreet 2005 NM- 9.2 value = $540. CGC census 9/05: 1 in 9.4, none higher.

2320 The Cisco Kid #7 (Dell, 1952) CGC NM 9.4 Off-white pages. Ernest Nordli cover. Overstreet 2005 NM- 9.2 value = $125. CGC census 9/05: 1 in 9.4, none higher.

2321 The Cisco Kid #19 (Dell, 1954) CGC NM 9.4 Off-white pages. Painted cover. Overstreet 2005 NM- 9.2 value = $110. CGC census 8/05: 1 in 9.4, none higher.

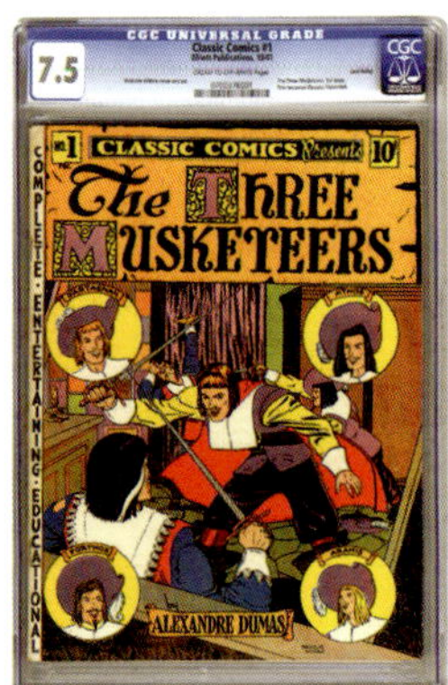

2322 Classic Comics #1 The Three Musketeers - Lost Valley pedigree (Elliott, 1941) CGC VF- 7.5 Cream to off-white pages. This is the Original Edition of this premiere issue, the first of a long, long series that soon changed its name to **Classics Illustrated** (and changed publishers from Elliott to Gilberton). For the Musketeers it was all for one and one for all, but in this auction, it's every man for himself — get your bid in early! Overstreet 2005 VF 8.0 value = $3,164. CGC census 8/05: 1 in 7.5, 3 higher.

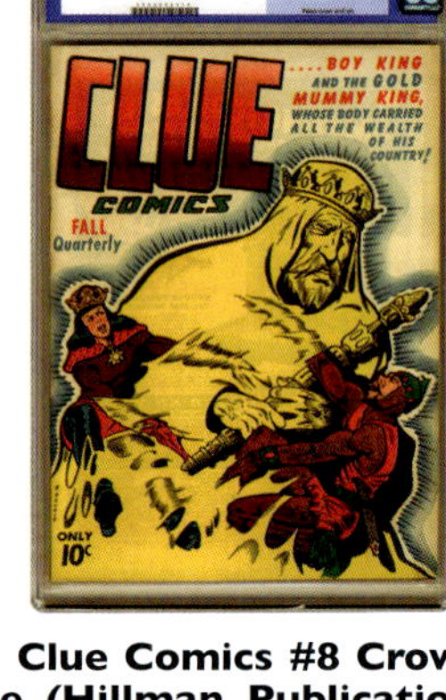

2323 Clue Comics #8 Crowley Copy pedigree (Hillman Publications, 1944) CGC NM- 9.2 Cream to off-white pages. One of the interesting things about the collection that Fawcett editor Wendell Crowley put together is that he didn't just set aside Fawcett books, but collected the work of the competition as well. This Hillman publication has Rudy Palais art. Overstreet 2005 NM- 9.2 value = $350. CGC census 9/05: 2 in 9.2, 1 higher.

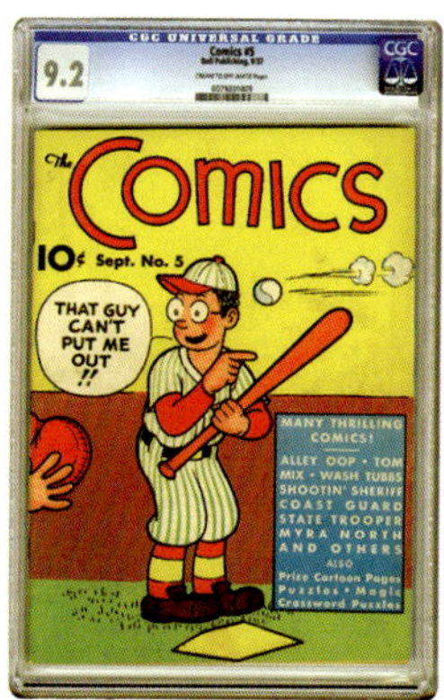

2324 The Comics #5 (Dell, 1937) CGC NM- 9.2 Cream to off-white pages. Dating from 1937, this book is from what many call the Platinum Age of comics (pre-Golden Age), making it all the more amazing that it's in NM- condition. Tom Mix, Alley Oop, and Wash Tubbs appear, among many other characters. This is the only copy of this issue that CGC has certified to date. Overstreet 2005 NM- 9.2 value = $860. CGC census 8/05: 1 in 9.2, none higher.

2325 Crime Must Pay the Penalty #33 (#1) (Ace, 1948) CGC Apparent VF/NM 9.0 Slight (A) Off-white to white pages. First issue of the title (numbering continued from **Four Favorites**). CGC notes, "Restoration includes: very small amount of color touch on cover." Overstreet 2005 GD 2.0 value = $35; VG 4.0 value = $70; FN 6.0 value = $105; VF 8.0 value = $198; VF/NM 9.0 value = $287.

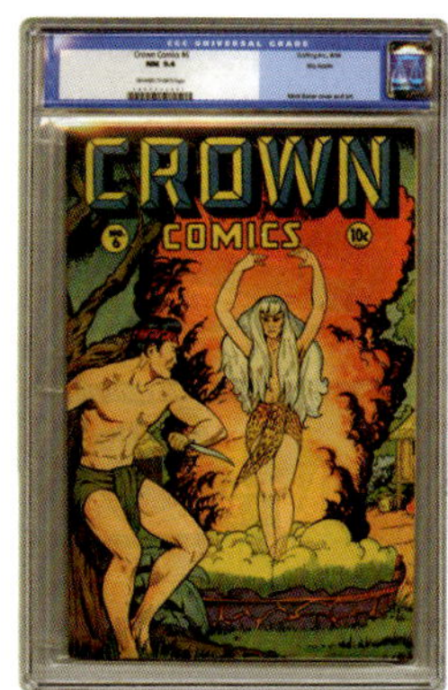

2326 Crown Comics #6 Big Apple pedigree (Golfing, Inc., 1946) CGC NM 9.4 Off-white to white pages. Highly collectable artist Matt Baker saw to both the cover and interior art for this issue. It's not a book that comes along often, and we've got the only copy graded above 6.0 by CGC as of this writing. Overstreet 2005 NM- 9.2 value = $310. CGC census 9/05: 1 in 9.4, none higher.

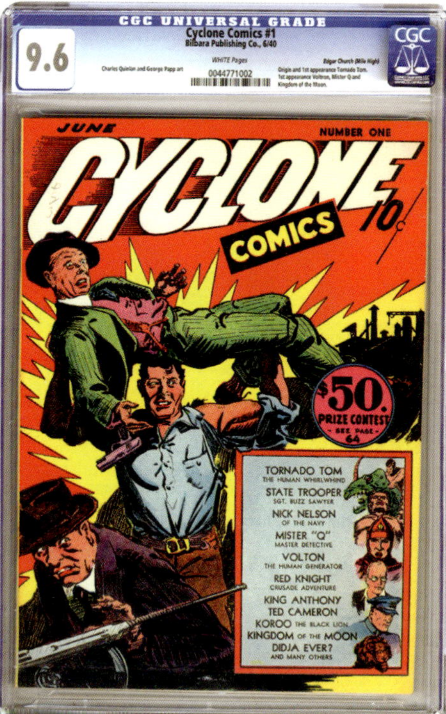

2327 Cyclone Comics #1 Mile High pedigree (Bilbara, 1940) CGC NM+ 9.6 White pages. This remarkable 1940-vintage comic book does not look its age; in fact, it looks so nice and fresh, one might think this is a modern-era reprint. Trust us, it's the real thing. Gerber refers to this first issue (featuring the origin and first appearance of Tornado Tom, as well as first appearances of Voltron, Mister Q, and Kingdom of the Moon, with art by Charles Quinlan and George Papp) as "uncommon;" that's what we say about the amazing cover color and gloss, and the incredible paper quality of this copy. Of course, it's from that most famous of all comic book collections, Edgar Church's Mile High hoard. And of course, this pedigreed copy currently ranks as "best" in CGC's census for this issue. Overstreet 2005 NM- 9.2 value = $2,000. CGC census 7/05: 1 in 9.6, none higher.

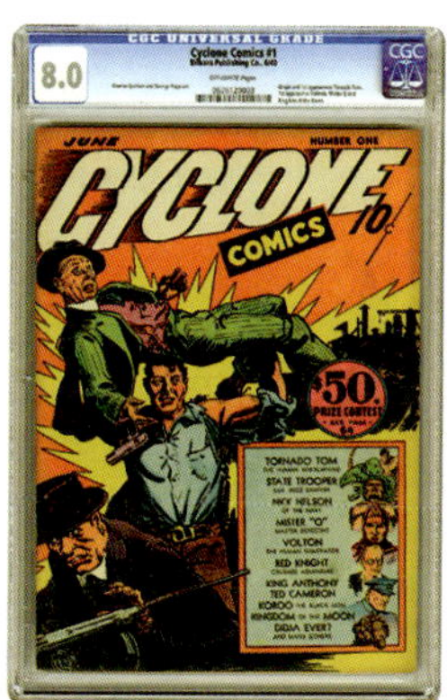

2328 Cyclone Comics #1 (Bilbara, 1940) CGC VF 8.0 Off-white pages. Tornado Tom and a host of other characters made their first appearances in this issue. The book features work by two notable artists in Charles Quinlan of **Catman** fame and future DC guy George Papp. Overstreet 2005 VF 8.0 value = $963. CGC census 8/05: 1 in 8.0, 4 higher.

2329 Daredevil Comics #2 (Lev Gleason, 1941) CGC FR 1.0 Brittle pages. Jerry Robinson, Reed Crandall, Charles Biro, and Dick Briefer art. Cover by Biro. CGC notes, "Moderate amount of tape on cover and interior." Overstreet 2005 GD 2.0 value = $303. CGC census 8/05: 1 in 1.0, 4 higher.

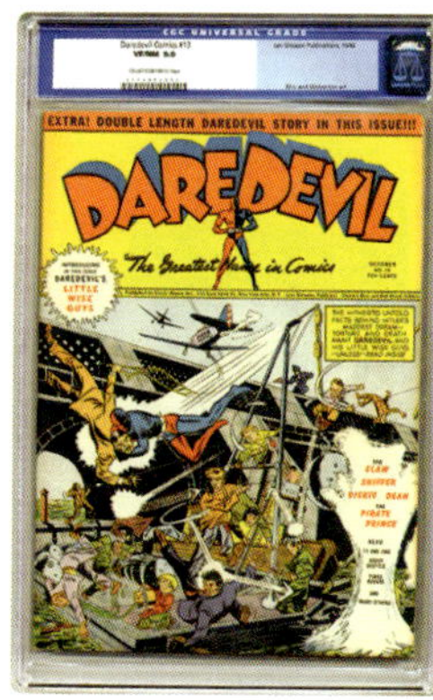

2330 Daredevil Comics #13 (Lev Gleason, 1942) CGC VF/NM 9.0 Cream to off-white pages. The Little Wise Guys made their first appearance in this issue. The group would become quite popular, in fact they would take over the starring role in this title just a few years down the road. The issue has Basil Wolverton interior art in addition to the work of Charles Biro, who contributed to almost every Lev Gleason comic. Overstreet 2005 VF/NM 9.0 value = $1,147; NM- 9.2 value = $1,550. CGC census 9/05: 1 in 9.0, none higher.

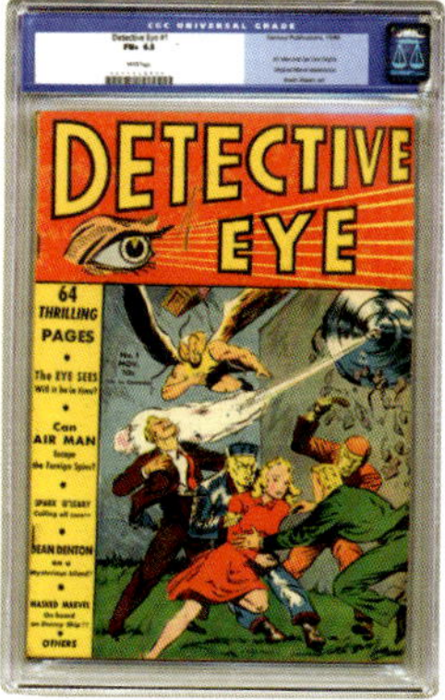

2331 Detective Eye #1 (Centaur, 1940) CGC FN+ 6.5 White pages. The Eye, Air Man, and the Masked Marvel, all former stars of **Keen Detective Funnies**, headlined the two-issue run of this title. The cover is by Lew Glanzman. Overstreet 2005 FN 6.0 value = $645; VF 8.0 value = $1,344. CGC census 9/05: 1 in 6.5, 4 higher.

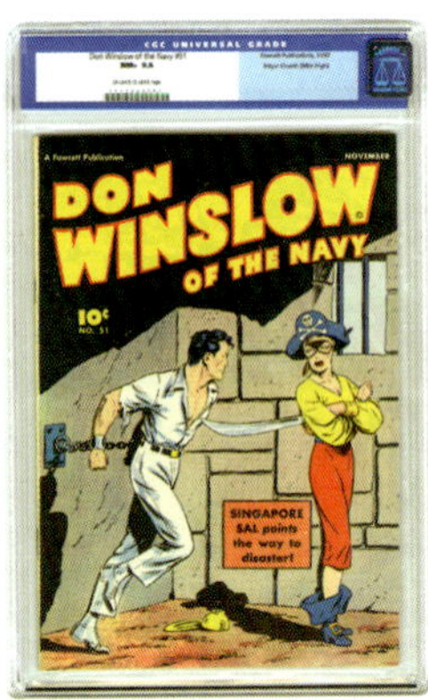

2332 Don Winslow of the Navy #51 Mile High pedigree (Fawcett, 1947) CGC NM+ 9.6 Off-white to white pages. Don Winslow was everywhere during the 1940s — there was the comic strip that started it all, plus a radio series, a 12-chapter movie serial, several boys' adventure novels and Big Little Books, as well as this long-running comic book published by Fawcett. You won't find many that look as good as this pedigreed copy, though. It beats the only other listed copy in the current CGC census (a 6.5) by a country mile! Overstreet 2005 NM- 9.2 value = $115. CGC census 9/05: 1 in 9.6, none higher.

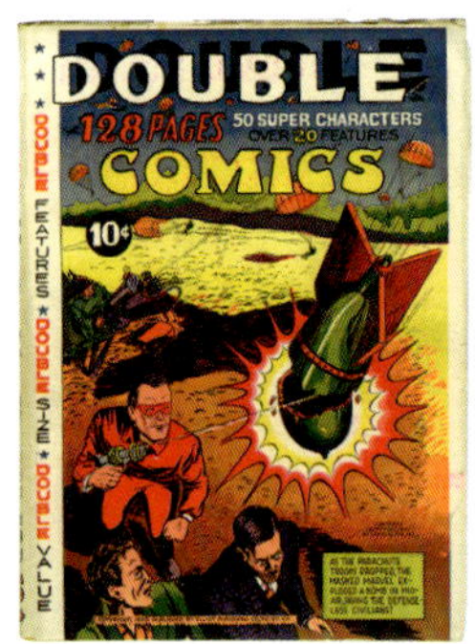

2333 Double Comics 1940 Edition (Elliot, 1940) Condition: VG/FN. Every issue of **Double Comics** was unique, as the contents were two always two remaindered, unsold comic books from other publishers, re-bound to make one 128-page issue. In this case, the contents are Fox's **Mystery Men** #5 and 6. Note that CGC could not encapsulate this comic due to a significant overhang at the top and side. While Overstreet lists a VG value of $476 and a FN value of $714 for 1940 issues, the Guide notes, "The actual contents would have to determine its price... value would be approximately 50 percent of contents," which in this case results in an approximate Overstreet value of $1,100.

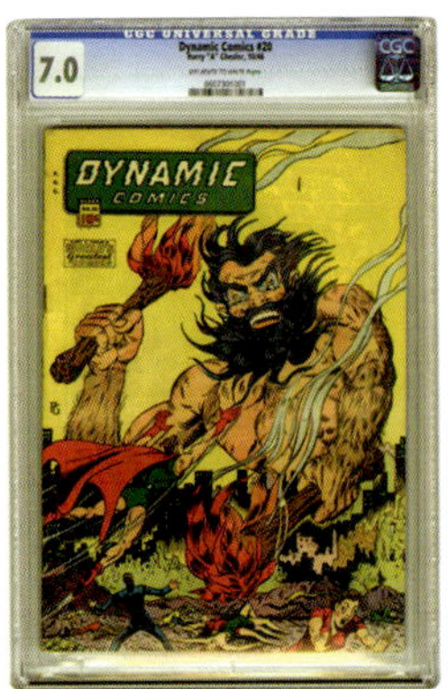

2334 Dynamic Comics #20 (Chesler, 1946) CGC FN/VF 7.0 Off-white to white pages. "Bare-breasted woman (on) cover," says Overstreet, and we high-minded comic fans didn't even notice it until we scrutinized the very bottom center of the cover image. Finished using your magnifying glass? OK, then we'll note that the cover is most likely the work of Chesler staff artist Paul Gattuso. Note that the only two copies graded higher than this one as of this writing are just a half-grade higher at 7.5. Overstreet 2005 FN 6.0 value = $207; VF 8.0 value = $431. CGC census 8/05: 1 in 7.0, 2 higher.

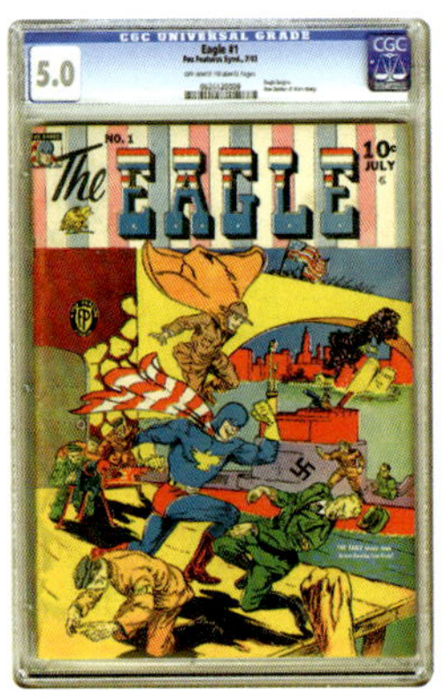

2335 The Eagle #1 (Fox, 1941) CGC VG/FN 5.0 Off-white to white pages. Only one copy of this issue has been graded higher by CGC to date; if you take a close look at our scan, we think you'll be pleased with this appealing mid-grade offering. The patriotic title character got his start in **Science Comics**, and what better way to start off his own book than by battling a Nazi sub off the coast of New York City? Among the backup features is a Rex Dexter of Mars tale with Dick Briefer art. Overstreet 2005 VG 4.0 value = $354; FN 6.0 value = $531. CGC census 8/05: 1 in 5.0, 1 higher.

2336 The Eagle #2 (Fox, 1941) CGC FN 6.0 Off-white pages. Origin and first appearance of the Spider Queen. Overstreet 2005 FN 6.0 value = $249. CGC census 8/05: 1 in 6.0, 1 higher.

2337 The Eagle #3 (Fox, 1941) CGC FN 6.0 Off-white to white pages. Origin of Joe Spook. Ramona Patenaude cover. Overstreet 2005 FN 6.0 value = $198. CGC census 8/05: 1 in 6.0, 2 higher.

2338 The Eagle #4 (Fox, 1942) CGC FN+ 6.5 Off-white pages. Note that the highest-graded copy as of this writing is just a half-grade higher at 7.0. Last issue of the title. Overstreet 2005 FN 6.0 value = $198; VF 8.0 value = $413. CGC census 8/05: 1 in 6.5, 1 higher.

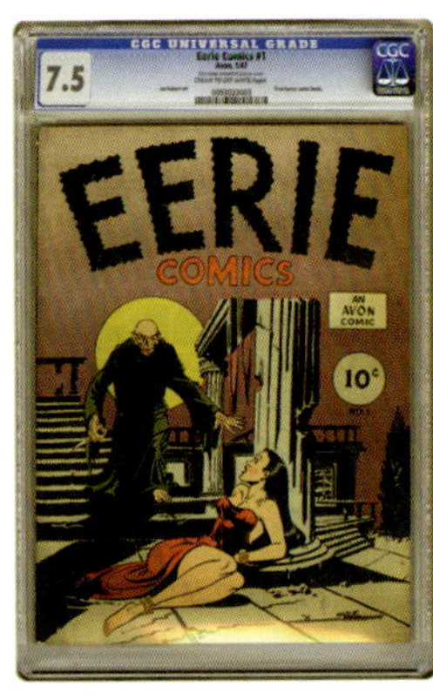

2339 Eerie #1 (Avon, 1947) CGC VF- 7.5 Cream to off-white pages. Many call this the first-ever horror comic book, so how can you have a horror comic collection without one? It's also "scarce," to use Overstreet's term. The artists include Joe Kubert and Bob Fujitani. CGC notes, "Very minor amount of glue on cover." Overstreet 2005 VF 8.0 value = $2,600. CGC census 9/05: 1 in 7.5, 3 higher.

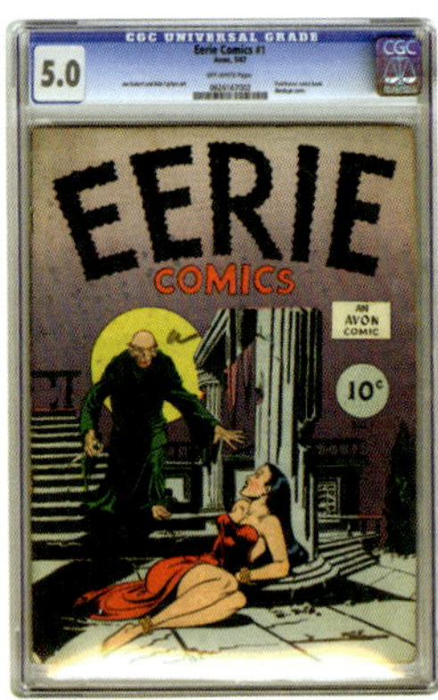

2340 Eerie #1 (Avon, 1947) CGC VG/FN 5.0 Off-white pages. This is the first-ever horror comic book according to CGC, while Overstreet dubs it the first "supernatural" comic. Either way, it's a milestone, and a hard-to-find one at that, earning Overstreet's "scarce" designation. The artists include Joe Kubert and Bob Fujitani. Don't forget the bondage cover, a motif that would crop up on many a horror cover to come. Overstreet 2005 VG 4.0 value = $800; FN 6.0 value = $1,200. CGC census 9/05: 2 in 5.0, 7 higher.

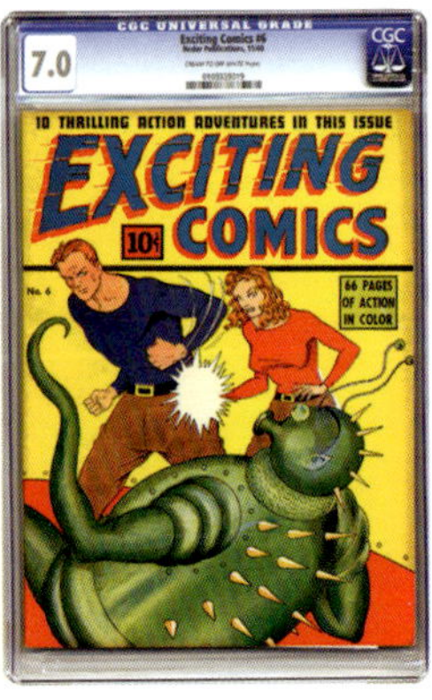

2341 Exciting Comics #6 (Nedor Publications, 1940) CGC FN/VF 7.0 Cream to off-white pages. Max Plaisted provided cover and interior art for this early issue. Overstreet 2005 FN 6.0 value = $231; VF 8.0 value = $481. CGC census 8/05: 1 in 7.0, none higher.

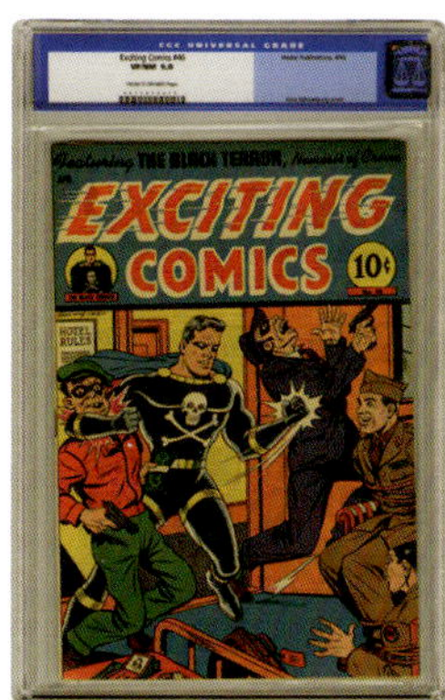

2342 Exciting Comics #46 (Nedor Publications, 1946) CGC VF/NM 9.0 Cream to off-white pages. The Black Terror takes matters into his own hands, literally, with two armed thugs, but is disappointed to find he's not saving a grateful (and preferably winsome) lass - "just" a couple of bound G.I.s! The Alex Schomburg cover comes to life on this offering which sports the highest grade CGC has certified to date for issue #46. Overstreet 2005 VF/NM 9.0 value = $548; NM- 9.2 value = $740. CGC census 9/05: 2 in 9.0, none higher.

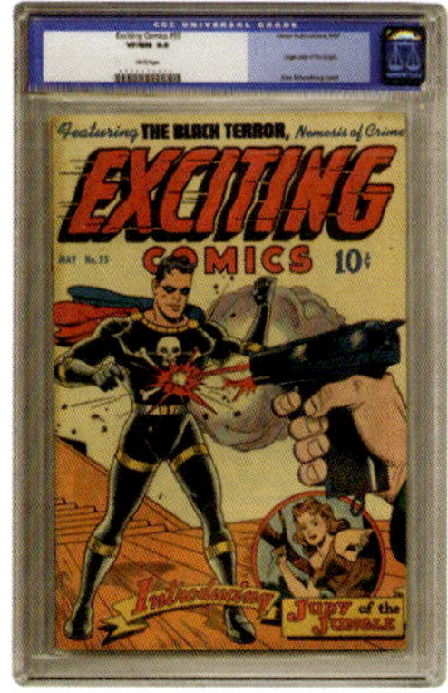

2343 Exciting Comics #55 (Nedor Publications, 1947) CGC VF/NM 9.0 White pages. Judy of the Jungle begins in this issue, but the Alex Schomburg cover is the main attraction. Well, that, and the fact that this is one of only two copies of #55 that CGC has certified to date. Check out the page quality on this one. Overstreet 2005 VF/NM 9.0 value = $511; NM- 9.2 value = $685. CGC census 9/05: 2 in 9.0, none higher.

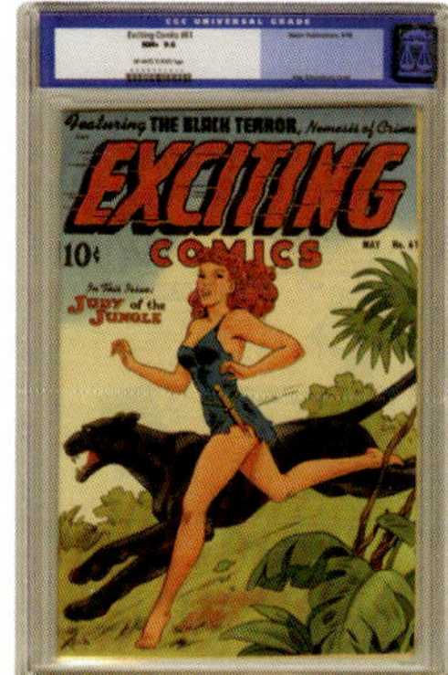

2344 Exciting Comics #61 (Nedor Publications, 1948) CGC NM+ 9.6 Off-white to white pages. Alex Schomburg's airbrushed cover technique fit this title, bringing a new dimension to his depiction of "good girls" like the lovely Judy of the Jungle. This copy is baaad - it's nationwide! It's the highest-graded copy of only three copies of #61 that CGC has certified to date. Overstreet 2005 NM- 9.2 value = $625. CGC census 9/05: 1 in 9.6, none higher.

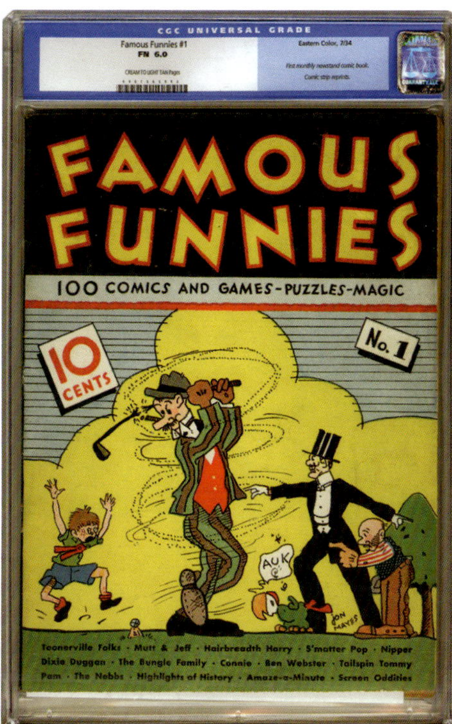

2345 Famous Funnies #1 (Eastern Color, 1934) CGC FN 6.0 Cream to light tan pages. This was the first comic book sold to the general public through newsstand distribution! You can't get much more historically significant than that. Just to run down the history for you: this comic's predecessors **Funnies On Parade**, **Famous Funnies: A Carnival Of Comics**, and a couple of other one-shots were giveaway premiums, the success of which indicated that there might be reader demand for the format. Then came **Famous Funnies, Series 1**, which was sold to the general public through chain stores. The new format having passed those tests, Eastern Color brought out this first issue of a monthly newsstand series. It would run for over twenty years. Like all early comic books, this contained comic strip reprints — the featured characters included Mutt and Jeff, Tailspin Tommy, and Joe Palooka (at the time, some naysayers wondered why anyone would pay 10 cents for the same strips they had already read for free in the newspapers). This comic is currently ranked #58 on Overstreet's list of the most valuable Golden Age comics — the only reason it's not much higher is that while most comics have NM- prices listed in the Guide, no NM- copy of this is known to exist. In fact, only two copies have received higher grades than our offering to date. And we shouldn't forget to mention that the issue is a Gerber "9" or "Very Rare," so forget about waiting for another one to come along! Overstreet 2005 FN 6.0 value = $9,129. CGC census 9/05: 1 in 6.0, 2 higher.

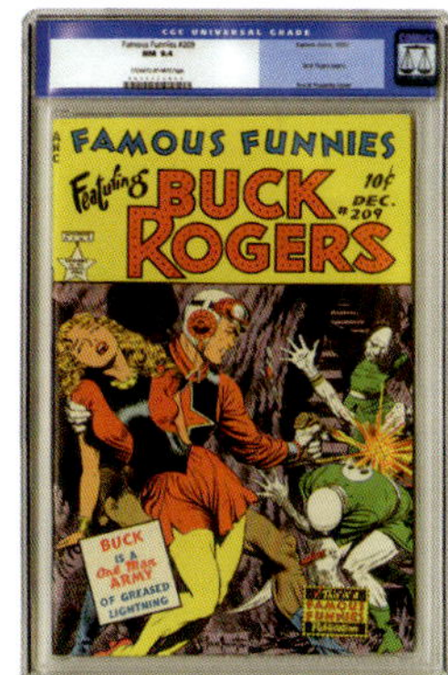

2346 Famous Funnies #209 (Eastern Color, 1953) CGC NM 9.4 Cream to off-white pages. This landmark title, launched way back in 1934, was nearing the end of its run when this issue came out in 1953. The Buck Rogers feature began with this issue, accompanied by some of the most dynamic covers in comic book history by the incomparable Frank Frazetta. For eight glorious issues, **Famous Funnies** was on top of the comics world. This wonderful copy shows clearly why Frazetta is so revered. Overstreet 2005 NM- 9.2 value = $1,600. CGC census 9/05: 2 in 9.4, 2 higher.

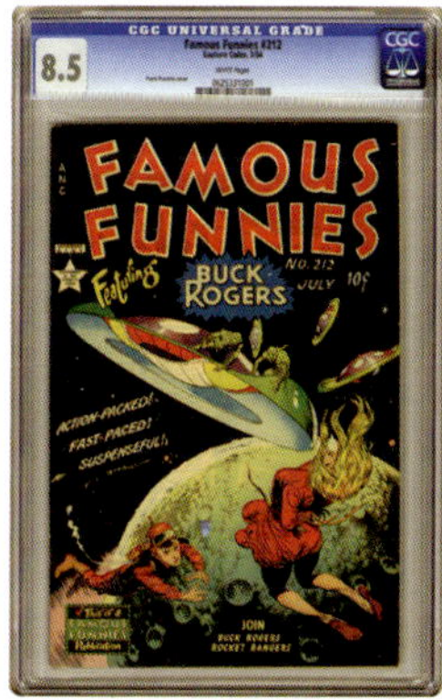

2347 Famous Funnies #212 (Eastern Color, 1954) CGC VF+ 8.5 White pages. This issue's Frank Frazetta cover featuring Buck Rogers speaks for itself, so we'll simply note that we seem to see this issue less here at Heritage than others in the famed #209-216 run. Understandably so — if *you* owned it, would *you* want to part with it? Overstreet 2005 VF 8.0 value = $769; VF/NM 9.0 value = $1,185. CGC census 9/05: 2 in 8.5, 3 higher.

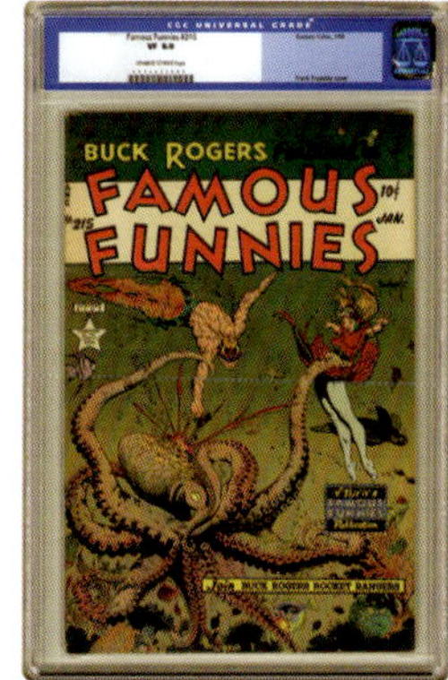

2348 Famous Funnies #215 (Eastern Color, 1955) CGC VF 8.0 Off-white to white pages. No one drew damsels in distress like Frank Frazetta... but nobody drew better heroes, monsters, or just about anything else either! If you're collecting the run with Frazetta's Buck Rogers covers, note that only one copy is ranked above this one in CGC's census as of this writing. Overstreet 2005 VF 8.0 value = $769. CGC census 9/05: 4 in 8.0, 1 higher.

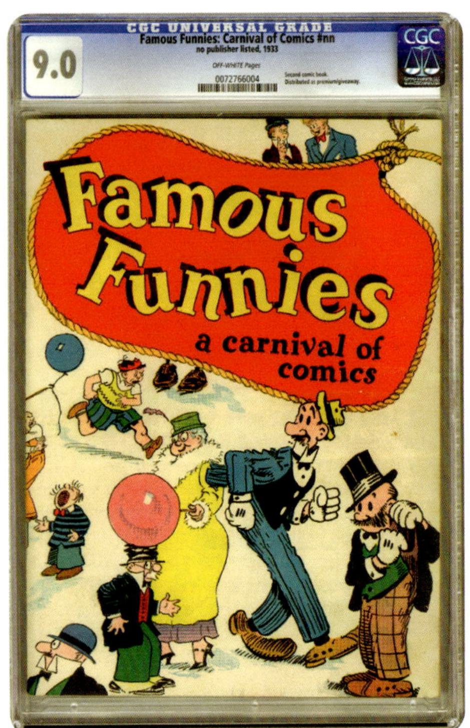

2349 Famous Funnies: A Carnival of Comics #nn (Eastern Color, 1933) CGC VF/NM 9.0 Off-white pages. Widely regarded as the second comic book ever published, this comic was marketed by M.C. Gaines to a host of retailers including Kinney Shoe Stores and Milk-O-Malt, all of whom used it as a promotional giveaway for their customers. Gaines was leading up to a key test for this new product: would anyone pay 10 cents for a comic book? This "carnival" contains reprints of strips starring Joe Palooka, Mutt and Jeff, Reg'lar Fellers, and other favorites. This historic item would be neat to have in any grade, and the fact that a VF/NM copy has survived is quite amazing — no copy has been graded higher by CGC to date. Overstreet 2005 VF/NM 9.0 value = $9,240; NM- 9.2 value = $13,000. CGC census 8/05: 3 in 9.0, none higher.

2350 Feature Books #2 Popeye (David McKay, 1937) Condition: VG. One of the nicest Popeye covers in comics, featuring Popeye and Swee'pea. Bottom staple rusted. Staining on front cover. Overstreet 2005 VG 4.0 value = $170.

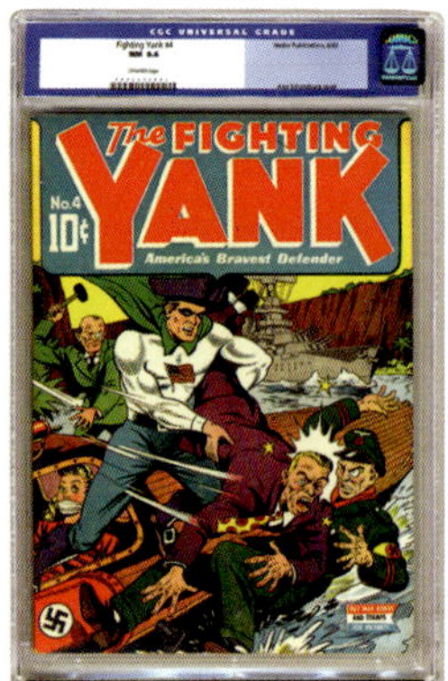

2351 Fighting Yank #4 (Nedor Publications, 1943) CGC NM 9.4 Off-white pages. This is Alex Schomburg's first cover for this title, and he got the Fighting Yank off to a great start here. Men who wear monocles are always evil, everyone knows that, and there's two of 'em here! No copy has been graded higher by CGC to date. Overstreet 2005 NM- 9.2 value = $1,050. CGC census 9/05: 2 in 9.4, none higher.

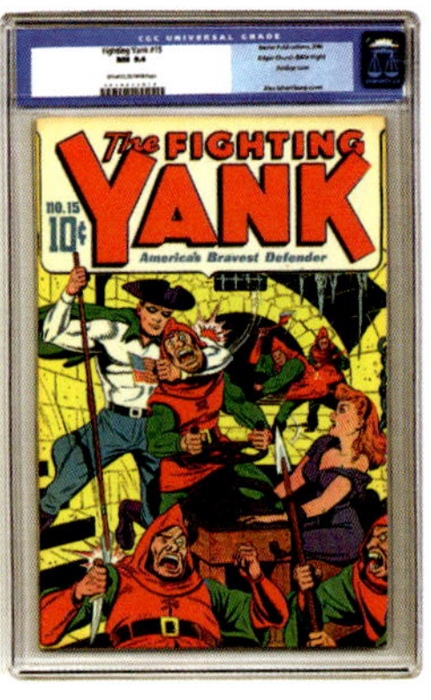

2352 Fighting Yank #15 Mile High pedigree (Nedor Publications, 1946) CGC NM 9.4 Off-white to white pages. A bondage and torture cover by Alex Schomburg graces this issue. Overstreet 2005 NM- 9.2 value = $650. CGC census 8/05: 2 in 9.4, none higher.

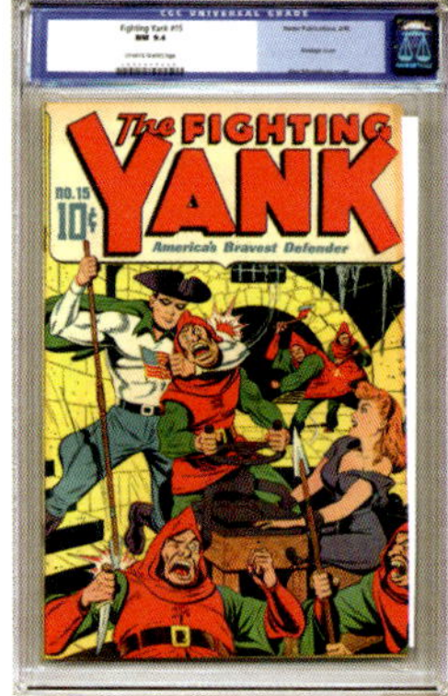

2353 Fighting Yank #15 (Nedor Publications, 1946) CGC NM 9.4 Off-white to white pages. This issue sports a bondage and torture cover by Alex Schomburg. Overstreet 2005 NM- 9.2 value = $650. CGC census 9/05: 2 in 9.4, none higher.

2354 No Lot.

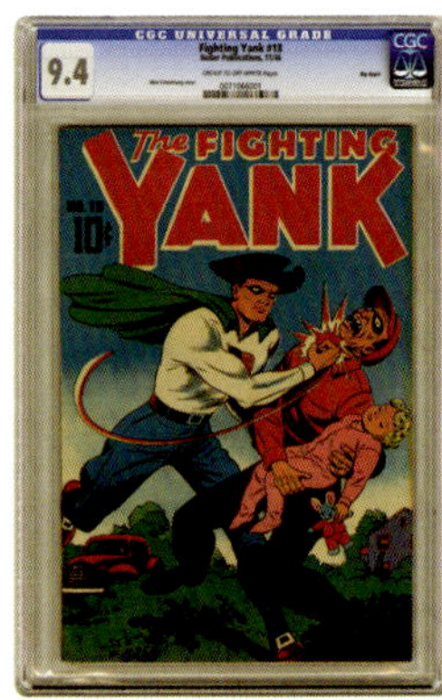

2355 Fighting Yank #18 Big Apple pedigree (Nedor Publications, 1946) CGC NM 9.4 Cream to off-white pages. A baby snatcher gets popped in the throat (ouch!) by the biggest patriot of all on this Alex Schomburg cover. There's no pain in looking at this pretty pedigreed copy, though. This one will make you get up and salute! Overstreet 2005 NM- 9.2 value = $650. CGC census 9/05: 4 in 9.4, none higher.

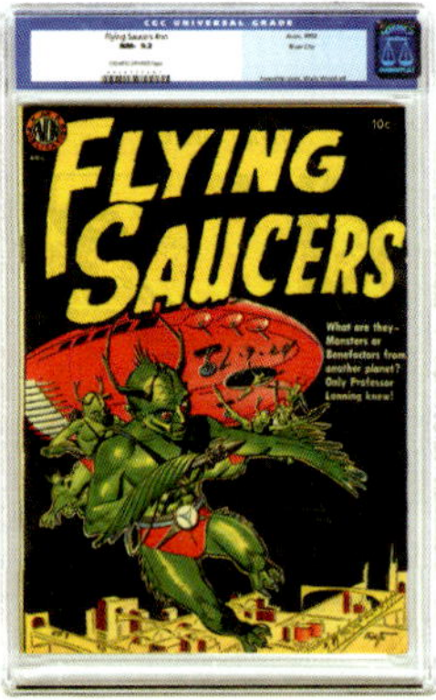

2356 Flying Saucers #nn River City pedigree (Avon, 1952) CGC NM- 9.2 Cream to off-white pages. Gene Fawcette's dynamic depiction of alien invaders is a textbook example of an effective cover; its limited color palette employs contrasting hues that spellbind the eye and refuse to let go. Interior art by Wally Wood is another bonus, as is its peerless River City pedigree. Overstreet 2005 NM- 9.2 value = $575. CGC census 9/05: 2 in 9.2, none higher.

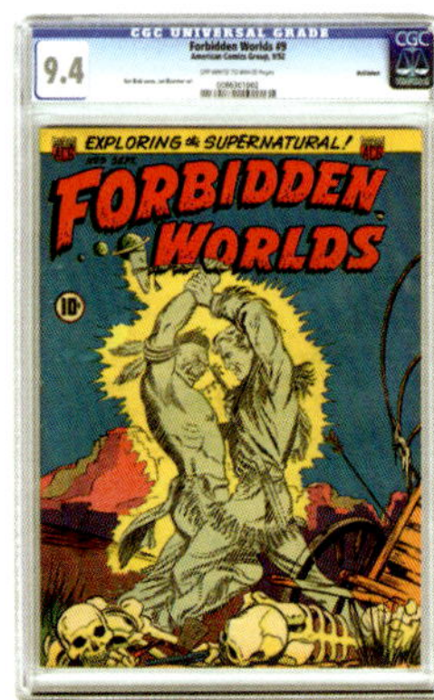

2357 Forbidden Worlds #9 Bethlehem pedigree (ACG, 1952) CGC NM 9.4 Off-white to white pages. Overstreet notes that there's an atomic explosion story in the pages of this issue. This high-grade Bethlehem pedigree comic is a choice one — to date, no copies of this issue have been graded higher by CGC. Overstreet 2005 NM- 9.2 value = $375. CGC census 9/05: 2 in 9.4, none higher.

2358 Four Color #167 The Lone Ranger (Dell, 1947) CGC VF/NM 9.0 Off-white pages. Overstreet 2005 VF/NM 9.0 value = $216; NM- 9.2 value = $290. CGC census 7/05: 4 in 9.0, 1 higher.

2359 Four Color #291 Donald Duck in "The Magic Hourglass" File Copy (Dell, 1950) CGC VF+ 8.5 White pages. Carl Barks art. Overstreet 2005 VF 8.0 value = $293; VF/NM 9.0 value = $459. CGC census 9/05: 1 in 8.5, none higher.

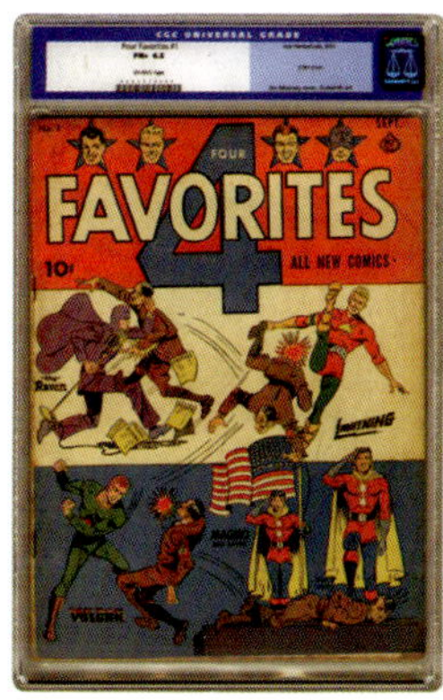

2360 Four Favorites #1 (Ace, 1941) CGC FN+ 6.5 Off-white pages. Hitler is pummeled in succession by all four favorite heroes — the Raven, Lightning, Vulcan, and Magno and Davey on this first issue cover, drawn by Jim Mooney. Overstreet 2005 FN 6.0 value = $507; VF 8.0 value = $1,056. CGC census 9/05: 2 in 6.5, 1 higher.

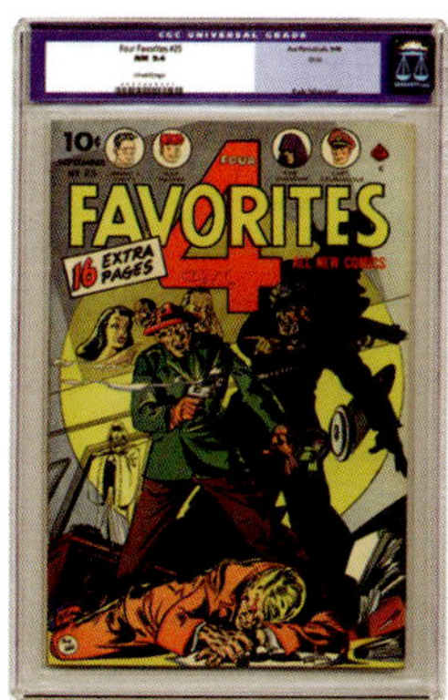

2361 Four Favorites #25 Ohio pedigree (Ace, 1946) CGC NM 9.4 Off-white pages. Rudy Palais' *noir*-ish cover gives us an unusual worm's-eye view of a crime scene. This crisp Ohio pedigree copy is outgraded by only one other copy according to CGC's current census report. Overstreet 2005 NM- 9.2 value = $260. CGC census 9/05: 1 in 9.4, 1 higher.

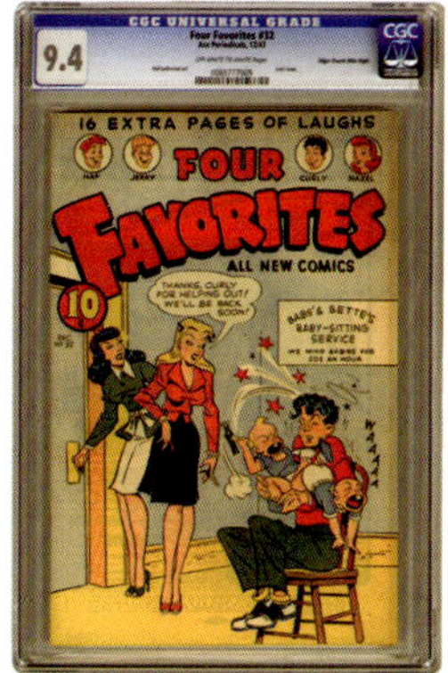

2362 Four Favorites #32 Mile High pedigree (Ace, 1947) CGC NM 9.4 Off-white to white pages. Last issue of the title, with art by Hal Lockwood. This gorgeous Edgar Church Mile High copy is currently the only one of this issue certified by CGC. Overstreet 2005 NM- 9.2 value = $150. CGC census 9/05: 1 in 9.4, none higher.

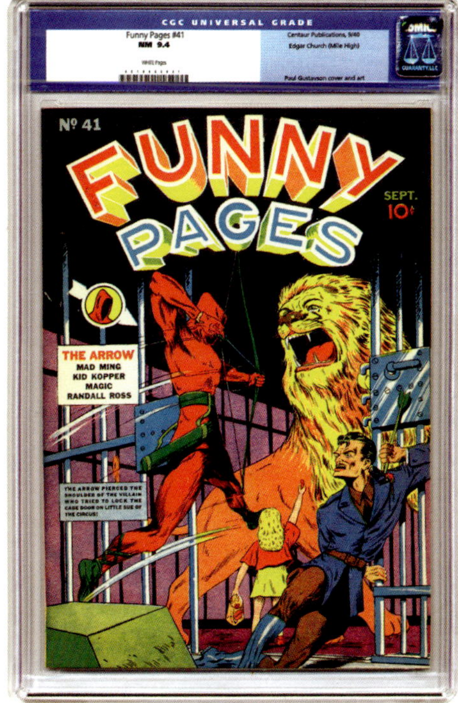

2363 Funny Pages #41 Mile High pedigree (Centaur, 1940) CGC NM 9.4 White pages. Here's a rarity for you — it's the only copy of the issue that CGC has certified to date, and the first one we've ever seen here at Heritage. It's also got a Gerber scarcity rating of "7." The cover and some of the interior art are by Paul Gustavson. Overstreet 2005 NM- 9.2 value = $2,350. CGC census 8/05: 1 in 9.4, none higher.

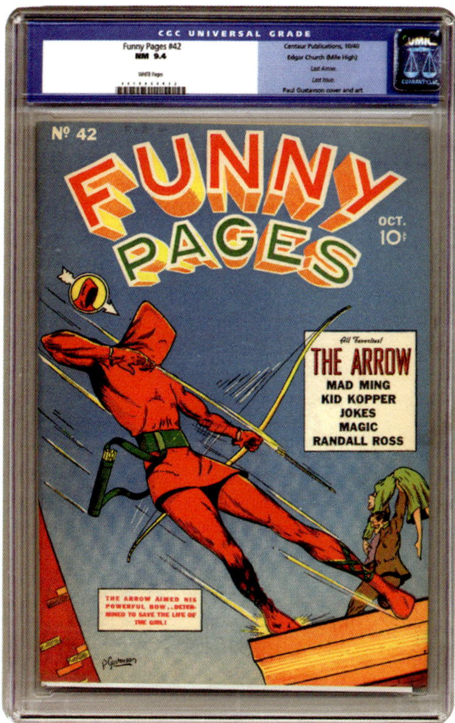

2364 Funny Pages #42 Mile High pedigree (Centaur, 1940) CGC NM 9.4 White pages. It's rated "scarce" by Overstreet, it's the only copy CGC has certified, the only one we've ever seen, and a Gerber "7"... what we're getting at is that this comic is hard to find! Paul Gustavson drew the issue's cover. Overstreet 2005 NM- 9.2 value = $2,450. CGC census 8/05: 1 in 9.4, none higher.

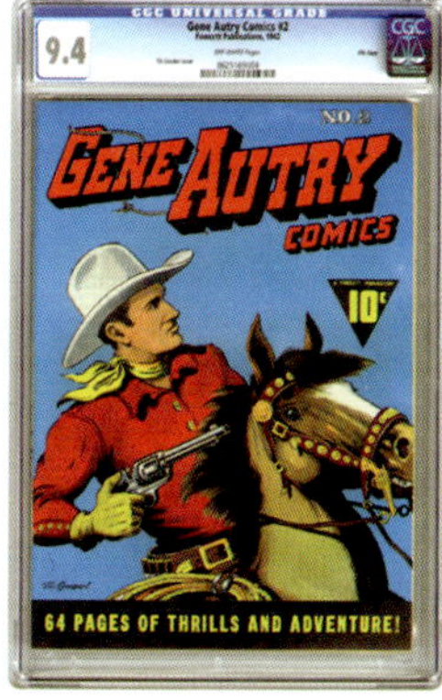

2365 Gene Autry Comics #2 File Copy (Fawcett, 1942) CGC NM 9.4 Off-white pages. In your quest for file copies, don't overlook those from Fawcett. This beauty copy beats the second-place contender in the CGC census by 9.4 to 8.0. Hardly a contest! Overstreet 2005 NM- 9.2 value = $2,100. CGC census 9/05: 1 in 9.4, none higher.

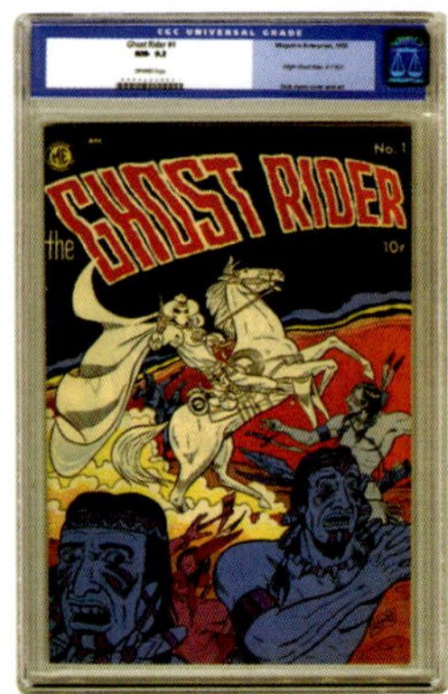

2366 Ghost Rider #1 (Magazine Enterprises, 1950) CGC NM- 9.2 Off-white pages. Inspired in part by the classic Vaughn Monroe hit recording "Ghost Riders in the Sky" comes the first issue of this wild Western title (actually, it's #27 of the series **A-1** — Magazine Enterprises' one-shot numbering system, similar to Dell's **Four Color** series). The Dick Ayers cover is moody and colorful with an all-white horse and rider set against a background that shifts from black to blue, yellow, and red; this copy displays plenty of great eye-appeal. Overstreet 2005 NM- 9.2 value = $1,400. CGC census 9/05: 1 in 9.2, 1 higher.

2367 Hit Comics #11 (Quality, 1941) CGC Apparent GD 2.0 Cream to off-white pages. Lou Fine cover ("classic" according to Overstreet). Jack Cole, Klaus Nordling, Nick Cardy, and Reed Crandall art. Note that CGC did not list a degree of restoration for this comic. CGC notes, "Centerfold trimmed. (Moderate amount of tape on cover)." Overstreet 2005 GD 2.0 value = $173.

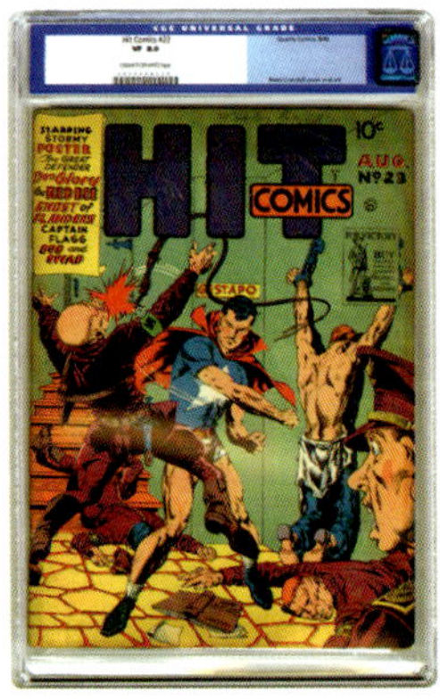

2368 Hit Comics #23 (Quality, 1942) CGC VF 8.0 Cream to off-white pages. Reed Crandall did his best Lou Fine impersonation on this cover, and we'd say he did a darn "fine" job of it! Overstreet 2005 VF 8.0 value = $600. CGC census 9/05: 1 in 8.0, none higher.

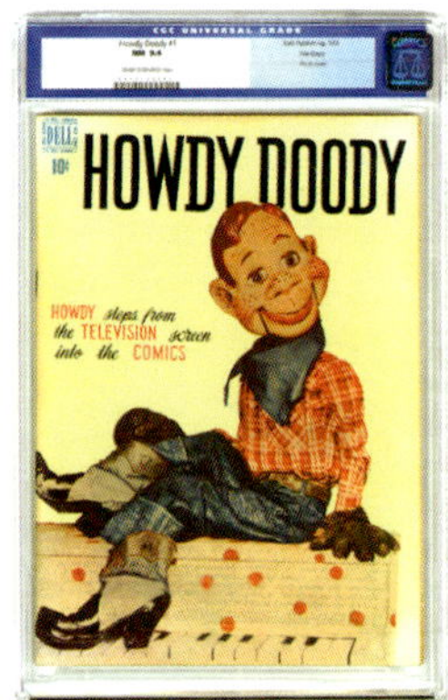

2369 Howdy Doody #1 File Copy (Dell, 1950) CGC NM 9.4 Cream to off-white pages. Cowabunga! You're looking at the very first TV comic book, tying in with the first really popular children's TV series. The star character poses for posterity on the photo cover. Overstreet terms the issue "scarce." Overstreet 2005 NM- 9.2 value = $1,600. CGC census 9/05: 2 in 9.4, none higher.

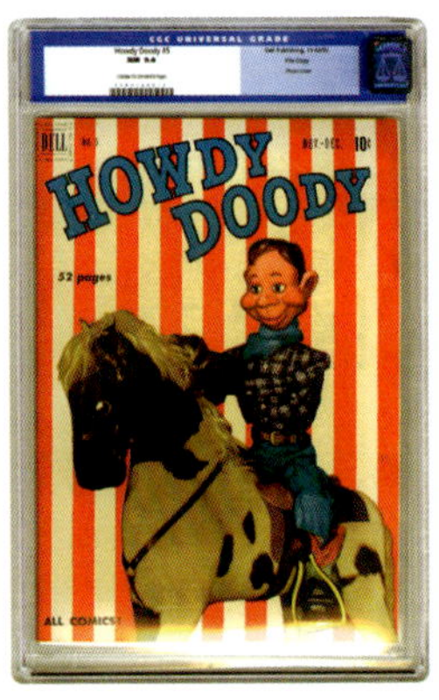

2370 Howdy Doody #5 File Copy (Dell, 1950) CGC NM 9.4 Cream to off-white pages. It's fitting that the first TV comic book tied in with the first really popular children's TV series. This was the last issue with a photo cover before a run of painted covers commenced. Only one copy of this issue has been certified with a higher grade by CGC to date. Overstreet 2005 NM- 9.2 value = $365. CGC census 9/05: 1 in 9.4, 1 higher.

2371 Jamboree Comics #1 (Round, 1946) CGC NM 9.4 Off-white to white pages. If you're looking for a nice high-grade generic humor comic book from the Golden Age for your collection, consider this little beauty. The flawless black background really makes the cartoon figures pop out on this JCA Studio cover. Overstreet 2005 NM- 9.2 value = $285. CGC census 8/05: 3 in 9.4, 1 higher.

2372 Jet Aces #1 Mile High pedigree (Fiction House, 1952) CGC NM- 9.2 Off-white pages. This is the only copy of this issue that CGC has certified as of this writing. Overstreet 2005 NM- 9.2 value = $170. CGC census 9/05: 1 in 9.2, none higher.

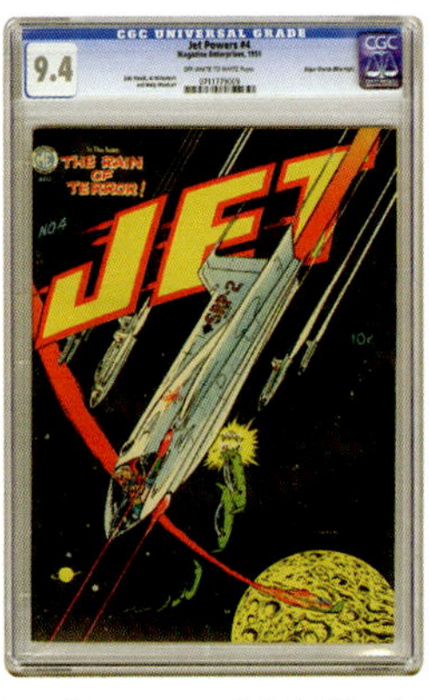

2373 Jet Powers #4 Mile High pedigree (Magazine Enterprises, 1951) CGC NM 9.4 Off-white to white pages. Features "The Rain of Sleep" drug story. Bob Powell, Al Williamson, and Wally Wood art. This is currently the highest grade awarded by CGC for this issue. Overstreet 2005 NM- 9.2 value = $475. CGC census 8/05: 1 in 9.4, none higher.

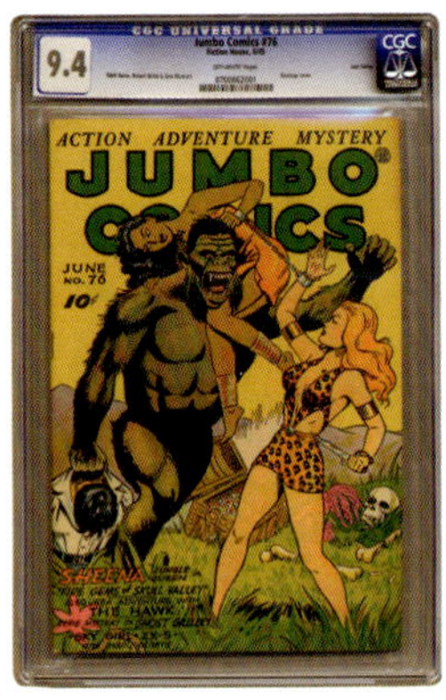

2374 Jumbo Comics #76 Lost Valley pedigree (Fiction House, 1945) CGC NM 9.4 Off-white pages. Bondage cover and gorilla cover enthusiasts alike will want to go after this Fiction House selection. It's got great Matt Baker interior art, filled with his trademark good girl images. A Lost Valley certificate of authenticity accompanies this lot. Overstreet 2005 NM- 9.2 value = $240. CGC census 9/05: 1 in 9.4, none higher.

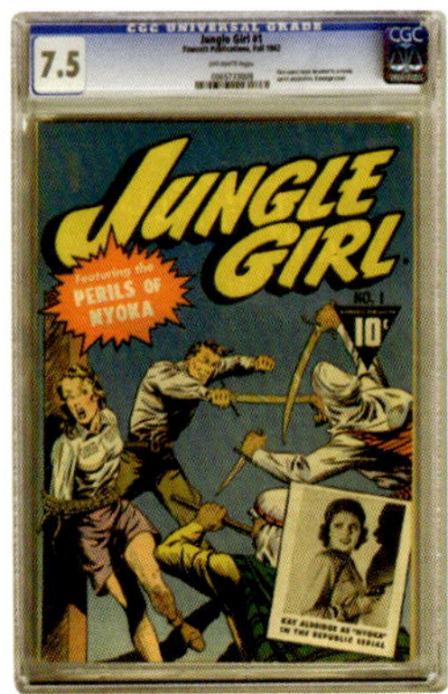

2375 Jungle Girl #1 (Fawcett, 1942) CGC VF- 7.5 Off-white pages. According to Overstreet, this is the first comic book to devote its entire contents to a movie serial adaptation. The character is perhaps better known to comic fans as Nyoka the Jungle Girl, and the series would be called by that name starting with the second issue. This first issue has a bondage cover as well as an inset photo of star Kay Aldridge. Overstreet 2005 VF 8.0 value = $819. CGC census 9/05: 1 in 7.5, 3 higher.

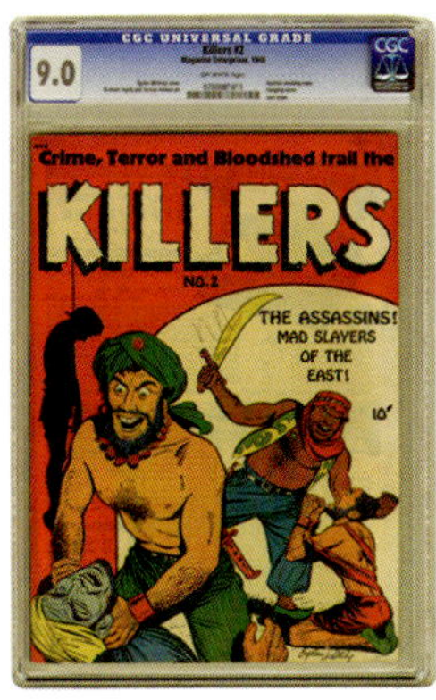

2376 Killers #2 (Magazine Enterprises, 1948) CGC VF/NM 9.0 Off-white pages. A comic that glorifies killers and touts "crime, terror, and bloodshed" is not exactly what Mom wanted to see Junior perusing. That's probably why this title disappeared from newsstands after two issues. This second issue is hard to find — both Overstreet and Gerber call it "scarce." The hanging (and strangling, and what looks like beheading) cover by Ogden Whitney is about as brutal as they come... compared to that, the "hashish smoking" story inside the comic doesn't sound so bad! Whitney contributed interior art as well, as did "Ghastly" Graham Ingels. Overstreet 2005 VF/NM 9.0 value = $853; NM- 9.2 value = $1,150. CGC census 8/05: 1 in 9.0, none higher.

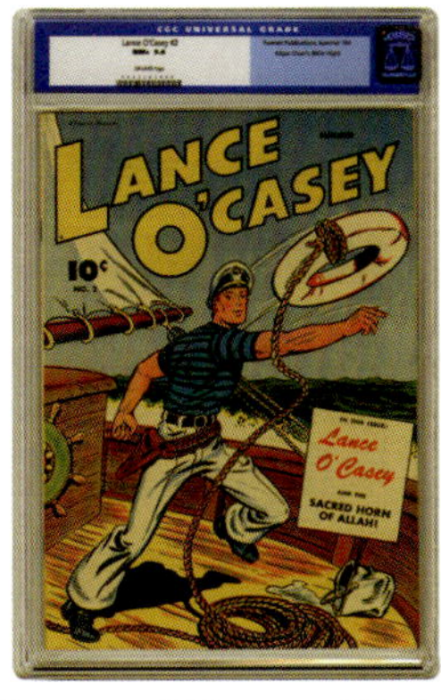

2377 Lance O'Casey #2 Mile High pedigree (Fawcett, 1946) CGC NM+ 9.6 Off-white pages. High seas adventurer Lance O'Casey is best known for starring in a longtime backup feature in **Whiz Comics**, but he did have his own title for a while — four issues to be exact. This beautiful copy isn't just the highest-graded that CGC has certified to date, it's the only one to receive a blue-label Universal Grade as of this writing. Overstreet 2005 NM- 9.2 value = $255. CGC census 9/05: 1 in 9.6, none higher.

2378 Large Feature Comic #1 Dick Tracy Meets The Blank (Dell, 1942) Condition: VG. The first Dell Dick Tracy comic book. Overstreet 2005 VG 4.0 value = $354.

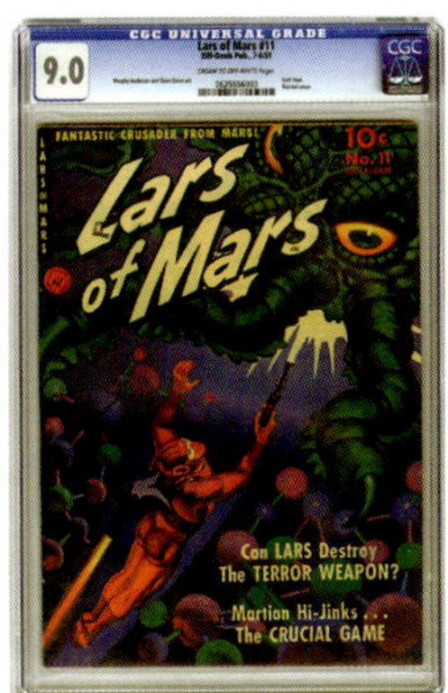

2379 Lars of Mars #11 (Ziff-Davis, 1951) CGC VF/NM 9.0 Cream to off-white pages. Comics from publisher Ziff-Davis are noted for their beautiful painted covers, and this comic, developed by **Superman** co-creator Jerry Siegel, is certainly no exception. It's the last of only two issues featuring the outer space adventurer; both issues feature covers considered "classic" by Overstreet. This one's a real doozy, featuring a hideous (for comic books, that's a good thing) green tentacled monster. The fun continues inside, with art by Gene Colan and Murphy Anderson. Overstreet 2005 VF/NM 9.0 value = $623; NM- 9.2 value = $840. CGC census 8/05: 3 in 9.0, none higher.

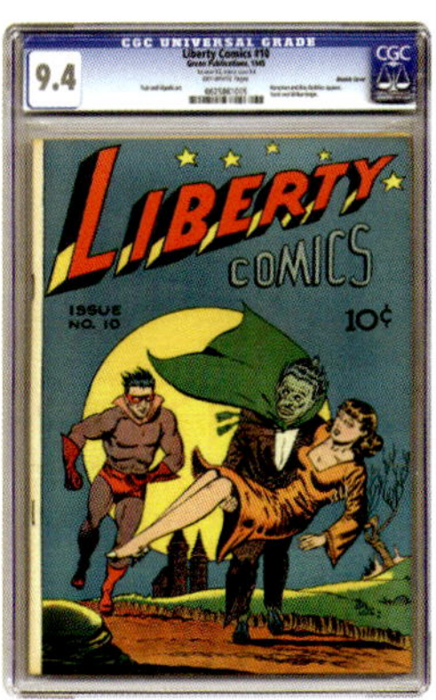

2380 Liberty Comics #10 Double Cover (Green Publishing Co., 1945) CGC NM 9.4 Off-white pages. This MLJ/Archie offshoot features appearances by the Hangman and the Boy Buddies, in three reprinted stories. But the real news here is the rare occurrence of a double cover. CGC notes, "First cover 9.2, interior cover 9.4." This one easily tops CGC's current census list for this issue. Overstreet 2005 NM- 9.2 value = $240. CGC census 8/05: 1 in 9.4, none higher.

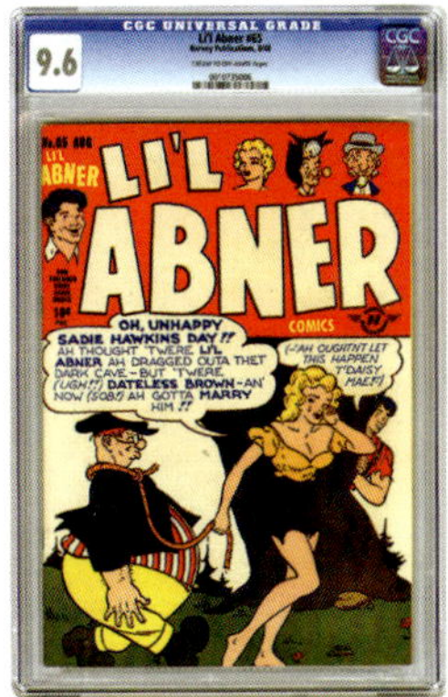

2381 Li'l Abner #65 (Harvey, 1948) CGC NM+ 9.6 Cream to off-white pages. Looks like Daisy Mae (inspiration for Daisy Duke in "Dukes of Hazzard," no doubt) roped herself a husband on Sadie Hawkins Day, but he's not Abner — it's (ugh!) Dateless Brown! Bob Powell art is featured. This incredible copy is far and away the highest-graded example currently found in CGC's census report for this issue. Overstreet 2005 NM- 9.2 value = $225. CGC census 8/05: 1 in 9.6, none higher.

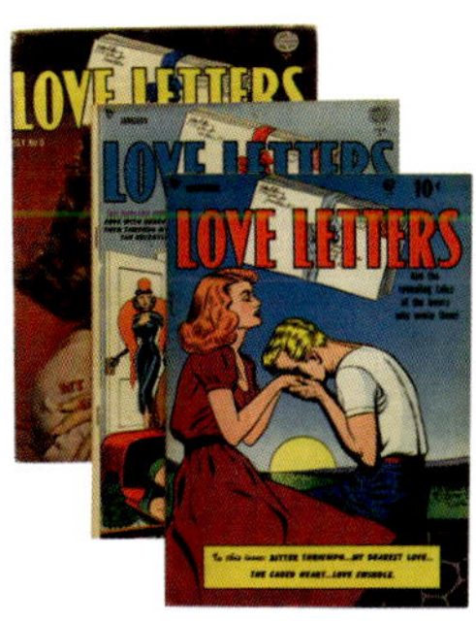

2382 Love Letters Group (Quality, 1949-53) Condition: Average VG/FN. The issues in this group include some line-drawn covers by Bill Ward as well as a number of photo covers. The most notable are the ones that depict Robert Mitchum (#9) and Jane Russell (#17)! Included here are #1 (FN+), 2, 5, 6, 7, 8, 9, 11, 12, 14, 15, 17, 19, 20, 22, 25, 27, 28, 29, 31, 36, and 41. Approximate Overstreet value for group = $500.

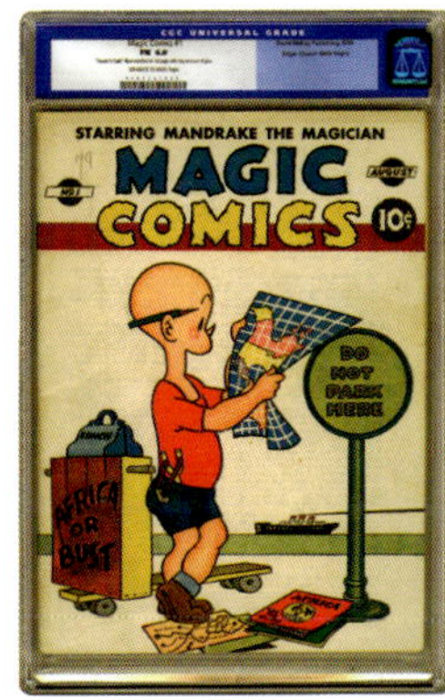

2383 Magic Comics #1 Mile High pedigree (David McKay Publications, 1939) CGC FN 6.0 Off-white to white pages. Just two unrestored copies of this premiere issue have been certified by CGC to date - no surprise, since Gerber rates it "scarce". CGC notes, "'Reader's Guild' flyer attached to 1st page with tiny amount of glue." Overstreet 2005 FN 6.0 value = $1,029. CGC census 9/05: 1 in 6.0, 1 higher.

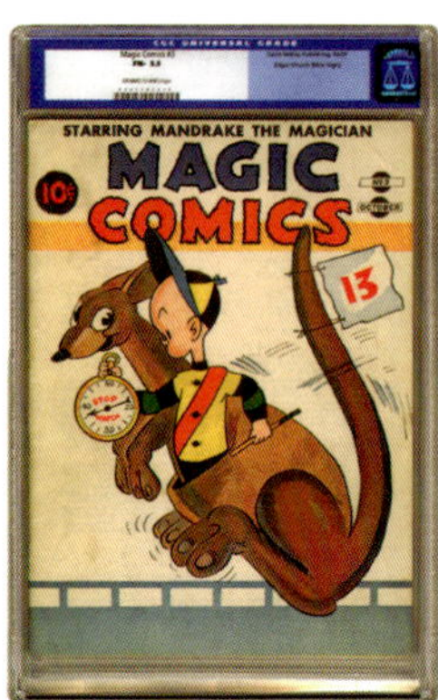

2384 Magic Comics #3 Mile High pedigree (David McKay Publications, 1939) CGC FN- 5.5 Off-white to white pages. Even at this grade, the book bears tell-tale characteristics of its peerless pedigree, including ranking as the finest copy CGC has certified to date for the issue. Overstreet 2005 FN 6.0 value = $270. CGC census 9/05: 1 in 5.5, none higher.

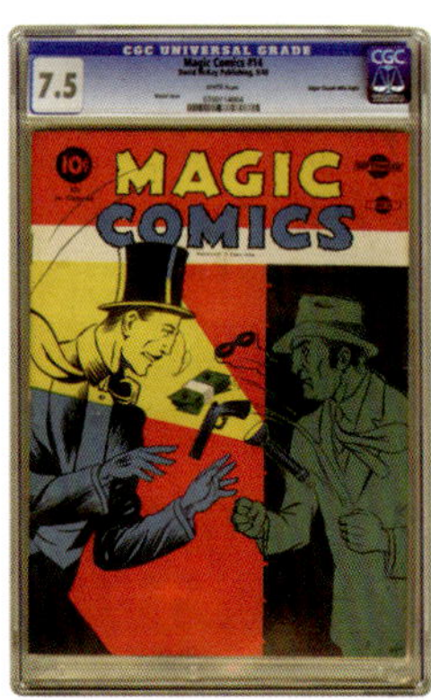

2385 Magic Comics #14 Mile High pedigree (David McKay Publications, 1940) CGC VF- 7.5 White pages. Mandrake the Magician gave this title its name, and he's among many characters featured inside the book. The cover is by Joe Musial. Overstreet 2005 VF 8.0 value = $209. CGC census 8/05: 1 in 7.5, none higher.

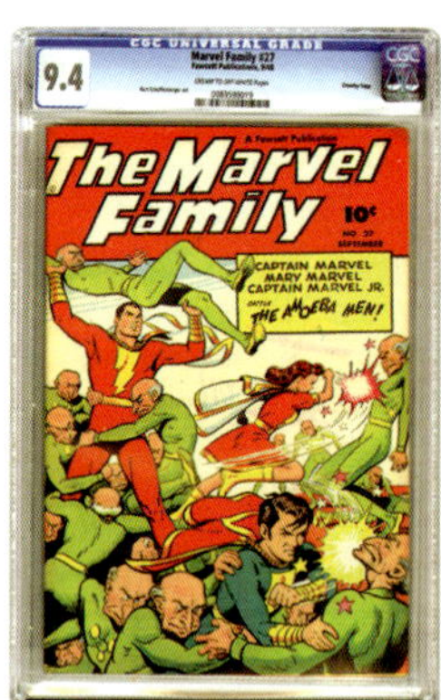

2386 The Marvel Family #27 Crowley Copy pedigree (Fawcett, 1948) CGC NM 9.4 Cream to off-white pages. The Marvel Family teams up to battle the Amoeba Men in this issue's lead story, and each of the big three (Cap, Junior, and Mary) stars in a solo adventure as well. Overstreet 2005 NM- 9.2 value = $275. CGC census 8/05: 1 in 9.4, none higher.

2387 The Marvel Family #62 Crowley Copy pedigree (Fawcett, 1951) CGC NM 9.4 Off-white pages. Dr. Sivana appears. Overstreet 2005 NM- 9.2 value = $160. CGC census 8/05: 1 in 9.4, 1 higher.

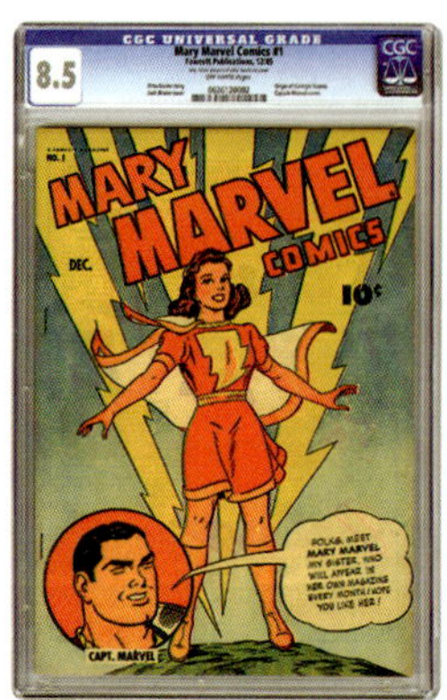

2388 Mary Marvel Comics #1 (Fawcett, 1945) CGC VF+ 8.5 Off-white pages. After starring in **Wow Comics**, Mary Marvel earned her own title, and not only did she have Captain Marvel introduce her on the cover, she got her very own archfoe in Georgia Sivana (daughter of Dr. Sivana), whose first appearance and origin are in these pages. The cover art is by Jack Binder. CGC notes, "Very minor amount of color touch on cover." Overstreet 2005 VF 8.0 value = $1,300; VF/NM 9.0 value = $2,000. CGC census 8/05: 2 in 8.5, 6 higher.

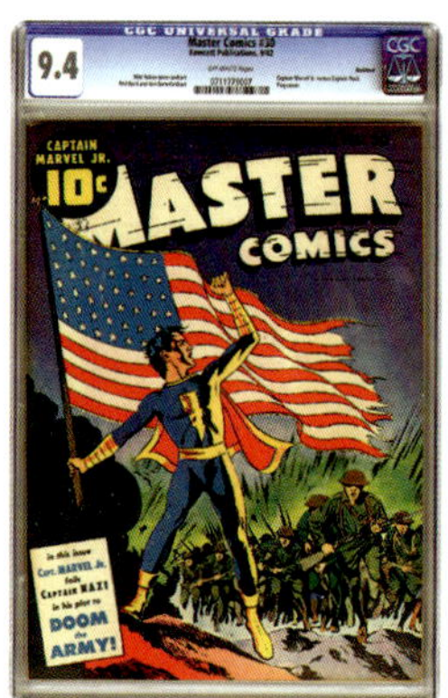

2389 Master Comics #30 Rockford pedigree (Fawcett, 1942) CGC NM 9.4 Off-white pages. If Captain Marvel Jr. is your thing, have we got a great comic for you! Check it out — a terrific early World War II flag cover featuring a charging line of soldiers; an appearance by Cap Jr.'s most hated foe, Captain Nazi; and beautiful Mac Raboy art. All this, plus a fantastic pedigreed copy, complete with certificate of authenticity — this one's got it all! Overstreet 2005 NM- 9.2 value = $1,125. CGC census 8/05: 1 in 9.4, 1 higher.

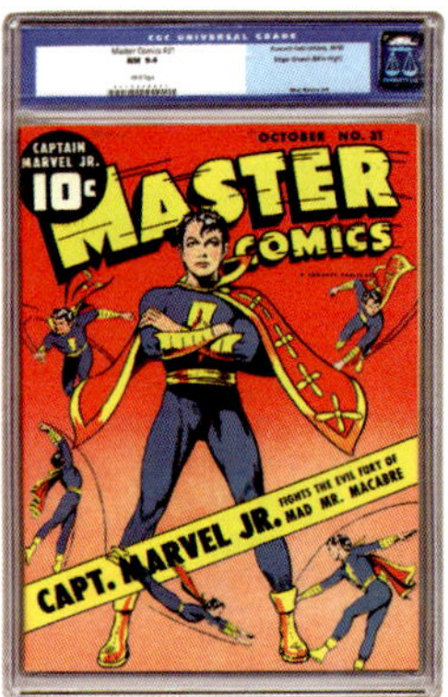

2390 Master Comics #31 Mile High pedigree (Fawcett, 1942) CGC NM 9.4 White pages. Great cover gloss, perfect edges, and white pages characterize this Mile High copy. It's one of only two that have been certified by CGC as of this writing, with the other far behind at 7.5. Captain Marvel Jr. is the star of the issue, drawn by his signature artist Mac Raboy. Overstreet 2005 NM- 9.2 value = $850. CGC census 7/05: 1 in 9.4, none higher.

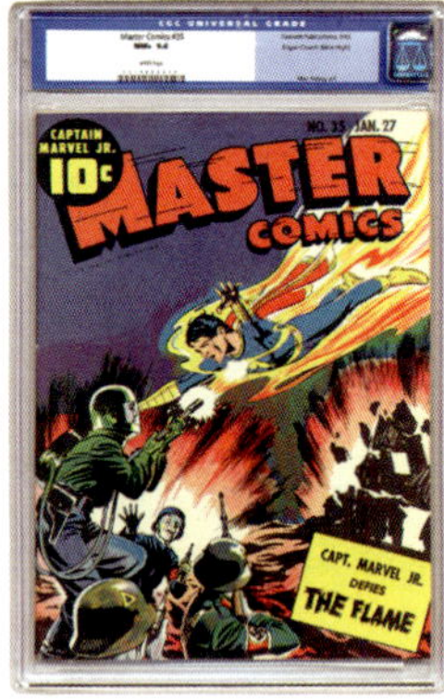

2391 Master Comics #35 Mile High pedigree (Fawcett, 1943) CGC NM+ 9.6 White pages. Midnight-blue covers were a specialty of this series, and the only problem with that is that the color exposes flaws much as a black cover would. No such worries with this Mile High copy, though! Captain Marvel Jr. (drawn by Mac Raboy) is the headliner, and Bulletman also appears. Overstreet 2005 NM- 9.2 value = $850. CGC census 7/05: 1 in 9.6, none higher.

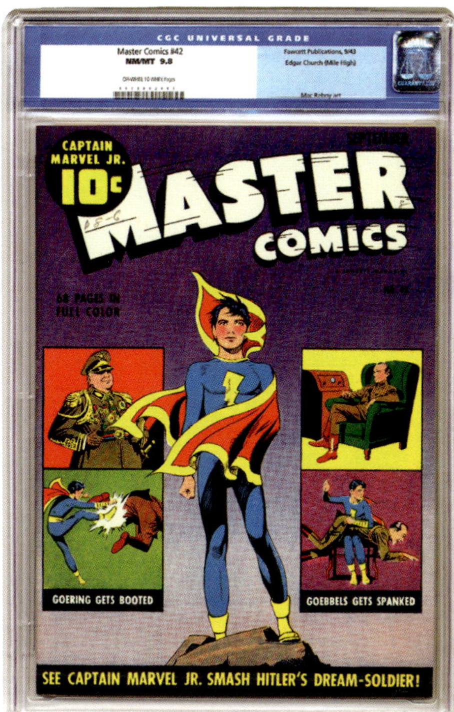

2392 Master Comics #42 Mile High pedigree (Fawcett, 1943) CGC NM/MT 9.8 Off-white to white pages. Josef Goebbels gets spanked and Hermann Goering gets a kick in the rear, that'll show Hitler's right-hand men the error of their ways! Speaking of Hitler, he joins the two other Nazis by appearing in the Captain Marvel Jr. story drawn by Mac Raboy. This Edgar Church copy comes as close to perfection as you're going to find. It's the only copy graded above 9.0 by CGC as of this writing. Overstreet 2005 NM- 9.2 value = $475. CGC census 7/05: 1 in 9.8, none higher.

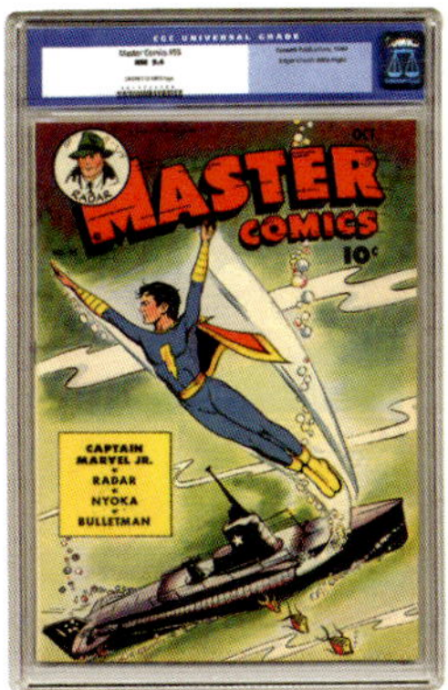

2393 Master Comics #55 Mile High pedigree (Fawcett, 1944) CGC NM 9.4 Off-white to white pages. Captain Marvel Jr. stars in this issue, which also has adventures of Radar, Nyoka the Jungle Girl, and Bulletman. Overstreet 2005 NM- 9.2 value = $265. CGC census 7/05: 3 in 9.4, 2 higher.

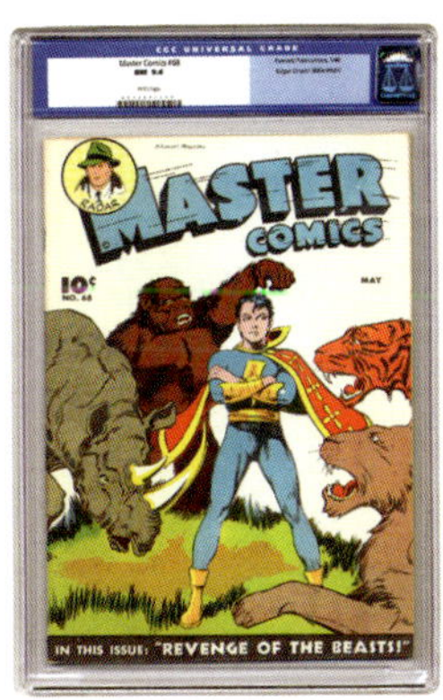

2394 Master Comics #68 Mile High pedigree (Fawcett, 1946) CGC NM 9.4 White pages. An umblemished white cover and of course white pages grace this lovely Mile High copy. The stars of the issue are Captain Marvel Jr., Bulletman, and Nyoka the Jungle Girl. Overstreet 2005 NM- 9.2 value = $200. CGC census 7/05: 1 in 9.4, none higher.

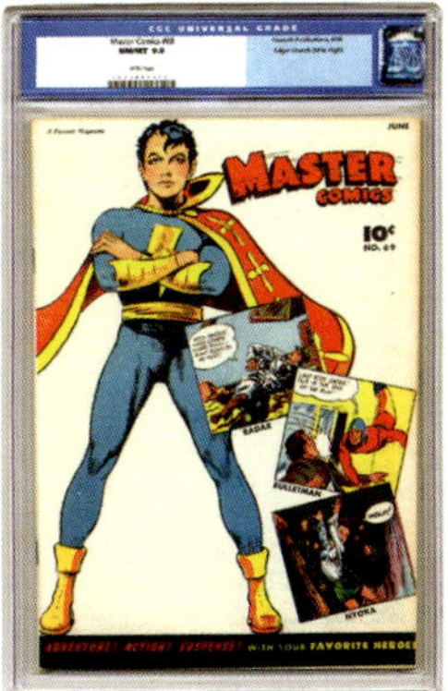

2395 Master Comics #69 Mile High pedigree (Fawcett, 1946) CGC NM/MT 9.8 White pages. This issue's white cover would usually be a collector's nightmare, but even after looking at it every which way, we don't see a blemish on this Edgar Church copy. This one doesn't even have the unobtrusive distributor pencil markings that some Mile Highs have! Our offering is the only copy of the issue to be graded above 9.0 by CGC as of this writing. Captain Marvel Jr., Bulletman, and Nyoka the Jungle Girl are the featured characters. Overstreet 2005 NM- 9.2 value = $200. CGC census 7/05: 1 in 9.8, none higher.

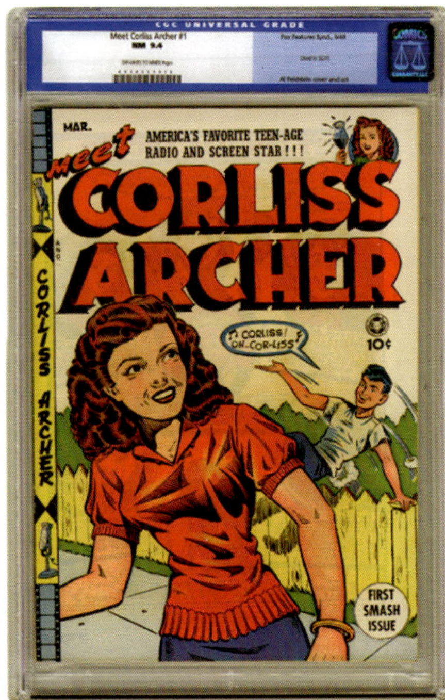

2396 Meet Corliss Archer #1 (Fox, 1948) CGC NM 9.4 Off-white to white pages. "America's Favorite Teen-Age Radio and Screen Star" was drawn so evocatively by (pre-EC days) Al Feldstein, that Dr. Frederic Wertham just had to make an issue of it in his diatribe **Seduction of the Innocent**. His concern is lost on us, and we appreciate Corliss' attributes, displayed nicely on the premiere issue's cover. CGC hasn't certified a higher grade to date for this issue. Overstreet 2005 NM- 9.2 value = $1,300. CGC census 9/05: 2 in 9.4, none higher.

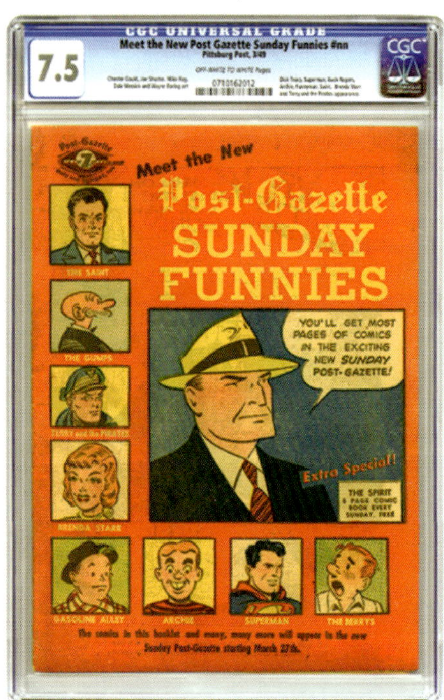

2397 Meet the New Post-Gazette Sunday Funnies #nn (Pittsburgh Post-Gazette, 1949) CGC VF- 7.5 Off-white to white pages. Superman, Archie, and Dick Tracy in the same comic book? That's something you won't find anywhere else but this hard-to-find promotional comic, which is called "rare" by Overstreet and is a Gerber "7." This 16-page comic with a paper cover was an insert in the newspaper, intended to drum up interest (and subscriptions) for the paper's revamping. In addition to the aforementioned features, there's Funnyman by Jerry Siegel and Joe Shuster, plus Buck Rogers, Gasoline Alley, Terry and the Pirates, Brenda Starr, and more. Overstreet 2005 VF 8.0 value = $4,500. CGC census 8/05: 1 in 7.5, 1 higher.

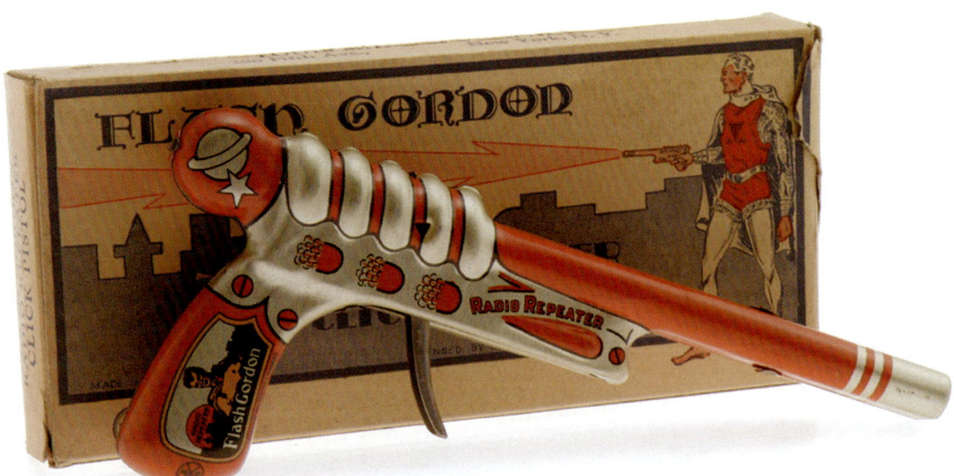

2398 Flash Gordon Radio Repeater Click Pistol with Original Box (Louis Marx, 1935). While it might seem otherwise, the ray gun market of the 1930s wasn't comprised of only Buck Rogers merchandise. Louis Marx Co. created the Flash Gordon Radio Repeater. A simpler pressing than the Buck guns, the toy made up for it with colorful lithography. The original box has a tear at the right side, but the colors are sharp, and it is in Very Good condition overall. The gun measures 10" long, and, aside from some light paint loss on the handle, is in Excellent condition.

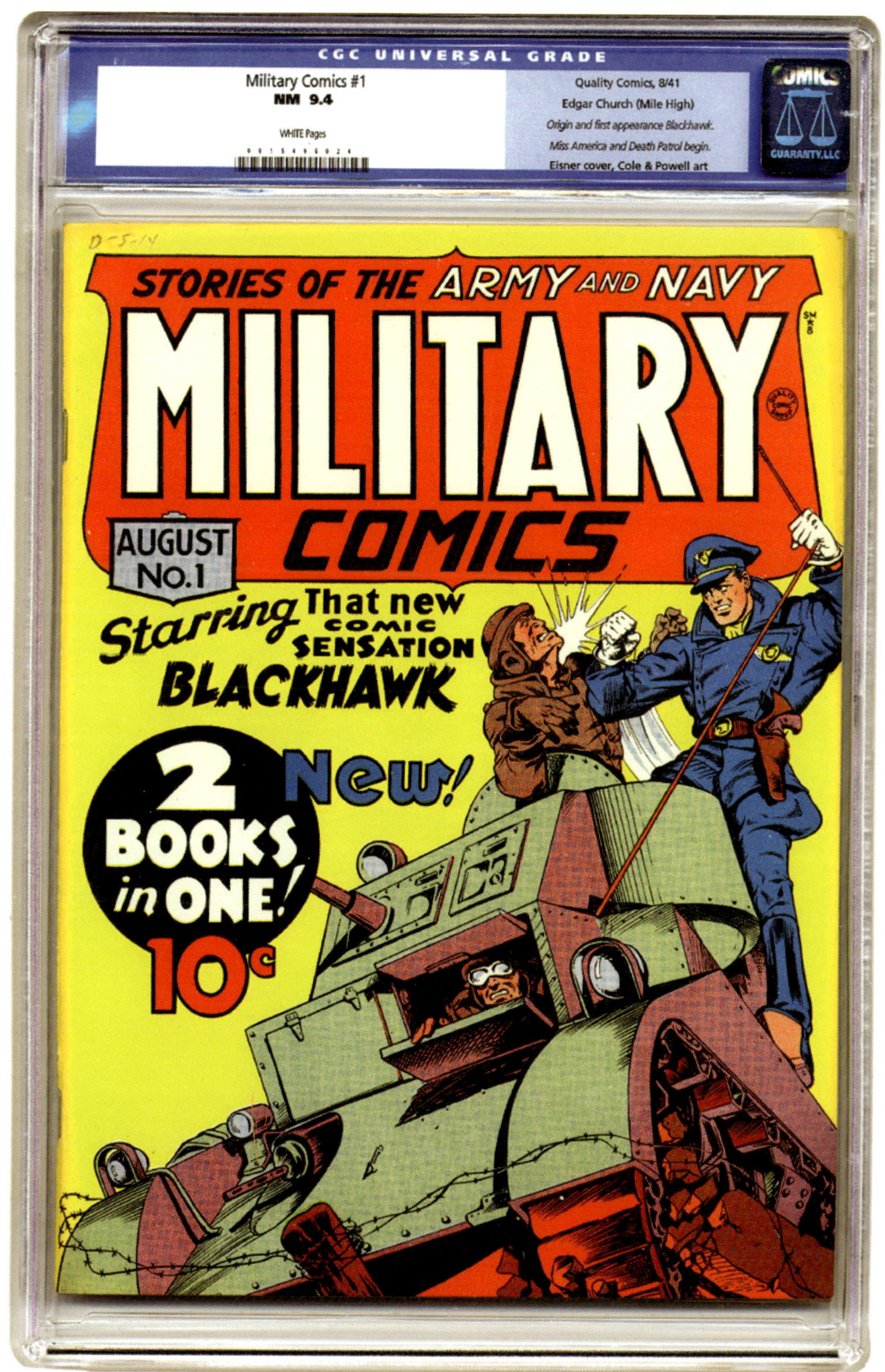

2399 Military Comics #1 Mile High pedigree (Quality, 1941) CGC NM 9.4 White pages. This issue features the origin and first appearance of one of the great heroes of the early days of comics, Blackhawk! That hero (and his supporting cast which debuted in later issues) endured all the way into the 1980s in various incarnations, being published by DC after Quality's demise. Will Eisner, who was reportedly a co-creator of the team, drew the cover. Inside the comic (which is divided into "Army Section" and "Navy Section"), Blackhawk is drawn by Chuck Cuidera. The other artists include Jack Cole, Fred Guardineer, and Klaus Nordling. Cole's feature, called "Death Patrol," is worthy of note, as it featured a "Dirty Dozen"-like concept decades before that movie was released. The group was aptly named, as one of its members died in every story! This Mile High copy is the only copy of the issue certified with a grade above VF/NM to date. Overstreet 2005 NM- 9.2 value = $14,500. CGC census 9/05: 1 in 9.4, none higher.

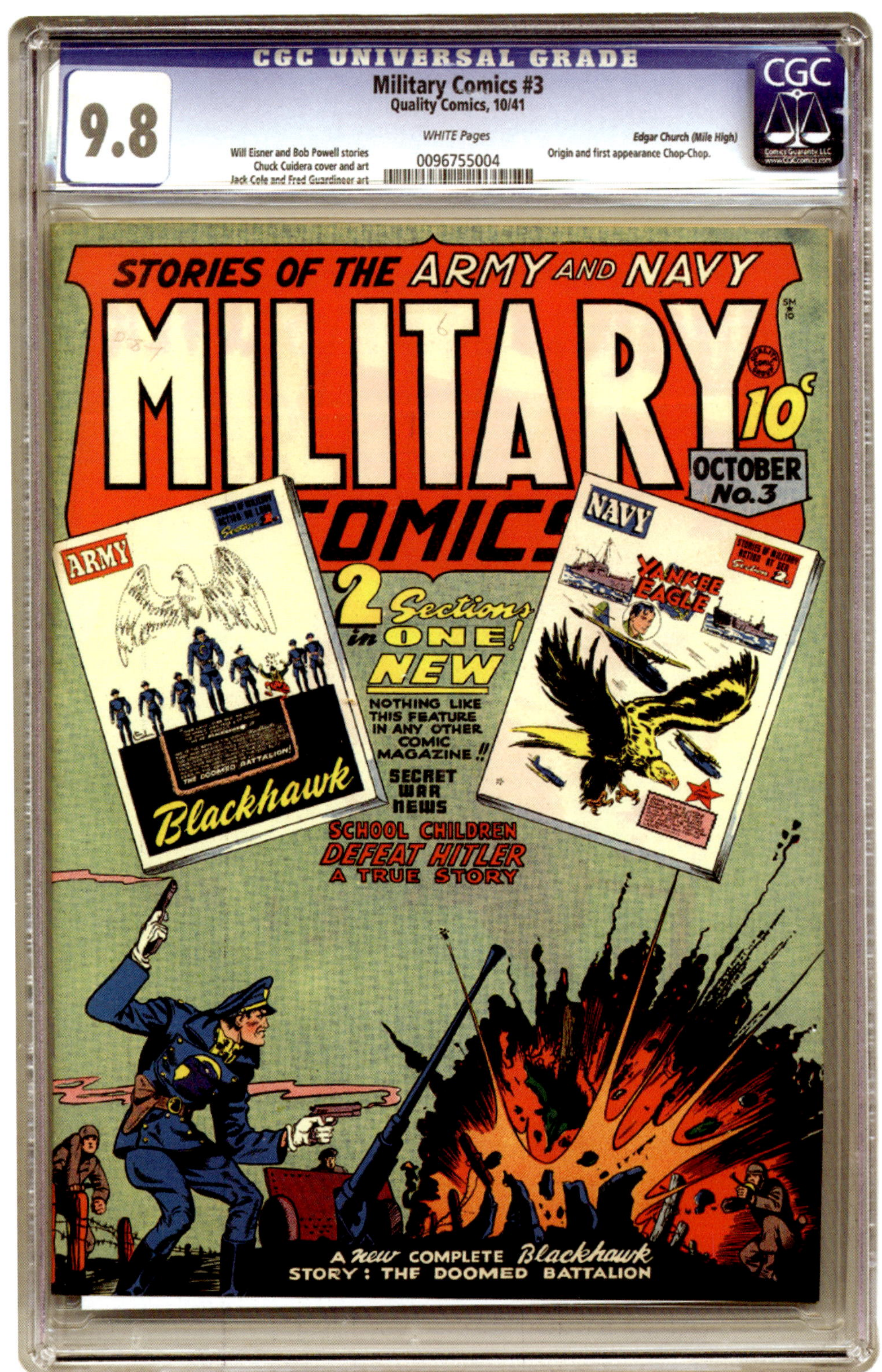

2400 Military Comics #3 Mile High pedigree (Quality, 1941) CGC NM/MT 9.8 White pages. The third appearance of the Blackhawks is the first appearance of Chop Chop! He's the comic relief member of the group, but also perhaps the bravest of the bunch. The Blackhawk story is just one of many tales of the Army and Navy in this issue. The book has a Chuck Cuidera cover, with interior art by Cuidera, Jack Cole, and Fred Guardineer. This is the highest-graded copy of the issue in CGC's census by far — in fact, as of this writing it's the only copy graded above VF/NM. Overstreet 2005 NM- 9.2 value = $3,050. CGC census 9/05: 1 in 9.8, none higher.

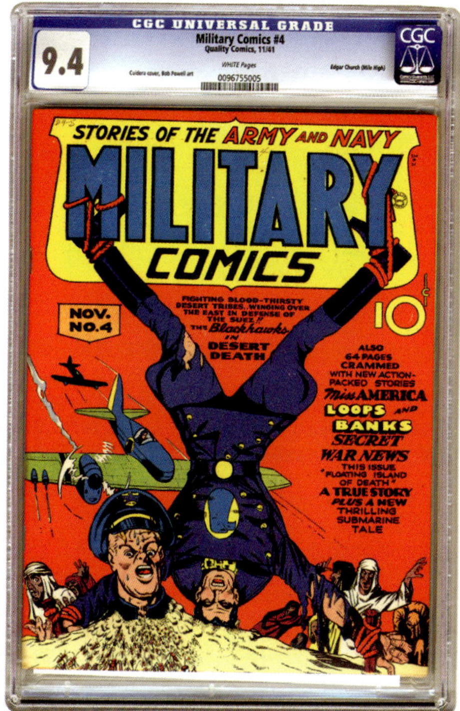

2401 Military Comics #4 Mile High pedigree (Quality, 1941) CGC NM 9.4 White pages. If you want a high-grade copy of this issue, it's this Mile High book or nothing — ours is the only copy certified above 5.5 by CGC to date! Chuck Cuidera drew the cover and the Blackhawk story, and Bob Powell and Dave Berg contributed art on backup features. Overstreet 2005 NM- 9.2 value = $2,450. CGC census 9/05: 1 in 9.4, none higher.

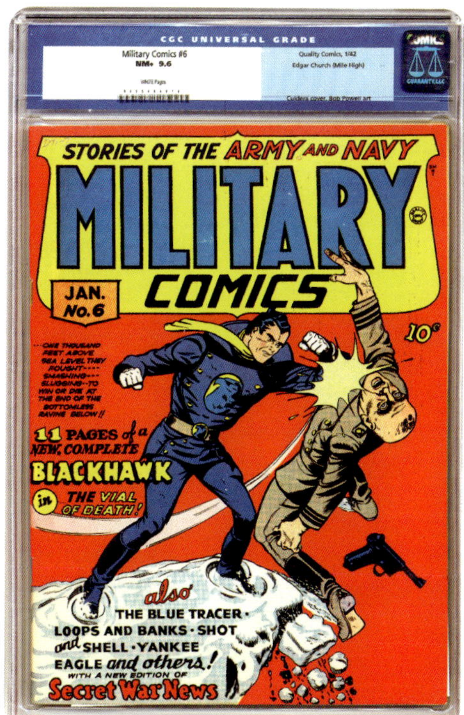

2402 Military Comics #6 Mile High pedigree (Quality, 1942) CGC NM+ 9.6 White pages. Here's a copy that looks like it just rolled off the printing press yesterday. The cover gloss and page quality are perfect! The star of the comic is, of course, Blackhawk. The issue's got a Chuck Cuidera cover, with interior art by Bob Powell, Klaus Nordling, and Dave Berg. Overstreet 2005 NM- 9.2 value = $1,475. CGC census 7/05: 1 in 9.6, none higher.

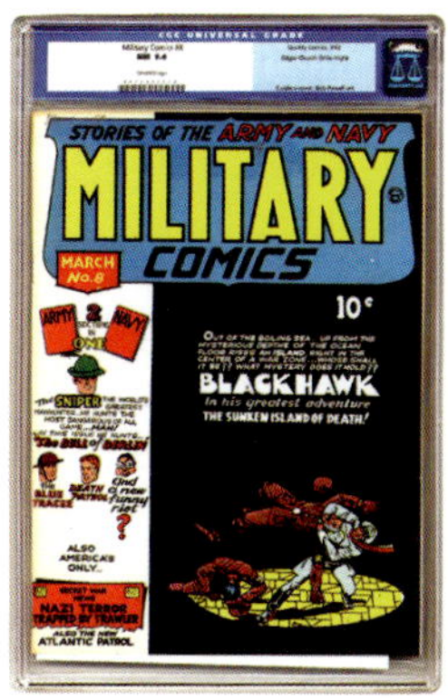

2403 Military Comics #8 Mile High pedigree (Quality, 1942) CGC NM 9.4 Off-white pages. A half-black, half-white cover adds up to a collector's nightmare, so if you want a top-grade copy of this issue, you'd best go after our amazingly preserved Mile High. The lead feature stars the Blackhawks, and it's a tale that sees Blackhawk about to be blown to bits, unless Chop Chop can save his bacon! Chuck Cuidera drew the cover as well as the Blackhawk story; there's also Bob Powell and Dave Berg art in the issue. Overstreet 2005 NM- 9.2 value = $1,475. CGC census 7/05: 1 in 9.4, none higher.

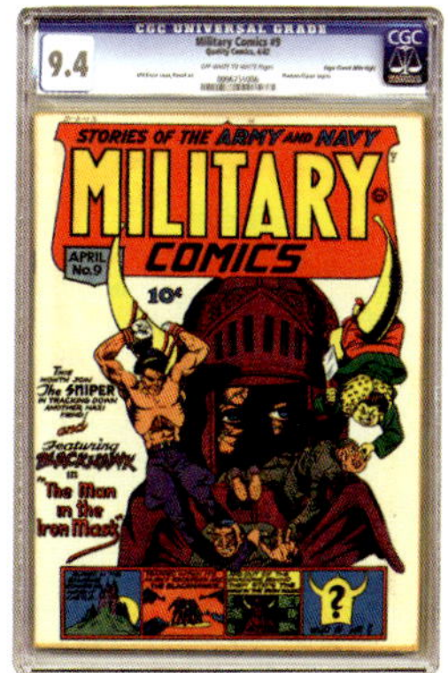

2404 Military Comics #9 Mile High pedigree (Quality, 1942) CGC NM 9.4 Off-white to white pages. This Edgar Church copy of the white-cover issue is the only copy graded above VF by CGC as of this writing. Overstreet credits the issue's cover to Chuck Cuidera. The issue stars Blackhawk; also of note is the first installment of the Phantom Clipper backup feature. Overstreet 2005 NM- 9.2 value = $1,475. CGC census 7/05: 1 in 9.4, none higher.

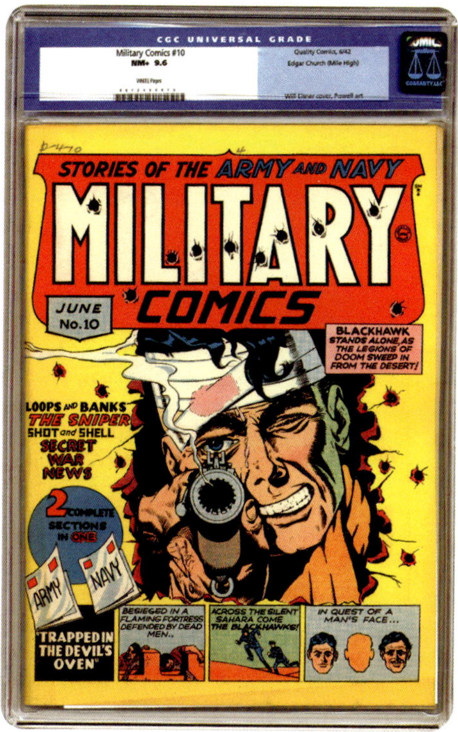

2405 Military Comics #10 Mile High pedigree (Quality, 1942) CGC NM+ 9.6 White pages. "Classic (Will) Eisner cover," says Overstreet, and how can you argue with that after having a look at it? And the image is best enjoyed on a NM+ copy like this Mile High gem. The issue's interior artists include Bob Powell. Overstreet 2005 NM- 9.2 value = $1,600. CGC census 7/05: 1 in 9.6, none higher.

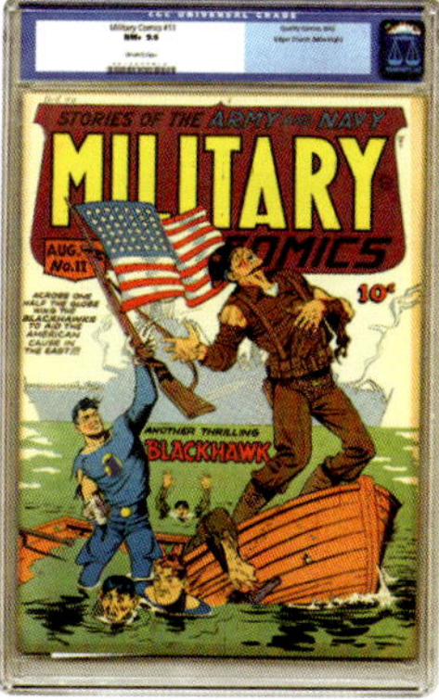

2406 Military Comics #11 Mile High pedigree (Quality, 1942) CGC NM+ 9.6 Off-white pages. Here's a World War II book featuring a great patriotic flag cover. This Edgar Church Mile high copy is by far the nicest of only three unrestored copies currently residing in CGC's census report for this issue. Overstreet 2005 NM-9.2 value = $1,200. CGC census 8/05: 1 in 9.6, none higher.

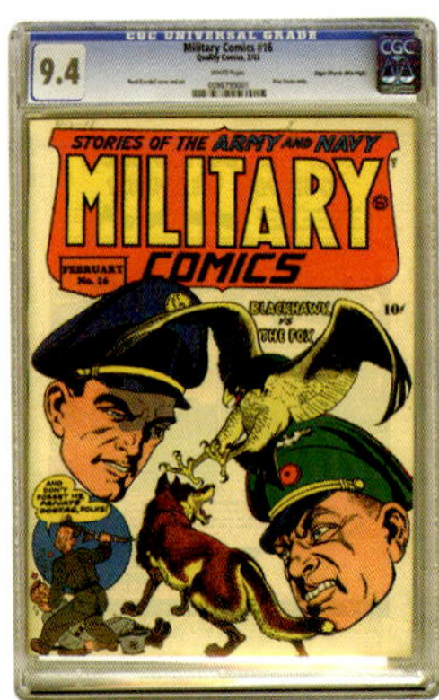

2407 Military Comics #16 Mile High pedigree (Quality, 1943) CGC NM 9.4 White pages. This handsome World War II comic is fronted by a great Reed Crandall cover illustration. The Blue Tracer feature ends with this issue. A comic this old and this fresh-looking could only be one thing — a book from the Mile High collection of Edgar Church. It's the best by far of only three copies of this issue currently graded by CGC. Overstreet 2005 NM- 9.2 value = $975. CGC census 8/05: 1 in 9.4, none higher.

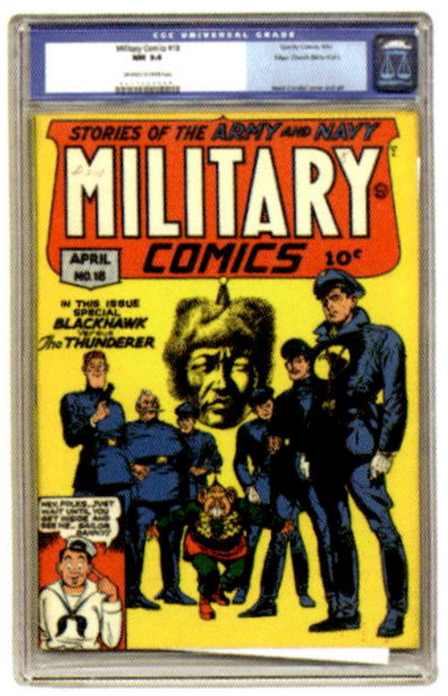

2408 Military Comics #18 Mile High pedigree (Quality, 1943) CGC NM 9.4 Off-white to white pages. In this issue's Blackhawk tale, when Olaf hears about a Tibetan menace named the Thunderer, he decides to go after him alone (well, alone except for Chop Chop)! Reed Crandall drew that story as well as the issue's cover. There are also a few laughs in the issue, courtesy of Sailor Danny and Private Dogtag. Our Mile High offering is the highest-graded copy in CGC's census report as of this writing. Overstreet 2005 NM- 9.2 value = $975. CGC census 7/05: 1 in 9.4, none higher.

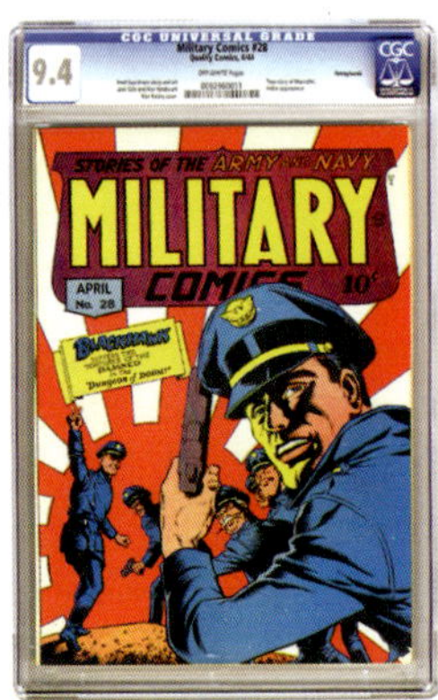

2409 Military Comics #28 Pennsylvania pedigree (Quality, 1944) CGC NM 9.4 Off-white pages. World War II buffs may want to pay close attention to this issue, as it features an appearence by Hitler, plus the "true" story of Italian dictator Mussolini. The cover illo by Alex Kotzky shows the team marching off towards the Japanese "rising sun" flag design, ready to take care of business. Jack Cole and Fred Guardineer art are also featured. This pedigreed copy is a real beauty, sharp and colorful. Overstreet 2005 NM- 9.2 value = $825. CGC census 7/05: 2 in 9.4, none higher.

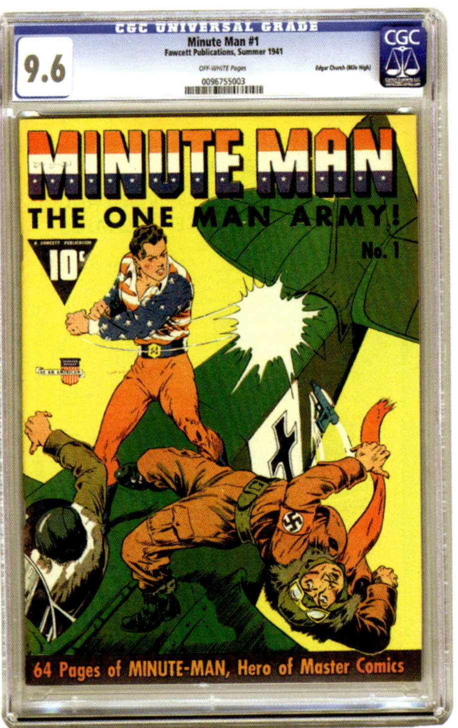

2410 Minute Man #1 Mile High pedigree (Fawcett, 1941) CGC NM+ 9.6 Off-white pages. Minute Man, who first appeared in **Master Comics**, popped up in a host of other Fawcett titles as well, including his own three-issue series. He was a private in the army who battled the enemy as a costumed hero, and if that reminds you of Steve Rogers/Captain America, we thought the same thing, except that Minute Man's first appearance was dated a month before Cap's! This impeccable Mile High copy is the only one to be certified with a grade above VG by CGC to date. Overstreet 2005 NM- 9.2 value = $2,700. CGC census 7/05: 1 in 9.6, none higher.

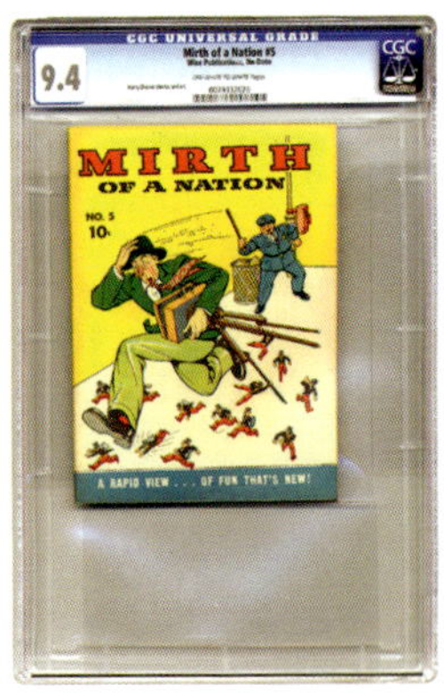

2411 Mirth of a Nation #5 (Wise Publications, circa 1940) CGC NM 9.4 Off-white to white pages. Here's a humor comic that's not in the Overstreet guide, and it's the only copy of the issue to be certified by CGC. The comic's in an unusual format, 5" by 7 1/2", with art credited to Harry "A" Chesler, who would go on to become a well-known editor and publisher. This is one for the comic collector who thought he had everything! Not listed in Overstreet. CGC census 7/05: 1 in 9.4, none higher.

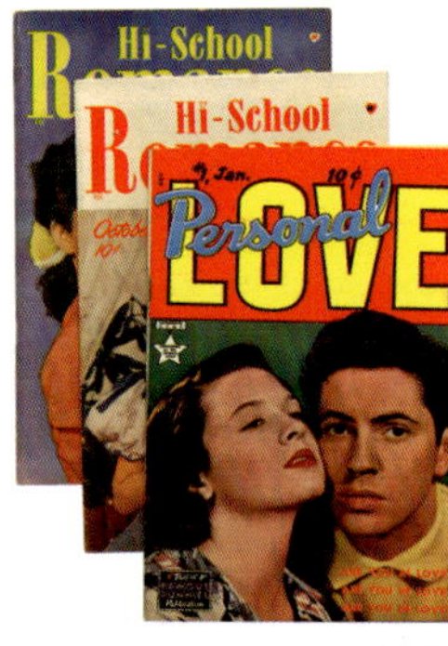

2412 Miscellaneous Golden Age Romance Group (Various Publishers, 1949-56) Condition: Average VG/FN. These love stories are from a mixed bag of publishers including Harvey, Fox, Avon, and Quality. Included here are **Hi-School Romance** #1, 2, 3, 5, 7, 8, 18, 19, and 38; **Realistic Romances** #4; **Personal Love** #1; **My Great Love** #1; **Movie Love** #11, 14, 15, and 17-22 (note that these **Movie Love** issues average FN+ condition); and **Love Secrets** #34, 35, 38, 39, 41, 42, 44-47, 49, 51, 53, and 56. Approximate Overstreet value for group = $700.

2413 Mister Mystery #2 Spokane pedigree (Aragon Magazines, Inc., 1951) CGC NM 9.4 Off-white pages. Overstreet calls a story in this issue "Kurtzmanesque", we would call the cover monster Gigeresque, and you can bet the result will be delightfully grotesque. The art is by Ross Andru and Mike Esposito. Overstreet 2005 NM- 9.2 value = $775. CGC census 9/05: 1 in 9.4, none higher.

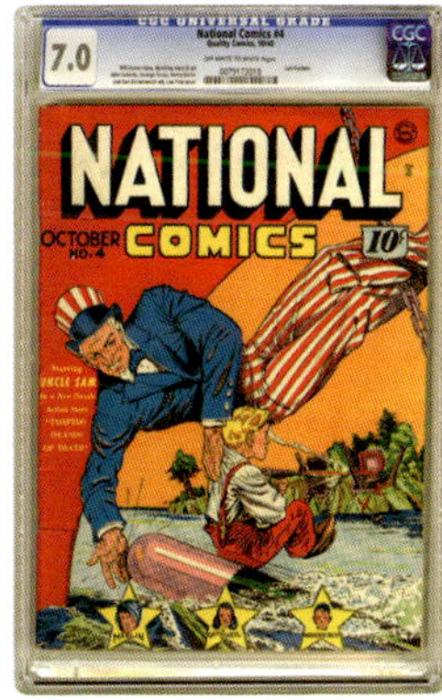

2414 National Comics #4 (Quality, 1940) CGC FN/VF 7.0 Off-white to white pages. The wonderful art of Lou Fine graces this cover, which features Uncle Sam. This issue's also got the last outing for the space pilot of the future known as the Cyclone. Overstreet 2005 FN 6.0 value = $405; VF 8.0 value = $844. CGC census 9/05: 1 in 7.0, 1 higher.

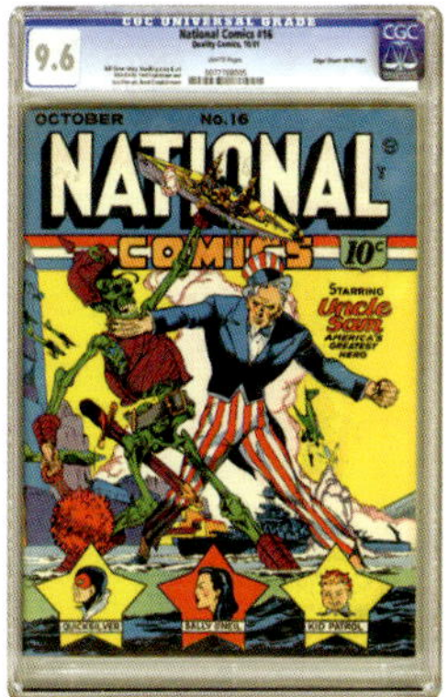

2415 National Comics #16 Mile High pedigree (Quality, 1941) CGC NM+ 9.6 White pages. Choosing Lou Fine's best cover would be a tall order indeed, but this one would have to be a candidate for the short list! Fine also handled the interior art on the Uncle Sam story; Nick Cardy and Fred Guardineer are among the other notables who contributed. Looking for a nice copy of the issue? Well, the second-best copy in CGC's census as of this writing is a 7.5... better go after this one. Overstreet 2005 NM- 9.2 value = $1,125. CGC census 8/05: 1 in 9.6, none higher.

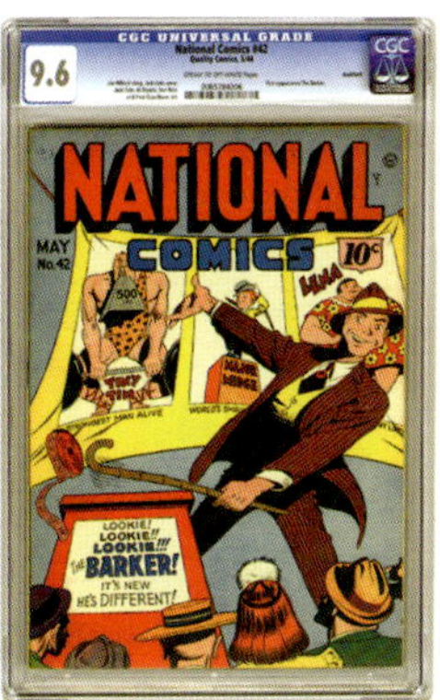

2416 National Comics #42 Rockford pedigree (Quality, 1944) CGC NM+ 9.6 Cream to off-white pages. Our one-stop shopping for top copies of **National Comics** continues with this beauty. While it may seem a bit bizarre that Uncle Sam was replaced as the cover star by the Barker (yes, he really is a carnival barker), it was a great excuse to get Jack Cole art on the cover. Overstreet 2005 NM- 9.2 value = $260. CGC census 9/05: 1 in 9.6, none higher.

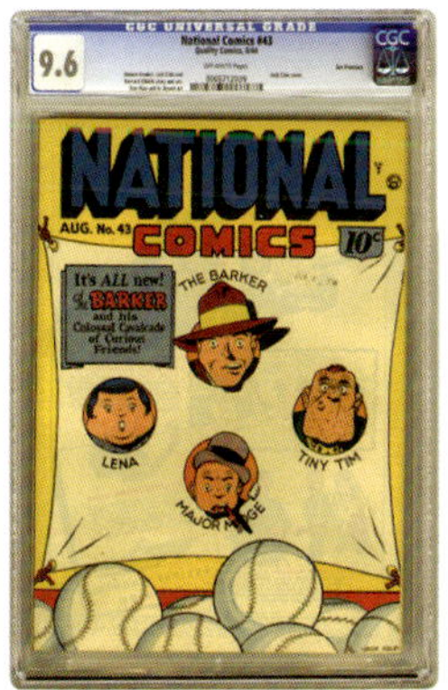

2417 National Comics #43 San Francisco (Quality, 1944) CGC NM+ 9.6 Off-white pages. This pedigree copy gazes down at all the others from atop CGC's census. It's got a Jack Cole cover; interior features include Uncle Sam, Quicksilver, and Chic Carter. Overstreet 2005 NM- 9.2 value = $260. CGC census 9/05: 1 in 9.6, none higher.

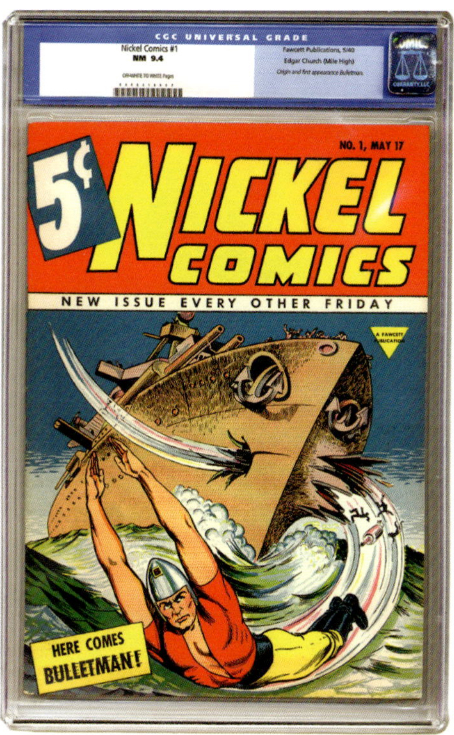

2418 Nickel Comics #1 Mile High pedigree (Fawcett, 1940) CGC NM 9.4 Off-white to white pages. The origin and first appearance of Bulletman puts this among the handful of key Fawcett issues. This series was quite an interesting experiment: half the price of the usual comic, half the content, and appearing twice as often (every two weeks). Alas, the title was short-lived, but Bulletman went on to be the star of **Master Comics** and even had his own title for a while. The cover of this premiere issue is by Jack Binder. Overstreet 2005 NM- 9.2 value = $5,800. CGC census 9/05: 2 in 9.4, 1 higher.

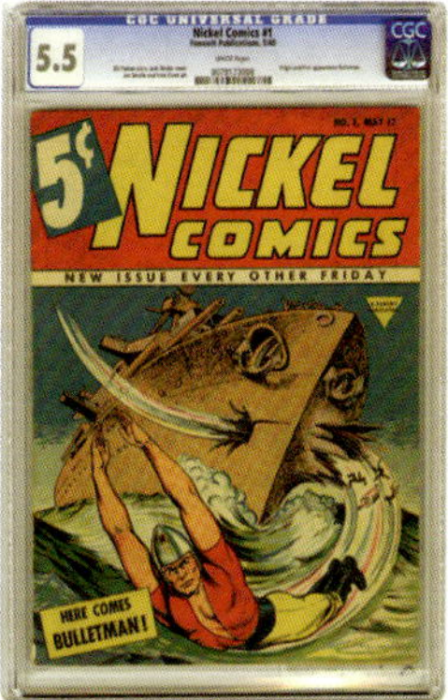

2419 Nickel Comics #1 (Fawcett, 1940) CGC FN- 5.5 White pages. Not only does this issue have the origin and first appearance of Bulletman, it's significant as the premiere of a unique format (a five-cent comic published bi-weekly). Overstreet 2005 FN 6.0 value = $1,200. CGC census 9/05: 1 in 5.5, 7 higher.

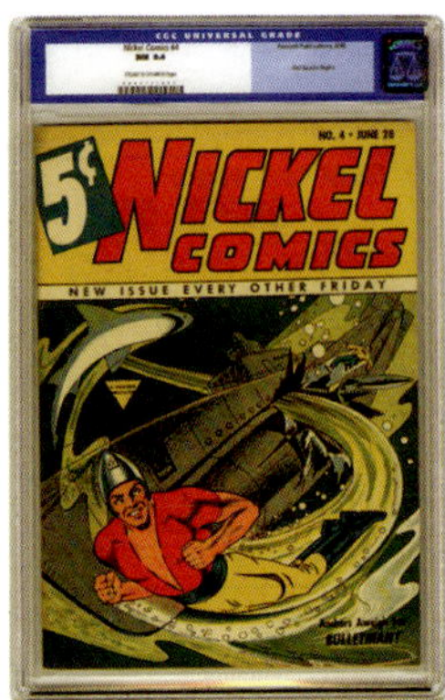

2420 Nickel Comics #4 (Fawcett, 1940) CGC NM 9.4 Cream to off-white pages. This 9.4 copy is tied for the highest grade that CGC has certified to date. Bulletman is the star of the book, which also has the first appearance of a Zorro-esque character called the Red Gaucho. Overstreet 2005 NM- 9.2 value = $1,050. CGC census 9/05: 3 in 9.4, none higher.

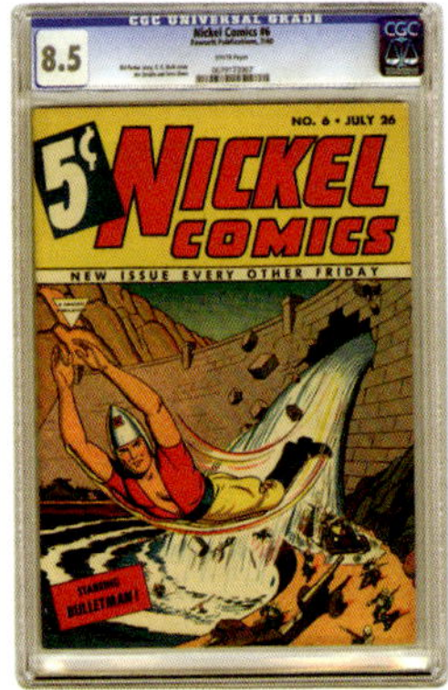

2421 Nickel Comics #6 (Fawcett, 1940) CGC VF+ 8.5 White pages. Fawcett ace C. C. Beck, best known for Captain Marvel, drew this issue's cover. And why exactly is the heroic Bulletman damaging a dam? Five cents would have bought you the answer back in '40 — this nice copy will prove to be quite a bit pricier. Overstreet 2005 VF 8.0 value = $481; VF/NM 9.0 value = $741. CGC census 9/05: 2 in 8.5, 2 higher.

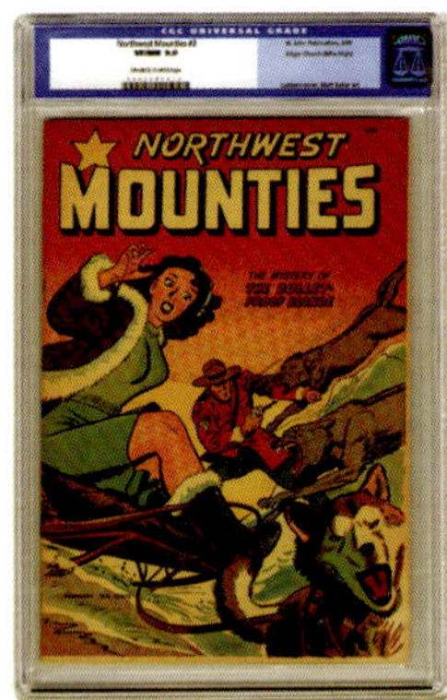

2422 Northwest Mounties #2 Mile High pedigree (St. John, 1949) CGC VF/NM 9.0 Off-white to white pages. This Mile High copy is the best one available, in fact it's the only copy of the issue graded above 8.0 by CGC to date. The book has Matt Baker interior art. Do not adjust your catalog — the cover advertising "The Bulletproof Blonde" does in fact feature a brunette, and she's lovingly rendered by Bob Lubbers. A mountie always gets his man, and you'd best make sure you get this Mile High! Overstreet 2005 VF/NM 9.0 value = $324; NM- 9.2 value = $425. CGC census 5/05: 1 in 9.0, none higher.

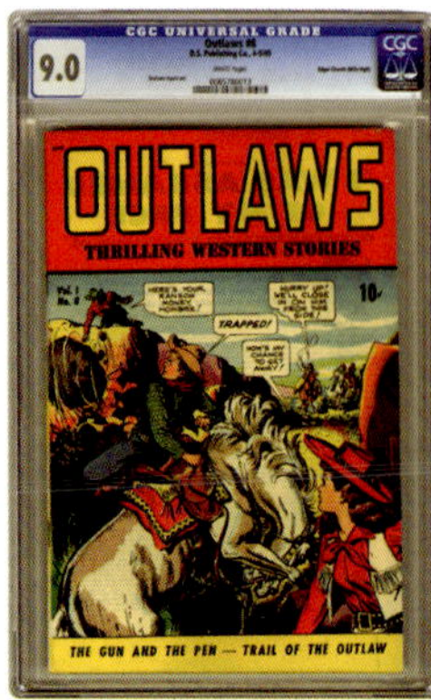

2423 Outlaws #8 Mile High pedigree (D.S. Publishing, 1949) CGC VF/NM 9.0 White pages. We know Graham Ingels as a horror artist, but before he turned "Ghastly" he was active in other genres as well, including creating great artwork for one of the tales of Wild West *banditos* in this book. This is the only copy of this issue that CGC has certified to date. Overstreet 2005 VF/NM 9.0 value = $211; NM- 9.2 value = $275. CGC census 9/05: 1 in 9.0, none higher.

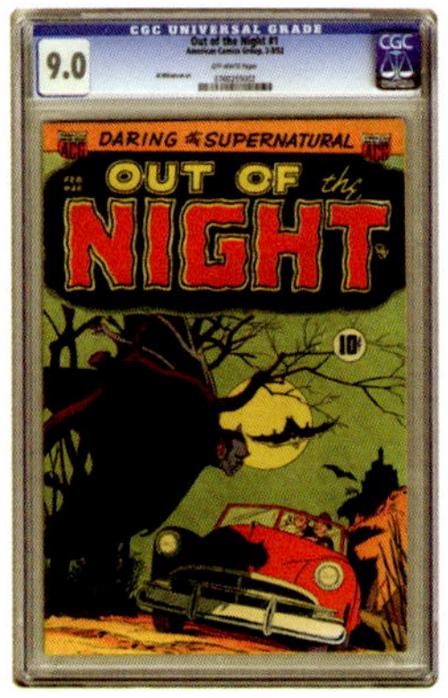

2424 Out of the Night #1 (ACG, 1952) CGC VF/NM 9.0 Off-white pages. Here's the highest-graded copy CGC has certified to date of this pre-Code issue. The great Al Williamson inked Ken LeDoux's pencils on one story. The cover's by Ken Bald. Overstreet 2005 VF/NM 9.0 value = $628; NM- 9.2 value = $850. CGC census 8/05: 1 in 9.0, none higher.

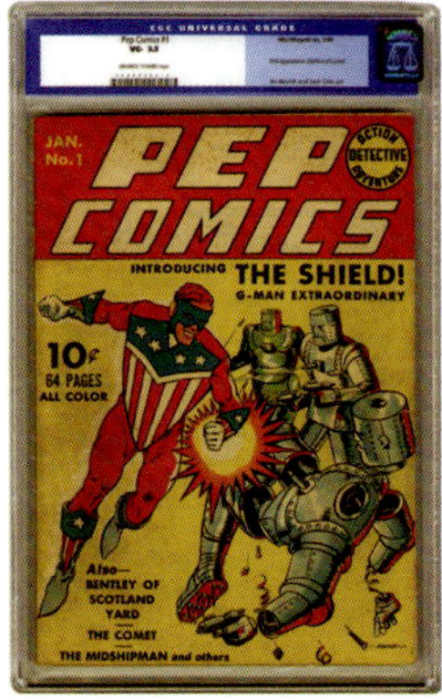

2425 Pep Comics #1 (MLJ, 1940) CGC VG- 3.5 Off-white to white pages. The Shield's first appearance in this issue predated the debuts of Captain America and other star-spangled types, making the Shield the first patriotic-themed superhero. Among many other features in the issue are the origin and first appearance of the Comet (by Plastic Man's creator Jack Cole) and the one and only Press Guardian (called the Falcon in this first appearance only), who did his part to protect the freedoms of the Fourth Estate. Irv Novick drew the robot cover as well as the Shield story inside the comic. Overstreet 2005 VG 4.0 value = $1,936. CGC census 9/05: 1 in 3.5, 6 higher.

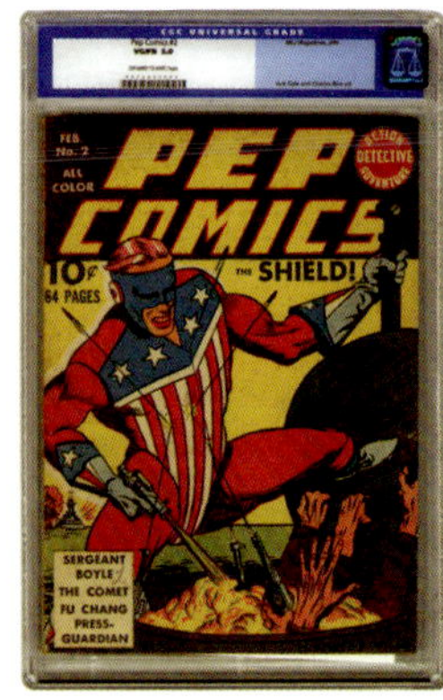

2426 Pep Comics #2 (MLJ, 1940) CGC VG/FN 5.0 Off-white to white pages. Here's the second outing for the Shield, who takes on some foes identified only as "Nordics" (but since the Nordics all speak German, readers got the message). This issue also had the origin of the Rocket, who had first appeared in the previous issue. There are contributions from some well-known artists in Irv Novick (the Shield), Jack Cole (the Comet), Charles Biro (Sergeant Boyle), and Mort Meskin (the Press Guardian). Overstreet 2005 VG 4.0 value = $500; FN 6.0 value = $750. CGC census 9/05: 2 in 5.0, 2 higher.

2427 Pep Comics #4 (MLJ, 1940) CGC VF- 7.5 White pages. Believe it or not, this issue's Shield story features an attack on Pearl Harbor, more than a year before the real-life tragedy! The attackers here are not the Japanese but the "Mosconians" (who all speak with German accents). And it may surprise some to know that comic book crossovers happened even in the Golden Age: the battle with the Mosconians was also being fought by the Wizard in the pages of **Top-Notch Comics**; the Wizard even appears in a few panels of this story to compare notes with the Shield! The Fu Chang backup feature is notable for having an early robot story. Also worth mentioning are artists Irv Novick (who drew the cover), Charles Biro, Jack Cole, and Mort Meskin. Overstreet 2005 VF 8.0 value = $938. CGC census 9/05: 1 in 7.5, none higher.

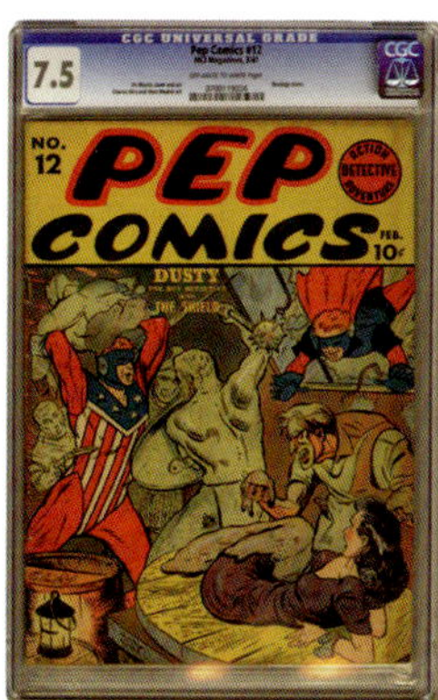

2428 Pep Comics #12 (MLJ, 1941) CGC VF- 7.5 Off-white to white pages. America's first flag-themed superhero, the Shield, has his work cut out for him on this bondage cover by Irv Novick — look at the creepy sculptor and what he's doing to the distressed damsel! At least the Shield's got some help from his sidekick Dusty the Boy Detective. In addition to the Shield story in this issue (also drawn by Novick), there's the work of Charles Biro and Mort Meskin, plus the origin and first appearance of Fireball, who was MLJ's answer to the Human Torch. Overstreet 2005 VF 8.0 value = $863. CGC census 8/05: 1 in 7.5, none higher.

2429 No lot.

2430 No lot.

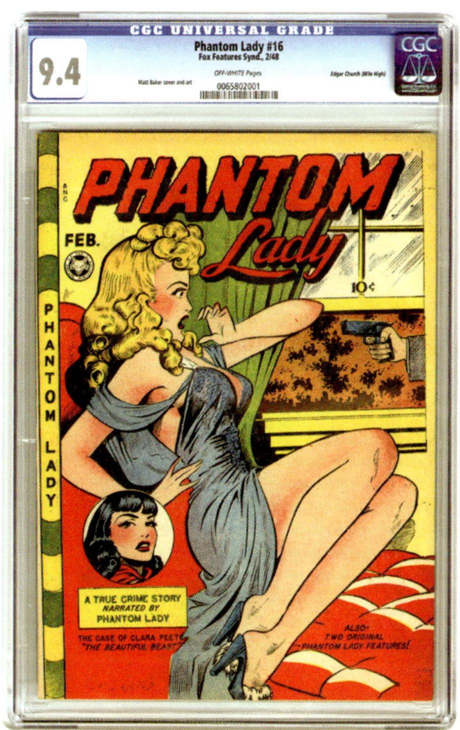

2431 Phantom Lady #16 Mile High pedigree (Fox Features Syndicate, 1948) CGC NM 9.4 Off-white pages. Matt Baker turned on the "headlights" for a truly memorable cover. And we'd be negligent if we didn't mention that negligee. A sexy classic! Even the title character, though relegated to an inset, adds a sultry gaze of her own. Inside the comic, true crime tales and, yes, even some negligee panels await. It's a must for Baker fans... and who isn't one? And if all of that isn't enough for you, it's the Mile High copy, for goodness' sake. Overstreet 2005 NM- 9.2 value = $3,300. CGC census 9/05: 2 in 9.4, none higher.

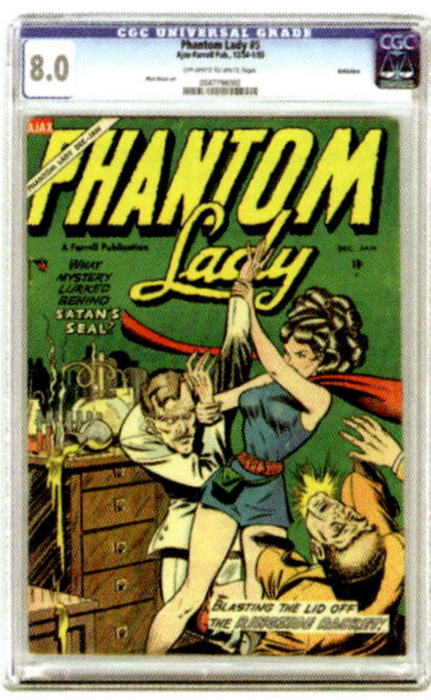

2432 Phantom Lady (second series) #5 (#1) Bethlehem pedigree (Ajax/Farrell, 1955) CGC VF 8.0 Off-white to white pages. Robert Farrell, a former editor for Holyoke, purchased the rights to some Fox characters after the latter publisher's demise, and one of them was Phantom Lady. This first issue of Ajax/Farrell's revival of the series even has art by the character's signature artist, Matt Baker. Overstreet 2005 VF 8.0 value = $719. CGC census 9/05: 2 in 8.0, none higher.

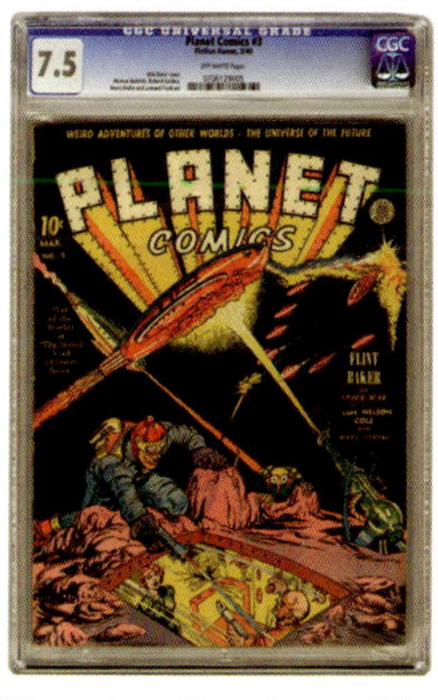

2433 Planet Comics #3 (Fiction House, 1940) CGC VF- 7.5 Off-white pages. A fantastic Will Eisner cover leads off this wonderful issue. An early issue of Fiction House's flagship science fiction comic series, and a companion to the pulp title of the same name, this series is a favorite among Golden Age comic fans. Flint Baker is the main star here, but it wouldn't be too long before others such as Gale Allen, the Star Pirate, and Mars God of War would join him. Overstreet 2005 VF 8.0 value = $1,908. CGC census 9/05: 2 in 7.5, 2 higher.

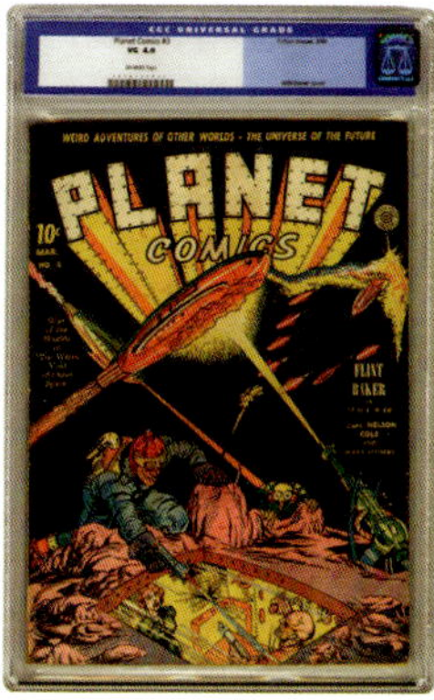

2434 Planet Comics #3 (Fiction House, 1940) CGC VG 4.0 Off-white pages. This issue's cover is by the late Will Eisner, who showed here that he could do science fiction just as well as the other genres he mastered! Overstreet 2005 VG 4.0 value = $600. CGC census 9/05: 2 in 4.0, 9 higher.

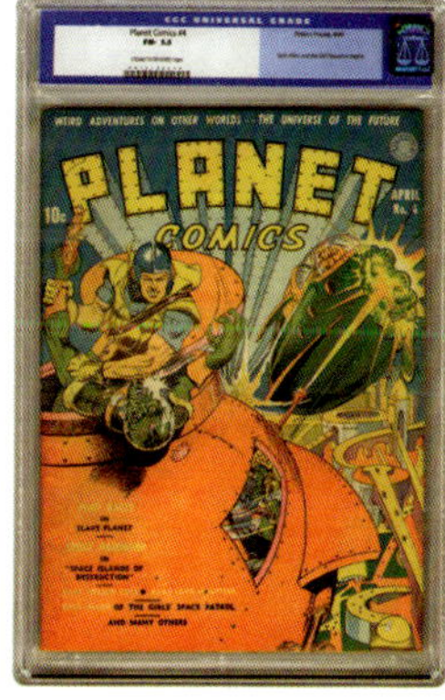

2435 Planet Comics #4 (Fiction House, 1940) CGC FN- 5.5 Cream to off-white pages. Gerber credits this issue's cover to Charles Sultan, and we credit Sultan with a creative idea — why zap an alien with a ray gun when you can just punch him out? Inside the comic is the first appearance of Gale Allen and the Girl Squadron; those ladies would be featured on many a cover of this title in years to come. Overstreet 2005 FN 6.0 value = $831. CGC census 9/05: 1 in 5.5, 4 higher.

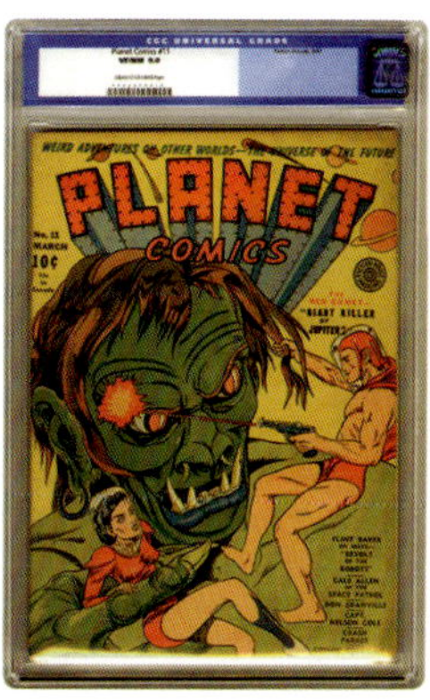

2436 Planet Comics #11 (Fiction House, 1941) CGC VF/NM 9.0 Cream to off-white pages. Gerber credits this issue's cover to Dan Zolnerowich. Our offering is bested by only one copy in CGC's current census, and it's also one of only two to be certified above 6.5 as of this writing. Overstreet 2005 VF/NM 9.0 value = $2,000; NM- 9.2 value = $2,700. CGC census 5/05: 1 in 9.0, 1 higher.

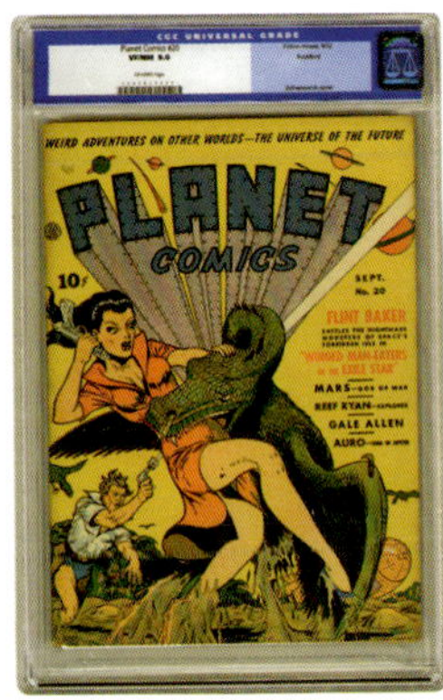

2437 Planet Comics #20 (Fiction House, 1942) CGC VF/NM 9.0 Off-white pages. Attributing Fiction House covers can be a tricky business, but this one actually bears the signature of Dan Zolnerowich. He delivered the combination of outer space, ray guns, and leggy ladies (in high heels on a swampy planet, no less) that Fiction House was famous for. Overstreet 2005 VF/NM 9.0 value = $1,316; NM- 9.2 value = $1,775. CGC census 9/05: 1 in 9.0, 1 higher.

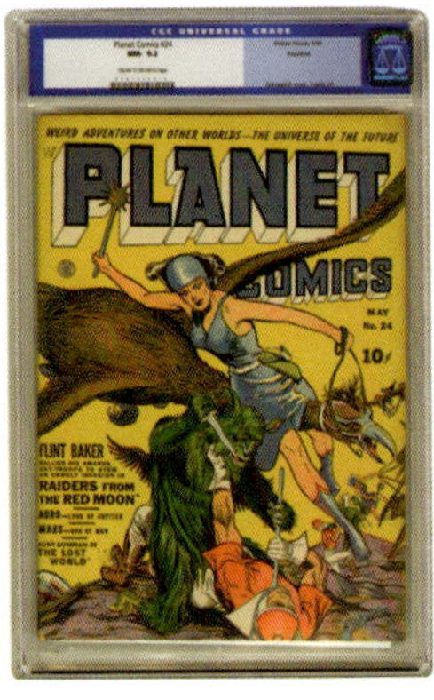

2438 Planet Comics #24 Rockford pedigree (Fiction House, 1943) CGC NM- 9.2 Cream to off-white pages. Flint Baker's Amazon Sky-Troops are not only fetching, they're quite adept at pummeling bad alien sorts. Dan Zolnerowich's masterful cover stands out on this pedigree copy. CGC has certified just one other with a higher grade for this issue - not surprising considering the book's a Gerber "7". Interior story art is provided by the likes of Graham Ingels, George Tuska, Lee Elias, and Joe Doolin - great early Golden Age fare. Overstreet 2005 NM- 9.2 value = $1,700. CGC census 9/05: 1 in 9.2, 1 higher.

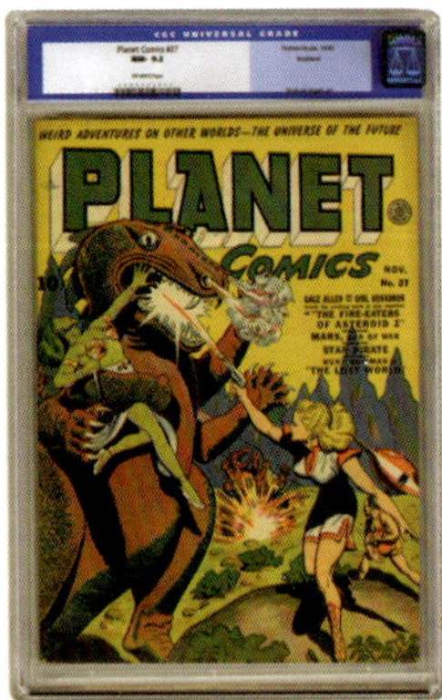

2439 Planet Comics #27 Rockford pedigree (Fiction House, 1943) CGC NM- 9.2 Off-white pages. Pedigree copy comes with a certificate from The Rockford Collection, and is CGC's second highest-graded copy to date. Joe Doolin's cover spotlights Gale Allen and the Girl Squadron. Interior artists include Doolin, Graham Ingels, and Lee Elias. Overstreet 2005 NM- 9.2 value = $1,350. CGC census 9/05: 1 in 9.2, 1 higher.

2440 Police Comics #42 (Quality, 1945) CGC FN/VF 7.0 Off-white to white pages. Jack Cole's Plastic Man and his pal Woozy headline this title. The Spirit, by Will Eisner and Lou Fine, is also featured. This attractive copy features a white cover. Overstreet 2005 FN 6.0 value = $159; VF 8.0 value = $323. CGC census 8/05: 1 in 7.0, 1 higher.

2441 Police Comics #45 (Quality, 1945) CGC FN 6.0 Off-white to white pages. Plastic Man, by Jack Cole, stretches the limits of imagination in this issue. A Lou Fine-illustrated episode of the Spirit is also included. Overstreet 2005 FN 6.0 value = $120. CGC census 8/05: 1 in 6.0, 2 higher.

2442 Police Comics #46 (Quality, 1945) CGC FN 6.0 Cream to off-white pages. Woozy has Plastic Man tied up in knots on the Jack Cole-illustrated cover to this issue. A Lou Fine Spirit story is also included. Overstreet 2005 FN 6.0 value = $120. CGC census 8/05: 1 in 6.0, 2 higher.

2443 Police Comics #47 (Quality, 1945) CGC VF- 7.5 Off-white pages. Jack Cole Plastic Man cover. Cole and Paul Gustavson art. Overstreet 2005 VF 8.0 value = $244. CGC census 8/05: 1 in 7.5, 2 higher.

2444 Police Comics #53 (Quality, 1946) CGC FN 6.0 Off-white pages. Plastic Man by Jack Cole. Overstreet 2005 FN 6.0 value = $108. CGC census 8/05: 1 in 6.0, 1 higher.

2445 Police Comics #58 (Quality, 1946) CGC VF- 7.5 Cream to off-white pages. Jack Cole's Plastic Man faces off against the Green Terror. This issue features the last appearance of the Human Bomb. Overstreet 2005 VF 8.0 value = $204. CGC census 8/05: 1 in 7.5, 1 higher.

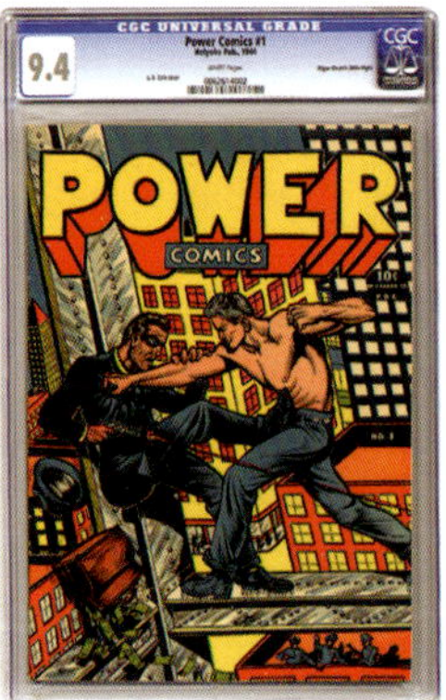

2446 Power Comics #1 Mile High pedigree (Holyoke Publications, 1944) CGC NM 9.4 White pages. This Edgar Church copy is the only one graded above 8.5 by CGC to date! Spectacular L. B. Cole covers are the reason for this series' popularity, and this one might be one of his best. Overstreet 2005 NM- 9.2 value = $1,925. CGC census 8/05: 1 in 9.4, none higher.

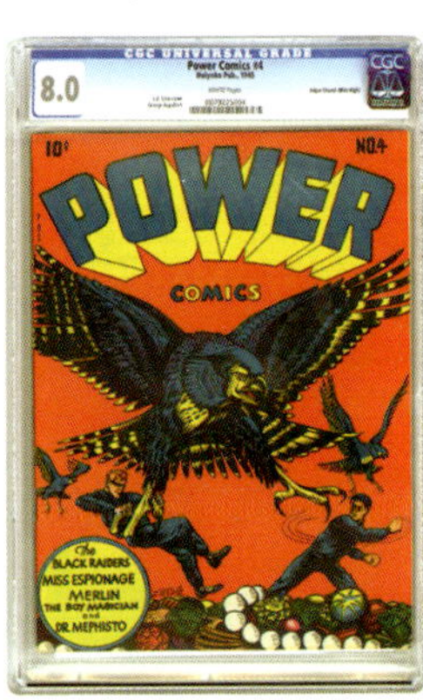

2447 Power Comics #4 Mile High pedigree (Holyoke Publications, 1945) CGC VF 8.0 White pages. The Black Raiders, Miss Espionage, Merlin the Boy Magician, and Dr. Mephisto make for an eclectic mix, but the real draw here is a sensational cover by L. B. Cole. Overstreet 2005 VF 8.0 value = $925. CGC census 9/05: 2 in 8.0, none higher.

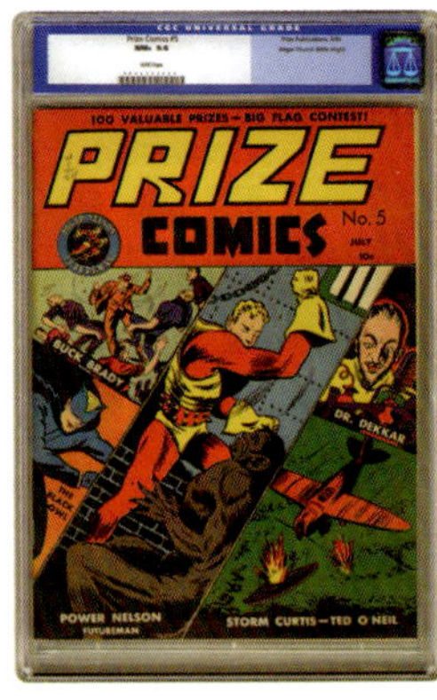

2448 Prize Comics #5 Mile High pedigree (Prize, 1940) CGC NM+ 9.6 White pages. This Mile High copy is the only copy graded above 7.5 by CGC to date. The roster of characters is led by the Flash Gordon-esque Power Nelson. Overstreet 2005 NM- 9.2 value = $1,125. CGC census 6/05: 1 in 9.6, none higher.

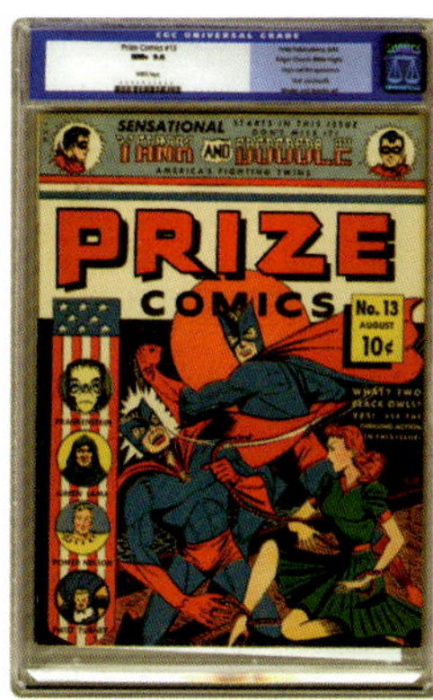

2449 Prize Comics #13 Mile High pedigree (Prize, 1941) CGC NM+ 9.6 White pages. This great Mile High offering is one of only two copies of the issue that CGC has certified as of this writing (we don't need to tell you it's the highest-graded copy, do we?). It features the origin and first appearance of kid superhero duo Yank and Doodle, who would be along for the remainder of the series' run. Also featured are an early appearance of Dick Briefer's Frankenstein as well as a Black Owl adventure with Jack Binder art. Overstreet 2005 NM- 9.2 value = $975. CGC census 6/05: 1 in 9.6, none higher.

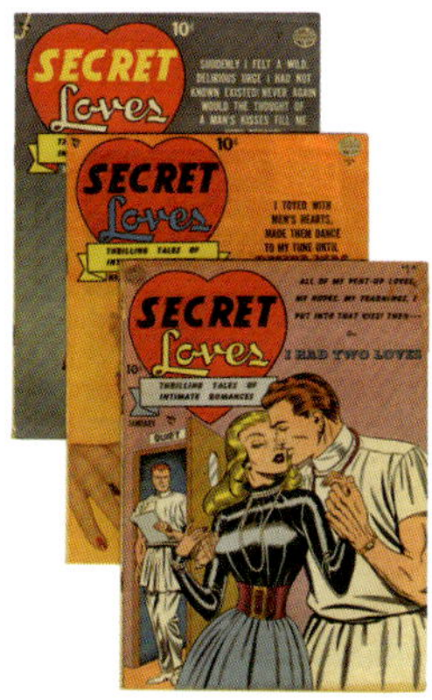

2450 Quality Comics Romance Group (Quality, 1949-50) Condition: Average VG/FN. Most of these issues have photo covers, and almost all of the line-drawn ones are by "good-girl" ace Bill Ward! Included here are **Secret Loves** #1-6; **Hollywood Diary** #1, 2, and 4; **Hollywood Secrets** #2-6 (#6 has extensive amateur tape repairs on the inside front cover); **Range Romances** #1 (Canadian edition published by Bell Features; has a paper cover but has the same cover and content as the Quality edition), 3, and 4; **Broadway Romances** #2 and 3; and **Untamed Love** #2, 3, 4, and 5. Approximate Overstreet value for group = $950.

2451 Red Seal Comics #17 Mile High pedigree (Chesler, 1946) CGC NM 9.4 Off-white to white pages. This mag from the Harry "A" Chesler publishing house features the likes of Lady Satan and Yankee Girl. The ageless George Tuska contributed art to the issue. Overstreet 2005 NM- 9.2 value = $600. CGC census 7/05: 1 in 9.4, none higher.

2452 Roy Rogers Comics #12 Mile High Comics (Dell, 1948) CGC VF 8.0 White pages. Photo cover. Overstreet 2005 VF 8.0 value = $102. CGC census 7/05: 1 in 8.0, none higher.

2453 Roy Rogers Comics #17 (Dell, 1949) CGC VF/NM 9.0 White pages. Photo cover. Overstreet 2005 VF/NM 9.0 value = $156; NM- 9.2 value = $210. CGC census 7/05: 1 in 9.0, 1 higher.

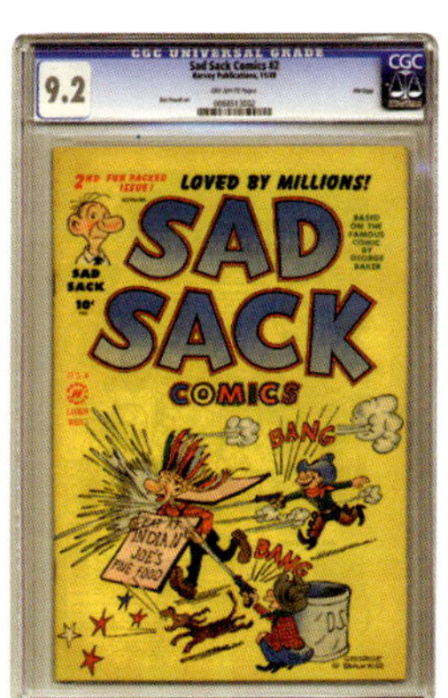

2454 Sad Sack Comics #2 File Copy (Harvey, 1949) CGC NM- 9.2 Off-white pages. This second issue, like all of the early ones, had Sad Sack trying to make a go of it in civilian life — he didn't return to the military until #22. Overstreet notes, "relatively few of the first 21 issues were ever collected and (they) remain scarce due to this." A backup feature in the issue has Bob Powell art. Overstreet 2005 NM- 9.2 value = $360. CGC census 7/05: 2 in 9.2, 2 higher.

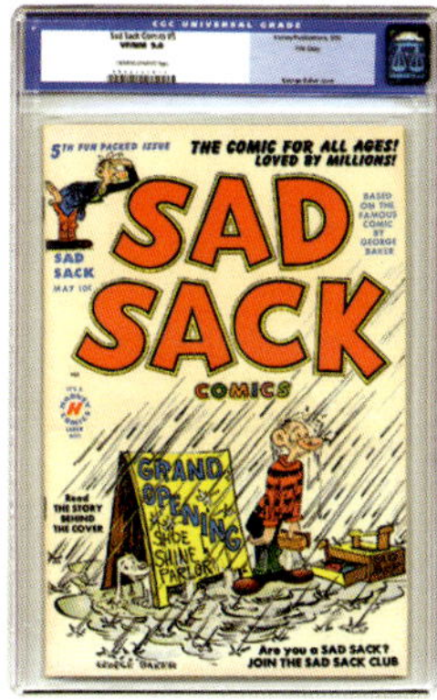

2455 Sad Sack Comics #5 File Copy (Harvey, 1950) CGC VF/NM 9.0 Cream to off-white pages. Sad Sack looks even sadder than usual on this George Baker cover! The issue's from the "Sad Sack goes civilian" era. Only one copy of the ish has been graded higher by CGC to date. Overstreet 2005 VF/NM 9.0 value = $114; NM- 9.2 value = $150. CGC census 7/05: 3 in 9.0, 1 higher.

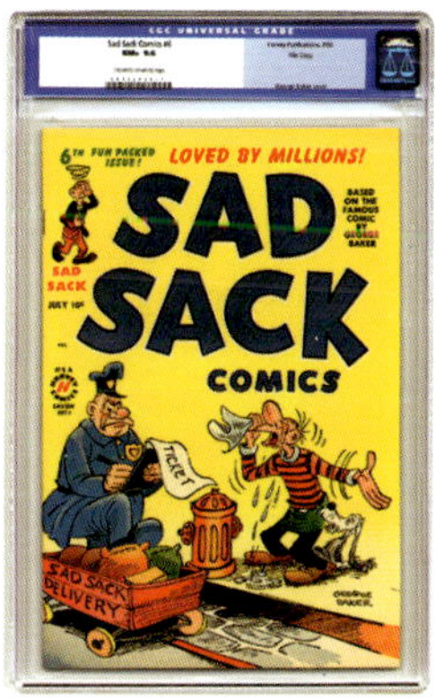

2456 Sad Sack Comics #6 File Copy (Harvey, 1950) CGC NM+ 9.6 Cream to off-white pages. Harveys in this grade are almost impossible to find "in the wild," luckily we've got a File Copy that never hit the spinner racks. The cover's by George Baker. Overstreet 2005 NM- 9.2 value = $150. CGC census 7/05: 4 in 9.6, 1 higher.

2457 Sad Sack Comics #9 File Copy (Harvey, 1951) CGC NM- 9.2 Cream to off-white pages. George Baker cover and art. Overstreet 2005 NM- 9.2 value = $150. CGC census 7/05: 2 in 9.2, none higher.

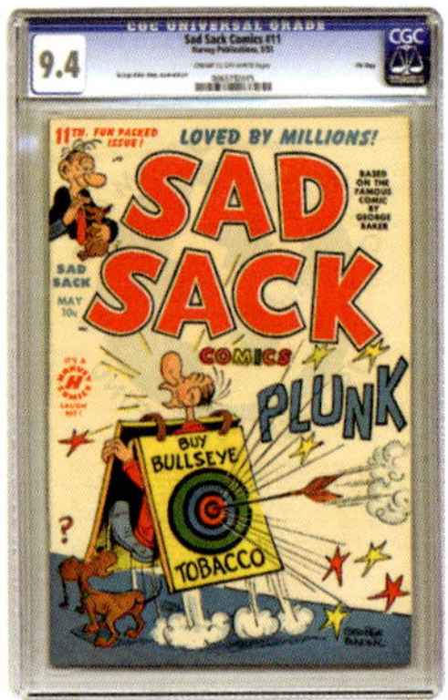

2458 Sad Sack Comics #11 File Copy (Harvey, 1951) CGC NM 9.4 Cream to off-white pages. A Harvey in high grade is always an eyebrow-raiser, all the more so in the case of this white-cover issue. The cover and interior art are by George Baker. Overstreet 2005 NM- 9.2 value = $100. CGC census 7/05: 1 in 9.4, none higher.

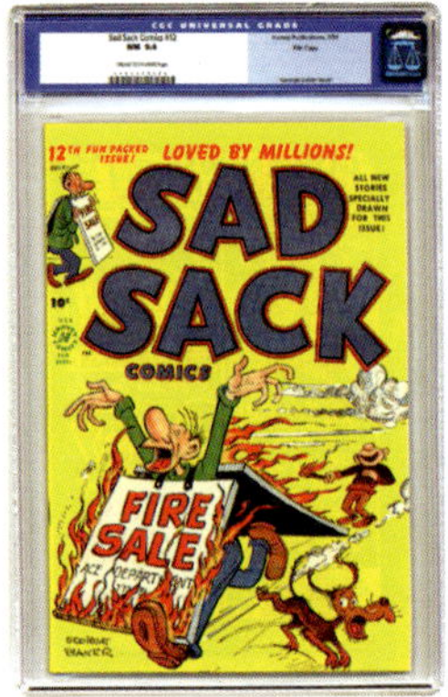

2459 Sad Sack Comics #12 File Copy (Harvey, 1951) CGC NM 9.4 Cream to off-white pages. Sad Sack can't get a break, but at least let us brighten up *your* day with this high-grade file copy. The cover is by George Baker. Overstreet 2005 NM- 9.2 value = $100. CGC census 7/05: 3 in 9.4, 1 higher.

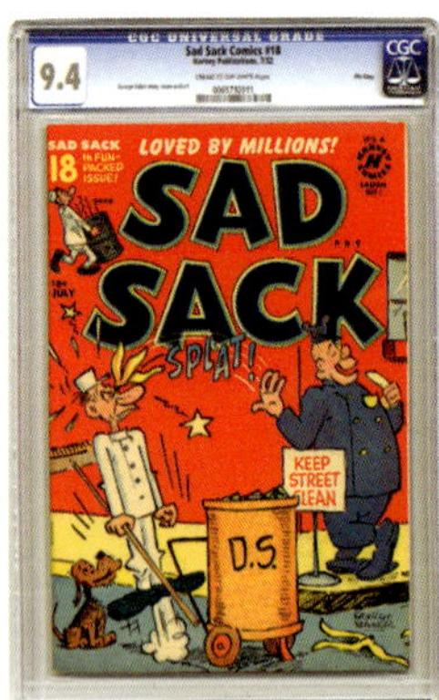

2460 Sad Sack Comics #18 File Copy (Harvey, 1952) CGC NM 9.4 Cream to off-white pages. This George Baker selection hails from the era when Sad Sack was giving civilian life a try. Our offering is the only copy of the issue that CGC has certified as of this writing. Overstreet 2005 NM- 9.2 value = $100. CGC census 7/05: 1 in 9.4, none higher.

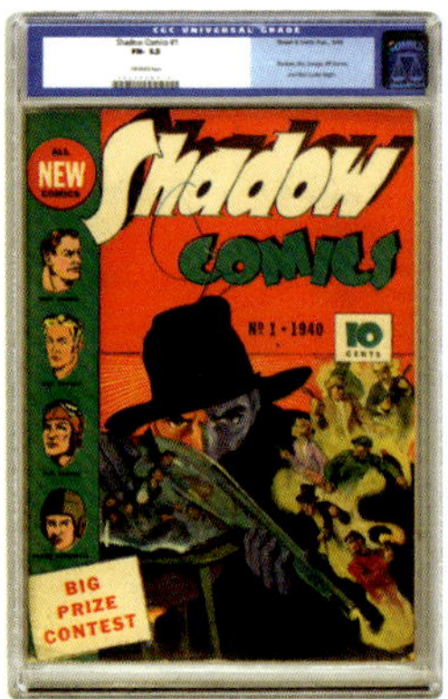

2461 Shadow Comics #1 (Street & Smith, 1940) CGC FN- 5.5 Off-white pages. The first comic book appearances of the Shadow and Doc Savage make this issue a milestone. On top of that, it's the very first comic book produced by publisher Street and Smith. In all, some of the most popular fictional characters of the first half of the 20th century fill this comic, with the aforementioned duo joined by Nick Carter, aviator Bill Barnes, and student-athlete Frank Merriwell, making for an unbeatable lineup. Overstreet 2005 FN 6.0 value = $1,356. CGC census 5/05: 1 in 5.5, 4 higher.

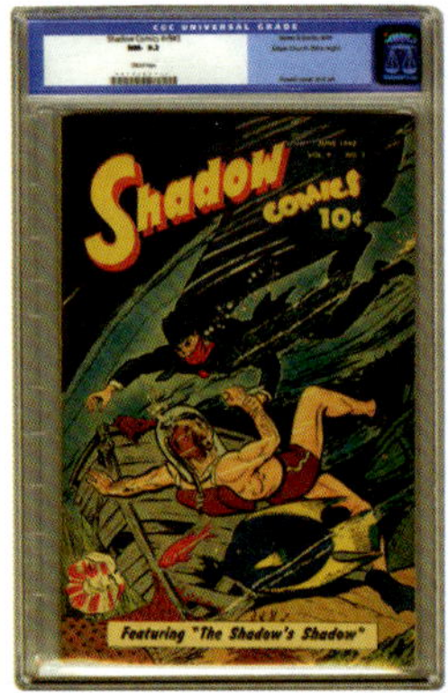

2462 Shadow Comics V9#3 Mile High pedigree (Street & Smith, 1949) CGC NM- 9.2 Cream pages. Bob Powell drew this issue's cover and contributed interior art as well. The Shadow isn't the only big name in these pages; there's also a Doc Savage backup feature. Overstreet 2005 NM- 9.2 value = $550. CGC census 5/05: 1 in 9.2, 1 higher.

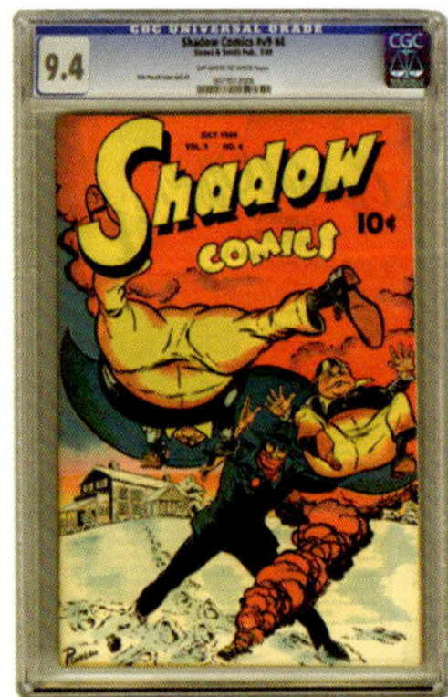

2463 Shadow Comics V9#4 (Street & Smith, 1949) CGC NM 9.4 Off-white to white pages. Walter Gibson meets... Lewis Carroll? Believe it, as the Shadow takes on Tweedledum and Tweedledee on this cover by Bob Powell. This issue, the title's second-to-last, also has a Doc Savage backup feature. Ours is the only copy that has been graded above 8.5 by CGC as of this writing. Overstreet 2005 NM- 9.2 value = $575. CGC census 5/05: 1 in 9.4, none higher.

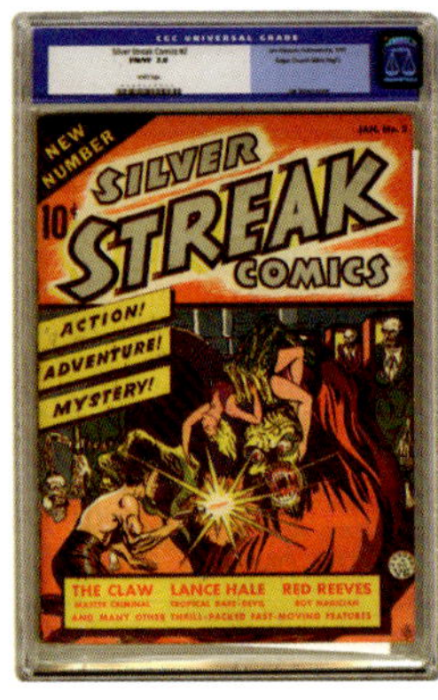

2464 Silver Streak Comics #2 Mile High pedigree (Lev Gleason, 1940) CGC FN/VF 7.0 White pages. The Claw was one of the most fearsome villains of the Golden Age, and in this comic he was drawn by two of the best artists of that era, Joe Simon (cover) and Jack Cole (interior story). If you're wondering where the title got its name, have a look at the metallic ink on the cover, a gimmick that looks neat even today! Overstreet 2005 FN 6.0 value = $1,158; VF 8.0 value = $2,509. CGC census 5/05: 1 in 7.0, 1 higher.

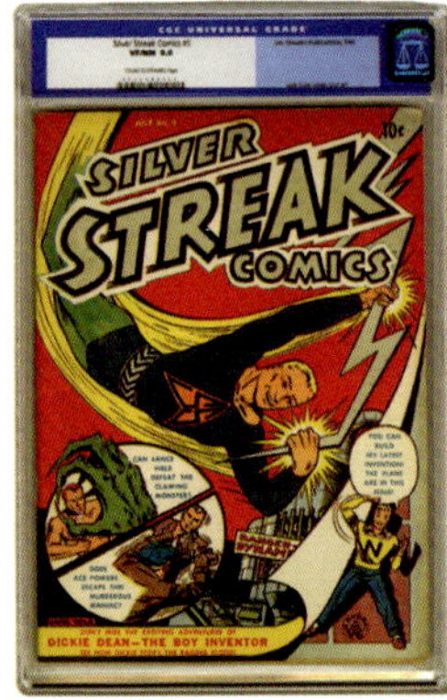

2465 Silver Streak Comics #5 (Lev Gleason, 1940) CGC VF/NM 9.0 Cream to off-white pages. Jack Cole, best known as the creator of Plastic Man, drew this issue's cover as well as two stories inside the comic. This is the last book in this title to feature the snazzy metallic ink on the cover. Overstreet 2005 VF/NM 9.0 value = $1,925; NM- 9.2 value = $2,600. CGC census 5/05: 3 in 9.0, none higher.

2466 Slick Chick Comics #1 (Leader Enterprises, 1947) CGC FN/VF 7.0 Off-white pages. Uncommon teen age humor comic with an emphasis on "good girl" art. This is currently the only copy certified by CGC. Overstreet 2005 FN 6.0 value = $36; VF 8.0 value = $71. CGC census 8/05: 1 in 7.0, none higher.

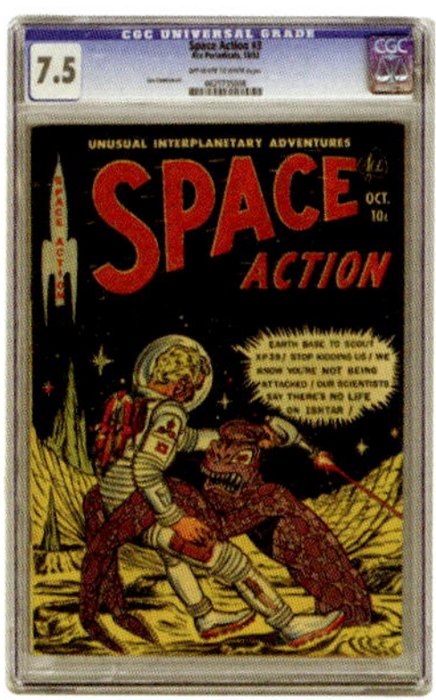

2467 Space Action #3 (Ace, 1952) CGC VF- 7.5 Off-white to white pages. The third and final issue of this short-lived series has a black outer space background, making it difficult to find in higher grades. Great artwork by Lou Cameron. Overstreet 2005 VF 8.0 value = $336. CGC census 9/05: 2 in 7.5, 4 higher.

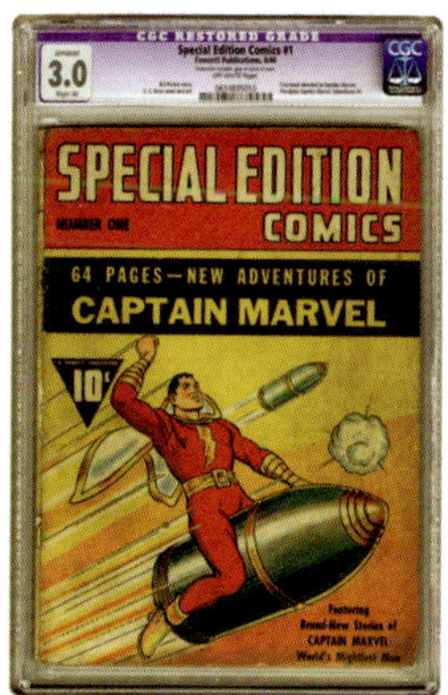

2468 Special Edition Comics #1 (Fawcett, 1940) CGC GD/VG 3.0 Slight (A) Off-white pages. Here's the first comic book entirely devoted to Captain Marvel! When this was published, Captain Marvel had starred in just a handful of issues of **Whiz Comics**; this one-shot appeared at the same time as **Whiz** #8. The cover art has been credited to C. C. Beck, and the clean, appealing style of Beck also graces the interior of this 64-page issue. CGC notes, "Restoration includes: glue on spine of cover." Overstreet 2005 GD 2.0 value = $839; VG 4.0 value = $1,678.

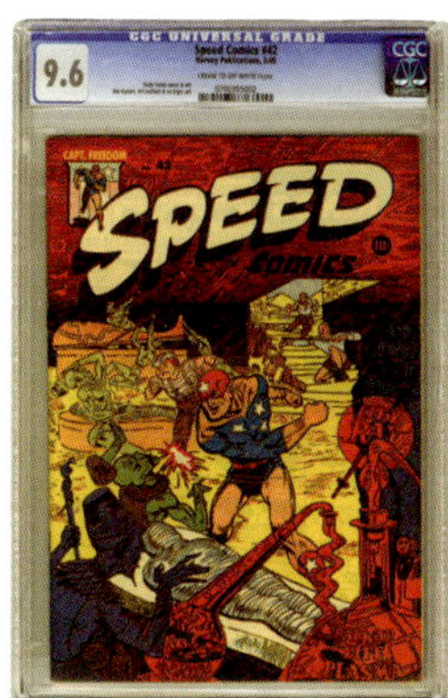

2469 Speed Comics #42 (Harvey, 1946) CGC NM+ 9.6 Cream to off-white pages. A great Captain Freedom cover by Rudy Palais gets this issue off to a flying start. Palais, Joe Kubert, Art Helfant, and Jill Elgin all contribute story art. Overstreet 2005 NM- 9.2 value = $550. CGC census 9/05: 1 in 9.6, none higher.

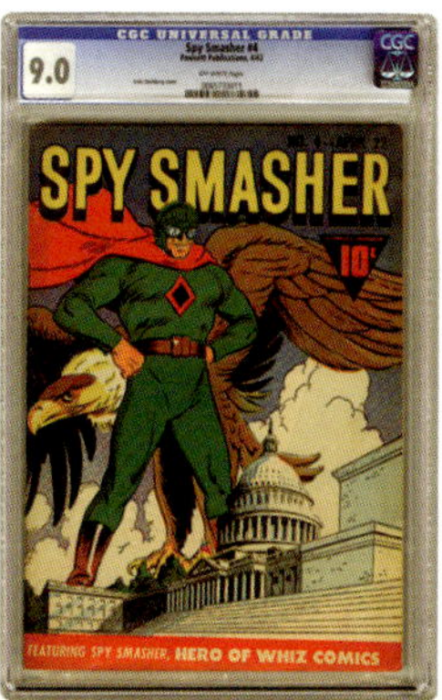

2470 Spy Smasher #4 (Fawcett, 1942) CGC VF/NM 9.0 Off-white pages. The Spy Smasher (alias wealthy playboy Alan Armstrong) is the scourge of Fifth Columnists everywhere! This issue's cover illustration has been credited to Irvin Steinberg. This is the highest-graded copy that CGC has certified to date. Overstreet 2005 VF/NM 9.0 value = $1,110; NM-9.2 value = $1,500. CGC census 6/05: 1 in 9.0, none higher.

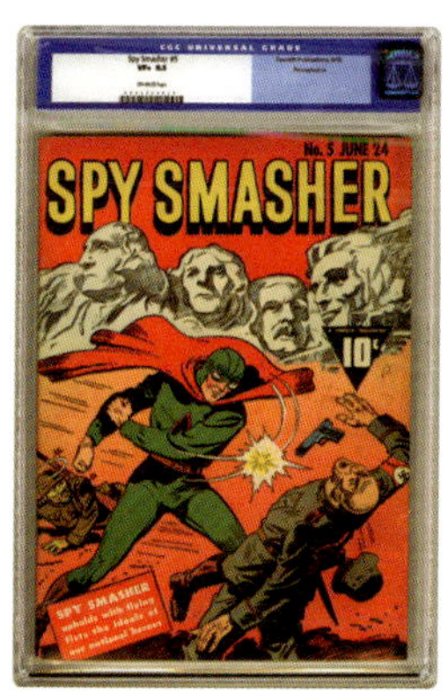

2471 Spy Smasher #5 Pennsylvania pedigree (Fawcett, 1942) CGC VF+ 8.5 Off-white pages. Less than a year after Mount Rushmore was completed, it found its way onto this cover as a stirring backdrop for Spy Smasher's punch-up with one Japanese and one German foe. Overstreet credits Mac Raboy with interior art for the issue. Overstreet 2005 VF 8.0 value = $625; VF/NM 9.0 value = $963. CGC census 6/05: 2 in 8.5, none higher.

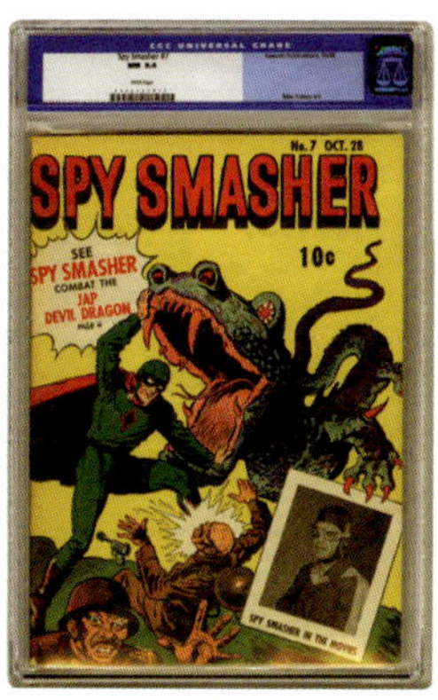

2472 Spy Smasher #7 (Fawcett, 1942) CGC NM 9.4 White pages. Spy Smasher's popularity was such that he was only the second comic book character (Captain Marvel being the first) to be adapted into a live-action movie. This partial photo cover shows actor Kane Richmond, the star of the Republic serial. The issue has Mac Raboy interior art. Overstreet 2005 NM-9.2 value = $1,300. CGC census 6/05: 1 in 9.4, none higher.

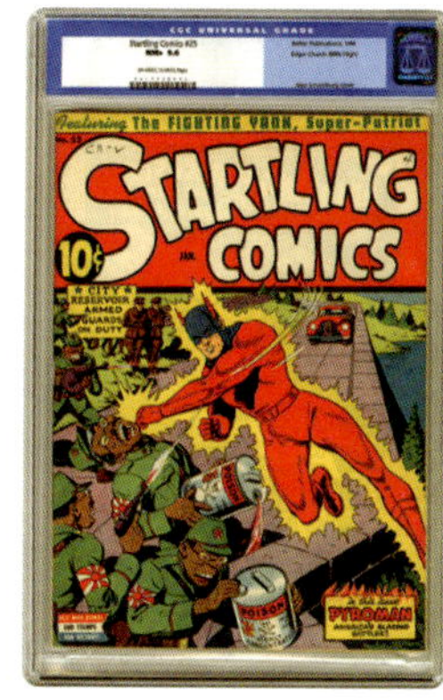

2473 Startling Comics #25 Mile High pedigree (Better Publications, 1944) CGC NM+ 9.6 Off-white to white pages. Pyroman stops the enemy from sabotaging the city's water supply in this wild World War II cover by Alex Schomburg. Search all you want; we doubt you'll encounter a nicer copy than this one, originally part of the famous Edgar Church Mile High collection. It's currently the only example of this issue to be graded by CGC. Overstreet 2005 NM- 9.2 value = $610. CGC census 8/05: 1 in 9.6, none higher.

2474 Straight Arrow #1 (Magazine Enterprises, 1950) CGC VF 8.0 Off-white pages. First mention of Sundown Valley and the Secret Cave. Ogden Whitney art. Overstreet 2005 VF 8.0 value = $281. CGC census 8/05: 1 in 8.0, none higher.

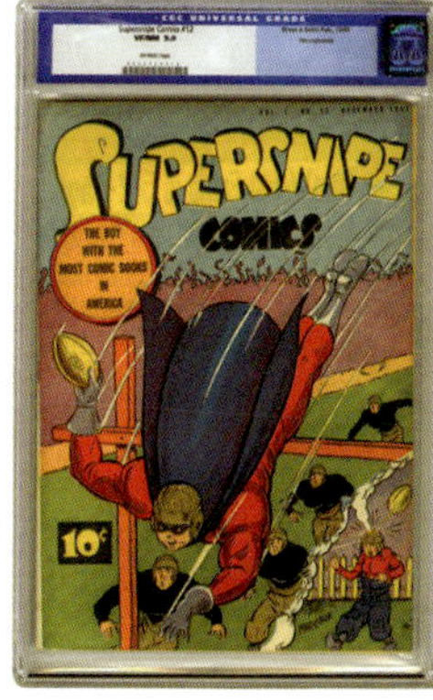

2475 Supersnipe Comics V1#12 Pennsylvania pedigree (Street & Smith, 1943) CGC VF/NM 9.0 Off-white pages. He's Koppy McFad, billed as "the boy with the most comic books in America," which officially makes him the original fanboy! This charming early parody of superhero comics is well-remembered by old-time fans and readers of **All In Color for a Dime**. Overstreet 2005 VF/NM 9.0 value = $476; NM- 9.2 value = $640. CGC census 7/05: 1 in 9.0, 1 higher.

2476 Suspense Comics #7 Mile High pedigree (Continental Magazines, 1944) CGC NM 9.4 White pages. The whole **Suspense** series continues to be in high demand, the main reason being striking L. B. Cole covers like this one. The book's interior artists include Rudy Palais. Our Mile High copy is the best one available, natch! Overstreet 2005 NM- 9.2 value = $2,150. CGC census 7/05: 1 in 9.4, none higher.

2477 Suspense Comics #11 Mile High pedigree (Continental Magazines, 1946) CGC NM 9.4 Off-white pages. One of the very best cover artists of the 1940s, L. B. Cole outdoes himself with this incredible Money Devil drawing. The only thing that can top this wild image (considered "classic" by Overstreet) is, of course, the fantastic condition of this Edgar Church Mile High example, which is fresh and sharp. Inside, there's stories featuring the Grey Mask and Mr. Nobody, but just try and tear yourself away from that vivid cover! Overstreet 2005 NM- 9.2 value = $4,550. CGC census 8/05: 2 in 9.4, none higher.

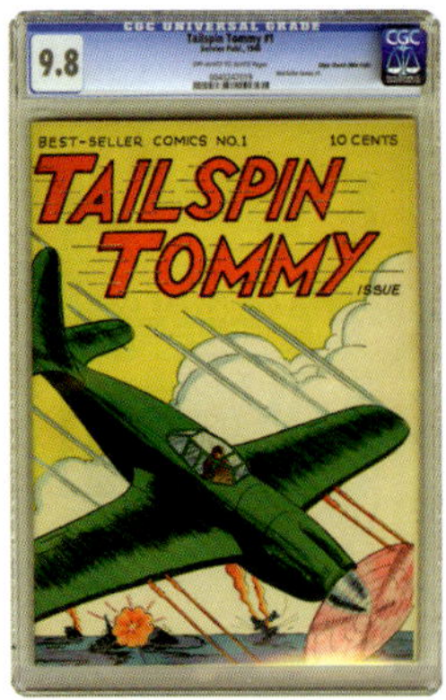

2478 Tailspin Tommy #1 Mile High pedigree (Service Publications, 1946) CGC NM/MT 9.8 Off-white to white pages. Tailspin Tommy had been appearing in a newspaper strip for almost twenty years when this one-shot (also known as **Best-Seller Comics** #1) was published, and Tommy starred in a movie serial as well, yet this was one of just a handful of comic book appearances for the aviator hero. This all but perfect Mile High copy is the only one graded higher than VF by CGC to date. Overstreet 2005 NM- 9.2 value = $160. CGC census 9/05: 1 in 9.8, none higher.

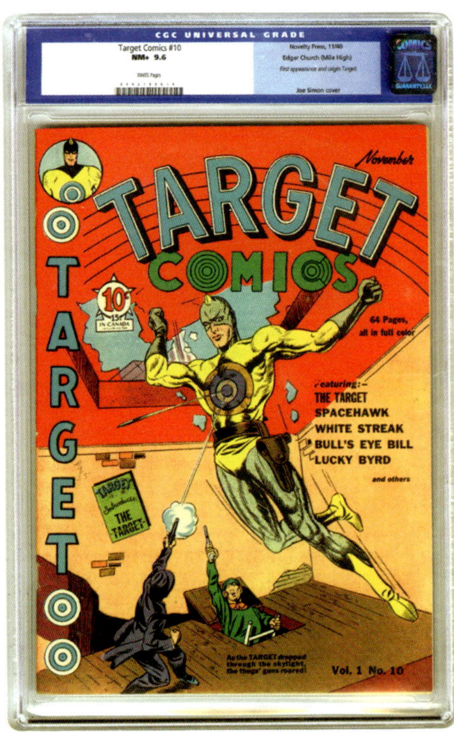

2479 Target Comics #10 Mile High pedigree (Novelty Press, 1940) CGC NM+ 9.6 White pages. This issue is notable for sporting perhaps the best-drawn cover of the title's run. Overstreet credits the cover to Joe Simon, Gerber to Jack Kirby... regardless, any S&K fan would love to add this "S *or* K" cover to his collection. Basil Wolverton, Carl Burgos, and Tarpe Mills are among those contributing interior features. As for the new hero on the block, **Target Comics**' name was, we presume, a nod to Bull's-Eye Bill, the first issue's coverboy, but since Bill had settled into more of a supporting role, it was time to introduce the Target! On the cover, the titular hero just dropped in to see what condition his condition was in. And we're happy to report that it's an amazing NM+. This comic is the highest-graded copy CGC has certified to date, and the only unrestored copy above 5.0. Take your best shot at this one! Overstreet 2005 NM- 9.2 value = $2,700. CGC census 9/05: 1 in 9.6, none higher.

2480 Tarzan #47 (Dell, 1953) CGC NM+ 9.6 Off-white to white pages. Photo cover featuring Lex Barker. Jesse Marsh and Russ Manning art. Overstreet 2005 NM- 9.2 value = $120. CGC census 8/05: 1 in 9.6, none higher.

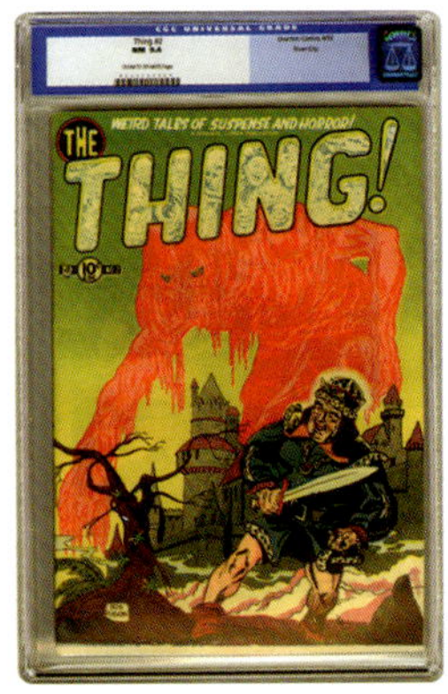

2481 The Thing! #2 River City pedigree (Charlton, 1952) CGC NM 9.4 Cream to off-white pages. What is the Thing? Something lurking in the shadows, waiting for a chance to attack? Something that exists only in the half-remembered world of bad dreams, shrouded in the misty areas of our fevered brains? We can't say, but this much is apparent: **The Thing!** was Charlton's creepiest comic book, published during the heyday of horrific titles like **Tales From the Crypt** and **This Magazine is Haunted**. This prime example carries a River City pedigree, as well as being the highest CGC-graded copy to date. Now that really *is* something! Overstreet 2005 NM- 9.2 value = $725. CGC census 9/05: 1 in 9.4, none higher.

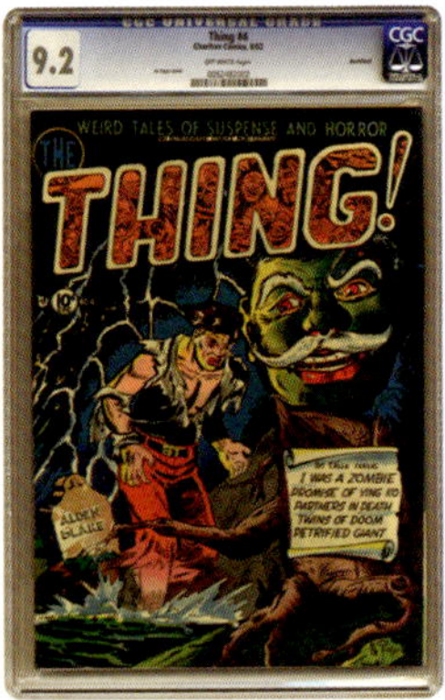

2482 The Thing! #4 Northford pedigree (Charlton, 1952) CGC NM- 9.2 Off-white pages. Artist Al Fago signed many a cover during the 1940s and '50s, usually drawing charming children's characters in titles like **Frisky Fables**. Here's another side to Al, depicting a red-eyed zombie marching through a graveyard in the middle of a dark and stormy night. It's wild and weird! This superb copy exhibits newsstand-fresh cover gloss, with fields of unbroken black ink backgrounds. Overstreet 2005 NM- 9.2 value = $640. CGC census 9/05: 1 in 9.2, none higher.

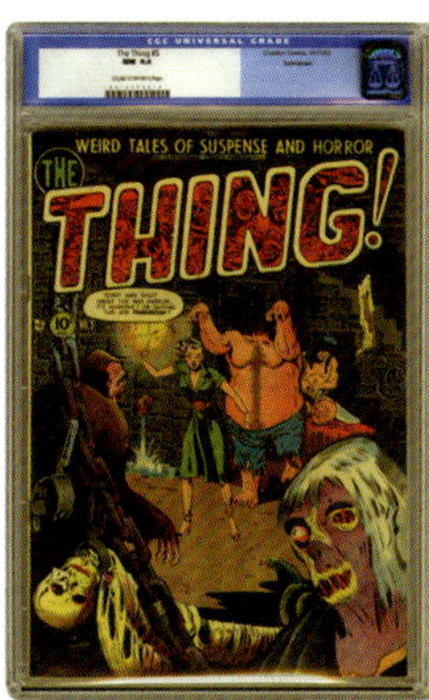

2483 The Thing! #5 Bethlehem pedigree (Charlton, 1952) CGC NM 9.4 Cream to off-white pages. Sometimes we find ourselves thinking that maybe Dr. Wertham (author of **Seduction of the Innocent**) was right. The good Dr. should have been warning parents about the kinds of comics their kids brought home if this particular issue was among the lot — the decapitation scene depicted on this Lou Morales cover will give anyone nightmares! Condition-wise, this one is so good, it's *scary*... and it has a pedigreed background, to boot! Put your fears behind you and bid! Overstreet 2005 NM-9.2 value = $640. CGC census 9/05: 2 in 9.4, none higher.

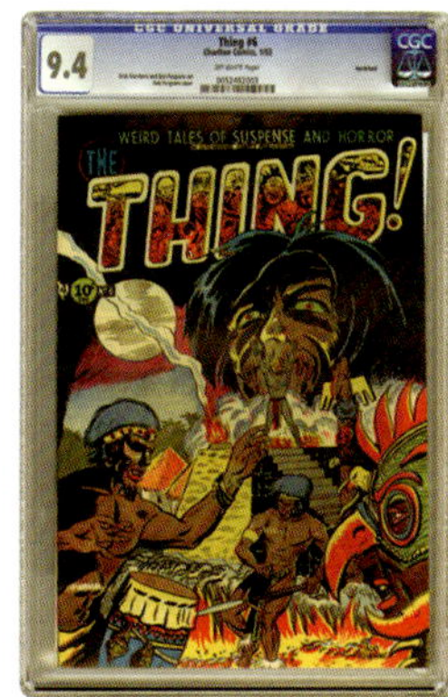

2484 The Thing! #6 Northford pedigree (Charlton, 1953) CGC NM 9.4 Off-white pages. A spooky-looking African voodoo ritual sets the tone for the horrific happenings inside the covers of this Charlton chiller. This incredible pedigreed copy features lush cover colors that are highlighted by plenty of deep black ink against white paper. Factor in the sharp corners and smooth surfaces; it all adds up to Near Mint. Now add up your resources and place that bid! Overstreet 2005 NM- 9.2 value = $640. CGC census 9/05: 2 in 9.4, none higher.

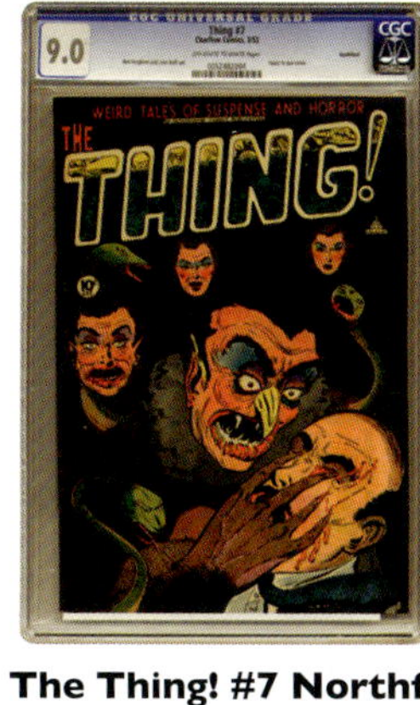

2485 The Thing! #7 Northford pedigree (Charlton, 1953) CGC VF/NM 9.0 Off-white to white pages. Lou Morales' cover to this issue of Charlton's **The Thing!** has to be one of the most unusual, and horrifying, images ever to grace a comic book. Against a pitch black background, we see a woman's face change into that of a harpy, who proceeds to claw a poor guy's eyes out — eeyow! Overstreet mentions that the "injury to eye" theme is carried over to an inside panel. Before we totally "creep you out," let us take a moment to observe the condition of this 52-year-old comic: it's terrific, with a ton of cover gloss. Overstreet 2005 VF/NM 9.0 value = $666; NM- 9.2 value = $900. CGC census 9/05: 1 in 9.0, 1 higher.

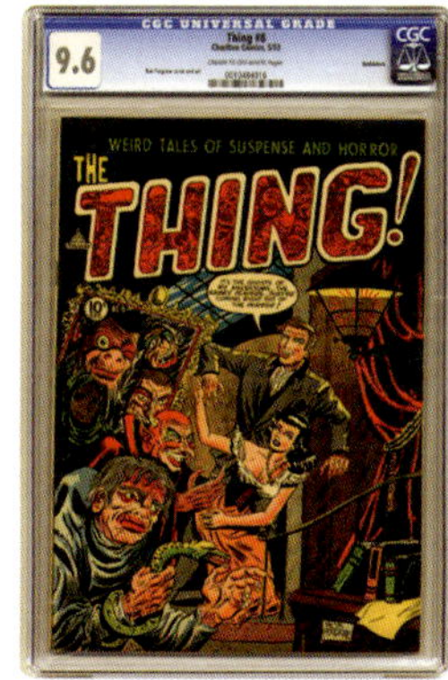

2486 The Thing! #8 Bethlehem pedigree (Charlton, 1953) CGC NM+ 9.6 Cream to off-white pages. While this title is noted for its often gruesome covers and violent content, this particular copy of issue #8 is noted for its extremely sharp condition. Only a light bit of paper toning keeps this cherry-picked copy from achieving gem-mint status. Overstreet 2005 NM-9.2 value = $735. CGC census 9/05: 1 in 9.6, none higher.

2487 The Thing! #17 Northford pedigree (Charlton, 1954) CGC NM 9.4 Off-white to white page. Rounding out our selection of pedigree issues of **The Thing!** is a beautiful, flawless black-background copy of this last issue. Steve Ditko provides a colorful sorcerer cover, which brings to mind his later work on Dr. Strange for Marvel. Inside, there's a classic parody of "Through the Looking Glass" by Bob Powell. Art by another future Marvel regular, Dick Ayers, is featured inside as well. Overstreet 2005 NM-9.2 value = $975. CGC census 9/05: 1 in 9.4, none higher.

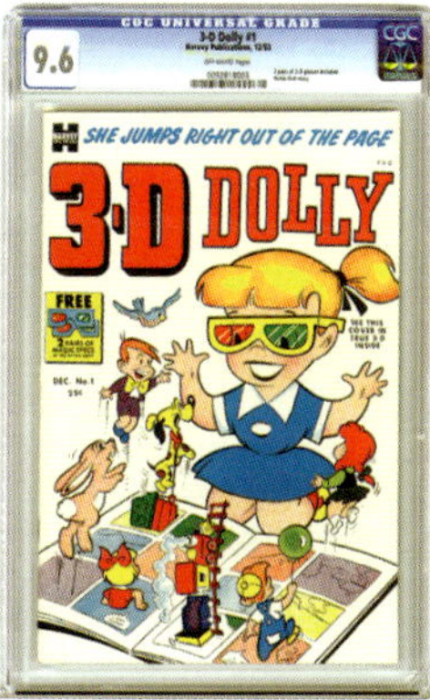

2488 3-D Dolly #1 (Harvey, 1953) CGC NM+ 9.6 Off-white pages. Both pairs of 3-D glasses are indeed included with this comic.... as if you needed any more proof that the thing's untouched after eyeing this copy's absolutely pristine white cover. Included in the issue is a redrawn version of the first appearance of Richie Rich in **Little Dot** #1. Overstreet 2005 NM- 9.2 value = $850. CGC census 7/05: 1 in 9.6, none higher.

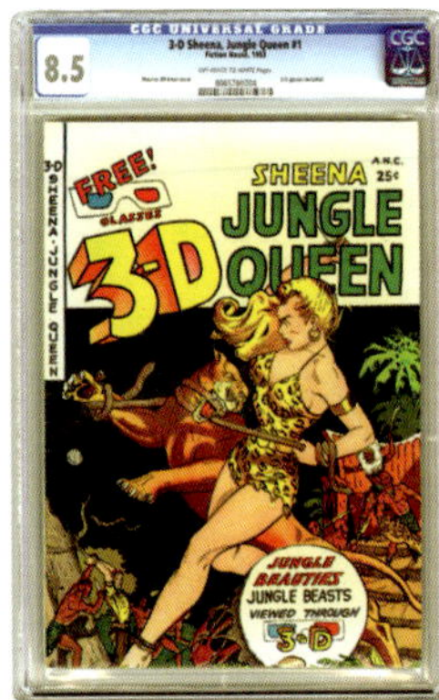

2489 3-D Sheena, Jungle Queen #1 (Fiction House, 1953) CGC VF+ 8.5 Off-white to white pages. This is the highest-graded copy CGC has certified to date, in fact it's the only one graded above 6.5. And yes, the 3-D glasses are included. The cover is by Maurice Whitman. Overstreet 2005 VF 8.0 value = $450; VF/NM 9.0 value = $695. CGC census 7/05: 1 in 8.5, none higher.

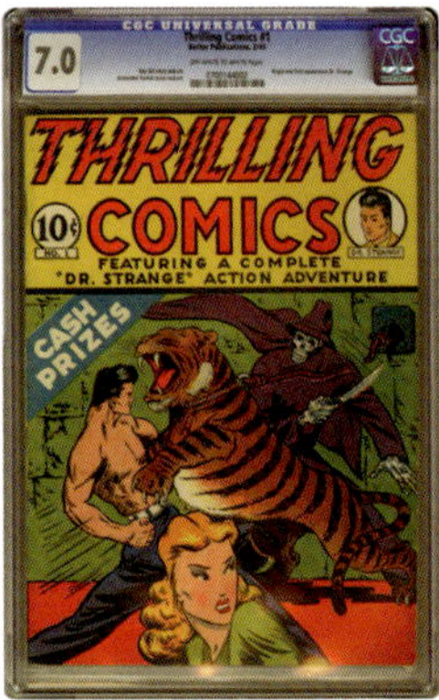

2490 Thrilling Comics #1 (Better Publications, 1940) CGC FN/VF 7.0 Off-white to white pages. It's the origin and first appearance of Doctor Strange! No hoary hosts of Hoggoth here, mind you — this is the adventurer who was more often called *Doc* Strange. Another feature that debuted here is Nickie Norton of the Secret Service. Overstreet 2005 FN 6.0 value = $900; VF 8.0 value = $1,892. CGC census 8/05: 1 in 7.0, 3 higher.

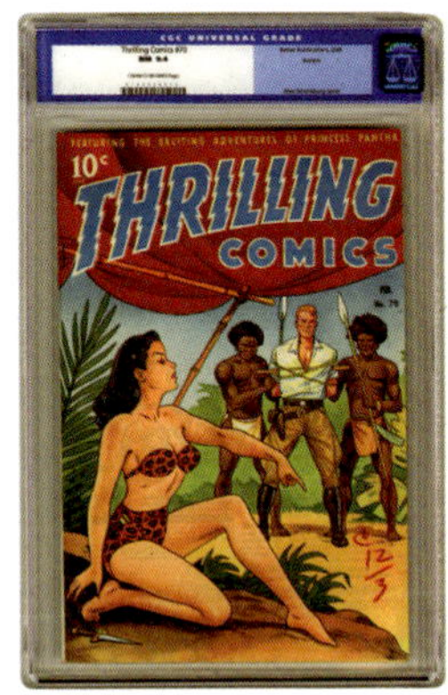

2491 Thrilling Comics #70 Aurora pedigree (Better Publications, 1949) CGC NM 9.4 Cream to off-white pages. The title featured "The Exciting Adventures of Princess Pantha," but we rarely get past the exciting cover by Alex Schomburg, whose airbrushed depictions of the Princess never fail to titillate! This copy is close to the finest specimen that CGC has certified to date of #70, edged out by only one copy at NM+ 9.6. If you need anything else to coax a bid out of you, how about seven pages of interior art by Frank Frazetta? Overstreet 2005 NM- 9.2 value = $575. CGC census 5/05: 1 in 9.4, 1 higher.

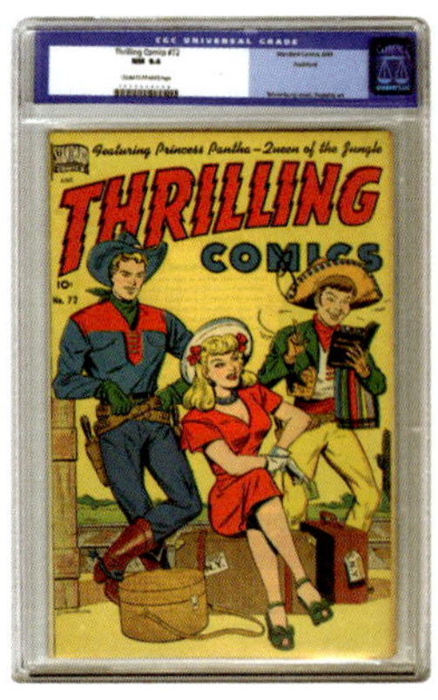

2492 Thrilling Comics #72 Rockford pedigree (Better Publications, 1949) CGC NM 9.4 Cream to off-white pages. An Alex Schomburg cover and Frank Frazetta interior art? Ahh, what a nice fantasy, if only there were such a com... waaait, we're wide awake, this comic's real! And we've got the only copy that CGC has certified to date. It doesn't get much more **Thrilling** than that for a comic fanboy or fangirl. Buck Ranger, Cowboy Detective, is the cover character. Overstreet 2005 NM- 9.2 value = $575. CGC census 7/05: 1 in 9.4, none higher.

2493 Tom Mix Comics #2 (Ralston-Purina Co., 1940) CGC VG 4.0 Cream to off-white pages. Ralston-Purina's mail-in comic books starring Western film star Tom Mix are quite scarce, and have been long sought-after by early comic collectors. This copy is currently the only unrestored CGC-graded example. Overstreet 2005 VG 4.0 value = $184. CGC census 8/05: 1 in 4.0, none higher.

2494 Tom Mix Comics #3 (Ralston-Purina Co., 1941) CGC VG 4.0 Cream to off-white pages. Solid copy of this scarce promotional comic. Overstreet 2005 VG 4.0 value = $116. CGC census 8/05: 1 in 4.0, 2 higher.

2495 Tom Mix Comics #4 (Ralston-Purina Co., 1941) CGC FN 6.0 Cream to off-white pages. Nice-looking copy of this sought-after promotional comic. Overstreet 2005 FN 6.0 value = $174. CGC census 8/05: 1 in 6.0, 2 higher.

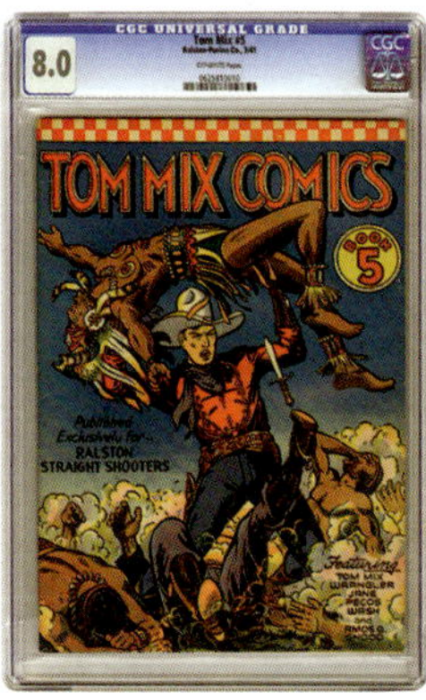

2496 Tom Mix Comics #5 (Ralston-Purina Co., 1941) CGC VF 8.0 Off-white pages. This very attractive copy currently tops the CGC census for this scarce issue. Overstreet 2005 VF 8.0 value = $363. CGC census 8/05: 1 in 8.0, none higher.

2497 Tom Mix Comics #6 (Ralston-Purina Co., 1941) CGC VG+ 4.5 Cream to off-white pages. This is currently the only unrestored CGC-graded copy of this issue. Overstreet 2005 VG 4.0 value = $116. CGC census 8/05: 1 in 4.5, none higher.

2498 Tom Mix Comics #7 (Ralston-Purina Co., 1941) CGC VG/FN 5.0 Cream to off-white pages. This seventh issue of the scarce promotional comic includes the beginning of the "Li'l Injun" feature. Overstreet 2005 VG 4.0 value = $116; FN 6.0 value = $174. CGC census 8/05: 1 in 5.0, 11 higher.

2499 Tom Mix Comics #8 (Ralston-Purina Co., 1942) CGC FN 6.0 Cream to off-white pages. Promotional comic featuring the cowboy film star. Overstreet 2005 FN 6.0 value = $174. CGC census 8/05: 1 in 6.0, 1 higher.

2500 Tom Mix Comics #9 (Ralston-Purina Co., 1942) CGC FN+ 6.5 Cream to off-white pages. Promotional comic; highest CGC-graded copy of this issue to date. Overstreet 2005 FN 6.0 value = $174; VF 8.0 value = $363. CGC census 8/05: 1 in 6.5, none higher.

2501 Tom Mix Comics #10 (Ralston-Purina Co., 1942) CGC FN/VF 7.0 Off-white pages. This World War II-era cereal giveaway reads "Tom Mix Commandos"; the origin of the Commandos is featured. Tom battles Japanese soldiers atop a submarine on the colorful cover. Back-up feature Speed O'Dare, Navy Flyer begins. Overstreet 2005 FN 6.0 value = $156; VF 8.0 value = $317. CGC census 8/05: 1 in 7.0, 1 higher.

2502 Tom Mix Comics #11 (Ralston-Purina Co., 1942) CGC VF- 7.5 Off-white pages. Promotional comic book with a World War II cover. Highest CGC-graded copy of this issue to date. Overstreet 2005 VF 8.0 value = $317. CGC census 8/05: 1 in 7.5, none higher.

2503 Tom Mix Comics #12 (Ralston-Purina Co., 1942) CGC VG+ 4.5 Cream to off-white pages. Last promotional issue, featuring a science fiction cover. CGC notes, "Original staples removed, 2 extra staples added, not from manufacturing." Overstreet 2005 VG 4.0 value = $104. CGC census 8/05: 1 in 4.5, none higher.

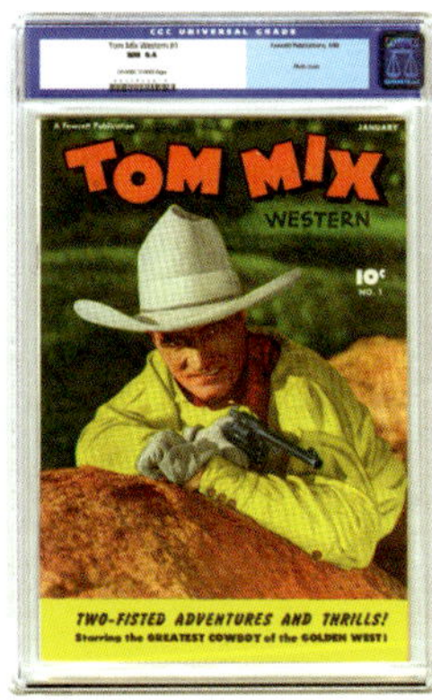

2504 Tom Mix Western #1 (Fawcett, 1948) CGC NM 9.4 Off-white to white pages. There's no better testament to Tom Mix's popularity than the fact that he starred in his own comic title which started almost eight years after his death! A photo from the archives graces this issue's cover. Overstreet 2005 NM- 9.2 value = $1,300. CGC census 9/05: 1 in 9.4, none higher.

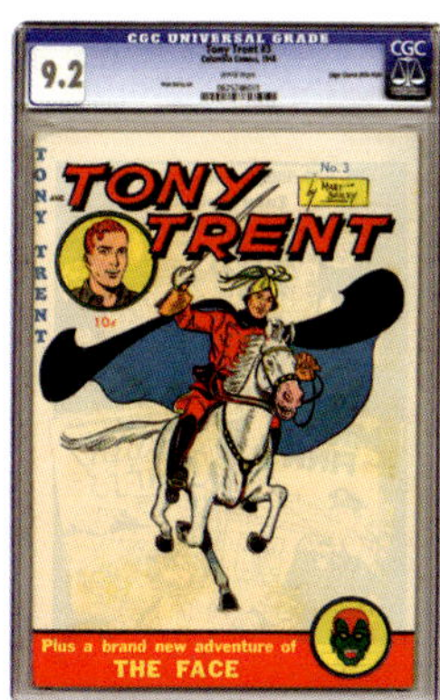

2505 Tony Trent #3 Mile High pedigree (Columbia Comic Corporation, 1948) CGC NM- 9.2 White pages. This issue's cover makes it look like the Face co-stars with Tony Trent, but in fact, the Face *is* Tony Trent! Yet this issue marked the last appearance of Tony's masked alter-ego. Mart Bailey handled art chores. Overstreet 2005 NM- 9.2 value = $200. CGC census 7/05: 1 in 9.2, none higher.

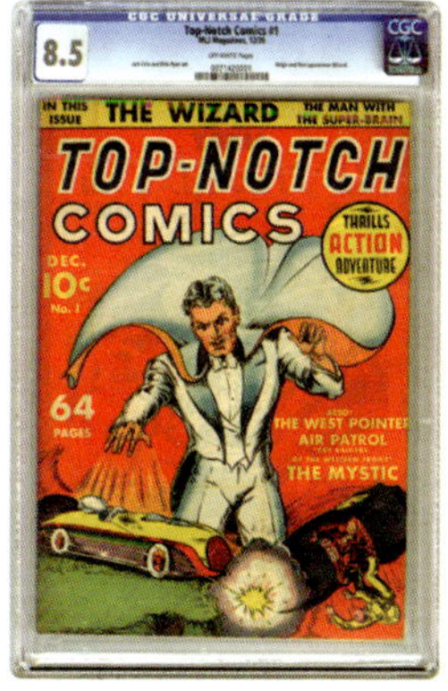

2506 Top-Notch Comics #1 (MLJ, 1939) CGC VF+ 8.5 Off-white pages. Only one copy of this book has been graded higher than our copy. The issue is best known for having the first appearance of the Wizard. It's one of the earliest comics from the publisher that would later be known as Archie. The book's interior artists include Jack Cole. Overstreet 2005 VF 8.0 value = $4,067; VF/NM 9.0 value = $6,534. CGC census 7/05: 2 in 8.5, 1 higher.

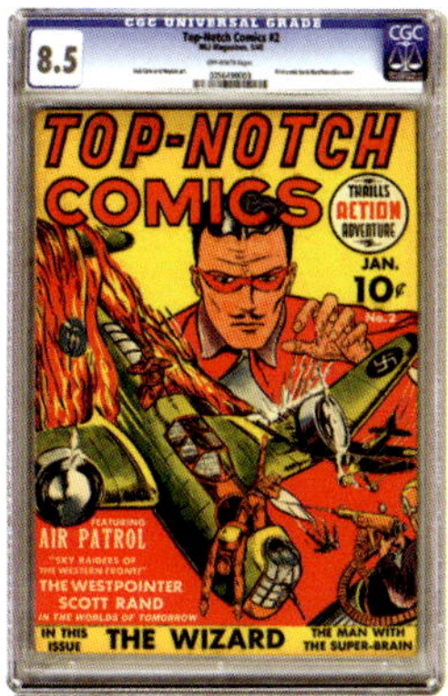

2507 Top-Notch Comics #2 (MLJ, 1940) CGC VF+ 8.5 Off-white pages. According to Overstreet, this was the first comic book to show a Nazi swastika on the cover! That's pretty amazing considering this comic's January 1940 cover date. The Wizard is the star of this issue, which has art by A-listers Jack Cole and Mort Meskin. Overstreet 2005 VF 8.0 value = $1,538; VF/NM 9.0 value = $2,369. CGC census 8/05: 1 in 8.5, 2 higher.

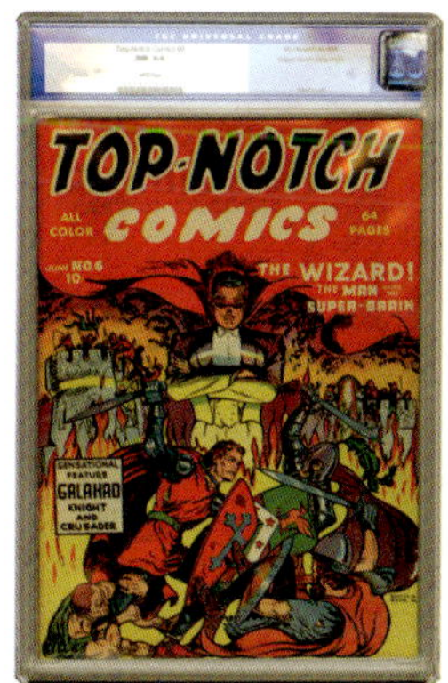

2508 Top-Notch Comics #6 Mile High pedigree (MLJ, 1940) CGC NM 9.4 White pages. Our Mile High offering is the only copy certified with a grade above 5.5 by CGC to date! The Wizard stars in the issue; he's drawn by Edd Ashe both on the cover and inside. The most notable of the issue's artists is Mort Meskin, who drew the tale of globetrotting adventurer Dick Storm. Overstreet 2005 NM- 9.2 value = $1,400. CGC census 8/05: 1 in 9.4, none higher.

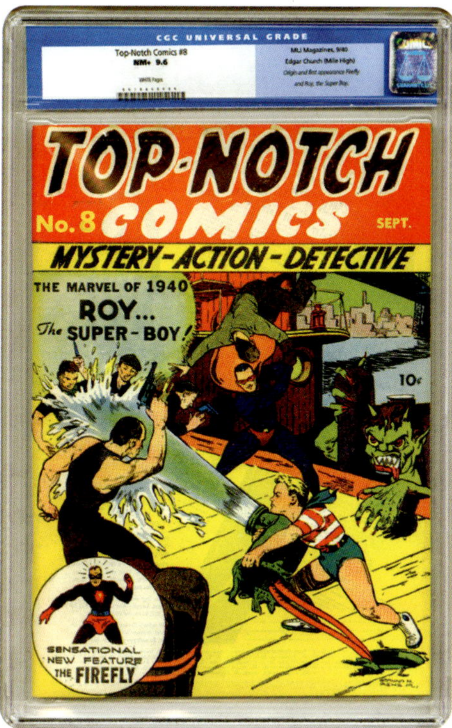

2509 Top-Notch Comics #8 Mile High pedigree (MLJ, 1940) CGC NM+ 9.6 White pages. One of the very first comic book sidekicks, Roy the Super Boy, made his first appearance in this issue. Overstreet speculates that Roy might be the second costumed boy hero in comics (trailing only Robin). Roy's origin is in this issue, and so are the origin and first appearance of Firefly, who was a regular in this title over the next couple of years. The issue's cover is by Edd Ashe; the interior artists include Mort Meskin. Overstreet 2005 NM- 9.2 value = $1,950. CGC census 8/05: 1 in 9.6, none higher.

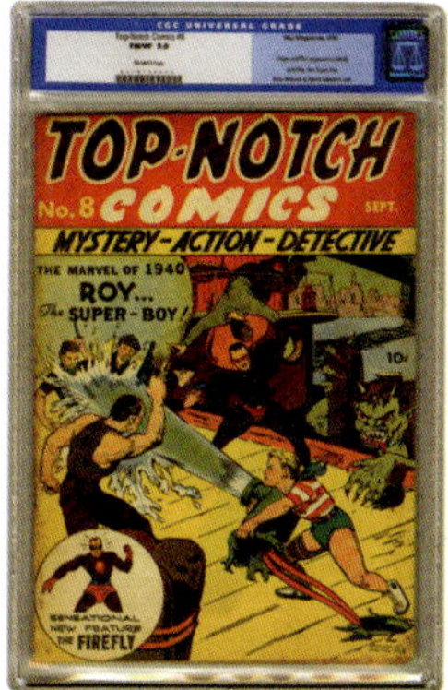

2510 Top-Notch Comics #8 (MLJ, 1940) CGC FN/VF 7.0 Off-white pages. Here's the origin and first appearance of Roy the Super-Boy. The Wizard and the Firefly also appear. The most notable artist is Mort Meskin, who drew the story starring adventurer Dick Storm. Overstreet 2005 FN 6.0 value = $450; VF 8.0 value = $938. CGC census 5/05: 1 in 7.0, 2 higher.

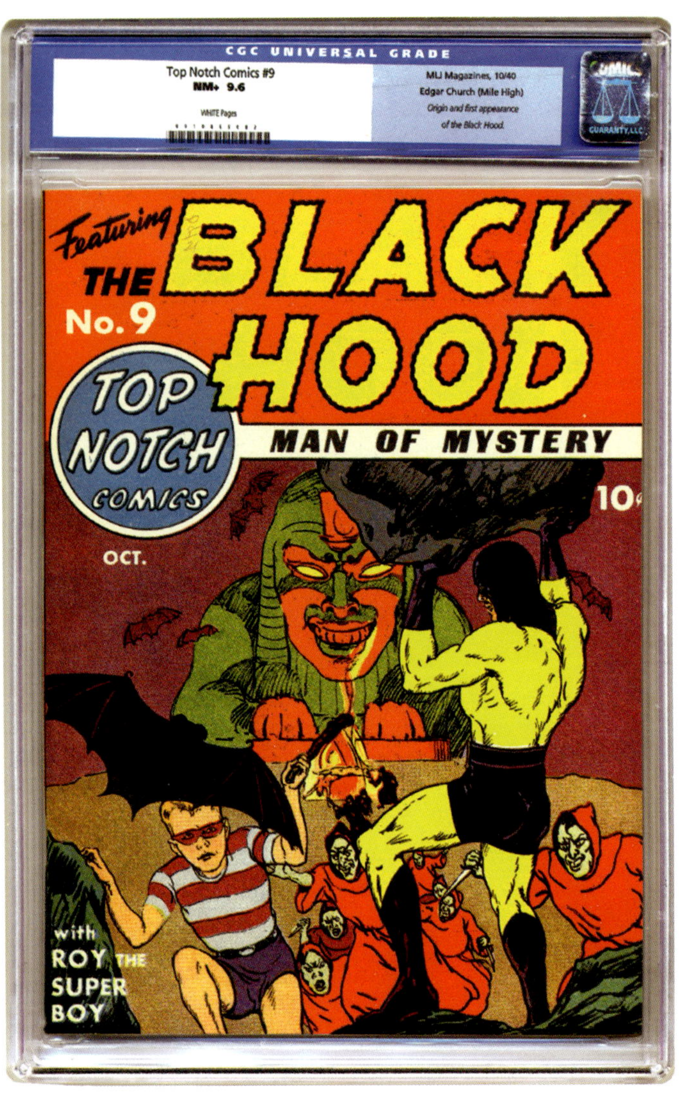

2511 Top-Notch Comics #9 Mile High pedigree (MLJ, 1940) CGC NM+ 9.6 White pages. MLJ was the publisher that became Archie, and this comic featured the origin and first appearance of one of their more prominent superheroes, the Black Hood. MLJ obviously expected big things from him, as he's billed above the actual title of the book! Youngster Roy the Super Boy, also seen on the cover, is actually the sidekick of this issue's other top hero, the Wizard. The book's artists include Irv Novick. Overstreet and Gerber both assigned their "scarce" rating to this issue. Overstreet 2005 NM- 9.2 value = $8,400. CGC census 9/05: 1 in 9.6, none higher.

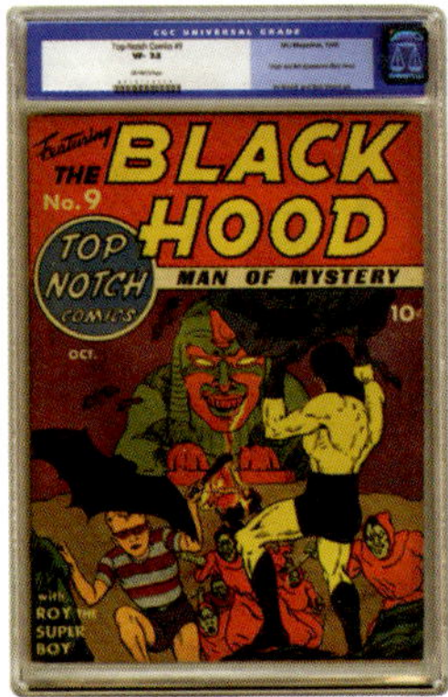

2512 Top-Notch Comics #9 (MLJ, 1940) CGC VF- 7.5 Off-white pages. This comic featured the origin and first appearance of the Black Hood - he gets a hand from the Wizard's sidekick, Roy the Super-Boy, on the cover. The book's artists include Irv Novick. Overstreet and Gerber both assign their "scarce" rating to this issue. Overstreet 2005 VF 8.0 value = $3,794. CGC census 5/05: 2 in 7.5, 3 higher.

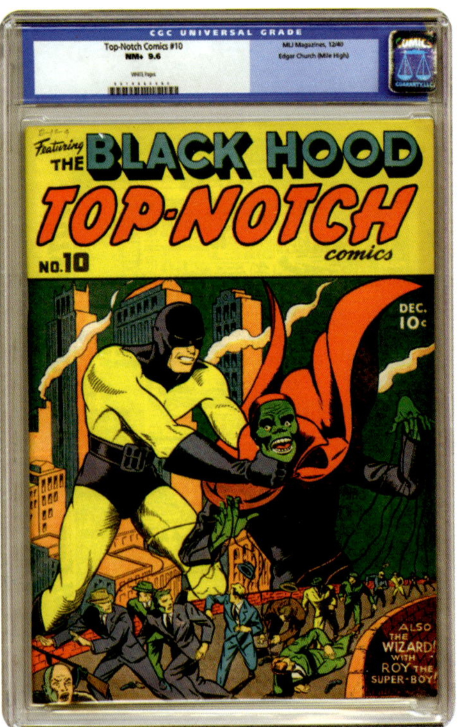

2513 Top-Notch Comics #10 Mile High pedigree (MLJ, 1940) CGC NM+ 9.6 White pages. This Mile High copy's the best one around by far, in fact it's the only one graded above FN by CGC as of this writing. In light of the Black Hood's above-the-title billing, you may be surprised to learn that this is only his second appearance! The cover is by Al Camy, who also drew both the accompanying story and a tale featuring the Wizard and sidekick Roy the Super-Boy. Overstreet 2005 NM- 9.2 value = $2,300. CGC census 8/05: 1 in 9.6, none higher.

2514 Top-Notch Comics #11 Mile High pedigree (MLJ, 1941) CGC NM+ 9.6 Off-white to white pages. This lovely Mile High book is the only copy of the issue graded above VF by CGC as of this writing. That's the Skull menacing the Black Hood on the cover, luckily our hero gets an assist from the Wizard and Roy the Super-Boy. The cover's by Al Camy. Overstreet 2005 NM- 9.2 value = $1,400. CGC census 8/05: 1 in 9.6, none higher.

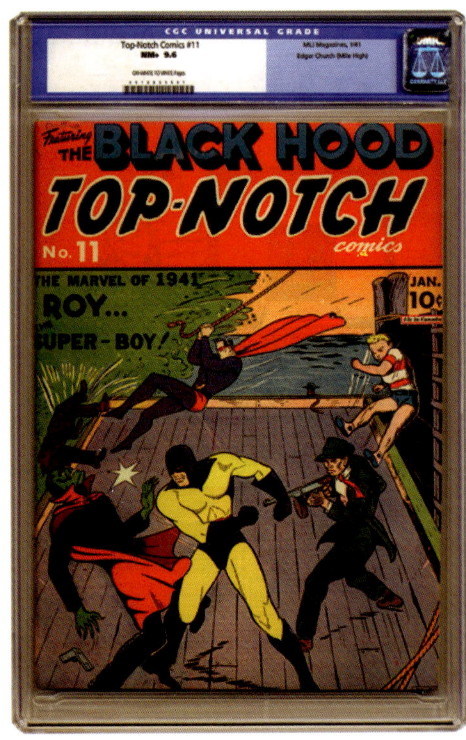

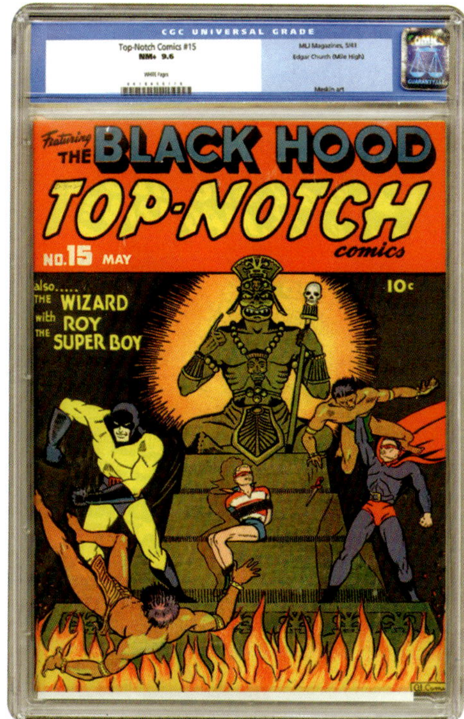

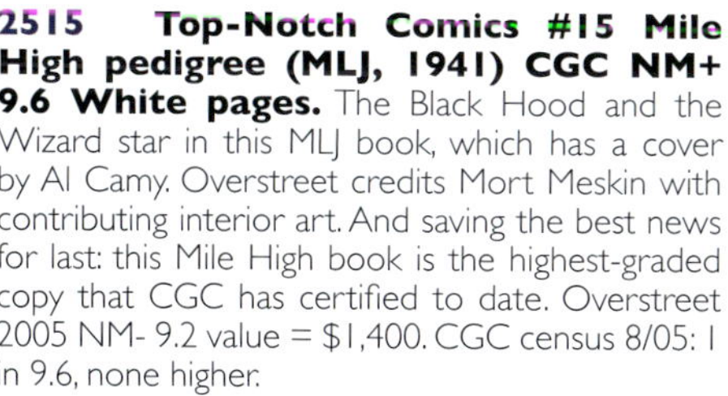

2515 Top-Notch Comics #15 Mile High pedigree (MLJ, 1941) CGC NM+ 9.6 White pages. The Black Hood and the Wizard star in this MLJ book, which has a cover by Al Camy. Overstreet credits Mort Meskin with contributing interior art. And saving the best news for last: this Mile High book is the highest-graded copy that CGC has certified to date. Overstreet 2005 NM- 9.2 value = $1,400. CGC census 8/05: 1 in 9.6, none higher.

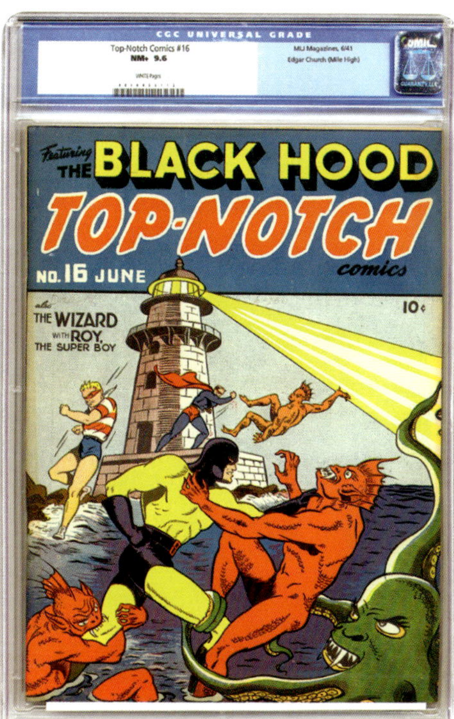

2516 Top-Notch Comics #16 Mile High pedigree (MLJ, 1941) CGC NM+ 9.6 White pages. It's always a thrill for us here at Heritage to see comic books that originally came from the celebrated Mile High (Edgar Church) collection. Having said that, let us add it's even more thrilling when the particular book is as nice as this incredible copy. This stunning example appears to have never been opened, let alone read! There is a hint of a dust shadow along the spine area, but that's the only real indication that this book is well over sixty years old. This comic features the Black Hood, the Wizard, and Roy the Super-Boy, MLJ's pre-Archie star attractions. But the real star here is Edgar Church — thank you, Mr. Church, for keeping your comics in such wonderful condition for so many years! Overstreet 2005 NM- 9.2 value = $1,225. CGC census 8/05: 1 in 9.6, none higher.

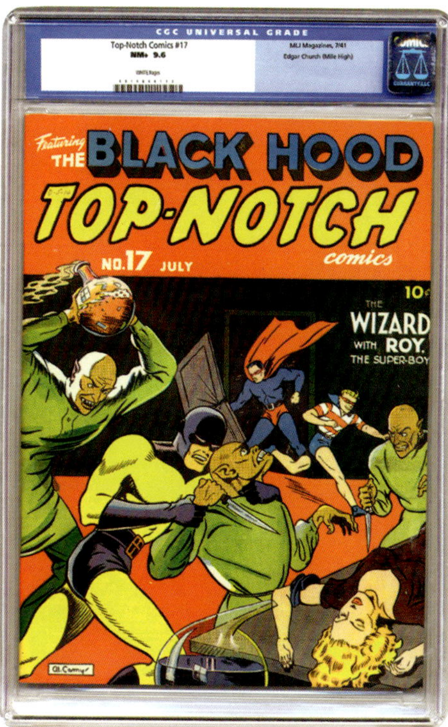

2517 Top-Notch Comics #17 Mile High pedigree (MLJ, 1941) CGC NM+ 9.6 White pages. This copy could literally pass for an issue that had just hit newsstands — it's that nice! There's not even a hint of a dust shadow or the like on this one. And it's the only copy certified above VG+ by CGC to date. The comic stars the Black Hood and the Wizard (and the latter's side-kick Roy the Super-Boy), as seen on the cover by Al Camy. Overstreet 2005 NM- 9.2 value = $1,225. CGC census 8/05: 1 in 9.6, none higher.

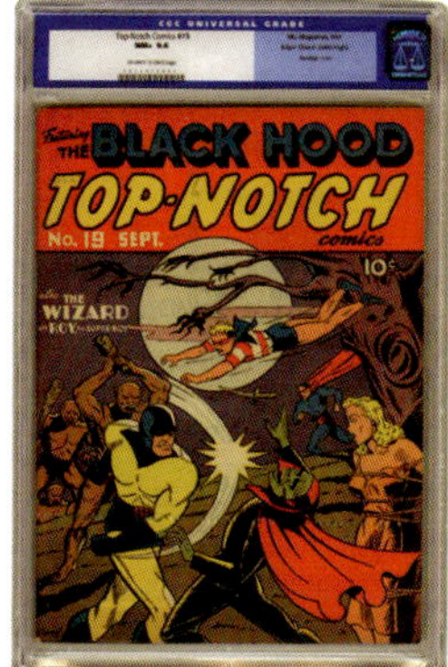

2518 Top-Notch Comics #19 Mile High pedigree (MLJ, 1941) CGC NM+ 9.6 Off-white to white pages. This isn't just the highest-graded copy of this issue that CGC has certified to date, it's the only one certified above 8.0! The villainous Skull, who appeared on several of this series' covers, is thwarted by the Black Hood, the Wizard, and Roy the Super-Boy on this bondage cover. Overstreet 2005 NM- 9.2 value = $1,225. CGC census 5/05: 1 in 9.6, none higher.

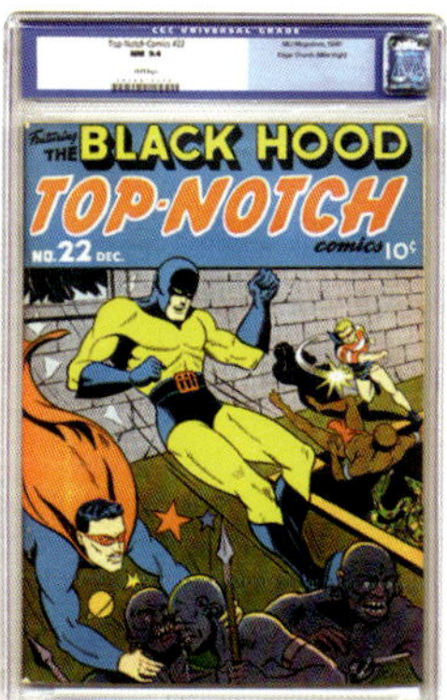

2519 Top-Notch Comics #22 Mile High pedigree (MLJ, 1941) CGC NM 9.4 White pages. Edgar Church did his usual beautiful job of preserving this comic, and he seems to be one of the few who saved the book at all; our offering is the only copy of the issue that CGC has certified to date. Al Camy is credited with the cover as well as the two features starring the Black Hood and the Wizard, respectively. Overstreet 2005 NM- 9.2 value = $900. CGC census 8/05: 1 in 9.4, none higher.

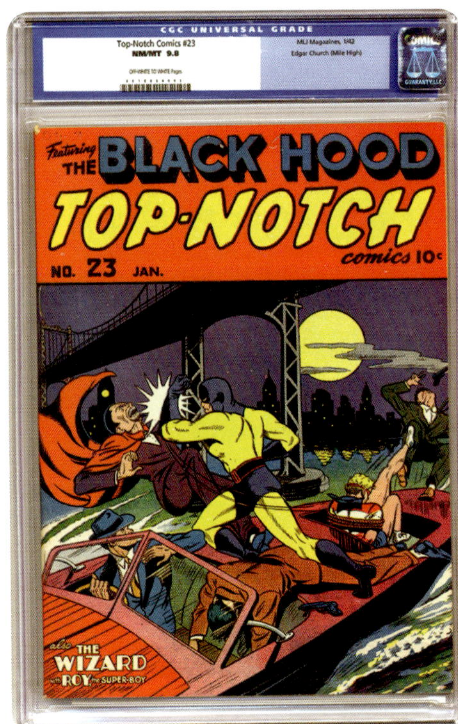

2520 Top-Notch Comics #23 Mile High pedigree (MLJ, 1942) CGC NM/MT 9.8 Off-white to white pages. Be prepared to be amazed by the remarkably fresh condition of this pre-World War II comic book, starring the Black Hood, the Wizard, and Roy, the Super-Boy. The book's got incredible gloss, rich color, and creamy smooth surfaces. You'll have to go back in time to ever find a better copy! Overstreet 2005 NM- 9.2 value = $900. CGC census 8/05: 1 in 9.8, none higher.

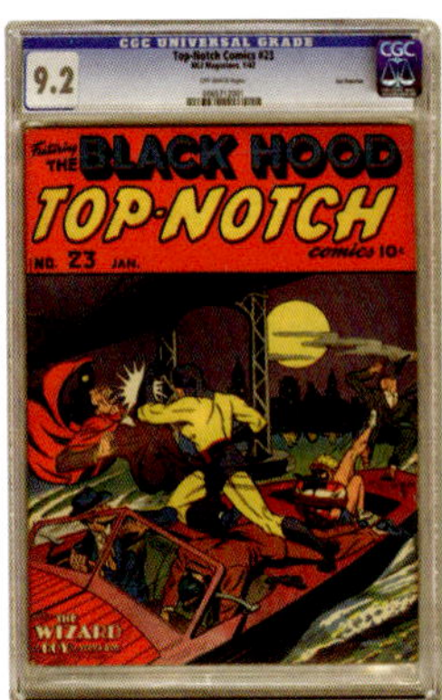

2521 Top-Notch Comics #23 San Francisco pedigree (MLJ, 1942) CGC NM- 9.2 Off-white pages. This NM- gem hails from the collection of Tom Reilly, one of the top two pedigree collections of all time according to most. MLJ heroes the Black Hood, the Wizard, Roy the Super-Boy, the Firefly, and others ply their crimefighting trade here. Overstreet 2005 NM- 9.2 value = $900. CGC census 5/05: 1 in 9.2, 1 higher.

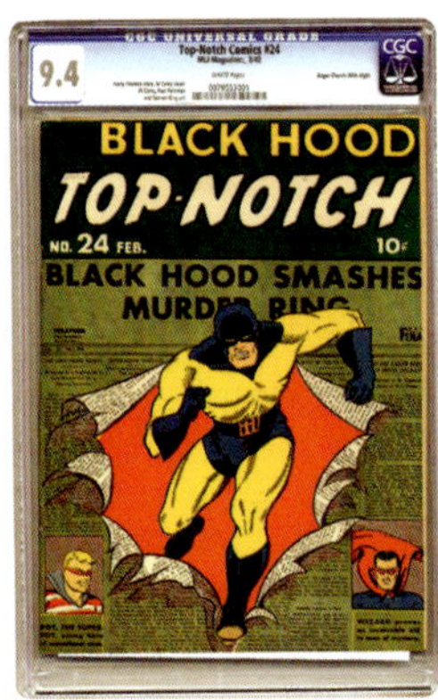

2522 Top-Notch Comics #24 Mile High pedigree (MLJ, 1942) CGC NM 9.4 White pages. Al Camy drew this issue's fake newspaper cover, which co-stars the Wizard and the latter's sidekick Roy the Super-Boy. This Mile High copy is the only one graded above 9.0 by CGC to date. Overstreet 2005 NM- 9.2 value = $900. CGC census 7/05: 1 in 9.4, none higher.

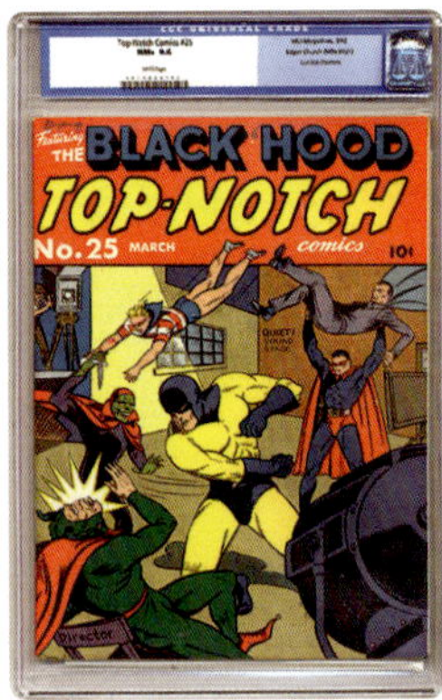

2523 Top-Notch Comics #25 Mile High pedigree (MLJ, 1942) CGC NM+ 9.6 White pages. This issue, starring the Black Hood, and featuring the last appearance of Bob Phantom, is considered "uncommon" by Gerber's **Photo-Journal Guide to Comic Books**. CGC bears out this fact; only two copies of issue #25 are listed in the current census: the Rockford pedigree copy in VF 8.0, and this magnificent Edgar Church example. Like most of the comics from the legendary Mile High pedigree, this is the one to own if only the best will do for your collection! Overstreet 2005 NM- 9.2 value = $900. CGC census 8/05: 1 in 9.6, none higher.

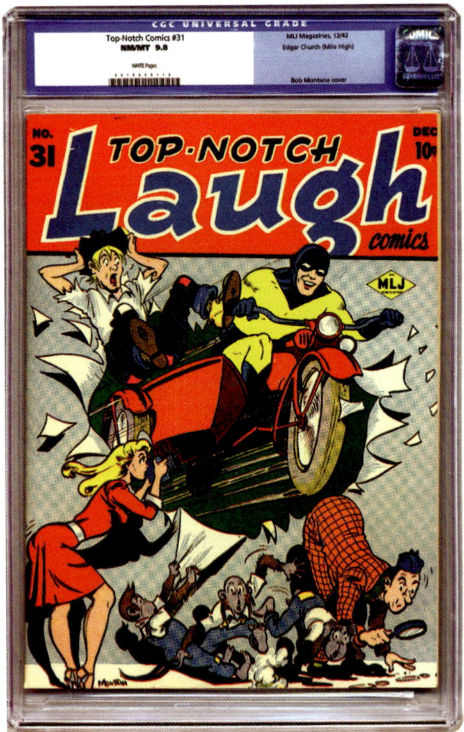

2524 Top-Notch Laugh Comics #31 Mile High pedigree (MLJ, 1942) CGC NM/MT 9.8 White pages. For some reason, these last few issues of **Top-Notch** haven't been dubbed "scarce" by the folks who assign such ratings, but we are prepared to do it for them — while we have seen the Mile High copies of some of the high-number issues, it seems that nobody *but* Edgar Church saved one! This is the only copy of the issue that has been slabbed to date by CGC, and it's a very collectible issue because it's so bizarre. Or what else would you call the Black Hood, a semi-grim hero, sharing a comic (and the cover) with Pokey Oakey the Funny Guy, the Three Monkeyteers, ditzy blonde Suzie, and Snoop McGook? The cover is by Bob Montana, the creator of Archie. Overstreet 2005 NM- 9.2 value = $475. CGC census 9/05: 1 in 9.8, none higher.

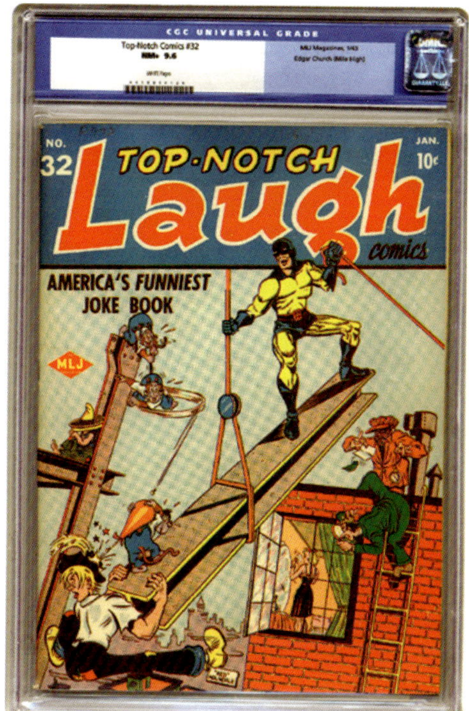

2525 Top-Notch Laugh Comics #32 Mile High pedigree (MLJ, 1943) CGC NM+ 9.6 White pages. Red Holmdale must have had as much fun drawing this cover as we do looking at it, though he did put MLJ's characters through plenty of humiliation here. How else do you explain masked crimefighter the Black Hood having to rescue backwoods hick Pokey Oakey? What else to call Suzie having to worry about a peeping tom, especially when it's Snoop McGook? As for the character Señor Siesta, we can only say "lo siento mucho." And regarding the Three Monkeyteers: Alexandre Dumas called, he wants his dignity back. Anyway, this is the only copy we've ever seen of this bizarre hero/humor hybrid, and the only copy that's been slabbed to date. Overstreet 2005 NM- 9.2 value = $475. CGC census 9/05: 1 in 9.6, none higher.

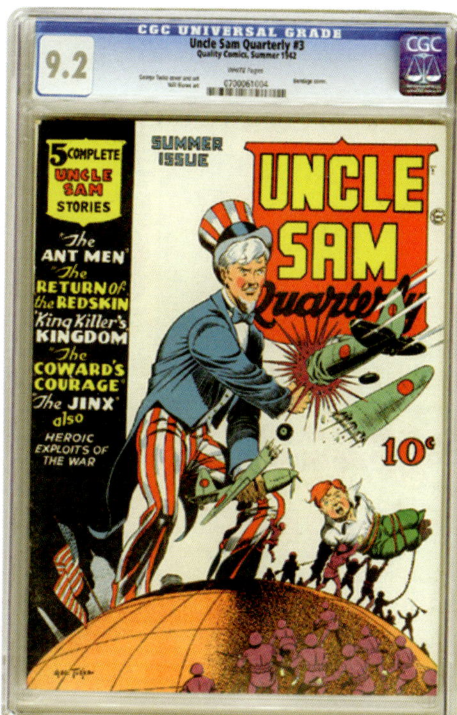

2526 Uncle Sam Quarterly #3 (Quality, 1942) CGC NM- 9.2 white pages. Here's the highest-graded copy of this issue, which stars the hero of **National Comics**. George Tuska contributed cover and interior art; according to Overstreet, Will Eisner added a two-pager. Overstreet 2005 NM- 9.2 value = $1,275. CGC census 1/05: 1 in 9.2, none higher.

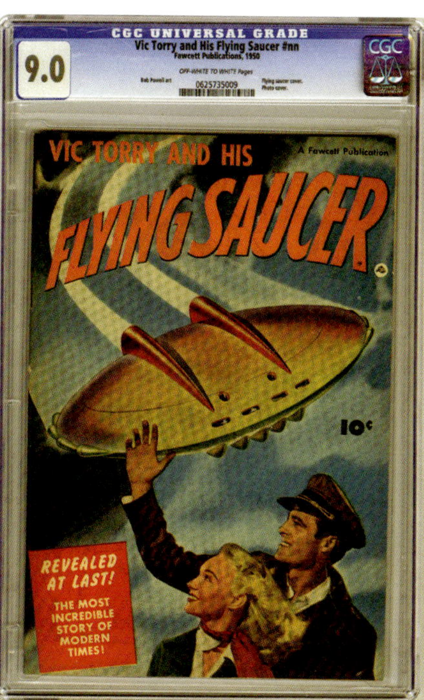

2527 Vic Torry & His Flying Saucer #nn (Fawcett, 1950) CGC VF/NM 9.0 Off-white to white pages. This UFO-themed one-shot has a colorized photo cover as well as book-length Bob Powell interior art. Overstreet 2005 VF/NM 9.0 value = $647; NM- 9.2 value = $875. CGC census 9/05: 2 in 9.0, 1 higher.

2528 Weird Comics #8 Mile High pedigree (Fox Features Syndicate, 1940) CGC NM 9.4 Off-white to white pages. This issue's the scarcest of the title's run according to Ernie Gerber, who gave the issue his "7" rating. And our copy is the only one that CGC has certified as of this writing. The comic stars the likes of the Dart, the Eagle, Dynamo, and Margo, the Panther Woman. Overstreet 2005 NM- 9.2 value = $1,250. CGC census 8/05: 1 in 9.4, none higher.

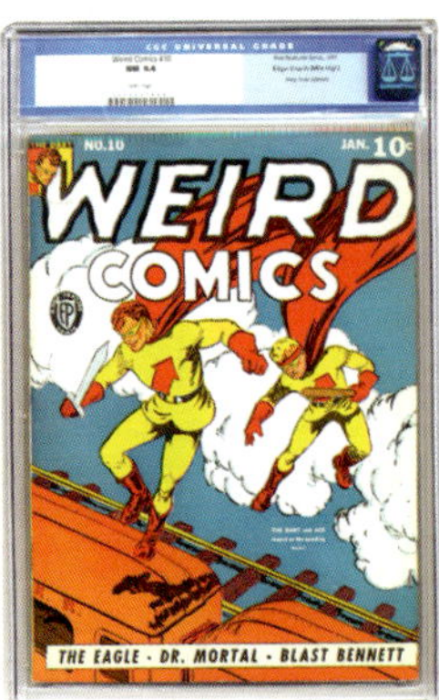

2529 Weird Comics #10 Mile High pedigree (Fox Features Syndicate, 1941) CGC NM 9.4 White pages. Even those few souls who lovingly preserved their DCs and Timelys weren't usually as gentle with their Fox comics, so it's quite amazing to see one in this condition. And our offering is the only copy of the issue that CGC has certified to date. Characters include the Dart, the Eagle, and Navy Jones. Overstreet 2005 NM- 9.2 value = $1,000. CGC census 8/05: 1 in 9.4, none higher.

2530 Weird Tales of the Future #4 (Aragon, 1952) CGC VF- 7.5 Cream to off-white pages. Basil Wolverton drew this issue's "Jumpin Jupiter" feature as well as part of the cover. Hmm, which part do you think he drew? If you guessed the far-out monsters, go to the head of the class. Overstreet 2005 VF 8.0 value = $756. CGC census 8/05: 2 in 7.5, 6 higher.

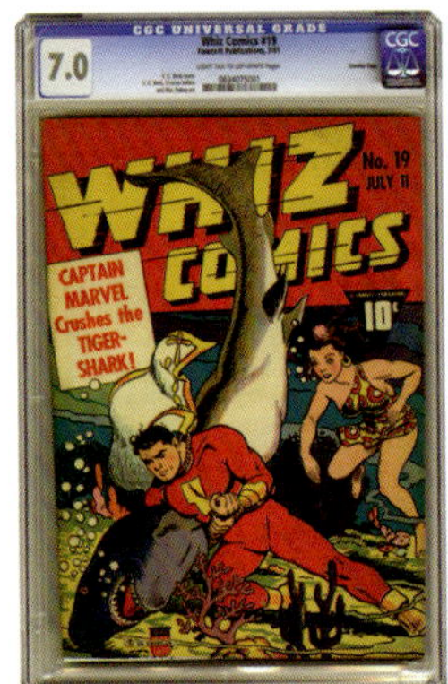

2531 Whiz Comics #19 Crowley Copy pedigree (Fawcett, 1941) CGC FN/VF 7.0 Light tan to off-white pages. C. C. Beck cover. Beck and Mac Raboy art. Overstreet 2005 FN 6.0 value = $261; VF 8.0 value = $544. CGC census 9/05: 1 in 7.0, 4 higher.

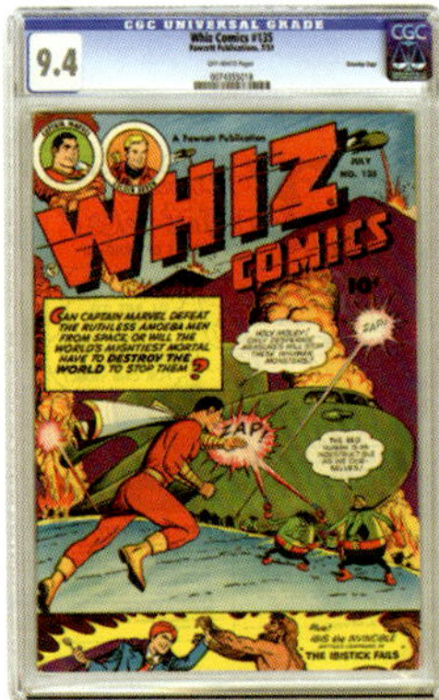

2532 Whiz Comics #135 Crowley Copy pedigree (Fawcett, 1951) CGC NM 9.4 Off-white pages. The Amoeba Men (whom Fawcett fans may recognize from **Marvel Family** #27) are back to menace Captain Marvel in this issue. The cover is by Kurt Schaffenberger. Overstreet 2005 NM- 9.2 value = $265. CGC census 8/05: 2 in 9.4, none higher.

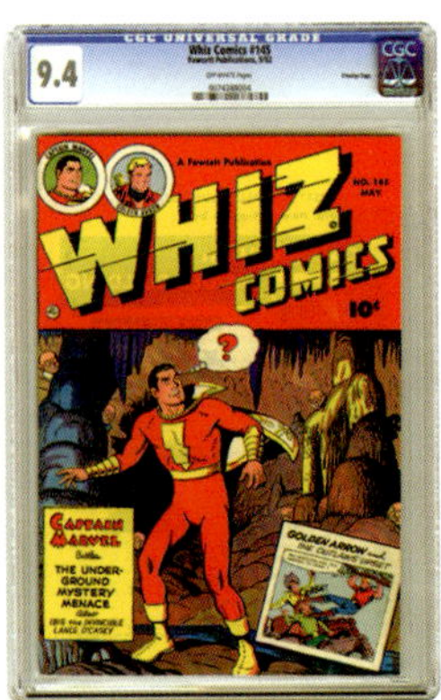

2533 Whiz Comics #145 Crowley Copy pedigree (Fawcett, 1952) CGC NM 9.4 Off-white pages. What's worse than being stuck in a cave with Sivana? Being stuck in a cave with *six* Sivanas, yikes! Kurt Schaffenberger provided interior art for the issue. Overstreet 2005 NM- 9.2 value = $265. CGC census 8/05: 2 in 9.4, none higher.

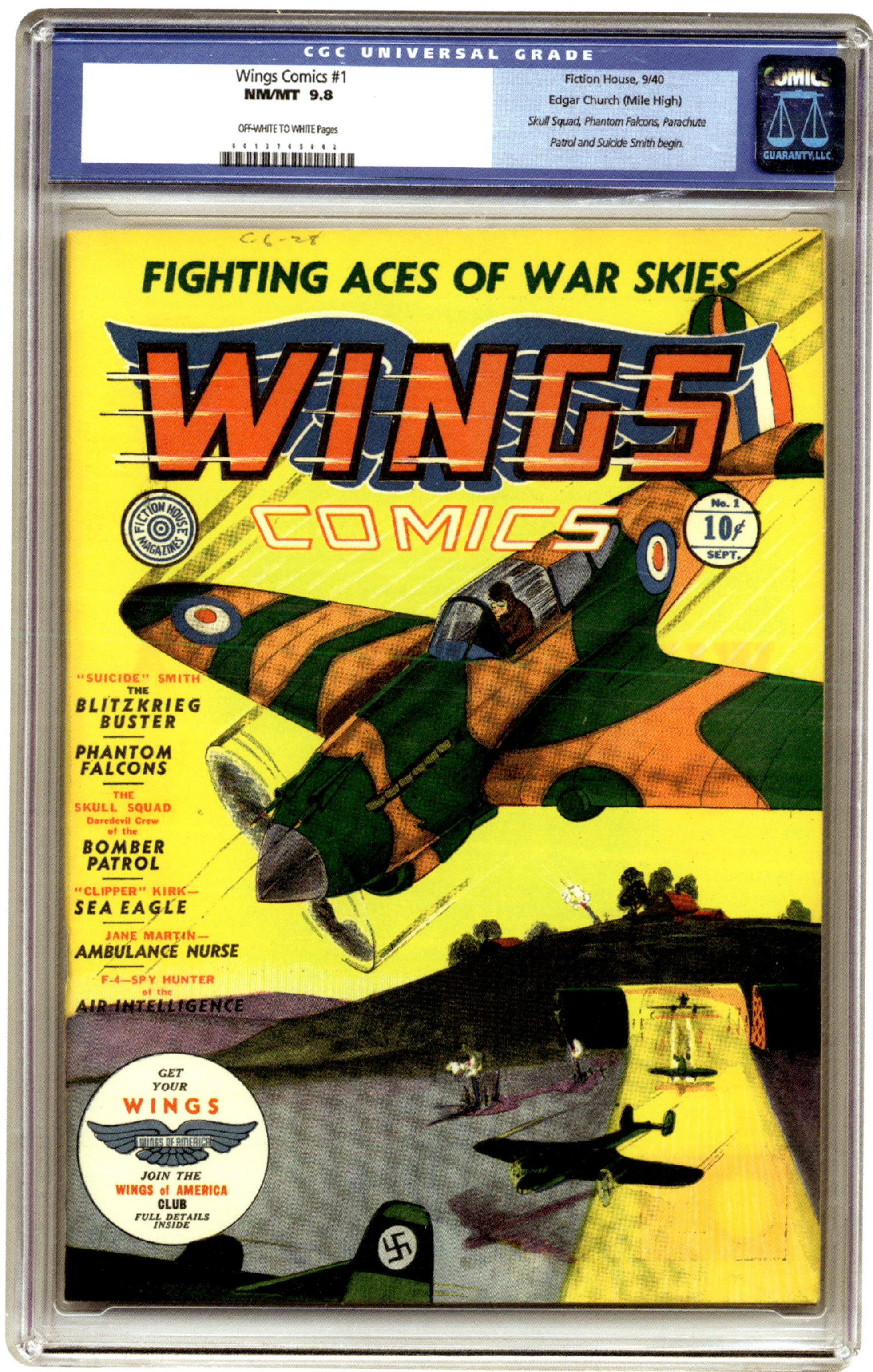

2534 Wings Comics #1 Mile High pedigree (Fiction House, 1940) CGC NM/MT 9.8 Off-white to white pages. If you collect Fiction House, it doesn't get much better than this A-plus copy of **Wings** #1, the first issue of a series that ran for 14 years and provided many thrills along the way. **Wings** was one of the earliest handful of comic book titles published by the company. It was produced by the Jerry Iger "shop" of writers and artists, and modeled closely on the **Wings** pulp magazine which was also published by Fiction House. A whole host of characters made their first appearances here, among them Suicide Smith (who appeared in the entire run of this series), Clipper Kirk, and "good girl" character Jane Martin, Ambulance Nurse. This debut issue's cover set the tone for the action-packed series; as Jim Steranko put it, "**Wings** covers attacked the reader. Thunderbolts, Wildcats, and Avengers roared right off the paper." And this grey tone example is certainly in that vein. The issue's interior artists include Klaus Nordling, George Tuska, and H. C. Kiefer. It's tough finding this issue at all (Gerber rates it a "7"), and of course this Mile High copy is the very best available. Overstreet 2005 NM- 9.2 value = $3,300. CGC census 8/05: 1 in 9.8, none higher.

2535 Wings Comics #24 (Fiction House, 1942) CGC VF/NM 9.0 Off-white to white pages. Gene Fawcette cover. Overstreet 2005 VF/NM 9.0 value = $342; NM- 9.2 value = $450. CGC census 9/05: 1 in 9.0, 2 higher.

2536 Wings Comics #30 (Fiction House, 1943) CGC VF 8.0 Off-white pages. Gene Fawcette cover. Bob Lubbers art. Overstreet 2005 VF 8.0 value = $233. CGC census 9/05: 2 in 8.0, 2 higher.

2537 Wings Comics #48 (Fiction House, 1944) CGC VF 8.0 Off-white pages. Artists include Lee Elias, Murphy Anderson, and Lily Renee. Overstreet 2005 VF 8.0 value = $164. CGC census 9/05: 2 in 8.0, none higher.

2538 Wings Comics #66 (Fiction House, 1946) CGC VF/NM 9.0 Cream to off-white pages. "Ghost Patrol" feature begins. Overstreet 2005 VF/NM 9.0 value = $191; NM- 9.2 value = $250. CGC census 9/05: 2 in 9.0, 1 higher.

2539 Wings Comics #73 (Fiction House, 1946) CGC VF/NM 9.0 Off-white pages. Overstreet 2005 VF/NM 9.0 value = $184; NM- 9.2 value = $240. CGC census 9/05: 2 in 9.0, none higher.

2540 Wings Comics #81 (Fiction House, 1947) CGC VF/NM 9.0 Off-white pages. Bob Lubbers cover. Lubbers and H. L. Larsen art. Overstreet 2005 VF/NM 9.0 value = $184; NM- 9.2 value = $240. CGC census 9/05: 1 in 9.0, 2 higher.

2541 Wings Comics #98 Mile High pedigree (Fiction House, 1948) CGC VF- 7.5 Cream to off-white pages. Bob Lubbers cover. George Evans art. Overstreet 2005 VF 8.0 value = $127. CGC census 9/05: 1 in 7.5, 4 higher.

2542 Wings Comics #104 (Fiction House, 1949) CGC VF/NM 9.0 Off-white to white pages. Bob Lubbers cover. John Celardo art. Overstreet 2005 VF/NM 9.0 value = $146; NM- 9.2 value = $190. CGC census 9/05: 1 in 9.0, none higher.

2543 Wings Comics #108 (Fiction House, 1949) CGC VF+ 8.5 Cream to off-white pages. Bob Lubbers cover. Lubbers and George Evans art. Overstreet 2005 VF 8.0 value = $102; VF/NM 9.0 value = $146. CGC census 9/05: 1 in 8.5, 1 higher.

2544 Wings Comics #109 (Fiction House, 1949) CGC VF+ 8.5 Cream to off-white pages. Bob Lubbers cover. Lubbers and George Evans art. Overstreet 2005 VF 8.0 value = $102; VF/NM 9.0 value = $146. CGC census 9/05: 1 in 8.5, 1 higher.

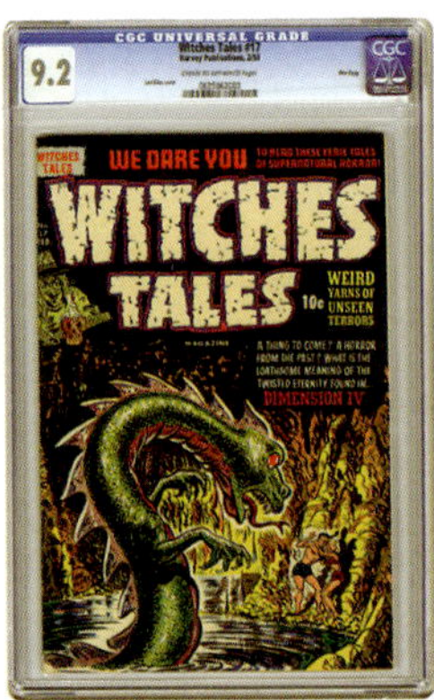

2545 Witches Tales #17 File Copy (Harvey, 1953) CGC NM- 9.2 Cream to off-white pages. Atomic disaster story. Lee Elias cover. Rudy Palais, Moe Marcus, and Manny Stallman art. This is currently the highest grade awarded by CGC for this issue. Overstreet 2005 NM- 9.2 value = $270. CGC census 8/05: 1 in 9.2, none higher.

2546 Witches Tales #20 File Copy (Harvey, 1953) CGC NM- 9.2 Cream to off-white pages. Lee Elias, Howard Nostrand, Bob Powell, and Jack Sparling art. This is currently the highest grade awarded by CGC for this issue. Overstreet 2005 NM- 9.2 value = $270. CGC census 8/05: 1 in 9.2, none higher.

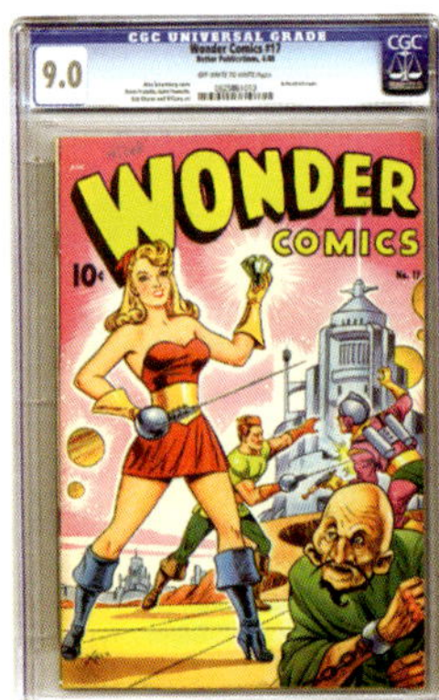

2547 Wonder Comics #17 (Better Publications, 1948) CGC VF/NM 9.0 Off-white to white pages. Now *here's* a real gem! This issue of **Wonder Comics** is a delight, starting with the wonderful airbrushed cover by "Xela" (better known to comic fans worldwide as Alex Schomburg), starring a sweetly smiling lady swashbuckler on some futuristic planet with a purple sky. Best of all are the distinctive touches of Frank Frazetta, who contributed to a couple of stories inside. Overstreet 2005 VF/NM 9.0 value = $594; NM- 9.2 value = $800. CGC census 8/05: 1 in 9.0, 1 higher.

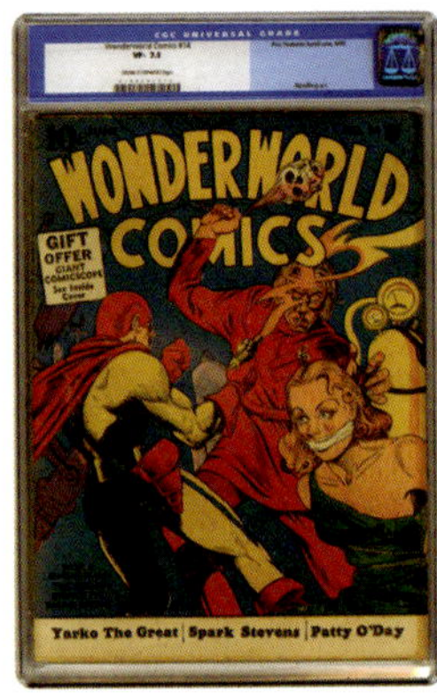

2548 Wonderworld Comics #14 (Fox, 1940) CGC VF- 7.5 Cream to off-white pages. One of the great comic book creators, Joe Simon, is among the contributors to this issue. Overstreet 2005 VF 8.0 value = $719. CGC census 8/05: 2 in 7.5, 1 higher.

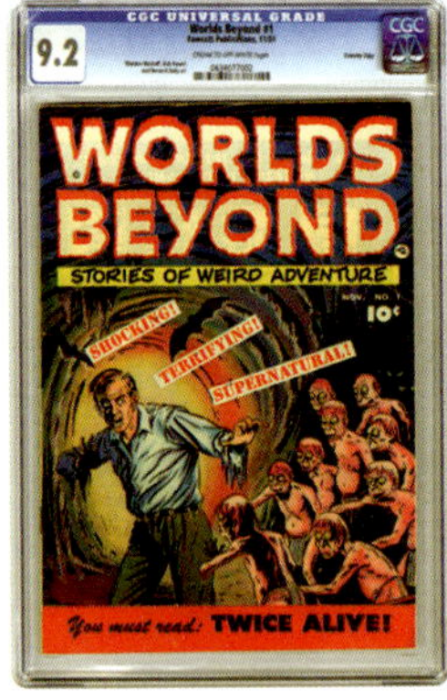

2549 Worlds Beyond #1 Crowley Copy pedigree (Fawcett, 1951) CGC NM- 9.2 Cream to off-white pages. This Pre-Code horror mag has cover art by Sheldon Moldoff, one of the originators of the horror comic genre. Bob Powell and Bernard Baily contributed interior art. Overstreet 2005 NM- 9.2 value = $560. CGC census 8/05: 3 in 9.2, 1 higher.

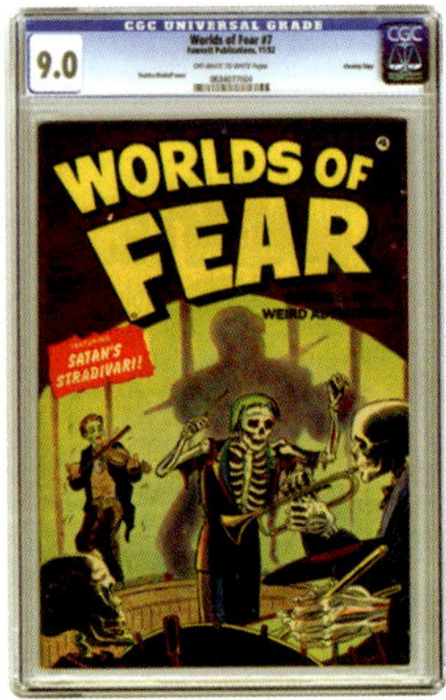

2550 Worlds of Fear #7 Crowley Copy pedigree (Fawcett, 1952) CGC VF/NM 9.0 Off-white to white pages. A great cover by Sheldon Moldoff kicks off a session of pre-Code creepiness! Overstreet 2005 VF/NM 9.0 value = $287; NM- 9.2 value = $375. CGC census 8/05: 1 in 9.0, 2 higher.

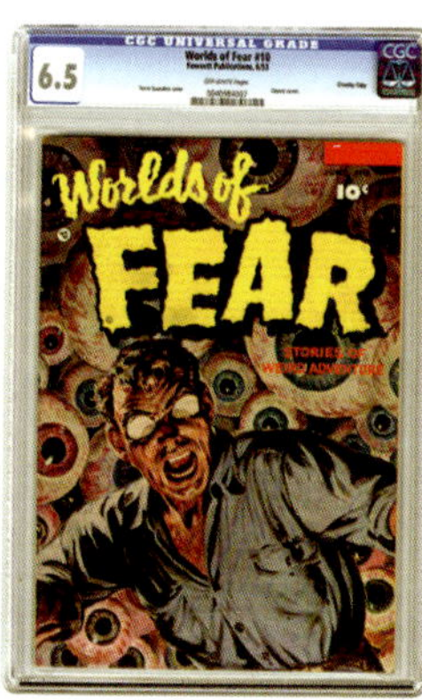

2551 Worlds of Fear #10 Crowley Copy pedigree (Fawcett, 1953) CGC FN+ 6.5 Off-white pages. A horrific painted cover by Norm Saunders makes this by far the most valuable issue of this pre-Code series' run! Overstreet 2005 FN 6.0 value = $231; VF 8.0 value = $481. CGC census 8/05: 1 in 6.5, 2 higher.

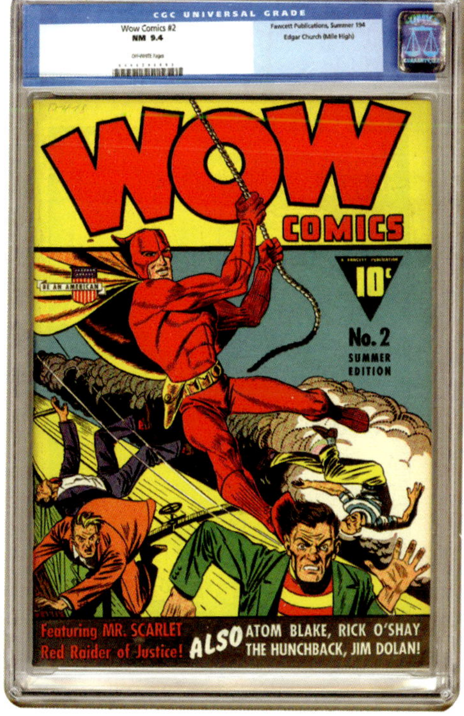

2552 Wow Comics #2 Mile High pedigree (Fawcett, 1941) CGC NM 9.4 Off-white pages. This issue's rated "scarce" by Overstreet, and we've got the highest-graded copy yet certified. Mr. Scarlet is the star of this issue (and the whole early run of the series). Premiering in this second issue is the Hunchback, a wealthy playboy who assumed the guise of a hunchback in order to — why else? — fight crime! Overstreet 2005 NM- 9.2 value = $3,200. CGC census 8/05: 1 in 9.4, none higher.

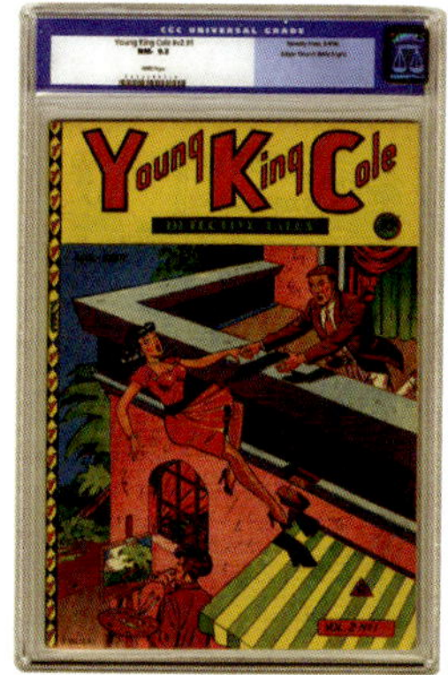

2553 Young King Cole V2#1 (Novelty Press, 1946) CGC NM- 9.2 White pages. Young King Cole was a bespectacled, harmless-looking fellow, but his appearance could be deceiving — he wasn't called the "Detective Agency Master Mind" for nothing! Oddly, the star of the comic doesn't appear on the cover, but some danger and a lovely lady make that omission excusable, we'd say. This is the only copy that CGC has certified to date of this issue of the detective series. Overstreet 2005 NM- 9.2 value = $105. CGC census 5/05: 1 in 9.2, none higher.

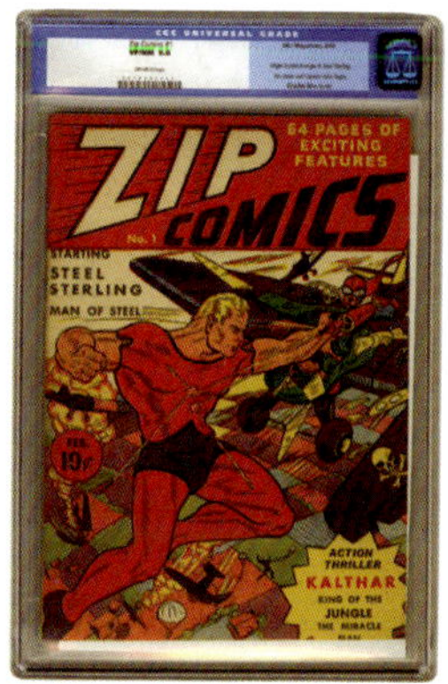

2554 Zip Comics #1 (MLJ, 1940) CGC VF/NM 9.0 Off-white pages. Steel Sterling made his first appearance in this issue! The book also has his origin story — as Ron Goulart wrote in **Comics Collector**, Steel "had an origin that was traumatic enough to have caused the average super-hero to call it quits right then and there." This issue also has the origin of the Scarlet Avenger (not to be confused with DC's Crimson Avenger). The most notable art in the issue is by Mort Meskin, who drew a story featuring the adventurer known as Captain Valor. Overstreet 2005 VF/NM 9.0 value = $5,661; NM- 9.2 value = $7,800. CGC census 5/05: 2 in 9.0, 1 higher.

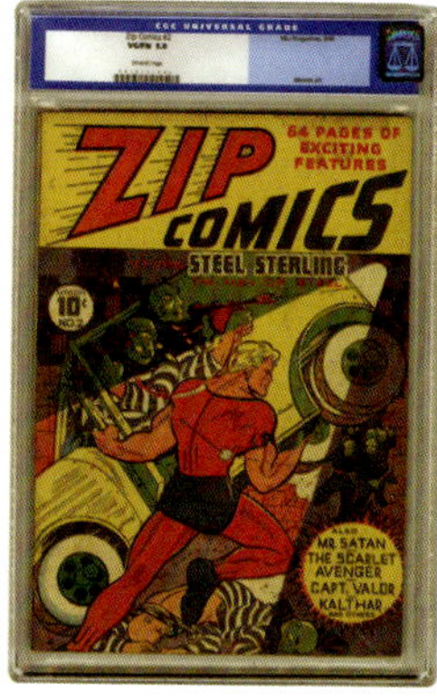

2555 Zip Comics #2 (MLJ, 1940) CGC VG/FN 5.0 Off-white pages. Steel Sterling, "The Man of Steel," was the star of this multi-character comic. There's also a Captain Valor story with Mort Meskin art, plus an adventure of Western hero Nevada Jones (who, we hasten to add, appeared more than 20 years before novelist Harold Robbins came up with Nevada *Smith*). While this copy's grade may seem to be nothing special, note that only one copy has been graded higher by CGC as of this writing. Overstreet 2005 VG 4.0 value = $476; FN 6.0 value = $714. CGC census 5/05: 1 in 5.0, 1 higher.

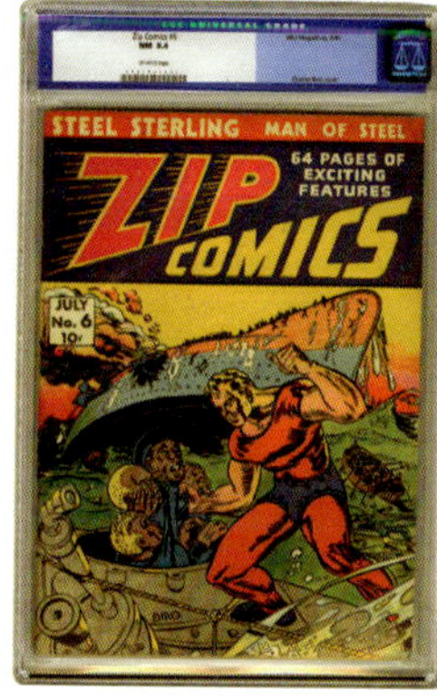

2556 Zip Comics #6 (MLJ, 1940) CGC NM 9.4 Off-white pages. Charles Biro drew Steel Sterling in action on this issue's cover as well as in the story featuring this "Man of Steel." Mort Meskin is among the other artists in this Archie superhero book. Overstreet 2005 NM- 9.2 value = $1,750. CGC census 5/05: 1 in 9.4, 1 higher.

2557 Zip Comics #6 (MLJ, 1940) CGC GD/VG 3.0 Slightly brittle pages. Charles Biro cover. Biro, Mort Meskin, and Irv Novick art. Overstreet 2005 GD 2.0 value = $135; VG 4.0 value = $270. CGC census 8/05: 1 in 3.0, 5 higher.

2558 Zip Comics #7 (MLJ, 1940) CGC VG/FN 5.0 Light tan to off-white pages. Charles Biro cover. Biro, Mort Meskin, and Irv Novick art. Overstreet 2005 VG 4.0 value = $270; FN 6.0 value = $405. CGC census 8/05: 1 in 5.0, 4 higher.

SESSION THREE

Public-Internet Auction #818
Saturday, October 15, 2005, 1:00 PM CT, Lots 3001-3492
Heritage Comic Auctions Dallas, Texas

Visit HeritageComics.com to view enlargeable color images and bid online.

THE AVIATOR COLLECTION

The following 86 Golden Age comic books offered as The Aviator Collection belonged to Gustave Schwartz, who was born in Schenectady, New York, and was a second generation U.S. citizen, son of German immigrants. When Gustave was 7 years old his father started buying him comic books. The young boy enjoyed them so much that in addition to what his father bought him, he would often spend a significant percentage of his 25 cent weekly allowance for comics. He would avidly read them, then share and trade them with friends. In mid-adolescence his attention was diverted toward other interests, such as Boy Scout activities, but Mr. Schwartz saved his comics, boxing them up in orange crates and storing them in the attic of his parents' home, where they remained for over half a century.

After high school he went to college, earning a Masters Degree in Aeronautical Engineering from Princeton University. Following college he joined the Air Force, where he got his training as a pilot. After his stint in the Air Force he found employment in the then burgeoning field of aviation. Around 1957 he hitched a trailer to his Ford and made the cross country drive to San Diego with his wife to start his new job.

When it came time to sell his home in Schenectady in the late 1990s he had his stored comics shipped out to him. They were placed in an airplane hangar where he worked. Not knowing what to do with the comics he gave them to his daughter, Cindy Schwartz, who was not a comic collector and didn't quite know what to do with the collection. However, after she overheard a co-worker, Steve Bergier, talking about his comic collecting hobby, she got an idea of the possible treasures in the four cases of comics she had. Enter Heritage Comic Auctions - now the collection is available for your bidding.

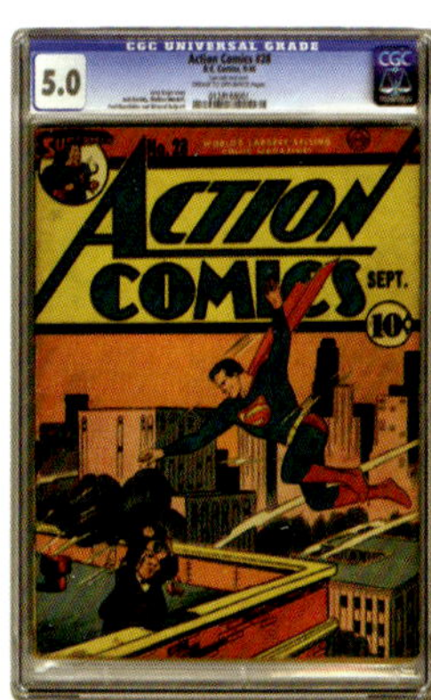

3001 Action Comics #28 (DC, 1940) CGC VG/FN 5.0 Cream to off-white pages. This modest mid-grade copy hasn't been bested by many other copies certified by CGC to date, only one of which earned a grade better than VF 8.0. DC Golden Age greats Jack Burnley, Sheldon Moldoff, Fred Guardineer, and Bernard Baily contributed interior art. The Grand Comics Database Project gives Paul Cassidy credit for the cover art. CGC notes, "Tape stain back cover." Overstreet 2005 VG 4.0 value = $508; FN 6.0 value = $762. CGC census 7/05: 1 in 5.0, 7 higher. *From the Aviator Collection.*

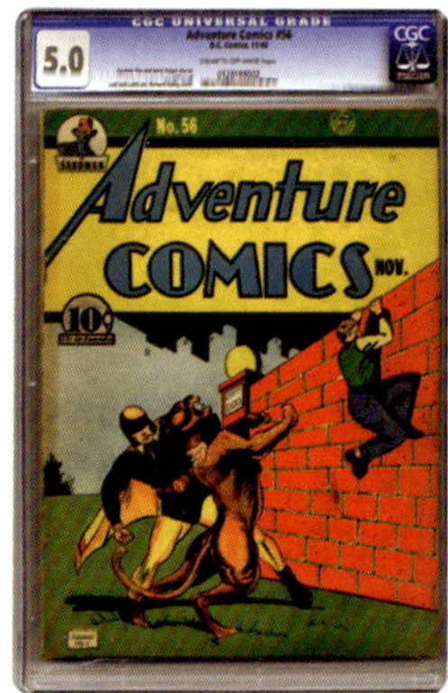

3002 Adventure Comics #56 (DC, 1940) CGC VG/FN 5.0 Cream to off-white pages. Hourman and Sandman are the featured attractions once again in this issue! The former is drawn by Bernard Baily (who also drew the cover) and the latter is rendered by Creig Flessel. Overstreet 2005 VG 4.0 value = $676; FN 6.0 value = $1,014. CGC census 8/05: 1 in 5.0, 7 higher. *From the Aviator Collection.*

3003 Adventure Comics #62 (DC, 1941) CGC FN/VF 7.0 Cream to off-white pages. Jack Burnley created the stylish cover, and also contributed interior art along with Creig Flessel. A Gerber "uncommon" issue. Overstreet 2005 FN 6.0 value = $576; VF 8.0 value = $1,200. CGC census 7/05: 1 in 7.0, 4 higher. *From the Aviator Collection.*

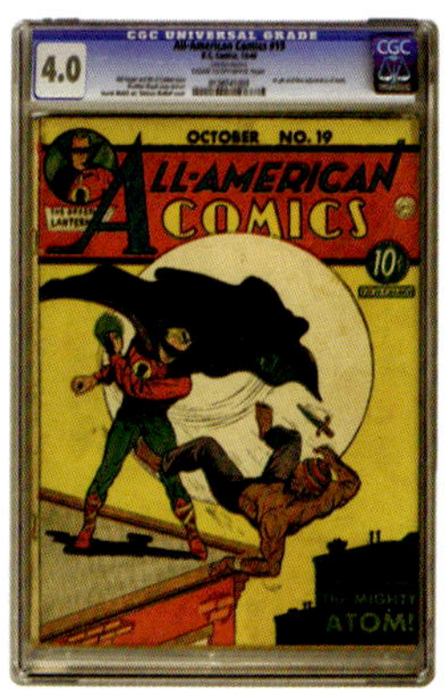

3004 All-American Comics #19 (DC, 1940) CGC VG 4.0 Cream to off-white pages. This is the second most valuable issue in the historic title's nine-year run. Three issues after the first appearance of Green Lantern, DC introduced the Atom here. Sheldon Moldoff is responsible for the neat cover, with Sheldon Mayer and Martin Nodell contributing interior art. If you think you'll hold out for a high-grade copy, good luck! Of the four copies that CGC has certified with higher grades to date, the best is a modest FN 6.0! Overstreet 2005 VG 4.0 value = $2,824. CGC census 7/05: 1 in 4.0, 4 higher. *From the Aviator Collection.*

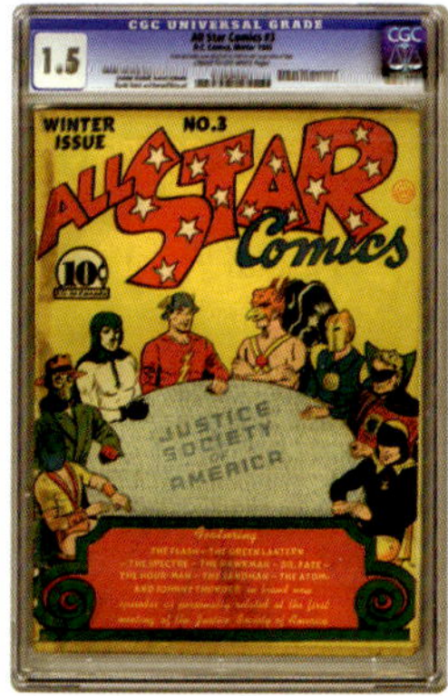

3005 All Star Comics #3 (DC, 1940) CGC FR/GD 1.5 Cream to off-white pages. Notoriously difficult to find in high grade (only two copies to date have been certified by CGC higher than FN/VF 7.0), this Gerber "uncommon" issue currently ranks as the 13th most valuable Golden Age comic book, befitting the significance of the origin and first appearance of the Justice Society of America. The cover is by E. E. Hibbard, with Hibbard, Bernard Baily, Sheldon Moldoff, and Martin Nodel providing interior art. CGC notes, "Front and back cover attached to interior with large piece of tape." Overstreet 2005 GD 2.0 value = $3,529. CGC census 7/05: 1 in 1.5, 17 higher. *From the Aviator Collection.*

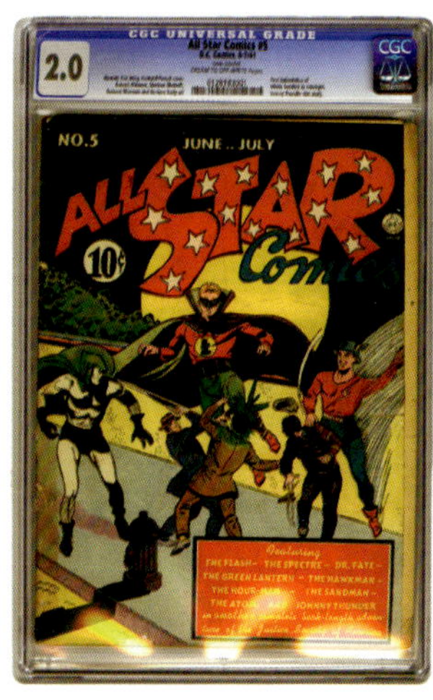

3006 All Star Comics #5 (DC, 1941) CGC GD 2.0 Cream to off-white pages. Considered the first costumed superheroine, Shiera Sanders makes her first appearance as Hawkgirl in this issue. Howard Purcell comes up with a nice action cover, while Sheldon Moldoff, Bernard Baily, Howard Sherman, and E. E. Hibbard help with interior art. Overstreet 2005 GD 2.0 value = $439. CGC census 7/05: 1 in 2.0, 22 higher. *From the Aviator Collection.*

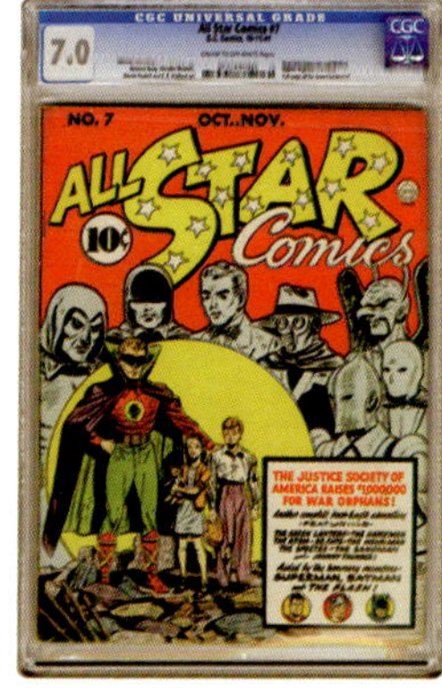

3007 All Star Comics #7 (DC, 1941) CGC FN/VF 7.0 Cream to off-white pages. Superman and Batman appeared together in a story for the very first time here, as Johnny Thunder made a wish that they would show up, and Johnny's powers being what they are, the two heroes suddenly appeared! The rest of the issue sees the Justice Society regulars doing their part to bring in humanitarian funds for war orphans. The issue has an E. E. Hibbard cover, with interior art by Hibbard, Martin Nodell, Bernard Baily, and Sheldon Moldoff to name but a few. Overstreet 2005 FN 6.0 value = $984; VF 8.0 value = $2,132. CGC census 9/05: in 7.0, higher.

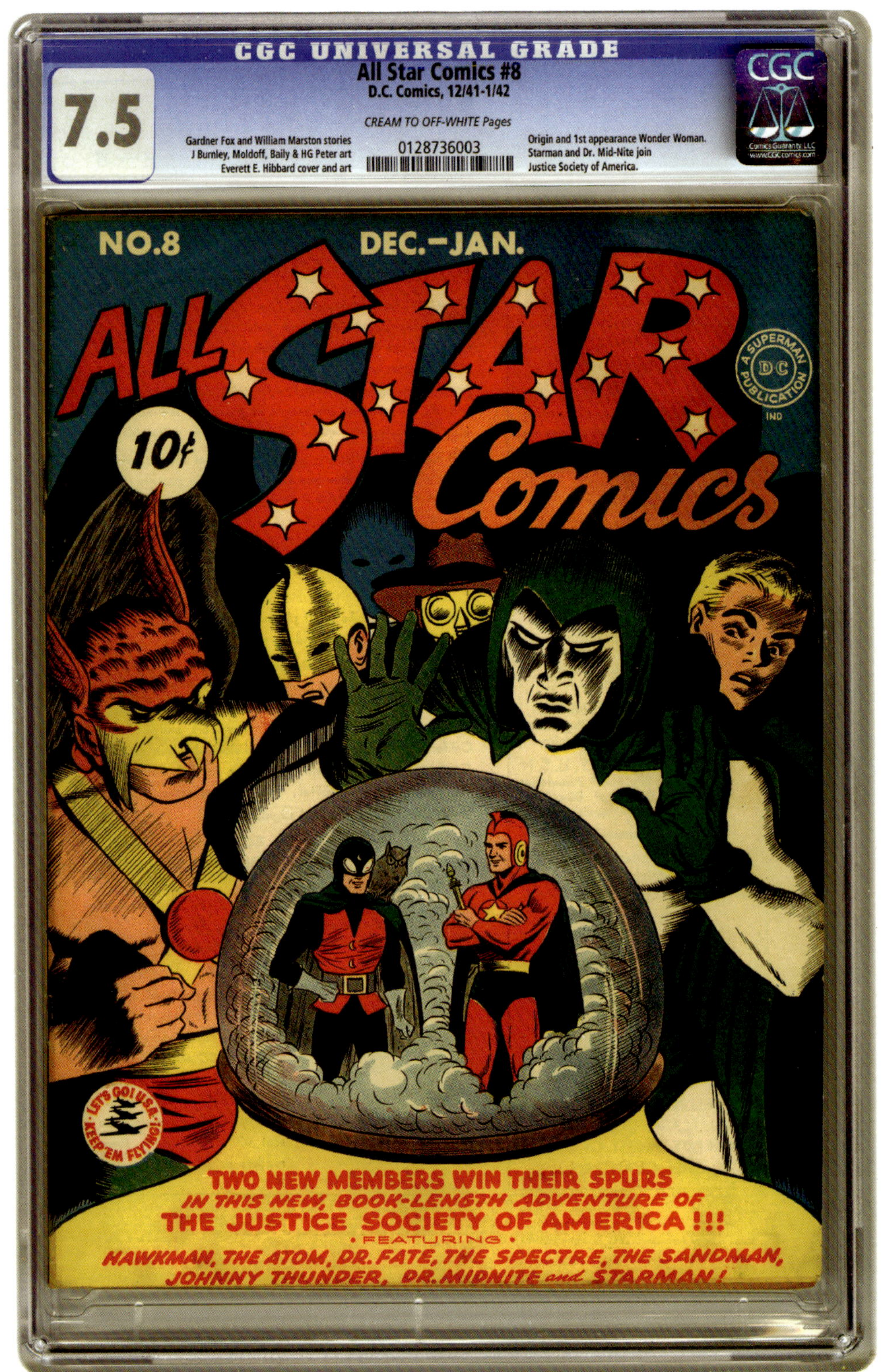

3008 All Star Comics #8 (DC, 1942) CGC VF- 7.5 Cream to off-white pages. The cover scene by artist E. E. Hibbard is seared into most serious Golden Age comic collectors' brains; this is truly one of the most important issues ever, and for multiple reasons. Foremost are the origin and first appearance of Wonder Woman, prime reasons this issue ranks 22nd in Overstreet's listing of the Top Golden Age Books. Other features include Starman and Dr. Mid-Nite becoming members of the JSA, Dr. Fate donning a new costume, and appearances by Shiera and Hop Harrigan. At VF- 7.5, our copy compares favorably to the finest copy CGC has certified to date, which registers VF+ 8.5. This is the finest copy of issue #8 that we have ever offered. Interior art is by Jack Burnley, Sheldon Moldoff, Bernard Baily, and H. G. Peter. Overstreet 2005 VF 8.0 value = $21,600. CGC census 7/05: 2 in 7.5, 2 higher. *From the Aviator Collection.*

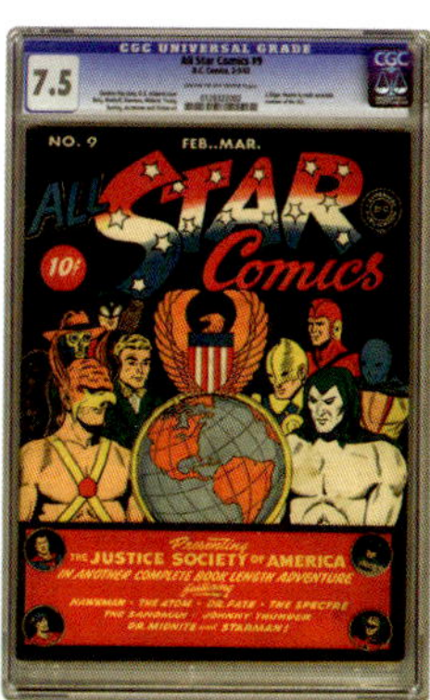

3009 All Star Comics #9 (DC, 1942) CGC VF- 7.5 Cream to off-white pages. J. Edgar Hoover is made an associate member of the JSA in this issue, deciding upon a traditional male dress suit over his more frilly suit dress for the occasion. E. E. Hibbard cover with Hibbard, Bernard Baily, Howard Sherman, Sheldon Moldoff, and Jack Burnley providing interior art. Overstreet 2005 VF 8.0 value = $1,825. CGC census 7/05: 4 in 7.5, 3 higher. *From the Aviator Collection.*

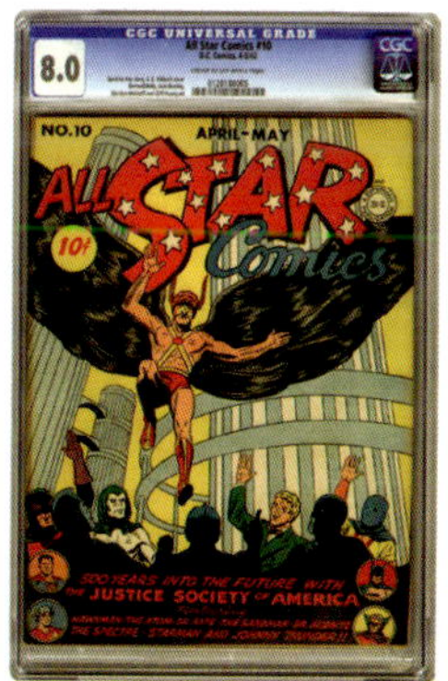

3010 All Star Comics #10 (DC, 1942) CGC VF 8.0 Cream to off-white pages. We've only offered a few copies of this issue previously, and this is one of the nicest you'll find. Only two copies have earned higher grades from CGC to date, just one of which graded higher than VF+ 8.5. The cover is by E. E. Hibbard, with interior art by Bernard Baily, Jack Burnley, and Sheldon Moldoff. Overstreet 2005 VF 8.0 value = $1,825. CGC census 7/05: 2 in 8.0, 2 higher.

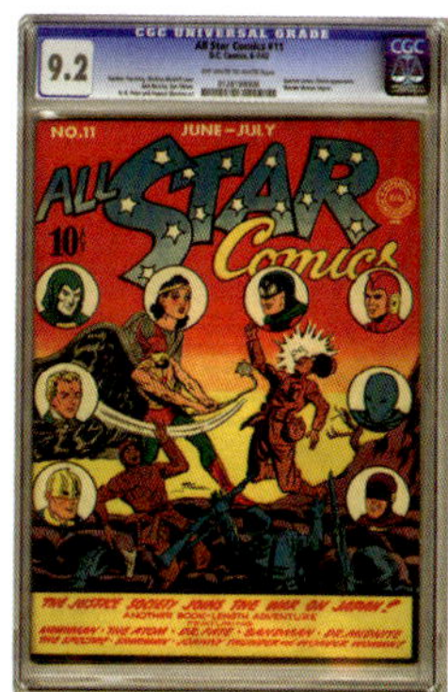

3011 All Star Comics #11 (DC, 1942) CGC NM- 9.2 Off-white to white pages. Stunning cover colors on this copy, which is close to the finest specimen CGC has certified yet for #11. Sheldon Moldoff created the nifty cover, which features an image of Wonder Woman for the first time in this title. Her feature also begins in this issue, which also has appearances by Shiera and the Spectre. Interior artists include Jack Burnley, H. G. Peter, and Howard Sherman. Overstreet 2005 NM- 9.2 value = $3,800. CGC census 7/05: 1 in 9.2, 2 higher. *From the Aviator Collection.*

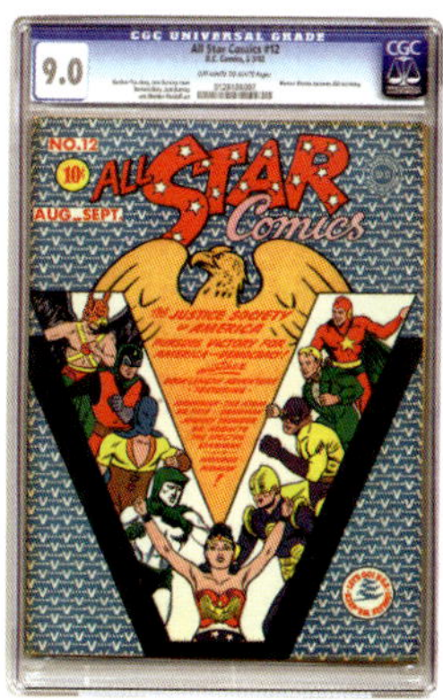

3012 All Star Comics #12 (DC, 1942) CGC VF/NM 9.0 Off-white to white pages. Only three copies of this issue have been graded higher by CGC as of this writing. This Justice Society tale has Wonder Woman being appointed the official secretary of the JSA and an honorary member of the group. The issue has a Jack Burnley cover and interior art by Burnley, Sheldon Moldoff, and Bernard Baily. Overstreet 2005 VF/NM 9.0 value = $2,519; NM- 9.2 value = $3,400. CGC census 7/05: 1 in 9.0, 3 higher. *From the Aviator Collection.*

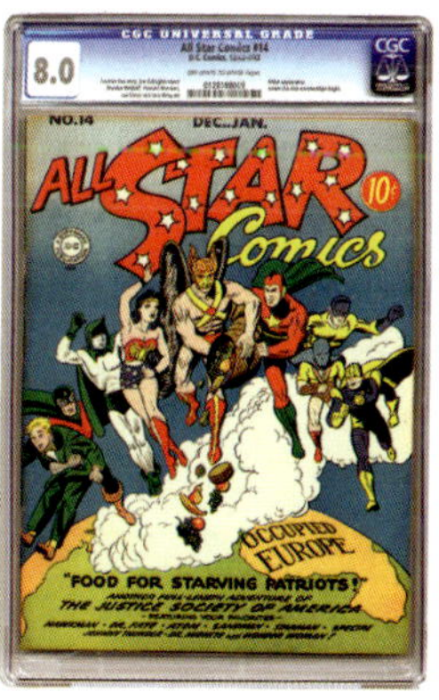

3013 All Star Comics #14 (DC, 1942) CGC VF 8.0 Off-white to white pages. The Justice Society sprang into humanitarian action in this issue, delivering food to the starving patriots in occupied Europe. Doctor Fate even visits a German concentration camp in this story, which is dated December 1942. Adolf Hitler appears in both the Doctor Fate and Sandman chapters. This was the first **All-Star** issue to have Simon and Kirby art — they produced the Sandman chapter, which also features the first appearance in this title of Sandy the Golden Boy. Sheldon Moldoff is among the issue's other artists; the book's cover is by Joe Gallagher. Overstreet 2005 VF 8.0 value = $1,563. CGC census 7/05: 1 in 8.0, 3 higher. *From the Aviator Collection.*

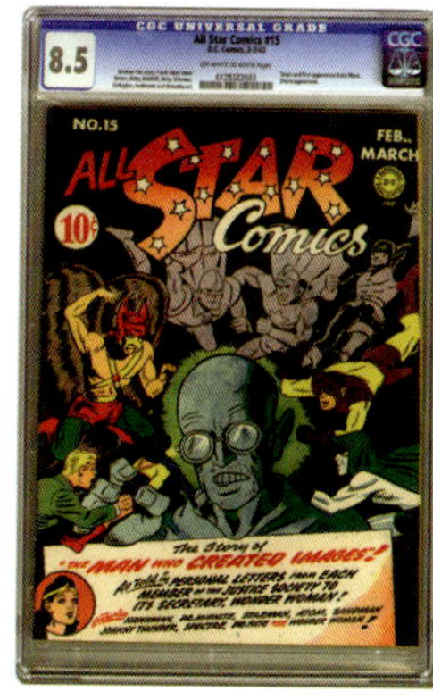

3014 All Star Comics #15 (DC, 1943) CGC VF+ 8.5 Off-white to white pages. This is one of the nicest known copies of one of the Golden Age's most desired titles. Highlights include the origin and first appearance of Brain Wave, and an appearance of Shiera. Artists include Frank Harry on the cover, with Simon and Kirby, Sheldon Moldoff, Bernard Baily, and Howard Sherman contributing interior art. Overstreet 2005 VF 8.0 value = $1,538; VF/NM 9.0 value = $2,369. CGC census 7/05: 2 in 8.5, 2 higher. *From the Aviator Collection.*

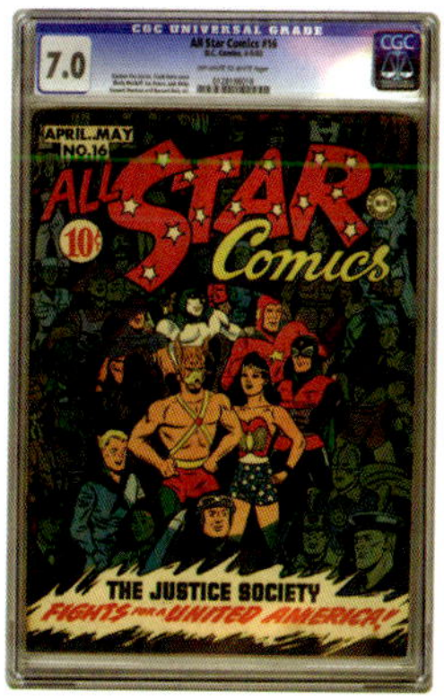

3015 All Star Comics #16 (DC, 1943) CGC FN/VF 7.0 Off-white to white pages. Frank Harry cover. Sheldon Moldoff, Joe Simon, Jack Kirby, Bernard Baily, and Howard Sherman art. Overstreet 2005 FN 6.0 value = $362; VF 8.0 value = $543. CGC census 7/05: 1 in 7.0, 3 higher. *From the Aviator Collection.*

3016 All Star Comics #24 (DC, 1945) CGC GD/VG 3.0 Off-white to white pages. Imaginative wartime cover (a Hitler cover) by Joe Gallagher who also provides story art, along with Martin Naydel and Joe Kubert. Flash and Green Lantern cameo. Wildcat and Mr. Terrific (his only) appearances. Overstreet 2005 GD 2.0 value = $158; VG 4.0 value = $316. CGC census 7/05: 1 in 3.0, 10 higher. *From the Aviator Collection.*

3017 All Star Comics #31 (DC, 1946) CGC VG 4.0 Cream to off-white pages. Martin Naydel cover. Naydel, Irwin Hasen, and Paul Reinman art. Overstreet 2005 VG 4.0 value = $242. CGC census 7/05: 3 in 4.0, 17 higher. *From the Aviator Collection.*

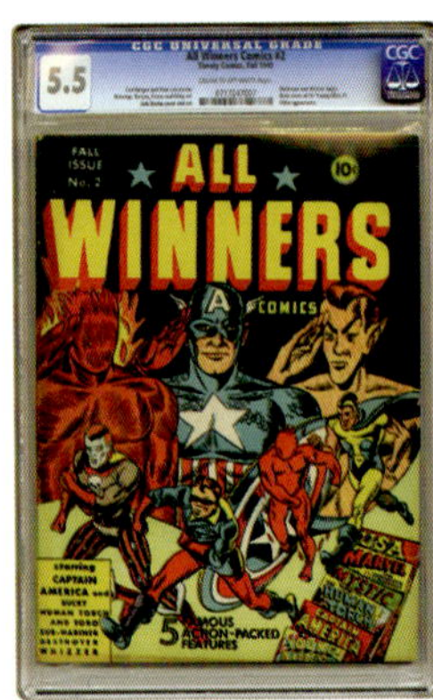

3018 All Winners Comics #2 (Timely, 1941) CGC FN- 5.5 Cream to off-white pages. Top heroes Human Torch, Captain America, and Sub-Mariner are joined by newcomers the Destroyer (from the pages of **Mystic Comics**) and the Whizzer (from **USA Comics**) here, as seen on the cover by Jack Binder. The impressive lineup of interior artists is headlined by Simon and Kirby (drawing their creation Captain America), Paul Reinman, and Carl Burgos, as well as Binder, whose Destroyer story has appearances by Hitler and fellow nefarious Nazi Rudolf Hess. Even the back cover is interesting, it's a full-page ad for **Young Allies** #1. Overstreet 2005 FN 6.0 value = $1,452. CGC census 9/05: 1 in 5.5, 4 higher. *From the Aviator Collection.*

3019 All Winners Comics #7 (Timely, 1942) CGC FN+ 6.5 Cream to off-white pages. Interesting cover by Alex Schomburg has the mighty Timely superheroes kicking Japanese *and* Nazi butt simultaneously. Oh, well, as great as Mr. Schomburg was, he never claimed to be historically accurate! Nice copy becomes even nicer when one reviews CGC's current census, which shows only three unrestored copies certified to date. Overstreet 2005 FN 6.0 value = $576; VF 8.0 value = $1,200. CGC census 7/05: 1 in 6.5, 1 higher. *From the Aviator Collection.*

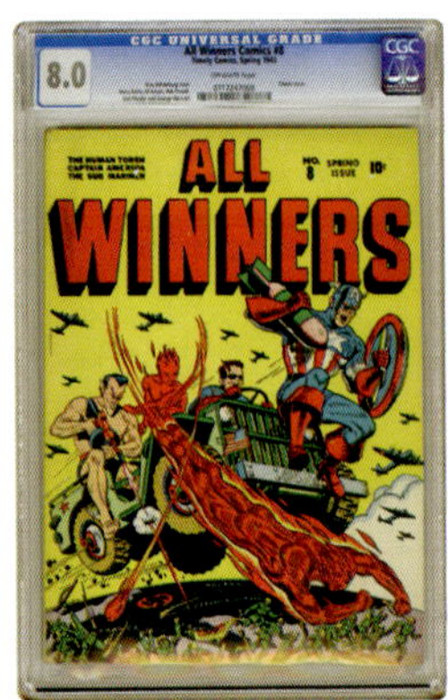

3020 All Winners Comics #8 (Timely, 1943) CGC VF 8.0 Off-white pages. Only one copy tops this one in CGC's latest census report, and that one's just a half-grade higher at 8.5! The issue's rousing war cover is the work of Alex Schomburg. Inside the comic, Timely's "Big Three" of Captain America, Sub-Mariner, and Human Torch (appearing in separate stories) are joined by the Whizzer and the Destroyer. Overstreet 2005 VF 8.0 value = $1,200. CGC census 9/05: 1 in 8.0, 1 higher.

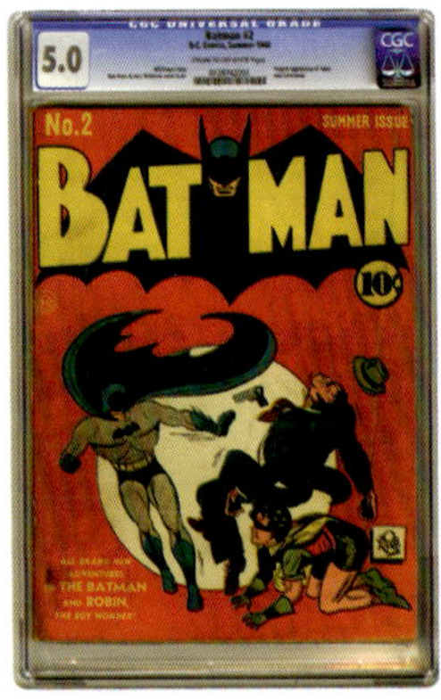

3021 Batman #2 (DC, 1940) CGC VG/FN 5.0 Cream to off-white pages. The second issue of the Caped Crusader's own title also occasions the second appearance of the Joker and Catwoman. Bob Kane and Jerry Robinson combine on both the cover and interior art for the definitive interpretation of the Golden Age Batman. Overstreet 2005 VG 4.0 value = $2,470; FN 6.0 value = $3,705. CGC census 7/05: 2 in 5.0, 6 higher. *From the Aviator Collection.*

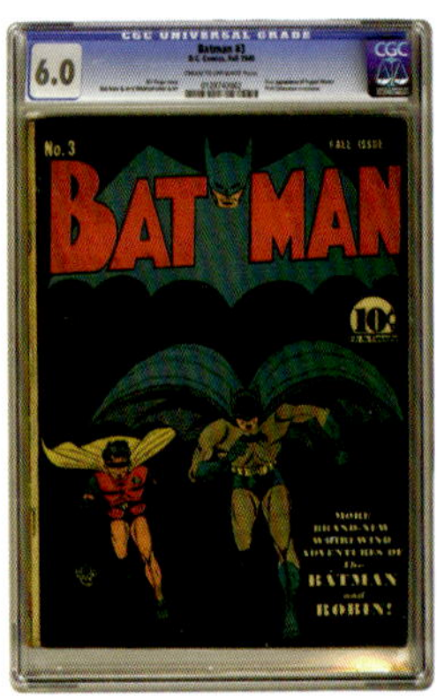

3022 Batman #3 (DC, 1940) CGC FN 6.0 Cream to off-white pages. Wonderful cover is deemed a "classic" by Overstreet, who attributes the art to Bob Kane and Sheldon Moldoff. CGC suggests Jerry Robinson is Kane's inker, and that the pair also did the interior art for this issue. The third appearance of Catwoman finds her in costume for the first time, and that makes her comic's first costumed villainess. Another first is the appearance of Puppet Master. Overstreet 2005 FN 6.0 value = $2,517. CGC census 7/05: 2 in 6.0, 20 higher. *From the Aviator Collection.*

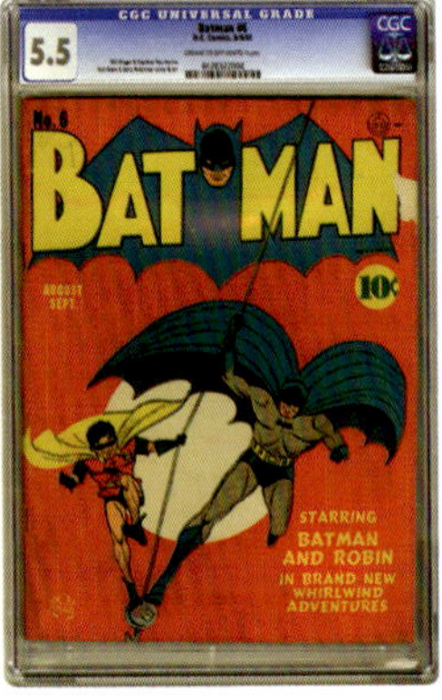

3023 Batman #6 (DC, 1941) CGC FN- 5.5 Cream to off-white pages. Co-creator Bob Kane gets assistance from Jerry Robinson on this brilliant cover, as well as on the interior art for this issue. Overstreet 2005 FN 6.0 value = $1,269. CGC census 7/05: 5 in 5.5, 30 higher. *From the Aviator Collection.*

3024 Batman #7 (DC, 1941) CGC VF 8.0 Off-white pages. The early issues of the title were characterized by some of the most dynamic covers in the entire run. This one's by Bob Kane, who also provided interior art, along with Jerry Robinson and George Roussos. The Joker makes his fourth appearance in seven issues. This is about as nice a copy as you'll find. Although a few copies rank ahead of our offering in CGC's current census, the highest grade yet assigned is a not-much-better VF/NM 9.0. Overstreet 2005 VF 8.0 value = $2,936. CGC census 7/05: 4 in 8.0, 6 higher. *From the Aviator Collection.*

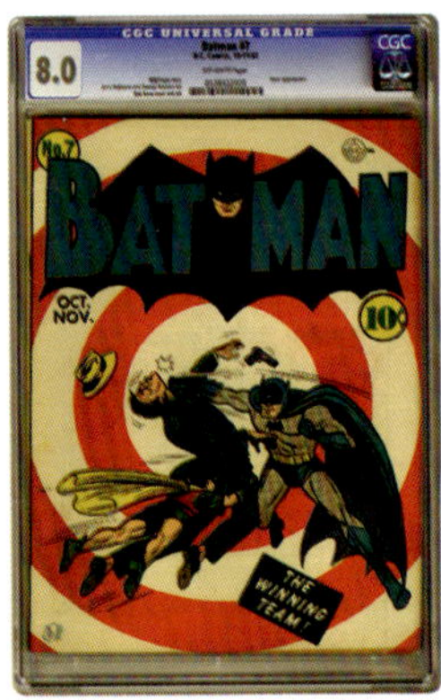

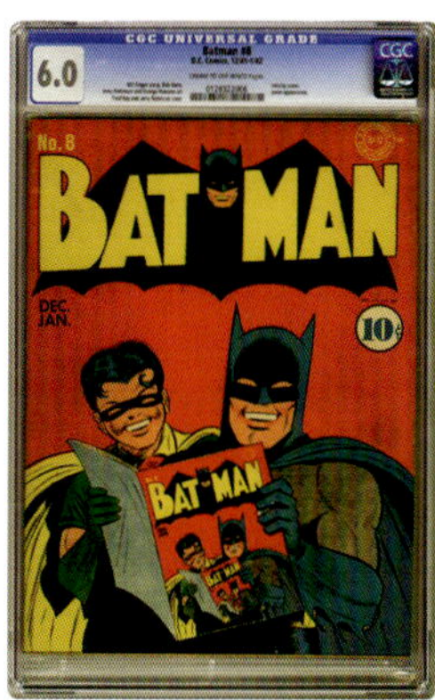

3025 Batman #8 (DC, 1942) CGC FN 6.0 Cream to off-white pages. Fred Ray does his first cover for this title, and it's an infinity cover... cover... cov... Ray, Jerry Robinson, Bob Kane, and George Roussos were the artists on the interior, where the Joker makes his usual (for the first several issues anyway) appearance. Overstreet 2005 FN 6.0 value = $1,077. CGC census 7/05: 3 in 6.0, 14 higher. *From the Aviator Collection.*

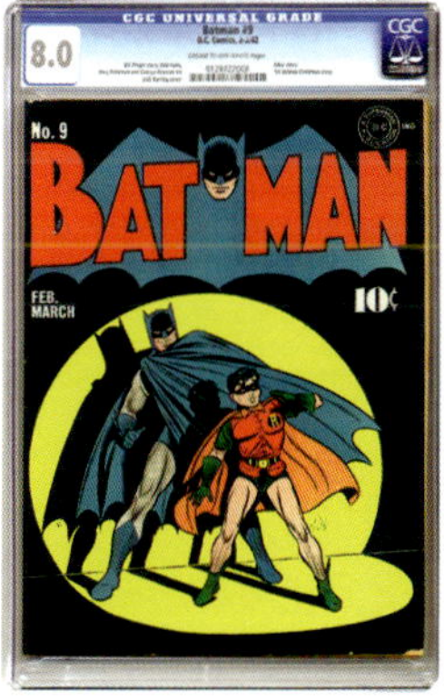

3026 Batman #9 (DC, 1942) CGC VF 8.0 Cream to off-white pages. One of the best-known Batman covers of all is this one here by Jack Burnley! Inside the issue, the Joker busts out of jail and wastes no time cooking up a money-laundering scheme which only the Dynamic Duo can (try to) foil. This issue also has the very first Batman Christmas story. The interior artists include Jerry Robinson and George Roussos. Overstreet 2005 VF 8.0 value = $2,243. CGC census 7/05: 6 in 8.0, 4 higher. *From the Aviator Collection.*

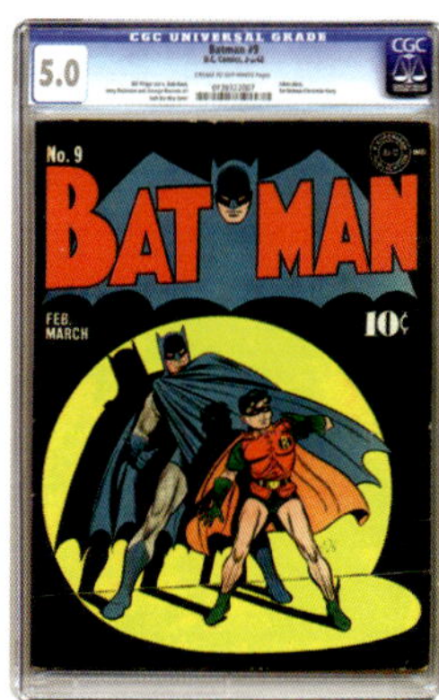

3027 Batman #9 (DC, 1942) CGC VG/FN 5.0 Cream to off-white pages. A classic cover by Jack Burnley leads off this issue; inside there's a Joker appearance as well as the first Batman Christmas story. Overstreet 2005 VG 4.0 value = $690; FN 6.0 value = $1,035. CGC census 7/05: 3 in 5.0, 22 higher. *From the Aviator Collection.*

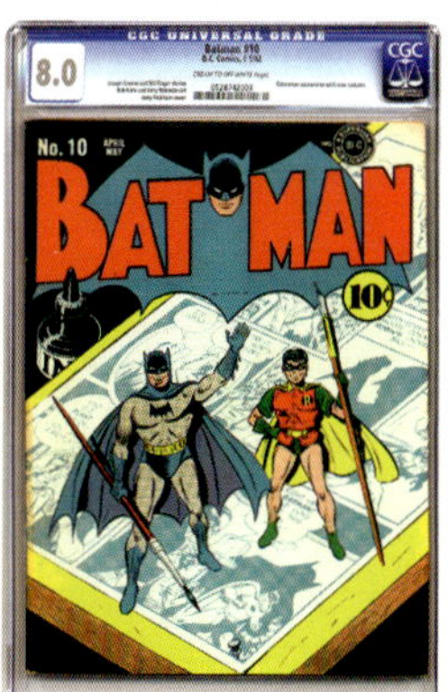

3028 Batman #10 (DC, 1942) CGC VF 8.0 Cream to off-white pages. Note that the highest grade yet assigned for this issue is just a half-grade higher at 8.5, so you'll be hard-pressed to find a nicer one than our offering here.In the issue, Catwoman appears sporting a new costume, but otherwise she hasn't changed — when she's caught, she gives Batman a big kiss, and what do you know, he lets her get away ... *again*! Overstreet 2005 VF 8.0 value = $2,243. CGC census 7/05: 3 in 8.0, 2 higher. *From the Aviator Collection.*

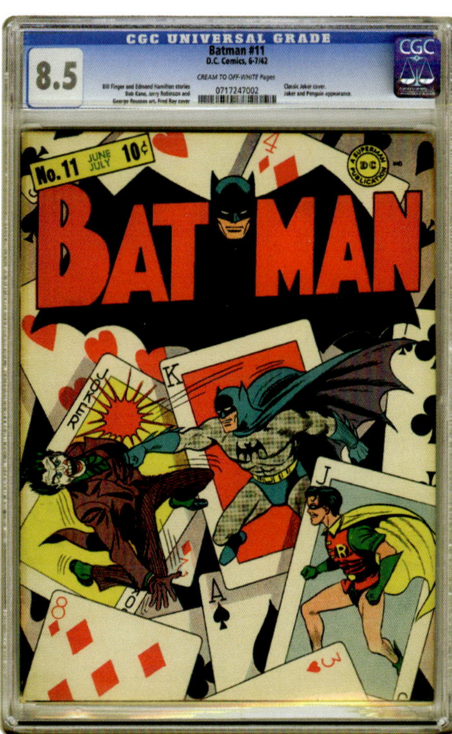

3029 Batman #11 (DC, 1942) CGC VF+ 8.5 Cream to off-white pages. The fact that the original art for this Fred Ray-Jerry Robinson cover recently sold at auction for a record price is evidence of how strongly collectors feel about this great image. The interior of the issue is equally memorable — it's got appearances by both the Joker and the Penguin. Overstreet 2005 VF 8.0 value = $4,739; VF/NM 9.0 value = $7,620. CGC census 9/05: 2 in 8.5, 4 higher.

3030 Batman #12 (DC, 1942) CGC VF 8.0 Cream to off-white pages. Jerry Robinson drew this issue's war bonds cover as well as contributing interior art. Jack Burnley and Bob Kane pitched in as well. The featured villain is none other than the Joker. Overstreet 2005 VF 8.0 value = $1,892. CGC census 9/05: 1 in 8.0, 3 higher. *From the Aviator Collection.*

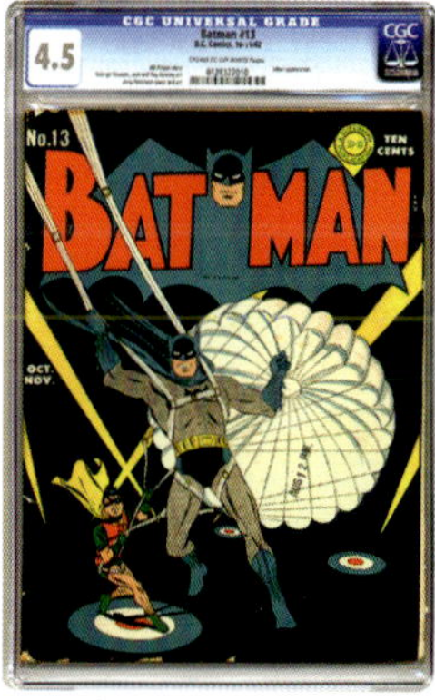

3031 Batman #13 (DC, 1942) CGC VG+ 4.5 Cream to off-white pages. The Joker has a new scheme to make loads of cash, and Batman readily gives him a check for $100,000! Has the Caped Crusader gone nuts? Find out in this issue, which has a Jerry Robinson cover and interior art by Robinson, George Roussos, Jack Burnley, and Ray Burnley. Overstreet 2005 VG 4.0 value = $600. CGC census 7/05: 3 in 4.5, 19 higher. *From the Aviator Collection.*

3032 Batman #15 (DC, 1943) CGC FN/VF 7.0 Off-white to white pages. Any comics fan could tell you that Batman never uses a gun... well, that's in *peacetime*. When the fate of the free world was at stake, he even manned a machine gun here on Jack Burnley's war cover! Inside the comic there's another major point of interest, as Catwoman appears in a new costume. The interior art is by Bob Kane, Jerry Robinson, and George Roussos. Overstreet 2005 FN 6.0 value = $900; VF 8.0 value = $1,892. CGC census 9/05: 4 in 7.0, 7 higher.

3033 Batman #28 (DC, 1945) CGC VG/FN 5.0 Off-white to white pages. Jack Burnley cover, with Jerry Robinson art. Joker appearance. Overstreet 2005 VG 4.0 value = $308; FN 6.0 value = $462. CGC census 7/05: 4 in 5.0, 33 higher. *From the Aviator Collection. From the Aviator Collection.*

3034 Batman #30 (DC, 1945) CGC VG- 3.5 Cream to off-white pages. Penguin story. Dick Sprang cover. Sprang, Jerry Robinson, and George Roussos art. Overstreet 2005 VG 4.0 value = $308. CGC census 7/05: 3 in 3.5, 27 higher. *From the Aviator Collection.*

3035 Batman #31 (DC, 1945) CGC FN- 5.5 Off-white to white pages. First appearance of Punch and Judy. Dick Sprang cover. Jerry Robinson and George Roussos art. Overstreet 2005 FN 6.0 value = $342. CGC census 7/05: 4 in 5.5, 20 higher. *From the Aviator Collection.*

3036 Batman #34 (DC, 1946) CGC VG/FN 5.0 Cream to off-white pages. Solid copy of an issue that features a Dick Sprang cover and interior art by Sprang and Jerry Robinson. Overstreet 2005 VG 4.0 value = $228; FN 6.0 value = $342. CGC census 9/05: 3 in 5.0, 20 higher. *From the Aviator Collection.*

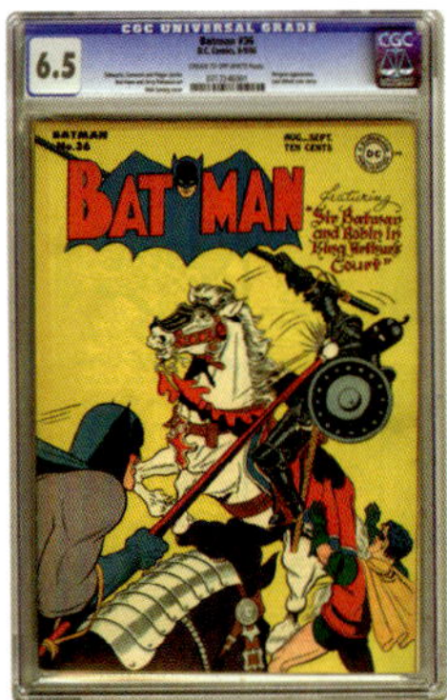

3037 Batman #36 (DC, 1946) CGC FN+ 6.5 Cream to off-white pages. Why is the Penguin *trying* to get sent to jail? That sort of behavior makes Batman pret-ty suspicious, as well he should be! In addition to tangling with the Man of a Thousand Umbrellas in the issue, Batman and Robin visit Prof. Carter Nichols and are sent back in time to King Arthur's day! There's also the last in the series of Alfred solo stories. The issue has a Dick Sprang cover, with interior art by Bob Kane, Jerry Robinson, and Ray Burnley. Overstreet 2005 FN 6.0 value = $342; VF 8.0 value = $713. CGC census 8/05: 2 in 6.5, 23 higher. *From the Aviator Collection.*

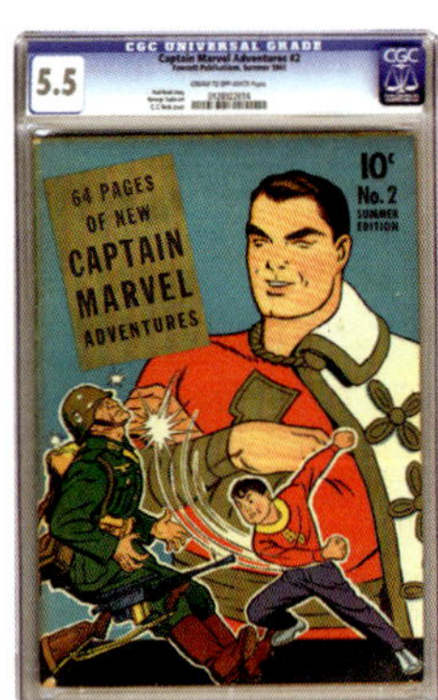

3038 Captain Marvel Adventures #2 (Fawcett, 1941) CGC FN- 5.5 Cream to off-white pages. Here's a tough find! Currently CGC has awarded a higher grade to just two other copies of #2, only one of which scored higher than FN 6.0 and neither above VF 8.0! C. C. Beck created a memorable cover, and George Tuska provided interior art. Overstreet 2005 FN 6.0 value = $1,269. CGC census 9/05: 1 in 5.5, 2 higher.

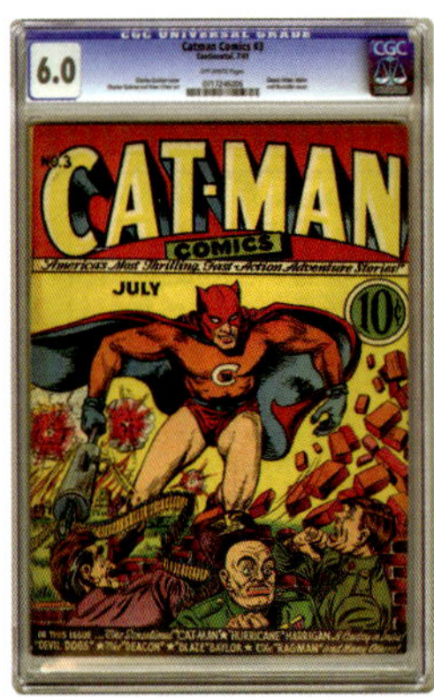

3039 Catman Comics #3 (Holyoke Publications, 1941) CGC FN 6.0 Off-white pages. Stalin, Mussolini, and Hitler, and Catman about to give 'em a whuppin'... that's the stuff of which great covers are made! Note that this one's one of the better copies available — the highest-graded one in CGC's current census report is a 7.0. A couple of details for accuracy's sake: this issue is also known as V1#8, and while the CGC slab lists the publisher as Continental, the company was still known as Holyoke at the time of this issue's publication. Overstreet 2005 FN 6.0 value = $351. CGC census 8/05: 1 in 6.0, 2 higher. *From the Aviator Collection.*

3040 Catman Comics #31 (Continental, 1946) CGC VG+ 4.5 Cream to off-white pages. L. B. Cole cover. Rudy Palais art. Second-to-last issue of the series. CGC notes, "10-inch tear on 5th page." Overstreet 2005 VG 4.0 value = $174. CGC census 8/05: 2 in 4.5, 12 higher. *From the Aviator Collection.*

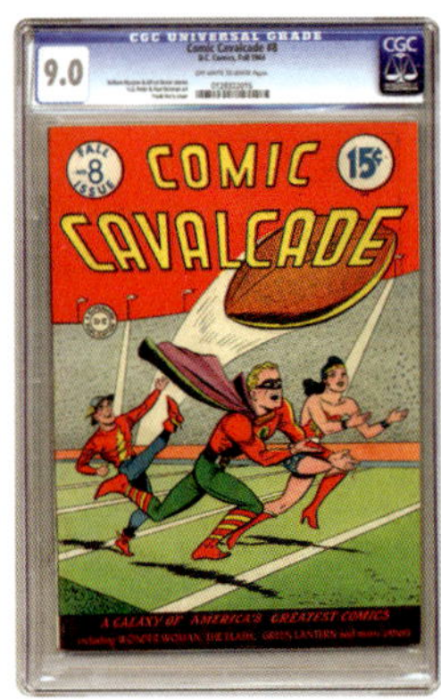

3041 Comic Cavalcade #8 (DC, 1944) CGC VF/NM 9.0 Off-white to white pages. Gorgeous copy of a book that may be rarer than its Gerber "4" would indicate. After all, CGC has certified just six unrestored copies to date. This one currently ranks as the second highest-graded. Frank Harry cover, with interior art by H. G. Peter and Paul Reinman. Overstreet 2005 VF/NM 9.0 value = $1,185; NM- 9.2 value = $1,600. CGC census 9/05: 1 in 9.0, 1 higher. *From the Aviator Collection.*

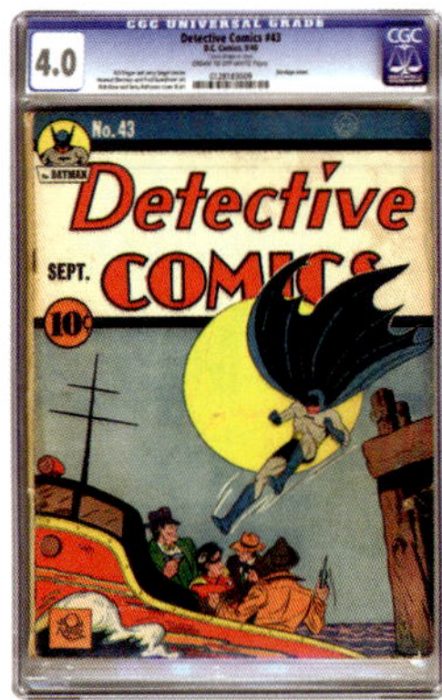

3042 Detective Comics #43 (DC, 1940) CGC VG 4.0 Cream to off-white pages. Here's a copy of an issue we have offered just a few times since our comic auctions began in 2001. The Robin-in-bondage cover is by Bob Kane and Jerry Robinson. Interior art was done by the same pair and by Fred Guardineer and Howard Sherman. Overstreet 2005 VG 4.0 value = $500. CGC census 9/05: 1 in 4.0, 10 higher. *From the Aviator Collection.*

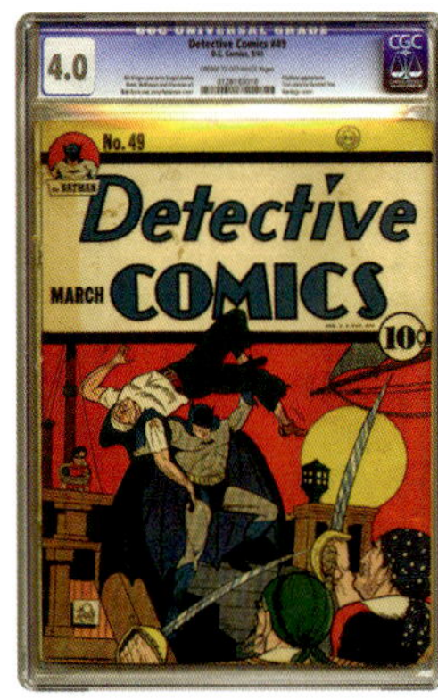

3043 Detective Comics #49 (DC, 1941) CGC VG 4.0 Cream to off-white pages. Clayface appears in this issue, which sports a cover (Robin in a typical rope-bound state) from Batman co-creator Bob Kane and Jerry Robinson, who also provided interior art. Howard Sherman also did some of the interior artwork for this issue. Overstreet 2005 VG 4.0 value = $462. CGC census 9/05: 1 in 4.0, 5 higher.

3044 Detective Comics #98 (DC, 1945) CGC FN+ 6.5 Cream to off-white pages. Dick Sprang cover. Sprang, George Roussos, and Louis Cazeneuve art. Overstreet 2005 FN 6.0 value = $231; VF 8.0 value = $481. CGC census 8/05: 1 in 6.5, 11 higher. *From the Aviator Collection.*

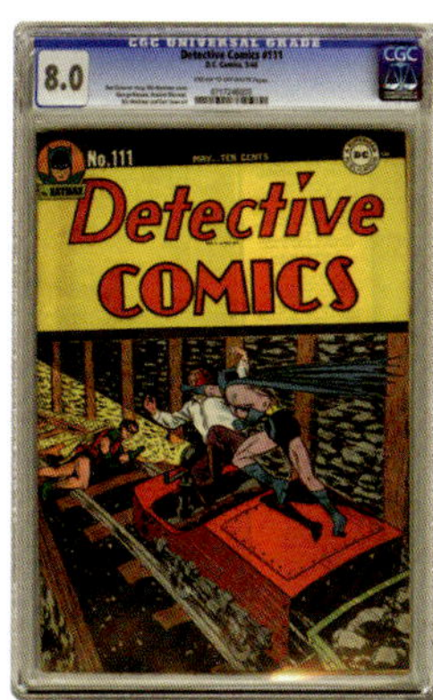

3045 Detective Comics #111 (DC, 1946) CGC VF 8.0 Cream to off-white pages. This cover's scene of mine shaft peril is a lead-in to Batman and Robin's visit to "Coaltown U.S.A.," in which they show a greedy mine owner the error of his ways. Win Mortimer drew the Dynamic Duo both on the cover and inside the comic. Backup features include Air Wave (with George Roussos art), the Boy Commandos (with Curt Swan art), and long-running Golden Age gumshoe Slam Bradley. Overstreet 2005 VF 8.0 value = $456. CGC census 8/05: 8 in 8.0, 11 higher. *From the Aviator Collection.*

3046 Detective Comics #116 (DC, 1946) CGC FN+ 6.5 Cream to off-white pages. Robin Hood appearance. Win Mortimer cover. Mortimer and Curt Swan art. Overstreet 2005 FN 6.0 value = $219; VF 8.0 value = $456. CGC census 8/05: 1 in 6.5, 7 higher. *From the Aviator Collection.*

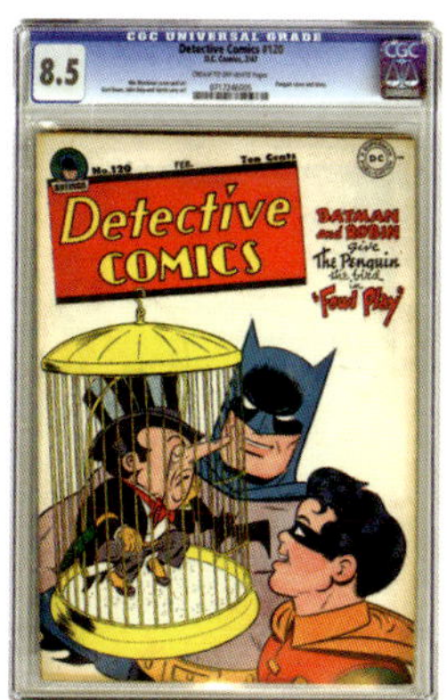

3047 Detective Comics #120 (DC, 1947) CGC VF+ 8.5 Cream to off-white pages. Overstreet says that this issue is "rare above fine" because of its white cover; well, here's a *VF+* copy just for you! It's no wonder most surviving copies have been sullied by multiple reads: in addition to the cover story with a Penguin appearance drawn by Win Mortimer (who also drew the cover), there's a Boy Commandos story with Curt Swan art as well as John Daly's rendition of the gumshoe who had been solving crimes since **Detective** #1, Slam Bradley. Overstreet 2005 VF 8.0 value = $1,056; VF/NM 9.0 value = $1,628. CGC census 8/05: 1 in 8.5, 2 higher.

3048 Detective Comics #122 (DC, 1947) CGC VG- 3.5 Cream to off-white pages. Robin finds another way to get hurt on this Bob Kane cover - scratching at the hands of Catwoman, who makes her first cover appearance. Interior art comes from Kane, Curt Swan, and Howard Sherman. Overstreet 2005 VG 4.0 value = $284. CGC census 9/05: 2 in 3.5, 17 higher. *From the Aviator Collection.*

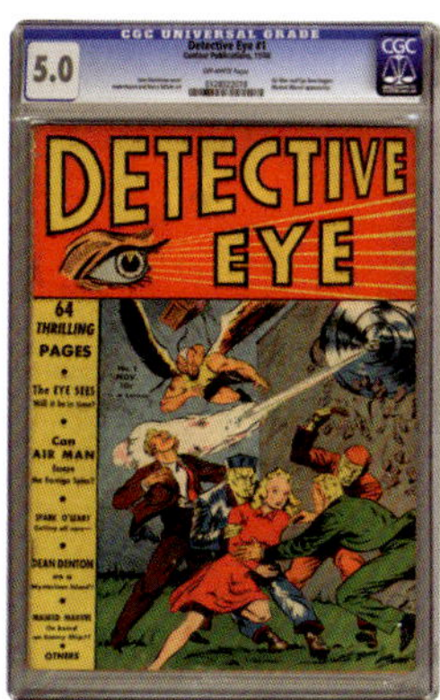

3049 Detective Eye #1 (Centaur, 1940) CGC VG/FN 5.0 Off-white pages. If you're lying awake nights wondering what happened to the stars of Centaur's **Keen Detective Funnies**, well, they continued their careers in this short-lived title. This issue has cover art by Lew Glanzman (brother of Sam) and interior art by Irwin Hasen and Harry Sahle. Overstreet 2005 VG 4.0 value = $430; FN 6.0 value = $645. CGC census 7/05: 1 in 5.0, 5 higher. *From the Aviator Collection.*

3050 Doc Savage Comics #2 (Street & Smith, 1940) CGC GD/VG 3.0 Cream to off-white pages. Origin and first appearance of Ajax the Sun Man. CGC notes, "Large piece off margin of 23rd, 24th, 25th, 26th & 28th page." Overstreet 2005 GD 2.0 value = $192; VG 4.0 value = $384. CGC census 8/05: 1 in 3.0, 2 higher. *From the Aviator Collection.*

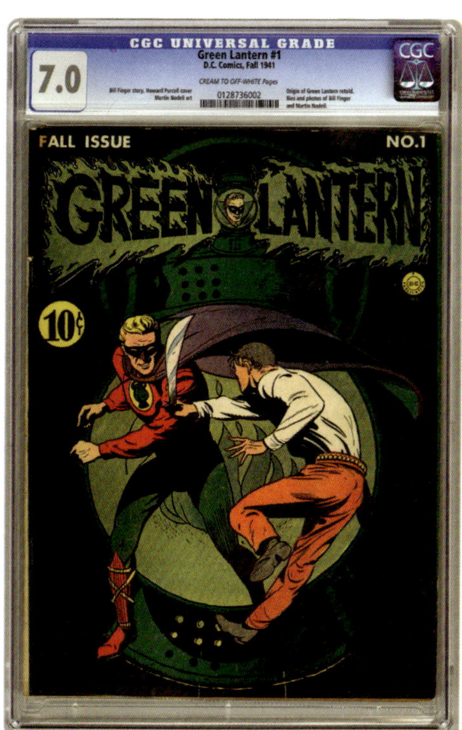

3051 Green Lantern #1 (DC, 1941) CGC FN/VF 7.0 Cream to off-white pages. Overstreet currently lists this issue in 16th place on its ranking of the most valuable comic books. It's the first issue of Green Lantern's solo title, which the character earned after his successful debut in **All-American Comics**. The origin of Alan Scott, the Golden Age bearer of the ring, is retold in this issue, which features a cover by Howard Purcell and interior art by GL's creator Martin Nodell. Overstreet 2005 FN 6.0 value = $8,925; VF 8.0 value = $23,800. CGC census 9/05: 5 in 7.0, 7 higher. *From the Aviator Collection.*

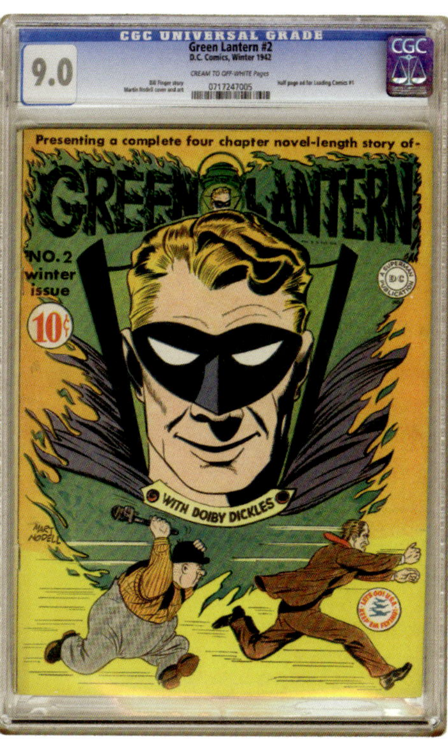

3052 Green Lantern #2 (DC, 1941) CGC VF/NM 9.0 Cream to off-white pages. It's the first book-length Green Lantern story! The hero's all smiles on the Martin Nodell cover, and why not — pal Doiby Dickles is wielding a mean monkey wrench. The interior art is also by Nodell, GL's creator. Overstreet 2005 VF/NM 9.0 value = $7,620; NM- 9.2 value = $10,500. CGC census 9/05: 1 in 9.0, none higher. *From the Aviator Collection.*

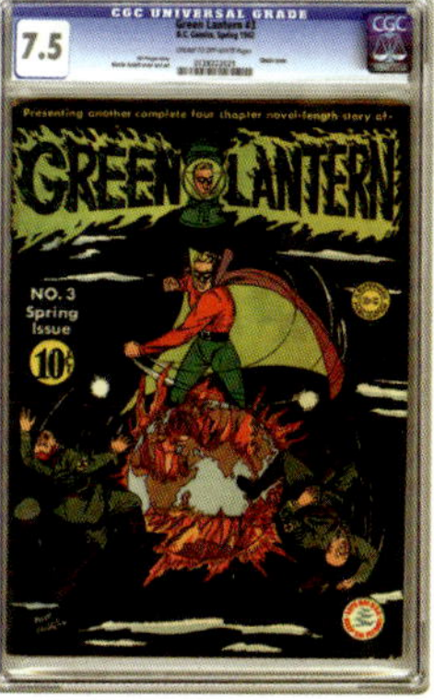

3053 Green Lantern #3 (DC, 1942) CGC VF- 7.5 Cream to off-white pages. Green Lantern doesn't even need his power ring to deal with some nefarious Nazis on this Martin Nodell cover, which earned Overstreet's "classic" designation. All of the interior art is also by Nodell, the character's creator. Overstreet 2005 VF 8.0 value = $3,388. CGC census 9/05: 1 in 7.5, 1 higher. *From the Aviator Collection.*

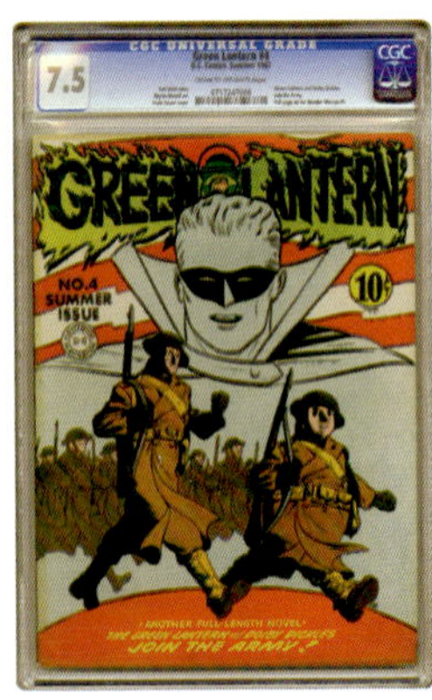

3054 Green Lantern #4 (DC, 1942) CGC VF- 7.5 Cream to off-white pages. Alan Scott, the original Green Lantern, was an upstanding guy who fought for what was right. So it's no surprise that Green Lantern joins the Army in this issue (with Doiby Dickles by his side as ever). The book has an Irwin Hasen cover and Martin Nodell interior art. Overstreet 2005 VF 8.0 value = $2,600. CGC census 9/05: 1 in 7.5, 2 higher. *From the Aviator Collection. From the Aviator Collection.*

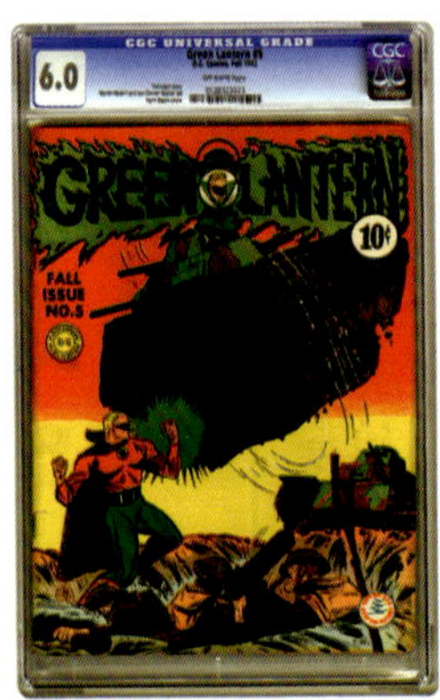

3055 Green Lantern #5 (DC, 1942) CGC FN 6.0 Off-white pages. Green Lantern says tanks but no tanks to a German armored assault on this rousing war cover by Irwin Hasen. The interior art is by Martin Nodell. Overstreet 2005 FN 6.0 value = $876. CGC census 9/05: 1 in 6.0, 2 higher.

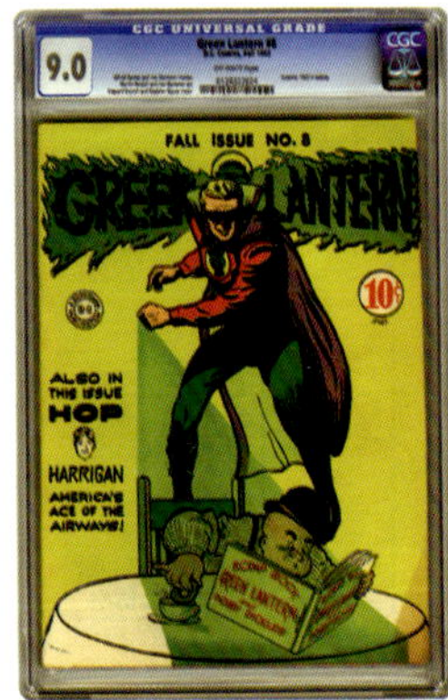

3056 Green Lantern #8 (DC, 1943) CGC VF/NM 9.0 Off-white pages. This Overstreet designated "classic" cover was created by Howard Purcell and Sheldon Mayer. Most issues of this title are elusive in high grade, and this beauty boasts the highest grade that CGC has awarded to date. Martin Nodell and Jon Blummer provided story art in this issue. Overstreet 2005 VF/NM 9.0 value = $2,222; NM- 9.2 value = $3,000. CGC census 7/05: 2 in 9.0, none higher. *From the Aviator Collection.*

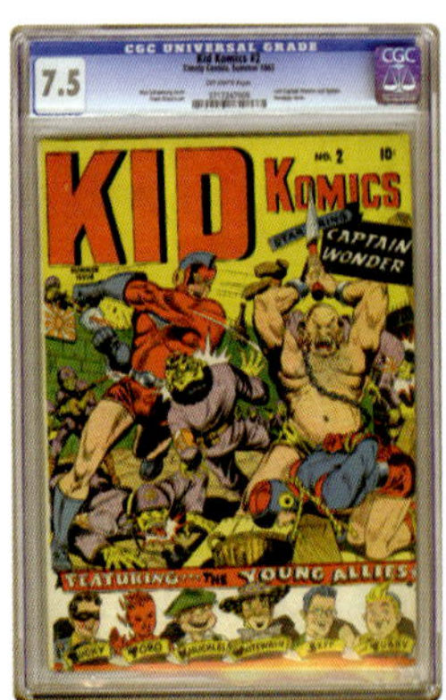

3057 Kid Komics #2 (Timely, 1943) CGC VF- 7.5 Off-white pages. While the Young Allies are the best-remembered characters of this series, top billing on this first issue went to Captain Wonder. It was the last appearance of the Captain, but at least he got a action-packed Alex Schomburg cover as a nice sendoff! The youngster in bondage is his sidekick, Tim. Also making his last appearance here was Subbie, a boy Sub-Mariner character. Overstreet 2005 VF 8.0 value = $1,225. CGC census 9/05: 2 in 7.5, 1 higher.

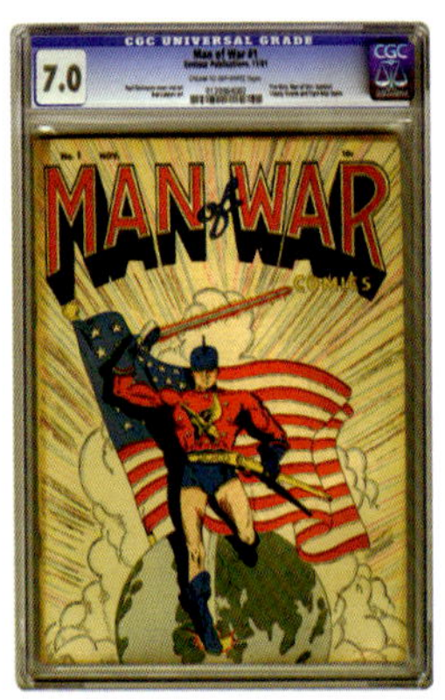

3058 Man of War #1 (Centaur, 1941) CGC FN/VF 7.0 Cream to off-white pages. Paul Gustavson's flag cover got this title off to a flying start — unfortunately, the run came to an end with the very next issue, and in fact, an Overstreet Guide of years past noted, "Conjecture is that Centaur itself expired with this book." This one's among the harder-to-find patriotic comics — it's a Gerber "scarce." Overstreet 2005 FN 6.0 value = $507; VF 8.0 value = $1,056. CGC census 9/05: 1 in 7.0, 4 higher. *From the Aviator Collection.*

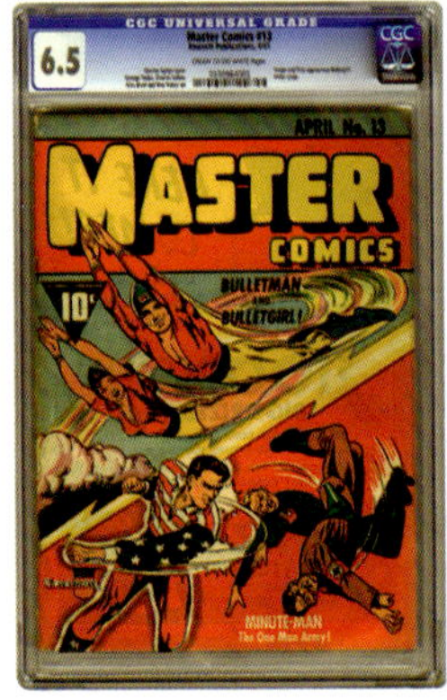

3059 Master Comics #13 (Fawcett, 1941) CGC FN+ 6.5 Cream to off-white pages. It's the first appearance of Bulletgirl, as Susan Kent, Bulletman's love interest, dons a costume for the first time. Her origin is also told in this issue — she was a police chief's daughter-turned-crime-fighter just like Batgirl a couple of decades later. Also worthy of mention is the cover showing Hitler getting punched out — at least as far as the cover date is concerned, this issue appeared just one month after **Captain America Comics** #1! That cover has been credited to Charles Sultan; contributing interior art are Mac Raboy and George Tuska among others. Overstreet 2005 FN 6.0 value = $606; VF 8.0 value = $1,263. CGC census 9/05: 1 in 6.5, 3 higher. *From the Aviator Collection.*

3060 Mystic Comics #5 (Timely, 1941) CGC VG+ 4.5 Off-white pages. Three new heroes, the Black Marvel, the Terror, and the Blazing Skull, made their debuts in this issue. The former stars on the Alex Schomburg cover. We also learn the Black Marvel's origin tale (Dan Lyons, who owes a debt to the Blackfoot Indians, passes their tribal tests to become their champion) courtesy of writer Stan Lee. Overstreet 2005 VG 4.0 value = $634. CGC census 7/05: 1 in 4.5, 4 higher. *From the Aviator Collection.*

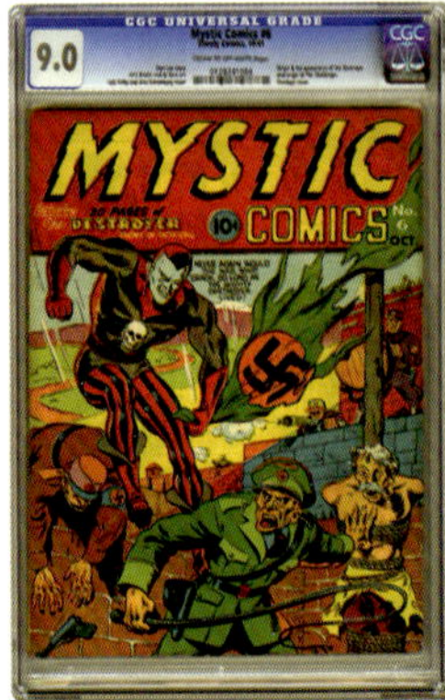

3061 Mystic Comics #6 (Timely, 1941) CGC VF/NM 9.0 Cream to off-white pages. There hasn't been a better copy of this issue certified by CGC as of this writing! This issue has the origin and first appearance of the Destroyer, who was the only one of the top Timely characters created by Stan Lee — he's been called Lee's most significant superhero creation prior to the Fantastic Four. Overstreet gives the cover the eyebrow-raising credit "Kirby/Schomburg"... if this is really a collaboration between those two, it's remarkable indeed. Overstreet 2005 VF/NM 9.0 value = $3,982; NM- 9.2 value = $5,500. CGC census 9/05: 2 in 9.0, none higher. *From the Aviator Collection.*

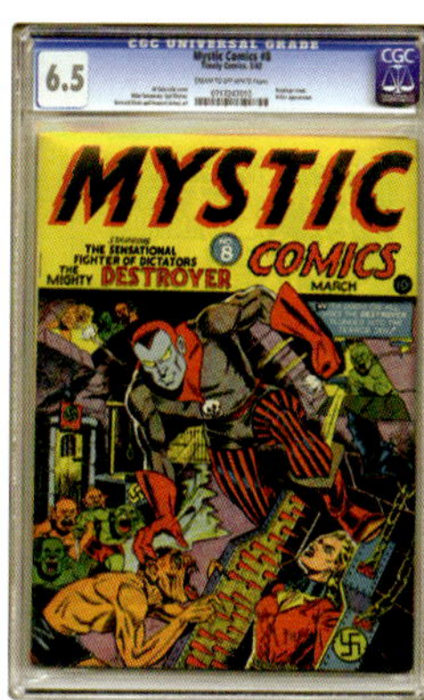

3062 Mystic Comics #8 (Timely, 1942) CGC FN+ 6.5 Cream to off-white pages. It's not apparent to us why this copy was only graded 6.5 — it's very nice-looking in our opinion, we say look at the scan and judge for yourself! Al Gabriele handled cover duties on the issue, and he wisely adhered pretty closely to the Alex Schomburg formula. There's a Hitler appearance inside the issue. Overstreet 2005 FN 6.0 value = $669; VF 8.0 value = $1,394. CGC census 9/05: 1 in 6.5, 6 higher. *From the Aviator Collection.*

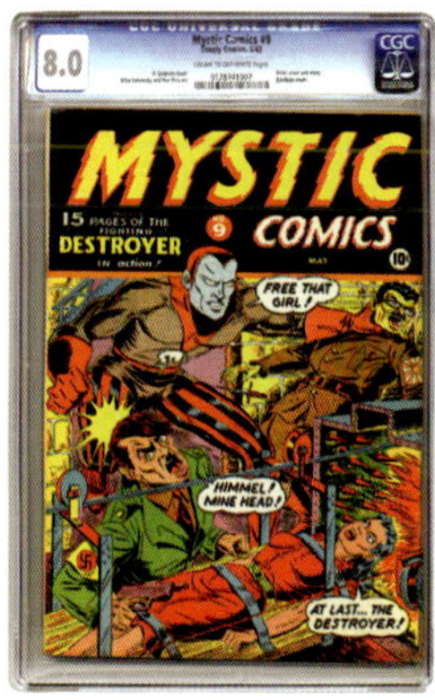

3063 Mystic Comics #9 (Timely, 1942) CGC VF 8.0 Cream to off-white pages. This frantic cover is not only a bondage scene, it features the villainy of Hitler himself — luckily the Nazi gets a well-deserved knock on the noggin courtesy of the Destroyer. This cover, drawn by Al Gabriele, is also notable for being one of very few Timely covers to have word balloons. The interior artists include Mike Sekowsky, who drew the Challenger story. This was the second to last issue of the title, and the last to feature characters the Black Marvel, Mystic, and Blazing Skull. Overstreet 2005 VF 8.0 value = $1,488. CGC census 7/05: 2 in 8.0, 1 higher. *From the Aviator Collection.*

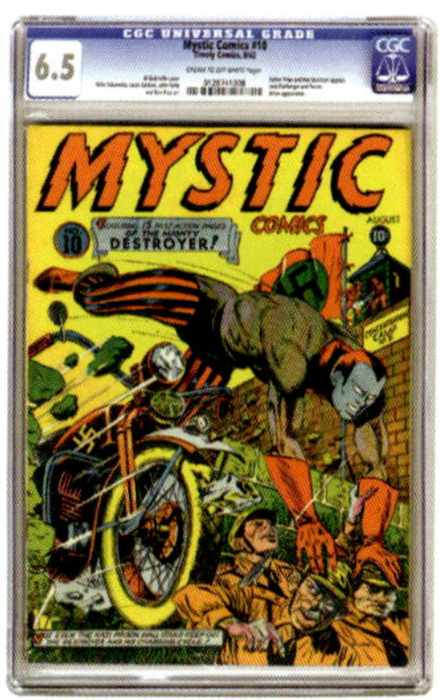

3064 Mystic Comics #10 (Timely, 1942) CGC FN+ 6.5 Cream to off-white pages. You gotta love this close-up of all-out Destroyer action, courtesy of Al Gabriele! Inside the issue, there's art by the like of Mike Sekowsky and Don Rico, an appearance of Red Skeleton (not to be confused with Red Skelton), and a Hitler appearance. Overstreet 2005 FN 6.0 value = $669; VF 8.0 value = $1,394. CGC census 7/05: 1 in 6.5, 2 higher. *From the Aviator Collection.*

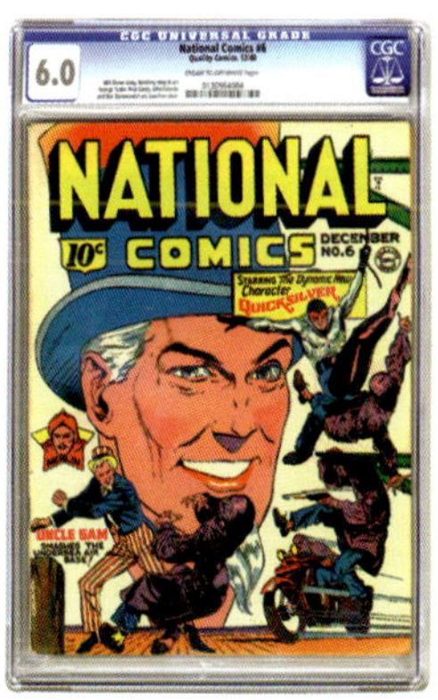

3065 National Comics #6 (Quality, 1940) CGC FN 6.0 Cream to off-white pages. Uncle Sam and speedster Quicksilver are just two of the stars of this issue. It sports a Lou Fine cover and has interior art by the likes of Nick Cardy, George Tuska, and Dan Zolnerowich. Overstreet 2005 FN 6.0 value = $387. CGC census 7/05: 1 in 6.0, 1 higher. *From the Aviator Collection.*

3066 No Lot

3067 No Lot

3068 Planet Comics #47 (Fiction House, 1947) CGC FN 6.0 Off-white pages. Lily Renee, George Evans, and Murphy Anderson art. Overstreet 2005 FN 6.0 value = $186. CGC census 8/05: 2 in 6.0, 10 higher. *From the Aviator Collection.*

3069 Planet Comics #48 (Fiction House, 1947) CGC FN+ 6.5 Cream to off-white pages. Robot cover. Murphy Anderson, George Evans, and Lily Renee art. Overstreet 2005 FN 6.0 value = $186; VF 8.0 value = $388. CGC census 9/05: 3 in 6.5, 16 higher. *From the Aviator Collection.*

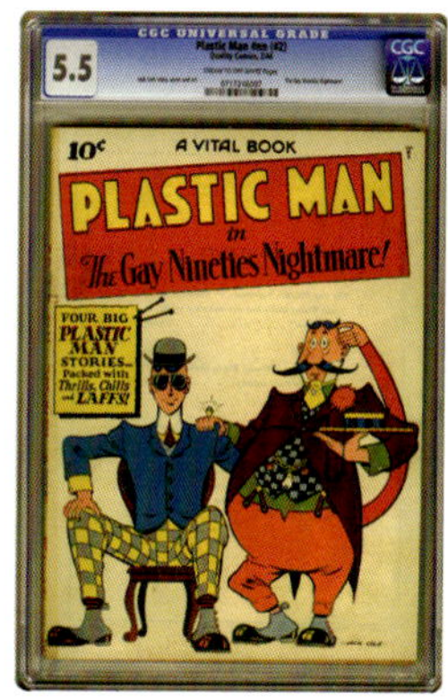

3070 Plastic Man #nn (#2) (Quality, 1944) CGC FN- 5.5 Cream to off-white pages. Some youngsters out there might not know that the 1890s were commonly known as the Gay Nineties — check out Plastic Man and Woozy Winks getting into the turn-of-the-century spirit on Jack Cole's cover! The interior story and art are also by Cole, the man who created Plas. Overstreet 2005 FN 6.0 value = $555. CGC census 8/05: 1 in 5.5, 6 higher. *From the Aviator Collection.*

3071 Police Comics #23 (Quality, 1943) CGC FN/VF 7.0 Cream to off-white pages. Last Phantom Lady story in this title. Jack Cole cover. Will Eisner art. Overstreet 2005 FN 6.0 value = $231; VF 8.0 value = $481. CGC census 9/05: 1 in 7.0, 2 higher. *From the Aviator Collection.*

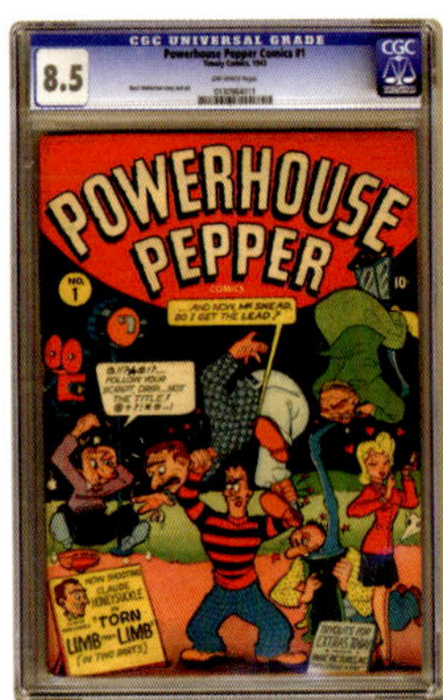

3072 Powerhouse Pepper Comics #1 (Timely, 1943) CGC VF+ 8.5 Off-white pages. Get ready for a laugh riot with this incredible comic! **Powerhouse Pepper** was the brainchild of Basil Wolverton, who poured plenty of rhyming gags, not to mention riotous renderings, onto every page (save the cover and a few ad pages) of this sixty-page pleaser. **Pepper** comics don't show up too often, so don't pass up this rare opportunity to own one of the funniest comics ever created... and not too shabby a copy, either! Overstreet 2005 VF 8.0 value = $1,156; VF/NM 9.0 value = $1,778. CGC census 9/05: 1 in 8.5, 3 higher. *From the Aviator Collection.*

3073 Powerhouse Pepper Comics #2 (Timely, 1948) CGC FN 6.0 Cream to off-white pages. With this second issue, Basil Wolverton takes over cover art duties as well as page after page of side-splitting art and story featuring bullet-headed tough guy, Powerhouse Pepper. Overstreet 2005 FN 6.0 value = $261. CGC census 9/05: 1 in 6.0, 3 higher. *From the Aviator Collection.*

3074 Shield-Wizard Comics #3 (MLJ, 1941) CGC VG+ 4.5 Cream to off-white pages. Irv Novick cover. Novick and Mort Meskin art. Overstreet 2005 VG 4.0 value = $300. CGC census 9/05: 1 in 4.5, 2 higher. *From the Aviator Collection.*

3075 Shield-Wizard Comics #7 (MLJ, 1942) CGC VG+ 4.5 Cream to off-white pages. Jack Kirby cover. Irv Novick art. Overstreet 2005 VG 4.0 value = $254. CGC census 8/05: 1 in 4.5, 5 higher. *From the Aviator Collection.*

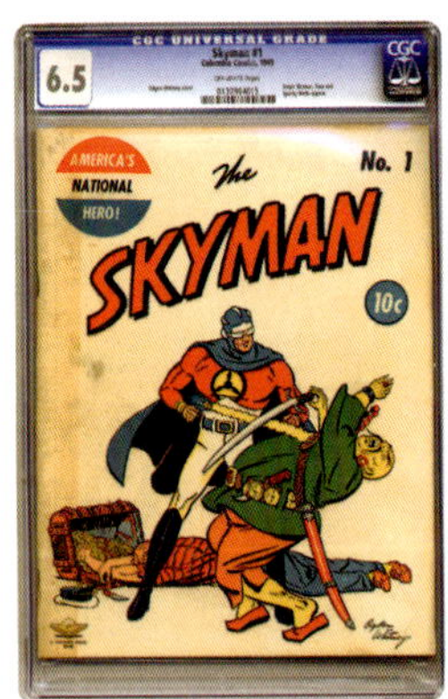

3076 Skyman #1 (Columbia, 1941) CGC FN+ 6.5 Off-white pages. Skyman of **Big Shot Comics** debuted in his own title here. The supporting cast includes another guy who starred in his own title, the Face (aka Tony Trent). The cover is by Ogden Whitney. Overstreet 2005 FN 6.0 value = $369; VF 8.0 value = $769. CGC census 7/05: 2 in 6.5, 3 higher. *From the Aviator Collection.*

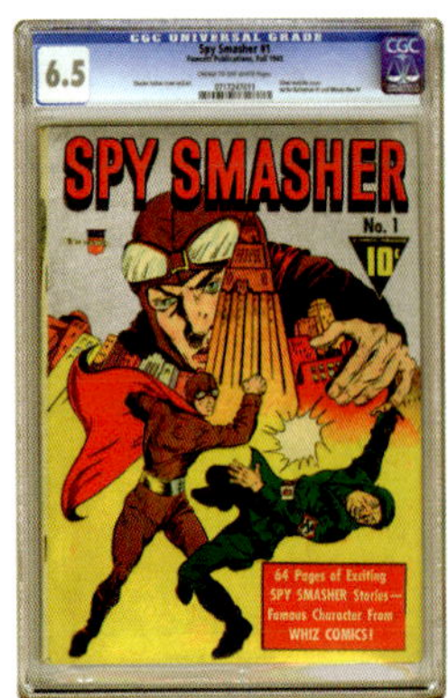

3077 Spy Smasher #1 (Fawcett, 1941) CGC FN+ 6.5 Cream to off-white pages. The unusual silver metallic cover sets this book apart, and may also be a reason why there don't seem to be high-grade copies around — no copy has been graded above VF by CGC to date. The title character got his own book after debuting in Whiz Comics (and continued to appear in both series). Overstreet 2005 FN 6.0 value = $1,116; VF 8.0 value = $2,418. CGC census 9/05: 1 in 6.5, 3 higher. *From the Aviator Collection.*

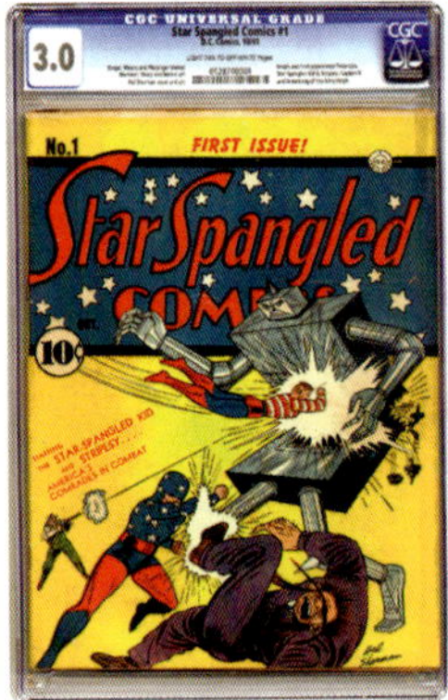

3078 Star Spangled Comics #1 (DC, 1941) CGC GD/VG 3.0 Light tan to off-white pages. The Star-Spangled Kid and Stripesy, having debuted in **Action Comics**, made their second appearance (and had the second half of their origin told) in this issue. That's them on Hal Sherman's robot cover. And if you thought wall-walking, web-shooting heroes didn't come along until the sixties, let us call your attention to the Tarantula, whose origin and first appearance are in this issue. The issue is a Gerber "scarce." Overstreet 2005 GD 2.0 value = $503; VG 4.0 value = $1,006. CGC census 8/05: 2 in 3.0, 16 higher. *From the Aviator Collection.*

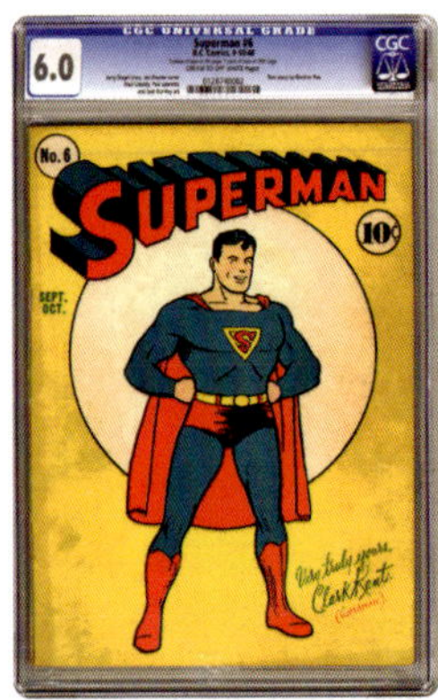

3079 Superman #6 (DC, 1940) CGC FN 6.0 Cream to off-white pages. This issue's Joe Shuster cover tells you all you need to know about the appeal of the character! There weren't planet-shattering super-battles in these early stories — in this issue, Superman solves a mystery, fights corruption, and even delivers humanitarian aid to a South American country. Overstreet notes that this issue has the first splash page in a Superman comic. The issue's artists include Jack Burnley and the late Paul Cassidy. CGC notes, "3 pieces of tape on 8th page, 1 piece of tape on 28th page." Overstreet 2005 FN 6.0 value = $909. CGC census 7/05: 1 in 6.0, 7 higher. *From the Aviator Collection.*

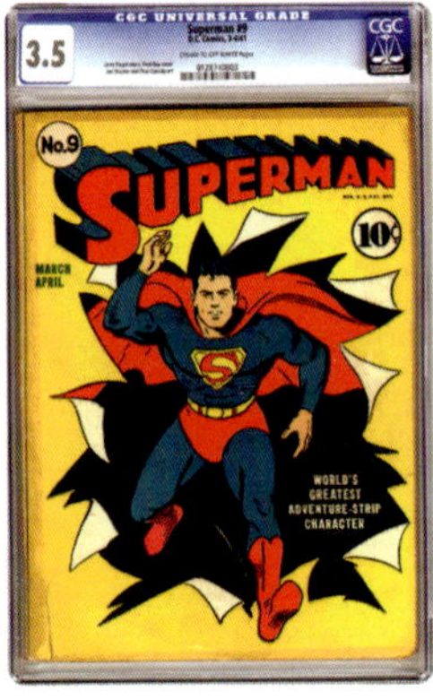

3080 Superman #9 (DC, 1941) CGC VG- 3.5 Cream to off-white pages. We love Fred Ray art — we might as well come out and admit it. He never made his covers more complicated than they had to be, and you can see right here how appealing he made the character of Superman. Inside the comic, the Man of Steel is drawn by his co-creator Joe Shuster as well as the late Paul Cassidy. Note that a small plastic stabilizing peg is loose inside the CGC holder, not affecting the integrity of the holder or the comic itself. Overstreet 2005 VG 4.0 value = $600. CGC census 7/05: 1 in 3.5, 29 higher. *From the Aviator Collection.*

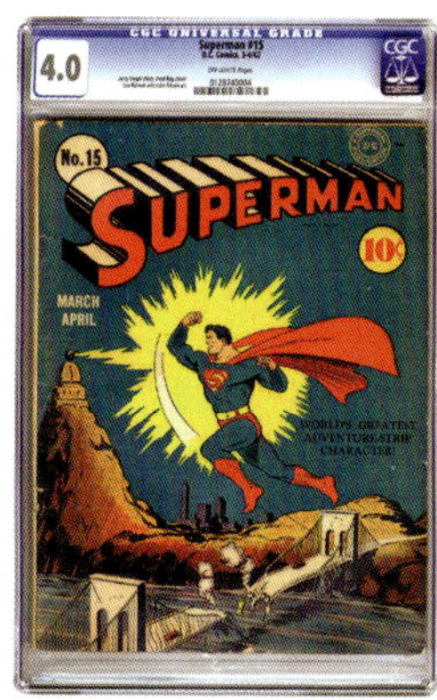

3081 Superman #15 (DC, 1942) CGC VG 4.0 Off-white pages. This Golden Age issue has a Fred Ray cover, with interior art by Leo Nowak and John Sikela. Overstreet 2005 VG 4.0 value = $462. CGC census 7/05: 2 in 4.0, 8 higher. *From the Aviator Collection.*

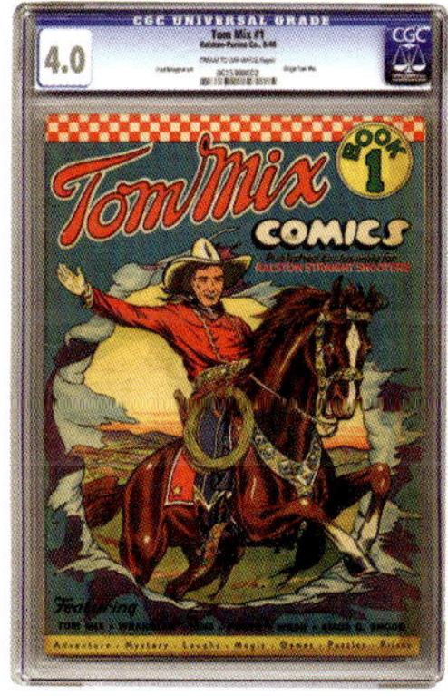

3082 Tom Mix Comics #1 (Ralston-Purina Co., 1940) CGC VG 4.0 Cream to off-white pages. Amazingly, only one copy of this issue has been graded higher by CGC to date. The reason for the lack of high-grade specimens is that these comics weren't set out at the newsstand, but rather sent through the U.S. Mail... and not in bags and boards, either! Originally offered as a mail-in premium by Ralston Wheat Cereal, this comic (a Gerber "8") is ranked among the 10 most valuable Western comic books by Overstreet. Overstreet 2005 VG 4.0 value = $600. CGC census 8/05: 1 in 4.0, 1 higher. *From the Aviator Collection.*

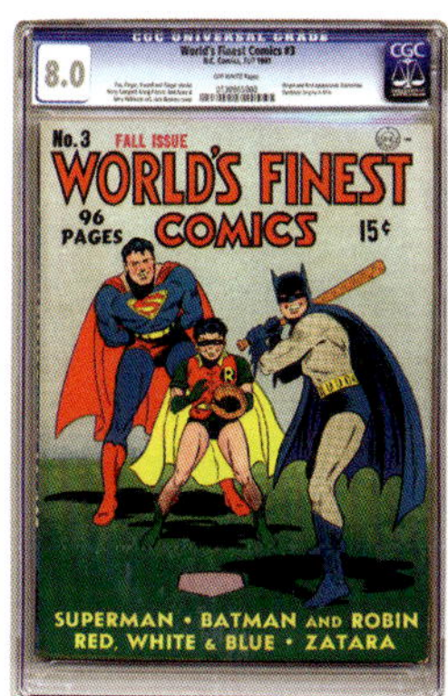

3083 World's Finest Comics #3 (DC, 1941) CGC VF 8.0 Off-white pages. Now that the Scarecrow has hit the big screen in the movie "Batman Begins," no Bat-Collector has an excuse not to have the baddie's first appearance. It's right here in this issue, as is the villain's origin. Bob Kane and Jerry Robinson drew the Batman tale. Other characters in this whopping square bound mag include the Sandman (his first outing in this series), Superman, and Johnny Thunder. While the CGC slab says "Jack Burnley cover," that's Fred Ray art if we've ever seen it, and Overstreet has our backs on that point. Only two specimens of the issue have been graded higher as of this writing, and they're both just half a grade higher at 8.5. Overstreet 2005 VF 8.0 value = $2,126. CGC census 7/05: 2 in 8.0, 2 higher. *From the Aviator Collection.*

3084 Wow Comics #4 (Fawcett, 1942) CGC Qualified FN- 5.5 Cream to off-white pages. Origin and first appearance of Pinky. CGC notes, "Half of 1st page missing, affects story. Incomplete." Overstreet 2005 GD 2.0 value = $121; VG 4.0 value = $242; FN 6.0 value = $363. *From the Aviator Collection.*

3085 X-Venture #1 (Victory Magazines, 1947) CGC VG 4.0 Cream to off-white pages. Atom Wizard and Mystery Shadow are featured. Overstreet 2005 VG 4.0 value = $224. CGC census 7/05: 1 in 4.0, 2 higher. *From the Aviator Collection.*

3086 Zip Comics #28 (MLJ, 1942) CGC VG+ 4.5 Cream to off-white pages. Bondage cover. Origin of the Web. Irv Novick and Paul Reinman art. Overstreet 2005 VG 4.0 value = $270. CGC census 7/05: 1 in 4.5, 3 higher. *From the Aviator Collection.*

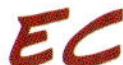

3087 Animal Fables #2 (EC, 1946) CGC FN/VF 7.0 Off-white to white pages. Aesop's fables are featured. CGC notes, "One-inch tear on last four pages." Overstreet 2005 FN 6.0 value = $93; VF 8.0 value = $175. CGC census 9/05: 1 in 7.0, 1 higher.

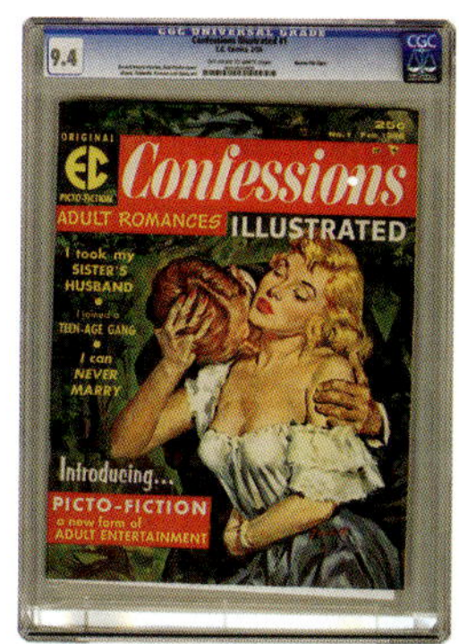

3088 Confessions Illustrated #1 Gaines File pedigree (EC, 1956) CGC NM 9.4 Off-white to white pages. Bud Parke cover. Wally Wood, Jack Kamen, Johnny Craig, and Joe Orlando art. Overstreet 2005 NM- 9.2 value = $275. CGC census 8/05: 2 in 9.4, 1 higher.

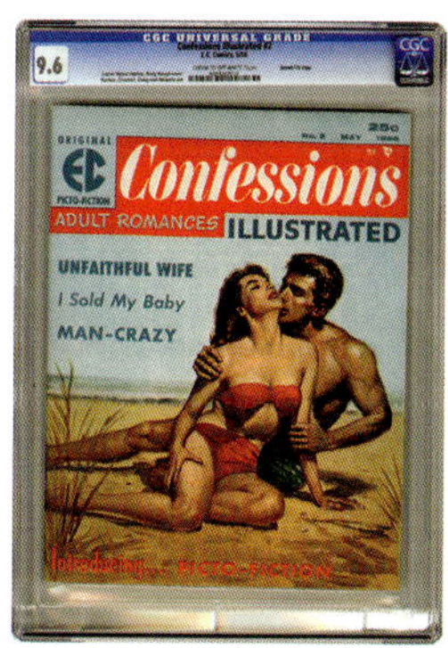

3089 Confessions Illustrated #2 Gaines File pedigree (EC, 1956) CGC NM+ 9.6 Cream to off-white pages. Rudy Nappi painted cover. Johnny Craig, Jack Kamen, Reed Crandall, and Joe Orlando art. This is currently the highest grade awarded by CGC for this issue. Overstreet 2005 NM- 9.2 value = $200. CGC census 8/05: 3 in 9.6, none higher.

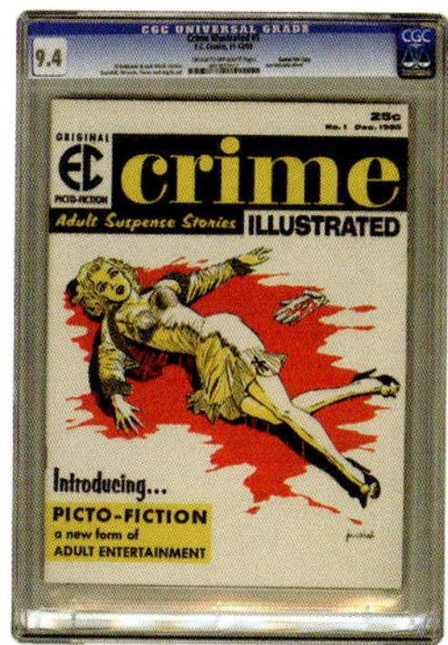

3090 Crime Illustrated #1 Gaines File pedigree (EC, 1955) CGC NM 9.4 Cream to off-white pages. Joe Orlando cover. Orlando, Crandall, George Evans, and Graham Ingels art. Al Feldstein is credited as "Alfred E. Neuman." Overstreet 2005 NM- 9.2 value = $175. CGC census 8/05: 4 in 9.4, 2 higher.

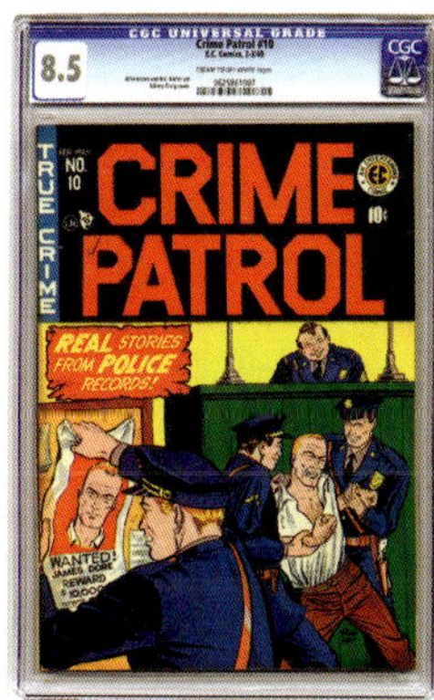

3091 Crime Patrol #10 (EC, 1949) CGC VF+ 8.5 Cream to off-white pages. Looks like the law has the the last laugh on this cool "pre-trend" Johnny Craig-illustrated cover. Other than a small dust shadow on the left side, this copy is a killer, with sharp corners and great cover color. Overstreet 2005 VF 8.0 value = $369; VF/NM 9.0 value = $565. CGC census 8/05: 1 in 8.5, 3 higher.

3092 Crime Patrol #11 (EC, 1949) CGC VF- 7.5 Cream to off-white pages. Johnny Craig cover. Al Feldstein, H. L. Larsen, and H. C. Kiefer art. Overstreet 2005 VF 8.0 value = $369. CGC census 9/05: 1 in 7.5, 1 higher.

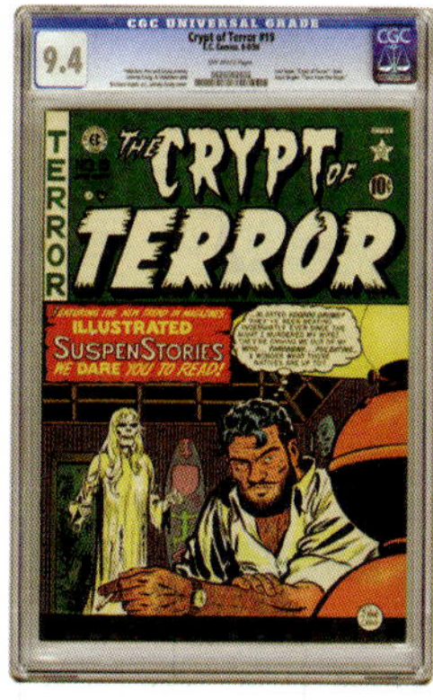

3093 Crypt of Terror #19 (EC, 1950) CGC NM 9.4 Off-white pages. Here's an absolutely beautiful copy of the last issue of this title — with #20, it became **Tales From the Crypt**. Johnny Craig's gruesome voodoo zombie cover is followed by interior work by Al Feldstein and Graham Ingels, as well as two tales drawn by Craig. Overstreet 2005 NM- 9.2 value = $2,300. CGC census 9/05: 1 in 9.4, 5 higher.

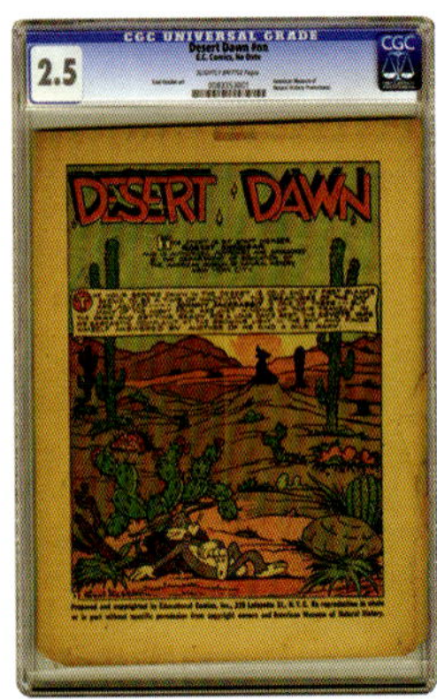

3094 Desert Dawn #nn (EC, circa 1935) CGC GD+ 2.5 Slightly brittle pages. Only three copies of this rarity are known to exist! EC lived up to its "Educational Comics" designation with this release, a promotional comic under the aegis of the American Museum of Natural History. The story was written by a museum staffer, while the art was in the hands of comics pro Saul Kessler. The star is the distinctly Bugs Bunny-like Johnny Jackrabbit. Not listed in Overstreet. CGC census 9/05: 1 in 2.5, 1 higher.

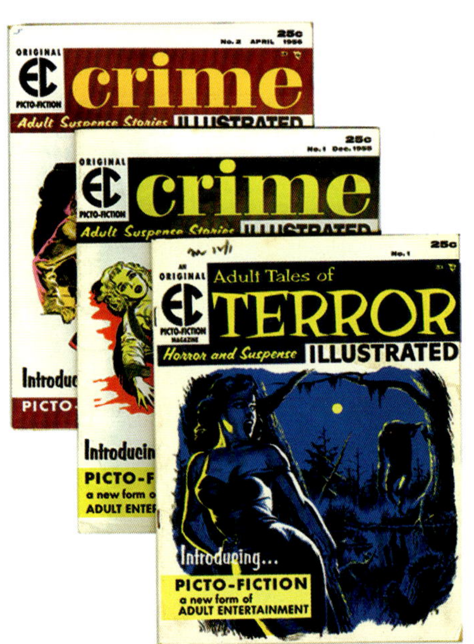

3095 EC Picto-Fiction Magazines Group (EC, 1955-56) Condition: Average FN. This is almost a full run of EC's short-lived "Picto-Fiction" magazines, in fact every issue that actually reached newsstands is included here (the rare **Shock Illustrated** #3 was produced in minuscule numbers but not officially released). The magazines in the group are **Adult Tales of Terror Illustrated** #1 and 2; **Crime Illustrated** #1 and 2; **Shock Illustrated** #1 and 2; and **Confessions Illustrated** #1 and 2. Jack Kamen, Wally Wood, Jack Davis, Johnny Craig, Graham Ingels, and the other EC regulars contributed art to these magazines. **Shock** #1 is in FR/GD condition; the others average FN. Approximate Overstreet value for group = $400.

3096 Haunt of Fear #15 (#1) (EC, 1950) CGC VF/NM 9.0 Off-white to white pages. This is the first issue of one of EC's famous horror titles, and it has the first story Harvey Kurtzman produced for EC (though not the first to make it into print). Johnny Craig's cover gave way to exquisite drawings by himself, Harvey Kurtzman, Al Feldstein, and the team of Harry Harrison and Wally Wood. Note that Overstreet lists the following issue as the first appearance of the Old Witch; while that does look like her on this issue's cover, some have speculated that that's her fellow GhouLunatic, the Vault Keeper. This is one of the hardest copies for Fan-Addicts to scare up — it's rated "scarce" by Overstreet. Overstreet 2005 VF/NM 9.0 value = $3,035; NM- 9.2 value = $4,000. CGC census 9/05: 1 in 9.0, 3 higher.

3097 Haunt of Fear #12 (EC, 1952) CGC NM+ 9.6 Off-white pages. Overstreet notes this Graham Ingels "walking corpse" cover as a "classic." An Al Feldstein biography is featured. Interior art by Ingels, Johnny Craig, Joe Orlando, and Jack Davis. For a copy that's *not* from the Gaines files, this one looks pretty sweet! Overstreet 2005 NM- 9.2 value = $490. CGC census 9/05: 3 in 9.6, 1 higher.

3098 Haunt of Fear #17 Gaines File pedigree, 6/12 (EC, 1953) CGC NM+ 9.6 White pages. Don't look too long at this classic cover by "Ghastly" Graham Ingels — you might get nightmares! Ingels, George Evans, Jack Kamen, and Jack Davis all contribute story art. Overstreet 2005 NM- 9.2 value = $475. CGC census 9/05: 4 in 9.6, 1 higher.

3099 Haunt of Fear #17 (#3) Gaines File pedigree (EC, 1950) CGC NM+ 9.6 White pages. No copy of this issue has been graded higher to date than our offering from the files of Bill Gaines! Speaking of Mr. Gaines, he makes an appearance in one of the stories along with Al Feldstein — we find out the origins of the **Crypt of Terror**, the **Vault of Horror**, and the **Haunt of Fear**, namely that the GhouLunatic narrators of those three comics captured Gaines and Feldstein and forced them to sign contracts to publish horror stories! Meanwhile, a character who happens to be named "John Severin" appears in the story "Nightmare, A Psychological Study," a tale taken to task in **Seduction Of The Innocent** because it "shows the same predilection for non-language expletives familiar in other comics." While we ponder what exactly that means, we'll mention that the issue has a Johnny Craig cover, with interior art by Craig, Al Feldstein, Harvey Kurtzman, and Graham Ingels. Note that while CGC has certified this comic as a Gaines File Copy, no certificate accompanies this lot. Overstreet 2005 NM- 9.2 value = $1,700. CGC census 9/05: 2 in 9.6, none higher.

3100 Haunt of Fear #21 Gaines File pedigree 1/10 (EC, 1953) CGC NM 9.4 White pages. Graham Ingels cover. Art by Ingels, Jack Davis, and Reed Crandall, plus a collaboration between Jack Kamen and Bill Elder. Overstreet 2005 NM- 9.2 value = $320. CGC census 8/05: 2 in 9.4, 1 higher.

3101 Impact #5 Gaines File pedigree (EC, 1955) CGC NM- 9.2 Off-white to white pages. Last issue of the title. Jack Davis cover. George Evans, Joe Orlando, Graham Ingels, and Bernie Krigstein art. Note that while CGC has certified this comic as a Gaines File copy, no certificate accompanies this lot. Overstreet 2005 NM- 9.2 value = $125. CGC census 9/05: 3 in 9.2, 2 higher.

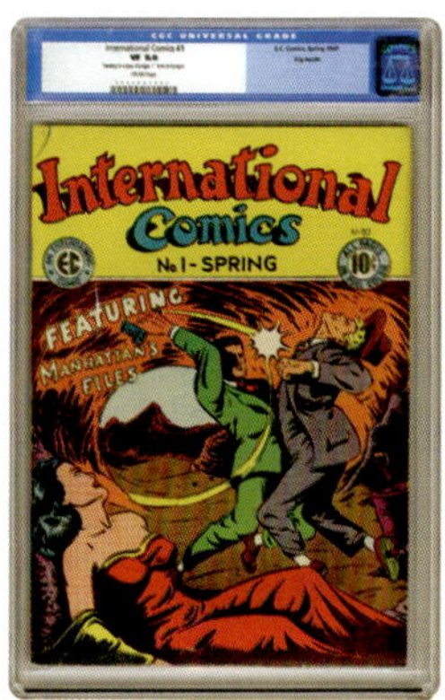

3102 International Comics #1 Big Apple pedigree (EC, 1947) CGC VF 8.0 Cream pages. The stars of this series included Van Manhattan (that's him getting decked on the Lee Bachelor cover) and French freedom fighter Madelon, both of whom would soon be part of a group called the Crime Patrol, and whose comic would become **International Crime Patrol** and then simply **Crime Patrol**. The issue's interior artists include Kurt Schaffenberger. CGC notes, "Tanning on edges of pages. One-inch tear on four pages." Overstreet 2005 VF 8.0 value = $375. CGC census 9/05: 1 in 8.0, 3 higher.

3103 Land of the Lost #1 (EC, 1946) CGC VF/NM 9.0 Light tan to off-white pages. Based on the Mutual Coast-to-Coast radio program. Overstreet 2005 VF/NM 9.0 value = $312; NM- 9.2 value = $410. CGC census 9/05: 2 in 9.0, none higher.

3104 Land of the Lost #6 (EC, 1947) CGC VF/NM 9.0 Cream to off-white pages. Based on the Mutual Coast-to-Coast radio program. Overstreet 2005 VF/NM 9.0 value = $161; NM- 9.2 value = $210. CGC census 9/05: 2 in 9.0, none higher.

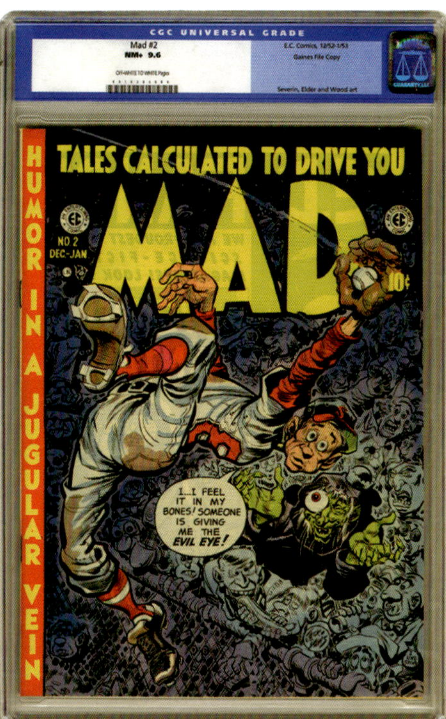

3105 Mad #2 Gaines File pedigree 3/12 (EC, 1952) CGC NM+ 9.6 Off-white to white pages. Here is the classic second issue of a title that has been going strong for 50 years. All of the comic-sized issues have become hard to find in any grade, making this gem a real treasure indeed. Jack Davis contributes the "evil eye" cover — looking through the crowd, there seems to be a *lot* of evil eye action going on! Davis, John Severin, Bill Elder, and Wally Wood supply the artistic thrills inside. This is one of the nicest copies of this issue we have seen. Overstreet 2005 NM- 9.2 value = $1,750. CGC census 9/05: 4 in 9.6, 1 higher.

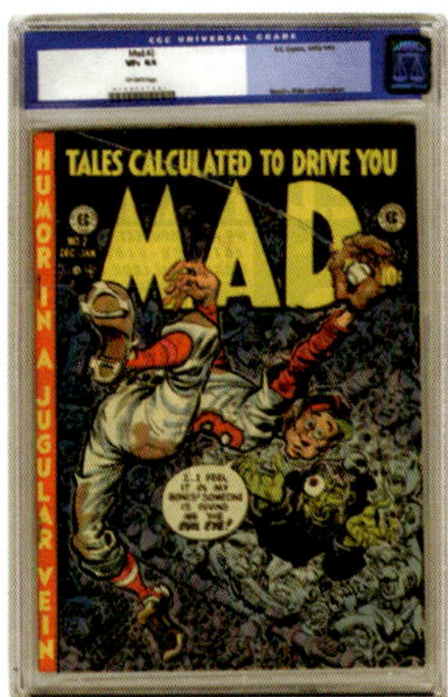

3106 Mad #2 (EC, 1952) CGC VF+ 8.5 Off-white pages. We're all used to the **Mad** style of humor by now, but back in 1952 there was nothing on the stands quite like this. Jack Davis' cover combined horror, humor, and baseball (as did the accompanying story). Another highlight is the John Severin-drawn Tarzan parody "Melvin!". Bill Elder and Wally Wood joined the fun by working under the pen names *Melvin* Elder and *Melvin* Wood for this issue. Overstreet 2005 VF 8.0 value = $908; VF/NM 9.0 value = $1,329. CGC census 6/05: 5 in 8.5, 13 higher.

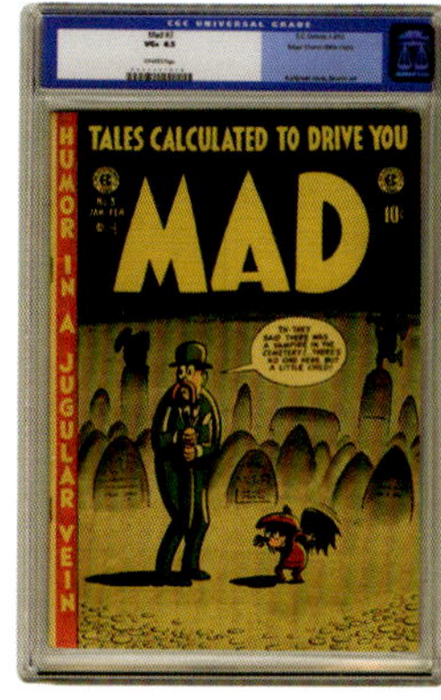

3107 Mad #3 Mile High pedigree (EC, 1953) CGC VG+ 4.5 Off-white pages. At first we were puzzled as to how this Mile High only graded out at VG+; the answer was provided by a subscription-type crease down the middle. Still and all, the Mile High of this early issue is a comic few collectors would pass by. Highlights of the issue include the "Lone Stranger" with Jack Davis art, "Dragged Net" with Bill Elder art, as well as the work of Harvey Kurtzman (cover), John Severin, and Wally Wood. Overstreet 2005 VG 4.0 value = $152. CGC census 5/05: 4 in 4.5, 34 higher.

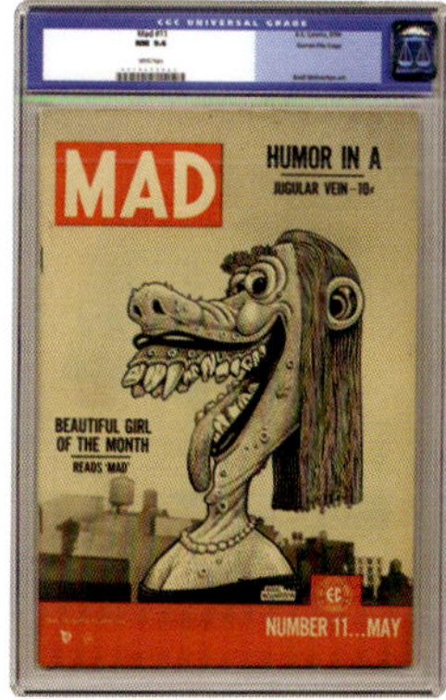

3108 Mad #11 Gaines File pedigree (EC, 1954) CGC NM 9.4 White pages. Here's one that warped a lot of young minds back in the good ol' innocent 1950s. Basil Wolverton's incredible "Life Magazine" parody cover is a real masterpiece of Ugly Art. And with interior art by Wolverton, Wally Wood (a funny *Flash Gordon* parody), Jack Davis, and Bill Elder, you can't go wrong. This white-page wonder is a real beauty, if something with a Wolverton "girl" on the cover can be called "beautiful." Although CGC recognizes this book as a Gaines File Copy, no certificate accompanies this lot. Overstreet 2005 NM- 9.2 value = $860. CGC census 6/05: 3 in 9.4, 1 higher.

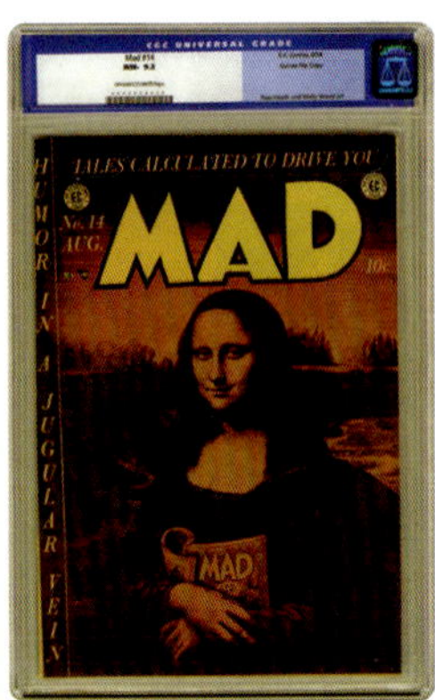

3109 Mad #14 Gaines File pedigree, 8/12 (EC, 1954) CGC NM- 9.2 Off-white to white pages. Mona Lisa finally reveals the source of her sly smile — she had been chuckling over a copy of **Mad**! Of course, it all makes sense now! Rewrite all the art history books! Art in this issue by Bill Elder (*Mandrake the Magician* parody), Wally Wood, Jack Davis, and Russ Heath (**Plastic Man** parody). Overstreet 2005 NM- 9.2 value = $675. CGC census 9/05: 2 in 9.2, 3 higher.

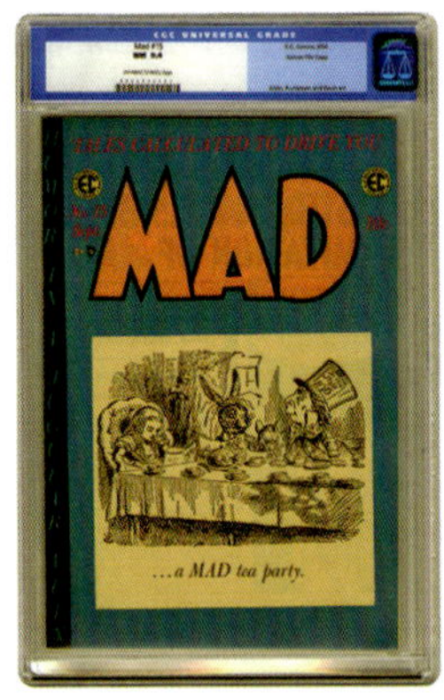

3110 Mad #15 Gaines File pedigree, 6/12 (EC, 1954) CGC NM 9.4 Off-white to white pages. Alice in Wonderland gets the **MAD**-treatment this issue, with a wonderful Jack Davis story. Other artists include Bill Elder, Harvey Kurtzman (with a great Pot Shot Pete reprint), and Wally Wood. Of course, this is one of publisher William Gaines' personal copies, stashed away for many years. Needless to say, it's a real beauty! Overstreet 2005 NM- 9.2 value = $675. CGC census 9/05: 4 in 9.4, none higher.

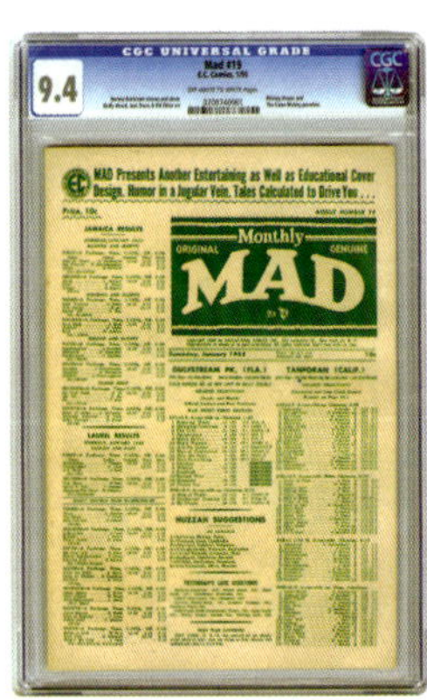

3111 Mad #19 (EC, 1955) CGC NM 9.4 Off-white to white pages. Harvey Kurtzman certainly gave readers plenty of humor for a dime — just reading the gag-filled fine print on the cover will take you a while. The issue's artists include Wally Wood, Jack Davis, and Bill Elder. Overstreet 2005 NM- 9.2 value = $575. CGC census 9/05: 3 in 9.4, 1 higher.

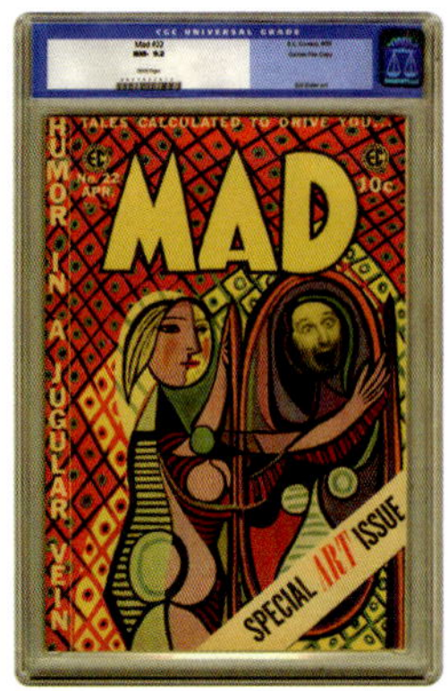

3112 Mad #22 Gaines File pedigree (EC, 1955) CGC NM- 9.2 White pages. This is the notorious "Special art issue," with a Picasso-like cover by Harvey Kurtzman, and all interior art by Bill Elder. Although CGC recognizes this book as a Gaines File Copy, no certificate accompanies this lot. Overstreet 2005 NM- 9.2 value = $575. CGC census 9/05: 2 in 9.2, 8 higher.

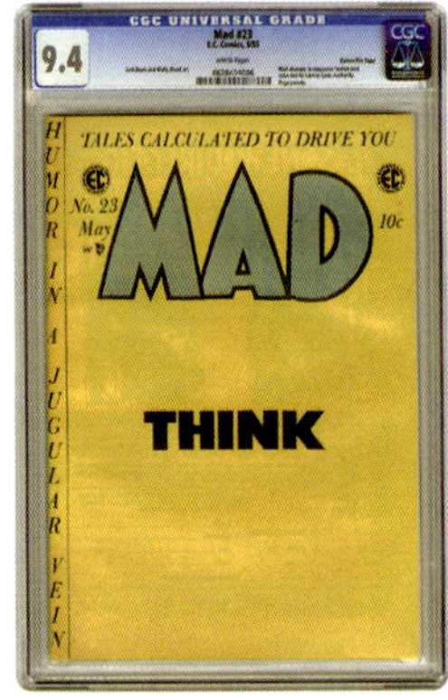

3113 Mad #23 Gaines File pedigree (EC, 1955) CGC NM 9.4 White pages. Here's the last comic book issue of **Mad**. While the comic book version of this classic satire title may have been too good to be true after a mere 23 issues, the magazine format continues to thrive today. This book may not make you "think" so much as cause you to laugh long and hard! Wally Wood and Jack Davis art is featured, and *Pogo* gets the **Mad** parody treatment. While CGC recognizes this as a Gaines file copy, no certificate accompanies the book. Overstreet 2005 NM- 9.2 value = $575. CGC census 8/05: 2 in 9.4, 1 higher.

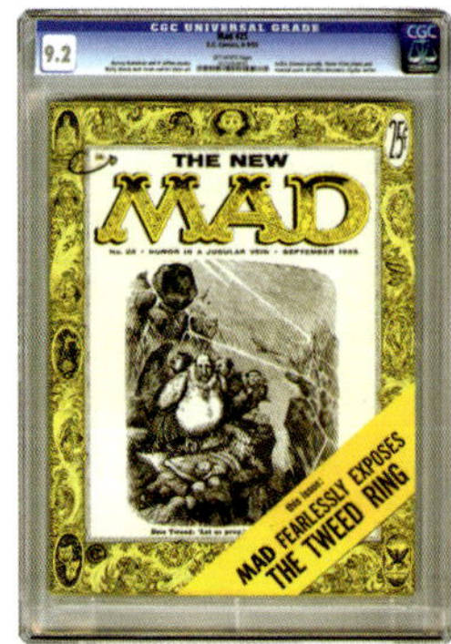

3114 Mad #25 (EC, 1955) CGC NM- 9.2 Off-white pages. Here is a stunning copy of the second magazine issue of **Mad**. The cover proclaims "**Mad** fearlessly exposes the Tweed Ring," while inside is a Jackie Gleason parody, plus a Steve Allen photo and musical score. Al Jaffee begins his run as a regular writer in this issue. Wally Wood, Jack Davis, and Bill Elder provide artwork. Overstreet 2005 NM- 9.2 value = $625. CGC census 9/05: 2 in 9.2, 1 higher.

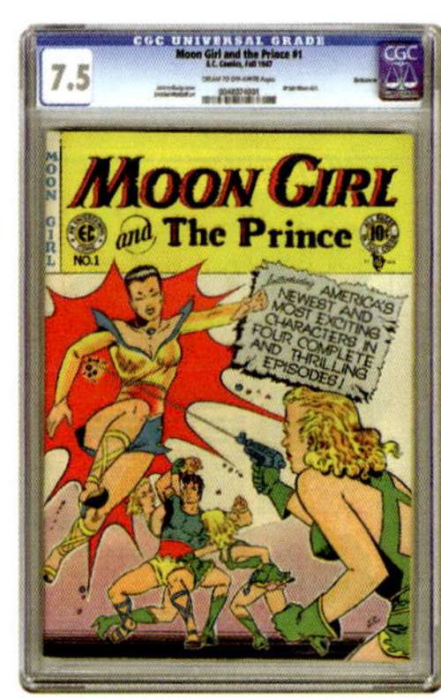

3115 Moon Girl and the Prince #1 Bethlehem pedigree (EC, 1947) CGC VF- 7.5 Cream to off-white pages. Here's the first issue of the title that was just plain **Moon Girl** from #2 on. The origin of the titular heroine is told in this issue. The cover is by Johnny Craig (in quite a different style than his later work), and the interior art's by Sheldon Moldoff. Note that the only copy that tops this one in CGC's census report (as of this writing) is just one grade higher at 8.5. Overstreet 2005 VF 8.0 value = $600. CGC census 7/05: 4 in 7.5, 1 higher.

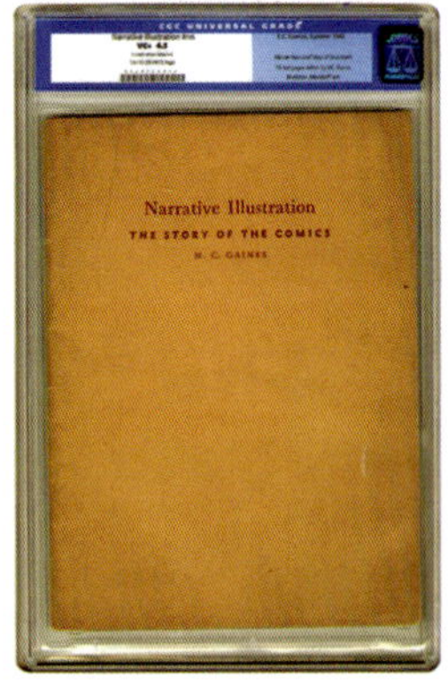

3116 Narrative Illustration: The Story Of The Comics #nn (EC, 1942) CGC VG+ 4.5 Tan to off-white pages. Overstreet calls this "very rare," and while we're among the biggest EC fans around, we had never seen a copy here at Heritage before now. This has 16 text pages by M. C. Gaines, whom some call the father of comics, and there's a 12-page comic insert. The comic material inside consists of "The Story of Saul" (which also saw publication in **Picture Stories from the Bible**) and "The Minute Man Answers The Call," the latter with art by Sheldon Moldoff. Note that Overstreet terms its stated value an "estimated value" and doesn't tie it to a specific grade. Overstreet notes, "3 center wraps detached." Overstreet 2005 "estimated value" (see note above) = $1,500. CGC census 9/05: 2 in 4.5, 1 higher.

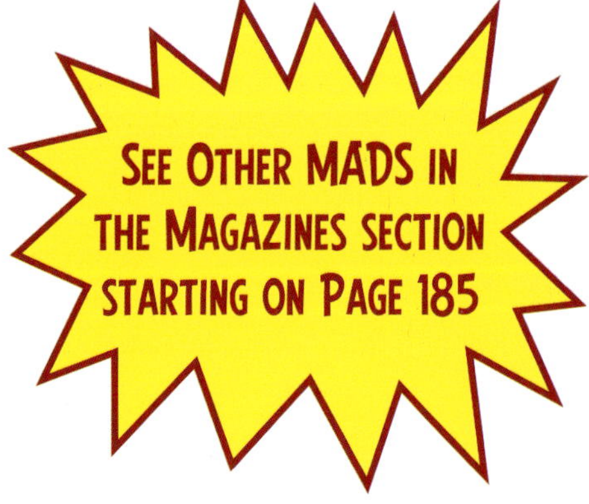

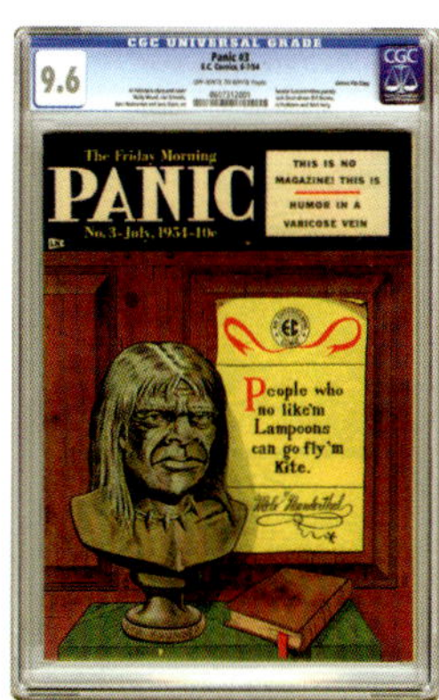

3117 Panic #3 Gaines File pedigree 8/12 (EC, 1954) CGC NM+ 9.6 Off-white to white pages. The EC crowd dished out plenty of zingers here: not only did they parody the Senate Subcommittee (the one that investigated comics), they lampooned Walt Kelly of "Pogo" fame and Li'l Abner's Al Capp. Also, a story drawn by Joe Orlando shows Old King Cole smoking... something (Overstreet says it's marijuana). The issue also has art by Jack Davis, Wally Wood, and Basil Wolverton. Overstreet 2005 NM- 9.2 value = $65. CGC census 9/05: 3 in 9.6, 2 higher.

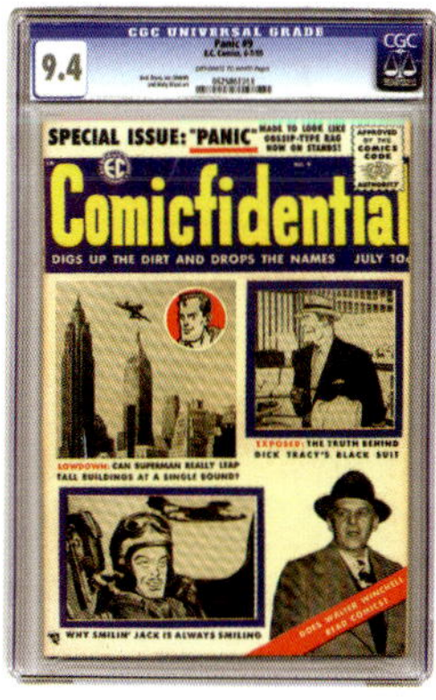

3118 Panic #9 (EC, 1955) CGC NM 9.4 Off-white to white pages. Superman, Dick Tracy, and Smilin' Jack all make a cover appearance on this wacky issue, disguised as a comic book version of the popular 1950s **Confidential** "gossip-type" magazine. Bill Elder, Jack Davis, Joe Orlando, and Wally Wood furnish the art. This exceptional copy ties with one other as highest-graded in CGC's current census report for issue #9. Overstreet 2005 NM- 9.2 value = $145. CGC census 8/05: 2 in 9.4, none higher.

3119 Picture Stories from the Bible New Testament 1 Gaines File pedigree (EC, 1946) CGC VF 8.0 Off-white pages. This is the 1946 EC reprint of an earlier DC edition. Although CGC recognizes this as a Gaines file copy, no certificate accompanies this book. Overstreet 2005 VF 8.0 value = $107. CGC census 9/05: 1 in 8.0, 1 higher.

3120 Piracy #5 Gaines File pedigree, 9/12 (EC, 1955) CGC NM- 9.2 Off-white to white pages. Bernie Krigstein's sketchy cover illustration for this issue looks incredible, thanks to some lovely color effects which faithfully mimic a turbulent ocean. Reed Crandall, Graham Ingels, Krigstein, and George Evans all contribute interior art. A beautiful copy of one of EC's better New Direction titles. Overstreet 2005 NM- 9.2 value = $190. CGC census 8/05: 2 in 9.2, 1 higher.

3121 Piracy #5 Gaines File pedigree (EC, 1955) CGC VF/NM 9.0 Off-white to white pages. An underwater scene by Bernie Krigstein graces this issue's colorful cover, the first to sport a Comics Code seal. Reed Crandall, Graham Ingels, Krigstein, and George Evans all supply story art. Although CGC recognizes this as a Gaines file copy, no certificate accompanies this book. Overstreet 2005 VF/NM 9.0 value = $144; NM- 9.2 value = $190. CGC census 9/05: 1 in 9.0, 3 higher.

3122 Piracy #5 Gaines File pedigree 12/12 (EC, 1955) CGC VF+ 8.5 White pages. Bernie Krigstein cover. Reed Crandall, Graham Ingels, Krigstein, and George Evans art. Overstreet 2005 VF 8.0 value = $98; VF/NM 9.0 value = $144. CGC census 7/05: 1 in 8.5, 4 higher.

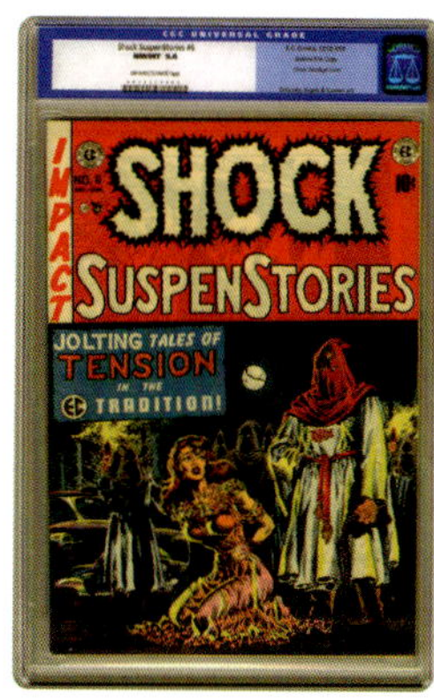

3123 Shock SuspenStories #6 Gaines File Copy 4/12 (EC, 1952) CGC NM/MT 9.8 Off-white to white pages. This title is rife with riveting covers, four earning "classic" designation by Overstreet. Moreover, most issues rate individual comments in the definitive price guide, with a select few garnering mention in **Seduction of the Innocent**, **Reader's Digest**, and the Senate investigation hearings of the mid-1950s. Even such a storied legacy fails to overshadow Wally Wood's hooded vigilante/bondage cover. The interior art by Wood, Jack Kamen, Joe Orlando, and Graham Ingels is no less classic. Overstreet 2005 NM- 9.2 value = $600. CGC census 8/05: 2 in 9.8, 1 higher.

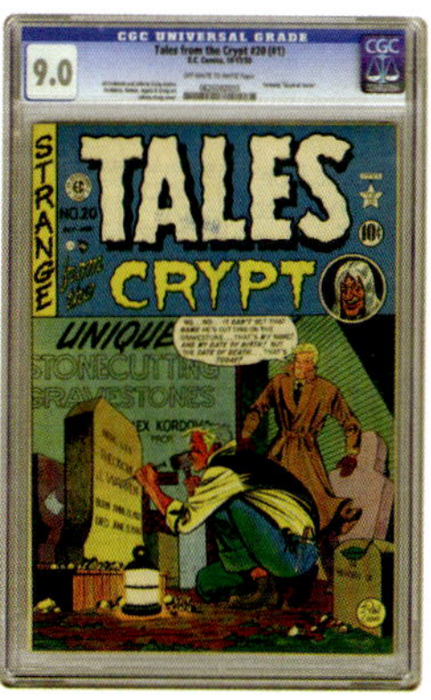

3124 Tales From the Crypt #20 (#1) (EC, 1950) CGC VF/NM 9.0 Off-white to white pages. The discovery of one's date of death has long been a popular theme in thriller fiction, and Johnny Craig employed the idea here with gloomy expertise! Artists Al Feldstein and Graham Ingels also contributed art to the issue. The cover's by Craig. This is the first issue as **Tales From the Crypt** — the series was formerly titled **The Crypt of Terror**. Overstreet 2005 VF/NM 9.0 value = $1,233; NM- 9.2 value = $1,625. CGC census 9/05: 1 in 9.0, 7 higher.

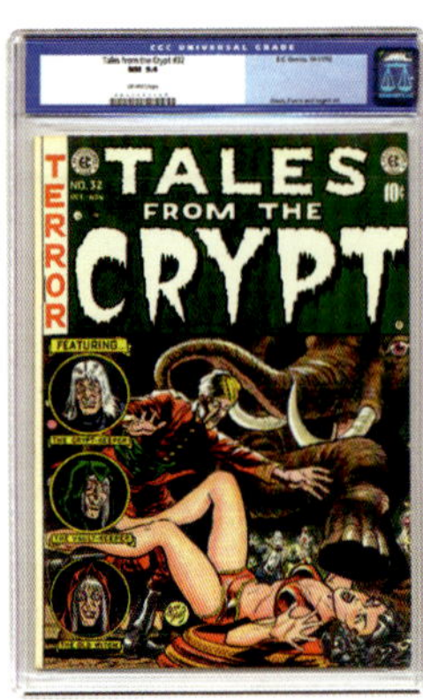

3125 Tales From the Crypt #32 (EC, 1952) CGC NM 9.4 Off-white pages. Jack Davis drew this issue's horror cover (demonstrating in the process that leggy ladies were well within his repertoire). The interior art is by Davis, George Evans, Fred Peters, and Graham Ingels. A writer to this issue's letters page summed up EC's appeal: "Your stories are the most revolting, the most repulsive, the most disgusting stories I have ever read... keep up the good work." Overstreet 2005 NM- 9.2 value = $565. CGC census 7/05: 5 in 9.4, 3 higher.

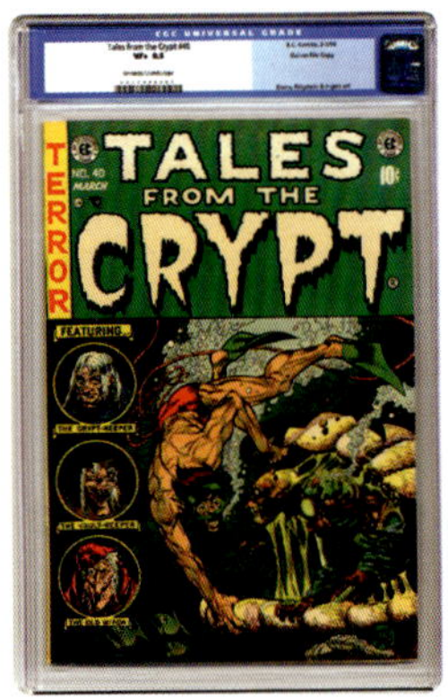

3126 Tales From the Crypt #40 Gaines File pedigree 9/12 (EC, 1954) CGC VF+ 8.5 Off-white to white pages. This comic was mentioned both in Senate hearings and in an anti-comics editorial in the *Hartford Courant*. Hmm, what could have caused all the fuss? The part where the guy gets eaten alive by a lion? Or the part where a guy gets buried alive only to be dug up and eaten by a gh... OK, we're starting to catch on. The issue has a Jack Davis cover, with interior art by Davis, George Evans, Bernie Krigstein, and Graham Ingels. Overstreet 2005 VF 8.0 value = $300; VF/NM 9.0 value = $433. CGC census 7/05: 3 in 8.5, 5 higher.

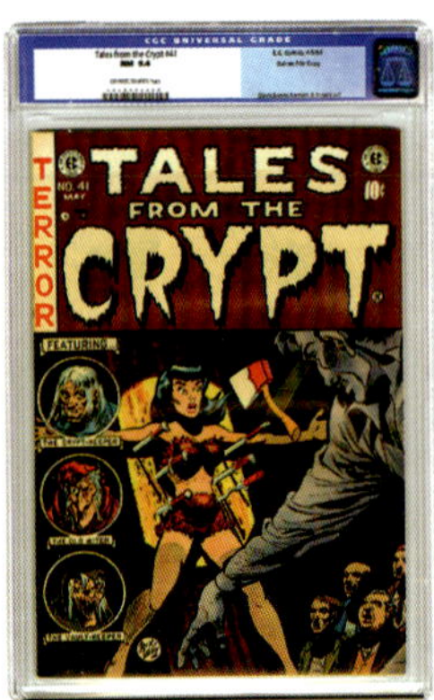

3127 Tales From the Crypt #41 Gaines File pedigree (EC, 1954) CGC NM 9.4 Off-white to white pages. Jack Davis' cover illustration gives us a glimpse of a carnival act about to go horribly wrong — looks like that knife thrower should have left the hatchet at home! Davis, George Evans, Jack Kamen, and Graham Ingels all contribute story art. While CGC recognizes this as a Gaines file copy, no certificate accompanies this book. At any rate, it's still a beautiful copy, sharp and glossy. Overstreet 2005 NM- 9.2 value = $560. CGC census 8/05: 3 in 9.4, none higher.

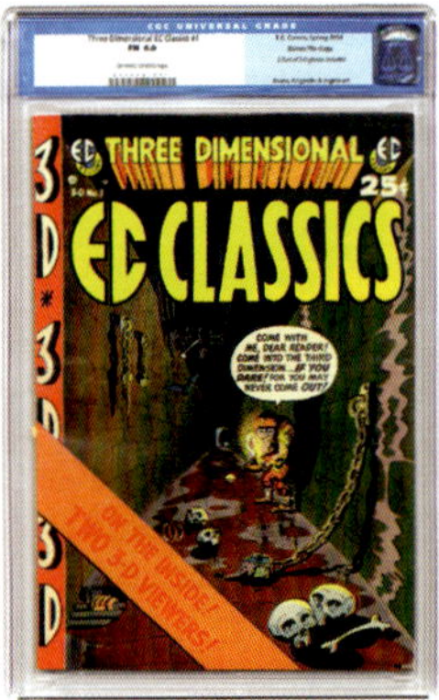

3128 Three Dimensional EC Classics #1 Gaines File pedigree 7/12 (EC, 1954) CGC FN 6.0 Off-white to white pages. This 3-D EC comic is a bit of an odd one; the stories were redrawn into the 3-D format, but not necessarily by the same artists who originally did the stories, and it's rare in high grades due to the unstable paper stock which was used. It has Wally Wood art on a story from **Mad** #3, Bernie Krigstein art on a story from **Weird Science** #7, George Evans art on a story from **Frontline Combat** #13, and Graham Ingels art on a story from **Crime SuspenStories** #5. The cover's by Harvey Kurtzman. CGC notes, "2 pairs of 3-D glasses included." Overstreet 2005 FN 6.0 value = $270. CGC census 7/05: 1 in 6.0, 8 higher.

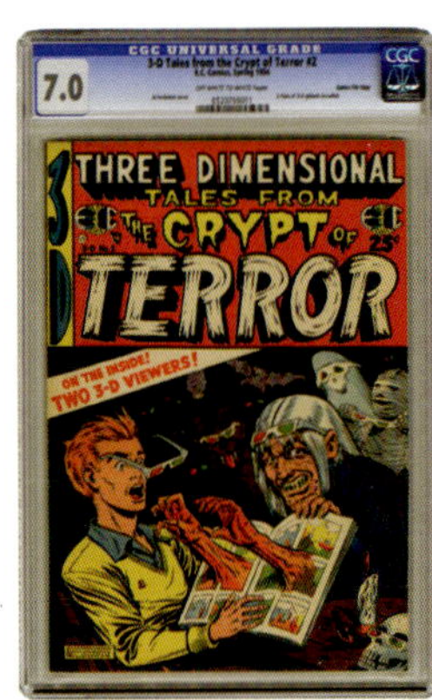

3129 Three Dimensional Tales from the Crypt of Terror #2 Gaines File pedigree (EC, 1954) CGC FN/VF 7.0 Off-white to white pages. This one-shot featured stories from **Tales From The Crypt** and **Vault of Horror** that were redrawn to the 3-D format by Jack Davis, Will Elder, Johnny Craig, and Joe Orlando. The cover is by Al Feldstein. And to our relief, CGC notes, "2 pairs of 3-D glasses included." Note that while CGC has certified this comic as a Gaines File copy, no certificate accompanies this lot. Overstreet 2005 FN 6.0 value = $267; VF 8.0 value = $556. CGC census 9/05: 1 in 7.0, 8 higher.

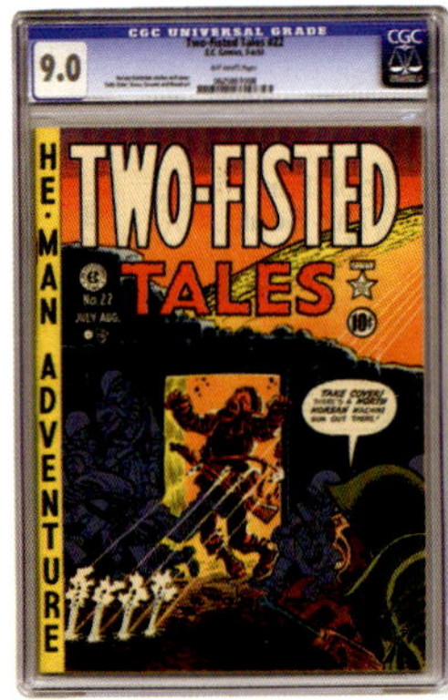

3130 Two-Fisted Tales #22 (EC, 1951) CGC VF/NM 9.0 Off-white pages. While many comic book stories of the early 1950s focused on the conflict in Korea, none could match the excitement and attention to detail found in writer/editor (and sometimes artist) Harvey Kurtzman's EC tales. This sharp-looking issue of **Two-Fisted** starts off with a real bang: Kurtzman's dynamic cover illustration. Inside, there's an unbeatable roster of artistic talent: Alex Toth, Jack Davis, Wally Wood, and the team of Bill Elder and John Severin. Overstreet 2005 VF/NM 9.0 value = $364; NM- 9.2 value = $480. CGC census 8/05: 1 in 9.0, 4 higher.

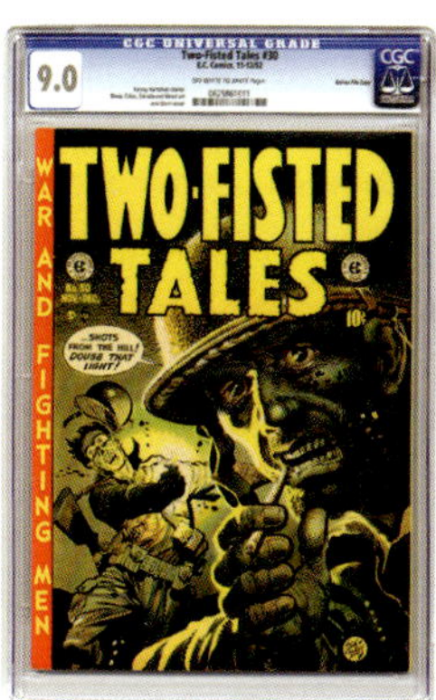

3131 Two-Fisted Tales #30 Gaines File pedigree (EC, 1952) CGC VF/NM 9.0 Off-white to white pages. The grim business of war gets the spotlight with this terrific issue. Writer/editor Harvey Kurtzman's stories are illustrated by cover artist Jack Davis, Gene Colan, Ric Estrada, and Wally Wood. While CGC recognizes this as a Gaines File copy, no certificate accompanies the book. Overstreet 2005 VF/NM 9.0 value = $212; NM- 9.2 value = $280. CGC census 8/05: 1 in 9.0, 4 higher.

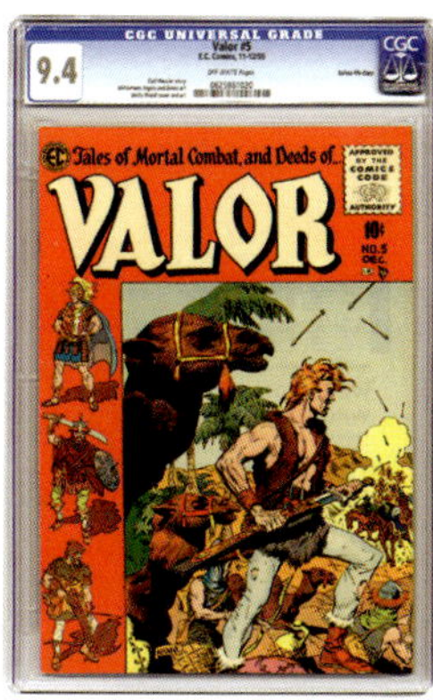

3133 Valor #5 Gaines File pedigree (EC, 1955) CGC NM 9.4 Off-white pages. This last issue of **Valor** signals the beginning of the end for EC's line of New Direction comics. They certainly went out with a bang with this great issue, loaded with exciting art by Wally Wood, Al Williamson, Graham Ingels, and George Evans. Although recognized by CGC as a Gaines File Copy, no certificate accompanies this book. Overstreet 2005 NM- 9.2 value = $210. CGC census 8/05: 1 in 9.4, 1 higher.

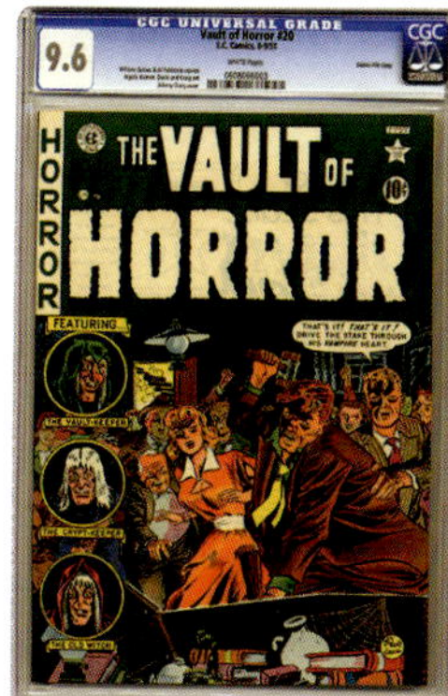

3136 Vault of Horror #20 Gaines File pedigree 2/12 (EC, 1951) CGC NM+ 9.6 White pages. Johnny Craig drew this issue's cover as well as the tale "About Face," in which a wealthy female lion tamer whose face has been scarred is duped by a man who says he loves her for her personality. But she's got a little trick up her sleeve... Jack Davis, Jack Kamen, and Graham Ingels also contributed art to the issue. Overstreet 2005 NM- 9.2 value = $535. CGC census 8/05: 2 in 9.6, 4 higher.

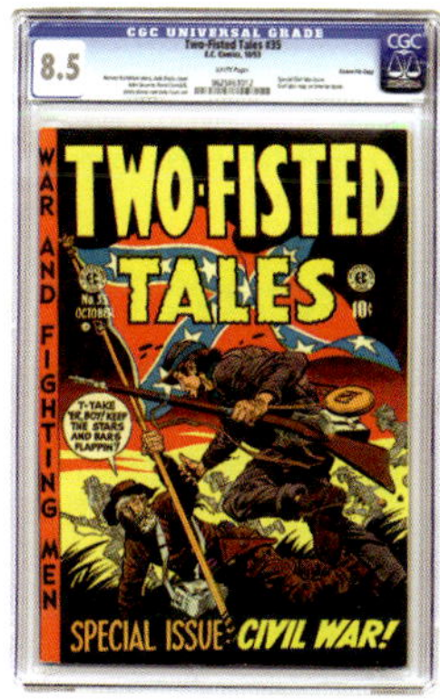

3132 Two-Fisted Tales #35 Gaines File pedigree, 6/11 (EC, 1953) CGC VF+ 8.5 White pages. Here's the third installment of writer/editor Harvey Kurtzman's ambitious Civil War Special Issues, this time focusing on the Confederate States. While additional war between the states specials were planned for **Two-Fisted** and **Frontline Combat**, this turned out to be the last. Artistic thrills are provided by John Severin, Wally Wood, Reed Crandall, and of course, Jack Davis, who contributed the "Stars and Bars" cover. This white-page wonder remains fresh and attractive. Overstreet 2005 VF 8.0 value = $113; VF/NM 9.0 value = $169. CGC census 8/05: 1 in 8.5, 1 higher.

3134 Vault of Horror #16 Gaines File pedigree (EC, 1950) CGC NM/MT 9.8 Off-white to white pages. If perfection is your goal as a collector, look no further than this magnificent file copy. The mostly black background fields on this incredible copy are flawless, the spine is unblemished, and the edges and corners appear razor-sharp. Johnny Craig's art adorns the spooky cover, while Graham Ingels, Jack Kamen, Craig, and Al Feldstein handle the interior art. While CGC recognizes this as a Gaines File copy, no certificate is included. Overstreet 2005 NM- 9.2 value = $825. CGC census 8/05: 1 in 9.8, none higher.

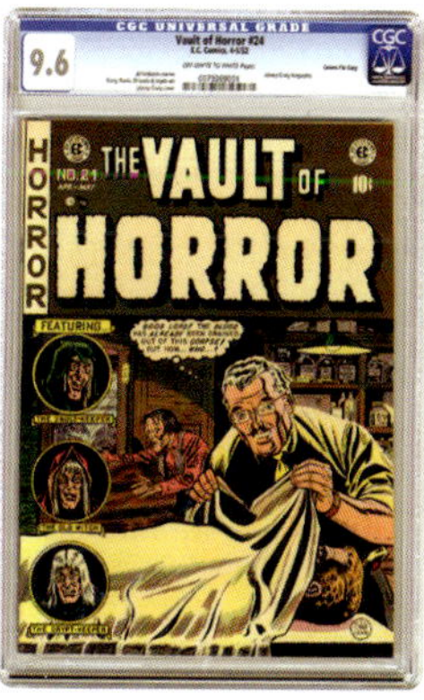

3137 Vault of Horror #24 Gaines File pedigree 4/11 (EC, 1952) CGC NM+ 9.6 Off-white to white pages. This issue spotlights Johnny Craig with a mini-biography and photo. Craig, who unlike most of the other EC regulars wrote his own stories, comes through with the cover of this issue as well as the lead story "A Bloody Undertaking." This issue also includes the artistic stylings of Graham Ingels, Joe Orlando, and Jack Davis. Overstreet 2005 NM- 9.2 value = $535. CGC census 7/05: 3 in 9.6, none higher.

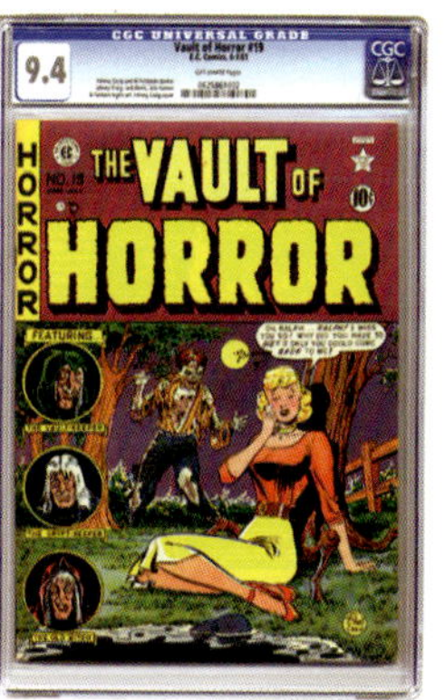

3135 Vault of Horror #19 Gaines File pedigree (EC, 1951) CGC NM 9.4 Off-white pages. Here's a sharp-as-a-tack copy of the eighth issue of this terror-filled title, looking for the most part as if it was just placed on a magazine rack down at the corner drug store, some fifty years earlier. The cover colors are so fresh, you can almost hear Perry Como on the radio as you scan your peepers across this pedigreed prize. The **Vault** art gang's all here: Johnny Craig, Jack Davis, Jack Kamen, and "Ghastly" Graham Ingels, and they're all waiting... for you! Although CGC recognizes this as a Gaines file copy, no certificate accompanies this book. Overstreet 2005 NM- 9.2 value = $650. CGC census 8/05: 1 in 9.4, 4 higher.

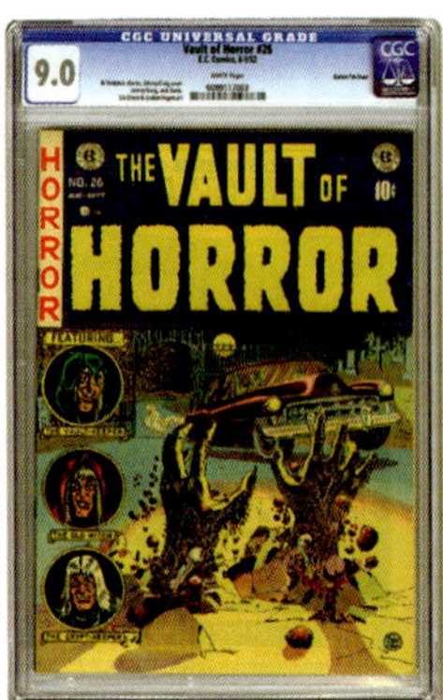

3138 Vault of Horror #26 Gaines File pedigree 9/11 (EC, 1952) CGC VF/NM 9.0 White pages. Two monstrous hands rip out of the ground on this great cover by Johnny Craig. Al Feldstein wrote the stories, with interior art by Craig, Jack Davis, Sid Check, and Graham Ingels. This issue also had black and white and color illustrations featured in **Parade of Pleasure**. Overstreet 2005 VF/NM 9.0 value = $407; NM- 9.2 value = $535. CGC census 8/05: 5 in 9.0, 3 higher.

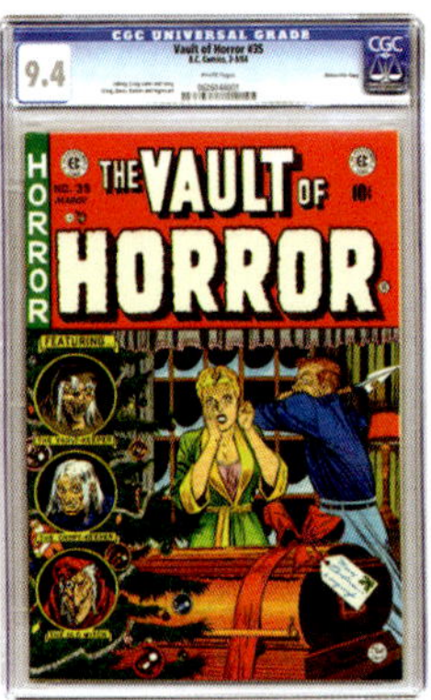

3139 Vault of Horror #35 Gaines File pedigree, 7/12 (EC, 1954) CGC NM 9.4 White pages. Merry Christmas, Darling! This has to be the most macabre holiday comic book cover ever! That Johnny Craig — what a cut-up! In addition to Craig's cover, there's more cool visuals by Jack Davis, Jack Kamen, and Graham Ingels. Overstreet 2005 NM- 9.2 value = $430. CGC census 9/05: 4 in 9.4, 2 higher.

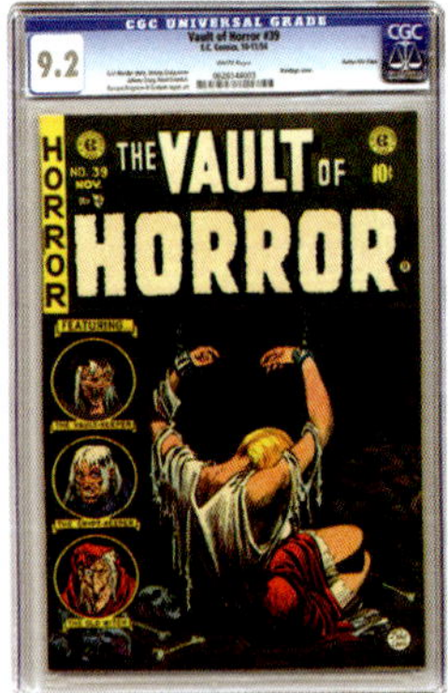

3140 Vault of Horror #39 Gaines File pedigree 11/12 (EC, 1954) CGC NM- 9.2 White pages. A Bondage cover by Johnny Craig is the highlight of this choice issue. Craig is joined by Reed Crandall, Bernie Krigstein, and Graham Ingels art inside. Although this copy doesn't top the CGC charts, it still looks incredibly nice, with great cover colors and sharp edges. Overstreet 2005 NM- 9.2 value = $415. CGC census 9/05: 1 in 9.2, 5 higher.

3141 War Against Crime #7 (EC, 1949) CGC VF 8.0 Cream to off-white pages. Johnny Craig cover. Al Feldstein art. Overstreet 2005 VF 8.0 value = $240. CGC census 9/05: 1 in 8.0, 1 higher.

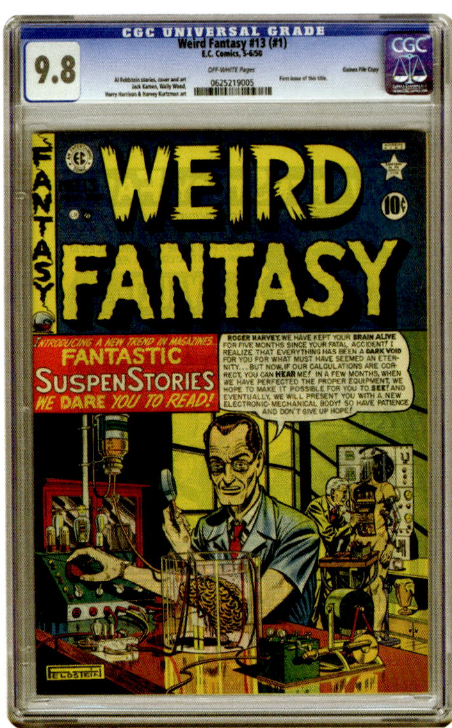

3142 Weird Fantasy 13 (#1) Gaines File pedigree (EC, 1950) CGC NM/MT 9.8 Off-white pages. The first issue of this title grabs your attention with cover art by Al Feldstein, who also provided it's stories. It would eventually become **Weird Science Fantasy** with #23. This stunning Gaines File copy contains interior art by Feldstein as well, along with Harry Harrison, Jack Kamen, and Harvey Kurtzman. This is currently the highest grade awarded by CGC for this issue, and the nicest copy we've offered so far. While CGC has certified this as a Gaines File copy, no certificate accompanies this lot. Overstreet 2005 NM- 9.2 value = $2,800. CGC census 8/05: 2 in 9.8, none higher.

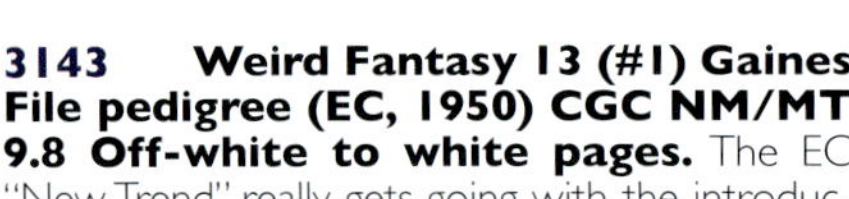

3143 Weird Fantasy 13 (#1) Gaines File pedigree (EC, 1950) CGC NM/MT 9.8 Off-white to white pages. The EC "New Trend" really gets going with the introduction of this groundbreaking title, and you couldn't ask for a nicer copy of the first issue than this stunning pedigreed example. Al Feldstein's cover theme was later echoed by the hit TV series "Six Million Dollar Man" — "we can rebuild him!" Feldstein, Harry Harrison, Jack Kamen, and Harvey Kurtzman are all featured artists. Although CGC recognizes this as a Gaines file copy, no certificate accompanies this book. Overstreet 2005 NM- 9.2 value = $2,800. CGC census 9/05: 2 in 9.8, none higher.

3144 Weird Fantasy #13 (#1) (EC, 1950) CGC NM 9.4 Off-white to white pages. EC introduced "a new trend in magazines" here, continuing the numbering from the bizarrely named **A Moon, A Girl ... Romance**. This premiere issue has an Al Feldstein cover, plus interior art by Feldstein, Jack Kamen, Harvey Kurtzman, and the team of Harry Harrison and Wally Wood. Overstreet 2005 NM- 9.2 value = $2,800. CGC census 9/05: 1 in 9.4, 3 higher.

3145 Weird Fantasy #13 (#1) (EC, 1950) CGC VF- 7.5 Cream to off-white pages. EC's "new trend in magazines" began here, and comics were never the same! This premiere issue (the numbering was continued from **A Moon, A Girl... Romance**) has an Al Feldstein cover, plus interior art by Feldstein, Jack Kamen, Harvey Kurtzman, and the team of Harry Harrison and Wally Wood. Overstreet 2005 VF 8.0 value = $1,448. CGC census 8/05: 2 in 7.5, 12 higher.

3146 Weird Fantasy #14 (#2) Gaines File pedigree (EC, 1950) CGC NM/MT 9.8 Off-white to white pages. This incredible copy of the second **Weird Fantasy** comic features a dynamic Atomic explosion cover, by Al Feldstein. Story art is by Feldstein (starring himself as a character, along with Bill Gaines), Wally Wood, Jack Kamen, and Harvey Kurtzman. This one's a dazzler — sharply cut, silky-smooth surfaces, rich, deep colors — *wow!* Although CGC recognizes this as a Gaines file copy, no certificate accompanies this book. Overstreet 2005 NM- 9.2 value = $1,300. CGC census 9/05: 2 in 9.8, none higher.

3147 Weird Fantasy 15 (#3) Gaines File pedigree (EC, 1950) CGC NM+ 9.6 Off-white to white pages. Take a trip in Outer Space, courtesy of this colorful Al Feldstein cover. Feldstein, Harvey Kurtzman, Jack Kamen, and Wally Wood all contribute story art. Although CGC recognizes this as a Gaines file copy, no certificate accompanies this book. Overstreet 2005 NM- 9.2 value = $870. CGC census 9/05: 1 in 9.6, 1 higher.

3148 Weird Fantasy 17 (#5) Gaines File pedigree (EC, 1951) CGC NM 9.4 White pages. Al Feldstein gives us a great "cigar"-shaped rocket ship cover for this fifth issue. Inside, Al's joined by Harvey Kurtzman, Wally Wood, and Jack Kamen on the story art. Although CGC recognizes this as a Gaines file copy, no certificate accompanies this book. Overstreet 2005 NM- 9.2 value = $725. CGC census 9/05: 1 in 9.4, 1 higher.

3149 Weird Fantasy #8 Gaines File pedigree (EC, 1951) CGC NM 9.4 Off-white to white pages. Those Al Feldstein-drawn space creatures on the cover of this issue look positively... *weird*! Feldstein, Wally Wood, Jack Kamen, and George Roussos story art is featured. Although CGC recognizes this as a Gaines File copy, no certificate accompanies the book. Overstreet 2005 NM- 9.2 value = $595. CGC census 9/05: 1 in 9.4, 2 higher.

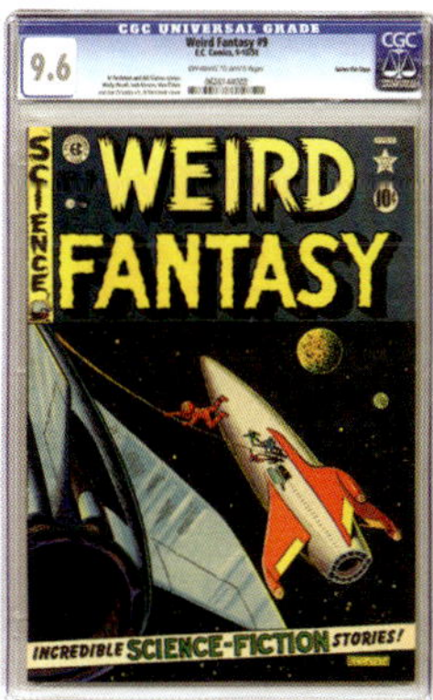

3150 Weird Fantasy #9 Gaines File pedigree (EC, 1951) CGC NM+ 9.6 Off-white to white pages. An Al Feldstein illustration of a rocket ship floating in an inky black space adorns this sparkling cover. Wally Wood, Jack Kamen, Marty Elkin, and Joe Orlando art is featured. Although recognized by CGC as a Gaines File copy, no certificate accompanies this book. Overstreet 2005 NM- 9.2 value = $595. CGC census 9/05: 2 in 9.6, none higher.

3151 Weird Fantasy #10 Gaines File pedigree (EC, 1951) CGC NM/MT 9.8 Off-white to white pages. This file copy looks about as nice as any you'll ever lay eyes on! The Al Feldstein cover illustration, depicting a cigar-shaped rocket ship zooming past Saturn, is a real grabber; you can almost get lost in the inky black outer space background! Interior art is by Wally Wood (two stories), Jack Kamen, and Joe Orlando. Although recognized as a Gaines file copy, no certificate accompanies this book. Overstreet 2005 NM- 9.2 value = $595. CGC census 9/05: 2 in 9.8, none higher.

3152 Weird Fantasy #10 (EC, 1951) CGC NM+ 9.6 Off-white pages. In this issue's story "A Timely Shock," drawn by Jack Kamen, an unwitting time-traveler meets a beautiful woman who immediately proposes marriage to him. This being an EC, there's a catch that he didn't know about, heh heh ... The book also features an Al Feldstein cover, two stories drawn by Wally Wood, and one story from the drawing board of Joe Orlando. Overstreet 2005 NM- 9.2 value = $595. CGC census 9/05: 1 in 9.6, 2 higher.

3153 Weird Fantasy #12 Gaines File pedigree (EC, 1952) CGC NM+ 9.6 Off-white to white pages. Al Feldstein's "rocket on another planet" cover is truly out of this world! Jack Kamen, Joe Orlando (also featured in the "Artist of the Issue" bio), and Wally Wood contribute story art. This is the famous issue featuring a cameo of the EC artists. Although CGC recognizes this as a Gaines file copy, no certificate accompanies this book. Overstreet 2005 NM- 9.2 value = $. CGC census 9/05: 2 in 9.6, 1 higher.

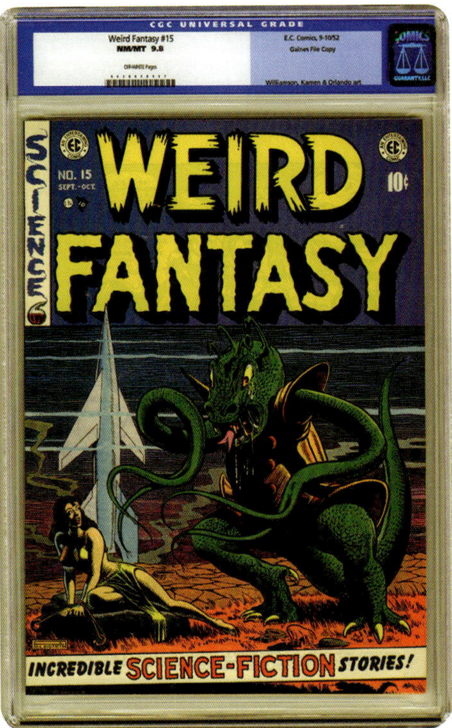

3154 Weird Fantasy #15 Gaines File pedigree (EC, 1952) CGC NM/MT 9.8 Off-white pages. Not only is this the only 9.8 in CGC's census as of this writing, the nearest runner-up is two notches down at 9.4! Al Williamson drew two stories for this issue, one with an assist by George Evans according to Overstreet. There are also stories drawn by Joe Orlando and Jack Kamen. The cover is by Al Feldstein. Note that while CGC has certified this comic as a Gaines File copy, no certificate accompanies this lot. Overstreet 2005 NM- 9.2 value = $870. CGC census 9/05: 1 in 9.8, none higher.

3155 Weird Fantasy #18 Gaines File pedigree (EC, 1953) CGC NM 9.4 Off-white to white pages. Al Williamson and Al Feldstein contribute a fantastic Space Station cover. A Ray Bradbury story, "Zero Hour," is given the EC treatment; plus, the classic Joe Orlando-illustrated story "Judgement Day" is featured. Al Williamson/Roy Krenkel, Jack Kamen, and John Severin/Bill Elder art also appears. Although CGC recognizes this copy as a Gaines File copy, no certificate accompanies this book. Overstreet 2005 NM- 9.2 value = $460. CGC census 9/05: 1 in 9.4, 2 higher.

3156 Weird Fantasy #19 Gaines File pedigree (EC, 1953) CGC VF/NM 9.0 White pages. This issue's cover announces another Ray Bradbury adaptation: "King of the Grey Spaces" was illustrated by the team of John Severin and Bill Elder. Other artists include Al Williamson (also featured in the "Artist of the Issue" bio), Jack Kamen, and Joe Orlando. Although CGC recognizes this as a Gaines file copy, no certificate accompanies the book. Overstreet 2005 VF/NM 9.0 value = $350; NM- 9.2 value = $460. CGC census 9/05: 1 in 9.0, 2 higher.

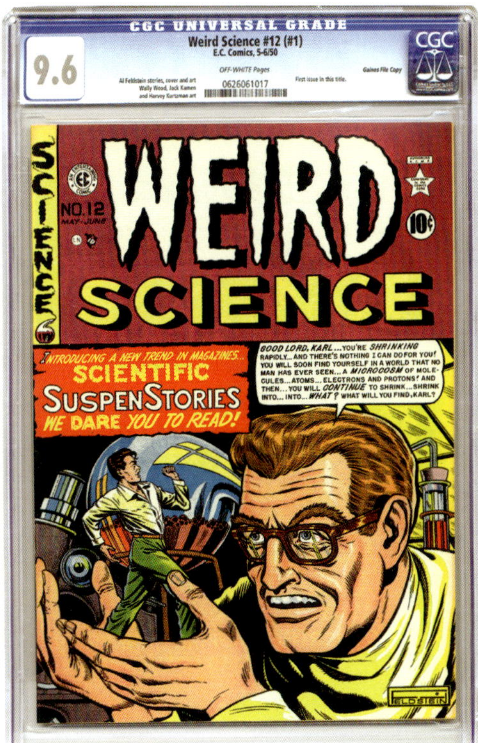

3157 Weird Science 12 (#1) Gaines File pedigree (EC, 1950) CGC NM+ 9.6 Off-white pages. Here's a pedigreed copy of the very first issue of this important title, in near-perfect condition. Al Feldstein's cover sets the tone, and interior art by Feldstein, Harvey Kurtzman (the classic story "Lost in the Microcosm"), Jack Kamen, and the team of Harry Harrison and Wally Wood keep things flying high. The Harrison/Wood story "Dream of Doom" parodies the entire EC staff. Although CGC recognizes this as a Gaines file copy, no certificate accompanies this book. Overstreet 2005 NM- 9.2 value = $2,800. CGC census 9/05: 1 in 9.6, none higher.

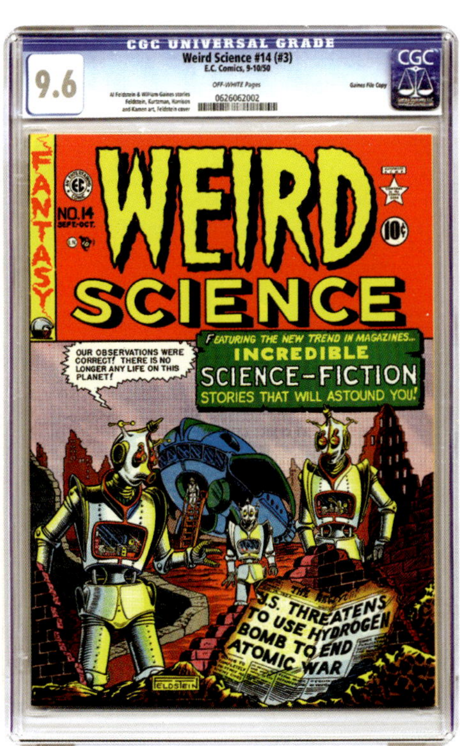

3158 Weird Science 14 (#3) Gaines File pedigree (EC, 1950) CGC NM+ 9.6 Off-white pages. Here's a beauty of a copy of this third issue, complete with an Al Feldstein robot cover. Feldstein (an "End of the World" tale), Harvey Kurtzman, Harry Harrison, and Jack Kamen all add story art. Although CGC recognizes this as a Gaines file copy, no certificate accompanies this book. Overstreet 2005 NM- 9.2 value = $1,225. CGC census 9/05: 3 in 9.6, 1 higher.

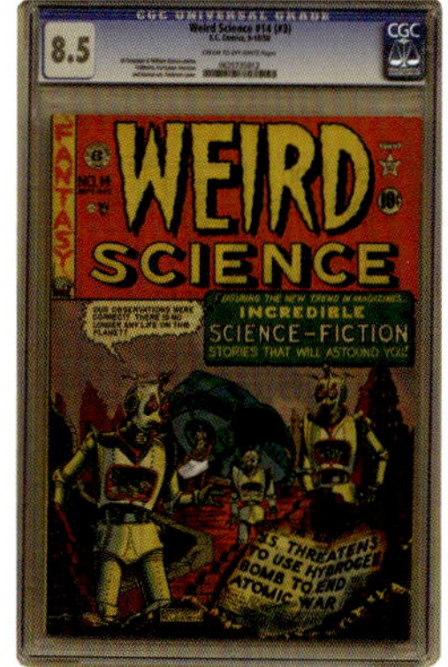

3159 Weird Science #14 (#3) (EC, 1950) CGC VF+ 8.5 Cream to off-white pages. Post-apocalyptic scenarios were revisited several times by EC's creators, with a powerful story the inevitable result. This time, it's Al Feldstein drawing the story (as well as the accompanying cover scene). This third issue also includes art by Harvey Kurtzman, Harry Harrison, and Jack Kamen. Overstreet 2005 VF 8.0 value = $630; VF/NM 9.0 value = $928. CGC census 9/05: 1 in 8.5, 6 higher.

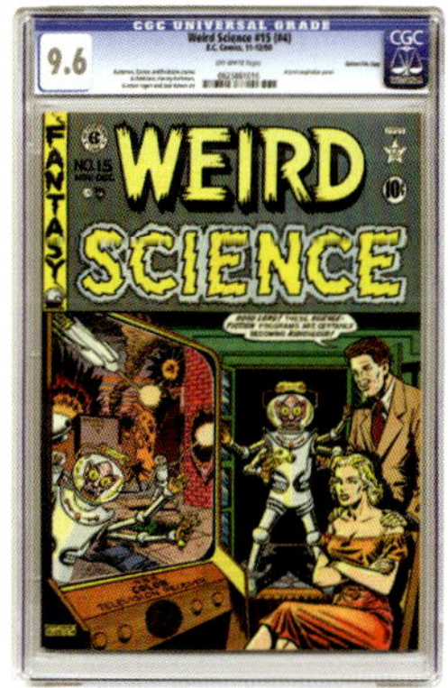

3160 Weird Science 15 (#4) Gaines File pedigree, 4/12 (EC, 1950) CGC NM+ 9.6 Off-white pages. Al Feldstein provides this early issue with a cover illustration that manages to be scary and funny and the same time! What a genius! And what a brilliant copy — sharp and sweet, with great cover color and near-flawless flat surfaces. Interior art is provided by Feldstein, Harvey Kurtzman ("The Radioactive Child"), Jack Kamen, and Graham Ingels (Ingels' only science story for EC). Overstreet 2005 NM- 9.2 value = $1,125. CGC census 8/05: 3 in 9.6, 1 higher.

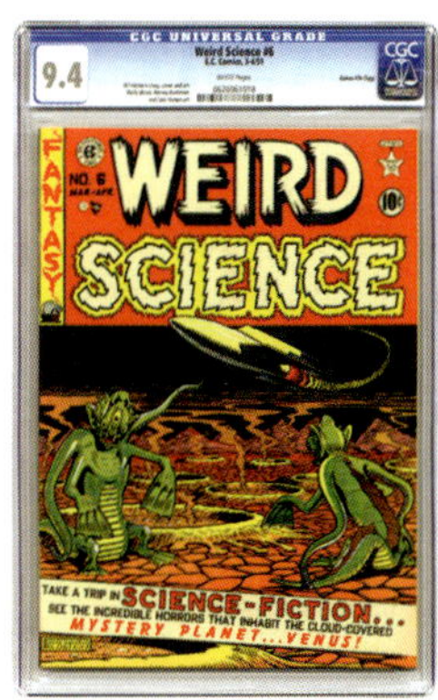

3161 Weird Science #6 Gaines File pedigree (EC, 1951) CGC NM 9.4 White pages. No one drew goofy-looking alien creature covers better than Al Feldstein, and here's one of his best! Inside, there's cool art by Wally Wood, Harvey Kurtzman, and Jack Kamen, plus Feldstein's classic "Spawn of Venus" story. Although CGC recognizes this as a Gaines File copy, no certificate accompanies the book. Overstreet 2005 NM- 9.2 value = $695. CGC census 9/05: 1 in 9.4, 1 higher.

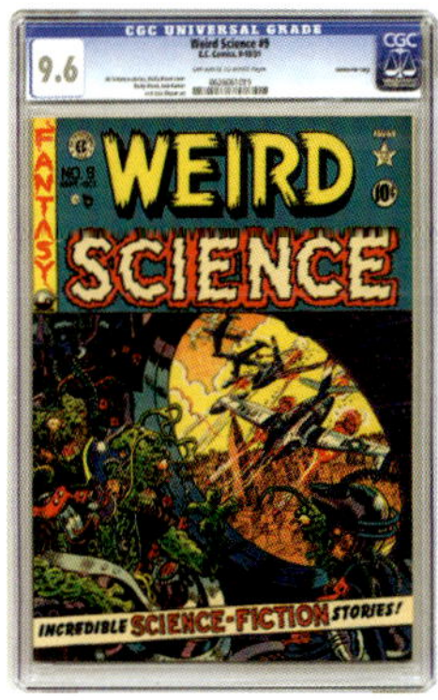

3162 Weird Science #9 Gaines File pedigree (EC, 1951) CGC NM+ 9.6 Off-white to white pages. Wally Wood turns in a great gruesome-looking alien invasion illustration for this cover, his first for EC. Interior art by Wood (two stories), Jack Kamen, and guest artist George Olesen. Although CGC recognizes this as a Gaines file copy, no certificate accompanies this book. Overstreet 2005 NM- 9.2 value = $695. CGC census 9/05: 5 in 9.6, none higher.

3163 Weird Science #12 Gaines File pedigree (EC, 1952) CGC NM 9.4 Off-white pages. A wild Wally Wood cover illustration shows the classic "inside the space ship" scene Wood became famous for. Interior stories include art by Wood (two stories), Jack Kamen, and Joe Orlando. Although recognized by CGC as a Gaines file copy, no certificate accompanies this book. Overstreet 2005 NM- 9.2 value = $490. CGC census 9/05: 1 in 9.4, none higher.

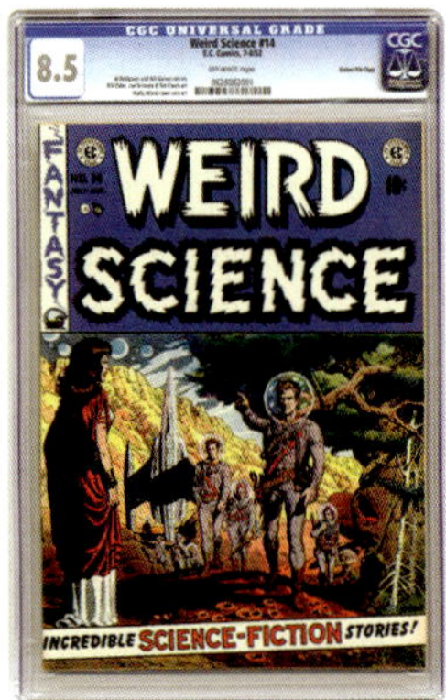

3164 Weird Science #14 Gaines File pedigree (EC, 1952) CGC VF+ 8.5 Off-white pages. For the life of us, we can't tell why this incredible file copy didn't receive a NM 9.4 or better grade, but who are we to argue? Check this one out closely! Wally Wood's gorgeous art adorns the cover; he was joined by Bill Elder, Sid Check, and Joe Orlando on the story art chores. Although CGC recognizes this as a Gaines file copy, no certificate accompanies this book. Overstreet 2005 VF 8.0 value = $255; VF/NM 9.0 value = $373. CGC census 9/05: 1 in 8.5, 6 higher.

3165 Weird Science #22 Gaines File pedigree (EC, 1953) CGC NM 9.4 Off-white to white pages. For Wally Wood fans, this final issue offers up something special. First, there's Wood cover, a colorful "creature in a castle" concept with an added Outer Space twist. But the real prize is inside: the "My World" story with Wood art, narrated by the artist. There's also art by Al Williamson (with help from Frank Frazetta and Roy Krenkel), George Evans, and Joe Orlando. Comics this good just weren't meant to last, it seems! Although CGC recognizes this as a Gaines file copy, no certificate accompanies this book. Overstreet 2005 NM- 9.2 value = $665. CGC census 9/05: 2 in 9.4, none higher.

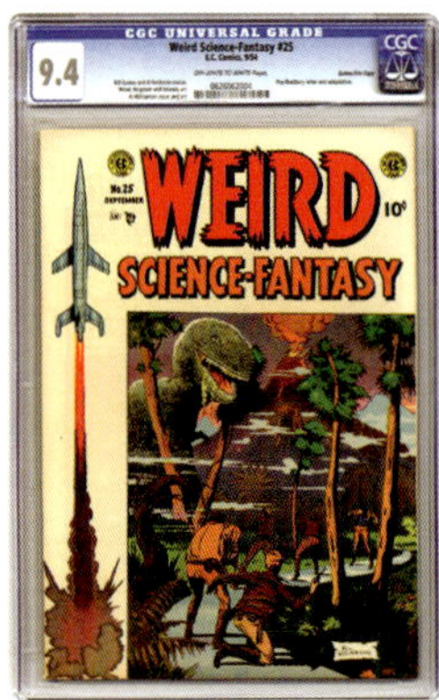

3166 Weird Science-Fantasy #25 Gaines File pedigree (EC, 1954) CGC NM 9.4 Off-white to white pages. Al Williamson scores a direct hit with this wild "Lost World cover, complete with a hungry dinosaur ready to pounce on the hapless humans who wandered in. This issue gets a jump-start on #26's "Flying Saucer Report" with one story. Williamson (doing a Ray Bradbury adaptation), Wally Wood, Marie Severin, Bernard Krigstein, and Joe Orlando are featured artists. Although CGC recognizes this as a Gaines file copy, no certificate accompanies this book. Overstreet 2005 NM- 9.2 value = $520. CGC census 9/05: 1 in 9.4, 1 higher.

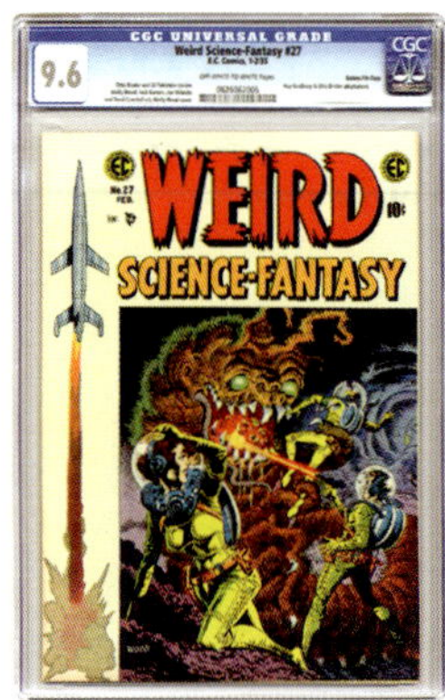

3167 Weird Science-Fantasy #27 Gaines File pedigree (EC, 1955) CGC NM+ 9.6 Off-white to white pages. It's time for some Bug Eyed Monster fun with this issue, courtesy of Wally Wood's great cover illustration. There's also art by Jack Kamen, Joe Orlando ("I, Robot," based on the "Adam Link" stories by Eando Binder), and Reed Crandall. Although CGC recognizes this as a Gaines file copy, no certificate accompanies this book. Overstreet 2005 NM- 9.2 value = $475. CGC census 9/05: 1 in 9.6, 1 higher.

3168 Weird Science-Fantasy #28 Gaines File pedigree (EC, 1955) CGC NM+ 9.6 Off-white pages. Al Feldstein's cover makes us wonder — is this Earth in the future, or some strange planet? At any rate, this is a sweet copy of this next-to-last issue (before the title changed to **Incredible Science Fiction**), which also includes an Adam Link story. Wally Wood, Al Williamson, Jack Kamen, and Joe Orlando all contribute interior art. Although CGC recognizes this as a Gaines file copy, no certificate accompanies this book. Overstreet 2005 NM- 9.2 value = $. CGC census 9/05: 2 in 9.6, 1 higher.

3169 Air Pirates Funnies (tabloid) #1 (Air Pirates, 1972) Condition: NM-. Extremely nice copy of this hard-to-find tabloid. Art by Bobby London, Shary Flenniken, and Dan O'Neill. Adult themes; not listed in Overstreet.

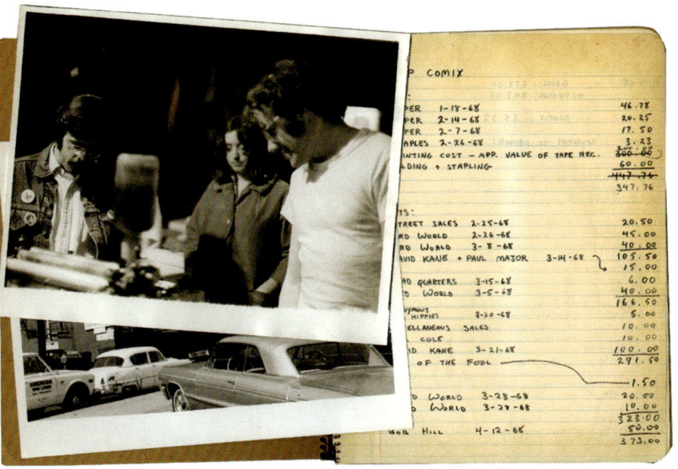

3170 Zap Comics #1 Publishing Archive Material (1968). The history of Underground Comix may have to be rewritten with this lot! From the archives of Apex Novelties founder and printer of the second edition copies of **Zap Comix** #1 comes this incredible treasure trove of information, receipts, notes, etc. from the Halcyon days of Underground Comix, circa 1968. Donahue traded Charles Plymell a tape recorder (valued at the time at $200) for the offset printing press Plymell used to print the book that started it all - Robert Crumb's **Zap** #1. The story that circulated for years was that Robert and his first wife, Dana, took the freshly-printed copies of **Zap** #1 from Plymell and hawked them on the streets of San Francisco's Height Asbury district from a baby carriage. We now know this is only partially true; it was actually Don Donahue, *not* Crumb, who was there with Dana. In fact, this lot includes the cash envelope from that day, with sales totals for Dana ($5.50), Don ($3.00 - slacker!) and Mimi ($12.00), dated 2/25/68. Also included in this historic lot is a photo of Donahue at his press, his receipts from various dealers for stacks of **Zap** #1, and copies of letters, photos, and a Jack Jackson eight-page comic story about the early days of Donahue's flat-mates, Rip Off Press (they all shared a loft in an old, condemned opera house in a bad part of town). Find out the costs of printing the second edition of **Zap**, and the share of the profits paid to Crumb (too little to print here without embarrassing the artist)! If the story of this fascinating chapter of comics history is your thing, here's a once-in-a-lifetime chance to own these rare archival items.

Certificate of Authenticity

This Certificate of Authenticity represents my guarantee that this is an original genuine Morse's Funnies.

This comic book was printed in the early 70s under my direction and is signed by me.

First Edition of first printing on card stock, consisting of 15 pages on one side.

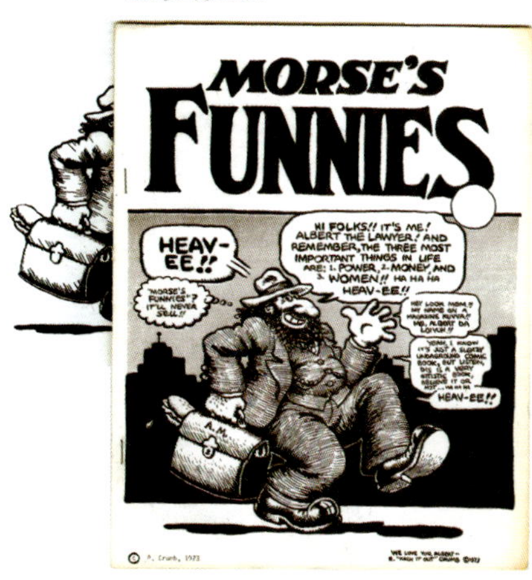

3171 Morse's Funnies #1 First Edition (Albert Morse, 1974) Condition: VF/NM. This is the super-rare edition of fifteen pages, each printed on one side only. Cover by Robert Crumb; other artists include Art Spiegelman and Trina Robbins. Signed by Albert Morse on the inside front cover; also includes a certificate of authenticity which was also signed by Morse. One of only 50 copies printed; this copy was purchased directly from Morse by the consignor. Adult themes; not listed in Overstreet.

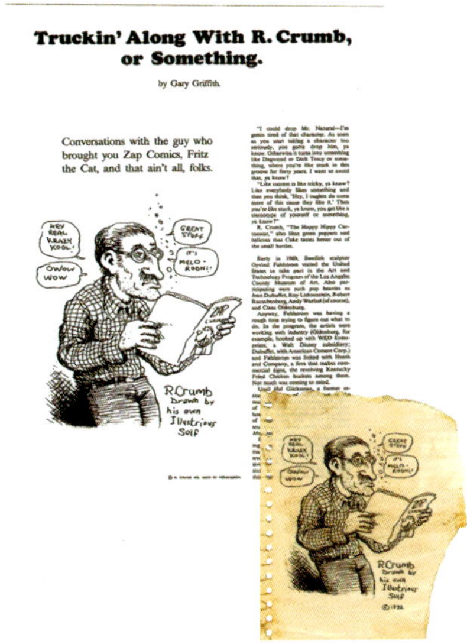

3172 Robert Crumb - Self Portrait Original Art (1972). This sketch shows Robert reading a copy of **Zap Comix**. As Crumb self-portraits go, this one is a little unusual, with extra emphasis given to his rather large (but noble) nose. This rare sketch of Crumb reading his own comic (his *only* self-portrait of this kind) was done during an interview conducted by Gary Griffith; Crumb then surprised Griffith by handing him the finished sketch, which was used in the article (a reprint is included with this lot). This sketchbook fragment measures approximately 4.5" x 5.5"; there are glue stains on the back that are beginning to show through, none of which really detract from the piece. Overall condition is very good.

3173 Tales from the Tube #1 Insert Edition (Surfer Magazine, 1972) Condition: NM. Hard to find 8.5" x 11" version of this classic Underground, originally published as an insert in **Surfer Magazine**. Art by Rick Griffin, Robert Crumb, S. Clay Wilson, and Robert Williams. This version rarely turns up in NM condition. Adult themes; not listed in Overstreet.

RANDOM HOUSE COMICS

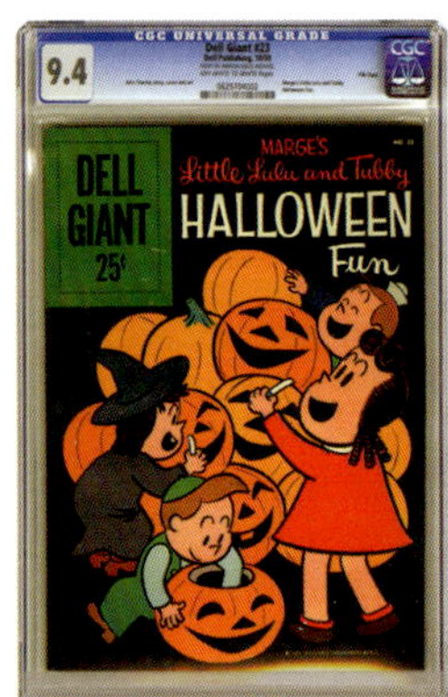

3174 Dell Giants #23 Marge's Little Lulu and Tubby Halloween Fun - File Copy (Dell, 1959) CGC NM 9.4 Off-white to white pages. CGC credits John Stanley with this issue's art, while Overstreet gives Irving Tripp the nod. Whatever the case, this copy of the square bound issue is tied for the highest grade that CGC has certified for the issue to date. Overstreet 2005 NM- 9.2 value = $210. CGC census 7/05: 3 in 9.4, none higher. *From the Random House Archives.*

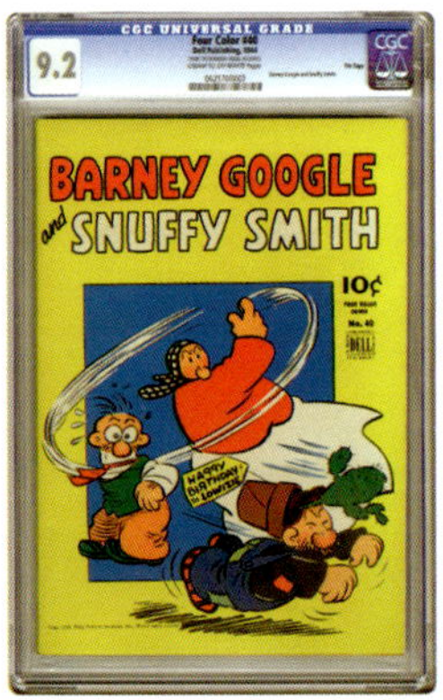

3175 Four Color #40 Barney Google and Snuffy Smith - File Copy (Dell, 1944) CGC NM- 9.2 Cream to off-white pages. This issue reprints Sunday pages by Billy DeBeck which appeared from 1939-42 (DeBeck was deceased by the time this comic hit the stands). Our offering is the highest-graded copy of the issue that CGC has certified to date. Overstreet 2005 NM- 9.2 value = $350. CGC census 7/05: 1 in 9.2, none higher. *From the Random House Archives.*

3176 Four Color #1008 Beep Beep the Road Runner - File Copy (Dell, 1959) CGC NM+ 9.6 Off-white pages. Overstreet 2005 NM- 9.2 value = $80. CGC census 7/05: 2 in 9.6, none higher. *From the Random House Archives.*

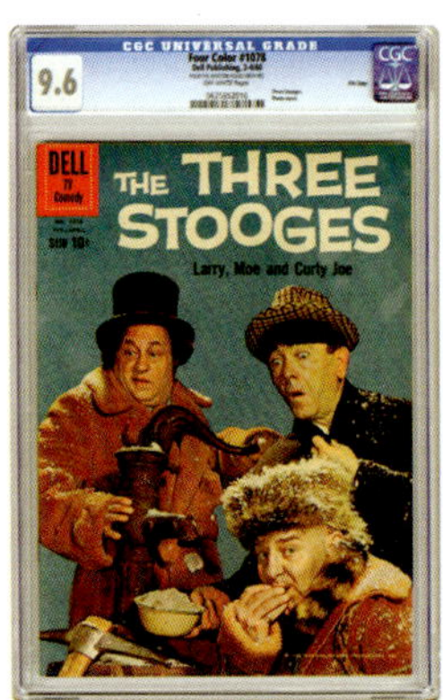

3177 Four Color #1078 The Three Stooges - File Copy (Dell, 1960) CGC NM+ 9.6 Off-white pages. Messrs. Howard, Fine, and DeRita star in this issue as well as on the photo cover. Our offering is the highest-graded copy of the issue that CGC has certified to date. Overstreet 2005 NM- 9.2 value = $200. CGC census 7/05: 1 in 9.6, none higher. *From the Random House Archives.*

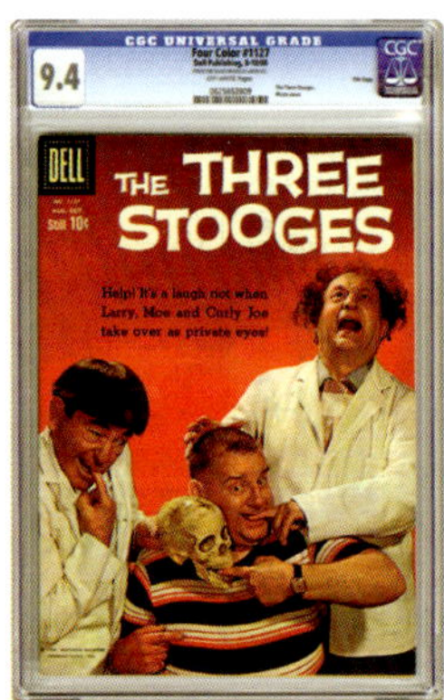

3178 Four Color #1127 The Three Stooges - File Copy (Dell, 1960) CGC NM 9.4 Off-white pages. It's "zany photo cover" time for the Three Stooges... gee, they're usually so dignified! Only one copy of the issue has been graded higher than this one by CGC to date. Overstreet 2005 NM- 9.2 value = $200. CGC census 7/05: 1 in 9.4, 1 higher. *From the Random House Archives.*

3179 Four Color #1129 Pollyanna - File Copy (Dell, 1960) CGC NM 9.4 Off-white pages. Hayley Mills photo cover. Overstreet 2005 NM- 9.2 value = $115. CGC census 8/05: 3 in 9.4, 1 higher. *From the Random House Archives.*

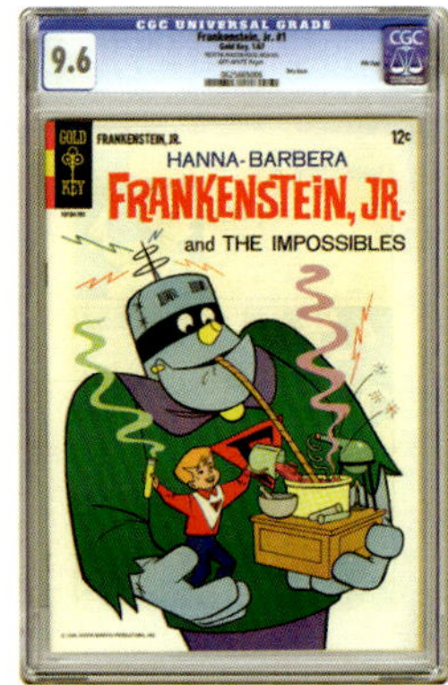

3180 Frankenstein, Jr. #1 File Copy (Gold Key, 1967) CGC NM+ 9.6 Off-white pages. Some of these 1960s Gold Key one-shots are the devil to get your hands on, and this one even earned Overstreet's "scarce" designation. Overstreet 2005 NM- 9.2 value = $170. CGC census 7/05: 6 in 9.6, 1 higher. *From the Random House Archives.*

3181 H.R. Pufnstuf #2 File Copy (Gold Key, 1971) CGC NM 9.4 Off-white to white pages. Photo cover. Overstreet 2005 NM- 9.2 value = $155. CGC census 7/05: 2 in 9.4, none higher. *From the Random House Archives.*

3182 H.R. Pufnstuf #3 File Copy (Gold Key, 1971) CGC NM 9.4 Off-white to white pages. Photo cover. Overstreet 2005 NM- 9.2 value = $155. CGC census 7/05: 2 in 9.4, 1 higher. *From the Random House Archives.*

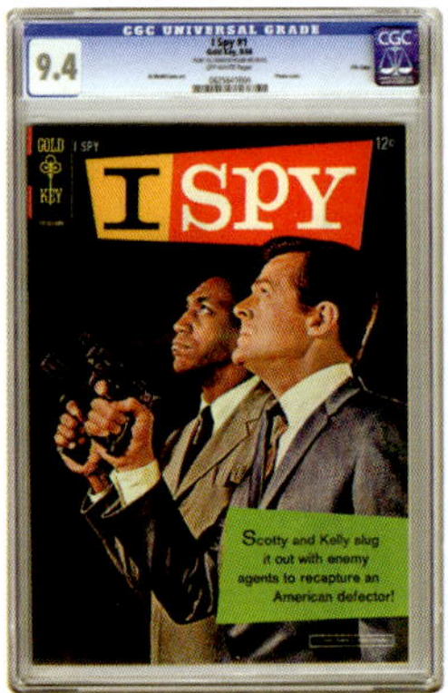

3183 I Spy #1 File Copy (Gold Key, 1966) CGC NM 9.4 Off-white pages. This issue's black cover makes it a tough find in high grade, luckily we've got a copy from the files of Western Publishing. Bill Cosby and Robert Culp star on the photo cover — why are they staring at the Gold Key logo, anyway? The issue's art is by Alden McWilliams. Overstreet 2005 NM- 9.2 value = $340. CGC census 7/05: 9 in 9.4, none higher. *From the Random House Archives.*

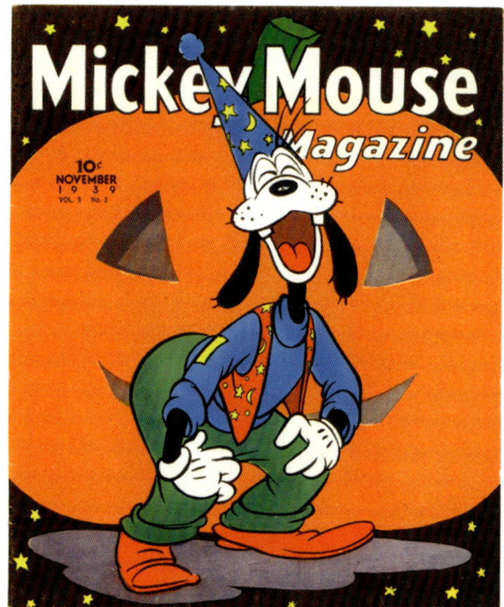

3184 Mickey Mouse Magazine File Copies Group (K. K. Publications, Inc., 1939-40). These are the final issues of the series that was the predecessor to **Walt Disney's Comics and Stories**, and the transition from this title's early format (magazine size with a couple of comic pages) to comic book format becomes apparent here, with V5#9 the first to be published in a narrower size and V5#12, the last issue of the title, the first to contain a significant amount of comic content (34 of 64 pages). Of special note is V5#2, as it's the first time Pinocchio appeared in a comic magazine. Alas, only the last three are complete, but that includes V5#12, the most valuable book of the bunch. The group includes V5#2 (PR, pages 19-24 missing, however the page with Pinocchio is present), V5#4 (PR, pages 17-20 missing), V5#6 (PR, pages 17-20 missing), V5#8 (PR, pages 17-20 missing), V5#9 (VG+), V5#10 (VG+), and V5#12 (VG; a Gerber "7"). The last three issues have gags created by Carl Barks. Approximate Overstreet value for group = $1,150. *From the Random House Archives.*

3185 Rawhide #1 File Copy (Gold Key, 1963) CGC NM- 9.2 Off-white to white pages. Photo cover featuring Clint Eastwood and Eric Fleming. Overstreet 2005 NM- 9.2 value = $200. CGC census 7/05: 1 in 9.2, none higher. *From the Random House Archives.*

RANDOM HOUSE ORIGINAL ART

3186 Pete Alvarado - Beagle Boys Versus Uncle Scrooge #1 Cover Original Art (Gold Key, 1979). In a race through the desert, Uncle Scrooge and the Beagle Boys compete to win "The Case of the Missing Nuggets" on this cover illustration from the first issue of this Gold Key series. The art has an image area of 10" x 11", and is in Excellent condition. *From the Random House Archives.*

3187 Pete Alvarado - Beagle Boys Versus Uncle Scrooge #12 Cover Original Art (Gold Key, 1980). Uncle Scrooge works night shift security in his vault, much to the surprise of some marauding Beagle Boys, in this cover illustration. The art has an image area of 10" x 11" and is in Excellent condition. *From the Random House Archives.*

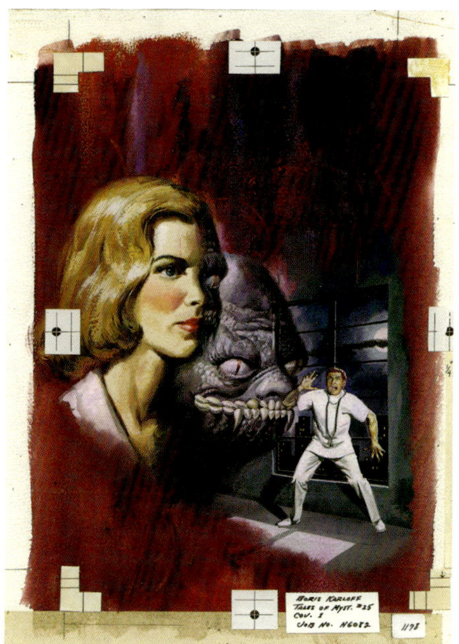

3188 Western Publishing Artist - Boris Karloff Tales of Mystery #25 Cover Original Art (Gold Key, 1969). She's a cold-hearted lizard woman in the guise of a lovely nurse, and the doctor is not happy! Here's a weird, wild illustration that covers the interior story, "The Thing Called Illona". Painted in watercolor on textured board, this art has an image area measuring 10.5" x 15" and is in Excellent condition. *From the Random House Archives.*

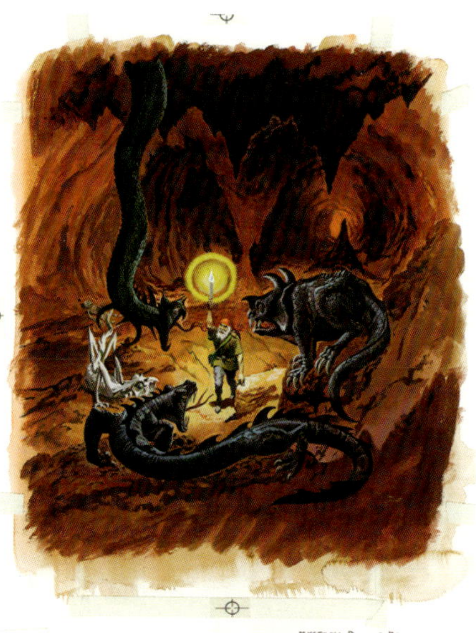

3189 Western Publishing Artist - Boris Karloff Tales of Mystery Story Digest #2 Cover Original Art (Gold Key, 1970). A lone explorer in a dimly lit cavern faces some monstrosities that won't be found in any zoo, in this cover illustration for an apparently unpublished second issue of **Boris Karloff Tales of Mystery Story Digest**. Painted in watercolor on illustration board, this art has an image area measuring 10.5" x 13" and is in Excellent condition. *From the Random House Archives.*

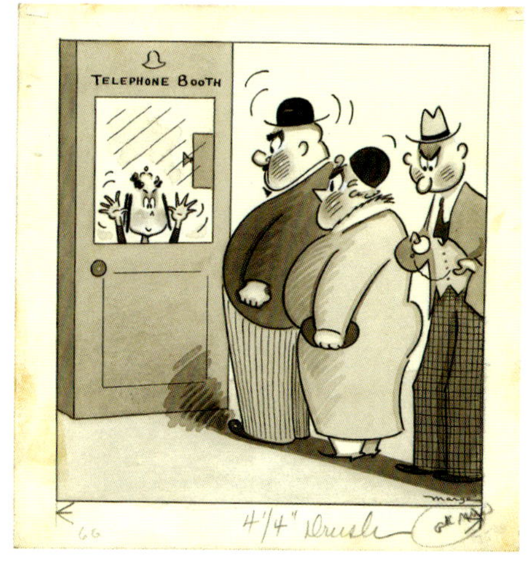

3190 Marge Buell - Little Lulu Panel Page Original Art (Saturday Evening Post, undated). In the days before cell phones, Little Lulu shows our bidders the number-one way kids used to annoy the public! *Little Lulu* was the brain-child of Marjorie Henderson Buell. The little moppet started out as a single-panel cartoon in the **Saturday Evening Post** on February 23, 1935. Dell Comics launched a title based on the merry prankster in 1945. This ink wash over pen and ink cartoon has an image area of 6.5" x 7", and the art is in Excellent condition. *From the Random House Archives.*

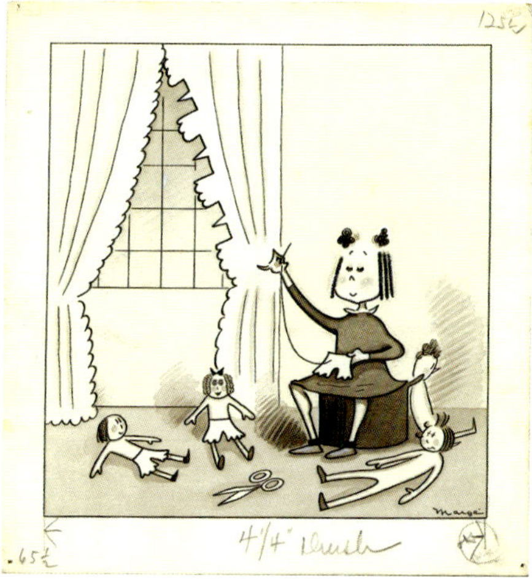

3191 Marge Buell - Little Lulu Panel Page Original Art (Saturday Evening Post, undated). While in a prim and proper mood, Little Lulu sews dainties for her dollies — but maybe she shouldn't make them from the curtain fabric! In a feature that often spotlighted children's ingenuity, Marge's Little Lulu established herself as a comedy starlet who was half-prankster and half free-thinker. *Little Lulu* took the country by storm in the mid-forties, and soon other cartoonists such as John Stanley and Roger Armstrong were tapped to draw her adventures for comic books and newspaper strips. This pen, ink, and grey tone wash illustration has an image area of 6.5" x 7". and the art is in Excellent condition. *From the Random House Archives.*

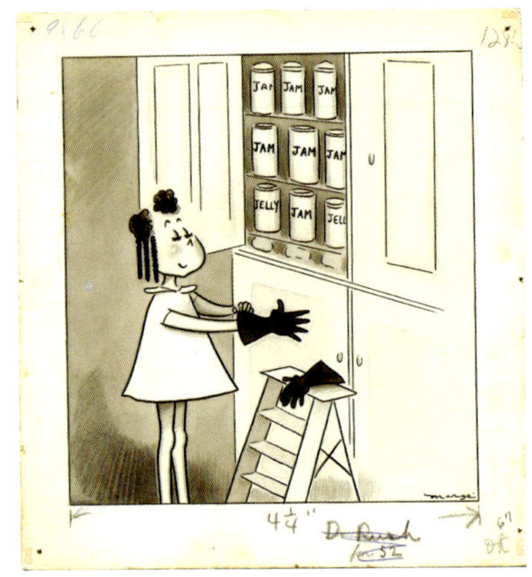

3192 Marge Buell - Little Lulu Panel Page Original Art (Saturday Evening Post, undated). Thinking ahead, Little Lulu protects herself from getting caught with sticky fingers! Little Lulu's devilish personality was rumored to have been based on "Marge" Henderson Buell's own mischevious youth. Marge created the Little Lulu character for the **Saturday Evening Post** as a replacement feature for the departing *Henry* strip. The image area of this knee-slapper measures 6.5" x 7" and the art is in Excellent condition. *From the Random House Archives.*

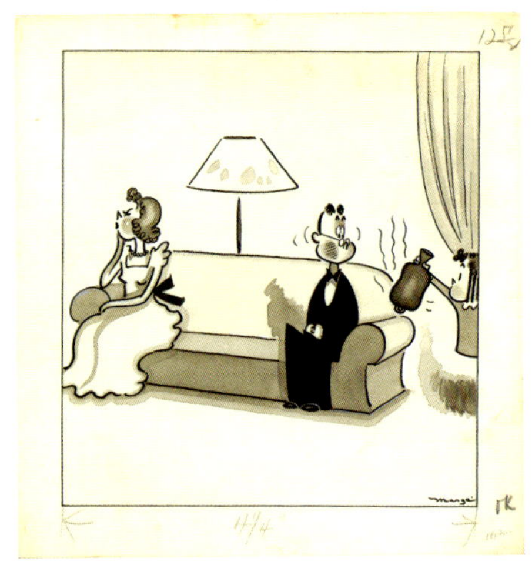

3193 Marge Buell - Little Lulu Panel Page Original Art (Saturday Evening Post, undated). Little Lulu offers her sure-fire solution to a suitor who is getting nothing but the "cold shoulder" from his date. This panel was drawn in ink and was given enhanced depth and mood lighting with greytone washes. The image area measures 6.5" x 7" and the art is in Excellent condition. *From the Random House Archives.*

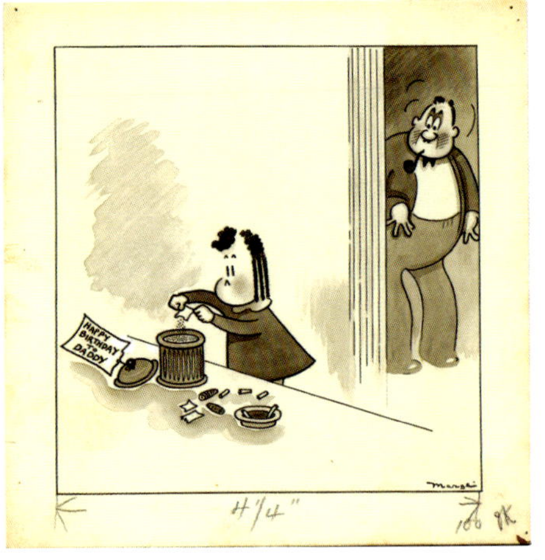

3194 Marge Buell - Little Lulu Panel Page Original Art (Saturday Evening Post, undated). One of the frequent highlights of Marge's **Saturday Evening Post** *Little Lulu* cartoons is watching the startled looks on the faces of the grown-ups after Lulu pulls one of her pranks. For a birthday gift, Lulu restocks her pop's pipe tobacco with a specially mixed blend! This pen and ink wash illustration has an image area of 6.5" x 7," and the art is in Excellent condition. *From the Random House Archives.*

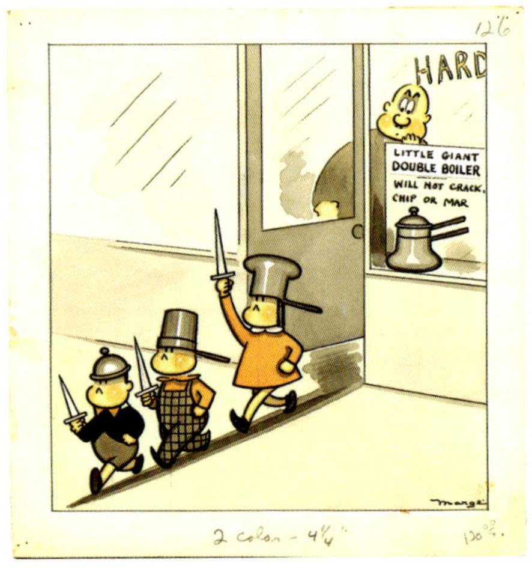

3195 Marge Buell - Little Lulu Panel Page Original Art (Saturday Evening Post, undated). Much to the astonishment of a frazzled hardware store clerk, Marge Buell's *enfant terrible*, Little Lulu, finds a new use for a giant double boiler — and one size fits all! Drawn in pen and ink with a red-orange wash on illustration board, this panel has an image area of 6.5" x 7," and the art is in Excellent condition. *From the Random House Archives.*

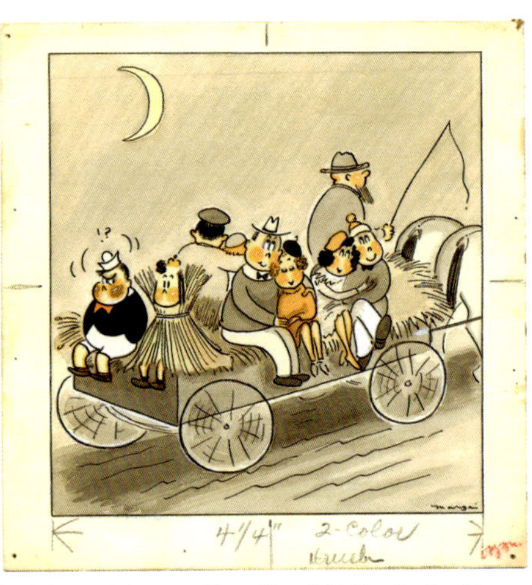

3196 Marge Buell - Little Lulu Panel Page Original Art (Saturday Evening Post, undated). Tubby's moves on a romantic hayride are foiled by Little Lulu's quick thinking — maybe when she's older, Lulu will agree to snuggle! This gag was drawn in grey and red-orange washes, and Marge's placement of the warmly colored accents in this panel is gorgeous. The image area of the drawing is 6.5" x 7", and the art is in Excellent condition. *From the Random House Archives.*

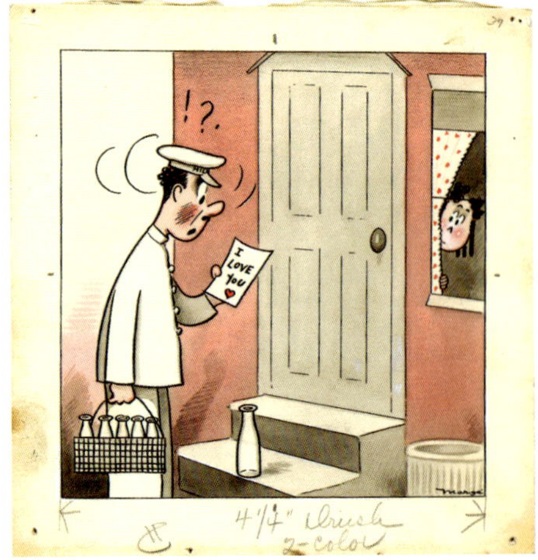

3197 Marge Buell - Little Lulu Panel Page Original Art (Saturday Evening Post, undated). This amusing milkman gag is among the cream of the crop! Lulu's note has the milkman totally flustered. This pen and ink illustration, enhanced with red washes, has an image area of 6.5" x 7", and is in Excellent condition. *From the Random House Archives.*

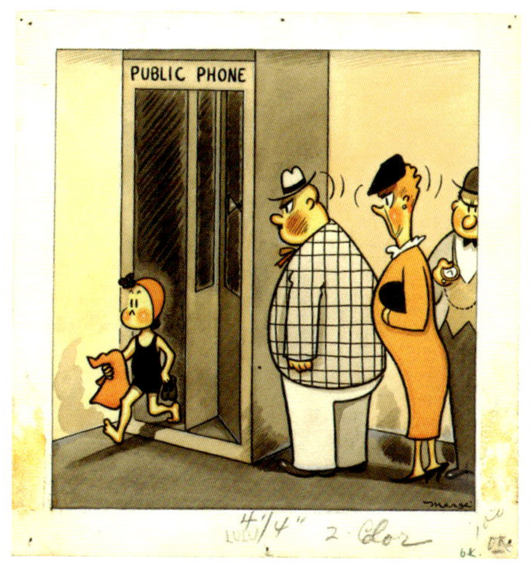

3198 Marge Buell - Little Lulu Panel Page Original Art (Saturday Evening Post, undated). Tsk, tsk! The things that people used to do in phone booths! Cell phones have all but eliminated a popular topic for panel cartoons. As for Lulu herself, she became the subject of children's books, games, puzzles, coloring books, activity books, greeting cards, dolls, and countless other merchandised items, and is still going strong today. With an image area of 6.5" x 7", and drawn using ink, and grey and orange washes, the art is in Excellent condition. *From the Random House Archives.*

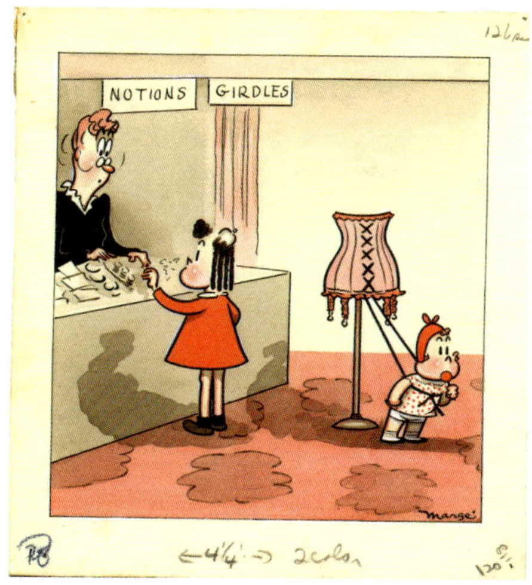

3199 Marge Buell - Little Lulu Panel Page Original Art (Saturday Evening Post, undated). Little Lulu has found a new use for the restraining power of the elastic girdle! Marjorie Buell, who signed her work simply as "Marge," has painted this hilarious piece using subtle and sublimely refined watercolor gradations of red and gray hues. Marge was a master at the art of pantomime humor and, the appeal of Little Lulu remains timeless. The image area of this panel measures approximately 6.5" x 7", and the art is in Excellent condition. *From the Random House Archives.*

3200 Western Publishing Artist - Bugs Bunny Cover Original Art, Group of 4 (Gold Key/Whitman, 1977-78). Here are more shenanigans from that smart aleck rabbit, Bugs Bunny, who, along with the perennially befuddled Elmer Fudd, is seen in these four cover illustrations. One cover also features an appearance by Yosemite Sam. This art appeared on the covers for **Bugs Bunny** #193, 198, 199, and 200. The image area of each cover is approximately 10" x 15", and the art is in Excellent condition. *From the Random House Archives.*

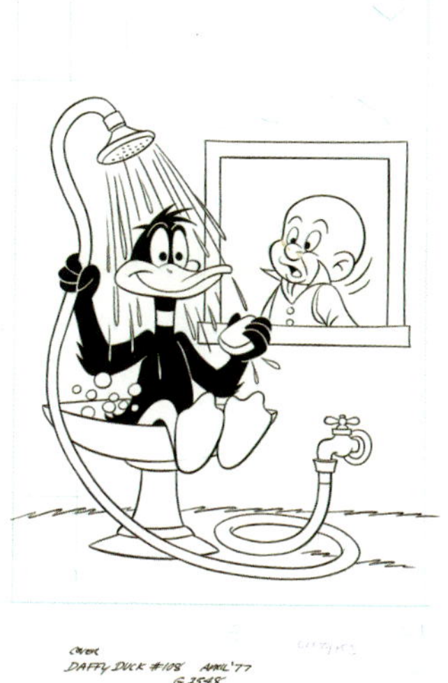

3201 Western Publishing Artist - Bugs Bunny Cover Original Art, Group of 4 (Gold Key, 1978). The cocky, wisecracking, good-hearted hare shares equal billing with that lovable dolt, Elmer Fudd, on these priceless cover illustrations. The art appeared on the covers for **Bugs Bunny** #202, 203, 204, and 205. The image area of each cover is approximately 10" x 15", and the art is in Excellent condition. *From the Random House Archives.*

3202 Western Publishing Artist - Bugs Bunny Cover Original Art, Group of 4 (Whitman, 1979-81). Bugs Bunny and Elmer Fudd mix it up on three laugh-filled covers, while Porky Pig makes an appearance on the fourth. The covers were printed for **Bugs Bunny** #213, 226, 228, and 229. The image area of each cover measures approximately 10" x 15", and aside from a few small stains on #213, mostly outside the image area, the covers average Excellent condition. *From the Random House Archives.*

3203 Western Publishing Artist - Bugs Bunny Cover Original Art, Group of 4 (Gold Key/Whitman, 1979-84). Cartoon legend, Bugs Bunny, and the simple-minded, good-intentioned, Elmer Fudd, are joined by Porky and Petunia Pig on these four cover illustrations. This art appeared on the covers for **Bugs Bunny** #216, 218, 219, and 248 (unpublished). The image area of each cover is approximately 10" x 15", and the art is in Excellent condition. *From the Random House Archives.*

3204 Western Publishing Artist - Bugs Bunny Cover Original Art, Group of 4 (Gold Key, 1979). That wascally wabbit, Bugs Bunny, the lispy liquidator, Elmer Fudd, and the explosive Yosemite Sam are front and center on these four endearing cover illustrations. This art appeared on the covers for **Bugs Bunny** #211, 212, 214, and 215. The image area of each cover is approximately 10" x 15", and the art is in Excellent condition. *From the Random House Archives.*

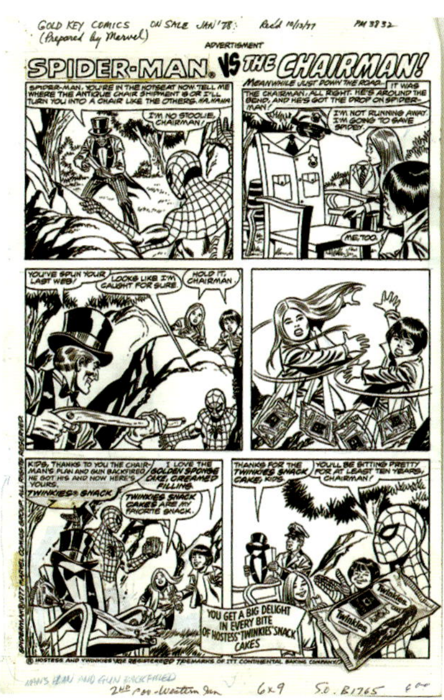

3205 Sal Buscema and Joe Sinnott (attributed) - Hostess Twinkie Ad/Story "Spider-Man vs. the Chairman" Original Art (1978). The Chairman's plan to turn Spider-Man into an antique rocker are unseated by two quick thinking kids who sacrifice their Twinkies to save Spidey. The image area of the page measures 10" x 15". Aside from a few paste-ups and several minor glue stains, the art is in Very Good condition. The color guide for the ad is also included in this lot. It has an image area of 6.5" x 10", and is also in Very Good condition. *From the Random House Archives.*

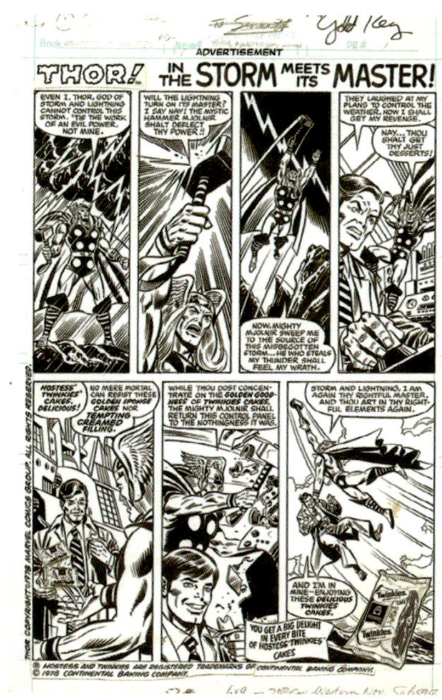

3206 Sal Buscema and Joe Sinnott (attributed) - Hostess Twinkie Ad/Story "Thor in the Storm Meets Its Master" Original Art (1978). Thor, the God of Thunder, sidetracks a mad weatherman with a heapin' helpin', handful of delicious Hostess Twinkies and then he throws a monkey wrench named Mjolnir into the madman's machine! The image area of the page measures 10" x 15". Aside from a few paste-ups and several minor stains, the art is in Excellent condition. The color key film for the ad is included in this lot. It has an image area of 5.75" x 9", and aside from pieces of cellophane tape around the borders, the color key is in Very Good condition. *From the Random House Archives.*

3207 Western Publishing Artist - Daffy Duck Cover Original Art, Group of 10 (Gold Key/Whitman, 1976-83). Certifiably silly Daffy Duck is up to more shenanigans, with the "help" of Elmer Fudd, in this "thtunning" selection of **Daffy Duck** cover illustrations, which includes issues #105, 108, 109, 110, 111, 112, 113, 114, 116, and 145 (the final issue). The image area of each cover measures approximately 10" x 13", and the art averages in Excellent condition. *From the Random House Archives.*

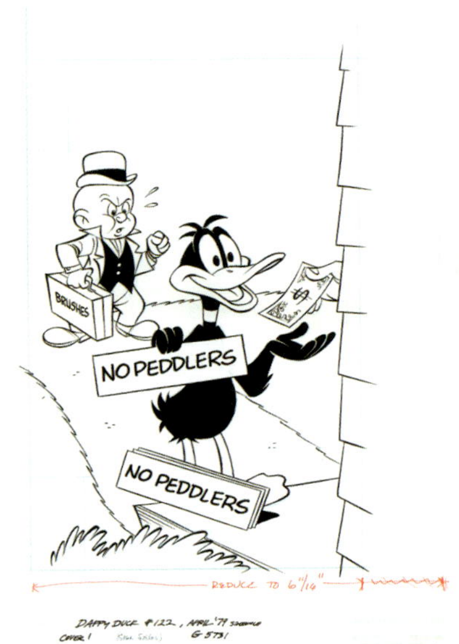

3208 Western Publishing Artist - Daffy Duck Cover Original Art, Group of 10 (Gold Key/Whitman, 1977-79). That frantic waterfowl, Daffy Duck, keeps the action uproarious with the help of his straight man, Elmer Fudd, in these ten **Daffy Duck** cover illustrations, including issues #122, 123, 124, 125, 126, 127, 128, 129, 130, and 131. The image area of each cover measures approximately 10" x 13", and the art is in Excellent condition. *From the Random House Archives.*

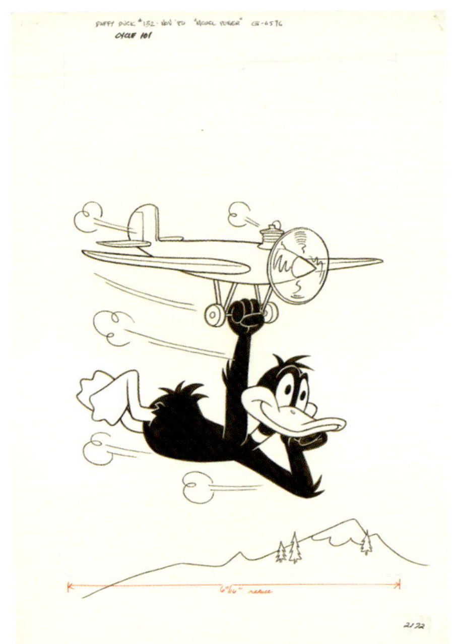

3209 Western Publishing Artist - Daffy Duck Cover Original Art, Group of 10 (Whitman, 1981-82). Crazy quacker, Daffy Duck, amuses and entertains in this great selection of **Daffy Duck** cover illustrations, including issues #132, 134, 135, 136, 137, 138, 141, 142, 143, and 144. The image area of each cover measures approximately 10" x 13", and the art is in Excellent condition. *From the Random House Archives.*

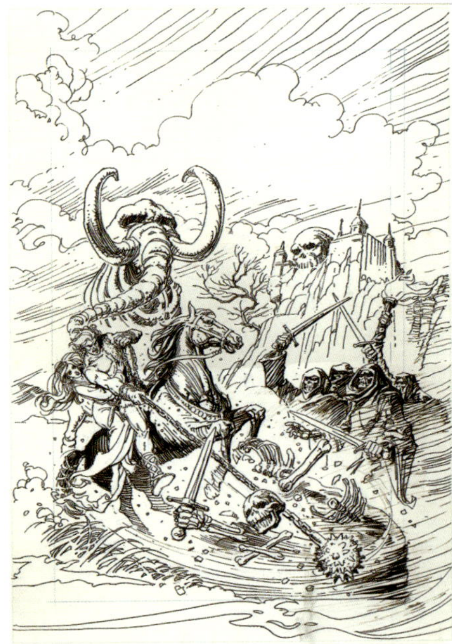

3210 Jesse Santos - Dagar the Invincible #1 Cover Layout Original Art (Gold Key, 1972). Dagar the Invincible was a original and well-written sword and sorcery series set in a mythical past of warriors and wizards. This series was competently written by Don Glut and beautifully drawn by Jesse Santos. Here, Santos creates an innovative pen and ink line drawing layout for the first issue, which another illustrator used to paint the cover art. The image area measures 12.5" x 18", and aside from one small smudge at the lower right, the art is in Excellent condition. *From the Random House Archives.*

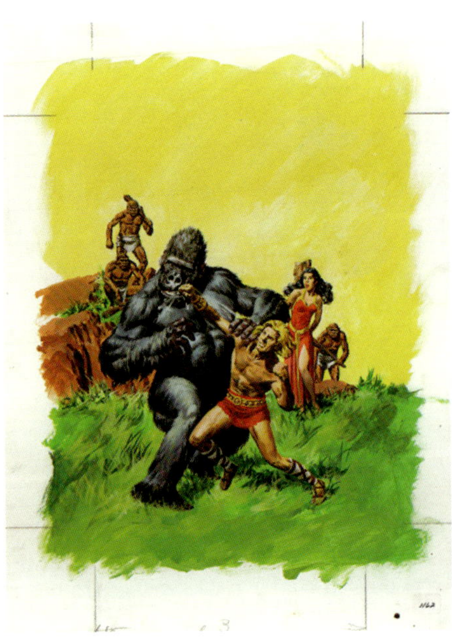

3211 Western Publishing Artist - Dagar, the Invincible #12 Cover Original Art (Gold Key, 1975). "Dagar battles a monstrous gorilla in the forest of fear!" The image area of this acrylic on board slug-fest measures 11" x 15", and the art is in Excellent condition. *From the Random House Archives.*

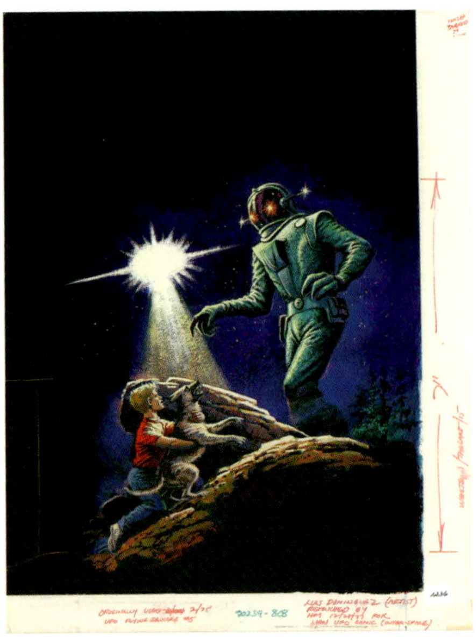

3212 Luis Dominguez - UFO Flying Saucers #5 Cover Original Art (Gold Key, 1975). A looming alien from space causes a watchdog to bark a warning in this stellar Luis Dominguez painting. The image area of this acrylic on board thriller measures 13" x 18.75" and the art is in Excellent condition. A production note at the bottom border indicates that Luis Dominguez retouched his cover at the end of 1977 for a new UFO comic, and indeed, this art was used for **UFO and Outer Space** #16 in 1978. *From the Random House Archives.*

3213 Robert Gregory (attributed) - Daisy and Donald Cover Original Art, Group of 3 (Gold Key, 1979). You can feel the love between Donald Duck and Daisy in these three cover illustrations. These covers appeared on **Daisy and Donald** #37, 38, and 41. The image area of each cover measures 10" x 12", and the art is in Excellent condition. *From the Random House Archives.*

3214 Robert Gregory - Daisy and Donald Cover Original Art, Group of 3 (Gold Key/Whitman, 1979-80). Three lighthearted scenes of Donald courting Daisy are spotlighted in this lot. These covers appeared on **Daisy and Donald** #39, 42, and 43. The image area of each cover measures approximately 10" x 15". The cover to #43 has three light creases horizontally through the cover; otherwise the covers average Very Good condition. *From the Random House Archives.*

3215 Robert Gregory (attributed) - Daisy and Donald Cover Original Art, Group of 3 (Gold Key, 1980). Daisy and her main squeeze, Donald Duck, waddle onto the main stage of these three cover illustrations. These covers appeared on **Daisy and Donald** #44 (special cameo by Gus Goose), 45, and 46. The image area of each cover measures 10" x 12", and the art is in Excellent condition. *From the Random House Archives.*

3216 Robert Gregory - Daisy and Donald Cover Original Art, Group of 3 (Whitman, 1980-81). Donald and Daisy Duck star on three side-splitting covers. The covers were printed for **Daisy and Donald** #47, 48 and 49. The image area of each cover measures approximately 10" x 15", and the art is in Excellent condition. *From the Random House Archives.*

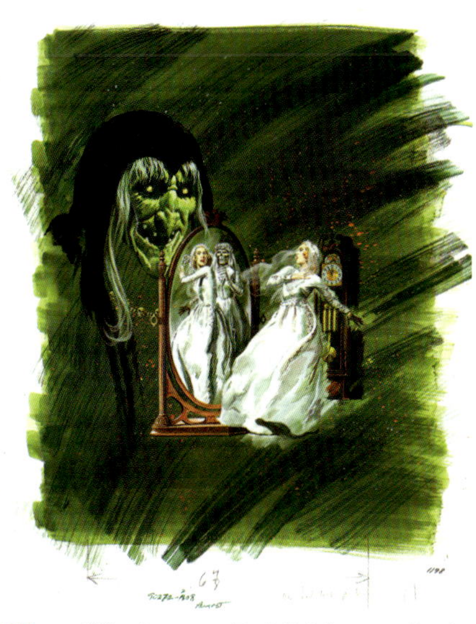

3217 Western Publishing Artist - Grimm's Ghost Stories #2 Cover Original Art (Gold Key, 1972). A lovely bride is haunted by an apparition in the mirror of a veiled horror, reaching out for her! The Grimm ghost with gleefully malevolent eyes hovers above her, a menacing, toothless grin breaking across its face. The artist of this terrifying tableau spared no expense with the deep, rich colors and stark stylization. The image area measures 12" x 16" and the art is in Excellent condition. *From the Random House Archives.*

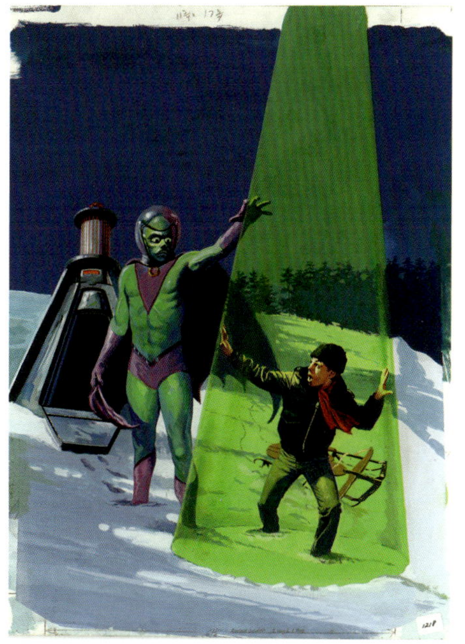

3218 Chuck Liese - UFO and Outer Space #21 Cover Original Art (Whitman, 1970). "Reader's report — I was frozen in my tracks, as the alien approached." Feets, don't fail me now! The image area of this acrylic on board scene measures 15" x 21", and the condition of the art is Excellent. *From the Random House Archives.*

3219 Jack Manning and Larry Mayer - Beagle Boys Versus Uncle Scrooge #6 Cover Original Art (Gold Key, 1979). Try to pick Uncle Scrooge's pocket and you're liable to get one right in your kisser! This Rube Goldberg-esque set-up needs no description, and has an image area of 10" x 11". In Excellent condition. *From the Random House Archives.*

3220 Jack Manning and Larry Mayer - Beagle Boys Versus Uncle Scrooge #11 Cover Original Art (Gold Key, 1980). The Beagle Boys spend a lazy afternoon fishing in Uncle Scrooge's vault, reeling in sacks of cash, while Scrooge frantically tries to save his money supply, in this cover illustration. The art has an image area of 10" x 11", and, aside from a slight stain at the bottom edge, the art is in Excellent condition. *From the Random House Archives.*

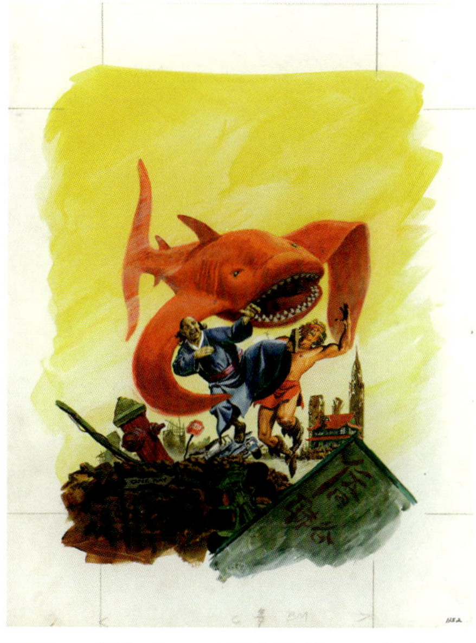

3221 Western Publishing Artist - Mighty Samson #24 Cover Original Art (Gold Key, 1974). "A powerful warrior pits himself against Mighty Samson — until a mutant killer strikes!" The image area of this acrylic on board battle royal is 10" x 15", and the art is in Excellent condition. *From the Random House Archives.*

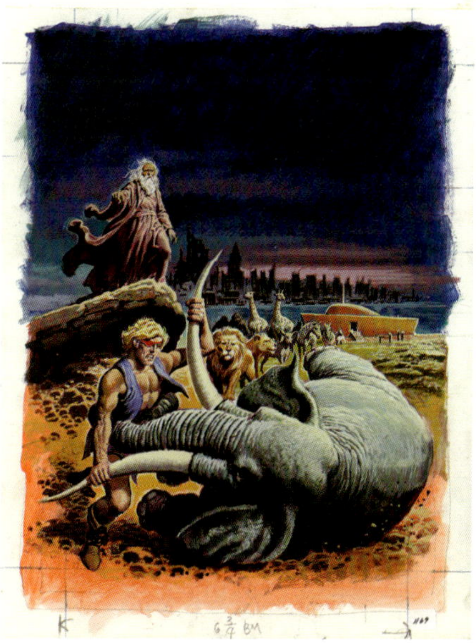

3222 Western Publishing Artist - Mighty Samson #27 Cover Original Art (Gold Key, 1975). "Old Noah wakes up to a violent new world... and decides to make it *his*!" It's a clash of the biblical titans as Samson battles Noah! The image area of this acrylic on board painting is 13" x 18", and the art is in Excellent condition. *From the Random House Archives.*

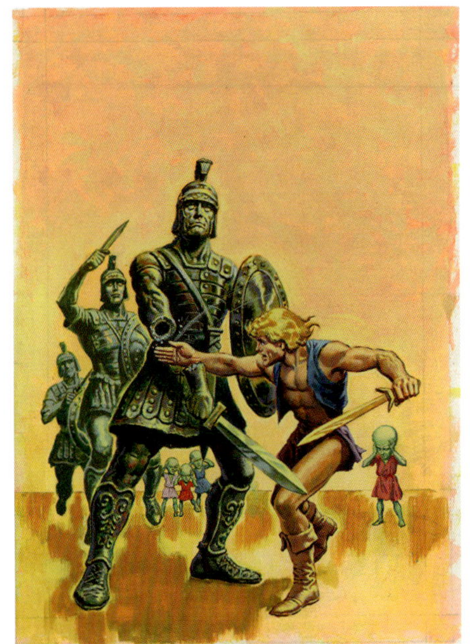

3223 Western Publishing Artist - Mighty Samson #28 Cover Original Art (Gold Key, 1975). "Statues become living weapons of war against Samson!" The image area of this acrylic on board blockbuster measures 11" x 16.5", and the art is in Excellent condition. *From the Random House Archives.*

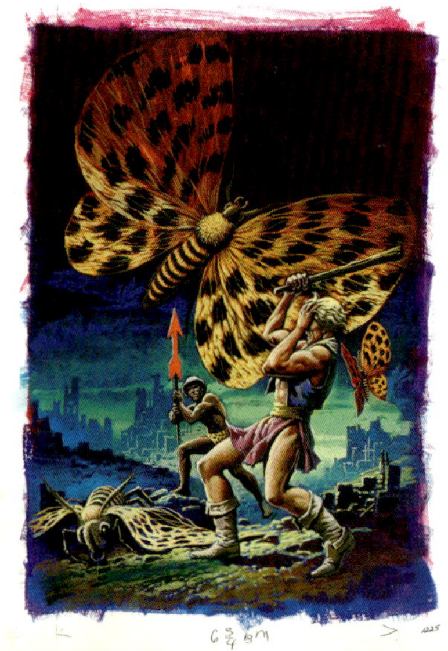

3224 Western Publishing Artist - Mighty Samson #31 Cover Original Art (Gold Key, 1976). "Giant moths spread their fearsome wings over N'Yark." Samson battles the menace of the Lepidop-Terror. The image area of this acrylic on board painting is 12" x 17", and the art is in Excellent condition. *From the Random House Archives.*

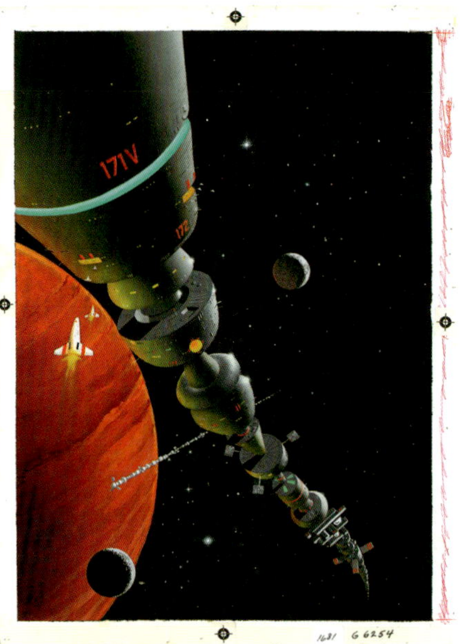

3225 Ron Miller - Questar Illustrated Science Fiction Classics #1 Cover Original Art (Golden Press, 1979). Ron Miller, widely regarded as a talented successor to astronomical painter Chester Bonestell, is noted for his works in William K. Hartmann's **Cycles of Fire: Stars, Galaxies and the Wonder of Deep Space**, the story of cosmic evolution. The image area of this acrylic on board painting measures 11.5" x 16.5", and the art is in Excellent condition. *From the Random House Archives.*

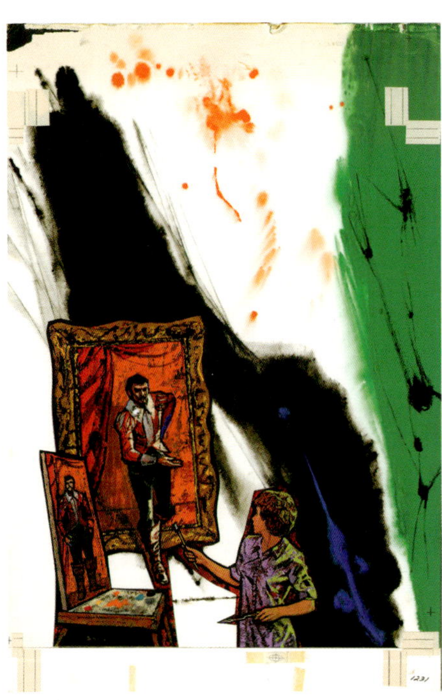

3226 Richard Powers (attributed) - Boris Karloff Thriller #2 Cover Original Art (Gold Key, 1963). A smiling cavalier steps out of a canvas in this surreal scene for **Boris Karloff Thriller**. Science fiction artist Richard Powers was an inspired choice to illustrate this cover. The image area of this acrylic on board scene measures 14" x 20". The foreground figures were glued onto the abstract background; otherwise the condition of the art is Excellent. *From the Random House Archives.*

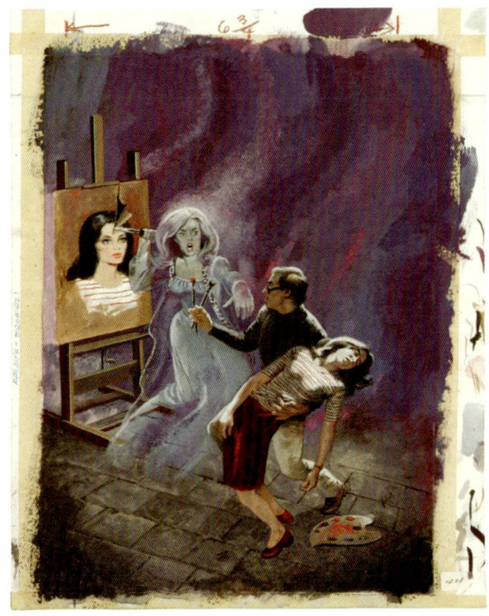

3227 Western Publishing Artist - Ripley's Believe It or Not True Ghost Tales #66 Cover Original Art (Gold Key, 1976). It seems *everyone's* an art critic — even in the afterlife! Armed with only a couple of brushes, we fear this painter doesn't stand a "ghost" of a chance when it comes to fending off an angry spirit! This weird, eerie cover illustration has an image area of 12.5" x 18" and is in Excellent condition. *From the Random House Archives.*

3228 Western Publishing Artist - The Road Runner, "The Super Beep Catcher," Page Original Art, Group of 120 (Whitman, 1968). Master spy, Mister B, and inventor, Wile E. Coyote, have their sights set on the big catch — the Road Runner Family! From the Big Little Book, **The Road Runner, The Super Beep Catcher**, published in 1968, come these approximately 120 black and white illustrations. Drawn on vellum, and glued onto a larger 6" x 7.5" sheet of illustration board, they include a Road Runner/Wile E. Coyote "flip-it" animation, which was photocopied into the upper right corner of each page. This lot also includes the original 95 animation drawings, which were used to make the "flip-it" section. The art averages Excellent condition. *From the Random House Archives.*

3229 Western Publishing Artist - Beep Beep, The Road Runner Cover Original Art, Group of 4 (Whitman, 1979-80). Wile E. Coyote gets outsmarted or outrun by the Road Runner on these four crash-bang covers. The covers were used for **Beep, Beep, The Road Runner** #85, 86, 87, and 88. The image area of each cover measures approximately 10" x 15.5", and aside from two tape residue stains on #87, the covers average Excellent condition. *From the Random House Archives.*

3230 Western Publishing Artist - Beep Beep, The Road Runner Cover Original Art, Group of 4 (Whitman, 1980-81). Doomed to forever try, but never succeed, the luckless Wile E. and his elaborate schemes to snag Road Runner are the *raison d'etre* of these fast and "furry-ous" cover scenes. The covers were drawn for **Beep, Beep, The Road Runner** #93, 95, 96, and 102. The image area of each cover is approximately 10" x 15", and the condition of art is Excellent. *From the Random House Archives.*

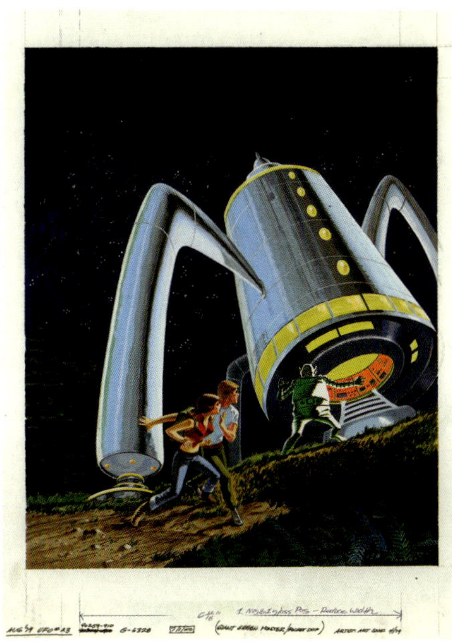

3231 Art Saaf - UFO and Outer Space #23 Cover Original Art (Gold Key, 1979). "Reader's report: tensely we stood, each waiting for the other to make the first move!" Art Saaf captures the drama of the uncomfortable moment between a close encounter of the third and fourth kind! The image area of this acrylic on board painting measures 13" x 16.5"and the art is in Excellent condition. *From the Random House Archives.*

3232 Jesse Santos - Swamp Creature Illustration Original Art (undated). Gold Key Comics, a nonsubscriber to the Comics Code, produced several horror titles including **Boris Karloff's Tales of Mystery** (1963), **Ripley's Believe It or Not! True Ghost Stories**, **The Occult Files of Dr. Spektor**, and **Grimm's Ghost Stories**. This Jesse Santos cover illustration is for an unidentified Gold Key publication, possibly unpublished. Although the color has been hand-painted on a sheet of illustration board, the line art is a touched-up photostat, and not original art. The image area measures 11" x 16" and the art is in Excellent condition. *From the Random House Archives.*

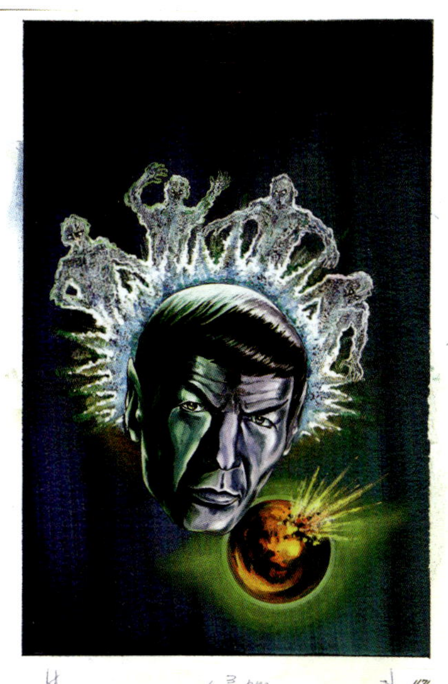

3233 Western Publishing Artist - Star Trek #35 Cover Original Art (Gold Key, 1975). An alien form invades the Enterprise through Spock's mind! This intense cover illustration featuring Captain Kirk's right hand man haloed by a quartet of strange, malignant energy forms, is certainly unforgettable! The art has an image area of 9.5" x 15" and is in Excellent condition. *From the Random House Archives.*

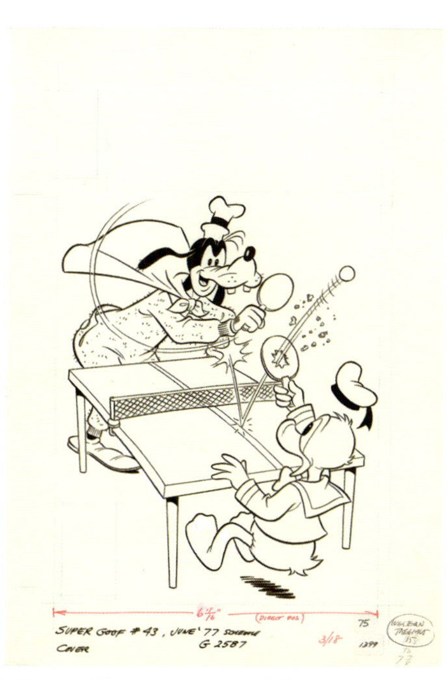

3234 Western Publishing Artist - Super Goof Cover Original Art, Group of 10 (Gold Key, 1977-79). Ka-Zip! Ka-Zap! Ka-Zowie! Super Goof is the super guy to beat on these ten scintillating covers! Included here are ten cover illustrations from **Super Goof**, including issues #43, 44, 47, 48, 49, 50, 51, 53, 54, and 55. The image area of each cover measures approximately 10" x 12", and the art is in Excellent condition. *From the Random House Archives.*

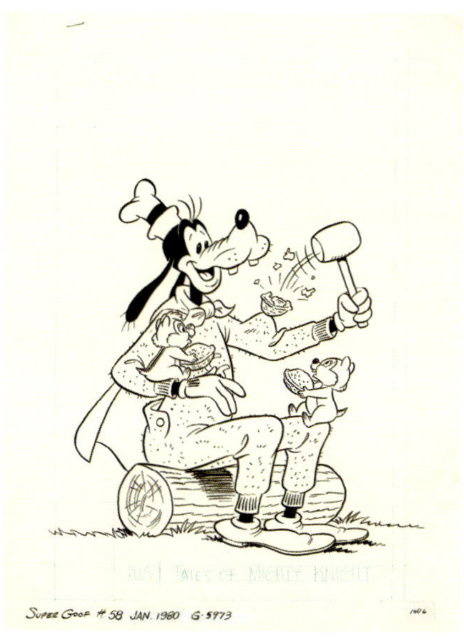

3235 Western Publishing Artist - Super Goof Cover Original Art, Group of 10 (Whitman, 1980-82). After popping a few magic goobers, Goofy becomes Super Goof, and is imbued with super strength, super breath, super telescopic vision, and super flight. For your enjoyment, we have ten cover illustrations from **Super Goof**, including issues #58, 59, 60, 61, 62, 63, 64, 65, 66, and 67. The image area of each cover measures approximately 10" x 12", and the art is in Excellent condition. *From the Random House Archives.*

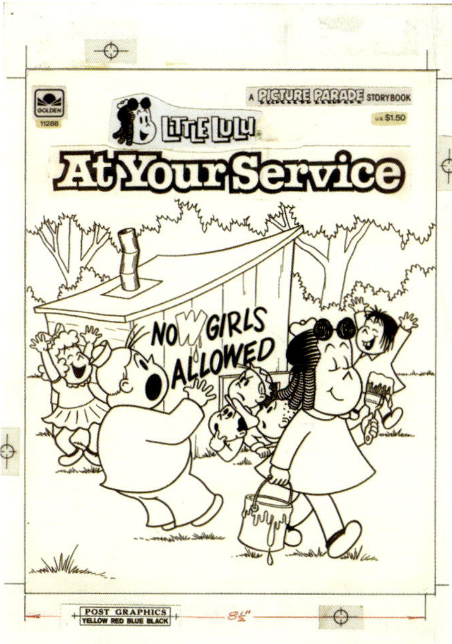

3236 Irving Tripp and Hy Eisman (attributed) - "Little Lulu at Your Service" Book Cover and Complete 16-page Story Original Art (Golden Press, 1983). In this story, Little Lulu's plan to raise money by performing personal services for neighbors is seriously compromised when Tubby and the boys get involved. The cover art has an image area of 9.5" x 12", while the interior pages measure 13" x 17". A few pieces of pasted-on type have slipped off the interior pages; otherwise the art averages Very Good condition. In addition to the previously described art, two photostat reproductions of the cover and an original 8.5" x 10.5" ink on vellum drawing are included. *From the Random House Archives.*

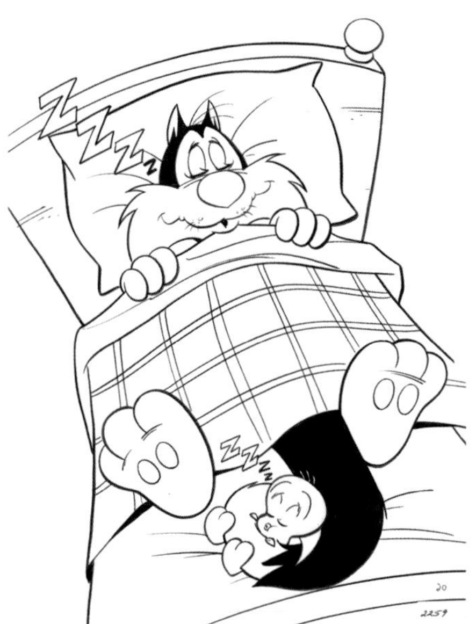

3237 Western Publishing Artist - Tweety and Sylvester Cover Original Art, Group of 5 (Gold Key, 1977-78). Five terrific covers capture the cat and canary hi-jinx of Sylvester and Tweety. These knee-slappers hail from **Tweety and Sylvester** #75, 76 (two fully inked versions of basically the same scene), 77, and 79. The image area of each cover measures approximately 10" x 15.5", and aside from two carefully pasted-in art corrections on #77 (on Sylvester's paws), and a small stain in the upper right of the cover for #79, all are in Excellent condition. Add a few to smiles your art collection with these charming pieces! *From the Random House Archives.*

3238 Western Publishing Artist - Tweety and Sylvester Cover Original Art, Group of 5 (Gold Key, 1977-78). You'll tink you taw a puddy tat, in these five splendid covers featuring Tweety and Sylvester. These side-splitters covered **Tweety and Sylvester** #72, 80, 81, 84, and 85. The image area of each cover measures approximately 10" x 15", and all are in Excellent condition. *From the Random House Archives.*

3239 Western Publishing Artist - Uncle Scrooge #147 Cover Original Art (Gold Key, 1977). Winter sports are a lot of fun, yet Uncle Scrooge manages to enjoy the thrill of sledding without leaving the premises of his fabulous money bin! The image area of this classic scene measures approximately 10" x 15", and the art is in Excellent condition. *From the Random House Archives.*

3240 Western Publishing Artist - Uncle Scrooge #156 Cover Original Art (Gold Key, 1978). There's nothing like a few cool Benjamins to take some of the heat off a hot summer day! Uncle Scrooge puts his money to good use in this cheerful cover illustration. The image area measures 10" x 13" and the art is in Excellent condition. *From the Random House Archives.*

3241 Western Publishing Artist - Beagle Boys Versus Uncle Scrooge #2 Cover Original Art (Gold Key, 1979). He may look like a panhandler, but Uncle Scrooge's scrounging proves that "There's Cash in Trash," in this cover illustration. The art has an image area of 10" x 11" and is in Excellent condition. *From the Random House Archives.*

3242 Western Publishing Artist - Beagle Boys Versus Uncle Scrooge #3 Cover Original Art (Gold Key, 1979). Uncle Scrooge and the Beagle Boys race for riches, in this cover which illustrates the interior story, "The Armored Car Caper". The art has an image area of 10" x 11" and is in Excellent condition. *From the Random House Archives.*

3243 Western Publishing Artist - Beagle Boys Versus Uncle Scrooge #4 Cover Original Art (Gold Key, 1979). The Beagle Boys never looked finer in their royal threads and regal dispositions. But can they outfox the wily Uncle Scrooge? This cover illustration spotlights the interior story, "The Great Gift Grab". The art has an image area of 10" x 11" and is in Excellent condition. *From the Random House Archives.*

3244 Western Publishing Artist - Beagle Boys Versus Uncle Scrooge #5 Cover Original Art (Gold Key, 1979). A time machine transports Uncle Scrooge to a treasure ship back in 1752, in this cover which illustrates the interior story, "The Buccaneer's Map". The art has an image area of 10" x 11" and is in Excellent condition. *From the Random House Archives.*

3245 Western Publishing Artist - Beagle Boys Versus Uncle Scrooge #7 Cover Original Art (Gold Key, 1979). Uncle Scrooge tempts the most notorious gang of thieves and thugs in Duckburg, The Beagle Boys, with a handful of jewels, in this cover illustration. The art has an image area of 10" x 11" and is in Excellent condition. *From the Random House Archives.*

3246 Western Publishing Artist - Beagle Boys Versus Uncle Scrooge #8 Cover Original Art (Gold Key, 1979). Uncle Scrooge encounters a group of deep sea raiders, The Beagle Boys, in this cover illustrating the interior story, "Danger At Fifty Fathoms". The art has an image area of 10" x 11" and is in Excellent condition. *From the Random House Archives.*

3247 Western Publishing Artist - Beagle Boys Versus Uncle Scrooge #9 Cover Original Art (Gold Key, 1979). Deep within Uncle Scrooge's money bin, a trio of sledding Beagle Boys find themselves faced with an alert Uncle Scrooge, who's not in a sporting mood! The art has an image area of 10" x 11" and is in Excellent condition. *From the Random House Archives.*

3248 Western Publishing Artist - Beagle Boys Versus Uncle Scrooge #10 Cover Original Art (Gold Key, 1979). An overjoyed Uncle Scrooge finds a money sack on his doorstep, believing it is full of cash! Of course, it's full of Beagle Boys instead! This classic Beagle Boys vs. Uncle Scrooge moment has an image area of 10" x 11". One small stain at the upper right edge, otherwise the art is in Excellent condition. *From the Random House Archives.*

3249 Western Publishing Artist - Beagle Boys Versus Uncle Scrooge #13 Cover Original Art (Gold Key, 1980). It's raining money, and the Beagle Boys are rolling in it, with Uncle Scrooge under the spell of "The Hypno Plot". Here is the cover art for **Beagle Boys Versus Uncle Scrooge** #13, which was never published. The art has an image area of 10" x 11" and is in Excellent condition. *From the Random House Archives.*

3250 Western Publishing Artist - Beagle Boys Versus Uncle Scrooge #14 Cover Original Art (Gold Key, 1980). The Beagle Boys will use any ruse to get their hands on Uncle Scrooge's money, and a Trojan piggy bank is just the thing to get his attention! This illustration was created for the cover to **Beagle Boys Versus Uncle Scrooge** #14, which was never published. The art has an image area of 10" x 11" and is in Excellent condition. *From the Random House Archives.*

3251 Western Publishing Artist - Beagle Boys Versus Uncle Scrooge #15 Cover Original Art (Gold Key, 1980). It's the old "money bag filled with water" trick, and the dim-witted Beagle Boys fall for it every time! This illustration was created for the cover to **Beagle Boys Versus Uncle Scrooge** #15, but was never published. The art has an image area of 10" x 11" and is in Excellent condition. *From the Random House Archives.*

3252 Western Publishing Artist - Uncle Scrooge #186 Cover Original Art (Whitman, 1981). Even in a simple game of tic-tac-toe, Uncle Scrooge ends up with all the dollar signs while Donald Duck gains nothing! The image area of this hilarious cover measures approximately 10" x 15", and it is in Excellent condition. *From the Random House Archives.*

3253 Western Publishing Artist - Uncle Scrooge #189 Cover Original Art (Whitman, 1981). Uncle Scrooge keeps cool by fanning himself with a breeze from a handful of moolah. The image area of this amusing scene measures approximately 10" x 15", and the cover is in Excellent condition. *From the Random House Archives.*

3254 Western Publishing Artist - Uncle Scrooge #193 Cover Original Art (Gold Key, 1982). The female octopus on this cover is all legs — tentacled legs, that is! Uncle Scrooge really makes some waves in this underwater illustration. The image area measures 10.5" x 11" and the art is in Excellent condition. *From the Random House Archives.*

3255 Western Publishing Artist - Uncle Scrooge #194 Cover Original Art (Gold Key, 1982). While Gyro Gearloose looks on, Uncle Scrooge barely manages to escape a river of molten gold, in this underground extravaganza which appeared on the cover of **Uncle Scrooge** #194. The image area measures 10" x 13" and the art is in Excellent condition. *From the Random House Archives.*

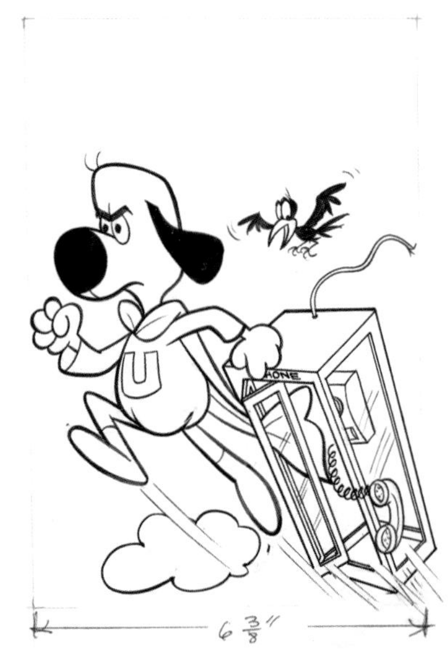

3256 Western Publishing Artist - Underdog #1 Cover Original Art (Gold Key, 1975). Have no fear — Underdog is here — in both a tightly penciled cover sketch and the finished inked illustration. The image area of each piece measures approximately 7" x 10.5", and both are in Excellent condition. *From the Random House Archives*

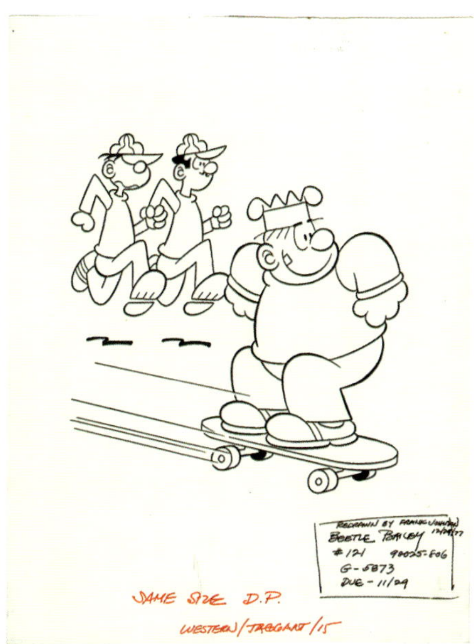

3257 Mort Walker Studio - Beetle Bailey Cover Original Art, Group of 12 (Gold Key, 1978-79). It's a battle of half-wits as Beetle Bailey and Sgt. Snorkel go at it on a dozen uproarious covers for **Beetle Bailey** #120, 121, 122, 123, 124, 126, 128, 129, 130, 131, 133, and an unidentified cover with the production note, "May sked." The image area of most of the covers is approximately 6.75" x 7.5", except for #120 which measures 10.5" x 14.5". The cover of #120 is made up of two collaged original art elements; otherwise the covers average Excellent condition. *From the Random House Archives.*

3258 Western Publishing Artist - Walt Disney Comics and Stories #399 Cover Original Art (Gold Key, 1973). There's nothing like a scary ghost story to shake things up, as Huey, Dewey and Louie soon find out. The image area of this chiller measures approximately 10" x 15", and the art is in Excellent condition. *From the Random House Archives.*

3259 Western Publishing Artist - Walt Disney Comics and Stories #435 Cover Original Art (Gold Key, 1976). Huey, Dewey, and Louie are caught with their sticky fingers in the cookie jar, thanks to Uncle Donald's home-made security camera. The image area of this freeze-frame crime scene measures approximately 10" x 15", and the cover is in Excellent condition. *From the Random House Archives.*

3260 Western Publishing Artist - Walt Disney Comics and Stories #438 Cover Original Art (Gold Key, 1977). They say imitation is the sincerest form of flattery, but Donald Duck doesn't seem too pleased with Huey, Dewey, and Louie's snowman. The image area of this ice-capade measures approximately 10" x 15", and the art is in Excellent condition. *From the Random House Archives.*

3261 Western Publishing Artist - Walt Disney Comics and Stories #444 Cover Original Art (Gold Key, 1977). A sleepy-eyed Donald Duck is forced to run away from home in order to get some relief from the boisterous marching band of Huey, Dewey, and Louie. The image area of this whooping hoedown measures approximately 10" x 15", and the art is in Excellent condition. *From the Random House Archives.*

3262 Western Publishing Artist - Walt Disney Comics and Stories #446 Cover Original Art (Gold Key, 1977). An eager beaver is a welcome addition to the rowing team of Huey, Dewey, Louie and Donald Duck. The image area of this whimsical gag measures approximately 10" x 15", and the art is in Excellent condition. *From the Random House Archives.*

3263 Western Publishing Artist - Walt Disney Comics and Stories #449 Cover Original Art (Gold Key, 1978). There's no waiting for a haircut when Donald Duck is the barber — he cuts all of his three nephews' mop-tops at once. The image area of this terrific scene measures approximately 10" x 15", and the art is in Excellent condition. *From the Random House Archives.*

3264 Western Publishing Artist - Walt Disney Comics and Stories #451 Cover Original Art (Gold Key, 1978). Donald Duck pulls the blind on his TV set so Huey, Dewey, and Louie will do their homework — that's "old school" parenting. The image area of this light-hearted cover measures approximately 10" x 15", and the condition of the art is Excellent. *From the Random House Archives.*

3265 Western Publishing Artist - Walt Disney Comics and Stories #452 Cover Original Art (Gold Key, 1978). Huey, Dewey, and Louie have found the ideal moving target for their indoor archery range! The image area of this uproarious cover gag measures approximately 10" x 15", and the art is in Excellent condition. *From the Random House Archives.*

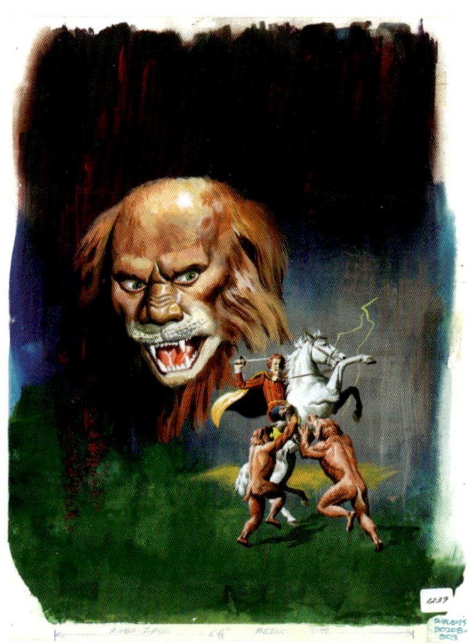

3266 George Wilson (attributed) - Ripley's Believe It or Not #7 Cover Original Art (Gold Key, 1967). "Strange! Shocking! The Werewolves of Poligny!" It's a scene featuring true demons and monsters— believe it, or not! The image area of this acrylic on board painting is 11" x 15.5", and the art is in Excellent condition. *From the Random House Archives.*

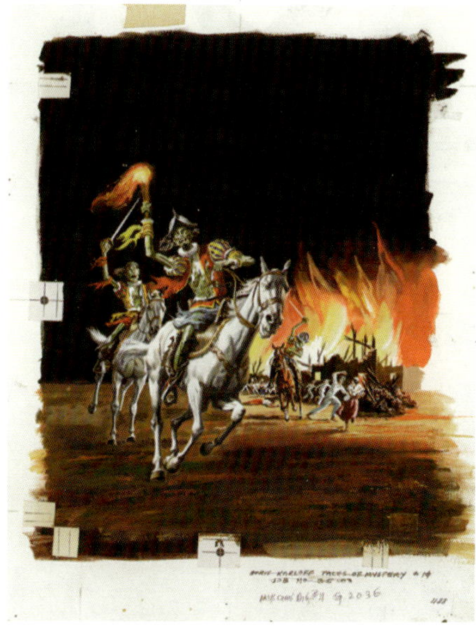

3267 George Wilson (attributed) - Boris Karloff Tales of Mystery #10 Cover Original Art (Gold Key, 1970). "Barbaric raiders, dead for centuries, come alive to spread panic in modern Peru!" Boris Karloff presents another chilling cover hook. The image area of this acrylic on board painting is 11.5" x 15.5", and the art is in Excellent condition. *From the Random House Archives.*

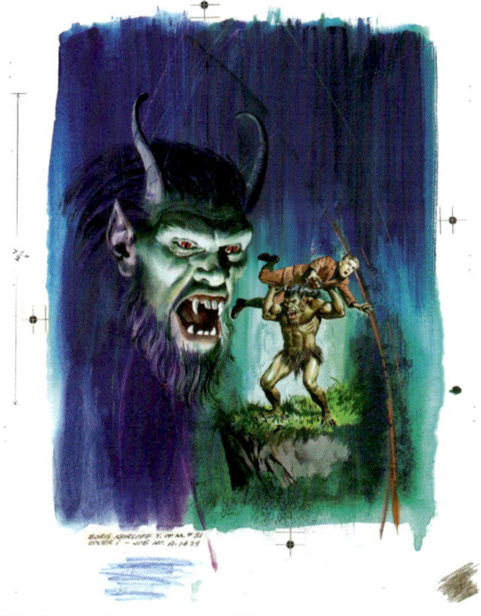

3268 George Wilson (attributed) - Boris Karloff Tales of Mystery #31 Cover Original Art (Gold Key, 1970). "His best friend — a killer monster!" With friends like that, who needs friends? The image area of this acrylic on board painting is 12" x 15.5", and the art is in Excellent condition. *From the Random House Archives.*

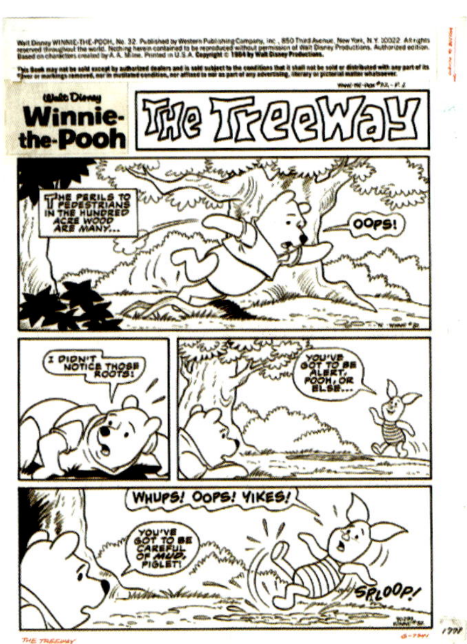

3269 Disney Studio Artist - Winnie-the-Pooh #32 Complete Story Original Art, Group of 4 (Whitman, 1984). Stuffed with fluff and ready for adventure, Winnie the Pooh, Piglet, Tigger, Rabbit, Eeyore, and all the other denizens of the Hundred Acre Woods are the stars of these four tales. Included here is the 8-page story, "The Treeway," the 9-page "Creep From the Deep," the 7-page "The Heffalump Search," and the 8-page "Polar Pilot". The pages have an image area of 12" x 18" and are all in Excellent condition. *From the Random House Archives.*

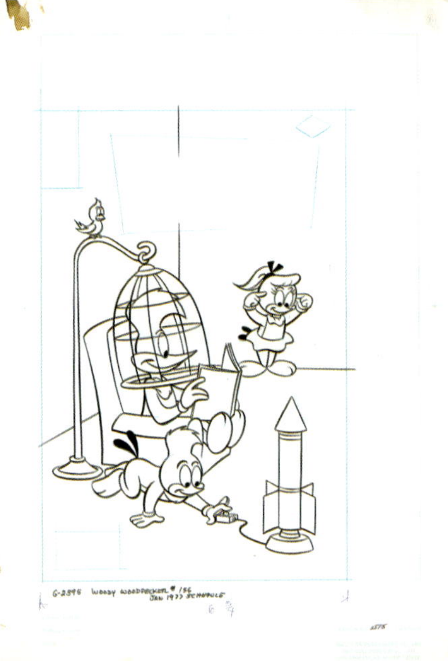

3270 Western Publishing Artist - Woody Woodpecker Cover Original Art, Group of 10 (Gold Key, 1977-79). Woody, Splinter and Knothead share fun and adventure in these ten **Woody Woodpecker** cover illustrations, including issues #156, 160, 167, 173, 175, 176, 177, 179, 180, and 181. The image area of each cover measures approximately 10" x 12", and the art is in Excellent condition. *From the Random House Archives.*

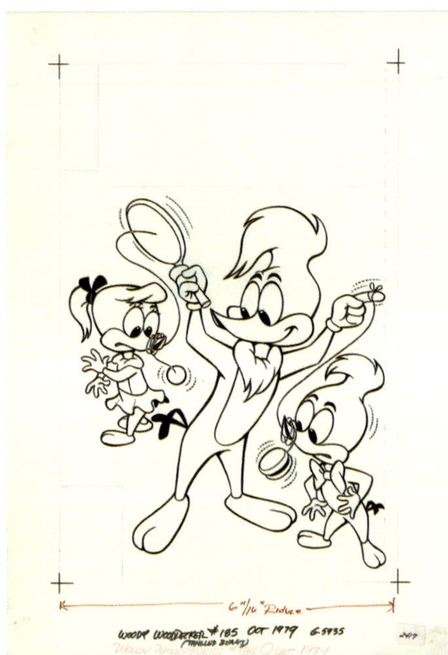

3271 Western Publishing Artist - Woody Woodpecker Cover Original Art, Group of 10 (Gold Key/Whitman, 1979-84). Splinter and Knothead keep Woody Woodpecker on his toes, in these ten cover illustrations. This lot includes **Woody Woodpecker** issues #185, 186, 188, 189, 193, 194, 199, 200, and the final issue of the series #201. Also included here is the front and back cover illustrations to **March of Comics** #478. The image area of each cover measures approximately 10" x 12", and the art is in Excellent condition. *From the Random House Archives.*

OTHER COOL STUFF FROM RANDOM HOUSE

3272 Kay Wright - Walt Disney's Comics and Stories #442 Cover Original Art (Gold Key, 1977). Huey goes long for a thick, juicy hamburger patty, in this backyard brouhaha by Karran "Kay" Wright. Director and producer Kay Wright worked for Disney, Warner Brothers, Wolff, Filmation, and Hanna-Barbera, and filled in on some Donald Duck dailies and Sundays. In 1988, he received the Motion Picture Screen Cartoonists Golden Award. This lively illustration has an image area of 11" x 16" and the condition is Excellent. *From the Random House Archives.*

3273 Golden Press Hardcovers-File Copies Group (Golden Press, 1958-61). This lot consists of Western Publishing file copies of 16 small-format hardcover books. All are devoted to themes from nature or the natural sciences. Condition ranges from Very Good to Excellent. Four are not numbered; the numbered books are 7707 (two different editions), 7708 (two different editions), 7712 (two different editions), 7716 (two different editions), 7807, 7821, 7822, and 8716. Not listed in Overstreet. *From the Random House Archives.*

3274 The Golden Magazine File Copies Box Lot (Golden Press, 1966-69) Condition: Average VF/NM. These could well be called "pay copies," as they have handwritten notations by Western Publishing staff regarding whether the rights to individual text and pictures were purchased outright or for a single use, and in some cases listing the amounts paid to the contributing creators. Approximately 70 issues of this "magazine for boys and girls" are included here, and they're not all different (there's only one pay copy of each issue, of course). The contents are educational children's fare (the only comic-type material we found are some Little Lulu strip reprints). Most average VF/NM condition, though there's one coverless one and a couple of other lower-grade specimens. Not listed in Overstreet. *From the Random House Archives.*

3275 Walt Disney and Other Paint Books Group (Whitman, 1942-52) Condition: Average VF. Eight unused coloring books taken from the Western Publishing files make up this lot. Books include: **Happy Hour Paint Book** #654; **Walt Disney's Snow White and the Seven Dwarfs Paint Book** #678-10; **Santa Claus Paint Book** #640-10; **Top Notch Paint Book** #675; three different **Whopper Paint Book**s, numbered #116015, #1160-15, and #1160; and **Top Notch Paint Book** #675 (a different book than above but with the same number). Not listed in Overstreet. *From the Random House Archives.*

3276 Disney Character Coloring Book Group (Whitman, 1954-61). Here's a big batch of Disney-related coloring books, all from the Western Publishing files. Some have production notes written and/or taped onto covers and interior pages. Included are: **Mousekartoon Coloring Book** #1150; **Uncle Scrooge** #2975-A (three copies from various printings); **Walt Disney's Coloring Book** (two different printings of same book with minor changes); **Pluto Pup and Other Disney Stories Cut-Out Coloring Book; Walt Disney's Cut-Out Coloring Book** (two different printings); **Johnny Tremain Cut-Out Coloring Book** (two copies); **Huey, Dewey and Louie Coloring Book** (with art by Tony Strobl); **Lady and the Tramp**; and **Snow White and the Seven Dwarfs Coloring Book**, with an embossed cover. Get this lot and get out the crayons! Not listed in Overstreet. *From the Random House Archives.*

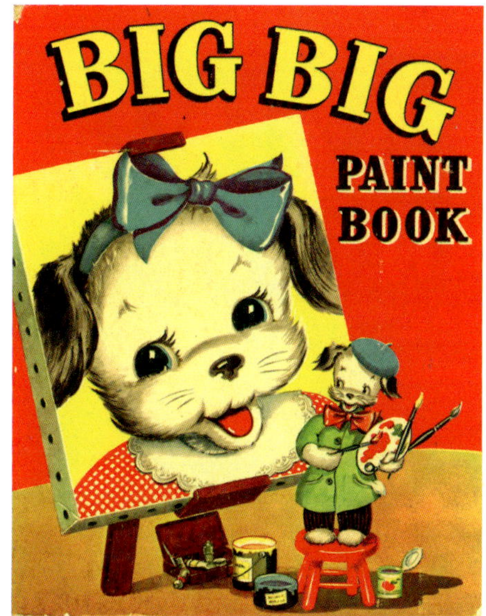

3277 Big Big Paint Book Group (Whitman, 1936-48) Condition: Average VF. Among the items found within the Western Publishing files held by Random House were these huge coloring books, designed for young children. Each book has extra-large page counts; the first two are massive, with over 400 pages. All are unused, and for the most part in remarkable condition; however, some minor dings and corner wear have occurred from storage. These items rarely turn up on the collector's market! Not listed in Overstreet. *From the Random House Archives.*

3278 Big Big Paint Book, Group of 3 (Whitman, 1941-48). Here are three wonderful **Big Big Paint Books** coloring books, with covers by Florence Kroger. Each measures approximately 8.5" x 11", and, aside from some paper aging, all three are in Excellent condition. *From the Random House Archives.*

3279 Whitman Paint Book, Group of 6 (Whitman, 1940-51). Another tremendous group of dazzling Whitman coloring books, including **Merry Christmas Paint Book** (1940, slight crease along the bottom); **Color Rhyme Paint Book** (1943); **Tracing Book to Paint and Color** (1944); **Paint Book** (1949); **Boys and Girls Paint Book** (1948); and **Paintless Paint** (1951). Measuring approximately 11" x 15" each, these delightful books are illustrated by Clarence Biers, Emma C. McKean, Ethel Bonnie Taylor, Eileen Fox Vaughan, and Luis M. Henderson. The bindings are tight and the edges are crisp, and they average Excellent condition. *From the Random House Archives.*

3280 Whitman Paint Book, Group of 6 (Whitman, 1940-51). You'll enjoy this sweet selection of coloring books, which include **Merry Christmas Paint Book** (1940, small amount of damage on upper spine); **Color Rhyme Paint Book** (1943); **Tracing Book to Paint and Color** (1944); **Paint Book** (1949); **Boys and Girls Paint Book** (1948); and **Paintless Paint** (1951). These colorful books measure approximately 11" x 15", and are filled with illustrations by Clarence Biers, Emma C. McKean, Ethel Bonnie Taylor, Eileen Fox Vaughan, and Luis M. Henderson. The colors are rich, and the average condition of the books is Excellent. *From the Random House Archives.*

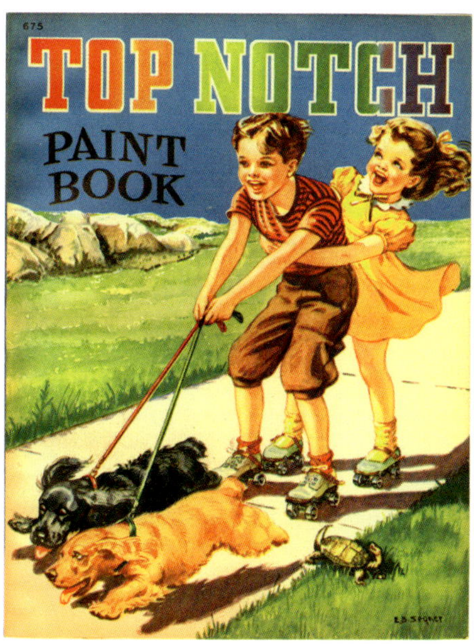

3281 Whitman Paint Book Group (Whitman, 1942-49) Condition: Average VF/NM. Here's a charming group lot of seven unused Paint and Coloring books from the 1940s, all taken from the Western Publishing files. Included in this lot are **Happy Hour Paint Book** (#654, 1942); two different **Top Notch Paint Books** (both numbered #675 and dated 1942); two copies of **Whopper Paint Book** (#1160, 1947); and two copies of a different **Whopper Paint Book** (#1160-15, 1949). Each book is filled with wonderful illustrations of children and animals from a bygone era. Not listed in Overstreet. *From the Random House Archives.*

3282 Whitman Coloring Books, Group of 9 (Whitman, 1952-51). Put on your artist's hat, 'cause here is a great group of coloring books, including **Basket Full of Fun** (1952); two sets of **Young Artist Coloring Kit** (1953); **My Color Kit** #3 (1956); two sets of **The ABC Rub-Off Coloring Pages** with Magic Slate Drawing Board (1959); **Bugs Bunny To Color** with Magic Slate Drawing Board (1959); **One Hundred and One Dalmatians To Color** with Magic Slate Drawing Board (1960); and **Merlin's Magic Duel** Color and Wipe-Off Book with Magic Crayons (1963). These books average in Excellent condition. *From the Random House Archives.*

3283 Whitman Coloring Kit Group (Whitman, 1953-59). From the Western Publishing files comes this group of five vintage coloring books, all complete with a small box of crayons attached. The books include: **My Color Kit** (1956; crayon box taped to cover, several pages have small tears); **Young Artist Coloring Kit** (1953); **Walt Disney's Sword in the Stone Merlin's Magic Duel** (1953; stamped File Copy on inside; light tape residue on cover & small tears along top of spine); **Bugs Bunny To Color - Wipe Off and Color Again** (1959, spiral bound book with Magic Slate); and **ABC Color - Wipe Off and Color Again** (1959; spiral bound with Magic Slate). Be a kid again and have fun with this nostalgic lot! Not listed in Overstreet. *From the Random House Archives.*

3284 Whitman Coloring Sets, Group of 4 (Various, 1953-74). Color your world with these four marvelous coloring sets, including a "Young Artist Coloring Kit," (1953); two "Color Go-Round" sets (1963), "Let's Go to the Farm!," and "Let's Play!"; and "Barbie Magic Window," (1964). The sets average in Excellent condition. *From the Random House Archives.*

3285 Bugs Bunny's Magic Rub-Off Pictures (Whitman, 1955). Activity set includes 14 re-usable pictures, a box of six crayons, and a package of wipe-off tissues. Unused with some very minor stress to the edges of the box lid, otherwise in great condition. *From the Random House Archives.*

3286 Flintstones Magic Rub-Off Coloring Kit (Whitman, 1962). Never used and in like-new condition; included are 14 re-usable pictures to color, a box of six crayons, and wipe-off tissues. *From the Random House Archives.*

3287 Paint With Water Set, Group of 7 (Whitman, 1976-82). From Whitman comes this group of 21 **Paint With Water** sets. Each set includes paintable pictures, a paintbrush, and a water tray. The sets include: "Sing-a-Song," "More Monsters," "Fun Faces," "Pizzazz," "Dragons 'n' Things," "Playtime Pals," "Mickey and Minnie Dancing Dazzle," "Shirt Tales," "Poochie," "Wonder Woman," "Walt Disney's All-Time Favorites," "Nursery Rhyme," "Daisy and Donald Good Sports," "Goofy the Great Magic Show," "Silly Animals," and "The Amazing Spider-Man". Also includes five "Color by Number" sets, including "Raggedy Ann & Andy," "The Pink Panther," "Barbie," "Tom and Jerry," and "Fairy Tales". All these sets are still in their original packaging, and in Excellent condition. *From the Random House Archives.*

3288 Paper Doll Kits, Group of 4 (Whitman, 1943-64). These are for the girls! Here are four unique paper doll sets, including: "3 Young Americans," (1943) which feature three lovely lady wood dolls with cloth-like dresses; "Three Little Girls... and How They Grew," (1943) (contains six stand-up dolls, three girls and three gorgeous young women, with paper accessories you can cut out and place on the figures); "Bunny Lou," (1960) (11" tall with real curls and 42 cut out costumes); and "Tammy and Her Family," (1964) (5 paper dolls with stands and "ready to punch out" clothes). Some light edge wear on the "Tammy" game, otherwise these items average in Excellent condition. *From the Random House Archives.*

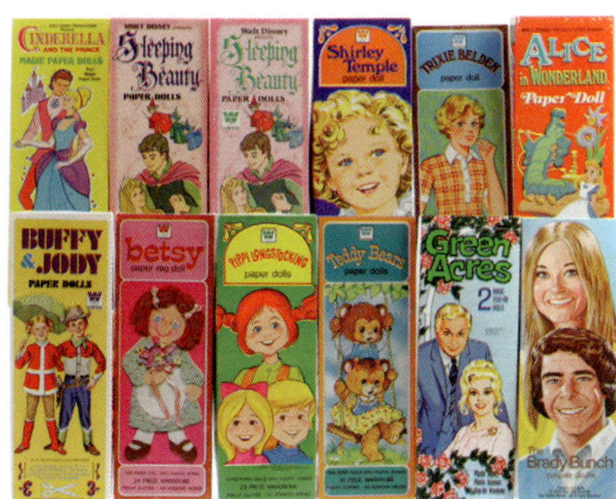

3289 Assorted Paper Dolls Group (Whitman, 1968-79). This group of 12 sets of paper dolls includes "Pippi Longstocking," "Buffy and Jody," "Green Acres," "The Brady Bunch," "Shirley Temple," "Sleeping Beauty" (two sets), "Teddy Bears," "Betsy," "Cinderella," "Alice in Wonderland," and "Trixie Belden." All are unused and in like-new condition. *From the Random House Archives.*

3290 Disney Paper Dolls Group (Whitman, 1969-79). Here are six sets of paper dolls based on Disney characters. Included are Cinderella, Snow White (two sets; one pre-cut, one with scissors), Alice in Wonderland, and Sleeping Beauty (two copies of the same set). Each is unused and in great condition. *From the Random House Archives.*

3291 Mickey Mouse Club Game in Disneyland (Whitman, 1955). "M-I-C-K-E-Y-M-O-U-S-E." This delightful **Mickey Mouse Club Game in Disneyland** board game contains a die and four playing pieces bearing images of Minnie Mouse, Donald Duck, Practical Pig and Little Bad Wolf. Manufactured by Whitman in 1955, the same year Disneyland opened in Anaheim, California, and "The Mickey Mouse Club" went on the air. In Excellent condition. *From the Random House Archives.*

3292 Disney Davy Crockett Board Game (Whitman, 1955). "Disneyland's Official Davy Crockett Indian Scouting Game." The first scout to make it to Army Headquarters wins. Never used; there is some minor stress to the box lid, otherwise the game is in great condition. *From the Random House Archives.*

3293 Walt Disney's World of Color Board Game (Whitman, 1961). "Be the first player to travel all six space orbits and collect the six different colored pieces to complete a TV screen." In great condition and never used, it contains all the original pieces. *From the Random House Archives.*

3294 Ludwig Von Drake Tiddly Winks (Whitman, 1961). Produced by Whitman in 1961, the box cover features Donald's three nephews (Huey, Dewey, and Louie) flipping tiddly winks at Ludwig Von Drake and trying to get them on the top of his mortar board. The directions for the game are on one side of the box. Inside is a target featuring a picture of Ludwig with the center goal being the top of his in which a marbleized plastic cup is placed. The set includes red, green, blue and yellow chips. This game is in Excellent condition. The colors are bright, the box is intact and the felt pieces and tiddly winks are all present. *From the Random House Archives.*

3295 Walt Disney Tiddly Winks Game (Whitman, 1963). The classic game got the Disney treatment in this 1963 edition. This set was never used (the pieces are still sealed in a plastic baggie) and, aside from some very minor wear tot eh box lid, is in great condition. *From the Random House Archives.*

3296 Disney Characters Board Game Group (Whitman, 1976-77). This group of seven children's board games by Whitman includes the Mickey Mouse Castle Escape Game, Chip 'N' Dale Nuts! Game, Mickey Mouse's Tree House Game, Pluto's Lost Bones Game, Goofy's Mad Maze Game, Goofy's Balloon Party Game, and Goofy's Jungle Safari Game. All are in like-new condition, have never been played, and include the orignal pieces. *From the Random House Archives.*

3297 Whitman Board Game and Coloring Sets Group (Whitman, 1965-72). This group lot features a Zorro board game, "Woody Woodpecker's crazy mixed-up Color Factory Game," a G. I. Joe color by number set (still sealed in original shrinkwrap), and Green Hornet, Tarzan, and Magilla Gorilla "Magic Rub-Off" coloring sets. All are in like-new condition and include their original pieces. *From the Random House Archives.*

3298 Little Lulu Doll, Group of Memorabilia Comic-related (Various, undated). Lovely group of Little Lulu dolls, including a 14" Horsman (an Irene Szor design), a 15" "La Pequena Lulu" doll, an unidentified 9" doll, a 6" Hallmark doll, and two 6.5" Gund dolls. The large Horsman doll is in its original packaging (package has some damage at the corners, doll is in Excellent condition, some light staining on the large Gund doll, otherwise they average in Excellent condition. *From the Random House Archives.*

3299 Little Lulu Style Manual (Western Publishing, 1972). This manual contains model sheets of the Little Lulu characters and a discussion of the characters and story situations. The model sheets are the definitive guide to the appearances of the characters. A great souvenir for fans of all things Lulu! The manual measures 9.5" x 11.5" and is in Excellent condition. *From the Random House Archives.*

BOUND COMIC VOLUMES

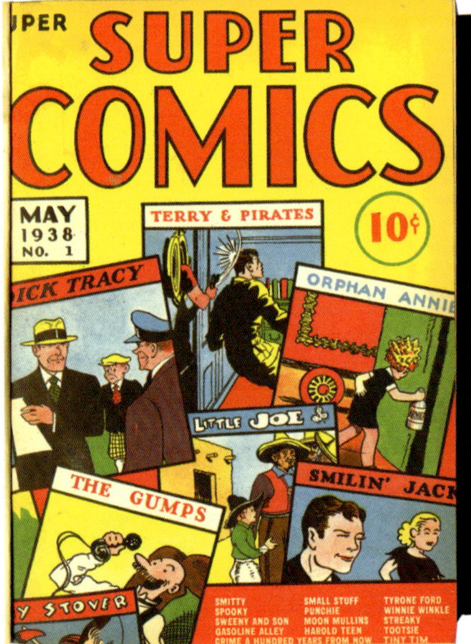

3300 Super Comics #1-12 File Copies Bound Volume (Dell, 1938-39). One of Western Publishing's first comic book titles was **Super Comics**. This title even pre-dates the "Dell" company logo, and features reprinted newspaper strips such as *Dick Tracy*, *Terry and the Pirates*, *The Gumps*, *Little Orphan Annie*, *Gasoline Alley*, *Smilin' Jack*, *Moon Mullins*, and more. This is one of the oldest bound volumes to come out of the Random House Archives; like others from that collection, it consists of file copies that were bound and trimmed into a hardback volume, designed for office reference use. This book has a few rough spots on the binding: there's a chunk missing from the spine of the book, and the back hinge is showing signs of beginning to come loose. But the comics inside still look pretty fresh, with colorful, matt-finish covers and supple pages. On the inside front cover is written "Property of Robert S. Callender", the former manager of Western Printing. A very historic volume! Overstreet 2005 VG 4.0 value for group = $2,074. *From the Random House Archives.*

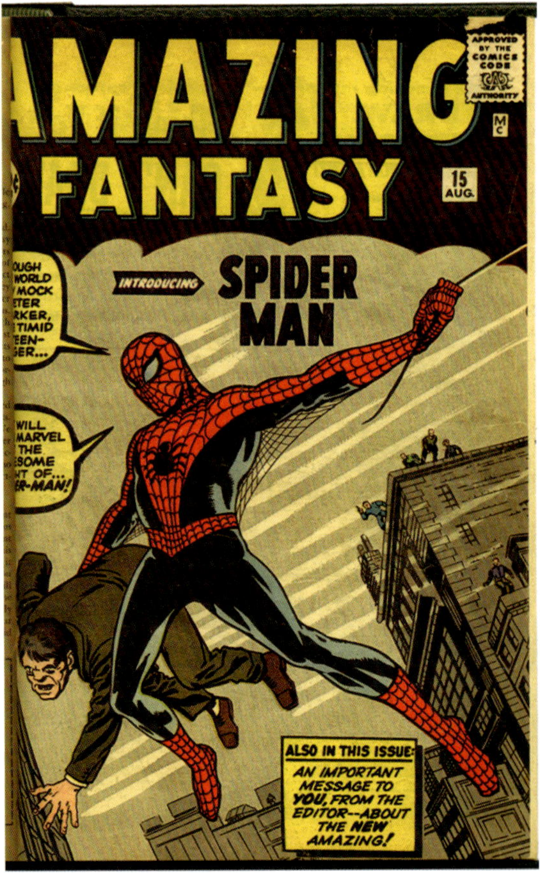

3301 Amazing Adventures, Amazing Adult Fantasy, and Amazing Fantasy #1-15 Bound Volume (Atlas/Marvel, 1961-62). When the first appearance of Spider-Man is only *one* of the highlights, you know you've got a special bound volume in your hands! Yes, **Amazing Fantasy** #15 is one of the comics in this handsome volume, which contains trimmed and bound copies of issues #1-15 (the series began as **Amazing Adventures**, becoming **Amazing Adult Fantasy** with #7, and of course #15 was the only issue to be called **Amazing Fantasy**). No doubt you already know all about the contents of #15, which is also described elsewhere in this catalog, but how about tons of Jack Kirby and Steve Ditko stories, many of which have never been reprinted anywhere (and the ones that did appear in reprints were usually cut down or altered)? In fact, looking through this treasure trove, we didn't see one single story that wasn't drawn by either Kirby or Ditko, and there are some classics in here like Kirby's "Sserpo, The Creature Who Crushed The Earth" and Ditko's "The Terror of Tim Boo Ba." The early issues combine monster yarns with tales of Dr. Droom, whom Overstreet calls the first Marvel Age superhero, making his first appearance in #1 a key issue in its own right. Also of note is a Ditko-drawn tale in #14 which is a prototype of the whole X-Men concept, with mutants who have special powers being hated and feared by their fellow man. These comics are fairly well-thumbed copies which evidently averaged approximately VG condition when bound, however it's amazing what preservation in a bound volume does for the page quality of a comic! The spine of the book is embossed with the title and issue numbers, and the previous owner's name is embossed on the front of the book. We will accept only one excuse for not bidding on this bound volume, and that's the highly unlikely event that you already own all of these issues. Anyone else who passes this by might as well turn in his M.M.M.S. card! Overstreet 2005 VG 4.0 value for group = $3,854.

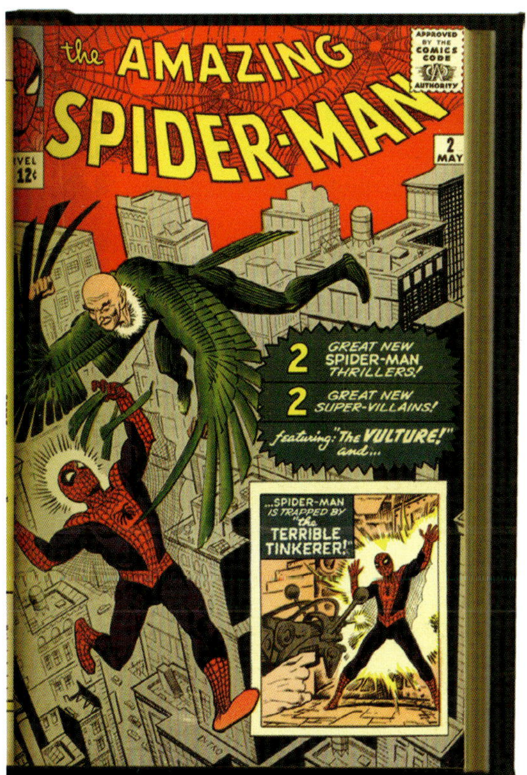

3302 The Amazing Spider-Man #1-20 Bound Volume (Marvel, 1963-65). These might be the best comic books ever produced, and there is *no* better way to enjoy them than by acquiring this bound volume. After all, even if you own every issue, your copies are either sealed up in slabs, or at the very least you have to handle them with kid gloves. And while we won't knock the **Marvel Masterworks**, those reprint books can't begin to compete with experiencing the original colors, Stan Lee's Bullpen Bulletins, the letters pages, and everything else that went into these classics. Trimmed and bound copies of issues #1-20 are contained in this handsome volume. *Note that #1 is the 1966 Golden Records reprint, but all of the other comics are the originals.* Most of the comics were evidently mid-grade copies when bound, but a chunk missing from the cover of #4 is the only serious defect of note. Some of the issues (including #2!) are *super*-nice, and the page quality will equal or beat any copies you would find "in the wild." The spine of the volume is embossed with the title and issue numbers, and the previous owner's name is embossed on the front of the book. So do you think you might like to have the first appearances of the Vulture, Doctor Octopus, the Sandman, Betty Brant, Liz Allen, the Lizard, Electro, Mysterio, the Green Goblin, Kraven the Hunter, Ned Leeds, and the Scorpion, all drawn by Steve Ditko?! We believe any comic fan with a pulse will answer that question with a resounding yes. Overstreet 2005 VG 4.0 value for group = $4,402.

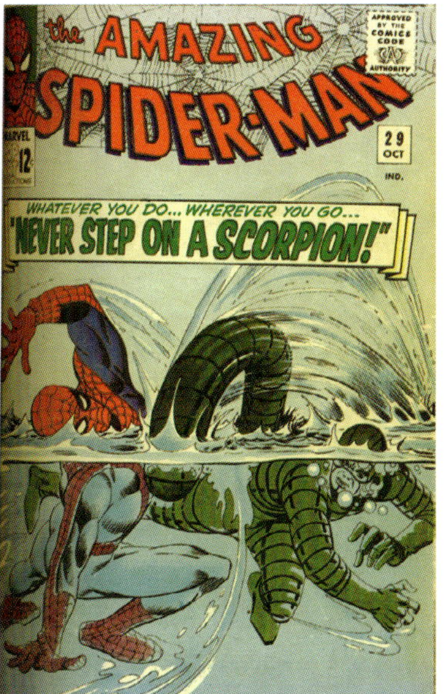

3303 The Amazing Spider-Man #21-40 Bound Volume (Marvel, 1965-66). Lots of Green Goblin tales are a highlight of this bound volume, which includes copies of issues #21-40 — that's the second half of the acclaimed Steve Ditko run and the first two issues of John Romita Sr.'s tenure as Spidey's artist. Note that these copies were not trimmed prior to binding, so they could conceivably be removed if a future owner sees fit to do so. The spine of the book is embossed with the title and issue numbers, and the previous owner's name is embossed on the front of the book. Overstreet 2005 VG 4.0 value for group = $1,268.

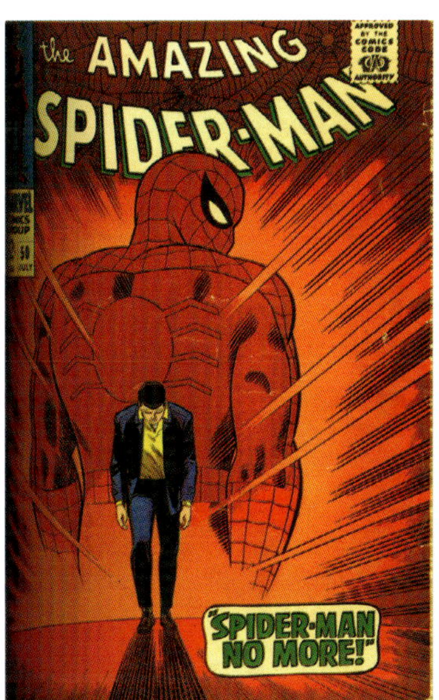

3304 The Amazing Spider-Man #41-60 Bound Volume (Marvel, 1966-68). The first appearance of the Kingpin and early appearances by Mary Jane Watson — and of course lots of John Romita Sr. art — are among the highlights of this part of the run. Note that these copies have not been trimmed prior to binding. Most of these issues were obviously in nice condition (some even VF or better) when bound; the only major defects of note are a water stain on #43 and a chunk missing from the cover of #60. The spine of the book is embossed with the title and issue numbers, and the previous owner's name is embossed on the front of the book. Overstreet 2005 VG 4.0 value for group = $654.

3305 The Amazing Spider-Man #61-80 Bound Volume (Marvel, 1968-70). Trimmed and bound copies of issues #61-80 are contained in this handsome volume (note that they were not trimmed prior to binding). The spine of the book is embossed with the title and issue numbers, and the previous owner's name is embossed on the front of the book. Overstreet 2005 VG 4.0 value for group = $358.

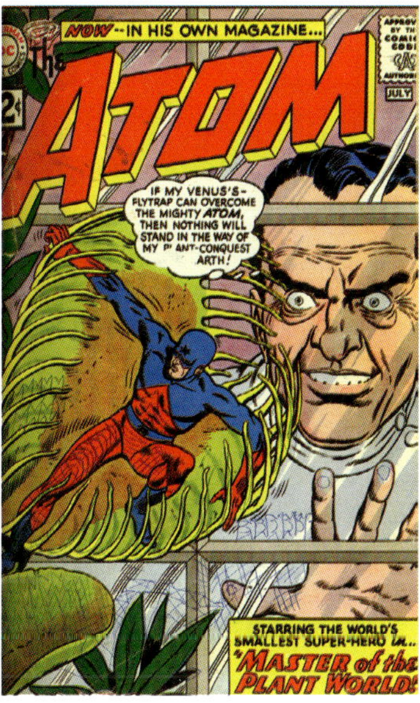

3306 The Atom #1-20 Bound Volume (DC, 1962-65). Highlights of this run include the first appearances of the Plant-Master (aka the Floronic Man), and Chronos, and of course lots of Gil Kane art. Trimmed and bound copies of issues #1-20 are contained in this handsome volume. The spine of the book is embossed with the title and issue numbers, and the previous owner's name is embossed on the front of the book. Overstreet 2005 VG 4.0 value for group = $662.

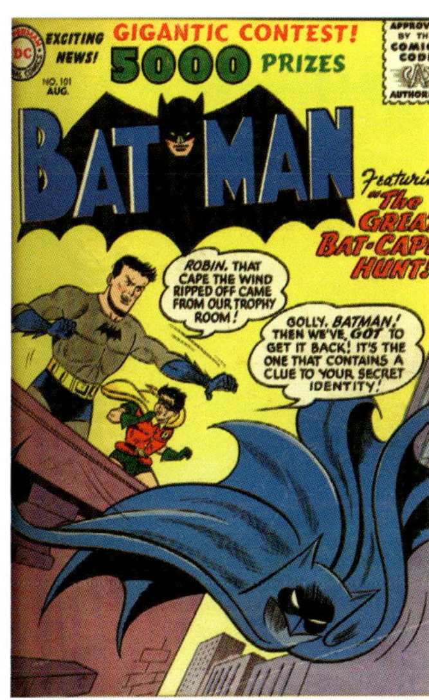

3307 Batman #101-120 Bound Volume (DC, 1956-58). Trimmed and bound copies of issues #101-120 are contained in this handsome volume. Sheldon Moldoff handled art chores on most of these issues, with Dick Sprang contributing as well. The spine of the book is embossed with the title and issue numbers, and the previous owner's name is embossed on the front of the book. Overstreet 2005 VG 4.0 value for group = $1,740.

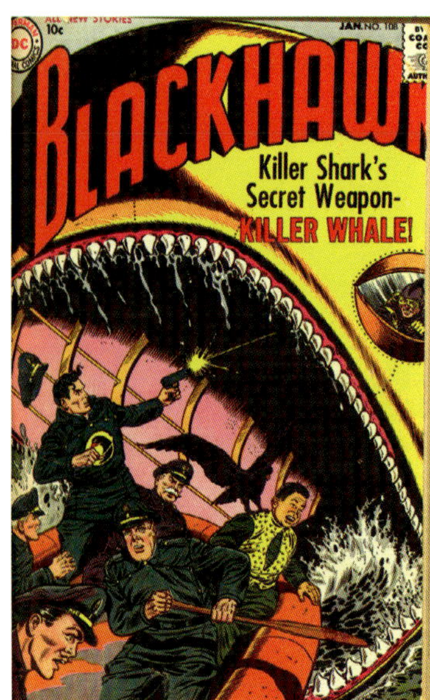

3308 Blackhawk #108-150 Bound Volumes (DC, 1957-60). This great run begins with the very first DC issue (#108, which continued the numbering from the Quality series)! Among many highlights are the first appearance of Lady Blackhawk (#133) and a feature with Frank Frazetta art (#118). In all, trimmed and bound copies of issues #108-150 are contained in these two handsome volumes. The spines of the books are embossed with the title and issue numbers, and the previous owner's name is embossed on the front of the books. Overstreet 2005 VG 4.0 value for group = $1,002.

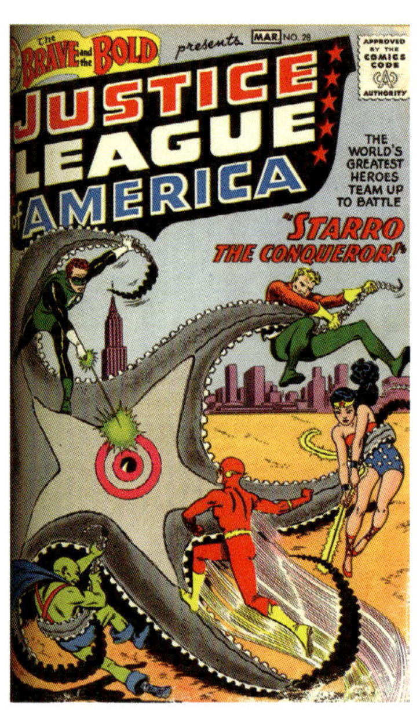

3309 The Brave and the Bold #11-30 Bound Volume (DC, 1957-60). The first appearance of the Justice League of America in #28 is the unquestioned highlight of this bound volume. Also in these pages are the second and third appearances of the group. But there's also the first appearance of the Suicide Squad as well as lots of Viking Prince stories with Joe Kubert art. In all, trimmed and bound copies of issues #11-30 are included here. The spine of the book is embossed with the title and issue numbers, and the previous owner's name is embossed on the front of the book. Aside from the occasional cover crease and a wee bit of edge chipping, the comics are in very nice condition; the page quality ranges from good to outstanding! Overstreet 2005 VG 4.0 value for group = $2,672.

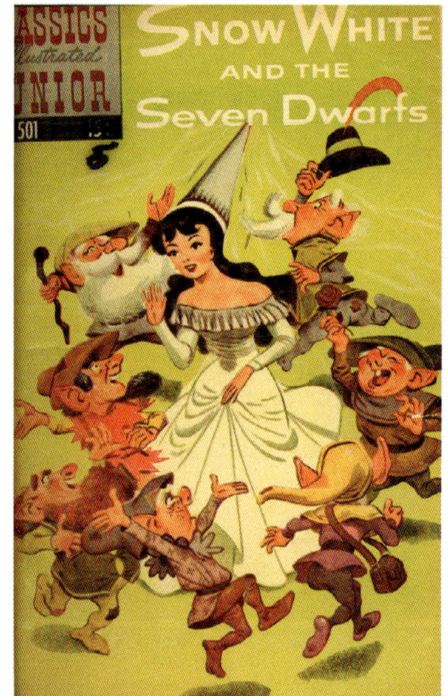

3310 Classics Illustrated Junior #501-577 Bound Volumes (Gilberton, 1953-69). These three bound volumes contain the entire run of this series! And it appears that every issue is an original edition. Note that almost every comic in this bound volume has the connect-the-dots puzzle on the inside front cover filled in (in pencil). Also, many of the comics, especially from the first half of the run, have a child's coloring on the black-and-white inside back cover. That said, the cover gloss and page quality of these issues is very impressive. The spine of the book is embossed with the title and issue numbers, and the previous owner's name is embossed on the front of the book. Approximate Overstreet VG 4.0 value for group = $1,000.

3311 Conan the Barbarian #1-25 Bound Volume (Marvel, 1970-73). Trimmed and bound copies of issues #1-25. Spine of the book is embossed with the title and issue numbers, and the previous owner's name is embossed on the front of the book. Art by Barry Smith, Gil Kane, and John Buscema. Overstreet 2005 VG 4.0 value for group = $256.

3312 Creepy #1-10 Bound Volume (Warren, 1964-66). Artists include Frank Frazetta, Al Williamson, Alex Toth, Johnny Craig, Gene Colan, and many more. Note that these magazines were not trimmed prior to binding. The spine of the book is embossed with the title and issue numbers, and the previous owner's name is embossed on the front of the book. Overstreet 2005 VG 4.0 value for group = $106.

3313 Eerie #2-10 and 1970 Yearbook Bound Volume (Warren, 1966-70). Artists include Frank Frazetta, Steve Ditko, Alex Toth, Johnny Craig, Gene Colan, and many more. Note that these magazines were not trimmed prior to binding. The spine of the book is embossed with the title and issue numbers, and the previous owner's name is embossed on the front of the book. Overstreet 2005 VG 4.0 value for group = $116.

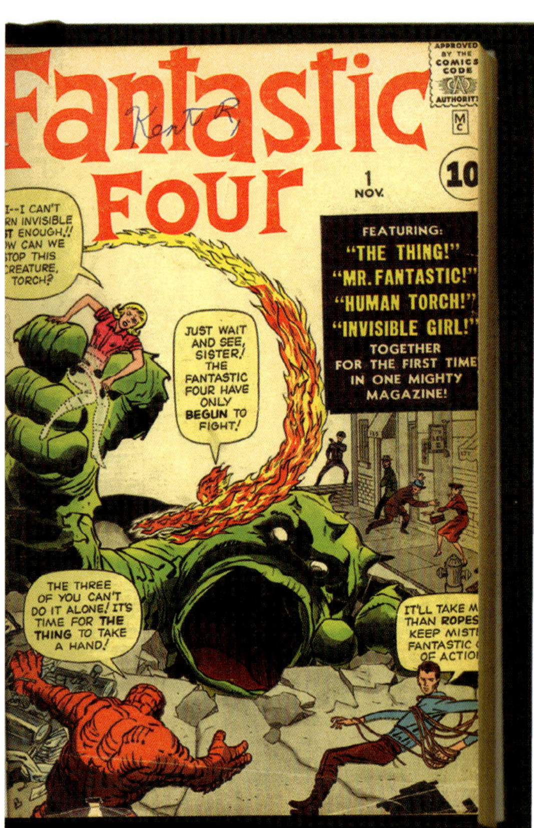

3314 Fantastic Four #1-20 and Annual #1 Bound Volume (Marvel, 1961-63). The first appearance of the Fantastic Four leads off this bound volume, but you also get the first appearances of the Skrulls, Dr. Doom, Alicia Masters, the Impossible Man, the Watcher, the Super Skrull, and more, plus the first Silver Age appearance of the Sub-Mariner! And to top it off, Stan Lee signed this book on the blank page across from the cover of #1. In all, trimmed and bound copies of issues #1-20 and Annual #1 are included here. The condition of the comics varies a bit, but the odd cover crease is the only defect of note (none of the comics was in less than VG condition when bound, and many are nicer than that). Try putting together 21 individual copies this nice — it would be an expensive venture indeed! The spine of the book is embossed with the title and issue numbers, and the previous owner's name is embossed on the front of the book. Overstreet 2005 VG 4.0 value for group = $6,528.

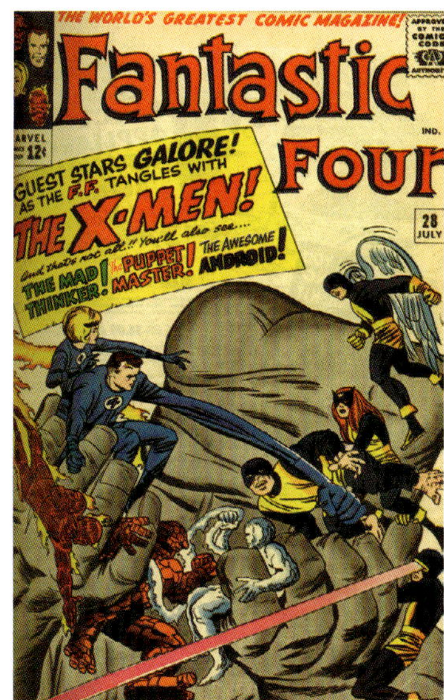

3315 Fantastic Four #21-40 Bound Volume (Marvel, 1963-65). This Stan Lee/Jack Kirby run on "The World's Greatest Comic Magazine" is a must-own, and there's no better way to enjoy it than by reading the original issues in this attractive bound volume. The spine of the book is embossed with the title and issue numbers, and the previous owner's name is embossed on the front of the book. Overstreet 2005 VG 4.0 value for group = $1,070.

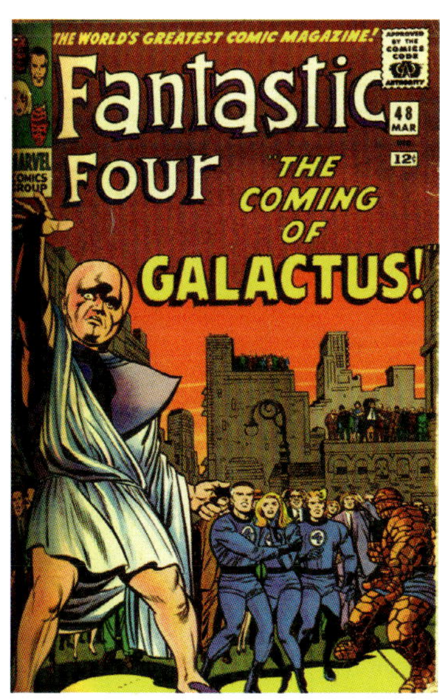

3316 Fantastic Four #41-60 Bound Volume (Marvel, 1965-67). If you're lucky enough to be the winning bidder for this lot, you'll be praying for a rainy weekend afternoon so you can engross yourself in one classic yarn after another. Need examples? Well, you'll meet the Inhumans, go right to the Galactus trilogy, in the very next issue experience the classic tear-jerker "This Man, This Monster," in the very next one after that see the first appearance of the Black Panther, and before you're done you'll also thrill to the epic three-parter in which Dr. Doom steals the Silver Surfer's powers! In all, bound copies of issues #41-60 are contained in this handsome hardcover volume. Note that unlike most bound volumes, this one contains comics that haven't been trimmed, so you could conceivably remove them from the book if you so desired. The condition of the comics varies a bit, but none is less than a VG-type copy, with many a lot nicer than that. The spine of the book is embossed with the title and issue numbers, and the previous owner's name is embossed on the front of the book. Overstreet 2005 VG 4.0 value for group = $694.

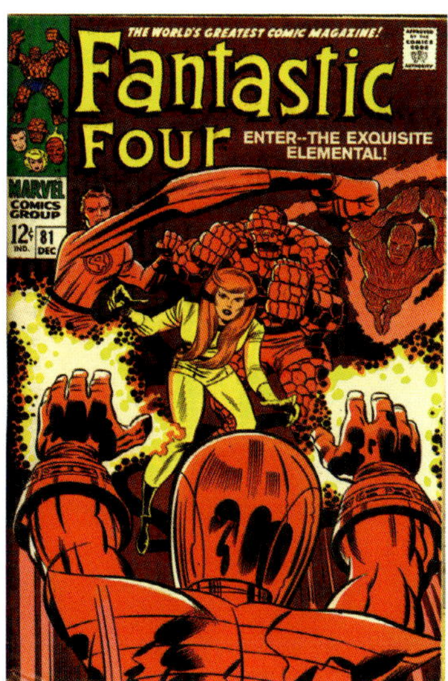

3317 Fantastic Four #61-100 Bound Volumes (Marvel, 1967-70). Every single issue in this bound volume has Jack Kirby art, and what memorable stories they are! In all, bound copies of issues #61-100 are contained in these two handsome hardcover volumes. Note that unlike most bound comic volumes (including most of the other ones in this auction), these contain copies which weren't trimmed prior to binding, meaning a future owner could conceivably remove the comics from the binding if he so desired. The spine of the book is embossed with the title and issue numbers, and the previous owner's name is embossed on the front of the book. Overstreet 2005 VG 4.0 value for group = $516.

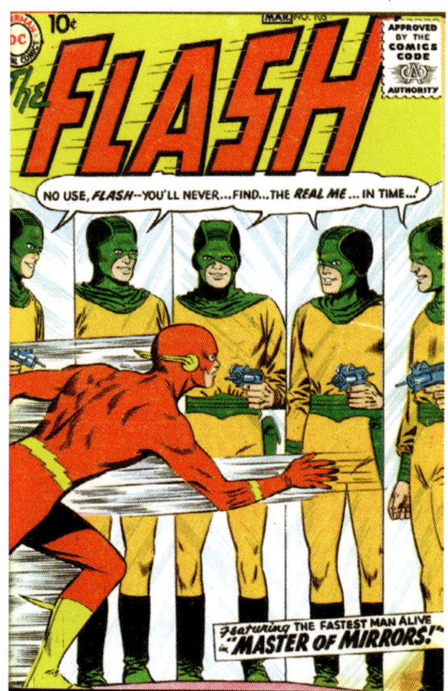

3318 The Flash #105-130 Bound Volume (DC, 1959-62). Two major highlights here are the first issue of the title (#105) and the key "Flash of Two Worlds" story (#123), but there's also much, much more in this awesome Silver Age run. There's the first appearances of Kid Flash, the Elongated Man, the Mirror Master, and the Top, just to name a few! In all, trimmed and bound copies of issues #105-130 are included here. What's really striking about this handsome volume is the superb page quality of the issues therein, making it the perfect way to enjoy these classic stories with Carmine Infantino art. The spine of the book is embossed with the title and issue numbers, and the previous owner's name is embossed on the front of the book. Overstreet 2005 VG 4.0 value for group = $2,904.

3319 Green Lantern #76-89 Bound Volume (DC, 1970-72). Contains trimmed and bound copies of issues #76-89 (the entire Neal Adams run). Includes card signed by Adams. Spine of book is embossed with the title and issue numbers. Previous owner's name is embossed on the front of the book. Overstreet 2005 VG 4.0 value for group = $256.

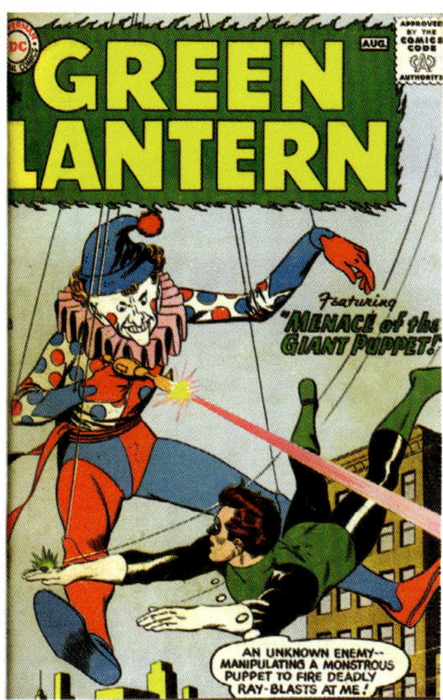

3320 Green Lantern #1-20 And More Bound Volume (DC, 1960-63). The key events in this superb run include the first appearances of the Guardians of the Universe, Sinestro, and Hector Hammond, plus Green Lantern's pal Thomas Kalmaku (aka Pieface). Also among the trimmed and bound comics in this handsome hardcover volume are the 80-pagers **Flash Annual** #1 and **Secret Origins** #1. If you're new to collecting bound volumes, you'll be amazed to see what preservation in this form does for the page quality of the comics, which is much nicer than on copies you'll find "in the wild." The spine of the book is embossed with the title and issue numbers, and the previous owner's name is embossed on the front of the book. Overstreet 2005 VG 4.0 value for group = $1,876.

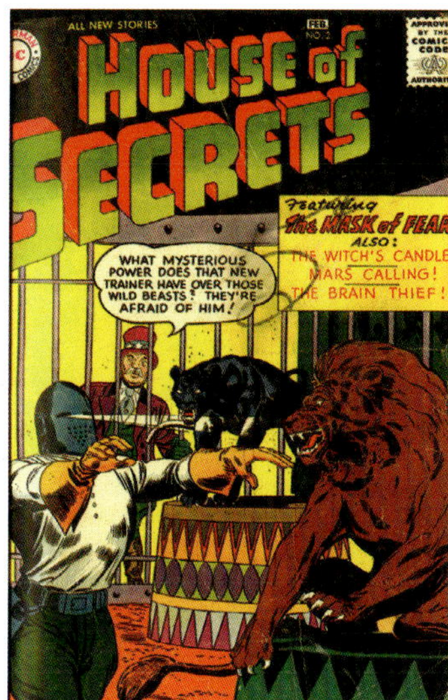

3321 House of Secrets #2-20 Bound Volume (DC, 1956-59). We rarely see extended runs of this title, and having the first few issues all together is especially nice, since many of them have Jack Kirby art! In all, trimmed and bound copies of issues #2-20 are contained in this handsome volume. The spine of the book is embossed with the title and issue numbers, and the previous owner's name is embossed on the front of the book. Overstreet 2005 VG 4.0 value for group = $724.

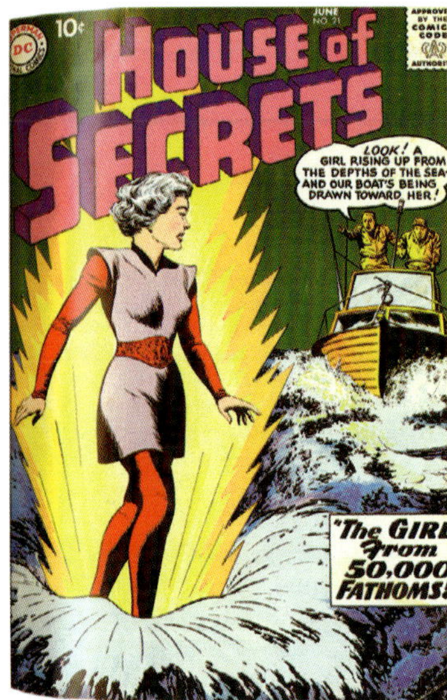

3322 House of Secrets #21-40 Bound Volume (DC, 1959-61). The first appearance of Mark Merlin in #23 is a highlight of this bound volume, which contains trimmed and bound copies of issues #21-40. The spine of the book is embossed with the title and issue numbers, and the previous owner's name is embossed on the front of the book. Overstreet 2005 VG 4.0 value for group = $422.

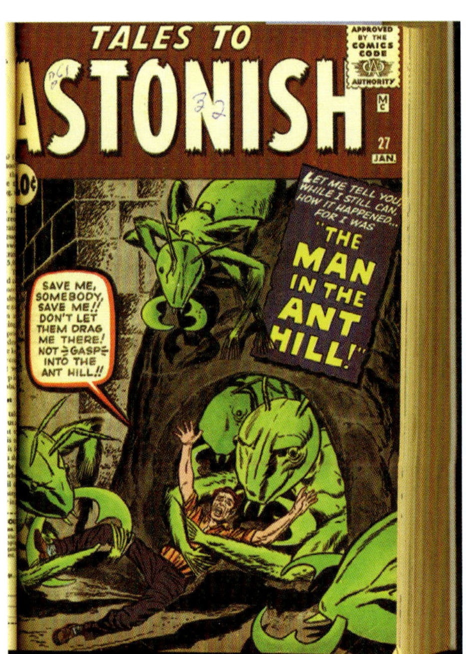

3323 The Incredible Hulk #1-6 and Tales To Astonish #26-40 Bound Volume (Marvel, 1962-64). This great-looking hardcover would be worth spending a pretty penny on just to get the first six **Hulk** issues alone, especially since #1 (the character's origin and first appearance) is autographed by Stan Lee, Jack Kirby, and even Dazzlin' Dick Ayers! But you also get the first appearance of Ant-Man in **TTA** #27, lots of other early Ant-Man stories, and lots of "mystery" tales with art by Kirby or Steve Ditko, some of which have never been reprinted! Note that the copies of **Tales To Astonish** #39 and 40 included here are the British editions (which are not reprints, but editions released at approximately the same time as the US versions); all other comics in this group are the original Marvel editions. The condition of these trimmed and bound copies varies a bit, but the only serious defects of note are handwriting on the front and back covers of **TTA** #27 and a one-inch tear through the last few pages of #26. The spine of the book is embossed with the title and issue numbers (mentioning only **Tales to Astonish**), and the previous owner's name is embossed on the front of the book. Overstreet 2005 VG 4.0 value for group = $4,774.

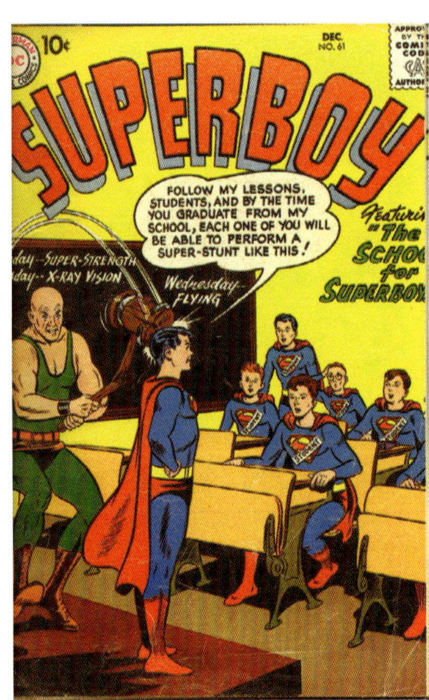

3324 Superboy #61-80 Bound Volume (DC, 1957-60). The origin and first appearance of Bizarro (#68) is a highlight of this Silver Age run. In all, trimmed and bound copies of issues #61-80 are contained in this handsome volume. The spine of the book is embossed with the title and issue numbers, and the previous owner's name is embossed on the front of the book. Overstreet 2005 VG 4.0 value for group = $728.

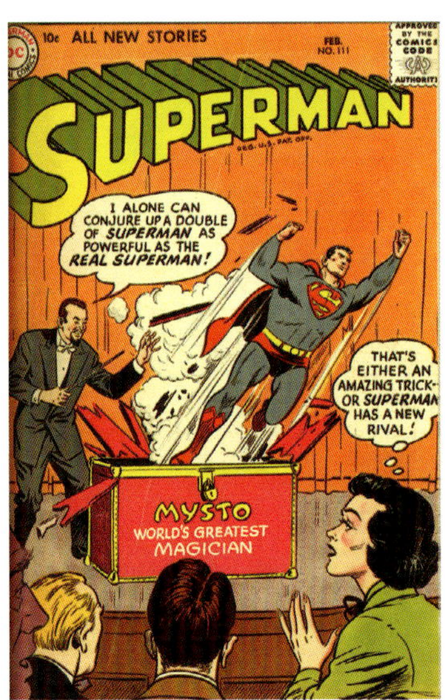

3325 Superman #111-125 Bound Volume (DC, 1957-58). The art of Wayne Boring and Curt Swan is on display in this handsome bound volume, which contains trimmed and bound copies of issues #111-125. The spine of the book is embossed with the title and issue numbers, and the previous owner's name is embossed on the front of the book. Overstreet 2005 VG 4.0 value for group = $1,066.

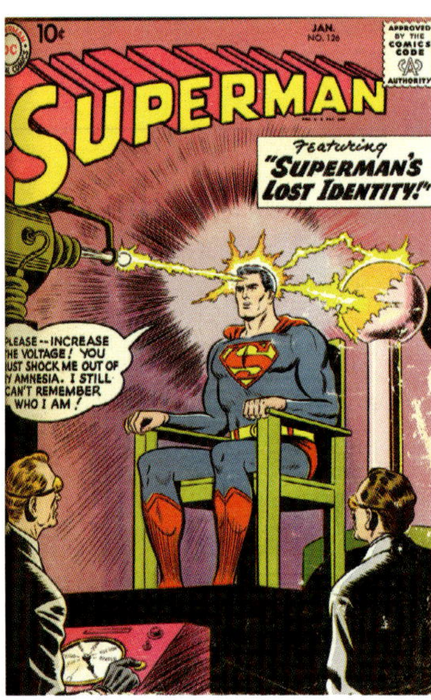

3326 Superman #126-140 Plus Bound Volume (DC, 1959-78). The first appearances of Titano the Super-Ape, Blue Kryptonite, and Bizarro Supergirl are among the highlights of this run. Also among the trimmed and bound comics in this handsome volume are **DC Special Series** #2 and 14 (featuring Swamp Thing). The spine of the book is embossed with the title and issue numbers, and the previous owner's name is embossed on the front of the book. Overstreet 2005 VG 4.0 value for group = $765.

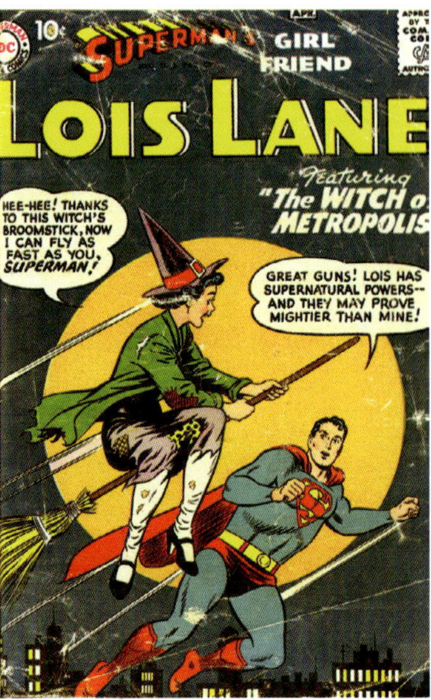

3327 Superman's Girl Friend Lois Lane #1-15 Bound Volume (DC, 1958-60). Trimmed and bound copies of issues #1-15 are contained in this handsome volume. The spine of the book is embossed with the title and issue numbers, and the previous owner's name is embossed on the front of the book. Except for issue #1 which has a heavily creased cover, the comics were obviously in very nice condition when bound, and the condition and page quality remain superb. Overstreet 2005 VG 4.0 value for group = $1,540.

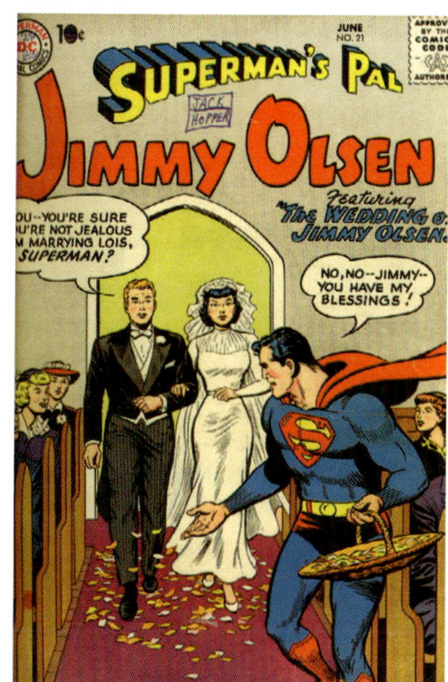

3328 Superman's Pal Jimmy Olsen #21-35 Bound Volume (DC, 1957-59). Trimmed and bound copies of issues #21-35 are contained in this handsome volume. The spine of the book is embossed with the title and issue numbers, and the previous owner's name is embossed on the front of the book. Issues #21, 22, and 32 have handwriting on the cover and/or the first page. Overstreet 2005 VG 4.0 value for group = $466.

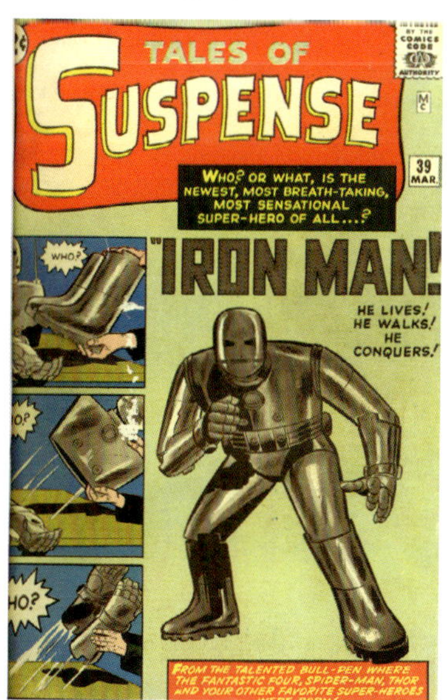

3329 Tales of Suspense #39-60 Bound Volume (Marvel, 1963-64). The origin and first appearance of Iron Man in #39 is only one of the key issues contained in this handsome bound volume. In all, trimmed and bound copies of issues #39-60 are included here. In addition to all of the earliest Iron Man stories, this group of issues includes the first appearances of the Black Widow (#52) and Hawkeye (#57), plus the first couple of Stan Lee/Jack Kirby Captain America backup features. And the icing on the cake comes in the form of lots of great "mystery" backup features with Steve Ditko art. The spine of the book is embossed with the title and issue numbers, and the previous owner's name is embossed on the front of the book. Overstreet 2005 VG 4.0 value for group = $2,474.

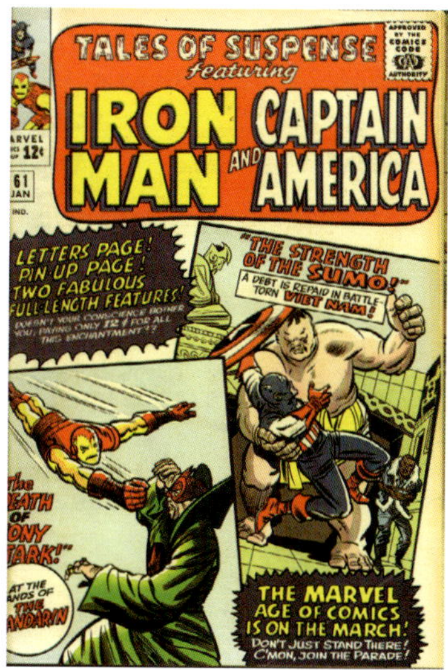

3330 Tales of Suspense #61-80 Bound Volume (Marvel, 1965-66). This volume contains bound copies of issues #61-80, which were all Iron Man/Captain America double-feature issues. The run of Cap stories culminates in the epic "Cosmic Cube" storyline. Note that unlike many bound volumes, this one has copies that have not been trimmed prior to binding. The spine of the book is embossed with the title and issue numbers, and the previous owner's name is embossed on the front of the book. Overstreet 2005 VG 4.0 value for group = $406.

3331 Tales of Suspense #81-99 Bound Volume (Marvel, 1966-68). All issues are Iron Man/Captain America double features. Comics not trimmed prior to binding. The spine of the book is embossed with the title and issue numbers, and the previous owner's name is embossed on the front of the book. Overstreet 2005 VG 4.0 value for group = $268.

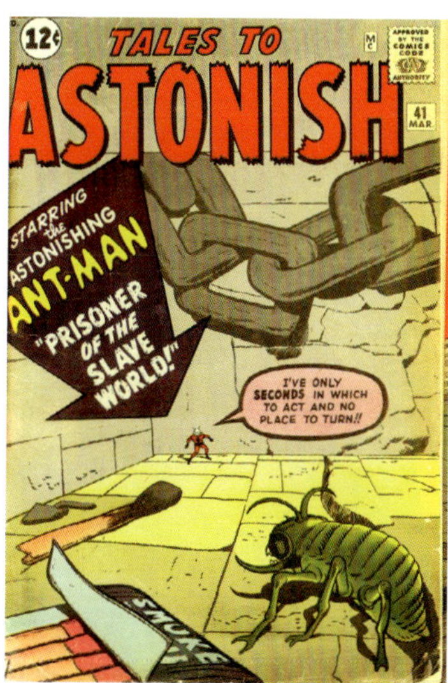

3332 Tales to Astonish #41-60 Bound Volume (Marvel, 1963-64). The issues in this bound volume are tales of Ant-Man and Giant-Man, plus the first couple of issues of the Giant-Man/Hulk double feature. These comics have not been trimmed prior to binding. The spine of the book is embossed with the title and issue numbers, and the previous owner's name is embossed on the front of the book. Overstreet 2005 VG 4.0 value for group = $836.

3333 Tales to Astonish #61-80 Bound Volume (Marvel, 1964-66). Double-feature issues star Hulk and Giant-Man (#61-69) and followed by Hulk and Sub-Mariner (#70-80). Comics were not trimmed prior to binding. The spine of the book is embossed with the title and issue numbers, and the previous owner's name is embossed on the front of the book. Overstreet 2005 VG 4.0 value for group = $322.

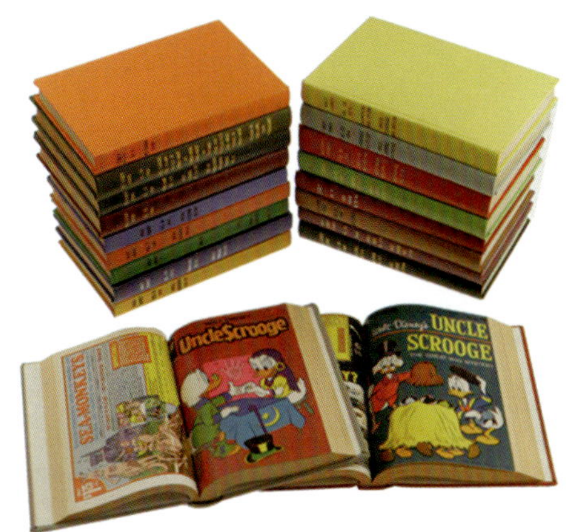

3334 Uncle Scrooge #47-209 and More Bound Volumes (Gold Key and Whitman, 1964-84). These 19 hardcover volumes from the files of Western Publishing contain trimmed and bound copies of every issue of **Uncle Scrooge** that Gold Key published over a span of 20 years, issues #47-209! Yes, even the hard to find Whitman "pre-pack only" issues are here, and yes, the ultra-tough #179 (one of the ten most valuable Bronze Age comic books) is among them! These copies were obviously in Near Mint condition when bound, and their cover gloss is still outstanding today. There's more than just **Scrooge** in this lot, by the way — there's also **Walt Disney Showcase** #7-33, **Donald Duck** #35-40, **Winnie the Pooh** #18-23, **Mickey Mouse** #128-133, **Super Goof** #12-15, and various other mini-runs and one-shots too numerous to mention. It's a whole bookshelf of pristine Disney! Approximate Overstreet VG 4.0 value for group = $2,400; approximate FN 6.0 value for group = $4,800; approximate VF 8.0 value for group = $7,500.

3335 Vampirella #1-10 And Other Magazines Bound Volume (Warren, 1969-81). Marvel and DC bonuses await the winning bidder for this handsome bound volume, which contains trimmed and bound copies of **Vampirella** #1-10, the Warren one-shot **On The Scene Presents Super-Heroes**, Marvel's **Bizarre Adventures** #27 (featuring the X-Men) and DC's **In The Days Of The Mob** (with Jack Kirby art, and with the pull-out poster included). The spine of the book is embossed with the title and issue numbers (only **Vampirella** is mentioned), and the previous owner's name is embossed on the front of the book. Overstreet 2005 VG 4.0 value for group = $354.

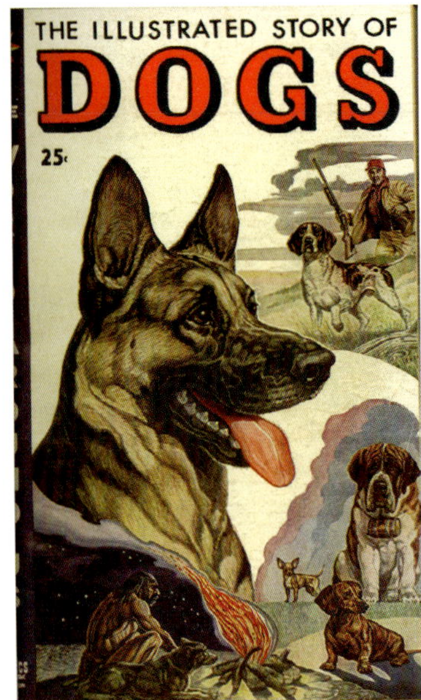

3336 World Around Us #1-36 Bound Volumes (Gilberton, 1958-61). The entire run of the series is collected in these three handsome bound volumes. The run includes work by an impressive roster of artists including L. B. Cole, Everett Raymond Kinstler, Graham Ingels, George Evans, Reed Crandall, Al Williamson, and even Jack Kirby (#31)! The issues were trimmed and bound for inclusion in this hardcover volume. Note that the last few issues in the third volume were bound out of order. The spine of the book is embossed with the title and issue numbers, and the previous owner's name is embossed on the front of the book. Overstreet 2005 VG 4.0 value for group = $570.

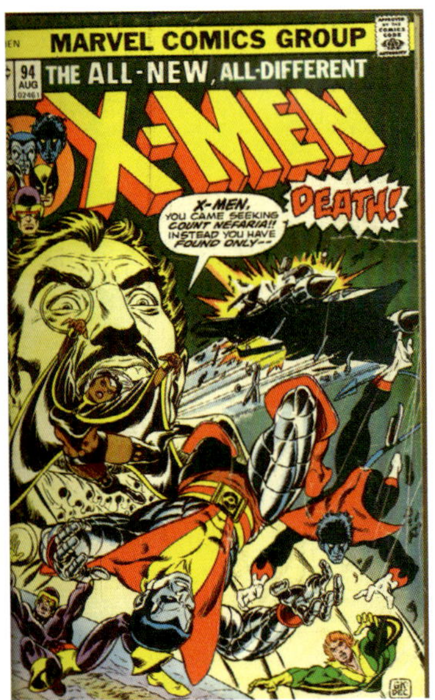

3337 X-Men #94-110, Giant-Size X-Men #1, And More Bound Volume (Marvel, 1972-78). Not only do you get the first appearance of the New X-Men and the first 17 issues of the team's regular series in this great bound volume, there's a special bonus for the winning bidder at the very end of this hefty hardcover. Enter the world of danger, drama, and death, the world of Linda Carter... **Night Nurse**! Yes, the full run of that series (#1-4) is also among the trimmed and bound copies here. The spine of the book is embossed with the title and issue numbers (only #94-110 are mentioned), and the previous owner's name is embossed on the front of the book. Overstreet 2005 VG 4.0 value for group = $536.

3338 X-Men #111-150 and Annuals 4-6 Bound Volumes (Marvel, 1978-82). Trimmed and bound copies of issues #111-150 and Annuals #4-6 are contained in these two handsome volumes. The spine of each the book is embossed with the respective title and issue numbers, and the previous owner's name is embossed on the front of each book. Overstreet 2005 VG 4.0 value for group = $289.

MAGAZINES

3339 Amazing World of DC Comics #15 (DC, 1977) CGC NM+ 9.6 White pages. Previously unpublished Wonder Woman story. Lynda Carter article and photos. Mike Nasser cover. Neal Adams and Dick Giordano art. CGC notes, "Don Rosa Collection." Overstreet 2005 NM- 9.2 value = $48. CGC census 7/05: 1 in 9.6, none higher.

3340 Amazing World of DC Comics #16 (DC, 1977) CGC NM 9.4 White pages. Special Golden Age issue. Wraparound cover by Marshall Rogers. CGC notes, "Don Rosa Collection." Overstreet 2005 NM- 9.2 value = $38. CGC census 7/05: 1 in 9.4, none higher.

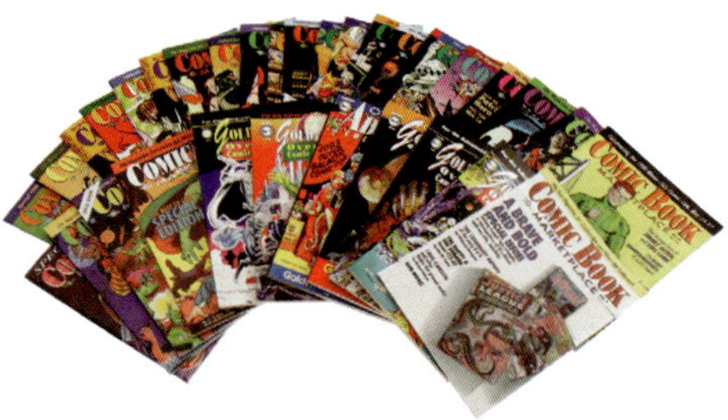

3341 Comic Book Marketplace Special Edition and Cover Variant Issue, plus Gold and Silver, Overstreet's Comic Book Quarterly Group (various, 1993-2000) Condition: Average VF+. This sensational lot includes the variant cover issues of **CBM** that were given away as a promotion at various comic conventions such as San Diego Comic Con, Chicago Comicon, Wondercon, and others. These variant issues include issue #25, 26, 34, 37, 41, 44, 46, 47, 48, 49, 58, 59, 60, 61, 62, 65, 67, 70, 77, 78, and 80 (two copies). Included along with those magazines are **CBM Special Edition** # 1, 2, 3, 4, and 5. As if that weren't enough comics history to boggle your brain, this lot also includes **Gold and Silver, Overstreet's Comic Book Quarterly** # 1, 2, 3, 4, 5, and 6. All in all, that's 33 issues of good reading fun! These magazines average VF+ condition.

3342 Creepy #7 Pacific Coast pedigree (Warren, 1966) CGC NM+ 9.6 Off-white pages. Frank Frazetta and Roy Krenkel cover. Frazetta, Alex Toth, Joe Orlando, Angelo Torres, Gray Morrow, Reed Crandall, and John Severin art. Overstreet 2005 NM- 9.2 value = $45. CGC census 7/05: 5 in 9.6, 2 higher.

3343 Creepy #8 Pacific Coast pedigree (Warren, 1966) CGC VF/NM 9.0 Off-white pages. Gray Morrow cover. Reed Crandall, George Evans, Johnny Craig, Gene Colan, and Joe Orlando art. Angelo Torres frontispiece. Overstreet 2005 VF/NM 9.0 value = $36; NM- 9.2 value = $45. CGC census 7/05: 2 in 9.0, 8 higher.

3344 Creepy #15 Pacific Coast pedigree (Warren, 1967) CGC NM- 9.2 Off-white pages. Classic cover by Frank Frazetta (legend has it it was painted on plywood when he found himself faced with a looming deadline and no canvas). Also featured is a 16-page time travel story with Neal Adams art; as well as art by Steve Ditko, Gil Kane, and Johnny Craig. Overstreet 2005 NM- 9.2 value = $45. CGC census 7/05: 3 in 9.2, 18 higher.

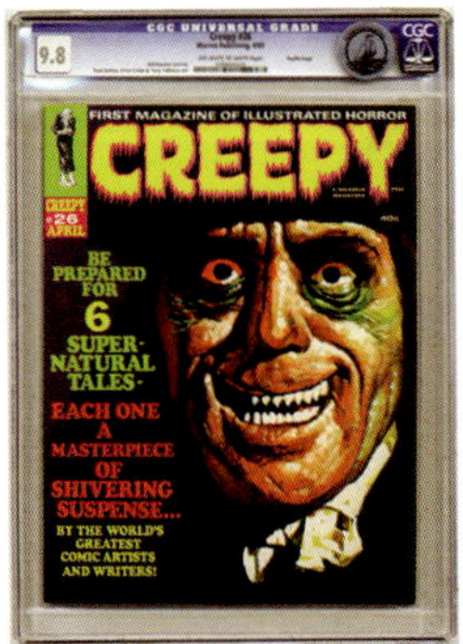

3345 Creepy #26 Pacific Coast pedigree (Warren, 1969) CGC NM/MT 9.8 Off-white to white pages. Cover by Basil Gogos. Art by Steve Ditko, Tom Sutton, Gray Morrow, Jerry Grandenetti, and Ernie Colon. Overstreet 2005 NM- 9.2 value = $35. CGC census 7/05: 2 in 9.8, none higher.

3346 Creepy #27 Pacific Coast pedigree (Warren, 1969) CGC NM 9.4 Off-white to white pages. Frank Frazetta cover. Steve Ditko, Reed Crandall, Tom Sutton, Angelo Torres, and Ernie Colon art. "Loathsome Lore" written by Forrest Ackerman. Overstreet 2005 NM- 9.2 value = $35. CGC census 7/05: 10 in 9.4, 11 higher.

3347 Creepy #40 (Warren, 1971) CGC NM+ 9.6 Off-white to white pages. Vaughn Bode and Larry Todd cover. Tom Sutton, Dave Cockrum, Pablo Marcos, and George Roussos art. CGC notes, "Don Rosa Collection." Overstreet 2005 NM- 9.2 value = $30. CGC census 7/05: 4 in 9.6, 2 higher.

3348 Creepy #91 (Warren, 1977) CGC NM/MT 9.8 White pages. 1977 Yearbook. Frank Frazetta cover. Bernie Wrightson, Wally Wood, John Severin, Alex Toth, Jeff Jones, Neal Adams, and Russ Heath art. Overstreet 2005 NM- 9.2 value = $14. CGC census 7/05: 4 in 9.8, none higher.

3349 Dracula Lives! #9 (Marvel, 1974) CGC NM/MT 9.8 Off-white to white pages. Bondage cover by Luis Dominguez. Ernie Chan and Alfredo Alcala art. CGC notes, "Don Rosa Collection." Overstreet 2005 NM- 9.2 value = $30. CGC census 7/05: 1 in 9.8, none higher.

3350 Dracula Lives! #11 (Marvel, 1975) CGC NM/MT 9.8 White pages. Tony DeZuniga and Dick Giordano art. Steve Fabian cover. CGC notes, "Don Rosa Collection." Overstreet 2005 NM- 9.2 value = $32. CGC census 7/05: 1 in 9.8, none higher.

3351 Dracula Lives! #12 (Marvel, 1975) CGC NM/MT 9.8 White pages. Ken Bald cover. Tom Sutton art. Biography of Christopher Lee. CGC notes, "Don Rosa Collection." Overstreet 2005 NM- 9.2 value = $32. CGC census 7/05: 1 in 9.8, none higher.

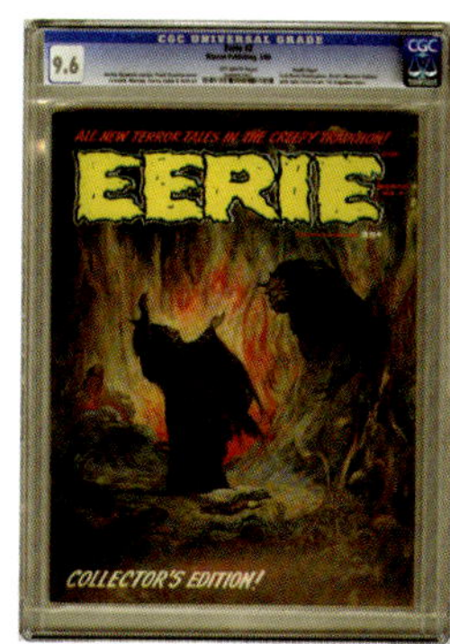

3352 Eerie #2 Pacific Coast pedigree (Warren, 1966) CGC NM+ 9.6 Off-white pages. The title's first newsstand issue, as well as the first appearance of Cousin Eerie. Cover by Frank Frazetta; interior art by Jack Davis, Alex Toth, Gene Colan, Reed Crandall, Angelo Torres, Johnny Craig, Gray Morrow, John Severin, and Joe Orlando. Overstreet 2005 NM- 9.2 value = $125. CGC census 7/05: 1 in 9.6, 1 higher.

3353 Eerie #3 (Warren, 1966) CGC NM 9.4 Off-white pages. Frank Frazetta cover. Interior art by Steve Ditko, Jack Davis, Alex Toth, Gene Colan, Johnny Craig (as "Jay Taycee"), Angelo Torres, Al Williamson, Joe Orlando, and Rocke Mastroserio. Debut of "Dear Cousin Eerie" letters page. Overstreet 2005 NM- 9.2 value = $90. CGC census 9/05: 3 in 9.4, 1 higher.

3354 Eerie #5 (Warren, 1966) CGC NM+ 9.6 Off-white pages. What an incredible line-up of talent for this issue — a Frank Frazetta cover; Steve Ditko, Gene Colan, Reed Crandall, Al Williamson, Joe Orlando, Angelo Torres, and Rocke Mastroserio interior art; even a Monster Gallery frontispiece by Wally Wood and Dan Adkins! On top of everything, this copy is a real beauty to boot! How can you go wrong? Bid! Overstreet 2005 NM- 9.2 value = $55. CGC census 8/05: 6 in 9.6, 1 higher.

3355 Eerie #6 Pacific Coast pedigree (Warren, 1966) CGC NM+ 9.6 Off-white pages. Cover by Gray Morrow, plus a Monster Gallery frontispiece by John Severin. The interior art is by Steve Ditko, Gene Colan, Reed Crandall, Angelo Torres, Johnny Craig (as Jay Taycee), and Rocke Mastroserio. Overstreet 2005 NM- 9.2 value = $55. CGC census 7/05: 2 in 9.6, none higher.

3356 Eerie #7 (Warren, 1967) CGC NM+ 9.6 Off-white to white pages. Frank Frazetta cover. Interior art by Gray Morrow, Gene Colan, Steve Ditko, Dan Adkins, Johnny Craig, and Jerry Grandenetti. Overstreet 2005 NM- 9.2 value = $55. CGC census 9/05: 7 in 9.6, 2 higher.

3357 Eerie #9 Pacific Coast pedigree (Warren, 1967) CGC NM- 9.2 Off-white pages. Includes an adaptation of "An Occurrence at Owl Creek Bridge" by Ambrose Bierce. Features a cover by Dan Adkins; art by Roy Krenkel, Steve Ditko, Neal Adams, Gene Colan, and Jerry Grandenetti. Overstreet 2005 NM- 9.2 value = $60. CGC census 7/05: 5 in 9.2, 5 higher.

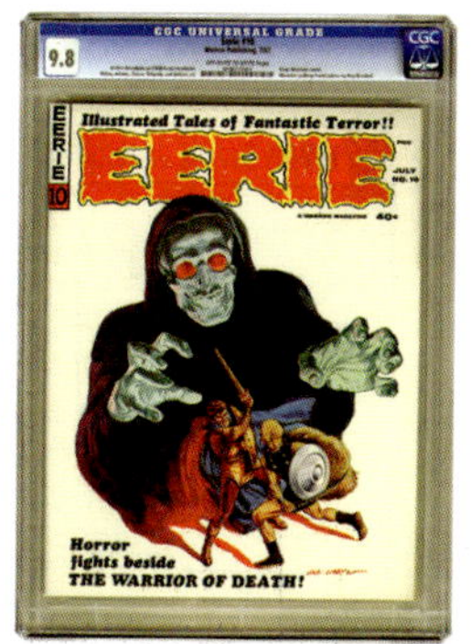

3358 Eerie #10 (Warren, 1967) CGC NM/MT 9.8 Off-white to white pages. The striking cover by Gray Morrow is enhanced by the pure white background of this exemplary copy, one of just four to have earned 9.8 status from CGC to date. Artists include Steve Ditko, Neal Adams, Gene Colan, Joe Orlando, Dan Adkins, and Roy Krenkel, who provided a monster gallery frontispiece. Overstreet 2005 NM- 9.2 value = $60. CGC census 9/05: 4 in 9.8, none higher.

3359 Eerie #10 Pacific Coast pedigree (Warren, 1967) CGC NM 9.4 Off-white pages. Gray Morrow cover; Roy Krenkel, Steve Ditko, Neal Adams, Gene Colan, Joe Orlando, and Dan Adkins art. Monster Gallery frontispiece with Krenkel art. Overstreet 2005 NM- 9.2 value = $60. CGC census 7/05: 18 in 9.4, 14 higher.

3360 Eerie #81 (Warren, 1977) CGC NM/MT 9.8 White pages. Frank Frazetta cover (all of the issue's stories are based on the cover illustration). Richard Corben and Carmine Infantino art. CGC notes, "Don Rosa Collection." Overstreet 2005 NM- 9.2 value = $24. CGC census 7/05: 5 in 9.8, none higher.

3361 Eerie #93 (Warren, 1978) CGC NM/MT 9.8 White pages. Alfredo Alcala and Alex Nino art. Don Maitz cover. CGC notes, "Don Rosa Collection." Overstreet 2005 NM- 9.2 value = $14. CGC census 7/05: 3 in 9.8, none higher.

3362 Eerie #108 (Warren, 1980) CGC NM/MT 9.8 White pages. Pablo Marcos, Val Mayerik, and Mike Zeck art. Jim Laurier cover. CGC notes, "Don Rosa Collection." Overstreet 2005 NM- 9.2 value = $14. CGC census 7/05: 2 in 9.8, none higher.

3363 Eerie #113 (Warren, 1980) CGC NM/MT 9.8 White pages. Jim Laurier cover. Alfredo Alcala and E. R. Cruz art. CGC notes, "Don Rosa Collection." Overstreet 2005 NM- 9.2 value = $14. CGC census 7/05: 3 in 9.8, none higher.

3364 Eerie Yearbook 1970 (Warren, 1970) CGC NM+ 9.6 Off-white pages. Art by Steve Ditko, Jack Davis, Gene Colan, Angelo Torres, Tom Sutton, Dan Adkins, and Rocke Mastroserio. Cover is a montage of Frank Frazetta images from other covers. Overstreet 2005 NM- 9.2 value = $60. CGC census 9/05: 4 in 9.6, 2 higher.

3365 Howard the Duck #8 (Marvel, 1980) CGC NM/MT 9.8 White pages. Batman parody. Gene Colan, Marshall Rogers, and Dave Sim art. John Pound cover. CGC notes, "Don Rosa Collection." Overstreet 2005 NM- 9.2 value = $5. CGC census 7/05: 1 in 9.8, none higher.

3366 Mad #27 (EC, 1956) CGC VF- 7.5 Cream to off-white pages. Al Jaffee's first issue as a staff artist. Cover by Jack Davis; interior art by Davis, Jaffee, Wally Wood, Russ Heath, and Bill Elder. Overstreet 2005 VF 8.0 value = $244. CGC census 7/05: 1 in 7.5, 6 higher.

3367 Mad #29 (EC, 1956) CGC VF+ 8.5 Light tan to off-white pages. Al Feldstein's first issue as editor. Don Martin's first issue as a regular. Also art by Jack Kamen, Basil Wolverton, Jack Davis, and Wally Wood. Overstreet 2005 VF 8.0 value = $213; VF/NM 9.0 value = $319. CGC census 9/05: 2 in 8.5, 3 higher.

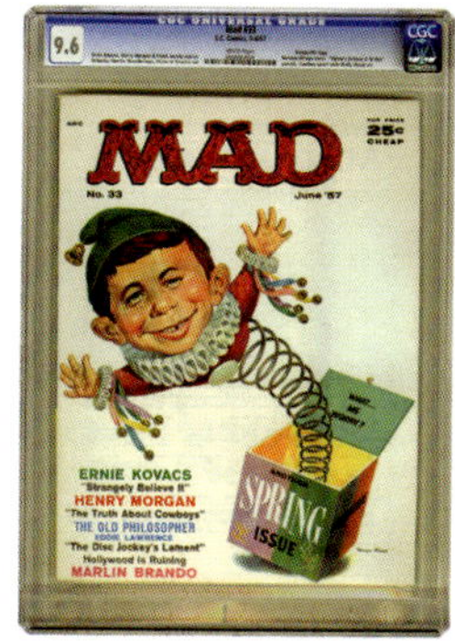

3368 Mad #33 Gaines File pedigree (EC, 1957) CGC NM+ 9.6 White pages. No copy of this issue has been graded higher by CGC to date, and considering the issue's white cover, it seems unlikely that one will be in the future! Not many people know that TV funnyman Ernie Kovacs contributed to the magazine in the early years, and he's joined by the Usual Gang of Idiots here. Wally Wood, Mort Drucker, and Joe Orlando are among the bigger names. The cover's by Norman Mingo. Overstreet 2005 NM- 9.2 value = $320. CGC census 9/05: 2 in 9.6, none higher.

3369 Mad #34 (EC, 1957) CGC VF/NM 9.0 Off-white to white pages. Parody of **Seduction of the Innocent** author Dr. Fredric Wertham. Norman Mingo cover. Interior art by Wally Wood, Kelly Freas, Don Martin, Mort Drucker, Joe Orlando, and Dave Berg (his first on the title). Overstreet 2005 VF/NM 9.0 value = $201; NM- 9.2 value = $270. CGC census 9/05: 5 in 9.0, 3 higher.

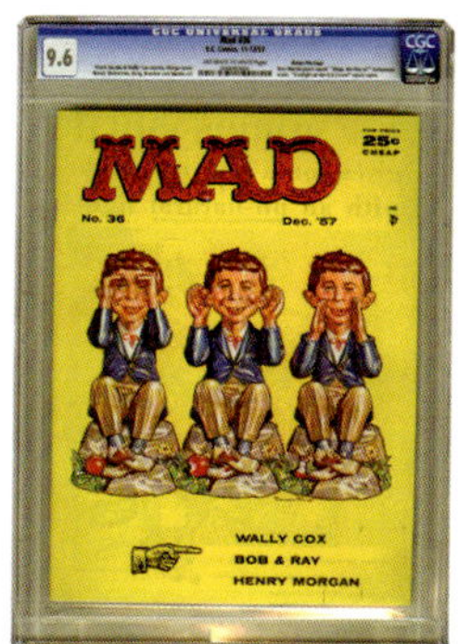

3370 Mad #36 Gaines File pedigree (EC, 1957) CGC NM+ 9.6 Off-white to white pages. Back in the day, who would have been able to resist cutting out the Alfred E. Neuman mask on this issue's back cover and clowning around as the What Me Worry Kid? Not many people, that's why a top-grade copy can only be had from the files of publisher Bill Gaines. Wally Wood and Basil Wolverton were among the contributors to this issue; the cover's by Norman Mingo. Overstreet 2005 NM- 9.2 value = $200. CGC census 9/05: 2 in 9.6, none higher.

3371 Mad #37 (EC, 1958) CGC NM- 9.2 White pages. Norman Mingo cover. Ernie Kovacs story. Wally Wood, Mort Drucker, Joe Orlando, Don Martin, and Dave Berg art. Overstreet 2005 NM- 9.2 value = $200. CGC census 9/05: 1 in 9.2, 2 higher.

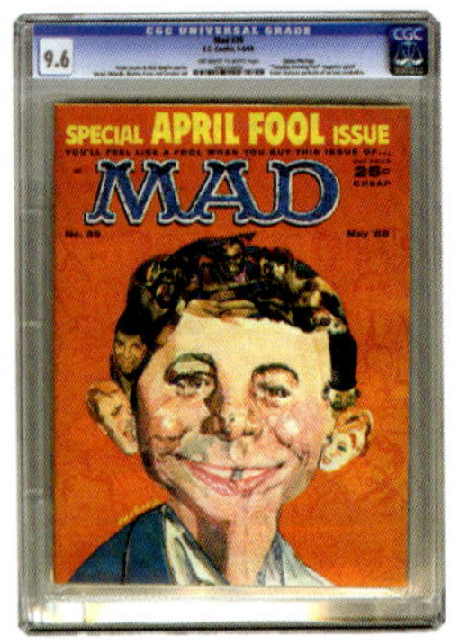

3372 Mad #39 Gaines File pedigree (EC, 1958) CGC NM+ 9.6 Off-white to white pages. And in this issue of that august American institution, **Collier's** magazine... wait a minute, this is **Mad**! What shmendrick got watercolorist C. C. Beall, Jr. to paint the cover showcasing famous Americans of the day? Ah, it all becomes clear when you find out that there's a **Saturday Evening Post** parody in the issue. The usual Gang of Idi... er, respectable artists are on hand, like Wally, uh, Wallace Wood, Mortimer Drucker, Joseph Orlando, Donald Martin, and Frank Kelly Freas. Overstreet 2005 NM- 9.2 value = $200. CGC census 9/05: 3 in 9.6, none higher.

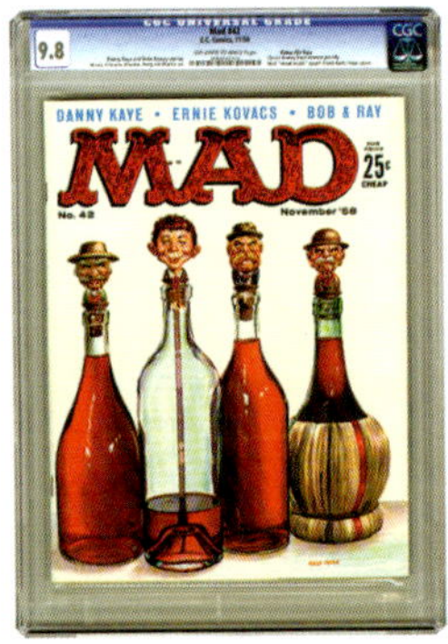

3373 Mad #42 Gaines File pedigree (EC, 1958) CGC NM/MT 9.8 Off-white to white pages. Kelly Freas painted this issue's cover, and regulars Wally Wood, Joe Orlando, Mort Drucker, Dave Berg, and Don Martin contributed interior art. CGC calls attention to a "classic Danny Kaye musical parody." Overstreet 2005 NM- 9.2 value = $165. CGC census 9/05: 3 in 9.8, none higher.

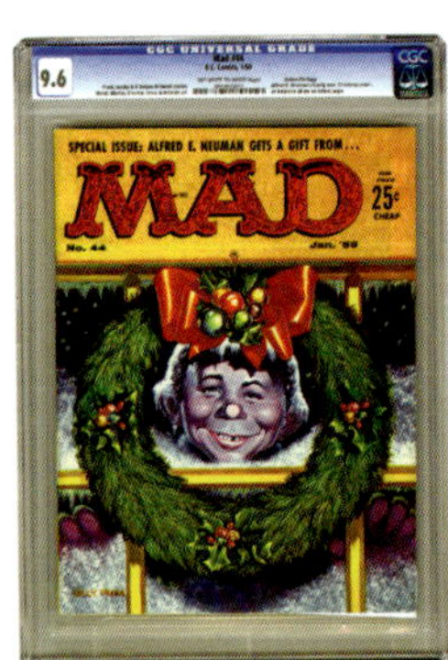

3374 Mad #44 Gaines File pedigree (EC, 1959) CGC NM+ 9.6 Off-white to white pages. Forget about the Christmas-themed cover by Kelly Freas, showing Alfred E. Neuman, and look at the Christmas-themed *back* cover, showing Alfred's *girlfriend* Moxie Cowznofski! Now, whether she's related to *Melvin* Cowznofski is something we haven't been able to determine, but we do believe this to be Moxie's first appearance. The issue's interior artists include Freas, Wally Wood, Don Martin, Mort Drucker, and Joe Orlando. Overstreet 2005 NM- 9.2 value = $165. CGC census 9/05: 3 in 9.6, 1 higher.

3375 Mad #45 Gaines File pedigree (EC, 1959) CGC NM- 9.2 White pages. Valentine's Day cover by Kelly Freas, featuring Alfred E. Neuman and Moxie Cowznofski. Interior art by Wally Wood, Joe Orlando, Mort Drucker, Dave Berg, and Don Martin. Overstreet 2005 NM- 9.2 value = $165. CGC census 9/05: 1 in 9.2, 3 higher.

3376 Mad #48 (EC, 1959) CGC VF+ 8.5 White pages. Uncle Sam cover by Kelly Freas. Perry Mason parody. Sid Caesar story. Art by Freas, Mort Drucker, Don Martin, Wally Wood, Bob Clarke, Dave Berg, and Joe Orlando. Overstreet 2005 VF 8.0 value = $81; VF/NM 9.0 value = $123. CGC census 9/05: 1 in 8.5, 5 higher.

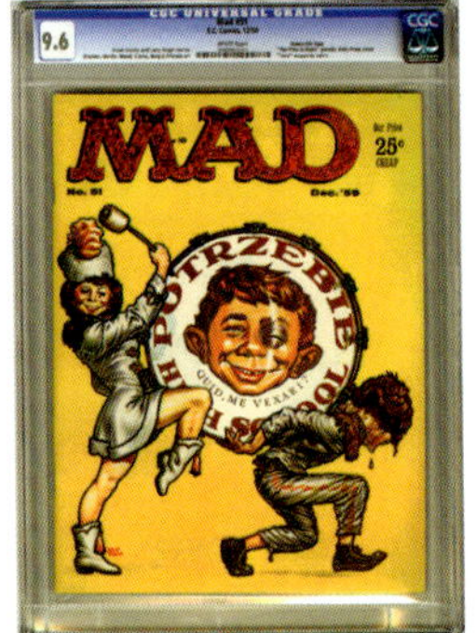

3377 Mad #51 Gaines File pedigree (EC, 1959) CGC NM+ 9.6 White pages. "The Price Is Right" is parodied in this issue, which dates from the pre-Bob Barker days when Bill Cullen was hosting the show! Kelly Freas drew the issue's cover. If you're not the winning bidder, we *don't* have any lovely parting gifts for you, so be sure to do what needs to be done to take home this fabulous prize. Overstreet 2005 NM- 9.2 value = $140. CGC census 9/05: 1 in 9.6, 1 higher.

3378 Mad #58 Gaines File pedigree (EC, 1960) CGC VF/NM 9.0 White pages. Kelly Freas cover. Joe Orlando back cover. Mort Drucker, Dave Berg, Wally Wood, Don Martin, and George Woodbridge art. Overstreet 2005 VF/NM 9.0 value = $105; NM- 9.2 value = $140. CGC census 9/05: in 9.0, 3 higher.

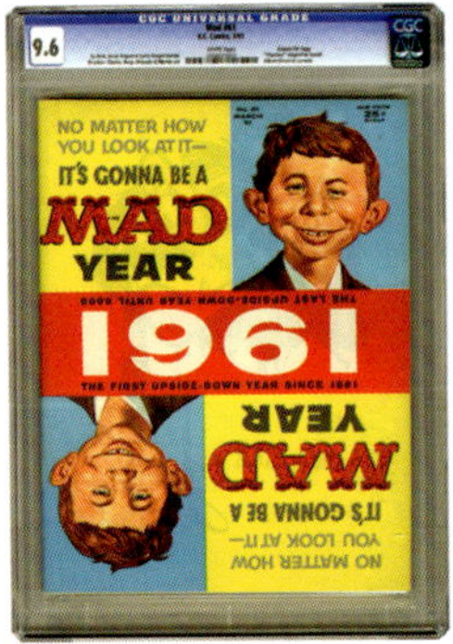

3379 Mad #61 Gaines File pedigree (EC, 1961) CGC NM+ 9.6 White pages. A "Playboy" spoof is a highlight of this issue, which has art by Mort Drucker, Bob Clarke, Dave Berg, Joe Orlando, and Don Martin. Overstreet 2005 NM- 9.2 value = $105. CGC census 9/05: 1 in 9.6, 2 higher.

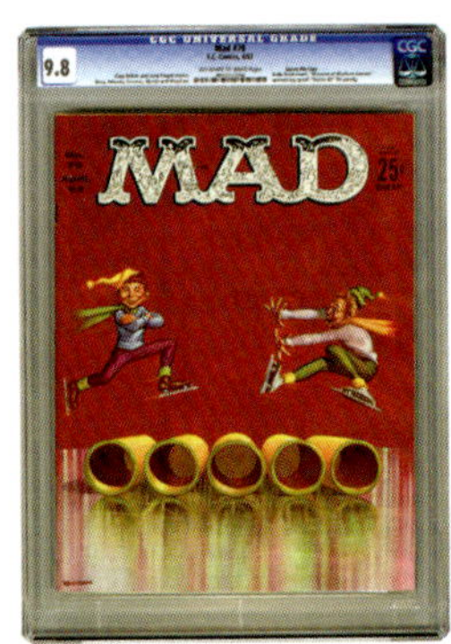

3380 Mad #70 Gaines File pedigree (EC, 1962) CGC NM/MT 9.8 Off-white to white pages. Here's a pristine copy from Bill Gaines' closet. The issue has a Kelly Freas cover and interior art by Dave Berg, Joe Orlando, Mort Drucker, Don Martin, and Wally Wood. Overstreet 2005 NM- 9.2 value = $105. CGC census 9/05: 2 in 9.8, none higher.

3381 Mad #85 Gaines File pedigree (EC, 1964) CGC NM+ 9.6 White pages. Dick Tracy and Popeye parodies. Norman Mingo cover. Mort Drucker, Jack Rickard, Joe Orlando, Don Martin, and Wally Wood art. Overstreet 2005 NM-9.2 value = $60. CGC census 9/05: 2 in 9.6, none higher.

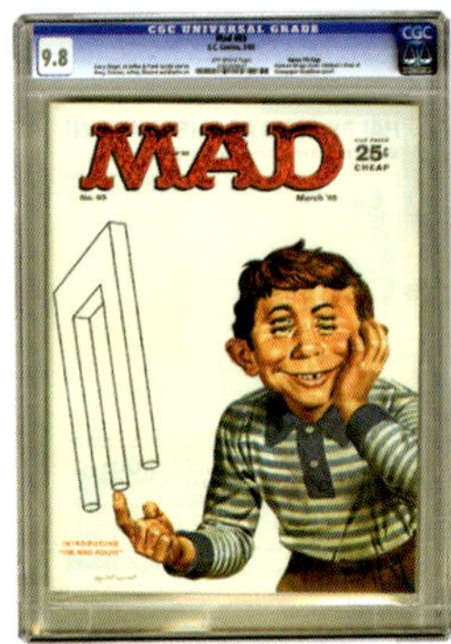

3382 Mad #93 Gaines File pedigree (EC, 1965) CGC NM/MT 9.8 Off-white pages. Even if you think M. C. Escher is a rapper, you'll probably enjoy this optical-illusion cover by Norman Mingo. The issue also has art by Dave Berg, Mort Drucker, Al Jaffee, Jack Rickard, and Don Martin. Overstreet 2005 NM- 9.2 value = $55. CGC census 9/05: 2 in 9.8, none higher.

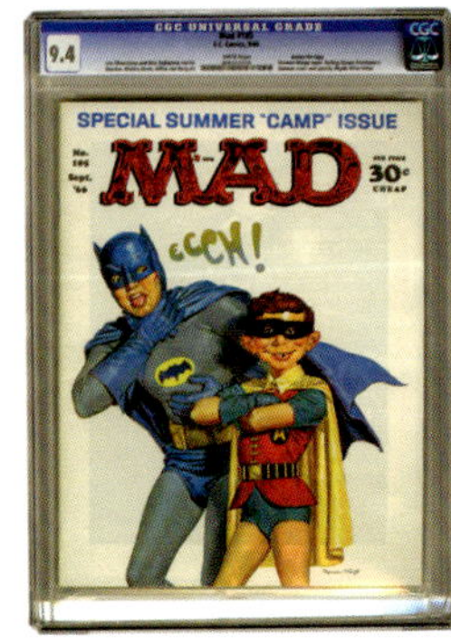

3383 Mad #105 Gaines File pedigree (EC, 1966) CGC NM 9.4 White pages. This issue's been changing hands at above Guide lately, and it could only be because of the "Batman" connection. That TV show is parodied in this issue. the mag has a Norman Mingo cover, and the interior artists include Mort Drucker, Don Martin, Jack

Davis, Al Jaffee, and Dave Berg. As Adam West once said on the TV show, "et cetera, et cetera, ad infinitum!" Overstreet 2005 NM- 9.2 value = $50. CGC census 9/05: in 9.4, higher.

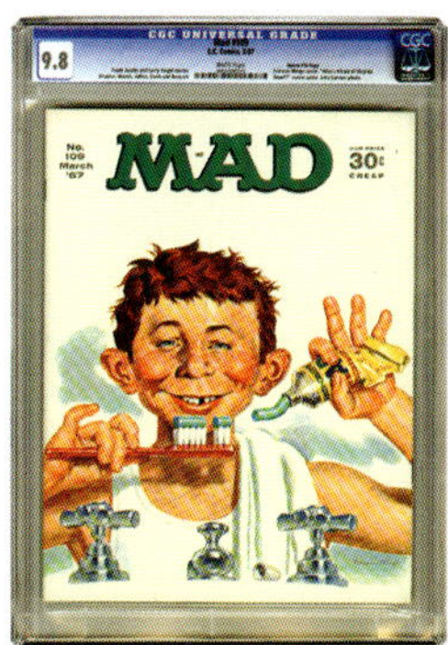

3384 Mad #109 Gaines File pedigree (EC, 1967) CGC NM/MT 9.8 White pages. Four out of five nudnicks recommend this dental-hygiene cover by Norman Mingo. The issue also has art by Mort Drucker, Don Martin, Al Jaffee, Jack Davis, and Dave Berg. Come to think of it, the magazines at our dentist's office are so old, there might be a Mad #109 in the stack somewhere! But we digress... get this 9.8 pedigree copy, no copy has been graded higher by CGC to date. Overstreet 2005 NM- 9.2 value = $38. CGC census 9/05: 3 in 9.8, none higher.

3385 Mad #110 Gaines File pedigree (EC, 1967) CGC NM/MT 9.8 Off-white to white pages. "Yellow Pages for Super-Heroes" article. Norman Mingo cover. Mort Drucker, Al Jaffee, Don Martin, Joe Orlando, and Dave Berg art. Overstreet 2005 NM- 9.2 value = $38. CGC census 9/05: 3 in 9.8, none higher.

3386 Mad #122 Gaines File pedigree (EC, 1968) CGC NM+ 9.6 White pages. Norman Mingo and Mort Drucker cover. Drucker, Don Martin, Al Jaffee, Joe Orlando, and Dave Berg art. Overstreet 2005 NM- 9.2 value = $28. CGC census 9/05: 3 in 9.6, none higher.

3387 Mad #132 Gaines File pedigree (EC, 1970) CGC NM+ 9.6 White pages. Photo cover. Christmas issue. Dave Berg, Mort Drucker, Jack Davis, Don Martin, and Angelo Torres art. Overstreet 2005 NM- 9.2 value = $28. CGC census 9/05: 2 in 9.6, none higher.

3388 Mad #133 Gaines File pedigree (EC, 1970) CGC NM/MT 9.8 White pages. "True Grit" movie parody. Dave Berg, Mort Drucker, Jack Davis, Don Martin, and Angelo Torres art. Overstreet 2005 NM- 9.2 value = $28. CGC census 9/05: 2 in 9.8, none higher.

3389 Mad #183 Gaines File pedigree (EC, 1976) CGC NM/MT 9.8 Off-white pages. "Dog Day Afternoon" and "Baretta" parodies. Norman Mingo cover. Mort Drucker, Don Martin, Dave Berg, Sergio Aragones, and Angelo Torres art. Overstreet 2005 NM- 9.2 value = $18. CGC census 9/05: 1 in 9.8, 1 higher.

3390 Marvel Comics Super Special #6 "Jaws 2" (Marvel, 1978) CGC NM/MT 9.8 White pages. Gene Colan art. Bob Larkin cover. CGC notes, "Don Rosa Collection." Overstreet 2005 NM- 9.2 value = $14. CGC census 7/05: 1 in 9.8, none higher.

3391 Marvel Preview #20 Bizarre Adventures (Marvel, 1980) CGC NM/MT 9.8 White pages. Howard Chaykin cover. Chaykin, George Perez, and Dave Cockrum art. CGC notes, "Don Rosa Collection." Overstreet 2005 NM- 9.2 value = $5. CGC census 7/05: 1 in 9.8, none higher.

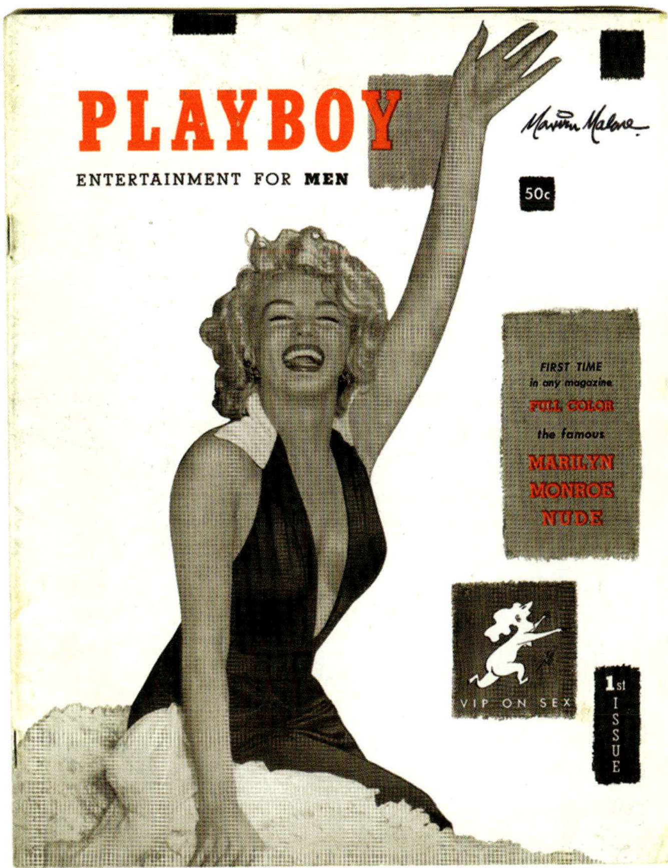

3392 Playboy #1 (HMH Publishing, 1953) Condition: FN. This issue started a multimedia phenomenon and made Hugh Hefner a household name. It's the very first **Playboy** magazine, which caused a splash by featuring some 1949 nude photos of Marilyn Monroe, but also held readers' interest thanks to a canny mix of features, including jokes, cartoons, and pictorials, but also a piece by Ambrose Bierce, a Sherlock Holmes story by Arthur Conan Doyle, a jazz article, and an article commending college football's return to the one-platoon system. The mag's introductory text says, "If we are able to give the American male a few extra laughs and a little diversion from the anxieties of the Atomic Age, we feel we've justified our existence." This is an attractive copy, with a three-inch crease on the back cover standing as the only negative. It's one of the better specimens we've seen of an issue that's not easy to find in any condition!

SEE PAGE 191 FOR A COPY OF PLAYBOY #2

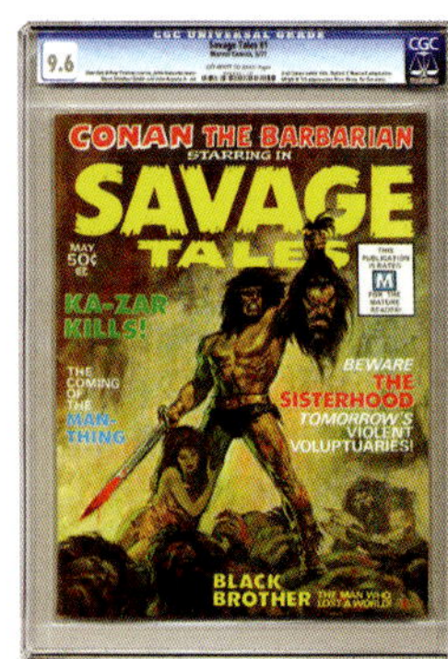

3393 Savage Tales #1 (Marvel, 1971) CGC NM+ 9.6 Off-white to white pages. While much has been written about the near-simultaneous debuts of Marvel's Man-Thing and DC's Swamp Thing, it should be noted that Man-Thing was the first to appear, and his origin and first appearance is in this very magazine. This black-and-white "adult" issue, which was not subject to the Comics Code, also has the first Conan comic story to appear outside of the main **Conan the Barbarian** title (with art by Barry Smith). The remaining artists are heavy-hitters one and all, with John Buscema (the cover and a Ka-Zar story), Gray Morrow, Gene Colan, and John Romita Sr. all contributing. Overstreet 2005 NM- 9.2 value = $225. CGC census 7/05: 6 in 9.6, 2 higher.

3394 Savage Tales #10 (Marvel, 1975) CGC NM+ 9.6 White pages. Boris Vallejo cover. Ka-Zar story with Russ Heath art, inked by Neal Adams and the "Crusty Bunkers." Shanna the She-Devil story with Ross Andru art. Original John Jakes text story. Overstreet 2005 NM- 9.2 value = $16. CGC census 1/05: 2 in 9.6, none higher. *From the collection of Chris Bell.*

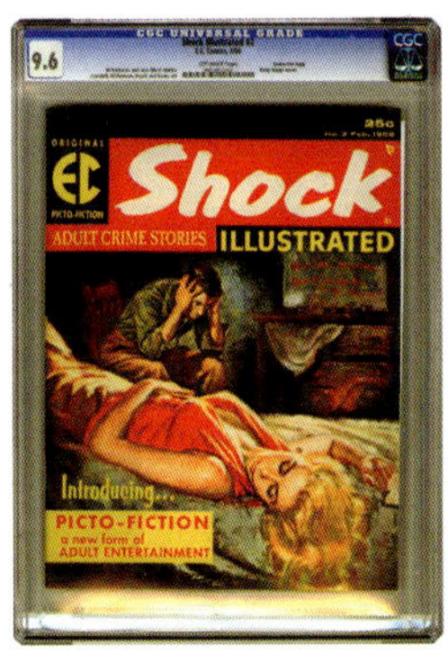

3395 Shock Illustrated #2 Gaines File pedigree (EC, 1956) CGC NM+ 9.6 Off-white pages. EC's magazine line was an idea ahead of its time. Here's a fantastic copy of this doomed series' second issue, with wonderful art by Reed Crandall, Al Williamson (with an Angelo Torres assist), Graham Ingels, and George Evans, plus a lush painted crime-scene cover by Rudy Nappi. Overstreet 2005 NM- 9.2 value = $190. CGC census 8/05: 4 in 9.6, none higher.

3396 Tales of Voodoo (Magazine) V4#3 (Eerie Publications, 1971) CGC NM+ 9.6 Off-white pages. CGC notes, "Don Rosa Collection." Overstreet 2005 NM- 9.2 value = $35. CGC census 7/05: 2 in 9.6, none higher.

3397 Terror Tales (Magazine) V4#6 (Eerie Publications, 1972) CGC NM+ 9.6 Off-white pages. CGC notes, "Don Rosa Collection." Overstreet 2005 NM- 9.2 value = $38. CGC census 7/05: 1 in 9.6, none higher.

3398 Trump #1 (HMH Publishing, 1957) CGC NM- 9.2 White pages. It's too bad this Hugh Hefner publication only lasted two issues, as the premise looked great — imagine **Mad Magazine** with the original writer/editor (Harvey Kurtzman) and **Playboy**-style production values! This first issue (of only two) features Li'l Abner and Rin-Tin-Tin spoofs, plus a "Hansel and Gretel" parody and the "Epic of Man" foldout centerfold. Kurtzman, Wally Wood, Bill Elder, and Jack Davis art. Overstreet 2005 NM- 9.2 value = $270. CGC census 8/05: 1 in 9.2, 1 higher.

3399 Unknown Worlds of Science Fiction #2 (Marvel, 1975) CGC NM/MT 9.8 Off-white to white pages. Mike Kaluta cover. Kaluta, Bruce Jones, Frank Brunner, and Alex Nino art. CGC notes, "Don Rosa Collection." Overstreet 2005 NM- 9.2 value = $16. CGC census 7/05: 4 in 9.8, none higher.

3400 Vampirella #3 (Warren, 1970) CGC VF+ 8.5 Off-white to white pages. "Vampi's Scarlet Letters" page begins in this issue. Cover by Larry Todd and Vaughn Bode. Billy Graham, Tom Sutton, and Dick Piscopo art. Overstreet notes "low distribution" for this issue. Overstreet 2005 VF 8.0 value = $270; VF/NM 9.0 value = $423. CGC census 9/05: 6 in 8.5, 10 higher.

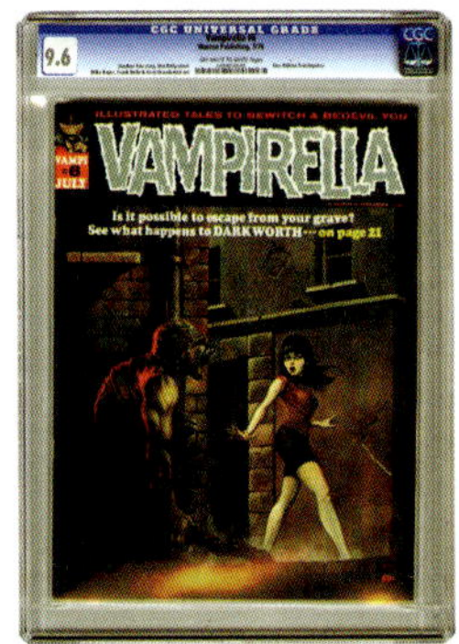

3401 Vampirella #6 (Warren, 1970) CGC NM+ 9.6 Off-white to white pages. The mag has a fantastic "good girl" horror cover by Ken Kelly, plus interior art by Jerry Grandenetti, Jack Sparling, Mike Royer, and Dan Adkins. Overstreet 2005 NM- 9.2 value = $145. CGC census 9/05: 7 in 9.6, 1 higher.

3402 Vampirella #6 (Warren, 1970) CGC NM 9.4 Off-white pages. Ken Kelly cover. Jerry Grandenetti, Jack Sparling, Mike Royer, and Dan Adkins art. CGC notes, "Don Rosa Collection." Overstreet 2005 NM- 9.2 value = $145. CGC census 7/05: 7 in 9.4, 8 higher.

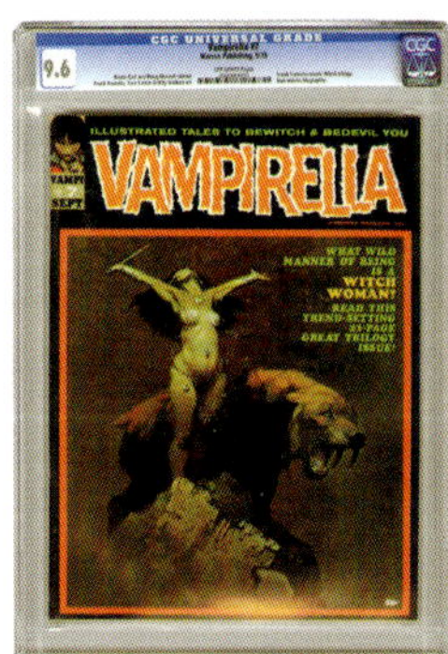

3403 Vampirella #7 (Warren, 1970) CGC NM+ 9.6 Off-white pages. Frank Frazetta's painting "Sun Goddess" adorns the cover of this issue. The magazine's interior art is by Frazetta (one illustration), Tom Sutton, Billy Graham, Ernie Colon, and Jerry Grandenetti. Overstreet 2005 NM-9.2 value = $150. CGC census 9/05: 6 in 9.6, none higher.

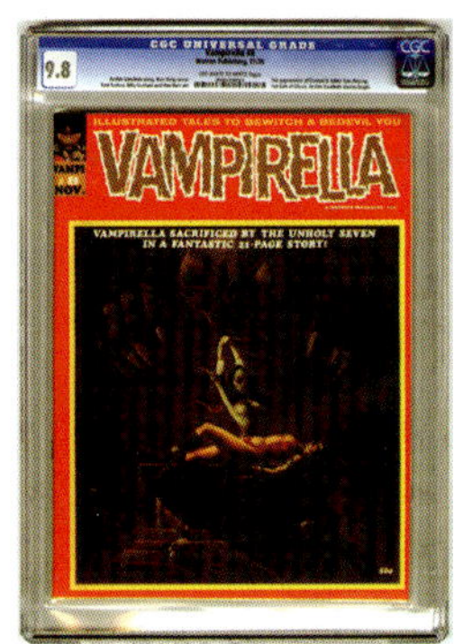

3404 Vampirella #8 (Warren, 1970) CGC NM/MT 9.8 Off-white to white pages. Vampirella, who had served as host of this title's horror tales, made her debut as a serious character in this issue, along with the first appearances of long-running characters Conrad and Adam Van Helsing, plus the Cult of Chaos. Another first here was Archie Goodwin's debut as writer — Goodwin's writing and editing would make quite an impact on the Warren line. The mag has a Ken Kelly cover, with interior art by Tom Sutton, Jack Sparling, George Roussos, Frank Frazetta (one page), and "Tony Williamsune" (Tony Tallarico and Bill Fraccio). Overstreet 2005 NM- 9.2 value = $160. CGC census 8/05: 2 in 9.8, none higher. *From the collection of Chris Bell.*

3405 Vampirella #15 (Warren, 1972) CGC NM+ 9.6 Off-white pages. 1971 Warren Creator Awards. Count Dracula cameo. Manuel Sanjulian cover. Richard Corben frontispiece. Luis Garcia, Jose Gonzalez, and Jose Bea art. Overstreet 2005 NM- 9.2 value = $90. CGC census 9/05: 3 in 9.6, 4 higher.

3406 Vampirella #19 (Warren, 1972) CGC NM+ 9.6 Off-white to white pages. Square bound. Text feature about the creation of Vampirella. Dracula appearance. Raquel Welch photo. 1972 yearbook. Jose Gonzalez cover. Gonzalez, Wally Wood, Neal Adams, Reed Crandall, Jerry Grandenetti, and Ernie Colon art. Overstreet 2005 NM- 9.2 value = $100. CGC census 9/05: 6 in 9.6, 2 higher.

3407 Vampirella #25 (Warren, 1973) CGC NM+ 9.6 Off-white pages. Vampi on cocaine story. Enrich Torres cover. Interior art by Esteban Maroto (color section) and Jose Gonzalez. Overstreet 2005 NM- 9.2 value = $80. CGC census 9/05: 5 in 9.6, 1 higher.

3408 Vampirella #30 Pacific Coast pedigree (Warren, 1974) CGC VF/NM 9.0 Cream to off-white pages. This issue features the first appearance of Pantha and an eight-page color story with art by Richard Corben. Cover by Enrich Torres, art by Neal Adams, Jose Gonzales, and Auraleon. Overstreet 2005 VF/NM 9.0 value = $40; NM- 9.2 value = $50. CGC census 7/05: 3 in 9.0, 1 higher.

3409 Vampirella #33 Pacific Coast pedigree (Warren, 1974) CGC NM 9.4 Cream to off-white pages. This issue features an eight-page color story with art by Richard Corben, as well as Bernie Wrightson's first work for Warren. The cover is by Enrich Torres; the interior art is by Wrightson, Jeff Jones, Jose Gonzalez, Rafael Auraleon, and Isidro Mones. Only one copy of this issue has been graded higher by CGC to date. Overstreet 2005 NM- 9.2 value = $50. CGC census 7/05: 2 in 9.4, 1 higher.

3410 Vampirella #41 Pacific Coast pedigree (Warren, 1975) CGC NM+ 9.6 Off-white pages. Cover by Enrich Torres. Esteban Maroto and Jose Gonzalez art. To date, only one copy of this issue has been certified with a higher grade by CGC. Overstreet 2005 NM- 9.2 value = $40. CGC census 7/05: 2 in 9.6, 1 higher.

3411 Vampirella #42 Pacific Coast pedigree (Warren, 1975) CGC NM 9.4 Off-white to white pages. Features a cover by Enrich Torres; a frontispiece by Jose Gonzalez; and interior art by Gonzalez, Esteban Maroto, and Luis Garcia. Overstreet 2005 NM- 9.2 value = $40. CGC census 7/05: 1 in 9.4, 2 higher.

3412 Vampirella #50 Pacific Coast pedigree (Warren, 1976) CGC NM 9.4 Off-white pages. This issue features a one-panel cameo by the Spirit, drawn by Will Eisner, and a 40-page Vampi story. Cover by Manuel Sanjulian; interior art by Jeff Jones, Jose Gonzalez, and Esteban Maroto. Overstreet 2005 NM- 9.2 value = $40. CGC census 7/05: 6 in 9.4, 2 higher.

3413 Vampirella #57 Pacific Coast pedigree (Warren, 1977) CGC NM+ 9.6 Off-white pages. Cover by Enrich Torres, art by Carmine Infantino, Esteban Maroto, Jose Gonzalez, and Dick Giordano. Overstreet 2005 NM-9.2 value = $28. CGC census 7/05: 7 in 9.6, 3 higher.

3414 Vampirella #61 Pacific Coast pedigree (Warren, 1977) CGC NM+ 9.6 Off-white pages. Enrich Torres cover. Russ Heath, Jose Gonzalez, Carmine Infantino, and Alex Nino art. Overstreet 2005 NM- 9.2 value = $28. CGC census 7/05: 4 in 9.6, 1 higher.

3415 Vampirella #112 (Warren, 1983) CGC NM 9.4 White pages. Last magazine published by Warren (tied with **Famous Monsters of Filmland** #191). Low print run. Pantha appearance. Martin Hoffman cover. Jose Gonzalez, Auraleon, and Esteban Maroto art. Overstreet 2005 NM-9.2 value = $75. CGC census 9/05: 8 in 9.4, 3 higher.

3416 Weird V10#2 (Eerie Publications, 1977) CGC NM+ 9.6 Off-white pages. Dick Ayers art. CGC notes, "Don Rosa Collection." Overstreet 2005 NM- 9.2 value = $42. CGC census 7/05: 1 in 9.6, none higher.

3417 Witches Tales V6#3 (Eerie Publications, 1974) CGC NM+ 9.6 Off-white to white pages. Decapitation cover. CGC notes, "Don Rosa Collection." Overstreet 2005 NM- 9.2 value = $35. CGC census 7/05: 1 in 9.6, none higher.

3418 Comic Book Marketplace #2-121 Group (Gary Carter/Gemstone, 1993-2005) Average Condition: VF+. Here's your chance to learn more about comics than 99.99 percent of the people in the free world! Simply study every page of this super-spectacular group lot. This stellar lot contains **Comic Book Marketplace** #2-121. The magazines average VF+ condition.

MEMORABILIA

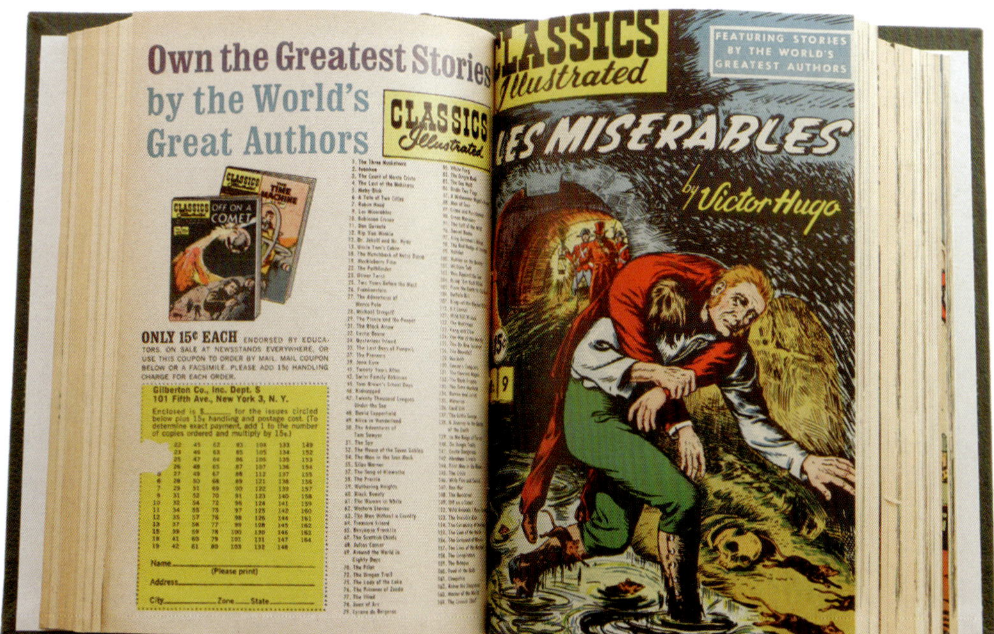

3419 Classics Illustrated #1-169 Bound Volumes (Gilberton). This incredible group of ten bound volumes brings together issues #1 through 169 of the **Classics Illustrated** series -- that's the title's full run! Also included are fifteen **Classics Illustrated Special Issues**. Most of the regular issues are not first printings -- approximately 50% range from HRN 161-169, but there are also quite a few in the 89-155 range, and a handful are original editions. Among the most notable gems are a HRN 15 copy of #14 and the Original Edition of #43. Each massive volume is attractively bound in a dark green leather-style cover, with titles stamped on the spine in gold. The name of the former owner is also stamped in gold on the front cover. All issues (most appearing in FN or better condition) have been trimmed in the binding process. Overstreet VG 4.0 value for group = $2,007.

3420 Carl Barks - Walt Disney's Uncle Scrooge Print (Another Rainbow, 1987). The cover from Carl Barks' **Uncle Scrooge** #39 (Sept. 1962) is the subject of this first-class print from Another Rainbow Publishing Company. Number 3 in the Comic Book Library series, this print measures 24" x 36" and is in Excellent condition.

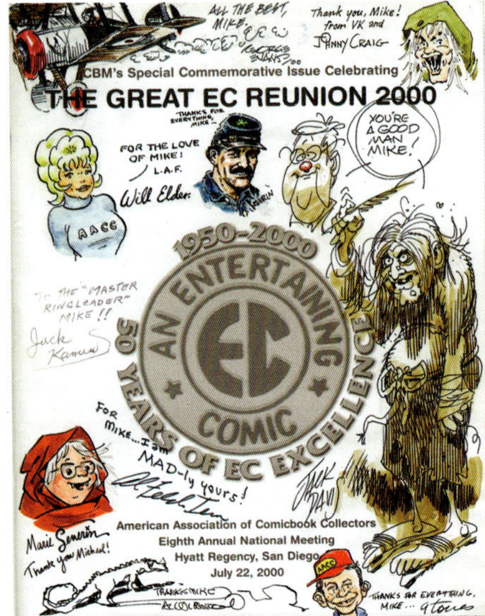

3421 Comic Book Marketplace #80 Personalized With Original Sketches and Autographs By EC Artists. Look at the cover of this special commemorative edition of **CBM**'s EC issue! Two sketches by Jack Davis (the Crypt-Keeper and a self-portrait), plus one drawing each by Johnny Craig (The Vault-Keeper), John Severin, George Evans, Will Elder (Little Annie Fanny), Marie Severin (a self-portrait as the Old Witch!), Al Williamson, and Angelo Torres (drawing Alfred E. Neuman, no less). Adding autographs were Al Feldstein and Jack Kamen. And what's really impressive is that the drawings by Davis, Severin, and Evans aren't "quickie" sketches but fairly meticulous drawings that really exhibit the signature style of those artists. We can't imagine that any EC Fan-Addict would pass on this one!

3422 Flintstone Jewelry in Display (Hanna-Barbera Productions, 1972). In this colorful Fred Flintstone stand-up display, you'll find thirty six rings of Fred, Wilma, Hoppy the Hopparoo, Pebbles, Dino, Bamm-Bamm, Barney and Betty! The rings are baked enamel, with adjustable bands, and sparkle like brand new! The display stands approximately 18" x 8" and is in Excellent condition.

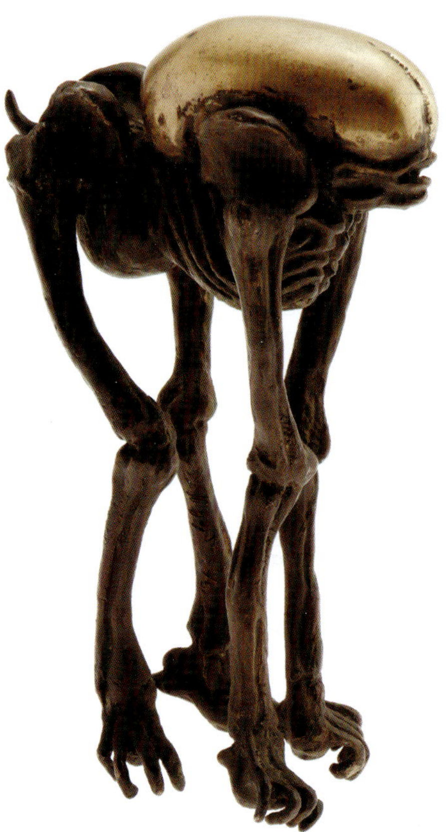

3423 H. R. Giger - "Baby" Alien III Silver Sculpture (early 1990's). H.R. Giger, one of the world's foremost artists of Fantastic Realism, studied architecture and industrial design at the Zurich School of Applied Arts, and had his first exhibit of drawings and paintings in 1966. His third and best-known book, **H.R. Giger's Necronomicon**, (1977) inspired the visuals for director Ridley Scott's blockbuster movie "Alien". Giger's "Alien" designs won him the 1980 Academy Award for Best Achievement in Visual Effects. This sculpture was originally purchased through the Alexander Galleries in New York, and was listed as one of five produced. The work is in Excellent condition.

3424 George Herriman The Lost Years Portfolio, Group of 2 (undated). George Herriman's *Krazy Kat* is a work of poetry and genius which is not easily described. In the early 1930s, there remained just a few newspapers still printing the strip, and by 1931, there was not a single paper which carried the Sunday page for the full year. These two portfolios reprint the missing years of *Krazy Kat* between 1931 and 1935, and the contents were painstakingly restored from microfilm with due attention to detail. Where there were altered pages available, they had to be reconstructed. The remaining Sundays were reproduced from existing newsprint or copies of the original artwork. It's full blown Coconino tomfoolery at its best! Each portfolio measures approximately 11" x 17" and they are both in Excellent condition.

3425 Mars Attacks Trading Cards Partial Set (Bubbles Inc., 1962). This is a partial set of Mars Attacks trading cards. There are 56 cards total. A few of them are in poor condition, but most look pretty nice. *From the Random House Archives.*

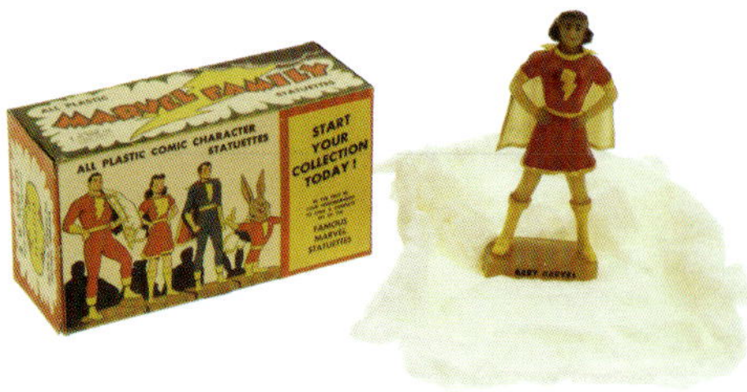

3426 Mary Marvel Statuette and Box (Kerr Co., 1946) Condition: NM-. This lovely Mary Marvel statuette with its original box was one of a set of four "All Plastic Marvel Family Statuettes" produced in 1946 which consisted of Captain Marvel, Captain Marvel Jr., Mary Marvel and Hoppy the Marvel Bunny. This painted solid plastic figure includes Mary's name on the front of the base and copyright Fawcett Publications Inc. on back. A fabulous C. C. Beck-designed box features a scene on one panel of Captain Marvel holding the Mary Marvel statue while one other panel depicts all four statuettes. The box measures 4" x 7" x 2.5", and the statuette measures 1.5" x 2.5" x 6.25" tall. There's been some minor repair work done to the ultra-delicate plastic cape, near the collar. There are probably less than 20 of these Mary Marvel statuettes in existence — don't miss this rare opportunity to own one!

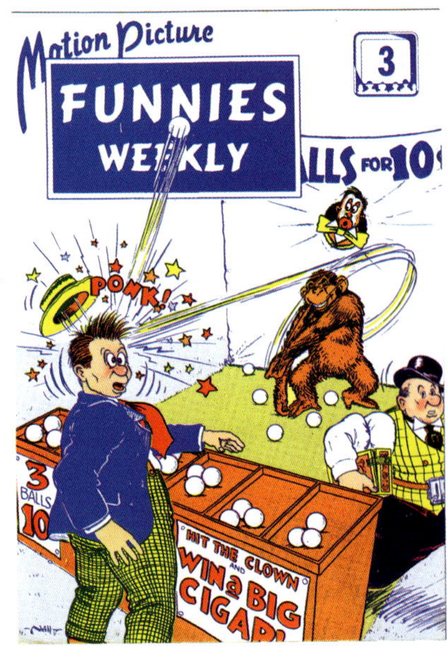

3427 Motion Picture Funnies Weekly #2-4 Covers Only (First Funnies, Inc., 1939). These covers for three planned but never-published issues are a real piece of comic book history. Of course, issue #1 is a legendary comic which never actually reached newsstands but featured the first printed appearance of the Sub-Mariner. The title actually wasn't intended for newsstands, but was to be distributed at movie theaters as a promotional giveaway. Alas, the concept never took off, and while a few copies of #1 survive, #2-4 were never finished at all. This title is also significant for being the first comic production of the Lloyd Jacquet shop, aka Funnies Inc., who went on to produce **Marvel Comics** #1 as well as many other key Golden Age comics. As for these items, the cover art for #3 is by Max Neill, whose work was later seen in Centaur comics among others, and the cover art for #2 and 4 is by Martin Filchock — if you were a kid in the 1970s you'll probably remember the "compare these two pictures" scenes Filchock drew for **Highlights** magazine. These covers are blank on the reverse. As for the condition, some minor dust shadows and a bit of foxing on #2 are the only negatives; overall, the items are in Excellent condition. Overstreet 2005 NM- 9.2 value for set = $1,000.

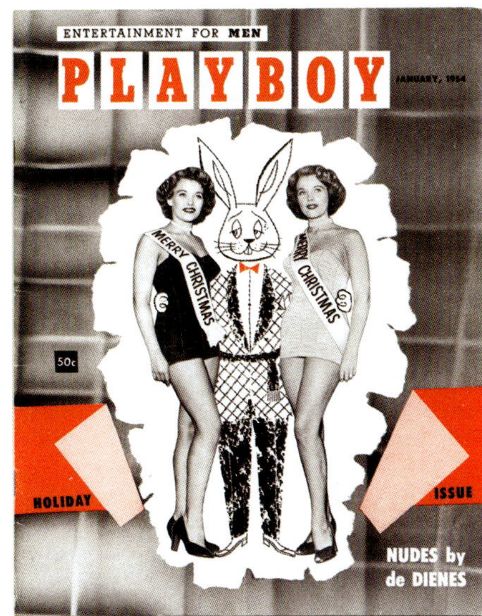

3428 Playboy #2 (HMH Publishing, 1954). Condition: VG. The second issue of Hugh Hefner's new magazine had a smaller print run than the first, making it even more scarce than the more famous Marilyn Monroe issue. Bidding for copies of #1 has been extremely competitive in recent auctions, setting new standards for the value of the trendsetting "Entertainment for Men" magazine, which suggests that values for #2 will follow suit. Although the Playmate of the Month feature still only commanded one color page, Hef was already complementing the undeniably sexy character of **Playboy** with fiction by well-known authors (in this issue, Sir Arthur Conan Doyle), pictorials of popular celebrities (Bob Hope), and a barrage of witty single-panel cartoons. The condition of this copy would be about Fine, but for what appears to be a subscription crease down the middle of the book. Interior pages are very nice ranging from off-white to white throughout.

3429 Vintage Superman Child's Costume (Superman Inc., circa 1940s-50s). If radio was good for the Superman franchise in the 1940s, then TV was even greater for him in the 1950s. "The Adventures of Superman" was the perfect TV embodiment of American society in the 50s, and was an immediate hit when it debuted, and it remained one of most popular and enduring of the early TV science-fiction showcases. Superman was also big with toy manufacturers at that time, because they could easily tie in with merchandising, starting at the very basic fantasy level of costumes for little boys to dress up like the Man of Steel. This costume includes blue and red pants and a cape, with a button up blue shirt which has a Superman logo on the chest. The original yellow belt is not included. There is an inscription on the bottom of the shirt which reads, "Remember — This suit won't make you fly — only Superman can fly." You'll find a bit of staining on several parts of the costume, but overall it is in Excellent condition.

BIG LITTLE BOOKS

3430 J. K. Potter - Surrealistic Print #21/100 (undated). Nothing is as it seems in the world of J. K. Potter. Always original, often eerily beautiful, and sometimes disturbing, the darkroom alchemy of his art has won him acclaim in many fields. This is the art of the bizarre, many of Potter's paintings "assault the eye". This image is as elegant as it is discomforting. Hand-printed on archival paper, this limited edition print is numbered 21 out of 100, and is signed by the artist at the bottom right. The image area measures 15.5" x 19.5", and, aside from a slight nick at the left middle, the condition is in Excellent.

3431 Big Little Book #1426 Brer Rabbit (Whitman, 1947) Condition: VF/NM. Hard cover, 288 pages. Adapted from the Walt Disney feature, "The Song of the South," by the artists of the Walt Disney Studios. Overstreet 2005 VF/NM value = $125.

3432 Big Little Book #1188 Buck Jones in the Fighting Rangers (Whitman, 1936) Condition: VF/NM. Hard cover, 240 pages. Adapted from an E. E. Rapp story. This book contains 68 motion picture stills from the Universal serial titled, "The Roaring West". Although Buck Jones was a right-handed cowboy who wore his holster on the right hip, the movie scenes in this book are printed backwards, converting Buck into a lefty! Overstreet 2005 VF/NM value = $90.

3433 Big Little Book #1404 Buck Jones and the Two-Gun Kid (Whitman, 1937) Condition: VF. About the time this Big Little Book was published, Buck Jones became the hero of a syndicated radio program titled "Hoofbeats". The program, sponsored by Grape Nuts Flakes, was a 15-minute, five-days-per-week action Western serial designed for a young audience. Hard cover, 432 pages. Written by Gaylord DuBois, and illustrated by Robert R. Weisman. Cover by Robert R. Weisman. Overstreet 2005 VF/NM value = $65.

3434 Big Little Book #nn Buck Rogers 25th Century A.D. (Whitman, 1933) Condition: VF+. Here is the first Buck Rogers Big Little Book. Hard cover, 320 pages. Written by Phil Nowlan, and illustrated by Lt. Dick Calkins. Cover art by Lt. Dick Calkins. This book reprints the first *Buck Rogers* daily series, 1932-33, strips #45 through #1300. Overstreet 2005 VF/NM value = $325.

3435 Big Little Book #1169 Buck Rogers and the Depth Men of Jupiter (Whitman, 1935) Condition: VG. Hard cover, 432 pages. Written by Phil Nowlan, with art by Dick Calkins. Reprint of first daily series (1933), strips #1393 through #1514. Looks VF, but many pages have been colored with yellow crayon. Overstreet 2005 GD value = $35; FN value = $95.

3436 Big Little Book #1474 Buck Rogers and the Overturned World (Whitman, 1941) Condition: FN/VF. Hard cover, 432 pages. Written by Phil Nowlan, with art by Lt. Dick Calkins. Reprint of the third daily *Buck Rogers* series, 1938-39, strips #445 through about #630. Includes a "flip-it" feature (A small elephant-like animal has its trunk bandaged after being stung by a bee). White pages. Overstreet 2005 FN value = $90; VF/NM value = 185.

3437 Big Little Book #1459 Charlie Chan Solves a New Mystery (Whitman, 1940) Condition: VF. Hard cover, 432 pages. Adapted from the work of Earl Derr Biggers, with art by Alfred Andriola. Overstreet 2005 VF/NM value = $85.

3438 Big Little Book #1446 Convoy Patrol (Whitman, 1942) Condition: VF. Specially created for the Whitman Better Little Book format, this thrilling U.S. Navy story was written by Russell R. Winterbotham, and illustrated by Erwin L. Hess. Hard cover, 432 pages. Includes a "flip-it" feature of airplanes dive bombing Navy ships. This is a hard-to-get book. Overstreet 2005 VF/NM value = $55.

3439 Big Little Book #1481 Dan Dunn and the Border Smugglers (Whitman, 1938) Condition: VF/NM. Written and illustrated by Norman Marsh. Hardcover, 432 pages. Overstreet 2005 VF/NM value = $75.

3440 Big Little Book #1446 Detective Dick Tracy and the Spider Gang (Whitman, 1937) Condition: NM. Hardcover. Includes scenes from the Republic Pictures movie serial, The Adventures of Dick Tracy. Overstreet 2005 VF/NM value = $165.

3441 Dick Tracy and the Blackmailers - Fast-Action Book (Dell, 1939) Condition: VF. Dell's response to Big Little Books was its series of Fast-Action Story books. This 196 page softcover has Chester Gould art. Overstreet 2005 VF/NM value = $260.

3442 Big Little Book #1482 Dick Tracy and the Wreath Kidnapping Case (Whitman, 1945) Condition: NM-. Hard cover, 352 pages. Written and illustrated by Chester Gould. Reprints the *Dick Tracy* daily strip beginning February 4, 1943 and ending April 14, 1943. Overstreet 2005 VF/NM value = $100.

3443 Big Little Book #1445 Dick Tracy and the Bicycle Gang (Whitman, 1948) Condition: VF/NM. Hard cover, 288 pages. Written by Helen Berke, and illustrated by Chester Gould. This book reprints the *Dick Tracy* daily strip beginning October 24, 1940 and ending December 19, 1940. The cover illustration was adapted from page 253 of **Dick Tracy and the Boris Arson Gang**. Overstreet 2005 VF/NM value = $100.

3444 Big Little Book #1124 Dickie Moore in the Little Red School House (Whitman, 1936) Condition: VF/NM. Hard cover, 240 pages. Written by Eleanor Packer — adapted from the Chesterfield Motion Pictures film. Includes 94 motion picture stills from the film. Overstreet 2005 VF/NM value = $75.

3445 Better Little Book #1404 Such a Life! Says: Donald Duck Better Little Book #1404 (Whitman, 1939) Condition: FN/VF. Hard cover, 432 pages. Written and illustrated by Al Taliaferro. Overstreet 2005 FN value = $35; VF/NM value = $70.

3446 Better Little Book #1430 Donald Duck Headed for Trouble (Whitman, 1942) Condition: VG+. Hard cover, 432 pages. Written and illustrated by Al Taliaferro. Includes a "flip-it" feature of Donald trying to carry a whipsaw. Overstreet 2005 GD value = $25; FN value = $80.

3447 Big Little Book #1489 Don Winslow of the U.S. Navy and the Great War Plot (Whitman, 1940) Condition: VF/NM. Hard cover, 432 pages. Written by Lt. Frank V. Martinek, with art by Leon Beroth. Overstreet 2005 VF/NM value = $90.

3448 Big Little Book #1418 Don Winslow Navy Intelligence Ace (Whitman, 1942) Condition: VF/NM. Hard cover, 432 pages. Includes a "flip-it" feature of Don Winslow rescuing a drowning man. Written by Lt. Frank V. Martinek, with art by Leon Beroth. Overstreet 2005 VF/NM value = $90.

3449 Big Little Book #1400 Dumbo, of the Circus - Only His Ears Grew! (Whitman, 1941) Condition: FN. Adapted from Walt Disney's feature film, "Dumbo," which was released on October 23, 1941. Hard cover, 432 pages. Includes a wonderful "flip-it" feature of Dumbo flying. Overstreet 2005 FN value = $80.

3450 Big Little Book #1465 Felix the Cat (Whitman, 1945) Condition: FN/VF. Otto Messmer is the artist of this whimsical book featuring Felix the Cat. Hard cover, 352 pages. Overstreet 2005 FN value = $65; VF/NM value = $130.

3451 Big Little Book #1164 Freckles and the Lost Diamond Mine (Whitman, 1937) Condition: VF/NM. Hard cover, 432 pages. Written and illustrated by Merrill Blosser. Overstreet 2005 VF/NM value = $70.

3452 Big Little Book 1433 Gang Busters (Whitman, 1939) Condition: VF/NM. This adaptation of the Phillip H. Lord "Gang Busters" radio program, was created specially for the Big Little Book format. Hard cover, 432 pages. Written by Isaac McAnally, with art by Henry E. Vallely. Overstreet 2005 VF/NM value = $75.

3453 Big Little Book #1402 Jackie Cooper in "Gangster's Boy" (Whitman, 1939) Condition: VF+. Hard cover, 240 pages. Written by Karl Brown and Robert Andrews. Contains 76 motion picture scenes from the Monogram film, "Gangster's Boy". Overstreet 2005 FN value = $40; VF/NM value = $80.

3454 Big Little Book #1409 Gene Autry and the Raiders of the Range (Whitman, 1946) Condition: VF+. First printing. Hard cover, 352 pages. Created by writer Till Goodman specially for the Whitman Big Little Book format. Overstreet 2005 VF/NM value = $75.

3455 Big Little Book #1577 Go Into Your Dance (Saalfield, 1935) Condition: VF-. Adapted from the novel by Bradford Ropes. Photo cover featuring Ruby Keeler and Al Jolson. Movies scenes with Al Jolson and Ruby Keeler. Overstreet 2005 VF/NM value = $80.

3456 Big Little Book #1432 Jack Armstrong and the Mystery of the Iron Key (Whitman, 1939) Condition: VF+. Hard cover, 432 pages. Written by Robert Hardy Andrews, and illustrated by the great Henry E. Vallely. Overstreet 2005 VF/NM value = $70.

3457 Big Little Book #1180 Jim Hardy, Ace Reporter (Saalfield, 1940) Condition: NM. Adapted from the famous newspaper comic strip by Dick Moores. Hard cover, 398 pages. Overstreet 2005 VF/NM value = $60.

3458 Big Little Book #1179 Zane Grey's King of the Royal Mounted and the Northern Treasure (Whitman, 1937) Condition: NM-. Hard cover, 432 pages. Written by Zane Grey and Romer Grey, and illustrated by Allen Dean and Charles Flanders. Overstreet 2005 VF/NM value = $80.

3459 Big Little Book #1441 Lightning Jim U.S. Marshal Brings Law to the West (Whitman, 1940) Condition: VF-. Adapted from radio program series, "The Adventures of Lightning Jim". Illustrated by Albert Micale. Hard cover, 432 pages. Overstreet 2005 FN value = $35; VF/NM value = $70.

3460 Big Little Book #1468 Little Orphan Annie and the Ancient Treasure of Am (Whitman, 1949) Condition: VF. This second printing is identified by its 288 page length, the publisher's number (#1468), and the cover illustration, otherwise it is identical to the first printing. It was also the last Better Little Book to be published. Written and illustrated by Harold Gray. Reprints the *Little Orphan Annie* daily strip beginning April 1, 1937 and ending June 10, 1937. Overstreet 2005 VF/NM value = $80.

3461 Big Little Book #1431 The Lone Ranger and the Secret Killer (Whitman, 1937) Condition: VF-. Over the years the masked man has become a popular American culture figure. Many people believe that the character really existed. This 432 page hard cover was created specially for the Big Little Book format by writer Buck Wilson and artist Herbert Anderson. Overstreet 2005 VF/NM value = $120.

3462 Big Little Book #1407 The Lone Ranger and the Dead Men's Mine (Whitman, 1939) Condition: FN. Hard cover, 432 pages. Probably written by Fran Striker, with art by Henry E. Vallely (not credited on title page). The story is adapted from the last Lone Ranger pulp, November 1937, titled "Death's-Head Vengeance". Overstreet 2005 FN value = $110.

3463 Better Little Book #1463 Mickey Mouse and the Pirate Submarine (Whitman, 1939) Condition: VF+. Hard cover, 432 pages. Written by Ted Osborne, with art by Floyd Gottfredson. This Better Little Book reprints from the *Mickey Mouse* daily strip beginning October 1, 1935 and ending January 4, 1935. Overstreet 2005 VF/NM value = $165.

3464 Big Little Book #1433 Mickey Mouse and the Lazy Daisy Mystery (Whitman, 1947) Condition: VF. This 288 page hardcover Better Little Book is written by author Bill Walsh, with art by Floyd Gottfredson. Reprinted from the *Mickey Mouse* daily strip, beginning March 5, 1945 and ending June 16, 1945. Some foxing on the edges and end papers. Overstreet 2005 VF/NM value = $110.

3465 Big Little Book #845 Walt Disney's Mickey Mouse the Miracle Maker (Whitman, 1948) Condition: NM. Mickey Mouse's second-hand store lamp has a genie inside it! Illustrated by the artists of the Walt Disney Studios. Overstreet 2005 VF/NM value = $70.

3466 Big Little Book #1411 Peggy Brown and the Mystery Basket (Whitman, 1941) Condition: VF+. Writer Kathryn Hiesenfelt, and artist, Henry E. Vallely, created this book especially for the Better Little Book format. Hard cover, 432 pages. Includes a "flip-it" feature (Peggy's dog is chased by a larger dog). Overstreet 2005 VF/NM value = $60.

3467 Big Little Book #1405 Popeye and the Jeep (Whitman, 1937) Condition: FN/VF. Hard cover, 432 pages. Written and illustrated by E. C. Segar. Reprinted from the *Popeye* daily strip beginning March 3, 1936 and ending in June, 1936. Overstreet 2005 FN value = $35; VF/NM value = $70.

3468 Big Little Book #1498 Radio Patrol and Big Dan's Mobsters (Whitman, 1940) Condition: VF/NM. Better Little Book. Hard cover, 432 pages. Written by Charlie Schmidt, and illustrated by Eddie Sullivan. Overstreet 2005 VF/NM value = $55.

3469 Big Little Book #1421 Roy Rogers and the Dwarf-Cattle Ranch (Whitman, 1947) Condition: VF+. Hard cover, 352 pages. Written by Don Middleton (pseudonym for Fran Striker), with art by the great Henry E. Vallely. Overstreet 2005 VF/NM value = $90.

3470 Big Little Book #1115 Shirley Temple in "The Littlest Rebel" (Saalfield, 1935) Condition: VF/NM. Softcover. Contains illustrations from the 20th Century Fox film, "The Littlest Rebel," starring Shirley Temple. Overstreet 2005 VF/NM value = $110.

3471 Big Little Book #1110 Tailspin Tommy and the Island in the Sky (Whitman, 1936) Condition: VF. Hard cover, 432 pages. Written and illustrated by Hal Forrest. Small water spot on back cover. Overstreet 2005 FN value = $35; VF/NM value = $70.

3472 Big Little Book #1102 The Return of Tarzan (Whitman, 1936) Condition: NM-. Adapted from the book by Edgar Rice Burroughs, with art by Rex Mason. Hard cover, 432 pages. Features 209 illustrations reprinted from the second *Tarzan* daily storyline. Overstreet 2005 VF/NM value = $130.

3473 Big Little Book #1452 Tarzan the Untamed (Whitman, 1941) Condition: FN. Better Little Book. Hard cover, 432 pages. Adapted from the book by Edgar Rice Burroughs, with art by Rex Maxon. Cover art by John Coleman Burroughs. Includes a "flip-it" feature drawn by John Coleman Burroughs (Tarzan battles a gorilla). Overstreet 2005 FN value = $120.

3474 Big Little Book #1453 Tarzan the Terrible (Whitman, 1942) Condition: VF. Hard cover, 432 pages. Adapted from the book by Edgar Rice Burroughs, with art by Rex Maxon. Cover art by John Coleman Burroughs. Includes a "flip-it" feature, which was drawn by John Coleman Burroughs (Tarzan fights a spotted leopard). Overstreet 2005 VF/NM value = $120.

3475 Big Little Book #1440 Zane Grey's Tex Thorne Comes Out of the West (Whitman, 1937) Condition: VF+. Based on the famous adventure strip. Hard cover, 432 pages. Written by Zane Grey's son, Romer Grey, with art by Allen Dean. Cover art by Hal Arbo. Overstreet 2005 VF/NM value = $55.

3476 Big Little Book #1461 Uncle Sam's Sky Defenders (Whitman, 1941) Condition: VF+. Created specially for the Big Little Book format by writer Peter A. Wyckoff, and illustrator Erwin L. Hess. Hard cover, 432 pages. Includes a "flip-it" feature (an airplane disperses soldiers on a battlefield). Overstreet 2005 VF/NM value = $55.

BOOKS

In the world of collecting, there are few universals. Every branch of collecting has its own grading terms and accepted customs for describing the condition of its collectibles. Thus the term "Very Good" in original art or book collecting means something entirely different than in comic book, card, or memorabilia collecting. Bearing that in mind, Heritage Auctions has adopted these four broad, overall grading terms for this auction's book lots:

Excellent - A copy that has terrific eye-appeal with only minimal signs of wear and use. A book in this condition has the appearance of being carefully handled, shelved, and stored.

Very Good - An above-average copy that is free of major creasing, spine problems, or other major defects. The book may show slight wear along the spine, or the edges and corners of its cover; overall eye-appeal may be reduced by an accumulation of very small defects.

Good - The average used and worn book that has all pages or leaves present, but shows considerable wear along the spine, edges, corners, and front and back covers. Books in this condition are often scuffed or lightly abraded. Often such copies are "ex-library" copies from a public library with their attendant markings, stamps, and labels.

Fair - The book has a complete, legible text, but has been very heavily used. It may have a damaged spine, a loose binding, heavy soiling, water staining, torn or heavily bent pages, loose joints, hinges, pages, etc. A book in this condition may be ragged and unattractive. Books in this condition are usually purchased as a "reading" or "research" copies because of price or scarcity considerations.

3477 Batman: The Dark Knight Returns Signed Hardcover 1321/4000 (DC and Graphitti Designs, 1986) Condition: Excellent. Hardcover with dust jacket. Signed and numbered by Frank Miller. Collects the entire limited series. Overstreet 2005 NM- 9.2 value = $250.

3478 Edgar Rice Burroughs - "Tarzan Triumphant," First Edition (Burroughs, 1932). The frontispiece and four full-page illustrations for the seventeenth novel in the Tarzan series were rendered by Studley Burroughs. This lot features an Excellent condition book with an Excellent condition dust jacket. A previous owner's name has been written on title page, and rather incredibly, it reads, "Herbert C. Hoover, Superior, Wis., June 10, 1934!"

3479 Edgar Rice Burroughs - "Tarzan the Invincible" (Burroughs, 1931). This copy has the original blue cloth binding, with its front and spine panels stamped in orange. This was the fifteenth Tarzan book and the first book to be published by Burroughs' own publishing company. The frontispiece and dust jacket illustrations are by Studley O. Burroughs. This is a Good condition book in a Good condition dust jacket.

3480 Edgar Rice Burroughs - "I Am A Barbarian," First Edition (Burroughs, 1967). The cover and frontispiece of this book both feature illustrations by Jeff Jones. This historical novel, set in ancient Rome, was one of Edgar Rice Burroughs' few stand-alone titles. The dust jacket blurb for the book notes, "Edgar Rice Burroughs wrote **I Am A Barbarian** while living in Honolulu. The story was completed only a few short months before Pearl Harbor. Burroughs was an eye-witness to the attack, and in the years that followed, the manuscript was all but forgotten." This copy is an Excellent condition book in an Excellent condition dust jacket.

3481 Edgar Rice Burroughs - "Tarzan and the Foreign Legion," First Edition (Burroughs, 1947). Illustrated by John Coleman Burroughs, this copy of the twenty-ninth novel in the Tarzan series is an Excellent condition book with an Excellent condition dust jacket. The endpaper has been embossed with a special seal which reads, "Burroughs-Tarzan Enterprises Inc., California, Incorporated October 4, 1934." In this thriller, Tarzan is in Sumatra after the war, still fighting the Japanese.

3482 Edgar Rice Burroughs - "The Return of Tarzan" (A.L. Burt, 1915). Published in March, 1915, with 365 pages, and the Popular Copyright Novels ads. The black and white decorations were drawn by J. Allen St. John, and the dust jacket was illustrated by N.C. Wyeth. This copy is a Very Good condition book in a Fair condition dust jacket (with large pieces out of the bottom edge and spine of the dust jacket).

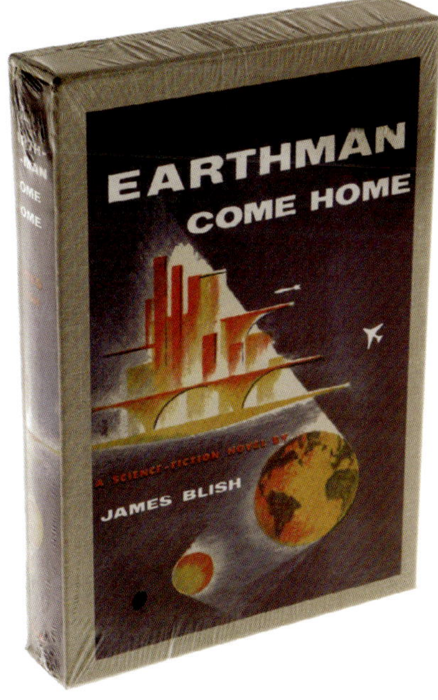

3483 First Edition Press Facsimile Edition Science Fiction Book Group (First Edition Press, 1975-92). Ever wanted to own first editions of great science fiction hardcover novels published during the 1940s, 50s, and 60s in perfect condition complete with mint dustjackets? How about copies with sturdy slipcovers, to keep the books like new? Here's your chance to own a number of wonderful books, all in mint, unread condition, at a fraction of the cost of obtaining the original editions. These are beautifully produced copies, with every attention paid to detail, of the following classics: **I, Robot** by Isaac Asimov; **Earthman Come Home** by James Blish; **Who Goes There?** by John W. Campbell; **The Golden Apples of the Sun** by Ray Bradbury; **Beyond the Horizon** by Robert A. Heinlein; **Shambleau and Others** by C. L. Moore; **Star Man's Son 2250 A.D.** by Andre Norton; **Tomorrow and Tomorrow/The Fairy Chessman** by Lewis Padgett; **Dreadful Sanctuary** by Eric Frank Russell; **Grey Lensman** by Edward E. Smith, Ph. D.; **The Weapon Makers** by A. E. van Vogt; and **The Legion of Space** by Jack Williamson. All copies are still in their original shrinkwrap.

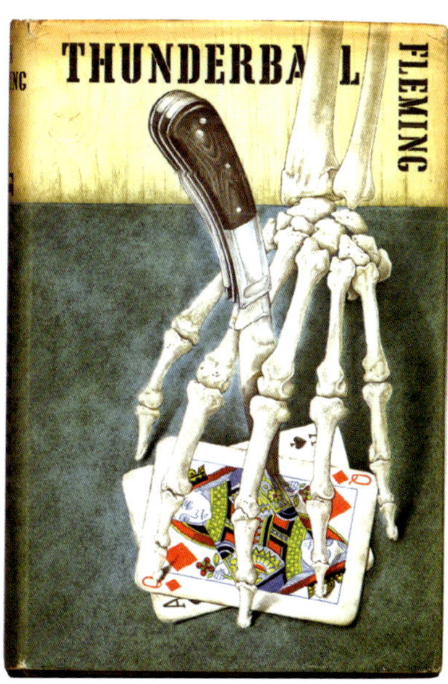

3484 Ian Fleming - James Bond Hardcover First Editions, Group of 7 (various). Here's a thrilling set of Ian Fleming first edition hardcovers, featuring James Bond, Agent 007 of Her Majesty's Secret Service. The group includes: **Dr. No** (Glidrose Productions, 1958), **For Your Eyes Only** (Glidrose Productions, 1960), **Thunderball** (Jonathan Cape, 1961), **On Her Majesty's Secret Service** (Glidrose Productions, 1963), **You Only Live Twice** (Jonathan Cape Ltd., 1964), **The Man with the Golden Gun** (Glidrose Productions, 1965), and **Octopussy and the Living Daylights** (Jonathan Cape, 1966). Original dust jackets are included, except for **Dr. No** and **For Your Eyes Only**. The books average Good condition; the dust jackets average Very Good.

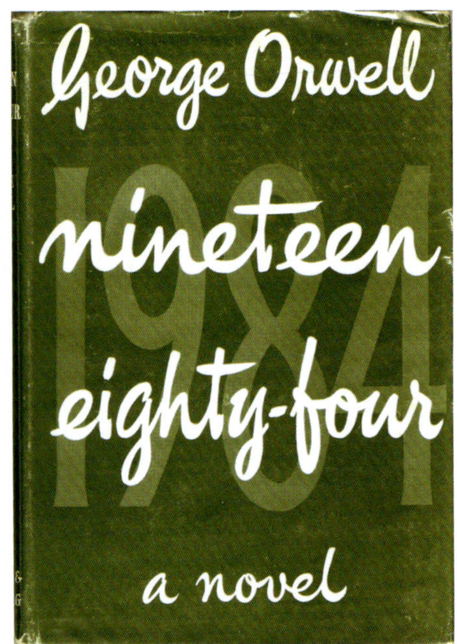

3485 George Orwell - "Nineteen Eighty-Four," First Edition (Secker and Warburg, 1949). This distopian classic is presented in its original green cloth binding with red lettering on the spine, and protected in a green dust jacket (the book was also produced with a red dust jacket). George Orwell started writing **Nineteen Eighty-Four** in 1945, and as he had found with **Animal Farm**, his new novel was in conflict with his previous publisher Gollancz's political leanings. So it was the firm of Secker and Warburg (publishers of **Animal Farm**) who first printed this timeless masterpiece. The dust jacket retains its publisher's price of 10s. at the bottom of its front flap. As the **Encyclopedia Britannica** has noted, "Orwell's warning of the potential dangers of totalitarianism made a deep impression on his contemporaries and upon subsequent readers, and the book's title and many of its coined words and phrases ('Big Brother is watching you,' 'newspeak,' 'doublethink') became bywords for modern political abuses." This is a Very Good condition book in a Very Good condition dust jacket.

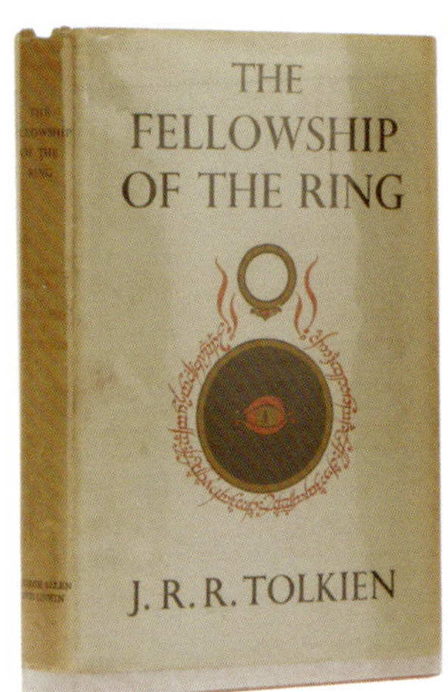

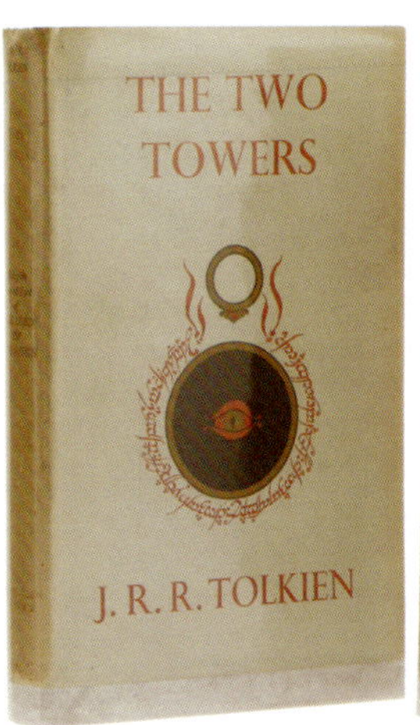

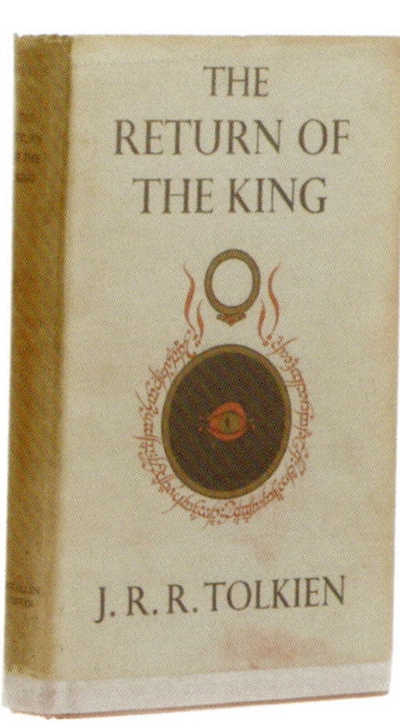

3486 J. R. R. Tolkien — "The Lord of the Rings," First Edition Set with Dust Jackets (George Allen & Unwin, 1954-55). After years of negotiating, it was eventually agreed that publisher Allen & Unwin would publish J. R. R. Tolkien's **The Lord of the Rings** in three volumes. After a long and difficult period of production, **The Fellowship of the Ring** was published on July 21, 1954. **The Two Towers** followed on November 11, 1954 and **The Return of the King** finally appeared on October 20, 1955. Presented here are first editions of each of these eventful books, including the dust jacket for each. The dust jackets show some aging along the edges, especially along the spines, with some ink loss on some of the type. Overall the jackets are in Good condition. The books have a bit of aging apparent, especially on the inside front and back covers. The previous owner's inscription is on the first page of each volume. The covers exhibit a bit of edge wear, and some light rubbing, but are in Very Good condition. Of this classic in world literature only 3500 sets were printed and no doubt fewer survived the past half century. Add this crown jewel to your collection with this remarkable offering!

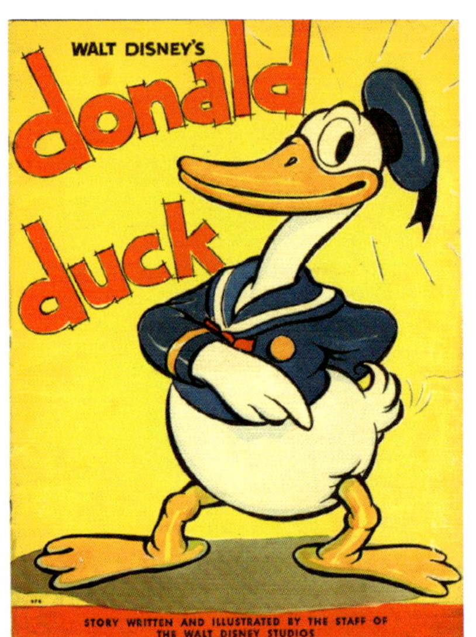

3487 Disney Linen-like Book Group (Whitman, 1935-37) Condition: Average VG. Two 9.5" x 13" Disney story books, both printed on linen-like stock, make up this lot: **Donald Duck** #978, the very first book completely devoted to this character; and **The Wise Little Hen** #888, which also features an early Donald appearance. The Donald book has a .75" tear visible on the cover and first page. Approximate Overstreet value for group = $800.

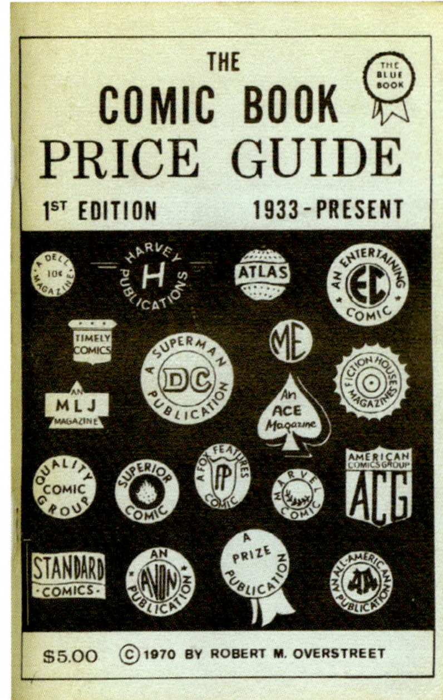

3488 Overstreet Comic Book Price Guide #1 Second Printing (Gemstone, 1970) Condition: FN. This is the blue-cover second printing of the very first Comic Book Price Guide... who could have dreamed back in 1970 that this guide to collectibles would itself become a collectible. After the first printing sold out, this second printing was released later the same year, with Bob Overstreet and his family collating and stapling every copy! The prices are, of course, an entertaining read for any comic lover of today — **Action Comics** #1 was priced at all of $300 in Mint condition, and we're really kicking ourselves for not stocking up on **Showcase** #4 ($12 in Mint) or **Suspense Comics** #3 ($5). Don't miss out on the book that helped make comic fandom what it is today. Overstreet 2005 FN value = $750.

SESSION FOUR

Public-Internet Auction #818
Saturday, October 15, 2005, 6:00 PM CT, Lots 4001-4535
Heritage Comic Auctions Dallas, Texas

Visit HeritageComics.com to view enlargeable color images and bid online.

ORIGINAL ART

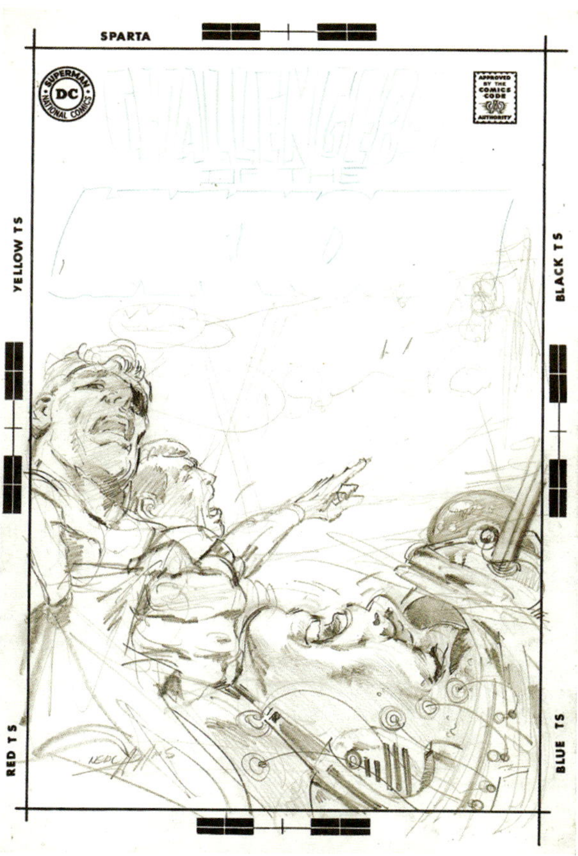

4001 Neal Adams - Challengers of the Unknown #67 Unpublished Cover Pencils Original Art (DC, circa 1969). Here's a wonderful opportunity to experience an expressive, unpublished, alternative Neal Adams "cover hook" for **Challengers of the Unknown** #67. The published cover has another take on the scene with a completely different layout. This terrific pencil piece offers a different conception for Robert Kanigher's yarn, "The Dream Killers." The image area measures 10" x 15" and the art is in Excellent condition.

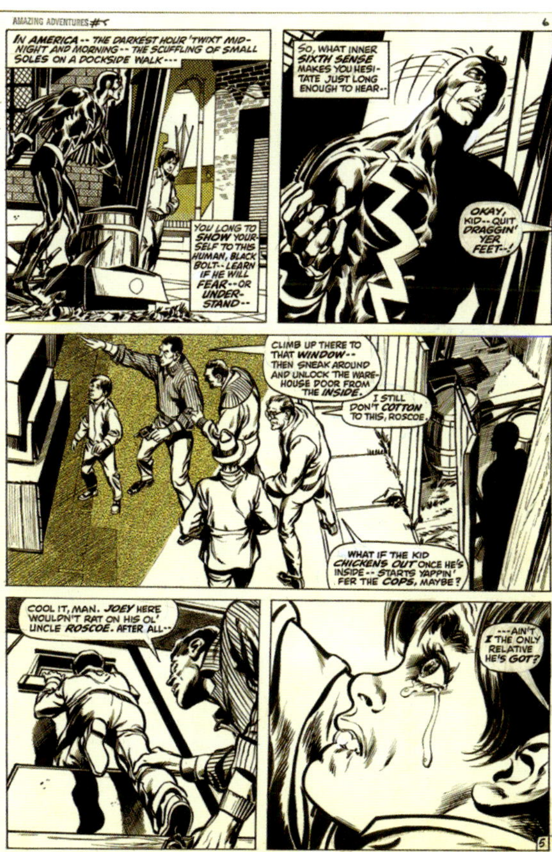

4002 Neal Adams and Tom Palmer - Amazing Adventures #5, page 5 Original Art (Marvel, 1971). What inner sixth sense makes Black Bolt hesitate while a young boy is coerced by his uncle into breaking into a warehouse? This page from Roy Thomas' story, "His Brother's Keeper," features dynamic Neal Adams pencils with hallmark inks by Tom Palmer. The image area measures 10" x 15" and the work is in Excellent condition.

ORIGINAL ART CONDITION

Excellent: Without flaws, or nearly so.

Very Good: One or two flaws, but no structural damage.

Good: Can have several flaws. Still complete and collectible. Could be missing one or two paste-up corrections.

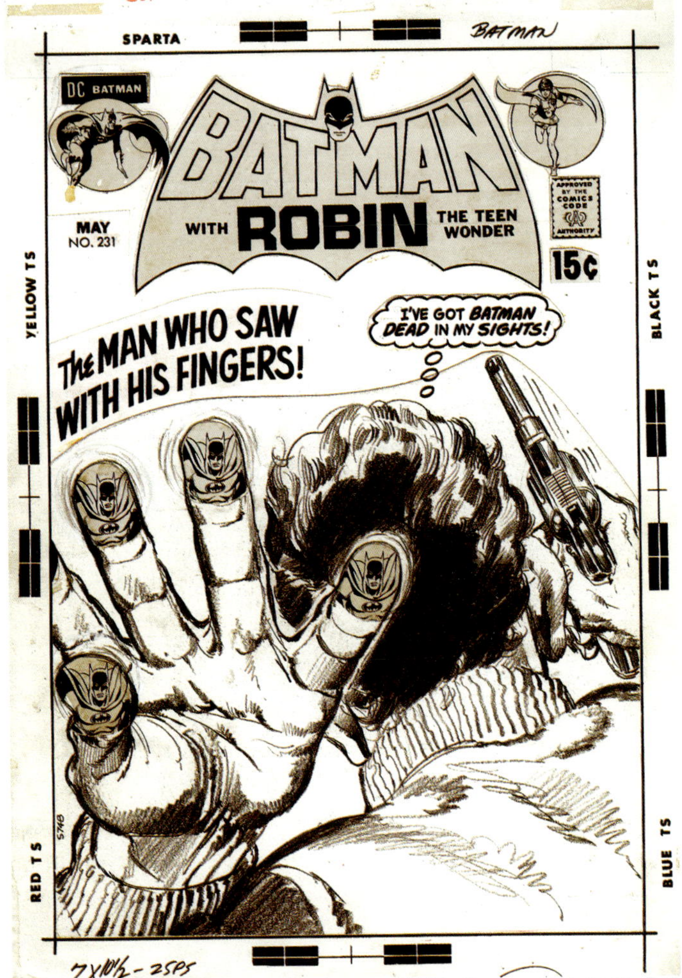

4003 Neal Adams - Batman #231 Cover Original Art (DC, 1971). "Ten-Eyed" Reardon let's his fingers do the watching as he sets his sights on Batman, in this bizarre cover illustration by Neal Adams. After a freak accident, former night watchman Reardon had a rogue doctor re-route his optic nerves to the sensory cells of his fingertips, giving him the awe-inspiring cognomen of "The Ten-Eyed Man," the man who saw with his fingers! Neal Adams pencils this "eye-catching" cover illustration, which has an image area of 10" x 15," and is in Excellent condition. This piece of cover art is notable for Adams' extremely tight pencils, which did not require inking — this IS the final cover artwork that the published art was shot from! Includes all the original logo and title type paste-ups.

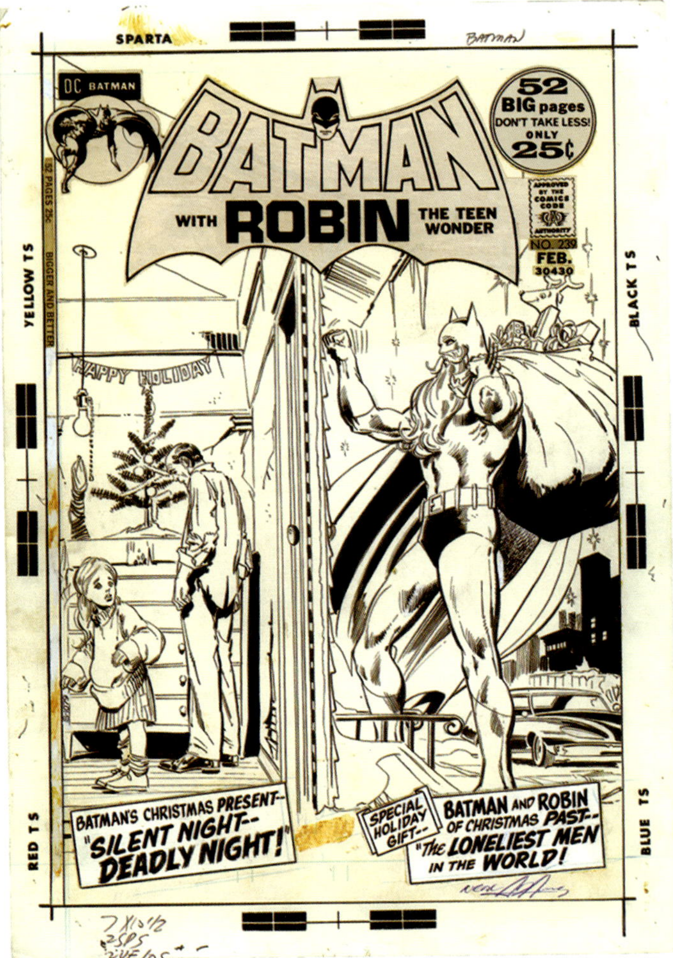

4004 Neal Adams - Batman #239 Cover Original Art (DC, 1972). With the first snowfall, Gotham is a different city. Everyday locales are changed into dazzling sights by the white snow. On this evening, the most wonderful, magical evening all year, the Masked Manhunter makes a special delivery to a down on his luck ex-convict and his daughter, in this cover illustrating the interior story, "Silent Night, Deadly Night," which was written by Denny O'Neil. A remarkable rendering by fan favorite Neal Adams, the art has an image area of 10" x 15", and, aside from some limited glue stains from a couple of missing paste-ups, is in Excellent condition. Signed by Neal Adams at the bottom right.

4005 Neal Adams and the Studio - Mr. T and the T Force #1, Splash Page 20 Original Art (Now, 1993). First name, Mr, middle name, period, last name T. The man that wears $80,000 worth of gold and fine silverware around his neck rules in this fool-pitying splash page by Neal Adams. American superstar actor, and cult hero, Mr. T and his T Force cleaned up the streets from drug dealers and other fools, making the inner city safe for decent folk once again. The image area measures 10" x 15" and the condition is Excellent. "Quit your jibber-jabbering and bid!"

4006 Arthur Adams and Terry Austin - Classic X-Men #20, page 1 Original Art (Marvel, 1988). While the X-Men recuperate at a local village in the Savage Land, Storm is attacked by the human pterodactyl, Sauron, in **Classic X-Men** #20, which was reprinted from **X-Men** #114. This frontispiece by penciler Arthur Adams, and inker, Terry Austin, includes the original title type paste-up art. The image area measures 10" x 5.5", and aside from some slight smudging along the center of the work, the art is in Excellent condition. Signed by Terry Austin.

4007 Dan Adkins - Silver Surfer Pin-Up Original Art (undated). Dan Adkins was one of big John Buscema's top inkers at Marvel during the Silver Age. And speaking of Silver, Adkins has recreated a John Buscema scene from one of the Silver Surfer's flights across the Manhattan skyline. The image area of this streamlined pin-up measures 8.75" x 15", and the art is in Excellent condition.

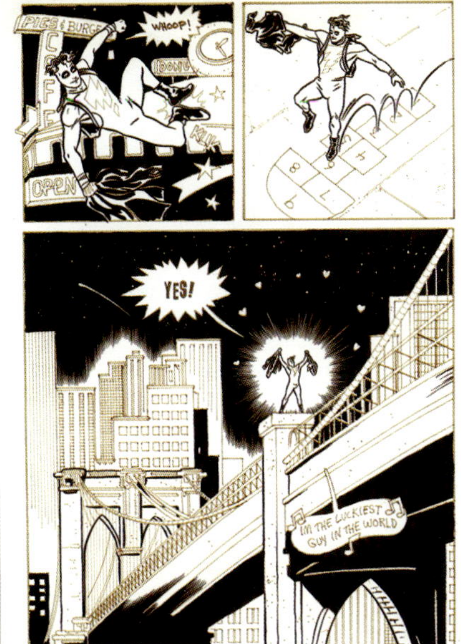

4008 Mike Allred - Madman Adventures #1, Page Original Art (Tundra, 1992). Mike Allred burst into the comics scene with **Madman**, published by Tundra in 1992, in a duo-tone comic book. From this humble beginning, the character has evolved from its small, cult status into a stylish, full-color book published by Dark Horse Comics. Here is a groovy panel page by Allred, featuring the world's snazziest hero! The image area measures 10.5" x 16.5". There is some slight fading to some of the linework (apparently Allred used delible ink, which has since faded), otherwise the work is in Excellent condition.

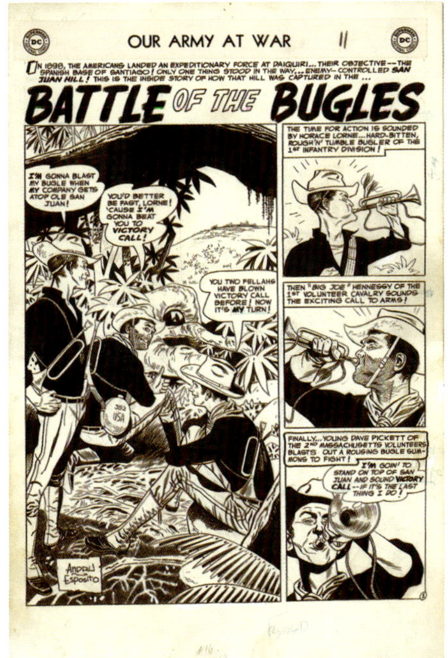

4009 Ross Andru and Mike Esposito - Our Army at War #16 Page Original Art, Group of 4 (DC, 1953). The DC war comics line fielded one of the most talented lineups of artists ever to work in comics. The supreme team of Ross Andru and Mike Esposito made their second appearance in the **Our Army at War** title with this yarn. The two proved themselves ideally suited for editor/writer Robert Kanigher's gritty, war-torn dramas. This lot features pages one, four, five, and six of "The Battle of the Bugles," a saga about the taking of San Juan Hill. The image area of each page measures 13" x 18", except for page six (which is a "half-page," with an image area of 13" x 11.75"). Aside from some minor aging, all of the pages are in Excellent condition.

4010 Ross Andru and Mike Esposito - The Flash #179, page 10 Original Art (DC, 1968). Barry Allen, the Flash, is knocked for a loop in this half-page from "The Flash — Fact or Fiction?" The team-supreme of penciler Ross Andru and inker Mike Esposito turned out countless classic pages for DC, Marvel, Standard, Skywald, and many other comic book companies. The overall size of this half-page measures 10.75" x 8.25". Three lettering corrections have slipped off of the word balloons; otherwise the art is in Very Good condition. This is a fun-tastic piece for a Silver Age Flash-fan!

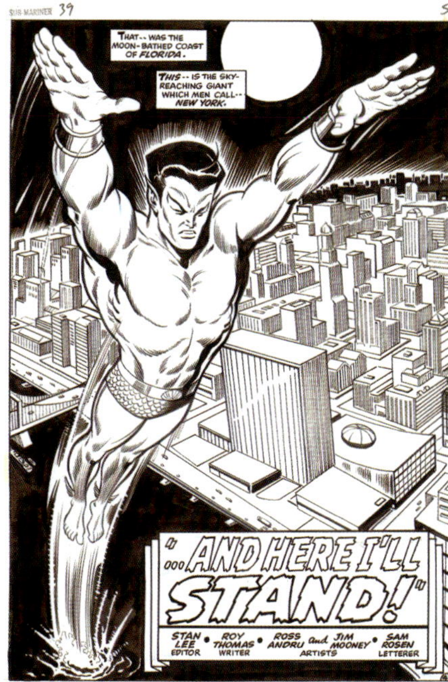

4011 Ross Andru and Jim Mooney - Sub-Mariner #39, Splash Page 4 Original Art (Marvel, 1971). Talk about a splash page! The Prince from Atlantis, makes his big city appearance in the sky-reaching giant men call New York, in this super-colossal splash page. Here is one of Marvel's mightiest mainstays, the short-fused Sub-Mariner, direct from the lost island of Atlantis, courtesy of penciler Ross Andru and inker Jim Mooney. The image area measures 10" x 15" and the work is in Excellent condition.

4012 Ross Andru and Mike DeCarlo - The Vigilante #7 Cover Original Art (DC, 1984). Unable to stand the frustration of watching criminals go free because of legal technicalities, attorney Adrian Chase learned combat skills and made himself a superhero outfit, fully equipped with heavy armament, to specialize in bringing justice to such cases. He called himself the Vigilante. From his bullet-ridden origin issue comes this formidable cover illustration by penciler Ross Andru and inker Mike DeCarlo. The image area measures 10" x 15" and the work is in Excellent condition.

4013 Jim Aparo - Aquaman, Batman, and Wonder Woman Page Original Art, Group of 2 (DC, 1975-76). The late, great Jim Aparo was renowned for his ability to finish a completely penciled, inked, and lettered page every day, day in and day out. After breaking into the comics field at Charlton, Aparo followed Dick Giordano over to the "big league" at DC, and he soon established himself as one of the company's best Bronze Age talents. **Brave and Bold** #131, page eight teams Batman with Wonder Woman, while **Adventure Comics** #443, page seven stars Aquaman, as he battles the menace of the Fisherman. Each page has an image area of 10" x 15", and aside from small areas of tape residue at the top and bottoms of the pages, both are in Excellent condition.

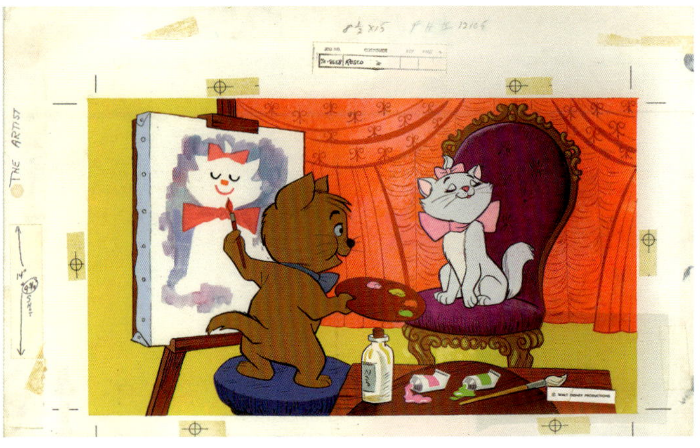

4014 Western Publishing Artist - The Aristocats Page Original Art (undated). Pedigreed kitten Toulouse paints a portrait of his sister, Marie, in this carefree illustration, titled "The Artist," painted for an unidentified publication. The image area measures 15.5" x 8.75", and, aside from some light spotting on Marie, the art is in Excellent condition.

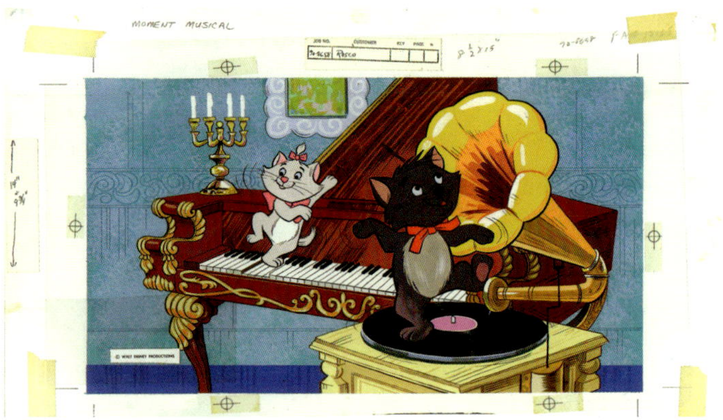

4015 Walt Disney Studio Artist - The Aristocats Picture Puzzle Cover Original Art (Jaymar, early 1970s). While Marie tickles the ivories, Berlioz kicks it old school, in this brilliant cover illustration for **The Aristocats Interlocking Picture Puzzle** #5047. This 100 piece interlocking picture puzzle was produced by Jaymar in the early 1970s. Spectacularly painted on heavy illustration board, the art has an image area of 15" x 9", and is in Excellent condition. Includes a **The Aristocats Interlocking Picture Puzzle** #5047.

4016 Rafael Auraleon - Creepy Magazine Splash Page Original Art (Warren, undated). This exceptional work of art by Rafael Auraleon is sweeping in its scope and dimensional representation. Despite the many character elements, it evokes a vastness of space which dwarfs the females in the foreground. A plethora of alien life forms adds a fun quality to the piece, and Uncle Creepy, himself, looks on in the upper right corner. Auraleon aptly handles the pen and ink with a variety of inking styles, conveying a wide range of textures. He uses ink wash to unify the composition. From an unidentified issue of **Creepy**, this page has an image area of approximately 12.25" x 17.5". The page has minor surface wear but, otherwise, is in Excellent condition.

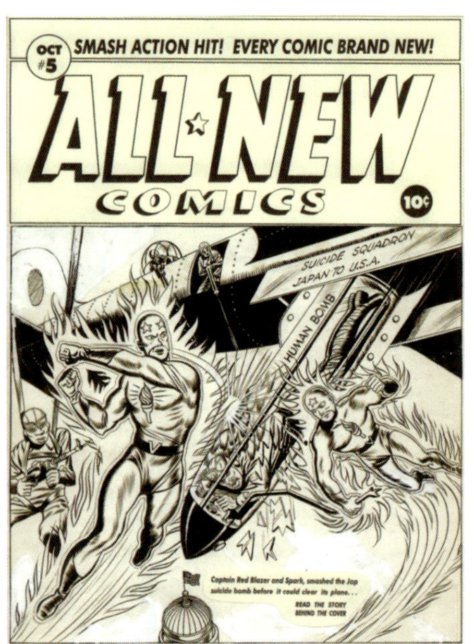

4017 Alex Schomburg - All-New Comics #5 Cover Original Art (Harvey, 1943). High above the U.S. Capitol, Captain Red Blazer and Spark smash a Japanese suicide bomb before it could even clear its plane, in this imaginative Alex Schomburg spectacle. Typical of Schomburg to label every bit of machinery, so that the kids would not misunderstand, the Japanese plane is labeled "Suicide Squadron Japan to U.S.A.," and the doomed kamikaze's deadly device has "Human Bomb" written on the side. These Eastern invaders are on a mission of death, and they don't won't anyone to think otherwise! The image area measures 11.5" x 16" and, aside from a bit of staining just over Captain Red Blazer's head, the work is in Excellent condition. The logo and masthead is recent photocopy replacement art.

4018 Dick Ayers and Paul Reinman - Tales to Astonish #57, page 13 Original Art (Marvel, 1964). Egghead pits Spider-Man against the Wasp and Giant-Man, and gleefully watches his plan unfold through a cybernetically-activated viewer. Dick Ayers pencils, and Paul Reinman inks, this titanic Silver Age Marvel team-up, and it's a real treat. The image area measures 12.5" x 18.5", and the condition is Excellent.

4019 Chris Bachalo and Mark Buckingham - Generation X #1, page 5 Original Art (Marvel, 1994). The Generation X drama begins almost immediately at Xavier's school, when Paige expresses a desire to be team leader, even though she may not be the best choice. Here is page 14 from the Scott Lobdell story, "Third Genesis," with pencils by Chris Bachalo and inks by Mark Buckingham. The image area measures 10" x 15" and the art is in Excellent condition.

4020 Chris Bachalo and Mark Buckingham - Generation X #1, page 14 Original Art (Marvel, 1994). The Generation X team of Husk, M, Jubilee, Skin, and Synch assembles at Xavier's school to begin their mutant education under the tutelage of Sean Cassidy and Emma Frost, in this first issue, written by Scott Lobdell. Here is page 14 from the story, "Third Genesis," with pencils by Chris Bachalo and inks by Mark Buckingham. The image area measures 10" x 15" and the art is in Excellent condition.

4021 Mark Bagley and Al Vey - Spider-Man Vs. Hammerhead Splash Page Original Art (undated). Spider-sense and spider-speed save the wondrous wall-crawler from a deadly crossfire unleashed by Hammerhead and a hovering helicopter. Mark Bagley captures the unique thrill of watching Spider-Man in action and Al Vey's inks add the perfect finish to this pulse-pounding drawing. The image area of the piece is 14" x 8", and the art is in Excellent condition. Mark Bagley has signed the art in the border at the lower right.

4022 Mark Bagley - Spider-Girl and Spider-Man Illustration Original Art (1999). The wildest (and cutest), web-slinger of all, May Parker, teams up with the original Webhead, in this illustration by Mark Bagley. Universes collide when Spider-Girl arrives in our "alternate" universe where she meets a much younger version of her father — Spider-Man! The image area measures 10" x 15" and the condition is Excellent. Signed by Mark Bagley along the bottom.

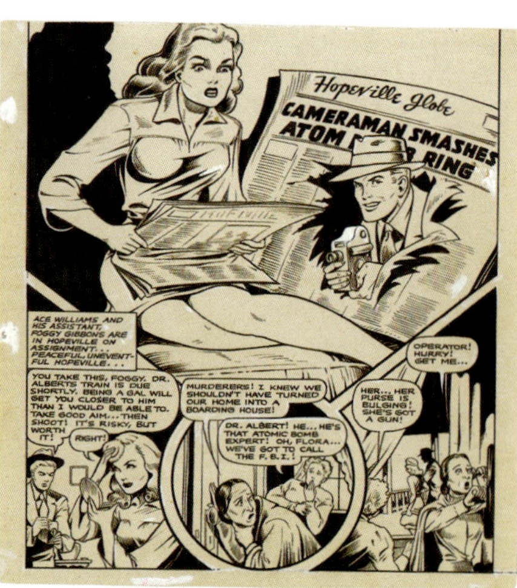

4023 Matt Baker - Crown Comics #5 Splash Page 1 Original Art (Golfing/McCombs, 1946). Photographer Ace Williams and his gorgeous assistant, Foggy Gibbons, are staying at a boarding house in Hopeville on a photography assignment. The landlady overhears their plan to "shoot" Dr. Albert, an atomic bomb expert. Call the FBI! The master of the female form, Matt Baker, starts this case of gross misunderstanding with a great cheesecake shot of reporter Foggy in the first panel! The image area measures 12.25" x 14.5", and, aside from some overall aging, and a missing logo section at the top, the condition is Excellent.

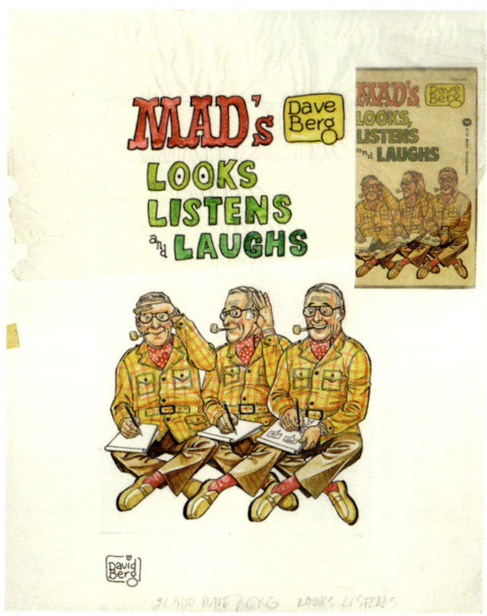

4032 Dave Berg - Mad's Dave Berg Looks, Listens and Laughs Paperback Book Cover Original Art (Warner Books, 1979). Dave Berg was best known as a cartoonist for **Mad** magazine where his comic illustrations are deeply embossed into our collective pop culture memory. He started the "The Lighter Side" cartoon in 1961, which would become his most famous creation. The strip often skewered Berg's own family, headed by his cranky alter-ego, Roger Kaputnik. Presented here is Berg's hand-painted cover art for the paperback **Mad's Dave Berg Looks, Listens and Laughs**. The image area measures 9" x 14" and the art is in Excellent condition. Includes a color photocopy of the book cover.

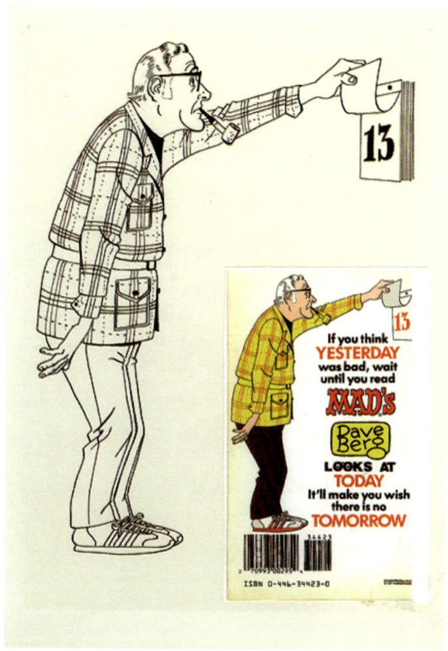

4033 Dave Berg - Mad's Dave Berg Looks at Today Paperback Book Back Cover Original Art (Warner Books, 1987). "He was not a cynic at all," said **Mad** magazine co-editor Nick Meglin about the talented Dave Berg, "It was just vignettes that he personally witnessed and did variations on of everyday life wherever it occurred." Dave Berg affectionately spoofed what he called "the human condition" in the pages of **Mad** for more than 40 years. His strips often featured the pipe-smoking "Roger Kaputnik" — his own alter-ego observer to help make Berg's points. This illustration was featured on the back cover of **Mad's Dave Berg Looks at Today**. It has an image area of 8" x 11" and is in Excellent condition. Includes a color photocopy of the book back cover.

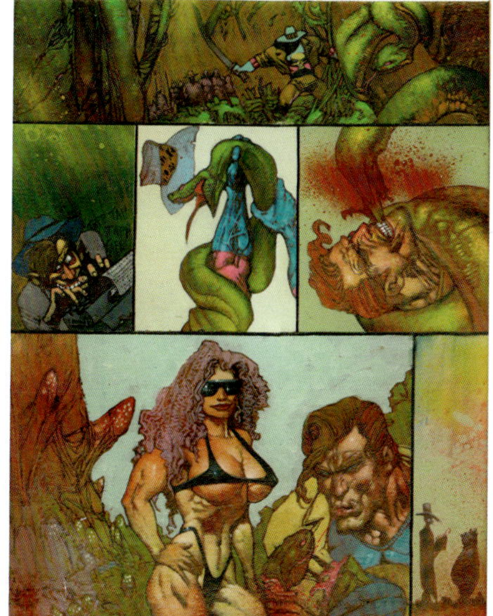

4034 Simon Bisley - Blast! #1, page 3 Original Art (John Brown Publishing, 1991). Dateline: darkest Africa. Reporter Danny Deadline follows the elusive monsterfighter, Mr. Monster, deep into the Congo to write a report on 24 hours in the life of the famous Dr. Stearn and his sharp, sexy gal Friday, Kelly. Simon Bisley bites off as much as he can chew in this blood spewn page, which features the good Doc, and his vivacious assistant in action. The image area measures approximately 11.5" x 15" and the art is in Excellent condition. The type and word balloons are attached to an acetate overlay, which is also included. Attractively matted in a 21" x 24.5" matte.

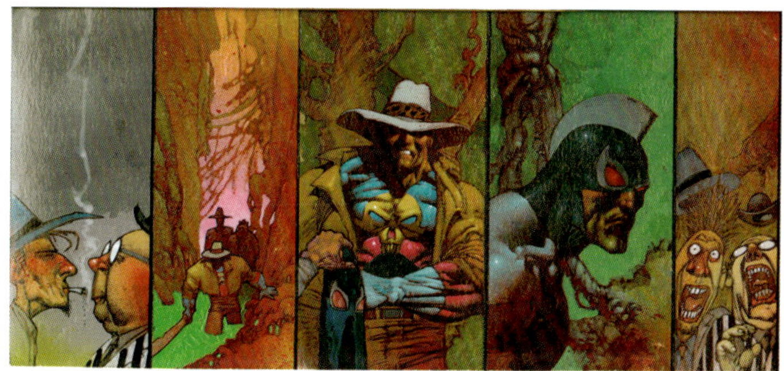

4035 Simon Bisley - Blast! #1, page 4 Original Art (John Brown Publishing, 1991). A grim-faced Dr. Strongfort Stearn dons his hood to become an even grimmer-faced Mr. Monster, in this fantastic page by Simon Bisley. Thickly painted with swashes of fluorescent colors, Bisley completes this stunning work in ink and acrylic on a sheet of illustration paper. The art has an image area of approximately 16.5" x 8" and the condition is Excellent. The art is beautifully matted in a 25" x 16.5" matte.

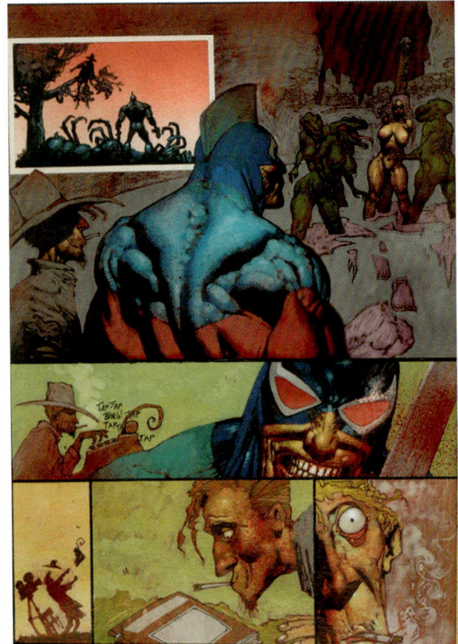

4036 Simon Bisley - Blast! #1, page 6 Original Art (John Brown Publishing, 1991). "Great Guns, Deadline! Lizard ladies! And they've got Kelly!" Mr. Monster takes the offensive, while reporter, Danny Deadline, chronicles his adventure, in this page by Simon Bisley. Spectacular and savage, Bisley pulls no punches in theses violent and sexy images. Painted with ink, acrylic and color pencil on illustration paper, the art has an image area of approximately 11.5" x 15" and the condition is Excellent. The type and word balloons are attached to an acetate overlay, which is also included. The art is beautifully matted in a 21" x 26" matte.

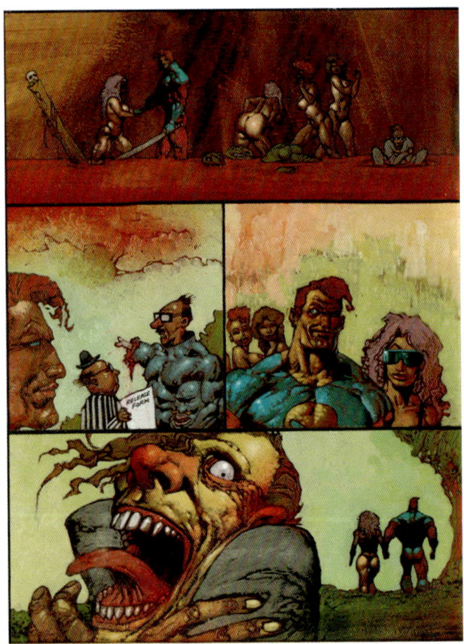

4037 Simon Bisley - Blast! #1, page 8 Original Art (John Brown Publishing, 1991). It's all in a day's work for the greatest monster fighter in the world — Mr. Monster! But his assignment to follow the elusive Dr. Stearn has driven reporter Danny Deadline to insanity! Simon Bisley painted this page with ink, acrylic and color pencil on illustration paper. The art has an image area of approximately 11.5" x 15" and the condition is Excellent. The type and word balloons are attached to an acetate overlay, which is also included. The art is beautifully matted in a 21" x 26" matte.

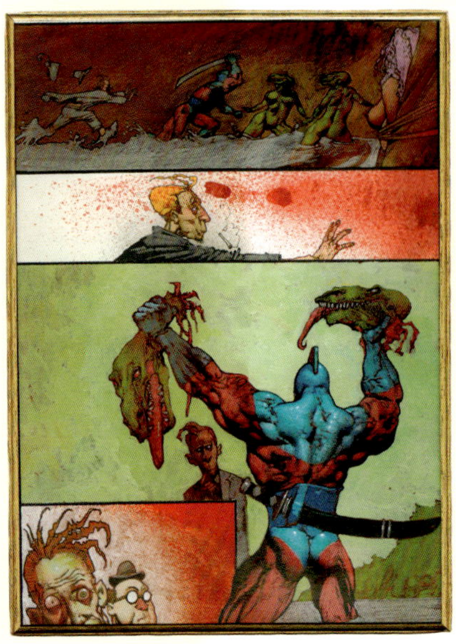

4038 Simon Bisley - Blast! #1, page 7 Original Art (John Brown Publishing, 1991). Deep within the Congo, Dr. Strongfort Stearn takes off the heads of two Hollywood actresses disguised as lizard women, before the startled eyes of reporter Danny Deadline. Riotous and raunchy, this Simon Bisley page is dark but delightfully rendered, in brilliant hues of red and green. The image area measures approximately 11.5" x 15" and the art is in Excellent condition. The type and word balloons are attached to an acetate overlay, which is also included. The art is beautifully matted in a 21" x 26" matte.

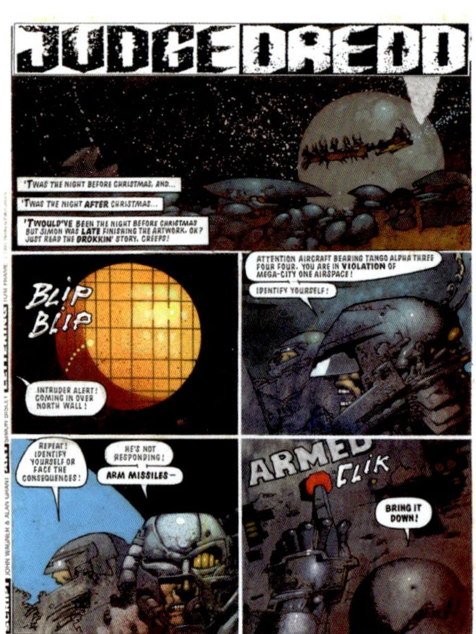

4039 Simon Bisley - Rock Power Magazine: Judge Dredd, page 1 Original Art (Fleetway, 1991). From the "Heavy Metal Dredd" series which first appeared in **Rock Power**, a metal music magazine, comes this *drokkin'* first page of the 6-page story, "The Night Before Christmas," written by John Wagner and Alan Grant, and painted by Simon Bisley. The image area measures 8" x 10.75" and the art is in Excellent condition.

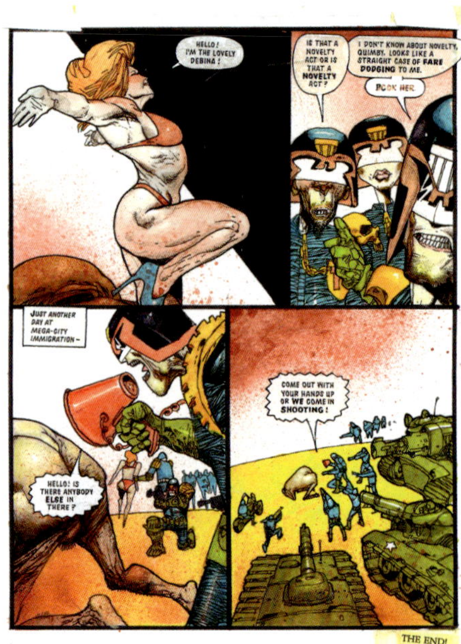

4040 Simon Bisley - Rock Power: Judge Dredd, page 6 Original Art (Fleetway, 1991). You are looking at an original page of art by Simon Bisley, which features one of the great characters of his career — Judge Dredd! From the "Heavy Metal Dredd" series, this art first appeared in **Rock Power** magazine, and was subsequently translated into many languages, before being reprinted in **Judge Dredd Megazine**. Painted in colored inks and marker on heavy illustration paper, the art has an image area of 8" x 11" and is in Excellent condition.

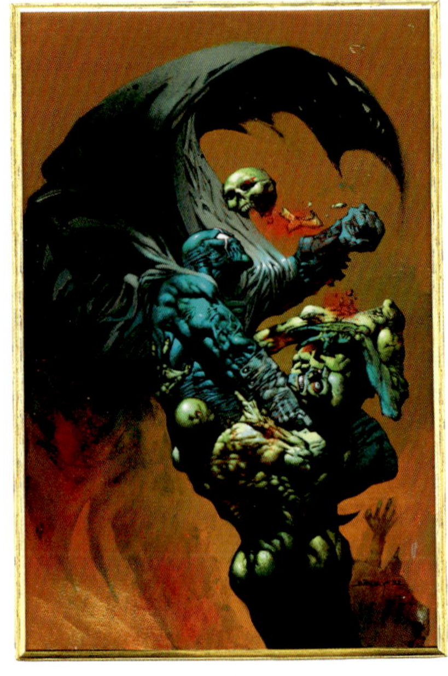

4041 Simon Bisley - Grendel: Warchild #2 Cover Original Art (Dark Horse, 1992). On a trip across the barren, deadly wasteland that is America, Grendel is beset by a plague of zombies, in this corpulent cover illustration by Simon Bisley. Painted with sombre earth tones in acrylic, and ink on illustration paper, the image area measures 11" x 17". This work is in Excellent condition, and is beautifully matted in a 18.5" x 24.5" matte.

4042 Simon Bisley - Max Carnage, page 2 Original Art (Heavy Metal, 1993). The demented cyborg, Thor, who calls himself Max Carnage, tangles with a couple of deadly black panthers, in this ultraviolent page by Simon Bisley. Originally presented in **Heavy Metal War Machine** Vol. 7 #1, Max Carnage is a superhero created by Dave Elliott and Simon Bisley, with everything that name implies. Bisley is one of the most insanely over the top artists you'll find, as you can see in this frenzied page. This exaggerated page has an image area of 11" x 17" and is in Excellent condition.

4043 Simon Bisley and Kevin Eastman - Melting Pot, Book One, page 1 Original Art (Kitchen Sink, 1994). With this page, the epic four-issue **Melting Pot** limited series gets off to an explosive start! A damaged starfighter makes an almost fatal crash landing on an unfamiliar planet. The pilot find herself alive, but what horrors are in store for her? Kevin Eastman's pencils are painted over by Simon Bisley, whose kinetic technique brings this page to smoking life. The art has an image area of 13.75" x 20" and is in Excellent condition.

4044 Simon Bisley and Kevin Eastman - Melting Pot, Book One, page 2 Original Art (Kitchen Sink, 1994). Her laser wounds the vicious little varmint who is intent on having her for lunch. Maybe this stranded pilot shouldn't count her blessing just yet, because this hostile planet has more menacing things in store for her! Here is the second page to the first issue of Kevin Eastman and Simon Bisley's epic four-issue series **Melting Pot**. Kevin Eastman pencils and Simon Bisley paints this intense multi-paneled page. The art has an image area of 13.75" x 21" and is in Excellent condition.

4045 Simon Bisley and Kevin Eastman - Melting Pot, Book One, page 3 Original Art (Kitchen Sink, 1994). It's survival of the fittest between the pilot of a crash-landed starfighter, and a rottweiler-sized alien creature, and only one will win! Kevin Eastman and Simon Bisley jump start this harrowing series with this early page, which is full of pure, thoughtless violence. Eastman is the penciler with Simon Bisley finishing the work with his overwhelming painting techniques. The art has an image area of 13.75" x 21" and is in Excellent condition.

4046 Simon Bisley and Kevin Eastman - Melting Pot, Book One, page 4 Original Art (Kitchen Sink, 1994). The deadly beast is upon her! She only has seconds to save herself! By the mother of all that's holy, what kind of hell has she been placed in? With a well aimed blast, the stranded starfighter pilot saves her own life — a short-lived moment brought to you by creator/penciler Kevin Eastman, and painter Simon Bisley. This page consists of many small panels, each lavished with lots of detail and textures by the hand of Bisley. The art has an image area of 13.75" x 20" and is in Excellent condition.

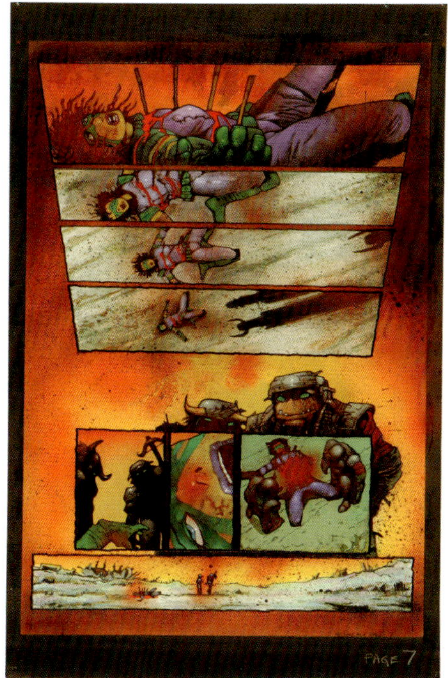

4047 Simon Bisley and Kevin Eastman - Melting Pot, Book One, page 7 Original Art (Kitchen Sink, 1994). The lone pilot of a battle-damaged starfighter takes her last breath, while her assassins gloat over their kill, in this cut-throat page from the Kevin Eastman/Simon Bisley collaboration. Simon Bisley attacks this page with his skilled brush, painting hues over Kevin Eastman's pencils. The art has an image area of 14" x 21.5" and is in Excellent condition.

4048 Simon Bisley and Kevin Eastman - Melting Pot, Book One, page 8 Original Art (Kitchen Sink, 1994). Two killers join an army of blood-thirsty soldiers making their yearly journey to the fortress of Shantarr, in this eighth page of the first issue of **Melting Pot**, Kevin Eastman and Simon Bisley's epic four-issue series. Kevin Eastman pencils, and Simon Bisley paints, this formidable multi-paneled page. The art has an image area of 13.75" x 21.5" and is in Excellent condition.

4049 Simon Bisley and Kevin Eastman - Melting Pot, Book One, Splash page 9 Original Art (Kitchen Sink, 1994). The border town of Juudas gets the Simon Bisley touch, in this remarkable, panoramic rendering. Created, written, and penciled by Kevin Eastman, the art was given a final painted polish by one of the most prolific painters in the "Biz"-ness, Simon Bisley! The art has an image area of 13.5" x 21" and is in Excellent condition.

4050 Simon Bisley and Kevin Eastman - Melting Pot, Book One, page 10 Original Art (Kitchen Sink, 1994). On their yearly pilgrimage to the city of Shantarr, two soldiers take in an death match between two deadly behemoths in the city of Juudas. This collaboration of Kevin Eastman's pencils and Simon Bisley's paints will set your teeth on edge, with its dynamic rendering and ferocious color. The art has an image area of 13.5" x 21" and is in Excellent condition.

4051 Simon Bisley and Kevin Eastman - Melting Pot, Book One, page 11 Original Art (Kitchen Sink, 1994). The mighty Gorr loses his battle in the arena at Juudas, leaving two soldiers broke, in this fatal page by Kevin Eastman and Simon Bisley. Eastman pencils, and Bisley paints, this bloody page from the first book of the **Melting Pot** series. The art has an image area of 13.5" x 21" and is in Excellent condition.

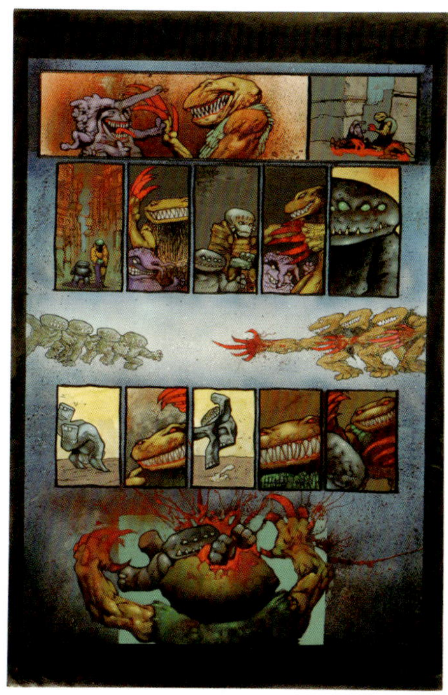

4052 Simon Bisley and Kevin Eastman - Melting Pot, Book One, page 13 Original Art (Kitchen Sink, 1994). A plague contaminates the border town of Juudas. Odin's protector, Zeek, faces a taloned killer and takes him down in an explosion of blood, in this page from Kevin Eastman and Simon Bisley's collaboration. Following Eastman's pencils, Bisley finishes off this page in rich, earthy hues, giving volume to the figures. Combined with his intense use of textures, the images fly off the page! This page has an image area of 14" x 21" and is in Excellent condition.

4053 Simon Bisley and Kevin Eastman - Melting Pot, Book One, page 14 Original Art (Kitchen Sink, 1994). More mayhem and malevolence from the minds of Kevin Eastman and Simon Bisley! In the mean streets of Juudas, the peace-seeking Odin stops his bodyguard, Zeek, from killing yet another creature, in this devastating delineation. The Biz lavishes his paint over Eastman's pencils to produce this deep, rich rendering. With an image area of 13.75" x 21.5", this art is in Excellent condition.

4054 Simon Bisley and Kevin Eastman - Melting Pot, Book One, page 15 Original Art (Kitchen Sink, 1994). While travelling through the devastated border town of Juudas, the ancient and wise Odin reminisces about the past to his protector, Zeek, in this page penciled by Kevin Eastman and painted by Simon Bisley. Bisley manages to keep the mood dark, with contrasting colors that make the page vibrate with intensity. The art has an image area of 13.5" x 21" and is in Excellent condition.

4055 Simon Bisley and Kevin Eastman - Melting Pot, Book One, page 16 Original Art (Kitchen Sink, 1994). Death comes very near Odin and his companion, Zeek, in the form of the evil Lord Tyler, astride his taloned flying creature, in this page penciled by Kevin Eastman, and painted by Simon Bisley. The page consists of numerous small panels, each lavished with lots of detail and textures by the hand of Bisley. The art has an image area of 13.75" x 21.5" and is in Excellent condition.

4056 Simon Bisley and Kevin Eastman - Melting Pot, Book One, page 19 Original Art (Kitchen Sink, 1994). Riding a horrid winged monstrosity, the malevolent Lord Tyler returns to his troops, who stand ready for battle. Simon Bisley paints over Kevin Eastman's pencils on this page from the four issue series. Bisley's tight ink and acrylic wash renderings nicely highlight the panels. The art has an image area of 14" x 21.5" and is in Excellent condition.

4057 Simon Bisley and Kevin Eastman - Melting Pot Book Two, page 22 Original Art (Kitchen Sink, 1994). Simon Bisley gets down to "Biz"-ness, in this eye-popping page from his collaboration with Kevin Eastman. Each panel was painted separately and then pasted on to a 15" x 20" illustration board. Textured borders were then added around the panels. When it comes to graphic violence, Bisley spares no intimate detail! The art is in Excellent condition.

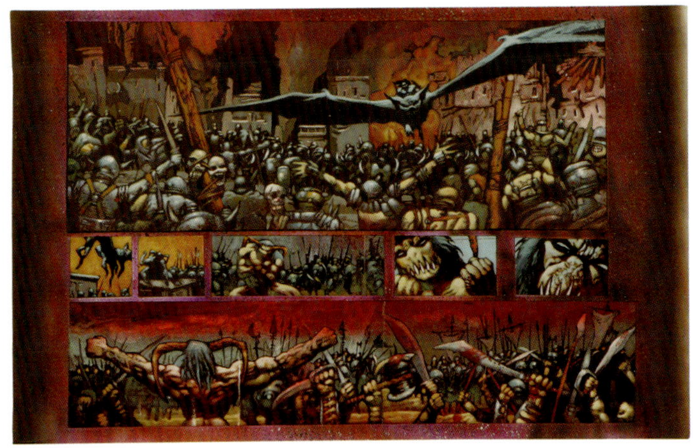

4060 Simon Bisley and Kevin Eastman - Melting Pot, Book Three, page 21 and 22 Original Art (Kitchen Sink, 1994). Lord Tyler returns to his soldiers and rallies them to prepare to march to the Holy Land for the final battle! Simon Bisley adds his lush painted hues over Kevin Eastman's pencils. The art has an image area of 14" x 21.5" and is in Excellent condition.

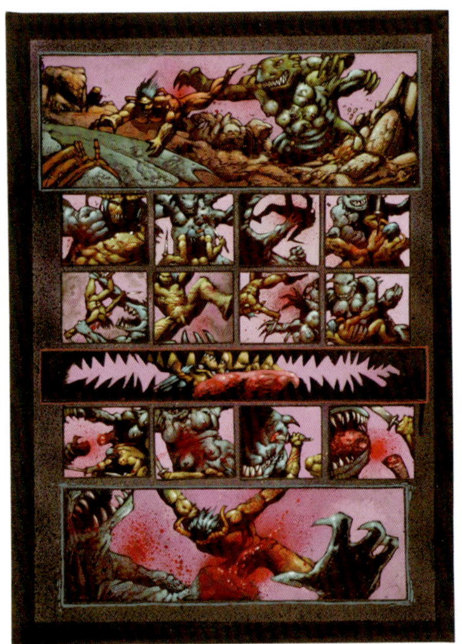

4058 Simon Bisley and Kevin Eastman - Melting Pot, Book Three, page 6 Original Art (Kitchen Sink, 1994). The evil Lord Tyler lashes out at a grotesque monstrosity, spewing blood and extremities all over this berserk page! This explosive scenario is given the full-blooded treatment by the amazing Simon Bisley, who paints over Kevin Eastman pencils. With an image area measuring 14" x 19.5" the art is in Excellent condition.

4059 Simon Bisley and Kevin Eastman - Melting Pot, Book Three, page 10 Original Art (Kitchen Sink, 1994). With a strangled tug on his leather harness, Lord Tyler guides his leather-winged transport high into the sky above Shantarr. This pestilent page, painted by Simon Bisley over Kevin Eastman's pencils, is a moody masterpiece rich in purple and blues. The art has an image area of 14" x 19.5" and is in Excellent condition.

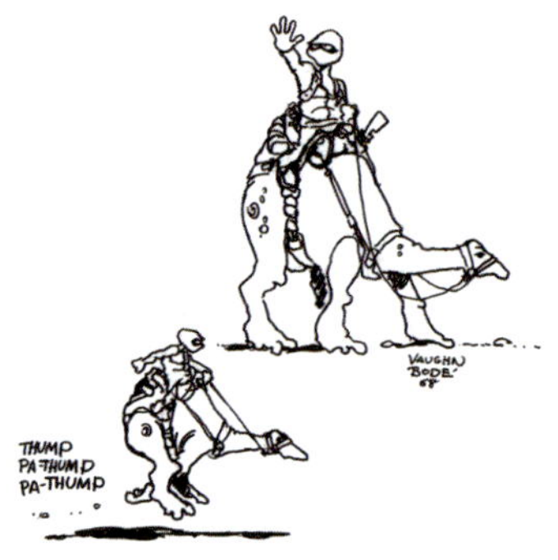

4061 Vaughn Bode - Cobalt-60 on his Grasser Illustration Original Art (1968). Next to the irascible Cheech Wizard, Cobalt-60 is the late Vaughn Bode's most enduring character. Cobalt-60 reveals the dark side of the peace and love generation's dreams, propelled into a future-tense apocalypse. Here is one of the earliest known drawings of Cobalt-60 on his Grasser, which was made famous in the seventh issue of the prozine, **Witzend**. Drawn in marker on a 8.5" x 11" sheet of vellum paper, it is signed by Vaughn Bode, and in Excellent condition.

4062 Mark Bode - Miami Mice #3, Splash Page 6 Original Art (Rip Off Press, 1986). Meet sexy Vermoosa Ratez, every mouse's dream! The Bode legacy continues in this slinky splash page by **Miami Mice** creator, Mark Bode, (son of the infamous Vaughn Bode), in his spoof of the "Miami Vice" television show. Mark's work has appeared in **Teenage Mutant Ninja Turtles**, the graphic novel **Cobalt 60**, **Heavy Metal**, **Epic Magazine**, **Hustler Comics**, and **Gauntlet** magazine. The image area measures 9.5" x 14" and is in Excellent condition.

4063 Brian Bolland - Animal Man #26 Cover Original Art (DC, 1990). Renowned cover artist, Brian Bolland, tackles this stunning image of Animal Man for the cover of issue #26. Covering the interior story, "Deus Ex Machina," written by Grant Morrison, this cover has an image area of 8.5" x 4", the background was a photograph which was added in production. Includes a black and white comp of the line art with an acetate overlay indicating the photo background. Signed by Brian Bolland at the bottom right.

4064 Daniel Brereton - Legends of the World's Finest #2, page 33 Original Art (DC, 1994). Daniel Brereton's evocative watercolored art is ideally suited for this scene of gritty, urban blight in the mean streets of Gotham City. Balloons or no balloons — there's fewer sights more unsettling than a nearby street performer dressed like the haughty Harlequin! The page has an image area of 12.5" x 18.5", and the art is in Excellent condition.

4065 Mark Bright and Bob Layton - Iron Man #215, page 23 Original Art (Marvel, 1987). Both new and old armor are featured on this page, as Tony Stark and Rhodes head into space to take on the evils of Advanced Idea Mechanics (A.I.M.) at Stark's new satellite. Unfortunately, Rhodey's armor malfunctions and he is gets burned during re-entry. **Iron Man** #215 features the return of writer David Micheline and artist Bob Layton for a second run on this series. This is penciler Mark Bright's second appearance as penciler for this title, and his layout is both dramatic and powerful. The image area measures 10" x 15" and the work is in Excellent condition. Signed by Bob Layton at the bottom right.

4066 Pat Broderick and Dick Giordano - The Fury of Firestorm #18 Cover Original Art (DC, 1983). Have penciler Pat Broderick and inker Dick Giordano got a cover for you! Henry Hewitt, who used a nuclear reactor to transform himself into the atomic super-villain, Tokamak, joins the Nuclear Man, Firestorm, and Martin Stein, on this incendiary illustration, which covers the interior story, "Squeeze Play," written by Gerry Conway. The image area measures 10" x 15", and, aside from one small glue stain from a missing title type paste-up, the work is in Excellent condition. The images of Martin Stein are photocopied onto an acetate overlay.

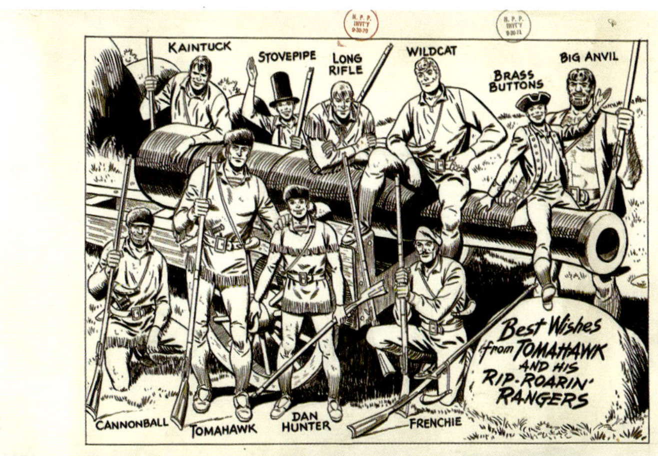

4067 Bob Brown - Tomahawk Unpublished Pin-Up Illustration Original Art (DC, circa 1967). Long-time Tomahawk artist Bob Brown drew this panoramic group portrait of Tomahawk and his Rangers posing with their big gun. The splash was written off and never used, most likely because the **Tomahawk** title changed directions in 1968 when Robert Kanigher came on board as the head writer. The image area of the art is 14.25" x 10.25", and the art is in Excellent condition.

4068 Bob Brown - The Brave and the Bold #78, page 21 Original Art (DC, 1968). While Batman, Batgirl and Wonder Woman act distracted, that snake in the grass, Copperhead, brazenly attempts to steal the Casque of Montezuma, his biggest prize yet, in this page from the Bob Haney story, "In the Coils of Copperhead". Penciled and inked by Bob Brown, this is the first comic book appearance of Copperhead. The image area measures 10" x 15", and, aside from some blue pencil editorial markings, the work is in Excellent condition.

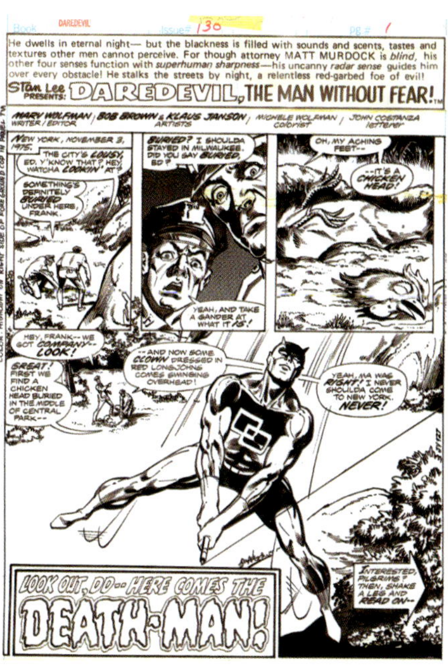

4069 Bob Brown and Klaus Janson - Daredevil #130, page 1 Original Art (Marvel, 1976). First they find a chicken head buried in the middle of Central Park, and now some clown dressed up in red long johns comes swinging overhead! All in a day's work for the New York City's finest! This is it, pilgrims, the first page of Marv Wolfman's story, "Look out, DD... Here Comes the Death-Man!," and believe us, it doesn't disappoint! The image area measures 10" x 15", and, aside from a bit of light staining in the second and third panels, and along the top just under the indicia, the work is in Very Good condition.

4070 Frank Brunner - Doctor Strange Illustration Original Art (1970s). This large illustration displays Frank Brunner's huge talent for expressive ink work. His ability to convey a variety of textures with many cross-hatching and line styles is all the more impressive because of the way that the imagery maintains its fluid essence. Brunner's work on the Doctor Strange universe of characters and backgrounds is milestone, and this piece exhibits many of those elements. The multi-planed imagery is successfully unified by the strong composition and use of line which centers on the serpent, spins to the eye, is shot across to the giant, led up the mace, to the thinking figure of Doctor Strange, across the void to the eclipse and back to the serpent. This piece includes some airbrush and pencil work that enhances the published art. Our research indicates that this piece saw publication in a fanzine just before or just after Brunner began his stint on the **Marvel Premiere** series. the image area measures 13" x 18" and the condition is Excellent.

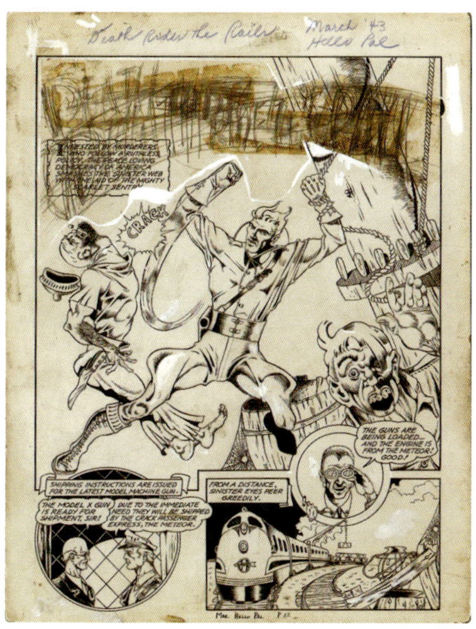

4071 Al Bryant (attributed) - Hello Pal #3 Complete 7-page Story "Death Rides the Rails" Original Art (Harvey, 1943). The influence of Lou Fine's approach to illustrating superheroic yarns can be seen throughout this slam-bang thriller. Nazi saboteurs attempt to heist the latest model machine gun from the Meteor, an express passenger train — only the derring-do and fisticuffs of the Scarlet Sentry foils their scheme! The image area of each page measures 13" x 17". The illustration boards show signs of aging and some surface wear. The title logo and a few art corrections have slipped off the pages; otherwise the art is in Good condition. Golden Age art has an unmatchable gusto and this romp has it in spades!

4072 Rich Buckler and Vince Colletta - Black Lightning #6 Cover Original Art (DC, 1978). On the trail of Peter Gambi's kidnappers, Black Lightning battles a villain by the name of Syonide and his two flunkies, who, as an inside joke, have the powers of Power Man and Iron Fist. This cover, penciled by Rich Buckler and inked by Vince Colletta, has an image area of approximately 10" x 15". Includes all the original logo and masthead paste-ups. There is are a few tiny stains, a paste-up discoloration on the word balloon, and a blue pencil editorial marking, otherwise the art is in Excellent condition. Signed by Rick Bucker along the left edge.

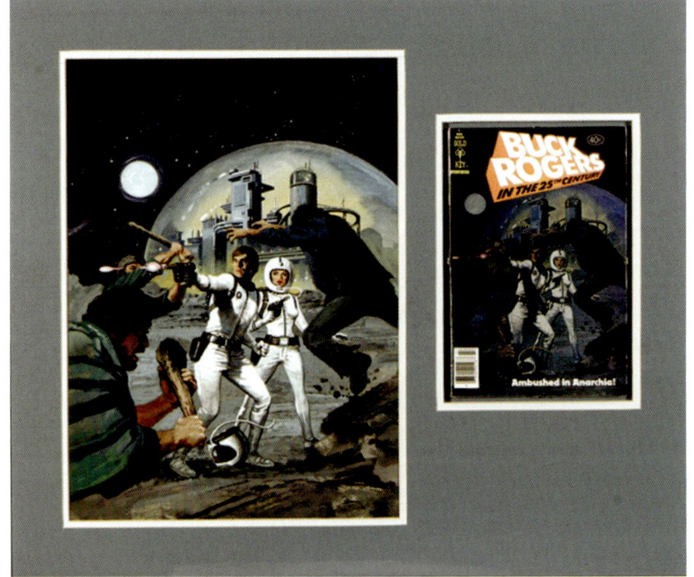

4073 Western Publishing Artist - Buck Rogers #4 Cover Original Art (Gold Key, 1979). Buck Rogers and Twiki stand ready to fight, while Wilma Deering leads Earth's Blue Squadron in an attack against a squadron of Draconian fighters, in this stunning cover illustration. Painted in watercolor on a 20" x 30" sheet of heavy illustration board, the art is in Excellent condition. Includes a copy of **Buck Rogers** #4.

4074 Western Publishing Artist - Buck Rogers in the 25th Century #6 Cover Original Art (Gold Key, 1980). Standing defiantly against the domed city of Anarchia, Buck Rogers and Wilma Deering face a group of club-carrying Anarchists, in this tremendous painted cover illustration. The image area of the art measures approximately 12" x 17" and the condition is Excellent. Includes a copy of **Buck Rogers in the 25th Century** #6.

4075 Western Publishing Artist - Bugs Bunny #136 Cover Original Art (Gold Key, 1971). Something fishy is going on at the fish store, as Bugs makes a lobster earn his keep in this "claw-some" cover illustration. This cover image has an image area of 10" x 11.5", and the art is in Excellent condition. This cover art was originally inspired by Dell's **Bugs Bunny** #32, and a copy of that issue is matted together with this piece.

4076 Western Publishing Artist - Yosemite Sam and Bugs Bunny #23 Cover Original Art (Gold Key, 1974). That rootin', tootin, rackin', frackin' gunslinger, Yosemite Sam, bait and tackles a mangy, fang-toothed critter, while Bugs captures the moment on film, in this captivating cover illustration. The image area measures 10.5" x 14.5" and the condition is Excellent.

4077 Bob Burden and Dave Sim - Flaming Carrot and Cerebus Sketch Original Art (1985). The Flaming Carrot debuted with a short story in **Visions**, a limited-run comic anthology, and later moved to his own title, **Flaming Carrot Comics** which was published by Dave Sim's company, Aardvark-Vanaheim in 1984. Here, Burden teams up with **Cerebus** creator Dave Sim, to produce this sketch, titled "Scratchy Ink Thing from Beyond the Star." Drawn in pencil and ink on a sheet of 14" x 17" illustration paper, this remarkable sketch features both of these creators' most famous characters. In Excellent condition.

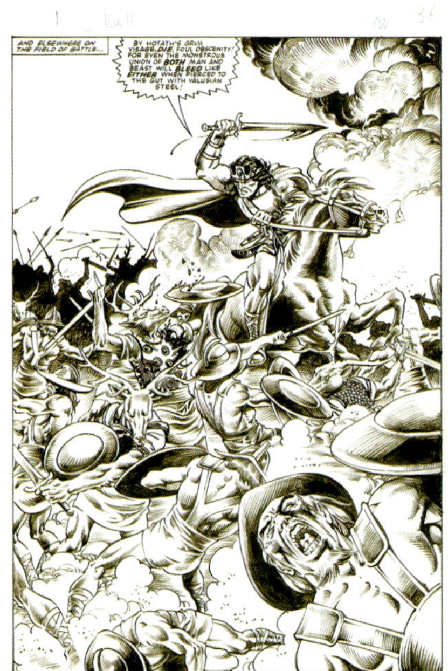

4078 John Buscema, Marie Severin, and Danny Bulanadi - Kull the Conqueror #1 Splash Page 36 Original Art (Marvel, 1982). Even before Marvel's first venture into the genre of sword and sorcery had proven successful with **Conan the Barbarian** a year earlier, Stan Lee had given Roy Thomas the green light to feature another barbarian hero from pulp writer Robert E. Howard's stable of literary characters — Kull! The King of Valusia delivers a taste of Valusian steel to an army of half men half beast warriors, in this page penciled by John Buscema and inked by Danny Bulanadi. Marie Severin also contributed with an art correction to Kull's face and a few touch-ups to the beast-men's costumes. The image area measures 10" x 15" and aside from touches of white-out on the art corrections, the art is in Excellent condition.

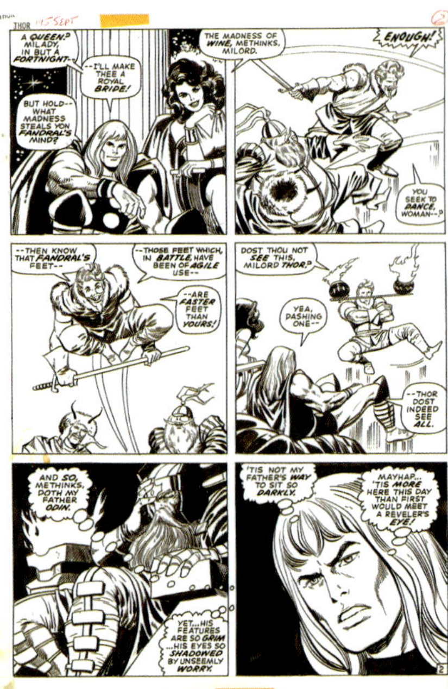

4079 John Buscema and Vince Colletta - Thor #195, pages 2 and 3 Original Art (Marvel, 1972). Most of the cast of the Mighty Thor saga star in two superb pages from "In the Shadow of Magog." The mighty Thor, fair Sif, Hogun the grim, the dashing Fandral, the voluminous Volstagg, and regal Odin - verily, the whole gang from beyond the Rainbow Bridge is here! John Buscema's talent for figure drawing is embellished with an old world flourish by Vince Colletta. The image area of each page measures 10" x 15" and aside from tape at the top and bottom of each page (outside the image area), the art is in Excellent condition.

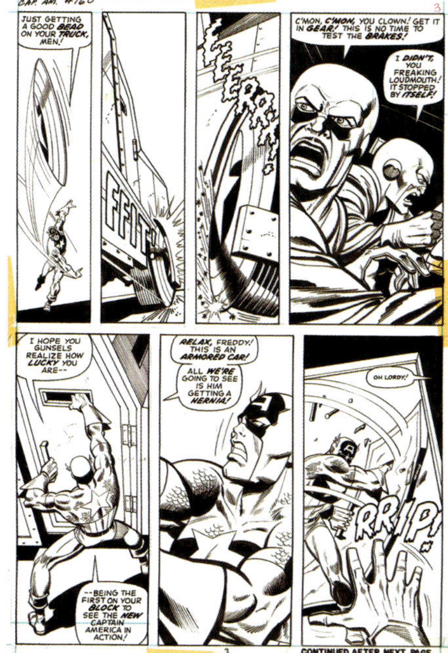

4080 Sal Buscema and Frank McLaughlin - Captain America #160, page 3 Original Art (Marvel, 1973). Rule number one: if you're a masked man and you've just stolen an armored car, don't use your first name under any circumstance! Rule number two: if you're a masked man and you've just stolen an armored car, don't try to outrun the Star-Spangled Captain America! Be the first on your block to witness the Shield-Slinger in action, as he lays down the law on a couple of career criminals, in this page from the Steve Englehart story, "Enter: Solarr!" The image area measures 10" x 15" and, aside from some tape staining on all four center edges, the work is in Very Good condition.

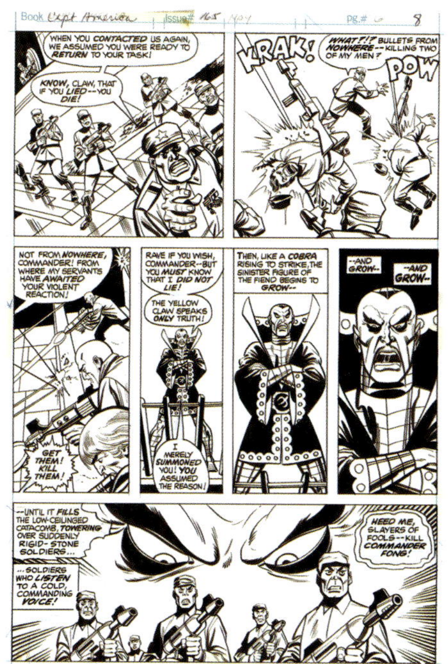

4081 Sal Buscema and Frank McLaughlin - Captain America #165, page 8 Original Art (Marvel, 1973). Commander Fong is not prepared to submit to the will of the Yellow Claw. Like a cobra rising to strike, the sinister figure of the Claw grows until it fills the low-ceilinged catacomb, towering over suddenly rigid-stone soldiers, hypnotizing them to kill their commander! Here is page 8 from "The Yellow Claw Strikes," written by Steve Englehart, which was penciled by Sal Buscema and inked by Frank McLaughlin. The art has an image area of 10" x 15" and is in Excellent condition.

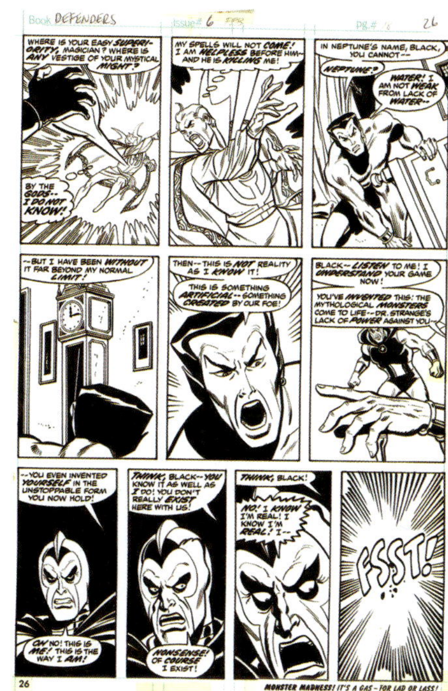

4082 Sal Buscema and Frank McLaughlin - The Defenders #6, page 18 Original Art (Marvel, 1973). He thinks, therefore he is! When Prince Namor realizes that he has been land-locked without water far beyond his normal limit, he understands that his foe, Cyrus Black, doesn't really exist! There's nothing more satisfying than watching a villain disappear to nothing! From the Steve Englehart story, "The Dreams of Death!," comes this page, which was penciled by Sal Buscema and inked by Frank McLaughlin. The art has an image area of 10" x 15", and, aside from some tape which extends into the image area, is in Excellent condition.

4083 Sal Buscema and Frank McLaughlin - The Defenders #6, page 5 Original Art (Marvel, 1973). Cyrus Black, the Devil Incarnate, has spent years studying, training himself to become a better sorcerer than Doctor Strange. His disciples attack Strange's stronghold, but face the warrior woman, Valkyrie, and the mighty Sub-Mariner! From the Steve Englehart's story, "The Dreams of Death!," comes this page, which was penciled by Sal Buscema and inked by Frank McLaughlin. The art has an image area of 10" x 15", and, aside from some light staining along the right edge, is in Very Good condition.

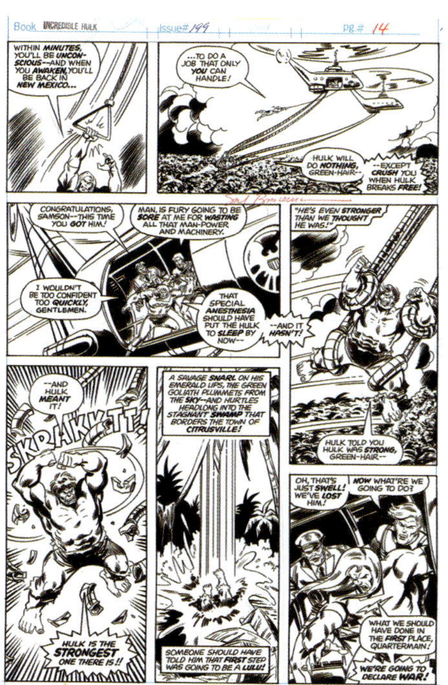

4084 Sal Buscema and Joe Staton - The Incredible Hulk #199, page 14 Original Art (Marvel, 1976). A savage snarl on his emerald lips, the Green Goliath breaks free of the bonds that Doc Samson and SHIELD have placed on him, and plummets from the sky headlong into the swamp that borders the once-placid town of Citrusville, in this page from the Len Wein story, "... and SHIELD Shall Follow!" The image area measures 10" x 15" and, aside from some blue pencil editorial markings, the work is in Excellent condition. Signed by Sal Buscema between the first and second tiers.

4085 Sal Buscema - Avengers #71 Cover Recreation Original Art (2003). The skies of Paris are filled with battling Golden and Silver Age heroes as Sal Buscema recreates his sensational Avengers vs. Invaders cover from the thriller, "Endgame." That yarn, set during World War II, featured the first appearance of the Invaders. Sal Buscema has signed his recreation at the lower left. A note penciled on the back of the page reads, "First time this cover was recreated," and is signed by Buscema's art representative and friend, Al Czarnecki. The image area of the recreation measures 9.75" x 15", and the art is in Excellent condition. O.K. Axis, here we come!

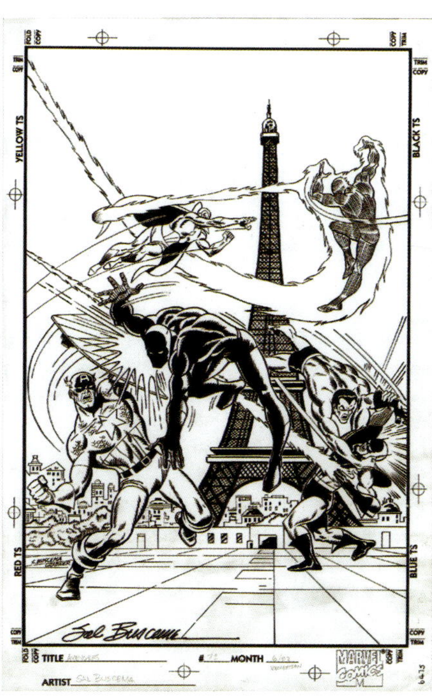

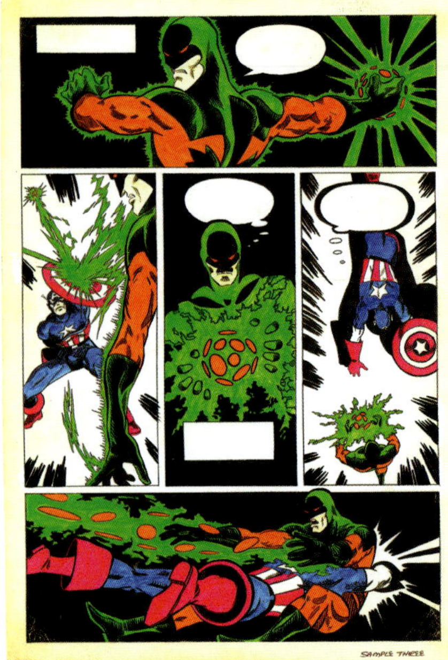

4086 John Byrne - Captain America and Vindicator Hand Colored Tryout Page Original Art (circa 1971). Here's proof that Vindicator of Alpha Flight was created years before John Byrne even joined Marvel! As Byrne explained in **The X-Men Companion**, published in 1982, "Vindicator goes back to my college days, when he was called the Sentinel, and then the Guardian... I created him in 1970 or 1971... In fact, somewhere Duffy Vohland, I think, has a badly colored page that has Vindicator battling Captain America that dates from those early days." That would put this page several years before Byrne's first published comic book work, and six or seven years before Vindicator made his first published appearance as "Weapon Alpha" in **X-Men** #109. The name Guardian, mentioned above by Byrne, later became the official name of the character when the **Alpha Flight** series began. The distinctive "Byrne cheekbones" are among the hallmarks evident on this early effort, which would have to be one of the earliest pieces of Byrne sequential art you'll find. The page has an image area of 10" x 15". Aside from paper creases in the center of the page and at the corners, the art is in Very Good condition.

4087 John Byrne - Fantastic Four Tryout, page 13 Original Art (unpublished, circa 1974). The ever-lovin' Thing plucks an extinguished Johnny Storm out of a freefall, hauling him, by the seat of his trunks, into the Fantasticar. The image area of this page measures 10" x 15", and the art is in Excellent condition. Marvel's favorite penciler from the Frozen North unleashes the mind-boggling talent that lifted him to super-star status.

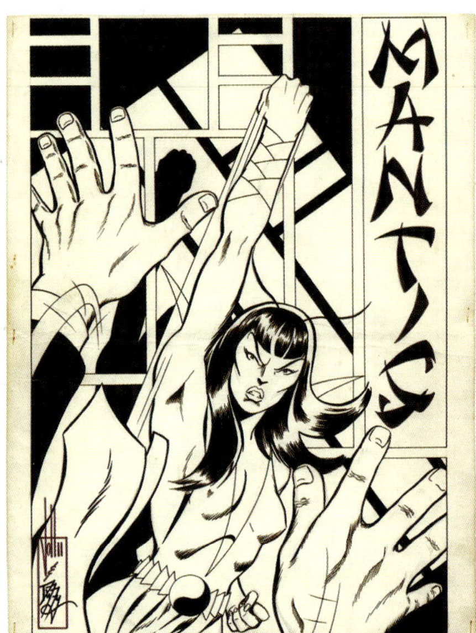

4088 John Byrne and Duffy Vohland - FOOM! #5 Back Cover Original Art (Marvel, 1974). The lucky winner of the FOOM! 1974 Irving Awards Questionnaire won this John Byrne/Duffy Vohland Mantis illustration which served as the back cover for FOOM! #5. Here is an example of very early Byrne work for Marvel, and it features a lovely lady to boot! The image area measures 10" x 15", and, aside from some slight creasing along the center, and some staple holes on the corners, the art is in Very Good condition. This lot includes the original Marvel congratulatory letter signed by FOOM! Editor, Scott Edelman, and Duffy Vohland, and a copy of **FOOM!** #5. Keep on FOOMin'!

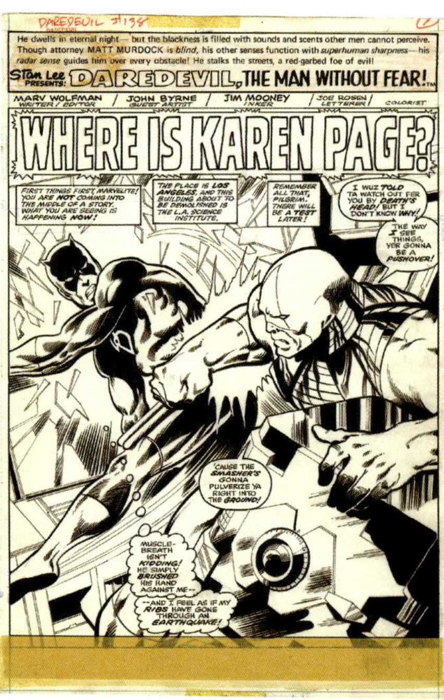

4089 John Byrne and Jim Mooney - Daredevil #139, Splash Page 1 Original Art (Marvel, 1976). The place is Los Angeles, and this building about to be demolished is the L. A. Science Institute. The Smasher simply brushed his hand against the Man Without Fear, and it feels like his ribs have gone through an earthquake! This pulverizing page is about to usher you into the Marv Wolfman story, "Where is Karen Page?," which is penciled by John Byrne, and inked by Jim Mooney. This art has an image area of 10" x 15", and, aside for a band of tape along the bottom edge, and a bit of discoloration in the indicia box at the top, is in Excellent condition. For magnificent Marvel action, look no further! *From the collection of "Mr. Ed" Lambert.*

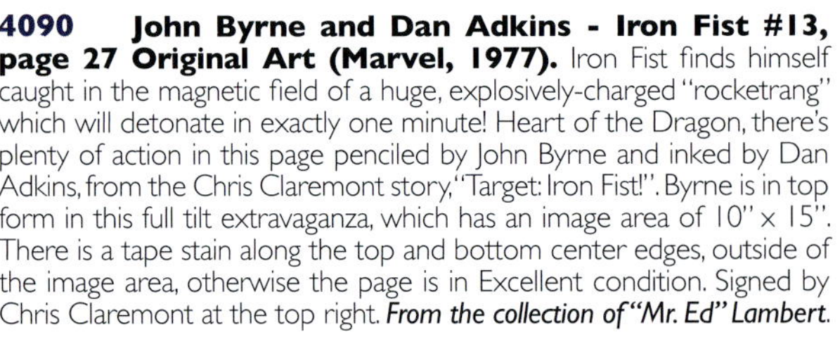

4090 John Byrne and Dan Adkins - Iron Fist #13, page 27 Original Art (Marvel, 1977). Iron Fist finds himself caught in the magnetic field of a huge, explosively-charged "rocketrang" which will detonate in exactly one minute! Heart of the Dragon, there's plenty of action in this page penciled by John Byrne and inked by Dan Adkins, from the Chris Claremont story, "Target: Iron Fist!". Byrne is in top form in this full tilt extravaganza, which has an image area of 10" x 15". There is a tape stain along the top and bottom center edges, outside of the image area, otherwise the page is in Excellent condition. Signed by Chris Claremont at the top right. *From the collection of "Mr. Ed" Lambert.*

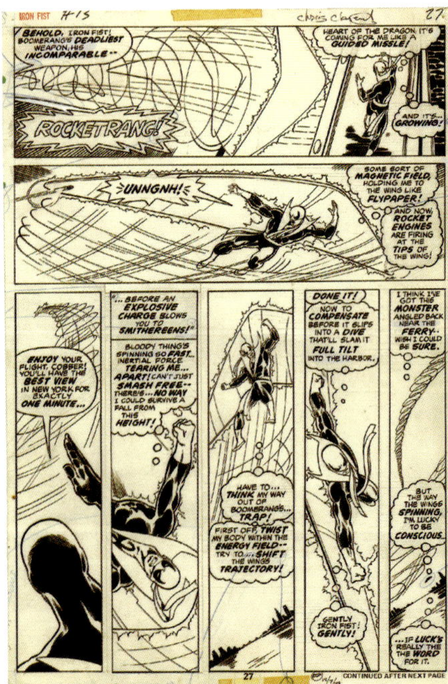

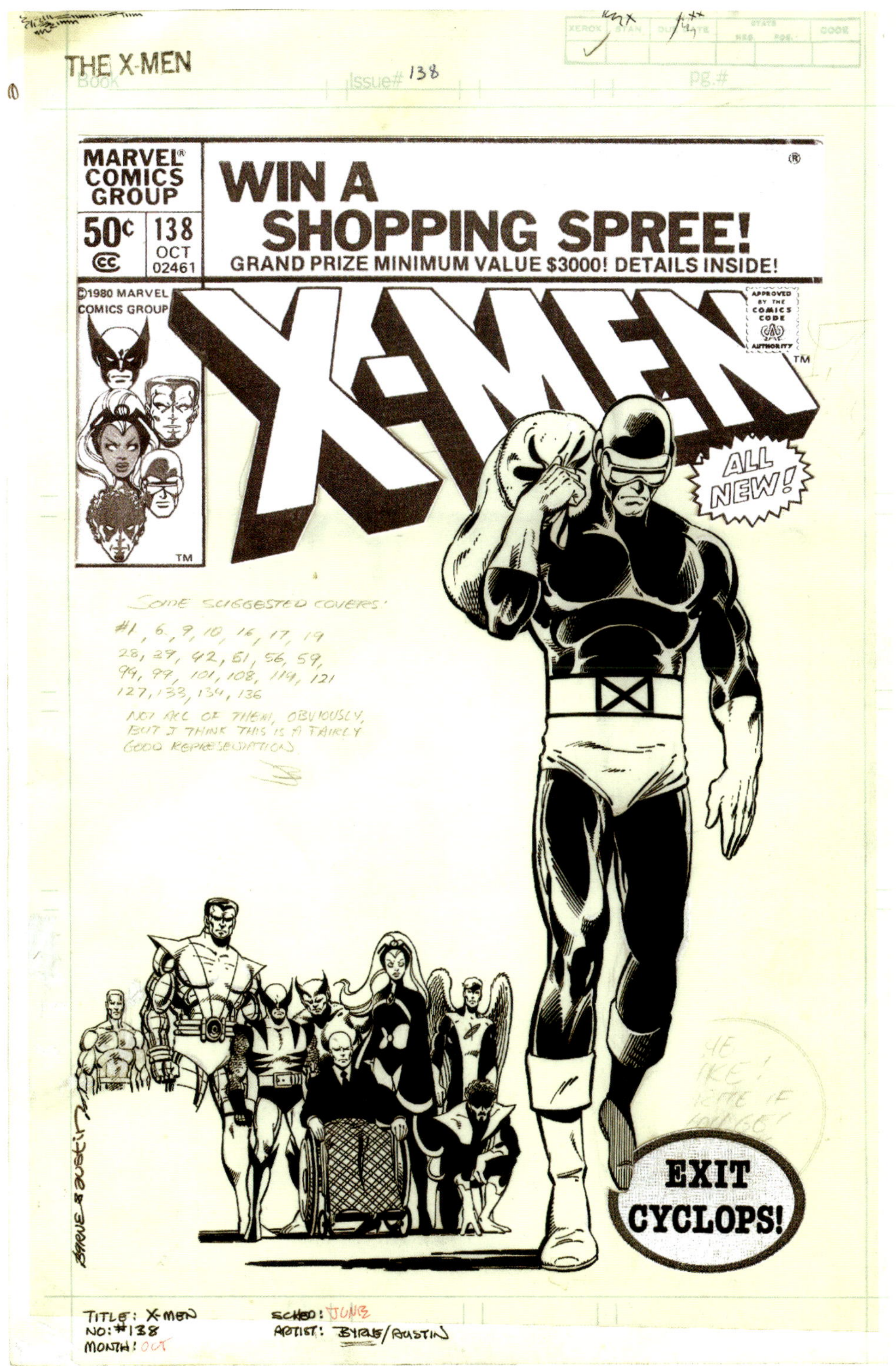

4091 **John Byrne and Terry Austin - X-Men #138 Cover Original Art (Marvel, 1980).** This cover packed a powerful emotional punch for every Marvel fan who saw it, as it came on the heels of the shocking death of Jean Grey in the previous issue. Scott Summers, aka Cyclops, opts to take a leave of absence from the X-Men in the story, but not before the readers share his poignant reminiscence about the X-Men's early years and Scott's love for Jean. In addition to its significance in terms of the storyline, this piece is notable for depicting all of the surviving original X-Men (Angel, Beast and Iceman in addition to Cyclops) along with the new team. In the final art, the covers of numerous past issues of **X-Men** were printed behind the figures, adding to the sense of history communicated in the story. You can see John Byrne's cover suggestions in pencil, just above the figures of Professor X and company. A little-known aspect of the issue's history is that in the original version of #137 Jean Grey did not die, and Byrne actually penciled a version of #138 that began with a romantic interlude between Jean and Scott. But according to lore, Marvel editor Jim Shooter decreed that #137 had to end with Jean being punished for her crimes, which resulted in the end of #137 and the beginning of #138 being re-drawn. And the rest is comic book history. Now, the issue stands as a watershed moment in the history of the new X-Men, as the Phoenix saga which had dominated the book for several years was brought to a close, and a new era began in this story, with young Kitty Pryde arriving at Professor Xavier's school to begin her tutelage as an X-Man. This image represents Byrne and Terry Austin at their best, and their best was powerful stuff indeed! The image area measures 10" x 15" and the work is in Excellent condition. The logo, masthead, and title type are recent photocopy replacement art. A copy of the published comic is included with this lot. ***From the collection of "Mr. Ed" Lambert.***

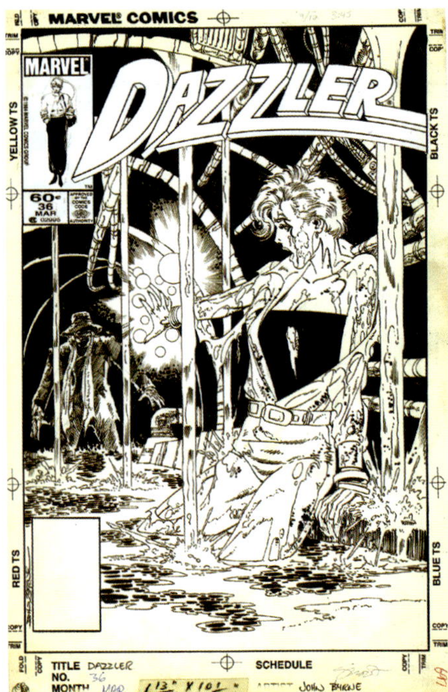

4092 John Byrne - Dazzler #36 Cover Original Art (Marvel, 1985). John Byrne was the first artist to draw the Dazzler (in the pages of **X-Men**) but this cover was his only contribution to the character's own title (except for inking the cover of #37). We'd say the ol' Byrne magic is exactly what that title was missing all along! Also, the well-traveled Marvel villain known as the Tatterdemalion has rarely looked as menacing as in this sewer scene. The cover has an image area of 10" x 15", and the art is in Excellent condition.

4093 John Byrne - Power Man and Iron Fist #114 Cover Original Art (Marvel, 1985). An exhausted white-collar type named Gordy is allegedly very, very dangerous. John Byrne has created an intriguing "cover hook" — what makes this guy so dangerous? And who but Marvel would dare to put out a cover that doesn't feature the title characters? The image area is 10" x 15", in Excellent condition. Byrne signed the art in the lower left.

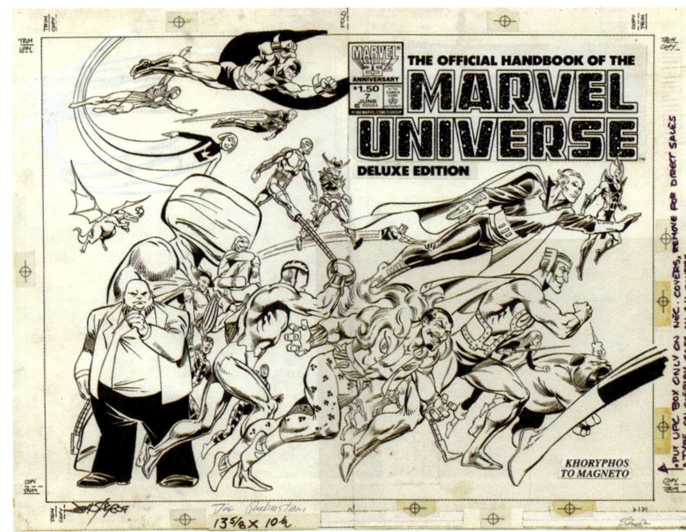

4094 John Byrne and Joe Rubinstein: The Official Handbook of the Marvel Universe Deluxe Edition #7 Wraparound Cover Original Art (Marvel, 1985). The Deluxe Edition of this series improved upon the original in nearly every way, including the assignment of Marvel's most popular artist, John Byrne, to draw the wraparound covers! The covers of each issue were designed to connect together (that's why Mister Fantastic's foot is seen here though the character wasn't featured till the following issue), and indeed, more than one young fan taped them all together to decorate his bedroom back in the day. We're struck by the fact that this issue's cover is the best of them all when it comes to ***villains***! You can't beat A-list evildoers Kingpin, Magneto, Loki, Kraven the Hunter, Klaw, and the Mad Thinker. They're joined by second-tier scofflaws Killer Shrike, Kurse, the Living Laser, Madcap, Maelstrom, and Lightmaster. The do-gooders include Machine Man, Madrox the Multiple Man, Longshot, Lightspeed (from the group Power Pack), the Inhuman Lockjaw, and three members of the X-Men family in Magik (aka Illyana Rasputin), Magma, and Lockheed. The image area measures 19.5" x 15," and, aside from a very light stain at the upper left and bottom right corners, the condition of the art is Excellent. Includes the original logo and masthead paste-ups. Signed by John Byrne and Joe Rubinstein at the bottom left edge.

4095 John Byrne and Keith Williams - Action Comics #591, page 5 Original Art (DC, 1987). How the H-E-double-hockey-sticks can Superman and Superboy be together in the same story? And for that matter, how can there ***be*** a Superboy since the **Crisis** revamping told readers that the Man of Steel didn't become a superhero till he was a grown-up? Superboy's pal Pete Ross is as confused as anybody in this page from the story "Superman vs. Superboy: Past Imperfect." Naturally, the always-creative writer and artist John Byrne managed to answer all of these questions. Byrne never let exposition get in the way of action and telling a good story, as this dramatic page illustrates. The page has an image area of 10" x 15", and the art is in Excellent condition. John Byrne has signed the page in panel three.

4096 John Byrne and Keith Williams - Action Comics #591, page 18 Original Art (DC, 1987). Superman has fought just about everyone over the years, but he never had to fight Superboy, Pa Kent and Krypto all in the course of a couple of pages! The former two are seen on this irresistible John Byrne page. It's part of a "Past Imperfect" story which explains how Superboy ties into post-**Crisis** DC continuity. John Byrne signed the art in panel three. The image area of this page measures 10" x 15" and the art is in Excellent condition.

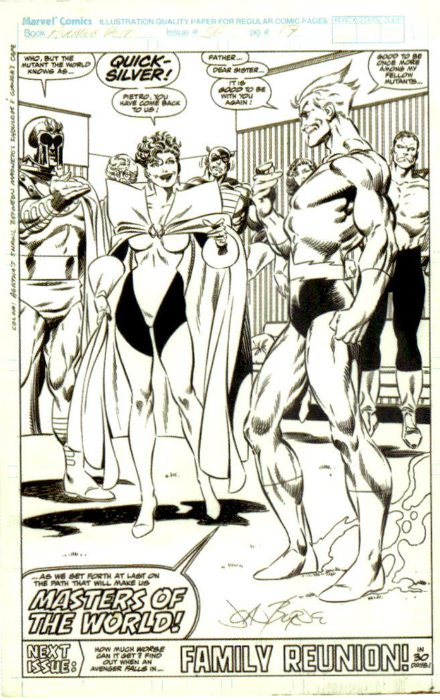

4097 John Byrne and Paul Ryan - Avengers West Coast #56, Splash Page 17 Original Art (Marvel, 1990). Like her brother, Quicksilver, The Scarlet Witch was first seen as a member of The Brotherhood of Evil Mutants, an alliance put together by Magneto for purposes of antagonizing the X-Men. History repeats itself in this final splash to John Byrne's story, "Darker Than Scarlet," as Magneto welcomes Quicksilver back amongst his fellow mutants, before an audience consisting of U.S. Agent, Wonder Man, and Agatha Harkness. The image area measures 10" x 15" and the condition is Excellent. Signed by John Byrne at the bottom.

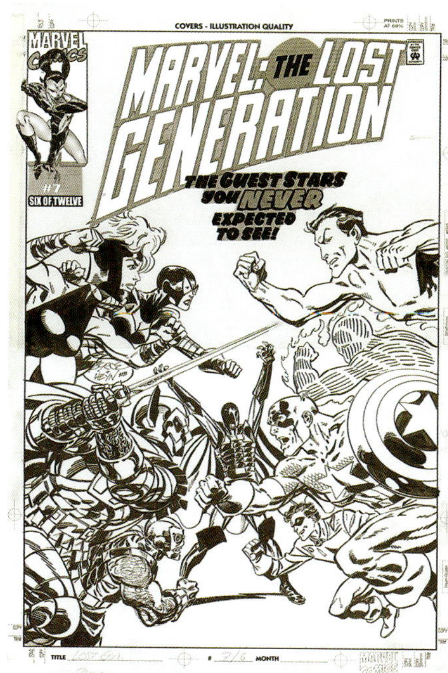

4098 John Byrne - Marvel: The Lost Generation #7 Cover Original Art (Marvel, 2001). John Byrne and Roger Stern's chance-taking 12-issue maxi-series, **Marvel: The Lost Generation**, was created with supreme care, with smart dialogue and great characterization. The title refers to Marvel's "lost generation" of Cold-War-era heroes — from the disappearance of Captain America at the end of World War II to just before Reed Richards and company became the Fantastic Four. The heroes are "lost" because most of them were created specifically for this series. This classically-designed cover art features Prince Namor, Captain America, the Human Torch and Bucky, as well as new characters such as Pixie, Knight Templar, Katyusha, Vulcan, and Nocturne. As for the signature "Byrne and Heyn": longtime Byrne enthusiasts will recall that one Bjorn Heyn is credited with inking JB's pencils now and then. Just rearrange the letters in "Bjorn Heyn," and you'll see that Mr. Byrne, a skilled inker in his own right, was just having a bit of fun with his legion of loyal fans. With an image area of 10" x 15," this art is in Excellent condition. The masthead is a recent photocopy replacement.

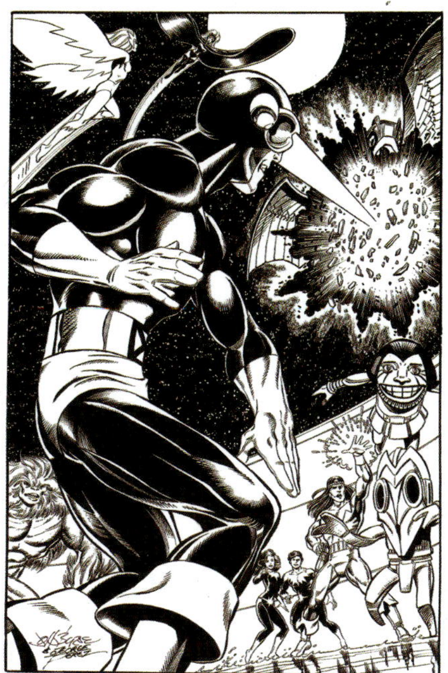

4099 John Byrne and George Perez - John Byrne X-Men Portfolio, X-Men and Alpha Flight Pin-Up Page Original Art (1983-2003). John Byrne and George Perez have both spoken admiringly of each other's work — here's a rare opportunity to get a collaboration between the two greats. This original piece was penciled by Byrne for the X-Men portfolio produced by Editions Deese, and appeared as plate 7 of the portfolio reproduced directly from Byrne's pencils. Subsequently, Perez inked the piece in 2003. A note detailing the history of the piece as noted above is written on the back of the page, signed by Byrne and dated April 15, 2004. A very sexy Aurora is joined by her brother Northstar as well as Alpha Flight mates Shaman, Sasquatch, and Snowbird, and X-Men Cyclops and Storm. It's a team-up not to be missed, and the same holds true for Byrne and Perez, two of the all-time fan favorites! The image area of the drawing measures 10.5" x 16" and the art is in Excellent condition.

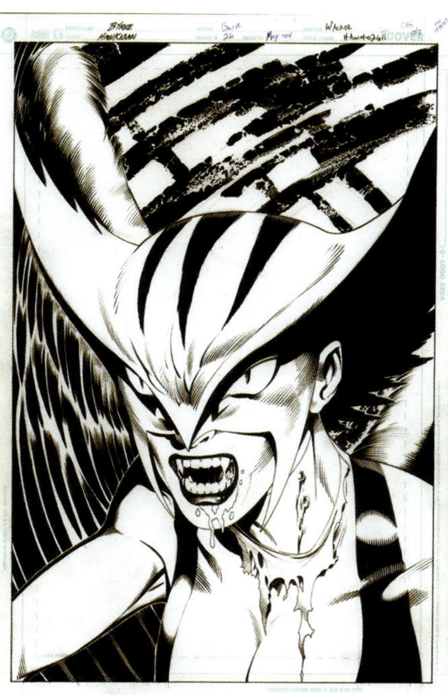

4100 John Byrne and Michael Bair - Hawkman #26 Cover Original Art, Group of 2 (DC, 2004). Ever a trailblazer on the comics landscape, John Byrne, who last graced the feathers of Hawkman and Hawkwoman in **Action Comics**, returns as the artist of this fill-in issue. Byrne goes right for the jugular in this solid take on a vampire bitten Hawkwoman, an incarnation of Kendra that is deadly earnest. The art has an image area which measures approximately 10" x 15" and the condition is Excellent. This lot also include Byrne's original cover sketch in pencil (10" x 15"), which has been signed by John Byrne.

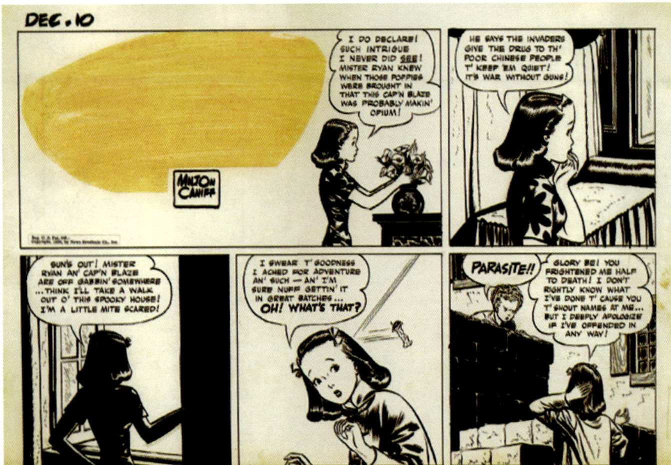

4101 Milton Caniff - Terry and the Pirates Partial Sunday Comic Strip Original Art, dated 12-10-39 (News Syndicate, 1939). Milton Caniff 's cast of characters for *Terry and the Pirates* has seldom been matched. Even with its exotic locales, bizarre villains, and luscious women, Caniff respected his players, and kept the stories believable. Intrigue and adventure aside, April Kane still has to deal with a disgruntled neighbor, in this upper portion of a Sunday from 1939. The image area measures 19" x 13". There is a glue stain from a missing logo photostat in the first frame, some slight aging along the extreme edges, and some light staining along the right edge, otherwise the art is in Excellent condition.

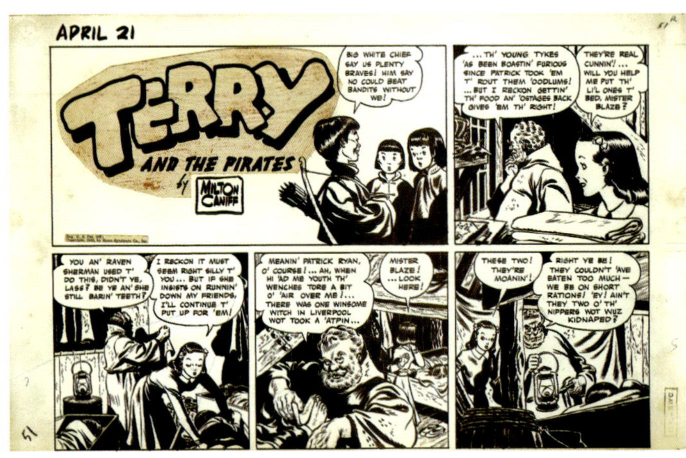

4102 Milton Caniff - Terry and the Pirates Partial Sunday Comic Strip Original Art, dated 4-21-40 (News Syndicate, 1940). Captain Blaze and April Kane prepare the children for bed, in the upper two tiers of this *Terry and the Pirates* Sunday from 1940. Milton Caniff suffuses this subtle scenario with a caring atmosphere. The image area measures of 19" x 12.5", and the art is in Excellent condition.

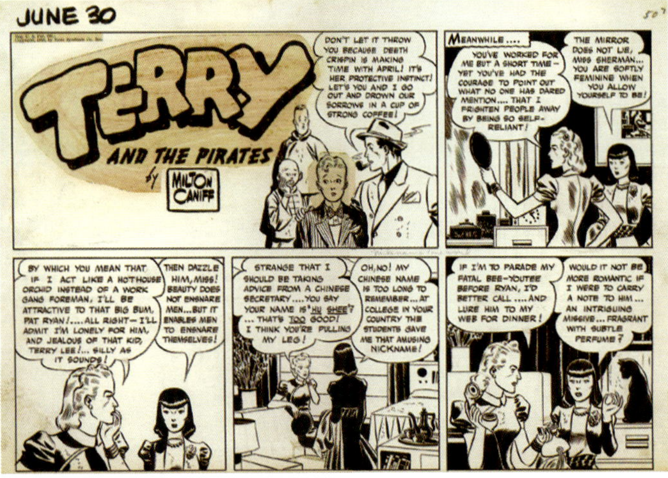

4103 Milton Caniff - Terry and the Pirates Partial Sunday Comic Strip Original Art, dated 6-30-40 (News Syndicate, 1940). The demure Chinese secretary, Hu Shee, convinces Miss Sherman to allow herself to be more feminine to attract "that big bum," Jim Ryan, in this upper portion of a Sunday strip from 1940. Wonderful work by the lighting and composition master, Milt Caniff — and some lovely ladies, too! The image area measures 19" x 13". There is a paste-over correction in the first panel, the logo photostat has yellowed, and you'll find some light smudging at the bottom left corner, otherwise the art is in Excellent condition.

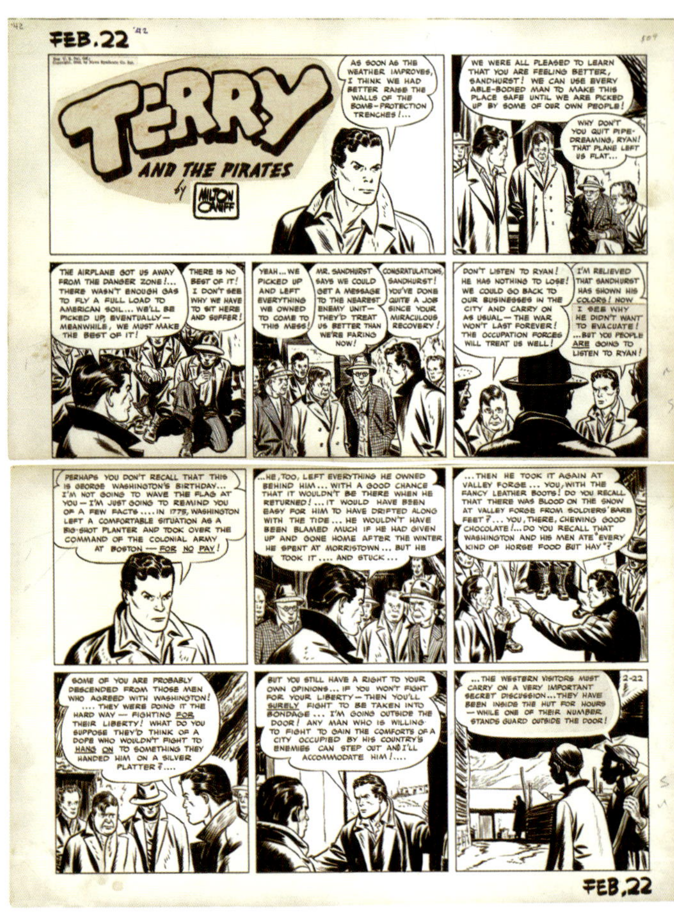

4104 Milton Caniff - Terry and the Pirates Sunday Comic Strip Original Art, dated 2-22-42 (Chicago Tribune, 1942). Pat Ryan tries to bolster his war-weary comrades' ***e'sprit de corps*** by contrasting their troubles with the tremendous sacrifices George Washington made on behalf of America — few cartoonists could wave the flag as well as Milton Caniff! The image area of the strip measures 19" x 26" and the strip was cut between panel tiers two and three. The title stat shows mild signs of aging and glue staining; otherwise the art is in Excellent condition.

4105 Art Capello - Just Married #107 Cover Original Art (Charlton, 1975). Their marriage is falling apart, why can't Carl see what's happening? Family ties are strangling two lovers' marriage vows, proving that the course set for this love story is not running smoothly. From the Bronze Age of Charlton Comics' romance titles, comes this lushly inked Pop Art melodrama drawn by Art Capello. The cover has a 10" x 15" image area which includes the original title logo paste-up. There is a stain from a missing indicia paste-up at the upper left, otherwise this work is in Excellent condition. A loving addition to your collection, not to be missed!

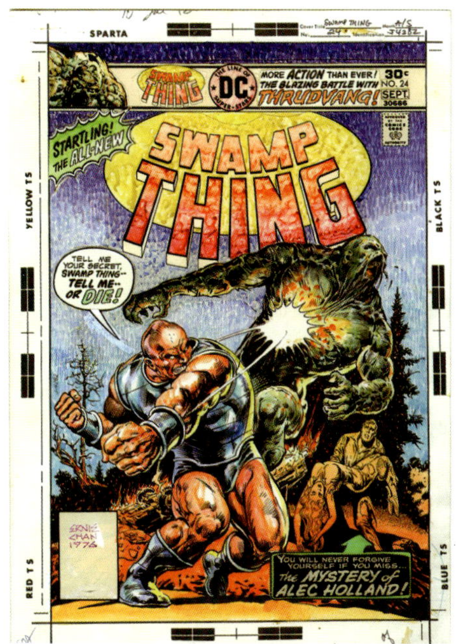

4106 Ernie Chan - Swamp Thing #24 Cover Hand Colored By the Artist Original Art (DC, 1976). More action than ever before — a blazing battle between the creature formerly known as Alec Holland, and Thrudvang, the Earth-Master, covers this 24th and final issue, with art by Ernie Chan! The image area measures 10" x 15" and the art is in Excellent condition. This muck-encrusted slug-fest comes complete with all original logo, masthead, and title type, and is signed by Ernie Chan at the lower left.

4107 Ernie Chan and Fred Carrillo - Swamp Thing #24, pages 8 and 9 Original Art (DC, 1976). He's unpredictable, his disposition is unstable, he's easily antagonized, and his potential for destruction is truly immense! He's Thrudvang and he's on a berserk rampage, in this earth-shaking, metal-twisting splash page from the final issue of the original **Swamp Thing** series. These two pages from the story, "The Earth Below," written by Len Wein, have a combined image area of 21" x 15". There are some editorial markings in blue pen, and a tape stain at the top of each page (outside of the image area), otherwise the art is in Excellent condition.

4108 Howard Chaykin and Bernie Wrightson - Eerie #72, pages 40 and 44 Original Art (Warren, 1976). Government agent, Reuben Youngblood, gets an undercover assignment that is way over his head, in these two pages from the Budd Lewis story, "Reuben Youngblood: Private Eye!: Beware The Scarlet Combine". Howard Chaykin and Bernie Wrightson work together to enliven this bewitching tale of booze and blood-suckers. The image area of each page measures 10.5" x 15". In pen and ink with marker gray tones, the word and type balloons are attached to an acetate overlay. There is some aging apparent in the type and word balloons, otherwise the pages are in Excellent condition.

4109 Western Publishing Artist - Chip 'n' Dale #23 Cover Original Art (Gold Key, 1973). When it rains it pours! Rodent rowdy, Chip, throws a little cold water on Dale, in this splashy cover illustration. The chipmunk pair were penciled, and inked by a Western Publishing artist, and then some enterprising painter carried this illustration a step further with watercolor! The image area measures 11" x 15.5" and the art is in Excellent condition. Includes a copy of **Chip 'n' Dale** #23.

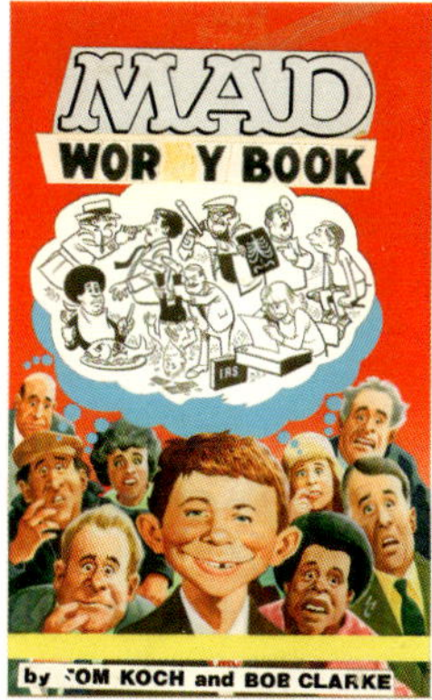

4110 Bob Clarke - The Mad Worry Book #2 Cover Original Art (Warner Books, 1980). Life is filled with threats, fears, and anxieties, and if you think you have good reason to worry — you're wrong! There are countless reasons you don't know about and this book is here to clue you in on 'em! Bob Clarke is responsible for painting this illustration which graced the cover of the second **The Mad Worry Book**, published in 1980. The art is painted on a sheet of 9" x 14.5" illustration board, and includes the logo and title type, which has been mounted onto a separate sheet of acetate. Although there is a missing letter in the title type, which has left a glue stain residue, the art is in Excellent condition. Includes a copy of **The Mad Worry Book** #2.

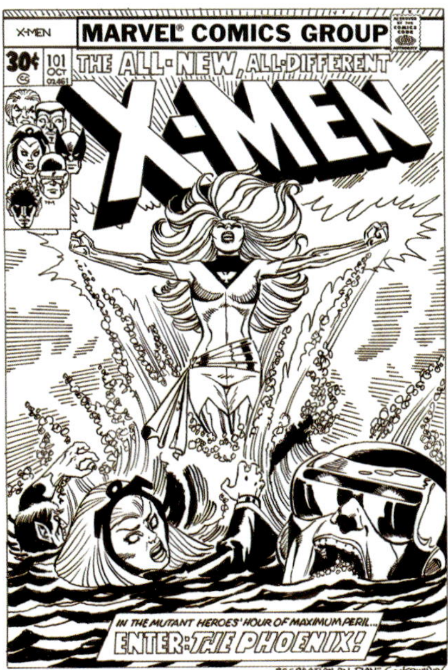

4111 Dave Cockrum - X-Men #101 Cover Recreation Original Art (2001). In the era of modern comics, few issues have had more industry-wide impact than that of **X-Men** #101. This landmark issue debuted Jean Grey's new incarnation in "Enter: The Phoenix!" Dave Cockrum's sensational talent for character and costume design is showcased in this dynamic recreation. The piece has an image area of 10" x 15" and the art is in Excellent condition. Dave Cockrum has signed and dated the page at the lower right. Excelsior!

4112 Gene Colan and Dick Ayers - Captain America #130, page 5 Original Art (Marvel, 1970). A sleepy little college town is the perfect place for Steve Rogers quit worrying about his past, present, or future. It's also a perfect place for Modok to fuel the already growing dissent amongst the student body, and stir up trouble! The Star-Spangled Avenger is in his civvies, although Gene Colan and Dick Ayers still deliver with high-octane excitement this page from the Stan Lee story, "Up Against the Wall!" The image area of this Bronze Age beauty measures 10" x 15", and aside from a few mild printer's oil stains, the art is in Excellent condition.

4113 Gene Colan and Dick Ayers - Captain America #130, page 7 Original Art (Marvel, 1970). When these college students riot, they don't kid around! Here's where Captain America should step in and make like a swingin' hero, but how does he decide whose side to take? More tense action and Mighty Marvel angst awaits you in this seventh page from Stan Lee's story, "Up Against the Wall!" Gene Colan takes charge, and Dick Ayers follows suit, in this thrilling page. The image area measures 10" x 15", and aside from some minor printer's oil stains, the art is in Very Good condition.

4114 Gene Colan and Dick Ayers - Captain America #130, page 20 Original Art (Marvel, 1970). The Hood's plan to ensnare the Shield-Slinger in his nefarious propaganda scheme falls through, and Batroc and his cohorts make their escape via a blast of Whirlwind, in this final page to Stan Lee's story, "Up Against the Wall!" The action comes fast and furious via penciler Gene Colan and inker Dick Ayers! The image area of the page is 10" x 15", and aside from some minor printer's oil stains, the art is in Very Good condition.

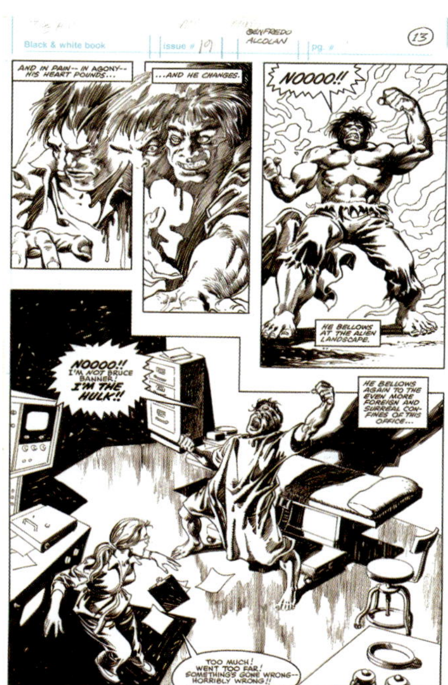

4115 Gene Colan and Alfredo Alcala - The Hulk Magazine #19, page 13 Original Art (Marvel, 1980). In pain and agony, his heart pounding, Bruce Banner transforms once again into Marvel's Mighty Man-Brute — Gene Colan and Alfredo Alcala style! A desperate search for a cure unleashes the power of the rampaging Hulk on a helpless New York City in this page from the story, "Master Mind," written by Doug Moench. The image area measures 10" x 15", and the condition is Excellent condition.

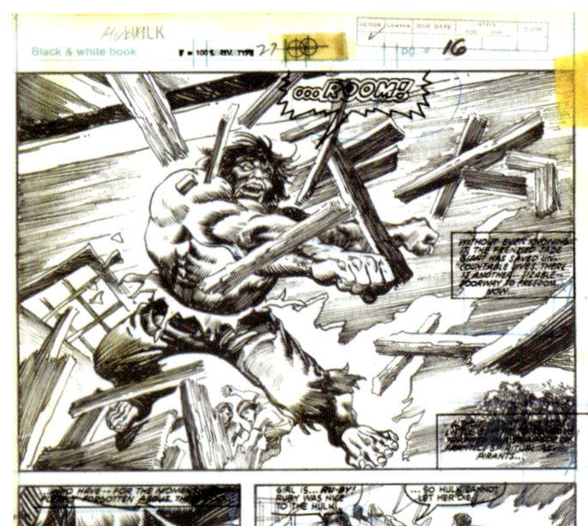

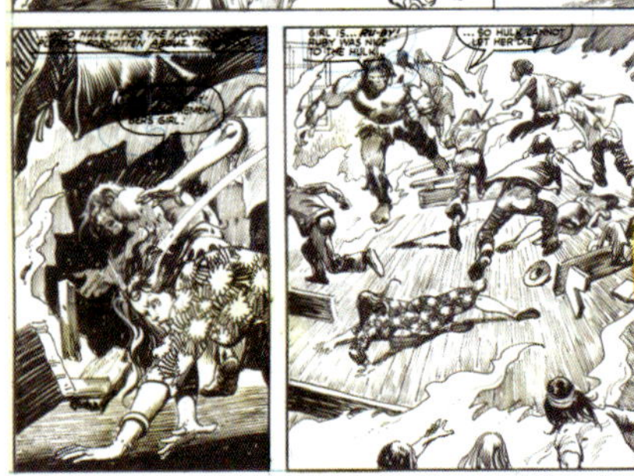

4116 Gene Colan and Dave Simons - The Rampaging Hulk #27, page 16 Original Art (Marvel, 1981). The frenzied jade giant known as the Hulk does what he does best - smash - in this page from Lora Byrne's story, "Feudin'". This final issue of the ongoing larger formatted magazine, **The Hulk**, returned once again to black and white interiors, allowing Gene Colan and Dave Simons' art to really sparkle. The type and word balloons have been inked onto a separate sheet of vellum paper, allowing you an unobstructed view of the Hulk in all his destructive glory! The image area measures 10.5" x 15", and the condition is Excellent.

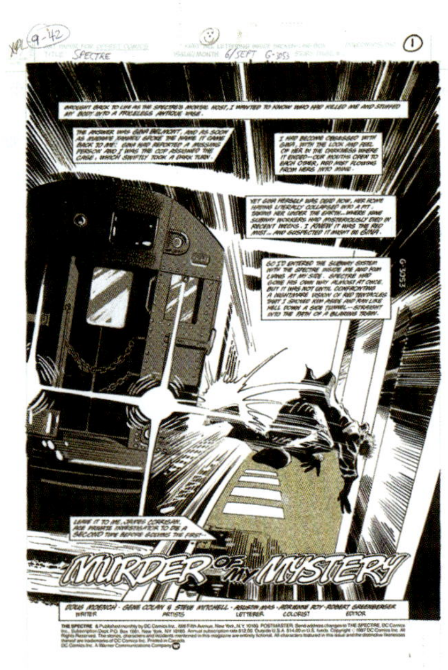

4117 Gene Colan and Steve Mitchell - The Spectre #6, Complete 23-page Story "Murder of My Mystery" Original Art (DC, 1987). Ace private investigator, James Corrigan, seeks to find the person who killed him and stuffed his body into a priceless antique vase, in this 23-pager, penciled by Gene Colan and inked by Steve Mitchell. Another "spook-tacular" Spectre story! The image area of each page measures 10" x 15" and the art is in Excellent condition.

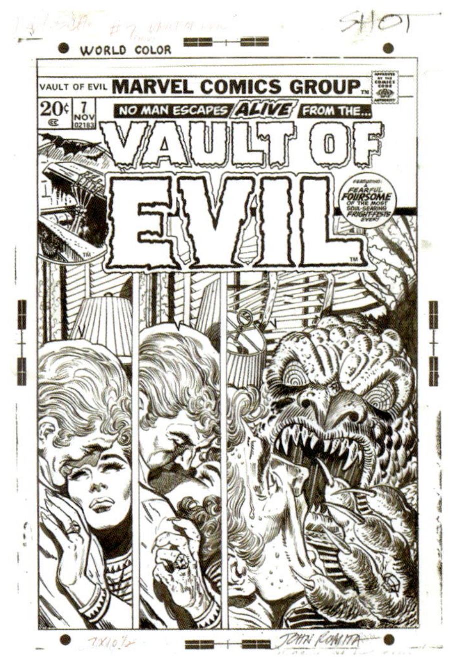

4118 Ernie Colon and John Romita Sr. (attributed) - Vault of Evil #7 Cover Original Art (Marvel, 1973). Here's a scene you've never seen in any romance comic! This fearful cover is one of the most soul-searing fright-fests ever, enough to make the hairs on the back of your head stand on end. Brought to you by Ernie Colon and John Romita, Sr., the image area measures 10" x 15". There is some slight scattered staining, otherwise the art is in Excellent condition. Includes the original masthead photostats. Signed by John Romita Sr.

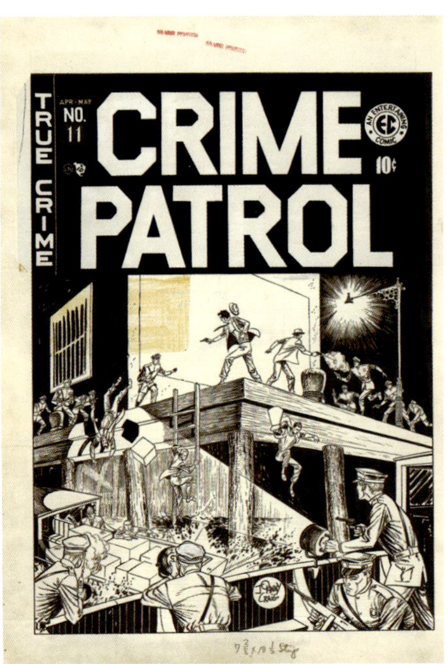

4119 Johnny Craig - Crime Patrol #11 Cover Original Art (EC, 1949). Johnny Craig offered up a sensational front row seat to a waterfront shootout on his panoramic tableau for **Crime Patrol** #11. Craig received the supreme compliment from fellow EC editor/writer artist Al Feldstein, "I always *admired* Johnny's work. He was the *ultimate* comic artist as far as I was concerned." A meticulous craftsman, Johnny Craig was nothing less than a perfectionist. The image area of this thriller measures 13.5" x 19". Aside from a missing caption box at the center left (which read "Real stories from police records"), the art is in Excellent condition.

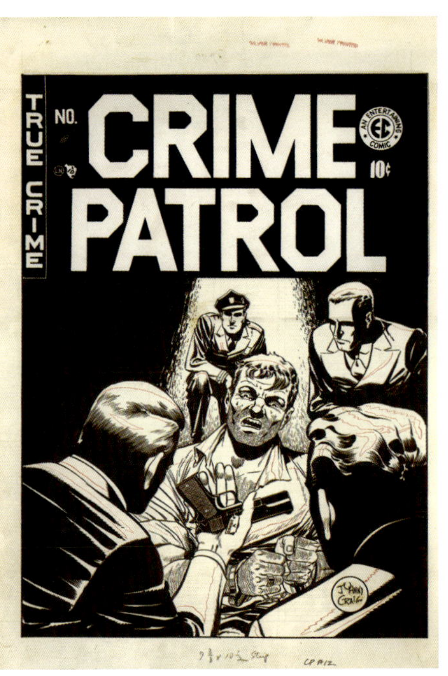

4120 Johnny Craig - Crime Patrol #12 Cover Original Art (EC, 1949). Few artists could capture a sweaty, fearful expression as convincingly as Johnny Craig — limning the peak moment of fear and loathing was one of Craig's hallmarks. Regarding Craig's renowned precision, William Gaines told **The Comics Journal**, "He would take an entire month to write and draw one story. It was just his nature. A lot of guys in comics bat stuff out; Johnny never did. Everything had to be perfect." The image area of this interrogation scene measures 13.5" x 19". Aside from a missing caption box at the center left (which read "Real stories from police records"), and a few missing elements such as the issue number, and a paste-over correction in Craig's signature circle, the art is in Excellent condition. A copy of the comic book is included in this lot.

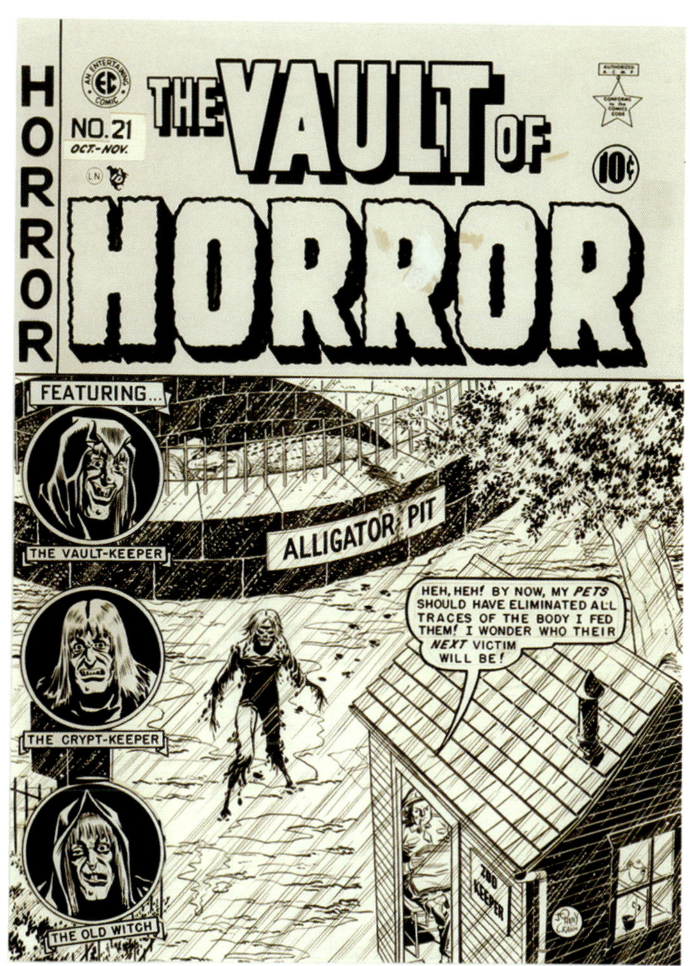

4121 Johnny Craig - Vault of Horror #21 Cover Original Art (EC, 1951). With his heart-stopping ability to create quiet, mounting terror, Johnny Craig was tapped by Bill Gaines to create the first cover of **Vault of Horror**, and every ensuing issue through the end of the run nearly five years later. In this particularly grisly cover by Johnny Craig, the remains of a psychotic zoo keeper's victim have emerged from an alligator pit to exact retribution. "He did some of our best covers," Gaines recalled. "Including the infamous severed head cover, which may be the most famous cover ever in comics, and certainly the only one ever to be the focus of an inquiry before the United States Senate." A slow, meticulous craftsman, in a career that spanned four decades, that Craig's relatively small body of work has been influential and well-remembered is testimony to his skill. The image area of this horrific masterpiece measures 13" x 18.5", and, aside from some light staining on the original logo stat, the art is in Excellent condition.

4122 Roy Crane and Hank Schlensker - Buz Sawyer Daily Comic Strip Original Art, Group of 8 (King Features Syndicate, 1976-78). *Buz Sawyer* is a powerful testament to the genius of Roy Crane, a master of the action-adventure comic strip. Crane's direct, simple style, and crisp, detailed line work, is accented by duotone to create depth of perspective, and new dimensions to lighting. Included are dailies from 5-24-76, 6-5-76, 1-3-77, 1-12-78, 1-16-78, 1-18-78, 1-19-78, and 2-6-78. This strips are signed Roy Crane, but assistant Hank Schlensker took most of the art responsibility for the strip after 1970. The strips have an image area of 15" x 4.75" and average in Excellent condition.

4123 Nicola Cuti - Captain Cosmos #0 Cover Original Art (Hamilton Comics, 1994). Many people know two-time Ray Bradbury Award of Excellence winner, Nicola Cuti, as co-creator of **E-Man**, and from his writing for such comics as **Creepy**, **Eerie**, and **Vampirella**. But he is also a talented artist. Here he paints the cover to the "ashcan" issue of his retro science fiction comic book, **Captain Cosmos**. This comic cover features the good Captain, based on Cuti himself, and was produced to be part of a proposed TV show in the tradition of the great TV programs of the 1950s. This issue includes a great black and white space opera story, titled " Never Leave Me," and discusses the format of the proposed TV series. The art has an image area of 16" x 20" and is in Excellent condition.

4124 Geof Darrow - Matrix Tattoo Illustration Original Art (undated). Damn! Those torpedoes! Evocative artist, Geof Darrow was credited as conceptual designer on all three "Matrix" movies. He has also contributed to both volumes of **The Matrix** comics, a series of short "Matrix" inspired comic stories. Darrow drops a couple of bombshells in this simply designed tattoo illustration. The image area measures 6" x 8" and the work is in Excellent condition. The image area was signed by Geof Darrow.

4125 Alan Davis - Batman and the Outsiders #22 Cover Original Art (DC, 1985). Batman, Black Lightning, Geo-Force, Katana, and Metamorpho face the hard vacuum of space, after a blast rips a hole in the JLA satellite, in this dramatic cover illustration by Alan Davis. This issue of **Batman and the Outsiders** concluded Outsider Halo's origin and brought top-notch Davis on as the artist. Covering the interior story, "The Truth About Halo, Part 3: What She Is and How She Came to Be," written by Mike W. Barr, Davis pencils and inks both the cover and the interior pages. The image area measures 10" x 15", and the condition is Excellent. The image of Halo has been photocopied onto a separate acetate overlay (not original art).

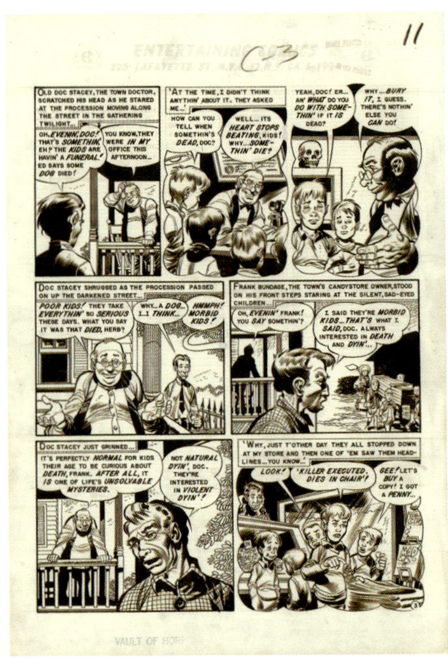

4126 Jack Davis - Vault of Horror #33, page 3 Original Art (EC, 1953). Jack Davis detailed this chilling page about a gang of kids' morbid fascination with crime and punishment. The tykes' mind-set seems to bother Frank Bundage, the local candystore owner who questions the gang's reading habits. Check out the comics rack shown in the final panel. There are copies of **Mad** and **Tales from the Crypt** on display, next to the newspaper. While the yarn was about the kids' own version of justice and capital punishment for a "crime," in a way this page foreshadows EC's own future troubles with the Senate Investigation, distributors, and the Comics Code Authority! The image area of the art is 13" x 18", and the art is in Excellent condition.

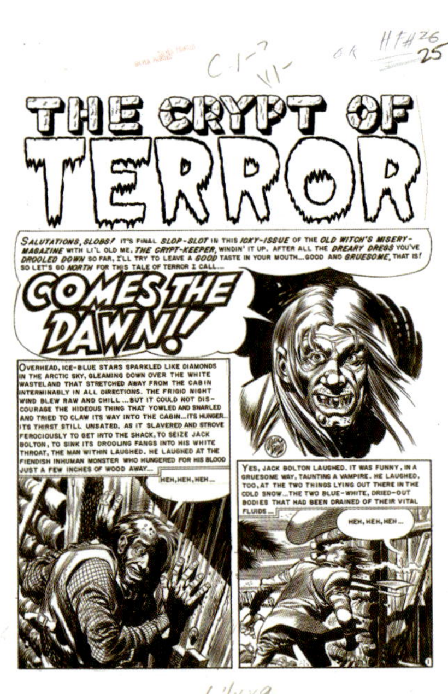

4127 Jack Davis - Haunt of Fear #26 Complete 7-page Story "Comes the Dawn!" Original Art (EC, 1954). This creepy high-concept vampire tale bears the unmistakable mark of EC stalwart Jack Davis, whose lushly detailed ink lines carve out a tale of terror to tingle the senses. A trio of prospectors head to the North Pole to look for uranium — they find a rich vein, but they also find a vampire. Narrator Jack decides to hoodwink his two buddies and claim it all for himself, but his plan goes south when he realizes just how far north he is... A classic even among the EC pantheon, this would make a great addition to any collection. The image area of each page measures 13" x 18" and the art is in Excellent condition.

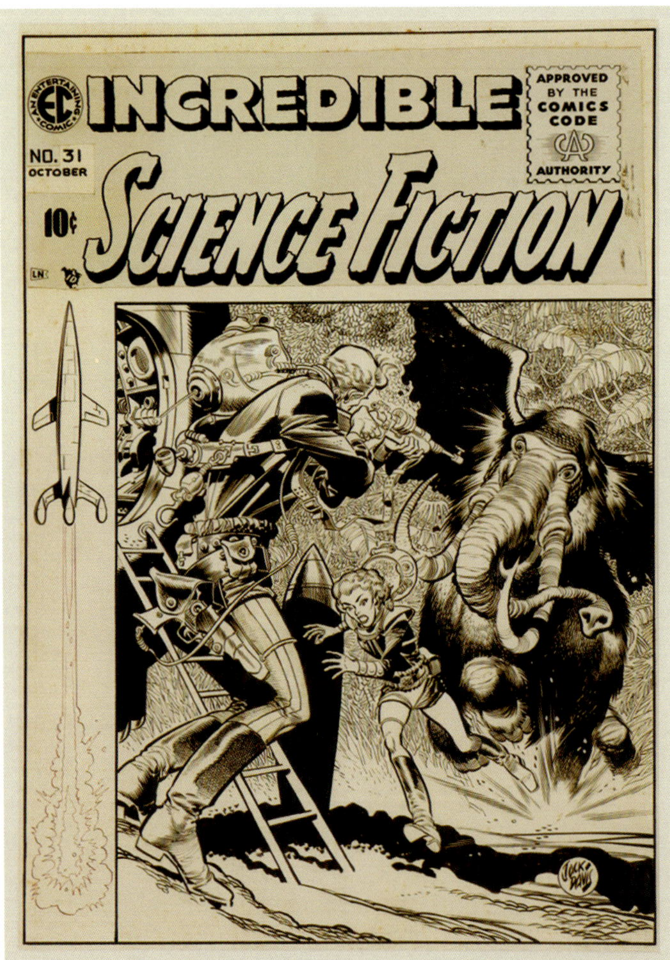

4128 Jack Davis - Incredible Science Fiction #31 Cover Original Art (EC, 1955). Jack Davis rarely drew covers for the EC science fiction titles. In fact he only drew *three*, for **Incredible Science Fiction** #30-32, so if you need one for your collection, don't delay in bidding! Davis is a master at drawing action and his dramatic inking insures that once seen, this "when alien animals attack" moment will burn itself into your memory banks. As EC historian Bill Spicer has pointed out, "A theme that got good mileage was the blending of primeval with future scenes that appeared in no less than seven EC science fiction covers. Davis' **Incredible Science Fiction** #31 was the last of that group to combine a prehistoric-like beast with science fictional trappings." The space costumes and futuristic hardware in this *mise en scene* show the unmistakable influence of EC's heralded science fiction master, Wally Wood. The cover has an image area of 13.5" x 19.5", and the art is in Excellent condition.

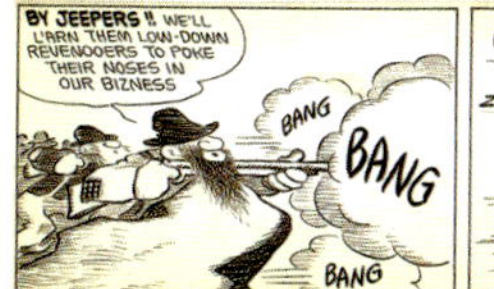

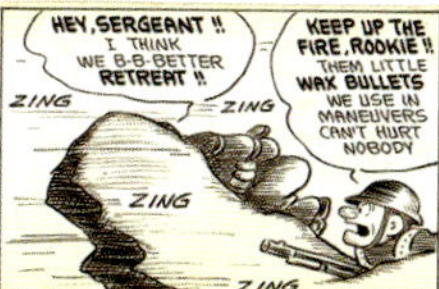

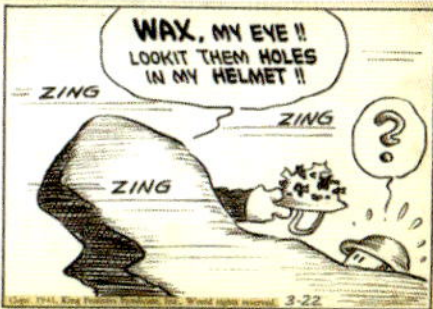

4129 Billy DeBeck - Barney Google and Snuffy Smith Daily Comic Strip Original Art, dated 3-22-41 (King Features Syndicate, 1941). Thar's a war goin' on in Hootin' Holler between the hill folks and them "revenooers". An amusing and spectacularly-drawn daily by Billy DeBeck. The image area measures 16.5" x 3.75" and the artwork is in Excellent condition, with only moderate aging overall.

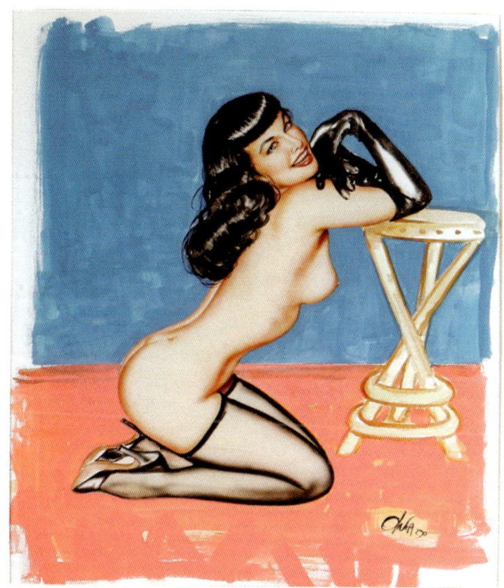

4130 Olivia de Berardinis - Bettie Page Painting Original Art (1990). This sensuous pin-up painting of famed model Bettie Page demonstrates how Olivia perfected her talent for capturing the female figure in its most erotic form. Without going over the top, this tasteful painting exudes the same sex-appeal that made Bettie irresistible to red-blooded males everywhere. Painted in mixed-media, this painting has an image area of 20" x 25" and is in Excellent condition. This sensational scene will be sure to attract "good girl" art collectors, so bid early and furiously.

4131 Sergio Aragones and Others - Alias the Owl Casting Illustration Original Art (1960s). Created as an in-house joke, this pen and ink illustration features Jerry De Fuccio casting the part of the Golden Age Owl, known to be a favorite of his. A long line waits, including caricatures of Sergio Aragones, and other Mad staffers, along with Charlie Brown and a number of strange birds. The image area measures 23" x 5" and the art is in Excellent condition.

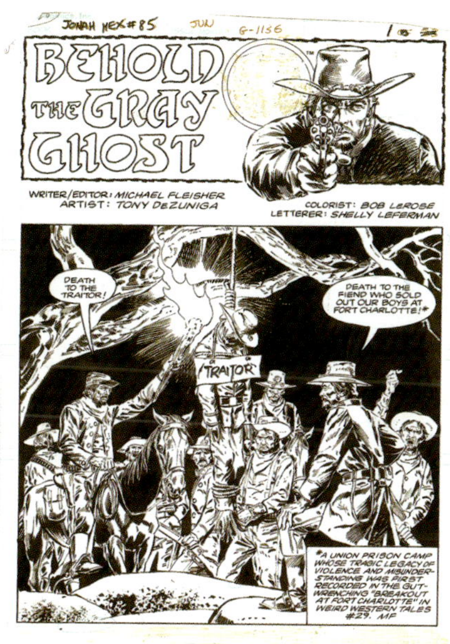

4132 Tony DeZuniga - Jonah Hex #85, Complete 23-page Story "Behold the Gray Ghost" Original Art (DC, 1984). Jonah Hex battles the menace of the Gray Ghost in this fast-moving Michael Fleisher story, beautifully illustrated by the talented Tony DeZuniga. As Shaun Clancy noted in his introduction for a Tony DeZuniga interview in **Comic Book Artist** V2#4, "Tony DeZuniga exploded on the scene at DC Comics in the early 1970s — the first of a tsunami of Filipino artists to arrive in the U.S. — most significantly as co-creator and artist of Jonah Hex, the 'Weird Western' anti-hero." The image area of each page is 10" x 15". The corners of the pages have been clipped outside the image area and there are a few missing pasted-on lettering corrections; otherwise the art is in Excellent condition. Here's a chance to win a great Tony DeZuniga story featuring one of his most famous co-creations!

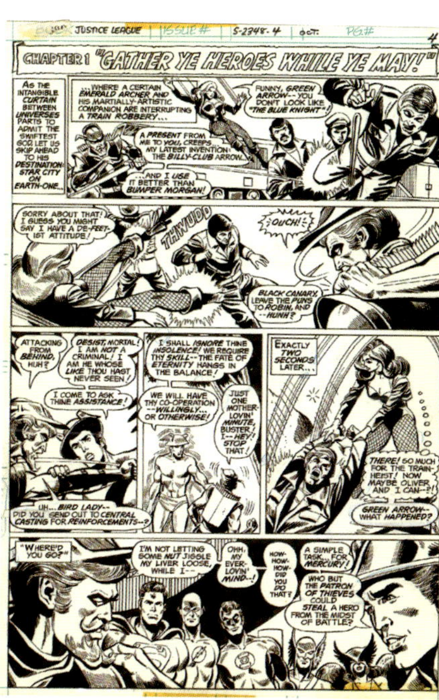

4133 Dick Dillin and Frank McLaughlin - Justice League of America #135, page 4 Original Art (DC, 1976). The Justice Leaguers of Earth One link up with the god Mercury, who looks an awful lot like the Flash of Earth Two, in this thrilling scene from "Crisis in Eternity." It gets mighty confusing when earths collide — do you need a heroes roll call? Starring on this page are Green Arrow, Black Canary, Superman, Flash (Barry Allen), Green Lantern (Hal Jordan), Hawkman, Hawkgirl, and Mercury! The page has an image area of 10" x 15", and aside from a small glue stain at the right, the art is in Excellent condition.

4134 Walt Disney Studios - The Tortoise and the Hare Animation Drawing Original Art (Disney, 1934). Directed by Wilfred Jackson, this Silly Symphony, "The Tortoise and the Hare," won an Academy Award for Best Cartoon. In his belief that he can win the race no matter what, overconfident Max Hare spends his time entertaining the female rabbits, while persistent Toby Tortoise comes from behind and wins the race. Here is a zippy animation drawing in graphite of Max Hare, drawn on a sheet of 9" x 11" animation bond paper. Aside from some overall aging, and some light staining along the left edge, this work is in Very Good condition.

4135 Walt Disney Studios - The Tortoise and the Hare Animation Drawing Original Art (Disney, 1934). Lessons in the pitfalls in overconfidence and the value of perseverance, are dished out Disney style in the short, "The Tortoise and the Hare". This short won Disney it's third straight Oscar for Animated Short, a category they maintained a death-grip on until the early 1940s. Here is a animation drawing in graphite of Toby Tortoise which was drawn on a sheet of 9" x 11" animation bond paper. Aside from some overall aging, it is in Excellent condition.

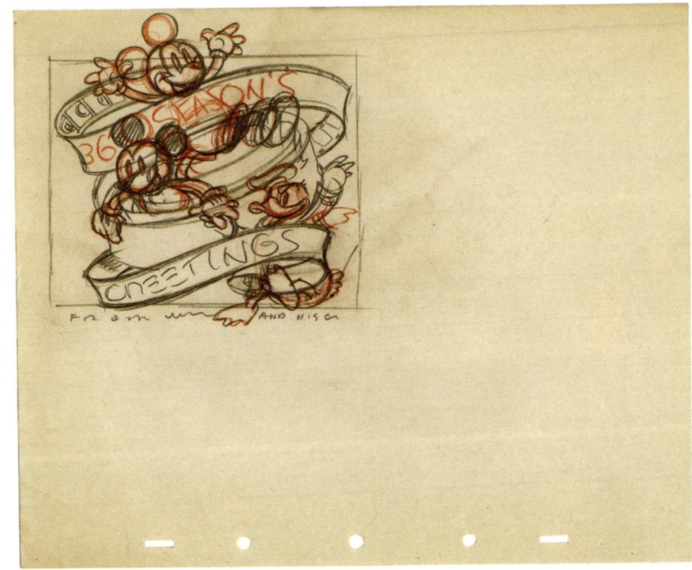

4136 Walt Disney Studios - Walt Disney Christmas Card Preliminary Pencil Sketch Original Art, Group of 47 (Disney, 1936). Offered here is a classy collection of 47 vintage pencil sketches, direct from the talented hands of Walt Disney artists. These are preliminary drawings for seasonal Christmas cards. The year that is indicated on these drawings is 1936. Drawn in graphite and red pencil, these boisterous sketches feature Mickey Mouse, Minnie, Donald Duck, and Pluto. The image area for each sketch ranges from 6" x 4.5" to 9" x 6", and, aside from some paper aging, they average Excellent condition.

4137 Disney Studio Artist - Winnie the Pooh Storyboard Original Art (undated). The best hopper at his family reunion, Rabbit, recounts his experience to Winnie the Pooh, Tigger, Eeyore, and Owl, in these three-paneled storyboard. Drawn in ink, and colored with marker, these boards have an image area of 22" x 4.5" and have the dialogue mounted in strips underneath the panels. There are two vertical fold lines in the art, between the first and second two frames; and some light soiling around the dialogue paste-ups, otherwise the work is in Excellent condition.

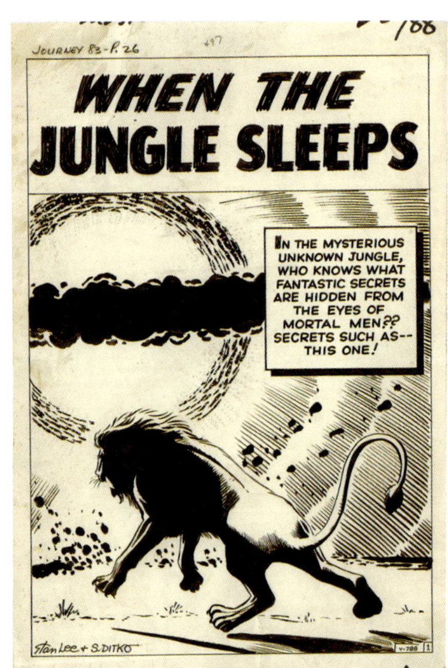

4138 Steve Ditko - Journey into Mystery #83 Splash Page 1 Original Art (Marvel, 1962). Steve Ditko's approach to fantasy art was so different, so sensational, Stan Lee soon assigned him to the art for *every* story in **Amazing Adult Fantasy**. Meanwhile, over at **Journey into Mystery**, while the Mighty Thor was battling "The Stone Men of Saturn" in his debut for the lead story of that historic issue, this lion was involved in mysterious doings in the back-up yarn, "When the Jungle Sleeps." The splash has an image area of 12.5" x 18.5", and the art is in Excellent condition.

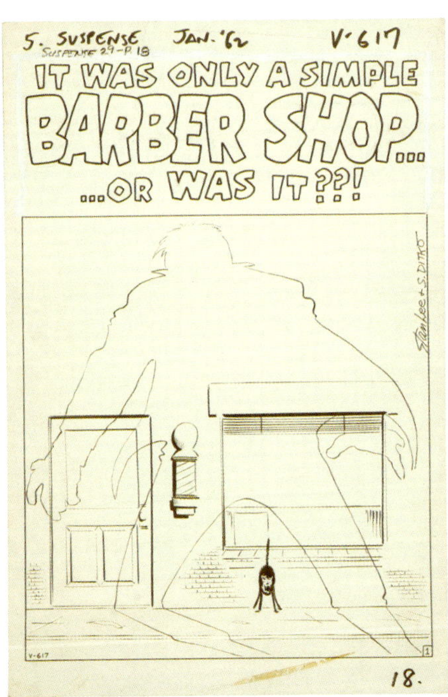

4139 Steve Ditko - Tales of Suspense #29, Splash Page 1 Original Art (Marvel, 1962). Steve Ditko brought a vigor and eccentric tone to his early 60s horror stories, and writer Stan Lee knew how to spur him to do his best work. Their twist-ending tales are drawn with the single-minded force of nightmares. This splash page from the story, "It Was Only a Simple Barber Shop... or Was It??!," is a highly stylized example of Ditko's talent, and is impossible to shake. The art has an image area of approximately 12" x 18" and, aside from a slight glue stain along the bottom, is in Excellent condition.

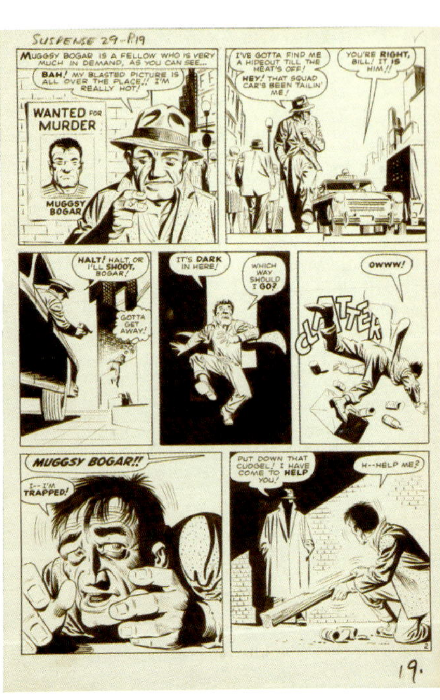

4140 Steve Ditko - Tales of Suspense #29, page 2 Original Art (Marvel, 1962). An extremely prolific creator, the reclusive and legendary Steve Ditko birthed many other comics projects outside of the famous wall-crawler, Spider-Man. His artwork is often understated and embroidered with detail. Here, wanted man, Muggsy Bogar, finds solace in a mysterious figure in an alleyway. Page 2 of the Stan Lee story, "It Was Only a Simple Barber Shop... or Was It??!" imprints upon the reader that fine Ditko style. The art has an image area of approximately 12" x 18" and is in Excellent condition.

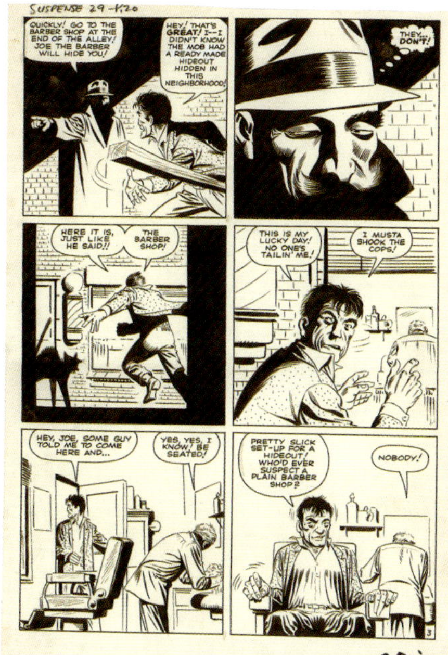

4141 Steve Ditko - Tales of Suspense #29, page 3 Original Art (Marvel, 1962). The idiosyncratic body language, odd hand positions, perfectly placed shadows, and treatment of surreal elements, all announce this piece as truly from Steve Ditko's pencil. Presented here is page three from "It Was Only a Simple Barber Shop... or Was It??!" a Stan Lee/Steve Ditko horror tale that shows a healthy knowledge of the dark corners of the human soul. The art has an image area of approximately 12" x 18" and the condition is Excellent.

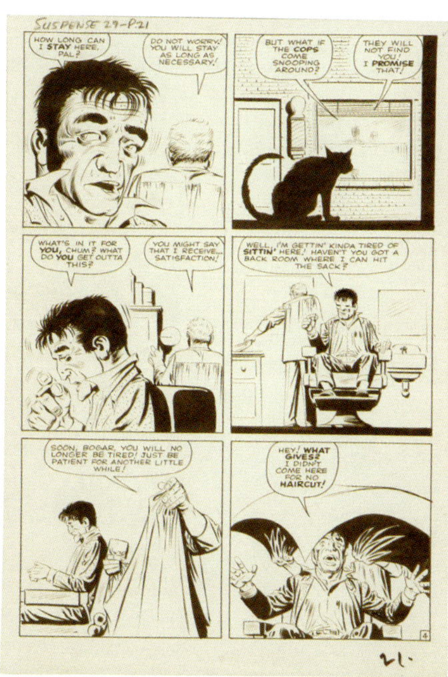

4142 Steve Ditko - Tales of Suspense #29, page 4 Original Art (Marvel, 1962). Steve Ditko's storytelling style and idiosyncrasies set his work apart from his peers in the world of comic book creation. His trippy, other-worldly approach balanced delicate detail with "cartoony" design. This page from the Stan Lee/Steve Ditko horror collaboration, "It Was Only a Simple Barber Shop... or Was It??!" consists of classic Ditko design work, including close-up shots of a distressed character, with little or no background, which makes the world he inhabits seem as suffocatingly terrifying as the scope of the story itself. The art has an image area of approximately 12" x 18" and is in Excellent condition.

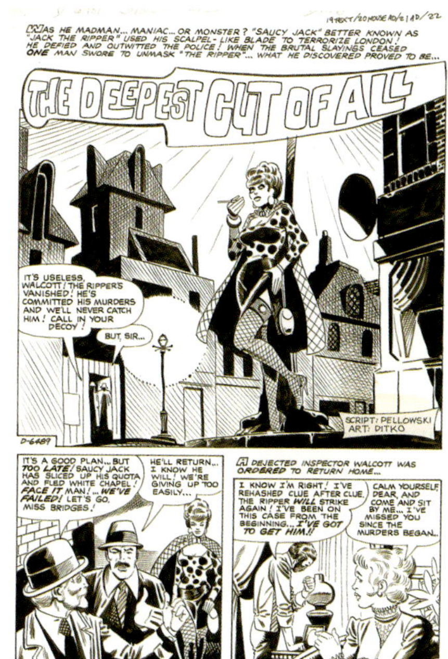

4143 Steve Ditko - Ghostly Haunts #46 Splash Page 1 Original Art (Charlton, 1975). A fetching streetwalker serves as the bait for Jack the Ripper in the atmospheric title page for "The Deepest Cut of All." The stage has been set for this gripping serial killer hunt by that master storyteller, Steve Ditko. Ditko's "good girl" art has seldomly looked more appealing. The splash has an image area of 12" x 18" and the art is in Excellent condition.

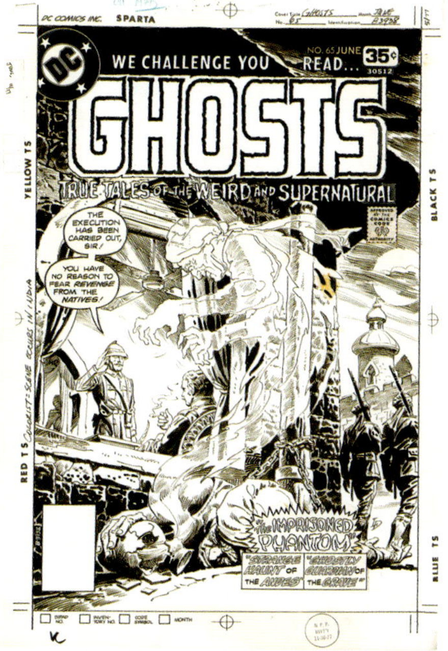

4144 Luis Dominguez - Ghosts #65 Cover Original Art (DC, 1978). The mysterious Far East serves as the backdrop for this haunting cover scene detailed by the talented Luis Dominguez. When DC ace cover artist Nick Cardy moved on to other venues, editor Murray Boltinoff, gave the nod to this master draftsman from Argentina. The image area of this chiller measures 9.75" x 15", and aside from a few small glue stains, the art is in Excellent condition.

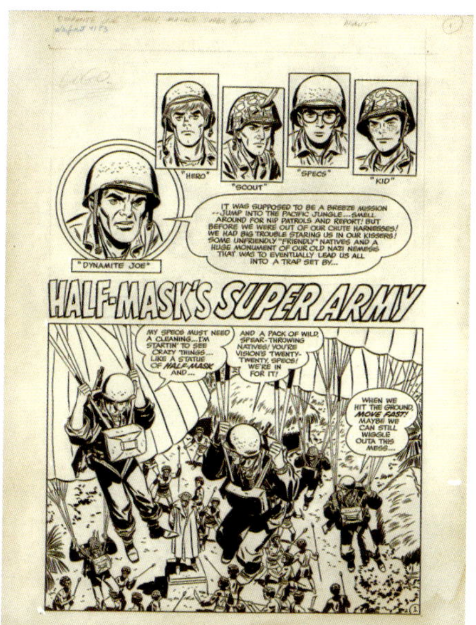

4145 Bill Draut - Warfront #41, Complete 16-page Story, "Half-Mask's Super Army" Original Art (Harvey, 1967). The war's weirdest villain, Half-Mask, is back with his deadly half-sub... it spells super bang-bang trouble for Dynamite Joe! America's explosive Marine faces his worst enemy, and an army of his "eye assassins," in this 16-page adventure by Bill Draut. The image area of each page measures 12" x 18", and, aside from some water damage along the bottom edge of the first four pages (outside of the image area), and some aging apparent along the extreme edges of each page, this slam-bang art averages in Excellent condition.

4146 Kieron Dwyer and Al Milgrom - The Official Marvel Index to the Avengers #4 Cover Original Art (Marvel, 1987). Kieron Dwyer and Al Milgrom present a formation of the Avengers for this cover, which includes Captain America, the Black Panther, Quicksilver, Vision, Scarlet Witch, Thor, Wasp, Yellowjacket, Goliath, and Iron Man. So much excitement couldn't be contained on one mere page, so the artists expanded it into a double-page spread! The back cover includes some of the Avengers' most nefarious foes, including Ultron, Enchantress, Kang the Conqueror, M'Baku the Man-Ape, The Sons of the Serpent, and Red Wolf. The image area measures 21" x 15", and the art is in Excellent condition. Signed by Kieron Dwyer at the bottom right.

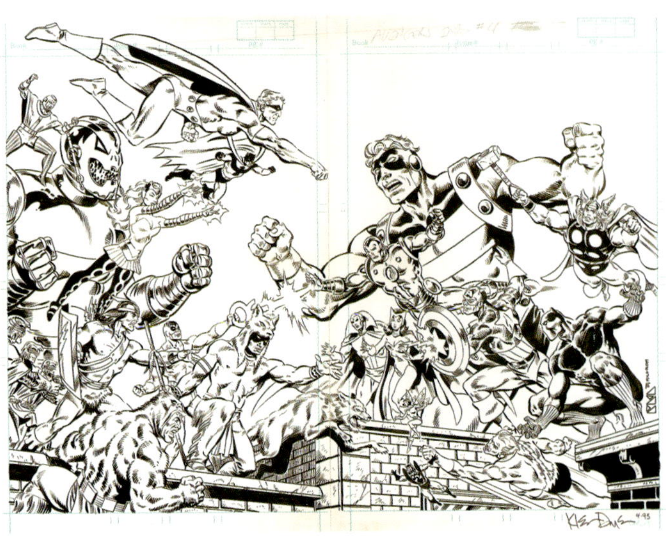

4147 Bob Eggleton - Saturn Starscape Sketch Original Art (undated). Hugo Award-winning artist Bob Eggleton began his career as a science fiction artist in 1984 with covers for Baen Books. He has since illustrated countless book covers and has created work for such magazines as **Astronomy** and **Sky and Telescope**. His technique uses dramatic angles and dazzling colors to create scenes both dreamlike and starkly realistic. Here is a color preliminary sketch created by Eggleton for an unidentified illustration, drawn in marker and ink on marker paper, which has been mounted onto heavy illustration board. The art has an image area of 6" x 9.5" and is in Excellent condition.

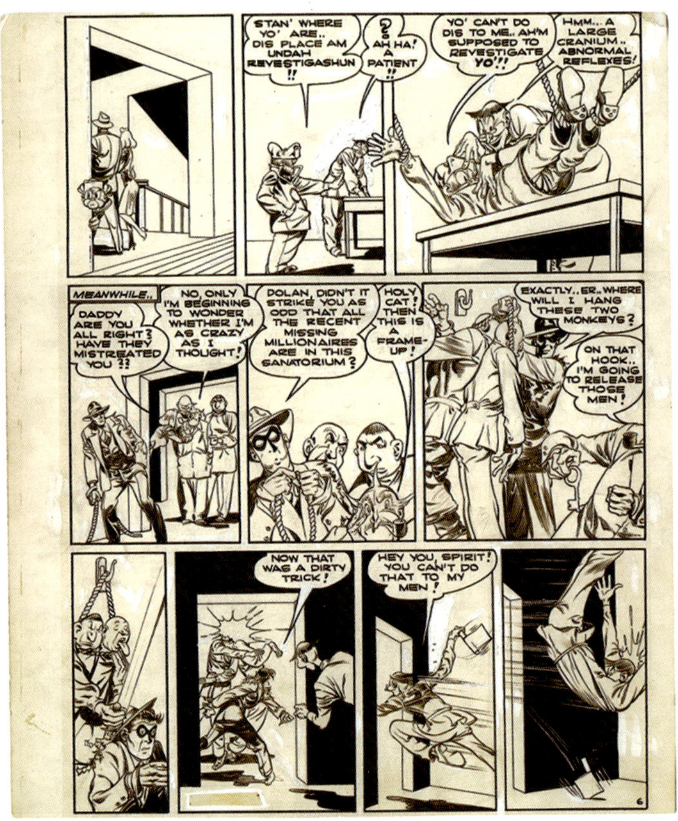

4148 Will Eisner Studio (with Lou Fine) - The Spirit, "Pink Elephants," page 6 Original Art, dated 9-6-42 (Des Moines Register and Tribune Syndicate, 1942). Will Eisner was that rarest of comics creators — in addition to being a superb writer and artist, he was also an astute business man, a talent scout, and a comic shop director. Eisner always staffed his shop with the comics industry's top talents, including artists such as Lou Fine, Bob Powell, Chuck Mazoujian, Jack Cole, and Alex Kotzky. Will Eisner was inducted into the Army in May, 1942, and eventually he was transferred to the Pentagon where he went on to pioneer a series of educational comics and teaching aids. As noted in **The Will Eisner Companion**, "Lou Fine was one of the assistants in Eisner's studio who worked on The Spirit, playing a particularly prominent role as artist and, for many of the stories while Eisner was in the army from 1942 to 1945, sometimes writing as well." Most of the major players in the Spirit feature put in an appearance on this page — Ebony White, Ellen Dolan, Commissioner Dolan, and of course, the Spirit himself. This page also features the humor and slam-bang action that were hallmarks of the strip. The page has an image area of 11.25" x 15.75", and the art is in Excellent condition.

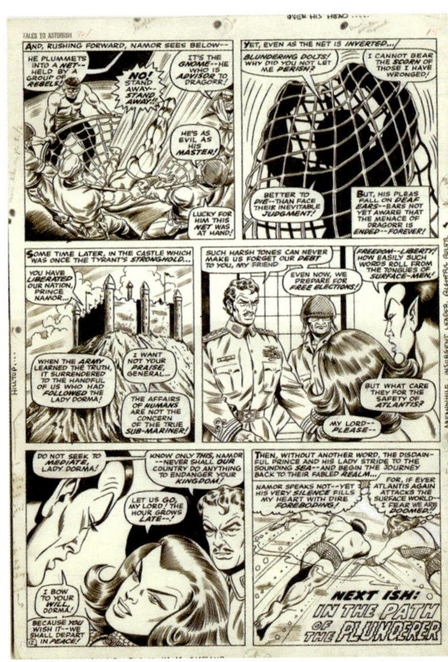

4149 Bill Everett - Tales to Astonish #94, page 12 Original Art (Marvel, 1967). The menace of Dragorr is ended, and a disdainful Prince Namor and his Lady Dorma have a few terse words with the General of a former dictatorial regime before beginning their journey back to the fabled realm of Atlantis, in this snazzy page from **Tales to Astonish** #94. This last page from the Roy Thomas story, "Helpless, at the Hands of Dragorr!," is drawn with imperial talent by original Namor creator, Bill Everett. The image area measures 12.5" x 18.5". Some story notations along the edges, outside the image area, and slight white-out usage, otherwise this scintillating page is in Excellent condition.

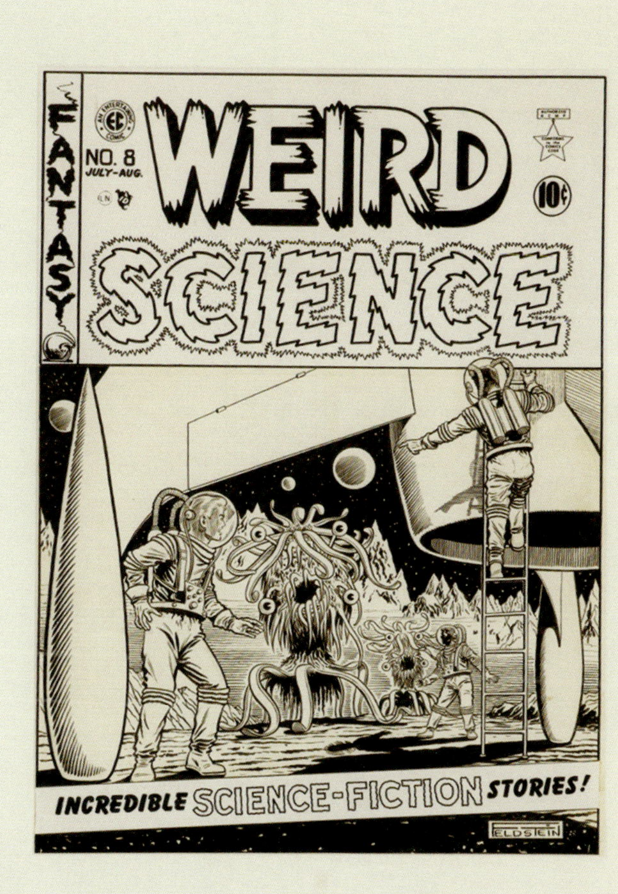

4150 Al Feldstein - Weird Science #8 Cover Original Art (EC, 1951). This wild and wooly cover scene has all of the Al Feldstein touches that a collector looks for in an EC science fiction cover. It has space-men, rocket ships in outer space, and horrific bug-eyed-monsters! The image area of this cover measures 13.5" x 19.5". The title logo and caption at the bottom are replacement stats; otherwise the art is in Excellent condition. The demand for EC covers continues to skyrocket and exceed the supply — don't miss this terrific opportunity to add a Feldstein science fiction classic to your collection.

4151 Al Feldstein - "Weird Science #8 Revisited" Painting Original Art (1992). Al Feldstein's eerie science fiction landscapes were influenced by the detailed, hard-edged astronomical paintings of Chesley Bonestell, but Feldstein also added his own knack for creating palpable scenes of unearthly terror to many of the EC incredible science fiction covers. This superb shocker displays the quintessential Feldstein hallmarks. Choke! The painting measures 24" x 20", and is in Excellent condition. This masterpiece would look fabulous on any EC fan-addict's wall, so bid now!

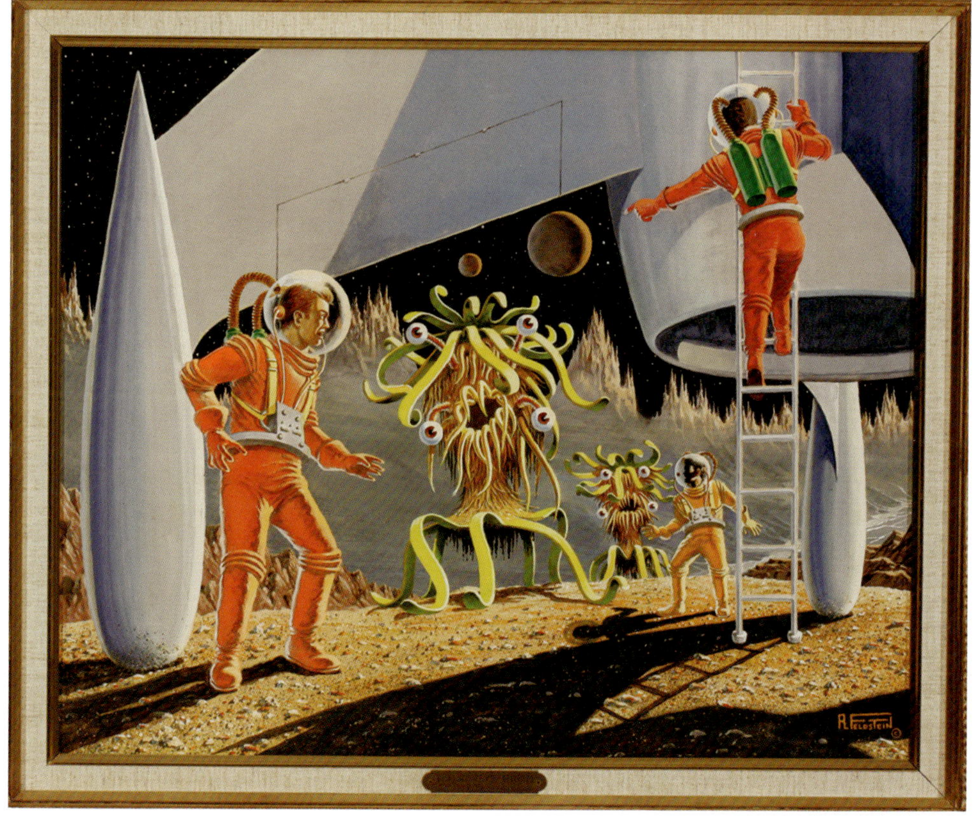

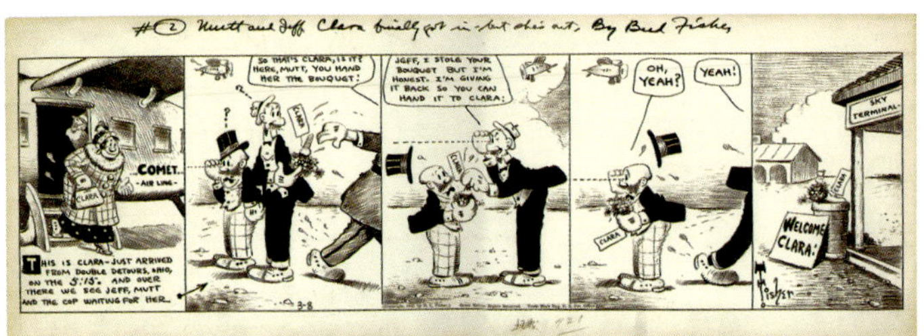

4152 **Bud Fisher Studio - Mutt and Jeff Daily Comic Strip Original Art, dated 3-8-32 (King Features Syndicate, 1932).** Clara from Double Detours, Ohio strikes out with her three would-be suitors as they each ditch her, one by one, after catching a glimpse of her bountiful beauty. First the cop, then Mutt, and finally Jeff — these boys hop away faster than frogs in a frying pan. The image area of this daily measures 29" x 8.5", and the art is in Excellent condition.

4153 **Four Star Artist - G.I. in Battle #6 Original Art (Four Star, 1958).** Pvt. Doyle has reached the limit of his endurance in hand-to-hand combat, and now he's a "Haunted Hero!" A well-rendered and dramatic cover from this rather obscure series, with the foreground figure giving the scene weight and emotion. The image area measures 11.5" x 16.5", and the art is in Very Good condition, with some creasing at the corners and overall wear.

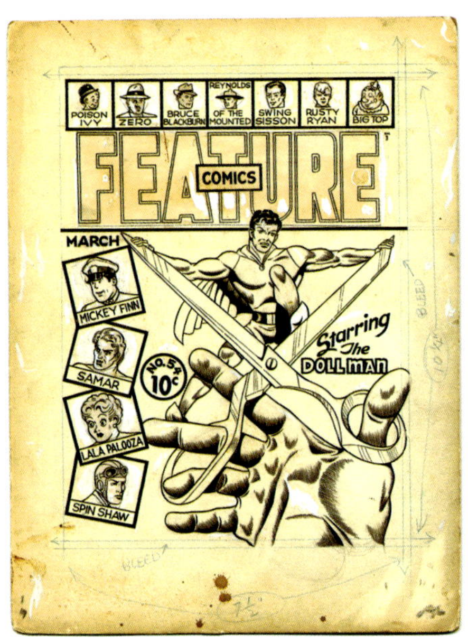

4154 **Gill Fox - Feature Comics #54 Cover Original Art (Quality Comics, 1942).** This historic Golden Age thriller was Gill Fox's *first* cover for Quality Comics. Gill recalled in a 2002 Jim Amash interview for **Alter Ego**, "The first cover I did completely was of Doll Man. Doll Man was holding a pair of scissors. I took artistic license with that because that would have cut his hands. We found out very early that Doll Man was popular. So he became the cover feature." Zero, Mickey Finn, Lala Palooza, and Poison Ivy also appear on this cover in cameo portraits. The image area of the cover is 8.75" x 12". The art is in Very Good condition, with only a few small stains, mostly outside of the image area. ***From the collection of Gill Fox.***

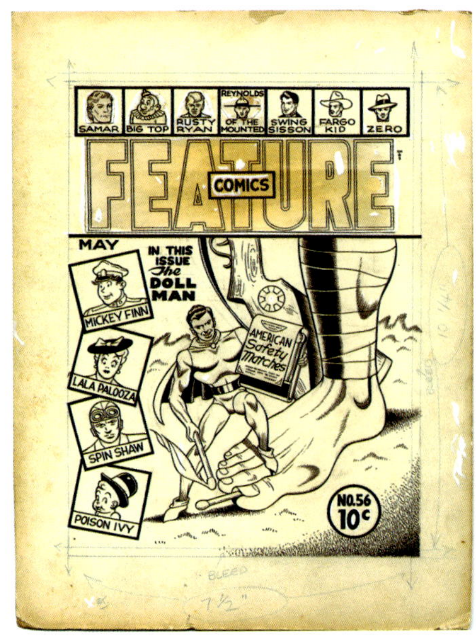

4155 **Gill Fox - Feature Comics #56 Cover Original Art (Quality Comics, 1942).** Doll Man brings his own brand of subversive warfare to World War II's Pacific Theatre in this red-hot cover gag. An all-star line-up of **Feature Comics'** players are spotlighted along the top and left borders. Notable characters answering the roll call include Samar, Mickey Finn, Lala Palooza, and Gill Fox's own unforgettable creation, Poison Ivy. When Editor Ed Cronin left Quality Comics to jump ship to another company, Gill Fox was promoted to editor and he drew many of the covers in office for the Quality titles. The cover art was routinely drawn at a smaller size than the interior pages. Fox explained why, "We had a lot of shields and titles, so it was different than the interior pages. The covers were made smaller for speed. That made them easier to color which we did by codes." The image area of the cover is 8.75" x 12". Aside from some slight paper aging and a bit of glue staining on the title logo, the art is in Very Good condition. ***From the collection of Gill Fox.***

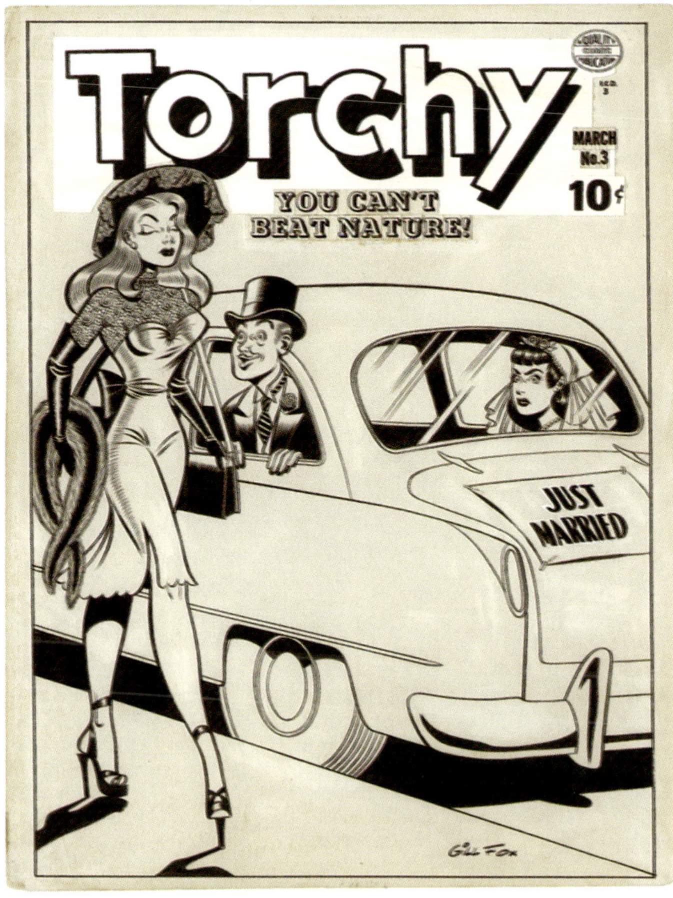

4156 Gill Fox - Torchy #3 Cover Original Art (Quality, 1950). Gill Fox did five **Torchy** covers, and every single one of them is a gem, so it is with great pride that we offer the extremely alluring cover artwork to issue #3, as Torchy inadvertently sends a couple down the road to divorce even as they depart for their honeymoon. Who could blame the hapless bridegroom for being dumbstruck by one of the sexiest women ever to grace a comic book cover? Not us! Beyond the amusing gag portrayed here, the actual rendering is absolutely stunning, with the intricate details of Torchy's dress, and the sultry pout of her mouth expertly fashioned by Fox, one of the top "good girl" artists ever to put pen to paper. Needless to say, **Torchy** covers are extremely rare, making this a rare opportunity to acquire a classic and sexy piece of original art. The image area measures 13.5" x 19", and includes all the original logo and masthead photostats. Aside from slight aging apparent, the art is in Excellent condition.

4157 Ramona Fradon - House of Secrets #136 Page Original Art, Group of 7 (DC, 1975). Little Paul Parker takes a strange and perilous voyage into the world of the unknown, passing a point beyond which man was never meant to travel, in these pages from the story, "Last Voyage of the Lady Luck," written by Maxene Fabe. Included here are pages 1, 3, 4, 5, 6, 7, and 8, penciled and inked by Ramona Fradon. The image area of each page measures 10" x 15". There is some light scattered staining on several of the pages, with blue line editorial markings, and tape stains at the upper and lower center edges of each page, otherwise the art is in Very Good condition.

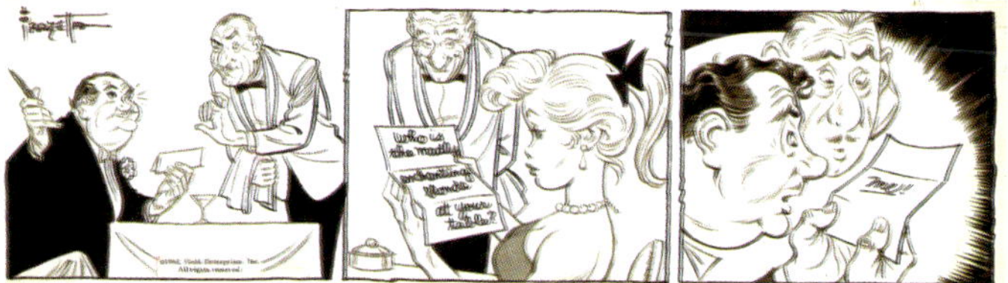

4158 Frank Frazetta - Sweet Adeline Daily Comic Strip Original Art (Field Enterprises, 1962). Frank Frazetta only drew one week of dailies for his try-out newspaper strip, *Sweet Adeline*. When it comes to drawing sensuous "good girl" scenes, Frank Frazetta has few, if any, serious artistic rivals! Able to work in a lighthearted manner as well as in his more celebrated, ultra-dynamic fantasy style, this daily is a whimsical delight! The daily was signed at the upper left. The strip has an image area of 16.5" x 4.5", and aside from a few small red spots in panels one and two, the art is in Very Good condition.

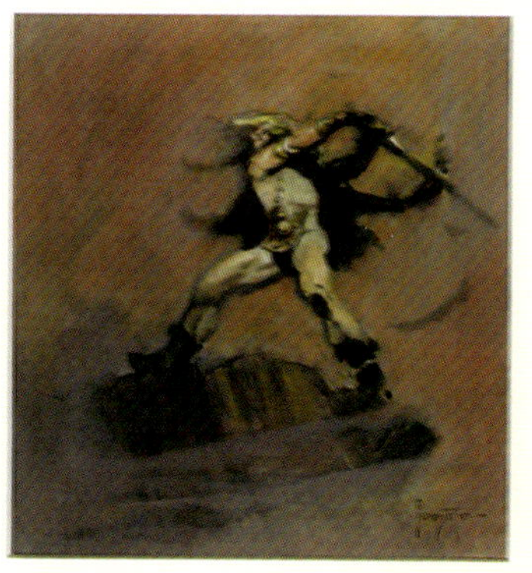

4159 Frank Frazetta - Warrior Color Preliminary Original Art (undated). A sword-slinging warrior prepares to strike in this spectacular color preliminary painting by master fantasy painter Frank Frazetta. The image area measures 6" x 6.5", and the piece is roughly twice the size of many of Frazetta's other color prelims. The figure unleashes his coiled fury, and the atmospheric background lends the scene an air of menace-laden mystery; it's nothing short of a gem-like masterwork by Frazetta. The artwork has been tastefully matted, and is in Excellent condition.

4160 Western Publishing Artist - Four Color #950 Frosty the Snowman Cover Original Art (Dell, 1958). Sizzlin' snowflakes, it's frost-filled fun as the button-nosed snowman takes to the ice, on this super-cool cover illustration. Hand-painted in watercolor on a sheet of heavy illustration board, this art includes all the original logo and masthead photostats, which are attached to a acetate overlay. The image area measures 8.5" x 11" and the art is in Excellent condition. Includes a color photocopy of the cover art, and a copy of **Four Color** #950.

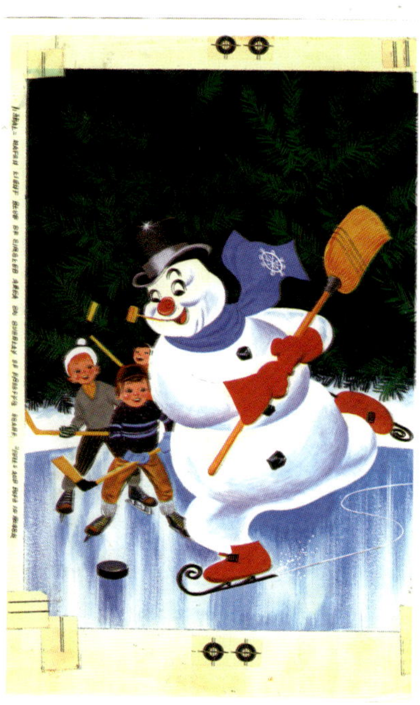

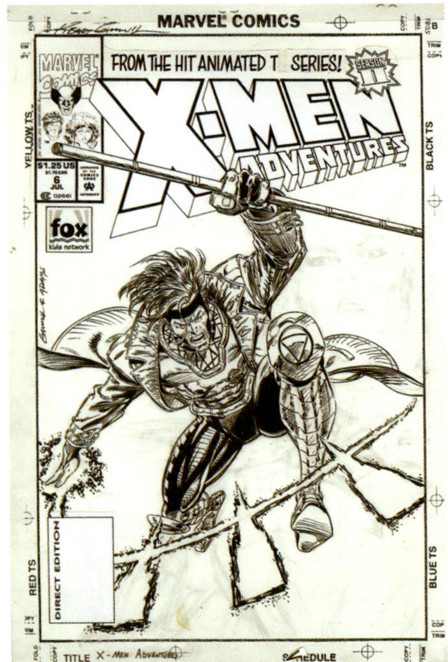

4161 Kerry Gammill and Greg Adams - X-Men Adventures Season II #6 Cover Original Art (Marvel, 1994). When the X-Men animated series came out, Marvel, never slow to miss a potential tie-in, put out the new title **X-Men Adventures**, which did adaptations of the cartoon series. Since the cartoon series itself was adapting three decades of X-Men stories, longtime readers tended to get odd feelings of deja vu. Gambit graces this over-the-top cover from the sixth issue, in a forceful image by Kerry Gammill and Greg Adams. The art has an image area of 10" x 15" and is in Excellent condition. Part of the art is on an acetate overlay. Includes the original masthead photostats. Signed by Gammill.

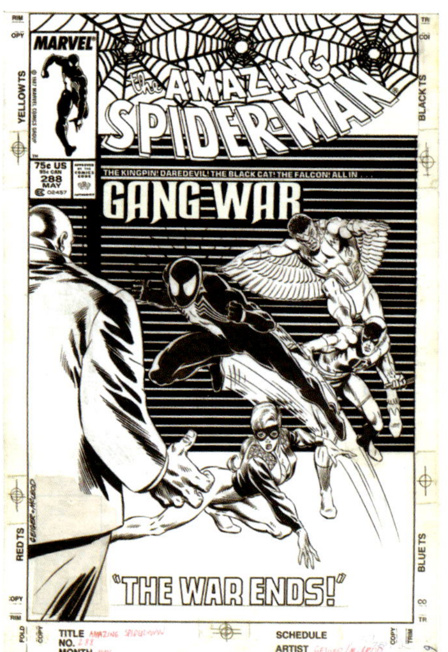

4162 Steve Geiger and Bob McLeod - The Amazing Spider-Man #288 Cover Original Art (Marvel, 1987). The Kingpin, Daredevil, the Black Cat, and the Falcon are all on this cover titled, "The War Ends!," which was penciled by Steve Geiger and inked by Bob McLeod. From the fifth chapter of the "Gang War" storyline (it began in issue #284), Kingpin is back after making a deal with the Feds, which involves sacrificing his lieutenants in the organization. The image area measures 10" x 15" and the art is in Excellent condition.

4163 Vincent Giarrano and Peter Gross - Doctor Fate #26 Cover Original Art (DC, 1991). Now in command of the Doctor Fate powers, Inza Nelson goes in search of the Lords of Order, on this spellbinding cover illustration by penciler Vincent Giarrano and inker Peter Gross. Inked on a sheet of acetate, which has been mounted onto a sheet of bristol board, the art has an image area of 10" x 15" and is in Excellent condition.

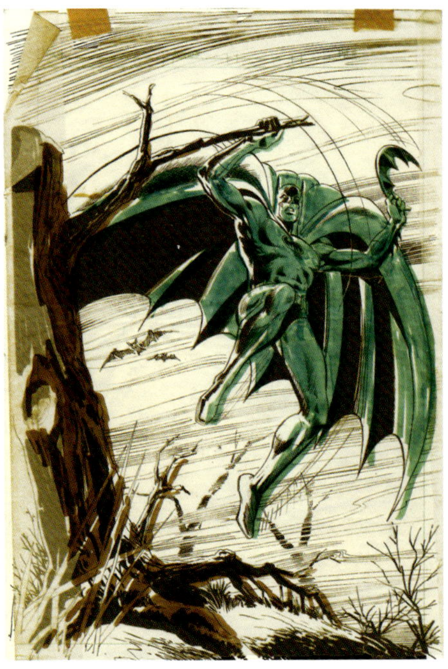

4164 Dick Giordano - Aurora Comic Scenes Batman Instruction Booklet Cover and Complete 5-page Story Original Art (Aurora, 1974). The darkest specter of every gangster's nightmare, Batman, takes down a group of kidnappers, (and believe us, it looks like it hurts), in this five-page tale. This cover and five pages were penciled and inked by one the most talented illustrators the field has ever seen, Dick Giordano. The image area of each page measures approximately 11" x 16", and, aside from some tape stains on the edges of several of the interior pages (outside of the image area), the pages average in Excellent condition.

4165 Dick Giordano - Wonder Woman #262 Cover Original Art (DC, 1979). Suffering Sappho — in this Bronze Age blockbuster Wonder Woman declares war on the street warriors — it's the social relevance of the seventies. What chance do such rowdy riff-raff stand against the Maid of Might? None at all. "Good girl" specialist Dick Giordano adds his own touch of stylish glamour to Wonder Woman's other amazing attributes! No Wonder Woman cover would be considered complete without the image of chains somewhere in the scene and this one has them, in the form of street weapons. The image area measures 10" x 15". The DC logo, issue number, and price tag stats have slipped off the page and the Wonder Woman logo is loose; otherwise the art is in Very Good condition.

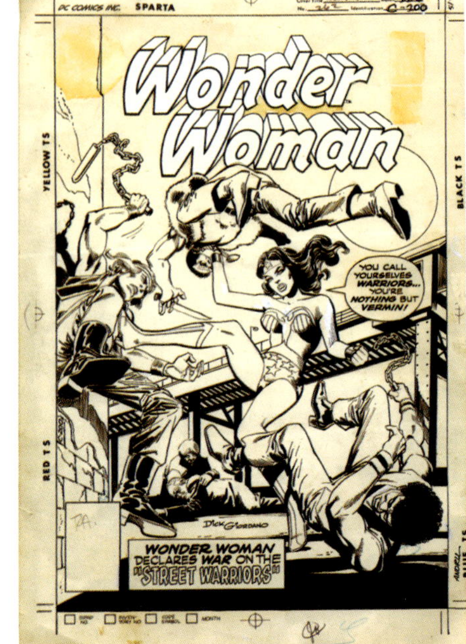

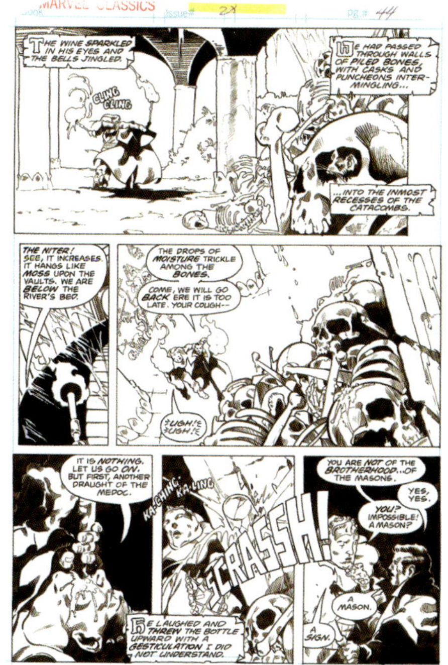

4166 Michael Golden - Marvel Classics #28, page 44 Original Art (Marvel, 1977). Writer Don McGregor and artist Michael Golden adapt Edgar Allan Poe's "The Cask of Amontillado" to the comics in this issue of **Marvel Classics**. Here is some nice, early work by Michael Golden, with a glimmer of the slick style that will one day make him a fan favorite. The image area measures 10" x 15". The corners have been trimmed during the production process, there is a tape stain at the top and bottom center edge, and some blue line editorial markings, otherwise the work is in Very Good condition.

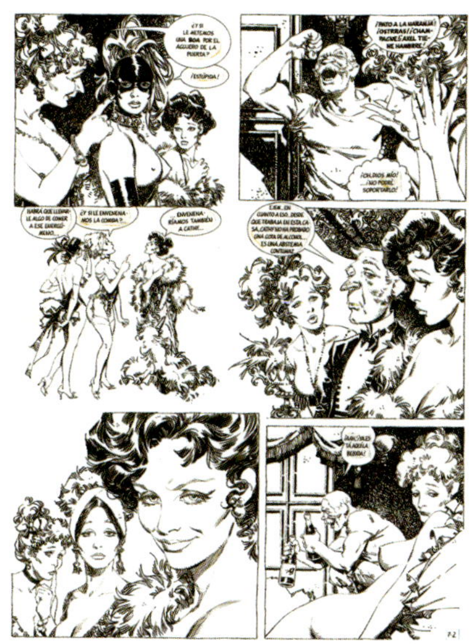

4167 Jose Gonzalez - Chantal Comic Page Original Art (Norma, circa 1980s). A great dose of eroticism can be found in this highly-textured page by Jose Gonzalez. Hailed as **Vampirella**'s greatest artist, Gonzalez was a maestro of the "Spanish School," which spear-headed the later period of the Warren horror era. This page was drawn for the Spanish publisher, Norma, and accomodates Gonzalez's natural pre-dilection for delineating the fairer sex. The image area measures approximately 14.5" x 20.5". The art has some light glue staining around several of the word balloon paste-ups, but is in otherwise Excellent condition.

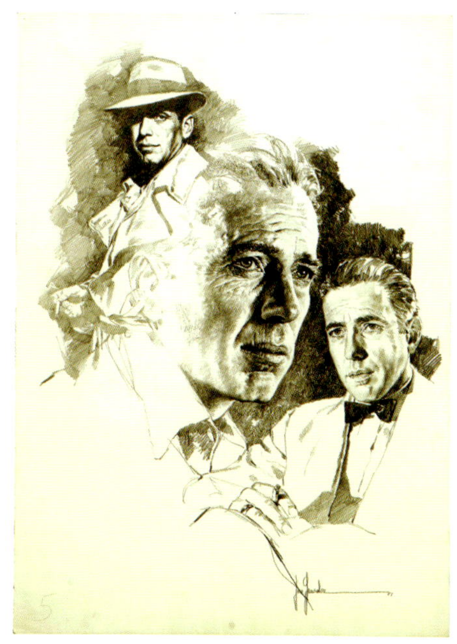

4168 Jose Gonzalez - Humphrey Bogart Portrait Original Art (1981). From hard boiled Sam Spade to cynical Rick Blaine, from wisecracking shamus Philip Marlowe to down-on-his-luck Fred C. Dobbs, Humphrey Bogart created a gallery of unforgettable characters. Appearing in over 75 films, spanning 26 years, Bogart left an indelible mark on American cinema. Jose Gonzalez has rendered this lavish graphite illustration of Bogart in his performance as Rick Blaine in the classic film, "Casablanca". Masterfully delineated with free-flowing lines and sensuous tones, this is the work of a draftsman without peer! The image area of the portrait measures approximately 19" x 26", and the art is in Excellent condition.

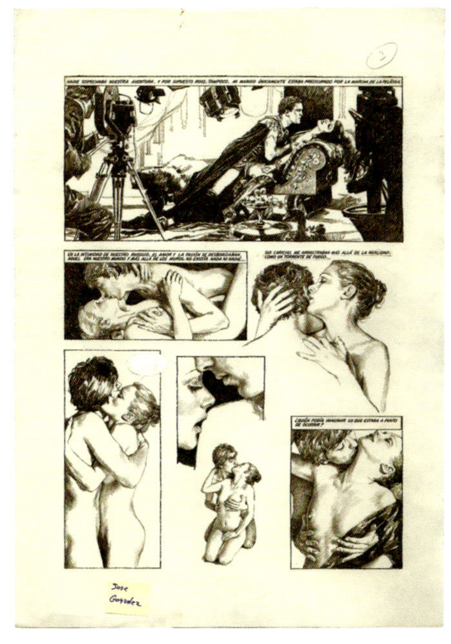

4169 Jose Gonzalez - "Nuestra Adventura" Page Original Art (undated). A Claudette Colbert look-a-like has an off-screen romp with her own personal Marc Antony (a Henry Wilcoxon doppelganger) in this beautifully penciled page by "good girl" master Jose Gonzalez. Erotic cartoon art has seldomly looked so romantic. The image area of the page measures approximately 16" x 23". The word balloon type is pasted-on lettering; otherwise the art is in Excellent condition.

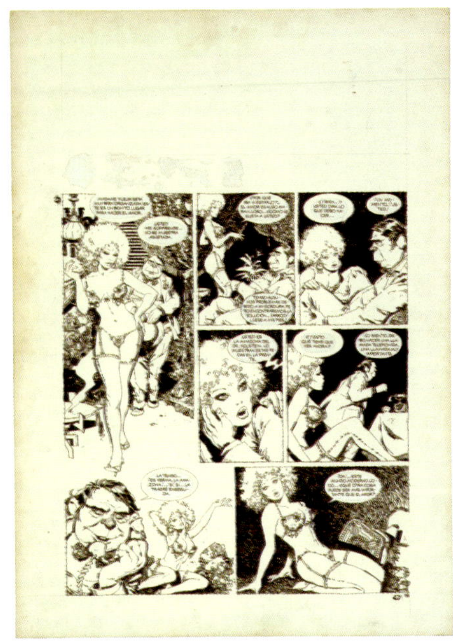

4170 Jose Gonzalez - European Erotic Comic Page Original Art (undated). The talented Jose Gonzalez was part of the wave of Spanish artists who came to dominate the American horror comics revival at Warren Publishing. Gonzalez's glamorous, exotic women and polished, ultra-slick inking are nowhere better demonstrated than in this luxurious page. Sensuous lines and scratchy textures hallmark this seven-paneled illustration. The art has an image area of approximately 16" x 22", and is in Excellent condition.

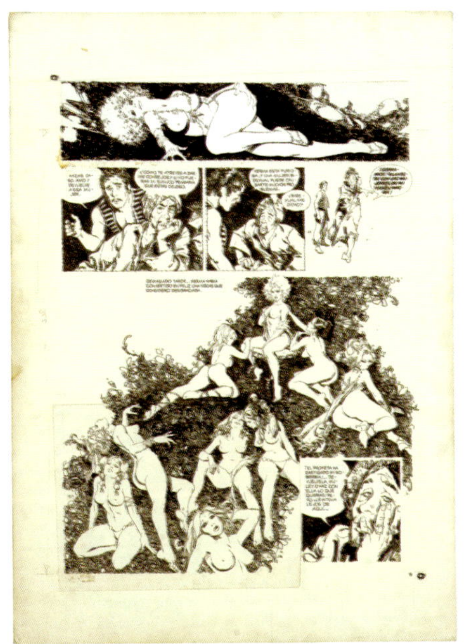

4171 Jose Gonzalez - European Erotic Comic Page Original Art (undated). International illustrator, Jose Gonzalez, is blessed with a remarkable artistic ability to imbue whatever he renders, be it clothing, or succulent female flesh, with a lifelike quality. Bordering on the psychedelic, Jose Gonzalez combines his very capable understanding of feminine anatomy with a flourish of texture, giving this page a pop art sensibility. The art has an image area of approximately 16" x 22". The top panel is photostat art, and there is a bit of slight glue staining; otherwise the art is in Excellent condition.

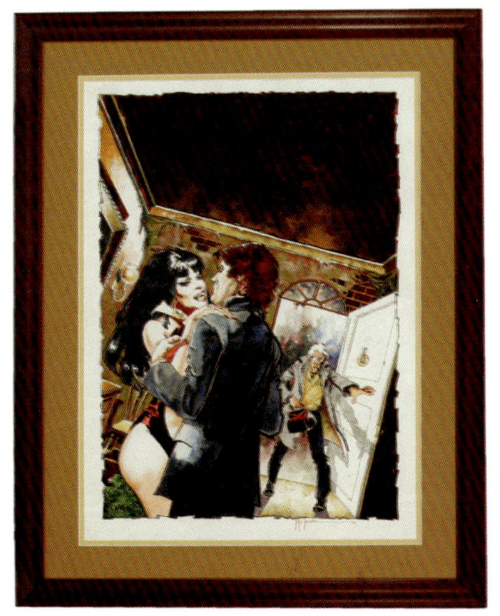

4172 Jose Gonzalez - Vampirella Illustration Original Art (2003). The sexy Drakulon is up to her old tricks, in this blood-freezing illustration by Jose Gonzalez, hailed by most as Vampirella's greatest artist. A simply stunning and perfect example of Vampirella art, which has been inked and hand-painted by Gonzalez, whose Vampi works are widely recognized by collectors as the most desirable and definitive images of Vampirella ever produced. Executed in ink, watercolor, and acrylic paint on white bristol, it is signed and dated 2003. The image area measures 19.5" x 28.5", and the work is in Excellent condition.

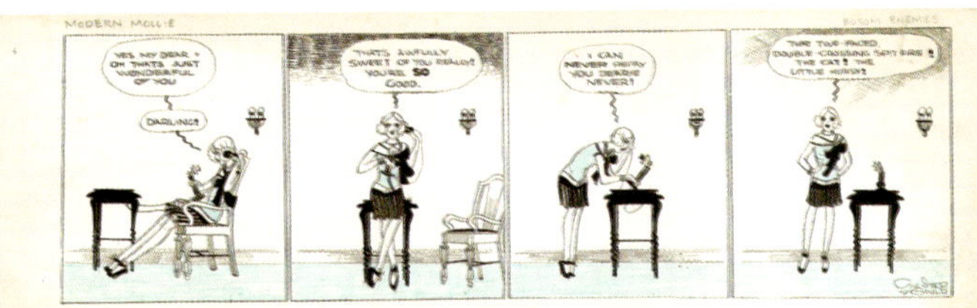

4173 Chester Gould - Modern Mollie Try-Out Daily Comic Strip Original Art (circa 1925). Chester Gould was driven to succeed as a cartoonist. After mastering the lessons set forth in W.L. Evans' famed mail-order cartooning course, Gould left Pawnee, Oklahoma to pursue his career in Chicago. Before he hit the big time with ***Dick Tracy***, Gould worked on humorous strips such as ***Fillum Fables***, ***Radio Lanes***, ***Radio Cats***, and ***The Girl Friends***. Light-hearted flapper fare such as this try-out strip, ***Modern Mollie***, went quickly out of fashion as soon as the Great Depression struck. Soon Gould had found his niche as ***Dick Tracy*** brought his brand of hard-hitting justice to the "dirty thirties." This daily gives a rare glimpse into an alternate facet of Chester Gould's cartooning talent. The daily has an image area of 20" x 6", and the art is in Excellent condition.

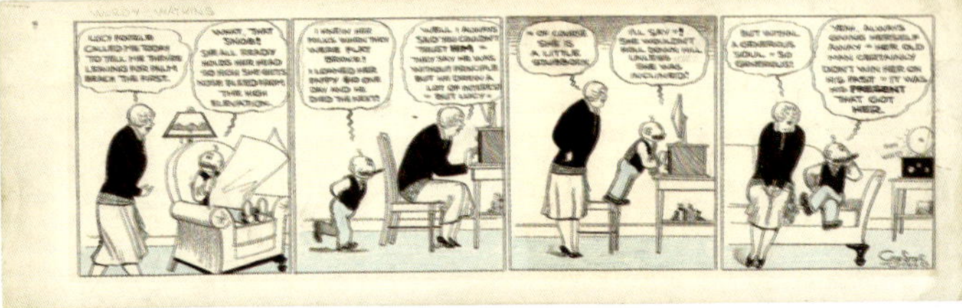

4174 Chester Gould - Wordy Watkins Try-Out Daily Comic Strip Original Art (circa 1925). Well before October 1931, when ***Dick Tracy*** first appeared in the pages of the Chicago Tribune, cartoonist Chester Gould struggled to make his mark in the burgeoning comic strip marketplace. Gould left Pawnee, Oklahoma to pursue his career in Chicago, where he produced numerous try-out strips, including ***Wordy Watkins***, a bubbly, domestic daily. This strip demos Gould's sense of humor, rarely seen in the more serious repertoire he was later to produce. The daily has an image area of 20" x 6", and the art is in Excellent condition.

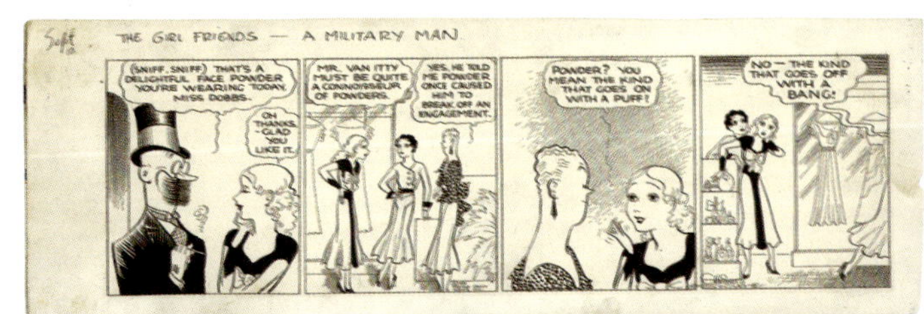

4175 Chester Gould - The Girl Friends Daily Comic Strip Original Art, dated 9-10-31 (Chicago Daily News, 1931). Chester Gould left his job at the **Evening American**, not wanting to get locked in to a five-year contract, and moved to the **Chicago Daily News**, where he was back to advertising art, some editorial cartoons, and this strip, ***The Girl Friends***. More lighthearted than his later, more famous strip, ***Dick Tracy***, here Gould shows a much softer side, in this daily, titled "A Military Man". On October 12, 1931, just about one month after this strip saw print, Dick Tracy was calling on the Truehearts for dinner, in his very first strip! The image area measures 20" x 6" and the condition is Excellent.

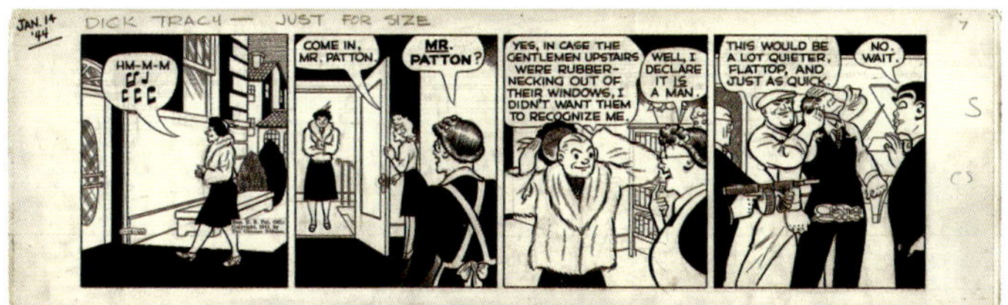

4176 Chester Gould - Dick Tracy Daily Comic Strip Original Art, dated 1-14-44 (Chicago Tribune, 1944). Shades of J. Edgar Hoover — Pat Patton has gone undercover, dressed as a woman, in a plan to rescue the kidnapped Dick Tracy. Meanwhile Dick nearly has his throat cut by Flattop's henchmen in the final panel — this daily is an all-around winner! The image area of the art measures 20" x 6", and it is in Excellent condition. ***From the collection of Larry Doucet.***

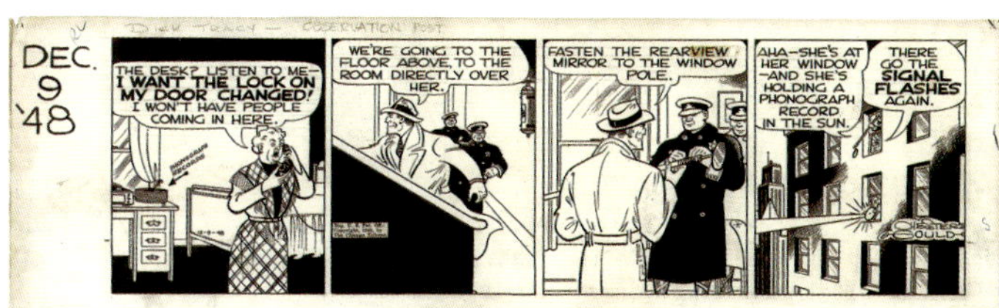

4177 Chester Gould - Dick Tracy Daily Comic Strip Original Art, dated 12-9-48 (Chicago Tribune, 1948). The ever-resourceful Dick Tray uses a makeshift mirror to uncover a suspect's game in this beautifully staged and drawn daily. Two first-rate portraits of Tracy at work are the highlights of the episode. The image area of the daily is 20" x 6", and the art is in Excellent condition. ***From the collection of Larry Doucet.***

4178 Chester Gould - Dick Tracy Daily Comic Strip Original Art, dated 3-22-52 (Chicago Tribune, 1952). Dick Tracy, Sam Catchem, and Junior can only stand and watch in this somber episode set in the intensive care unit of a hospital. The death watch for Model Jones ends in tragedy. Chester Gould created his tender, sad scenes with as much skill and detail as he did his slam-bang action sequences. The image area of the daily measures 16.5" x 5", and the art is in Excellent condition. ***From the collection of Larry Doucet.***

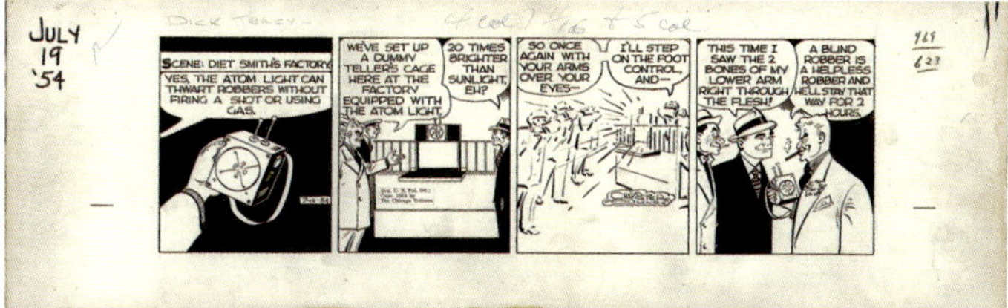

4179 Chester Gould - Dick Tracy Daily Comic Strip Original Art, dated 7-19-54 (Chicago Tribune, 1954). Diet Smith demonstrates one of his most famous crime-stopping inventions — the atom light. Sam Catchem and Dick Tracy appear in the final panel for a group portrait with Diet Smith. The image area of the daily measures 16.5" x 5", and the art is in Excellent condition. ***From the collection of Larry Doucet.***

4180 Chester Gould - Dick Tracy Daily Comic Strip Original Art, dated 6-3-54 (Chicago Tribune, 1954). Open-Mind Monty's game of possum ends when Dick Tracy soaks him with a towel filled with ice — a lighthearted moment for the boys in blue! Expressive linework and snappy patterns in the art add to the overall sense of fun. The daily has an image area of 16.5" x 5", and the art is in Excellent condition. ***From the collection of Larry Doucet.***

4181 Chester Gould - Dick Tracy Daily Comic Strip Original Art, dated 7-21-54 (Chicago Tribune, 1954). Dick Tracy unveils another crime-fighting gizmo — an early form of "caller identification!" Dick Tracy had more tools than any crimefighter this side of Batman! Tess, Bonnie Braids, and Junior also cameo. The image area of the daily is 16.5" x 5", and the condition of the art is in Excellent. ***From the collection of Larry Doucet.***

4182 Chester Gould - Dick Tracy Daily Comic Strip Original Art, dated 12-11-54 (Chicago Tribune, 1954). Dick Tracy has brought in another criminal's corpse for the boys in the crypt room to finger print; meanwhile Rughead senses the writing is on the wall! The strip has an image area of 16.5" x 5", and the art is in Excellent condition. ***From the collection of Larry Doucet.***

4183 Chester Gould - Dick Tracy Daily Comic Strip Original Art, dated 12-28-59 (Chicago Tribune, 1959). Flyface, his mom, and Willie the Fifth all co-star in this star-studded daily from the fifties. Dick Tracy shoots off a pistol in panel one — "Little Doc's" water pistol! The image area of the daily measures 16.5" x 5". The strip has several stains at the bottom of the page, mostly outside of the image area, and a pasted-on lettering correction in panel two; otherwise the art is in Very Good condition. ***From the collection of Larry Doucet.***

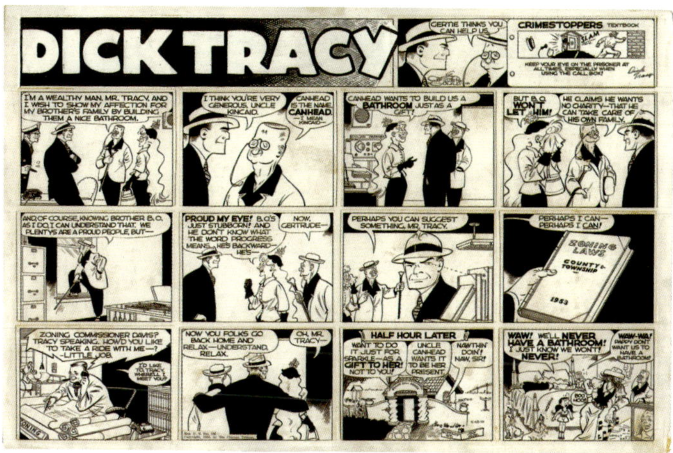

4184 Chester Gould - Dick Tracy Sunday Comic Strip Original Art, dated 6-28-53 (Chicago Tribune, 1953). B.O. Plenty wants no part of his brother's (Kinkaid "Canhead" Plenty) plan to add a bathroom onto his Sunny Dell Acres estate. This droll strip spotlights many of the features headliners — Dick Tracy, Chief Patton, Canhead, Gravel Gertie, Little Wingy, Sparkle Plenty, and B.O. Plenty. The image area of the strip is 27" x 18". Each panel of the Sunday was affixed to a larger support page; otherwise the condition of the art is Excellent.

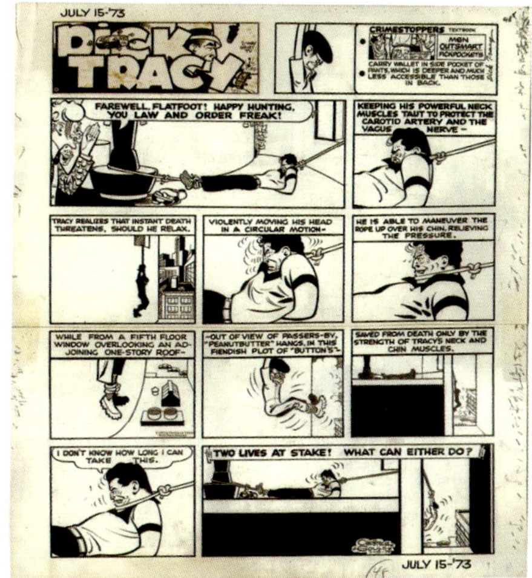

4185 Chester Gould - Dick Tracy Sunday Comic Strip Original Art, dated 7-15-73 (Chicago Tribune, 1973). Buttons has Dick Tracy and Peanutbutter tied together in a terrible deathtrap. However, the resourceful flatfoot manages to work the rope noose from around his neck and onto his chin — but he'd best be careful — his razor-sharp jaw line might slice through that hemp! The image area of the strip is 19.5" x 23.75". The Sunday was cut between panel tiers three and four and has since been taped together on the back of the paper, and the title logo stat has some mild glue staining; otherwise the condition of the art is Very Good.

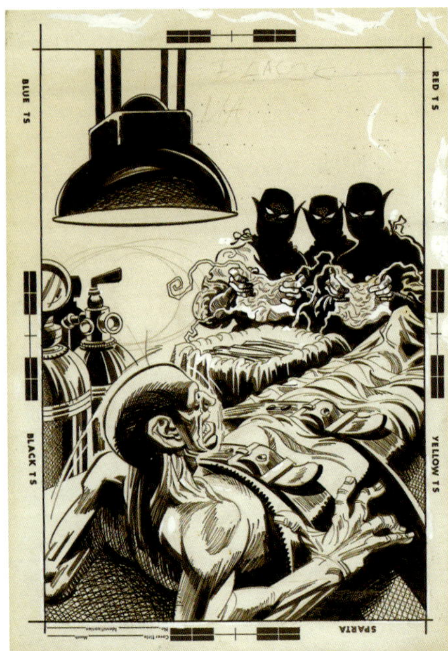

4186 Jerry Grandenetti (attributed) - Black Magic #3 Cover Original Art (DC, 1974). One of the great individual stylists of comic books, Jerry Grandenetti established himself as an innovator in the field, and was especially suited for stories in the war, mystery, and horror genres. He excelled at creating dramatic scenes from unusual angles and skewed perspectives, while still maintaining a realistic style. A panic-stricken patient discovers that his cure may be worse than his disease, on this cover from 1974. The image area measures 10" x 15" and the art is in Excellent condition.

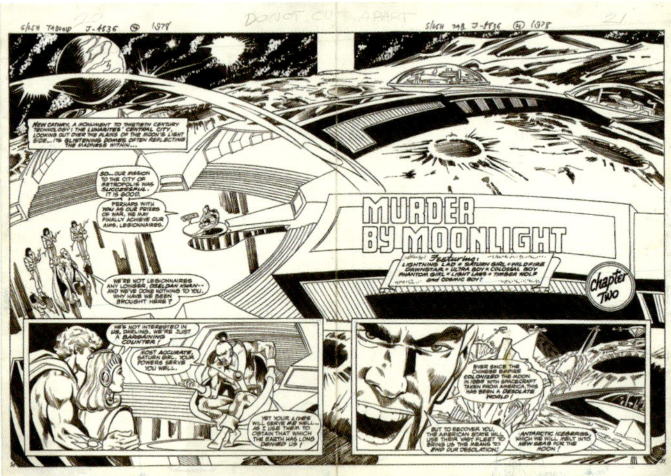

4187 Mike Grell and Vince Colletta - All New Collectors' Edition #C-55 Superboy and the Legion of Super-Heroes, Splash pages 20 and 21 Original Art (DC, 1978). The peaceful lunar setting of New Cathay, a monument to thirtieth century technology, is contrasted with the mad ravings of Oseldan Khan, who has taken Saturn Girl, and Lightning Lad as bargaining chips in his insane plan to restore water to the moon. Here are pages 20 and 21 from the Paul Levitz story, "The Millennium Massacre Chapter 2: Murder by Moonlight". The image area measures 22" x 15", and, aside from some slight soiling along the center of the two conjoined pages, and a minor glue stain in the final panel, the condition of the work is Excellent.

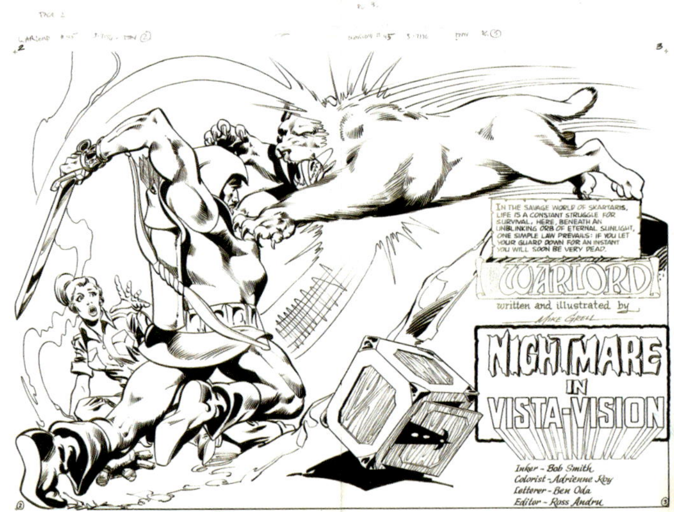

4188 Mike Grell and Bob Smith - The Warlord #45, Splash Pages 2 and 3 Original Art (DC, 1981). A unique series in the DC Comics firmament of stars, **The Warlord** chronicled the adventures of Air Force pilot, Travis Morgan, and his incredible descent into the lost world of Skartaris, hidden beneath the Earth's crust. It contained all the typical trappings of the sword and sorcery genre — prehistoric beasts, scantily clad women, high adventure and plenty of magic. Its hidden weapon was Mike Grell, creator, writer and penciller. Grell brought a degree of sophistication to the series, utilizing intelligent panel layouts and unpredictable narratives to tell his story. It turned conventional sword and sorcery on its axis. This double-page splash page has an image area of 21.5" x 15" and is in Excellent condition.

4189 Mike Grell, Lurene Haines, and Julia Lacquement - Green Arrow: The Longbow Hunters, page 12 Original Art (DC, 1987). Crime fighting stops being a game, and becomes deadly serious in writer/artist Mike Grell's remake of Oliver Queen in the stunning **Green Arrow: The Longbow Hunters** mini series. Skillfully portraying the humanity of the main characters, Grell spent a year putting together the three-issue, hand painted mini-series with artist Lurene Haines for what has become destined to be known by many modern Green Arrow fans as one of the best "Green Arrow Stories" ever. The image area of this page measures 11.5" x 16.5" and the art is in Excellent condition.

4190 Tom Grummett and Karl Kesel - Superboy #19 Cover Original Art (DC, 1995). Holding an ailing Valor in his arms, the Boy of Steel and the voluptuous, but volatile Knockout stand side by side against an entire army battalion, in this cover illustration for **Superboy** #3. Tom Grummett and Karl Kesel continue their "Kirby-esque" style in the life of Kon-El. The image area measures 10.5" x 15.5", and the work is in Excellent condition.

4191 Paul Gulacy and Sal Trapani - Master of Kung Fu #25, page 11 Original Art (Marvel, 1975). On a path deep within the jungle, along the Amazon River, Shang Chi is led by a group of Jivaro tribesmen to the center of their compound, where bound to a stake is a member of Chi's father's cult of Si-Fan assassins. Here is the eleventh page of Doug Moench's "Rites of Courage, Fists of Death!," penciled by Paul Gulacy and inked by Sal Trapani. The image area measures 10" x 15", and, aside from a small stain in the fourth panel, the art is in Excellent condition.

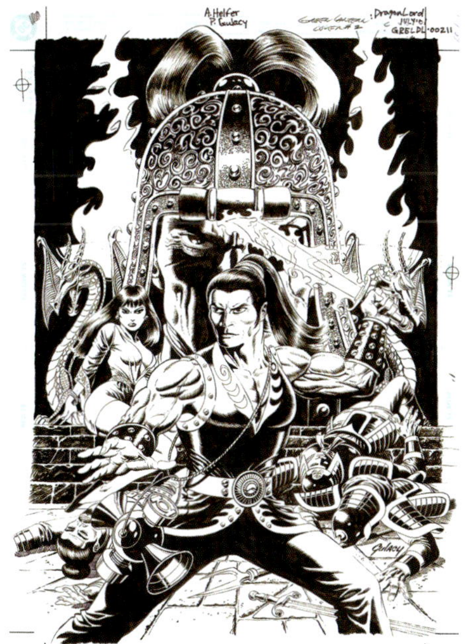

4192 Paul Gulacy - Green Lantern: Dragon Lords #2 Cover Original Art (DC, 2001). Let no evil escape your sight — ancient China served as the backdrop for this exotic addition to the traditional Green Lantern mythos. Paul Gulacy's detailed cover montage is brimming with finely rendered patterns and flickering shadows and one of Gulacy's hallmarked "good girls" flashes some decolletage— keep your eyes on the prize! The cover has an image area of 10.5" x 15.5" and the art is in Excellent condition.

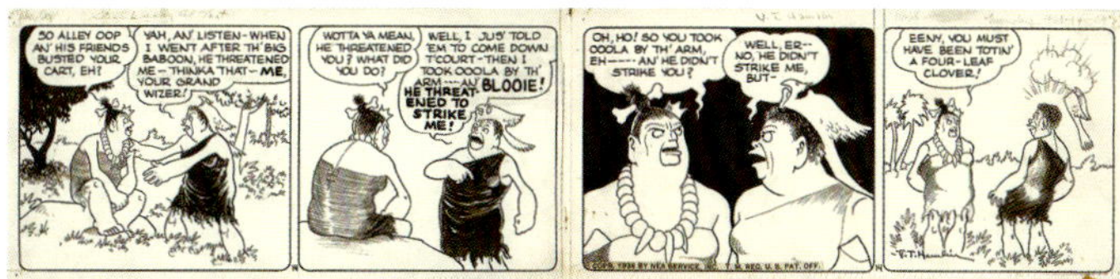

4193 Vincent T. Hamlin - Alley Oop Daily Comic Strip Original Art, dated 2-14-38 (NEA Service, 1938). Queen Oompa explains to Eeny, the Grand Wizer, that Alley Oop let her off easy, in this boisterous *Alley Oop* daily from 1938, titled "She's Luck at That". This art has an image area of 21" x 4.5". It has been folded in half and there are some pencil notations along the edges, outside of the image area. Aside from some very light scattered stains along the center, this strip is in Excellent condition.

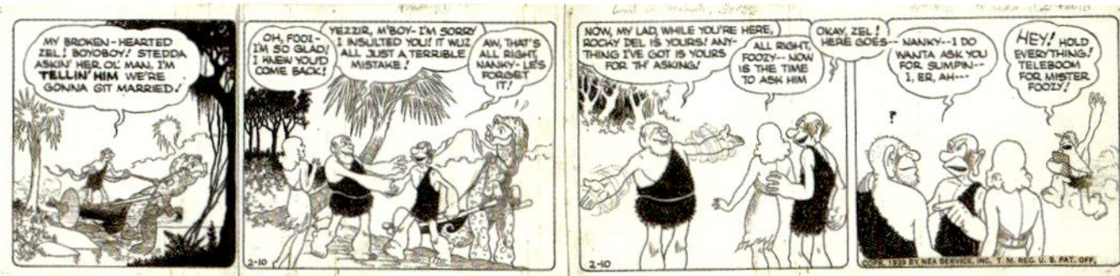

4194 Vincent T. Hamlin - Alley Oop Daily Comic Strip Original Art, dated 2-10-39 (NEA Service, 1939). Racing back to Rocky Del, Foozy is determined to ask Nanky for permission to marry his daughter, Zel. But wait, there's a teleboom for Mister Foozy! This daily is titled, "Wait a Minute Foozy," and has a 20.25" x 4.5" image area. You'll find some slight vertical stains running through several of the frames, and a fold along the center, otherwise the work is in Good condition.

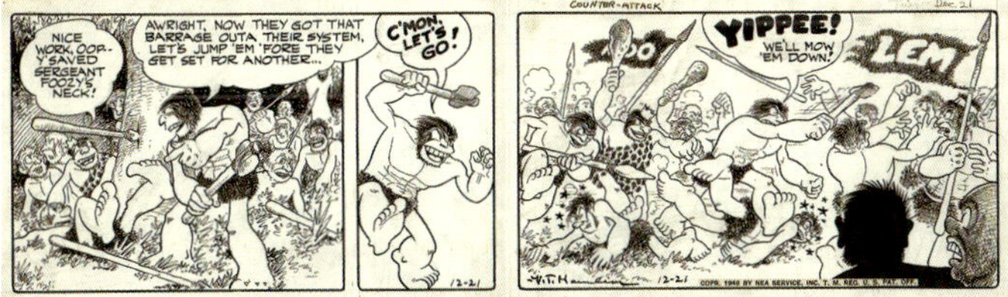

4195 Vincent T. Hamlin - Alley Oop Daily Comic Strip Original Art, dated 12-21-48 (NEA Service, 1948). If it's Alley Oop action you're craving, this strip has more than you can shake a club at! V.T. Hamlin's prehistoric protagonist, Alley Oop, King Guz, and the men of Moo, give their rival nation, Lem, a run for their money, in this daily titled, "Counter-Attack". The strip has a 20.5" x 5.75" image area. You'll find some slight soiling in the final frame, and a light fold along the center, otherwise the work is in Very Good condition.

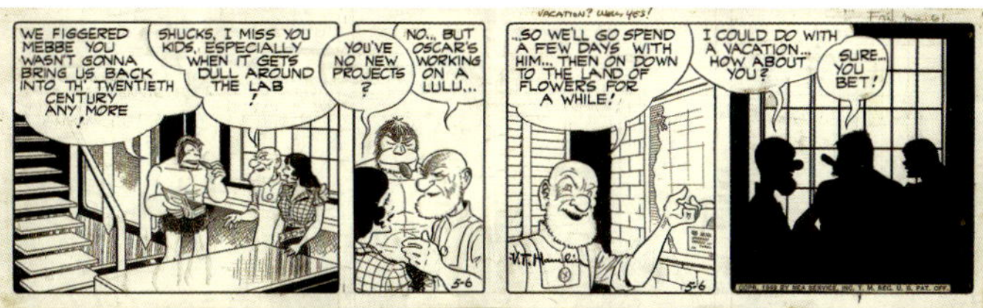

4196 Vincent T. Hamlin - Alley Oop Daily Comic Strip Original Art, dated 5-6-49 (NEA, 1949). As if going from prehistoric times to the twentieth century wasn't vacation enough! Doc Wonmug invites Alley and Ooola to take a trip with him down the the land of flowers, in this fine daily. Beautifully detailed art by Vincent T. Hamlin. The image area measures 20" x 5.75", and aside from a fold in the panel gutter between panels two and three, and some mild paper aging, this daily is in Excellent condition.

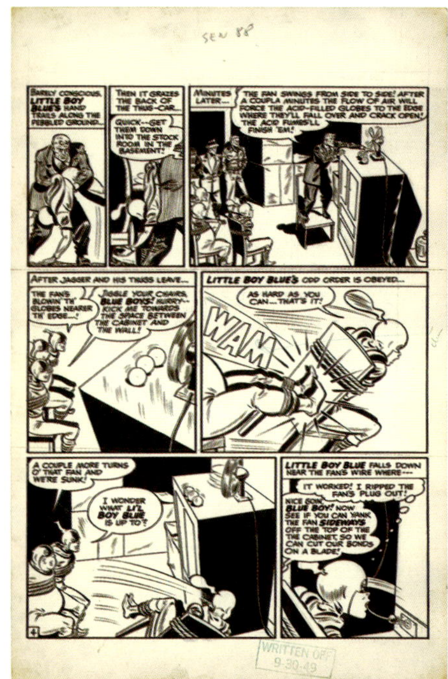

4197 Frank Harry - Golden Age Little Boy Blue and the Blue Boys Unpublished page 4 Original Art (DC, 1949). Their names are Tommy Rogers, Tubby, and Toughy, and together they are Little Boy Blue and the Blue Boys. This page was slated for **Sensation Comics** #88, although Boy Blue and the Boys made their final appearance in issue #82, in 1948. There is a production note on the page, "written off 9-30-49," which indicates that this page was never published. During the 70s, DC staffers were ordered to cut up older pages and they did as ordered, only they carefully cut each page between the panel gutters when possible and saved the art from destruction. The image area of this page measures 13" x 18". Although conjoined with tape on the back of the art, the art is in Excellent condition.

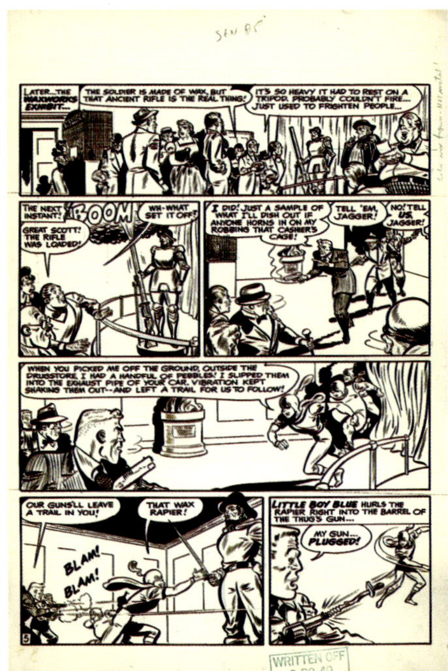

4198 Frank Harry - Golden Age Little Boy Blue Unpublished Page 5 Original Art (DC, 1949). When a waxwork museum exhibit is terrorized by Jagger and his thugs, it's Little Boy Blue and his Blue Boys to the rescue! This Golden Age page was originally slated for **Sensation Comics** #88, but was "Written Off 9-30-49," and never published. DC staffers were ordered to cut up older pages in the 1970s and they did as ordered, but they carefully cut each page between the panel gutters when possible and saved the art from oblivion. The image area of this page measures 13" x 18". The three tiers were cut from the page and later conjoined with tape on the back of the art; otherwise the art is in Excellent condition.

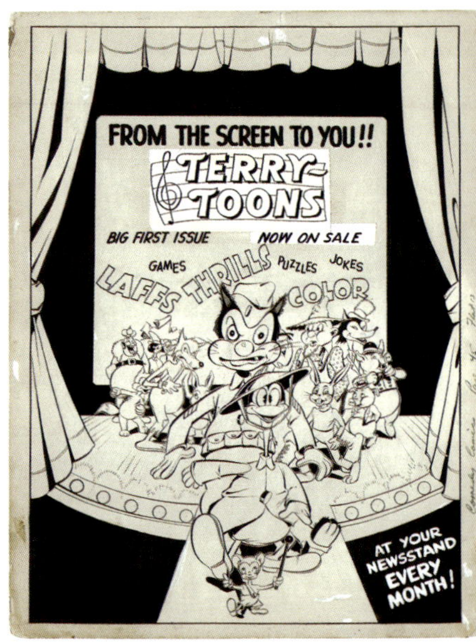

4199 Ernie Hart - Terry-Toons Comics #1 Ad Splash Page Original Art (Timely, 1942). The funny animals go to World War II on this patriotic full-page ad for the premiere issue of **Terry-Toons Comics**. Gandy Goose and Sourpuss lead the parade. Production notes indicate this ad page may have appeared in **Comedy Comics** #11 or 12. The odd mixture of war-time blood and thunder and funny animal characters had a real impact on at least one notable, youthful reader — Underground comix guru Robert Crumb. The image area of the page is 13.5" x 19" and the art is in Excellent condition.

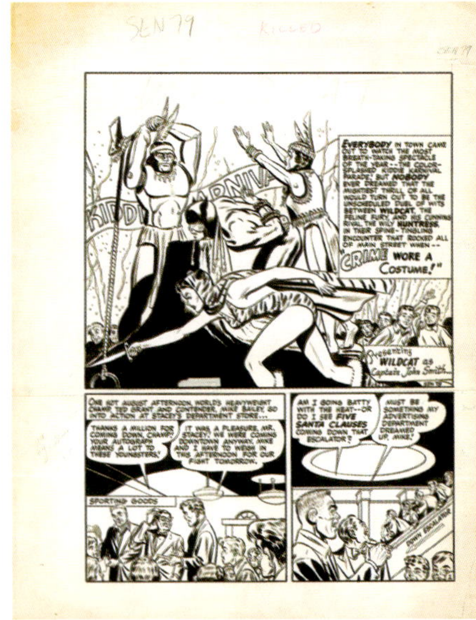

4200 Irwin Hasen (attributed) - Wildcat Complete 7-page Story "Crime Wore a Costume!" Original Art (DC, 1949). Originally slated for **Sensation Comics** #79, this Golden Age Wildcat story was subsequently "written off" and was slated to be destroyed, but the pages were cut horizontally into tiers instead. The feline fury, Wildcat, faces a duel of wits with his cunning rival, the wily Huntress, in this six-page story. The image area measures 13" x 18". The tiers have been taped together on the back of the art, there are some blue pencil line editorial notations, and edge wear (outside of the image area), otherwise the pages are in Excellent condition.

4201 Russ Heath - Our Army at War #263 Complete 12-page Story "The Cage" Original Art (DC Comics, 1973). Even a German POW camp can't keep Rock and the boys of Easy Company down! From the legendary team of Bob Kanigher and Russ Heath, this hard-hitting story is masterfully rendered and evocatively drawn. Each page has an image area of 10" x 13.5", and the art is in Excellent condition, with minor tape stains in the margins. This is a fabulous, almost cinematic, example of Russ Heath's work, and will make a worthy addition to any collection.

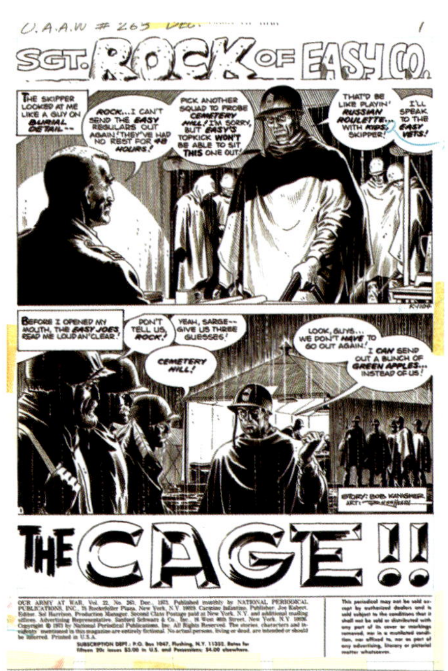

4202 Don Heck - Heart Throbs #146 Cover Original Art (DC, 1972). Love is no laughing matter for the blonde on this cover illustration, whose date has just received a note from the admiring brunette at the next table! Succinctly staged, this scintillating scenario from the seventies was made possible by the titanically talented Don Heck. The issue number is #146, the last **Heart Throbs** published. The image area measures 10" x 15", and, although there is an overall aging apparent and some white-out usage, the art is in Very Good condition. Includes all the original logo and masthead paste-ups. A copy of the cover book is included in this lot.

4203 Ralph Heimdahl - Looney Tunes #249 Cover Original Art (Dell, 1962). Have carrot, will travel! Bugs packs only the basic bunny essentials, (an oversized carrot), for his bus trip with Elmer Fudd, in this riotous cover for **Looney Tunes** #249. The image area measures 10" x 13", and although the paper has a bit of aging overall, and there is a horizontal crease along the bottom portion, and a stain along the right edge (outside of the image area), the art is in Very Good condition. Includes a copy of **Looney Tunes** #249.

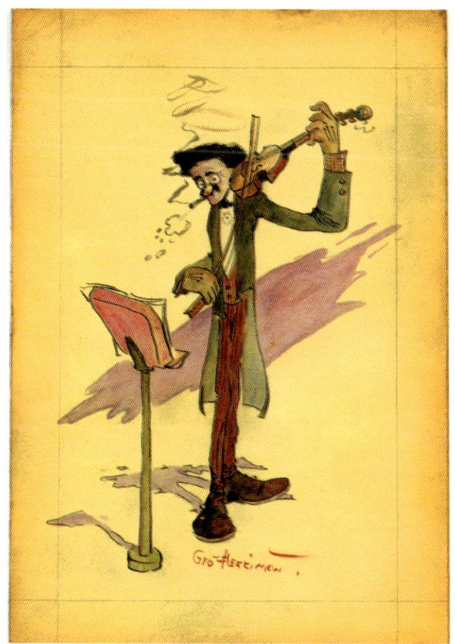

4204 George Herriman - Color News Weekly Illustration Original Art (circa 1902-03). Offered here is one of the earliest George Herriman originals known to exist, in fact, it may be *the* earliest! Herriman started his cartooning career in 1901, working for numerous weeklies, and he eventually joined the **New York World** (arguably the most important newspaper in America). If ever a comic strip was to be acknowledged as being "Art-with-a-capital-A," his immortal classic, *Krazy Kat*, is certainly one of the few candidates for such a lofty honor. A unique amalgam of humor, poetry, line, tone, and color, this illustration has an image area of 9" x 14.5" and, aside from some aging to the paper, its condition is Excellent. Signed by George Herriman at the bottom.

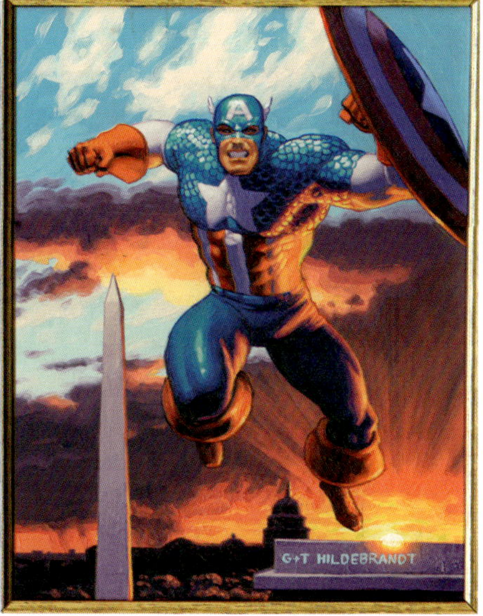

4205 Greg and Tim Hildebrandt - "Captain America" Painting Original Art (1994). Tim and Greg Hildebrandt have honed their imaginations into a superior art form, and as The Brothers Hildebrandt they are perhaps the world's finest living fantasy illustrators. America's Sentinel of Liberty has never looked more patriotic than in this painting, created by the Hildebrandts for the Marvel Masterpieces trading card set, one of Fleer's best sellers of 1994. Painted in acrylics on a sheet of 11" x 15" masonite, the art is in Excellent condition. Attractively matted in a 18" x 22" matte.

4206 Mike Hoffman - "Octavia" Illustration Original Art (2003). Whether scouring nightmare dungeons, or blasting fearsome monsters, the mysterious, white-haired beauty who haunts the dungeons of the Marquessa Octavia's remote Spanish Castle always looks sensational! Mike Hoffman delivers with this sexy and erotic rendering of his latest femme fatale, Octavia. Hoffman's surging popularity is a testament both to his ability and the power of his talent. This graphite illustration has a 9" x 12" image area, and is in Excellent condition.

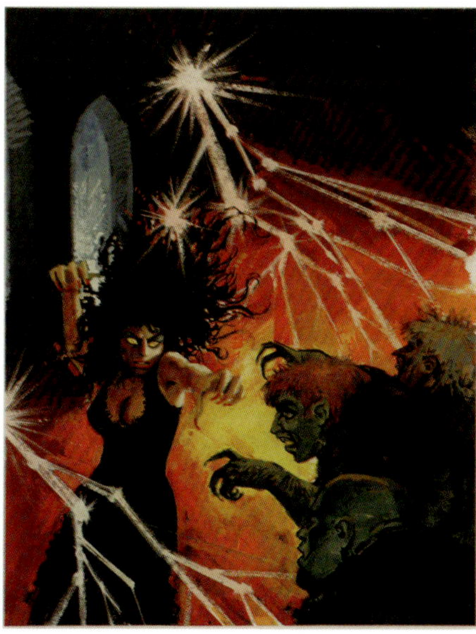

4207 Bill Hughes - Vampirella #2 Cover Preliminary Original Art (Warren, 1969). Meet Evily, Vampirella's bombshell cousin, the weirdest, wildest witch ever to cast a spell, in this color cover preliminary by Bill Hughes. Check your heartbeat before you check out Hughes' dark Princess of Vaalgania, a deadly color study for his cover to Vampi's second issue ever! The image area measures 9.5" x 12" and the work is in Excellent condition.

4208 Carmine Infantino and Bernard Sachs - Golden Age Flash Unpublished Partial Page Original Art (DC, 1948). As was noted in Roy Thomas' **Alter Ego** #12 article, "Written off 9-30-49, Part II, "In 1949 National Comics Publications, Inc. (a.k.a. DC), elected to "write off" what may be amounted to hundreds page of unpublished comic art and story, no doubt in order to get a one-time tax break. Many of these pages were stamped 'Written Off - 9-30-49" or later. During 1967-68, Marv Wolfman, an intern at the time, was ordered by production chief Sol Harrison to cut the pages of art into three pieces. Wolfman did as ordered, but he cut many of them carefully between panel tiers and he was allowed to cart off hundreds of the pages and demi-pages, dated from the 1940-60 era. In this bottom tier from an unpublished page, the Flash has to make a quick stop — at a traffic light! The image area is 13" x 6" and the art is in Excellent condition.

4209 Carmine Infantino and Bernard Sachs - Golden Age Flash Unpublished Partial Page Original Art (DC, 1949). This zippy, fast-paced partial Flash page is from a never-published, "written off" story, which was slated to be destroyed, but the page was cut horizontally into tiers instead. It's the Scarlet Speedster in action, a fast and furious slice of Golden Age glory! The image area is 13" x 6" and, aside from the top of the panels being trimmed very close to the line, the art is in Excellent condition.

4210 Carmine Infantino - Golden Age Flash Unpublished Partial Page 4 Original Art (DC, 1949). Slip-sliding your way is this terrific Golden Age Flash page, featuring the Scarlet Speedster in action! Never published, this art was stamped "written off 9-30-49" and was originally slated to be destroyed. But as fate would have it, the art was cut horizontally into tiers by a DC staffer and saved. These bottom two tiers show the Flash hydroplaning into unconsciousness, while the Thinker makes his escape. The image area measures 13" x 12" and the art is in Excellent condition.

4211 Carmine Infantino and Bernard Sachs - Golden Age Flash Unpublished Partial Page Original Art (DC, 1949). This bottom tier of a Golden Age Flash page was stamped, "Written Off 9-30-49," and slated to be destroyed, but the page was cut horizontally into tiers instead. In these two thrilling panels, the Scarlet Speedster zips up the side of a building to see through a skylight! The image area is 13" x 5.75" and, aside from the top of the panels being trimmed, and a blue pencil editorial marking in the final panel, the art is in Excellent condition.

4212 Carmine Infantino and Bernard Sachs - Golden Age Flash Unpublished Partial Page Original Art (DC, 1949). Jay Garrick, the Fastest Man Alive, has a brush with a deadly giant magnet, in this bottom tier of an unpublished Flash page. This Golden Age page was "Written Off 9-30-49," and slated to be destroyed, but the page was cut horizontally into tiers instead. The art has an image area of 13" x 6" and is in Excellent condition.

4213 Carmine Infantino - Golden Age Flash Unpublished Partial Page 8 Original Art (DC, 1949). The Flash continues to trail the Thinker in this partial page from 1949. The art was stamped "written off 9-30-49" and was originally slated to be destroyed. But as fate would have it, the art was cut horizontally into tiers by a DC staffer and saved. The image area measures 13" x 6" and, aside from a blue line editorial marking in the first panel, the art is in Excellent condition.

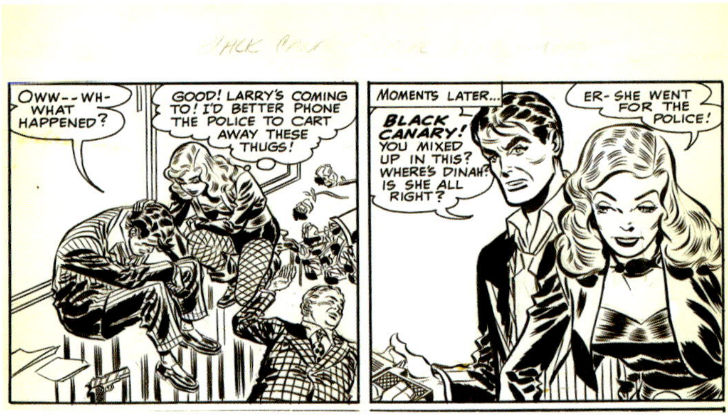

4214 Carmine Infantino - Golden Age Black Canary Unpublished Partial Page Original Art (DC, 1949). The Black Canary explains to Larry that Dinah Drake has gone for the police, in this top tier to an unpublished page from the story, "Special Delivery... Death!" Gorgeous work by the legendary Carmine Infantino, with two fabulous portraits of the Canary. "Written off" by DC editors in 1949, this art was saved from destruction in the 1960s by some DC staffers who, ordered to dispose of the old artwork, cut the pages horizontally in the spaces between the panels, rather than diagonally. The image area measures 13" x 6" and, aside from some moderate aging, the work is in Excellent condition.

4215 Klaus Janson - World's Finest Comics #304 Cover Original Art (DC, 1984). One has the power of nulling light and sound, and the other has mastered the art of teleportation — together they are Null and Void. The long-awaited origin of Superman and Batman's nastiest nemeses is the cover feature for this issue of **World's Finest Comics**, which was illustrated by Klaus Janson. The image area measures 10" x 15", and the art includes the original logo and masthead paste-up photocopy art. There is one small stain at the top right corner, otherwise the work is in Excellent condition.

4216 Western Publishing Artist - The Jetsons #21 Cover Original Art (Gold Key, 1966). When Rosie, the stainless steel maid-servant of the Jetsons household, says "pick up your feet," she's not fooling around! The first family of the future is featured on this cover illustration, which has an image area of 10" x 11". In Excellent condition. Includes a copy of **The Jetsons** #21.

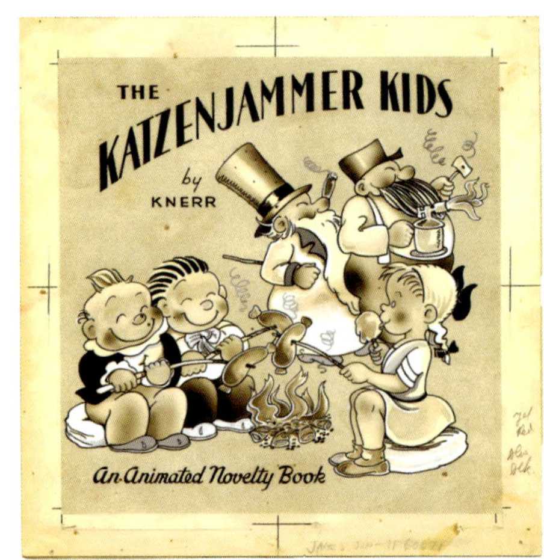

4217 James Jon - The Katzenjammer Kids by Knerr An Animated Novelty Book Cover and Production Original Art, Group of 4 (John Martin's House, 1945). Here's a selection of enchanting black and white and color illustrations for this rare, and hard to find spiral-bound book. Includes a mock-up of the book, with a hand-painted cover in full-color on a sheet of vellum paper, two hand-painted interior page mock-ups, and the original hand-painted black and white cover art (this was the initial plate that the colorist used to strip in the color). The image area of the mock-up measures approximately 8" x 8.5" (roughly the size of the actual book), and the art is in Excellent condition.

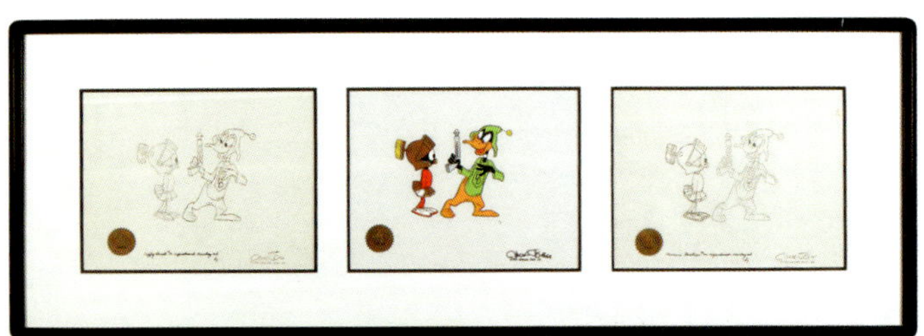

4218 Chuck Jones - Duck Dodgers and Marvin the Martian Pencil Drawing and Hand Painted Cel, Group of 3 (Warner Bros., 1980). Duck Dodgers demonstrates the proper use of a disintegrator ray gun, in this delightful set, consisting of three pieces. Linda Jones Enterprises produced this snazzy selection of original pencil drawings, combined with their photocopies on acetate (which, in production, would later be painted on the back), and a hand inked and hand painted cel of the combined scene, all signed by Chuck Jones. The image area of each individual piece measures 12" x 9" and the condition is Excellent.

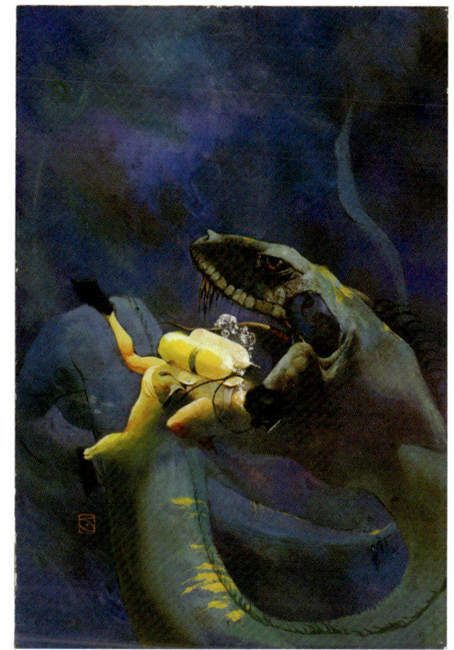

4219 Jeff Jones - "Sea Siege" Paperback Book Cover Painting Original Art (Ace Books, 1971). After breaking into the comics field in the early 1970s, Jeff Jones soon reduced the amount of his sequential art assignments in order to focus his efforts more on the illustration and fine art markets. Celebrated as a modern successor to the masters of classical illustration, Jones ranks among the top artists in the field. Powerful yet subtle, this cover painting is a superb example of Jones' paperback cover approach, capturing a mood and a moment perfectly. The oil on masonite painting has an image area of 20" x 30", and the art is in Excellent condition. A printer's proof of the paperback cover is included in this lot.

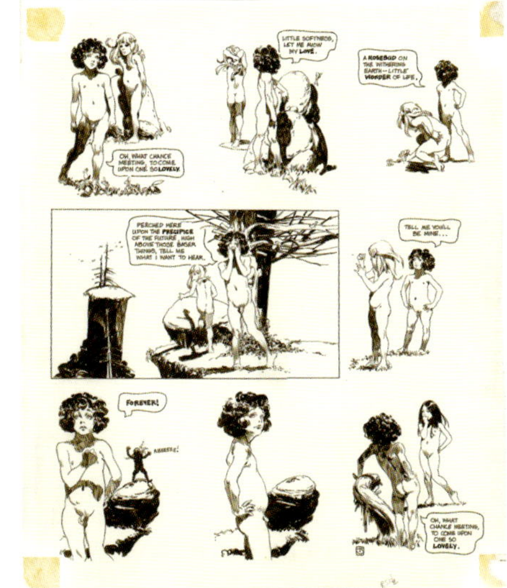

4220 Jeff Jones - "Idyl" Page Original Art (National Lampoon 1972). Jeff Jones explores the fickle sentiments of ever-lasting love, as a young lad sweet-talks two young ladies. From the infamous "Idyl" strip in the October, 1972 issue of **National Lampoon**. The image area of the art measures 18" x 23", and the art is in Excellent condition.

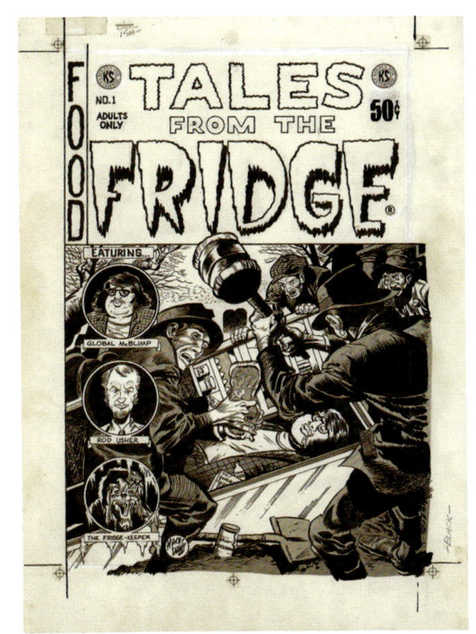

4221 Russ Jones and Bhob Stewart - Tales From the Fridge Cover Original Art (Kitchen Sink, 1973). From the halcyon years of Underground Comix comes this cool cover, giving a hint to just how important the EC line of comics were to the Underground scene of the late 1960s and '70s. Written by long-time EC fan and Wally Wood associate Bhob Stewart, and illustrated in a dead-on imitation of Jack Davis (this cover is signed "Hack Davis") by **Creepy** artist Russ Jones, this parody of **Tales From the Crypt** boils down to a series of "fat jokes" starring the man in glasses (looking a little like a young Bill Gaines) having a "steak" driven into his heart. The page measures 13" x 18" with an image area of 10.5" x 15". Other than a bit of light soiling along the outside borders, this piece is in Excellent condition. Dig in, and pass the mayo!

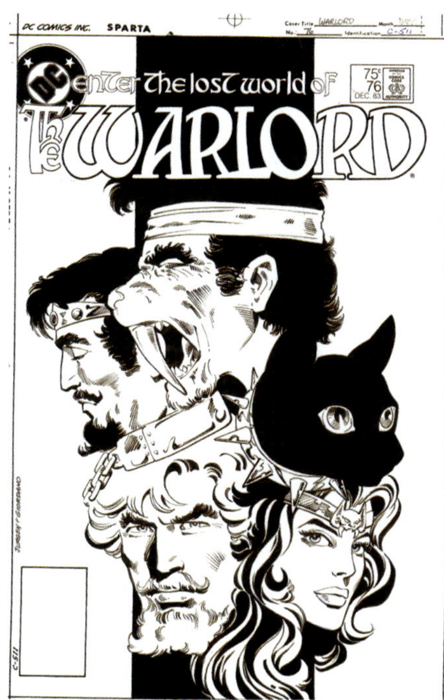

4222 Dan Jurgens and Dick Giordano - The Warlord #76 Cover Original Art (DC, 1983). Along with the luscious art by Dan Jurgens and Dick Giordano, you get a picture of Travis Morgan, along with his Shamballah allies, Tara, Queen of Shamballah and the Warlord's love, and Shakira the Cat-woman. The forces of Saber-Tooth have conquered Shamballah, and Travis Morgan and his allies try to cope in the interior story, "Aftermath," which was written by Cary Burkett. The image area measures 10" x 15", and the condition of the art is Excellent. Includes all the original logo and masthead photostat art.

4223 Dan Jurgens and Dan Adkins - The Warlord #83, Page Original Art, Group of 9 (DC, 1984). In year is 2303, Travis Morgan and his band of time-travelers face the totalitarian government of the United States of the 24th Century, while Tara fights the New Atlanteans in Skartaris. Penciler Dan Jurgens and inker Dan Adkins continue the Mike Grell legacy in pages 1, 2, 3, 4, 5, 6, 7, 8, and 9 of the Cary Burkett story, "Revolution!" The image area of each page measures 10" x 15", and although the edges of almost every page has been trimmed during the printing process, the work averages Excellent condition.

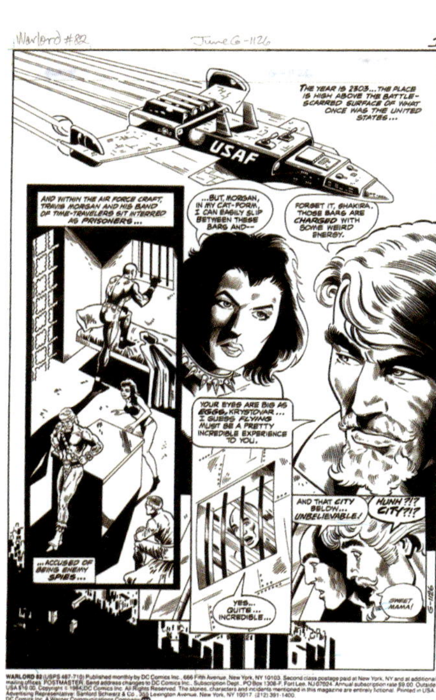

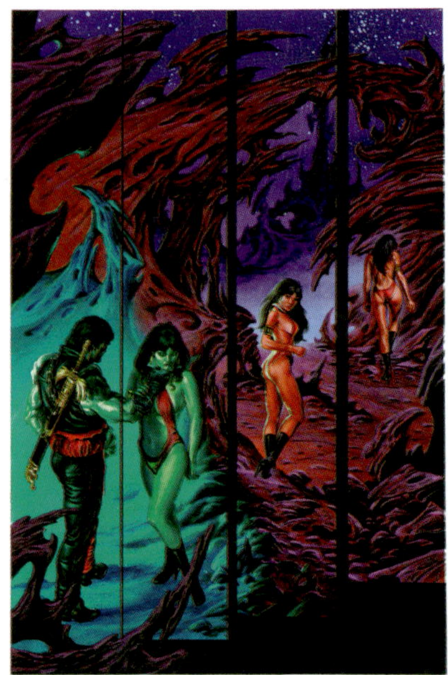

4224 Joe Jusko - Vampirella: Blood Lust #1, page 19 Original Art (Harris Comics, 1997). That vivacious vixen, Vampirella, gives a longing look over her shoulder, as she turns and walks out of a tender embrace. This is a fully finished, painted piece of comic art by Joe Jusko, featuring intense color and sensuous lighting effects on the Drakulon darling's perfect-10 figure. The overall size of the work is 12.5" x 18", and it's in Excellent condition. Includes a photocopy of the original page pencils. This painting will make your blood run hot — for Vampi.

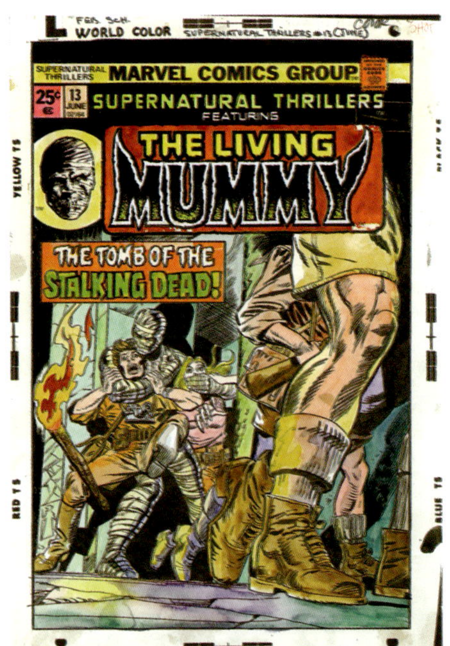

4225 Gil Kane - Supernatural Thrillers #13 Hand Colored Cover Original Art (Marvel, 1975). From the seventh issue of the "Living Mummy" storyline comes this captivating cover, in which two members of an ill-fated expedition find themselves wrapped up in the mummified grip of an ancient evil. A spectacular spectrum of color has been added by artist Gil Kane to the original art, bringing a sparkle to this work. The image area measures 9.5" x 15", and the work is in Excellent condition.

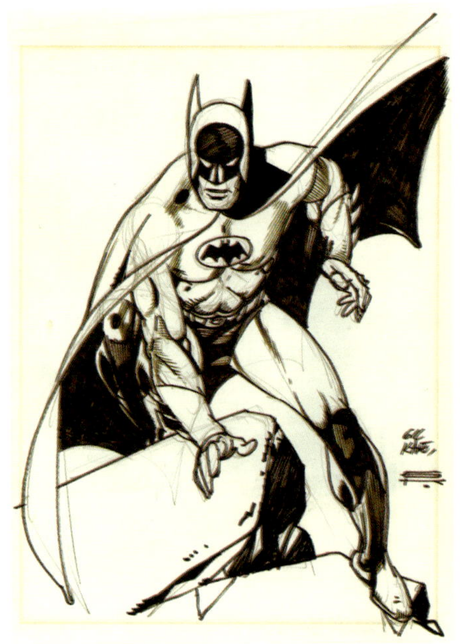

4226 Gil Kane - Batman Sketch Original Art (1977). Gotham City's guardian never looked so dynamic, than in this pencil and marker sketch by legendary Gill Kane. Drawn on the back of a promotional flyer for NEA, this interesting item also features a large photo of Kane himself, set against some of his ***Star Hawks*** daily comic strips. At the time of this drawing, Kane was the recent winner of the National Cartoonist Society's Reuben Award for "Story Strip" category for his illustration of ***Star Hawks***, the first two-tier strip for daily he co-created with Ron Goulart. The art has an image area of 11" x 16.5" and, aside from a slight discoloration from former matting, the art is in Excellent condition.

4227 Gil Kane - Anatomy Sketches Original Art (undated). Gil Kane has drawn countless comics series for Marvel, DC, and many other publishers during his 30-plus years in the business. He has always brought to his work a distinctive personality, an intelligence that gives his work a consistent quality above and beyond his amazingly skillful command of the craft. Kane filled this double-sided 17" x 13.5" sketch with numerous figure and head studies, which he drew directly in marker, without any pencil underdrawing. The paper exhibits a bit of aging, otherwise the work is in Excellent condition.

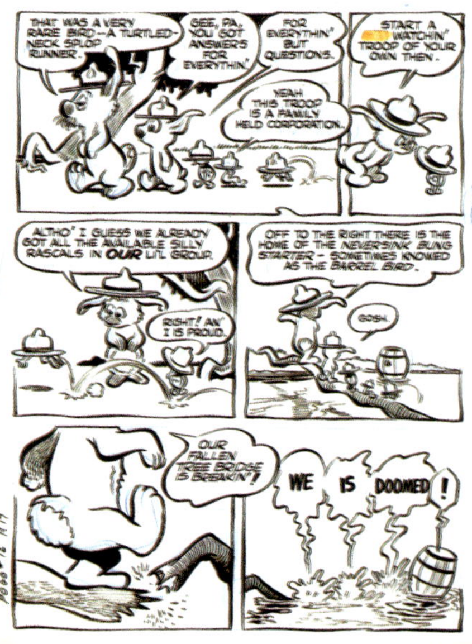

4228 Walt Kelly - Pogo Possum #12, page 12 Original Art (Dell, 1953). The Boy Bird Watcher's troop takes an unexpected detour into the river while searching for the Neversink Bung Starter, sometimes "knowed" as the Barrel Bird, in this Walt Kelly **Pogo Possum**, published by Dell Comics. The image area measures 9.5" x 13" and, aside from a missing word in the balloon in the second panel, the art is in Excellent condition.

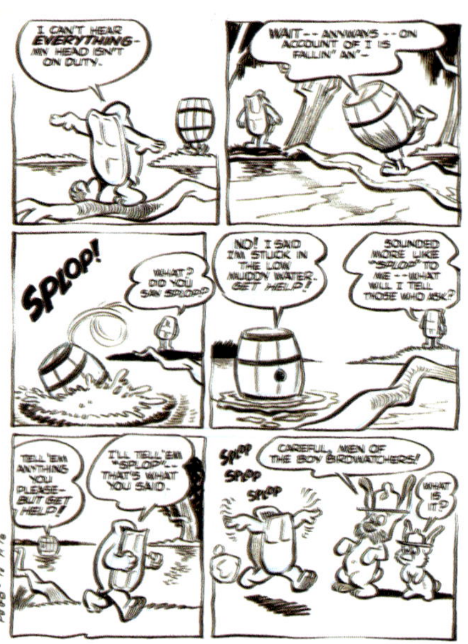

4229 Walt Kelly - Pogo Possum #12, page 16 Original Art (Dell, 1953). Churchy La Femme can't hear much because his head isn't on duty, in this "barrel of fun" panel page from Walt Kelly's Dell series. Kelly's blue pencil sketch lines are visible underneath the inks of this appealing page. The image area measures 9.5" x 13" and the art is in Excellent condition.

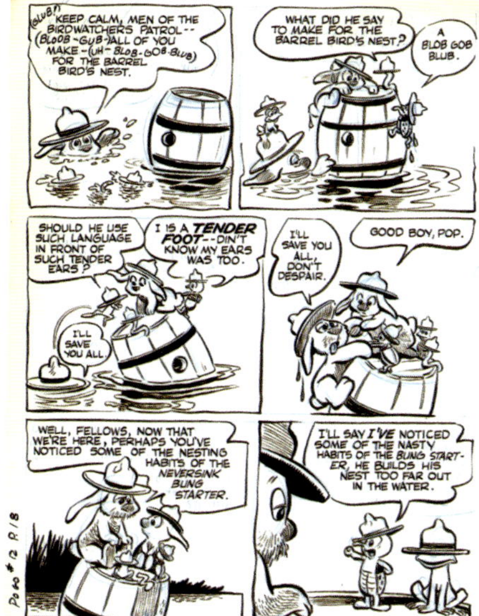

4230 Walt Kelly - Pogo Possum #12, page 18 Original Art (Dell, 1953). The men of the Boy Birdwatcher's Patrol get a soggy look at the nesting habits of the Neversink Bung Starter, in this waterlogged page from the Walt Kelly comic book series. Kelly's animated blue pencil lines show under his beautiful inks. The image area measures 9.5" x 13" and the art is in Excellent condition.

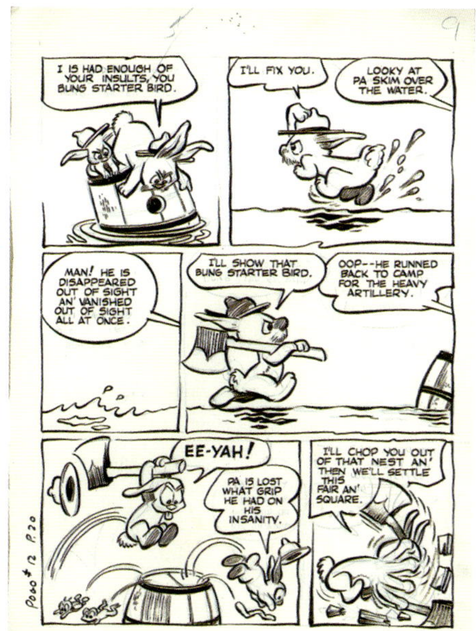

4231 Walt Kelly - Pogo Possum #12, page 20 Original Art (Dell, 1953). Pa Rabbit has lost what grip he had on his insanity! A boisterous bird in a barrel sends this mustachioed marsupial into madness, in this cute and hilarious page from the short-lived comic book series. The image area measures 9.5" x 13" and the art is in Excellent condition. These don't turn up often, so don't let this nice page pass by without a bid!

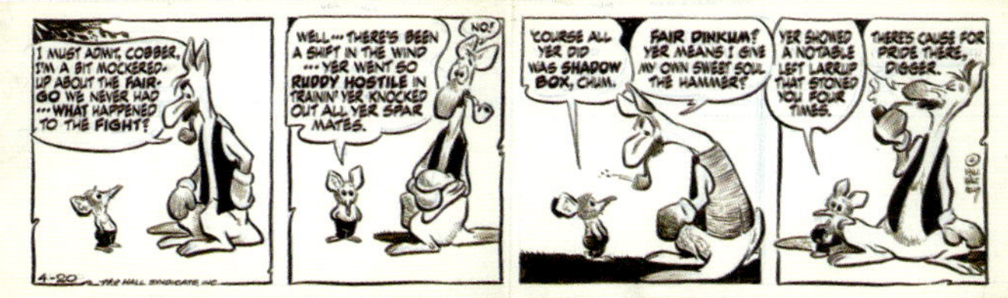

4232 Walt Kelly - Pogo Daily Comic Strip Original Art, dated 4-20-61 (Hall Syndicate, 1961). Besides being a skilled illustrator, former Walt Disney Studio animator, Walt Kelly, had a good ear for language, and often created new words to fit his characters. You can tell by the exuberance of this daily, that Kelly was certainly having fun writing this strip! Kelly's blue penciling can be seen beneath his inks. The image area is 18.5" x 5", and the art is in Excellent condition.

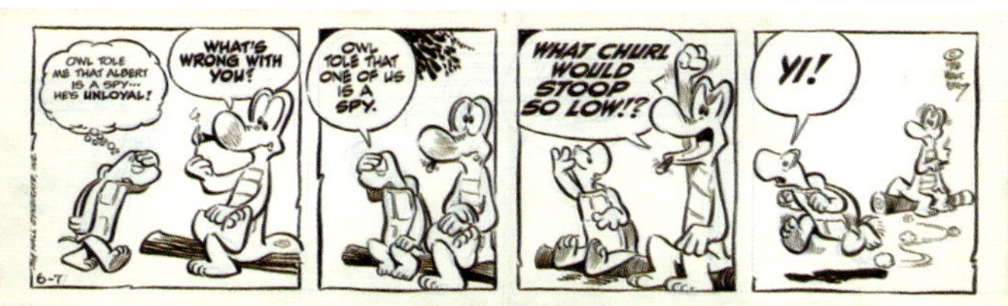

4233 Walt Kelly - Pogo Daily Comic Strip Original Art, dated 6-7-61 (Hall Syndicate, 1961). What churl would stoop so low? More verbal bombast from Walt Kelly comes your way in this daily, when Churchy Le Femme gets the word that Albert is an unloyal spy! With it's lovable characters, and engaging social and political satire, Kelly's *Pogo* belongs among a canon of classics comic strips. Kelly's blue penciling can be seen beneath his inks. The image area is 20" x 5.5", and the art is in Excellent condition.

4234 Walt Kelly - Pogo Daily Comic Strip Original Art, dated 4-19-68 (Hall Syndicate, 1968). Howland Owl goes into a panic after swallowing an "eminently edibobble" "Pogo for Pres" campaign button. Walt Kelly's ever-popular *Pogo* was a witty, political kick in the shins, brought to life by a comedy master. Kelly's blue penciling can be seen beneath his inks. The image area is 20" x 5.5", and the art is in Excellent condition.

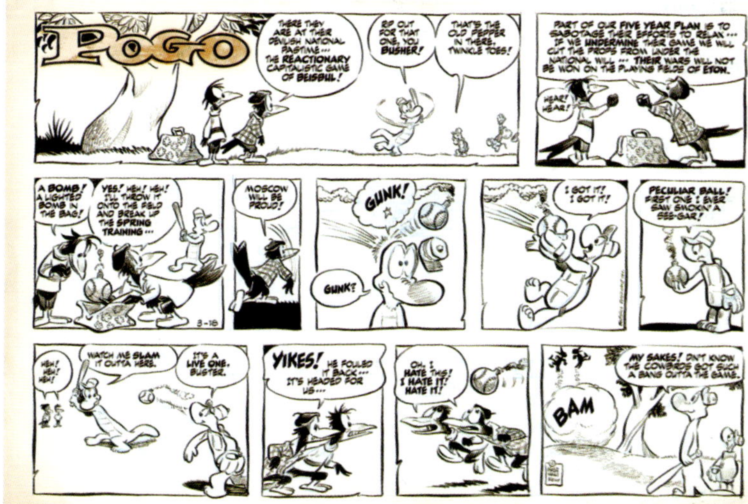

4235 Walt Kelly - Pogo Sunday Comic Strip Original Art, dated 3-18-62 (Hall Syndicate, 1962). You'll get a bang outta this animated *Pogo* Sunday, as two Moscow cowbirds make an effort to sabotage Pogo and his pals at their "devilish national pastime," the "reactionary capitalistic game of ***beisbul***!" Walt Kelly's lines ebb and flow, along with his easy-going story-telling style. As in many of Kelly's work, you can see his blue penciling underneath the inks. The image area is 23.5" x 16", and the art is in Excellent condition.

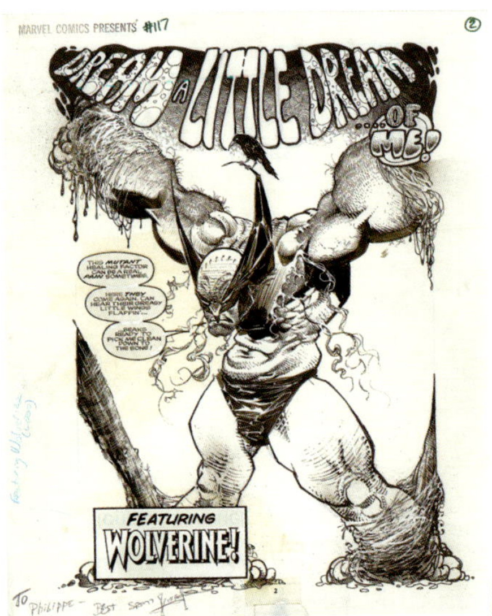

4236 Sam Kieth - Marvel Comics Presents #117, Splash Page 2 Original Art (Marvel, 1991). With an innovative design approach, and luscious pen and ink work, Sam Kieth garnered popular and critical acclaim for his Wolverine series from **Marvel Comics Presents**. Intricately rendered, Kieth's dynamic style can only fully be appreciated in the original; too much detail was obscured in the less-than-perfect printing process used in the early 1990s. This splash page to the story, "Dream a Little Dream," written by Howard Mackie, has an image area of 10.5" x 15.5". Aside from some light staining around the word balloons, and at the bottom around the title type, the art is in Excellent condition. Signed and inscribed the Sam Kieth at the bottom left.

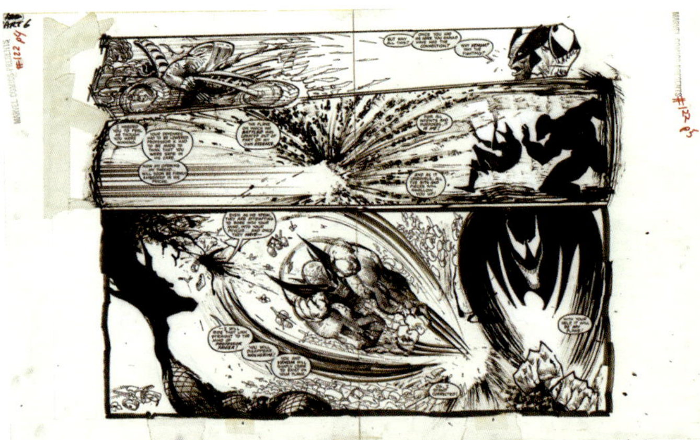

4237 Sam Kieth - Marvel Comics Presents #122 pages 4 and 5 Original Art (Marvel, 1993). Wolverine versus Venom — the mere concept guaranteed a wild and wooly *battle royale*, and Sam Kieth delivered the goods with verve. His manic double-page showdown for "Nightmares End (Claws and Webs)" was nothing less than a modern Marvel milestone. The image area of these conjoined pages is 20" x 15". The pages were taped together on the back, and the word balloons and captions are stick-ons; otherwise the art is in Excellent condition.

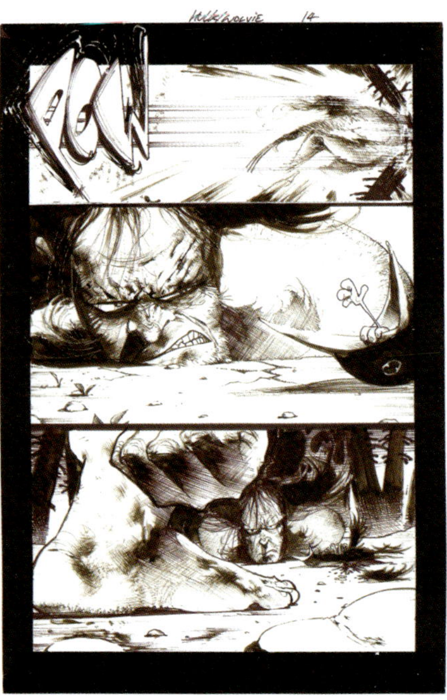

4238 Sam Kieth - Wolverine/Hulk, page 14 Original Art (Marvel, 2002). When Marvel Comics introduced the world to Wolverine in **The Incredible Hulk** #181 in 1974, it unleashed a multifaceted character that still captivates readers over 30 years later. In 2002, the adamantium-clawed X-Man and the Green-skinned Goliath crossed paths again, courtesy of Sam Kieth, in a four-issue mini-series, **Wolverine/Hulk**. Kieth wrote and illustrated this series, which had readers recalling his Wolverine art from **Marvel Comics Presents**. This page has an image area of 10" x 15.5" and the condition is Excellent.

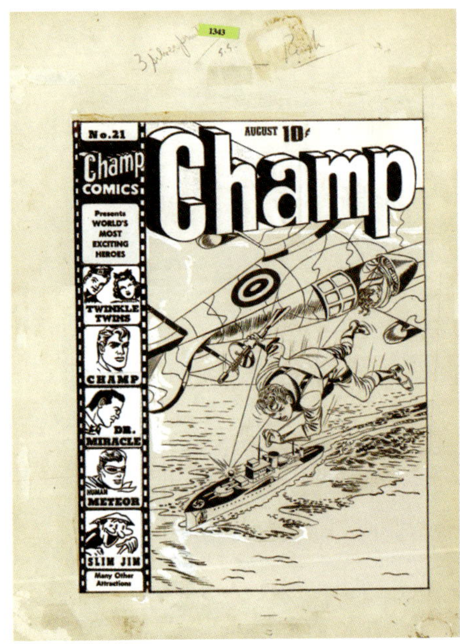

4239 Jack Kirby and Joe Simon - Champ Comics #21 Cover Original Art (Harvey, 1942). This is a terrific WWII propaganda cover, with an American Liberty Lad bailing out of a British plane, ready to take on the Nazi warship below, with nothing but a tommy-gun! The logo and masthead elements are recent photocopy replacements. The art has an image area of 10.5" x 14.5". There are small touches of white-out, and some wear, to the lower right corner of the art paper, well outside the art area, otherwise the art is in Very Good condition.

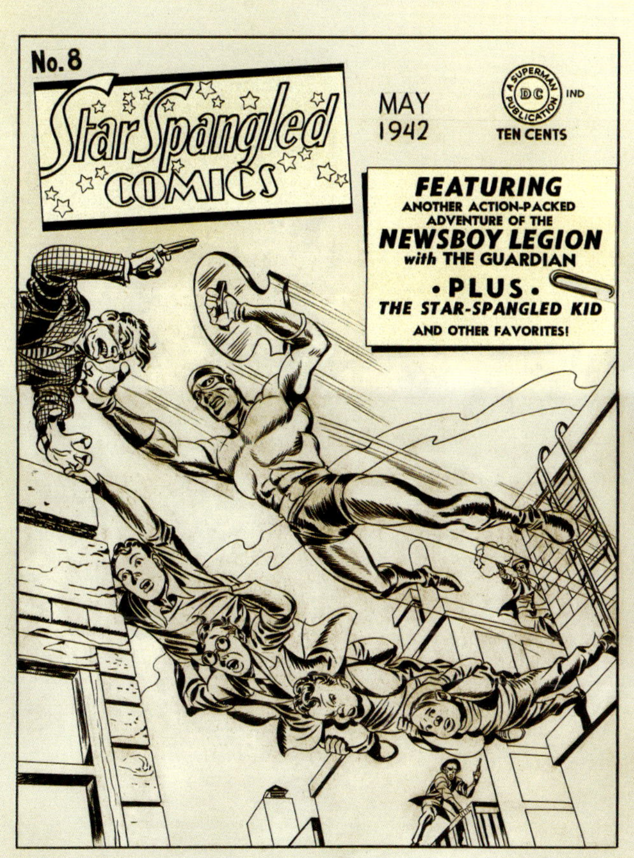

4240 Jack Kirby and Joe Simon - Star-Spangled Comics #8 Cover Original Art (DC, 1942). The Newsboy Legion and the Guardian, in their second appearance, are featured on this fantastic Joe Simon and Jack Kirby cover illustration. The Newsboys were one of S&K's great "Dead End"-style kid gangs; teamed with policeman-turned masked hero, the Guardian, they inhabited over fifty issues of this long-running title. This cover may make you a little dizzy; it's a wild perspective view of the gang straddling two tall buildings, making a human bridge for the Guardian as he battles two gun-wielding bad guys. The shot of the Guardian, sailing through the air, is Jack Kirby at his Golden Age best. Illustrated on a sheet of 16" x 21" illustration board, the art has an image area of 12.5" x 17", and has been professionally restored, leaving it in Excellent condition. The logo and titles are recent photocopy replacements. It's a very beautiful piece, one that is sure to be the highlight of some lucky bidder's collection!

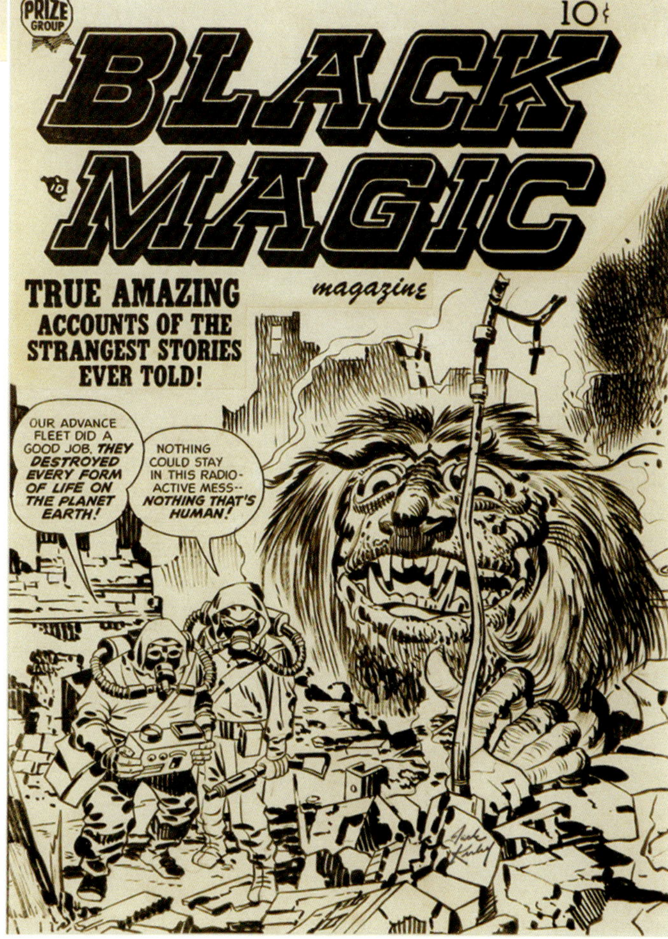

4241 Jack Kirby and Joe Simon - Black Magic Unused Cover Original Art (Prize, circa 1952). The Simon and Kirby team's work for Prize was the refined culmination of their long partnership in comics — their hard-hitting artwork was more detailed than their 1940s work and more finished as well. This wild and woolly scene (perhaps deemed too intense by the newly established Comics Code Authority) has been regarded by many Kirby aficionados as a precursor to the "prehero" Marvel monster books that Kirby is celebrated for. This unused **Black Magic** shocker finally saw print in Kirby's 1971 portfolio **Kirby Unleashed**. The image area of the cover measures 12.5" x 17.5". The logo is a carefully color-matched replacement; otherwise the art is in Excellent condition.

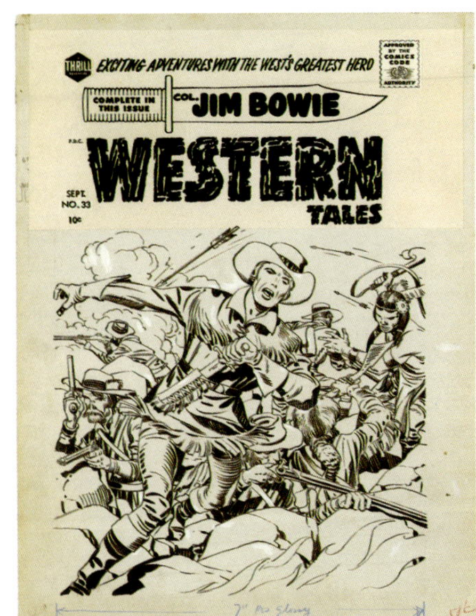

4242 Jack Kirby and Joe Simon - Western Tales #33 Jim Bowie Cover Original Art (Harvey, 1956). Jim Bowie leads a desperate break-out charge in this heated battle scene — but what's with that puny pig-sticker he's drawing? — it must be his back-up blade! Jack Kirby loved drawing Westerns and it shows in the power of this rousing cover. The image area of the page measures 12" x 18.5". The logo is a replacement; otherwise the art is in Excellent condition. This spectacular piece is sure to be a welcome addition to any Simon and Kirby fan's cover collection!

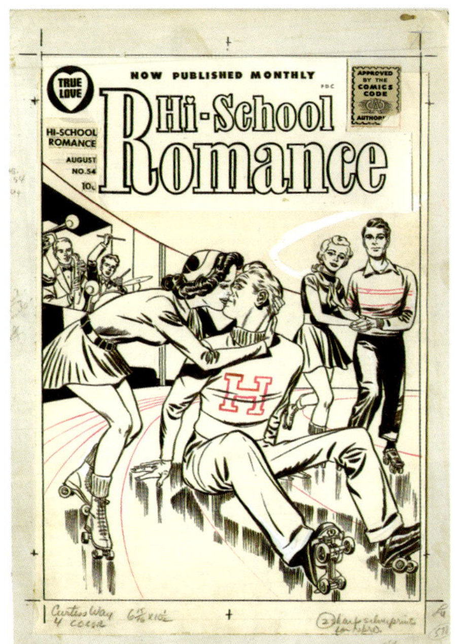

4243 Jack Kirby - Hi-School Romance #54 Cover Original Art (Harvey, 1956). It's easy to take a hard fall in matters of the heart, but this lucky hi-school letter-man is comforted with a kiss from his gal-pal after a spill at the roller-rink. With his work in the romance genre, Jack "King" Kirby proved he could handle tender romance scenes with as much aplomb as he did all-out action slugfests. The image area of this cover measures 12" x 17.5". The main image area of the cover was drawn on bristol paper which was then mounted to a support board, the title logo is a recent replacement, and part of the Comics Code Authority stamp has worn away; otherwise the cover is in Very Good condition.

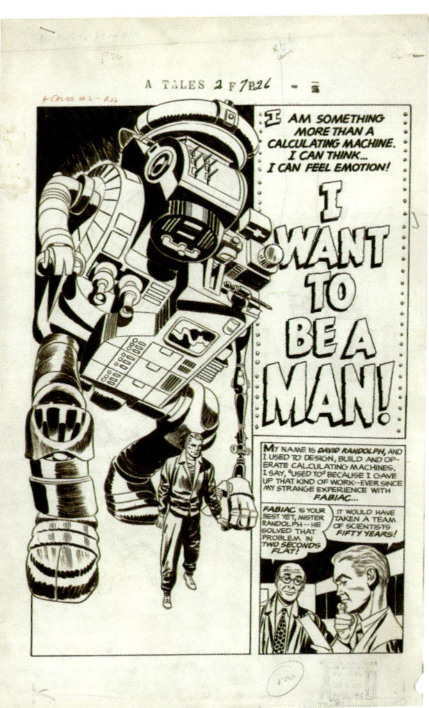

4244 Jack Kirby - Alarming Tales # 2, Complete 5-page Story "I Want To Be a Man" Original Art (Harvey, 1957). A scientist encounters a giant robot in this five page Silver Age Harvey science fiction tale. The pages have an image area of 12" x 18". There is some white-out use and minimal paper aging throughout, otherwise the art is in Very Good condition. A great example of Kirby technology!

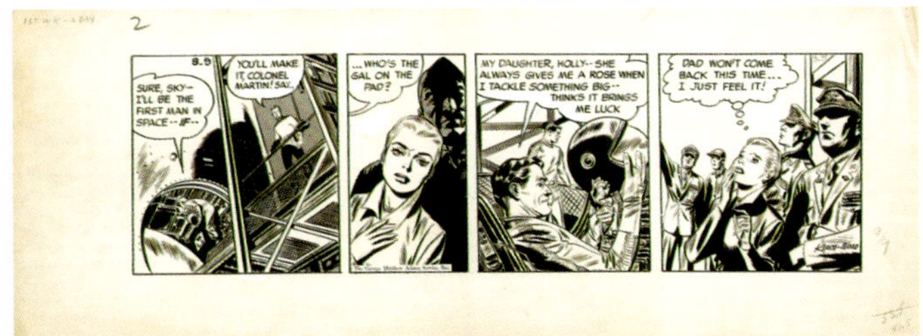

4245 Jack Kirby and Wally Wood - Sky Masters of the Space Force Daily Comic Strip Original Art, dated 9-9-58 (The George Matthew Adams Service, Inc., 1958). Two titans of the comic book field, Jack "King" Kirby and Wally Wood, joined forces on this stellar, yet short-lived science fiction strip from the late 1950s and early 1960s. This handsome daily was only the second one published! The amalgamation of Kirby's dynamic pencils with Wood's lustrous inks resulted in a look that is hard to match for drama and beauty. The strip has an image area of 18" x 5.5" and the art is in Excellent condition.

4246 Jack Kirby and Wally Wood - Sky Masters Daily Comic Strip Original Art, dated 11-26-58 (George Matthew Adams Service, 1958). A dire warning is written across a solar mirror in this suspenseful daily drawn by two supreme masters of the comic book arts — Jack Kirby and Wally Wood. Wood's addition of starkly shadowed accents to Kirby's dramatic pencils creates a remarkable depth to each scene. The strip has an image area of 18" x 5.5", and the art is in Excellent condition.

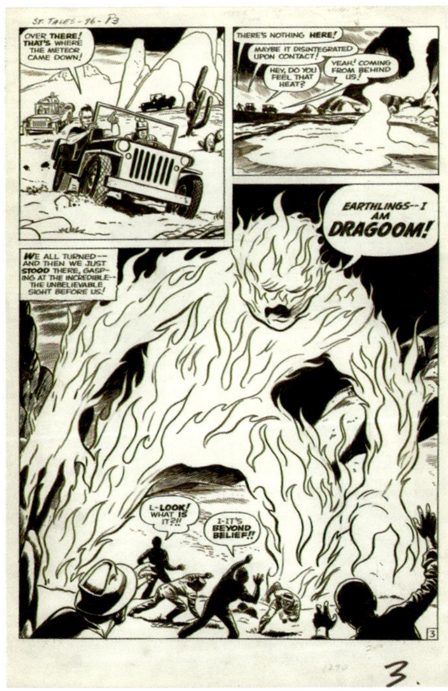

4247 Jack Kirby and Dick Ayers - Strange Tales #76, page 3 Original Art (Marvel, 1960). Dragoom, the flaming invader announces his spectacular arrival on Earth in this pyrotechnic two-thirds page splash panel. No one could top Jack "King" Kirby at creating appealing monsters. The image area of the art measures 12.5" x 18.5", and it is in Excellent condition.

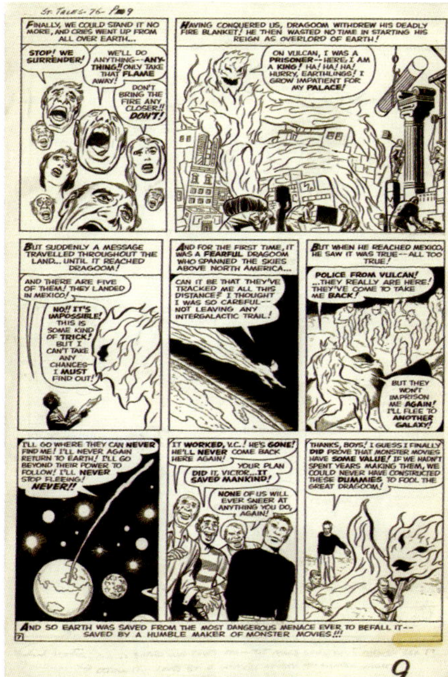

4248 Jack Kirby and Dick Ayers - Strange Tales #76, page 7 Original Art (Marvel, 1960). The fearsome Dragoom is tricked by a few slick Hollywood prop men in this wild and wonky yarn from the House of Ideas. The image area of the page measures 12.5" x 18.5" and the art is in Excellent condition. Demand for Silver Age Marvel art from the "King" is always at a fever pitch; so don't let this smokin' hot page slip by, Marvel monster fans!

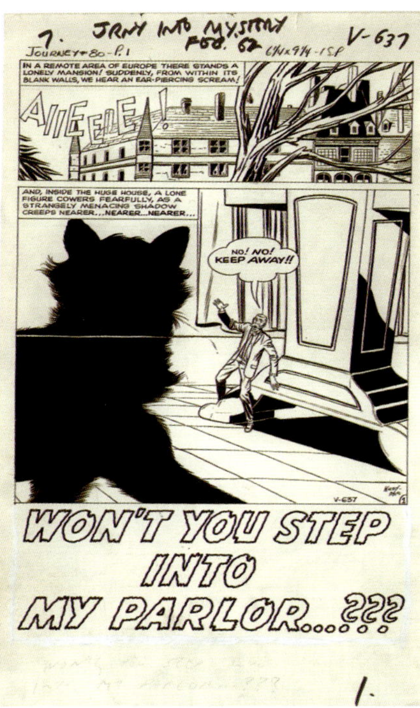

4250 Jack Kirby and Dick Ayers - Journey into Mystery #80 Splash Page 1 Original Art (Marvel, 1962). I taught I saw a puddy tat— hey, it's no laughing matter when you are only six inches tall! Jack Kirby and Dick Ayers open "Won't You Step Into My Parlor" with an absolutely riveting "story hook." This splash has an image area of 12.5" x 18.5", and the art is in Excellent condition.

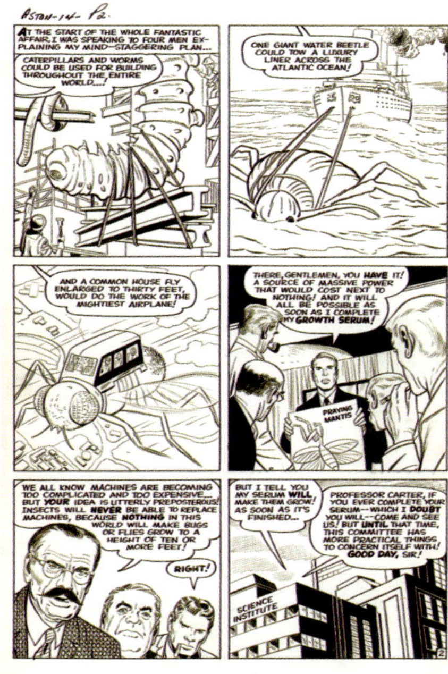

4249 Jack Kirby and Dick Ayers - Tales to Astonish #14, page 2 Original Art (Marvel, 1960). A wacky inventor details his nutty scheme to use a growth serum on insects in order to transform them into beasts of burden in "I Created Krang!" — but what would happens if a giant ant was to turn on his human "masters?" Mass carnage, that's what! Jack Kirby makes it all seem possible with his unparalleled storytelling. This sensational Marvel "monster-piece" has an image area of 12.5" x 18.5", and the art is in Excellent condition.

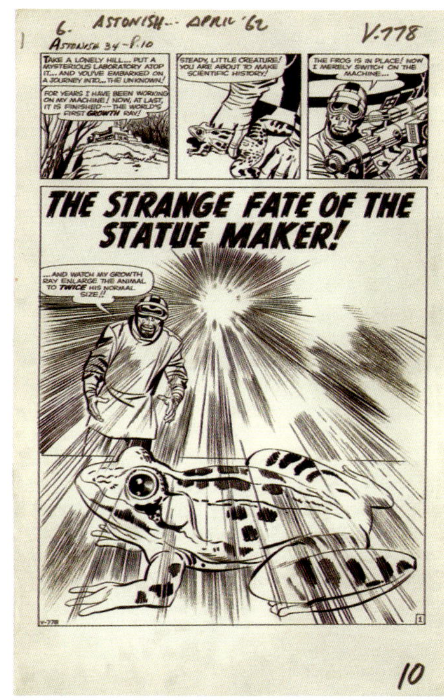

4251 Jack Kirby and Paul Reinman - Tales to Astonish #34 Complete 6-page Story "The Strange Fate of the Statue Maker" Original Art (Marvel, 1962). When greedy inventor Luther Benedict finds out his growth machine transmutes living flesh into stone, his plans for cashing in change in an unexpected manner. Will a lovely model fall victim to his insidious machine? Jack Kirby dramatized this clever variation on the story of Pygmalion and Galeta for the House of Ideas. Each page has an image area of 12.5" x 18.5", and other than a carefully taped in panel six art correction on page six, the art is in Excellent condition.

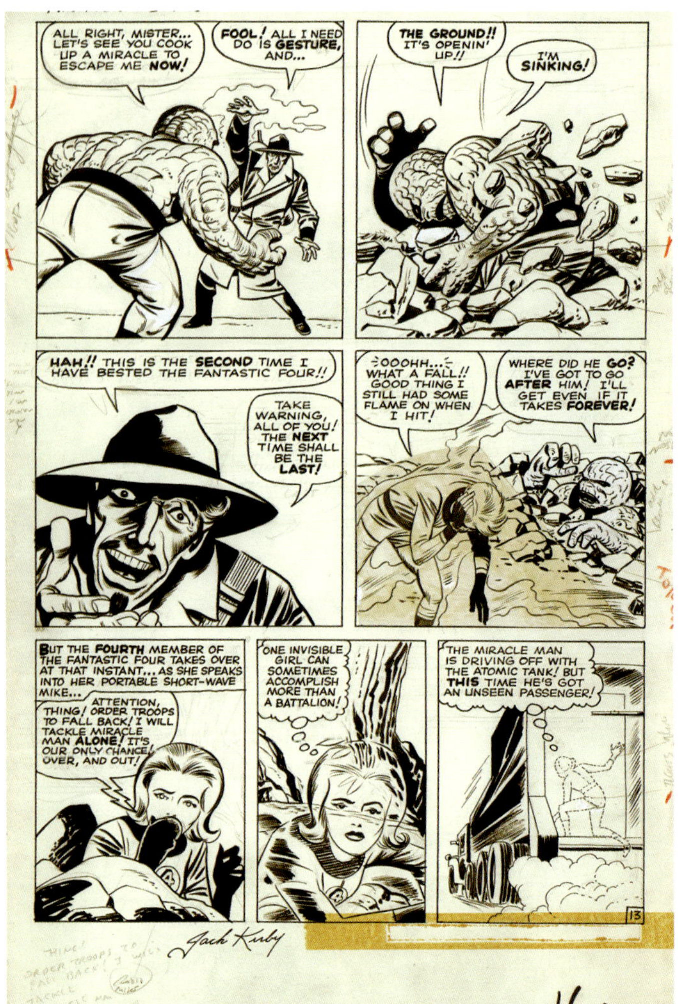

4252 Jack Kirby and Sol Brodsky (attributed) - Fantastic Four #3, page 13 Original Art (Marvel, 1963). Face front, true believers — here's the *earliest* Fantastic Four page to ever reach the marketplace! "The Menace of the Miracle Man" was the milestone yarn in which the Fantastic Four first donned their costumes — and they were designed by Sue Storm herself. Just two pages prior to this one, the ever-lovin' Thing modified his costume for battle by throwing away a fancy helmet and tearing off his shirt, bellowing, "I'm gettin' outta this monkey suit so I can *move*!" The Thing wasted no time, charging hard at the Miracle Man, who gestured hypnotically — and suddenly the ground seemed to swallow bashful Benjamin up. A flamed-out Johnny Storm was drawn as an original art paste-on, done as a correction, in panel four. Sue Storm starred throughout the final panel tier and her scene featured her as the Invisible Girl fading away and tagging along with the fleeing Miracle Man. The page has an image area of 12.5" x 18.5". Aside from the pasted-on original art in panel four, some touches of white-out on the Thing's face in the same panel, and a tape residue stain at the lower right of the page, the art is in Excellent condition. Jack Kirby signed the page in black ink in the lower left border. Don't miss out on this early piece of Marvel lore!

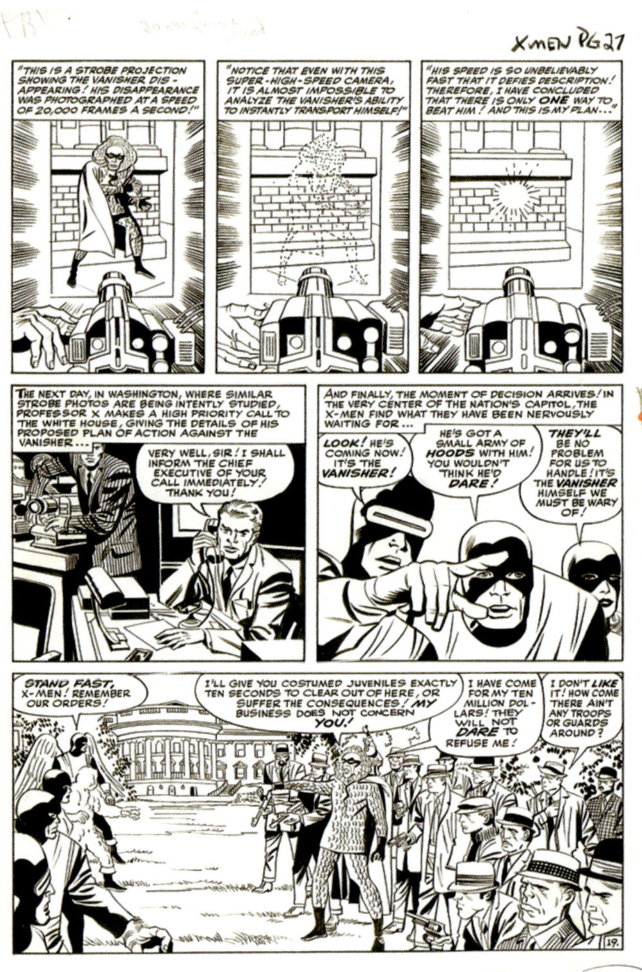

4253 Jack Kirby and Paul Reinman - X-Men #2, page 19 Original Art (Marvel, 1963). This block-busting issue of **X-Men** marked the first appearance of the villainous Vanisher, and his mutant powers are showcased in this spectacular scene, penciled by Jack "King" Kirby. The X-Men force a showdown in the last two panels and the entire teen-team is featured. This Marvel milestone is classic Kirby all the way, and it's especially thrilling since it hails from only the second issue of the trend-setting title. The page has an image area of 12.5" x 18.5", and the piece is in Excellent condition.

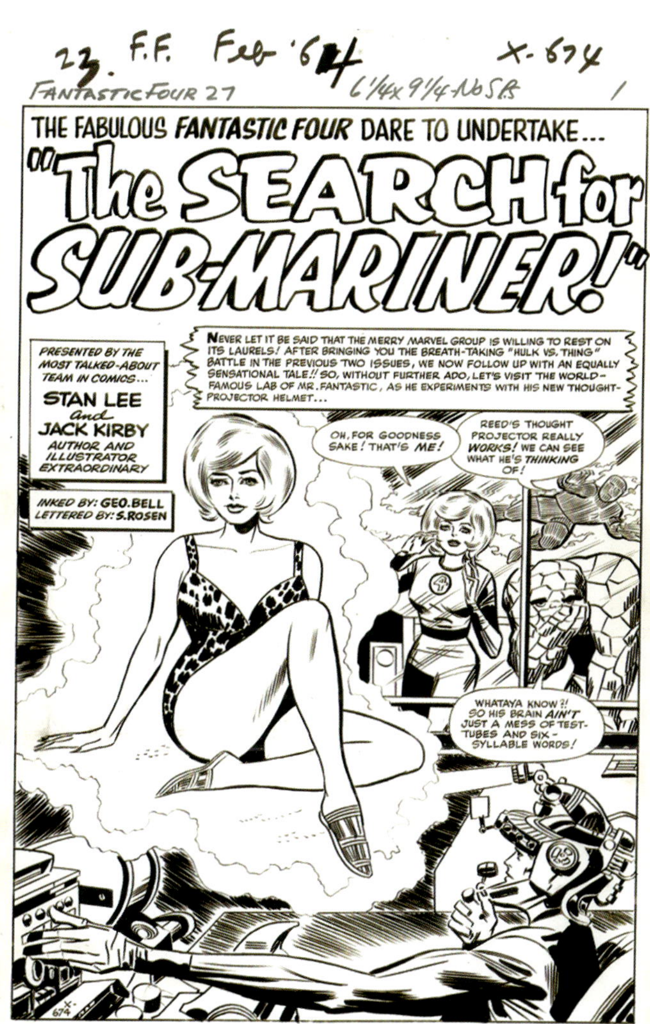

4254 Jack Kirby and George Roussos (as George Bell) - Fantastic Four #27 Splash Page 1 Original Art (Marvel, 1964). Va-va-voom — no wonder Mr. Fantastic and the Sub-Mariner are fighting to win the heart of the Invisible Girl. Reed Richards shows exactly what's on his wandering mind with this daydream image of Sue Storm in her beach wear. Jack Kirby's women had a special zaftig quality and a vitality that no other cartoonist's' "good girl" art could match. Besides a double-portrait of Sue Storm, the Invisible Girl, this gorgeous splash also spotlights the rest of the Fantastic Four team — the Human Torch, the Thing, and Mr. Fantastic. The scene even includes some of Mr. Fantastic's "Kirbytech" gizmos. This beauty has an image area of 12.5" x 18.5", and the art is in Excellent condition.

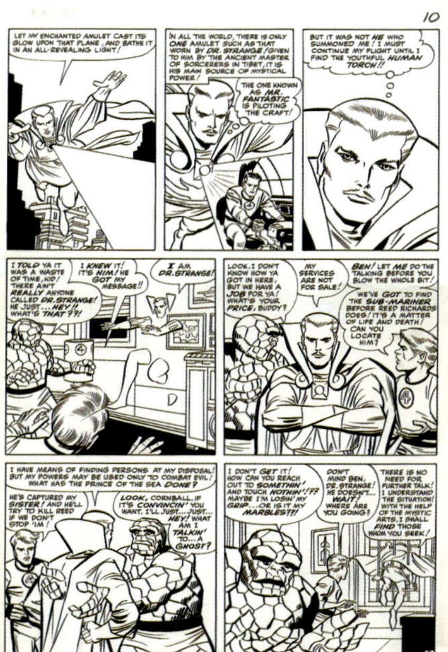

4255 Jack Kirby and George Roussos (as George Bell) - Fantastic Four #27, page 9 Original Art (Marvel, 1964). The Human Torch called in Dr. Strange, master of the mystic arts, to help the Fantastic Four in "The Search for the Sub-Mariner." The good Doctor appears in every panel of this page and the "King" captures all of the appeal of Steve Ditko's unique character design. Cross-overs such as this forged the mighty Marvel Universe and made for genuine excitement amongst the True Believers. This scene features great portraits of the Human Torch, the Thing, and Doctor Strange. This action-packed page has an image area of 12.5" x 18.5", and the art is in Excellent condition.

4256 Jack Kirby and Chic Stone - Journey into Mystery #109, Thor page 12 Original Art (Marvel, 1964). The mighty Thor, in his mortal guise at Don Blake, scrambles to survive an all-out assault by the leader of the Evil Mutants, the malevolent Magneto. Only Jack "King" Kirby could choreograph action like this! Jack Kirby signed the art in panel one. The image area of this slam-bang romp is 12.5" x 18.5", and the art is in Excellent condition. Make yours Marvel, True Believer, with this spectacular Kirby masterwork!

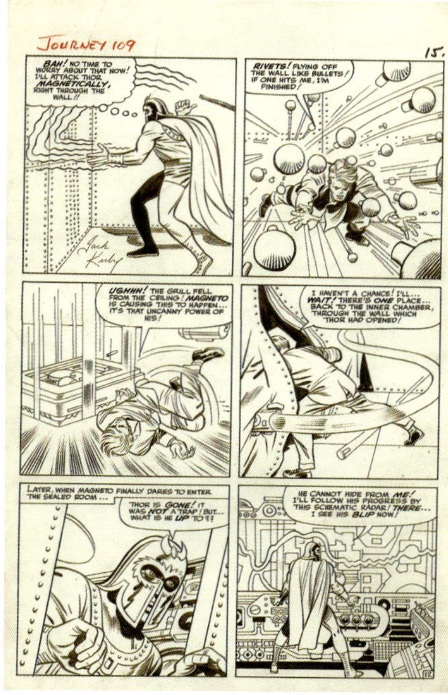

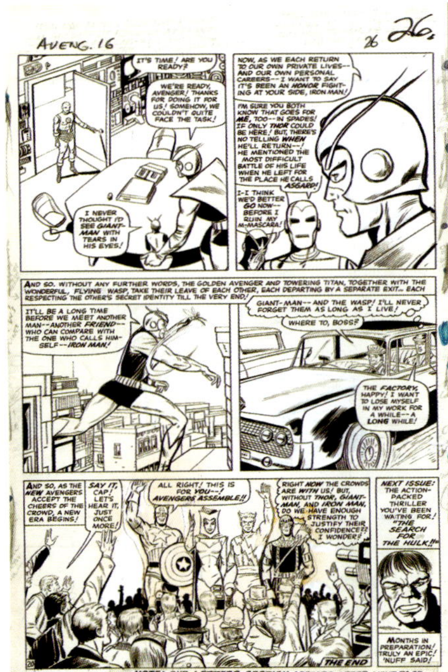

4257 Jack Kirby and Dick Ayers - Avengers #16, page 14 Original Art (Marvel, 1965). Working from Jack Kirby's spectacular "layouts," Dick Ayers tightened-up and inked this story in the tried and true Mighty Marvel manner. Iron Man, Giant Man, and the Wasp step down from the Avengers to make room for the new line-up featuring Scarlet Witch, Quicksilver, and Hawkeye. Thus, in "The Old Order Changeth," three ex-supervillains became America's highest profile superheroes - it was a thrilling moment in Marvel lore! And, as if Captain America didn't have enough to worry about, he planned to add muscle to the squad by recruiting the Hulk (who makes a cameo appearance in the final panel). There are heavy touches of white-out correction, and the Captain America and Hawkeye figures in panel five are taped-in art corrections; otherwise the art is in Very Good condition.

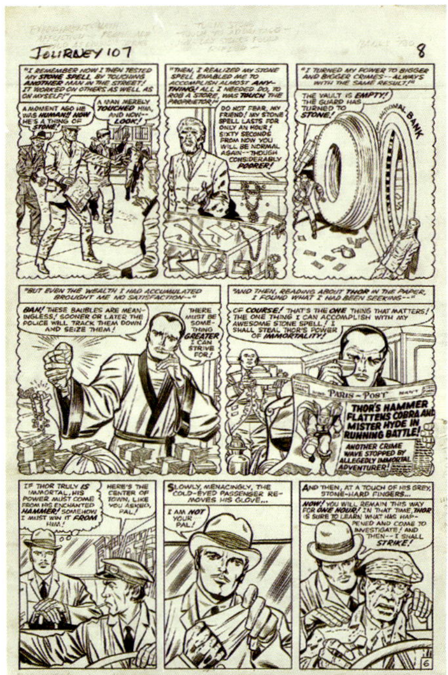

4258 Jack Kirby and Chic Stone - Journey Into Mystery #107, Thor page 6 Original Art (Marvel, 1965). He's one stone crazy dude, and he's got his sights set on Thor's enchanted hammer! Once a lowly research chemist, an accident granted Paul Duval the ability to transform any object into stone with a touch of his hand! Adopting the identity of the Grey Gargoyle, Duval embarked on a criminal quest for wealth and power! From his first appearance in the story, "The Grey Gargoyle Strikes!," written by Stan Lee, Duval comes to terms with his tremendous power, and sets his nefarious plan into motion. The art measures 12.5" x 18.5" and is in Excellent condition. A key page from the Marvel Age of comics!

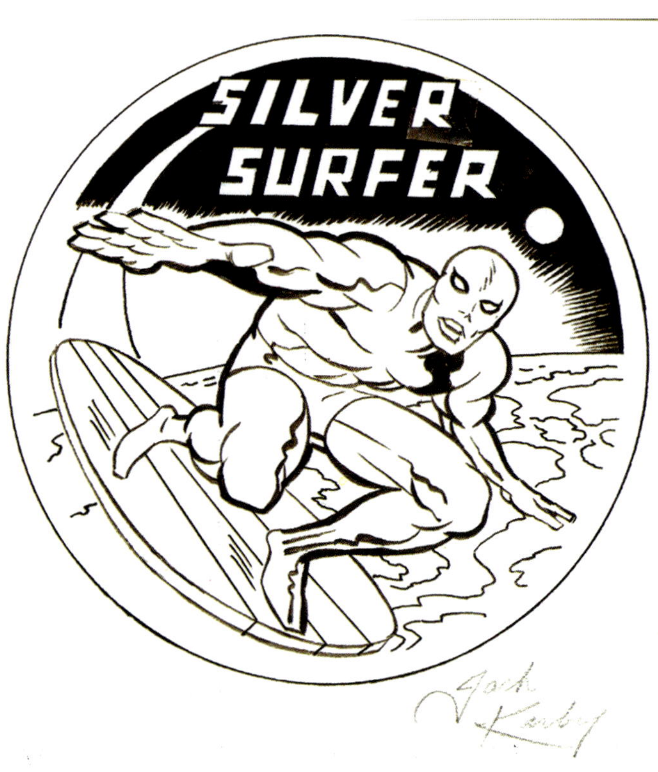

4259 Jack Kirby - Silver Surfer Marvelmania/Merry Marvel Marching Society Button Illustration Original Art (circa 1967). One of Jack Kirby's most spectacular creations was the super-streamlined traveler of the cosmos — the Silver Surfer. Since his first appearance in 1966, the Surfer has become a pop culture icon who has transcended his comic book origins. The Jack Kirby-drawn Silver Surfer appeared only on eight **Fantastic Four** covers and **Silver Surfer** #18. As a result, "King" Kirby Silver Surfer art is incredibly scarce and desirable. The Surfer's "cult figure" status was highlighted in this line of dialogue from the film "Crimson Tide": "Now everyone who reads comic books knows that the Kirby Silver Surfer is the only true Silver Surfer, now am I right or wrong?" In another movie, "Breathless," Richard Gere's character muses over a Silver Surfer yarn and equates his own alienation with the Surfer's profound cosmic aloneness. The image area of this circular design has a diameter of 5.5". The letter "r" on the word Silver is a pasted-on correction; otherwise the art is in Excellent condition. The piece was signed in pencil by Jack Kirby at the lower right. There is little doubt — no Jack Kirby art collection could be considered complete without a shining example spotlighting the sensational Silver Surfer!

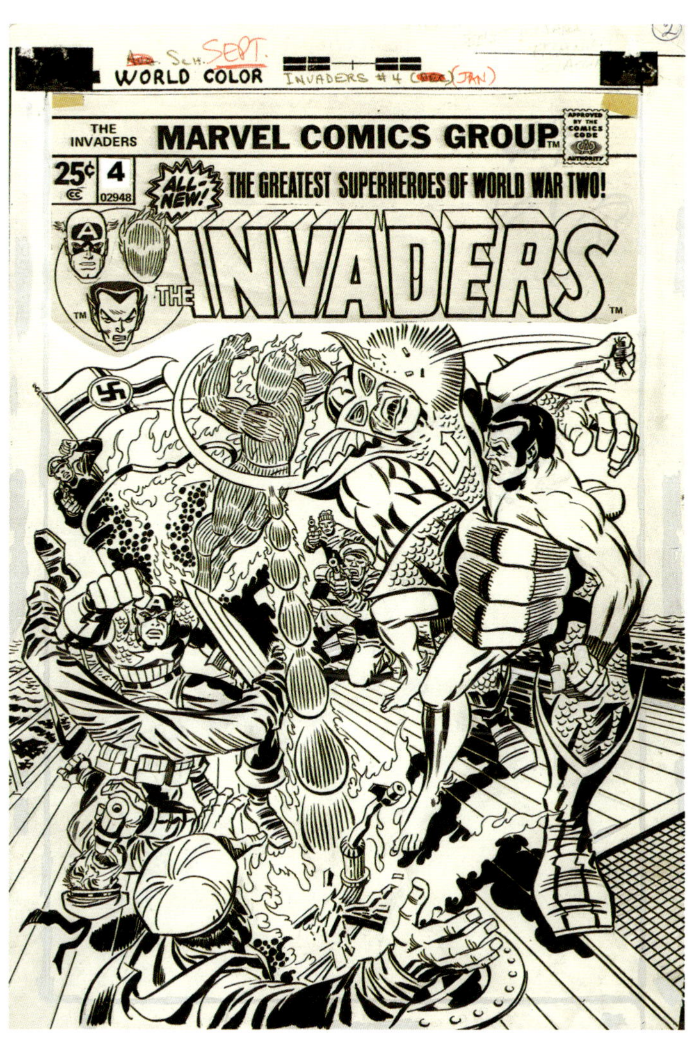

4260 Jack Kirby and Frank Giacoia - The Invaders #4 Cover Original Art (Marvel, 1976). "U-Man Must be Stopped", and the "big three" of Marvel Comics' Golden Age — Captain America, the Human Torch, and the Sub-Mariner — are just the heroes to do it! Jack "King" Kirby brings his unparalleled talent for penciling powerhouse action to this jam-packed World War II thriller, and Frank Giacoia finished the art with his silky-smooth inks. John Romita Sr. might have had a hand in this scene as well, as the Sub-Mariner's head and right arm have a hint of blue under-penciling showing, and Namor's grimace shows Jazzy Johnny's influence. Frank Giacoia inscribed and signed the piece in marker in the upper border, but his writing has faded and can be scarcely seen. His inscription reads, "To Steve, Best Wishes Frank Giacoia." In addition to that signature, Captain America's co-creator, Joe Simon, has signed the art on the back of the page. The image area of the cover measures approximately 11.25" x 16". The title logo is a recent replacement, and the ruled border lines on the left, right, and bottom borders were whited-out, and the original art extended to those three edges of the paper. The lower right corner is trimmed in at an angle ever so slightly; otherwise the art is in Excellent condition.

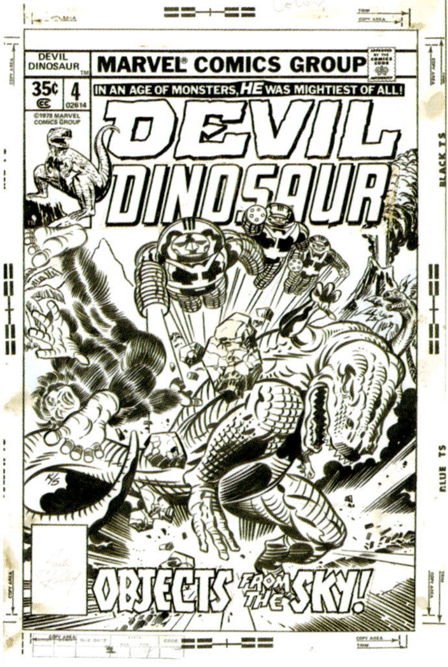

4261 Jack Kirby and Joe Sinnott - Devil Dinosaur #4 Cover Original Art (Marvel, 1978). The Valley of Flame is invaded by aliens intent on killing all the dinosaurs and protohumans. Moon Boy and Devil Dinosaur take the brunt of an alien attack, on this cover from Jack Kirby's late period. Using basic geometric shapes and sparse line work, Kirby brings a monumental solidity and presence to this work that makes it leap right off the page. The image area measures 10" x 15". Includes all the original logo and masthead photostats. Some light glue stains are apparent, otherwise the art is in Very Good condition. Signed by Jack Kirby at the bottom left.

4262 Jack Kirby - Super Powers #2, page 12 Pencils Original Art (DC, 1985). Kirby is "King!" Hawkman and Red Tornado star in this pulse-pounding masterwork from the thriller, "When Past and Present Meet." Kirby inker Greg Theakston inked the finished art for the **Super Powers** series using a lightbox and thus Kirby's peerless pencils were preserved for posterity! The page has an image area of 10" x 15", and the art is in Excellent condition. Here's a chance to experience pure, unadulterated Kirby!

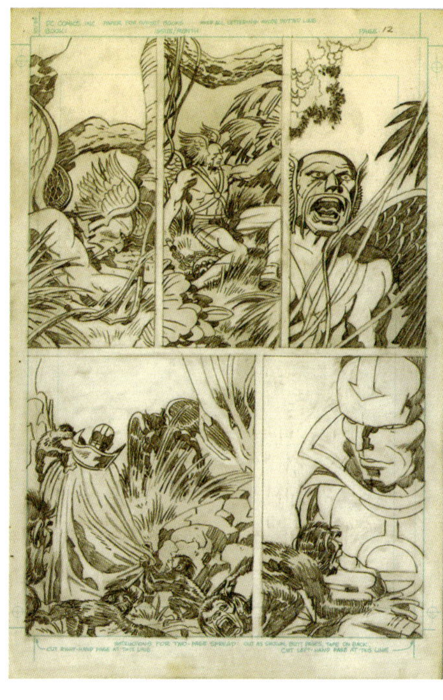

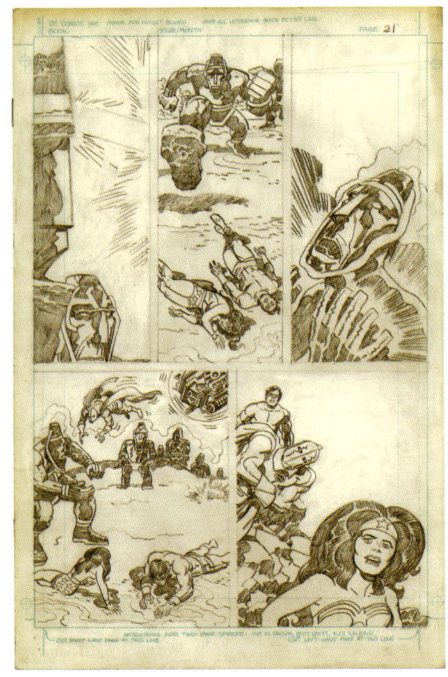

4263 Jack Kirby - Super Powers #3, page 21 Pencils Original Art (DC, 1985). The DC superhero icons experience a dynamic Jack "King" Kirby makeover, as the "King" spotlights Superman, Wonder Woman, Green Lantern and Dr. Fate in this raucous rumble from "Time Upon Time Upon Time." Inker Greg Theakston finished the art using a lightbox so as to save Kirby's penciled page. Theakston recalled in **The Jack Kirby Collector** #17, "Working with Kirby was a dream come true. Some kids fantasized about being a major ball player, or an astronaut, or a rock star, but never realized their dreams. As a child I fantasized about working with Kirby, and being his friend, and ultimately my dream came true — a rare thing in the real world." The page has an image area of 10" x 15", and the art is in Excellent condition.

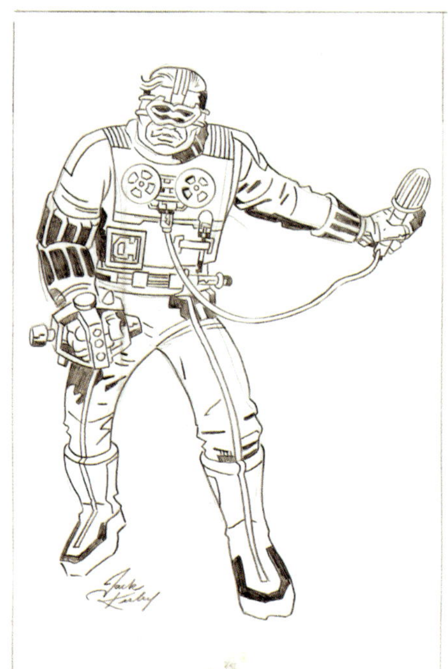

4264 Jack Kirby - The Recorder Character Design Sketch Original Art (undated). From the fertile imagination of Jack Kirby comes this character design for "the Recorder." In the later years of his career, Kirby worked in the animation field, creating scores of "concept drawings", and this may be one of them. This traveling documentarian comes armed with a set of Kirbytech brass knuckles. Talk about the power of the press — the man's a walking lawsuit, waiting to happen! The image area of this graphite pencil on paper drawing measures 9.75" x 15", and the art is in Excellent condition.

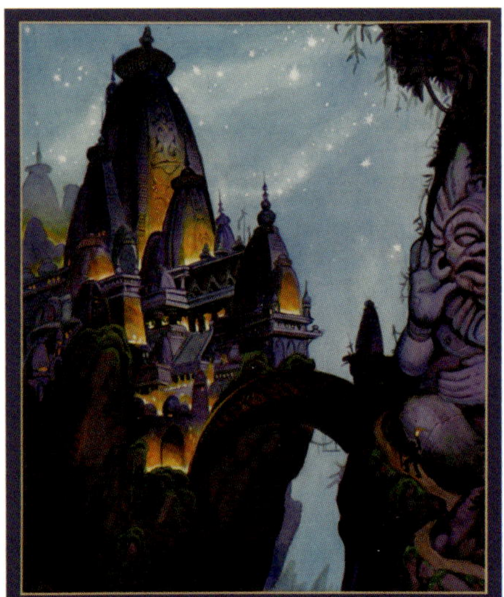

4265 Tim Kirk - Tales of the Three Hemispheres Cover Original Art (1976). The early stories and novels of Lord Dunsany laid the foundations of modern fantasy literature, and yet, despite the profound influence of his exotic and highly polished writings upon the genre, he remains, paradoxically, a neglected and under-appreciated writer. Originally published in 1919, **Tales of Three Hemispheres** evokes a richly-imagined, dream like landscape far removed from Edwardian England. Fantasy artist, Tim Kirk, builds on Dunsany's rich, and descriptive writings to produce this scintillating cover illustration. The image area measures approximately 10" x 18.5", and is in Excellent condition.

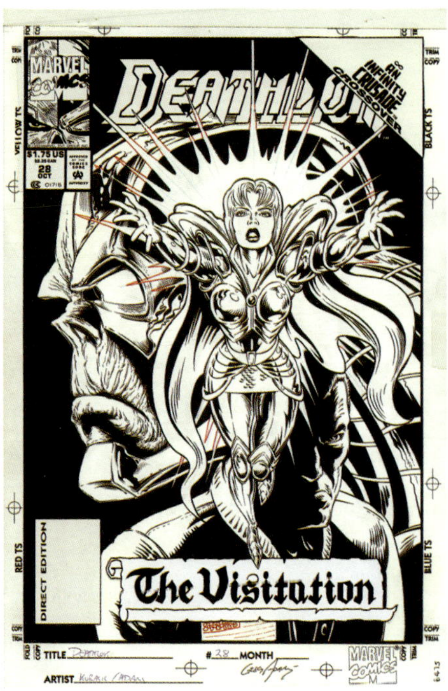

4266 Kevin Kobasic and Greg Adams - Deathlok #28 Cover Original Art (Marvel, 1992). The Infinity Crusade dealt with the battle against Warlock's repressed feminine, "good" side, the Goddess, who started a religious crusade with the purpose of destroying the universe. She enlists several noble and spiritual heroes to her cause, leaving it up to the hard cases to save the universe — meaning they have to fight teammates and friends in the Goddess' army. In this issue of **Deathlok** #28, the Goddess attempts to recruit Deathlok, in "The Visitation". The art has an image area of 10" x 15" and is in Excellent condition. Signed by Greg Adams.

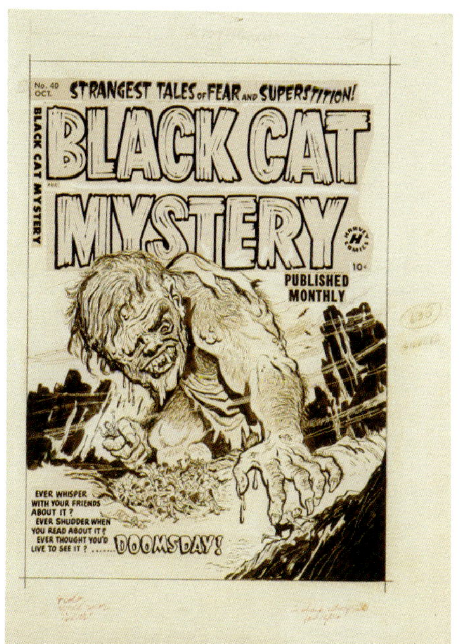

4267 Warren Kremer (attributed) - Black Cat Mystery #40 Cover Original Art (Harvey, 1952). It doesn't get more gruesome than in this pre-code horror cover by Warren Kremer! A giant, slavering monster snatches up villagers on this macabre masterpiece from 1952. Kremer's most notorious assignments were the shocking horror covers he drew for Harvey Comics. His organic style suited the macabre work that was Harvey's stock-in-trade during the fifties. Kremer had a way of making creepy things ooze right off the page, as this dreadful delineation will attest. The image area measures 11.5" x 16.5" and the art is in Excellent condition. Includes the original logo and masthead paste-up art. The type at the bottom is recent photocopy replacement art.

4268 Warren Kremer - Little Dot #7, Complete 5-page Story "Water Baby" Original Art (Harvey, 1954). It's a bloomin' fight for survival, when Little Dot falls asleep before she gives the poor flowers a drink! Warren Kremer's line work is a pure joy, in these five lushly illustrated pages. The image area of each page measures 12" x 18" and the art is in Excellent condition.

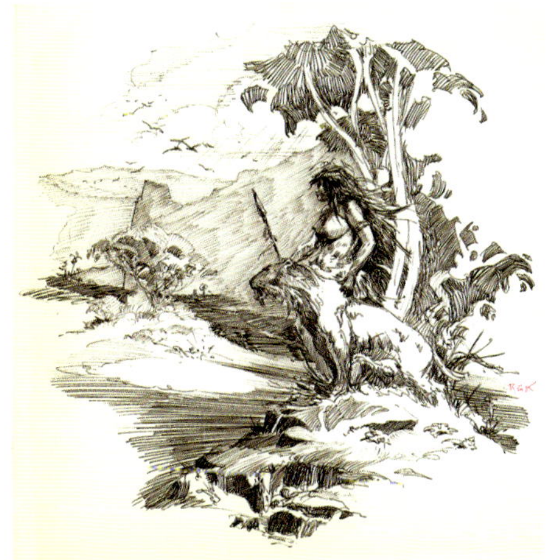

4269 Roy Krenkel - Cavewoman with Sabre-Toothed Tiger Illustration Original Art (undated). Roy G. Krenkel was known for the almost obsessive amount of detail work he added to each of his creations. After a limited time in the comics field, Krenkel devoted himself to illustrating, most notably cover illustrations for books by Edgar Rice Burroughs and Otis A. Kline. Krenkel lavishes this fine pen and ink illustration with layers of expressive line work, culminating in yet another extraordinary masterpiece. This art has an image area of 11" x 11" and the condition is Excellent. Signed with the "RGK" monograph at the right.

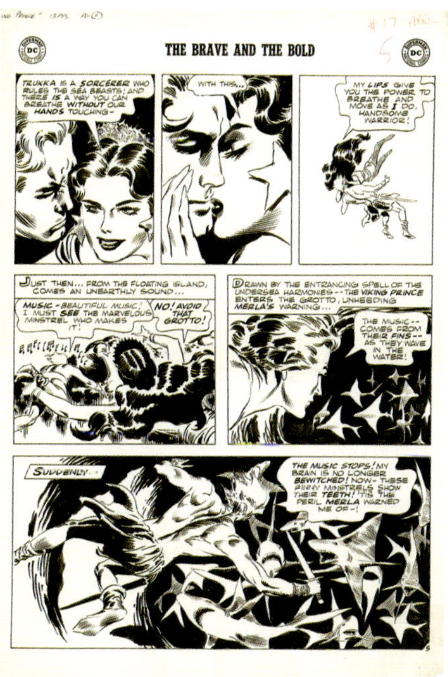

4270 Joe Kubert - Brave and the Bold #17, page 5 Original Art (DC, 1957). Thrill to the heroic feat of Jon, the Viking Prince, as the Princess of the Lake, Merla, leads him into her underwater canyon to face the evil sorcerer, Trukka, in this page from the Bob Haney story, "The Lady of the Lake". You'll be drawn into Joe Kubert's entrancing spell in this Silver Age showcase. With an image area of 13" x 18", and the art is in Excellent condition.

4271 Joe Kubert - G.I. Combat #56, page 3 Original Art (DC, 1958). The D.I. rides the "sand flea" in this thriller by the K-K team of Robert Kanigher and Joe Kubert. This yarn is cited by DC war aficionados as a highly significant step in the evolution and creation of the Sgt. Rock character. Kubert's expressive inks are even more gorgeous when drawn on the larger paper size of the early Silver Age stories. The image area of the page is 13" x 18". The paper shows mild signs of aging; otherwise the art is in Excellent condition.

4272 Joe Kubert and Jack Abel - Our Army at War #192 Splash Pages 5 and 6 Original Art (DC, 1968). Sgt. Rock and the men of Easy Company wade into a Nazi squad in a bare-knuckles donnybrook. Joining heavyweight champion Jackie Johnson in this knuckle-duster are Bulldozer, Wild Man, Ice Cream Soldier, and Little Sure Shot. Joe Kubert landed the ***Tales of the Green Berets*** strip around this time and so DC war comic veteran Jack Abel was recruited to ink Kubert's pencils. These two splash pages combine to create an overall image area of 20" x 15". The pages were taped together on the back of the pages. There are pieces of tape at the tops and bottoms on the fronts of the pages; otherwise the art is in Very Good condition. Nothin's ever easy for Easy!

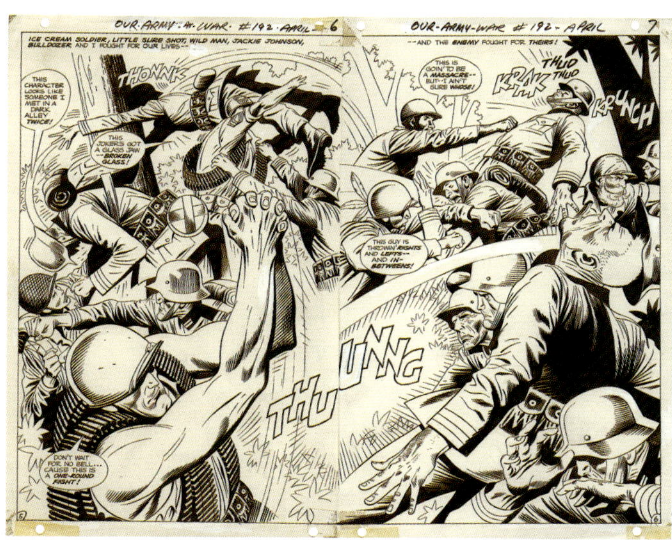

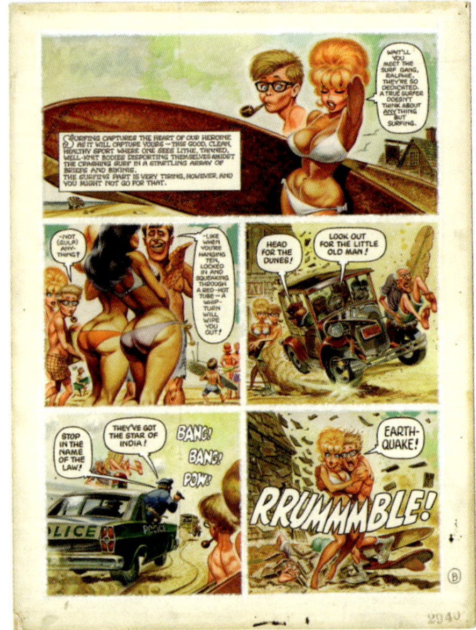

4273 Harvey Kurtzman, Bill Elder, Frank Frazetta, and Jack Davis - Playboy, July, 1965, Little Annie Fanny, "Surfers," page 1 Original Art (Playboy, 1965). Harvey Kurtzman assembled the *creme de la creme* of his former **Mad** collaborators for the beautifully rendered *Little Annie Fanny* feature. This spectacular page has a wealth of hall-of-fame comic book talent working on it. "Good girl" specialist Frank Frazetta painted the smokin' hot babes-in-bikinis, Jack Davis handled the zany beach "extras," Bill Elder painted the Annie and Ralphie faces and added his hallmarked background gags, and Harvey Kurtzman wrote and laid out the whole fershlugginer yarn. It's a testament to these artists' monumental talents that the result of the diverse hands is a masterpiece of humor art. The image area of the mixed-media on board painting is 14" x 20", and the art is in Excellent condition.

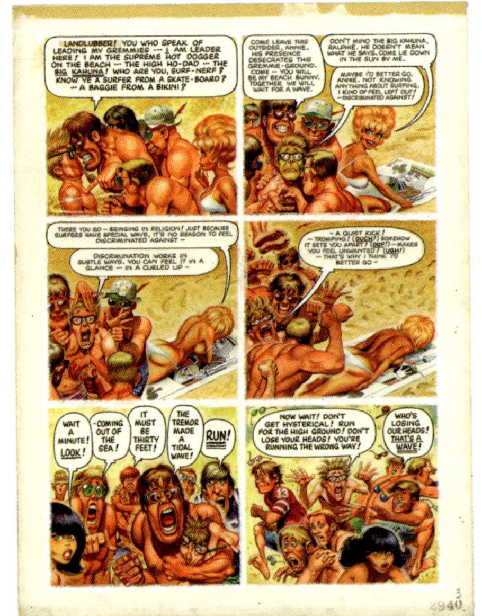

4274 Harvey Kurtzman, Bill Elder, Frank Frazetta, and Jack Davis - Playboy, July, 1965, Little Annie Fanny, "Surfers," page 3 Original Art (Playboy, 1965). This boisterous beach scene benefits from a synergy of humor, as each former **Mad**-man adds his own superb touches to this *Annie Fanny* tale. Check out Bill Elder's hilarious beach blanket gag in panels two through four. Of course, you'll have a devil of a time tearing your eyes away from Frank Frazetta's sensuous renderings of Annie's young, nubile curves. Jack Davis adds a manic energy to the whole mise-en-scene, while Harvey Kurtzman keeps the lampoon racing along at a rapid-fire clip with his razor-sharp dialogue and storytelling. The image area of this mixed-media on board painting measures 14" x 20", and the art is in Excellent condition. This laugh-riot is a delightful smorgasbord of comic art!

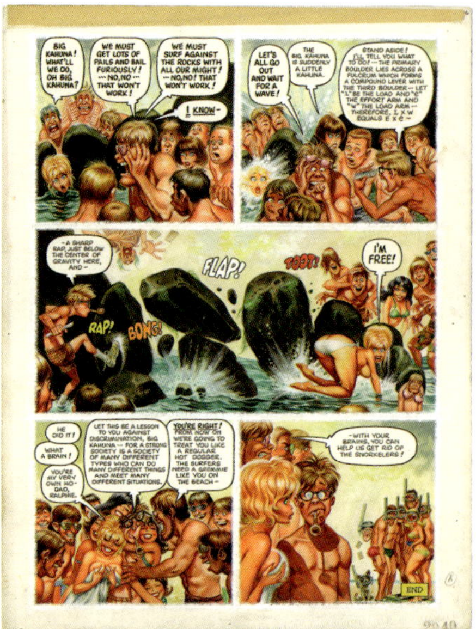

4275 Harvey Kurtzman, Bill Elder, Frank Frazetta, and Jack Davis - Playboy, July, 1965, Little Annie Fanny, "Surfers," page 5 Original Art (Playboy, 1965). Ralphie's crusade against discrimination at the beach is only partially successful as the surfers transfer their wrath away from "gremmies" like Ralphie and towards a new group — snorkelers! The satirical twist to Ralphie's plea for tolerance is pure Harvey Kurtzman. Bill Elder, Jack Davis, and Frank Frazetta's art make this page a feast for the eyes. The image area of this mixed-media on board painting is 14" x 20", and the art is in Excellent condition. Hang ten, bidders!

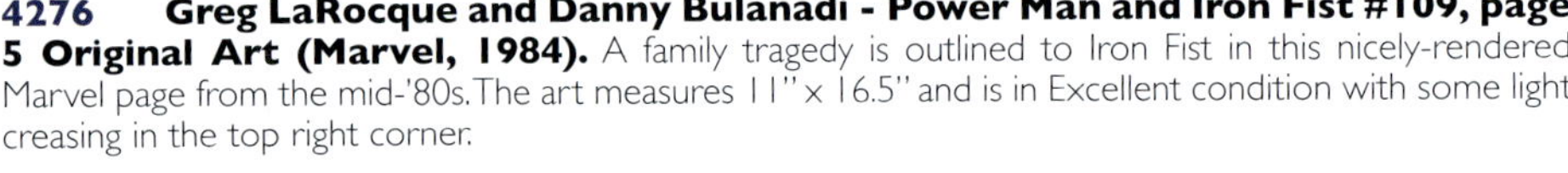

4276 Greg LaRocque and Danny Bulanadi - Power Man and Iron Fist #109, page 5 Original Art (Marvel, 1984). A family tragedy is outlined to Iron Fist in this nicely-rendered Marvel page from the mid-'80s. The art measures 11" x 16.5" and is in Excellent condition with some light creasing in the top right corner.

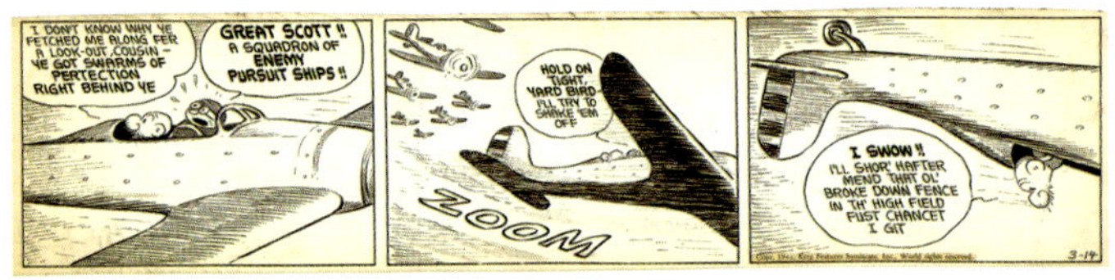

4277 Billy DeBeck - Barney Google and Snuffy Smith Daily Comic Strip Original Art, dated 3-14-41 (King Features Syndicate, 1941). Snuffy Smith and his cousin are being pursued by a squadron of enemy ships, and all Snuffy can think about is that he needs to fix his fence! This topsy-turvy daily by Billy DeBeck has an image area measuring 16.5" x 3.75" and the artwork is in Excellent condition.

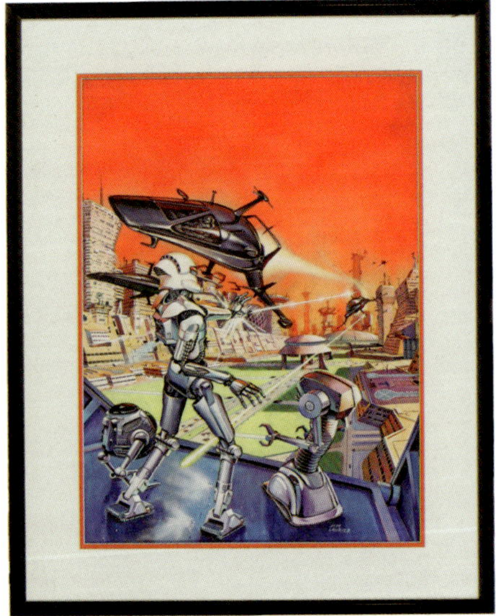

4278 Jim Laurier - Creepy #121 Cover Original Art (Warren, 1980). Jim Laurier's highly polished tribute to the space epic, is methodically rendered in this stellar cover illustration for **Creepy** #121. Laurier, currently one of the most celebrated aviation artists in the U.S., has worked as a free-lance illustrator since 1978, completing numerous illustration assignments on wide-ranging subjects including science fiction, medical, technical, advertising, and editorial illustration. Realism has become the trademark of Laurier's work, whether he's painting space invaders, or a Grumman F6F-3 Hellcat. The image area of this art measures 17.5" x 24.5" and the condition is Excellent.

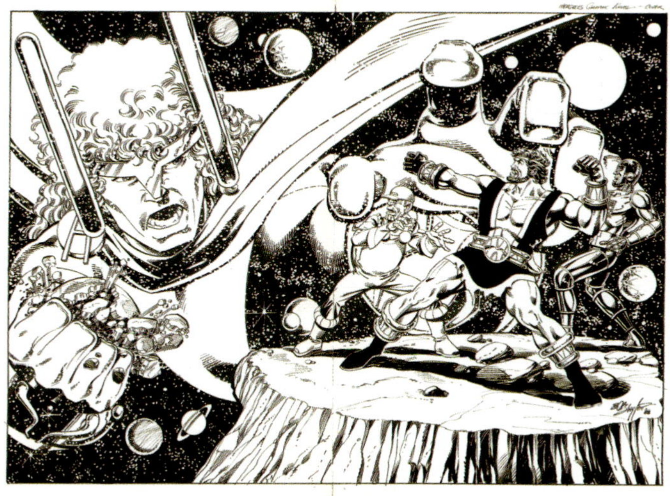

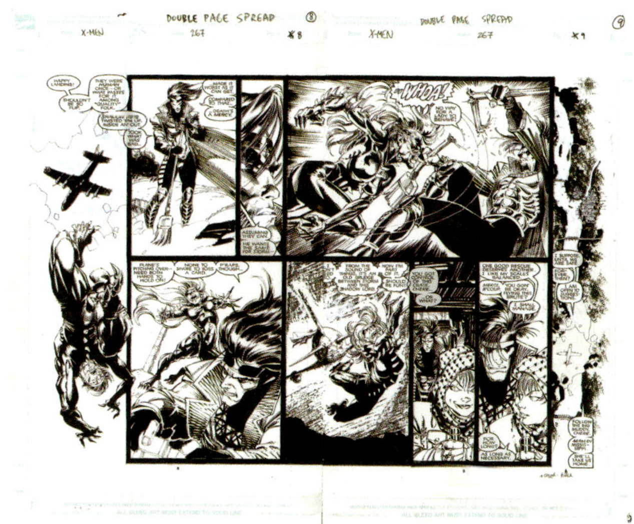

4279 Bob Layton - Hercules: Full Circle Graphic Novel Cover Original Art (Marvel, 1988). After Bob Layton had completed this cover for his first **Hercules** graphic novel, Marvel broke the bad news to him that he was not allowed to do wrap-around covers on graphic novels. Layton wrote:" After I lamented the enormous waste of time, I tossed it into a box and went on with the show. And there it sat — until today. All in all, I personally like this cover better than the final, published version". This original cover features a different take on the published cover, featuring The Lion of Olympus, and his pals, Skyppi, and Recorder #417. The image area measures 21" x 15" and the art is in Excellent condition.

4280 Jim Lee, Whilce Portacio, and Scott Williams - The Uncanny X-Men #267, Double Page Spread, pages 8 and 9 Original Art (Marvel, 1990). Minions of the Shadow King try to put the moves on Gambit, in this double-page spread from the Chris Claremont story, "Nanny: Into the Fire". Known for his stylized, detailed and dynamic style, penciler Jim Lee remains one of the most popular illustrators in comics, and with help by fellow penciler Whilce Portacio, and inker Scott Williams, we have the makings of two classic pages. These pages hail from Jim Lee's first issue as regular penciler on the series. The image area of the combined pages measures 21.5" x 15" and the work is in Excellent condition.

4281 Larry Lieber, Frank Giacoia, and Vince Colletta - Marvel Super-Heroes #20, page 7 Original Art (Marvel, 1969). Two of the Fantastic Four's most fearsome foes, Dr. Doom and Diablo, battle it out in this action-packed Silver Age thriller from "This Man, This Demon." The page has an image area of 10" x 15", and the art is in Excellent condition.

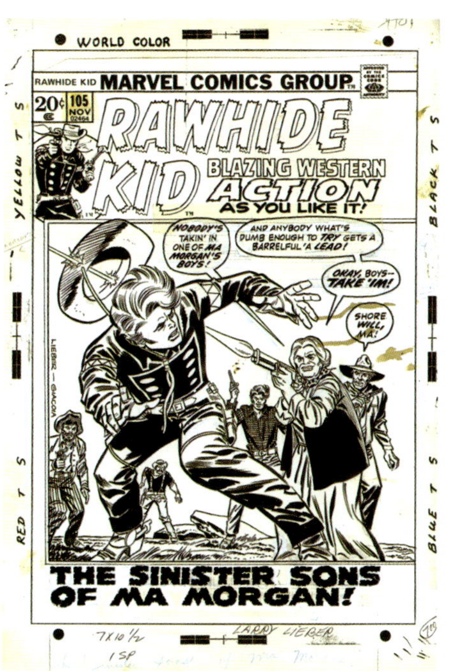

4282 Larry Lieber - Rawhide Kid #105 Cover Original Art (Marvel, 1972). Pa Morgan lived an honest life, and died broke! That's a mistake that Ma Morgan and her sinister sons are gonna rectify! Have a looksee at this gun-barrelful 'a fun featuring Ma and her boys tag-teaming against the Rawhide Kid, illustrated by the great Larry Lieber! Blazing your way with an image area of 10" x 15", the art has some printer's oil staining along the right edge, and a piece of tape attached along the bottom of the logo photostat, otherwise it's in Very Good condition.

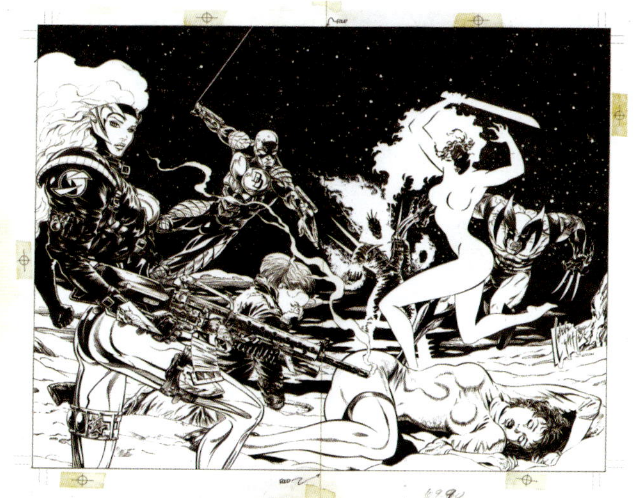

4283 Steve Lightle - Marvel Comics Presents #150 Cover Original Art (Marvel, 1994). The mutant empath, Jessie, is at the center of this incredible double-page cover spread by Steve Lightle. Wolverine, aided by Typhoid Mary, Daredevil, and Vengeance attempt to rescue Jessie, while sexy marksman, Steel Raven occupies most of the back cover, courtesy of the talented Lightle. The image area measures 19" x 15" and is in Excellent condition. The original logo, title, and masthead photostats are on a separate cel overlay.

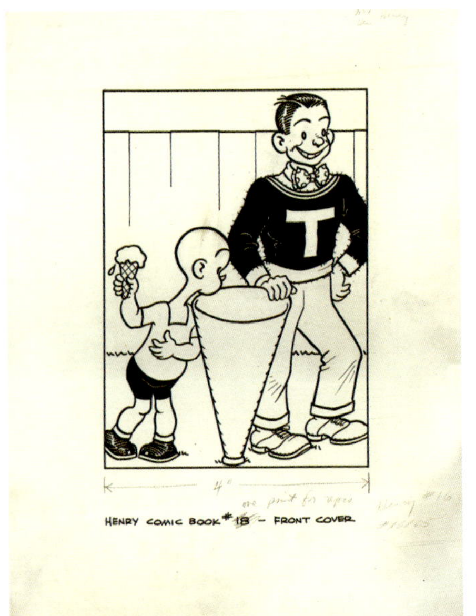

4284 John Liney - Henry #16 Cover Original Art (Dell, 1950). Carl Anderson's popular pantomime comic strip character was also the star of a long-running series of comic books published from 1948 to 1961, after a couple of **Four Color** one-shot try-outs. Anderson, already in his seventies when he created the character in 1932, retired in 1942 and handed over the *Henry* daily strip his assistant, John J. Liney. Although the strip and book continued to carry Anderson's by-line long after his death in 1948, Liney was the artist on all the Dell **Henry** comic books, including this cover illustration. Drawn in pencil and india ink on a 14" x 19" piece of bristol board, the piece has an image area of 8" x 11.5" and is in Very Good condition. A copy of **Henry** #16 accompanies this lot.

4285 Joe Linsner - Daredevil Sketch Original Art (1988). Michael Joseph Lisner's striking art, incomparable symbolism and dialogue, provocative enough to startle, enhance this epic rendition of the Man Without Fear. Drawn in colored marker, and colored pencil, the image area measures 6" x 9.5" and the work is in Excellent condition.

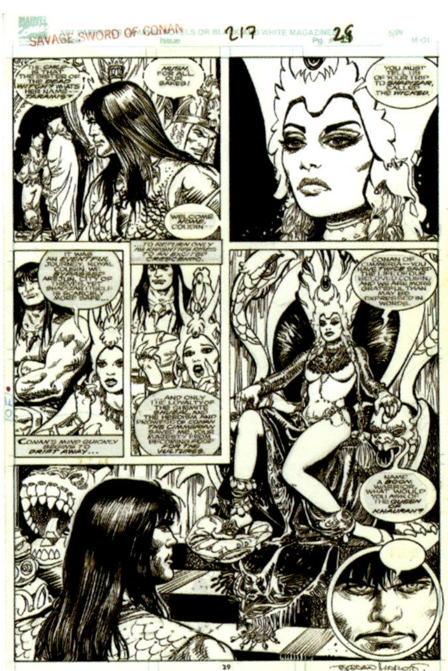

4286 Esteban Maroto - Savage Sword of Conan #217, page 29 Original Art (Marvel, 1994). By Crom, here is some good stuff by the great Spanish artist, Esteban Maroto, a man who knows a thing or two about sensuous art and irresistible women. Maroto's distinctive flowing style has been seen everywhere from the Warren heyday, to DC and Image today. The Cimmerian stands mute before the ravishing Queen of Khauran, in this splendid page from the Roy Thomas story, "For the Soul of a Cimmerian". The image area measures 10" x 15" and the work is in Excellent condition. Signed by Esteban Maroto at the bottom right.

4287 Fran Matera - Daily Comic Strip Original Art, Group of 4 (undated). Considered by his peers to be an accomplished artist of considerable range, Fran Matera has an incredible body of work in comic strips, and comic book art. His career began upon his return to civilian life from the Marines in 1947, when he was assigned to draw the action strip *Dickie Dare*, created by Milton Caniff, and he has been busy ever since. Here are four daily try-out strips by Matera, including *O. Macdonald*, *Classified Clarence*, *For Students Only*, and *Lucky*. The strips range in size from 14" x 4" to 18.5" x 5.5". Aside from some overall aging apparent, and some slight staining, the strips average in Very Good condition.

4288 Val Mayerik - Conan Annual #8, Page Original Art, Group of 8 (Marvel, 1983). By Crom, Mitra, and Ishtar! King Kull and the Cimmerian, Conan, encounter evil, sorcerous doings, in these pages from the James Christopher Owsley story, "Dark Night of the White Queen". Included here are pages 3, 5, 6, 11, 12, 16, 17, and 18. The edges have been trimmed during the production process, otherwise the art averages in Excellent condition.

4289 Val Mayerik - Ka-Zar the Savage Complete Story Original Art, Group of 2 (Marvel, 1984). Here are two "Tales of Zabu" yarns written by Bruce Jones and illustrated by Val Mayerik. The first is a 3-page story, "Freefall," from **Ka-Zar the Savage** #22. The second is the 5-page story, "A Savage is Born!" from **Ka-Zar the Savage** #24. Some of the type box photostats exhibit a bit of aging, some of the title type is missing from the first page of the "Freefall" story, and the edges of each page have been clipped during the production process, otherwise the art is in Very Good condition.

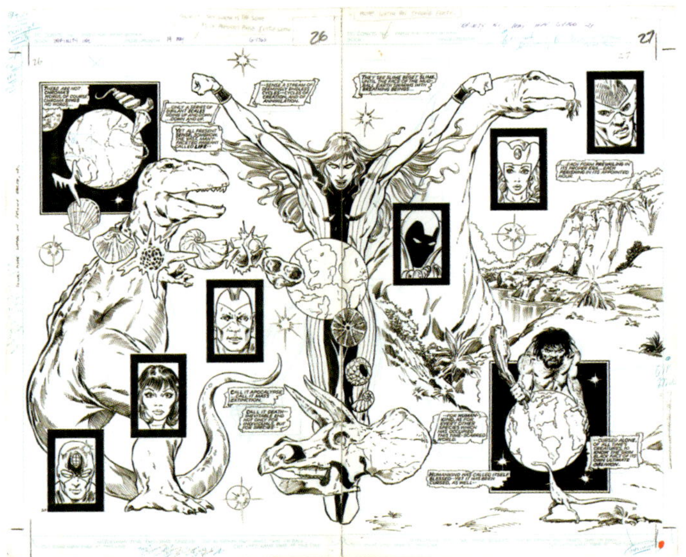

4290 Todd McFarlane and Tony DeZuniga - Infinity, Inc. #14, Splash Pages 20 and 21 Original Art (DC, 1985). While providing security at a rock concert, everyone in the audience, including Infinity, Inc., is affected when an alien being called Chroma sings a strange song that seems to envision the Earth's birth, life, and death. This time-spanning double page splash represents pages 20, and 21 of Roy and Dann Thomas' story, "Concert In the Key of... Chroma". These pages are an early example of Todd McFarlane's art, and aptly display his ability to render detail and characters into his pages. This page has an image area of 23" x 17.5", and is in Excellent condition.

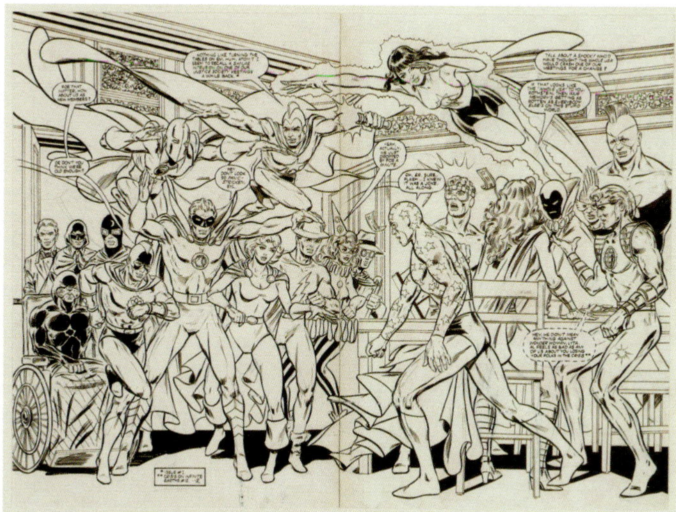

4291 Todd McFarlane and Tony DeZuniga - Infinity, Inc. #25, Splash Pages 2 and 3 Original Art (DC, 1986). This great splash features all of the members of the Justice Society of America and Infinity, Inc. on two separate pages. This is an early example of Todd McFarlane's art which displays his ability to render a lot of detail and characters into his pages. This piece would make an awesome addition to any DC comic fan's wall. This double-page spread has an image area of 23" x 17" and is in Excellent condition.

4292 Todd McFarlane and Tony DeZuniga - Infinity, Inc. #30, Splash Page 28 Original Art (DC, 1986). Here's a spectacular pin-up by Todd McFarlane showing the entire Infinity, Inc. team of Brainwave Jr., Fury, Jade, Nuklon, Obsidian, Silver Scarab, Star-Spangled Kid, and Northwind. This is a fitting tribute to these second-generation heroes by a first-rate artist. Covering McFarlane's potent pencils is Tony DeZuniga's fine inking, which give the art a life all its own. With an image area of 10" x 15", this page is a beauty, and in Excellent condition. Signed by both artists in the middle right area.

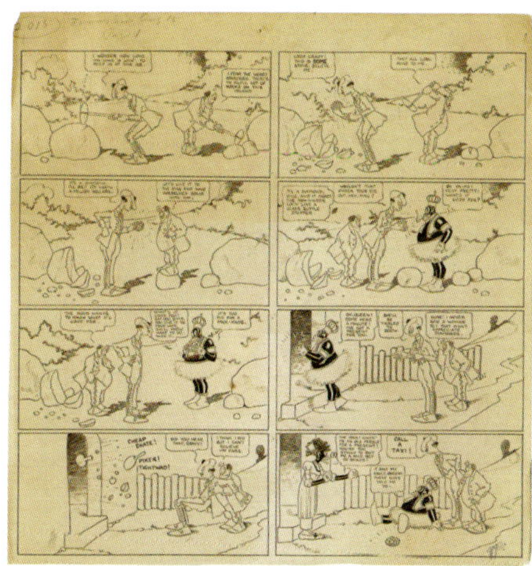

4293 George McManus - Spare Ribs and Gravy Sunday Comic Strip Original Art, dated 8-18-12 (NY World, 1912). Fans of George McManus' wonderful art deco "clear line" cartooning style will be hard-pressed to find an earlier example than this side-splitting Sunday. To paraphrase an old saying, "One man's treasure is another man's trash." Spare Ribs and Gravy can scarcely believe their eyes when a giant diamond they've unearthed fails to impress the Queen of a remote kingdom. *Spare Ribs and Gravy* was a lampoon of the exploits of scientific explorers and these two adventurers were often caught up in hilarious cultural misunderstandings. Note that George McManus signed this Sunday "Carm'l." He often signed his strips with the name of a town he was visiting when he drew something while out of town and thus, he signed this episode "Carm'l," instead of with his regular McManus signature. The Sunday has an image area of 18" x 18" and aside from some mild signs of paper aging and edge wear, this early original is in Very Good condition.

4294 Mell Lazarus - Miss Peach Daily Comic Strip Original Art, dated 3-23-57 (New York Herald Tribune, 1957). America's favorite schoolmarm and her classroom rascals fill this early daily from 1957. Dated just over a month from the strip's first publication, this charming single-panel strip has an image area of 17.5" x 5". Signed and inscribed "To Jerry, with all good wishes, Mel Lazarus," along the lower edge.

4295 Dale Messick - Brenda Starr Sunday Comic Strip Original Art, dated 8-31-41 (Chicago Tribune, 1941). Just arrived from Sucatash, Indiana, it's Brenda's cousin — Abretha Breeze! This big, corn fed gal has a lot of love to give her big city cousin, but first the girl's gotta eat! More delight and drama is here in this engaging installment of the long-running series, gorgeously rendered by creator Dale Messick. This Sunday strip is in two pieces, both of which have been assembled by gluing various panels to a common backing board. There is moderate aging apparent, a few small pin-holes, and some staining, especially around the panel paste-ups, but overall the artwork is in Very Good condition.

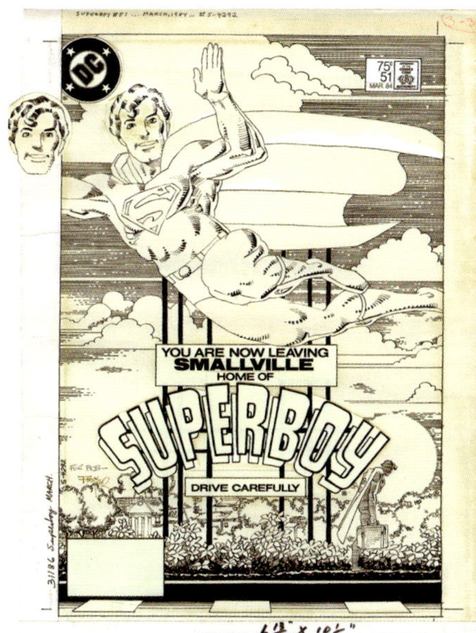

4296 Frank Miller - The New Adventures of Superboy #51 Cover Original Art (DC, 1984). You are now leaving Smallville, the home of Superboy — *fly carefully*! Frank Miller's superb cover illustration has a jewel-like quality — sinewy lines accentuated with bullets of pure ink — making for an artistic expression all Miller's own. There is an extra Superboy head, also hand-drawn by Miller, that had been attached to the left edge of the art, leaving a slight bit of glue residue on the page. The image area measures 10" x 15", and the art is in Excellent condition. Signed by Frank Miller at the lower left.

4297 Ian Miller - A Tolkien Bestiary, pages 100 and 101 Original Art (Mitchell Beazley, 1979). Since its publication, writer David Day's **A Tolkien Bestiary** has sold more than 350,000 copies in nine languages. This lavishly illustrated book on myth and fantasy lore, includes tales of the castles of Middle Earth. This double page illustration, exquisitely illustrated in pen and ink and watercolor by Ian Miller, filled pages 100 and 101. The image area measures 15" x 9.5" and the condition of the work is Excellent. Signed by Ian Miller at the bottom right.

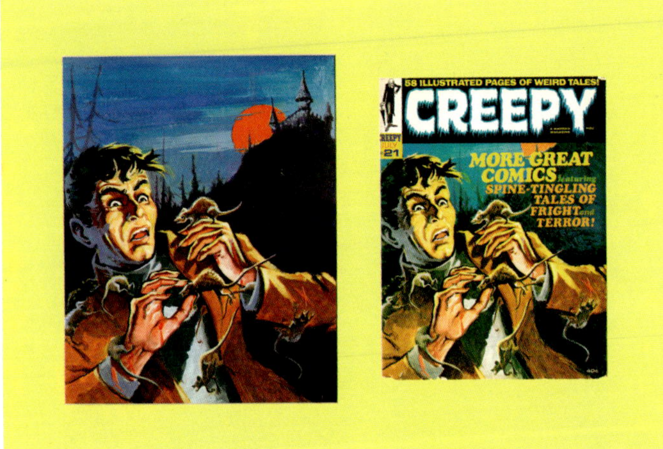

4298 Gutenberg Monterio - Creepy #21 Cover Original Art (Warren, 1968). The hapless gentleman on this **Creepy** cover never suspected that a visit to castle Dracula included lunch with rats! But these aren't ordinary rats, they're vicious vermin with a lust for blood — human blood! Gutenberg Monterio painted only two covers for Warren, and this is his first. The image area measures approximately 10" x 12.5" and the art is in Excellent condition. Includes a copy of **Creepy** #21.

4299 Bill Montes and Dick Giordano - Judomaster #93, Sarge Steel Page Original Art, Group of 3 (Charlton, 1967). She has blackmailed nations, seated a king, destroyed a prime minister, and, for amusement, looted half a dozen private art collections, and now she's set her sights on Ambassador Bruyden! Her name is Santana Noir — the Devil's Bride, and Sarge Steel has his work cut out for him in this Joe Gill tale, "Case of the Devil's Wife". Here are pages 2, 3, and 4 of the seven-page story. The image area of each page measures 12" x 18" and the work is in Excellent condition.

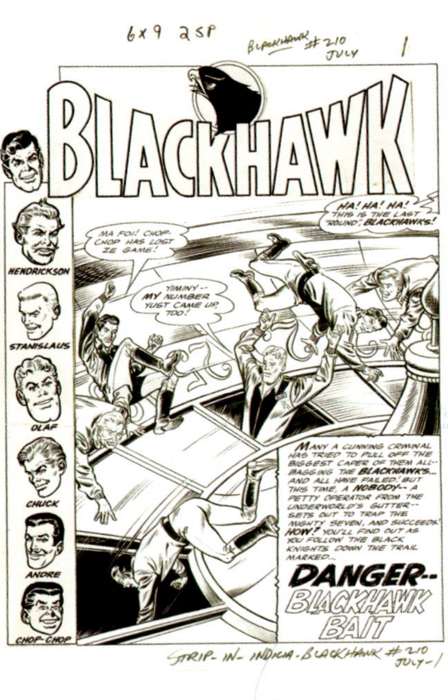

4300 Jim Mooney and Charles Cuidera - Blackhawk #210, Splash Page 1 Original Art (DC, 1965). A petty operator from the underworld's gutter steps out to trap the Mighty Seven and succeeds! Join the Black Knights on the first page to the story, "Danger — Blackhawk Bait". Jim Mooney pencils this image of the Blackhawks taking a ride on a gigantic roulette wheel, together with classic inks by Charles Cuidera, making this is a truly memorable splash page from DC Silver Age. The art includes the original logo and masthead paste-ups. The image area measures 13" x 17", and, aside from a pencil editorial marking, and some light glue staining, the condition is Excellent.

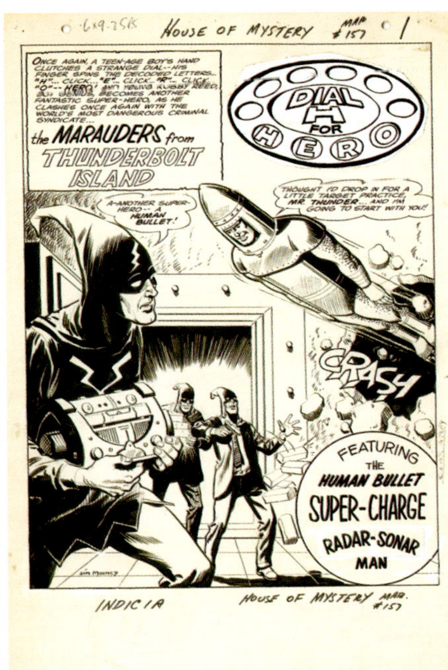

4301 Jim Mooney - House of Mystery #157, "Dial H for Hero" Splash Page 1 Original Art (DC, 1966). Robby Reed, in his newest guise as the Human Bullet, crashes in on the nefarious Mr. Thunder and his gang in the explosive splash for "The Marauders From Thunderbolt Island." Nothing shouts Silver Age like a way-out and wonky splash page from a sixties DC story! Jim Mooney captures the offbeat scene with a dramatic, yet convincing flair. To top it all off, this splash hails from the second "Dial H for Hero" yarn. The image area of the page measures 12" x 16" and aside from some mild paper aging, this big and bold scene is in Excellent condition. Dial H for Heritage!

4302 Jerome Moore - Star Trek: The Next Generation #4 Cover Original Art (DC, 1990). An away team lead by Lt. Riker is trapped aboard a derelict starship, which was designed to collect biological samples. Worf and chief engineer McRobb are the only two members who were not placed in stasis, and must battle the ship for their freedom. Jerome Moore's highly individual style graces this cover illustrating the interior story, "The Hero Factor," written by Michael Jan Friedman. The image area measures 10" x 15" and the condition is Excellent. Includes the original logo and masthead art.

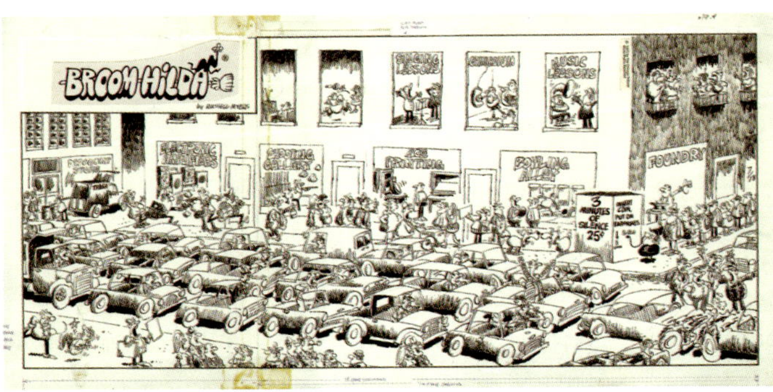

4303 Russell Myers - Broom-Hilda Sunday Comic Strip Original Art, dated 7-18-71 (The Chicago Tribune, 1971). Silence is not only golden, it's a golden opportunity for Russell Myers to amuse and amaze us with this wordless masterpiece, which was published on July 18, 1971. Myers' *Broom-Hilda* maintains a standard of madness where total irrelevance is the only relevancy. This panoramic pantomime is bewitchingly entertaining, and has an image area of 12" x 27". There is a vertical tape residue stain at the left portion, just to the right of the logo photostat, which runs the length of the artwork, and a smudge at the extreme left edge, otherwise the art is in Very Good condition.

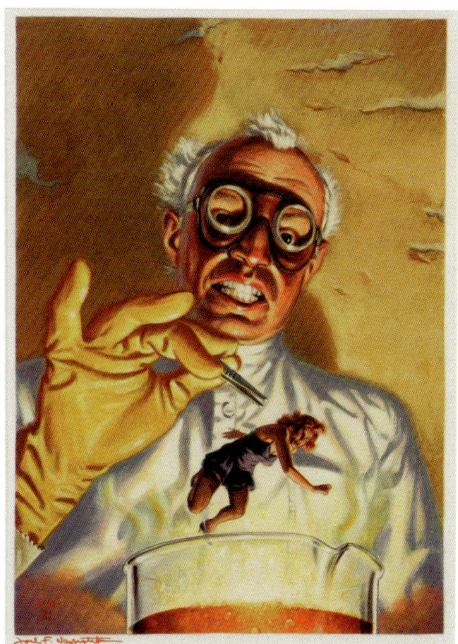

4304 Joel Naprstek - Science Fiction Age Magazine Cover Original Art (Sovereign Media Company, 1991). Here's a weird, wild cover painting courtesy of fan favorite, Joel Naprstek, for the now-defunct **Science Fiction Age Magazine**. **SFAM** was a mag for the serious sci-fi reader, each issue featuring fiction from the foremost authors with art by the day's leading artists including Naprstek, who's illustrations graced this 1991 issue. Vivid, over-the-top colors and shocking displays of light and shadows intensify this bizarre scenario. The image area measures 9" x 13" and the work is in Excellent condition. Signed by Joel Naprstek.

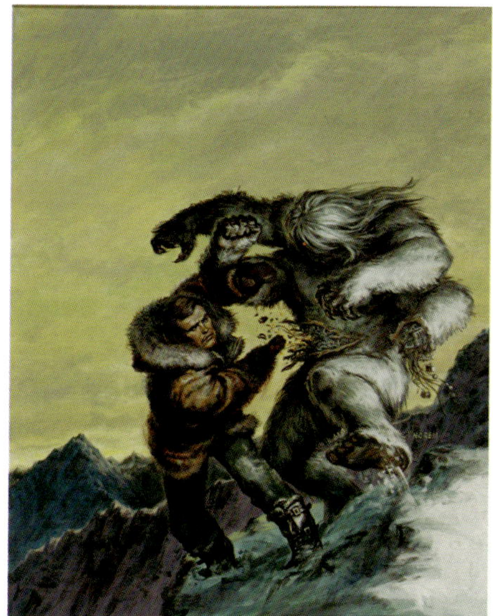

4305 Earl Norem - The Six Million Dollar Man #5 Cover Original Art (Charlton, 1977). It's bionic man vs. bionic yeti at the top of the world... and only one can survive! One of the best-loved and best-remembered TV shows of the 1970s, "The Six Million Dollar Man" was brought to full-color life by Charlton, with covers by some of the industry's greatest talents, including Earl Norem, as in the example offered here. Measuring a big 26" x 20" overall, with an approximate image area of 21" x 16", this piece is in Excellent condition and has been signed by the artist.

4306 Irv Novick and Tex Blaisdell - The Joker #9, page 19 Original Art (DC, 1976). Will the real Joker please stand up? Catwoman witnesses an interesting scenario, when the movie comedian Benny Springer, disguised as the Joker, and the real Joker, battle for the title of "real clown". Here is page 19 from the Elliot S! Maggin story, "The Cat and the Clown," illustrated by penciler Irv Novick and inker Tex Blaisdell. The image area measures 10" x 15", and, aside form some blue line editorial markings, and tape stains at the top and bottom center edges, the work is in Very Good condition.

4307 Tom Palmer - Star Wars #71, page 24 Original Art (Marvel, 1983). Tom Palmer brought continuity to the look of Marvel's **Star Wars** series, inking Howard Chaykin, Carmine Infantino, and Walt Simonson among others in the course of the run. Here, Palmer provided finished pencils over Ron Frenz's breakdowns in addition to inking the story. This issue came out about a half a year before "Return of the Jedi" was released, so Han Solo was still frozen in carbonite. Luke Skywalker recapped events from "Star Wars" and "The Empire Strikes Back" here — as if any kid in '83 didn't know it all by heart! With Chewbacca, Leia, and C-3PO on hand as well, this page has got all of the principals of George Lucas' galaxies-spanning saga. The page has an image area of 10" x 15" and the art is in Excellent condition.

4308 George Perez and Mike Esposito - Deadly Hands of Kung Fu #9, page 15 Original Art (Marvel, 1975). Hard on the heels of the successfully launched **Master of Kung Fu** monthly comic came the black and white **Deadly Hands of Kung Fu** magazine, featuring (throughout the greater portion of its enviable run) two essential strips, "Master of Kung Fu," and the "B"-movie flavored "The Sons of the Tiger". The "Sons of the Tiger" was everything a low budget, "high concept" martial arts movie should be, really. Three wildly disparate martial arts students — philosophical Lin Sun; street-hardened Abe Brown; and smug, shallow film star, Bob Diamond, are improbably thrown together when their aged sensei is brutally slain by a clandestine ninja cult. This ambitiously-staged drama sequence by George Perez and Mike Esposito is immediate and visceral. The image area measures 10" x 15," and the art is in Excellent condition.

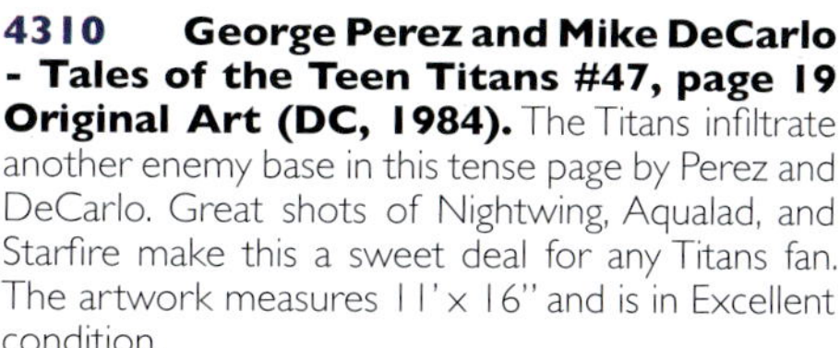

4310 George Perez and Mike DeCarlo - Tales of the Teen Titans #47, page 19 Original Art (DC, 1984). The Titans infiltrate another enemy base in this tense page by Perez and DeCarlo. Great shots of Nightwing, Aqualad, and Starfire make this a sweet deal for any Titans fan. The artwork measures 11' x 16" and is in Excellent condition.

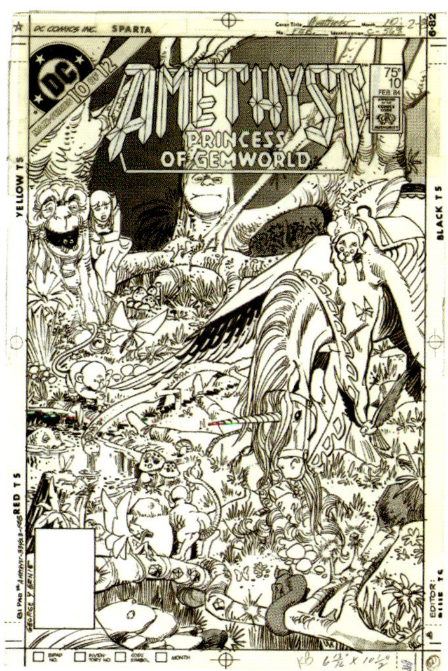

4309 George Perez and Ernie Colon - Amethyst, Princess of Gemworld #10 Cover Original Art (DC, 1984). This expansive landscape, filled with a dozen delectably detailed cast members, is brought to you courtesy of George Perez and Ernie Colon. Working in a whimsical style (yet still filled with all the ravishing detail he is famous for), George Perez pencils this magnificent fantasy setting, complete with Amethyst and her winged unicorn. The sterling artwork of Ernie Colon brought this series to life, and he proved his versatility with his imaginative interpretations of an otherworldly magical realm and its denizens. Here, he inks this grand illustration, which has an image area of 10" x 15" and is in Excellent condition. Includes the original logo and masthead paste-ups.

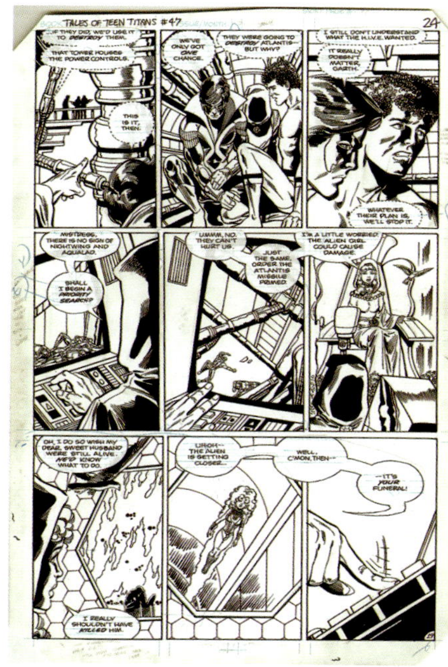

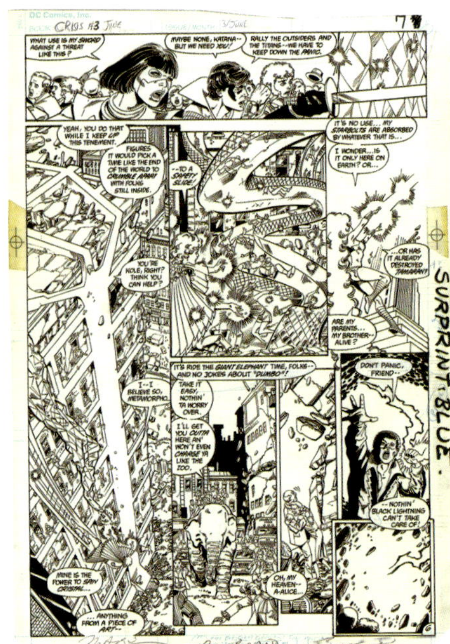

4311 George Perez and Dick Giordano - Crisis on Infinite Earths #3, page 6 Original Art (Marvel, 1985). Kole and Metamorpho help the residents of a crumbling tenement building, while Katana, Nightwing, Starfire, Jericho, Black Lightning, and Changeling rally to keep down the panic, in this tense page from **Crisis on Infinite Earths** #3. This 12-part mini-series featured nearly every DC character and redefined the DC universe. The image area measures 15" x 21", and, with some edge cuts and tape stains outside the image area, is still in Excellent condition. Signed by Marv Wolfman, George Perez and Dick Giordano along the bottom edge.

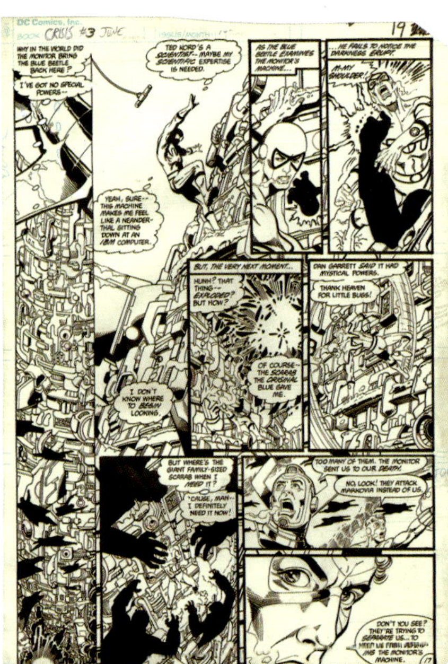

4312 George Perez and Dick Giordano - Crisis on Infinite Earths #3, page 17 Original Art (Marvel, 1985). DC editors bestowed four-color godhood upon Marv Wolfman, when they approved his proposal to revamp the company's incomprehensible 50-year history in the early 1980s. And, like an angry deity come judgment day, Wolfman waved his hand and wiped countless redundant universes from existence, making the DC universe a more accessible place for new readers. This page from Marv Wolfman's "Oblivion Upon Us," features the Blue Beetle battling a brood of shadow demons, in lavish George Perez style. The image area measures 15" x 21", and, aside from some edges trimmed during the production process, the art is in Excellent condition. Signed by Marv Wolfman, George Perez and Dick Giordano along the bottom edge.

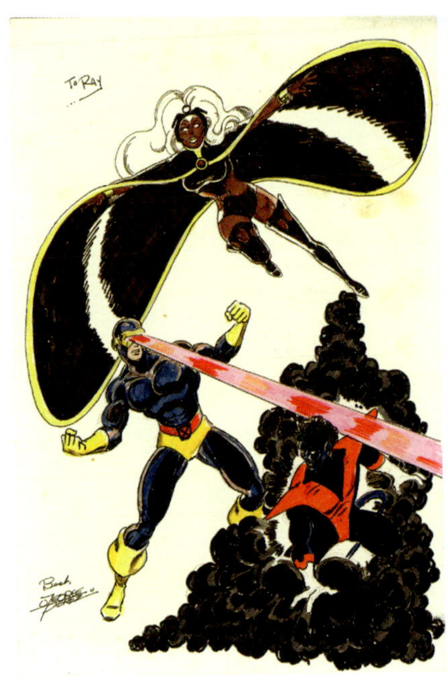

4313 George Perez - X-Men Hand Colored Pin-Up Original Art (undated). George Perez proved himself to be a master of the team-up books early on with stints on **The Avengers** and of course the **The New Teen Titans**. But the X-Men weren't on his resume in those early years (his **X-Men** debut wasn't till Annual #3 in 1979), so it's a real treat to see his version of the team. Nightcrawler had best watch where he teleports, Cyclops' eyebeams are dangerous! Storm rounds out this mutant trio. The overall size of the hand colored pin-up measures 11" x 17". There is some light wear and mild staining on the paper; otherwise the art is in Very Good condition.

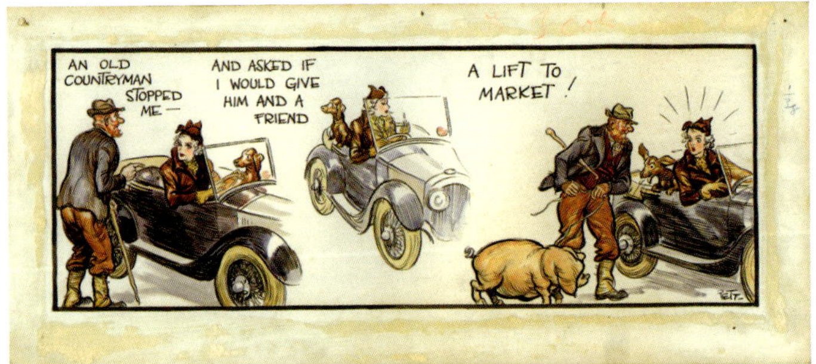

4314 Norman Pett - Hand Colored Jane Daily Comic Strip Original Art (undated). *Jane* was an English strip that ran from 1932-59, mainly in England. It was syndicated in the USA for a short period after World War II, circa 1945-46. The feature was often rather risque, but it was toned down for its American audience. Jane debuted in 1932, when *Jane's Journal, the Diary of a Bright Young Thing* was published in London's **Daily Mirror**. When the war broke out, Jane (said to be modeled after Pett's wife), was pictured wearing less and less of her clothes, thus boosting the morale of the fighting men abroad. In 1948, Pett devoted himself to a new feature, *Susie*, which appeared in the **Sunday Dispatch**. Finally, in 1959, Jane's adventures (now continued by Pett's former assistant) ended after she married her long time boyfriend. The image area of this handsome daily measures 5.5" x 15", and aside from paper "pulls" around the borders, outside the image area, the art is in Excellent condition.

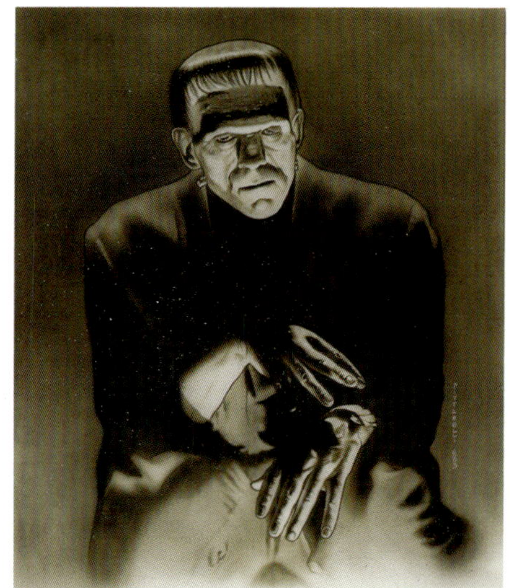

4315 Jeff Pittarelli - Boris Karloff as Frankenstein Illustration Original Art (2003). A self-professed illustrator of the unreal, Jeff Pittarelli's monochromatic creations give a timeless quality to their subjects. Pittarelli has been painting for nearly 20 years in the realm of horror, sci-fi and fantasy, and worked for just about everyone including Chaos Comics, Image and Marvel. Painted and airbrushed in pencil and ink, this electrifying image measures 14" x 17" and is in Excellent condition. Signed by Jeff Pittarelli at the right.

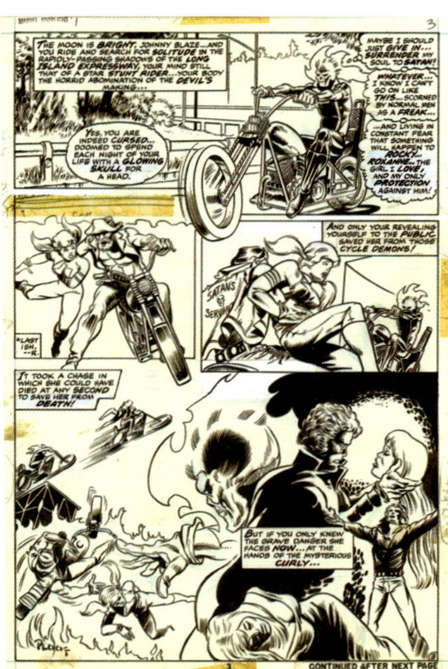

4316 Mike Ploog and Frank Chiaramonte - Marvel Spotlight #7, page 3 Original Art (Marvel, 1972). The Ghost Rider heads out onto the Long Island Expressway, in search of solitude. His mind is still that of star stunt rider, Johnny Blaze, but his body is a horrid abomination of the devil's making. His thoughts turn to the girl he loves — Roxanne Simpson, his only protection against the master of all evil! Here is page three from "Die, Die My Daughter," written by Gary Friedrich, penciled by acclaimed artist Mike Ploog, and inked by Frank Chiaramonte. The image area measures 10" x 15," and, aside from tape stains in all four center edges, and a missing type balloon, the art is in Excellent condition. Signed by Mike Ploog in the final panel.

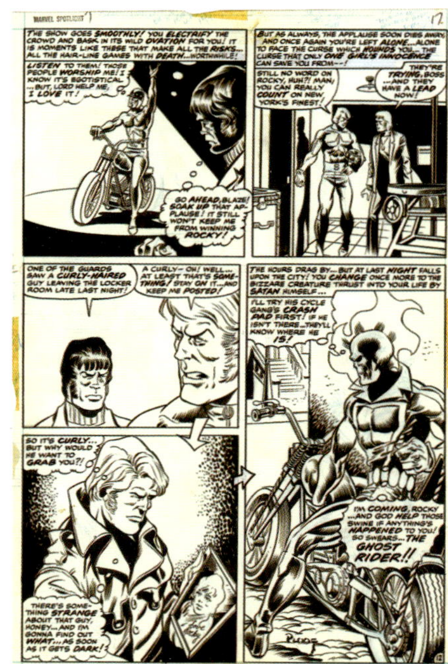

4317 Mike Ploog and Frank Chiaramonte - Marvel Spotlight #7, page 12 Original Art (Marvel, 1972). Johnny Blaze's girlfriend, Roxanne Simpson, is missing! As night falls, the Ghost Rider begins his date with vengeance against the might of the Devil and his minions, with Rocky's soul hanging in the balance. Page 12 from "Die, Die My Daughter," written by Gary Friedrich, is penciled by one of the finest artists of the Bronze Age, Mike Ploog, and inked by Frank Chiaramonte. The image area measures 10" x 15," and, aside from tape stains in all four center edges, and a trimmed top edge, the art is in Excellent condition. Signed by Mike Ploog in the final panel.

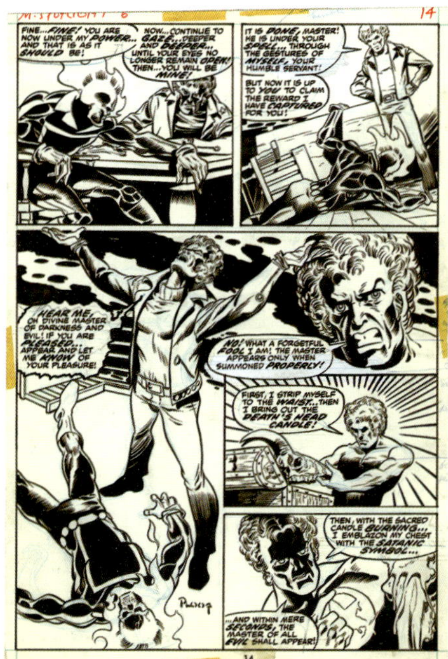

4318 Mike Ploog and Frank Chiaramonte - Marvel Spotlight #7, page 14 Original Art (Marvel, 1972). Curly Samuels, humble servant to the divine master of darkness — Satan — has cast a spell on the Ghost Rider, and now summons his boss to finish the job, in this page from "Die, Die My Daughter," written by Gary Friedrich. The horror artist of the Bronze Age, Mike Ploog, penciled this supernatural thriller, which was inked by Frank Chiaramonte. The image area measures 10" x 15," and, aside from tape stains in all four center edges, and a trimmed top edge, the art is in Excellent condition. Signed by Mike Ploog in the third panel.

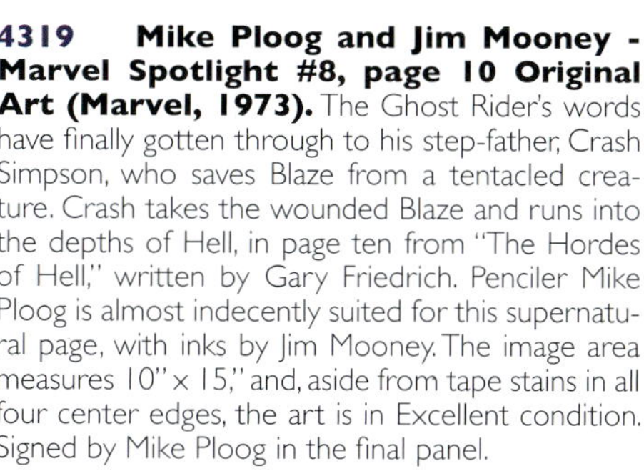

4319 Mike Ploog and Jim Mooney - Marvel Spotlight #8, page 10 Original Art (Marvel, 1973). The Ghost Rider's words have finally gotten through to his step-father, Crash Simpson, who saves Blaze from a tentacled creature. Crash takes the wounded Blaze and runs into the depths of Hell, in page ten from "The Hordes of Hell," written by Gary Friedrich. Penciler Mike Ploog is almost indecently suited for this supernatural page, with inks by Jim Mooney. The image area measures 10" x 15," and, aside from tape stains in all four center edges, the art is in Excellent condition. Signed by Mike Ploog in the final panel.

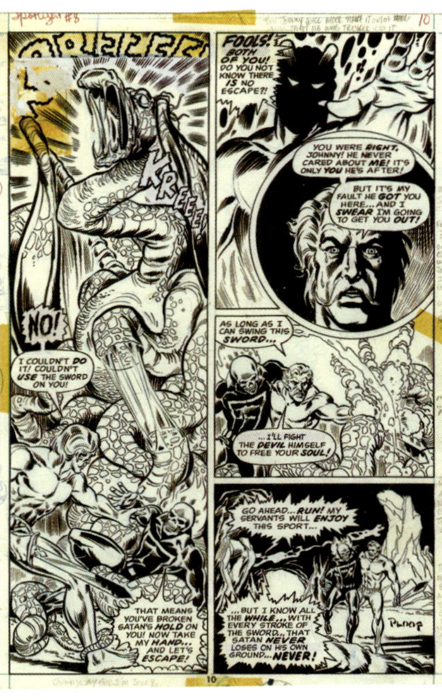

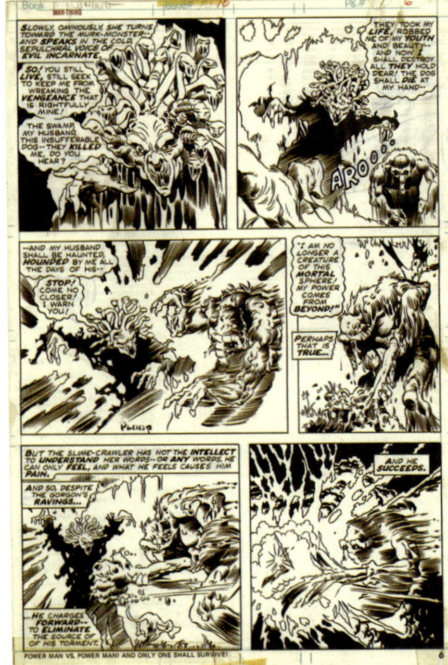

4320 Mike Ploog and Frank Chiaramonte - Man-Thing #10, page 6 Original Art (Marvel, 1974). In January 1974, Steve Gerber began writing the **Man-Thing** series, which became Marvel's chief non-superhero fantasy title. The shambling, mindless guardian of the "nexus of all realities," maintained a distinct atmosphere of dread, courtesy of Gerber, and Mike Ploog, the definitive artist of the character. In this page from the story, "Nobody Dies Forever," the slime-crawler faces a malevolent force that was once Maybelle Tork, a story tailor-made for Ploog, a master of the incredible and the macabre. The image area measures 10" x 15," and, aside from several light stains along the right edge, and a tape stain along the bottom, the art is in Excellent condition. Signed by Mike Ploog in the third panel.

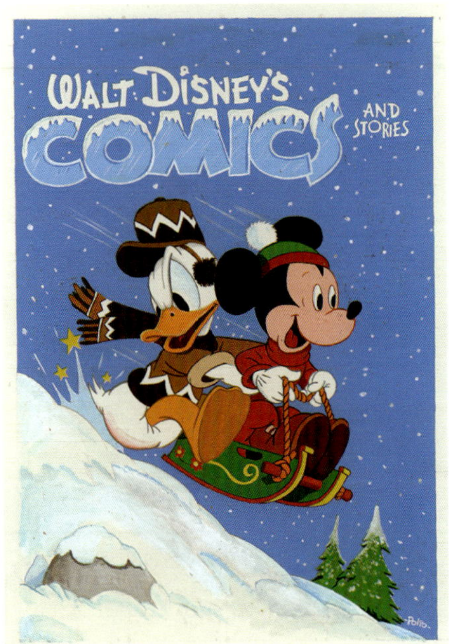

4321 Bob Polio - Walt Disney's Comics and Stories #41 Cover Recreation Original Art (undated). Bob Polio, art director for New England Comics' **The Tick** comic line, produced this recreation of Walt Kelly's original cover art from **Walt Disney's Comics and Stories** #41. This colorful offering by Polio adds dimension to Kelly's original animated masterpiece with this dimensional hand-painted watercolor on illustration board. The image area measures 11" x 15", and, aside from some slight scattered spotting, the art is in Very Good condition. Includes a copy of **Walt Disney's Comics and Stories** #41, and two copies of **Mickey and Donald** #2, which feature a reprint of Walt Kelly's original cover.

4322 Keith Pollard and Kim DeMulder - Nick Fury, Agent of SHIELD #4 Cover Original Art (Marvel, 1986). The menace of the Death's Head Squad brings Nick Fury out of a one year secluded retirement to investigate the assassination of various intelligence operatives, in this series which began in the late 80s. Deep within their lair, Fury and his agents face the deadly threat of the Death's Head, in this cover penciled by Keith Pollard and inked by Kim DeMulder! The image area measures 10" x 15", and the work is in Excellent condition.

4323 Western Publishing Artist - Porky Pig #72 Cover Original Art (Dell, 1960). That sputtering swine, Porky Pig, applies his handypig skills using poor Cicero's head, in this st-st-st-stupend, er, exciting cover illustration for **Porky Pig** #72. The image area measures 11" x 12", and, aside from a tape stain at the upper right corner, the art is in Excellent condition. Includes a copy of **Porky Pig** #72.

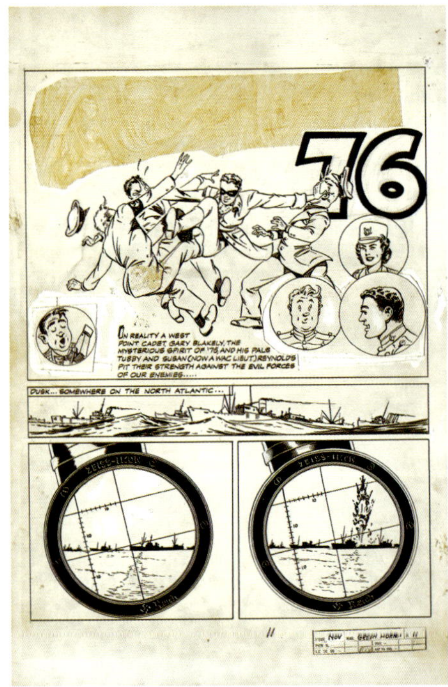

4324 Bob Powell - Green Hornet Comics #21, Complete 8-page Story "The Crooner's Code" Original Art (Harvey, 1944). West Point cadet, Gary Blakely — the mysterious Spirit of '76 — and his pals, Tubby, and Lieutenant Susan Reynolds, pit their strength against a smooth-crooning spy named Hank Wonatra, who's passing out secret military information via his radio broadcasts, in these eight Golden Age pages. Bob Powell handles the drama as easily as he does the weaponry, and the image area of each page measures 12" x 18". Aside from some overall apparent aging, a missing logo paste-up in the first frame, and a small glue stain in the first panel, the art averages in Excellent condition.

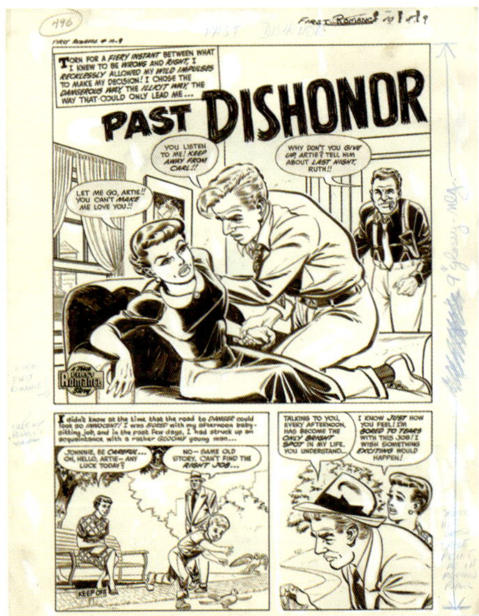

4325 Bob Powell - First Romance Magazine #10 Complete 6-page Story "Past Dishonor" Original Art (Harvey, 1951). Torn between what she knew to be wrong and right, Ruth recklessly allows her wild impulses to make a dangerous decision that leads to shame, scandal, and jail! Bob Powell's dramatic design work here is stunning. The image area of each page measures 12" x 18", and the art is in Excellent condition.

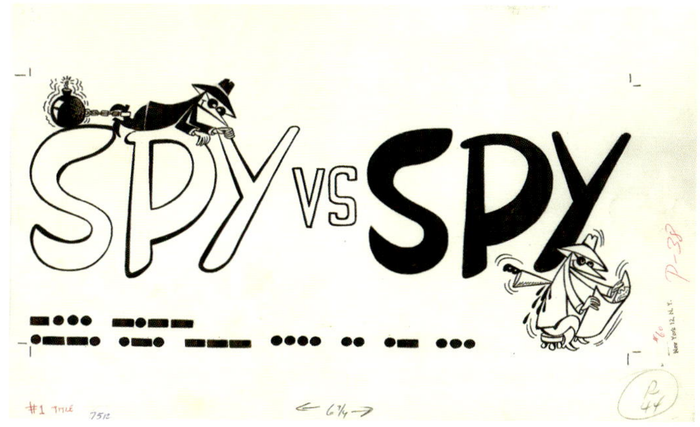

4326 Antonio Prohias - Mad #60 "Spy vs. Spy" Page Original Art (EC, 1961). "The sweetest revenge," Antonio Prohias told a **Miami Herald** reporter in 1983, "has been to turn Castro's accusation of me as a spy into a money-making venture". Prohias, one of Cuba's premier editorial cartoonists before the revolution, fled to the U.S. in 1960, his anti-Castro cartoons earning him international awards — and the enmity of his government, which accused him of working for the CIA. About to turn forty, with a family to support, he had to take work in a New York City sweatshop before stumbling into **Mad** magazine's offices, where in January, 1961, they began to publish his masterful series, "Spy vs Spy." Since then, the Spies have done battle more than 500 times and their spirited rivalry continues to surprise, deceive and revolt. Here is their very first American appearance, from **Mad** #60. In three decades with the magazine, Prohias produced over two hundred of the self-contained gags. There are two pieces here — the logo art, and the panel strip, both have an image area of approximately 16" x 10", and their condition is Excellent. Signed by Prohias in the final panel.

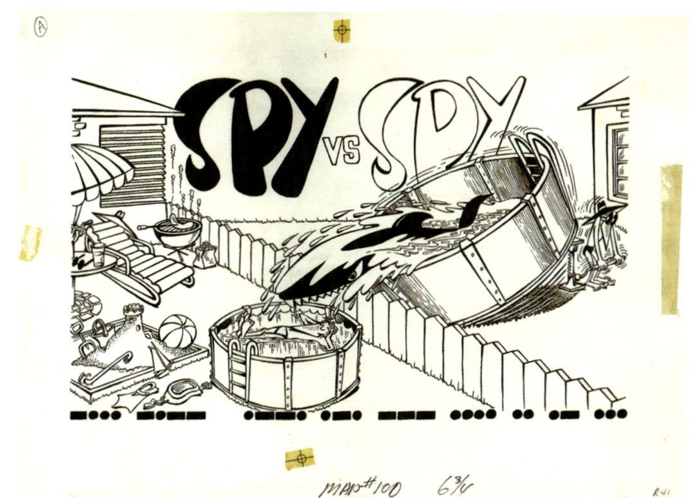

4327 Antonio Prohias - Mad #100 "Spy vs. Spy" Page Original Art (EC, 1966). Three days before Fidel Castro's henchmen took over what remained of Cuba's free press, famous Cuban artist, Antonio Prohias, fled to New York City stone broke. Once here, he came directly to **Mad** with his captivating gag series, "Spy vs Spy." This sequence is from **Mad** #100, one of the over 200 strips he created in his thirty year tenure with the magazine. There are two pieces here — the logo art, and the panel strip, both have an image area of approximately 16.5" x 12", and their condition is Excellent. Signed by Prohias in the final panel.

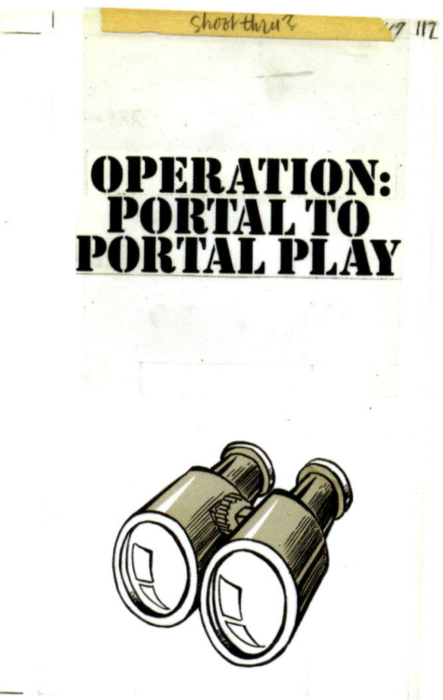

4328 Antonio Prohias - Spy vs. Spy, Complete 14-page story "Operation: Portal to Portal Play" Original Art (undated). From 1960 until his retirement in 1990, Antonio Prohias' unique, wordless Cold War feature, "Spy vs. Spy" ran in **Mad** magazine. With the help of some sophisticated television equipment, Black sends White on a sky-scraping wild goose chase, in this episode. Each page has an image area of 6.5" x 11.5", and the pages are in Excellent condition.

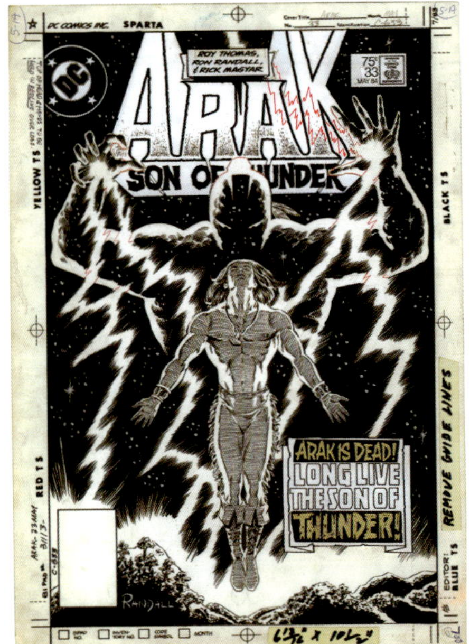

4329 Ron Randall and Rick Maygar - Arak, Son of Thunder #33 Cover and Panel Page Original Art, Group of 14 (DC, 1984). Arak is dead! Long live the Son of Thunder! From the thirty third issue of the historic fantasy title, **Arak, Son of Thunder**, comes this mesmerizing cover illustration by Ron Randall. This group also includes 13 pages from Roy Thomas' story, "To Your Sky-Born Father Go!," an origin of sorts featuring Arak and his heavenly father, He-No. Seeking his American roots, Arak was killed, but after a direct meeting with He-No himself, he is resurrected, and becomes both a physical warrior and a mystical shaman. The image area of these pieces measures approximately 10" x 15". There is some tape along the edges of each of the interior pages, and the corners have been trimmed during the production process, otherwise the work averages in Very Good condition.

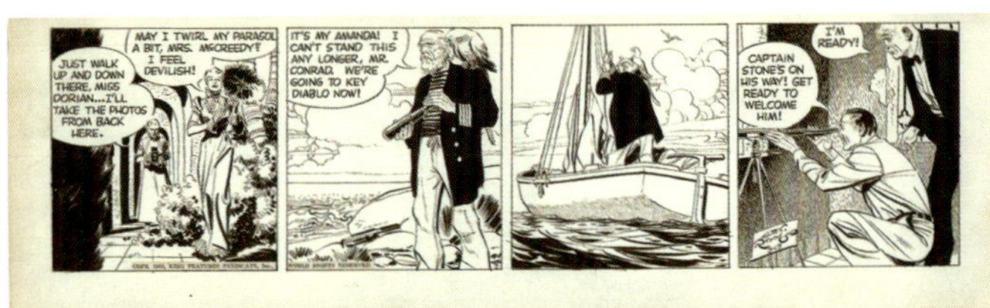

4330 Alex Raymond - Rip Kirby Daily Comic Strip Original Art, dated 3-13-53 (King Features Syndicate, 1953). One look at this gorgeous daily from 1953, and you'll understand why Alex Raymond is considered one of the all-time greats. Mrs. McCreedy, Captain Stone, and the lovely Miss Honey Dorian all figure into this beautifully-drawn daily by the modern master. The image area measures 22" x 6.75", and the art is in Excellent condition.

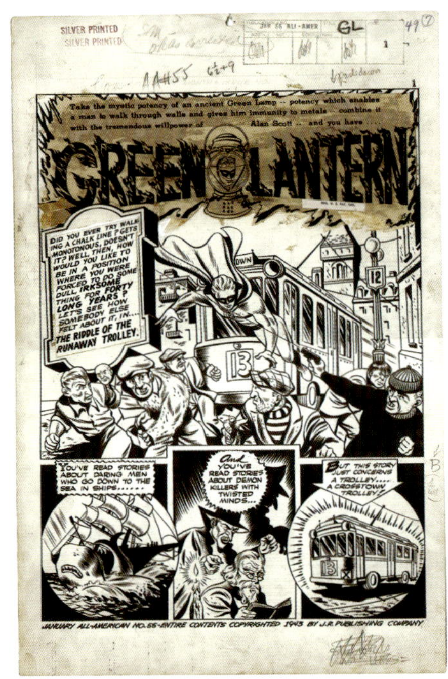

4331 Paul Reinman and Sam Burlockoff - All-American Comics #55, Splash Page 1 Original Art (DC, 1944). Green Lantern takes the offense on a gang of pistol-packing ruffians, in this daring splash page penciled by Paul Reinman and inked by Sam Burlockoff. Presented here is the first page to the 13-page story, "The Riddle of the Runaway Trolley," which was written by Bill Finger. The image area measures 13" x 18", and aside from a discolored logo photostat, and some light glue staining, the art is in Good condition.

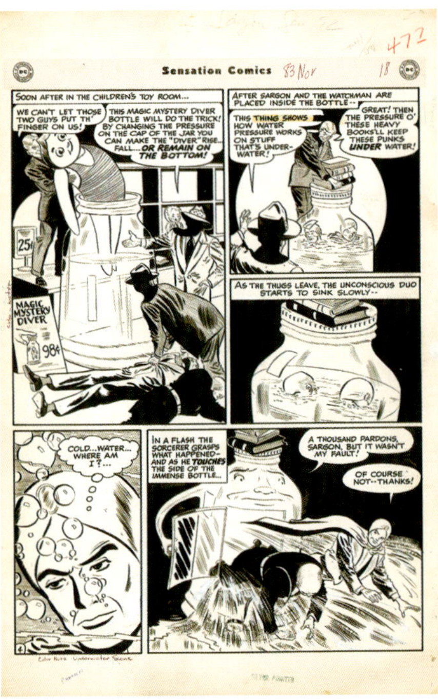

4332 Paul Reinman - Sensation Comics #83 Sargon Page Original Art, Group of 2 (DC, 1948). Golden Age Sargon the Sorcerer originals are harder to catch to than a dove flying out of a magician's hat! They are scarcely, if ever, offered in the marketplace. Paul Reinman's Golden Age art, with its dramatic angles and deeply shadowed figures, inspired the "new wave" of young comic books artists who went directly from their New York City art high schools into the industry in the late forties. Alex Toth in particular enjoyed Reinman's approach. Sargon the Sorcerer works his marvelous magic in pages four and five from "The Man From Nowhere." Each page has an image area of 13" x 18" and aside from two small lettering corrections that have slipped off the pages, the art is in Excellent condition.

 Visit HeritageComics.com to view enlargeable images and bid online.

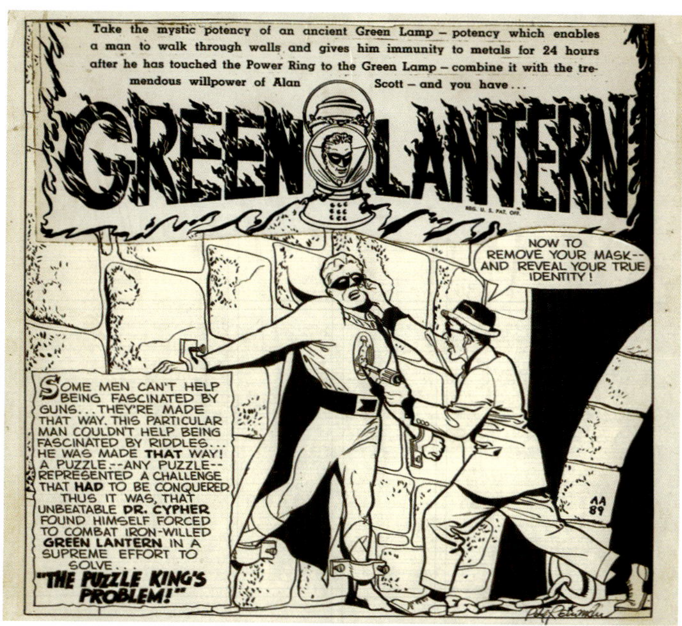

4333 Paul Reinman - Golden Age Green Lantern Unpublished Partial Page Original Art (DC, 1949). The iron-willed Green Lantern finds himself forced to combat the unbeatable Dr. Cypher, in this partial first page of "The Puzzle King's Problem!" Apparently slated for **All-American Comics** #89, this Golden Age Green Lantern story was subsequently "written off" and was slated to be destroyed, but the page was cut horizontally into tiers instead. The image area measures 13" x 12.5" and the art is in Excellent condition. Signed by Paul Reinman at the lower right.

4334 Paul Reinman - Golden Age Green Lantern Unpublished Partial Page Original Art (DC, 1949). Happy Valley has no crime problem? How come nobody has ever heard of the place? That's just what the Green Lantern wants to know! This Golden Age treasure was "written off" and scheduled to be destroyed, but the page was cut horizontally into tiers by a forward thinking DC staffer, and saved instead. Contains great shots of the Green Gladiator! The image area measures 13" x 9" and the art is in Excellent condition.

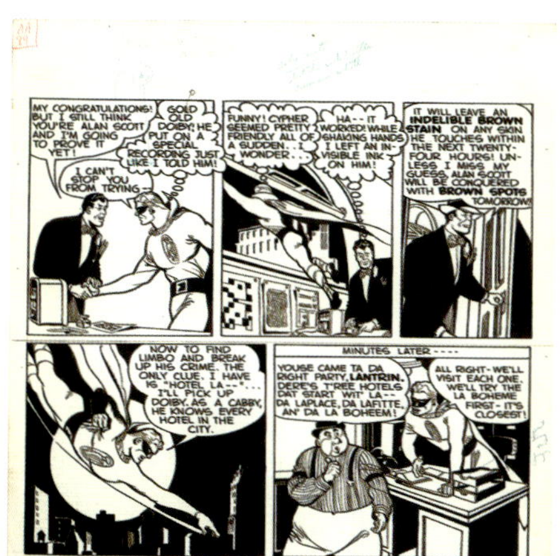

4335 Paul Reinman - Golden Age Green Lantern Unpublished Partial Page Original Art (DC, 1949). The Green Gladiator gets a dose of Dr. Cypher's double-dealings in this never published page from the story, "The Puzzle King's Problem!," which was apparently slated for **All-American Comics** #89. This Golden Age treasure was "written off" and scheduled to be destroyed, but the page was cut horizontally into tiers by a DC staffer, and saved instead. A beautiful page containing fabulous panels of the Green Lantern and Doiby! The image area measures 13" x 12" and the art is in Excellent condition.

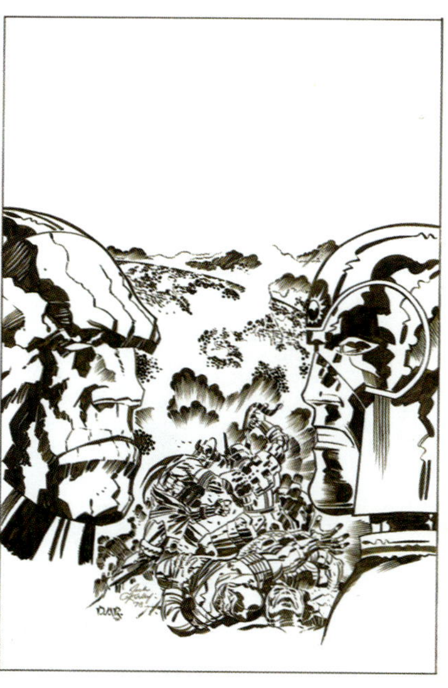

4336 David Roach (attributed) - Unpublished Jack Kirby Tribute, New Gods Cover Original Art (1994) Darkseid and Orion face off as the New Gods battle, between their profiles. Working from a photocopy of a Jack Kirby 1978 pencil drawing, artist David Roach inked Kiby's tableau onto a sheet of a paper with the help of a lightbox in 1994. Thus, there are no pencils under these inks and the page is super-clean. "Posthumous collaborations" such as this one have become commonplace since Kirby's death in 1994, thanks to tribute magazines, repackaging efforts, "inking contests" and fanzines dedicated to "the King." As often is the case, the piece even has an inked facsimile of Jack Kirby's signature dated "'78." The image area of the cover is 10" x 15", and the art is in Excellent condition.

4337 Disney Studios Artist - Robin Hood Picture Puzzle Cover Original Art (Jaymar, 1973). Legendary outlaws, Robin Hood and Little John, compete at the padded feet of Prince John, while Maid Marion looks on, in this illustration for the cover of this 100 piece interlocking picture puzzle produced by Jaymar. The art consists of a photocopy, which has been hand-painted in watercolor, and mounted onto a sheet of 18" x 15.5" illustration board. The image area measures 13.5" x 10.5" and the art is in Excellent condition. Includes a **Robin Hood Picture Puzzle**.

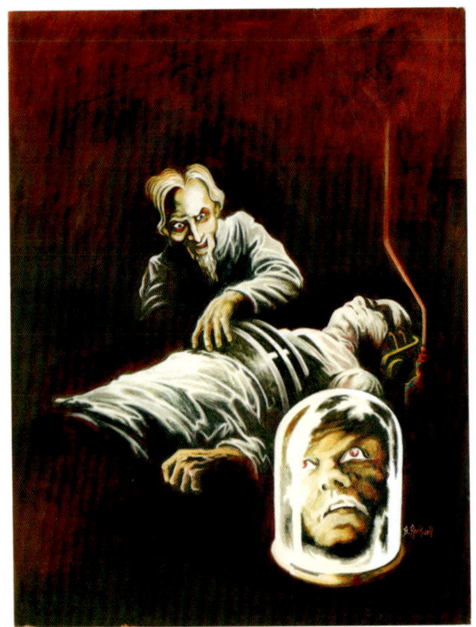

4338 Barry Rockwell - Eerie #16 Cover Original Art (Warren, 1968). Beware the diabolically wicked genius, Doctor Felix, and his gruesome experiments! This mind-shattering image of the deadly doctor is the one and only Warren cover illustration created by Barry Rockwell. It's a classic, campy cover with brilliant detail and terrific colors, painted in oils on a sheet of 16" x 21" illustration board. Although there is a bit of wear along the edges, well outside of the image area, the condition of the work is Excellent. The artist has signed the painting "B. Rockwell" in the lower right. This lot includes a copy of **Eerie** #16.

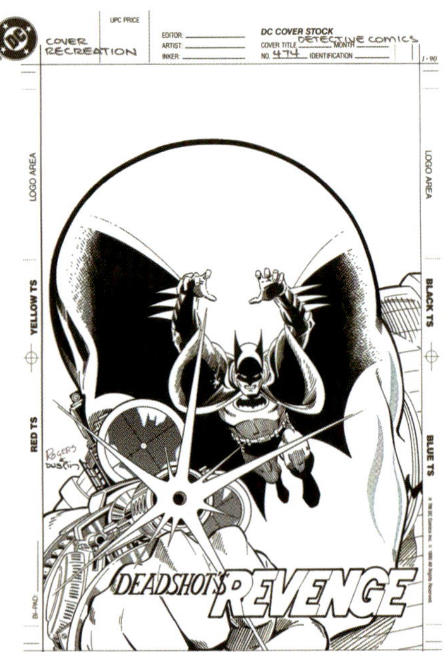

4339 Marshall Rogers and Terry Austin - Detective Comics #474 Cover Recreation Original Art (undated). Deadshot has Batman dead-center in his crosshairs in this beautifully finished recreation of the cover for the yarn "Deadshot's Revenge." Terry Austin's inks add a silky-smooth finish to Marshall Roger's superbly designed montage. The image area of the art measures 10" x 15" and the piece is in Excellent condition.

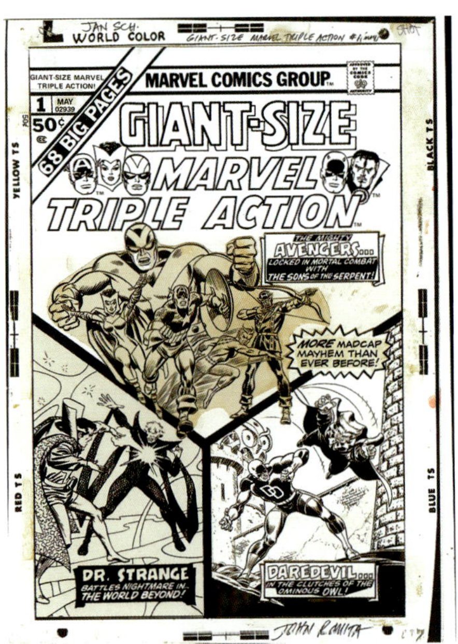

4340 John Romita Sr. - Giant Size Marvel Triple Action #1 Cover Original Art (Marvel, 1975). All three panels in this dynamic tryptic were drawn by Jazzy John Romita Sr., but only the center section is original art; the two lower images are both photostats. The center image, of the Mighty Avengers springing into action, was rendered on vellum and then cut to fit the layout on this backing board. A truly terrific piece by one of the most beloved artists in the Marvel bullpen. The art measures 11.5" x 16.5" and is in Very Good condition, with some discoloration in the borders. The piece was signed by the Jazzy One himself in the lower right corner.

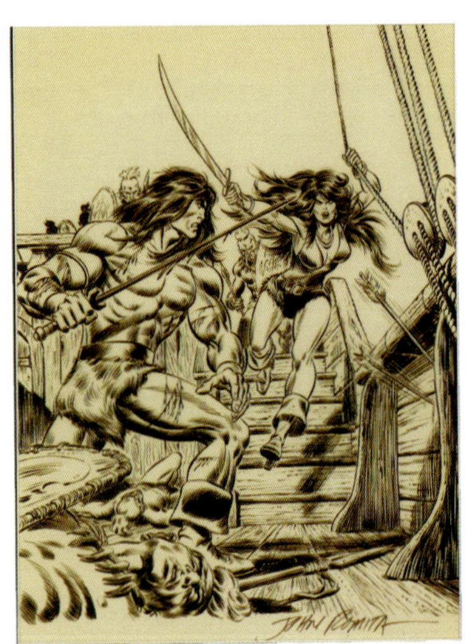

4341 John Romita Sr. and John Buscema - Conan the Barbarian #58 Cover Original Art (Marvel, 1976). Conan faces off against Belit, Queen of the Black Coast. Working from a John Buscema design, John Romita Sr. inked this cover image directly onto translucent vellum paper, so there are no signs of Buscema's under-penciling on the art. There are no title logos or type stats on the art, and it is very clean. The vellum paper is a cream color. John Romita Sr. has signed the art in the lower border of the vellum. The image area measures 10" x 14", and the art comes with a copy of the comic book. The piece is in Excellent condition. "Jazzy" John Romita Sr. is in full command of his lush inking style on this gorgeous Bronze Age Conan masterwork.

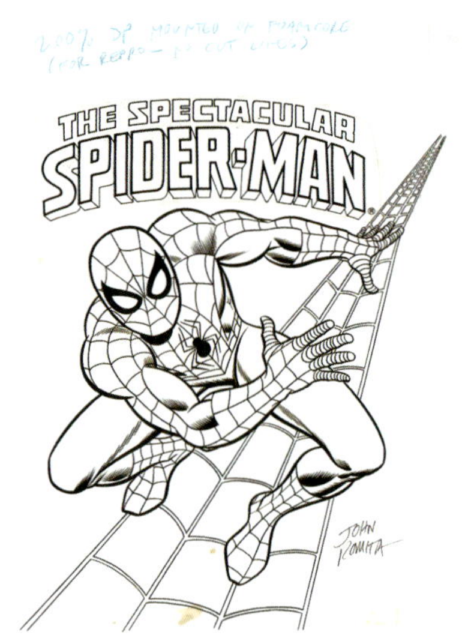

4342 John Romita Sr. - Spider-Man Poster Original Art (Marvel, 1978). Hey there Marvelite, shake hands with your friendly neighborhood Spider-Man! John Romita Sr.'s masterwork, drawn for a Marvel poster is nothing less than a Silver Age web-swinging wonder! The art has an image area of 11.5" x 15". There are a few small stains at the bottom of the drawing; otherwise the art is in Excellent condition. John Romita Sr. signed the art at the lower right. A folded copy of the printed, full-color poster is included in this lot.

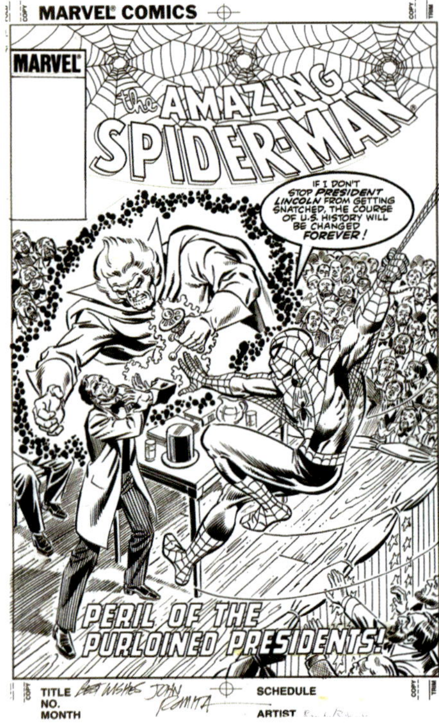

4343 John Romita Sr. and Joe Rubinstein - Unpublished Spider-Man Cover Original Art (circa 1984). The Collector has his heart set on adding President Abraham Lincoln to his showroom. Only Spider-Man stands in the way of history being changed forever. A wild and wacky concept, this John Romita Sr. cover never saw print. Unlike many Romita Sr. covers, this one was drawn on comic book cover stock, not vellum. The page has an image area of 9.75" x 15" and the art is in Excellent condition. John Romita Sr. signed the art at the lower left. Hang loose, heroes and bid!

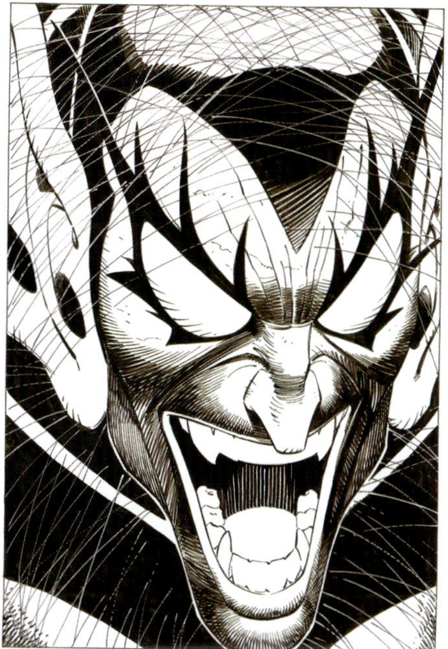

4344 John Romita Jr. and Scott Hanna - Peter Parker: Spider-Man #98 Splash Page 1 Original Art (Marvel, 1998). It's a case of delusion for Norman Osborne, in the aftermath of his final battle with Spider-Man. As the story opens, the Green Goblin screams that Spider-Man is dead, of course we realize that this raving lunatic is wrong, as the next page reveals Spider-Man standing triumphantly over a webbed up Green Goblin. From the first page to the last issue of **Peter Parker: Spider-Man** comes this extravaganza penciled by John Romita Jr. and inked by Scott Hanna. The image area measures 10" x 15" and the art is in Excellent condition. Signed by John Romita Jr. at the bottom.

4345 Alex Ross - Marvels, Dr. Doom and Thing Preliminary Sketch Original Art (undated). Alex Ross is one of the most gifted talents in comic art today, and the demand for his work continues to grow steadily. "I do the gigs I do because I care about the material," Ross says. "In some cases, it's because I like the character. In some cases, I have a vision in my head of something I must do. It all involves artistic expression. If I can't get into the work on some artistic level, I can't do it." Here, Ross presents this color preliminary sketch of two of Marvel's most significant characters, Doctor Doom and Ben Grimm, in marker and colored pencils on marker paper, for the **Marvels** mini-series. The image area measures 8" x 11.5" and, aside from some edge wear and creasing, the art is in Good condition. Signed by Alex Ross at the lower right.

4346 Alex Ross - Terminator: The Burning Earth V2#3, page 1 Original Art (Now Comics, 1990). Here's a page from one of the first comic books Alex Ross ever drew (the now-legendary artist's first published comic work was V2#1 of this series)! Here, the war between man and machine is about to reach its brutal conclusion and only one side will survive! This mini-series for Now Comics was based on the popular "Terminator" films. The image area of this page measures 10" x 15" and the art is in Excellent condition. The word and type balloons are on an acetate overlay, and the art has been signed by Alex Ross at the lower left.

4347 Vince Colletta - Popular Romance #29 Complete Original 8-page Story "Don't Play at Love" Original Art (Standard, 1954). Romance fans are unlikely to find a lovelier Vince Colletta story than this beauty! Standerd's master of romance, Alex Toth, revolutionized the comics industry with his elegant and design-oriented storytelling. His work bloomed in the fifties. Soon art director (and inker) Mike Peppe was encouraging the other artists at Standard to adapt Toth's approach and as a result, many Standard stories had the same sharp look, and especially so in the romance line. Vince Colletta, Ross Andru, Mike Esposito, Art Saaf, Nick Cardy, Gene Fawcette, and others proved themselves quite capable of delivering this streamlined "house style." In this melodrama, although college co-ed Josie is insecure about her humble family income level, in the end her sterling character wins the heart of her well-to-do beau. The image area of each page is 12" x 18", and the art is in Excellent condition.

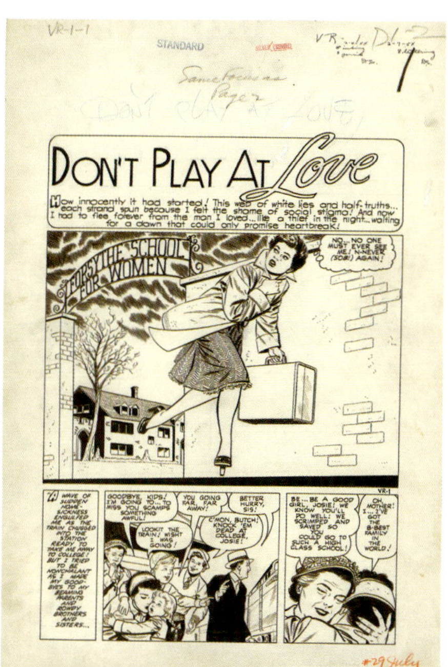

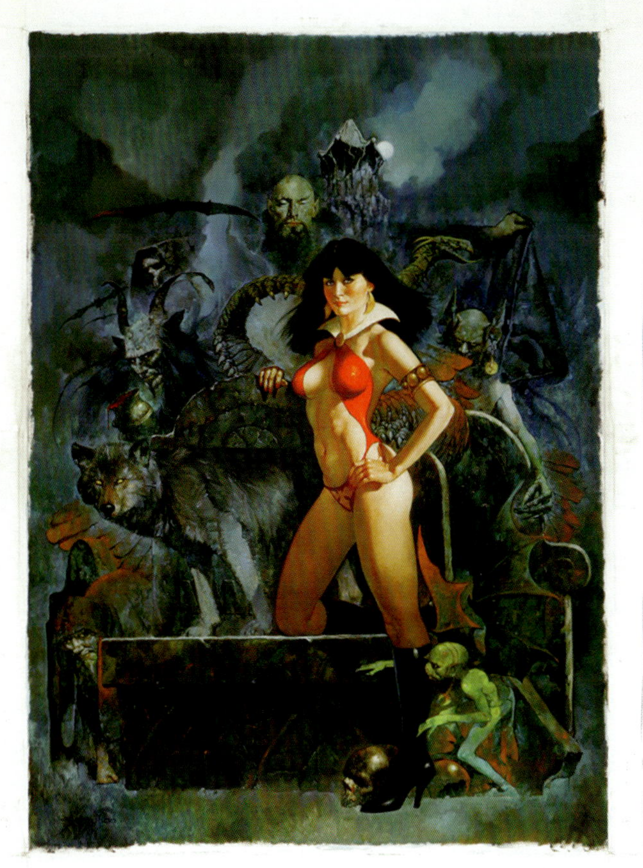

4348 Manuel Sanjulian - "The Horde of Chaos" Vampirella Painting Original Art (undated). Manuel Sanjulian is a celebrated talent in the realm of painted fantasy art. His skilled use of color and light infuse his haunting images with an air of suspense and electric tension. Contrasting warm and cool color variations in the hues give this art exceptional eye-appeal. This full-length portrait of Vampirella, with all things vampire, recalls the same spine-tingling mood found in his fan-favorite cover for **Eerie** #41. The image area of this painting measures approximately 36" x 50", and the piece is in Excellent condition. Very few paintings could sate the forbidden desires of a thrall of Vampirella's as fully as this moody masterpiece!

4349 Kurt Schaffenberger and Bob Wiacek - Shazam! #31, page 17 Original Art (DC, 1977). One of the six female warriors known as the Rainbow Squad clobbers Minute Man, who has returned after a 33 year absence. But does that stop him? Heck, no! Now he knows what he's been missing all these years... ***excitement!*** This page features great shots of the World's Mightiest Mortal, plus Mr. Mind! Here is page 17 from the E. Nelson Bridwell story, "The Rainbow Squad". The image area measures 10" x 15", and, aside from a tape stain at the upper and lower center edges, and some blue pencil editorial notations, the art is in Excellent condition.

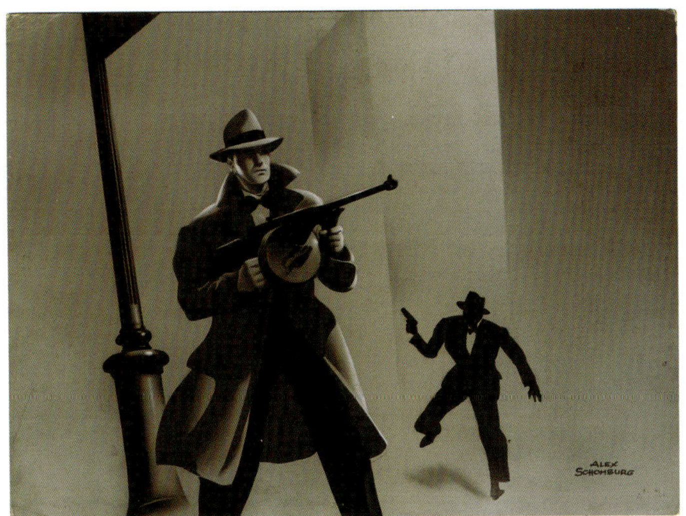

4350 Alex Schomburg - Gunman Airbrushed Illustration Original Art (circa 1940s). Before he launched his legendary career in comics, Alex Schomburg worked as a commercial artist for National Screen Service. In the monograph **Chroma: The Art of Alex Schomburg**, the talented artist recalled his days there, "National is where I learned most of my craft. We did a lot of art of all different kinds. Most of the illustrations were done in black and white and with the aid of an airbrush. This gave me a chance to really learn to operate an airbrush; I became pretty good at it." That's an understatement! The main figure in this scene, with his snap brim hat, overcoat, and Thompson machine gun bears more than a passing resemblance to the legendary crime stopper, Dick Tracy — is this fellow a gangster or a G-Man? The overall size of the illustration measures 20" x 15" and aside from some light edge wear, the art is in Excellent condition. This is a superb piece!

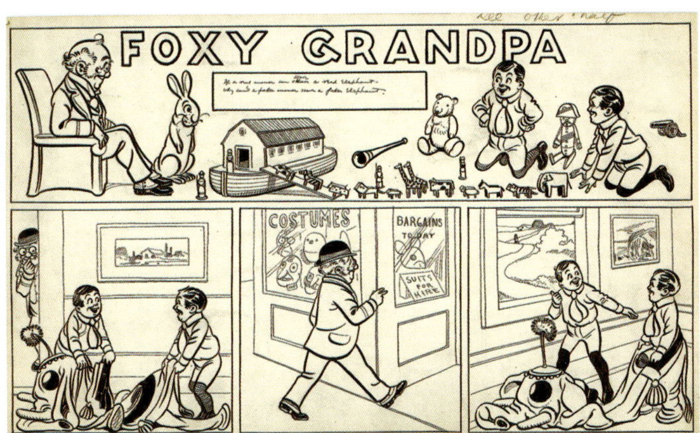

4351 Carl E. "Bunny" Schultze - Foxy Grandpa Partial Sunday Comic Strip Original Art (undated). Foxy Grandpa was nothing like the curmudgeonly old geezers often portrayed in popular comics. No, he was quite the opposite — a sprightly, stout gent full of wily cunning, who always managed to keep a few steps ahead of his folly-filled nephews. In this partial Sunday strip, the nephews plan to scare Grandpa with an elephant costume, but Grandpa is one step ahead of 'em! The image area measures 19.25" x 11.5" and the art is in Excellent condition.

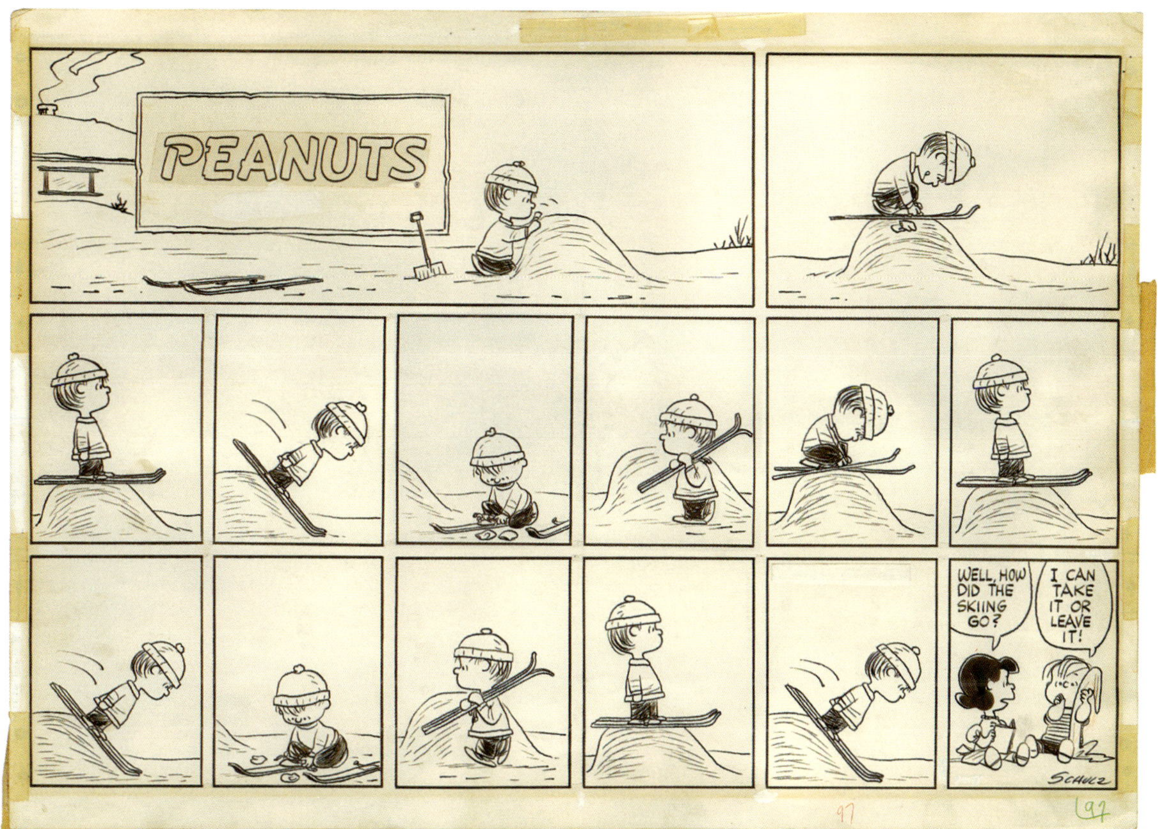

4352 Charles Schulz - Peanuts Sunday Comic Strip Original Art, dated 1-8-61 (United Feature Syndicate, 1961). Lucy's little brother, Linus, tackles a ski slope in this mostly silent Sunday from 1961. A truly classic, mostly wordless work of whimsy by a master of the comic strip, Charles Schulz! The image area of the strip measures 22.5" x 15". There is a bit of aging apparent along the very edges of the strip, some very slight staining in several of the panels, and aged tape pieces along the edges (outside of the image area), otherwise this genius piece is in Very Good condition. This strip has been confirmed by the Schulz Museum to have been printed in January 1961. ***Peanuts*** art from the sixties is highly prized among collectors, and this pleasing piece from 1961 is sure to win a special place in someone's collection.

4353 Mike Sekowsky - Informer #5, page 4 Original Art (Feature Television Productions, 1954). Mike Sekowsky's thrilling subway scene for "Death Travels North" captures the same big city excitement pioneered by crime dramas such as TV's "Dragnet." The page has an image area of 12" x 18" and the art is in Excellent condition.

4354 Mike Sekowsky and Sid Greene - Justice League of America #60, page 17 Original Art (DC, 1968). JLAers Superman and the Flash are transformed into worker bees at the behest of the mesmeric, but malicious, Queen Zazzala, in order to do her evil bidding, in this page from the classic Gardner Fox story "Winged Warriors of the Immortal Queen". Mike Sekowsky and Sid Greene create a snazzy Silver Age page, which has an image area of 10" x 15". The art has an image area of 10.5" x 16" and is in Excellent condition. Although there are punch-holes in the margins, outside of the image area, and some blue pencil editorial markings, the condition of the art is Excellent.

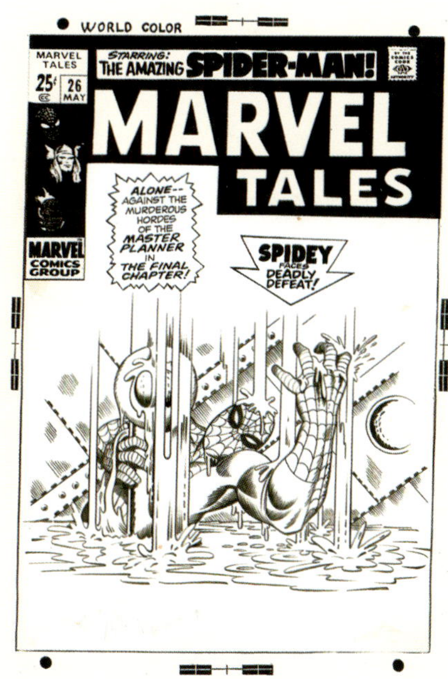

4355 Marie Severin - Marvel Tales #26 Cover Original Art (Marvel, 1970). Marie Severin's cover drawing for **Marvel Tales** #26 recalls one of the most dramatic tests in Spider-Man's early life. In a three-issue story arc, originally drawn by sturdy Steve Ditko, the wall-crawler battled Doctor Octopus (as the Master Planner) for possesion of a cannister of rare radioactive isotopes. Spider-Man needed the isotopes in order to formulate a serum designed to save Aunt May's ebbing life. In the build-up to the conclusion of "The Final Chapter" (originally printed in **Amazing Spider-Man** #33) Spider-Man was trapped beneath a huge block of wrecked machinery in Doc Ock's flooding, underwater lair, with time running out for both Spider-Man and Aunt May. Summoning a herculean reserve of strength, and pushed to his limits, Spidey threw off the dead-weight in one of the greatest sequences of storytelling in comic book history. This Marie Severin scene was originally used for the top half of the cover for **Marvel Tales** #26 (the bottom half was composed of panels of Thor and the Human Torch). The drawing has since been mounted to a facsimile of Marvel cover stock, with recreated logo and caption blocks added. Thus, the drawing is now presented as a single-image cover. This cover has an image area of 11.5" x 17", and other than a few small stains, the art is in Very Good condition.

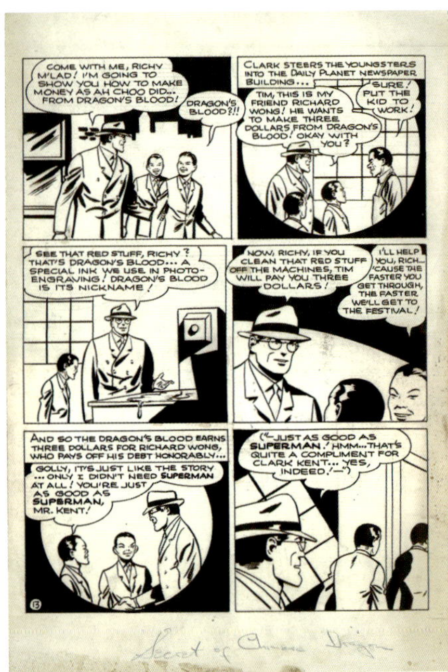

4356 Joe Shuster Studio - Superman, page 13 Original Art (DC, circa 1945). Clark Kent lends a helping hand to young Richard Wong, with the aid of "dragon's blood," a special ink used in photoengraving, in this page from the story, "Secret of the Chinese Dragon." Notes indicate that this page was unpublished and created by the artists at the Joe Shuster studio sometime in the mid-1940s. The image area measures 13" x 18" and, aside from some light apparent aging, and some slight soiling along the right edge, the art is in Very Good condition.

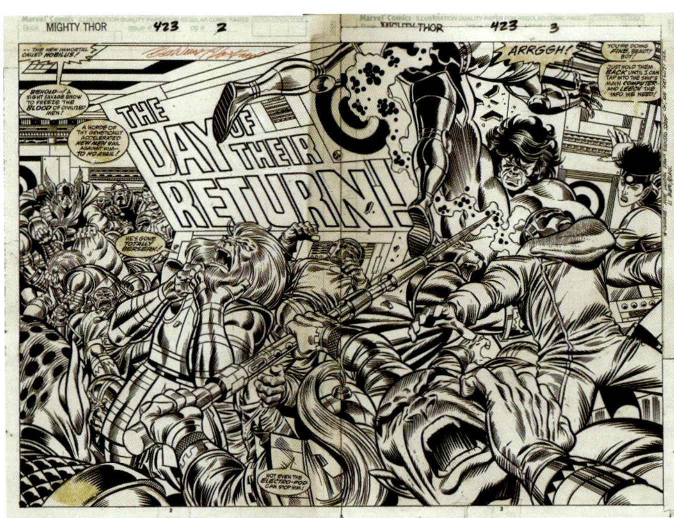

4357 Joe Sinnott and Ron Frenz - Thor #423, pages 2 and 3 Original Art (Marvel, 1990). From the Black Galaxy saga comes this outstanding Kirby-esque title splash by the legendary Joe Sinnott (from layouts by Ron Frenz). The Thunder God watches in horror as the unstoppable Nobilus makes mincemeat of a corridor-load of genetically accelerated "New Men." Bold lines and frantic action make this double-page spread a wonder to behold. Consisting of two 11" x 17" pages taped together at the back, this is in Excellent condition overall with minor edge wear; the word balloons are paste-ups, some of which are slightly discolored and/or missing their tails. Signed by Frenz near the top of the left-hand page. Mighty Marvel action doesn't get much better than this.

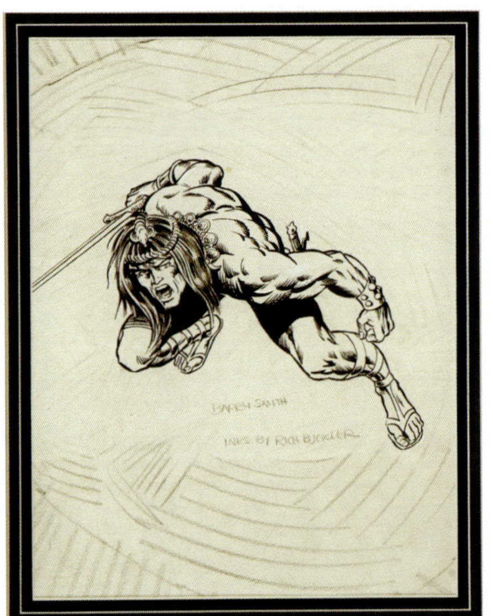

4358 Barry Smith and Rich Buckler - Conan Sketch Original Art (undated). Barry Smith has penciled a pulse-pounding portrait of Conan, the Cimmerian — the brawling barbarian has his sword drawn, and stands ready to crush his enemies, see them driven before him, and hear the lamentation of their women. Smith signed his drawing beneath the figure and a note was written below that in pencil, "inks by Rich Buckler." The background texture was left uninked and part of it was erased to give more contrast to the figure, to separate it visually from the patterned background. The image area of this work measures approximately 8.5" x 11", and there are a few touches of white-out; otherwise the art is in Excellent condition. Don't miss out on this fabulous portrait by one of Conan's finest interpreters.

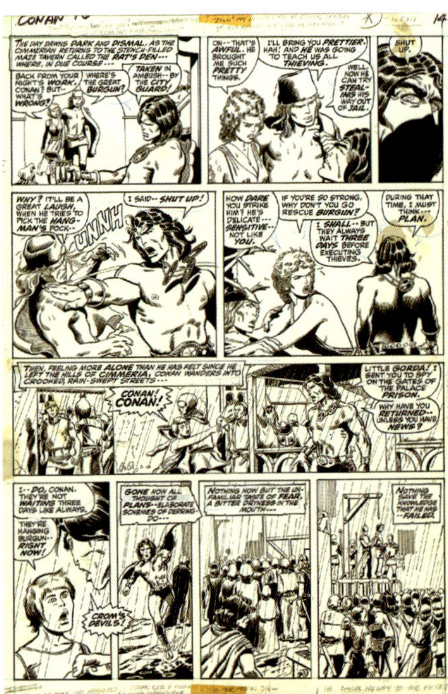

4359 Barry Smith and Sal Buscema - Conan the Barbarian #10, page 13 Original Art (Marvel, 1971). Barry Smith was just rounding into form as an artist when this issue was released, and he was well on his way to becoming a fan favorite! And his collaborator Roy Thomas delivered a fantastic original story here, as Conan, who was not infallible, is too late to save his ally Burgun the Gunderman. The other character of note is Jenna, another Thomas creation who appeared in multiple issues as a quasi-love interest for the Cimmerian. It's a powerful page from "Beware the Wrath of Anu." The page has an image area of 10" x 15". Aside from a few printer's oil stains and tape reside stains at the top and bottom of the page (outside the image area), the art is in Very Good condition.

4360 Barry Smith and Frank Brunner - Marvel Premiere #4, page 22 Original Art (Marvel, 1972). Writers Roy Thomas and Archie Goodwin pit Dr. Strange against "the forces of the world-devouring Shuma-Gorath," in this story, "The Spawn of Sligguth". Especially calling to mind the works of Lovecraft, Shuma-Gorath was a titanic slumbering beast-god whose minions include the snake-like people of Starkesboro. This "sssatisssfying" page is penciled by Barry Smith, and inked by Frank Brunner. The image area measures 10" x 15", and, aside from some tape stains in the four center edges, and few mild printer's oil stains, the art is in Very Good condition.

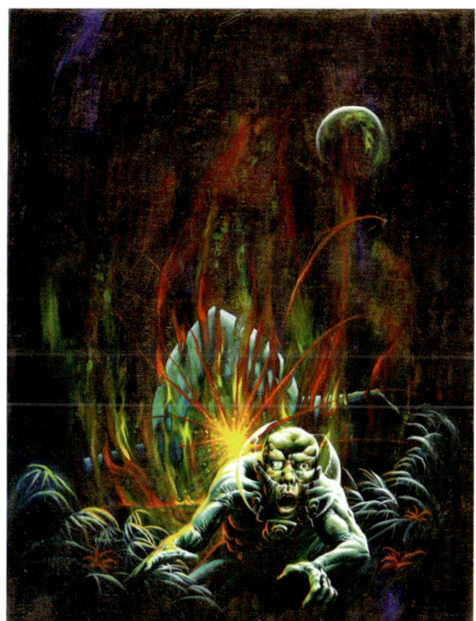

4361 Kenneth Smith - Eerie Annual 1971 Cover Original Art (Warren, 1971). Few fantasy artists can create a whole nether world more effectively than Kenneth Smith, whose distinctive style is instantly recognizable, and a most ideal match for Warren Publishing. Smith was one of the great stars of illustration art of his day, though his long-standing policy of rarely parting with his originals has made them virtually absent from the marketplace. His original Warren cover paintings, among his most highly regarded works, were finally sold directly by Smith in the early 1990s, in response to collector enthusiasm. This unsettling image features one of Kenneth Smith's highly stylized creatures, clearly from another world, apparently running away from danger. His expression registers unmistakable terror, and this alien figure seems poised to jump right out of the painting! Painted in oil on a 12" x 16" canvas board, and signed by the artist at the lower left, the condition is Excellent. On the reverse are notations in Kenneth Smith's hand, including his original Connecticut address and phone number, and the date he finished the painting (February 1970). An exceptional example of Kenneth Smith's cover artistry, and one of only five Warren cover paintings by this very significant artist.

4362 Todd Smith - Omega Men Annual #1 Cover Original Art (DC, 1984). Harpis leads the star-spanning hero team, the Omega Men, including Nimbus, Kalista, Primus, Broot, and Tigorr, to the deadliest planet in the star system, in this metagalactic masterpiece by Todd Smith. The image area measures 10" x 15" and the work is in Excellent condition.

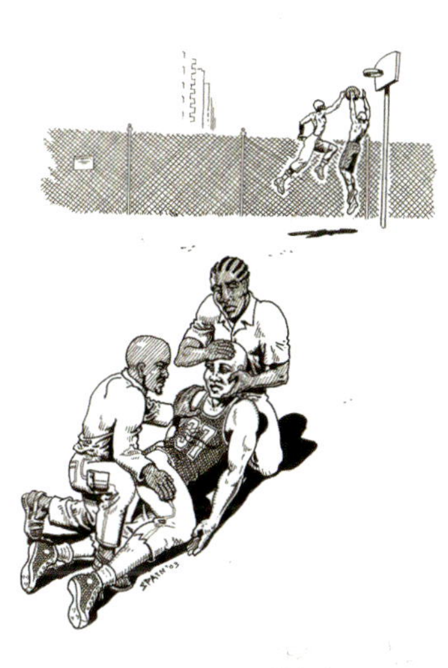

4363 Spain Rodriguez - Planet Medicine: Modalities Illustration Original Art (Pub Group West, 2003). Writer Richard Grossinger's book, **Planet Medicine: Modalities**, explores the history of medicine and healing from its earliest socio-cultural roots, discussing shamanism in the light of its medical traditions, image and process, origins, and ethnocultural backgrounds. **Trashman** creator, Spain Rodriguez, contributes this heartfelt illustration, which has an image area of 7" x 10". In Excellent condition.

4364 Spain Rodriguez - San Diego Reader Cover Original Art (San Diego Reader, 2003). San Diego Reader is a weekly publication that covers San Diego life in general, with emphasis on local arts and entertainment, politics and events. This nicely detailed editorial cover illustration is by legendary **Zap Comix** artist Spain, created for the August 21, 2003 edition. The image area measures approximately 8.5" x 6" and is in Excellent condition.

4365 Spain Rodriguez - San Francisco Bay Guardian Cover Original Art (San Francisco Bay Guardian, 2004). Underground Comix legend, Spain Rodriguez contributed this dynamic illustration for the April 6, 2004 edition of the **San Francisco Bay Guardian** for their "Super List Issue". The image area measures approximately 11" x 9" and is in Excellent condition.

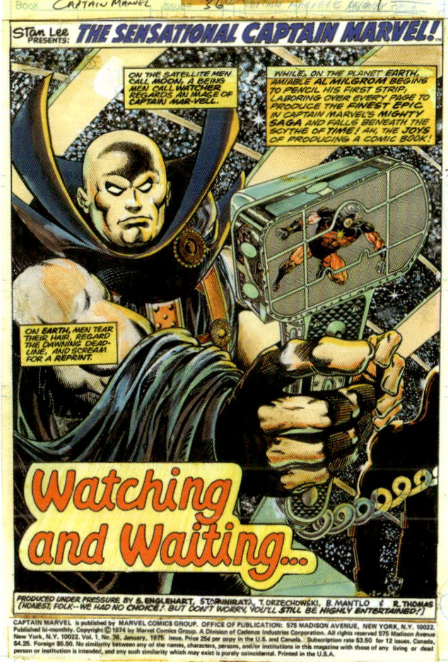

4366 Jim Starlin - Captain Marvel #36, Hand Colored Splash Page 1 Original Art (Marvel, 1974). Take a good look at this stellar, hand-painted splash — the only **Captain Marvel** series page one splash penciled, inked, and painted by Jim Starlin — as the Watcher regards an image of Captain Mar-vell on his hand-held viewer. This scintillating first page framed this issue's story, "The Coming of Captain Marvel!," which reprinted the first appearance of Captain Marvel, from **Marvel Superheroes** #12. Writer Steve Englehart titled this short sequence "Watching and Waiting...," and he poked fun at artist Al Milgrom for missing his deadline, forcing Marvel to have to pull this story out of the files. The image area measures 10" x 15" and aside from some glue and tape stains, mostly outside of the image area, the art is in Very Good condition.

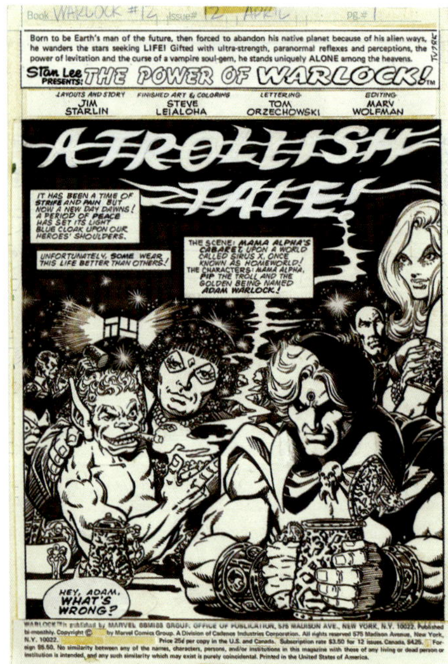

4367 Jim Starlin and Steve Leialoha - Warlock #12 Splash Page 1 Original Art (Marvel, 1976). The scene: Mama Alpha's Cabaret, upon a world called Sirus X, once known as Homeworld. The characters: Mama Alpha, Pip the Troll and the golden being named Adam Warlock. This celestial splash page is from 1976, and writer/artist Jim Starlin was at his absolute best, elevating Warlock to an utterly unique, compelling character with gripping characterization, thought provoking philosophy and theology, and good old superhero bustem' up action. Starlin's art here is superb, heavy on brooding shadows, with a striking panel composition and an enthralling set. The art has an image area of 10" x 15," and is in Excellent condition.

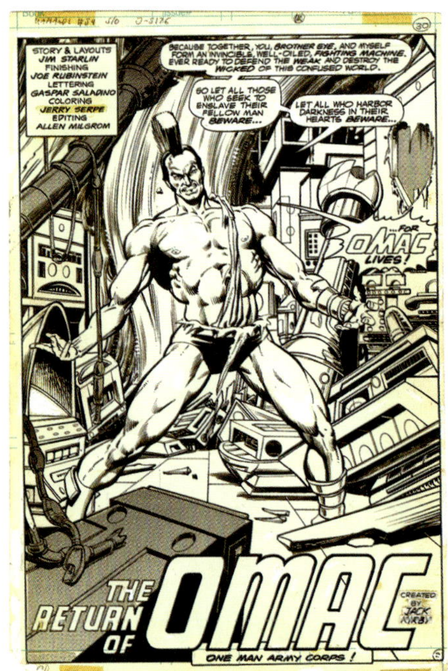

4368 Jim Starlin and Joe Rubinstein - Kamandi, the Last Boy on Earth #59, Splash Page 2 Original Art (DC, 1978). Brother Eye and OMAC form an invincible, well-oiled, fighting machine, ever ready to defend the weak and destroy the wicked of this confused world. Jim Starlin writes and pencils another finely-crafted, star crossed story, "The Return of OMAC," for the final issue of **Kamandi**. The image area measures 10" x 15", and, although there is a bit of glue and tape staining along the edges, and the bottom left edge has been trimmed during the production process, the art remains in Excellent condition. Let all who harbor darkness in their hearts beware... OMAC lives!

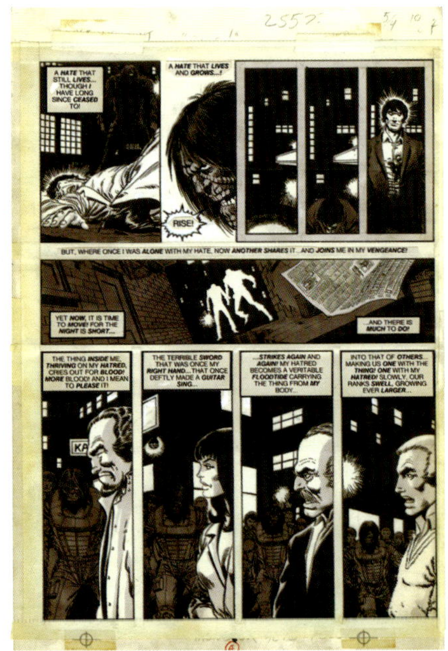

4369 Jim Starlin - Eerie #72, pages 48, 49, and 50 Original Art (Warren, 1982). An army of pure hatred has gathered to overrun the entire world, in these three pages from the Archie Goodwin story, titled "Avenger". Originally intended for inclusion in **Creepy** #64, some panels throughout the story were inked by Neal Adams, and other Continuity Studio members. The image area of each page measures 10.5" x 15". In pen and ink with ink wash, the word and type balloons are attached to an acetate overlay. There is some aging apparent in the type and word balloons, otherwise the pages are in Excellent condition.

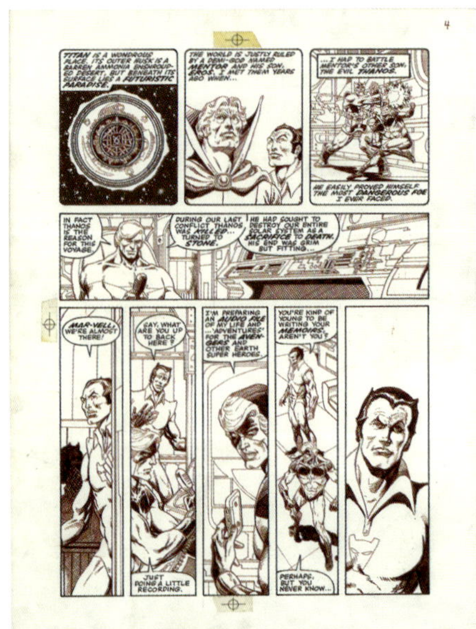

4370 Jim Starlin - Death of Captain Marvel Graphic Novel, page 4 Original Art (Marvel, 1982). The straight from the heart **Death of Captain Marvel** storyline was inspired by the death of writer/artist Jim Starlin's own father, who died from cancer. An exposure to a form of nerve gas several years before has given Captain Marvel cancer, and realizing that it's only a matter of time before he succumbs to it, he begins to record his memoirs. With an image area measuring 12" x 17.5" this page is in Excellent condition.

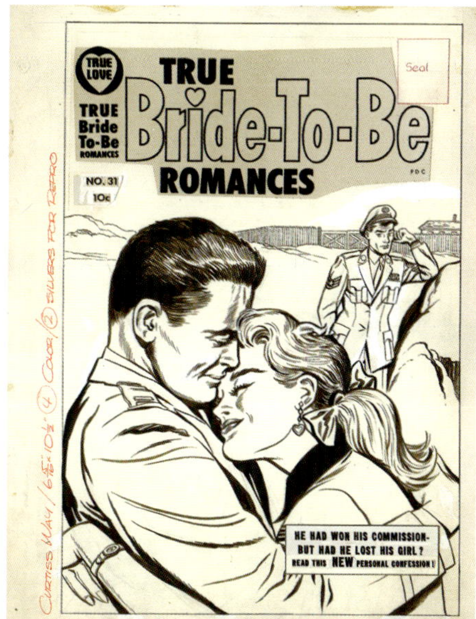

4371 Marvin Stein (attributed) - Unpublished True Bride-To-Be Romances #31 Cover Original Art (Harvey, circa 1958). This up-close and personal clutch scene was slated for the cover of **True Bride-To-Be Romances** #31, but according to Overstreet, #30 was the last issue published. This bold and beautiful cover has an image area of 12" x 18", and aside from some aging of the title logo stat and a missing Comics Code Authority stamp stat, the art is in Excellent condition. A touch of romance to your collection.

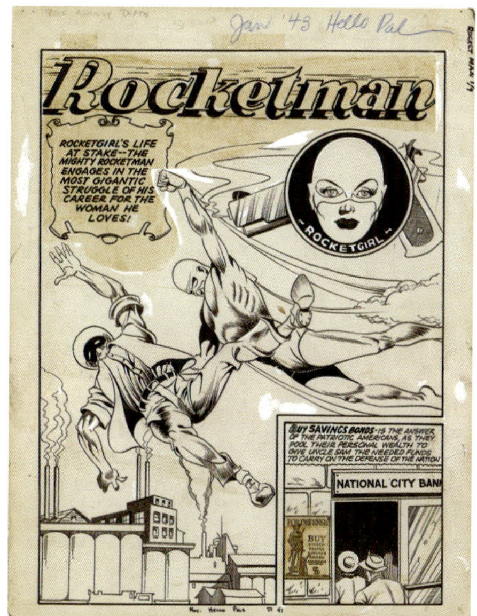

4372 Charles Sultan (attributed) - Hello Pal Comics #1, Complete 7-page Story "Rocketman" Original Art (Harvey, 1943). The mighty Rocketman engages in the most gigantic struggle of his career for the woman he loves, when Rocketgirl's life is at stake, in this seven page story, the duo's first appearance in comics! The Golden Age never looked more golden, as Rocketman races against the clock, in this breakneck tale by Charles Sultan. The image area of each page measures 13" x 18", and, aside from some overall aging, the pages are in Excellent condition.

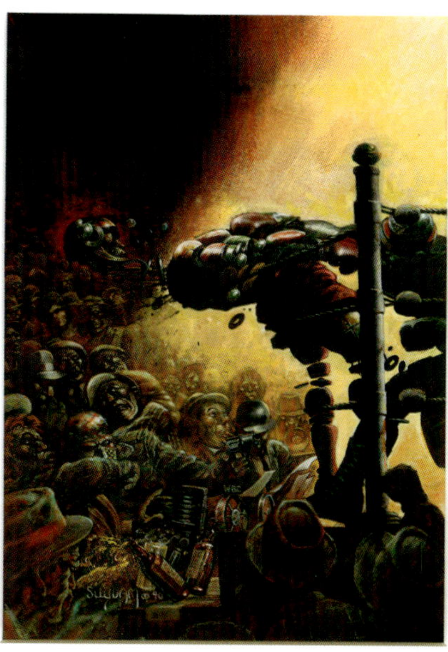

4373 Arthur Suydam - The New Adventures of Cholly and Flytrap: Till Death Do Us Part #2 Cover Original Art (Epic, 1991). The main event of the evening comes to a crashing finale as Stanley Yablowski, the killing machine known as the Champ, takes yet another opponent to pieces before a stunned crowd, in this smoky, hooch-filled illustration by Arthur Suydam. This stupendous display of Suydam's mastery of brushwork, shading, composition, and color has an image area of 13.5" x 19". Attractively matted for an overall size of 23.5" x 29".

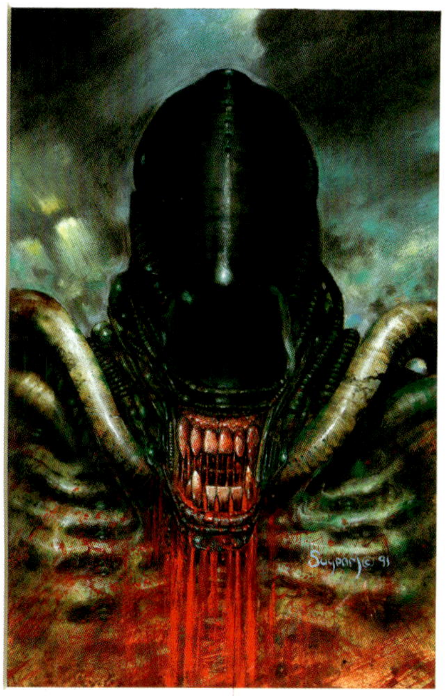

4374 Arthur Suydam - Aliens: Genocide #1 Cover Original Art (Dark Horse, 1991). Few fantasy artists can successfully match the technique and skill of Arthur Suydam. Since he burst on the scene in the 1970s, Suydam has been building a body of work with a distinct and evocative style that is second to none. Terrifying in its raw painterly effect, this Suydam original features the last thing you will ever see, if you ever find yourself faced with an Alien. Suydam also chose this image to be the cover for his career retrospective book, **Visions: The Art of Arthur Suydam**, which was published by Dark Horse in 1995. The image area measures 10.5" x 16.5" and is in Excellent condition. Attractively matted in a 20.5" x 26.5" matte.

4375 Western Publishing Artist - Tom and Jerry Comics Cover Original Art (Dell, circa 1950). Here's ink in your eye, Tom! Jerry and Tuffy take to the skies to prove that the pen is mightier than the sword, in this animated cover illustration. The image area measures 11" x 16" and the art is in Excellent condition. The logo and masthead is recent photocopy replacement art.

4376 Western Publishing Artist - Tom & Jerry Comics #204 Cover Original Art (Dell, 1961). Slurpp! Tom, Jerry and Tuffy enjoy a double dose of double-dip ice cream, on this delicious cover illustration from 1961. The image area measures 11" x 13.5", and the art is in Excellent condition.

4377 Pines Artist - Tom Terrific #1 Cover Original Art (Pines Comics, 1957). The wee superhero in the magic, funnel-shaped hat, Tom Terrific, and his "ever-faithful companion," the big, baggy-eyed pooch, Mighty Manfred the Wonder Dog, play pirate on this imaginative cover illustration. Drawn in the same clean, stylized line of the animated cartoon, this inventive cover art has an image area of 11.5" x 17", and is in Excellent condition. Includes the original logo and masthead paste-up art. A copy of **Tom Terrific** #1 is included in this lot.

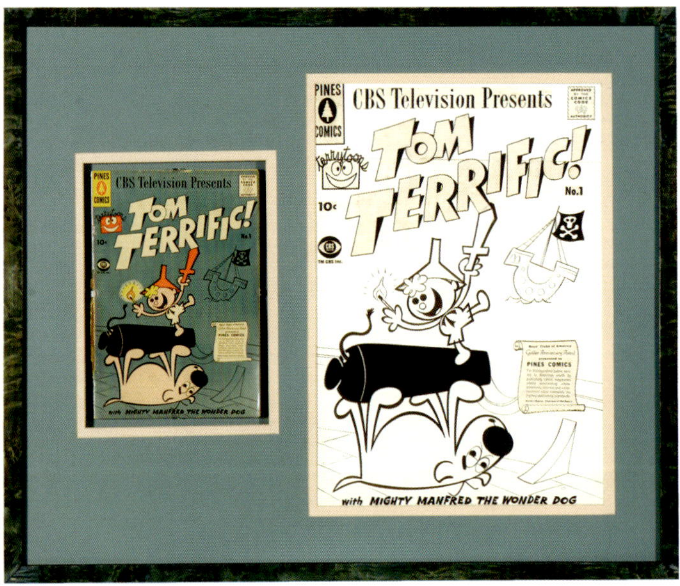

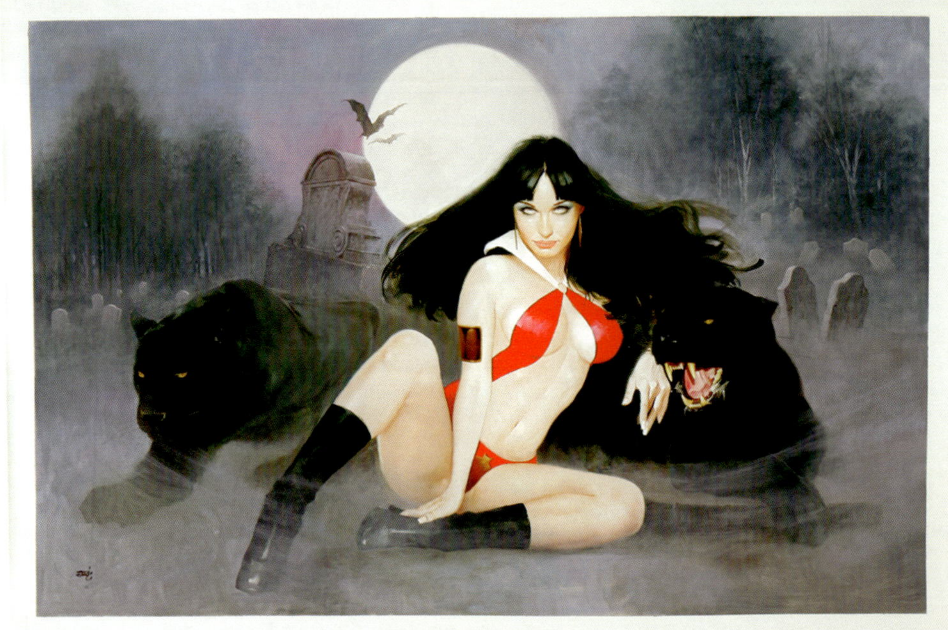

4378 Enrique Torres - "The Night Awaits" Vampirella Painting Original Art (undated). Rendered in lush, atmospheric layers of luminous color, this work is nothing short of a senses-shattering spectacular by a modern master of fantasy art. Enric (Enrique Torres) is considered by fans and pros alike to be among the top Vampirella artists, a ranking reinforced by the exquisite quality of this sensuous scene. Measuring approximately 60" x 40", the painting is in Excellent condition. This tantalizing treasure will make a first-rate acquisition for any fan of the Queen of Drakulon!

4379 John Totleben - Swamp Thing Illustration Original Art (1986). The legendary creative team of Alan Moore, Stephen Bissette, and John Totleben redefined the Swamp Thing as a powerful elemental being, with a potential as vast as the Earth itself. This visceral pen and ink sketch by Totleben brims with a slushy elegance, as the earth element emerges into the sunlight from a dark place hidden in the swamp. This art has an image area of 10.5" x 15", and was drawn in marker by John Totleben during the "glory days" of the series. In Excellent condition and signed by John Totleben at the lower right.

4380 John Totleben - Vermillion #10 Cover Original Art (Helix, 1997). John Totleben graces the cover of issue #10 of Lucius Shepard's limited issue series, **Vermillion**, with this striking cover illustration. After a technological event transforms the universe into a single vast city known as Vermillion, only one man remembers that things were once different — Jonathan Cave. Totleben's decisive line and woodcut-like technique perfectly captures the baroque and exotic mood of this alternative reality. From the cover story, "Lord Iron and Lady Manganese, Part Two: A Little Light Reading," this art has an image area of 10" x 15" and is in Excellent condition.

4381 Herb Trimpe - The Further Adventures of Indiana Jones #15 Cover Original Art (Marvel, 1984). The famed archaeologist, Indiana Jones, faces danger from above, in this kinetic cover image by Herb Trimpe. Attempting to photograph an abandoned Chinese temple deep in the Aleutian islands, Indy hires a ship, the Bantu Wind, to take him there. But someone is determined to stop him! The image area measures 9.5" x 15", and, aside from a bit of very light staining on Indy's right leg, and on the logo paste-up, the art is in Excellent condition. Includes all the original logo and masthead paste-up art.

4382 Western Publishing Artist - Marge's Tubby #22 Cover Original Art (Dell, 1957). Tubby's fishing lure draws a crowd — unfortunately it's a brace of ducks, not a school of fish! The image area of this laugh-riot measures 7.25" x 10.25", and the art is in Excellent condition. A copy of the comic book is included in this lot.

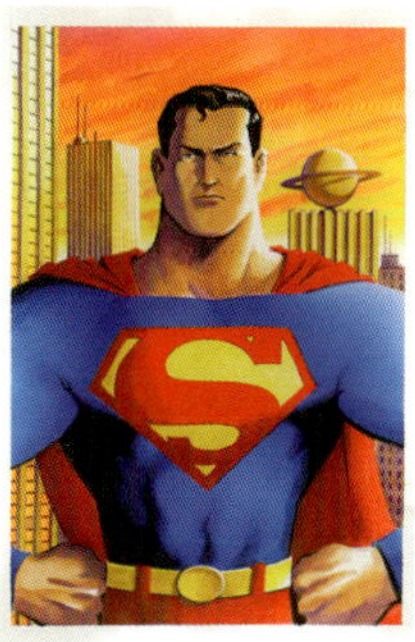

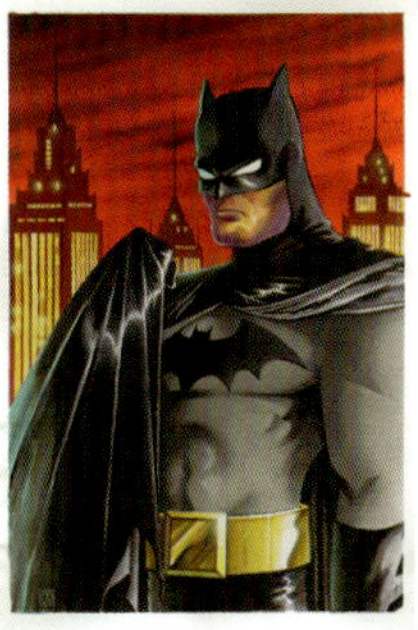

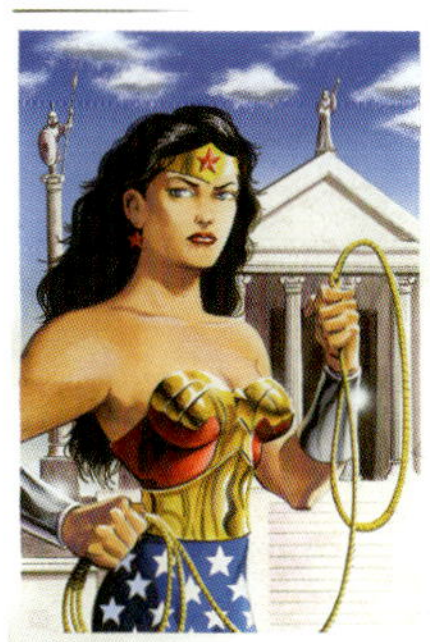

4383 **Matt Wagner - Trinity Covers Original Art, Group of 3 (DC, 2003).** Matt Wagner tackled three of the mainstream's most powerful heroes in his **Trinity** mini-series, which chronicled Wonder Woman's first meeting with Batman and Superman. Here Wagner captures the three icons of comicdom in paint, in three illustrations which were featured on the covers of these heroes's regular monthly titles. Published the same month that the **Trinity** hardcover collection was released, these covers consist of **The Adventures of Superman** #628, **Wonder Woman** #204, and **Batman** #627. With dynamic flair, and skillful use of color, Wagner brings these towering figures to life on three pieces of illustration board. The image area of each illustration measures 10" x 15.5" and the work is in Excellent condition. Includes a copy of the **Trinity** hardcover, which has been signed by Matt Wagner and customized with an original sketch of the three heroes.

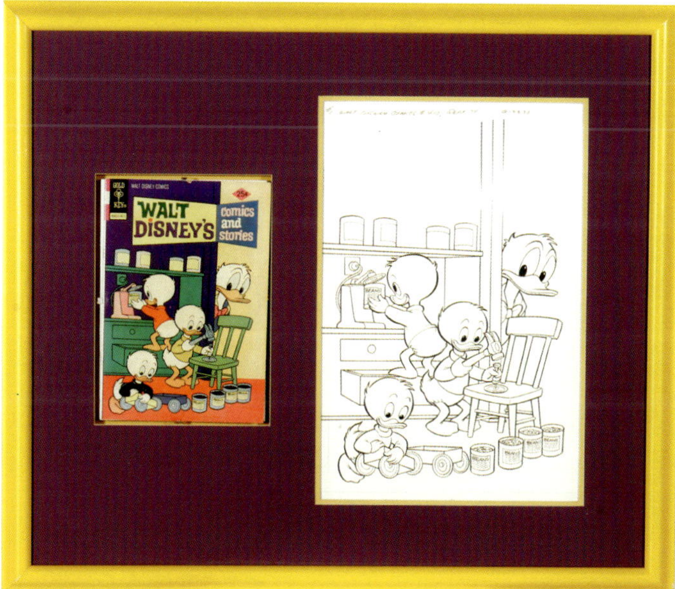

4384 **Western Publishing Artist - Walt Disney's Comics and Stories #410 Cover Original Art (Gold Key, 1974).** Uncle Donald's nephews, Huey, Dewey and Louie, put their mechanic skills to good use with a few cans of beans and a couple of cigar boxes, in this cover illustration for **Walt Disney's Comics and Stories** #410. The image area measures approximately 10" x 15", and the art is in Excellent condition. A copy of the comic book is included in this lot.

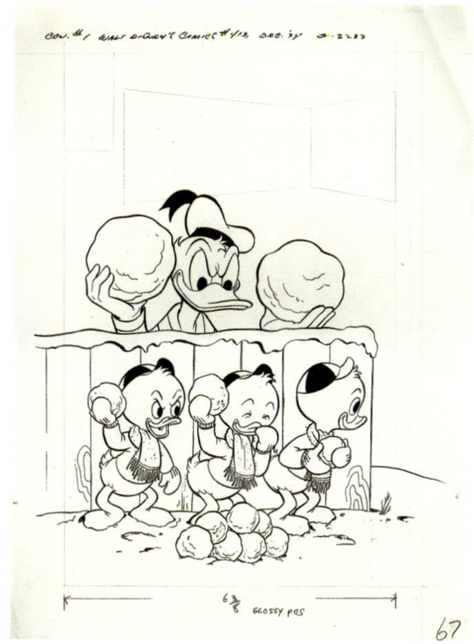

4385 **Western Publishing Artist - Walt Disney's Comics and Stories #413 Cover Original Art (Gold Key, 1975).** Huey, Dewey, and Louie don't stand a snowball's chance against the two snow boulders their Uncle Donald has whipped up, in this cover illustration for **Walt Disney's Comics and Stories** #413. The image area measures approximately 10.5" x 11", and the art is in Excellent condition. A copy of the comic book is included in this lot.

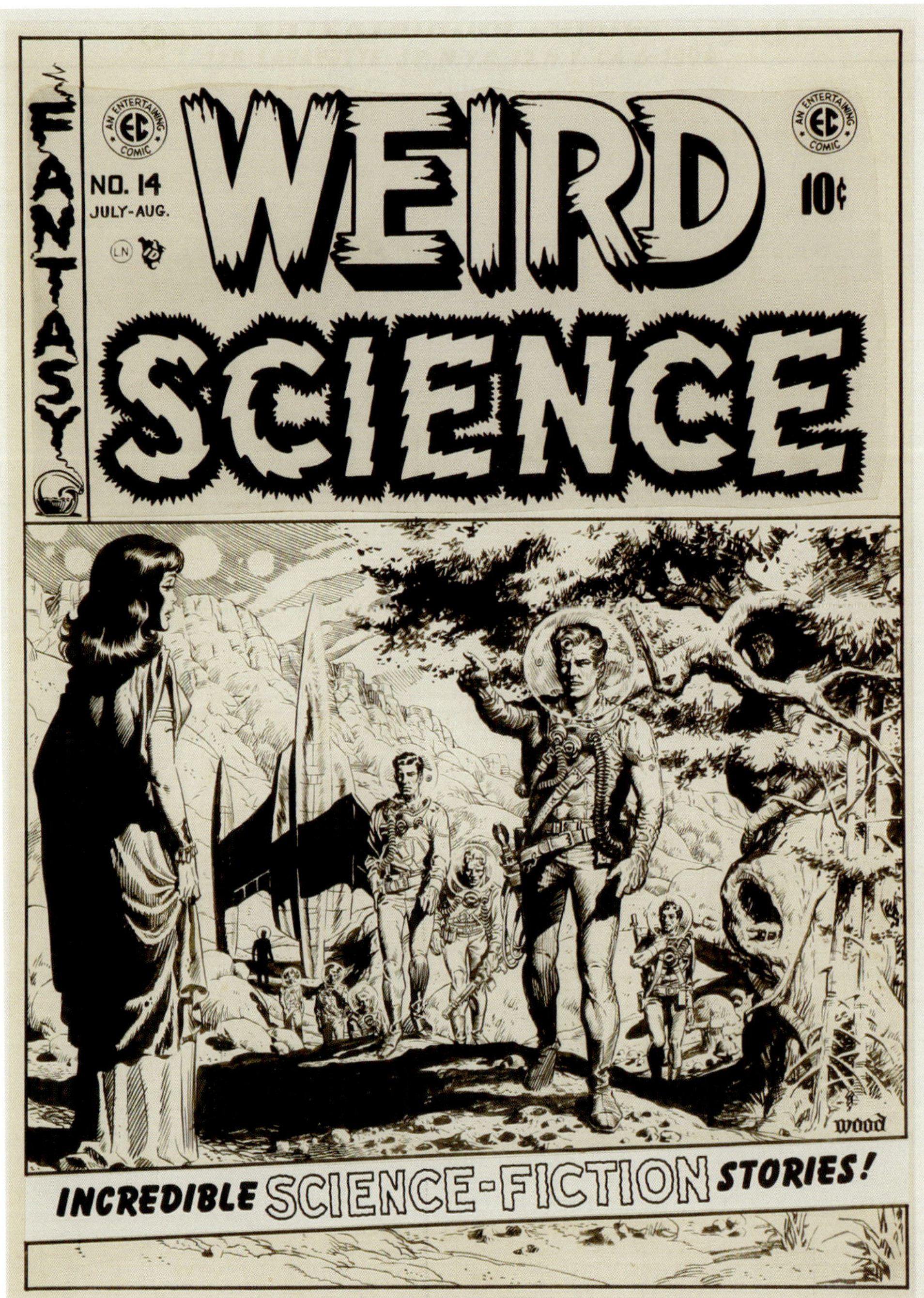

4386 Wally Wood - Weird Science #14 Cover Original Art (EC, 1952). Many of the top comic artists of the 1950s gravitated to EC, as Bill Gaines' outfit had established a reputation for rewarding quality. The three EC editor/writer/artists allowed their pool of artists to ink their own pencils, and never fretted over maintaining a homogenized "house style." Within the superb roster of all-stars assembled for Bill Gaines' imprint, the title of "top science fiction artist" was awarded to Wally Wood. Even so, his slick, hyper-realistic style lent itself to virtually every EC story, be it horror, humor, war, or science fiction. Without a doubt, Wood's science fiction covers remain among the best the genre has ever produced. Here is one of his masterpieces — an erotically charged scene, showing the electrifying contact between two alien cultures, as detailed in the shocker, "There'll Be Some Changes Made." Beautifully drawn, this stellar cover has an image area of 13" x 19", and the art is in Excellent condition.

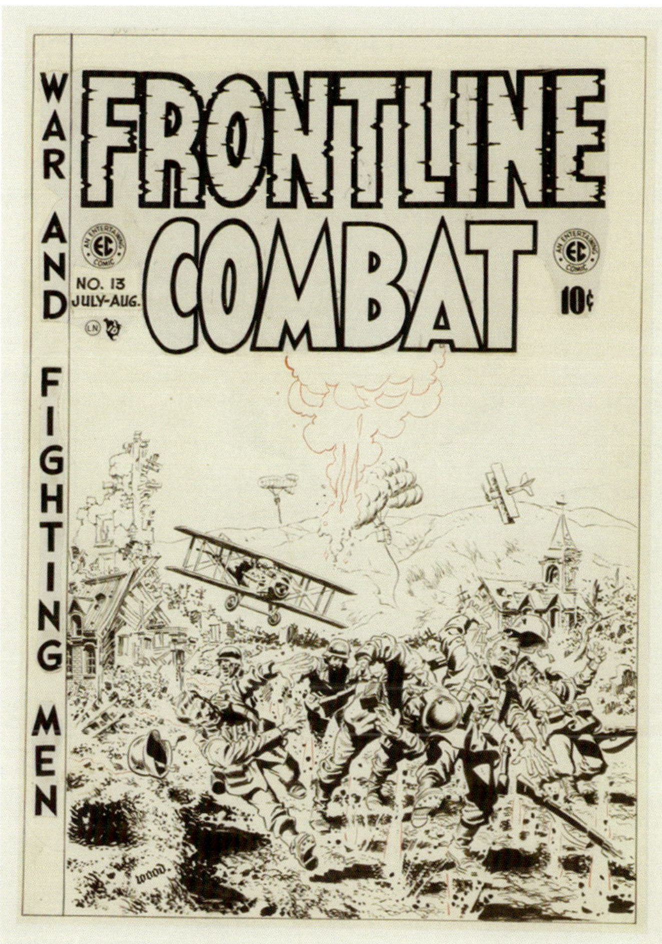

4387 Wally Wood - Frontline Combat #13 Cover Original Art (EC, 1953). One of the most celebrated artists to illustrate the pages of EC Comics, Wally Wood's work is still eagerly sought out by a legion of fans. Whether he was drawing incredible science fiction tales or, as in this cover, frontline combat scenes, Wood always delivered, with a bravura and attention to detail that few cartoonists, if any, could match. Called upon to work in every genre that EC published, Wood's visions of war were just as compelling as those he created for the crime, humor, or horror yarns. This cover was the first of only three covers that Wood drew for **Frontline Combat** — in fact, he only did a total of five covers for EC's war titles, so bid accordingly! This superb cover has an image area of 13.5" x 19.5", and the art is in Excellent condition.

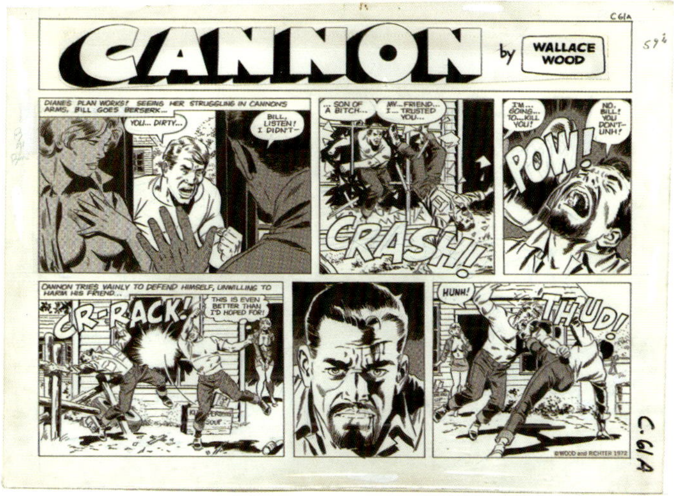

4388 Wally Wood - Cannon Comic Strip #C61 Original Art (Wood and Richter, 1972). Wally Wood proved himself one of the most talented and hard-working artists of the Silver Age. From 1970-74 Wood wrote and drew *Cannon*, an adventure strip designed for a newspaper distributed exclusively to military bases. Cannon is a dehumanized killer "wet-works" agent for the US government, and most of his adventures were spiced with beautiful, busty women, hard drinking men, fast cars, big guns and a supreme knack for the manly art of self-defense. This continuity features Cannon being led to a near-certain deathtrap by two buxom *femmes fatales*. The strip was drawn on two boards, each with an image area measuring 17" x 10.25", and both pieces are in Excellent condition.

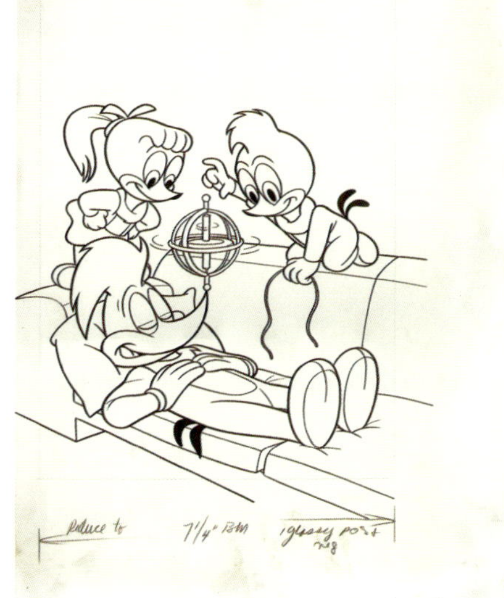

4389 Western Publishing Artist - Woody Woodpecker Comics #53 Cover Original Art (Dell, 1959). Splinter and Knothead put a spin on Uncle Woody's bill, in this hypnotic cover image from **Woody Woodpecker** #53. It's interesting to see the original spinner was a gyroscope, which was obviously revised in the final art. This cover image was reprinted in Gold Key's **Woody Woodpecker** #100, in 1968. The image area measures 13" x 13", and the art is in Excellent condition. Includes a copy of **Woody Woodpecker** #53, and **Woody Woodpecker** #100.

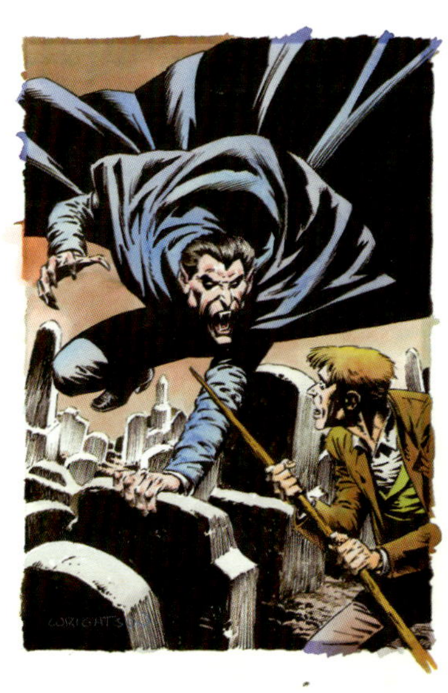

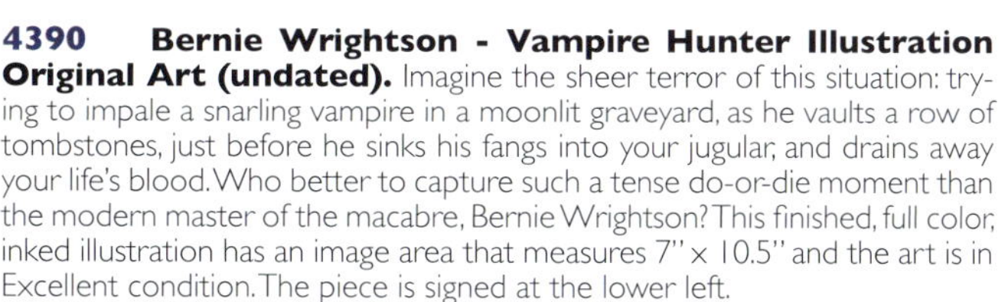
4390 Bernie Wrightson - Vampire Hunter Illustration Original Art (undated). Imagine the sheer terror of this situation: trying to impale a snarling vampire in a moonlit graveyard, as he vaults a row of tombstones, just before he sinks his fangs into your jugular, and drains away your life's blood. Who better to capture such a tense do-or-die moment than the modern master of the macabre, Bernie Wrightson? This finished, full color, inked illustration has an image area that measures 7" x 10.5" and the art is in Excellent condition. The piece is signed at the lower left.

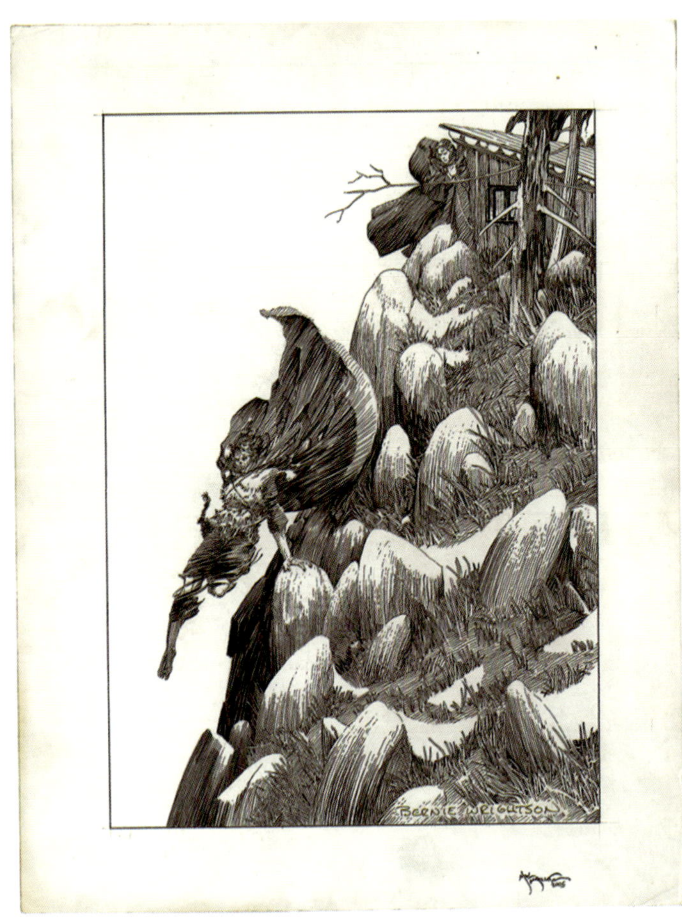

4391 Bernie Wrightson and Mike Kaluta - Frankenstein Illustration Original Art (circa 1980s-2005). Bernie Wrightson's life-long fascination with the Frankenstein story has been a constant source of inspiration for the artist. Wrightson commented in Christopher Zavisa's book, **Berni Wrightson: A Look Back**, "Ever since I first started working professionally I drew the monster into various things. You can find him in just about everything from fanzines to **Swamp Thing**. It seems as though my whole career up to this point has been in preparation for an illustration of the novel." In 1974, the collaboration of Bernie Wrightson and Mike Kaluta in DC Comics' **The Shadow** #3 resulted in an incredible story, "The Kingdom of the Cobra." Pages from this thriller are highly sought-after by fans. This piece reunites the talents of these two greats — Bernie Wrightson penciled this scene in the 1980s and Mike Kaluta inked it in 2005. Kaluta did not miss a fine line in this drawing — his detailed inking is magical. The illustration has an image area of 11" x 16", and the art is in Excellent condition. This finished work is a masterpiece and it is sure to be a stand-out in any collection!

4392 George Wunder - Terry and the Pirates Sunday Comic Strip Original Art, dated 11-12-50 (Chicago Tribune, 1950). Terry and Hot-Shot Charlie prepare for guerrilla skirmishes in this starkly shadowed Sunday. George Wunder moves the points of view around in his "staging" of each panel of this dramatic episode, continuing a storytelling tradition established for *Terry* by Milton Caniff and Noel Sickles. The image area of the Sunday is 25.5" x 17". The logo stat has some glue staining and each panel of the strip has been carefully glued to the support paper; otherwise the art is in Excellent condition.

4393 George Wunder - Terry and the Pirates Sunday Comic Strip Original Art, dated 12-31-50 (Chicago Tribune, 1950). George Wunder had the unenviable task of succeeding Milton Caniff on *Terry and the Pirates*, but he passed muster with flying colors and went on to have a 27-year run on the feature. George Wunder displays his hallmarked, boldly detailed brushwork. Terry and Hot Shot Charlie star in this episode. The image area of the strip measures 25.5" x 17". The logo stat has some glue staining and each panel of the Sunday has been carefully glued to the support paper; otherwise the art is in Very Good condition.

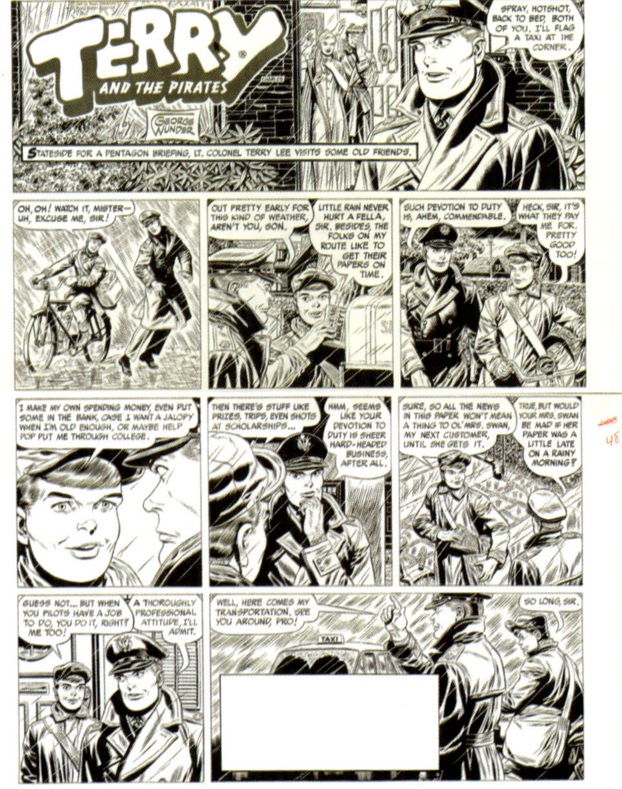

4394 George Wunder - Terry and the Pirates Promotional Comic Strip Original Art (Chicago Tribune, 1967). Terry Lee nearly gets run down by an industrious paper boy on a bike, but soon the two are chewing the fat about "taking care of business," regardless of time or weather. Hot Shot Charlie makes a cameo appearance in panel one. This page was most likely done as a promotional piece for a newspaper and the caption box in the final panel was left open for type. As always, George Wunder packs each panel with detail and starkly shadowed patterns. The image area of the strip measures 19" x 26" and the strip was cut between panel tiers two and three. The top half of the page shows mild signs of paper aging; otherwise the art is in Excellent condition.

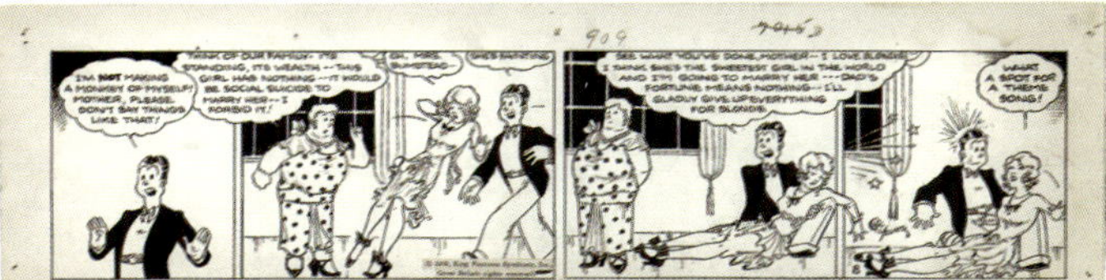

4395 Chic Young - Blondie Daily Comic Strip Original Art, dated 9-16-30 (King Features Syndicate, 1930). In this very early strip, Chic Young's *Blondie* was not yet the level-headed housewife readers would come to know in later years, but was instead a carefree flapper girl who spent her days in dance halls. Her boyfriend's upper-crust family were adamant that their son, Dagwood, would be committing social suicide if he married this girl who has nothing! But Dagwood was determined to marry her, even if he had to give up everything! A sweet, funny daily from the eighth day of the strip's publication, this art has an image area measuring 18" x 4" and is in Excellent condition.

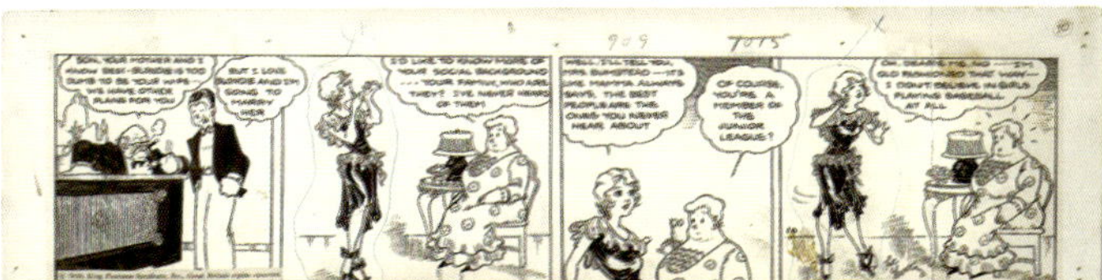

4396 Chic Young - Blondie Daily Comic Strip Original Art, dated 9-18-30 (King Features Syndicate, 1930). In spite of his father's objections to her lowly social status, Dagwood is determined to marry Blondie Boopadoop. Of course, Blondie's not winning any popularity contests with Dagwood's mother, when she is quizzed about her social connections! This daily is for the tenth day of the strip, and gives us an early insight into the Bumstead/Blondie dynamic. The image area measures 18" x 4", and, aside from some light staining, soiling, a blue line editorial notation in the second panel, and a crease along the art in last panel, the condition of the art is Good.

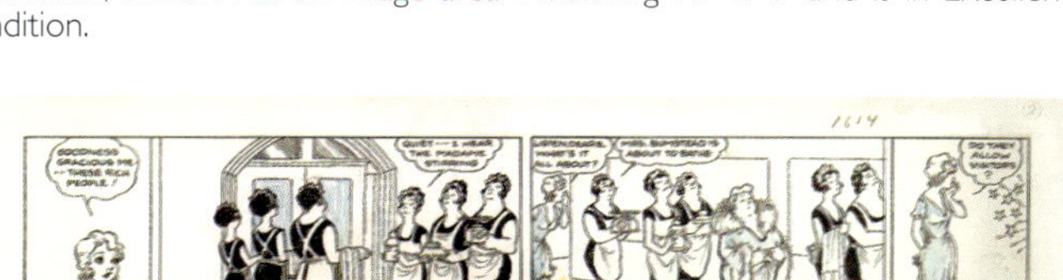

4397 Chic Young - Blondie Daily Comic Strip Original Art, dated 9-23-30 (King Features Syndicate, 1930). First appearing at the outset of the Great Depression, *Blondie* retains its status as one of the most widely read comic strips in the history of the genre. Blondie Boopadoop entered the world over seventy years ago, on September 15, 1930, the featured character of a new comic strip by Murat "Chic" Young. A flighty flapper, at first she dated playboy Dagwood Bumstead, son of the millionaire, J. Bolling Bumstead, a railroad magnate, along with several other boyfriends. The comic strip floundered, however, until Young decided to have the couple fall deeply in love. This superb daily dates a little more than one week from the very first *Blondie*, and gives us an early glimpse at the charming bachelorette! The image area measures 18" x 4", and, aside from some very light staining, the condition of the art is Excellent.

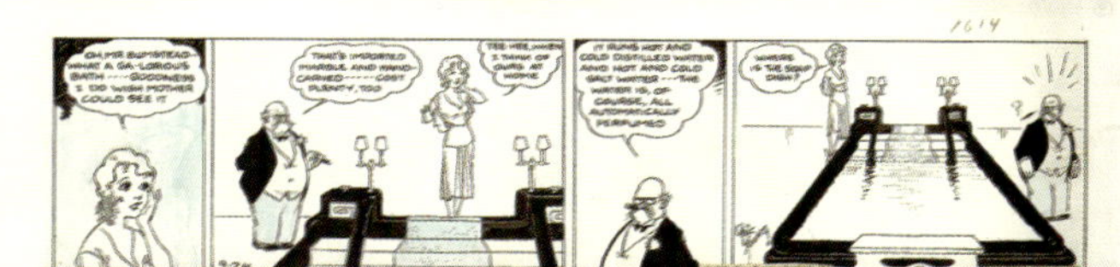

4398 Chic Young - Blondie Daily Comic Strip Original Art, dated 9-24-30 (King Features Syndicate, 1930). Americans, caught up in the woes of the Great Depression, immediately took to Chic Young's humorous daily reminders that love, not money, conquers all. In this daily, dating a little more than one week from the very first *Blondie*, the flighty flapper, Blondie Boopadoop, gets a tour of the Bumstead bath, much to the chagrin of the elder Bumstead! The image area measures 18" x 4", and the art is in Excellent condition.

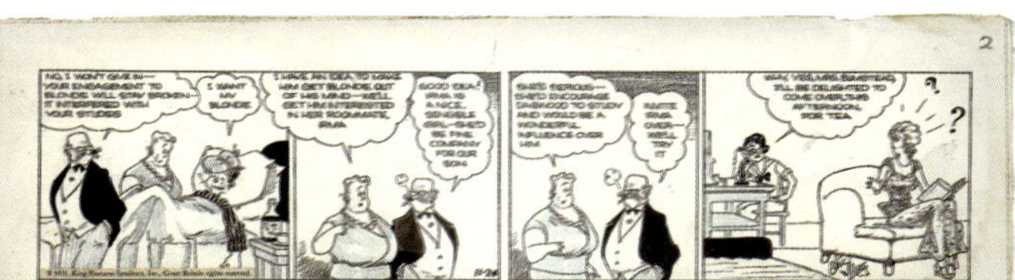

4399 Chic Young - Blondie Daily Comic Strip Original Art, dated 11-24-31 (King Features Syndicate, 1931). She was a flighty flapper called Blondie Boopadoop with a short skirt, a cute curl and a passion for her millionaire beau. He was Dagwood Bumstead, not the harried suburbanite we know today, but a rich playboy so in love with Blondie that he defied his wealthy father and gave up a fortune to marry her in 1933. Here, once again, the elder Bumsteads make yet another effort to separate the young lovers, by inviting Blondie's homely roommate to tea, in this daily from 1931. This art has an image area of 18" x 4" and is in Excellent condition.

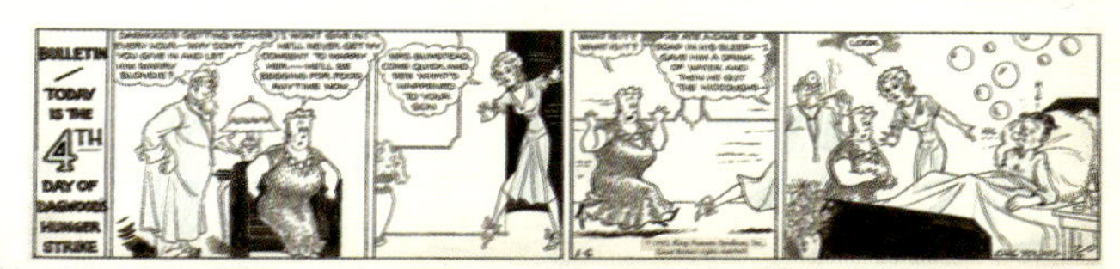

4400 Chic Young - Blondie "Hunger Strike" Daily Comic Strip Original Art, dated 1-6-33 (King Features Syndicate, 1933). Desperate to wed Blondie, in spite of his father's objections to her lowly social status, Dagwood went on a hunger strike until the elder Bumstead grudgingly acknowledged their relationship but refused to continue to support his son. This daily, from the fourth day of Dagwood's hunger strike, bubbles over with drama, when Mrs. Bumstead finds her son has eaten a cake of soap, and gotten the hiccoughs. The image area measures 19.5" x 4.25", and the art is in Excellent condition.

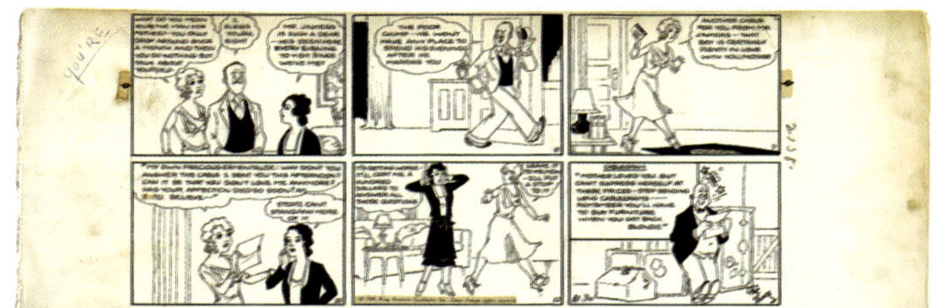

4401 Chic Young - Blondie Partial Sunday Comic Strip Original Art, dated 11-30-30 (King Features Syndicate, 1930). Mr. Jinkers is certainly plenty in love with Blondie's mother, Ermentrude! But to answer his cablegram is going to cost her a fortune! It helps that Blondie doesn't mince words, and in returning the cable, she gets right down to business! Maybe the Bumsteads think of her as just a flighty flapper, not suitable for their playboy son, Dagwood, but if they could see her now they might change their tune! This sensational Sunday dates a little more than two months from the very first *Blondie*, and gives us an early glimpse into Blondie's pre-Dagwood family life. The image area measures 16.5" x 7.5" and although the top two tiers are missing, the condition of the art is Excellent.

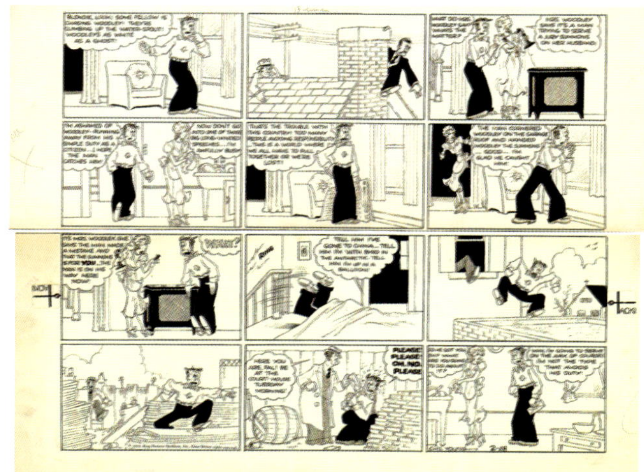

4402 Chic Young - Blondie Sunday Comic Strip Original Art, dated 2-18-34 (King Features Syndicate, 1934). Dagwood's high-falutin' attitude about the duties of citizens goes right out the window, when he finds out that the jury summons his neighbor is running from is for him! It's impossible to read this side-splitting Sunday without a smile on your face! The image area measures 17" x 13.5" and although there is a bit of aging overall, the art is in Excellent condition.

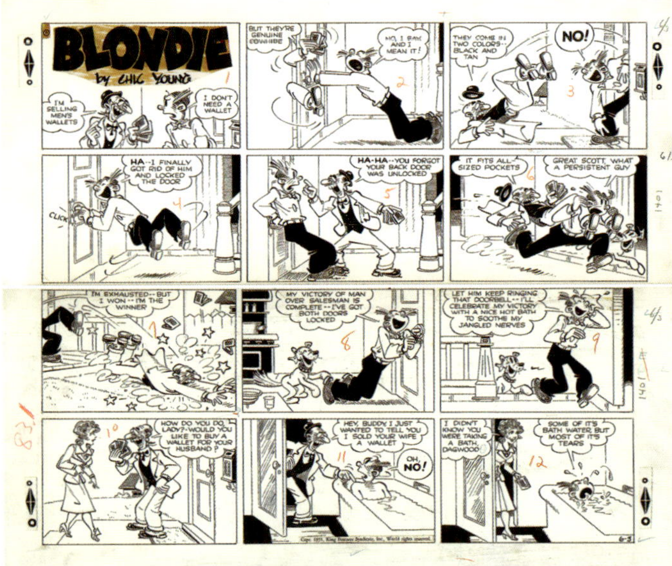

4403 Chic Young Studio - Blondie Sunday Comic Strip Original Art, dated 6-3-51 (King Features Syndicate, 1951). A pesky, but persistent, men's wallet salesman has Dagwood in a tub of tears by the end of this exhilarating Sunday from 1951. This strip also contains cameos by Blondie and Daisy. The image area is 17" x 14.75". There is some very slight discoloration between the second and third tiers (the upper and lower portions of the strip are not attached), and along the extreme outside edges. You'll also find some red editorial markings in each panel, but overall the strip is in Very Good condition.

4404 Mike Zeck and Frank McLaughlin - Captain America #263, page 2 Original Art (Marvel, 1981). Now that the Red Skull has destroyed Captain America's reputation, he plans to kill him and record the event on film for the world to see. In a dusty soundstage on a long-abandoned movie studio lot, Cap's deadliest adversary elaborates on the evil plan that he has lead up to this moment, with Captain America helpless to stop him! The image area measures 10" x 15", and, aside from the upper left edge trimmed during the printing process, the art is in Excellent condition.

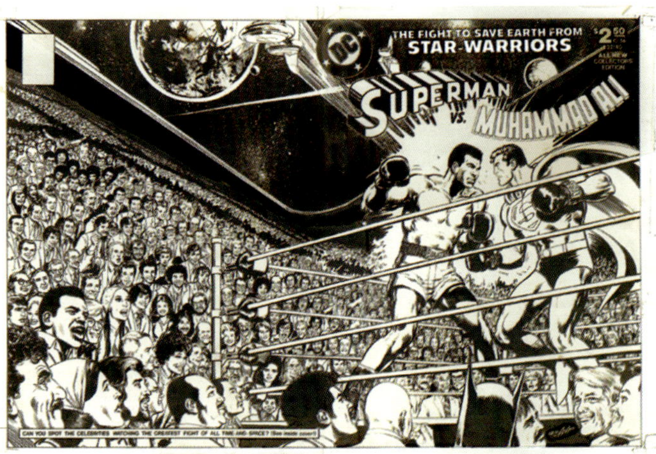

4405 Neal Adams - All-New Collectors' Edition #C-56 "Superman vs. Muhammad Ali" Cover Stat (DC, 1978). Only Neal Adams could detail the epic clash between the Man of Steel and a real-life hero like Muhammad Ali with the photo-realism that the assignment demanded. Joe Kubert originally had the assignment, but some objections to his expressionistic approach ended with Adams taking over the job. This is the "photo-ready" cover stat/paste-up used to print the wrap-around cover. Several elements were carefully pasted together and then touched up with black ink. The cover has an image area of 20.5" x 13.75". There is some slight fading on some of the photostat lines, and the caption "The Fight to Save Earth from Star-Warriors" is affixed to a small acetate overlay; otherwise the photostat layout is in Excellent condition.

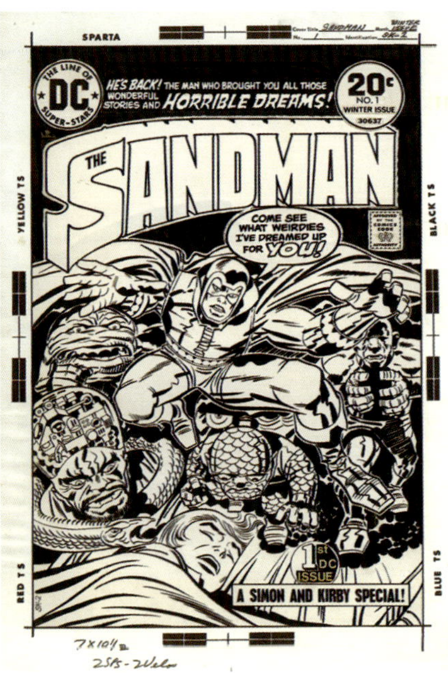

4406 Jack Kirby and Mike Royer - The Sandman #1 Cover Stat (DC, 1974). Originally scheduled as a one-shot, Joe Simon and Jack Kirby reunite for a last collaboration with this revamp of the Sandman. Speculators drove the sales of this single issue up so high that a series was scheduled. Simon and Kirby's **Sandman** was an otherwise unnamed hero who operated out of a place called the "Dream Dome," and was assisted by two grotesque "nightmare monsters" named Brute and Glob. This insomnia-charged cover is not original art, but "photo-ready" cover stat/paste-up art used to print this issue. The image area measures 10" x 15" and the work includes the original logo and masthead paste-up art. There is some slight water damage to the extreme left edge, outside of the image area, otherwise this photostat layout is in Excellent condition.

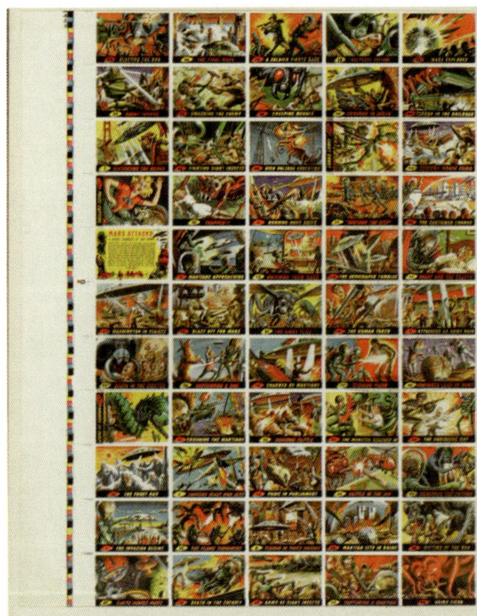

4407 Mars Attacks Trading Cards Color Proof (Topps, 1962) Planning to conquer the Earth, Mars sends flying saucers through space carrying deadly weapons. The Martians destroy much of Earth's population, and those that are left go into hiding. Despite its losses, Earth launches a counter-attack that shatters the Martians on their home planet, Mars! Topps' 1962 **Mars Attacks** set is one of the collecting hobby's most coveted non-sports series. The set consists of 55 cards in all, 54 are painted images, and one card features a synopsis of the story. We are proud to present this original color proof, which features the color images printed onto a sheet, with the black line art on a separate acetate overlay. The image area measures approximately 17" x 27", and the condition is Excellent. A unique bit of **Mars Attacks** memorabilia!

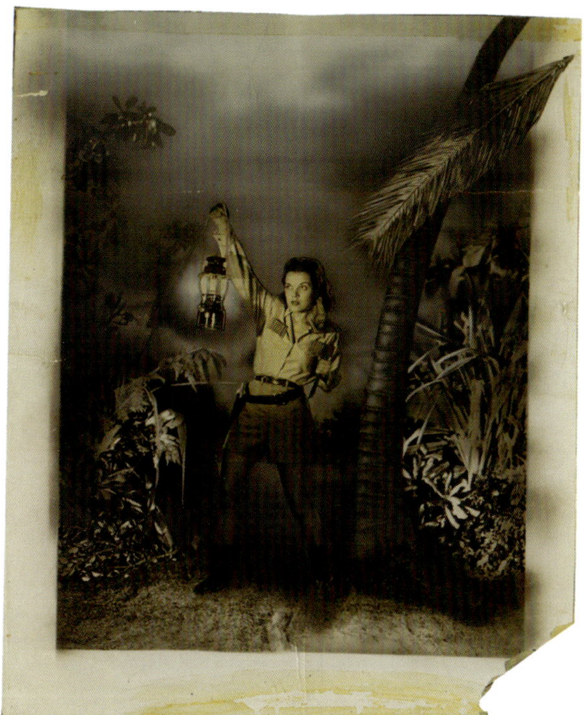

4408 Fawcett Comics Artist - Nyoka the Jungle Girl #57 Cover Photo Montage Art (Fawcett, 1951). A photomontage was retouched with an airbrush to create the dramatic cover scene for **Nyoka the Jungle Girl** #57 A photograph of Nyoka holding a lantern was carefully cut out and placed atop a background photograph. Airbrush paint was used to lighten areas in the background and also used to create a glow around Nyoka's lantern. The photomontage has an image area of 12.5" x 17". The lower right corner of the photo paper was torn off, mostly outside of the image area; otherwise the art is in Excellent condition. A copy of the comic book is included in this lot.

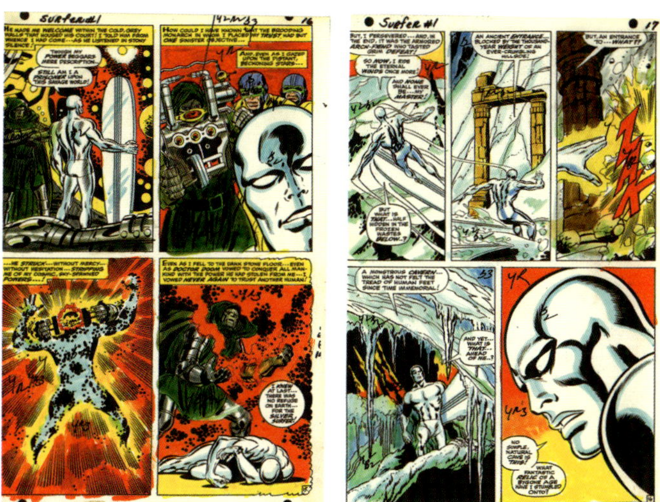

4409 Silver Surfer #1 Color Guide, Group of 38 (Marvel, 1968). Behold the sky-born spanner of a trillion galaxies — the restless, streaking stranger from the farthest reach of space! This glistening, gleaming seeker of truth, whom men call — the Silver Surfer! From one of comicdom's greatest collaborations comes the color guide to the entire first issue of **Silver Surfer** #1, written by Stan Lee, with art by John Buscema and Joe Sinnott. The art has been reduced to close to published size (6" x 8.25"), and each photocopied page has been hand-colored with vivid washes of watercolor, with numbered color indications throughout. Vibrant and educational, these pages are in Excellent condition, and allow us to see behind the scenes of the Mighty Marvel production machine!

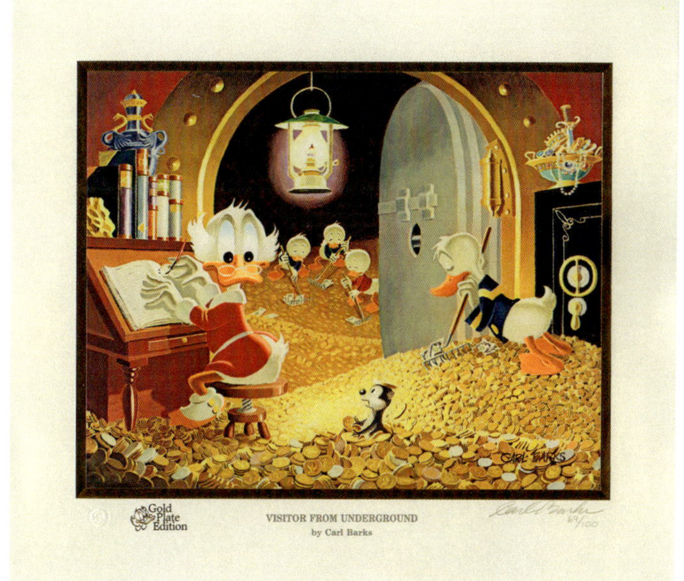

4410 Carl Barks - "Visitor From Underground," Gold Plate Edition Miniature Lithograph, numbered 69/100 (Another Rainbow, 1991). The Duck clan toils away in Uncle Scrooge's money bin. Donald Duck, Huey, Dewey, and Louie are exhausted but Uncle Scrooge is still going strong, working at his ledger. Meanwhile, a frisky gopher digs his way to the surface of the lucre pile! This was the second miniature lithograph issued by Another Rainbow. The lithograph is numbered 69/100. The print has an overall size of 13.5" x 11". The Gold Plate Edition of this print features a gold trim border and a drawing by Barks stamped in gold in the lower left margin. Carl Barks signed and numbered the lithograph at the lower right, and the print is in Excellent condition. A numbered Certificate of Authenticity is included in the lot.

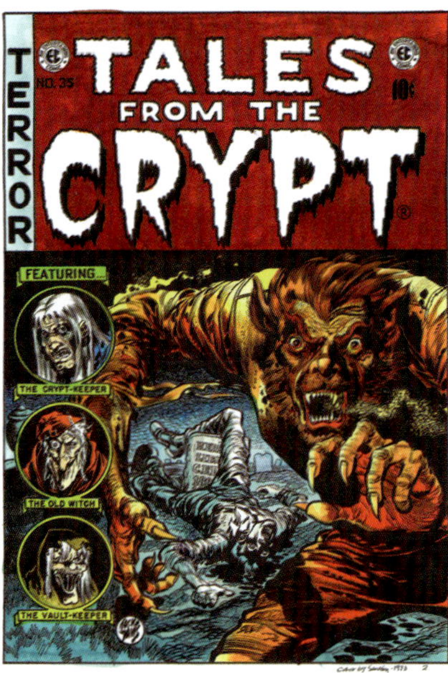

4411 Jack Davis and Marie Severin - Tales From the Crypt #35 Hand Colored Print (EC, 1973). Creep around the graveyard at night under a full moon, and you're likely to find yourself face to snout with this wild and wooly creature, courtesy of Jack Davis. E.C.'s most versatile artist was assigned cover duties on its most recognizable horror title for 18 consecutive issues. This print was hand colored by Marie Severin, and is number 2 in a series, each colored by Severin. The image area measures 10" x 14.5" and is in Excellent condition.

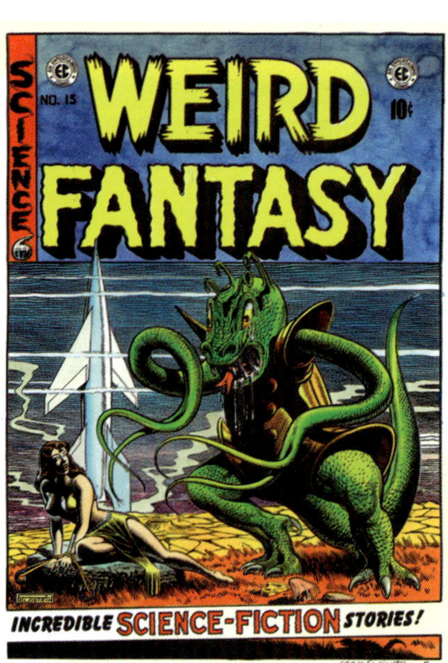

4412 Al Feldstein and Marie Severin - Weird Fantasy #15 Hand-Colored Print (EC, 1973). Al Feldstein's lovestruck monster/girl-in-bondage cover print is even more enthralling with its hand-coloring by Marie Severin. This print is #2 in a series, and was lovingly colored by Severin. The image area measures 10" x 14.5" and, aside from a light dust shadow outside of the image area, the work is in Excellent condition.

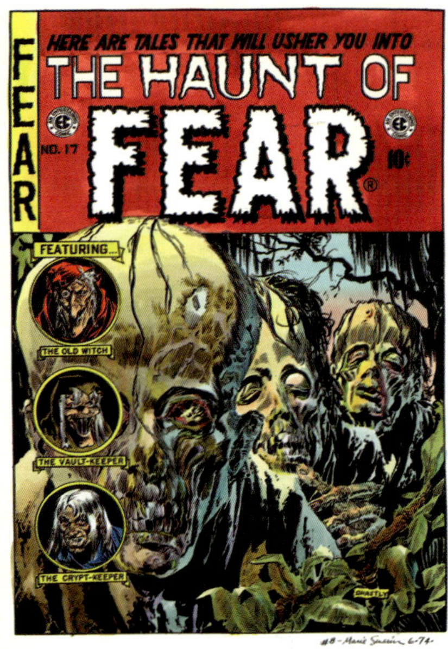

4413 Graham Ingels and Marie Severin - The Haunt of Fear #17 Hand Colored Print (EC, 1974). This cover from the pen of the otherworldly Graham "Ghastly" Ingels, is one of the four that Ingels created for **The Haunt of Fear** that has received the "classic" designation from Overstreet. Hand colored by Marie Severin, this print is number eight in a series, each colored by Severin. The image area measures 10" x 14.5" and is in Excellent condition.

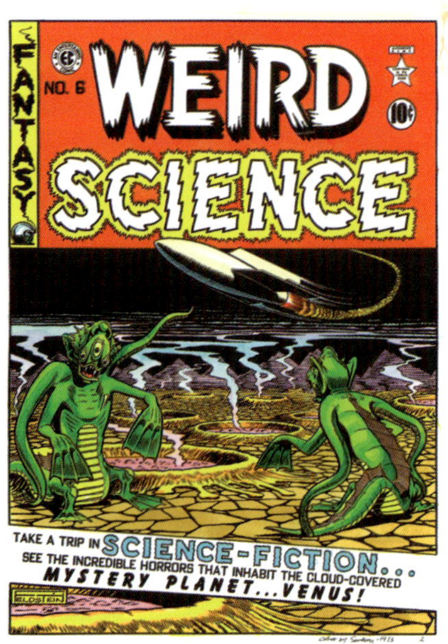

4414 Al Feldstein and Marie Severin - Weird Science #6 Hand-Colored Print (EC, 1973). See the incredible horrors that inhabit the cloud-covered mystery planet Venus! This print of Al Feldstein's classic cover for **Weird Science** #6 was hand-colored by Marie Severin, and is #2 in a series. The image area measures 10" x 14.5" and, aside from some slight staining at the upper right, the work is in Excellent condition.

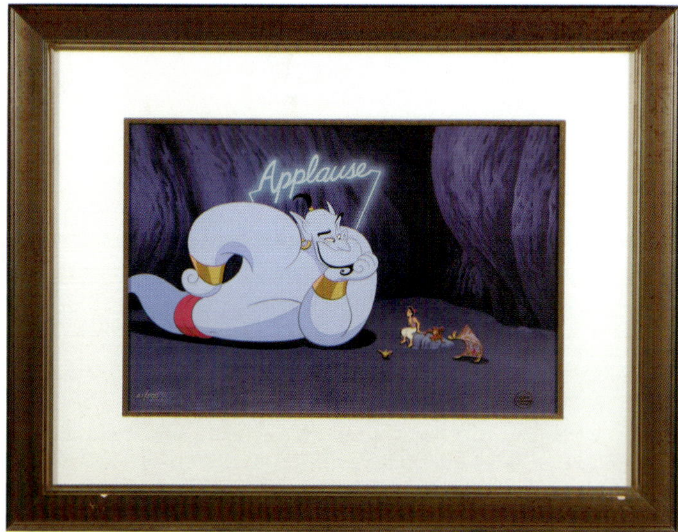

4415 Aladdin Limited Edition Hand-Painted Cel Set-Up #21/500 (The Walt Disney Company, 1993). This recreated cel set-up, "Applause," is from Sequence 11, Scene 110.2 of "Aladdin". Genie has been freed from the lamp by Aladdin and has just finished singing "Friend Like Me!" Disney artists have recreated this artwork from "Aladdin" using traditional animation techniques. Original animation drawings were transferred to acetate cels by a special six-step xerographic process. These cels were enhanced with hand-inked lines, and then hand-painted. This is number 21 from a limited edition of 500 hand-painted character cel set-ups. With an image area measuring 13" x 10", this cel set-up is in Excellent condition, and includes a certificate of authenticity.

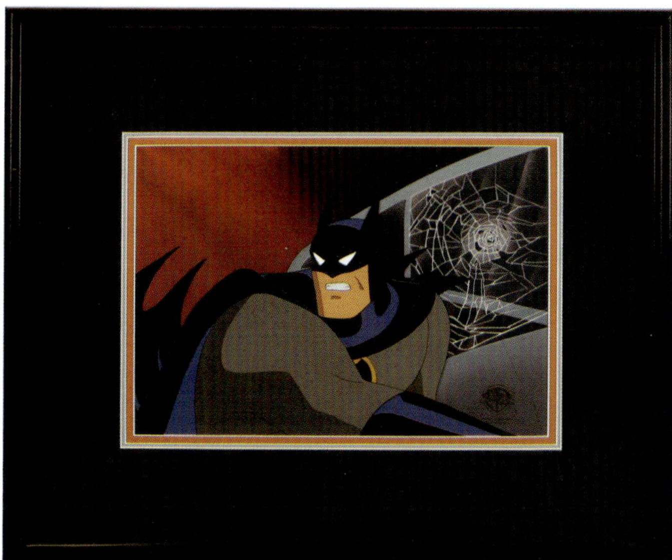

4416 Batman: The Animated Series Production Cel (Warner Bros., 1992). The Riddler lures Batman into a riddle-solving contest inside a computer game of virtual reality. Batman learns that he is able to manipulate the virtual reality landscape much like the Riddler does. With this newfound power Batman causes the Riddler to lose his concentration. As the virtual reality background collapses on the Riddler, his "superior" mind is thrown into a state of catatonia, perhaps for all time. This cel set-up, which consists of one cel, and a photograph of the original production background, is from the episode "What is Reality?" This hand-painted production cel has an image area of 11.5" x 8" and is in Excellent condition. Includes a certificate of authenticity.

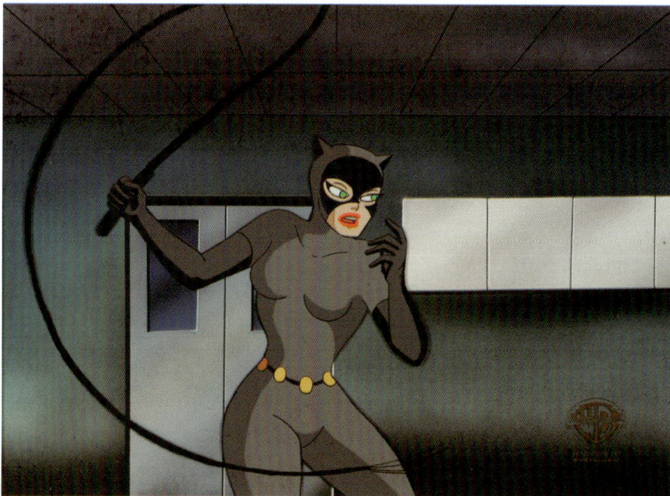

4417 "Batman: The Animated Series" Catwoman Production Cel and Background (Warner Bros., 1992). Selina Kyle uncovers a plot by industrialist Roland Daggett and his company scientist, Professor Milo, to infect animals with a disease that will spread through the city's strays and eventually affect the human populace as well. Daggett has the only cure which he plans to introduce onto the market. Catwoman pulls out the claws to stop them in this episode of "Batman: The Animated Series", titled "Cat Scratch Fever". This hand-painted production cel set-up consists of an original production cel featuring Catwoman, plus a photocopy of the original production background. With an image area of 11.5" x 8.5", the art is in Excellent condition. Includes a certificate of authenticity.

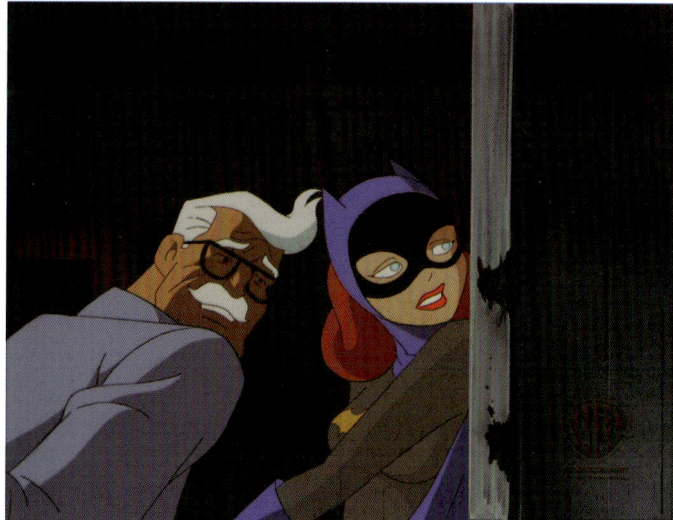

4418 "Batman: The Animated Series" Commissioner Gordon and Batgirl Production Cel (Warner Bros., 1992). At Bayshore Wharf, Batgirl attempts to save her father, Commissioner Gordon, from his imminent execution by Two-Face! Taken from the "Batman: The Animated Series" episode titled "Shadow of the Bat - Part II," this hand-painted production cel set-up consists of one cel and a photocopy of the original production background. With an image area of 9.5" x 7.5", the art is in Excellent condition. Includes a certificate of authenticity.

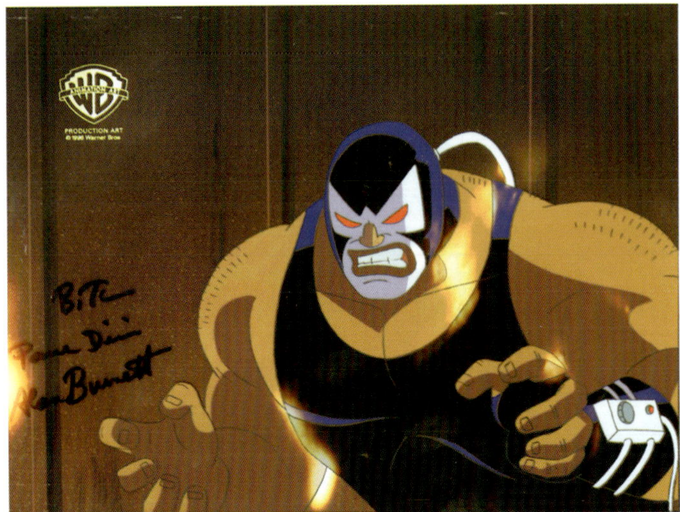

4419 "Batman: The Animated Series" Bane Production Cel (Warner Bros., 1996). It's a fight to the death with all of Gotham in the balance, as Batman takes on his most powerful adversary yet, the chemically-charged assassin, Bane. This hand-painted production cel from Warner Bros. successful "Batman: the Animated Series," features the man who has vowed to "Break the Bat!" This cel set-up, which consists of one cel, and a photocopy of the original production background, has an image area of 9.5" x 7.5" and is in Excellent condition. Signed by Bruce Timm, Alan Burnett, and Paul Dini, the chief producers of "Batman: The Animated Series," and its sequels. Includes a certificate of authenticity.

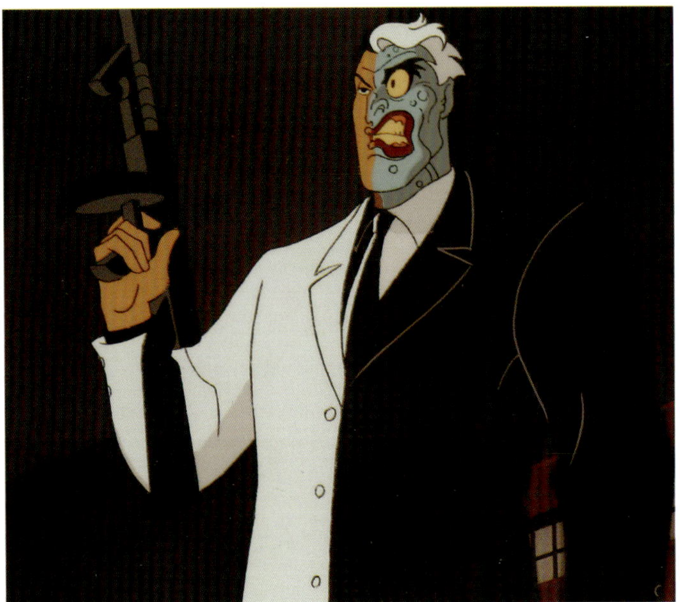

4420 "Batman: The Animated Series" Two-Face Production Cel (Warner Bros., 1992). In the episode, "Two-Face: Part II," Bruce Wayne's former best friend, Harvey Dent (Two-Face), begins an aggressive campaign against his hated rival, Rupert Thorpe, who puts out a two million dollar contract on him. Batman intervenes to keep the peace, and finally Two-Face is taken to the prison hospital accompanied by his former fiancee, Grace. Taken from the "Batman: The Animated Series," this hand-painted production cel set-up consists of one cel featuring a frightening visage of Two-Face, and a photocopy of the original production background. With an image area of 11.5" x 8.5", the art is in Excellent condition. Includes a certificate of authenticity.

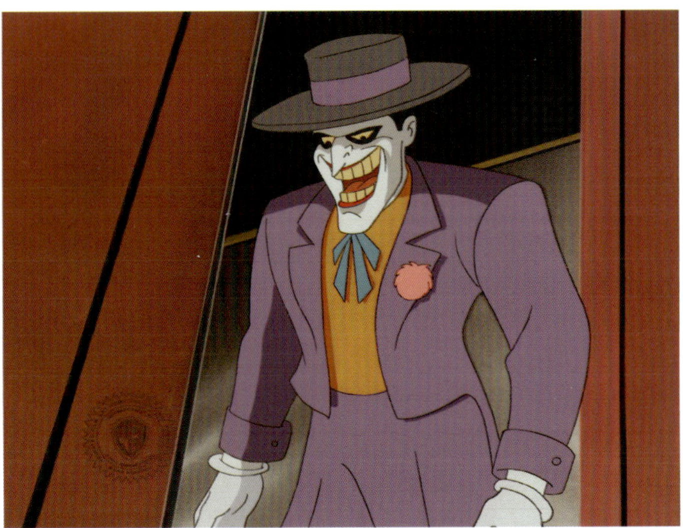

4421 "Batman: The Animated Series" Joker Production Cel (Warner Bros., 1992). This richly-produced production cel possesses the same mystique, "Dark Deco" look, and bizarre villains that epitomizes Warner Bros. successful "Batman: the Animated Series". Charlie Collins, a nondescript accountant, accidently runs afoul of the Joker, who makes Charlie promise to do him a favor. Charlie must distract Batman while the Joker plants a bomb at a testimonial dinner from Commissioner Gordon. But Charlie decides he has had enough, and takes on the Joker man to man. This cel set-up, which consists of one cel, and a photograph of the original production background, is from the episode "Joker's Favor". This hand-painted production cel has an image area of 11.5" x 8" and is in Excellent condition. Includes a certificate of authenticity.

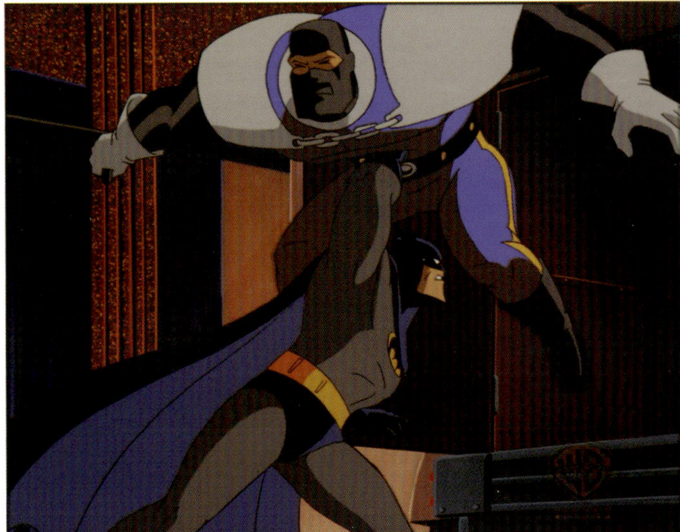

4422 "Batman: The Animated Series" Batman Production Cel (Warner Bros., 1992). When Arkham asylum's sadistic chief of security, Lyle Bolton, is fired, he vows revenge against Gotham city officials, including Commissioner Gordon, and Mayor Hill, and locks them away on an abandoned prison ship. This cel set-up, which consists of one cel, and a photocopy of the original production background, features Batman in action, from the episode "Lock-Up" This hand-painted production cel has an image area of 11.5" x 8" and is in Excellent condition. Includes a certificate of authenticity.

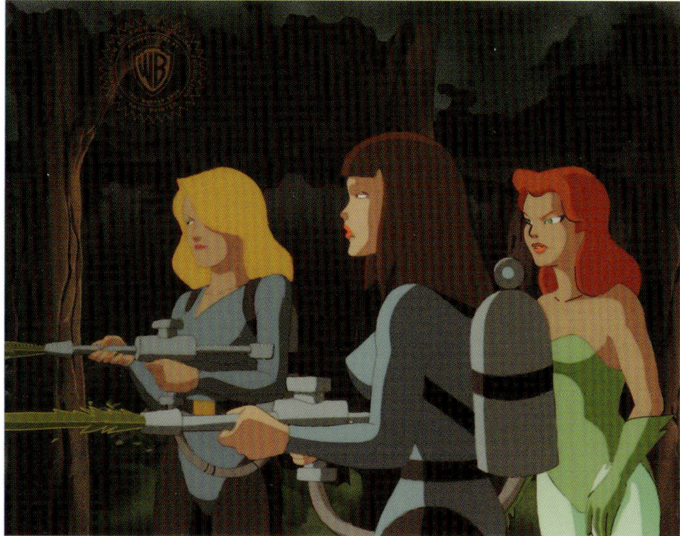

4423 "Batman: The Animated Series" Poison Ivy Production Cel (Warner Bros., 1992). Alfred and his friend, Maggie Paige, are lured to a health spa which advertises "back to nature" rejuvenating potions, but it's a scam run by Poison Ivy to turn people into trees! Batman investigates, and is nearly transformed into a tree himself, in this episode of "Batman: the Animated Series," titled "Eternal Youth". This cel set-up, which consists of one hand-painted cel, and a photocopy of the original production background, has an image area of 10" x 8" and, although there is some fading to the inked character lines, the work is in Excellent condition. Includes a certificate of authenticity.

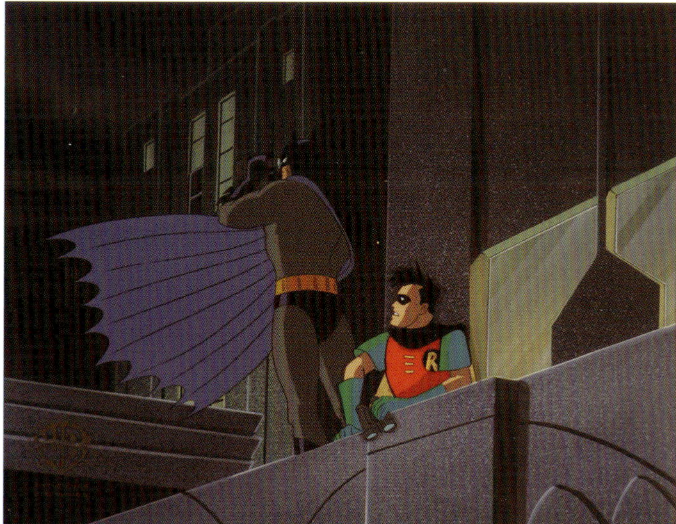

4424 "Batman: The Animated Series" Batman and Robin Production Cel and Background (Warner Bros., 1992). In the "Batman: The Animated Series" episode, "Riddler's Reform," the Riddler challenges Batman to a deadly battle of wits, in which he plans to get rid of his opponent and end the riddle games once and for all. This hand-painted production cel set-up consists of an original production cel featuring the Dark Knight and Robin, plus the original production background. With an image area of 11.5" x 8.5", the art is in Excellent condition. Includes a certificate of authenticity.

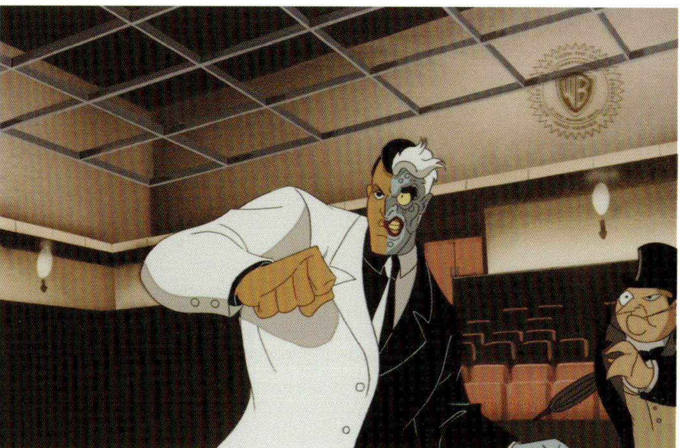

4425 "Batman: The Animated Series" Two-Face Production Cel (Warner Bros., 1992). When Judge Vargas, a good friend of Commissioner Gordon's and Bruce Wayne's, is blackmailed by Dr. Hugo Strange, Bruce journeys to Strange's health resort in Yucca Springs to investigate. Strange has invented a machine that can see people's thoughts, and he uses this on Bruce to discover that Bruce Wayne is Batman. He then attempts to auction Batman's secret identity to the Joker, Two-Face, and the Penguin. This incredible production cel features Two-Face and the Penguin. This cel set-up, which consists of one cel, and a photocopy of the original production background, is from the episode "The Strange Secret of Bruce Wayne". It is a hand-painted production cel with an image area of 11" x 7.5", and is in Excellent condition. Includes a certificate of authenticity.

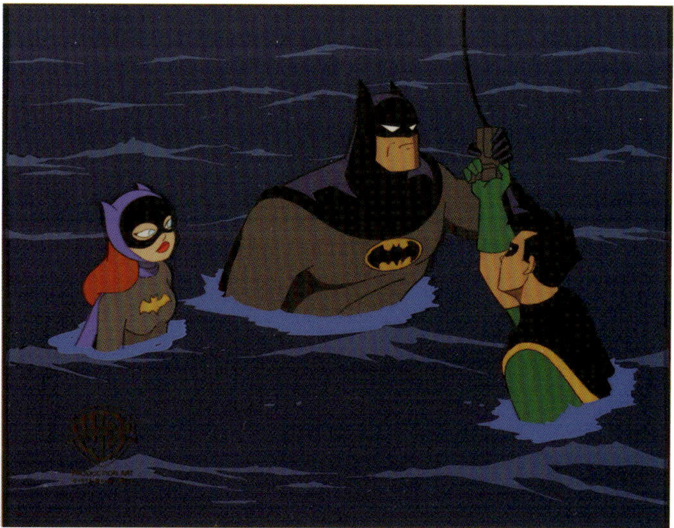

4426 "Batman: The Animated Series" Batman, Robin, and Batgirl Production Cel (Warner Bros., 1992). Batman steps in to save Robin and Batgirl, after Two-Face floods the subway tunnel they are trapped in, in this episode of "Batman: The Animated Series," titled "Shadow of the Bat - Part II". This hand-painted production cel set-up consists of one cel and a photocopy of the original production background. With an image area of 9.5" x 7.5", the art is in Excellent condition. Includes a certificate of authenticity.

4427 Western Publishing Artist - Bugs Bunny Frame-Tray Puzzle Illustration Original Art (Whitman, 1977). "Overture, curtains, lights! This is it. The night of nights. No more rehearsing and nursing a part. We know every part by heart!" You can almost hear the theme song of "The Bugs Bunny Show", as Bugs and Porky pull out all the stops in this foot-tapping musical masterpiece! Painted on illustration board, the art has an image area of 8" x 10", and is in Excellent condition. Includes a copy of the **Bugs Bunny Frame-Puzzle**.

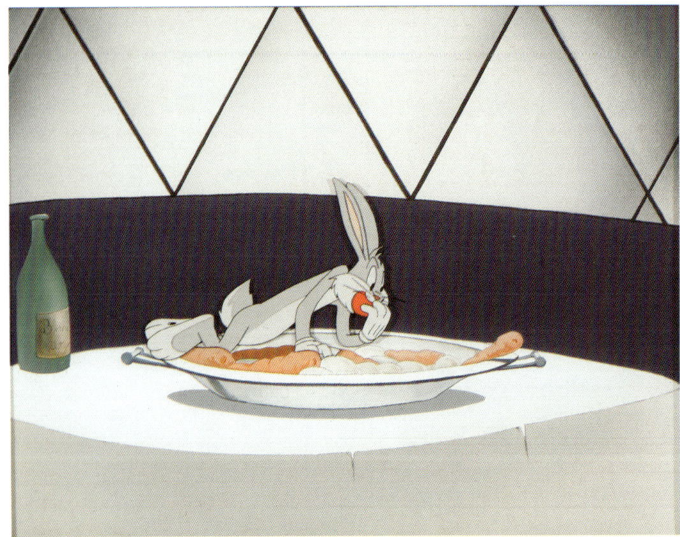

4428 "Slick Hare" Bugs Bunny Production Cel (Warner Bros., 1947). Here is an original hand inked and hand painted cel featuring Bugs Bunny, which was used in the production of this timeless classic, along with a hand painted recreation of the original production background. Elmer, running a swanky restaurant, tries to catch Bugs for an order of fried rabbit for a very important customer, Bogart's companion, "Baby" Bacall, in the Warner Bros. animated short, "Slick Hare" (1947). This original production cel has an image area of 11.5" x 9" and is in Excellent condition. Includes a certificate of authenticity.

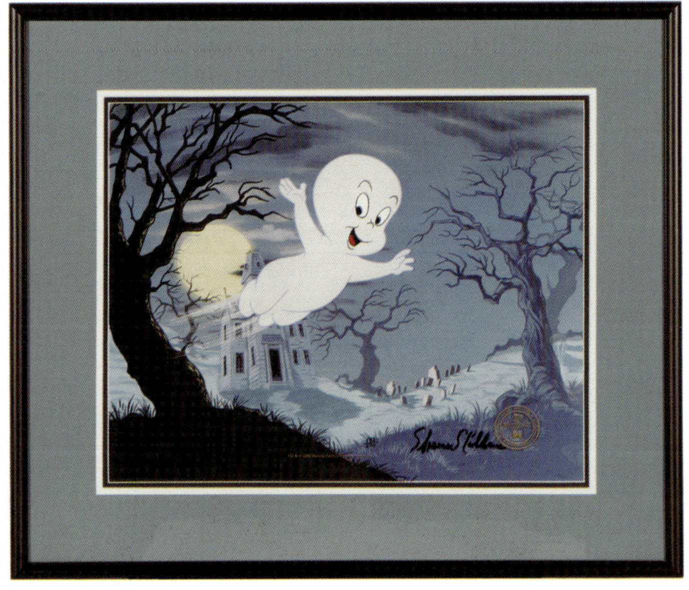

4430 Casper Hand-Painted Limited Edition Cel #132/250 (Harvey Comics Entertainment, 1992). This hand-inked and hand-painted character cel of Casper is number 32 in a limited edition of 250. Original animation drawings were transferred to acetate cels with colored inks, and were then hand-painted. With an image area measuring 16" x 13", this cel set-up is in Excellent condition, and includes a certificate of authenticity. Signed by industry legend Shamus Culhane.

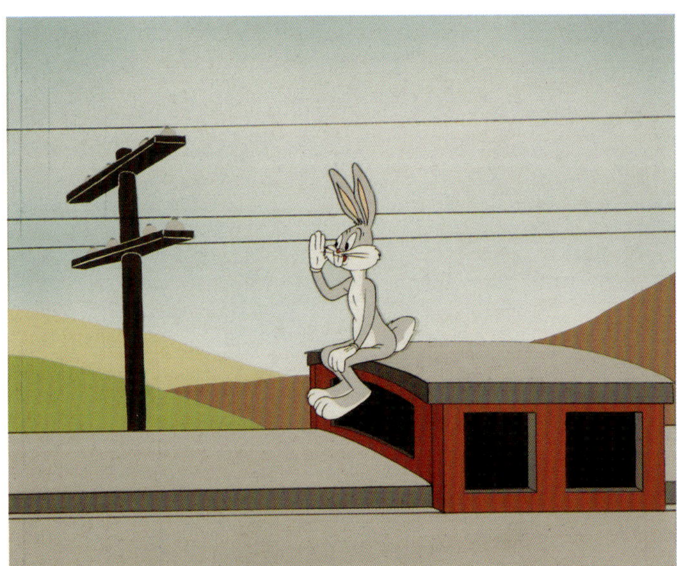

4429 "Half-Fare Hare," Bugs Bunny Production Cel (Warner Bros., 1956). "So long screwy, see you in Saint Louie!" Bugs Bunny delivered this immortal line in the final scene of "Half-Fare Hare," right before the "That's All Folks" ending. When Bugs Bunny hops the Chattanooga Choo-Choo to get carrots, he finds himself in a car with Ralph Crumden and Ned Morton — bums who want a rabbit dinner! Here is a cel set-up featuring Bugs atop the train from the Warner Bros. animated short, "Half Fare Hare" (1956). This lot includes an original hand-inked and hand-painted cel, along with a hand-painted recreation of the original production background. This original production cel has an image area of 11.5" x 9" and is in Excellent condition. Includes a certificate of authenticity.

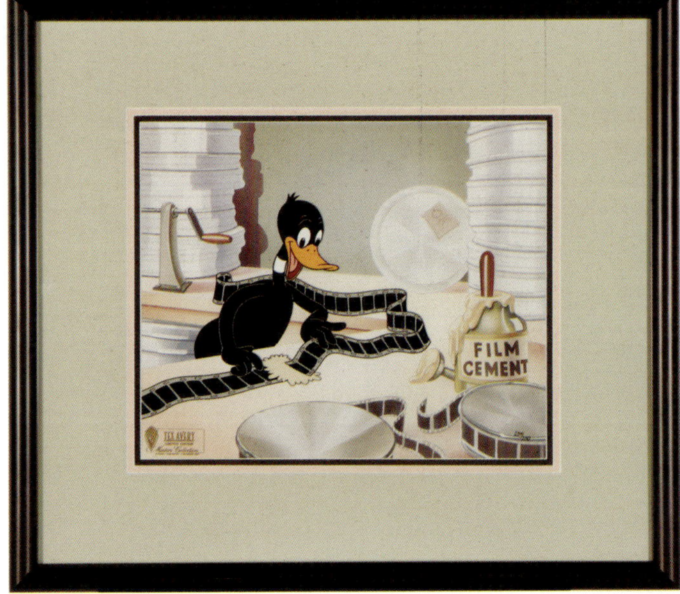

4431 "Daffy Duck in Hollywood" Tex Avery Masters Collection Hand-Painted Limited Edition Scene Cel #234/150 (Warner Bros., 1994). This hand-inked and hand-painted cel was created by Warner Bros. Animation. Inspired by a scene from Tex Avery's "Daffy Duck in Hollywood" (1938), this limited edition cel is part of the Masters Collection. With an image area measuring 12" x 10", the condition is Excellent.

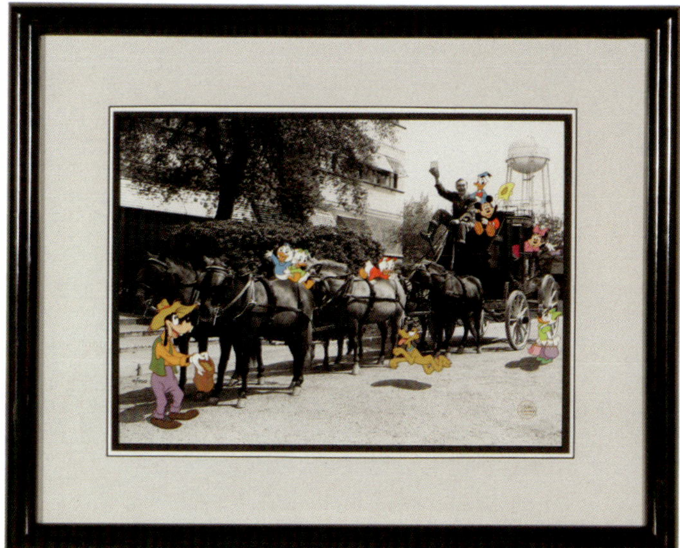

4432 Walt's Stagecoach Hand-Painted Character Cel Set-up #9/950 (The Walt Disney Company, 1993). This is number 9 in a limited edition of 950 hand-painted character cels combined with a photograph taken in April, 1954 of Walt Disney showing off a new stagecoach built at the Walt Disney Studios, and later taken to Disneyland where it was used as an attraction. This cel set-up, "Walt's Stagecoach," features Walt Disney with his most famous characters as he hitches up for the wildest ride in the west! Disney artists have created this artwork using traditional animation techniques. Original animation drawings were transferred to acetate cels by a special six-step xerographic process, which were then hand-painted. The photographic background was produced using the original black and white negative, which has been conserved at the Disney Photo Library. With an image area measuring 15" x 11", this cel set-up is in Excellent condition, and includes a certificate of authenticity.

4433 Walt Disney Studios - Dopey Hand-Painted Limited Edition Scene Cel (Walt Disney Art Classics, 1997). This classic portrait of Dopey is from Sequence 5A, Scene 19 of "Snow White and the Seven Dwarfs" (1937). Disney artists have recreated this artwork using six hand-inked line colors, then hand-painted the cel using 16 acrylic colors. The background is actual wood veneer recreating the unique presentation style used on many of the fine art edition Disney celluloids released in the late 1930s. This edition consists of 750, and includes a certificate of authenticity.

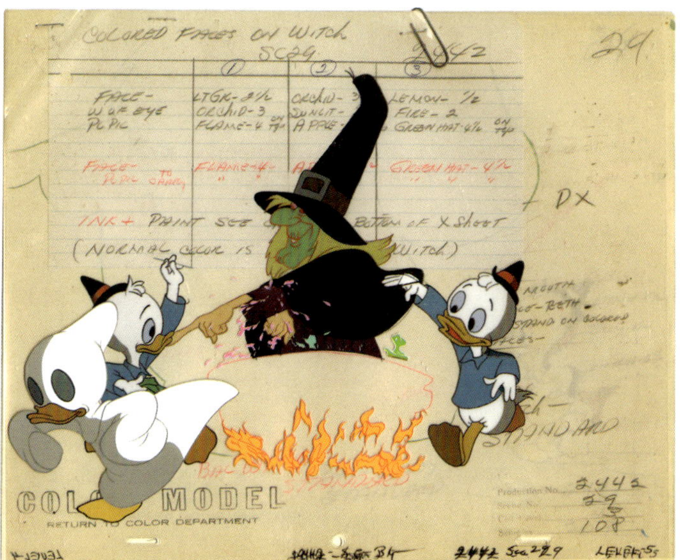

4434 "Trick or Treat" Huey, Dewey, and Louie Color Model Cel Set-Up (Disney, 1952). After Donald steals Huey, Dewey, and Louie's Halloween candy, they enlist the help of Witch Hazel to get back at him, in this short film from 1952. This amazing color model set up features all three of the nephews and Witch Hazel, all hand-inked and hand-painted on numerous cel layers, along with their original pencil animation drawings. There are six cels, and seven multi-colored pencil drawings here, and this group also includes the special effects layers. A dazzling display of Disney animation artistry! Both the cels and the original drawings have a 12" x 10" image area, and are all in Excellent condition.

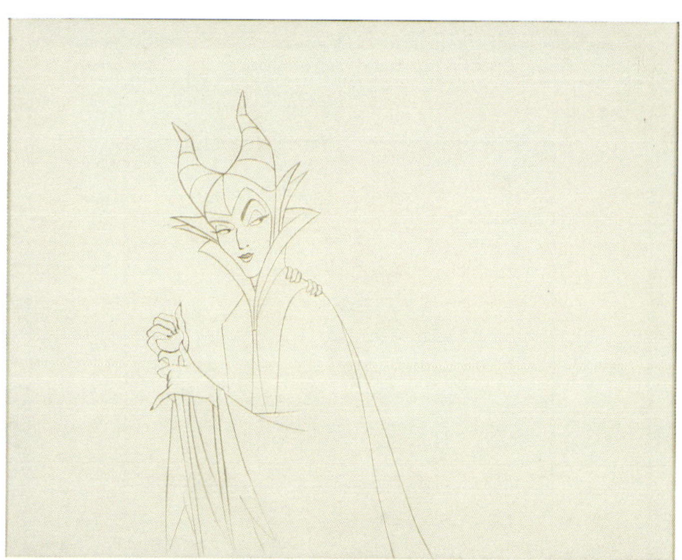

4435 "Sleeping Beauty" Maleficent Pencil Animation Drawing Original Art (Walt Disney, 1959). She is called Maleficent, a name for a witch, if there ever was one. The mistress of all evil will cast her spell on you in this magnificent pencil sketch from the final fairy tale to be produced by Walt Disney himself, "Sleeping Beauty". Here is an original animation pencil drawing of the bad fairy, created in graphite by Disney animators. This pencil sketch has an image area of 9" x 8", and is in Excellent condition. Includes a certificate of authenticity.

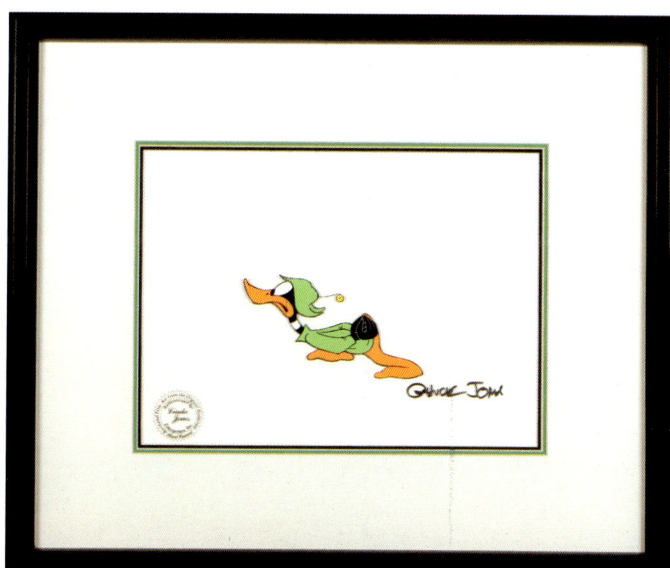

4436 Duck Dodgers and the Return of the 24 1/2 Century Production Cel (Warner Bros., 1980). This original production animation cel featuring Daffy Duck as Duck Dodgers appeared in the Warner Bros. short, "Duck Dodgers and the Return of the 24 1/2 Century". This one of a kind hand-painted cel was filmed in a studio and actually appeared in the cartoon. The image area of this cel measures 14" x 10", and the condition is Excellent. Signed by Chuck Jones. This lot also includes a certificate of authenticity.

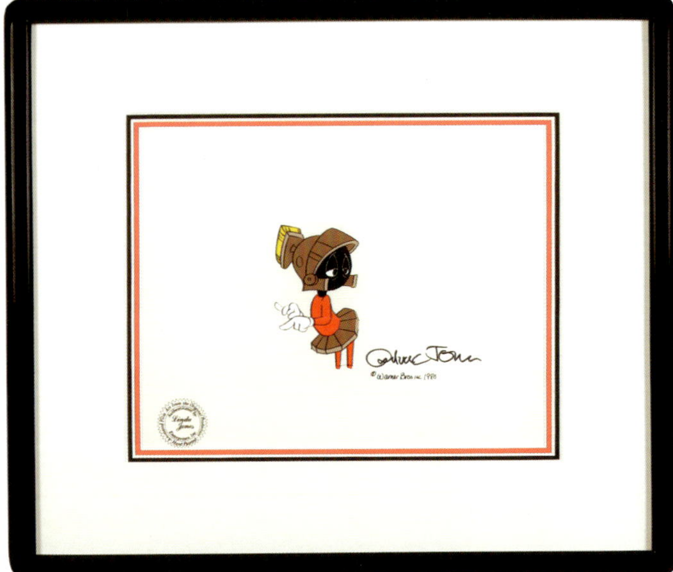

4437 Duck Dodgers and the Return of the 24 1/2 Century Production Cel (Warner Bros., 1980). This original hand-painted production animation cel featuring Marvin the Martian appeared in the Warner Bros. short, "Duck Dodgers and the Return of the 24 1/2 Century". This one of a kind painting was filmed in a studio and actually appeared in the cartoon. The image area of this cel measures 14" x 10", and the condition is Excellent. Signed by Chuck Jones. This lot also includes a certificate of authenticity.

4438 Duck Dodgers and the Return of the 24 1/2 Century Production Cel (Warner Bros., 1980). From the Warner Bros. short, "Duck Dodgers and the Return of the 24 1/2 Century," here is an original hand-painted production animation cel featuring Space Cadet Porky Pig. This one of a kind painting was filmed in a studio and actually appeared in the cartoon. The image area of this cel measures 14" x 10", and the condition is Excellent. Signed by Chuck Jones. This lot also includes a certificate of authenticity.

4439 Snidely Whiplash, Dudley Do-Right, Nell, and Horse Hand-Painted Scene Cel (Jay Ward Productions, 1990). This hand-inked and hand-painted cel was created by Jay Ward Productions. With an image area measuring 12" x 9.5", the condition is Excellent. This lot also includes a certificate of authenticity.

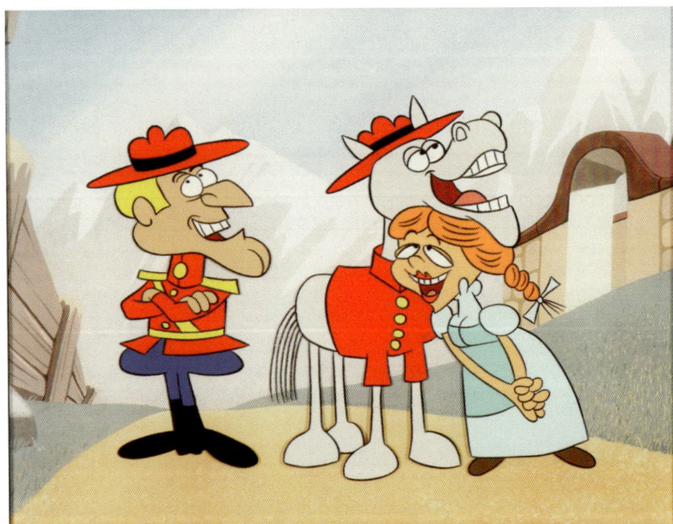

4440 Dudley Do-Right, Nell and Horse Hand-Painted Scene Cel (Jay Ward Productions, undated). Dudley Do-Right of the Mounties, that lonely defender of justice and fair play, spends some quality time with his girl, Nell, and his horse. This hand-inked and hand-painted cel sits atop a facsimile background, and was created by Jay Ward Productions. With an image area measuring 11" x 9", the condition is Excellent. This lot also includes a certificate of authenticity.

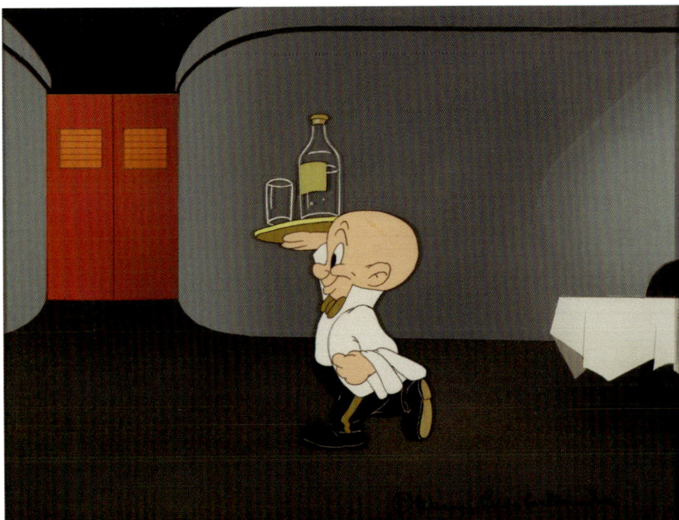

4441 "Slick Hare" Elmer Fudd Production Cel (Warner Bros., 1947). Waiter Elmer Fudd is at a loss when his famous customer, Humphrey Bogart, gives him twenty minutes to prepare rabbit. With time running out, Fudd tries to get Bugs Bunny into the pot, in the Warner Bros. animated short, "Slick Hare" (1947). Here is an original hand inked and hand painted cel featuring Elmer Fudd, which was used in the production of this timeless classic, along with a hand painted recreation of the original production background. This original production cel has an image area of 11.5" x 9" and is in Excellent condition. Includes a certificate of authenticity.

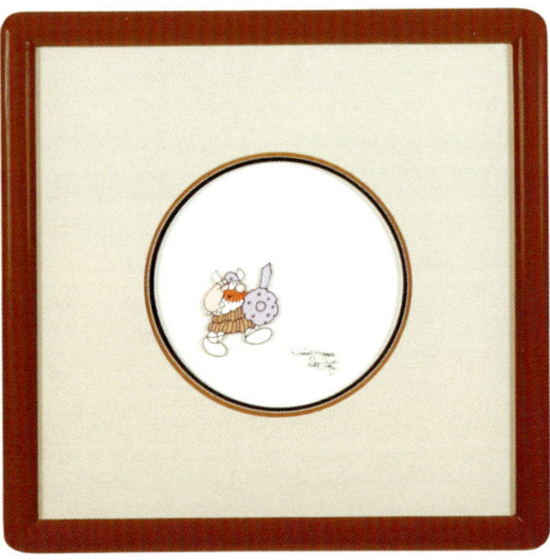

4442 King Features' 25th Anniversary Special "Hagar the Horrible" Production Cel (King Features, undated). Dick Browne's bumbling barbarian, Hagar the Horrible, is the subject of this original hand-inked, and hand-painted, production cel. Autographed by producers Daniel Hunn and Ron Fritz. The art has an image area of 6" x 6" and is in Excellent condition. Includes a certificate of authenticity.

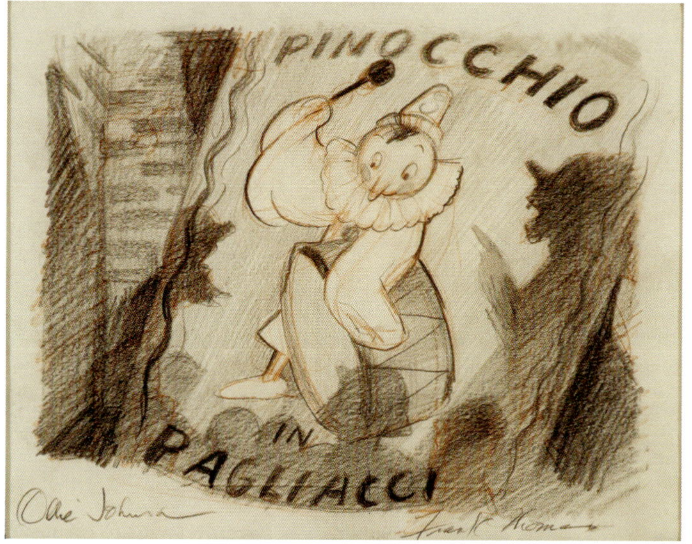

4443 Frank Thomas and Ollie Johnston - "Pinocchio" Production Design Drawing Original Art (Disney, 1940). Pinocchio is seduced away by two villains who sell him to the greedy puppetmaster, Stromboli, who makes Pinocchio a prisoner and forces him to perform in his puppet show. Truer to the original Collodi version, this graphite and red pencil inspiration sketch was created to visualize Pinocchio's scenes in the marionette theatre. This delightful sketch is signed by two of Disney's "Nine Old Men," animators Frank Thomas and Ollie Johnston. The image area of this graphite sketch measures 10" x 8.5" and the art is in Excellent condition. Signed by Frank Thomas and Ollie Johnston at the bottom.

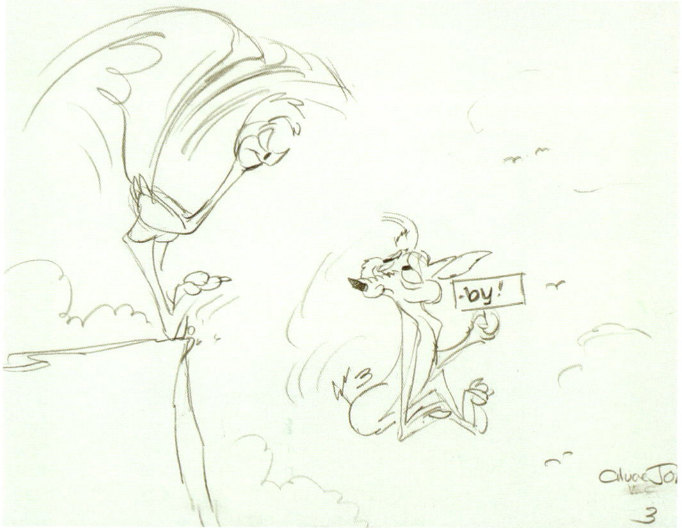

4444 Chuck Jones - Road Runner and Wile E. Coyote Pencil Sketch Original Art (Linda Jones Enterprises, 1998). Throughout Road Runner and Wile E. Coyote's careers in over two dozen Warner Bros. cartoons chronicling the duo's encounters, their classic chase formula has never lost its tension. The calamitous Wile E.'s seemingly foolproof scheme to snag Road Runner fails miserably once again, in this authentic pencil sketch by Chuck Jones. The image area measures 12" x 9.5" and the work is in Excellent condition. Signed by Chuck Jones. Includes a certificate of authenticity.

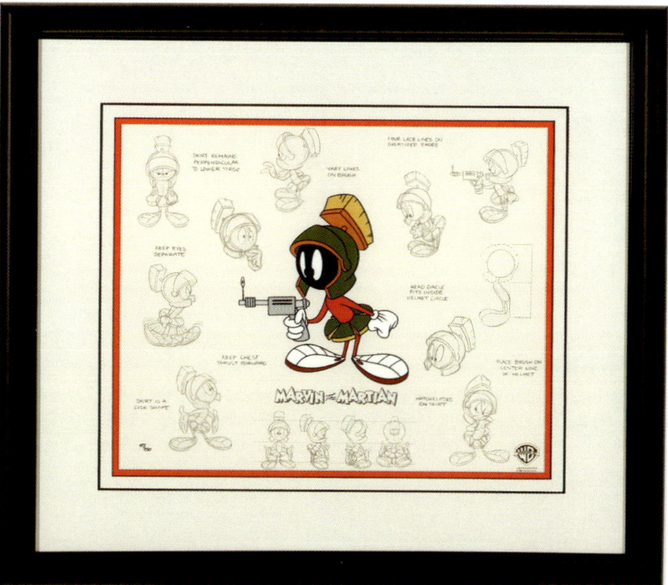

4445 Model Sheet: Marvin the Martian Limited Edition Hand-Painted Cel #187/750 (Warner Bros., 1996). In 1948, Chuck Jones directed the classic Looney Tunes cartoon, "Haredevil Hare," which introduced this world to that intrepid space traveler Marvin the Martian. This hand-painted limited edition animation cel was produced by Warner Bros. Animation Art using the same methods employed in preparing cels for actual production. The background drawings were adapted from an original Marvin the martian model sheet from Warner Bros. Classic Animation, and special attention was paid in the printing in order to capture the delicate line quality. This art measures 16" x 13," and is in Excellent condition. Includes a certificate of authenticity.

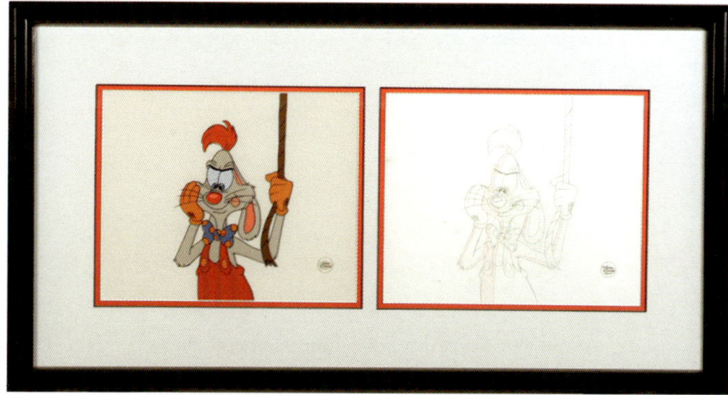

4446 Mickey's 60th Birthday Special Animation Drawing and Production Cel (Walt Disney Company, 1988). Roger Rabbit shows the audience the ropes, in this one of a kind cel that was used in the production of the "Mickey's 60th Birthday Special," which aired on NBC on November 13, 1988. In honor of Mickey's 60th birthday, this television special was produced by Murakami Wolf Swenson Inc. with The Walt Disney Studios, and incorporated live action and animation. Included here is the original pencil animation sketch, along with a hand-inked and hand-painted cel. The sketch and cel both have an image area of 11" x 9" and are in Excellent condition. Includes a certificate of authenticity.

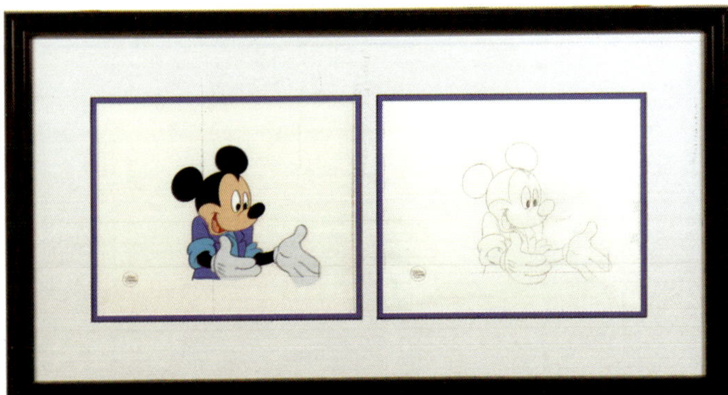

4447 Mickey's 60th Birthday Special Animation Drawing and Production Cel (Walt Disney Company, 1988). In honor of Mickey Mouse's 60th birthday, NBC aired the "Mickey's 60th Birthday Special," on November 13, 1988. Produced by Murakami Wolf Swenson Inc., with The Walt Disney Studios, this television special incorporated live action and animation. Included here is the original pencil animation sketch, along with a hand-inked and hand-painted cel. The sketch and cel both have an image area of 11" x 9" and are in Excellent condition. Includes a certificate of authenticity.

4448 Sorcerer Mickey Pencil Animation Drawing (undated). Animator Eric Scales is responsible for this magical rendition of Mickey Mouse, inspired by the "Sorcerer's Apprentice" from Walt Disney's "Fantasia". The art is drawn in two tones of blue pencil, and has a 9.5" x 9" image area. This work is in Excellent condition, and is signed by Eric Scales.

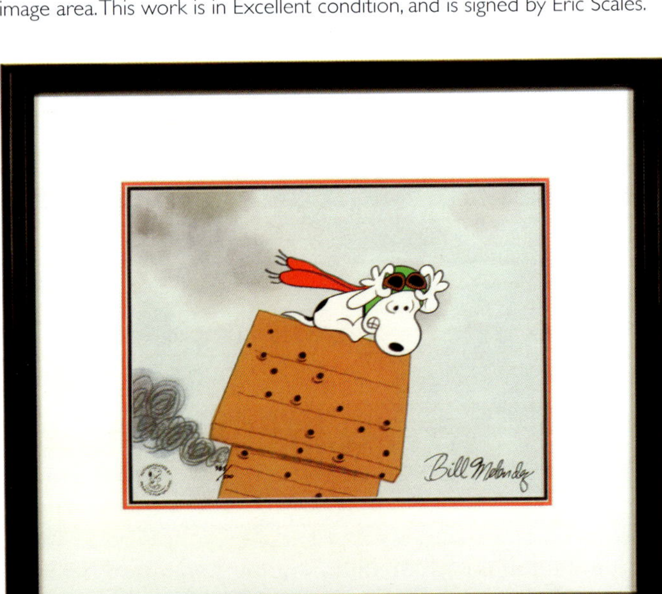

4449 It's the Great Pumpkin, Charlie Brown Limited Edition Production Cel (Bill Melendez Productions, 1966). This is an original hand-painted animation cel from "It's the Great Pumpkin, Charlie Brown," which originally aired on October 27, 1966. This television special was produced by Bill Melendez Productions, in association with Lee Mendelson Productions, and ***Peanuts*** creator Charles M. Schulz. Titled "Losing Altitude: Snoopy as the Flying Ace," this is a hand-painted cel with background, numbered 385 out of 500. Each and every Limited Edition is individually numbered, and features the signature of Bill Melendez and bears the Peanuts Film Gallery seal of authenticity. The art has an image area of 11.5" x 8" and is in Excellent condition. Includes a certificate of authenticity.

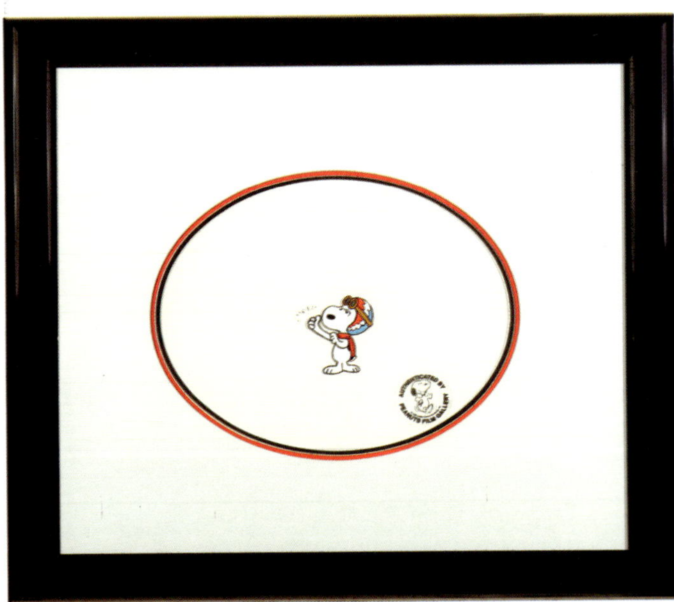

4450 You're a Good Sport, Charlie Brown Limited Edition Production Cel (Bill Melendez Productions, 1975). This is an original hand-painted animation cel from the 1975 television special, "You're a Good Sport, Charlie Brown," which was produced by Bill Melendez Productions, in association with Lee Mendelson Productions. This is a hand-painted cel features a star-spangled Snoopy. The art has an image area of 11.5" x 8" and is in Excellent condition. Includes a certificate of authenticity.

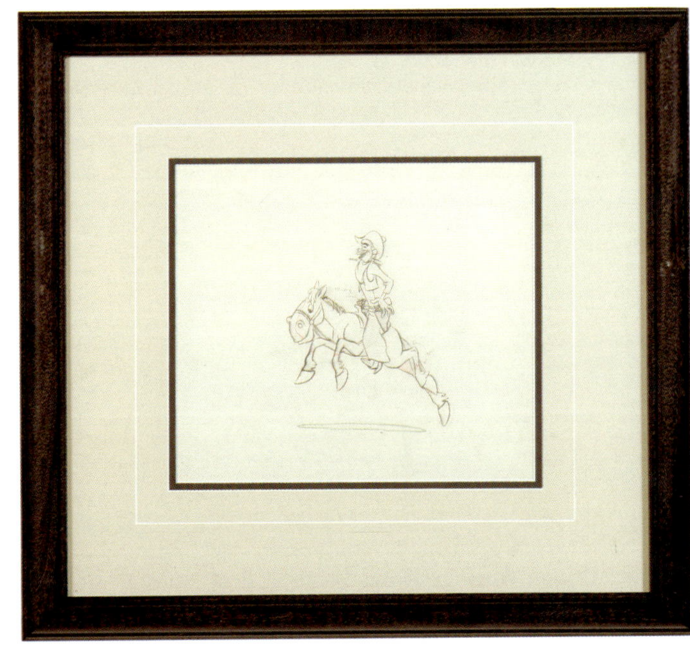

4451 Pecos Bill Original Pencil Animation Drawing (Walt Disney, 1948). Here is an original animation pencil drawing from the "Pecos Bill" section of Walt Disney's feature film, "Melody Time". Created by Disney animators, this lively drawing was created in multi-color pencil and has an image area of 9" x 8", and is in Excellent condition. Includes a certificate of authenticity.

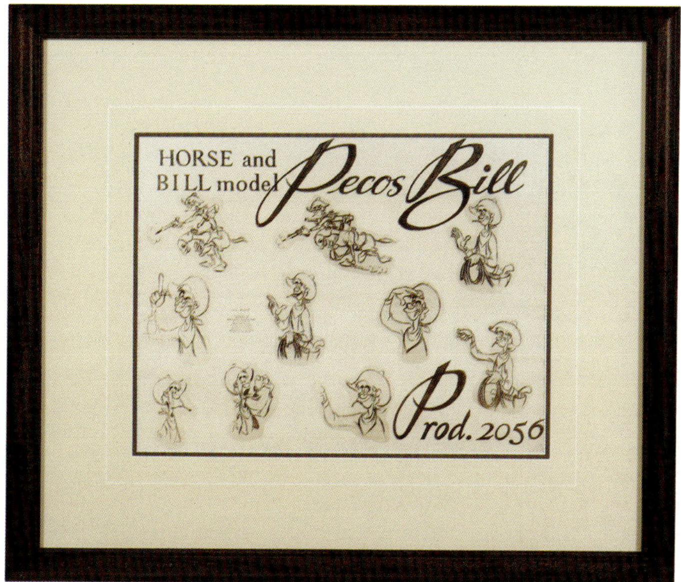

4452 Pecos Bill Model Sheet (Disney, 1946). "Pecos Bill" appeared in Walt Disney's 10th animated feature film, "Melody Time," which appeared in theaters on May 27, 1948. This character model sheet features Pecos Bill, the biggest, bestest cowboy there ever was, and his horse, Widowmaker. The image area measures 13.5" x 10" and the art is in Excellent condition.

4453 Animaniacs Production Cel (Warner Bros., 1993). The Brain is missing one important ingredient in his plan to take over the world — $99,000! So, disguising himself in a mechanical human suit, he becomes a contestant on "Gyp-Parody" and employs his incredible knowledge to try and win the money. This genuine hand-painted production cel was used in the episode, "Win Big," from the original Warner Bros. animated television series, "Animaniacs". This cel has an image area of 11.5" x 8.5" and is in Excellent condition. Includes a certificate of authenticity.

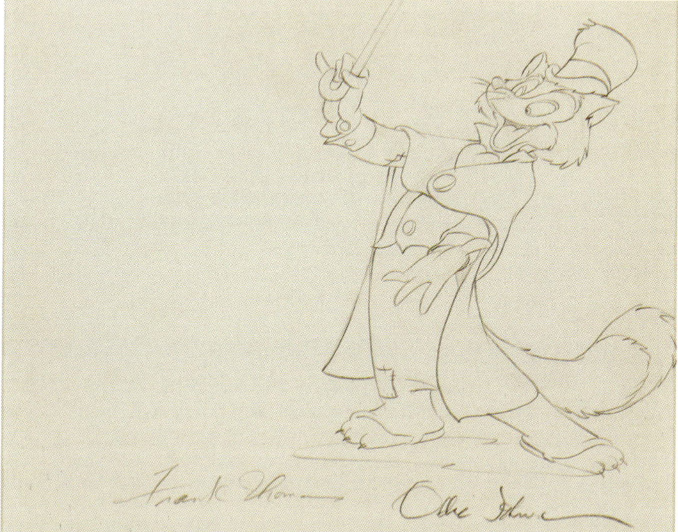

4454 Frank Thomas and Ollie Johnston - "Pinocchio" Honest John Model Drawing Original Art (Disney, 1940). When Pinocchio is waylaid by Honest John Fox and Giddy Cat, it is his innocence and naivete that allows them to convince him to try "an actor's life", and then to accept the "free ticket" on the coach to Pleasure Isle. Walt Disney's film version of this Italian folk tale was released in 1940, and featured animation by two of Disney's "Nine Old Men," animators Frank Thomas and Ollie Johnston. The image area of this graphite sketch measures 11" x 9" and the art is in Excellent condition. Signed by Frank Thomas and Ollie Johnston at the bottom.

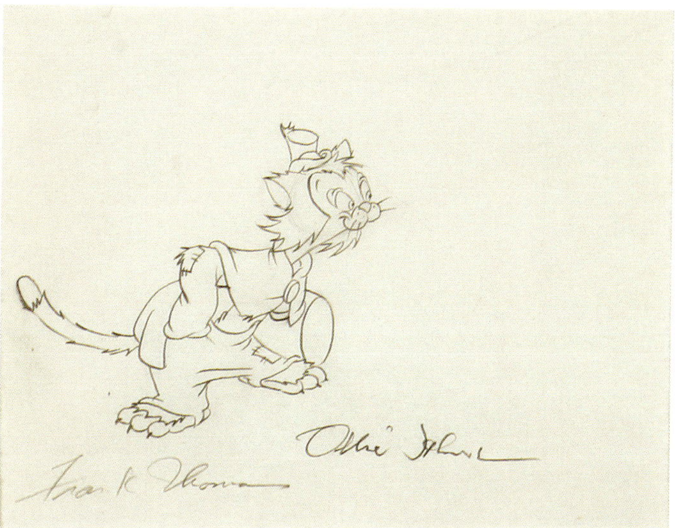

4455 Frank Thomas and Ollie Johnston - "Pinocchio" Gideon Model Drawing Original Art (Disney, 1940). Relive the wonder of Walt Disney's story of the wooden puppet, Pinocchio, brought to life by the Blue Fairy, in this lively original model drawing. Pinocchio is led astray by the wicked Honest John and his companion, Gideon, who turn him over to an evil puppeteer, Stromboli. Animators Frank Thomas, and Ollie Johnston produced this wonderful 9" x 7" graphite sketch of Gideon, which, aside from some light smudging along the left edge, is in Excellent condition. Signed by Frank Thomas and Ollie Johnston at the bottom. Includes a certificate of authenticity.

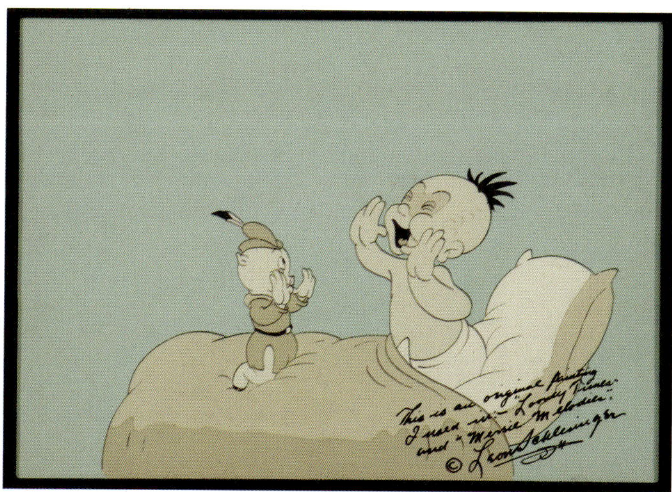

4456 "Porky the Giant Killer" Porky Pig Production Cel (Warner Bros., 1939). Porky Pig enchants a giant baby in this vintage hand-inked, and hand-painted black and white animation production cel. This has an image area of 11" x 8" and is in Excellent condition. Signed and inscribed by Leon Schlesinger. Includes a certificate of authenticity.

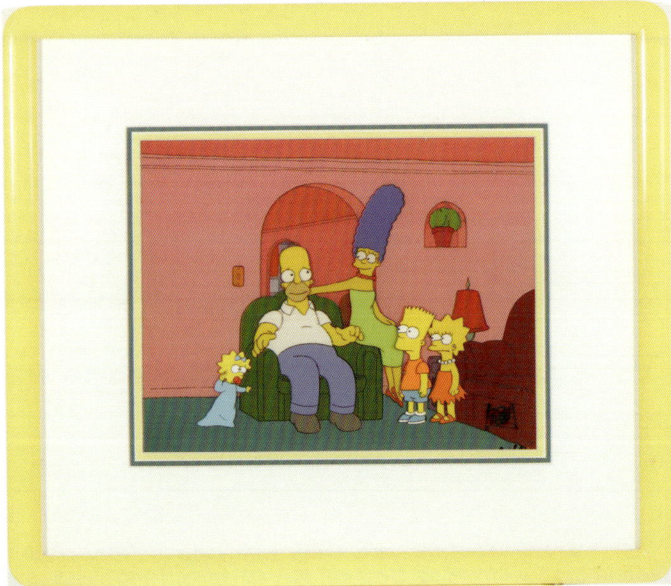

4457 The Simpsons Hand-Painted Cel Set-Up (20th Century Fox, undated). America's first family of ink and paint has gone from one minute shorts on "The Tracy Ullman Show" to one of the highest rated shows on television. This cel set-up features the entire Simpson clan, Homer, Marge, Bart, Lisa, and Maggie in their living room, courtesy of "The Simpsons" animation artists. The image area measures 12" x 9.5". Attractively matted for an overall size of 18" x 15.5".

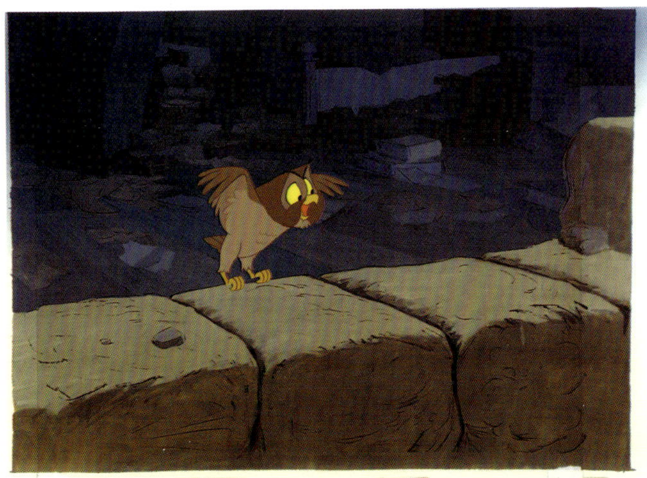

4458 Sleeping Beauty Production Cel (Walt Disney, 1959). This is an original production cel of the owl from Walt Disney's 1959 animated feature "Sleeping Beauty". This cel sits against a photocopy of the original production background. The art has an image area of 12.5" x 10.5" and, aside from some slight ink loss at the top of the owl's head, the art is in Excellent condition.

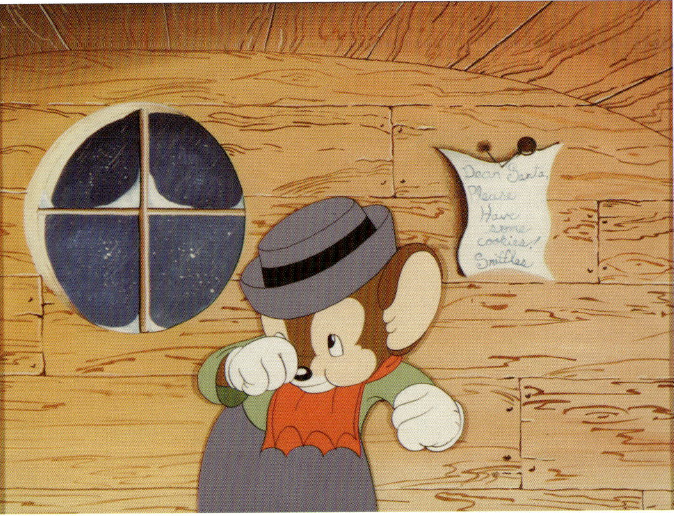

4459 "Bedtime For Sniffles" Sniffles the Mouse Production Cel (Warner Bros., 1940). Here is a cel set-up featuring one of Chuck Jones' greatest creations, the cute little Sniffles, from the Warner Bros. animated short, "Bedtime For Sniffles" (1940). Ben Mankiewicz selected this cartoon for a showing on Turner Classics Movies' "Cartoon Alley Christmas Special." This lot includes an original hand-inked and hand-painted cel, along with a hand-painted recreation of the original production background. This original production cel has an image area of 11" x 8.5" and is in Excellent condition. Includes a certificate of authenticity.

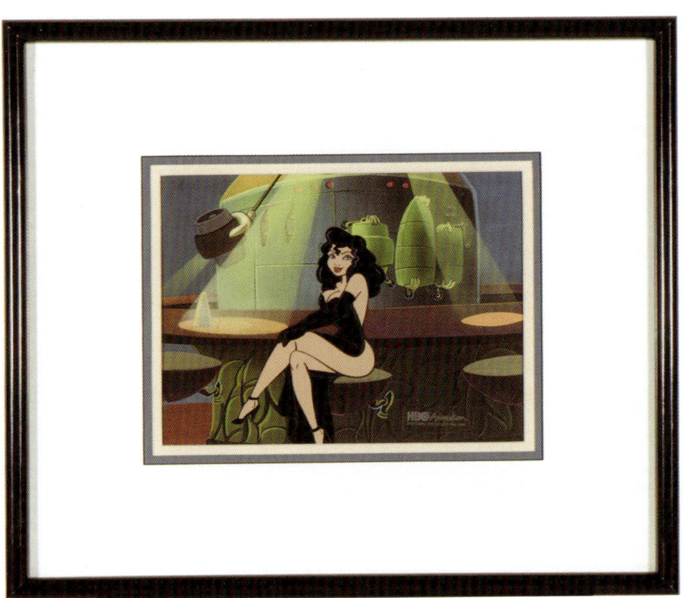

4460 "Spicy City" Raven Production Cel (HBO Animation, 1997). This sleek, sexy original hand-painted animation cel is from director Ralph Bakshi's cyberpunk noir animated series, "Spicy City," which was created for HBO. This cel sits against a photograph of the original production background. The art has an image area of 10" x 7.5" and is in Excellent condition.

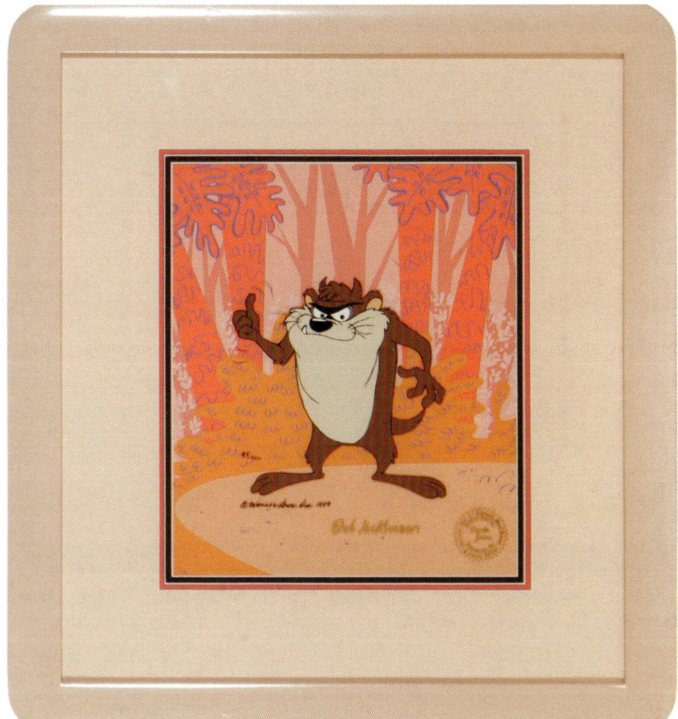

4461 Tasmanian Devil Hand-Painted Limited Edition Cel (Linda Jones Enterprises, 1989). As an animator, Bob McKimson's ability to draw a character quickly, cleanly, and accurately, earned him the positions of senior model sheet artist, troubleshooter, and animation supervisor at the studio. He is responsible for the creation of the Tasmanian Devil, one of his best-loved characters. This fine art limited edition hand-painted cel measures approximately 9.5" x 11.5", and is limited to only 500 works of art in the edition. Signed by Bob McKimson.

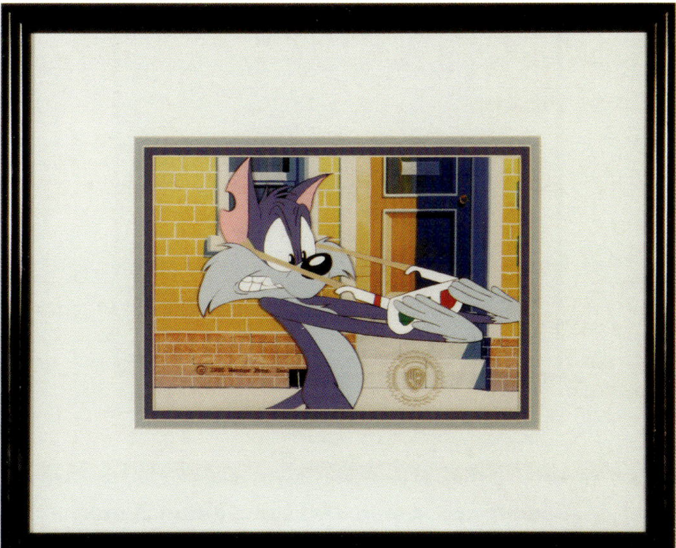

4462 Tiny Toons Adventures Production Cel (Warner Bros., 1990). This cel set-up, which consists of one cel and a photograph of the original production background, features Furrball trying to remove a menacing pair of 3-D glasses which have inadvertently become glued to his face in "Optical Intrusion," from "Tiny Toons Adventures" episode #406113, "The Wheel of Comedy". This hand-painted production cel has an image area of 11.5" x 8.5" and is in Excellent condition. Includes a certificate of authenticity.

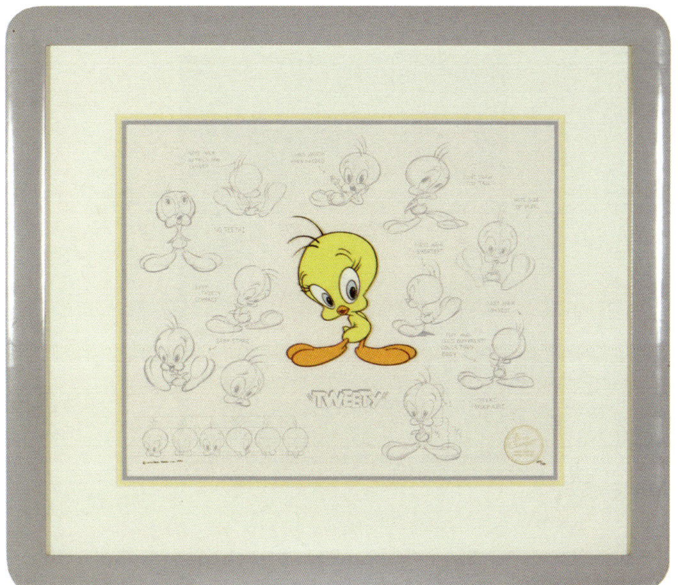

4463 The Model Series: Tweety Bird Limited Edition Hand-Painted Cel #329/500 (Warner Bros., 1991). This hand-painted limited edition animation cel was produced by the Bob Clampett Animation Art studio using the same methods employed in preparing cels for actual production. The pose was adapted from director Bob Clampett's original character models and animation, and the background lithography was printed on a premium stock. This art measures 16" x 13," and is in Excellent condition. Includes a certificate of authenticity.

4464 Warner Bros. Animation - Native American on Horseback Animation Drawing Original Art (Warner Bros., undated). A snappy pencil drawing, courtesy of the fine artists at the Warner Bros. Animation Department, is presented here in this original pencil animation sketch. This vintage image may have possibly been created for the short, "Sweet Sioux," directed by Isadore "Friz" Freleng, which was released in 1937. Drawn on a sheet of 9" x 8" animation paper, the work is in Excellent condition.

4465 Yosemite Sam Hand-Painted Cel Original Art (Warner Bros., 1982). There is some speculation that Yosemite Sam was based on director/creator Friz Freleng himself — both being short, red-haired chaps with risable tempers. This charming cel measures 12" x 9.5" and is in Excellent condition. Signed by Friz Freleng at the bottom left.

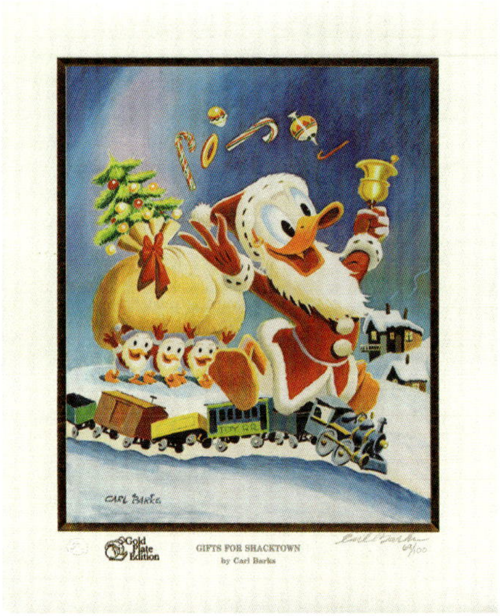

4466 Carl Barks - "Gifts For Shacktown", Gold Plate Edition Miniature Lithograph, numbered 69/100 (Another Rainbow, 1991). Donald Duck, dressed as Santa Claus, rings a bell signaling good cheer as he rides a toy train. Huey, Dewey, and Louie play Santa's tiny helpers, and they tote a giant sackful of toys for the unfortunate children of Shacktown. This was the third miniature lithograph issued by Another Rainbow. The lithograph is numbered 69/100. The print has an overall size of 11" x 13.5". The Gold Plate Edition of this print has a gold trim border and a drawing by Barks stamped in gold in the lower left margin. Carl Barks signed and numbered the lithograph at the lower right, and the print is in Excellent condition. This scene was a recreation of the cover for **Four Color** #367, published with a cover date of January 1952. A numbered, full-color, spiral-bound reprint of the cover story, "A Christmas for Shacktown," and a numbered Certificate of Authenticity are also included in this lot.

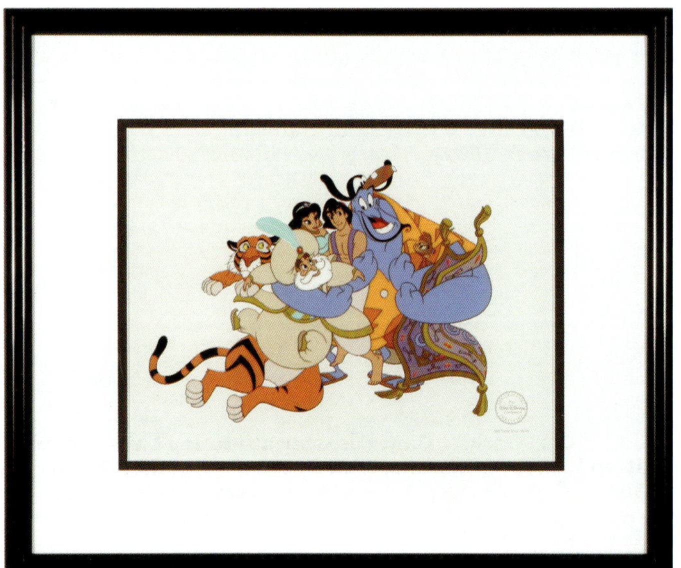

4467 Aladdin Limited Edition Sericel (The Walt Disney Company, 1993). This limited edition sericel depicts Rajah the tiger, the Sultan, Princess Jasmine, Aladdin, the Genie, Abu, and the magic carpet joining in for a group hug to celebrate Princess Jasmine's announcement that she has chosen Aladdin to become her husband. Disney artists, working from the original animation drawings used in the production of "Aladdin," have translated the original image to a hand-inked and hand-painted cel. That cel was used in the production of this screen-printed sericel. It is from a limited edition of 5,000, and includes a certificate of authenticity. With an image area measuring 13" x 10", this sericel is in Excellent condition.

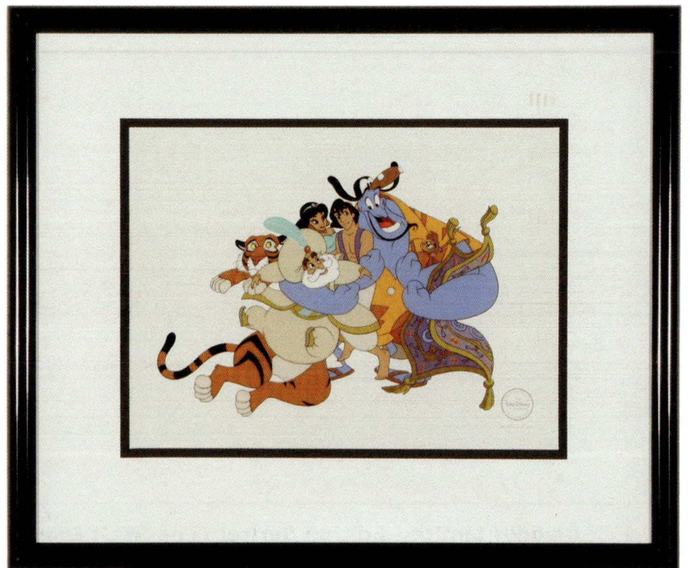

4468 Aladdin Cast Limited Edition Sericel (The Walt Disney Company, 1993). Princess Jasmine's announcement that she has chosen Aladdin to become her husband is a joyous occasion for all, in this limited edition sericel. Rajah the tiger, the Sultan, Aladdin, Princess Jasmine, the Genie, Abu, and the magic carpet join in for a group hug to celebrate. Working from the original animation drawings used in the production of "Aladdin," Disney artists have translated the original image to a hand-inked and hand-painted cel. That cel was used to produce of this fine art screen-printed sericel, which is limited to an edition of 5,000. With an image area measuring 13" x 10", this sericel is in Excellent condition. Includes a certificate of authenticity.

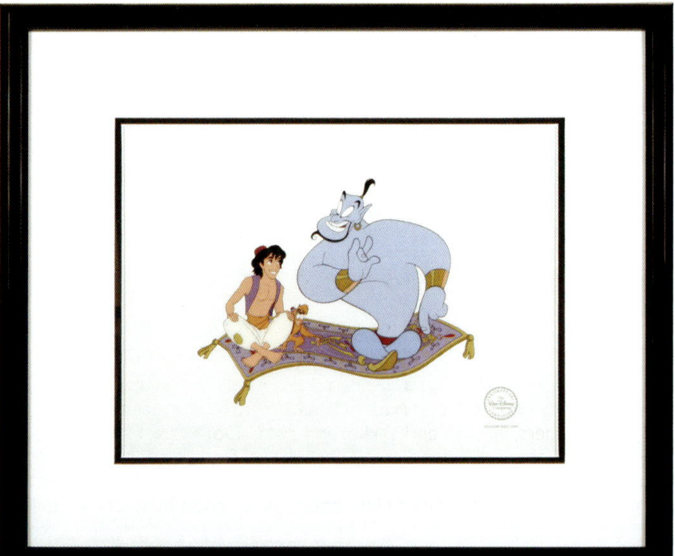

4469 Aladdin and Genie Limited Edition Sericel (The Walt Disney Company, 1992). This limited edition sericel depicts Aladdin, Abu, and the Genie from Walt Disney's animated feature "Aladdin". Walt Disney artists created this character image using the fine art screen-printing process of color reproduction known as serigraphy. Limited to an edition of 2,500, this sericel has an image area measuring 13" x 10", and the condition is Excellent. This lot also includes a certificate of authenticity.

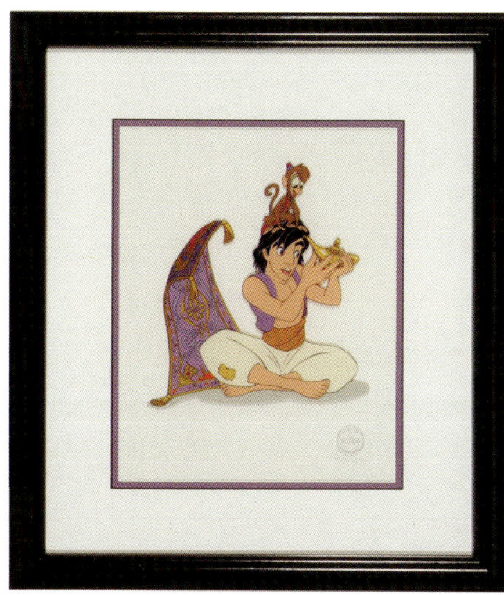

4470 Aladdin Limited Edition Sericel (The Walt Disney Company, 1992). This limited edition sericel, "No Ordinary Lamp," is from Sequence 11, Scene 7 of Walt Disney's 31st animated feature "Aladdin". Aladdin discovers that although he is trapped in the Cave of Wonders, Abu has managed to steal a lamp from Jafar. Little does he know the surprise that awaits him after he rubs the "worthless piece of junk"! Walt Disney artists created this character image using screen-printing process known as serigraphy. Limited to an edition of 5,000, this sericel has an image area measuring 10" x 13", and is in Excellent condition. This lot also includes a certificate of authenticity.

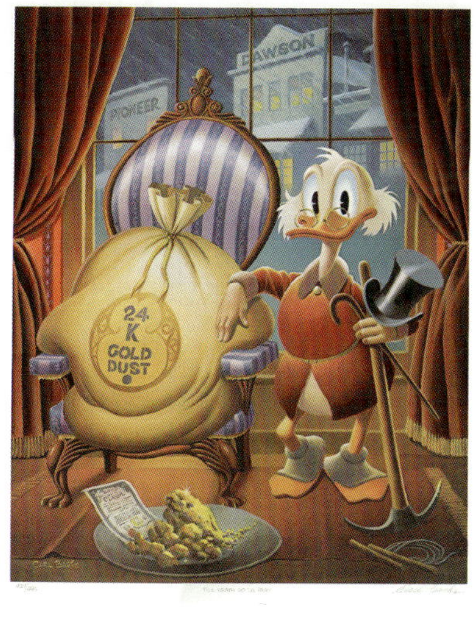

4472 Carl Barks - Till Death Do Us Part, Regular Edition Lithograph, numbered 427/495 (Another Rainbow, 1983). Based on a sketch done in 1961 for Michael J. Cronin of the Harvard Business School, the third lithograph from Another Rainbow featured Uncle Scrooge posing with a huge sack of 24 karat gold dust! The overall size of this lithograph is 20" x 24". The print is numbered 427/495, Carl Barks signed the print, in pencil, at the lower right, and the condition of the print is Excellent. Also included in the lot is the print's numbered Certificate of Authenticity.

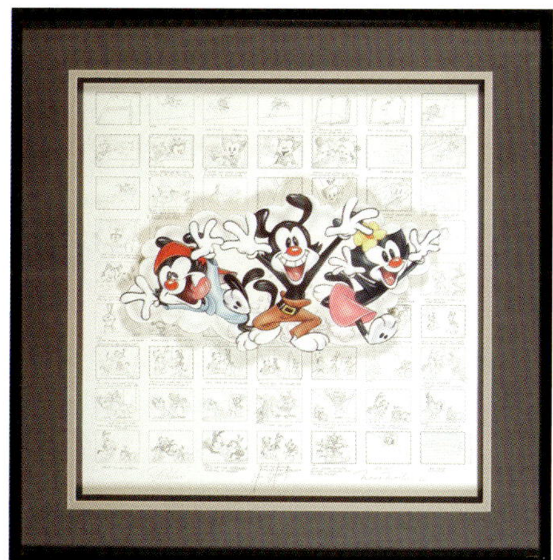

4471 Animaniacs Storyboard Limited Edition Lithograph Print #1189/2500 (Warner Bros., 1994). The central image of Warner Brothers, Wakko and Yakko, and sister, Dot were expertly die-cut and mounted above a lithographic print created from the final scene storyboard sequence used by Warner Bros. animators to create the episode, "I'm Cute!" Each of these storyboard lithographs was signed by voice artists Rob Paulson (Yakko), Jess Harnell (Wakko), and Tress McNeille (Dot). This print is number 1,189 out of an edition of 2,500. The image area measures 21" x 22", and the condition is Excellent. Includes a certificate of authenticity.

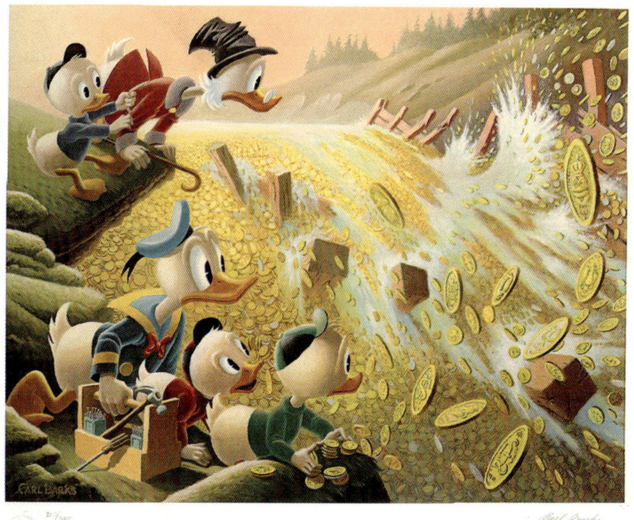

4473 Carl Barks - Dam Disaster at Money Lake, Regular Edition Lithograph, numbered 210/345 (Another Rainbow, 1986). This scene shows a battered-but-not-beaten Uncle Scrooge with Donald Duck, Huey, Dewey, and Louie as the Beagle Boys have succeeded in bursting the dam at Money Lake to wash Scrooge's life savings downstream and into the lowlands. The overall size of this lithograph measures 25" x 21.5". The lithograph is numbered 210/345. Carl Barks signed the lithograph at the lower right, and the condition of the print is in Excellent. Also included in this lot is a numbered Certificate of Authenticity and also a matching, numbered special edition reprinting of **Uncle Scrooge** #1.

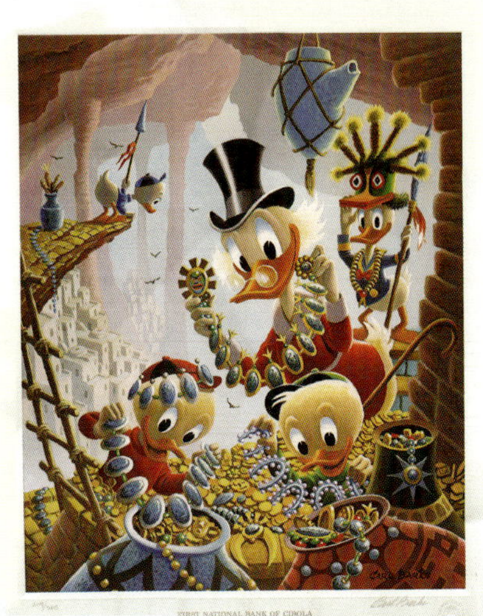

4474 Carl Barks - First National Bank of Cibola, Regular Edition Lithograph, numbered 209/345 (Another Rainbow, 1987). Somewhere in the parched deserts of the Southwest — among the canyons, mesa, arroyos and cacti, and not too far east of the Colorado River — Uncle Scrooge, with nephews Donald Duck, and siblings Huey, Dewey and Louie find the ancient Indian ruins of the fabled Seven Cities of Cibola. The overall size of this opulent lithograph is 21" x 25.5". The print is numbered 209/345, Carl Barks signed the print, in pencil, at the lower right, and the print is in Excellent condition. Also included in the lot is the matching, numbered Certificate of Authenticity.

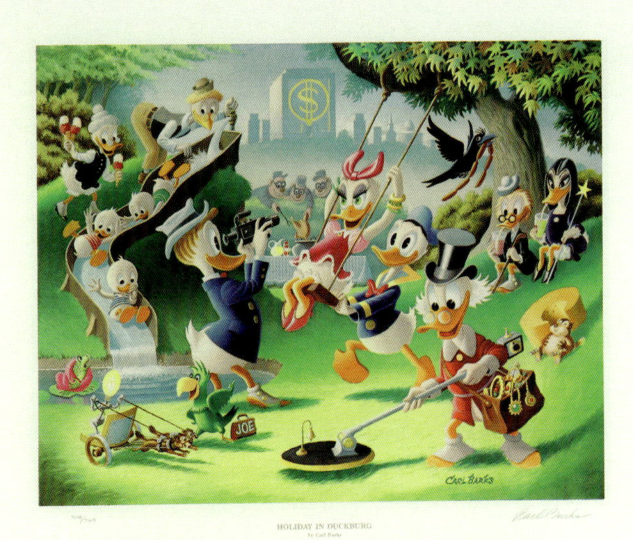

4475 Carl Barks - Holiday in Duckburg, Regular Edition Lithograph, numbered 304/345 (Another Rainbow, 1989). Twenty-one fowl townsfolk and other assorted characters frolic in Duckburg's city park. Uncle Scrooge, patriarch of the clan, appears center stage with Donald, Daisy, and Gladstone Gander. Lurking in the background are the notorious Beagle Boys and Magica De Spell. The image area of this lithograph is 20" x 15.5". The lithograph is numbered 304/345. Carl Barks signed the lithograph at the lower right, and the print is in Excellent condition. Included in this lot is the print's numbered Certificate of Authenticity.

4476 Carl Barks - An Astronomical Predicament, Regular Edition Lithograph, numbered 161/345 (Another Rainbow, 1990). The way-out sixties found Uncle Scrooge and Donald taking part in the space race. This image, based on the yarn "Island in the Sky" from **Uncle Scrooge** #29, shows Uncle Scrooge, Donald, Huey, Dewey, and Louie as they are confronted by the hungry inhabitants of a barren asteroid. The image area of this lithograph is 15.5" x 20". The lithograph is numbered 161/345. Carl Barks signed the lithograph at the lower right, and the condition of the print is in Excellent. Also included in this lot is a numbered Certificate of Authenticity and a small 5.5" x 7.5" booklet reprinting the original story in black and white.

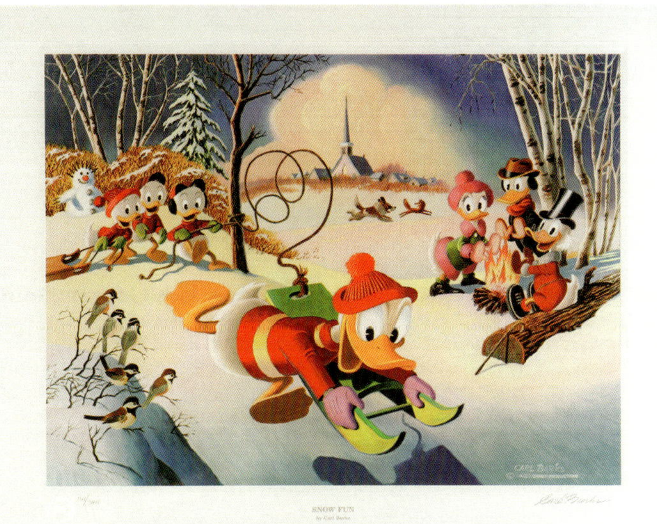

4477 Carl Barks - Snow Fun, Regular Edition Lithograph, numbered 161/345 (Another Rainbow, 1990). Carl Bark's **Snow Fun** was inspired by the cover to **Walt Disney's Comics and Stories** #89. The original scene, showcasing Donald Duck , Huey, Dewey, and Louie, has been expanded to include Uncle Scrooge, Gladstone Gander, and Daisy. Also, Bolivar the Saint Bernard is shown chasing a fox across a frozen pond in the background. The image area of this lithograph is 20" x 15.5". The lithograph is numbered 161/345. Carl Barks signed the print, in pencil, at the lower right, and the condition of the print is Excellent. Also included in the lot is the numbered Certificate of Authenticity for the print.

4478 Carl Barks - A Hot Defense 10th Anniversary Edition Lithographic Print #AR19/50 (Another Rainbow, 1990). "A Hot Defense" was the first in a series of miniature Carl Barks lithographs issued alternately with Another Rainbow's regular large series. It was been produced in eleven continuous-tone colors, picturing Donald Duck battling well-fortified nephews Huey, Dewey and Louie. The complete story, "The Duck in the Iron Pants," is told in an accompanying, like-numbered, full color 8.5" x 11" spiral-bound comic book story. The print measures 13" 11.5" and is in Excellent condition. The print is signed and numbered by Carl Barks. This print is from the special 10th Anniversary edition (limited to 50 prints) and includes a certificate of authenticity.

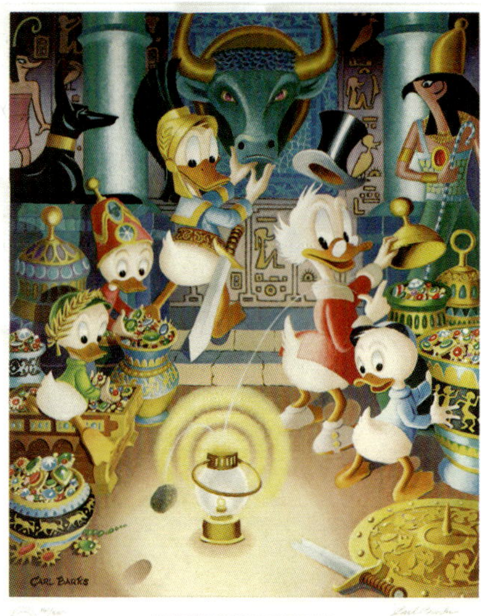

4479 Carl Barks - The Stone That Turns All Metals Gold, Regular Edition Lithograph, numbered 161/350 (Another Rainbow, 1991). As the certificate of authenticity for this superb lithograph notes, "Carl Barks' legendary 1955 comic book story, 'The Fabulous Philosopher's Stone' tells of the fantasticatillionare, Uncle Scrooge McDuck, who researches a myth in in ancient books of bygone pagan kings and an alchemist who fused four metals into a ball of mother-of-gold, thereby making a true Philosopher's Stone that — by touch — turns all metals into pure gold!" The overall size of the print is 21" x 25.5". The print is numbered 161/350, Carl Barks signed the print, in pencil, at the lower right, and the print is in Excellent condition. Also included in the lot is the numbered Certificate of Authenticity, and a copy of an **Uncle Scrooge** #253 comic book, which reprinted the original yarn.

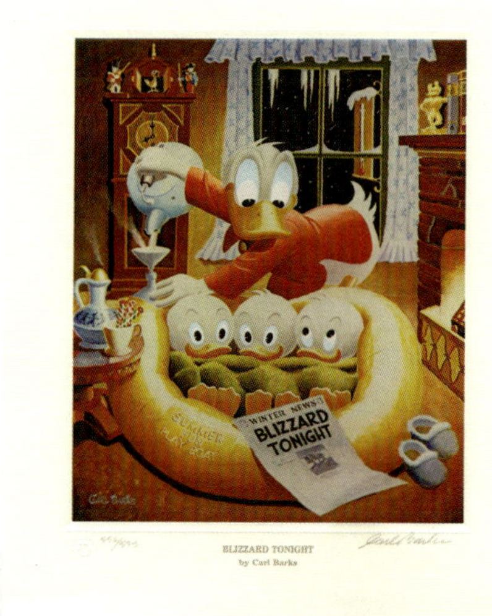

4480 Carl Barks - "Blizzard Tonight", Regular Edition Miniature Lithograph, numbered 552/595 (Another Rainbow, 1993). The weather outside leaves no doubt as to the newspaper's forecast accuracy that there is, indeed, a blizzard tonight. Thanks to Donald Duck's inspired use of a rubber "summer fun play boat" as a hot water bottle, Huey, Dewey, and Louie will remain comfy! This was the fifth miniature lithograph issued by Another Rainbow. The lithograph is numbered 552/595. The print has an overall size of 11" x 13.5". Carl Barks signed the lithograph at the lower right, and the print is in Excellent condition. Also included in this lot is a numbered Certificate of Authenticity.

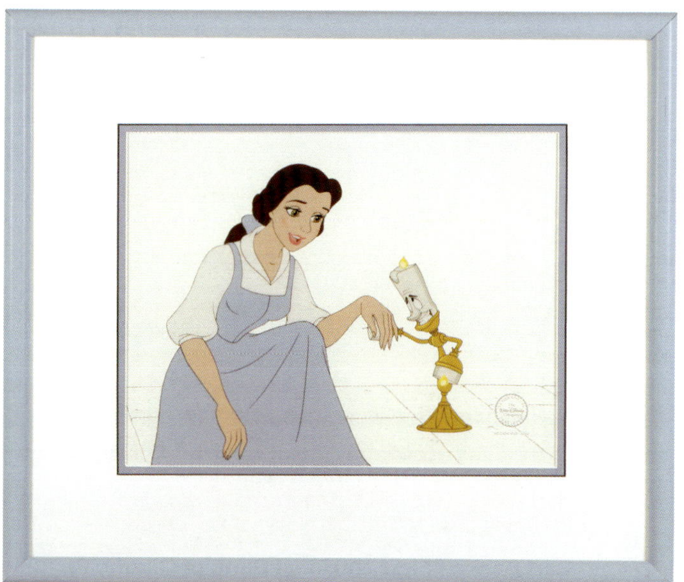

4481 Beauty and the Beast Limited Edition Sericel (The Walt Disney Company, 1993). "Ah... *enchanté*, cherie". This limited edition sericel is from Sequence 10, Scene 27 of "Beauty and the Beast," and features the always charming Lumiere suavely introducing himself to Belle. Disney artists recreated this scene from the classic film and hand-inked and hand-painted the art onto a master cel from which the serigrapher used to create this special sericel, from a limited edition of 5,000. With an image area measuring 13" x 10", this sericel is in Excellent condition, and includes a certificate of authenticity.

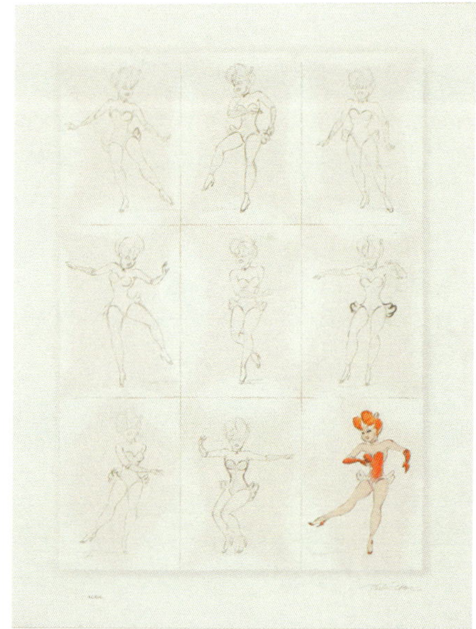

4482 Preston Blair - Nine Times the Heat Limited Edition Serigraph #42/500 (Warner Bros., 1995). The always alluring Red Hot was created by director Tex Avery in 1943 for the MGM short cartoon, "Red Hot Riding Hood". The wartime siren went on to star in several other MGM films, including "Uncle Tom's Cabana," and "Swingshift Cinderella". The design of Red Hot, however, is the unmistakable masterwork of classic animator Preston Blair. This edition is limited to 500 pieces, and was silk-screened with the Hanna-Barbera Seal of Authenticity, and Preston Blair's signature, onto an acid-free rag paper stock. This serigraph measures 27.5" x 36.5" and is in Excellent condition. Includes a certificate of authenticity.

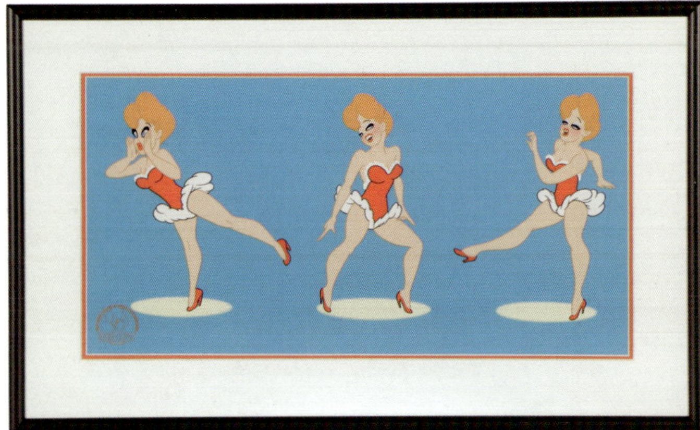

4483 "The Lady Known as Lou" Limited Edition Sericel #158/2500 (Hanna-Barbera, undated). This limited edition sericel, titled "The Lady Known as Lou," was produced using designer Preston Blair's original production art for the 1945 MGM cartoon, "The Shooting of Dan McGoo," which was directed by Tex Avery. This sericel was created from the original inking by Helene Hunter, and the Hanna-Barbera Animation Art, using the fine art process of serigraphy. With an image area measuring 19" x 9.5," the condition is Excellent. Also includes a certificate of authenticity.

4484 "Special Delivery from Mars" Limited Edition Sericel #2120/5000 (Warner Bros., 1994). Marvin the Martian and K-9 get a special delivery by similarly dressed non-Martian, Bugs Bunny, in number 2120 of a limited edition of 5,000 sericels. Created by Warner Bros. Animation, the image was hand-inked onto a master cel from which the serigrapher then creates silkscreened lines for this special edition. Hand cut screens are created for each of the vibrant colors. This sericel has an image area measuring 14" x 10". The condition is Excellent, and this lot also includes a certificate of authenticity.

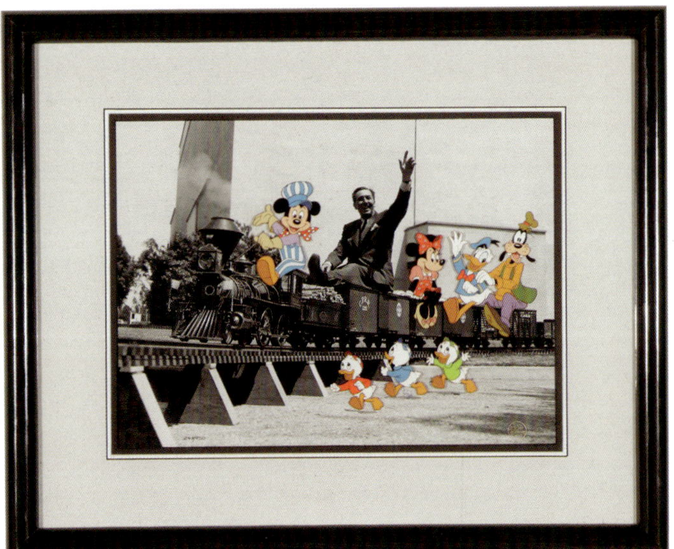

4485 Walt's Train Hand-Painted Character Cel Set-up #248/950 (The Walt Disney Company, 1993). This is number 248 in a limited edition of 950 hand-painted character cels combined with a photograph taken in 1951 of Walt Disney on his newly-built miniature railroad at the Disney Studio in Burbank, California. This cel set-up, "Walt's Train," features Walt Disney along with Mickey Mouse who assumes the role of the engineer as Minnie, Donald and Goofy join the both of them in an afternoon train ride. Original animation drawings were transferred to acetate cels by a special six-step xerographic process, which were then hand-painted. The photographic background was produced using the original black and white negative, which has been conserved at the Disney Photo Library. With an image area measuring 15.5" x 11.5", this cel set-up is in Excellent condition, and includes a certificate of authenticity.

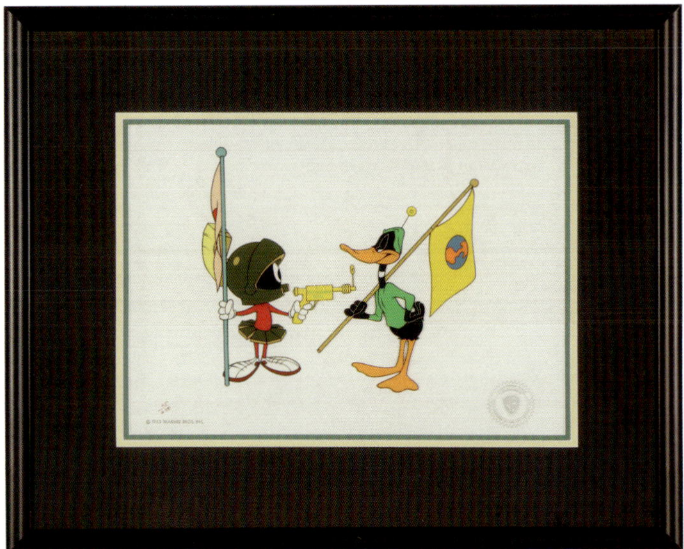

4486 Duck Dodgers in the 24 1/2 Century Limited Edition Sericel #25/250 (Warner Bros., 1991). This limited edition sericel captures the initial confrontation between the mockingly confident Duck Dodgers and his adversary, Marvin the Martian for the right to colonize Planet X. The talented artists of Warner Bros. Animators have recreated this image directly from the classic film through the fine art of serigraphy. This is number 25 out of an edition of 250. This sericel has an image area measuring 14" x 10", and the condition is Excellent. This lot also includes a certificate of authenticity.

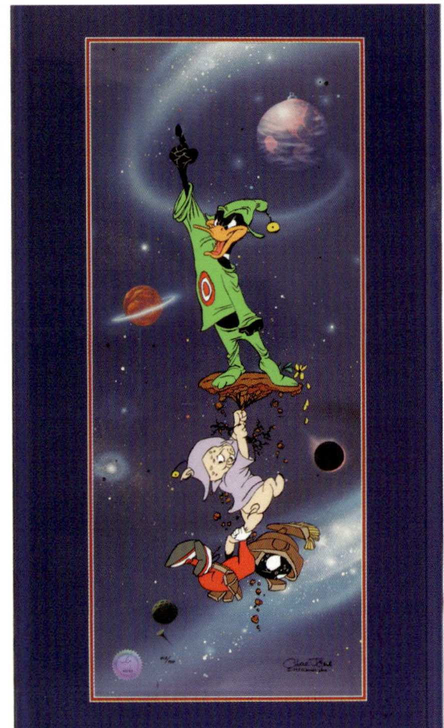

4487 Duck Dodgers in the 24 1/2 Century Limited Edition Sericel #412/750 (Warner Bros., 1993). In this finale to Chuck Jones' 1953 cartoon short, the planet that Duck Dodgers and Marvin the Martian are fighting over has been destroyed, and the remaining area claimed by Dodgers at the end is barely more than a pebble in size. The dismissive attitude to Dodger's pyrrhic victory is epitomized by Porky's cynical response to his boss' overblown proclamation, "B-B-Big deal." This limited edition sericel is number 412 out of 750. Warner Bros. Animation artists have recreated this image directly from the classic film through the fine art of serigraphy. This sericel has an image area measuring 13" x 32", and the condition is Excellent.

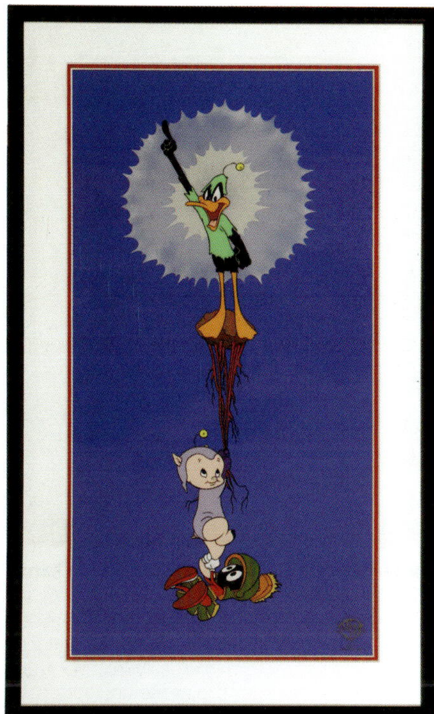

4488 Duck Dodgers in the 24 1/2 Century Limited Edition Sericel (Warner Bros., 1996). "This planet ain't big enough for the two of us!" This limited edition sericel captures the defiant Duck Dodgers, his eager young space cadet, Porky Pig, and Marvin the Martian in the final moment of this classic cartoon. Warner Bros. Animation artists have recreated this image directly from the classic film through the fine art of serigraphy. This sericel has an image area measuring 10" x 19.25", and the condition is Excellent. This lot also includes a certificate of authenticity.

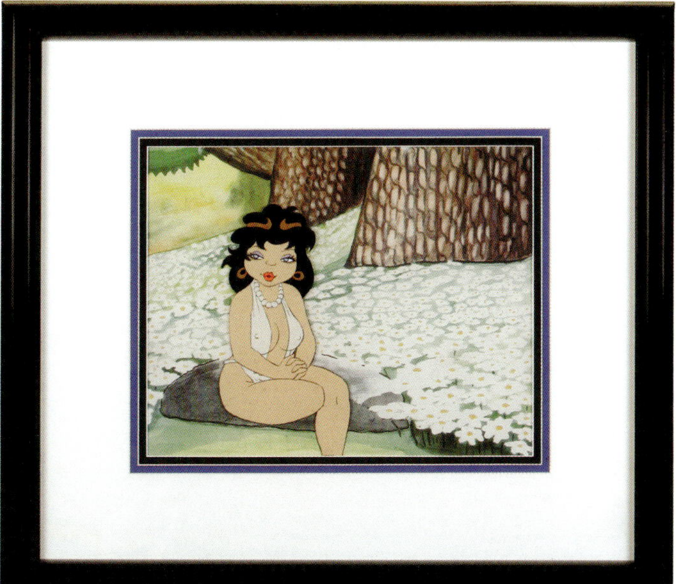

4489 Wizards Production Cel (Bakshi Productions, 1977). This is an original hand-painted animation cel from producer/director Ralph Bakshi's 1977 feature film, "Wizards," featuring Princess Elinore. This cel sits against a photograph of the original production background. The art has an image area of 11.5" x 9" and is in Excellent condition.

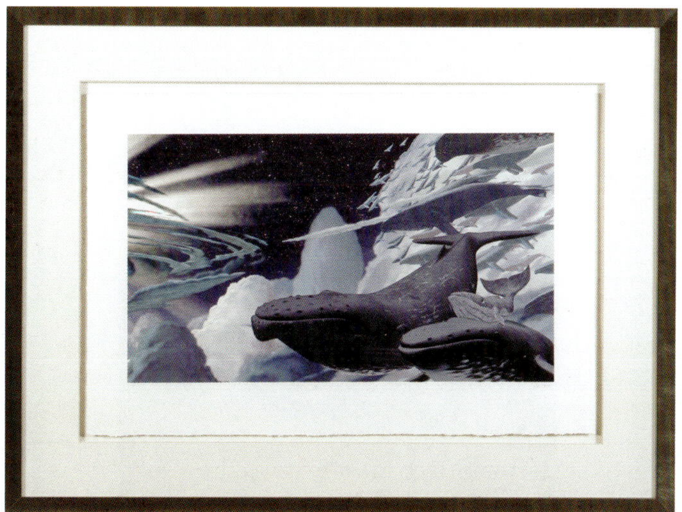

4490 Fantasia/2000 Limited Edition Giclee Print #200/300 (Disney Enterprises, 2000). This limited edition Giclee print depicts a scene from the Disney animated featured, "Fantasia/2000". This edition, "Taking Flight," recreates Sequence 10, Scenes 5 and 65 in which a pod of whales rise and soar as if lifted by currents of song, embodying the spirit of wonder in a place where the sea meets the sky. This computer-based digital file was printed using the Giclee process on premium-quality, acid-free paper with an enhanced printer, specially modified for fine art reproduction. This print is #200 from a limited edition of 500, and includes a certificate of authenticity. With an image area measuring 19" x 11", it is in Excellent condition.

4491 Garfield "Playful" Limited Edition Sericel (Jim Davis, 1993). This limited edition of Jim Davis' curmudgeonly cat, Garfield, was produced in 1993, and is comprised of 9,500 serigraph cels. Jim Davis and his studio artist colleagues created this art using the fine art process of serigraphy. With an image area measuring 14" x 10," the condition is Excellent. Also includes a certificate of authenticity.

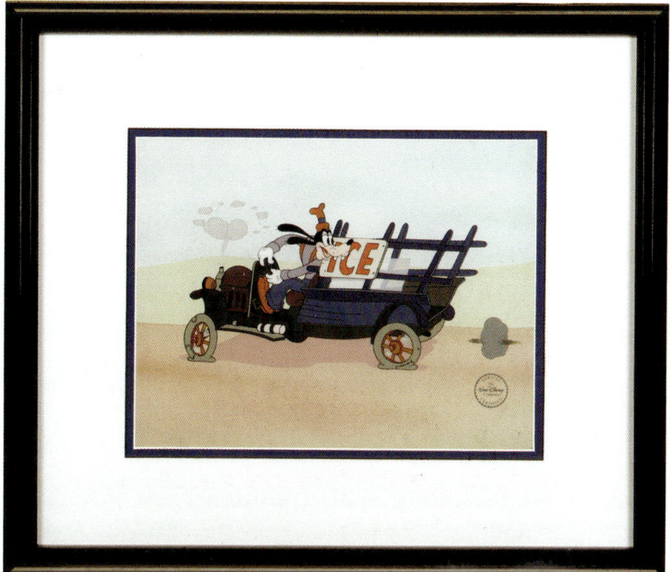

4492 Moving Day "Goofy Delivery" Limited Edition Sericel (The Walt Disney Company, 1997). This limited edition sericel recreates Scene 18 from the film, "Moving Day" (1936), as ever loyal Goofy is ready to help his pals Mickey Mouse and Donald Duck haul their belongings on moving day. Walt Disney artists worked from the original animation drawings used for the production, translating these images to a hand-inked and hand-painted cel, which was used in the production of this sericel. Limited to an edition of 1,500, this sericel has an image area measuring 11.5" x 9". The condition is Excellent, and this lot also includes a certificate of authenticity.

4493 Jessica Rabbit Poster (Disney, undated). Roger Rabbit's impossibly buxom wife is the Toontown star of this grand poster, which has an image area of 19" x 19". Sultry Jessica Rabbit's voluptuousness makes this show-stopping poster a must-have! Beautifully framed, and in Excellent condition.

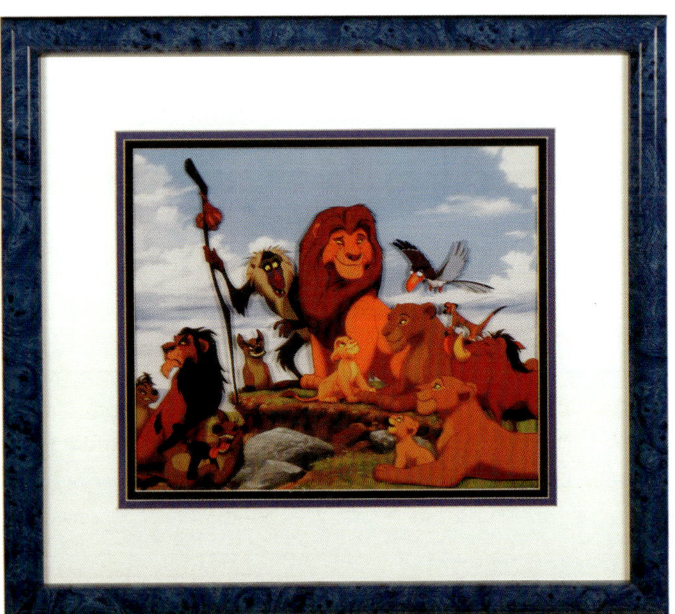

4494 The Lion King Commemorative Sericel (The Walt Disney Company, undated). This limited edition sericel depicts the opening sequence from the Disney animated feature, "The Lion King". This computer-based digital file was printed onto acetate with an enhanced printer, specially modified for fine art reproduction. With an image area measuring 12" x 10.5", it is in Excellent condition. Includes a certificate of authenticity.

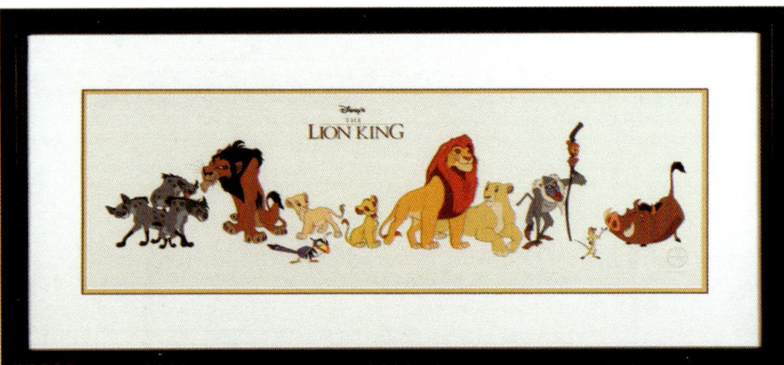

4495 The Lion King Sericel (The Walt Disney Company, 1994). This limited edition sericel depicts characters from Disney's 32nd animated feature, "The Lion King". Disney artists created this "Cast of Characters" from original pre-production and production art used by animators during the making of "The Lion King," translating these images to a hand-inked and hand-painted cel, which was used in the production of this sericel. The image area measures 30.5" x 9.5", and the sericel is in Excellent condition. Includes a certificate of authenticity.

4496 The Lion King Special Edition Print (The Walt Disney Company, 1995). Timon and Pumbaa attend to their future king, Simba, in this special edition print, which depicts characters from Disney's animated feature, "The Lion King". In stunning color, the image area measures 7" x 8.5", and, aside from some slight buckling to the paper, the condition is Excellent.

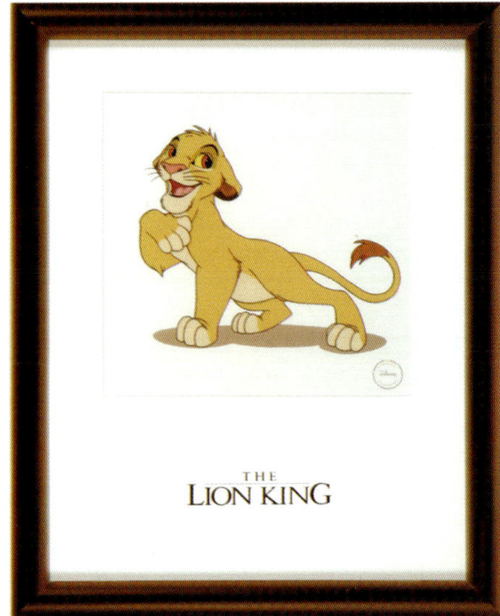

4497 Simba Sericel (The Walt Disney Company, 1994). This sericel depicts Simba, the lead lion from Disney's 32nd animated feature, "The Lion King". Disney artists created this sericel from original production art used by animators during the making of "The Lion King," through the fine art process of serigraphy. The image area measures 7" x 7", and the sericel is in Excellent condition.

4498 The Lion King Limited Edition Sericel (The Walt Disney Company, 1994). Simba and Nala frolic in the Pride Lands, as Simba muses about his future as the King. This limited edition sericel, titled "Simba and Nala," is from Sequence 5, Scene 1 of Walt Disney's "The Lion King". Disney artists created this image using the original animation drawings used for the production of "The Lion King," translating these images to a hand-inked and hand-painted cel, which was used in the production of this sericel. The image area measures 13" x 10", and the sericel is in Excellent condition. Includes a certificate of authenticity.

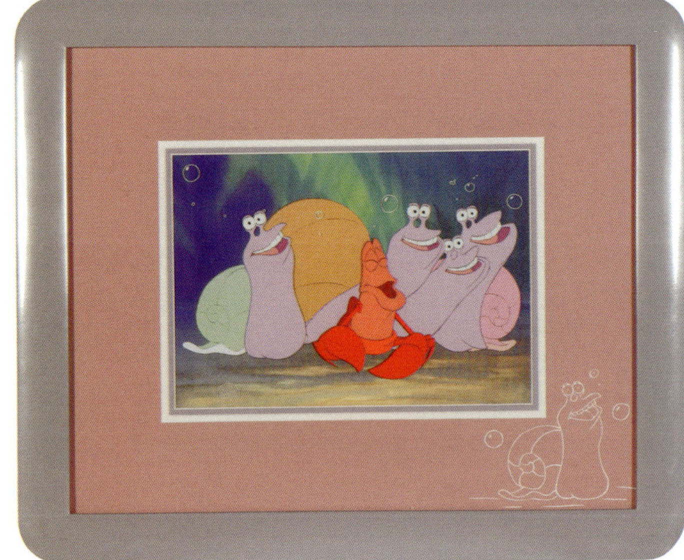

4499 The Little Mermaid "Sebastian" Sericel (The Walt Disney Company, undated). This limited edition sericel depicts Sebastian singing the Academy Award nominated song, "Kiss the Girl," from Disney's animated feature, "The Little Mermaid". Disney artists used animation production art, translating this image using the fine art of serigraphy. The image area measures 10.5" x 7.5", and this sericel comes complete with a hand-carved customized mat, featuring one of the singing snails, both are in Excellent condition.

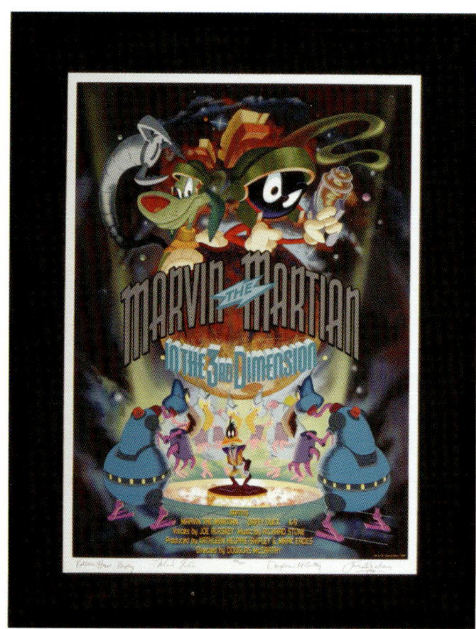

4500 Marvin the Martian in the 3rd Dimension Limited Edition Serigraph Print #242/500 (Warner Bros., 1996). This is a limited edition fine art serigraph print based on the 1996 Warner Bros. 3-D animated cartoon, "Marvin the Martian in the 3rd Dimension". Hilarity and havoc ensue as Marvin the Martian, his faithful lieutenant, K-9, and Daffy Duck engage in a game of mistaken identities. This print is beautifully reproduced on archival paper using 95 colors and personally hand signed by producers Kathleen Helppie-Shipley, and Mark Eades; director Doug McCarthy, and voice talent, Joe Alaskey. The image area measures 18.5" x 26" and the print is in Excellent condition. Includes a certificate of authenticity.

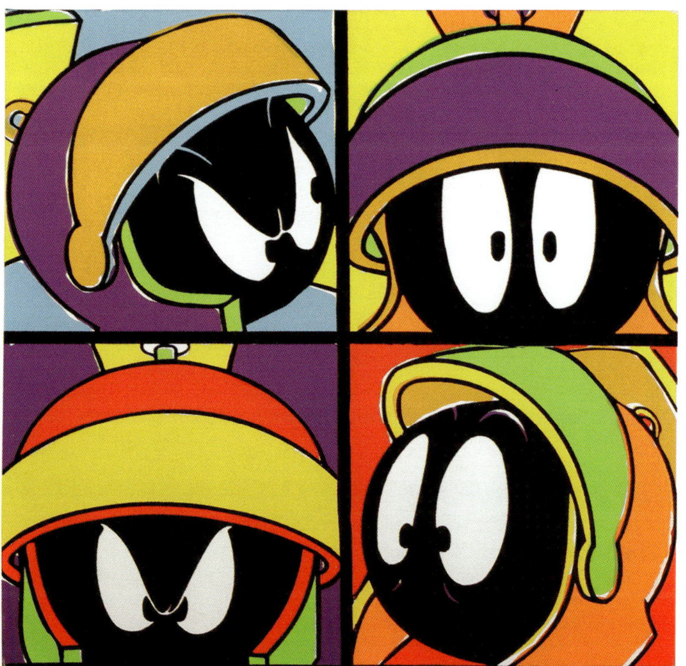

4501 Steve Kaufman - Marvin the Martian "Attitudes" Print on Canvas #55/100 (Warner Bros., undated). World renowned Pop Art artist Steve Kaufman was commissioned by the Warner Brothers Studio Store chain to do a series of iconic silkscreens of the famous Warner Brothers characters. This work features Marvin the Martian, and is titled "Attitudes". Measuring 32.5" x 32", this colorful item is screenprinted with oils and acrylics on canvas, and has a clean, modern art look. This print is number 55 out of 100, and is in Excellent condition. Signed by Steve Kaufman on the inside of the canvas. Includes a certificate of authenticity.

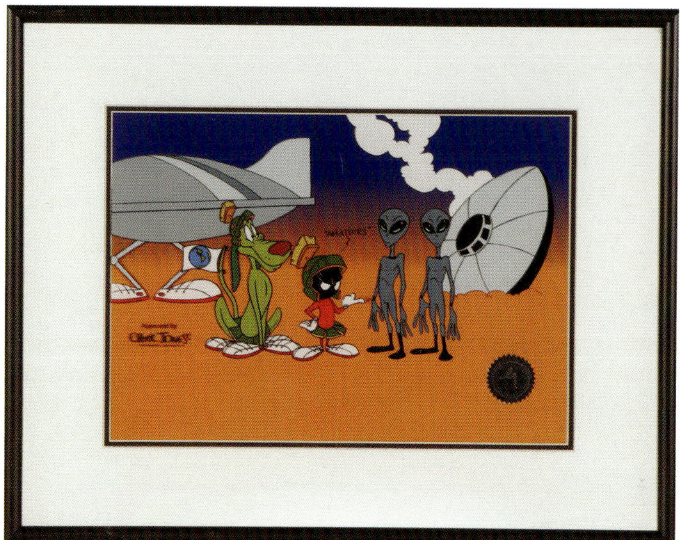

4502 "Amateurs" Limited Edition Sericel (Linda Jones Enterprises, 1997). To help commemorate the 50th anniversary of the Roswell Incident, Linda Jones Enterprises presents to this limited edition sericel. Marvin the Martian, and his companion, K-9 meet the occupants of the "flying disk" which crash landed near Roswell, New Mexico in July, 1947, in this sericel titled "Amateurs". Limited to an edition of 5,000, this sericel has an image area measuring 14" x 10". The condition is Excellent, and this lot also includes a certificate of authenticity.

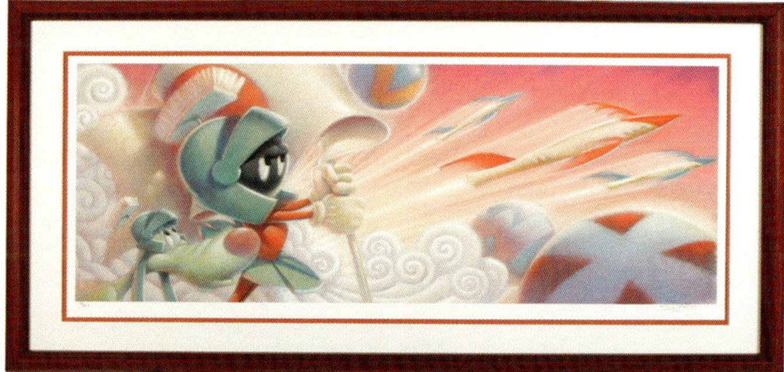

4503 Le Sortie Dans La Blue De Ciel Limited Edition Print #25/350 (Warner Bros., 1999). Artist Scott Seeto brings his distinctive pastel rendering style to this limited edition print, capturing a rare moment of Martian grandeur as Marvin the Martian, and his faithful lieutenant K-9, serve as standard bearers at the launching of a new fleet of Martian space ships. This print, reproduced in the Giclee process on archival paper stock, is number 25 in an edition of 350. The image area measures 37" x 15" and is signed by the artist. This lot also includes a certificate of authenticity.

4504 Marvin the Martian and Bugs Bunny Print (Warner Bros., undated). That persistent ambassador from the Planet Mars, Marvin the Martian, holds his weapon on that "naughty earth specimen," Bugs Bunny in this print illustrated by Chuck Jones. This image has an image area of 9" x 7", and is in Excellent condition.

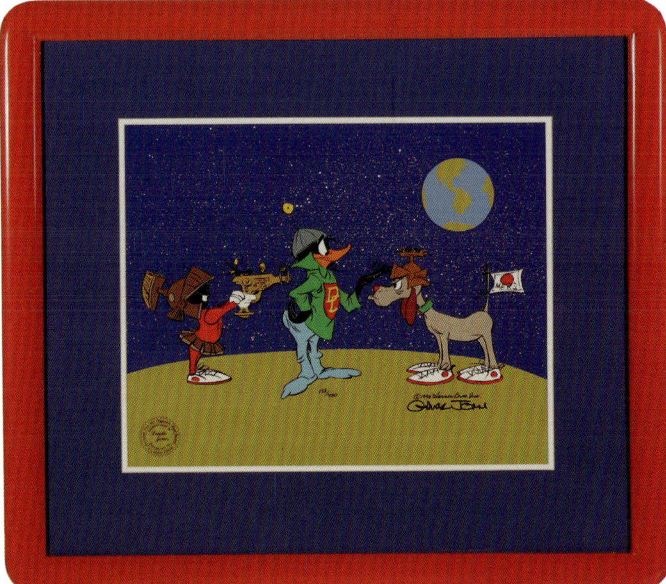

4505 Marvin the Martian, Duck Dodgers, and K-9 Limited Edition Sericel #158/750 (Linda Jones Enterprises). While Duck Dodgers takes time to bond with K-9, Marvin the Martian moves in with his weapon ready, in this limited edition sericel. Linda Jones Enterprises has become a leader in the publication and distribution of animation art throughout the world. This sericel has an image area measuring 15.5" x 13", and its condition is Excellent.

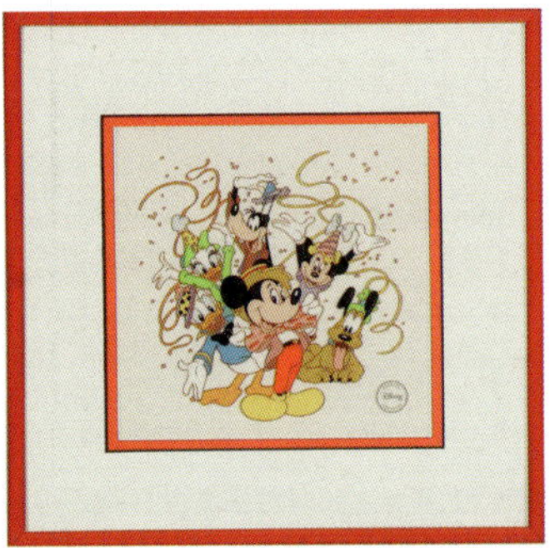

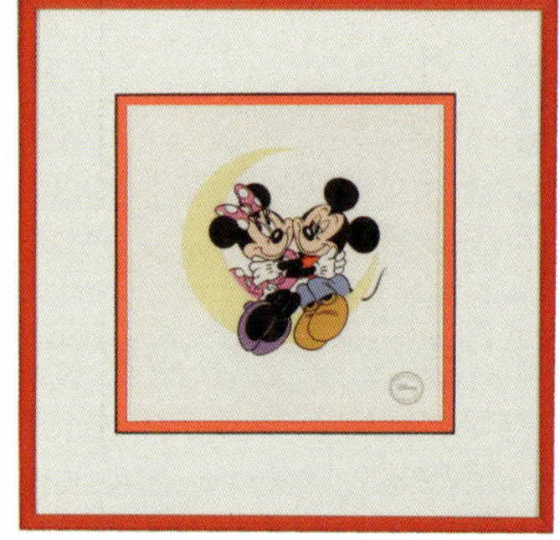

4506 "Moonlight Romance," and "Party Time" Limited Edition Sericel (The Walt Disney Company, 1994-95). "Moonlight Romance" features Mickey and Minnie embracing in the romantic light of a crescent moon, and "Party Time" features Mickey, Minnie, Goofy, and Pluto jovially celebrating a festive occasion with streamers and confetti. Limited to an edition of 7,500 each, these sericels have an image area measuring 6.5" x 6.5". Both are in Excellent condition, and each includes a certificate of authenticity.

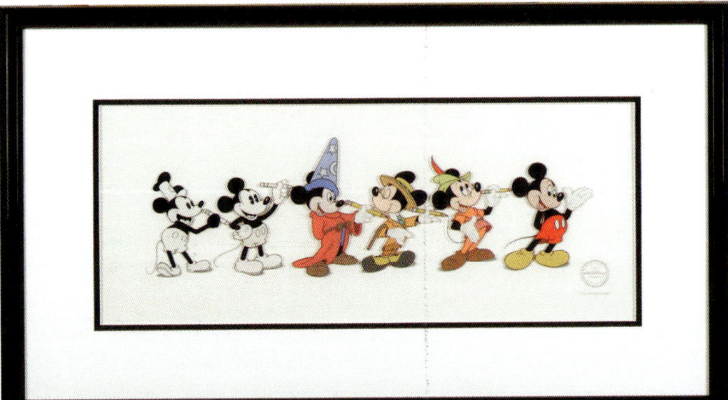

4507 Mickey Through the Years Limited Edition Sericel (The Walt Disney Company, 1993). Walt Disney artists, in celebration of Mickey Mouse's 65th birthday, created this commemorative sericel, "Mickey Through the Years," in 1993. These artists, working from specially created drawings, have translated original images to a hand-inked and hand-painted cel. The cel was used in the production of this set of sericels. Limited to an edition of 5,000, this sericel has an image area measuring 20" x 8". The condition is Excellent, and this lot also includes a certificate of authenticity.

4508 Mickey and Pluto Sericel (The Walt Disney Company, undated). This delightful sericel is a real piece of Disney animation history and features both Mickey and Pluto, two of Disney's best loved characters! The image area measures 13" x 10" and the art is in Excellent condition.

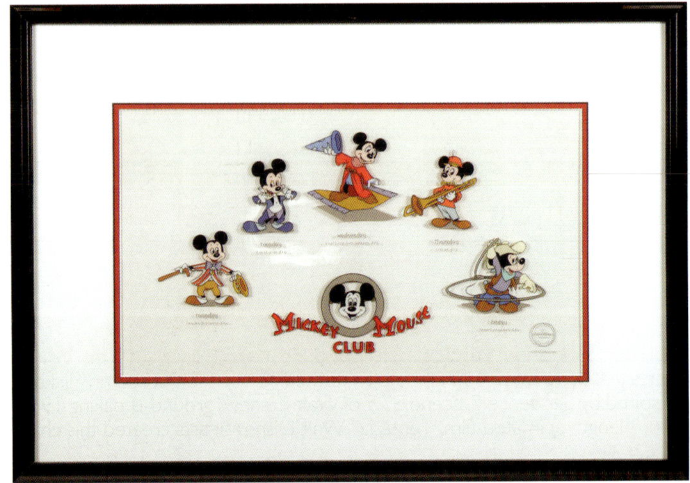

4509 Mickey Mouse Club Limited Edition Sericel (The Walt Disney Company, 1995). This sericel, titled "Hi, Mouseketeers!," recreates five character images from the introduction segments of "The Mickey Mouse Club" television series. Mickey wore a different costume each day to reflect the show's subject, Monday was "Fun with Music Day," Tuesday was "Guest Star Day," Wednesday was "Anything Can Happen Day," Thursday was "Circus Day," and Friday ended with "Talent Round-Up Day". Walt Disney artists, working from the original animation drawings used for the production of "The Mickey Mouse Club," translated these images to a hand-inked and hand-painted cel. That cel was used in the production of this set of sericels. Limited to an edition of 5,000, this sericel has an image area measuring 19" x 11", and is in Excellent condition. This lot also includes a certificate of authenticity.

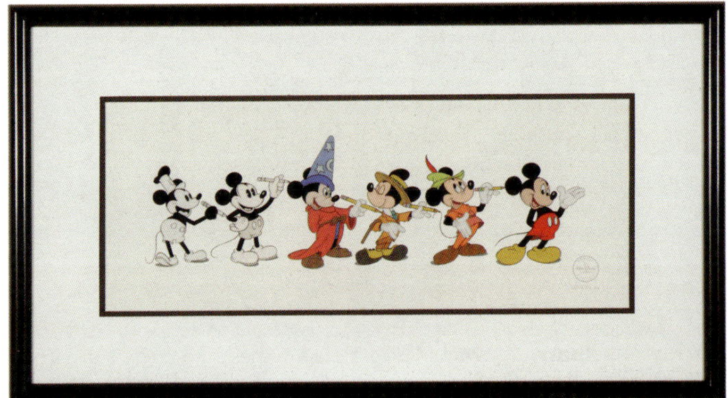

4510 Mickey Through the Years Limited Edition Sericel (The Walt Disney Company, 1993). This beautiful commemorative sericel, "Mickey Through the Years," was created by Walt Disney artists in celebration of Mickey Mouse's 65th birthday. Working from specially created drawings, this limited edition sericel was created using the fine art screen-printing process of serigraphy. Limited to an edition of 5,000, this sericel has an image area measuring 20" x 8". The condition is Excellent, and this lot also includes a certificate of authenticity.

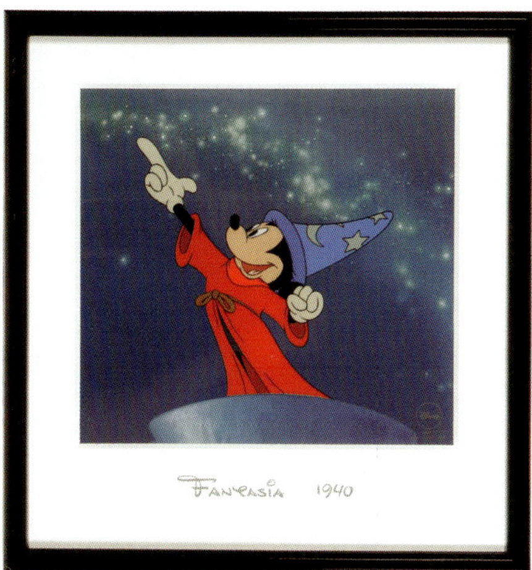

4511 Sorcerer Mickey Limited Edition Sericel (The Walt Disney Company, 1998). This limited edition sericel, "Sorcerer Mickey," is inspired by Sequence 7, Scene 37.5 of Walt Disney's ground-breaking 1940 feature-length animated film, "Fantasia". Walt Disney artists created this character image using the fine art of serigraphy. Limited to an edition of 5,000, this sericel has an image area measuring 10" x 11", and is in Excellent condition. This lot also includes a certificate of authenticity.

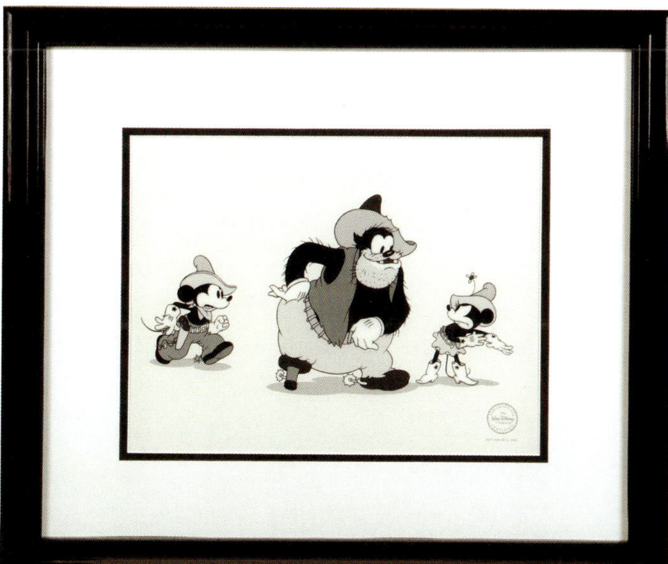

4512 Two Gun Mickey Limited Edition Sericel (The Walt Disney Company, 1994). Mickey Mouse rushes in to save Minnie from Peg Leg Pete, in this limited edition sericel. This sericel, titled "To the Rescue," is from Scene 11 of the Disney short, "Two Gun Mickey". Disney artists, working from the original animation drawings, have translated this scene using the fine-art screen-printing process of color separation known as serigraphy. Limited to an edition of 5,000, this sericel has an image area measuring 13" x 10", and is in Excellent condition. This lot also includes a certificate of authenticity.

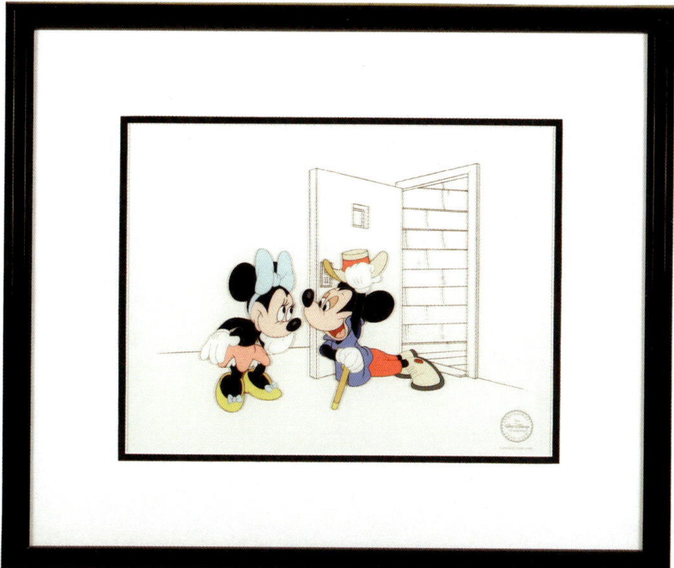

4513 Mickey's Birthday Party Limited Edition Sericel (The Walt Disney Company, 1993). This limited edition sericel depicts a scene from Walt Disney's animated short, "Mickey's Birthday Party," which was originally released in 1942. From Scene 5, Minnie's beauty captures Mickey's heart as he dreamily asks: "How about a little kiss?" Walt Disney artists created this sericel using the screen-printing process of color reproduction known as serigraphy. Limited to an edition of 5,500, this sericel has an image area measuring 13" x 10", and is in Excellent condition. This lot also includes a certificate of authenticity.

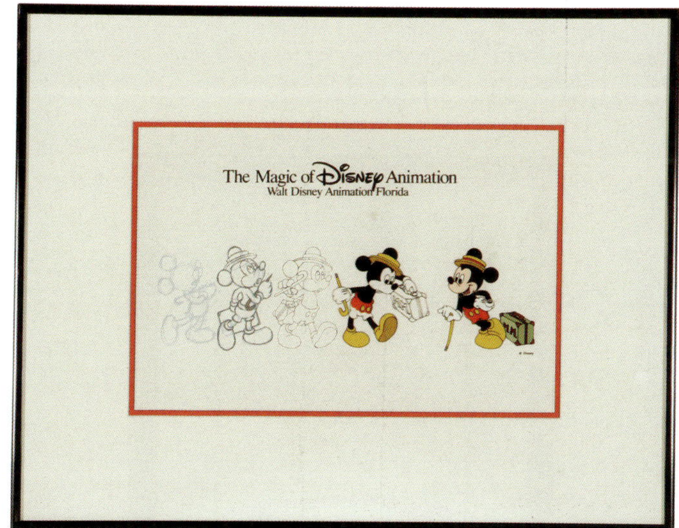

4514 The Magic of Disney Animation Sericel (The Walt Disney Company, undated). This progressive Mickey Mouse cel shows the basic steps to bringing an animated character to life on the screen. These five poses were taken from the short film, "Mr. Mouse Takes a Trip" (1940), and this same art is displayed in the animation production area of The Walt Disney Animation Florida Studio, where the original cel was created. Animators have created this image through the fine art of serigraphy. With an image area measuring 11.5" x 7.5", this cel is in Excellent condition.

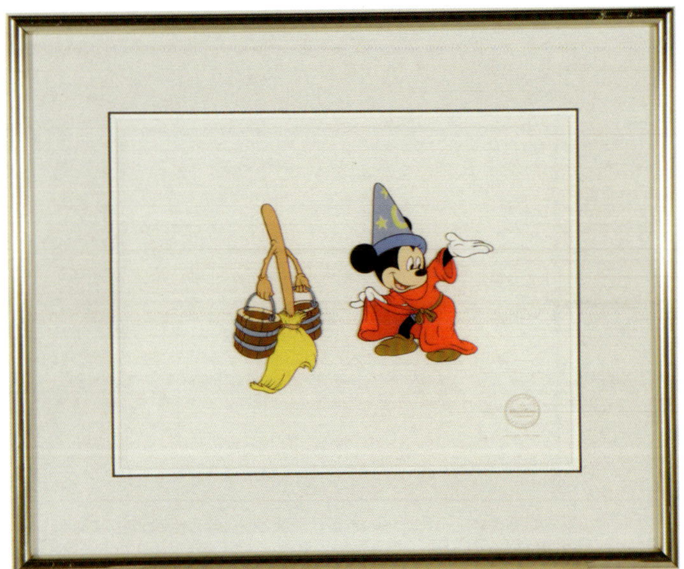

4515 The Sorcerer's Apprentice Limited Edition Sericel (The Walt Disney Company, 1990). This limited edition sericel, from "The Sorcerer's Apprentice" sequence of "Fantasia," was recreated by Disney artists, working from the original animation drawings. These craftsmen translated the original image to a hand-inked and hand-painted cel, which was used in the production of this screen-printed sericel. It is from a limited edition of 2,500, and includes a certificate of authenticity. With an image area measuring 13" x 10", this sericel is in Excellent condition.

4516 The Cat's Bah Lobby Card (Warner Bros., 1954). Pepe le Pew was an imitation of Charles Boyer in "Algiers," a 1938 remake of "Pepe Le Moko". Director Chuck Jones, and writer Michael Maltese not only satirize "Algiers," but "Casablanca," as well, in the short, "The Cat's Bah". Chuck Jones said Pepe was "what I wanted to be and what I think every man would like to be: irresistible, at least in one's own eyes." With an image area measuring 9" x 7.5", this lobby card is in Excellent condition.

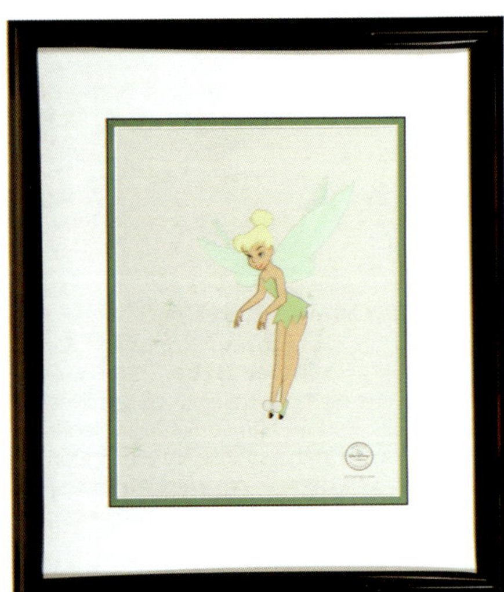

4517 Peter Pan "Playful Pixie" Limited Edition Sericel (The Walt Disney Company, 1996). This limited edition sericel recreates Sequence 11, Scene 48 from Walt Disney's "Peter Pan". Titled "Playful Pixie," this scene features Tinker Bell, who is angry with her friend, Peter Pan, and offers to lead the villainous Captain Hook to the hiding place of Wendy Darling. Walt Disney artists created this character image using the fine art screen-printing process of color reproduction known as serigraphy. Limited to an edition of 5,000, this sericel has an image area measuring 10" x 13", and the condition is Excellent. This lot also includes a certificate of authenticity.

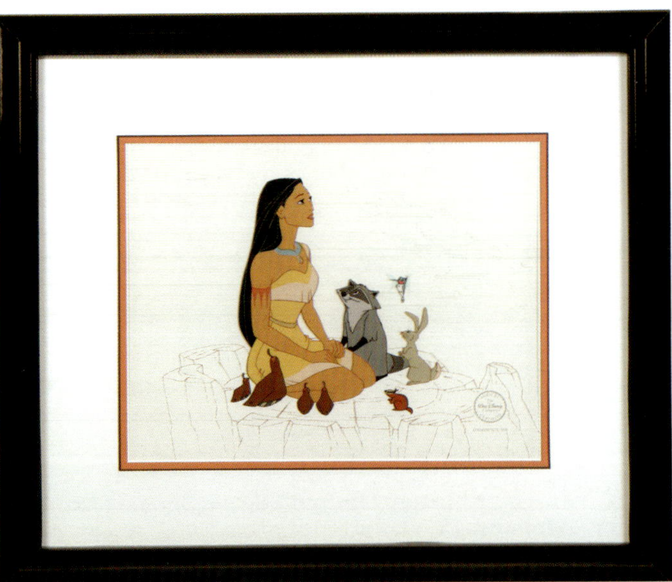

4518 Pocahontas Limited Edition Sericel (The Walt Disney Company, 1992). This limited edition sericel, "Woodland Friends," recreates Sequence 5.5, Scene 37.5 of Walt Disney's 33rd feature-length animated film, "Pocahontas". Pocahontas' woodland friends look on as she asks the wise Grandmother what her path in life is and how she will find it. Walt Disney artists created this character image using the fine art screen-printing process known as serigraphy. Limited to an edition of 5,000, this sericel has an image area measuring 13" x 10", and is in Excellent condition. This lot also includes a certificate of authenticity.

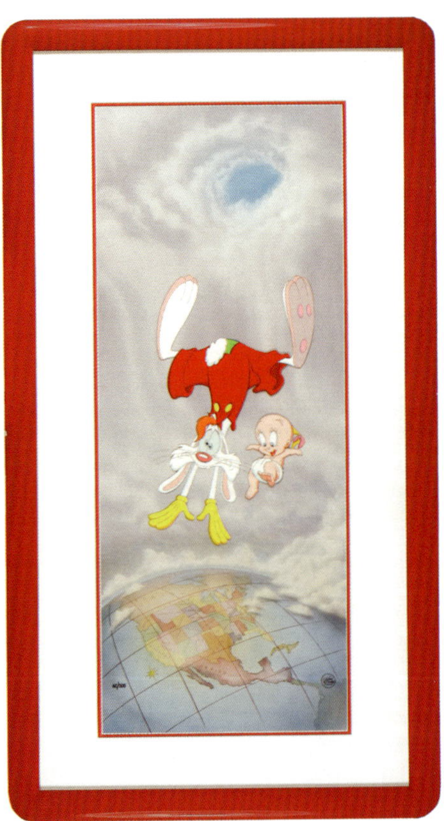

4519 Tummy Trouble Limited Edition Hand-Painted Cel (Disney, 1989). Roger Rabbit and Baby Herman find themselves close to the stratosphere in this incredible, hand-painted limited edition vertical pan cel from "Tummy Trouble". The first of three Roger Rabbit theatrical cartoons, this short was originally shown together with "Honey, I Shrunk the Kids!" This cel set-up includes a hand-painted cel, and a photographic reproduction of the original background. This art measures 11.5" x 30," and is in Excellent condition.

4520 Who Framed Roger Rabbit Limited Edition Sericel (The Walt Disney Company, 1994). This limited edition sericel, "My Honey Bunny," is from Sequence 235, Scene 20 of Touchstone/Amblin Entertainment's feature "Who Framed Roger Rabbit" (1988). Jessica and Roger, who have just been saved from the "dip," happily embrace. Walt Disney artists created this character image using the fine art screen-printing process known as serigraphy. Limited to an edition of 5,000, this sericel has an image area measuring 13" x 10", and is in Excellent condition. This lot also includes a certificate of authenticity.

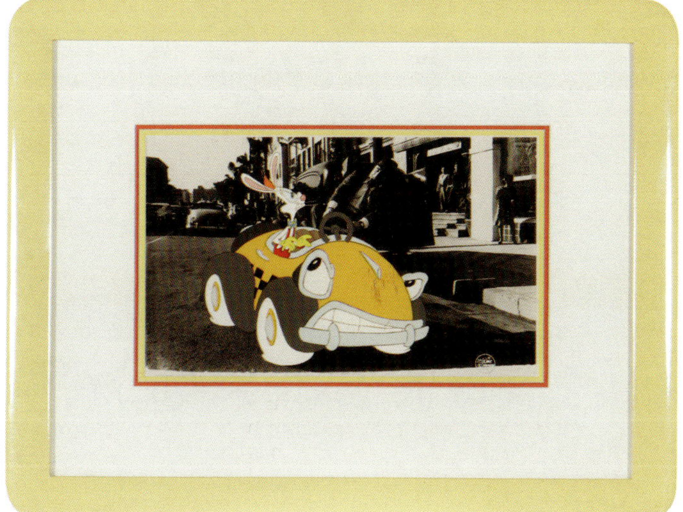

4521 Who Framed Roger Rabbit Serigraph (The Walt Disney Company, undated). This sericel is based on a scene taken from the technically-marvelous landmark film, "Who Framed Roger Rabbit" (1988), which blended animated, ink-and-paint cartoon characters with flesh-and-blood live actors. In this scene hapless, no-nonsense private eye, Eddie Valiant, hops into Benny the Cab, where Roger waits. The sericel is placed on top of a photo image of Eddie Valiant (Bob Hoskins), which was taken from the film. The image area measures 13" x 8" and the art is in Excellent condition.

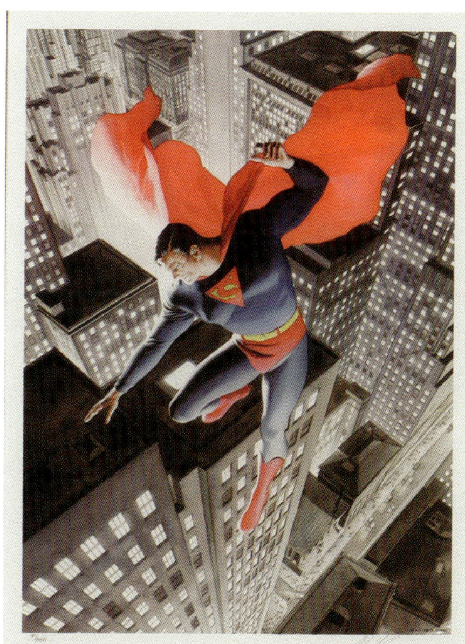

4522 Alex Ross - Superman: Twentieth Century Limited Edition Print #84/350 (Warner Bros., 1998). Superman takes to the skies in this limited edition lithograph illustrated by Alex Ross. This classic image, inspired by the cover of **Superman** #1, originally published in the summer of 1939, captures the Man of Tomorrow against a backdrop of Metropolis. Ross draws inspiration for his interpretation of Superman from the Man of Steel's classic comics of the 1940s, 50s, and 60s, as well as the Max Fleischer animated Superman cartoons. Measuring 16" x 23", this print is number 84 in a series of 350, and is signed by Alex Ross. The condition of this print is Excellent, and it includes a certificate of authenticity.

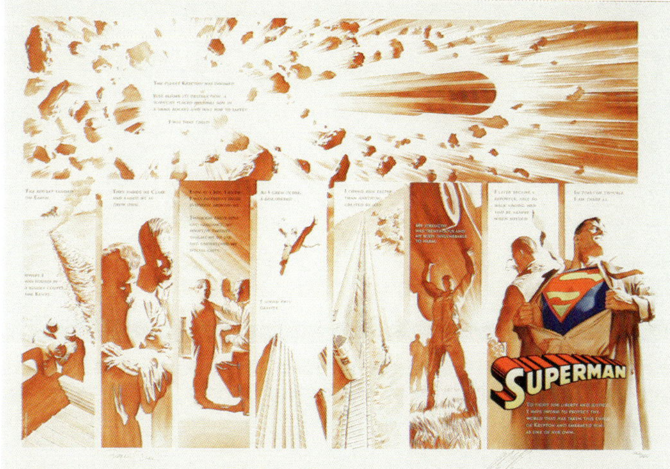

4523 Alex Ross - Superman: Peace On Earth Limited Edition Print #142/350 (Warner Bros., 1998). The unforgettable origin and amazing powers of Superman are recounted in this spectacular limited edition lithograph. This image is taken from the groundbreaking graphic novel, **Superman: Peace On Earth**, published by DC Comics in 1998, which combined the talents of Alex Ross, and Paul Dini, producer of the award-winning "Superman" animated television series. Measuring 27" x 20", this print is number 142 in a series of 350 and is signed by Alex Ross and Paul Dini. In Excellent condition, it also includes a certificate of authenticity.

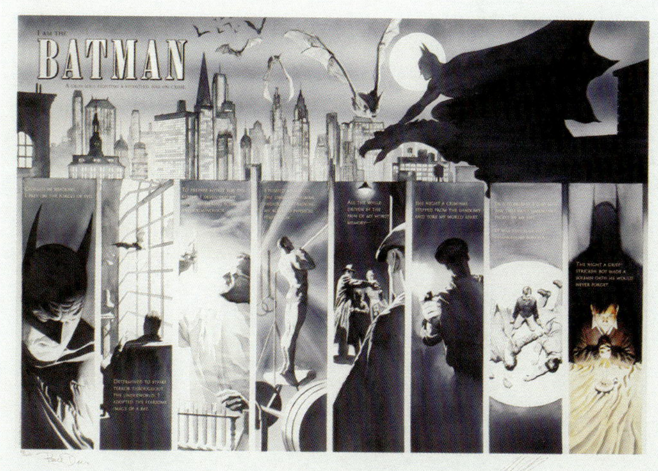

4524 Alex Ross - Batman: War On Crime Limited Edition Print #93/250 (Warner Bros., 2000). Driven by the pain of his worst memory — the night a criminal took the lives of the two most important people in his life — the Batman fights a relentless war on crime. His solemn origin is recounted in this striking limited edition lithograph. Taken from the graphic novel, **Batman: War On Crime**, published by DC Comics in 1999, it combines the talents of Alex Ross, and Paul Dini, co-creator of "Batman: The Animated Series". This print is number 93 in a series of 250 and measures 27" x 20". Signed by Alex Ross and Paul Dini, the condition is Excellent.

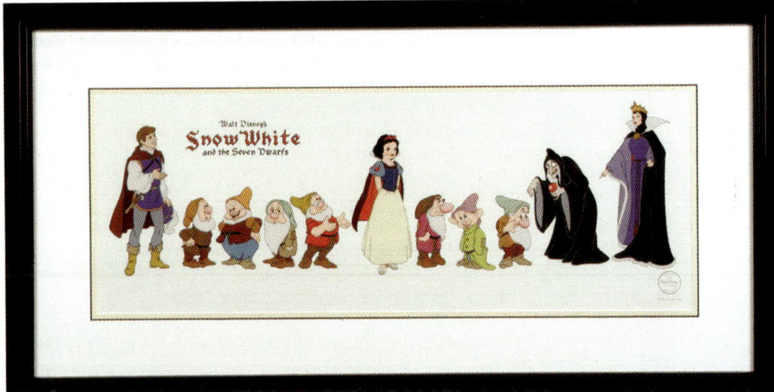

4525 Snow White and the Seven Dwarfs Limited Edition Sericel (The Walt Disney Company, 1994). This sericel depicts characters from Walt Disney's first feature-length animated film "Snow White and the Seven Dwarfs". This "Cast of Characters" features the Prince, Sneezy, Happy, Sleepy, Doc, Snow White, Grumpy, Dopey, Bashful, the Witch, and the Queen. Walt Disney artists, working from the original model sheets used by animators during the film's production, translated these images to a hand-inked and hand-painted cel, which was used in the production of this sericel. Limited to an edition of 5,000, this sericel has an image area measuring 26" x 9.5". The condition is Excellent, and this lot also includes a certificate of authenticity.

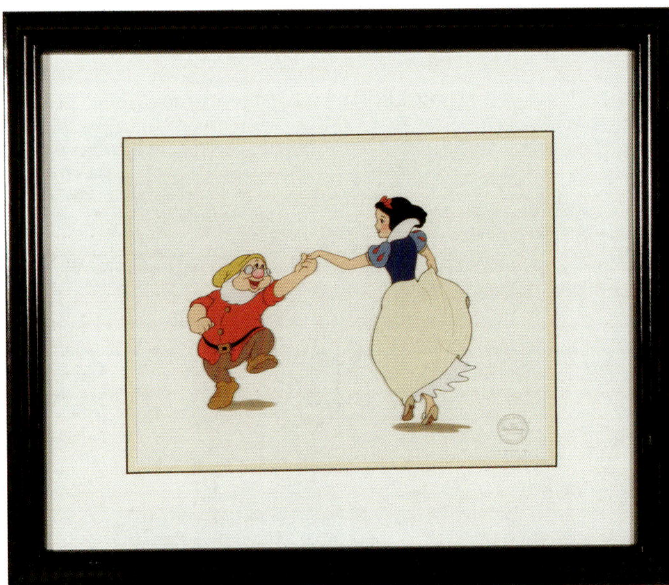

4526 Snow White and Doc Limited Edition Sericel (The Walt Disney Company, 1994). This limited edition sericel, titled "Snow White and Doc," is from Sequence 8A, Scene 23 of "Snow White and the Seven Dwarfs," as the dwarfs entertain Snow White with their yodel song she decides to join in and dances with Doc. Disney artists, working from the original animation drawings, have translated the original image to a hand-inked and hand-painted cel. That cel was used in the production of this screen-printed sericel. It is from a limited edition of 5,000, and includes a certificate of authenticity, which was signed by animator Marc Davis. With an image area measuring 13" x 10", this sericel is in Excellent condition.

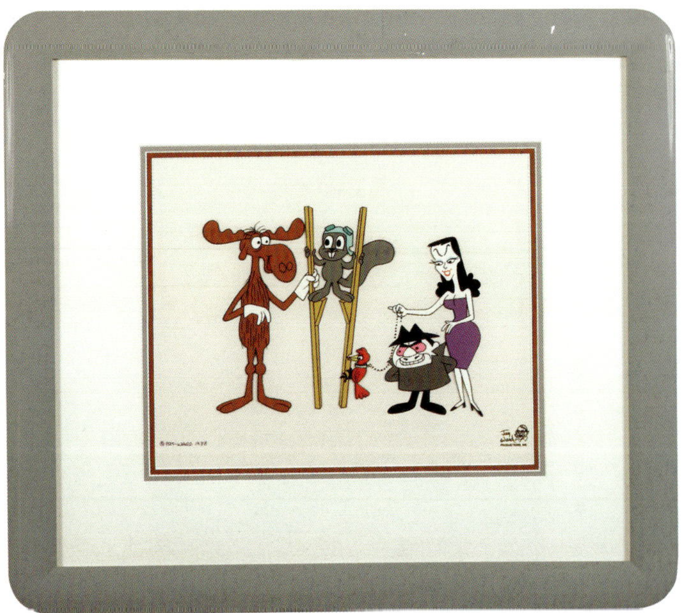

4527 Bullwinkle, Rocky, Boris, and Natasha Hand-Painted Scene Cel (Jay Ward Productions, 1988). This hand-inked and hand-painted cel was created by Jay Ward Productions. With an image area measuring 12" x 9.5", the condition is Excellent. This lot also includes a certificate of authenticity.

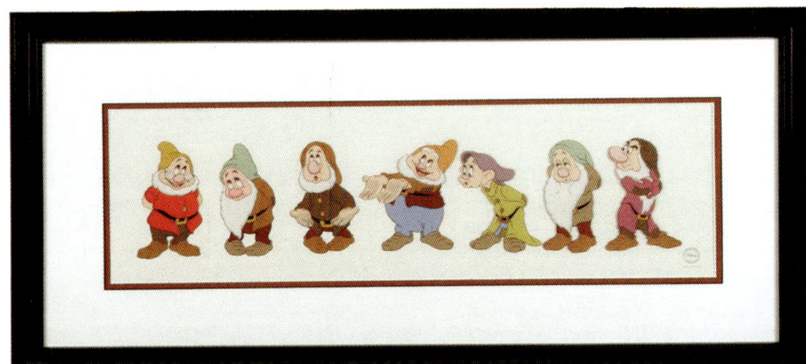

4528 Snow White and the Seven Dwarfs "Time to Wash Up" Limited Edition Sericel (The Walt Disney Company, 1996). This sericel depicts characters from Walt Disney's first feature-length animated film "Snow White and the Seven Dwarfs". Snow White makes the seven dwarfs line up for a pre-supper "dirty hands inspection" which, sadly, they fail. "Time to Wash Up" recreates Sequence 5B, Scenes 13B and 16 from Disney's classic animated feature. Walt Disney artists, working from the original animation drawings, translated these images to a hand-inked and hand-painted cel, which was used in the production of this sericel. Limited to an edition of 5,000, this sericel has an image area measuring 26" x 7.5". The condition is Excellent, and this lot also includes a certificate of authenticity.

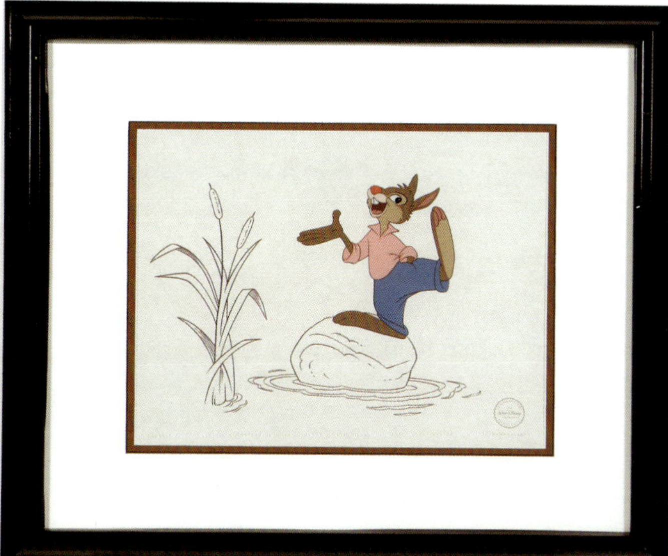

4529 Song of the South Limited Edition Sericel (The Walt Disney Company, 1994). This is a sericel from Walt Disney's full-length feature film "Song of the South," which was released in 1946. This limited edition sericel, "Brer Rabbit," recreates Sequence 52, Scene 727 of "Song of the South". Brer Rabbit springs into the live-action portion of the film with his characteristic bravado and ceaseless energy, as Uncle Remus begins to tell Johnny another fable. Walt Disney artists created this character image using a fine art screen-printing process called serigraphy. Limited to an edition of 5,000, this sericel has an image area measuring 13" x 10", and is in Excellent condition. This lot also includes a certificate of authenticity, which was signed by Marc Davis.

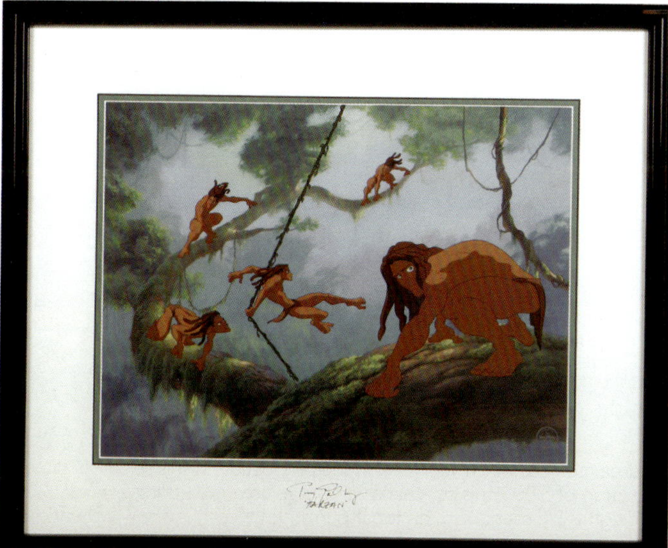

4530 Surfing on a Vine Limited Edition Sericel (The Walt Disney Company, 1993). This limited edition sericel depicts five poses of the star of Walt Disney Pictures' "Tarzan". Titled "Surfing on a Vine," the art was inspired by Sequence 8.4, Scene 69.50 of the 1999 animated feature. Walt Disney artists created this character image using the fine art screen-printing process of color reproduction known as serigraphy. Limited to an edition of 2,500, this sericel has an image area measuring 17" x 13", and is signed by "Tarzan" voice artist, Tony Goldwyn. The condition is Excellent, and this lot also includes a certificate of authenticity.

4531 Royal Embrace Limited Edition Sericel (The Walt Disney Company, 1993). This limited edition sericel depicts Prince Ali and Jasmine embracing after she has announced to her father the Sultan that she has chosen the prince to be her husband. Titled "Royal Embrace," the art was inspired by Sequence 17, Scene 81 of "Aladdin". Walt Disney artists created this character image using the fine art of screen-printing process of color reproduction known as serigraphy. Limited to an edition of 5,000, this sericel has an image area measuring 10" x 13", and is in Excellent condition. This lot also includes a certificate of authenticity.

4532 "Get a Gremlin" Print (Warner Bros., undated). In the Warner Bros. short, "Russian Rhapsody," (based on the Roald Dahl novel, "The Gremlins"), Bob Clampett introduced us to those "Gremlins from the Kremlin," who attack a plane piloted by Hitler in an effort to defend their Russian homeland. This reproduction was taken from a scene from that hysterical film, and has an image area of 9" x 7". In Excellent condition.

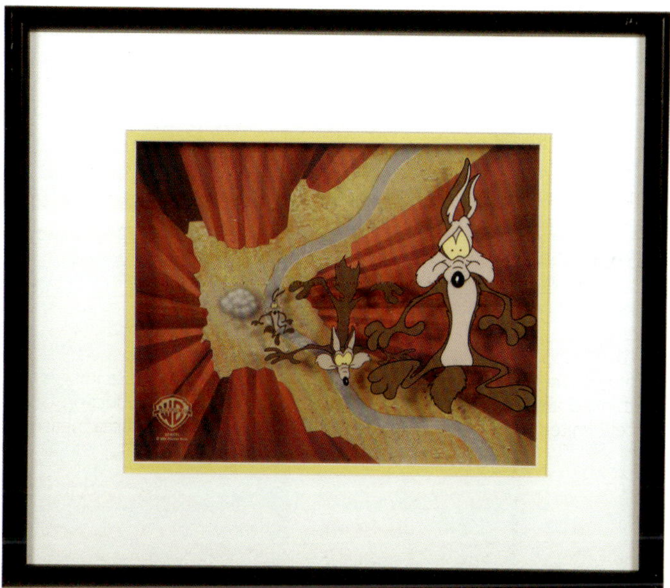

4533 Coyote Falling Limited Edition Dimensional Sericel #244/1000 (Warner Bros., 1994). This dimensional image captures the sinking sensation as Wile E. Coyote fails at another attempt to capture the Road Runner. Titled "Coyote Falling," this multi-image, multi-layered sericel was created by Warner Animation artists using a four-color lithography process. This is number 244 out of 1000 sericels. The image area measures 10" x 7.5" and the art is in Excellent condition.

4534 Wizards "Princess Elinore" Model Sheet, Group of 2 (Bakshi Productions, 1975). The full-figured form of Princess Elinore fills these two model sheets, which were used in the production of Ralph Bakshi's 1977 feature film, "Wizards". Photocopied onto acetate, these two pieces measure approximately 12.5" x 8.5" and are in Excellent condition.

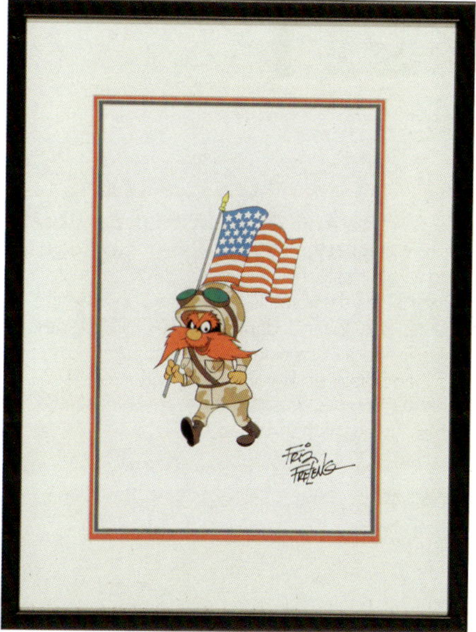

4535 Yosemite Sam Salutes the U.S. Limited Edition Lithograph #219/1000 (Warner Bros., undated). This limited edition lithograph was created in honor of U.S. troops by Academy Award-winning animator and director, Friz Freleng. A label on the back of the art indicates that this is number 219, out of 1000 prints. The image area measures 10" x 14" and the art is in Excellent condition.

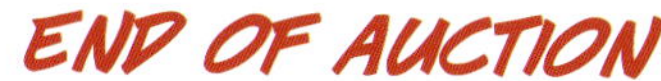